COST ACCOUNTING
Planning and Control
Seventh Edition

Adolph Matz, PhD
Professor Emeritus of Accounting
The Wharton School
University of Pennsylvania

Milton F. Usry, PhD, CPA
Regents Professor of Accounting
College of Business Administration
Oklahoma State University

A86

Published by

SOUTH-WESTERN PUBLISHING CO.

CINCINNATI   WEST CHICAGO, ILL.   DALLAS   PELHAM MANOR, N.Y.   PALO ALTO, CALIF.

Preface

Management's efforts to achieve company objectives rest upon the twin functions of planning and control. The *planning function* is essentially a decision-making process dealing with the establishment of a desired profit; the preparation and availability of materials, labor force, and plant and equipment for the anticipated volume; and the creation of a communication system that permits reporting and controlling actual results against predetermined plans. The *control function* deals with management's task of organizing and marshaling natural forces, human behavior, and material objects into a coordinated unit in order to attain the desired results. The connecting link between the originating planning function and the terminating control function is the cost accounting information system, rightly termed a tool of management, that permits effective communication, continuous feedback, responsibility accounting, and managerial flexibility.

The processing and reporting of a firm's historical and projected microeconomic data assist management in developing new potentials, improving present opportunities, establishing more aggressive yet flexible control of operations, and enhancing the management process through objective evaluation of the feedback data.

The importance of cost accounting to the performance and success of any level of management in both problem identification and problem solving is emphasized throughout this edition. While *planning* is essentially a decision-making activity, *control* intends to ensure realization of the planner's goals. Although the information and underlying data required for these two functions are often quite different, one expects the cost accounting system to provide the answers and respond to the needs of both functions. This dual responsibility of the cost accounting information system to both functions strongly influenced the authors in structuring the presentation followed in this textbook.

Parts One and Two of the textbook fuse planning and control into a harmonious whole by first presenting the cost data accumulation methods. The study of a job order or a process cost system might be considered a mechanical exercise by some accounting instructors; yet in any cost system they deserve primary attention if routine employee performance and computerized accounting are to furnish reliable data for management's tasks and decisions. The need for improving cost accounting instruction is recognized; but an orderly growth is still necessary, and the value of established practices as well as the lessons of the past should not be discarded.

Part Three deals essentially with the planning and control of factory overhead and responsibility accounting. The text discussion shows that these steps outlined for a manufacturing concern are equally important and adaptable to nonmanufacturing businesses and nonprofit organizations.

Part Four considers the other two cost elements, materials and labor, from both the planning and cost control phases.

Part Five is the heart of the planning function — budgeting. Long- and short-range budgets as well as the flexible budget are discussed.

Part Six treats not only standard costs basic to the control of costs and profits but also gross profit analysis and direct costing.

Part Seven, the final section, covers the entire spectrum of cost and profit analysis, culminating in a chapter on linear programming for planning and decision making.

The concepts and techniques presented in this textbook are mainly in the context of manufacturing business organizations. However, it is important to note their wide, virtually universal applicability to many dimensions of organizations including (1) small business organizations of all types; (2) nonmanufacturing businesses such as wholesale and retail stores and such service organizations as banks, insurance companies, hotels, and motels; and (3) nonprofit institutions such as churches, fraternal and charitable organizations, hospitals, libraries, public school systems, colleges and universities, and local, county, state, and federal government units and agencies. Indeed, any organization charged with the responsibility of efficient use of resources could and should utilize cost accounting concepts and techniques.

Like many other disciplines, cost accounting has been influenced by the development of quantitative management techniques and decision models. New topics and topics retained from earlier editions include such techniques as the method of least squares for regression analysis, the discounted cash flow method, PERT/cost, probability analysis, decision trees, risk and sensitivity analysis, correlation analysis, and the simplex method for profit maximization and cost minimization. These techniques and their applications are presented in a clear and concise manner.

As in previous editions, cost accounting topics of current interest have been included where appropriate. These topics include computerized budgeting and materials and payroll procedures, human resource accounting, learning curve theory, the Pension Reform Act of 1974, zero-base budgeting, probabilistic budgets, transfer pricing theory, and segment reporting.

The presentation of the fundamental theoretical and practical aspects of cost accounting and relevant behavioral science concepts provide wide flexibility for classroom usage. In addition to its applicability to the traditional two-semester or three-quarter course, the textbook may be used in a one-semester cost course or in a managerial accounting course with emphasis on profit planning and cost analysis. For these alternative courses, a suggested outline, by chapter numbers, follows:

Cost Accounting (one semester)	Profit Planning and Cost Analysis (one semester)
Chapters 1–15	Chapters 1–4
Chapters 18–20	Chapter 13
	Chapters 16–28

Many other chapter combinations can be used effectively, depending on students' needs. The Instructors' Manual includes an outline of possible variations.

End-of-chapter materials total 400 discussion questions, 274 exercises, 213 problems, and 55 cases. These materials include over 200 questions, exercises, problems, and cases from the examinations administered by the American Institute of Certified Public Accountants (designated AICPA adapted), the Institute of Management Accounting of the National Association of Accountants (designated CMA adapted), the Canadian Institute of Chartered Accountants (designated CICA adapted), and the Certified General Accountants' Association of Canada (designated CGAA adapted). The authors are indebted to these organizations for the use of their materials.

Most of the end-of-chapter materials are new or revised. Exercises and problems included for each topic afford coverage of relevant concepts and techniques at progressive levels in the learning process, thereby providing a significant student-learning benefit.

Three separately printed practice cases are available, coauthored by John H. McMichael of the Wharton School, University of Pennsylvania. Each case — a job order cost case, a process cost case, and a standard cost analysis case — acquaints students with basic procedural characteristics without involving time-consuming details.

New with this edition is a student study guide, prepared by Edward J. VanDerbeck of Xavier University, Cincinnati. This study guide contains a brief summary of each chapter, as well as questions and exercises with answers, thus providing students with immediate feedback on their comprehension of material.

Instructors adopting this edition are supplied with a manual that has been carefully prepared to improve the effective use of the textbook, to reduce the time spent in checking problems, and to help plan class periods more efficiently. The major portion of this manual is devoted to detailed solutions of the end-of-chapter materials. Wherever computations, supporting entries, schedules, or analyses are of a detailed or involved nature, the computations are given in full. Instructors are also entitled to practice case solutions, an Examinations Booklet (including both multiple-choice questions and problems), and multiple copies of Student Check Sheets for the problems.

The authors wish to express appreciation to the many users of the previous editions who offered helpful suggestions. Special thanks are given the students and teachers of the Wharton School of the University of Pennsylvania and of Oklahoma State University who class-tested the new exercises, problems, and cases and made suggestions for improvements.

Finally, we wish to express our heartfelt appreciation to our wives, Trean Benfer Matz and Dona White Usry, for their assistance in the preparation and completion of this edition.

Adolph Matz
Milton F. Usry

Contents

PART 2 THE COST INFORMATION SYSTEM AND COST ACCUMULATION PROCEDURES

PART 3   PLANNING AND CONTROL OF FACTORY OVERHEAD

PART 5 PLANNING OF PROFITS, SALES, AND COSTS

PART 6 CONTROLLING COSTS AND PROFITS

PART 7 COST AND PROFIT ANALYSIS

Part One Cost Accounting — Concepts and Objectives

1

Concept of Management and Function of the Controller

The management of a business enterprise is based upon a structure of individuals who belong to one of three groups: (1) the operating management group, consisting of foremen and supervisors; (2) the middle management group, represented by department heads, division managers, and branch managers; and (3) the executive management, consisting of the president, the executive vice-presidents, and the executives in charge of the various functions of marketing, purchasing, engineering, manufacturing, finance, and accounting. The existence of these three levels suggests that management consists basically of people whose activities must be planned and controlled through top-level directives, decisions, and instructions. Plans and directives should be considered under the all-inclusive term "planning," and the continuous observation of the plans under the term "control." *Planning* refers to the construction of an operating program, comprehensive enough to cover all phases of operations and detailed enough so that specific attention may be given to the program's fulfillment in controllable segments. *Control* is that force which guides management in achieving objectives by comparing performance with policies and decisions. Planning is basically an executive management responsibility. Control, however, requires participation of all levels of the management team.

Management needs systematic, comparative cost information as well as analytical cost and profit data to manage an enterprise. This information is needed to assist in (1) setting the company's profit goal by executive management, (2) establishing departmental targets which direct middle and operating management toward the achievement of the final goal, (3) measuring and controlling departmental and functional activities with the aid of budgets and standards, and (4) analyzing and deciding on adjustments and improvements to keep the entire organization moving forward in balance toward established profit and other company objectives.

THE CONCEPT "MANAGEMENT"

A comprehensive explanation of the concept "management" poses innumerable difficulties. Invariably it leads to descriptive phrases such as "making decisions, giving orders, establishing policies, providing work and rewards, and hiring people to carry out policies." Management sets certain objectives which it tries to accomplish through the efforts of the people it directs. In this sense, it looks toward a final goal through a series of steps and processes. To be successful, management requires the integration of its own knowledge, skills, and practices with the know-how and experience of those who are entrusted with the task of carrying out the objectives. These objectives can be achieved by management, together with the efforts of all employees, through performance of the two basic management functions — planning and controlling — both of which are basic to this textbook.

Planning
Planning is fundamental to the management process, a process of sensitizing an organization to external opportunities and threats, of determining desirable and possible objectives, and of deploying resources to match the objectives. Without planning there is no basis for controlling, for planning provides the foundation upon which the control function operates. Effective corporate planning is based on facts collected and analyzed. Reflective thinking, imagination, and foresight are of invaluable help. The planner should be able to visualize the proposed pattern of activities individually and collectively, internally and externally. Planning is looking ahead — preparing for the future. It involves a choice of several possible alternatives, a matter of making a decision. Planning must precede the doing.

One kind of plan, among several, is the budget. The budget is not only the most important plan of an enterprise, but also the basic link of cost accounting with management. The use of budgets, particularly in connection with the control phase of management, has been termed "budgetary control." In a budget, anticipated results, as envisioned by the planners, are expressed in quantitative data such as dollars, labor hours, number of employees, units of input and output, and products made and sold.

For the budget or any other kind of plan to operate effectively, an integrated balance must be maintained among the various plans and programs.

Engineering, manufacturing, marketing, research, finance, and accounting participate in the establishment of the corporate plan. No single function should plan and act individually or independently from other functions, for all are interdependent. Failure to recognize this fundamental truth can cause unnecessary complexity and difficulty in planning and can result in disaster for the organization.

Closely allied with proper planning are the determination and establishment of company objectives. An objective is a target, an end result. Corporate planning includes such areas of investigation as the nature of the company's business, its objectives and major policies, the timing of major steps in the plan, and other factors related to long-range plans.

When asked to state the objectives of a business enterprise, many people point to the need for realizing a profit. However, in the last few years business people have tended more frequently to soft-pedal profit maximization and to emphasize the modern corporation's growing list of social obligations. Yet, the phrase "social responsibilities," rarely defined, remains a hazy concept. Profits are the indispensable element in a successful business enterprise. A firm making inadequate profits will not only not survive but will perhaps become a social or economic disaster to the very society it is expected to support. Social responsibility is a fair-weather concept; management cannot begin to think in terms of philanthropy unless profits are adequate. However, profit cannot remain the sole objective of the company and its management. It is a limited concept in today's economic society and does not give the whole answer. Management must execute a series of thinking processes and actions which will guide it to produce specific products or render service in a definite manner or method, in a volume, at a time, at a cost, and at a price that will, in the long run, assure a profit and also win the cooperation of employees, gain the goodwill of customers, and meet social responsibilities.[1] Such a company will be able to make the strongest case for profit maximization. Business logic and changing public expectations suggest that plans should be formulated within a framework of four major parameters — economic, technological, social, and political. Organizational objectives and performance criteria must be broader and more sophisticated.

Controlling

Management control is the systematic effort by business management to compare performance to plans. The control function is of prime importance in the accomplishment of objectives. The need for control increases with the size and complexity of the organization. Continuous supervision of an activity, task, or job is required to keep it within previously defined boundaries. These boundaries, termed "budgets" and/or "standards," are set up for manufacturing, marketing, finance, and all other activities. Actual results are measured against plans; and if significant differences are noted, remedial actions

---

[1]"The Executive As Social Activist," *Time*, Vol. 96, No. 3, pp. 62–68.

are taken. Diagrammatically, the control process can be pictured in the manner illustrated by the chart below:

Control
Circuit

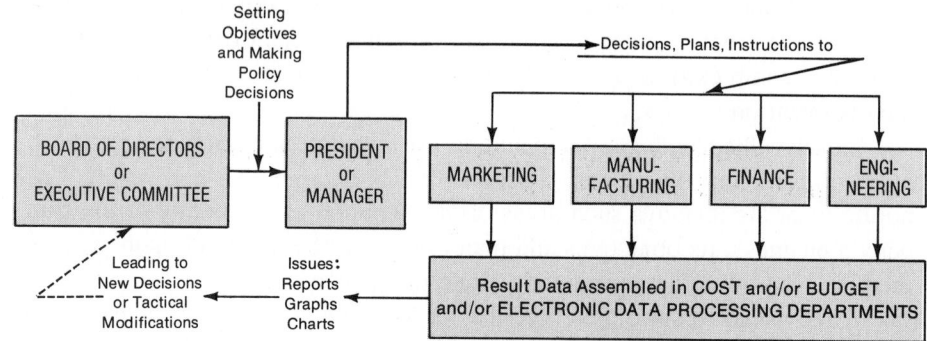

Planning and Control Responsibilities of Middle and Operating Management Levels

In a small company, planning and control activities often tend to be performed by one person. The owner or the general manager of a small company can often perform these tasks without elaborate fact-finding and analysis due to intimate knowledge of employees, materials, money, and customers. In a large concern with numerous divisions and a variety of products or services, planning and control responsibilities are not combined in the same person or group of persons. In fact, the larger the business organization the greater the problem of planning, and the more involved the process of controlling the activities of individual units scattered throughout the United States and foreign countries. For this reason many firms have initiated the decentralization of certain planning and control functions in order to place the reports and necessary corrective actions closer to the scene of activity.

Overall responsibility for control rests with executive management or, in the final analysis, with the president of the company. Because the president cannot attend to every aspect of the control program, authority and responsibilities must be assigned to middle and operating echelons of management in order to assure the success and control of management's plans.

Authority is the key to the managerial job and the basis for responsibility. It is not only the force that binds the organization together, but also the power to command others to perform or not perform certain activities. Managers work through people. Authority vested in a division manager, a department head, or a supervisor enhances compliance with the plans and objectives of the organization. Authority originates with executive management which delegates it to the various managerial levels. Delegation of authority is essential to the existence of an organizational structure. By means of delegation, the chief executive extends the area of operations, but must always retain the overall authority for the assigned functions, since delegation does not mean a permanent release from obligations.

Closely related to authority is responsibility. The essence of *responsibility* is obligation. It arises particularly in the superior-subordinate relationship due to the fact that the superior has the authority to require specified work or services from other people. As these other people accept the obligation to perform the work, they create their own responsibility. However, since responsibility cannot be delegated, the superior is, in the last analysis, responsible for performance or nonperformance by the individual.

Responsibility is often considered to have two facets. In addition to securing results, another aspect of responsibility is *accountability* — reporting results achieved back to higher authority. The reporting phase is an important function of budgetary control and standard cost accounting. It makes possible the comparison of actual performance with predetermined plans and the measurement — in terms of quantity, quality, time, and cost — of the extent to which objectives were reached.

Accountability is basically an individual rather than a group problem, and the principle of single accountability has become well established in profit and not-for-profit organizations. Divided authority and responsibility result in divided accountability. The organizational structure must avoid duality or pooling of judgment, for this diffuses responsibility and nullifies accountability. Without single accountability, control reports would not only be meaningless, but corrective actions would be delayed or not forthcoming at all.

ORGANIZING

Organizing is essentially the establishment of the framework within which required activities are to be performed and by whom. Without proper organization a person cannot function as a manager.

The terms "organize" or "organization" refer to the systematization of various interdependent parts and units into one whole. Considered in this sense, organizing requires (1) bringing the many functional units of an enterprise into a well-conceived structure and (2) assigning authority and responsibility to certain individuals. These organizational efforts include the task of getting people to work together for the good of the company. Because of the attitudes, ambitions, and ideas of the many persons involved, indoctrination, instruction, and patience are needed to arrive at the desired organizational structure.

Creation of an organization involves the establishment of organizational or functional units generally known as divisions, departments, sections, or branches. These units are created for the purpose of dividing tasks into workable parts leading to specialization of labor. A manufacturing enterprise usually consists of at least three large, fundamental activities: manufacturing, marketing, and administration. Within these three basic organizational units, numerous departments or sections are formed according to the nature and the amount of work, the degree of specialization, the number of employees, and the location of the work.

After organizational units have been created, management must assign the work to be done within each unit. Appropriate division and distribution of work among the employees combined in organizational units are vital to the attainment of company objectives. Of still greater importance are the relationships between superior and subordinate on the one hand and among managers within the management team on the other. For ultimate success, the authority relationship binds the units into one whole.

THE ORGANIZATION CHART

The *organization chart* sets forth each principal management position and helps to define authority, responsibility, and accountability. The accountant's reports must help management evaluate the effectiveness of its plans, must pinpoint successes or failures in terms of specific responsibilities, and must establish the conditions that will lead to corrective action. The coordinated development of a company's organization with the cost and budgetary system will lead to an approach to accounting and reporting called "responsibility accounting" (Chapter 11).

An organization chart is essential to the development of a cost system and cost reports which parallel the responsibilities of individuals for implementing management plans. Generally, an organization chart is shown in the form illustrated below.

Organization
Chart Based on
Line-Staff
Concept

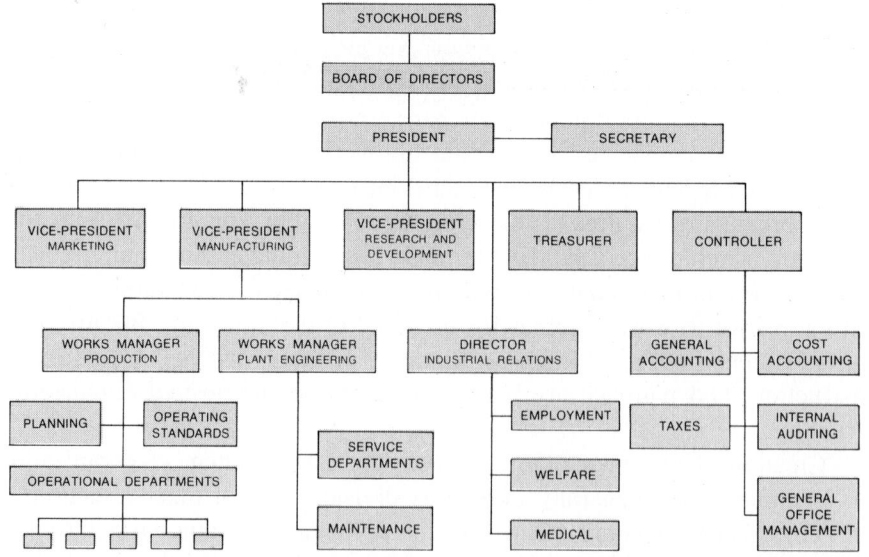

This type of organization chart is based on the line-staff concept, a concept that is particularly useful when a company's product lines are simple and not subject to frequent changes over the years. The fundamental assumption is that all positions or functional divisions can be simply categorized into two groups: one group — the line — makes decisions and performs the true management functions; the other group — the staff — gives advice or performs any technical functions.

Another type of organization chart, based on the functional-teamwork concept of management, appears below. The functional-teamwork concept is structured to place proper emphasis and balance on the truly important functions of any enterprise.[2] These business functions can be grouped around resources, processes, and human interrelations. The *resources* function involves the acquisition, disposal, and husbanding of a wide variety of resources — tangible and intangible, human and physical. The *processes* function deals with activities such as product design, research and development, purchasing, manufacturing, advertising, marketing, and billing. The *human interrelations* function directs the company's effort toward the behavior of people inside and outside the company.

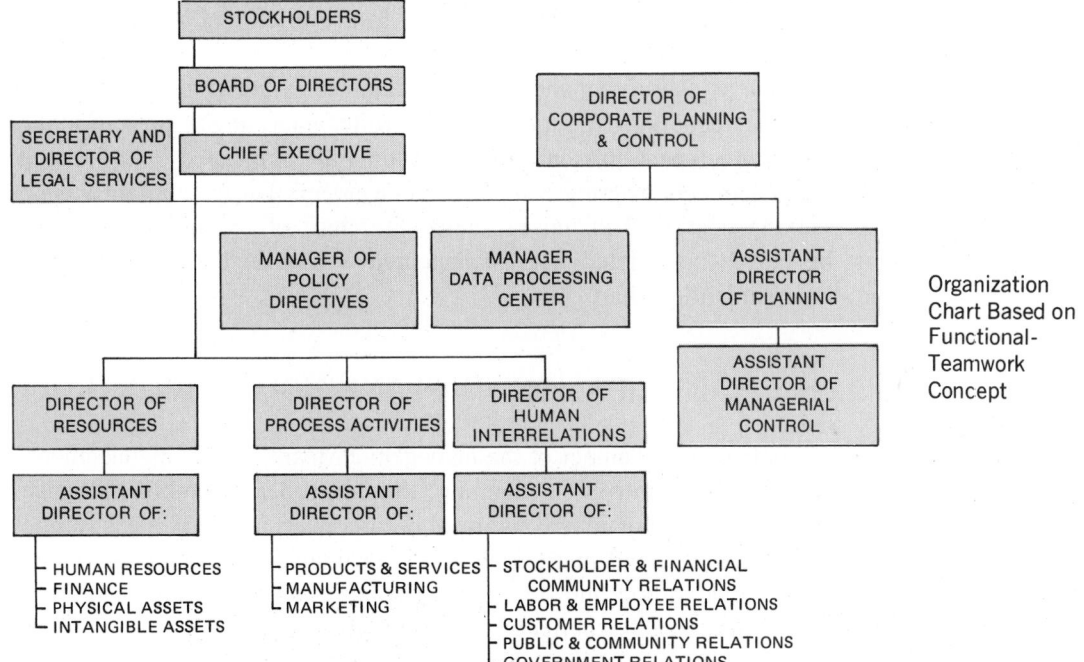

Organization Chart Based on Functional-Teamwork Concept

ACCOUNTING — THE FRAMEWORK FOR PLANNING AND CONTROLLING MANAGEMENT ACTIVITIES

The effective use of company capital is one of management's chief concerns. This capital is invested in the form of productive facilities such as factory buildings, factory machinery, tools, and equipment as well as in the form

---

[2]Gerald G. Fisch, "Line-Staff Is Obsolete," *Harvard Business Review*, Vol. 39, No. 5, pp. 67–79.

of circulating capital called current assets. The use of this capital is determined by management's plans for the immediate future and by long-range plans. The budget, emerging as the result of management's planning, plays an important role in controlling operations. Constant comparison of the budget plan with actual results not only provides a measure of the amount of deviation but also reflects the reasons for variances or differences.

The effectiveness of the control of costs depends upon proper communication through control and action reports from the accounting function to the various levels of management. Accounting and cost control reports are directed to three levels of management: executive, middle, and operating. Each managerial level requires data for deciding and solving varied and difficult problems, and data assembled for one purpose may not be usable for another purpose. For example, figures collected and assembled for measuring and reporting to operating management the past use of materials, labor, machines, and money are often irrelevant for future price and output decisions made by executive management.

Inasmuch as classifying and reporting data are essential to the proper discharge of the accounting function, the controller must devise an information system into which past, present, and future data are marshaled to fit the multitude of problems confronting company management. The accountant's means of classifying costs and expenses, called the chart of accounts (Chapter 4), must be closely associated with management's own fundamental classification, the organization chart.

THE CONTROLLER'S PARTICIPATION IN PLANNING AND CONTROL

The controller, a member of the management team, assists management in both planning and control. In planning, the controller assembles, classifies, and presents the economic and financial data concerning employees, money, materials, machines, and methods into a coordinated plan or plans for management's consideration and decisions. The data are based on (1) the company's own historical, experienced, or past costs and revenue modified by management's own evaluation of the future and (2) other economic forecast information originating outside the company. To coordinate the internal and external information and to chart for management a course of expected trend levels constitutes the controller's most important contribution to planning.

In recent years the controller and staff have become the nerve centers of many large corporations. Their knowledge and control of the basic communication network — the electronic data processing system — permit them to extract diverse data from computer storage and to suggest to executive management alternative plans and sound decisions in crucial areas of operations.

In the control phase, the controller's function is the result of a need for checks and balances within the business. Actually, the controller does not control but, through the issuance of performance reports, advises all levels of mangement where and what activities require corrective action. These reports should make possible *management by exception*. Emphasizing the exceptions to or deviations from a predetermined plan expedites managerial control.

The functions of the controllership sector of a business are depicted in the diagram illustrated below.

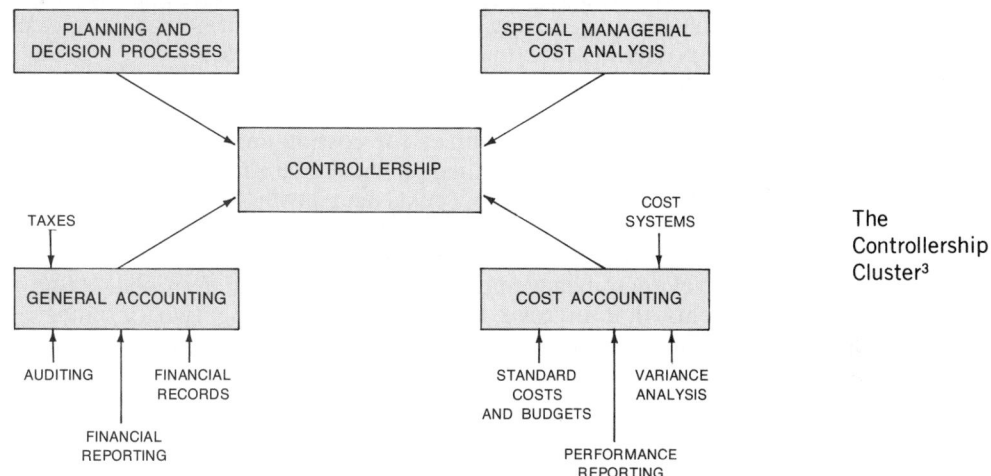

The Controllership Cluster[3]

THE NATURE OF COST ACCOUNTING

Cost accounting, sometimes called management or managerial accounting, should be considered the key managerial partner, furnishing management with the necessary accounting tools to plan and control activities.

In the planning phase, cost accounting deals with the future. It helps management to budget the future or predetermined materials costs, wages and salaries, and other costs of manufacturing and marketing products. These costs might be used to assist in setting prices and disclosing the profit that will result, considering competition and other economic conditions. Cost information is also provided to aid management with problems such as capital expenditure decisions, expansion of facilities for increased sales or production, make-or-buy decisions, or purchase-or-lease decisions.

In the control phase, cost accounting deals with the present, comparing current results with predetermined standards and budgets. Cost control, to be effective, depends upon proper cost planning for each activity, function, and condition. Via the cost accounting media, management is informed frequently of those operating functions that fail to contribute their share to the total profit or that perform inefficiently, thereby leading to profit erosion.

---

[3]Adapted from John P. Fertakis, "Toward a Systems-Oriented Concept of Controllership," *Management Accounting*, Vol. L, No. 6, p. 8.

Periodically, generally at the end of the fiscal period, cost accounting deals with past costs for the purpose of profit determination and thereby with the allocation of historical costs to periods of time. At this point, cost accounting procedure is particularly concerned with the application of manufacturing cost to units of products to be capitalized in the ending inventory and transferred to cost of goods sold as shipments are made.

More specifically, cost accounting is charged with the tasks of:

1. Establishing costing methods and procedures that permit control and, if possible, reduction or improvement of costs.
2. Aiding and participating in the creation and execution of plans and budgets.
3. Creating inventory values for costing and pricing as described by law and, at times, controlling physical quantities.
4. Determining company costs and profit for an annual or shorter accounting period, in total or by segment, as determined by management or required by governmental regulations.
5. Providing management with cost information in connection with problems that involve a choice from among two or more alternative courses, that is, decision making. The decision may be to enter a new market, develop the costs for a new product, discontinue a product line, buy or lease equipment, or take other actions to increase profits or solve problems.

SCOPE OF COST ACCOUNTING

Cost accounting is generally considered applicable only to manufacturing operations. This opinion is not valid in today's economy; every type and kind of activity, regardless of size, in which monetary value is involved should consider the use of cost accounting concepts and techniques. Nonmanufacturing activities of manufacturing firms, wholesale and retail businesses, banks and other financial enterprises, insurance companies, transportation companies, railroads, airlines, shipping companies, bus companies, schools, colleges and universities, hospitals, governmental units on local, state, or federal levels, churches, and welfare organizations — all should employ cost accounting in order to operate efficiently. These many types are not considered individually in this text; however, at appropriate places, mention will be made regarding the use of specific costing concepts and techniques in certain of these activities. In other cases it is a matter of recognition by the management and its accounting staff of the applicability of these concepts and techniques to their own special nonmanufacturing and nonprofit fields of endeavor.

THE COST DEPARTMENT

The cost department is responsible for keeping records associated with the accounting for manufacturing and nonmanufacturing activities. To attain the greatest usefulness, the cost department must not only record but also analyze all costs of manufacturing, marketing, and administration for use by management in planning and control. It must, in addition, issue significant control reports and other decision-making data to executives, superintendents, and department heads, who assist in controlling and improving costs and operations. The need for the prompt issuance of reports and statements must alert the accountant to modern developments and techniques in the field of communications. Information transmittal problems have too often been overlooked or neglected. Cost control needs or profit opportunities have been delayed or missed because of poor communication. The analysis of costs and the preparation of reports are greatly facilitated through proper sectioning of functions generally listed under the cost department. Proper coordination is also needed with other functions closely allied with cost accounting, for which separate departments or sections are often set up; namely, planning and cost analysis and general accounting activities. These functional units should come under the supervision of the controller.

The performance of the functions of the cost department involves the past, present, and future. In profit measurement, as evidenced in the income statement, the accountant is primarily concerned with the proper recording and presentation of costs and revenue for operations and transactions already experienced. When issuing cost control reports, the accountant is working in the present rather than in the past. In developing costs for planning and decision-making purposes, the accountant is concerned with the future.

RELATIONSHIP OF THE COST DEPARTMENT TO OTHER DEPARTMENTS

The *manufacturing departments*, under the direction of factory superintendents and engineers, design, plan, and control products to their finished stage. In research and design, cost estimates are needed for each type of material, each item of labor, and each machine process before an intelligent decision can be reached in accepting or rejecting a design. Likewise, the scheduling, producing, and inspecting of jobs and products by the manufacturing departments are measured for efficiency in terms of the costs incurred.

The *personnel department* interviews, screens, and selects employees for various job classifications. It keeps workers' personnel records and is interested in keeping efficient and satisfied employees. The wage rates and the methods of remuneration agreed upon with the employee form the basis for the computation of the payroll.

The *treasury department*, responsible for the financial administration, relies upon accounting, budgeting, and related reports in scheduling cash requirements and expectations.

The *marketing department* needs a good product at a competitive price in its dealings with customers. While prices should not be set merely by adding a predetermined percentage to cost, cost cannot be ignored. Pertinent cost data give marketing managers information as to which products are most profitable and assist them greatly in determining sales policies.

The *public relations department* has the primary function of maintaining good relations between the company and the public in general, especially customers, stockholders, and employees. Points of friction are most likely to be prices, wages, profits, and dividends. The cost department is often called on to provide basic information for public releases concerning these policies and practices.

The *legal department* finds cost accounting helpful in keeping many affairs of the company in conformity with the law. The Federal Wage and Hour Law, terms of industry-wide union contracts, the Robinson-Patman Act, social security taxes, unemployment compensation taxes, the Employee Retirement Income Security Act of 1974, as well as income tax, are some of the areas where the legal and cost departments need to cooperate.

SOURCES OF COST ACCOUNTING DATA

Much of the source data for cost accounting originates outside the accounting function. In addition to invoices and documents supporting transactions of materials purchased, consumed, or transferred between departments, the accountant requires reports of time studies, records of workers' actual time, bills of material, and lists of operating and planning schedules. Capacity studies, machine-tool requirements, and statistics regarding floor space, machine capacities, and power ratings or power consumption constitute additional source data required. The accountant's dependence upon information furnished by outsiders necessitates source data that are accurate, reliable, and available at the proper time.

The accountant evaluates and uses such data in a manner that will channel out essential facts for management. Since these cost data depend upon proper, correct, and timely information from all levels of the organization, cost accounting becomes a cooperative venture involving all departments of the company. It is an educational problem of executive management, the controller, and the controller's staff to make all employees cost conscious. Employees must be taught to observe and execute cost procedures to promote cost control.

INFORMATION SYSTEM

With the aid of the supervisors in charge of the functions shown on page 9, the controller coordinates participation in planning and control by consulting with various segments of management concerning any phase of the operation of the business as it relates to the attainment of objectives, the effectiveness of policies, and the creation of organizational structures and procedures. It is also the controller's responsibility to observe the method of planning and control throughout the enterprise in order to propose improvements in the planning and control system. To discharge these duties, the controller's function is immeasurably assisted by an electronic data processing system. Depending on the progress made in the use of computers, the assistance offered will generate the effective development of a new information technology which requires the use of these modern computer-communication facilities.

An integrated and coordinated information system should provide exactly the data and other information needed, and no more, to all responsibility heads in accordance with their needs. A good information system requires the establishment of (1) long-range objectives, (2) an organization plan showing delegated responsibilities in detail, (3) detailed plans for future operations, both long- and short-term, and (4) procedures for implementing and controlling these plans.

A comparison of the characteristics of the three management levels highlights the similarities, differences, and interrelationships among these groups. Executive management is principally concerned with long-range decisions, middle management with decisions of medium-range impact, and operating managers with short-range decisions. The information requirements for each level of planning and control vary significantly. Executive management, engaged in strategic planning, sets objectives and determines the resources to be applied in meeting these objectives. For these tasks essential information ingredients should consist of long-term trends, extensive staff studies, external situation information, and reports of achievements. The middle management, engaged in tactical planning and control decision making, relies upon summaries, exceptions, operating results, and estimates relating to internal information of the enterprise. The operating management requires data on internal events relating to daily, weekly, or monthly transactions to fulfill its operational duties and responsibilities.

DISCUSSION QUESTIONS

1. Webster includes in the definition of management "judicious use of means to accomplish an end;" planning is described as "the establishment of goals, policies, and procedures for a social or economic unit;" and control is defined as "to exercise restraining or directing influence." In today's economy

these definitions might be paraphrased to describe management planning and control as a concept of doing business.

(a) State the premises on which these management functions might be based.

(b) Why does the concept of management planning and control vary among companies?

2. (a) State the fundamental task in planning and controlling the activities of a company.

(b) A sound organization is often the product of a positive and dynamic program of planning and control. Name some fundamental steps needed to achieve a sound organization.

3. Enumerate some social responsibilities of which management should be aware.

4. What is the meaning of assignment of responsibility?

5. Explain the relationship between assignment of responsibility and control.

6. When an organization or business outgrows direct supervision and management by its owner, authority must be delegated to subordinate managers, and some form of accountability on their part must be provided. Discuss.

7. (a) What is meant by responsibility accounting?

(b) Is responsibility accounting identical with the concept of accountability?

8. As a member of the management advisory service division of a certified public accounting firm, you visit a client's office and find the following situation:

Sam McGinnis is President and Sales Manager of the company. Ruby Cunningham is Vice-President in Charge of Purchasing, preparing weekly production schedules and maintaining inventories of materials and work in process. Dan Troop is the Assistant Purchasing Agent; John Coors is Vice-President in Charge of Sales; and Pedro Gonzalez, the Product Engineer, is responsible for design and engineering development. The Accounting Department and General Office are under the supervision of Peggy Van Housen, who reports directly to the President. Office help consists of two full-time and one part-time bookkeeper, one typist, and one clerk. The company's factory is divided into four producing departments employing about 175 workers. The President requests:

(a) An organization chart.

(b) An opinion regarding certain duties that apparently have not been sufficiently delegated.

(c) A report as to additional information needed to prepare a more satisfactory organization chart.

9. The number of factory workers mentioned in Question 8 indicates that this company falls into the category of small business.

(a) Would the consultant's answer be different if the company employs 2,000 factory workers?

(b) What additional managerial positions might have to be set up?

(c) In what manner would the Accounting Department and General Office have to be reorganized?

10. The management of the Kringle Company, interested in an improved organization, created a Control Division with a controller as its chief executive. The

controller prepared the organization chart below and invited staff members to comment on the chart with respect to:

(a) Organization.
(b) Possible improvements.
(c) A new chart.

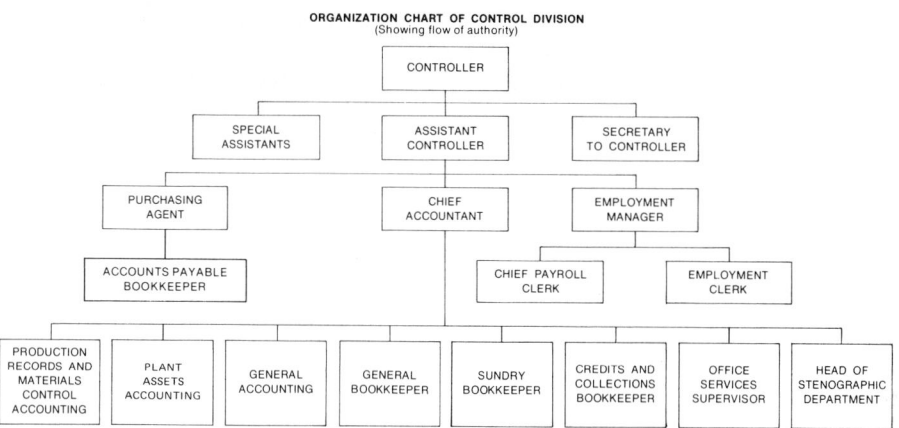

ORGANIZATION CHART OF CONTROL DIVISION
(Showing flow of authority)

11. Why has the budget been cited as the most essential tool in cost planning?

12. In what manner does the controller exercise control over the activities of other members of management?

13. The principle of management by exception is followed by a company in which a major item showed the following percentage relationship to the budgeted figures for six consecutive months: 92%, 95%, 96%, 99%, 103%, 108%. Does the item need attention?

14. Discuss the functions of the cost department.

15. Why must the controller be aware of the latest developments in the field of communications?

16. Numerous nonaccounting departments require cost data and must also feed basic data to the cost department. Discuss.

17. Enumerate the requirements of a good information system.

2

Financial Statements
The Bases for Planning and Control

The controller, as the chief executive officer of the accounting function, is responsible for the reporting of financial, cost, and economic data to enable executive management to plan the company's future and to control its day-by-day activities. The accounting division must establish communication with other departments and functions in order to fulfill its obligations to all parties concerned. Internally, these parties consist of the three levels of management as explained in Chapter 1. Externally, they comprise stockholders, future investors, government agencies, and other interested parties who receive their information generally via the annual report of the company as well as quarterly statements.

THE REPORTING FUNCTION

Accounting information is the chief means of communicating the results of management's stewardship to external and internal users. There is no need to argue the relative importance of external and internal reporting. Basically, both are needed and both emanate from a single accounting system. The external users receive their information in annual and quarterly reports, which include the balance sheet, the income statement, and the statement of changes in financial position. These reports often lack a considerable amount of explanatory detail, since it is impossible to include all the data relevant to the external users' many needs.

Additionally, effects of price-level changes and/or current values have been presented as supplemental information to these historical-dollar financial statements. In recent years considerable debate has been centered about inflation accounting. These arguments have ranged from price-level adjusted financial statements to so-called "current value accounting" variously based on current reproduction costs, current replacement costs, net realizable values, liquidation values, and discounted future cash flows. However, such requested and perhaps even desirable reporting aids are neither found in nor based on the books and records of the general and/or cost accounting departments nor have they been accumulated in the data processing system.

The internal users, executive management and all other levels of management, have access to many sources of information required for the execution of the planning and control tasks. Management needs are answered by information provided by the conventional accounting system models — balance sheet, income statement, statement of changes in financial position — and by information outside these models most easily and quickly obtainable from the total computerized information system.

FINANCIAL STATEMENTS IN THE ANNUAL REPORT

The reporting function is initially illustrated here with two historical-dollar financial statements based on the published report of a manufacturing company: the balance sheet, also called the statement of financial position, and the income statement, often labeled the earnings statement. These published statements and their individual items are analyzed primarily to help the external users to appraise a company's overall performance and financial position. Within a company, a wealth of internal data gives the managers not only an opportunity for using more valuable ratios but also additional assistance in the planning and control phases. Not mentioned here is the statement of changes in financial position, which is also found in published annual financial reports to stockholders. Such a statement is designed to "(1) summarize the financing and investing activities of the entity, including the extent to which the enterprise has generated funds from operations during the period, and (2) complete the disclosure of changes in financial position during the period."[1]

Although the balance sheet of The Klondike Manufacturing Company is utilized in the discussion of financial ratios beginning on page 22, it is not discussed in as much depth as the income statement because, as with the statement of changes in financial position, any in-depth discussion is better left to financial accounting textbooks.

The income statement, however, is supported with schedules of cost of goods sold, marketing (sometimes called selling or distribution) expenses, and administrative expenses. These supporting statements are generally made available to executive management, not to external users. They are included here to (1) indicate the difference existing in the information provided and (2) permit the subsequent discussion of additional cost accounting theory, pro-

---

[1]*Opinions of the Accounting Principles Board, No. 19*, "Reporting Changes in Financial Position" (New York: American Institute of Certified Public Accountants, 1971), par. 4.

cedures, analytical steps, and methods necessary to succeed in the planning and control task.

The Balance Sheet

The balance sheet of The Klondike Manufacturing Company is a systematic exhibit based upon the general ledger account balances at the end of the accounting period after adjustment and closing; it is a statement of financial position.

The Klondike Manufacturing Company
Balance Sheet
December 31, 19--

Assets

Current assets:

Cash		$ 2,320,000
Marketable securities		820,000
Accounts receivable (net)		2,661,000
Inventories (finished goods, work in process, materials)		3,231,800
Prepaid insurance, taxes, and miscellaneous expenses		220,000
Total current assets		$ 9,252,800

Property, plant, and equipment:

Land		$ 289,000	
Buildings	$ 3,406,100		
Machinery and equipment	12,529,000	$15,935,100	
Less accumulated depreciation	8,118,000	7,817,100	
Total property, plant, and equipment			8,106,100
Total assets			$17,358,900

Liabilities

Current liabilities:

Accounts payable		$ 990,800
Accrued payroll, taxes, interest, etc.		1,045,000
Estimated income tax		190,700
Due on long-term debt		200,000
Total current liabilities		$ 2,426,500
Long-term debt		2,677,500
Total liabilities		$ 5,104,000

Stockholders' Equity

Common stock	$ 4,258,000	
Retained earnings	7,996,900	
Total stockholders' equity		12,254,900
Total liabilities and stockholders' equity		$17,358,900

The Income Statement

The income statement of The Klondike Manufacturing Company is based upon the revenue, costs and expenses of manufacturing, marketing, and administration, other income and expense items, and income tax. The income statement is complementary to the balance sheet. Neither statement alone offers a sufficiently clear picture of the status and progress of a company; for most purposes they should be presented together as a unit.

The Klondike Manufacturing Company
Income Statement
For Year Ended December 31, 19--

Sales (4,500,000 units @ $5.50 per unit)		$24,750,000	100.0%
Less cost of goods sold (Schedule 1)..		21,285,000	86.0
Gross profit...		$ 3,465,000	14.0%
Less commercial expenses:			
Marketing expenses (Schedule 2)...........................	$580,000		
Administrative expenses (Schedule 3)	533,750	1,113,750	4.5
Income from operations		$ 2,351,250	9.5%
Other income and expense items:			
Royalties and dividends...	$167,000		
Gain from sales of plant assets....................................	12,000		
	$179,000		
Interest and debt expenses.....................................	129,500		
Net addition		49,500	0.2
Income before estimated income tax		$ 2,400,750	9.7%
Less estimated income tax		1,064,250	4.3
Net income...		$ 1,336,500	5.4%

The Cost of Goods Sold Statement. In the income statement, the cost of goods sold is shown in one figure, which is also the general procedure in a published report. However, for internal uses, additional information is necessary for future planning and for evaluation of the past. Schedule 1, on page 20, offers the assistance needed for other analytical applications.

The cost of goods sold section of the income statement of The Klondike Manufacturing Company or of any other manufacturing business can be divided into five distinct parts:

1 Direct materials section, comprised of beginning inventory, purchases, any purchases returns or allowances, and ending inventory.

2 Direct labor section, indicating the cost of those employees whose work can be identified directly with the product manufactured.

3 Factory overhead, comprised of all those costs that assist in an indirect manner in the manufacturing of the product, e.g., factory supplies and depreciation of machinery. The factory overhead section does not indicate the amount of fixed and variable factory overhead, an extremely important requisite in the analytical uses of cost data. Furthermore, it must be assumed that the items are stated at actually experienced costs. Generally, as introduced in Chapter 4 and discussed in detail in the factory overhead Chapters 9, 10, and 11, a predetermined factory overhead rate is used to charge overhead to work in process. For example, The Klondike Manufacturing Company might apply fac-

The Klondike Manufacturing Company

Cost of Goods Sold Statement
For Year Ended December 31, 19--

1 Direct materials:

Materials inventory, January 1, 19--.............................		$1,572,400	
Purchases	$8,420,000		
Less purchases returns and allowances...	42,000	8,378,000	
Materials available for use..		$9,950,400	
Less materials inventory, December 31, 19--.............		1,270,600	
Direct materials consumed..			$ 8,679,800
2 Direct labor...			7,346,400

3 Factory overhead:

Indirect labor	$1,329,300	
Salaries..	972,000	
Payroll taxes	489,000	
Power	112,000	
Heat	69,200	
Light	44,300	
Factory supplies..	50,000	
Depreciation — factory building	68,300	
Depreciation — machinery....................................	403,000	
Repairs and maintenance....................................	145,800	
Patent amortization..	33,200	
Tools and dies used	178,600	
Insurance on building and machinery....................	21,200	
Total factory overhead		3,915,900

Total manufacturing cost...		$19,942,100
4 Add work in process inventory, January 1, 19--............		2,338,000
		$22,280,100
Less work in process inventory, December 31, 19--......		1,303,200
Cost of goods manufactured	(4,430,000 units)	$20,976,900
5 Add finished goods inventory, January 1, 19--......	(210,000 units)	966,100
Cost of goods available for sale	(4,640,000 units)	$21,943,000
Less finished goods inventory, December 31, 19--...	(140,000 units)	658,000
Cost of goods sold...	(4,500,000 units)	$21,285,000

tory overhead on a unit of production basis. Factory overhead could also be applied as a rate based on percentage of direct labor cost, or on direct labor hours or some other representative method. With 4,430,000 units being manufactured and assuming a factory overhead rate of $.90 per unit ($3,960,000 predetermined factory overhead ÷ 4,400,000 planned units), total applied factory overhead would amount to $3,987,000. Deducting the actual overhead of $3,915,900 shows that $71,100 was overapplied; i.e., actual factory overhead was less than the overhead charged to production. In The Klondike Manufacturing Company's cost of goods sold statement, the accountant might have shown the difference in this manner:

Applied factory overhead.......................... $3,987,000
Less overapplied factory overhead 71,100

Actual factory overhead, as per schedule.. $3,915,900

4 Work in process inventories, representing costs in process at the beginning and costs still in process at the end of the fiscal period.

5 Finished goods inventories, beginning and ending.

Schedules of Marketing and Administrative Expenses. Schedules 2 and 3 depict detailed information concerning marketing and administrative expenses.

The Klondike Manufacturing Company

Schedule 2

Marketing Expenses
For Year Ended December 31, 19—

Sales salaries and commissions	$330,500
Travel expenses	43,000
Payroll taxes	16,850
Advertising	125,000
Telephone and telegraph	11,800
Entertainment	21,000
Donations and dues	4,000
Depreciation — furniture and fixtures	7,500
Stationery and office supplies	13,500
Postage	6,850
Total	$580,000

The Klondike Manufacturing Company

Schedule 3

Administrative Expenses
For Year Ended December 31, 19—

Salaries — officers and executives	$290,200
Salaries — general office employees	77,250
Travel expenses	22,450
Payroll taxes	17,500
Depreciation — furniture and fixtures	6,200
Stationery and office supplies	5,450
Telephone and telegraph	7,800
Postage	3,650
Subscriptions, dues, and association activities	4,750
Legal and accounting fees	46,000
Donations	52,500
Total	$533,750

These schedules should be further detailed to identify costs related to individual products and areas of management responsibility.

EVALUATING ANNUAL RESULTS TO ORIENT THE OUTSIDER

The income statement (page 19) follows a functional classification. Costs incurred are grouped according to the function served by their incurrence: manufacturing, marketing, administrative, and nonoperating. The relationship between the various items in the income statement is a criterion for judging the efficiency with which the profit-earning process is conducted. Using the sales figure as a base, or 100 percent, absolute differences become more meaningful when they are reduced to percentage relationships, as indicated in the final column of the statement. Today's annual reports have been made more useful by adding financial ratios which in combination with a ratio or trend analysis program would be beneficial for judging operations in their final results. Only a sample of the more prevalent ratios based on the data available in the preceding financial statements is illustrated.

1. Current ratio $= \dfrac{\text{Current assets}}{\text{Current liabilities}} = \dfrac{\$9,252,800}{\$2,426,500} = \underline{3.81}$,

   indicating that $3.81 is available in current assets for every $1 of current liabilities; it is a guide to the magnitude of the financial margin of safety.

2. Acid-test ratio $= \dfrac{\$5,801,000}{\$2,426,500} = \underline{2.39}$,

   computed by omitting inventories and prepaid items, $2.39 in current assets is available for every $1 of current liabilities.

3. (a) Income before estimated income tax $= \underline{9.7\%}$,

   calculated as a percentage of sales $\left(\dfrac{\$\ 2,400,750}{\$24,750,000}\right)$.

   (b) Net Income $= \underline{5.4\%}$,

   calculated as a percentage of sales $\left(\dfrac{\$\ 1,336,500}{\$24,750,000}\right)$.

   The difference of 4.3% between the two percentages indicates the portion of income claimed by the government and unavailable to the stockholder.

4. Ratio of gross profit to sales $= \underline{14\%}$

   This ratio indicates the percentage available for operating expenses (marketing and administrative), other income and expense items, income tax, and net income. The thinner the margin, the more vulnerable the profit position usually is. The gross profit and its percentage are significant to management's planning and are discussed in depth in Chapter 21.

5. Rate of return on capital employed $= \dfrac{\text{Net income}}{\text{Capital employed (total assets)}}$

   $= \dfrac{\$\ 1,336,500}{\$17,358,900} = \underline{7.7\%}$

   This ratio reveals the percentage earned on the assets employed in the business. It should not be confused with the income to sales ratio of

No. 3 above. The numerator may be more generally described as "profit." The rate of return on capital employed is presented in detail in Chapter 27.

EVALUATING RESULTS TO ORIENT THE INSIDER

The ratios illustrated on page 22 will, of course, also aid the management team. However, the availability of the detailed schedules and other pertinent nonaccounting information permits the insider to make comparative studies of the company's experience over the years. Comparison is an important analytical process, because it focuses attention on deviations from normal. Comparison can be made against actual company experience or against a standard, budget, or forecast. Much data on which to base comparison and evaluation can be obtained from a company's accounting, sales, production, purchasing, or other functional departments.

One of the purposes of cost accounting is the determination of a unit cost figure to be utilized in assigning costs to inventories included in the balance sheet and in the income statement. For example, using the illustrative statements and assuming that 4,500,000 units were sold and 4,430,000 manufactured, with 210,000 units in the beginning inventory of finished goods and 140,000 units in the ending inventory of finished goods, the following unit costs can be calculated:

$$\frac{\text{Cost of goods manufactured}}{\text{Units manufactured}} = \frac{\$20,976,900}{4,430,000} = \$4.735 \text{ average cost per unit manufactured}$$

$$\frac{\text{Cost of beginning finished goods inventory}}{\text{Units in beginning finished goods inventory}} = \frac{\$966,100}{210,000} = \$4.60 \text{ average cost per unit in beginning finished goods inventory}$$

$$\frac{\text{Cost of ending finished goods inventory}}{\text{Units in ending finished goods inventory}} = \frac{\$658,000}{140,000} = \$4.70 \text{ average cost per unit in ending finished goods inventory}$$

$$\frac{\text{Cost of goods sold}}{\text{Units sold}} = \frac{\$21,285,000}{4,500,000} = \$4.73 \text{ average cost per unit sold}$$

Such calculations merely fill the gaps in financial accounting created by the fact that an enterprise seldom sells all the goods manufactured during the year. Financial statements are basically of a long-run nature based on historical or past costs. The insiders (the various levels of management) also need present and future costs for planning and control.

THE FLOW OF COSTS

Cost accounting neither adds new steps to the familiar accounting cycle nor does it discard the principles and procedures studied in financial accounting. Cost accounting consists of a system which is concerned with a more adequate, detailed, and precise recording and measurement of cost elements as they originate and flow through the productive processes. The accounting cycle in such a system is illustrated below:

Flow of
Manufacturing
Costs

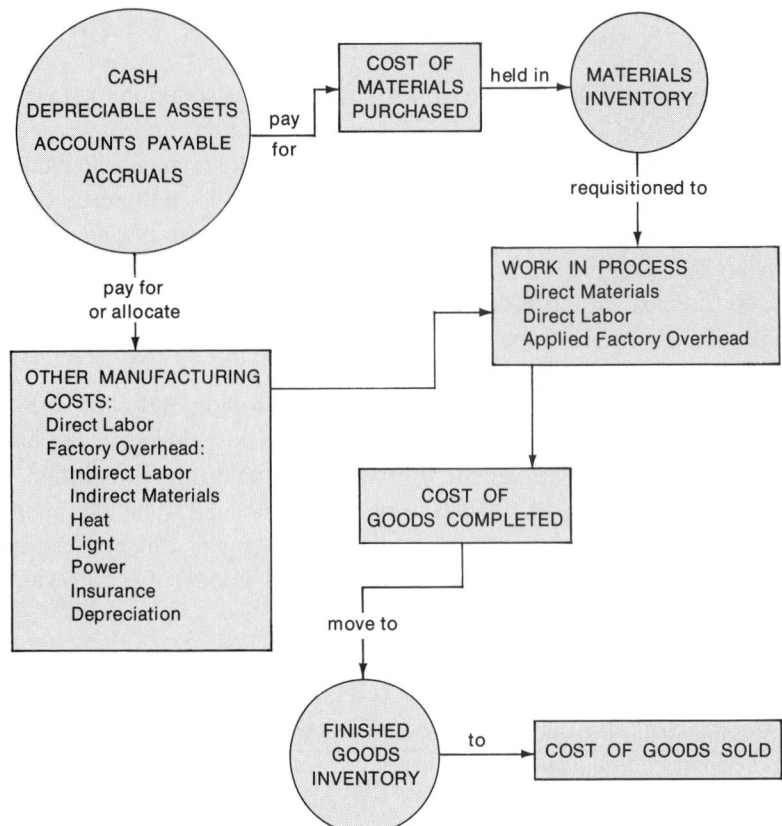

As materials are purchased, they are first held in the inventory account, an asset, from which they move as needed to the work in process account, an asset. There labor and factory overhead are added. When completed, these costs move into the finished goods inventory account, an asset. When sold, the asset, finished goods, moves to the income statement as costs of goods sold.

PLANNING AND CONTROL MODELS

While financial accounting with its annual report relates to the overall progress of the enterprise, cost accounting must aid and fulfill management's needs for planning and control information. It must concern itself with the details of the progress and the contributive efforts and effect of the enterprise's divisions, departments, and manufacturing/marketing units and centers. The form of assistance offered to management has been labeled "models," meaning a framework which allows a compact approach to the solution of management's problems. The budget constitutes the basic model to attain that goal.

Conventional accounting models — namely, the balance sheet and the income statement — used to evaluate the past, are also useful in planning the future of the enterprise. As explained in the budget chapters, the planning process is best started by examining the past, particularly with regard to trends and directions, and then forecasting the future course by projecting and predetermining costs, revenue, profits, and rates of return based on numerous alternatives. The projected data, as well as the process of setting long- and short-term goals for the subdivisions of the enterprise, allow management to test the feasibility and degree of possible success of the forecast outcome of the operations. The budget is not only the widely used instrument for mangement planning but is also the fundamental accounting model for management control. The development of the budget requires the participation of many individuals who are made responsible for the control of their planned costs within a company. This phase of cost planning is expressed as *responsibility accounting*, details of which are reserved for Chapter 11. Since plans are based primarily on forecasts of future conditions, it is necessary to consider costs as they most likely will be at such times. For planning purposes, costs must be considered in terms of their relationship to volume as well as in terms of future prices, plant capacities, and labor efficiencies.

The Budget — A Planning and Control Model

The ever-increasing use of standard costs provides a necessary measure of what costs should be. These standard costs permit an early preparation and presentation of short-run cost reports to operating management and summary statements to executive and middle management, highlighting deviations from the planned goals. Reports comparing actual results with planned or budgeted figures based on standard costs bring to management not only the information regarding the profits already made, but also those that should have been made. Standard costs should ideally be an integral part of the budget in its preparation as well as in its use as a control device.

Standard Costs for Planning and Control

Cost accounting can assist management levels in planning and control duties by providing information via analytical tools that express more vividly and forcefully the multidimensional aspects of managerial problems. The return-on-capital-employed ratio has been illustrated in connection with the analysis of the financial statements. Break-even analysis offers another method that permits management to judge the overall plan on a pragmatic and convenient basis. To calculate the break-even point, it is first necessary to observe the behavior of costs as to their fixed or variable nature. For the present, it suffices to say that direct materials and direct labor are fundamen-

Break-Even Analysis — A Check on Planning

tally considered variable costs. Factory overhead, as well as marketing and administrative expenses, contains elements of fixed and variable costs. These costs must be analyzed to establish a clear-cut division between fixed and variable components. Detailed procedures and mathematical and statistical methods to establish cost variability are described in Chapter 18.

The break-even point can be computed by the following formula:

$$\text{Break-even sales volume in dollars} = \frac{\text{Fixed costs}}{1 - \dfrac{\text{Variable costs}}{\text{Sales}}}$$

Other variations used to compute the break-even point are discussed in Chapter 24. Assume, for the sake of illustration, that the budgeted fixed and variable operating costs and the forecast sales dollar volume of The Klondike Manufacturing Company are:

Fixed costs .... $ 2,500,000
Variable costs.. 20,400,000
Forecast sales dollar volume 25,300,000

The break-even sales dollar volume would be calculated as follows:

$$\frac{\$2,500,000 \text{ fixed costs}}{1 - \dfrac{\$20,400,000 \text{ variable costs}}{\$25,300,000 \text{ sales volume}}} = \frac{\$2,500,000}{1 - .806} = \frac{\$2,500,000}{.194} = \underline{\$12,886,597}$$

The break-even sales dollar volume indicates the amount of sales needed to break even, i.e., to make neither a profit nor a loss. The result can be checked by making this statement:

Break-even sales volume $12,886,597
Variable costs (80.6% of break-even sales volume) 10,386,597
Contribution margin to cover fixed costs and profit...................... $ 2,500,000
Fixed costs 2,500,000
Profit or (loss)... 0

The answers to break-even calculations suggest to management the level of operations at which it is profitable to operate. The above illustration indicates that a level above $12,886,597 sales is needed if the company is to make a profit. Expressed in terms of units, the break-even point would be approximately 2,343,017 units ($12,886,597 ÷ $5.50, the unit sales price).

COST-AND-PROFIT ANALYSIS

Break-even techniques provide but one example of the ever-widening application of cost-and-profit analysis and an understanding of the behavior of costs in the use of making rational decisions. Decisions involving cost-profit-price-volume levels offer still another example of meaningful analysis. The multiplicity of causes and effects of these four factors is dramatically emphasized with the aid of electronic computers that quickly and economically collect and process data from a variety of sources for a variety of end products. These mechanical influences, together with inventory models to project future materials requirements based on orderly planning and control procedures, the use of time-adjusted cash flow projections for capital expenditures, and the techniques of linear programming for profit maximization or cost minimization, are examples of an ever-growing number of decision-aiding models that have become part and parcel of the information system available to management for the execution of its planning and control responsibilities.

OPERATIONS RESEARCH

The techniques of linear programming involve the application of scientific methods to the study of planning and controlling the operations of complex organizations and/or activities. Many operations research concepts and techniques are relevant and applicable to numerous phases of cost accounting and are discussed in this text. For instance, OR working tools are applied in inventory control models, statistical cost analysis, probability theory, learning curve theory, PERT/cost, and present value analysis. The last chapter of this text deals entirely with linear programming in connection with both the graphic and simplex methods.

GOVERNMENTAL AND PRIVATE ORGANIZATIONS INFLUENCING GENERAL AND COST ACCOUNTING PRINCIPLES AND PRACTICES

The previous discussion emphasized the primary uses of financial and cost accounting information by management. The internal reporting and assistance phase is by nature the realm and prerogative of the company management team. Closely allied with the internal reports are the external reports, basically the financial statements consisting of the balance sheet, income statement, and statement of changes in financial position. These reports issued to outsiders have received greater attention and have been substantially influenced by many groups and organizations in recent years.

In the public sector, financial or external reporting has been influenced significantly by the Securities and Exchange Commission (SEC), the Internal Revenue Service (IRS), the Treasury Department, and Congress in creating the Cost Accounting Standards Board (CASB), which is discussed in Chapter 3. Furthermore, federal, state, and local governments prescribe certain accounting-related regulations that must be observed and often embodied in the accounting system.

In the private sector, professional organizations include the American Institute of Certified Public Accountants (AICPA) which sponsored the formation of the Financial Accounting Standards Board (FASB); the National Association of Accountants (NAA); the American Accounting Association (AAA); and the Financial Executives Institute (FEI). Research and pronouncements by these groups contribute to the development, improvement, and revision of both financial and cost accounting theory and practice. Contributions have also been made by companies, nonprofit organizations, public accounting firms, and individuals.

Securities and Exchange Commission's Pronouncements

The federal government, through the actions of the SEC and other regulatory agencies, is showing an increasing interest and influence in companies' external reports. These reports are addressed basically to the investing public, the company's shareholders, and the financial community. However, any additional and required accounting and cost data demand a consistent and unified information system to allow prompt response to legitimate inquiries and outside interests. The most useful form for financial information still remains the annual report of the company.

The preparation of the financial statements that appear in the annual report is the responsibility of company management. The SEC sets forth the requirements for financial statements filed with the Commission in its publication, *Form and Content of Financial Statements*, known as Regulation S-X. Of interest for this textbook is the income statement, which forms the basis for the discussion of revenue and expenses in subsequent chapters.

Besides these annual report requirements, additional rules have been issued in recent years; e.g., the inclusion of quarterly data for each of the quarters of the two most recent years in the annual report (Accounting Series Release No. 177), and the line-of-business or segment disclosures (Securities Act Release Nos. 8650, 9000, and 10591). The quarterly reporting must be included in Form 10-Q and requires comparative balance sheets, income statements (quarterly and year-to-date), and statements of changes in financial position. For each of the quarters of the two most recent years, the quarterly data should show sales or revenue, gross profit, income before extraordinary items, the cumulative effect of an accounting change, per share data based upon such income, and net income.

The SEC has adopted amendments to synchronize its rules on line-of-business disclosure with the provisions of FASB Statement No. 14, "Financial Reporting for Segments of a Business Enterprise." These provisions require line-of-business disclosures when sales, profit, or assets attributable to a line of business are 10 percent or more of the respective total company amounts. The SEC requires some information beyond that required by the FASB with respect to (1) intersegment transfers and (2) the interim performance of industry segments and geographic areas under certain circumstances. The SEC also requires a textual discussion of the registrant's business and property, which includes competitive factors, major customers, sales backlog, materials sources, research and development costs, and other factors.

The National Association of Accountants and the Financial Executives Institute sponsored separate research studies on segment reporting. Published in 1968, the objectives of these studies were very similar: (1) to evaluate the need and desirability of segment reporting by diversified companies; (2) to identify the kinds of segment information that can best serve the needs of creditors and investors; and (3) to ascertain the major limitations and inherent disadvantages of such reporting.[2] The Federal Trade Commission requires businesses to furnish information covering a wide range of specific product categories.

Undoubtedly, the promotion of segment reporting seems essential for fair presentation of financial position and results of operations. However, the subject matter is made part of this cost accounting textbook because of the critical implementation problems for such reporting. One of the chief difficulties connected with segment reporting is the basis used to segment the business or firm. Other difficulties include the allocation of common and/or joint costs among segments and products and the pricing of intersegment transfers. These and numerous others constitute troublesome areas for which equitable and acceptable procedures must be found to make segment reporting meaningful.

Internal Revenue Service

IRS regulations are designed primarily to determine federal income tax liability, yet their influence on financial statements and on cost accounting methods and procedures cannot be ignored. Likewise, any meaningful analysis for planning and decision making must carefully consider federal as well as applicable state and local income tax consequences, because they constitute the very essence of intelligent tax and profit planning.

U.S. Treasury

The Treasury Department has many times in the past issued so-called Treasury Decisions (TDs) that have the effect of law and must be strictly followed. During World War II, Treasury Decision 5000 played a significant part in determining costs in connection with defense and war contracts. TD5000 spelled out the admissible and inadmissible costs and expenses that a contractor was allowed or disallowed in the performance of a government contract. The Cost Accounting Standards Board promulgates in an elaborate and diversified manner the cost and profit requirements to be followed by businesses in connection with government bids and contract performance.

The scope of this textbook does not permit a detailed discussion of the innumerable governmental rules, regulations, and requirements; however, the business community, management, the controller and staff, and the practicing accountant must study and observe these pronouncements.

---

[2]Morton Backer and Walter B. McFarland, *External Reporting for Segments of a Business* (New York: National Association of Accountants, 1968). Robert K. Mautz, *Financial Reporting by Diversified Companies* (New York: Financial Executives Research Foundation, 1968).

DISCUSSION QUESTIONS

1. The balance sheet and the income statement complement each other. Discuss, with an illustration.

2. A corporation's annual financial statements and reports were criticized because it was claimed that the income statement does not by any means give a clear picture of annual earning power, and the balance sheet does not disclose the true value of the plant assets. Considering the criticism made, offer an explanation of the nature and purpose of the income statement and of the balance sheet, together with comments on their limitations.

3. The president of the New Haven Products Co. requests your advice with respect to the following situation:

   The company's chief accountant has been telling the president each year that "the business has just about been breaking even." This statement has been puzzling to the president because inventories, receivables, and payables have not varied much since the company was organized over ten years ago. In fact, cash has been increasing constantly. The president thinks that the business has been making money and that the chief accountant is wrong. Furthermore, no sale of assets, no refinancing of indebtedness, nor any change in the corporate structure, such as a sale of stock, has taken place in these years.

   Explain to the president the continued increase in cash, giving illustrative examples of transactions, as well as a recommendation for any additional financial statements which may be of use to the president.

   (AICPA adapted)

4. Enumerate the five parts of the cost of goods sold section of the income statement.

5. Distinguish between actual and applied factory overhead.

6. The gross profit of the Girard Company for 19–– is $56,000; the cost of goods manufactured is $300,000; the beginning inventories of work in process and finished goods are $18,000 and $25,000, respectively; and the ending inventories of work in process and finished goods are $28,000 and $30,000, respectively. Determine the company's sales for 19––.

7. State some ratios that assist outsiders in evaluating a company's annual results.

8. Give the formula to calculate the break-even point in dollars.

9. Define the term operations research; give examples of OR techniques.

10. Name governmental and private groups whose pronouncements influence accounting methods and procedures.

11. Explain the requirements of line-of-business or segment reporting.

12. Select the answer which best completes the statement:
    (a) An understatement of work in process inventory at the end of a period will: (1) understate cost of goods manufactured in that period; (2) overstate current assets; (3) overstate gross profit from sales in that period; (4) understate income for that period.

(b) If the work in process has increased during the period: (1) cost of goods sold will be greater than cost of goods manufactured; (2) cost of goods manufactured will be greater than cost of goods sold; (3) manufacturing costs for the period will be greater than cost of goods manufactured; (4) manufacturing cost for the period will be less than cost of goods manufactured.

(c) The following information is available for the Gant Company: freight in, $20,000; purchases returns and allowances, $80,000; marketing expenses, $200,000; finished goods inventory, ending, $90,000. The cost of goods sold is equal to 700% of marketing expenses. The cost of goods available for sale is: (1) $1,390,000; (2) $1,490,000; (3) $1,500,000; (4) $1,590,000.

(d) Cost of goods available for sale for the Green and Gold Sporting Goods store was $400,000; gross profit was 25% of sales; sales were $480,000. The amount of the ending inventory was: (1) $20,000; (2) $40,000; (3) $60,000; (4) $80,000.

(e) Information concerning 19A projections of the Elston Company are: net sales of $1,000,000; fixed cost of goods sold of $100,000; 60% increase in variable cost of goods sold for each dollar increase in net sales. The projected 19A cost of goods sold is: (1) $700,000; (2) $600,000; (3) $400,000; (4) $300,000.   (AICPA adapted)

EXERCISES

Round off all amounts to three decimal places.

1. Inventory calculation. On January 1, the finished goods inventory of the Manuel Company was $300,000. During the year Manuel's cost of goods manufactured was $1,900,000, sales were $2,000,000 with a 20% gross profit.

Required: The cost assigned to the December 31 finished goods inventory.

(AICPA adapted)

2. Manufacturing costs; cost of goods manufactured; cost of goods sold. The December 31, 19B trial balance of the Balkwell Company showed:

Sales	$4,000,500	Sales returns and allowances	$ 25,200
Purchases (net)	2,400,000	Transportation in	32,000
Direct labor	3,204,000	Factory overhead	1,885,600
Sales salaries	200,000	Advertising expense	155,000
		Delivery expense	65,000

Inventories:

	DECEMBER 31, 19B	DECEMBER 31, 19A
Finished goods	$467,400	$620,000
Work in process	136,800	129,800
Materials	196,000	176,000

Required:
(1) Total manufacturing cost.
(2) Cost of goods manufactured.
(3) Cost of goods sold.

(CGAA adapted)

3. Cost of goods sold statement; income statement. The accounting department of the Ruthven Company provided the following data for May: sales, $72,000; marketing expenses, 5%; administrative expenses, 1%; other expenses, .5% of all sales; purchases, $36,000; factory overhead, ⅔ of direct labor; direct labor, $15,000.

Beginning inventories:	
Finished goods	$ 7,000
Work in process	8,000
Materials	8,000
Ending inventories:	
Finished goods	$10,200
Work in process	15,000
Materials	8,500

Required:
(1) Cost of goods sold statement.
(2) Income statement.

(CGAA adapted)

4. Income statement. Crowley, Inc., submits the following data for September:

Direct labor cost, $30,000.
Cost of goods sold, $111,000.
Factory overhead is applied at the rate of 150% of direct labor cost.

Inventory accounts showed these beginning and ending balances:

	SEPTEMBER 1	SEPTEMBER 30
Finished goods	$15,000	$17,500
Work in process	9,600	13,000
Materials	7,000	7,400

Other data:

Marketing expenses	$ 14,100
General and administrative expenses	22,900
Sales for the month	182,000

Required: An income statement with schedule showing cost of goods manufactured and sold.

5. Income statement; profit percentage. The Shelikoff Company submits the following information on December 31, 19--:

Sales for the year	$314,000
Inventories at the beginning of the year:	
Finished goods	5,900
Work in process	4,600
Materials	3,800
Purchases of materials for the year	140,000
Direct labor	67,350
Factory overhead: 50% of labor cost	
Inventories at the end of the year:	
Finished goods	9,270
Work in process	6,200
Materials	4,300
Other expenses for the year:	
Marketing expenses	23,115
Administrative expenses	17,650

Required:
(1) An income statement for the year ended December 31, 19--.
(2) The percentage of income to sales, before income tax.

6. Cost of goods sold statement. The following data are provided by the controller of the Metaxen Corporation:

Cash	$240,000
Accounts receivable	348,000

Inventories:

	JANUARY 1	DECEMBER 31
Finished goods	$44,200	$66,000
Work in process	29,800	38,800
Materials	88,000	64,000

Materials purchased	$ 366,000
Sales discount	8,000
Factory overhead (excluding depreciation)	468,400
Marketing and administrative expenses (excluding depreciation)	344,200
Depreciation (90% manufacturing, 10% marketing and administrative expenses)	116,000
Sales	1,844,000
Direct labor	523,600
Freight on materials purchased	6,600
Rental income	64,000
Interest on bonds payable	16,000

Required: Cost of goods sold statement.

(CGAA adapted)

7. Cost of goods sold statement. The following data relate to the Brockway Corporation:

	INVENTORIES	
	Ending	Beginning
Finished goods	$95,000	$110,000
Work in process	80,000	70,000
Direct materials	95,000	90,000

Costs incurred during the period:

Costs of goods available for sale	$684,000
Total manufacturing cost	584,000
Factory overhead	167,000
Direct materials used	193,000

Required: Cost of goods sold statement.

(AICPA adapted)

8. Cost of goods sold statement; unit cost. The records of Reinecke, Inc., show the following information as of March 31, 19B:

Materials used	$440,000
Direct labor	290,000
Indirect labor	46,000
Light and power	4,260
Depreciation	4,700
Repairs to machinery	5,800
Miscellaneous factory overhead	29,000
Work in process inventory, April 1, 19A	41,200
Finished goods inventory, April 1, 19A	34,300
Work in process inventory, March 31, 19B	42,500
Finished goods inventory, March 31, 19B	31,500

During the year, 18,000 units were completed.

Required:
(1) A cost of goods sold statement for the year ended March 31, 19B.
(2) The unit cost of goods manufactured.
(3) The amount of over- or underapplied factory overhead if the company applies factory overhead on the basis of 30% of direct labor cost.

9. Unit cost; inventory valuation; cost of goods sold. The cost department of the White Corporation prepared the following data and costs for the year 19--:

Inventories:

	JANUARY 1	DECEMBER 31
Finished goods..	$48,600	?
Work in process	81,500	$ 42,350
Materials	34,200	49,300
Depreciation — factory equipment		21,350
Interest earned		6,300

Finished goods inventory: January 1: 300 units; December 31: 420 units, all
   from current year's production.
Sold during 19--: 3,880 units at $220 per unit.

Materials purchased	$364,000
Direct labor..	162,500
Indirect labor...	83,400
Freight in	8,600
Miscellaneous factory overhead	47,900
Purchases discount	5,200

Required:
  (1) The unit cost of the finished goods inventory, December 31.
  (2) The total cost of the finished goods inventory, December 31.
  (3) The cost of goods sold.
  (4) The gross profit total and the gross profit per unit.

10. Rate of return on capital employed. During the past year, a company had net income,
$40,000; sales, $200,000, and total capital employed, $400,000.

Required: Rate of return on capital employed.

11. Income statement. In an accounting conference, discussion turned to the possibility of preparing financial statements from a few key accounts, together with financial or cost ratios.
    The assistant controller of a participating firm provided the following data: pretax income for
the year, $1,200,000; pretax income rate on sales, 10%; gross profit rate, 40%; rate of marketing
expenses to sales, 15%; 5% bonds payable represent 37.5% of the total liabilities of $2,000,000.

Required: An income statement for the year based on the above information.

12. Income statement; cost and profit ratios. The records of the Yukon Refrigerator Company
show the following information for the three months ended March 31, 19--:

Materials purchased	$1,946,700
Inventories, January 1, 19--:	
Finished goods (100 refrigerators)	43,000
Materials	268,000
Direct labor..	2,125,800
Factory overhead (40% variable)..	764,000
Marketing expenses (all fixed)..	516,000
General and administrative expenses (all fixed)..........................	461,000
Sales (12,400 refrigerators)..	6,634,000

Inventories, March 31, 19--:
  No unfinished work on hand.
  Finished goods (200 refrigerators), costed at $395 each.

Materials	167,000

Required:
  (1) An income statement for the period.
  (2) The number of units manufactured.
  (3) The unit cost of refrigerators manufactured.
  (4) The gross profit per unit sold.
  (5) The income per unit sold.
  (6) The ratio of gross profit to sales.
  (7) The income to sales percentage.
  (8) The break-even point in sales dollars.

Round off all amounts to three decimal places.

2-1. Manufacturing costs. The payroll records of the Weber Company show payments for labor of $400,000, of which $80,000 is indirect labor. Materials requisitions show $300,000 for materials used, of which $280,000 represents direct materials. Other manufacturing expenses total $124,000. Finished goods on hand at the end of the period are stated at cost, $176,000, of which $40,000 is direct materials cost. Factory overhead is allocated on the basis of direct labor cost.

Required: The amount of direct labor and the amount of factory overhead in Finished Goods.

2-2. Manufacturing costs. The Klaassen Company reports the following data for September:

	PRODUCT A	PRODUCT B
Production	10,000 units	8,000 units
Per unit production costs applicable to beginning inventories and September production:		
Direct materials	$ 4	$ 3
Direct labor	10	20
Applied factory overhead..	7	14
	$21	$37
Sales price per unit	$30	$50
Beginning inventories...	1,000 units	900 units
Ending inventories	2,000	100

Actual factory overhead was $180,000; factory overhead is applied at a rate of $.70 per direct labor dollar. Over- or underapplied factory overhead is closed to the cost of goods sold account. Marketing and administrative expenses were $100,900.

Required:
(1) Over- or underapplied factory overhead.
(2) Cost of goods manufactured.
(3) Cost of goods sold.
(4) Operating income.

2-3. Income statement. Morimatsu, Inc., produces a household appliance that sells for $90. The basic patent is held by the inventor, who is paid a royalty of $5 on each unit sold. The royalty is considered a marketing expense.

The data taken from the books and other records of the company on December 31, 19--, are shown below and on the following page:

Inventories:

	JANUARY 1	DECEMBER 31
Finished goods...	$4,584	$ 7,518
Work in process	8,159	4,002
Materials	3,420	7,130

Sales..	$387,000
Materials purchased	90,563
Freight in	477
Direct labor..	62,522
Indirect labor...	5,026
Depreciation — factory equipment	2,135
Miscellaneous factory overhead	17,908
Rent..	5,000
Sales salaries..	28,000
Royalties paid...	21,500
Freight out..	1,860
Miscellaneous marketing expenses	11,380
Office salaries..	24,790

Uncollectible accounts expense	$ 280
Miscellaneous administrative expenses	8,700
Interest earned	130
Purchases discount	840

There were 120 units in the inventory of finished goods on January 1 and 179 in the inventory on December 31. All units held on January 1 were sold during the year. Rent is to be apportioned 80% to manufacturing, 10% to marketing, and 10% to administration.

Required:
(1) An income statement for the year ended December 31, 19--, supported by a schedule of cost of goods sold.
(2) Figures to prove the cost of the inventory of finished goods on December 31, 19--.

2-4. Income statement; cost of goods sold statement; factory overhead analysis. On October 1, 19--, the accountant of the Melbourne Company prepared a trial balance from which these accounts were extracted:

Finished Goods (2,800 units)	$ 9,800	
Work in Process (1,200 units)	4,070	
Materials and Supplies	40,700	
Buildings	48,000	
Accumulated Depreciation — Buildings		$ 6,000
Machinery and Equipment	96,000	
Accumulated Depreciation — Machinery and Equipment		37,500
Office Equipment	3,200	
Accumulated Depreciation — Office Equipment		1,000
Accrued Payroll		650

The following transactions and other data have been made available for October:

Purchased materials and supplies	$ 24,800
Paid factory overhead	20,100
Paid marketing expenses	25,050
Paid administrative expenses	19,700
Requisitions for:	
Direct materials	29,800
Indirect materials	3,950
Depreciation:	
Building, 5% (75% to manufacturing, 15% to marketing, and 10% to administrative expenses)	
Machinery and equipment, 10%	
Office equipment, 15% (40% to marketing and 60% to administrative expenses)	
Sales on account (20,700 units)	144,900
Sales returns and allowances	1,300
Cash payments for:	
Accounts payable	75,000
Payroll	21,800
Distribution of payroll earned:	
Direct labor	18,600
Indirect labor	4,400
Cash collected from customers	116,900
Applied factory overhead	27,450

Units transferred to finished goods, 20,400.
Cost of goods sold figure is calculated on the fifo basis.
Work in process inventory on October 31, 19--, $4,440.

Required:
(1) The cost of goods sold section of the income statement in detail, assuming that over- or underapplied factory overhead is deferred until the end of the fiscal period.
(2) The income statement for October.
(3) The amount of over- or underapplied factory overhead.

2-5. Profit planning via income statement. The controller of Prescott Products, Inc., presented the following income statement for the year ending June 30, 19A, to the board of directors:

Sales		$12,000,000
Cost of goods sold:		
Direct materials	$3,800,000	
Direct labor	2,900,000	
Factory overhead	2,450,000	9,150,000
Gross profit		$ 2,850,000
Commercial expenses:		
Marketing expenses	$1,350,000	
Administrative expenses	1,000,000	2,350,000
Operating income		$ 500,000

The board discussed the ratio of operating income to sales and decided that for the year ending June 30, 19B, an increase of at least 25% of the present profit was desirable. While the sales volume is expected to increase about 20%, all costs and expenses point to considerable increases in costs; e.g., direct materials, 8%; direct labor, 10%; factory overhead, 3%; marketing expenses, 4%; and administrative expenses, 2%. The 3% increase in factory overhead applies to the variable factory overhead only. Fixed factory overhead is considered to remain at the present level of $1,250,000. Volume will not cause an increase in marketing and administrative expenses. Ignore income tax.

Required:
(1) A forecast income statement for the year ending June 30, 19B, incorporating all cost increases as well as management's goal for a higher operating income.
(2) The change from the previous year in the percentage of operating income to sales.

2-6. Ratio and break-even analyses. The condensed financial statements of the Buffalo Bill Company for the year ended December 31, 19––, appeared as:

Buffalo Bill Company
Condensed Balance Sheet
December 31, 19––

Assets		Liabilities and Capital	
Cash	$ 750,000	Accounts and notes payable	$1,494,000
Receivables	3,508,000	Accruals payable	368,000
Inventories	2,217,000	Common stock	4,387,000
Plant and equipment	1,353,000	Retained earnings	1,579,000
	$7,828,000		$7,828,000

Condensed Income Statement
For Year Ended December 31, 19––

Sales	$6,491,000
Cost of goods sold	4,676,000
Gross profit	$1,815,000
Marketing and administrative expenses	804,000
Operating income	$1,011,000

Required:
(1) The current ratio.
(2) The acid-test ratio.
(3) The operating income as a percentage of sales.
(4) The rate of return on capital employed.
(5) The break-even point in dollars if 75% of the cost of goods sold figure consists of variable costs, and 80% of the marketing and administrative expenses consists of fixed costs.

2-7. Balance sheet; income statement. On December 31, 19A, the Sea Isle Canning Company with outstanding common stock of $30,000 had the following assets and liabilities:

Cash	$ 5,000
Accounts receivable	10,000
Finished goods	6,000
Work in process	2,000
Materials	4,000
Prepaid expenses	500
Property, plant, and equipment (net)	30,000
Current liabilities	17,500

During 19B, the retained earnings account increased 50% as a result of the year's business. No dividends were paid during the year. Balances of accounts receivable, prepaid expenses, current liabilities, and common stock were the same on December 31, 19B, as they had been on December 31, 19A. Inventories were reduced by exactly 50%, except for the finished goods inventory, which was reduced by 33⅓%. Plant assets (net) were reduced by depreciation of $4,000, charged ¾ to factory overhead and ¼ to administrative expenses. Sales of $60,000 were made on account of finished goods costing $38,000. Direct labor cost was $9,000. Factory overhead was applied at a rate of 100% of direct labor cost, leaving $2,000 underapplied that was closed into the cost of goods sold account. Total marketing and administrative expenses amounted to 10% and 15%, respectively, of the gross sales.

Required:
(1) A balance sheet as of December 31, 19B.
(2) An income statement for the year 19B, with details of the cost of goods manufactured and sold.

(AICPA adapted)

3

Costs
Concepts, Uses, and Classifications

Cost accounting measures cost in accordance with the plans and needs of management. Costs must be based on relevant facts, competently observed and significantly measured to enable management to make valid decisions. A diagnosis of this requirement reveals a wide diversity in the use of terms and concepts employed in cost computations resulting from a variety of causes. Costs may have to be computed under different conditions, for different purposes, by different people. Cost accounting is a means to an end, not an end in itself.

THE CONCEPT "COST"

Accountants, economists, engineers, and others facing cost problems have developed cost concepts and cost terminology according to their needs. Basically, a concept should be stated in the terms in which it has become generally familiar. It is not easy to define or explain the term "cost," leaving no doubt concerning its meaning. The Committee on Cost Concepts and Standards of the American Accounting Association wrote: "Cost is a forgoing, measured in monetary terms, incurred or potentially to be incurred to achieve a specific objective."[1] In "A Tentative Set of Broad Accounting Principles for Business Enterprises," cost is defined as "an exchange price, a forgoing, a sacrifice made to secure benefit. In financial accounting, the forgoing or sacrifice at date of acquisition is represented by a current or future diminution in cash or other assets."[2] This same AICPA study considers expense to be:

[1] Report of the Committee on Cost Concepts and Standards, *The Accounting Review*, Vol. XXVII, No. 2, p. 176.
[2] Robert T. Sprouse and Maurice Moonitz, *Accounting Research Study No. 3*, "A Tentative Set of Broad Accounting Principles for Business Enterprises" (New York: American Institute of Certified Public Accountants, 1962), p. 25.

. . . the decrease in net assets as a result of the use of economic services in the creation of revenues or of the imposition of taxes by governmental units. Expense is measured by the amount of the decrease in assets or the increase in liabilities related to the production and delivery of goods and the rendering of services. . . .*Expense* in its broadest sense includes all expired costs which are deductible from revenues. In income statements, distinctions are often made between various types of expired costs by captions or titles including such terms as cost, expense, or loss, e.g., cost of goods or services sold, operating expenses, selling and administrative expenses, and loss on sale of property.[3]

Frequently the term "cost" is used synonymously with the term "expense" and means an expired cost. Yet the term "cost" is used for both assets and expenses. The term "expense" refers to the sacrifice, the renouncing aspect of the revenue transaction. Expenses are the measured outflow of goods and services that are matched with revenue to determine income.

When the term "cost" is used specifically, it should be modified with reference to the object costed, using such descriptions as direct, prime, conversion, indirect, fixed, variable, controllable, product, period, joint, estimated, standard, future, replacement, opportunity, imputed, sunk, differential, and out-of-pocket. Each modification implies a certain attribute which is important in computing and measuring the cost which is to serve the management levels in achieving their basic objectives of planning and control.

These modifications or cost attributes are, as the text will show, applicable to many objectives. A definition of each will not be offered at this point but will be found at the appropriate place within the textbook. Many of these cost attributes are used in connection with the accumulation of cost data necessary for the assignment of costs to inventories, the preparation of general financial statements, and the planning and control of costs by the various levels of management. In most cases they find their way into the books and records and as such constitute typical cost attributes. However, for planning, analytical, and decision-making purposes, the accountant often must abandon "book" costs and deal with future, imputed, differential, or opportunity costs, which must be based on other than the recorded past costs. It is a fundamental axiom that a cost must be understood in its relationship to the aims or purposes which it is to serve. A request for cost data must be accompanied by a description of the situation in which the data are to be used, for the same cost data cannot serve all purposes equally well.

USES OF COST DATA

The collection, presentation, and analysis of cost data should serve the following essential uses or aims:

1. Planning profit by means of budgets.
2. Controlling costs via responsibility accounting.

---

[3]*Ibid.*, p. 49.

3. Measuring annual or periodic profit, including inventory costing.
4. Assisting in establishing selling prices and a pricing policy.
5. Furnishing relevant cost data for analytical processes for decision making.

The planning phase deals with the future — the next year or years — of **Planning** the company. Cost accounting provides or budgets the contemplated materi- **Profit by** als costs, wages and salaries, and other costs of producing and marketing the **Means of** products. Management is concerned with the ultimate profit arising from these **Budgets** costs and planned revenue or sales. *Budgeting* is the forecast of the effects on profits of varying volumes of activity. Budgeted materials costs and quantities and labor costs and predetermined quantities of time required to manufacture each product are basic for these cost elements. These costs plus all factory overhead and nonmanufacturing costs that fluctuate with activity must be determined first in order to establish the profit base for budgeted sales. Some operating costs vary directly in relationship to volume; other costs and expense items are either wholly or partially fixed in character. The final budget should represent a conservative operating forecast, including all these costs. If the contemplated volume seems attainable and management decides to operate on such a cost-volume-profit relationship, it becomes imperative for all levels of management to strive to control their costs accordingly.

To control costs, these fundamentals should be observed: (1) fixing re- **Controlling** sponsibility for control, (2) limiting the individual's control effort to controll- **Costs via** able costs, and (3) reporting the performance of the individual. **Responsibility**

Fixing responsibility for the control of costs requires the establishment of **Accounting** definite lines of authority. The organization chart presents the organizational structure and, following these lines of authority, allows the assignment of cost control responsibility to specific individuals. These individuals should also have had a hand in determining the planned or budgeted costs under their control. Not only costs but also sales revenue and profits are made the responsibility of certain managers. Cost and revenue responsibility becomes profit responsibility.

Limiting the individual's control effort to controllable costs is a necessary aspect of responsibility accounting. Any report should specifically identify the manager's controllable costs. Of course, each cost should be someone's responsibility. This responsibility phase often becomes lost in a maze of cost classifications as shown later in the chapter.

The reporting and measuring phase has already been mentioned. It is important that each individual's budget be considered an integral part of the overall company budget. The greater each supervisor's effort and success in controlling the costs for which each is responsible, the greater the chance for the entire company to reach the planned profit goal.

The control of costs requires a basis for comparison. Budgeted costs constitute one basic foundation for comparison; standards or predetermined costs and expenses provide the cornerstone for cost control procedures. A comparison of actual or experienced costs and expenses with these standards reveals an out-of-line performance. These exceptions form the basis for an investigation into the reasons, hopefully resulting in remedy and correction.

Measuring Annual or Periodic Profit, Including Inventory Costing

The measuring of an annual or periodic profit for the entire enterprise involves the matching of expired costs with revenue on some consistent basis. This matching process requires distinguishing between short-run and long-run costs. The longer the period, the greater the accuracy of the matching process. A company's financial statements reflect the results of separating the costs applicable to the units sold from the costs applicable to the units in inventories. This separation procedure has always been a distinctive feature of cost accounting. The costs reported thereby are *historical* or past costs. Short-run, interim, or periodic detailed reports are especially useful for purposes of internal control and for the solution of particular managerial problems.

Variable manufacturing costs are assigned first to the units manufactured and then matched with the units sold; variable nonmanufacturing costs typically are matched initially with the units sold. Fixed (capacity) costs require an arbitrary allocation to the units and consequently lead to the possibility of three alternative matching processes:[4]

1. To match fixed (capacity) costs assigned to each period in total with revenue of that period (direct costing).
2. To match manufacturing fixed (capacity) costs on a product unit basis and to match all other fixed costs in total each period (absorption costing, the generally accepted method).
3. To match all fixed (capacity) costs, manufacturing as well as nonmanufacturing, on a long-run sales unit basis.

Over a long enough period, these methods give the same result but yield a different profit for individual short periods when cost-incurring activities are out of phase with revenue. Because all methods are arbitrary to some extent, no one method gives consistently useful results under all conditions. Different circumstances may call for different methods.[5]

Assisting in Establishing Selling Prices and a Pricing Policy

The establishment of a profitable sales price workable over a period of time requires the combined knowledge of costs and their volume. In the planning phase, a knowledge of future costs and allowances for fluctuating production and sales might permit management to agree on a pricing policy that assures not only the recovery of all costs but also the securing of a profit even under adverse conditions. Supply and demand are still considered the corner-

---

[4]Walter B. McFarland, *Concepts for Management Accounting* (New York: National Association of Accountants, 1966), p. 134.
[5]*Ibid.*, pp. 134–135.

stones for pricing. However, costs and their proper application to the company's pricing efforts must never be forgotten.

Managerial planning as evidenced by long-range budgeting involves business strategies covering one or more years. To implement long-range strategy, management must make tactical changes and decisions involving a choice of alternative courses of action. Different costs and different revenues may have to be determined and presented by the accountant. Changes in production methods, making or buying a component part, replacing equipment, substituting materials, accepting or rejecting a price or an order — each situation calls for new expected actual costs and a new set of revenues related to these specific situations.

Furnishing Relevant Cost Data for Analytical Processes for Decision Making

COST DATA: IMPORTANCE OF PAST, PRESENT, FUTURE

Measuring annual or periodic profit, including inventory costing, pertains mainly to events of the past. Cost control relates to the present. Planning, pricing, and analyzing data for decision making are future-oriented. These time-frame-oriented views of cost data intertwine; e.g., (1) inferences may be drawn from the past as plans and decisions are made about the future and (2) cost control should be designed to monitor the accomplishments of plans.

Ranking these time-frame categories as to their relative importance would certainly place the organization's future as most important, followed by what is presently occurring, and lastly, by what has happened in the past. This ranking does not mean that data about the past are unimportant or that they should be neglected, because past data may aid in present cost control and in future decision making. Past performance must be reported to internal management as well as to external groups such as stockholders, creditors, the Internal Revenue Service, and the general public. The point is not that past performance is unimportant but rather that the cost accounting information system often does little more than account for the past without being adequately designed and utilized to focus on the present and future time frames.

Optimum attention to the past, present, and future at a reasonable cost should be the primary objective of the cost data provided by the information system.

CLASSIFICATIONS OF COSTS

Cost classifications are needed for the development of cost data that are useful to management with regard to the five purposes or aims described on pages 40–43. Therefore, costs are classified:

1. By the nature of the item (a natural classification).
2. With respect to the accounting period to which they apply.

3. By their tendency to vary with volume or activity.
4. By their relation to the product.
5. By their relation to manufacturing departments.
6. According to their nature as common and/or joint costs.
7. For planning and control.
8. For analytical processes.

Natural Classification of Costs

The process of classifying costs and expenses can begin with *total cost*, which may be considered as all costs or deductions from sales revenue before income tax. In a manufacturing concern, total operating cost is divided into (1) manufacturing cost and (2) commercial expenses.

Manufacturing cost, often named *production cost* or *factory cost*, is the sum of three cost elements: direct materials, direct labor, and factory overhead. During the accounting period, that part of manufacturing cost which represents work completed is transferred to Finished Goods, while incomplete work remains in Work in Process.

Commercial expenses also fall into two large classifications: (1) marketing (distribution or selling) expenses and (2) administrative (general and administrative) expenses. Marketing expenses begin at the point where the factory costs end; that is, when manufacturing has been completed and the product is in salable condition. *Marketing expenses* cover the expenses of making sales and delivering products. *Administrative expenses* include expenses incurred in the direction, control, and administration of the organization. Some of these items, such as executive salaries, are often allocated to manufacturing and marketing and included in factory and marketing cost. The sum of the expired factory cost and commercial expenses is the cost to make and sell.

This basic classification of costs must be expanded into numerous subclasses, groups, or divisions. The chart on the following page illustrates the further division of the total operating cost and individual cost elements.

Costs with Respect to the Accounting Period to Which They Apply

Expenditures can be divided into two broad classes: (1) capital expenditures and (2) revenue expenditures. A *capital expenditure* is intended to benefit future periods and is classified as an asset; a *revenue expenditure* benefits the current period and is termed an expense. An expenditure classified originally as an asset will ultimately flow into the expense stream when the asset is either consumed or charged off.

The distinction between capital and revenue expenditures is essential to the proper matching of costs and revenue and to the accurate measurement of periodic income. While the distinction between a capital or revenue expenditure is generally observed, a precise interpretation and application is not always feasible or practical. The initial classification depends in many cases upon (1) the attitude and action taken by the management toward these expenditures and (2) the character of the company's operations. Management's decision on classification is often influenced by the ease and accuracy with which costs may be allocated among products, departments, territories, or

ANALYSIS OF TOTAL OPERATING COST

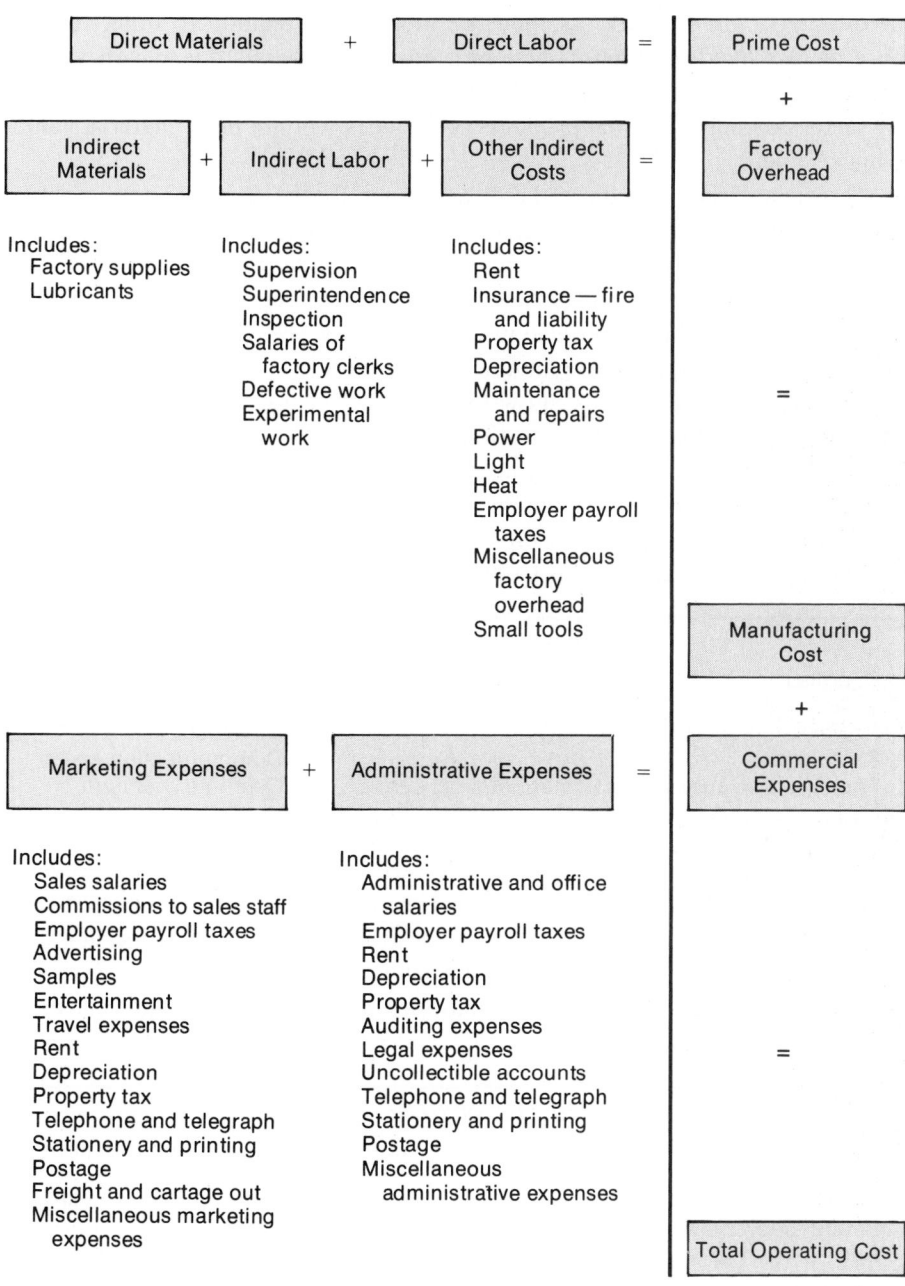

any other desirable division. The amount of the expenditure and the number of detailed records and underlying documents required are also factors that determine the distinction between these two basic classes of costs. Whatever classification is decided upon can and does affect the computed unit costs and reported profit figures of a fiscal period.

**Costs in
Their
Tendency
to Vary with
Volume or
Activity**

Some costs vary directly in relation to changes in the volume of output (production), while others, as they are incurred in relation to time, remain more or less fixed in amount. Unless a cost system pays due regard to this distinction, costs accumulated and reported for planning the company's strategy or for costing individual products or services will not be of material value to management.

Direct materials and direct labor are generally listed among the variable costs. Factory overhead and nonmanufacturing costs, however, must be examined with regard to items of a variable and fixed nature. It is impossible to budget and control these costs successfully without regard to their tendency to be fixed or variable; the division is a necessary prerequisite to successful budgeting and intelligent cost planning and analysis.

In general, *variable costs* show the following characteristics: (1) variability of total amount in direct proportion to volume, (2) comparatively constant cost per unit in the face of changing volume within a relevant range, (3) easy and reasonably accurate assignments to operating departments, and (4) control of their incurrence and consumption by the responsible department head. The following costs fall into this category:

VARIABLE FACTORY OVERHEAD	
Supplies	Receiving costs
Fuel	Hauling within plant
Power	Royalties
Small tools	Communication costs
Spoilage, salvage, and reclamation expenses	Overtime premium

The characteristics of *fixed costs* are: (1) fixed amount within a relevant output range, (2) decrease of fixed cost per unit with increased output, (3) assignment to departments often made by arbitrary managerial decisions or cost allocation methods, and (4) control for incurrence resting in most cases with executive management rather than operating supervisors. The following are examples of fixed costs:

FIXED FACTORY OVERHEAD	
Salaries of production executives	Wages of security guards, janitors, and fire fighters
Depreciation	
Property tax	Maintenance and repairs of buildings and grounds
Patent amortization	
Rent	Insurance — property and liability

Whether or not a cost is classified as fixed or variable may well be the result of management decision. For example, management may decide to (1) rent a truck at a rate per mile (a variable cost) or (2) buy a truck and depreciate it by the straight-line method (a fixed cost).

Some factory overhead items are *semivariable* in nature, containing both fixed and variable elements. A semivariable expense is often characterized by a fixed dollar element below which it will not fall, at all relevant levels of output. The variable element, as defined above, changes at a constant amount per unit of output within a relevant range. Electricity cost, for example, may be used to furnish both lighting for the plant as well as power to operate the equipment. The electricity used for lighting tends to be a fixed cost because, if the plant is in use, the building will be lighted regardless of the level of output. Conversely, electricity used to operate the equipment will vary depending on how much use is made of the equipment.

The following items generally contain both fixed and variable elements:

SEMIVARIABLE FACTORY OVERHEAD

Supervision	Maintenance and repairs of machinery and equipment
Inspection	
Payroll department services	Compensation insurance
Personnel department services	Health and accident insurance
Factory office services	Payroll taxes
Materials and inventory services	Industrial relations and employees' welfare expenses
Cost department services	
	Heat, light, and power

For practical purposes it is desirable to classify all manufacturing and nonmanufacturing costs as fixed and variable costs. Semivariable expenses must therefore be divided into their fixed and variable elements. Methods to accomplish this are discussed in Chapter 18.

Costs in Their Relation to the Product

The elements of manufacturing costs are direct materials, direct labor, and factory overhead. Direct materials and direct labor are combined into another classification called *prime cost*. Direct labor and factory overhead can be combined into a classification called *conversion cost*, representing the costs of converting direct materials into finished products.

Direct materials are all materials that form an integral part of the finished product and that can be included directly in calculating the cost of the product, such as the lumber to make furniture, the steel to make automobile bodies, and the crude oil to make gasoline. The ease and feasibility with which the materials items can be traced to the final product are major considerations in their designation as direct materials. Glue and tacks to build furniture form part of the finished product, but for costing purposes such items may be classified as indirect materials for expediency.

Direct labor is labor applied directly to the materials comprising the finished product. The cost of wages paid to skilled or unskilled workers and assignable to the particular unit produced is termed direct labor.

Factory overhead — also called *manufacturing overhead*, *manufacturing expenses*, or *factory burden* — may be defined as the cost of indirect materials, indirect labor, and all other manufacturing costs that cannot conveniently be charged to specific units, jobs, or products. Simply stated, factory overhead includes all manufacturing costs except direct materials and direct labor.

Indirect materials are those needed for the completion of the product but whose consumption with regard to the product is either so small or so complex that it would be futile to treat them as direct materials. Glue, thread, nails, tacks, rivets, and other such items usually belong in this category. *Factory supplies*, a form of indirect materials, consist of items such as lubricating oils, grease, cleaning rags, and brushes needed to maintain the working area and machinery in workable and safe condition.

Indirect labor may be defined, in contrast to direct labor, as that labor which does not directly affect the construction or the composition of the finished product. The term includes the labor cost of supervisors, shop clerks, general helpers, cleaners, and those employees engaged in maintenance work or other service work not directly related to physical production.

Costs in Their Relation to Manufacturing Departments

A factory is generally organized along departmental lines for production purposes. This factory departmentalization is the basis for the important classification and subsequent accumulation of costs by departments to achieve (1) cost budgeting with responsibility accounting and control and (2) a greater degree of reliable costing.

Producing and Service Departments. The departments of a factory generally fall into two categories: (1) producing departments and (2) service departments.

A *producing department* is one in which manual and machine operations are performed directly upon any part of the product manufactured. More specifically, producing departments are those whose costs may be charged to the product because they have contributed directly to its production, such as the machining, forming, upholstering, or assembling departments.

In many cases, producing departments are further subdivided into *cost centers*, or *cost pools*. Where two or more different types of machines perform operations on a product within the same department, a breakdown into cost centers increases the accuracy of product costs. For example, in the manufacture of cotton yarn and cloth, the producing department "Carding" can be broken up into the cost centers: opening cotton bales, picking, carding, drawing, and slubbing.

A *service department* is one that is not directly engaged in production but renders a particular type of service for the benefit of other departments. In some instances these services benefit other service departments as well as the producing departments. The cost incurred in the operation of service departments represents a part of the total factory overhead and must be absorbed in the cost of the product by means of the factory overhead rate. Some service departments common to many industrial concerns are receiving, inspection, storeroom, maintenance, timekeeping, payroll, cost accounting, budgeting, data processing, general office, cafeteria, and plant protection.

Departmentalization for Product Costing and Responsibility Accounting. The organization chart divides a business into departments, segments, or functions. Although the division is often made primarily for administrative purposes, departmentalization or segmentation is significant and important for (1) the costing of a product and (2) the control of costs by means of departmental budgets.

For product costing, the factory may be divided into departments, and departments may be further subdivided into cost centers. As a product passes through a department or cost center, it is charged with direct materials, direct labor, and a share of factory overhead on the basis of a departmental factory overhead rate.

For cost control, budgets are established for departments and cost centers with the active participation of operating management in order to achieve a sense of commitment on the manager's part. Managers should be made to feel responsible for the control of those costs they helped to develop. The crux of the matter rests in controllability. A departmental budget should clearly identify those costs about which the manager can make decisions. This identification of costs by areas of responsibility and therewith of their controllability depends on the time frame and the level in the organization, i.e., the degree of segmentation reported. All costs should be controllable at some level of management over some time frame; no cost can remain in a noncontrollable category. The comparison of actual costs with budget allowances at the end of a weekly, monthly, or annual reporting period permits evaluation and judgment regarding the efficiency of a department or cost center and measures the manager's success in controlling the expenses for which responsibility has been accepted.

Direct and Indirect Departmental Charges. In connection with the charging of expenses to departments, it is important that the term "direct" as applied to factory overhead be clearly understood. In the preceding discussion of production costs, the terms direct materials and direct labor were introduced. The word "direct," in that discussion, referred to costs which were chargeable directly to the product produced and which, therefore, needed no further allocation.

Factory overhead is considered indirect with regard to a product or job. However, as actual factory overhead expenses are incurred and charged to either a producing or a service department, the expense is referred to as a *direct* departmental charge if it is readily identifiable with the originating department. Expenses such as rent and depreciation of a building may be shared by several departments; they are described as *indirect* or *common costs* because they must be prorated to benefiting departments. The same notion of direct and indirect charges is equally applicable to nonmanufacturing activities and organizations.

Service department expenses are prorated to producing departments and/or service departments. These prorated costs are also termed *indirect departmental charges.* When all service department expenses have been prorated to the producing departments, each producing department's overhead will consist of its own direct and indirect departmental expense and the prorated or apportioned charges from service departments to form the total factory overhead for the department. This total actual cost is then compared with the amount charged to production on the basis of each producing department's predetermined factory overhead rate.

Care must be taken to avoid charging indirect costs as direct costs to a department, product, or job while at the same time allocating them via the overhead rate. This procedure is referred to as *double counting.* For example, double counting is charging product inspection costs directly to a producing department, yet, at the same time, allocating inspection costs in the charging rate of a factory overhead service department to all producing departments. In 1972, the Cost Accounting Standards Board (CASB) issued Standard No. 402, "Consistency in Allocating Costs Incurred for the Same Purpose," which deals with this problem in accounting for governmental contracts to which CASB regulations apply.

Departmentalization of a factory is of even greater importance in connection with budgeting and control of costs. Factory overhead is charged to the product on the basis of a predetermined departmental overhead rate based on budgeted or estimated costs and planned production. During the year, it becomes quite necessary for all individuals to make every effort to keep costs within the predetermined budget level. Department heads are made responsible and accountable for the actual controllable costs incurred in their departments. Direct materials and direct labor may also be departmentalized. Cost responsibility is assigned to operating managers in accordance with the authority delegated to them. Keeping actual costs in line with budgeted costs aids in attaining the organization's profit objective.

Common and/or Joint Costs

Considerable confusion exists with regard to the correct usage of these two cost classifications. *Common costs* are costs of facilities or services employed in two or more accounting periods, operations, commodities, or services. For example, a capital expenditure, intended to benefit future periods, is classified as an asset. Subsequently, the cost of the asset flows into the expense stream as the asset is consumed or charged off. Since the asset benefits several accounting periods, the cost must arbitrarily be allocated or shared among the periods. Depreciation of a building is a good example.

Common costs are particularly prevalent in organizations with many departments or segments. The degree of segmentation increases the tendency of costs to be common costs. For example, the salary of the marketing vice-president is direct, or not commonly shared, as long as the segment is the entire marketing function; when the marketing function becomes segmented by regions, the vice-president's salary becomes a common cost to the various regions.

Joint costs occur when the production of one product may be possible only if one or more other products are manufactured at the same time. The meat-packing industry, the oil and gas industry, the liquor industry, and refineries are excellent examples of industries in which joint costs are significant. Joint costs can only be allocated to joint products by an arbitrary procedure that is often based on a cost-causing characteristic. Care must be taken to recognize the resulting restriction on the use of such data. Erroneous analyses and decisions may result therefrom. The problem of joint cost allocation is particularly difficult in connection with product-line or segment reporting.

A company's cost information system provides the data required for the preparation and operation of a budget and for establishing standard costs.

Costs for Planning and Control

Budgets. In many companies, predetermining or estimating factory overhead constitutes the initial step toward a budget program. When all phases of a business — sales, engineering, manufacturing, marketing, and administration — have been coordinated into a well-thought-out budget program, the budget becomes the written expression of management's plan for the future. The budget program enlists all members of management in the task of creating a workable and acceptable plan of action, welds the plan into a homogeneous unit, communicates to all managerial levels differences between planned activity and actual performance, and points out unfavorable conditions which need corrective actions. No person intimately connected with the affairs of a company in which budgeting is used can be unaffected or disinterested. The budget will not only help promote coordination of people, clarification of policy, and crystallization of plans, but with successful use will create greater internal harmony and unanimity of purpose among managers and workers.

Standard Costs. Closely allied with the budget are *standard costs*, which are predetermined costs for direct materials, direct labor, and factory overhead. They are established by using information accumulated from past experience and data secured from research studies. The established standard costs for materials, labor, and factory overhead form the foundation for the budget. Since standard costs are an invaluable aid in the process of setting prices, it is essential to set these standard costs at realistic levels.

A standard states the costs under given conditions which are held constant in order to observe and measure fluctuations. The measurement of deviations from established standards or norms is accomplished with the aid of *variance* accounts. These deviation measurements are similar to budget comparisons in that they compare actual with predetermined data. The deviation measurements and budget comparisons are also alike in that both relate to the idea of responsibility accounting. It should be noted, however, that standards with their variance analyses go beyond the mere comparative level.

Standard costs constitute a basic accounting tool which aids in the solution of managerial problems. The accounting measurement of variances provides management with necessary information; and to be complete, standard costs' service to management should include systematic, day-by-day reports relaying deviation information which requires the attention of management.

Costs for Analytical Processes

Costs as a basis for analysis are estimated costs which may be incurred if any one of several alternative courses of action is adopted. Different types of costs involve varying kinds of considerations in managerial analysis for decision making. For example, *differential* and *out-of-pocket* costs are types of costs which attempt to envision and evaluate future conditions in the light of the current situation. When management is faced with the problem of abandoning one product and substituting another, the decision will demand the consideration of *opportunity* costs. If expansion of operating facilities is contemplated, the *relevant* costs are future costs to be incurred. Should a project be abandoned or capital costs never fully recovered through revenues, the company's management will face a cost situation that is termed a *sunk* cost. The measure of a sunk cost is the difference between book value at any time and the disposal value of the facilities.

While these isolated illustrations stress the managerial aspect of accounting, it must be realized that, in the final analysis, all accounting is management accounting. For a long time, the major reporting emphasis was on the balance sheet, but more and more importance has been placed on the income statement. The rapid rise and growth of business units into large-scale enterprises caused cost accounting to develop as a separate, yet integral division of the accounting function. Cost accounting should be regarded as the first step in distinguishing a major part of accounting as managerial accounting. It institutes the concepts of cost planning and cost control, both of which are essential to managing successfully the multiple divisions and interests of a modern organization. Cost accounting's importance necessitates the establishment of that type of cost system which best fulfills the needs of management.

FACTORS INFLUENCING RESPONSIBLE COST CONTROL

The statement was made on page 41 of this chapter that the fundamental tenet of responsibility accounting limits the individual's control effort to controllable costs. Analyses have shown that environmental influences have a substantial impact on the performance of departmental tasks. Furthermore, actual costs are often caused by an interdependent relationship between departments or centers. The more complex this relationship, the greater the influence on the performance and the costs incurred by a particular unit. Therefore, as far as responsibility accounting and budgeting are concerned, the question to be addressed is the extent of controllability.

A recent study by David C. Hayes points out that the effectiveness of individual departments may be influenced by (1) internal departmental factors,

(2) interdependency with other departments, and (3) environmental factors (interactions external to the firm). These factors can be viewed as comprising a performance model.

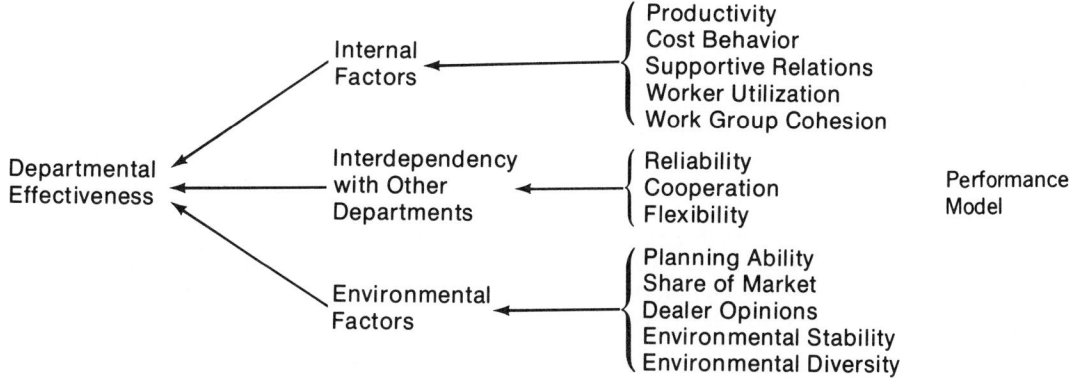

The research study found evidence that manufacturing departments are greatly influenced by internal factors, with interdependency of secondary importance. Research and development departments are influenced by interdependency factors, and marketing departments by environmental variables, with interdependency factors of less importance.[6]

Accounting data can never serve as a surrogate for all factors that influence and measure performance effectiveness. A well-designed accounting system should place emphasis on controllability of cost via responsibility accounting and should be aware of the overall need for relevant cost accounting data. The system should afford a positive influence in enhancing the performance effectiveness of subunits as well as of the entire organization.

COST ACCOUNTING STANDARDS BOARD

While the Securities and Exchange Commission and the Financial Accounting Standards Board have been making headlines for years, the Cost Accounting Standards Board is not well known to the business community. This lack of familiarity is regrettable, since many people in public and private sectors predict that the CASB will have considerable impact on business in general in the years ahead.

Created as an agent of Congress, the Board was established by Public Law 91-379, August 15, 1970, an amendment of Section 719 of the Defense Production Act of 1950, and was formally organized in January, 1971. The Comptroller General of the United States serves as chairperson of the five-member board and appoints the other members, who serve four-year terms.

---

[6]David C. Hayes, "The Contingency Theory of Managerial Accounting," *The Accounting Review*, Vol. LII, No. 1, pp. 22–39.

The purpose of the Board is outlined in parts (g) and (h) of Section 719 and is stated as follows:

> The Board shall from time to time promulgate cost-accounting standards designed to achieve uniformity and consistency in the cost-accounting principles followed by defense contractors and subcontractors under Federal contracts. Such promulgated standards shall be used by all relevant Federal agencies and by defense contractors and subcontractors in estimating, accumulating, and reporting costs in connection with the pricing, administration, and settlement of all negotiated prime contract and subcontract national defense procurements with the United States in excess of $100,000, other than contracts or subcontracts where the price negotiated is based on (1) established catalog or market prices of commercial items sold in substantial quantities to the general public, or (2) prices set by law or regulation. In promulgating such standards . . . the Board shall take into account the probable costs of implementation . . . compared to the probable benefits. . . . Such regulations shall require defense contractors and subcontractors as a condition of contracting to disclose in writing their cost-accounting principles, including methods of distinguishing direct costs from indirect costs and the basis used for allocating indirect costs, and to agree to a contract price adjustment, with interest, for any increased costs paid to the defense contractor by the United States because of the defense contractor's failure to comply with duly promulgated cost-accounting standards or to follow consistently his disclosed cost-accounting practices in pricing contract proposals and in accumulating and reporting contract performance cost data.

The CASB defines a cost accounting standard as a formal statement that (1) enunciates a principle or principles to be followed, (2) establishes practices to be applied, or (3) specifies criteria to be employed in selecting from alternative principles and practices in estimating, accumulating, and reporting costs of contracts subject to the rules of the Board. A cost accounting standard may be stated in terms as general or as specific as the CASB considers necessary to accomplish its purpose.

To achieve increased uniformity and consistency in accounting for costs of negotiated defense contracts, cost accounting standards should provide criteria for the allocation to cost objectives of the cost of resources used. *Cost* in this discussion is the monetary value of the resources used. As defined by the Board, a *cost objective* is "a function, organizational subdivision, contract, or other work unit for which cost data are desired and for which provision is made to accumulate and measure the cost of processes, products, jobs, capitalized projects, etc." Standards deal with all aspects of cost allocability, including:

1. The definition and measurement of costs which may be allocated to cost objectives.
2. The determination of the cost accounting period to which such costs are assignable.
3. The determination of the methods by which costs are to be allocated to cost objectives.

The Board will adhere to the concept of full costing whenever appropriate. Full allocation of all costs of a period, including general administrative expenses and all other indirect costs, is generally considered by the Board to be the basis for determining the cost of negotiated defense contracts.

The CASB's pronouncements thus far have been in general harmony with sound accounting concepts and techniques and with generally accepted accounting principles. Yet, the CASB has not hesitated to tackle controversial issues that many felt would be in the domain of the Financial Accounting Standards Board. Accordingly, the CASB's influence might be all the more significant and far-reaching.

Contractor's Coverage

The Board is directed to promulgate standards that will ensure uniformity and consistency in the cost accounting principles which defense contractors and subcontractors follow in estimating, accumulating, and reporting costs under negotiated contracts. The statute says that only defense contracts are covered by the CASB's standards. Nevertheless, these standards have been adapted as part of the procurement regulations that apply to civilian contracts as well. Although the statute creating the CASB applies to defense contracts, all nondefense agencies have implemented the CASB's standards, rules, and regulations. This means that most negotiated contracts and subcontracts in excess of $100,000 with any governmental agency are subject to cost accounting standards.

On January 1, 1975, an amendment removed from the CASB's coverage smaller contractors and business units with insignificant amounts of government business. Coverage now extends only to business units (segments or profit centers) of a contractor that has received a covered prime or subcontract in excess of $500,000. Once having received such an award, a business unit must comply with applicable standards for all subsequently awarded prime and subcontracts in excess of $100,000 unless otherwise exempt. The CASB's coverage ceases only when all covered contracts in excess of $100,000 are completed by a contractor. Coverage becomes operative again for contracts in excess of $100,000 upon acceptance of an award exceeding $500,000. A firm qualifying as a small business under the regulations of the Small Business Administration (SBA) is exempt from CASB requirements.

In 1978, the Board issued a rule exempting contracts and subcontracts awarded to foreign concerns and governments from most CASB standards. The exemptions are intended to remove impediments to efficient and successful contracting with the foreign groups.

Statement of Disclosure

As a condition of contracting, the CASB can also require contractors to disclose in writing their cost accounting practices. For this purpose, the Board has provided a 42-page Disclosure Statement. The instructions pertaining thereto indicate that a contractor must state the practices of each profit center, division, or similar organizational unit. A *profit center* is defined as "the smallest organizationally independent segment of a company which has been charged by management with profit and loss responsibility."

A detailed presentation of the Disclosure Statement does not seem advisable here; however, it should be noted that the statement requires information regarding the three major elements of direct costs, i.e., direct materials, direct labor, and other direct costs; the methods used to charge-out materials (fifo, lifo, standard costs, or others); the accumulation of variances; the method of charging direct labor (individual/actual rates, average rates, standard cost rates, or others) and a description of the types of variances; the method used to cost interorganizational transfers; and the allocation bases used for charging indirect costs to government contracts or similar cost objectives. There are many more questions dealing with cost phases that must be answered in the Disclosure Statement. It should be noted that these practices and procedures are discussed in appropriate places in subsequent chapters.

Significant Standards Issued

The Board has issued several standards governing the determination and allocation of specific costs. Many of the subjects have been difficult and highly controversial.

Two relatively recent standards have the potential for impact far beyond the government contracting area, i.e., Standard No. 409 and Standard No. 414. Standard No. 409 requires contractors to depreciate their assets for contract costing purposes over useful lives based on documented historical usefulness, irrespective of the lives used for either financial or income tax purposes. Standard No. 414 recognizes as a contract cost the imputed cost of capital committed to facilities, thereby overturning the government's long-standing practice of disallowing interest and other financing-type costs.

Need to Observe CASB's Pronouncements

Since many firms engage in federal contract work in today's economy, the CASB's pronouncements become more and more important in terms of their impact on a firm's cost accounting system and procedures. In the past, state and local governments have prescribed certain accounting-related regulations. Now the possibility exists that eventually the CASB's cost accounting standards might be adopted by state and local governments in their contract solicitations. Furthermore, federal regulatory agencies might require the companies they regulate to adopt specific standards promulgated by the Cost Accounting Standards Board.

DISCUSSION QUESTIONS

1. Enumerate the various classifications of costs.
2. The statement has often been made that an actual product cost does not exist in the sense of absolute authenticity and verifiability. Why?

3. The division of costs between inventory charges and profit and loss charges is not uniform throughout industries.
   (a) Name these two costs.
   (b) Give reasons for the existence of the different treatment of these costs.

4. Expenditures may be divided into two general categories: capital expenditures and revenue expenditures.
   (a) Distinguish between these two categories of expenditures and their treatment in the accounts.
   (b) Discuss the impact on both present and future balance sheets and income statements of improperly distinguishing between capital and revenue expenditures.
   (c) What criteria do firms generally use in establishing a policy for classifying expenditures under these two general categories?

5. (a) What is a service department? Name a few.
   (b) What are some characteristics of a service department in connection with the establishment of a product cost?

6. The board of directors of Mission Viejo, Inc., has just received the company's financial statements. While reading them, one director asked, "What are the precise meanings of the terms 'cost,' 'expense,' and 'loss'? These terms sometimes seem to identify similar items and other times dissimilar terms."
   (a) Explain the meanings of the terms (1) "cost," (2) "expense," and (3) "loss," as used for financial reporting in conformity with generally accepted accounting principles. The explanation should indicate distinguishing characteristics of the terms, their similarities and interrelationships.
   (b) Classify each of the following items as a cost, expense, loss, or other category, with an explanation of how the classification of each item may change: (1) cost of goods sold; (2) uncollectible accounts expense; (3) depreciation expense for plant machinery; (4) organization costs; (5) spoiled goods.
   (c) The terms "period cost" and "product cost" are sometimes used to describe certain items in financial statements. Define these terms and distinguish between them. To what types of items does each apply?
                                                                    (AICPA adapted)

7. Select the answer which best completes the statement:
   (a) Conversion cost is equal to the total of: (1) direct labor and raw materials; (2) direct labor and factory overhead; (3) indirect labor and factory overhead; (4) factory overhead and raw materials.
   (b) The best example of a variable cost is: (1) property tax; (2) the corporate president's salary; (3) the controller's salary; (4) interest charges; (5) materials in a unit of product.
   (c) Prime costs are: (1) the first costs incurred on a job; (2) indispensable as distinguished from avoidable costs; (3) direct materials and direct labor; (4) costs incurred in service departments.
   (d) Depreciation based on the number of units produced would be classified as: (1) out-of-pocket cost; (2) differential cost; (3) variable cost; (4) fixed cost.
   (e) The costing of inventories on a prime cost basis would: (1) achieve the same results as direct costing; (2) exclude all factory overhead from re-

ported inventory costs; (3) always be achieved when standard costing is adopted; (4) be achieved when the lifo cost flow assumption is adopted.

(f) The statement best describing cost allocation is: (1) a company can minimize or maximize total company income by selecting different bases to allocate indirect costs; (2) a company should select an allocation base to raise or lower reported income on given products; (3) except for the effect of inventory changes, a company's total income will remain unchanged no matter how indirect costs are allocated; (4) as a general rule, a company should allocate indirect costs randomly or based on an ability-to-bear criterion.

(AICPA and CMA adapted)

EXERCISES

1. Classify the following costs as fixed, variable, or semivariable. Explain the reasons for your classification of the semivariable costs.

(a) Depreciation — straight-line method
(b) Direct materials
(c) Factory insurance
(d) Heat, light, and power
(e) Indirect labor
(f) Rent
(g) Repairs to machinery
(h) FICA tax
(i) Superintendence
(j) Washroom supplies

2. Under which subheading of the elements of cost should each of the following costs be classified?

(a) Cutting tools
(b) Depreciation of factory
(c) Earnings of machinist
(d) Supervisors' wages
(e) Maintenance parts for factory equipment
(f) Inspector's salary
(g) Legal expenses
(h) Lubricating oil
(i) Salary of factory stores clerk
(j) Wages of factory crane operator

3. Classify the following items as direct or indirect materials:

(a) Ailerons on an airplane
(b) 1-oz. perfume bottle
(c) Sanding material in furniture making
(d) Bags in flour mills
(e) Ingots used by a foundry for making castings
(f) Seats to be installed in a railway car
(g) Stainless steel cone that holds the mirror in a color television set
(h) Milk to make ice cream

4. Bid calculations. The Shepard Company is to submit a bid on the production of 10,000 ceramic salad bowls. It is estimated that the cost of materials will be $7,500 and direct labor, $10,100. Factory overhead is applied at $5 per direct labor hour in the Molding Department and at 120% of the direct labor cost in the Finishing Department. It is estimated that 800 direct labor hours will be required in Molding and that direct labor cost in Finishing will be $4,300. The company wishes a bid price consisting of a markup of 40% of its total production costs.

Required:

(1) Estimated cost to produce.
(2) Estimated prime cost.
(3) Estimated conversion cost.
(4) Bid price.

5. Cost computations. Messersmith, Inc., submits the following data on October 31, 19——: materials put into process, $42,300; direct labor is paid at the rate of $7.80 and $8.40 per hour in Departments A and B respectively; Department A worked 6,125 hours and Department B reported 9,875 hours. Factory overhead is applied on the basis of direct labor hours at the rate of $5 per hour in Department A and $4.20 per hour in Department B.

	INVENTORIES	
	Oct. 1	Oct. 31
Finished goods..	$11,300	$ 9,400
Work in process	17,300	19,425
Materials	15,000	19,200

Required: Without preparing a formal income statement, determine:
(1) Total manufacturing costs.
(2) Cost of goods manufactured.
(3) Cost of goods sold.

6. Cost computations. On October 1, the Florida Company had the following inventories: materials, $24,000; work in process, $12,000; and finished goods, $36,000. During the month, materials purchases totaled $56,000. Direct labor for October was $40,000, at a uniform wage of $6.40 per hour. Marketing and administrative expenses for the month amounted to 10% of net sales. Inventories on October 31 were as follows: materials, $20,000; work in process, $8,000; and finished goods, $40,000. Net sales for October totaled $200,000. Factory overhead is applied on the basis of $8 per direct labor hour.

Required:
(1) Prime cost.
(2) Conversion cost.
(3) Cost of goods manufactured.
(4) Cost of goods sold.
(5) Income from operations.

7. Gross profit determination. The Davidson Corporation manufactures a kitchen appliance to sell for $280. Last year the company sold 2,000 of these appliances, realizing a gross profit of 25% of the cost of goods sold. Of this total cost of goods sold, materials accounted for 40% of the total and factory overhead for 15%.

During the coming year, it is expected that materials and labor costs will each increase 25% per unit and that factory overhead will increase 12½% per unit. To meet these rising costs, a new sales price must be set.

Required: The number of units that must be sold to realize the same total gross profit in the coming year as realized last year if the new selling price is set at: (1) $300; (2) $325; (3) $350.

8. Sales price computation. In June, Steinhardt, Inc., sold 50 air conditioners for $200 each. Costs included materials costs of $50 per unit, direct labor costs of $30 per unit, and factory overhead at 100% of direct labor cost. Interest expense on an 8% bank loan was equivalent to $2 per unit. Federal income tax at a 30% rate was equivalent to $15 per unit.

Effective July 1, materials costs decreased 5% per unit and direct labor costs increased 20% per unit. Also effective July 1, the interest rate on the bank loan increased from 8% per annum to 9% per annum.

Assume in requirements (1) and (2) that the expected July sales volume is 50 units, the same as for June.

Required:
(1) The sales price per unit that will produce the same ratio of gross profit, assuming no change in the rate of factory overhead in relation to direct labor costs.
(2) The sales price per unit that will produce the same ratio of gross profit, assuming that $10 of the June factory overhead consists of fixed costs and that the variable factory overhead ratio to direct labor costs is unchanged from June.

(AICPA adapted)

9. Fire loss calculation. Robidaux Products, Inc., a small manufacturing company, produces a highly flammable cleaning fluid. On May 31, 19F, the company had a fire which completely destroyed the processing building and the work in process inventory; some of the equipment was saved.

After the fire, a physical inventory was taken. The materials were valued at $30,000, the finished goods at $60,000, and supplies at $5,000.

The inventories on January 1, 19F, consisted of:

Finished goods	$ 70,000
Work in process...	50,000
Materials	15,000
Supplies..	2,000
Total	$137,000

A review of the accounts showed that the sales and gross profit for the last five years were:

	SALES	GROSS PROFIT
19A	$300,000	$ 86,200
19B	320,000	102,400
19C	330,000	108,900
19D	250,000	62,500
19E	280,000	84,000

The sales for the first five months of 19F were $150,000; materials purchases were $50,000; freight on purchases was $5,000; direct labor for the five months was $40,000. For the past five years, factory overhead was 50% of direct labor cost.

Required: The value of the work in process inventory lost by fire.

(AICPA adapted)

PROBLEMS

3-1. Bid calculations. The Davies Equipment Company manufactures machines to customers' specifications. Two requests for bids have been received, each calling for the delivery of one machine with the following shop and cost specifications:

	BID NO. 1	BID NO. 2
Parts to be purchased	$550	$900
Materials: bar, strip, and sheet metal.....................................	130	190
Pig metal for castings...	56	80

	DIRECT LABOR HOURS	
	Bid No. 1	*Bid No. 2*
Foundry...	6 hrs.	8 hrs.
Machining..	8	20
Electroplating and painting	6	12
Assembly...	40	70
Installing	0	16

Labor and overhead hourly rates:

	FOUNDRY	MACHINING	E & P	ASSEMBLY	INSTALLING
Direct labor rate per hour	$8.25	$7.50	$8.40	$8.00	$7.00
Factory overhead rate per direct labor hour....	3.25	3.00	2.50	2.60	1.80

Allowance for spoilage and estimating error, 5% of direct labor and materials cost (including parts purchased).

Allowance for marketing and administrative expenses and profit, 35% of sales.

Required: The bids for the two possible orders.

3-2. Influence of fixed and variable costs on price and profit. In 19A, the Velasquez Products Company produced a machine that sold for $600, of which $450 represented cost of goods sold and $50 represented marketing and administrative expenses. The cost of goods sold was comprised of 40% materials cost, 40% labor cost, and 20% factory overhead. During 19A, 2,000 machines were sold. During 19B, increases of 20% in the cost of materials and 25% in the cost of labor are anticipated. The company plans to raise the selling price to $675 per unit with a resulting decrease of 40% in the number of units to be sold.

Required:
(1) An income statement for the year 19B, indicating the new costs per unit. Assume that materials and labor costs will still equal 80% of the cost of goods sold for 19B and marketing and administrative expenses are still $50 per unit.
(2) A revised income statement for 19B, disregarding the 80% relationship of materials and labor costs to cost of goods sold. After the statement required in (1) was prepared, it was ascertained that the 20% factory overhead in 19A consisted of $100,000 fixed and $80,000 variable expenses. The decrease in the number of units to be sold in 19B does not influence the fixed costs.

3-3. Price determination. Strabone, Inc., produces a single product which is sold to fabricators of electronic equipment. Since the company is relatively small, it does not utilize involved cost accounting techniques in determining inventory values. Direct materials and direct labor are identified with specific lots of product. Factory overhead rates are not used; the company waits until the end of the accounting period for which statements are required and then assigns overhead to inventory and to cost of goods sold on a unit of production basis.

During 19--, the company produced its regular year's output by December 15, at which time it planned to shut down for the last two weeks of the year, reopening after the new year. As of December 15, the following income statement, which included all 19-- costs, was prepared:

Strabone, Inc.
Income Statement
For the Year Ended December 31, 19--

Sales (20,000 units)		$100,000
Cost of goods sold:		
Inventory, January 1, 19--	-0-	
Production costs for an output of 22,000 units:		
Direct materials	$13,500	
Direct labor	30,500	
Factory overhead	35,200	
Total	$79,200	
Inventory, December 31, 19-- (2,000 units)	8,220	70,980
Gross profit		$ 29,020
Marketing and administrative expenses (all fixed)		10,000
Income (before income tax)		$ 19,020

On December 18, 19--, a department of the United States government placed an order with the company for 4,000 units of product. The company accepted the order, which stipulated that delivery be made by December 31, 19--, and that the company should be permitted to earn a gross profit on the order calculated at 20% of selling price. The company called back its production personnel and, by the end of the year, completed 2,000 units which, with the inventory, comprised the government's total order. During this period, it expended additional costs as follows: direct materials, $1,300; direct labor, $2,800; and factory overhead, $800.

In accordance with the terms of the order, the government was billed at a price of $4.85 per unit. The government auditor who reviewed the company's invoice complained that at this price the company would earn a profit of 32.4% on sales and that the unit sales price should be $4.10 in order to comply with the terms of the order.

Required:

    (1) Calculations to show (a) the method used by the company to arrive at its price of $4.85 and (b) the method used by the government to reach a price of $4.10.

    (2) A critical evaluation of the two pricing methods. Could acceptable accounting procedures be utilized to arrive at a third price for the order? Explain this third method and indicate which of the three methods is preferable in this instance.

CASE

    Government contracts and CASB regulations. The Cost Accounting Standards Board issued two standards that require (1) consistency in estimating, accumulating, and reporting costs (Standard No. 401) and (2) consistency in allocating direct and indirect costs incurred for the same purpose (Standard No. 402).

    Part 1. The Otani-Smith Company sells products in excess of $30 million a year to the United States Government. As a separate cost center of its parent company, the O-S Company must file a Disclosure Statement describing in detail the company's cost accounting system.

    On January 1, 19--, the company was awarded a firm fixed-price contract which called for 1,000 units of product MAC. The performance period was one year and the total price of the contract was $8,058,000. When the government auditor analyzed the contract six months later, inconsistencies were found between the company's methods of estimating direct labor costs and the method described in its disclosed accounting practices. In the proposal (Exhibit 1) which resulted in the contract, manufacturing labor was estimated as a total dollar amount which included significant, disparate elements or functions of manufacturing labor. Manufacturing labor was calculated by using a plant-wide labor rate multiplied by the estimated manufacturing hours. The auditor found that the company's cost accounting system, budget procedure, and reporting methods provided for the breakdown of manufacturing costs into functional levels, using the individual worker or functional average labor rates.

Exhibit 1

CONTRACT PROPOSAL		
	RATES	ESTIMATES
Manufacturing labor (400 hours)	$5.45/hr.	$ 2,180
Manufacturing overhead (based on direct labor dollars)	180%	3,924
Total		$ 6,104
General and administrative expenses	20%	1,221
Total cost		$ 7,325
Profit	10%	733
Contract price per unit		$ 8,058
Total contract price, 1,000 units		$8,058,000

Required: A new unit cost and total dollar difference due to the above stated inconsistency between pricing and costing:

    (1) Using the new rate of $5.10 for manufacturing labor, developed by the auditor, and

    (2) Revising all other factors stated incorrectly.

    Part 2. In a second contract, the company prepared the proposal shown on page 63. In reviewing the contract, the auditor found that warranty costs were stated as direct costs in the contract. When examining the manufacturing overhead and its 180% rate, the auditor discovered that warranty costs of the same nature were also charged to the manufacturing overhead expense pool as indirect expenses. These costs were therefore subject to adjustment for double counting.

Exhibit 2

CONTRACT PROPOSAL		
	RATES	ESTIMATES
Manufacturing labor	$5.45/hr.	$ 2,180
Manufacturing overhead	180%	3,924
Materials		4,800
Other direct costs		976
Warranty		700
Total		$ 12,580
General and administrative expenses	20%	2,516
Total cost		$ 15,096
Profit	10%	1,510
Total contract price per unit		$ 16,606
Total contract price, 1,000 units		$16,606,000

Required: A revised cost and price estimate by:
(1) Computing a new manufacturing overhead charging rate, omitting the total warranty cost of $10,000 included in the $360,000 originally forecast for overhead, and assuming that the labor cost forecast was $200,000 ($360,000 ÷ $200,000 = 180%).
(2) Applying the new rate to the revision and calculating a new unit and total cost of the contract.

(Based on an article in *Management Accounting*)

Part Two

The Cost Information System and Cost Accumulation Procedures

4

The Cost Accounting System
Design and Operation

Timely and meaningful information on revenue, costs, and profit is vital for management's effective and competent planning and control. The cost accounting information system — a part of the total integrated, computerized type of information developed by accounting techniques — should give executive management significant planning data to aid in understanding the specific problems facing the company, indicating alternative ways and methods for the best possible solutions. Periodically, information must be communicated to middle and operating management in the form of control reports to show the individual manager, department head, or supervisor the success or failure of the objective and the cost of accomplishment. These cost reports should motivate responsible people to corrective action and new decisions. The accumulation of accounting data requires many forms, methods, and systems due to the varying types and sizes of businesses. A successful system is tailored to give the blend of sophistication and simplicity that is most efficient and economical for a specific organization. In recognition of these facts, this chapter is divided into six parts:

1. Fundamentals of a cost accounting information system.
2. Chart of accounts.
3. Data processing by means of the journal voucher control system.

4. The manufacturing cost accounting cycle.
5. The factory ledger.
6. The electronic data processing and information system.

FUNDAMENTALS OF A COST ACCOUNTING INFORMATION SYSTEM

The construction of a cost accounting information system requires a thorough understanding of (1) the organizational structure of the company, (2) the manufacturing procedure or processes, and (3) the type of cost information desired and required by all levels of management.

Management is responsible for setting objectives and goals and measuring performance with the aid of the cost accounting information system. The interface between the system and the managers at all levels is fraught with behavioral implications. The system could enhance or thwart achievement of desired results, depending on the extent to which sound behavioral judgment is applied in developing, administering, and improving the system.

The cost accounting information system with its operating accounts must correspond to the organizational division of authority so that the individual manager can be held accountable for the cost incurred in each department. The concept of authority and responsibility is closely allied with accountability, which recognizes the need for measuring a manager's discharge of responsibilities. The organization charts on pages 6 and 7 depict the authority and responsibility relationships between managers, superintendents, and department heads who are responsible for:

1. Providing detailed information needed by the accounting department in order to install a successful system.
2. Incurring expenditures for materials, labor, and other costs which the accountant must segregate and report to those in charge.

The system must reflect the manufacturing procedures, processes, shop methods, and the marketing and administrative organization and processes of the particular company for which it is designed. The accountant designing the system must know the type of pay plan (piece-rate, incentive, day-rate, etc.); the method of collecting hours worked; the control of inventories; the costing of tools and machinery; and other information related to operations.

A satisfactory system results from a meeting of minds between the accountant and management. The service rendered by the accountant is judged by prompt presentation of meaningful cost reports and statements to management. These reports indicate the success or failure of a preestablished course of action. Deviations from the course, if significant, are of interest to management. The cost control presentation should be made so that management by exception is possible; that is, it should enable management to take prompt remedial action based on compact information regarding the activities of the various divisions and departments of the company.

While details for analyzing and reporting may be different for different businesses, each system should be perfected in a manner that will:

1. Aid in planning the future and controlling the present.
2. Provide a means of costing inventories.
3. Compute the cost of sales.
4. Measure the efficiency of employees, materials, and machines.
5. Aid in establishing selling prices.
6. Furnish data for various other analytical processes.

Accounting records do not provide all the information necessary for effective management. Other quantifiable as well as nonquantifiable information, much of which may involve estimates as to the future, may provide vital information especially with respect to the decision-making process. With the use of electronic computers and their large memory storage, all data — past, present, and future, accounting and nonaccounting — will be stored for quick retrieval in a total information system.

It is equally important to weigh the cost of the system against its value. There are certain external requirements imposed on an organization that necessitate the establishment of minimum systems requirements. For example, the Internal Revenue Code prescribes certain record-keeping and reporting requirements, as does the Federal Insurance Contributions Act, the 1974 Pension Reform Act, the Securities and Exchange Commission, the Cost Accounting Standards Board, the Federal Power Commission for public utilities, and various other governmental regulatory agencies and taxing authorities at local, state, and federal levels. Also stockholders, creditors, labor unions, and others may impose requirements on the information system. These many legal or contractual requirements must be met, but in meeting them the system should be designed in a cost-conscious manner. Beyond these external requirements, any additional sophistication in the system should be justified solely on the basis of its value to management.

CHART OF ACCOUNTS

Every organization, irrespective of its size and complexity, whether organized for profit or nonprofit, must maintain some type of general ledger accounting system. Data must be collected, identified, and coded for recording in journals and posting to ledger accounts for subsequent reporting. The prerequisite for accomplishing these tasks is a properly established account structure. A company's chart of accounts is the fundamental means for budgetary and control accounting. It provides control accounts for the recognized elements of cost, and it segregates and details all expenses not included in prime cost. The coding system should permit the flow and charge of costs and expenses directly to the individual responsible and accountable for their incurrence.

In constructing a chart of accounts, the following basic considerations should be observed:

1. Accounts should be arranged and designated to give maximum information with the least need for supplementary analysis consistent with a reasonable degree of economy in performing the accounting function.
2. Account titles should reflect as far as possible the purpose rather than the nature of the expenditure.
3. Manufacturing, marketing, and administrative cost accounts should receive particular attention because these accounts are used to bring efficiency variations to management's attention. These costs should be classified further so as to identify them with the responsible department managers. Discussion of this added dimension of cost accumulation is illustrated in subsequent chapters.

A chart of accounts is divided into (1) balance sheet accounts for assets, liabilities, and capital and (2) income statement accounts for sales, cost of goods sold, factory overhead, marketing expenses, administrative expenses, and other expenses and income. A typical chart of accounts for a manufacturing concern is shown on pages 68 and 69.

Assignment of codes in the form of numbers, letters, or other symbols is essential to facilitate the processing of the information. Modern data processing equipment makes coding an essential technique. The rapid handling of data by accounting machines, tabulating equipment, and electronic computers necessitates a high degree of planning, organizing, and integrating of the classification and coding of business data.

DATA PROCESSING BY MEANS OF THE JOURNAL VOUCHER CONTROL SYSTEM

Every company designs an accounting system that will meet its own particular needs. Since a knowledge of costs is of key importance to management, the system should make pertinent cost information available to the right person at the right time. To assure the flow of needed cost information into control accounts and subsidiary records, the original transaction must first be account-classified and coded.

Throughout the fiscal year, the accounting staff assembles and analyzes source documents related to numerous financial transactions. Source documents, often referred to as transaction documents, are the fundamental evidence for an accounting event. Source documents — such as sales slips, checks received, checks mailed out, purchase invoices, payroll clock or time cards, materials requisitions, production reports, and shipping records — indicate the occurrence of a transaction. Properly approved transaction documents generate the flow of accounting events into the accounting system. The system itself then depends upon the type and size of a business and the part accounting plays in its management.

CHART OF ACCOUNTS FOR A MANUFACTURING BUSINESS

BALANCE SHEET ACCOUNTS (100–299)
Assets (100–199)

Current Assets (100–129)

101	Cash in Bank
102	Cash on Hand
103	Petty Cash
104	Marketable Securities
106	Notes Receivable
106.1	Notes Receivable Discounted
109	Accounts Receivable
109.1	Allowance for Doubtful Accounts
115	Finished Goods
116	Work in Process
117	Materials
117.1	Inventory Adjustments
120	Prepaid Property Tax
121	Prepaid Insurance
122	Miscellaneous Prepaid Items

Property, Plant, and Equipment (130–159)

130	Land
132	Buildings
132.1	Accumulated Depreciation — Buildings
135	Machinery and Equipment — Factory
135.1	Accumulated Depreciation — Machinery and Equipment — Factory
143	Automobiles
143.1	Accumulated Depreciation — Automobiles
146	Office Furniture and Fixtures
146.1	Accumulated Depreciation — Office Furniture and Fixtures

Intangible Assets (170–179)

170	Goodwill
171	Patents
172	Franchises, Licenses, and Other Privileges

Other Assets (180–189)

Sinking Funds (190–199)

Liabilities and Capital (200–299)

Current Liabilities (200–219)

201	Notes Payable
203	Accounts Payable
206	Accrued Payroll
207	Accrued Interest Payable
208	Accrued Sales Tax
209	Other Accrued Liabilities
210	Employees Income Tax Payable
211	FICA Tax Payable
212	Federal Unemployment Tax Payable
213	State Unemployment Tax Payable
214	Estimated Federal Income Tax Payable
215	Estimated State Income Tax Payable
216	Long-Term Debt (due within one year)
218	Dividends Payable

Long-Term Liabilities (220–229)

220	Bonds Payable
222	Mortgage Payable
224	Other Long-Term Debt
226	Deferred Income Tax Payable

Capital (250–299)

250	Common Stock
250.1	Treasury Stock
255	Paid-In Capital in Excess of Par
260	Retained Earnings

INCOME STATEMENT ACCOUNTS (300–899)

Sales (300–349)

301	Sales
301.1	Sales Returns
301.2	Sales Allowances
301.3	Sales Discount

Cost of Goods Sold (350–399)

351	Cost of Goods Sold
356	Materials Price Variance
357	Materials Quantity Variance
358	Purchases Discount
366	Labor Rate Variance
367	Labor Efficiency Variance
372	Applied Factory Overhead
376	Factory Overhead Spending Variance
377	Factory Overhead Idle Capacity Variance
378	Factory Overhead Efficiency Variance
379	Over- or Underapplied Factory Overhead

(Continued)

CHART OF ACCOUNTS FOR A MANUFACTURING BUSINESS
(Concluded)

Factory Overhead (400–499)

400	Factory Overhead Control
401	Salaries — Factory
411	Indirect Materials
412	Indirect Labor
414	Freight In
417	Training
420	Overtime Premium
422	FICA Tax
423	Federal Unemployment Tax
424	State Unemployment Tax
425	Vacation Pay
427	Workmen's Compensation
434	Fuel — Factory
436	Light and Power
438	Telephone and Telegraph
440	Tools
442	Defective Work
450	Insurance Expense
460	Depreciation Expense — Buildings
461	Depreciation Expense — Machinery and Equipment
462	Repairs and Maintenance of Buildings
463	Repairs and Maintenance of Roads
464	Repairs and Maintenance of Transportation Facilities
465	Repairs and Maintenance of Machinery and Equipment
480	Rent of Equipment
485	Property Tax
486	Amortization of Patents

Marketing Expenses (500–599)

500	Marketing Expenses Control
501	Salaries — Sales Supervision
503	Salaries — Salespeople
504	Salaries — Clerical Help
507	Sales Commissions
515	Freight Out
522	FICA Tax
523	Federal Unemployment Tax
524	State Unemployment Tax
530	Supplies
534	Fuel
536	Light and Power
538	Telephone and Telegraph
546	Postage
548	Travel Expenses
550	Insurance Expense
560	Depreciation Expense — Buildings
561	Depreciation Expense — Automobiles
562	Repairs and Maintenance of Buildings
565	Advertising
567	Display Materials
568	Conventions and Exhibits
580	Rent of Equipment
585	Property Tax

Administrative Expenses (600–699)

600	Administrative Expenses Control
601	Salaries — Administrative
604	Salaries — Administrative Clerical Help
620	Overtime Premium
622	FICA Tax
623	Federal Unemployment Tax
624	State Unemployment Tax
630	Supplies
634	Fuel
636	Light and Power
638	Telephone and Telegraph
646	Postage
648	Travel Expenses
650	Insurance Expense
660	Depreciation Expense — Buildings
661	Depreciation Expense — Furniture and Fixtures
662	Repairs and Maintenance of Buildings
670	Legal and Accounting Fees
680	Rent of Equipment
685	Property Tax
691	Donations
693	Uncollectible Accounts Expense

Other Expenses (700–749)

701	Interest Paid on Notes Payable
703	Interest Paid on Mortgage
707	Interest Paid on Bonds
731	Operating Expenses on Excess Facilities

Other Income (800–849)

801	Income from Investments
816	Interest Earned
817	Rental Income
818	Miscellaneous Income

Income Deductions (890–899)

890	Federal Income Tax
891	State Income Tax

Accounting systems often facilitate the flow of accounting by the use of the *journal voucher control system*, consisting of journal vouchers supported by the original transaction documents.[1] In such systems, journal entries are made via the journal voucher, which represents the transactions that have occurred during a given period and that have been identified with the chart of accounts. Essential to a journal voucher control system is the voucher itself. Whether a manual, mechanized, or computerized accounting information system is utilized, the journal voucher is prepared for the purpose of summarizing the transactions in journals and posting them to the accounts.

The journal voucher format used is generally quite similar among organizations. Basically, it should indicate the voucher number, the date, the accounts with their account numbers or codes, the amounts to be debited and credited, and approval (as illustrated below). When subsidiary ledgers or cost ledgers are involved, columns are added to meet the needs of the detailed expense and cost subsidiary ledger requirements at the same time; subsidiary details may also be posted directly from the transaction documents.

Journal
Voucher
Evidencing
Purchase of
Materials on
Account

DATE		JOURNAL VOUCHER	NO. **123**		
MONTH	DAY				
MAR.	31		APPROVED *E g y*		
ACCOUNT		ACCT. NO. OR CODE	AMOUNT		
			DEBIT	CREDIT	
Materials		117	25,000		
Accounts Payable		203		25,000	

THE MANUFACTURING COST ACCOUNTING CYCLE

The manufacturing process and the physical arrangement of a factory are the skeleton upon which the cost system and cost accumulation procedures for the manufacturing function are built. A knowledge of the flow of products through their various productive steps determines the nature of the costing techniques. Since cost accounts are an expansion of general accounts, they should, as a basic accounting procedure, be related to them. This relationship leads to the concept of the tie-in of cost accounts with general accounts as illustrated on page 71.

Accounts describing manufacturing operations are: Materials, Payroll, Factory Overhead Control, Work in Process, Finished Goods, and Cost of

---

[1]The journal voucher control system should not be confused with the voucher register, a basic journal for classifying and summarizing expenditures. The voucher register, also called an accounts payable register, could be a part of the system, particularly under a manual system. Mechanization and computerization have eliminated the need for the voucher register; therefore it is not presented in this textbook.

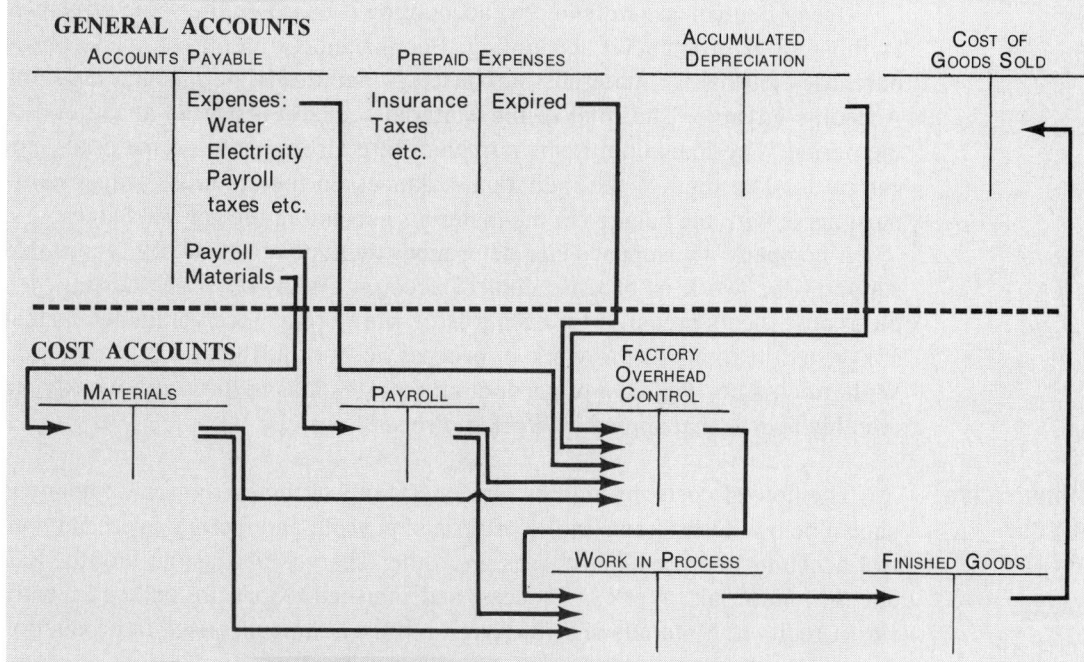

Relationship Between General Accounts and Cost Accounts

Goods Sold. Each fiscal period, these accounts recognize and measure the flow of costs — from the acquisition of materials, through factory operations, to the cost of products sold. The CASB's Disclosure Statement requires that covered federal government contractors disclose the type of cost accounting system in use and the extent of integration of the cost system with the general accounts.

Cost accounting makes extensive use of control accounts. To illustrate, the materials account controls hundreds of different materials, and the factory overhead account controls indirect labor, supplies, rent, insurance, taxes, repairs, and other factory expenses. The following schedule lists the generally used control accounts with their subsidiary ledgers or records:

CONTROL ACCOUNT	SUBSIDIARY LEDGER OR RECORD
Materials	Materials ledger cards — perpetual inventory
Factory Overhead	Expense ledger or departmental expense analysis sheets
Work in Process	{ Cost sheets — job order costing { Production reports — process costing
Finished Goods	Finished goods ledger cards
Machinery and Equipment	Plant or equipment ledger

The control account-subsidiary record format is used when it is desirable to maintain detailed information about general ledger accounts.

Use of control accounts in cost accounting is based on the same principles as those used in financial accounting. For instance, an entry is made in the purchases journal for materials purchased — debiting Materials and crediting Accounts Payable. The total of the Materials column is posted at the end of the period. The individual items purchased are also entered on materials ledger cards. The total of the individual balances on the materials ledger cards must agree with the balance in the materials account in the general ledger.

A company's cost procedure determines the type of subsidiary record that supports the work in process control account. With job order costing, job order cost sheets prepared for each job (or work order) receive the details that are posted in totals to the work in process account at the end of the month. With process costing, cost of production reports indicate the daily, weekly, or monthly figures that appear in Work in Process.

Illustrative Cycle Problem

The flow of costs through factory operations of the Fairbanks Company is shown below. Debit items in the materials, payroll, and factory overhead control accounts represent purchases and other charges during the month. Balances in Materials, Work in Process, and Finished Goods are ending inventories. Credits to Materials and to Payroll represent amounts used in production during the period. In the factory overhead control account, actual expenses

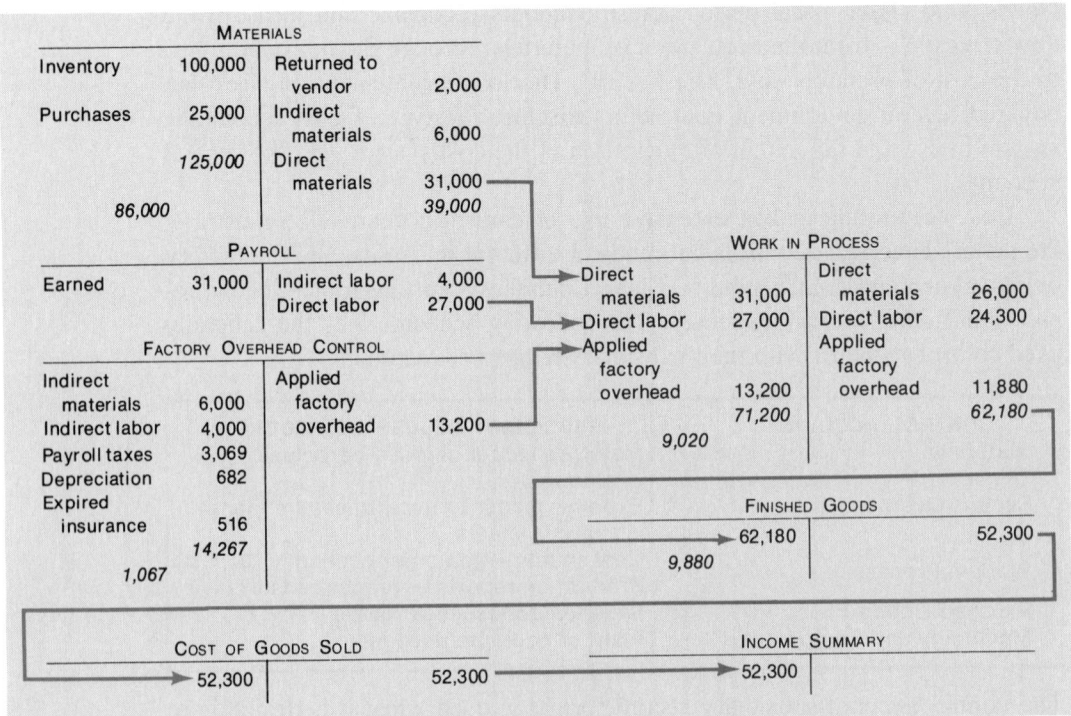

Flow of Costs Through Factory Operations

incurred — including indirect materials, indirect labor, employer payroll taxes,[2] depreciation, and other prepaid items and accruals (expired insurance in this illustration) — comprise the total debit of $14,267.

By means of a predetermined factory overhead rate, it is estimated that for each direct labor hour used in production, $2.20 of factory overhead should be charged to production. The credit of $13,200, based on 6,000 direct labor hours, is the factory overhead charged to production during the month. The debit balance of $1,067 in Factory Overhead Control represents the amount of underapplied factory overhead. The significance and disposition of such a balance, either over- or underapplied, are discussed in Chapter 9.

Cost of all production during the month consists of direct materials, $31,000; direct labor, $27,000; and applied factory overhead, $13,200 — a total production cost of $71,200. Units completed during the period cost $62,180 (direct materials, $26,000; direct labor, $24,300; and applied factory overhead, $11,880). The total cost of goods completed, $62,180, is transferred from the work in process account to the finished goods account. Finally, cost of goods sold of $52,300 is transferred from Finished Goods to Cost of Goods Sold. At the end of each accounting period, Cost of Goods Sold is closed to Income Summary.

The ledger accounts with the transactions posted therein should be looked upon as the storage space or data bank mentioned in computerized accounting systems. The flow of costs to these memories is based on originating documents that must be verified, vouchered, journalized, and posted. Documents may be for:

Underlying Documents

> *Materials* — purchase invoices, materials requisitions, materials returned slips, etc.
>
> *Labor* — time tickets or time sheets, clock cards, job tickets, etc.
>
> *Factory overhead* — vouchers prepared to set up depreciation or prepaid expenses; vendors' invoices, utility bills, etc.

THE FACTORY LEDGER

The accounting system, and especially the cost accounting cycle problem based on the factory operations of the Fairbanks Company, assumes that the entire business is under one roof or that little distance separates the factory and the general offices. It is not uncommon for administrative, marketing, and

---

[2]The amount of $3,069 for payroll taxes consists of:

    $2,015 — 6.5% FICA tax on $31,000 ($27,000 direct labor plus $4,000 indirect labor)

       217 — .7% federal unemployment tax on $31,000

       837 — 2.7% state unemployment tax on $31,000

    $3,069 — total payroll taxes

accounting offices to be far removed from factory sites; and, of course, the same company may operate several factories or marketing offices in different parts of the country. If the factory is some distance from the general or home office or if the manufacturing requires many accounts, it is practical to do some accounting at the factory.

Transactions recorded at the factory should be posted to a *factory ledger*. The factory ledger includes a control account entitled General Ledger that shows the equity of the general office in the factory. A reciprocal control account entitled Factory Ledger is maintained in the accounting records kept at the general office. When General Ledger is debited in the factory books, Factory Ledger is credited in the general office books; when General Ledger is credited, Factory Ledger is debited.

Just how much of the accounting may be done at the factory depends upon the organization and operation of a business. If sales are made, invoices prepared, and statements rendered from the factory, Cash, Accounts Receivable, Sales, and related accounts may appear in the factory ledger. If sales invoices, billings, and collections are made at the general office, only a petty cash account along with the various manufacturing accounts would be needed on the factory books.

At one factory it may be advantageous to meet payrolls locally, thereby requiring a bank account and payroll accounts. In another factory, the payroll summary might be sent to the general office, which would prepare the payroll checks or envelopes and mail or deliver them to the factory. The liability for payroll taxes and income tax withheld from employees is either kept in the general ledger or transferred from the factory ledger to the general ledger. For efficient management and control, one firm may keep detailed equipment accounts in the factory books, while another may keep them with accumulated depreciation accounts in the general office books. Similar procedures would be followed in the case of several factory sites or other functions physically separated from the general offices, e.g., a marketing branch office with reciprocal control accounts at the home office and the separate factory sites.

Illustrative Problem

With the data of the Fairbanks Company (page 72) as the basis for the illustration, the entries on pages 75 and 76 would be recorded, assuming that (1) the materials account is kept at the factory while all invoices are vouchered and paid from the general office, (2) the payroll with its deductions is prepared at the factory while paychecks and tax liabilities are the treasurer's responsibility at the main office, and (3) the finished goods account is kept at the factory and the cost of goods sold account at the general office.

In this illustrative problem, subsidiary record detail is shown for factory overhead only. Similar detail, often posted to subsidiary records directly from transaction documents, must be available for all ledger accounts for which subsidiary records are maintained, e.g., materials and finished goods.

GENERAL OFFICE			FACTORY OFFICE		
				SUBSIDIARY	
	DR.	CR.		RECORD	DR.	CR.

Entries for the purchase of the materials:

| Factory Ledger .... | 25,000 | | Materials .... | | 25,000 | |
| Accounts Payable .... | | 25,000 | General Ledger .... | | | 25,000 |

Entries for the requisitioning of direct and indirect materials:

NO ENTRY			Work in Process................		31,000	
			Materials			31,000
NO ENTRY			Factory Overhead Control ..		6,000	
			Indirect Materials........	6,000		
			Materials			6,000

Entries for the return of materials to the vendor:

| Accounts Payable .... | 2,000 | | General Ledger................. | | 2,000 | |
| Factory Ledger .... | | 2,000 | Materials .... | | | 2,000 |

Entries to prepare the payroll at the factory and to set up payroll liability and pay employees at the main office (employees' payroll deductions consist of 15% for income taxes and 6.5% for FICA taxes; the tax liabilities are transferred to the general office):

Factory Ledger	24,335		Payroll		31,000	
Accrued Payroll		24,335	General Ledger			24,335
Accrued Payroll	24,335		Employees Income Tax			
Cash		24,335	Payable			4,650
			FICA Tax Payable..........			2,015
Factory Ledger	6,665		Employees Income Tax			
Employees Income			Payable		4,650	
Tax Payable.........		4,650	FICA Tax Payable.............		2,015	
FICA Tax Payable ...		2,015	General Ledger			6,665

Entries for the company's payroll tax liability:

Factory Ledger	3,069		Factory Overhead Control ..		3,069	
FICA Tax Payable ...		2,015	FICA Tax Expense	2,015		
Federal			Federal Unemployment			
Unemployment			Tax Expense	217		
Tax Payable.........		217	State Unemployment			
State Unemployment			Tax Expense	837		
Tax Payable.........		837	General Ledger			3,069

Entries to distribute payroll to work in process for direct labor and to factory overhead control for indirect labor:

NO ENTRY			Work in Process................		27,000	
			Factory Overhead Control ..		4,000	
			Indirect Labor	4,000		
			Payroll			31,000

Entries to charge factory overhead to work in process based on 6,000 direct labor hours worked at a factory overhead rate of $2.20 per hour:

NO ENTRY			Work in Process................		13,200	
			Factory Overhead			
			Control......................			13,200

| GENERAL OFFICE | | | FACTORY OFFICE | | | |

Entries to charge expense accounts in the factory office with credits in the general office books for writing off prepaid insurance and accumulating depreciation (prepaid expenses and accumulated depreciation accounts are kept in the general office ledger):

	DR.	CR.		SUBSIDIARY RECORD	DR.	CR.
Factory Ledger	1,198		Factory Overhead Control ..		1,198	
Prepaid Insurance....		516	Expired Insurance	516		
Accumulated			Depreciation Expense ..	682		
Depreciation........		682	General Ledger.............			1,198

Entries to transfer work in process to finished goods:

			SUBSIDIARY RECORD	DR.	CR.
No Entry		Finished Goods.................		62,180	
		Work in Process.............			62,180

Entries to transfer the cost of the goods sold to the general office books when notice is received that shipments were made to customers:

	DR.	CR.			DR.	CR.
Cost of Goods Sold	52,300		General Ledger		52,300	
Factory Ledger		52,300	Finished Goods..............			52,300

In the general office, a second entry is necessary for the sales transaction. Entry assuming the above shipment was sold for $88,000:

	DR.	CR.		
Accounts Receivable...	88,000		No Entry	
Sales....................		88,000		

ELECTRONIC DATA PROCESSING

The term *data processing* applies to the accumulation, classification, analysis, and summary reporting of large quantities of information. The procedures, forms, and equipment used to process and communicate data are called a *data processing unit*. Any accounting system, even a cash register in a supermarket, is basically a data processing system designed to make pertinent and timely information available to the personnel responsible for various functions. Every purchase transaction requires a purchase requisition, a purchase order, verification of receipt of the order, voucher preparation, journalizing, posting, and a check to make payment. Multiple copies of the forms are prepared for the departments concerned, and it is necessary to rewrite the data perhaps several times — a time-consuming procedure almost certain to generate errors.

Electronic data processing is a system for recording and processing information without rerecording of repetitive data. For instance, payables data of all kinds — purchase orders, receiving reports, credits and allowances, cash discounts, invoices, and payrolls — can be processed through the accounting procedures with summary reports monthly, weekly, and daily where needed. The results of computer processing are verification of accuracy, automatically written checks and remittance statements, classified and stored data files, preparation and posting to general and subsidiary records, and analytical reports.

The transition from often vaguely existing rules of procedure to stringent computer instructions is one of the most interesting aspects of programming. *Programming* in a broad sense involves the analysis of the job to be converted to electronics, the preparation of extensive flowcharts, the detailed instruction coding for the computer, the debugging process, and the necessary trial runs. Generally, to program an accounting procedure for an electronic computer requires:

1. A detailed analysis of the accounting procedure to be converted.
2. The reduction of the accounting procedure to a logical design for the computer.
3. The writing of a series of instructions for the logical operations that the computer is to perform.

The punched card can be used to process source information. Depending upon the procedures, the original punched cards are prepared from either transaction documents or from journal vouchers showing the details provided by the source documents. After verification for accuracy, the punched cards are entrusted to extremely fast, accurate, and self-verifying machines for further processing. For business uses, the processing is usually done by a digital computer, which basically is a calculating machine with extraordinary capabilities. At very high speeds it can perform basic arithmetic functions, compare numbers as to size, and make many yes or no decisions as called for in solving problems or processing an established routine. In addition, the computer can communicate with other machines in a system, such as a magnetic ink reader, or another computer, which could be located in another city.

In the course of recording and evaluating information, the computer will recognize and report any circumstances deviating from the routine or standard. This makes possible more efficient use of the concept of management by exception. Executives can examine and act upon only those situations requiring attention, allowing all normal operations to flow unimpeded.

Major Computer Activities

All digital computers provide for four major activities: (1) *input-output* for transferring information into and out of the computer, (2) *storage* or *memory* where figures and facts are accessible, (3) *processing* or *calculating*, the *arithmetic and logic unit*, where operations are performed on the stored data, and (4) *control* for coordinating other units in the system to perform the instructions and desired sequence of operations. The diagram shown on page 78 illustrates these activities.

Major Activities
of a Computer
System

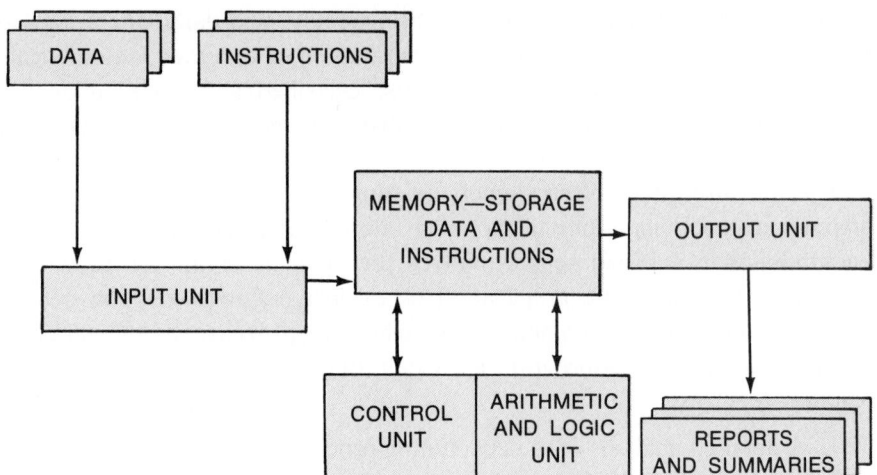

Input-Output. An input unit working from punched cards, punched paper tape, magnetic tape, magnetic ink, or other media feeds the data and processing instructions into the storage unit. The original data may come from purchase requisitions, invoices, time tickets, and sales tickets as well as from journal vouchers. The output system, a printer, prints out results at the conclusion of processing as instructed in the program, thereby providing feedback to managerial personnel.

Storage. The computer stores information on magnetic tapes, magnetic cores, or magnetic disks. Computer storage can be regarded as a completely indexed electronic filing cabinet in many cases instantaneously accessible to the computer. Characters or digits of information are stored on tiny magnetized spots or cores in code form, and the data are processed electronically at very high speed to provide the computer with the information it seeks.

Arithmetic and Logic Unit. From its almost unbelievably complete electronic filing cabinet, the arithmetic and logic unit of a computer system follows programmed instructions to select data from storage and to make desired computations or arrangements. This is done by electronic circuits at the speed of light.

Control Unit. A control panel or unit reads instructions and informs the computer where the desired data are stored, what data are required, and which sequence to follow. The computer can guide itself through a continuous series of instructions or programs, call data from storage and process it, return it to storage, and direct the output printer to print out the final results or report as directed. A console permits the operator to communicate with and manually control certain functions of a digital computer, such as starting and stopping the machine, regulating input and output units, and directing other operations of the system.

In essence, a computer system immediately converts the original transaction document to computer language and files it. Then, as instructed, the computer reaches into its file and completes all further actions required in connection with the transaction, along with summary reports of all transactions classified in a way most useful to management.

Large businesses have converted their basic data accumulation procedures to an electronic system of some sort. Ledgers are now replaced by cards, reels of magnetic tape, or disks as media for recording and storing account data. Ledgers in the form of punched cards, for example, offer a high degree of economy and flexibility; i.e., posting can be accomplished simply by merging accounts payable cards into a master file (arranged in sequence by account number) at machine speeds. The same cards can be converted into the accounts payable ledger file by the computer. Any card that goes into the file is prepared and verified from the source document. The card is immediately available for use in any phase of the accounting procedures. None of the accounts or documents needs to be handled individually (except source documents); and each item of data can be used as a unit, rather than as a fixed part of a rigid record.

As an example, at the end of each week or month, the accounts payable cards accumulated from daily processing of invoices or other source documents are withdrawn from the file, machine sorted into account number sequence, and then listed by a printer to produce the accounts payable distribution summary. These same cards can be machine sorted into categories of purchases and expenses. Summaries can be prepared for each class of expenditure or for each department manager responsible for cost control.

Electronic Data Processing and the Information System

Successful management of a business is essentially a continuous process of decision making. The decision making becomes even more complex with multiple plants located throughout the nation and in foreign countries; multiple product lines with an array of sizes, colors, and options; reports necessary for taxing authorities, regulatory agencies, employees, and stockholders; and the necessity to communicate policies and objectives from executive management to all operating levels. With the speed and flexibility of computers, an information system may collect and analyze business data into categories for different levels of management, such as (1) data from routine business transactions, (2) control totals, (3) control ratios, and (4) statistically tested mathematical models or simulations.

Data from Repetitive Transactions. These data originate with the source documents necessary to verify the transaction in accordance with good business practice or to comply with legal requirements. Clock cards or time tickets, purchase orders and invoices, sales invoices, and derived documents (such as journal vouchers, materials cards, FICA tax records, employees' earnings records, payrolls, checks, production reports, inventory records, and other prepared documents and reports) constitute routine business data. Each document serves a simple and specific purpose, without which a business cannot operate. Approximately 75 percent of all digital computers are utilized for handling routine business data.

Control Totals. Control totals arise because a business functions through departments, branches, and operating divisions; and data generated in one phase of operations flows into another phase. Or for internal control it may be necessary for different individuals or departments to report on the same transactions. Checks written in payment to creditors must show a total that agrees with amounts recorded in the cash payments journal; the total of materials purchased must agree with combined entries on materials cards; daily receipts from credit customers must show a total in agreement with amounts deposited and credited to customer accounts; materials issued totals need to agree with amounts entered on job or production cost sheets; and so on. In each case there is an accounting control total, and the separately derived totals must be identical. A person with even a slight familiarity with business and accounting knows of the time and effort often required to locate errors in order to bring control totals into agreement. The electronic computer readily provides control totals, and its use often releases supervisory personnel for more creative effort.

Control Ratios. Control ratios provide management with information necessary for decisions and action. Cost control is basically a process of watching figures and taking action that will increase or decrease the figures if they become too small or too large. These figures may be totals of sales, materials cost, labor hours, labor cost, overhead, variable cost, or spoilage cost. For management purposes, control totals are obtained each day, week, month, and quarter, and are compared with previous time periods, with budgets, and with standards. From control totals, other ratios meaningful to management are possible, such as inventory turnover, sales per dollar of variable cost, sales per dollar of assets, earnings per dollar of sales, and each cost element as a ratio to sales or to total costs.

Mathematical Models. Mathematical models are now used by management as a tool to describe and help control operations. For example, models or simulations make it possible to test out various inventory control policies and forecasting techniques based on past experience and to select the method that best meets management objectives. By using the computer, it is possible to simulate a complete operating budget and manipulate product mix, price, cost factors, and the marketing program. By studying alternative combinations of the variables, it is possible to reduce uncertainty in making decisions.

The linear programming chapter (Chapter 28) presents problems that can be attacked effectively by computer programming. These illustrations are realistic to the extent that management does face such problems, but often with more complexities and variables. Imagine an oil refinery that blends some combination of materials to produce a considerable array of products. If the goal is maximum earnings per barrel of crude refined and there are dozens of products and product variations with possibly 50 constraints, a computer solution is the only accurate and feasible way. Naturally, oil refineries were in operation before computers came into being, and refinery managers have been making decisions on these matters for years. The value of computer solutions in such work lies in the substantial financial effect of small improvements. The managers' decisions reached by previous methods may have been close to the optimum, but a few cents a barrel is a great deal of money when multiplied by production runs in the tens of thousands of barrels per day.

The amazing speed of the computer as a data processing device and its value in an updating or posting application (payrolls, accounts receivable, inventories, etc.) can readily be seen. The opportunities and applications in preparation and analysis of operating and financial information are not so obvious. Program libraries exist in machine-readable form for various related companies where the data for each company, plant, or operating division appear in standardized format. It is feasible to have computer programs which will analyze data for all or any part of the related companies for any number of accounting periods.

DISCUSSION QUESTIONS

1. Define a cost system.

2. A principal factor in the creation of a cost system is a knowledge of the company's plant, machinery, methods, layout, and flow of work. With this knowledge, the accountant possesses the essential background information to develop the necessary cost procedures. Explain how the accountant would use this information.

3. A chart of accounts, accompanied by adequate instructions, is a great aid to better accounting, costing, and controlling. Explain.

4. The journal voucher control system is said to be one of the most effective means of internal control when designed to fit a specific enterprise and properly administered.
   (a) Explain how the voucher can be a means of internal control.
   (b) How does a voucher serve as a connecting link between general accounting and cost accounting?

5. If a factory is located in one city or state and the general office in another, it is desirable to separate a portion of the records.
   (a) Name four control accounts and the subsidiary ledgers that would likely be kept at the factory.
   (b) How are ledgers kept in balance between the factory and the general office?

(c) What entry would be made on the factory books when goods are shipped directly to a customer? Assume that inventory records are maintained at the factory.

(d) What entry would be made on the home office books for transaction (c)?

(e) A factory sends goods it has produced to another branch factory. What entry would be made on the producing factory's books?

6. (a) When a portion of the accounting is done at the factory and a factory ledger is maintained, what accounts are most likely to be in the factory ledger?

(b) What is the principal reason for maintaining accounts at the factory?

7. Explain the term "programming."

8. What are the four major activities provided by a digital computer?

9. Draw up a flowchart with the functional parts of a computer system.

10. A computer system may collect and analyze business data in different ways for different levels of management. Discuss.

11. State some advantages which the electronic data processing system offers for cost accounting record-keeping.

EXERCISES

1. Cost accounting cycle entries. The following accounts were taken from the ledger of the Arlington Company:

A. Accounts Receivable
B. Accrued Payroll
C. Cash
D. Cost of Goods Sold
E. Applied Factory Overhead
F. Factory Overhead Control
G. Employees Income Tax Payable
H. Federal Unemployment Tax Payable
I. FICA Tax Payable

J. Finished Goods
K. Materials
L. Payroll
M. Sales
N. Marketing and Administrative Expenses
O. State Unemployment Tax Payable
P. Accounts Payable
Q. Work in Process

Required: The correct debit(s) and credit(s) for each of the following transactions, selecting the appropriate letter(s) from the list above:

(1) Paid accounts payable due.
(2) Issued direct materials and factory supplies from the storeroom.
(3) Recorded payroll, including employee FICA contributions and income tax withheld.
(4) Distributed the payroll, which consisted of direct labor, indirect labor, and sales salaries.
(5) Recorded employer payroll tax liability. Payroll taxes for factory workers are treated as factory overhead.
(6) Applied factory overhead.
(7) Completed Job 501.
(8) Shipped Job 500 to customer on account.

2. T accounts showing flow of cost. The Seitz Company had the following inventories on September 1:

Materials	$60,000	Work in process — labor	$36,000
Finished goods	50,000	Work in process — factory	
Work in process — materials	30,000	overhead	27,000

During September, the cost of materials purchased was $200,000, direct labor cost incurred was $180,000, and factory overhead applicable to production was 75% of the direct labor cost. The September 30 inventories were as follows:

Materials.....................................	$30,000	Work in process — labor............	$20,000
Finished goods	47,000	Work in process — factory	
Work in process — materials.....	12,000	overhead	15,000

Required: T accounts showing the flow of the cost of goods manufactured and sold, using three accounts for work in process.

3. Factory overhead rate and relationship of cost elements. A schedule of cost of goods manufactured shows:

Materials used	$300,000
Direct labor	800,000
Overhead costs...	640,000
Work in process, ending inventory..	140,000

Required:
(1) The rate of factory overhead to direct labor cost.
(2) The cost of direct materials included in the work in process ending inventory, assuming that the direct labor cost included in the inventory of work in process is $50,000.

4. Journal entries for the cost accounting cycle. On May 1, the trial balance of the Endeavor Company showed:

Cash...	25,800	
Accounts Receivable...	47,740	
Allowance for Doubtful Accounts		2,825
Finished Goods...	78,700	
Work in Process..	85,400	
Materials...	44,880	
Building	120,000	
Accumulated Depreciation — Building		48,000
Equipment...	237,240	
Accumulated Depreciation — Equipment....................................		115,210
Accounts Payable..		54,270
Accrued Payroll...		6,600
Common Stock		80,000
Retained Earnings		332,855
	639,760	639,760

During May, these transactions took place:

(a)	Materials purchased on account...	$ 40,000
(b)	Direct materials issued..	65,000
	Indirect materials issued	3,500
(c)	Materials returned to supplier	900
(d)	Total payroll (direct labor)	80,000
	Total payroll (indirect labor)	9,500
	(Assume that there are no payroll deductions)	
(e)	Wages paid..	75,000
(f)	Sundry manufacturing expenses incurred	42,000
(g)	Marketing and administrative expenses incurred......................	8,500
(h)	Accounts receivable collected..	300,000
(i)	Accounts payable paid..	135,000
(j)	Depreciation to be provided for May at the rate of 2% per annum on building; 10% per annum on equipment.................	?
(k)	Factory overhead applied to production at 60% of direct labor cost..	?
(l)	Work in process, May 31..	75,000
(m)	Cost of goods sold..	205,000
(n)	Sales on account	285,000

Required: Journal entries for the above transactions.

5. Cost accounting cycle entries in T accounts. At the beginning of September, the ledger of the MacFarland Company contained (among other accounts) the following: Cash, $23,000; Finished Goods, $25,000; Work in Process, $40,000; Materials, $35,000. During September, the following transactions were completed:

(a) Materials were purchased on account at a cost of $48,500.

(b) Materials in the amount of $62,000 were issued from the storeroom for use in production.

(c) Requisitions for indirect factory materials and supplies totaled $6,000.

(d) The total payroll was $85,000, including sales salaries of $20,000 and office salaries of $15,000. Labor time tickets show that $40,000 of the payroll was direct labor. Income tax was withheld at the rate of 10% of wages earned, and employee FICA tax, at a 6.5% rate, was deducted. The payroll due the employees was paid during the month.

(e) The employer payroll taxes for all categories of employees consist of the same rate of FICA, 1.4% state unemployment insurance, and .7% federal unemployment insurance tax.

(f) Sundry manufacturing expenses of $12,600 were paid.

(g) Factory overhead of 80% of the direct labor cost is charged to production.

(h) Cost of production completed for the month totaled $155,000, and finished goods in the warehouse at the end of September totaled $20,000.

(i) Customers were billed $222,000 for shipments made during September.

(j) Customers paid $168,000 on account.

Required:
   (1) T accounts for the transactions for September, using one work in process account.
   (2) Income statement accounts closed to Income Summary; underapplied factory overhead closed to Cost of Goods Sold.

6. Factory ledger entries. Farrell and Harrell, Inc., uses a general ledger and a factory ledger. Inventory accounts, a payroll clearing account for factory employees, and Factory Overhead Control are kept at the factory; plant asset accounts and Accounts Payable are part of the general office books. The following transactions took place:

Mar. 2. Purchased materials for the factory, $20,000. Terms 1/10, n/60.

      4. Requisitions of $4,000 of direct materials and $2,000 of indirect materials were filled from the stockroom.

      8. Factory payroll of $2,000 ($1,880 direct labor; $120 indirect labor) for the week was made up at the home office; $1,690 in cash was sent to the factory. FICA tax was $130 and income tax was $180.

   14. Depreciation of $200 for factory equipment was recorded. (Assets and accumulated depreciation accounts are kept on the general office books.)

   14. A job was completed in the factory with $960 direct labor and $450 of materials being previously charged to the job. Factory overhead is to be applied at a rate of 66⅔% of direct labor.

   15. Miscellaneous factory overhead of $800 was paid by the home office and transferred to the factory.

   16. The job completed on the 14th was shipped to Brill Bros. on instructions from the home office. Customer was billed for $2,800.

Required: Journal entries on the factory books and the general office books.

7. Factory ledger entries. Plastic Design has its general office in Philadelphia, but its plant is in Montgomeryville. A separate set of records is kept at the home office and at the factory. On November 1, the factory trial balance showed the following:

Finished Goods	6,400	
Work in Process	7,800	
Materials	3,500	
General Ledger		17,700
Total	17,700	17,700

For November, the following transactions occurred:

(a) Materials purchased on account, $33,000.
(b) Direct materials of $22,000 were requisitioned, along with indirect materials of $6,500 and $2,500 of supplies.
(c) Total payroll was $30,000. The home office prepared the payroll and the checks and deducted 6.5% for FICA tax and 10% for federal income tax. The liability for employer payroll taxes is kept on the home office books. The state unemployment insurance tax rate is 2.1%; the federal unemployment insurance tax rate is .7%. The payroll consisted of office salaries of $3,000, sales salaries of $8,000, indirect labor of $4,000, and direct labor of $15,000.
(d) Factory overhead is applied at a rate of 110% of direct labor cost.
(e) Materials costing $275 were defective and were returned to the supplier.
(f) Payments made to vendors on account, $31,500.
(g) Various factory overhead expenses totaled $2,000, including $400 depreciation on factory machinery.
(h) Goods completed totaled $48,300.
(i) Goods costing $45,000 were sold for $65,000.

Required: Journal entries on the books of the general office and the factory to record the above transactions.

8. Factory ledger entries. Electronics Incorporated maintains its factory in Stillwater, Oklahoma, but its main office is in Tulsa. On September 1, the factory trial balance appeared as follows:

Finished Goods..	23,000	
Work in Process...	68,250	
Materials...	19,500	
Factory Overhead Control..	540,000	
Factory Machinery...	120,000	
Accumulated Depreciation — Factory Machinery.........................		36,000
Applied Factory Overhead		536,400
General Ledger		198,350
Total..	770,750	770,750

The following transactions were completed during September:

(a) Direct materials of $120,000 were purchased on terms of 2/10, n/30.
(b) The factory payroll for $45,000 direct labor and $9,000 indirect labor was mailed to the home office. The home office payroll was $15,000 for sales salaries and $21,000 for office salaries. Employee payroll deductions were recorded at the home office at these rates: 6.5% of gross earnings for FICA tax; 18% of gross earnings for federal income tax.
(c) Indirect factory materials and supplies amounting to $26,250 were purchased; terms 2/10, n/30.
(d) Employer payroll tax expense is recorded on the home office books. State unemployment rate, 1.8%; federal unemployment, .7%; FICA tax, 6.5%.
(e) Analysis of the materials requisitions (all supplies are kept at the factory):

Production orders...	$60,000
Indirect factory materials and supplies...............................	15,000
Shipping supplies	4,500

(f) Defective shipping supplies of $900 were returned to the vendor.
(g) Accounts payable totaling $142,500, including the accrued payroll, were paid.
(h) Depreciation at an annual rate of 10% of the original cost was recorded on the factory machinery.
(i) Sundry factory expenses of $6,900 were recorded as liabilities.
(j) Factory overhead was applied to production at the rate of $6 per direct labor hour; the factory worked 6,000 hours.
(k) Goods completed with a total cost of $126,000 were transferred to finished goods.
(l) Sales were $150,000 and cost $96,000 to produce.

Required:

    (1) Journal entries to record the transactions on the general office books and on the factory books.

    (2) The two factory overhead accounts, in which applicable transactions are posted; the transfer of any over- or underapplied overhead to the cost of goods sold account, and the closing of all factory overhead accounts.

PROBLEMS

4-1. Manufacturing costs. The following information is available for March:

Accounts payable, March 1	$ 6,000
Work in process, March 1	30,000
Finished goods, March 1	50,000
Materials, March 31	15,000
Accounts payable, March 31	10,000
Finished goods, March 31	60,000
Actual factory overhead	150,000
Cost of goods sold	300,000
Payment of accounts payable (assume this account is used for materials only)	35,000

Factory overhead is applied at 200% of direct labor cost. Jobs still in process on March 31 have been charged $6,000 for materials and $12,000 for direct labor (1,500 hours). Actual direct labor hours, 10,000 at $8 per hour.

Required:

    (1) Materials purchased.
    (2) Cost of goods manufactured.
    (3) Applied factory overhead.
    (4) Work in process, March 31.
    (5) Materials used.
    (6) Materials, March 1.
    (7) Over- or underapplied factory overhead.

(CGAA adapted)

4-2. Factory ledger entries. The following transactions were completed by Busch Corporation, which maintains both a factory ledger and a general ledger:

    (a) Materials purchased and received at the factory $13,500
    (b) Requisitions received and filled in the storeroom:

For direct materials	$12,300
For manufacturing supplies	4,000

    (c) Factory payroll paid for the week, as follows:

Direct labor	$10,000
Indirect labor	3,200
Superintendence	1,000

(A factory payroll book is maintained at the factory. At the end of each week, the factory payroll is reported to and paid by the general office. Provision for employee FICA tax in the amount of $923 and 10% income tax is made on the general office books. The only payroll entry on the factory books is one distributing the payroll to the appropriate accounts and crediting General Ledger. The employer factory payroll taxes are treated as factory overhead. The state unemployment insurance rate is 1.8%, the federal unemployment insurance rate is .7%, and the employer FICA tax is $923.)

(d) Direct materials returned to the storeroom, $800.

(e) A transfer voucher from the general office showed the following expenses to be recorded:

Insurance on factory building and equipment (prepaid account on general books)...............	$ 250
Heat, light, and power..	325
Property tax on factory building	75
Depreciation of machinery	240
Depreciation of factory building	100
	$ 990

(f) Factory overhead is applied to production at the rate of 125% of direct labor cost.

(g) Work completed during the week, $28,000.

(h) Goods costing $32,500 to produce were sold for $42,000.

Required: Journal entries to record the above transactions on the general office books and on the factory books, using only one work in process account and assuming that all inventory accounts and Factory Overhead are a part of the factory ledger, while liability accounts, Sales, and Cost of Goods Sold are a part of the general ledger.

4-3. Factory ledger entries. Spacecraft Corporation has its general office in Princeton, N.J., and its factory in nearby Trenton. A separate set of records is kept at the general office and at the factory.

On January 1, the Trenton factory trial balance showed the following:

Finished Goods	19,000	
Work in Process	28,500	
Materials	49,000	
General Ledger...		96,500
Total	96,500	96,500

The following transactions were completed at the factory during the month:

(a) Materials purchases..	$55,000
(b) Materials requisitions:	
Direct	67,000
Indirect..	10,000
(c) Return of materials to suppliers...	950
(d) Payments to vendors (before 2% discount)	55,000
(e) Payrolls for the month:	
Direct labor ($6 per hour)...	26,400
Indirect labor...	6,400
Sales salaries	2,800
Office salaries	2,300

        (Deduct 6.5% for FICA tax and 10% for federal income tax. Liability for payrolls and payroll taxes is kept on the home office books.)

(f) Workers are paid and employer payroll taxes are recorded. The state unemployment insurance rate is 2%, the federal unemployment insurance rate is .7%, and employer FICA tax is 6.5%.

(g) Sundry factory overhead expenses, $32,000.

(h) Factory overhead is applied to production at $5 per direct labor hour.

(i) Goods completed amounted to 80% of the total cost in the work in process account.

(j) Finished goods amounting to $114,000 were shipped to customers. (A gross profit of 25% is made on these shipments.)

Required: Entries in journal form to record the January transactions, using one work in process account and two parallel vertical columns headed General Office and Trenton Plant.

4-4. Factory ledger accounts, journal entries, and trial balances. The Nevada Company's cost accounting system uses both general and factory ledgers. On December 31, 19A, after closing, the ledgers contained the following account balances:

Cash	$20,000	Accounts Payable	$15,500
Accounts Receivable	25,000	Accrued Payroll	2,250
Finished Goods	9,500	Common Stock	60,000
Work in Process	4,500	Retained Earnings	21,250
Materials	10,000	Factory Ledger	24,000
Machinery	30,000	General Ledger	24,000

Inventory accounts are kept in the factory ledger.

During January, 19B, the following transactions were completed:

(a) Materials purchased, $92,000.
(b) Factory overhead incurred, $18,500.
(c) Labor was consumed as follows: for direct production, $60,500; indirect labor, $12,500; sales salaries, $8,000; administrative salaries, $5,000. Credit Accrued Payroll for total gross wages. The employer payroll tax cost is based on labor purchased. The state and federal unemployment insurance tax rates are 1.6% and .7%, respectively; the employer FICA tax is $5,590. Of the FICA tax, $480 pertained to sales and $325 to administrative salaries.
(d) Gross payrolls totaling $75,750 were paid (10% of wages paid was withheld for income tax, and $4,923.75 for FICA tax). Debit Accrued Payroll for total gross wages of $75,750. Credit Accounts Payable for employee earnings after deductions; then record the cash payment to employees.
(e) Materials were consumed as follows: direct materials, $82,500; indirect materials, $8,300.
(f) Factory overhead applied to production was 76% of the direct labor cost.
(g) Work finished and placed in stock cost $188,000.
(h) All but $12,000 of the finished goods were sold, terms 2/10, n/60. The markup was 30% above production cost.
(i) Of the accounts receivable, 80% was collected, less 2% discount.
(j) A liability was recorded for various marketing and administrative expenses amounting to $30,000. Of this amount, 60% was marketing and 40% was administrative.
(k) The check register showed payments of $104,000 for liabilities other than payrolls.

Required:
(1) Trial balances of the general ledger and of the factory ledger as of January 1, 19B.
(2) General ledger and factory ledger accounts, with balances from the January 1 trial balances.
(3) January transactions posted directly into the ledger accounts, without journal entries and with new accounts opened whenever necessary.
(4) Trial balances of the general ledger and the factory ledger as of January 31, 19B.

4-5. Cost accounting cycle; cost of goods sold and income statements. Baker Co. had these beginning and ending inventories at the end of its current year:

	BEGINNING	ENDING
Finished goods	$25,000	$18,000
Work in process	40,000	48,000
Materials	22,000	30,000

During the year the following transactions occurred:

Materials purchased	$300,000
Indirect materials and supplies purchased	50,000
Direct labor cost	120,000*
Indirect factory labor	60,000*
Property tax and depreciation on factory building	20,000
Property tax and depreciation on salesroom and office (shared equally)	15,000

*Assume no payroll deductions are made.

Utilities (60% to factory, 20% to salesroom, and 20% to office)	$50,000
Indirect materials issued to factory	40,000
Factory overhead applied on the basis of 120% of direct labor cost	?
Salespersons' salaries	40,000*
Office salaries	24,000*
Sales on account	730,000

Over- or underapplied factory overhead is deducted from or added to cost of goods sold.

*Assume no payroll deductions are made.

Required:
(1) T accounts with the data posted therein. (Purchases and payroll to be credited to Accounts Payable.)
(2) A cost of goods sold statement.
(3) An income statement.

(AICPA adapted)

CASE

Chart of accounts — coding system. Robert B. Mace has recently been appointed controller of a family-owned manufacturing enterprise. The firm, S. Dilley & Co., was founded by Samuel Dilley about 20 years ago, is 78% owned by Dilley, and has served the major automotive companies as a parts supplier. The firm's major operating divisions are Heat Treating, Extruding, Small Parts Stamping, and Specialized Machining. Sales last year from the several divisions ranged from $150,000 to over $3,000,000. The divisions are physically and managerially independent except for Dilley's constant surveillance. The accounting system for each division has evolved according to the division's own needs and to the abilities of its accountants. Mace is the first controller in the firm's history to have responsibility for overall financial management. Dilley expects to retire within six years and has hired Mace to improve the firm's financial system.

Mace decides to design a financial reporting system that will:
1. Give managers uniform, timely, and accurate reports on business activity. Monthly divisional reports should be uniform and available by the 10th of the following month. Company-wide financial reports also should be prepared by the 10th.
2. Provide a basis for measuring return on investment by division. Divisional reports should show assets assigned each division and revenue and expense measurement in each division.
3. Generate meaningful budget data for planning and decision-making purposes. The accounting system should provide for the preparation of budgets which recognize managerial responsibility, controllability of costs, and major product groups.
4. Allow for a uniform basis of evaluating performance and quick access to underlying data. Cost center variances should be measured and reported for operating and nonoperating units, including headquarters. Also, questions about levels of specific cost factors or product costs should be answerable quickly.

It appears to Mace that a new chart of accounts is essential to attacking other critical financial problems. The present account codes used by divisions are not standard. Mace sees a need to divide asset accounts into six major categories, i.e., current assets, plant and equipment, etc. Within each of these categories, no more than 10 control accounts are needed, and 100 subsidiary accounts seem more than adequate for each control account.

No division now has more than five major product groups. The maximum number of cost centers within any product group is six, including operating and nonoperating groups. General divisional costs are considered as a nonrevenue-producing product group. Altogether, about 44 natural expense accounts plus about 12 specific variance accounts would be adequate.

Mace is planning to implement the new chart of accounts in an environment that at present includes manual records systems and one division which is using an EDP system. In the near future most accounting and reporting for all units will be automated. Therefore, the chart of accounts should facilitate the processing of transactions manually or by machine. Efforts should be made to restrict the length of the code for economy in processing and convenience in use.

Required:
  (1) A new chart of accounts coding system that will meet the new controller's requirements, beginning with a digital layout of the coding system; an explanation of the coding method chosen and the reason for the size of the code elements, and an explanation of the code as it would apply to asset and expense accounts.
  (2) Use of the new chart of accounts coding system to illustrate the application of the code for the following data:
    (a) In the Small Parts Stamping Division, $100 was spent on cleaning supplies by Supervisor Bill Shaw in the Polishing Department of the Door Lever Group. Code the expense item using the new code.
    (b) A new motorized sweeper has been purchased for the Maintenance Department of the Extruding Division for $3,450. Code this asset item using the code developed above.

(CMA adapted)

5

Job Order Costing

An enterprise seeks to profit by providing customers with goods and services. To realize this profit, it is necessary to make decisions based upon appropriate and timely information provided by accounting reports. In fulfilling the needs of management, cost accounting consists of three basic phases: (1) cost determination and measurement, (2) cost planning and control through budgets and standards, and (3) cost analysis for decision-making purposes.

The previous chapter presented an overall view of the flow of costs and expenses, generally known as the manufacturing cost accounting cycle for cost determination. The greater part of this chapter is devoted to the cost accumulation procedures utilized in job order costing. Before entering into this discussion, it seems advisable to differentiate briefly between cost systems and cost accumulation procedures.

COST SYSTEMS: ACTUAL OR STANDARD

Determination of a product's cost is a basic objective of cost accounting. After the cost unit has been selected (see discussion on page 93), the obvious question arises: How are these costs accumulated? A decision must be made whether to compile and allocate actual costs to the units of production or to assign costs on a standard cost basis. If the latter method is chosen, variance accounts will set off the difference between actual costs and standard costs.

An *actual* or *historical* cost system collects the costs as they occur but delays the presentation of results until manufacturing operations have been performed or services rendered. While the job or the process is charged with the actual quantities and costs of materials used and labor expended, the factory overhead in many cases is allocated on the basis of a predetermined overhead rate. Thus, even a so-called ''actual'' cost system is not predicated entirely on actual costs.

In a *standard* cost system, unit costs are predetermined in advance of production. Products, operations, and processes are costed using standards for both quantity and dollar amounts. Accounts are designed to collect actual costs. Differences between actual costs and standard costs, called *variances*, are collected in separate accounts. These variances are analyzed, and management is expected to move quickly to check unfavorable trends and departures from predetermined standards as well as from the desired overall profit goal.

COST ACCUMULATION PROCEDURES: JOB ORDER OR PROCESS

Both the actual cost system and the standard cost system may be used in connection with either job order or process costing.

The Job Order Cost Procedure

The job order cost procedure keeps the costs of various jobs or contracts separate during their manufacture or construction. The method is applicable to job order work in factories, workshops, and repair shops as well as to work by builders, construction engineers, shipbuilders, and printers. The cost unit is the job, the work order, or the contract; and the records will show the cost of each. The method presupposes the possibility of physically identifying the jobs produced and of charging each with its own cost.

A variation of the job order cost method is that of costing orders by lots. A lot is the quantity of product that can conveniently and economically be produced and costed. For example, in the shoe manufacturing industry a contract is divided into lots, each lot being from 100 to 250 pairs of one size and style of shoe. The costs are then accumulated for each lot.

The Process Cost Procedure

The process cost procedure discussed in Chapters 6, 7, and 8 consists of computing an average unit cost for production by dividing the total manufacturing cost by the total number of units produced in the factory over a specific period of time. This method is used when units are not distinguishable from one another during one or more manufacturing processes. The following conditions may also exist:

1. The product of one process becomes the material of the next process.
2. Different products, or even by-products, are produced by the same process.

The process cost method is applicable to industries such as flour mills, breweries, chemical industries, textile factories, and many others. Because of the nature of the output, it is necessary to compute a unit cost for each process. A process is often identifiable with a department. Such a computation is prepared on a process cost sheet or a cost of production report.

Many companies use both the job order and the process cost method in their product costing. For example, a company manufacturing a railway car built according to the customer's specifications uses job order costing to collect the cost per railway car. However, the multiple small metal stampings required are manufactured in a department which uses fast and repetitive stamping machines. The cost of these stampings is accumulated by the process cost method.

Both the job order and process costing procedures can also be used by service organizations. For example, an automobile repair shop uses job order costing to accumulate the costs associated with work performed on each automobile. An airline or a hospital can utilize the notion of process costing to accumulate costs per passenger mile or per patient day, respectively. The textbook discussion of job order and process costing emphasizes manufacturing activity; however, the broad applicability of cost accumulation methods, including both actual and standard costs, should be understood.

Cost Units

Determination of unit costs and assignment of inventory costs for the purpose of profit determination is fundamental to cost accounting. The accumulation of costs poses a problem regarding the unit in which the product cost is to be stated. Because the total cost figure is considered unsatisfactory from a control point of view, a cost unit must be found that most adequately conforms both to the type of product and the manufacturing processes. The cost unit used is by no means uniform. While coal is measured by the ton, oil by the barrel, and lumber by board feet, products such as machines, airplanes, automobiles, shoes, shirts, suits, or dresses are measured either by the individual unit or by multiples thereof, such as a dozen or a gross.

In selecting the cost unit, care must be taken that it is neither too large nor too small. If the unit is too large, significant cost trends may pass unnoticed due to averaging of costs. If the unit is too small, it may necessitate detailed and expensive clerical work. After the cost unit has been established, data can be marshaled to determine unit costs and to assign inventory costs.

JOB ORDER COST ACCUMULATION PROCEDURES

Job order and process costing procedures are employed by many types of manufacturing and service businesses. It should be remembered that job order and process costing represent two methods of cost accumulation, both of which follow the basic manufacturing cost cycle.

**Job Order
Cost
Sheets**

In job order costing, each job is an accounting unit to which materials, labor, and factory overhead costs are assigned by means of job order numbers. The cost of each order produced for a given customer or the cost of each lot to be placed in stock is recorded on a summary sheet called a *job order cost sheet*, or merely a *cost sheet*. This master sheet is designed to collect the costs of materials, labor, and factory overhead applicable to a specific job.

Cost sheets differ in form, content, and arrangement in each business. The illustrations below and on page 95 show simple forms. In each form, the upper section provides space for the job number, the name of the customer, a description of the items to be produced, the quantity, the date started, and the date completed. In factories with departmentalized operations (page 95), the cost sheet will show the materials, labor, and factory overhead applied in each department or cost center.

Cost Sheet
for a
Nondepartmen-
talized Plant

Delta Manufacturing Co.   JOB ORDER NO. **978**

FOR: Evans Construction Company   DATE ORDERED: 3/10/--

PRODUCT: #14 Maple drain boards   DATE STARTED: 3/14/--

SPECIFICATION: 12' x 20" x 1" clear finished   DATE WANTED: 3/22/--

QUANTITY: 10   DATE COMPLETED: 3/20/--

MATERIALS		DIRECT LABOR		APPLIED FACTORY OVERHEAD RATE: 125% of direct labor cost	
DATE	AMOUNT	DATE	AMOUNT	DATE	AMOUNT
3/14	$420.00	3/14	$78.00	3/20	$305.00
3/19	78.00	3/17	56.00		
3/20	62.00	3/18	56.00		
		3/19	24.00		
		3/20	30.00		
TOTAL ⟶	$560.00	TOTAL ⟶	$244.00	TOTAL ⟶	$305.00

MATERIALS .... $ 560.00   SELLING PRICE $1,850.00

DIRECT LABOR 244.00

APPLIED FACTORY OVERHEAD .... 305.00   FACTORY COST $1,109.00

            MARKETING EXPENSES ...   176.00

TOTAL FACTORY COST .... $1,109.00   ADMIN. EXPENSES 125.00

            COST TO MAKE AND SELL 1,410.00

            PROFIT ....$ 440.00

modern furniture company

JOB ORDER NO. **2706**

FOR: Federated Department Stores

PRODUCT: #120--recliners

SPECIFICATIONS: Attached drawings & blueprints

QUANTITY: 100

DATE ORDERED: 9/22/--

DATE STARTED: 11/21/--

DATE WANTED: 12/10/--

DATE COMPLETED: 12/5/--

DIRECT MATERIALS

DATE	DEPARTMENT	REQ. NO.	DESCRIPTION OR STORES NO.	QUANTITY	COST PER UNIT	TOTAL
11/12	Cutting	2947	Support lumber oak, 10 feet	100 pieces	$10.80	$1,080.00
		2948	Support lumber pine, 8 feet	50 pieces	7.00	350.00
11/15	Assembly	3080	Glue, pegs, and screws (standard)	500	3.00	1,500.00
11/27	Upholstery	3407	Upholstery cloth	1,000 yds.	6.50	6,500.00
			Total Materials Cost			$9,430.00

DIRECT LABOR

DATE	DEPARTMENT	TIME REPORT NO.	DESCRIPTION OF LABOR OR PROCESS	HOURS	RATE	COST
11/12-14	Cutting	867-901	Power saw cutting	20	$6.75	$ 135.00
11/14	Planing	1125-1130	Planing	50	7.50	375.00
11/15-21	Assembly	1360-1397	Assembling frames	100	7.25	725.00
11/25-27	Upholstery	1480-1505	Padding and upholstery	150	8.00	1,200.00
			Total Labor Cost			$ 2,435.00

APPLIED FACTORY OVERHEAD

DATE	DEPARTMENT	BASIS OF APPLICATION	HOURS	RATE	COST
11/15	Cutting	$3 per direct labor hour	20	$3.00	$ 60.00
11/15	Planing	$4 per direct labor hour	50	4.00	200.00
11/22	Assembly	$2 per direct labor hour	100	2.00	200.00
11/29	Upholstery	100% of direct labor cost	--	--	1,200.00
		Total Applied Factory Overhead			$ 1,660.00

Departmentalized Cost Sheet

DIRECT MATERIALS .... $ 9,430.00
DIRECT LABOR................................ 2,435.00
APPLIED FACTORY OVERHEAD 1,660.00

TOTAL FACTORY COST $13,525.00

SELLING PRICE $21,000.00

FACTORY COST $13,525.00
MARKETING EXPENSES 2,206.00
ADMIN. EXPENSES 1,905.00

COST TO MAKE AND SELL 17,636.00

PROFIT .... $ 3,364.00

Several jobs or orders may be going through a factory at the same time. Each cost sheet is given a job number which is placed on each materials requisition and labor time ticket used in connection with the job. These forms used for materials and labor, numbered for the job to which they apply, are totaled daily or weekly and entered on the cost sheets. The cost sheet eventually becomes a summary of all the costs, including factory overhead, involved in completing a job. The cost sheets are subsidiary records and are controlled by the work in process account.

Jobs performed on the basis of customer specifications allow the computation of a profit or loss on each order. If jobs constitute production of a specific quantity for inventory, job order costing permits computation of a unit cost for inventory costing purposes.

The discussion that follows deals with job order cost accumulation procedures using the data of the Fairbanks Company presented on pages 72 and 75. The data are expanded in this chapter for purposes of introducing the many detailed procedures that are so essential to an adequate accounting for costs.

Cost Accounting Procedures for Materials

Merchandise Inventory and Purchases are familiar accounts in trading concerns. In manufacturing enterprises, it is common practice to record all materials and supplies in one control account, Materials. Procedures that affect the materials account involve the:

1. Purchase of materials.
2. Issuance of materials for factory use.

These procedures are discussed in greater detail in Chapters 12 and 13.

Recording the Purchase of Materials. Accounting techniques used for the purchase of materials vary little from those studied in general accounting. The account debited is Materials or Materials Inventory (now used in place of Purchases), and the credit is made to Accounts Payable as materials are received. However, a posting to the materials account is not sufficient. Each purchase is also entered on an individual materials ledger card (a separate card being used for each materials item) showing quantity received, unit cost, and total amount. The posting to each materials ledger card is added to the previous balance, which provides a perpetual inventory.

When materials are purchased, the approved invoice is recorded as:

Materials	25,000	
Accounts Payable...		25,000

Materials returned to the vendor are recorded as follows:

Accounts Payable...	2,000	
Materials		2,000

An entry for the returned materials is also made on the appropriate materials ledger cards.

Recording the Issuance of Materials. When a job is started, the materials necessary for the work are issued to the factory on the basis of materials requisitions prepared by production scheduling clerks or other employees. A copy of the requisition goes to the storekeeper, who assembles the materials called for on the requisition. The materials requisition bears the job order number and specifies the type and quantity of materials required. The quantity, unit cost, and the total cost of each of the materials are entered later on the requisition and posted to the materials ledger card.

The flow of materials from storeroom to factory results in a transfer of materials from the materials account to the work in process account. Essentially, each requisition results in a debit to Work in Process and a credit to Materials. Materials requisitions are summarized and recorded as follows:

Work in Process	31,000	
Materials		31,000

A copy of each requisition goes to the cost department. These requisitions are sorted by job numbers, totaled, and entered in the materials section of the cost sheet bearing the same number. This basic costing technique accumulates the quantity and cost of materials used in each job.

When materials originally requisitioned for a job are not used and are returned to the storeroom accompanied by a returned materials report, Materials is debited and Work in Process is credited. This requires entries on the materials ledger card as well as on the job order cost sheet.

Materials requisitions are also used to secure indirect materials or factory supplies from the storeroom. At the time of purchase, indirect materials are charged to Materials or to separate accounts such as Indirect Materials or Factory Supplies. When indirect materials are issued, the requisitions are charged to the factory overhead control account and are recorded in departmental expense analysis sheets, which constitute a subsidiary ledger for the departments using the supplies. Supplies used in marketing or administrative activities are charged to marketing or administrative expense accounts. The entry for indirect materials requisitions is shown as follows:

	SUBSIDIARY RECORD	DR.	CR.
Factory Overhead Control		6,000	
Indirect Materials	6,000		
Materials (or Indirect Materials or Fac			
tory Supplies).................................			6,000

The effect of these transactions on the materials account is shown below.

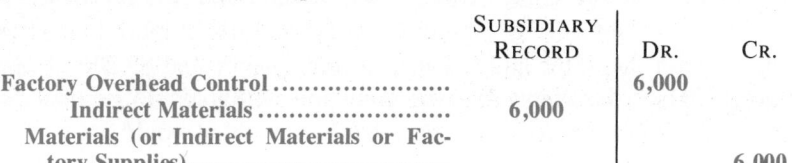

				MATERIALS			
Mar.	1	Inventory		100,000	Mar. 31	Return	2,000
	31	Purchase		25,000	31	Direct materials	
			86,000	125,000		requisitions	31,000
					31	Indirect materials	
						requisitions	6,000
							39,000

Cost Accounting Procedures for Labor

The entire payroll procedure may be divided into two distinct phases:

1. Collection of payroll data, computation of earnings, calculation of payroll taxes, and payment of wages.
2. Distribution and allocation of labor costs to jobs, departments, and other cost classifications.

To compute the labor cost of a given order, the time spent on each job during a day must be recorded on each worker's time ticket. The time tickets, in turn, are priced in the payroll department to permit computation of employees' gross earnings.

In most factories the worker punches a time clock when entering and leaving the plant. The timekeeper makes periodic checks and records the days or hours worked by each employee. The clock card registers time In and Out. Clock card hours should be reconciled with time ticket hours. When wages are paid on an hourly basis, the employee's clock card is often used by payroll clerks to compute gross earnings.

For each payroll period — weekly, every two weeks, or monthly — a record of the labor cost and the liability for payment is summarized by journalizing and posting to the general ledger accounts. Time tickets for the various jobs worked on each day are sorted, priced, and summarized; at regular intervals, usually at the end of the payroll period, the labor time and labor cost for each job are entered in the space provided on the job order cost sheets. Posting to the cost sheets constitutes the distribution of the direct labor payroll. A summary of time ticket data facilitates journalizing, general ledger posting, and preparation of reports. A full explanation of labor costing and payroll accounting is deferred to Chapters 14 and 15.

To simplify this discussion, reference will be made only to deductions from the gross earnings of employees for federal income tax and for the employees' share of FICA (Federal Insurance Contributions Act) tax.[1] However, it should be realized that an employee's gross earnings may be subject to other deductions, such as state income tax, city earnings tax, pension payments, savings bonds, union dues, and United Fund contributions.

To illustrate the recording of labor cost, assume that the Fairbanks Company met two payrolls during the month: $12,000 of direct labor and $1,800 of indirect labor on the 15th; and $15,000 of direct labor and $2,200 of indirect labor on the 31st. Assuming that the company withholds 15 percent for income tax and 6.5 percent for FICA tax, the journal entry would be:

15th			31st		
Payroll	13,800		Payroll	17,200	
Employees Income			Employees Income		
Tax Payable........		2,070	Tax Payable........		2,580
FICA Tax Payable ..		897	FICA Tax Payable ..		1,118
Accrued Payroll......		10,833	Accrued Payroll......		13,502

[1]For convenience in computations, a rate of 6.5 percent on annual wages up to $25,000 paid each employee is used for FICA tax (Old Age, Survivors, and Disability Insurance and the Hospital Insurance Plan, or Medicare) in the illustrations and problems of this textbook.

At each payroll date, the entry to record the payment to the workers would be:

15th			31st		
Accrued Payroll.........	10,833		Accrued Payroll.........	13,502	
Cash		10,833	Cash		13,502

The employer's payroll taxes are commonly recorded at the end of each month or sooner if necessary. For convenience, the FICA tax liability of both the employer and the employees is recorded in one account, FICA Tax Payable. Assuming a 6.5 percent FICA tax, a 2.7 percent state unemployment tax, a .7 percent federal unemployment tax, and that payroll taxes for direct and indirect factory labor are treated as factory overhead, the entry would be:[2]

	SUBSIDIARY RECORD	DR.	CR.
Factory Overhead Control		3,069	
Payroll Taxes	3,069		
FICA Tax Payable			2,015
State Unemployment Tax Payable...........			837
Federal Unemployment Tax Payable			217

Payroll is the labor cost clearing account kept in the records as a convenience, pending analysis of the labor time tickets and distribution of the labor cost to the proper accounts. To distribute the total cost incurred, the following month-end summary entry would be in order:

	SUBSIDIARY RECORD	DR.	CR.
Work in Process		27,000	
Factory Overhead Control		4,000	
Indirect Labor	4,000		
Payroll			31,000

Distribution entries are usually recorded on a weekly basis, so that labor cost remains current on the job order cost sheets and available to operating management. The details supporting the $27,000 Work in Process debit should be found in the labor cost section of the job order cost sheets.

Indirect labor is also accounted for through the use of time tickets and clock cards and entered in the factory overhead control account and on the departmental expense analysis sheets in the same manner as indirect materials. The payroll account and employer payroll taxes accounts may also include amounts applicable to marketing and administrative personnel. Such costs would be charged to marketing and administrative expense accounts. A summary of the entries required in recording labor cost is on page 100. Stage 1 represents the record for each payroll period. Stage 2 shows the cost accounting phase resulting from the labor used.

---

[2]A maximum state unemployment tax of 2.7 percent and a federal unemployment tax of .7 percent on annual wages up to $6,000 are used in this textbook.

STAGE 1 PAYROLL COMPUTED AND PAID	STAGE 2 PAYROLL COSTS DISTRIBUTED

Journal Entries:

15th

Payroll	13,800	
Employees Income Tax		
Payable		2,070
FICA Tax Payable		897
Accrued Payroll		10,833
Accrued Payroll	10,833	
Cash......................................		10,833

31st

Payroll	17,200	
Employees Income Tax		
Payable		2,580
FICA Tax Payable		1,118
Accrued Payroll		13,502
Accrued Payroll	13,502	
Cash......................................		13,502
Factory Overhead Control		
(Payroll Taxes)	3,069	
FICA Tax Payable.............		2,015
State Unemployment Tax		
Payable........................		837
Federal Unemployment		
Tax Payable		217

General Ledger:

FACTORY OVERHEAD CONTROL

3,069 |

Subsidiary Records:

Employees' earnings records, tax, and other deduction records.

DEPARTMENTAL EXPENSE ANALYSIS SHEETS[1]	
Classification	Amount
FICA tax...	$2,015
State unemployment tax..............	837
Federal unemployment tax..........	217

Journal Entries:

31st

Work in Process	27,000	
Factory Overhead Control		
(Indirect Labor)....................	4,000	
Payroll.................................		31,000

General Ledger:

WORK IN PROCESS

27,000 |

FACTORY OVERHEAD CONTROL

3,069 |
4,000 |

Subsidiary Records:

JOB ORDER COST SHEETS[2]		
Direct Labor Section		
Date	Hours	Amount
31	xx	$27,000

DEPARTMENTAL EXPENSE ANALYSIS SHEETS	
Classification	Amount
Indirect Labor......................................	$4,000

[1]There is an analysis sheet for each department or cost center.
[2]There is a separate cost sheet for every job. Entries in the direct labor section of all jobs worked on during the period total $27,000 as shown by the work in process account.

Entries Required in Recording Labor Cost

The quantity and the cost of materials and labor used on a given order can generally be measured in a straightforward and reasonably exact manner. The remaining cost element, factory overhead, presents a more involved problem.

Cost Accounting Procedures for Factory Overhead

If a planing mill contracts to make fifty cabinet assemblies for an apartment complex, the materials used and the labor expended can be entered on the requisitions and time tickets. But how much depreciation of the factory building should be charged to the fifty cabinet assemblies; how much depreciation of saws, planers, and sanders; how much lubricating oil for the machines; how much power, light, heat, insurance, property tax, machine repairs, cutting tools, idle time, security guard's salary, janitor's wages, plant manager's salary, payroll taxes, and cost accountant's salary; and how much for other costs necessary to productive operations? A contributing difficulty is the fact that some of the expenses, such as rent, insurance, property tax, and security guard's salary, are fixed regardless of the amount of production, while other expenses, such as lubricating oil, power, and cutting tools, vary with the quantity of goods manufactured. How, then, is it possible to charge a finished job at the time of completion with a reasonable share of factory overhead when the actual amount of these expenses is often not known until the end of the fiscal period?

Estimated Factory Overhead. Factory overhead is entered on the job order cost sheets on the basis of a predetermined factory overhead rate based on direct labor hours, direct labor cost, machine hours, or other appropriate base. Although a comprehensive study of estimating factory overhead is presented in Chapters 9, 10, and 18, a brief explanation of the procedure is advisable here to complete the picture of the cost cycle. In principle, the accountant determines a causal relationship between two factors, such as the direct labor hours and factory overhead, and uses this relationship as the means of charging factory overhead to jobs. For example, suppose that the Fairbanks Company's direct labor hours for the month were estimated to be 7,000 hours and factory overhead was estimated to be $15,400. These estimates lead to the assumption that for each hour of direct labor there is $2.20 ($15,400 ÷ 7,000 hours) of factory overhead. The job order cost sheet for any job done during the period would disclose the factory overhead applicable to the job (direct labor hours worked on the job times the factory overhead rate).

Applied Factory Overhead Account. The applied factory overhead entered on the job order cost sheet for each job is the basis for the following entry. Again, figures used are from the illustration on page 72.

Work in Process	13,200	
Applied Factory Overhead (6,000 direct labor hours ×		
$2.20)...		13,200

The applied factory overhead account is closed to the actual factory overhead control account at the end of the accounting period by the entry shown at the top of the following page.

| Applied Factory Overhead .... | 13,200 | |
| Factory Overhead Control .... | | 13,200 |

It is common practice to use an applied factory overhead account because it keeps applied costs and actual costs in separate accounts. Some companies do not use the applied factory overhead account and post the credit directly to Factory Overhead Control:

| Work in Process .... | 13,200 | |
| Factory Overhead Control .... | | 13,200 |

This entry eliminates the transfer of applied expenses to actual expenses.

Actual Factory Overhead. While job order cost sheets receive factory overhead on the basis of a predetermined factory overhead rate, actual factory overhead (consisting of indirect materials, indirect labor, payroll taxes, invoices received for overhead items, and the monthly adjusting entries such as depreciation and expired insurance) is charged to Factory Overhead Control and to departmental expense analysis sheets. These procedures are discussed in greater detail in the factory overhead chapters.

Representative examples of factory overhead costs involving adjusting entries are given below.

	SUBSIDIARY RECORD	DR.	CR.
Factory Overhead Control		682	
Depreciation Expense — Machinery..	682		
Accumulated Depreciation — Machinery .			682
Factory Overhead Control		516	
Insurance Expense	516		
Prepaid Insurance..............................			516

For the Fairbanks Company, $6,000 of indirect materials were requisitioned from storerooms, $4,000 of indirect labor was used, and payroll taxes on factory labor totaled $3,069. Other factory expenses comprised of depreciation ($682) and insurance ($516) were prorated through month-end adjusting entries. The factory overhead control account would reflect these facts as shown below.

FACTORY OVERHEAD CONTROL

Mar.	31	Indirect materials	6,000	Mar.	31	Overhead applied	13,200
	31	Indirect labor	4,000			to work in	
	31	Payroll taxes	3,069			process	
	31	Depreciation —					
		machinery	682				
	31	Insurance expense	516				
			1,067				14,267

The balance of $1,067 in the factory overhead control account indicates that actual expenses exceeded the overhead applied to the job orders; stated differently, overhead was underapplied. The above control account was debited with all actual factory overhead items and credited with the applied factory overhead amount. In practice, the details of the actual factory overhead items are recorded in a subsidiary ledger called *departmental expense analysis sheets* or *factory overhead analysis sheets*.

The flow of factory overhead through accounting records is illustrated below. In Stage 1, actual factory overhead is recorded. In Stage 2, overhead is applied to specific jobs.

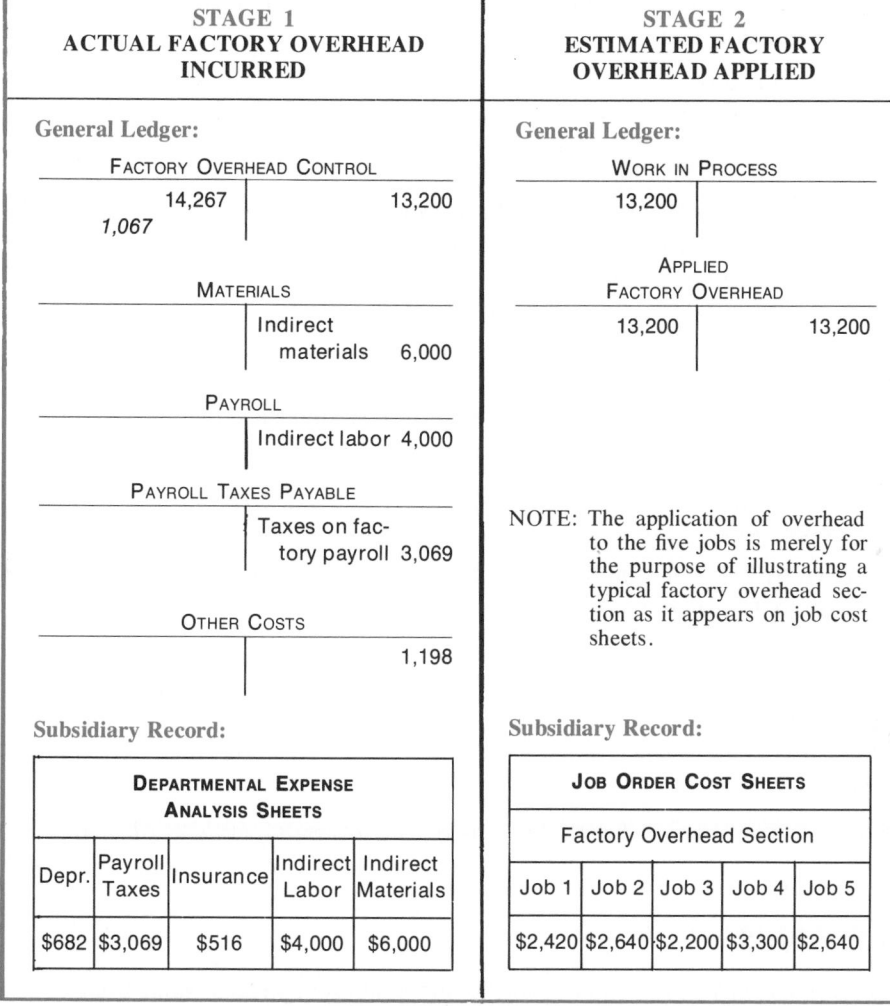

STAGE 1 ACTUAL FACTORY OVERHEAD INCURRED	STAGE 2 ESTIMATED FACTORY OVERHEAD APPLIED
General Ledger:	**General Ledger:**
FACTORY OVERHEAD CONTROL 14,267 | 13,200 1,067	WORK IN PROCESS 13,200 |
MATERIALS | Indirect materials 6,000	APPLIED FACTORY OVERHEAD 13,200 | 13,200
PAYROLL | Indirect labor 4,000	
PAYROLL TAXES PAYABLE | Taxes on factory payroll 3,069	NOTE: The application of overhead to the five jobs is merely for the purpose of illustrating a typical factory overhead section as it appears on job cost sheets.
OTHER COSTS | 1,198	
Subsidiary Record:	**Subsidiary Record:**

DEPARTMENTAL EXPENSE ANALYSIS SHEETS

Depr.	Payroll Taxes	Insurance	Indirect Labor	Indirect Materials
$682	$3,069	$516	$4,000	$6,000

JOB ORDER COST SHEETS

Factory Overhead Section

Job 1	Job 2	Job 3	Job 4	Job 5
$2,420	$2,640	$2,200	$3,300	$2,640

Flow of Factory Overhead Through Accounting Records

During a month's operations, the materials placed in process are accounted for through materials requisitions for the jobs, the labor in process is evidenced by time tickets, and the factory overhead is applied. The figures charged to the work in process account represent the total factory cost for a month's operations.

As jobs are completed, cost sheets are moved from the in-process category to a finished work file. Completion of a job results in a debit to Finished Goods and a credit to Work in Process. If the completed job is undertaken for the purpose of replenishing stock, quantity and cost are recorded on finished

Accounting Procedures for Jobs Completed and Products Sold

goods ledger cards, which are the subsidiary record of the finished goods account. The journal entry to record all the work completed during the month for the Fairbanks Company is:

Finished Goods..	62,180	
Work in Process		62,180

Or, if a separate work in process account is used to accumulate each cost element, the entry is:

Finished Goods..	62,180	
Work in Process — Materials.....................................		26,000
Work in Process — Labor		24,300
Work in Process — Factory Overhead...........................		11,880

In factories with departmentalized operations, separate work in process accounts may be maintained for each producing department, and accumulated costs may be transferred from one department to the next, based on the sequential work flow. Another possible procedure is to accumulate costs but not transfer them to subsequent departments until the job or the work is completed.

When finished products are delivered or shipped to customers, sales invoices are prepared, leading to an entry:

Accounts Receivable..	88,000	
Sales		88,000

Each delivery or shipment necessitates a debit to Cost of Goods Sold and a credit to Finished Goods, using the cost figures recorded on the ledger cards:

Cost of Goods Sold...	52,300	
Finished Goods...		52,300

DISCUSSION QUESTIONS

1. Cost accounting is said to consist of three different phases. Name them.

2. Name four control accounts concerned primarily with cost determination.

3. What subsidiary record or ledger supports each of the control accounts mentioned in answering Question 2?

4. What is the primary objective in job order costing?

5. What is the rationale supporting the use of process costing instead of job order costing for product costing purposes?

(AICPA adapted)

6. What is a cost sheet?

7. How is control over prime costs achieved in job order costing?

8. What is the function of the work in process account in job order costing?

9. What is factory overhead?

10. Explain briefly: (a) actual factory overhead; (b) applied factory overhead.

11. When a sale is made, an asset is debited and Sales is credited. If a cost system, including perpetual inventory accounts, is used, what additional entry is required for this transaction?

12. Select the answer which best completes the statement:
    (a) Of the following production operations, the one most likely to employ job order cost accumulation is: (1) soft drink manufacturing; (2) shipbuilding; (3) crude oil refining; (4) candy manufacturing.
    (b) Under job order cost accumulation, the dollar amount of the entry involved in the transfer of inventory from Work in Process to Finished Goods is the sum of the costs charged to all jobs: (1) started in process during the period; (2) in process during the period; (3) completed and sold during the period; (4) completed during the period.

Unless otherwise directed, use these rates in the exercises, problems, and cases that follow: FICA tax, 6.5%; federal unemployment insurance tax, .7%; state unemployment insurance tax, 2.7%.

EXERCISES

1. **Cost accumulation procedure determination.** Classify these industries with respect to the type of cost accumulation procedure generally used — job order costing or process costing.

(a) Meat
(b) Sugar
(c) Steel
(d) Breakfast cereals
(e) Paper boxes
(f) Wood furniture
(g) Toys and novelties
(h) Coke
(i) Cooking utensils
(j) Caskets
(k) Pianos
(l) Linoleum
(m) Leather
(n) Nylon
(o) Baby foods
(p) Locomotives
(q) Office machines and equipment
(r) Luggage
(s) Paint
(t) Tires and tubes

2. **Job order cost sheet.** Forge Machine Works collects its cost data by the job order cost accumulation procedure. For Job 642, the following data are available:

DIRECT MATERIALS	DIRECT LABOR
9/14 Issued........... $1,200	Week of Sept. 20 — 180 hrs @ $6.20/hr
9/20 Issued........... 662	Week of Sept. 26 — 140 hrs @ 7.30/hr
9/22 Issued........... 480	

Factory overhead is applied at the rate of $3.50 per direct labor hour.

Required:
(1) The appropriate information entered on a job order cost sheet.
(2) The sales price of the job, assuming that it was contracted with a markup of 40% of cost.

3. **Job order costing.** The Cambridge Company uses job order costing. At the beginning of May, two jobs were in process:

	JOB 369	JOB 372
Materials...	$2,000	$700
Direct labor	1,000	300
Applied factory overhead...	1,500	450

There was no inventory of finished goods on May 1. During the month, Jobs 373, 374, 375, 376, 378, and 379 were started.

Materials requisitions for May totaled $13,000, direct labor cost, $10,000, and actual factory overhead, $16,000. Factory overhead is applied at a rate of 150% of direct labor cost.

The only job still in process at the end of May is No. 379, with costs of $1,400 for materials and $900 for direct labor.

Job 376, the only finished job on hand at the end of May, has a total cost of $2,000.

Required:

  (1) T accounts for Work in Process, Finished Goods, Cost of Goods Sold, Factory Overhead Control, and Applied Factory Overhead.

  (2) General journal entries to record:

    (a) Cost of goods manufactured.

    (b) Cost of goods sold.

    (c) Closing of over- or underapplied factory overhead to Cost of Goods Sold.

(CGAA adapted)

4. Job order cycle entries. Beaver Products, Inc., provided the following data for January, 19B:

Materials and supplies:

Inventory, January 1, 19B	$10,000
Purchases on account	30,000

Labor:

Accrued, January 1, 19B	$ 3,000
Paid during January (ignore payroll taxes)	25,000

Factory overhead costs:

Supplies (issued from materials)	$ 1,500
Indirect labor	3,500
Depreciation	1,000
Other factory overhead costs (all from outside suppliers on account)	14,500

Work in process:	JOB 1	JOB 2	JOB 3	TOTAL
Work in process January 1, 19B	$1,000	—	—	$ 1,000
Job costs during January, 19B:				
Direct materials	4,000	$6,000	$5,000	15,000
Direct labor	5,000	8,000	7,000	20,000
Applied factory overhead	5,000	8,000	7,000	20,000

Job 1 started in December, 19A, finished during January, and sold to a customer for $21,000 cash.

Job 2 started in January, not yet finished.

Job 3 started in January, finished during January, and now in the finished goods warehouse awaiting customer's disposition.

Finished goods inventory, January 1, 19B	–0–

Required: Journal entries, with detail for the respective job orders and factory overhead subsidiary records, to record the following transactions for January:

  (1) Purchases of materials on account.

  (2) Labor paid.

  (3) Labor cost distribution.

  (4) Materials issued.

  (5) Depreciation for the month.

  (6) Acquisition of other overhead costs on credit.

  (7) Overhead applied to production.

  (8) Jobs completed and transferred to finished goods.

  (9) Sales revenue.

  (10) Cost of goods sold.

5. Job order for a municipality. The Intragovernmental Service Fund of Jackson Township manufactures (1) street and traffic signs for the Sanitation and Street Funds and (2) historical markers, information signs, and danger signs for the General Fund and Utility Fund. Each job is charged to

these funds at prime costs (materials and labor) plus applied overhead of 12% of prime costs. On November 1, there were no jobs in process. During November these transactions occurred:
  (a) Materials purchased on account from nongovernmental agencies, $8,000; materials transferred in from the Special Revenue Fund, $2,000 (credit Due to Special Revenue Fund).
  (b) Actual overhead vouchered, $1,500. (The account is called Job Overhead Control instead of Factory Overhead.)
  (c) Total production costs incurred on jobs during November:

JOBS FOR	MATERIALS	LABOR
Sanitation and Street Fund	$5,000	$7,500
General Fund	3,000	4,500
Utility Fund	1,000	2,000

  (d) From the payroll in (c), these deductions were made: FICA tax, $910; employees' federal income tax, $1,600; union dues, $100; and employees' group insurance, $100.
  (e) Recorded the employer's payroll taxes for November. The city has achieved a merit rating that enables it to pay only 1.5% for state unemployment tax.
  (f) All jobs were completed and billed to the proper funds (for receivables, debit Due from _____ Fund).
  (g) Close over- or underapplied factory overhead to Cost of Jobs Billed.
  (h) Paid amount owed to the Special Revenue Fund.
  (i) Collected $10,000 from the Sanitation and Street Fund; $5,000 from the General Fund; and $3,000 from the Utility Fund.

Required: General journal entries for the preceding transactions, using separate jobs in process accounts for each fund.

PROBLEMS

5-1. Job order cost sheet. Tedyuscung Company produces special machines made to customer specifications. The following data pertain to Job 1106:

Customer: Markem Machine Shop
Customer's Order No.: C696
Dated: October 27
Description: 18 drilling units

Date started: 11/4/19--
Date finished: 11/18/19--
Total cost to manufacture: ?
Sales price: $20,425

	WEEK ENDING 11/11	WEEK ENDING 11/18
Materials used, Dept. 1	$2,400	$1,300
Direct labor rate, Dept. 1	$8.20 per hour	$8.20 per hour
Labor hours used, Dept. 1	300	200
Direct labor rate, Dept. 2	$8.00 per hour	$8.00 per hour
Labor hours used, Dept. 2	150	70
Machine hours, Dept. 2	200	120
Applied factory overhead, Dept. 1	$4.00 per labor hour	$4.00 per labor hour
Applied factory overhead, Dept. 2	$1.80 per machine hour	$1.80 per machine hour

Marketing and administrative costs are charged to each order at a rate of 25% of the cost to manufacture.

Required: A suitable cost sheet showing the above data. Did the company make an adequate profit margin on this order?

5-2. Job orders; factory overhead subsidiary ledger; cost of goods manufactured statement. At the beginning of September, certain ledger accounts in the books and records of the Ambler Products Company had these balances:

	DR.	CR.
Work in Process	$2,020	
Materials	7,380	
Accrued Payroll		$1,436

The balance in the work in process account is supported by these details appearing in the job order cost sheets:

Direct materials	$ 640
Direct labor (150 hours)	900
Applied factory overhead	480
Total	$2,020

Certain columnar totals in the accounts payable register at the end of September show:

Accounts Payable	$13,820 (credit)
Discounts Lost	108 (debit)
Materials	10,600 (debit)
Accrued Payroll	8,704 (debit)
Employees Income Tax Payable	956 (credit)

Materials requisitions indicate:

For production	$ 8,540
For repairs and maintenance	500
For factory supplies	1,200

The labor distribution sheet shows:

Direct labor (for job orders), 2,000 hours		$12,000
Factory overhead:		
Supervisor's salary	$ 1,600	
Repairs and maintenance	360	
Indirect labor	1,200	3,160
Total		$15,160

The finished orders for the month consist of:

Direct materials	$ 8,060
Direct labor (1,910 hours)	11,460
Applied factory overhead	6,112
Total	$25,632

The following subsidiary accounts and their balances controlled by the factory overhead control account appear in the ledger as of September 30:

Supervisor's Salary	$1,600	Factory Insurance	$ 300
Repairs and Maintenance	860	Light and Power	320
Indirect Labor	1,200	Water and Heat	300
Factory Supplies	1,200	Payroll Taxes	1,500
Depreciation—Factory Equipment	240	Rent — Factory	400

At the end of the month, the three incomplete production (job) orders can be summarized as follows:

Materials	$1,120
Direct labor (240 hours)	1,440
Applied factory overhead	768
Total	$3,328

Required:
(1) A statement of the cost of goods manufactured for September.
(2) A calculation of the over- or underapplied factory overhead for September.

5-3. Job order costing. Williams, Inc., had the following inventories on March 1:

Finished goods	$15,000
Work in process	19,070
Materials	14,000

The work in process account controls three jobs:

	Job 621	Job 622	Job 623
Materials	$2,800	$3,400	$1,800
Labor	2,100	2,700	1,350
Applied factory overhead	1,680	2,160	1,080
Total	$6,580	$8,260	$4,230

The following information pertains to March operations:

(a) Materials purchased and received, $22,000; terms, n/30.
(b) Materials requisitioned for production, $21,000. Of this amount, $2,400 was for indirect materials; the difference was distributed: $5,300 to Job 621; $7,400 to Job 622; and $5,900 to Job 623.
(c) Materials returned to the storeroom from the factory, $600, of which $200 was for indirect materials, the balance from Job 622.
(d) Materials returned to vendors, $800.
(e) Payroll, after deducting 6.5% for FICA tax and 12% for employees' income tax, was $30,970. The payroll amount due the employees was paid during March.
(f) Of the payroll, direct labor represented 55%; indirect labor, 20%; sales salaries, 15%; and administrative salaries, 10%. The direct labor cost was distributed: $6,420 to Job 621; $8,160 to Job 622; and $6,320 to Job 623.
(g) An additional 9.9% was entered for employer payroll taxes, representing the employer's 6.5% FICA tax, 2.7% state unemployment insurance tax, and .7% federal unemployment insurance tax. Employer payroll taxes related to direct labor are charged to the factory overhead control account.
(h) Factory overhead, other than any previously mentioned, amounted to $5,500. Included in this figure were $2,000 for depreciation of factory building and equipment and $250 for expired insurance on the factory. The remaining overhead, $3,250, was unpaid at the end of March.
(i) Factory overhead applied to production: 80% of the direct labor cost to be charged to the three jobs based on the labor cost for March.
(j) Jobs 621 and 622 were completed and transferred to the finished goods warehouse.
(k) Both Jobs 621 and 622 were shipped and billed at a gross profit of 40% of the cost of goods sold.
(l) Cash collections from accounts receivable during March were $69,450.

Required:
(1) Job order cost sheets to post beginning inventory data.
(2) Journal entries to record the March transactions with current postings to general ledger inventory accounts and to job order cost sheets.
(3) A schedule of inventories on March 31.

5-4. Journal entries and ledger accounts covering cost accounting cycle. During November, these transactions took place in Singer, Inc., a company that uses job order costing:

(a) Materials purchased on account, $35,600.
(b) Materials issued: to fill requisitions on job orders, $25,250; factory supplies, $1,300.
(c) Materials issued to complete defective units, $200.
(d) Freight paid for materials received, $850. (Freight is not added to unit costs on materials inventory cards.)
(e) Materials returned to the vendor, $225.
(f) Scrap materials received in the storeroom were set up at a value of $175, and credit was given to Factory Overhead Control for that amount. (A separate general ledger account, Scrap Materials, is used.)
(g) Materials returned to the storeroom: from job orders, $1,090; factory supplies, $125.
(h) Total payroll was as follows:
Recorded and then paid liability for net pay to workers, $72,054.
Withheld for employees' income tax, $7,780.

Withheld for hospitalization plan, $950.
Withheld for FICA tax, $5,616.
(i) The employer's FICA tax was recorded. State unemployment tax for Singer is 1.5% of total payroll, and the federal unemployment tax rate is .7%. These taxes were charged to Factory Overhead Control.
(j) The payroll was distributed as follows: direct labor, $75,600; indirect labor, balance of payroll.
(k) Depreciation for the month: buildings, $750; machinery, $800.
(l) Property tax accrued, $750; insurance expired with a credit to the prepaid account, $850.
(m) Factory overhead is charged to production at a rate of $1.20 per direct labor hour. Records show 18,900 direct labor hours worked during the month.
(n) Close out the over- or underapplied factory overhead to Cost of Goods Sold.
(o) Cost of goods completed, $122,020.
(p) Goods costing $108,300 were sold on account at a sales price of $159,750.

Required:
(1) Journal entries to record these transactions, indicating the subsidiary records to which the entries would also be posted.
(2) Ledger accounts for Work in Process, Factory Overhead Control, Materials, and Finished Goods. The November 1 balances were: Finished Goods, $5,660; Work in Process, $9,750; Materials, $6,180. Perpetual inventory procedures are used.
(3) What is the effect of closing the over- or underapplied factory overhead to Cost of Goods Sold?

5-5. Ledger accounts covering cost accounting cycle and job cost accumulation. The following is information regarding the March operations of the Better Products Company:
The books show these account balances as of March 1:

Finished Goods...	$ 78,830
Work in Process..	292,621
Materials...	65,000
Over- or Underapplied Factory Overhead	12,300 (cr.)

The work in process account is supported by these job order cost sheets:

JOB	ITEM	DIRECT MATERIALS	DIRECT LABOR	FACTORY OVERHEAD	TOTAL
204	80,000 Balloons	$ 15,230	$ 21,430	$ 13,800	$ 50,460
205	5,000 Life Rafts	40,450	55,240	22,370	118,060
206	10,000 Life Belts	60,875	43,860	19,366	124,101
		$116,555	$120,530	$ 55,536	$292,621

During March these transactions occurred:

(a) Purchase of materials, $42,300.
(b) Purchase of special materials for new Job 207, $5,800, which calls for 4,000 life jackets.
(c) Payroll data for March:

JOB	AMOUNT	HOURS
204	$26,844	6,711
205	22,750	6,500
206	28,920	7,230
207	20,370	5,820

Indirect labor cost, $9,480; factory superintendence, $3,000.
Payroll deductions: FICA tax, 6.5%; employees' income tax, 12%.
(d) Employer's payroll taxes: FICA, 6.5%; state unemployment, 1.6%; federal unemployment, .7%. These taxes are charged to Factory Overhead Control.
(e) Materials issued:

Job 204..............................	$ 9,480
Job 205..............................	11,320
Job 206..............................	10,490

Job 207............................. $16,640   (excluding special purchase of $5,800
                                                which is also issued at this time)

(f) Other factory overhead incurred or accrued (credit Various Credits):

Insurance on factory...............................	$ 830	Coal expense...	$1,810
Tax on real estate....................................	845	Power	3,390
Depreciation — machinery......................	780	Repairs and maintenance........................	2,240
Depreciation — factory building.............	840	Indirect supplies.....................................	1,910
Light...	560		

(g) Factory overhead is applied at the rate of $1.15 per direct labor hour.

(h) Shipped and billed Job 204 at a contract price of $117,500.

Required:

(1) Ledger accounts, inserting beginning balances and entering transactions for March. (Factory overhead is to be posted to the control account only.)

(2) In itemized form, the total cost of each job at the end of March.

(3) The amount remaining in the over- or underapplied factory overhead account.

5-6. General and subsidiary ledger accounts covering cost cycle using job order cost accumulation. The Starter Company makes two types of storage batteries: Dependable Senior and Dependable Junior. General and subsidiary ledger balances as of May 1 were:

Cash...	$ 35,000	
Accounts Receivable..	25,000	
Finished Goods	25,000	
Work in Process	15,000	
Materials..	35,000	
Factory Equipment...	20,000	
Accumulated Depreciation — Factory Equipment....................		$ 4,000
Accounts Payable...		46,000
Common Stock..		80,000
Retained Earnings..		25,000
Total	$155,000	$155,000

Materials:		Finished goods inventory:	
Cases	$17,500	Dependable Senior............	$15,000
Zinc.....................................	12,000	Dependable Junior	10,000
Fluid...................................	5,500		
		Total	$25,000
Total	$35,000		

	DEPENDABLE SENIOR JOB 84 FOR STOCK	DEPENDABLE JUNIOR JOB 85 FOR STOCK
Work in process inventory:		
Materials	$5,000	$4,000
Labor..	2,500	1,500
Factory overhead	1,250	750
Total	$8,750	$6,250

The figures in the subsidiary ledgers are expressed in dollars only. The company buys cases, zinc, and fluid but assembles the batteries.

(a) Summary of accounts payable register:

Materials purchases:		
Cases	$10,000	
Zinc...	5,000	
Fluid..	5,000	$20,000
Payroll		18,000
Factory overhead..		3,000
Marketing expenses..		20,000
Administrative expenses...		10,000
Financial expenses..		4,000
		$75,000

(b) Summary of materials requisitions:

	TOTAL	JOB 84	JOB 85
Cases	$21,000	$11,000	$10,000
Zinc	16,000	8,000	8,000
Fluid	8,000	5,000	3,000
	$45,000	$24,000	$21,000

(c) Payroll analysis:

Direct labor:

Job 84	$7,000	
Job 85	7,500	$14,500
Indirect factory labor		3,500
		$18,000

(d) The overhead rate is 50% of direct labor cost. Charge the two orders.
(e) Job 84 is finished.
(f) Summary of sales on account:

	SALES PRICE	COST PRICE
Dependable Senior	$ 80,000	$45,000
Dependable Junior	22,000	8,000
Total	$102,000	$53,000

(g) Summary of cash transactions:

Received on account	$118,000
Paid creditors and other liabilities	105,000

(h) Depreciation on factory equipment is $1,250.

Required:
(1) The posting of all transactions to general ledger and inventory subsidiary ledger accounts to record the above data.
(2) The amount of over- or underapplied factory overhead, transferring the balances to the cost of goods sold account.
(3) The checking of the control account balances with the balances of the related subsidiary ledger balances.
(4) A trial balance.

CASES

A. Job order costing; general and factory ledger. On December 31, 19A, after closing, the ledgers of the Vilas-LaMesa Company contained these accounts and balances:

Cash	$47,000	Accounts Payable	$ 59,375
Accounts Receivable	50,000	Common Stock	100,000
Finished Goods*	32,500	Retained Earnings	34,925
Work in Process*	7,500	Factory Ledger	62,000
Materials*	22,000	General Ledger*	62,000
Machinery	35,300		

*Maintained in the factory ledger.

Details of the three inventories are:

Finished goods inventory: Item X — 1,000 units @ $12.50	$12,500
Item Y — 2,000 units @ 10.00	20,000
Total	$32,500

Work in process inventory:		Job 101	Job 102
Direct materials:			
500 units of A @ $5.00		$2,500	
200 units of B @ 3.00			$ 600
Direct labor:			
500 hours @ $4.00		2,000	
200 hours @ 5.00			1,000
Factory overhead applied at the rate of $2.00/hour		1,000	400
Total		$5,500	$2,000

Materials inventory:	Material A — 2,000 units @ $5.00	$10,000
	Material B — 4,000 units @ 3.00	12,000
	Total	$22,000

During January, 19B, these transactions were completed:

(a) Purchases on account: Material A, 10,000 units @ $5.20; Material B, 12,000 units @ $3.75; indirect materials, $17,520.
(b) Payroll totaling $110,000 was paid. Of the total payroll, $20,000 was for marketing and administrative salaries. Payroll deductions consisted of $15,500 for employees' income tax and 6.5% for FICA tax.
(c) Payroll to be distributed as follows: Job 101, 5,000 direct labor hours @ $4.00; Job 102, 8,000 direct labor hours @ $5.00; Job 103, 6,000 direct labor hours @ $3.00; indirect labor, $12,000; marketing and administrative salaries, $20,000. Employer's payroll taxes are: FICA, 6.5%; state unemployment, 2.7%; federal unemployment, .7%.
(d) Materials were issued on a fifo basis as follows: Material A, 10,000 units (charged to Job 101); Material B, 12,000 units (charged to Job 102); Material A, 1,000 units, and Material B, 2,500 units (charged to Job 103). (*Note*: Transactions are to be taken in consecutive order.) Indirect materials amounting to $7,520 were issued.
(e) Factory overhead was applied to Jobs 101, 102, and 103 based on a rate of $2 per direct labor hour.
(f) Jobs 101 and 102 were completed and sold on account for $120,000 and $135,000, respectively.
(g) After allowing a 5% cash discount, a net amount of $247,000 was collected on accounts receivable.
(h) Marketing and administrative expenses (other than salaries) paid during the month amounted to $15,000. Miscellaneous factory overhead of $10,800 was paid and transferred to the factory. Depreciation on machinery was $2,000.
(i) Payments on account, other than payrolls paid, amounted to $85,000.
(j) The over- or underapplied factory overhead is to be closed to the cost of goods sold account.

Required:
(1) Trial balances of the general ledger and of the factory ledger as of January 1, 19B.
(2) General ledger and factory ledger accounts opened and balances recorded from the January 1 trial balances.
(3) Journal entries to record the January transactions.
(4) The posting of January transactions to the general ledger, factory ledger, and subsidiary ledgers for materials, work in process, finished goods, and factory overhead incurred.
(5) Trial balances of the general ledger and the factory ledger as of January 31, 19B, reconciling control accounts with subsidiary ledgers.
(6) A statement of cost of goods sold for January, 19B.

B. Determination of cost. The president of the Nola Cola Bottling Company has heard rumblings of dissatisfaction among the board of directors about the relatively low net earnings of the company. Several directors are not satisfied with the accounting reports being issued.

They believe, it appears, that the shipping and delivery expenses are reasonable, that advertising is in line, and that administrative expenses, although possibly somewhat above normal, are not out of control. Their primary criticism seems leveled at manufacturing costs.

Consequently, a meeting of the board of directors has been called in order to examine critically the accounting system in use for determining manufacturing costs; that is, in essence, the cost of a Nola Cola bottle ready for delivery as it comes from the last operation of the bottling process.

Sensing some of the problems involved, the president has adopted a recognized technique of executive strategy. Before having the controller explain the accounting system in use, the president has decided to ask for an opinion as to what items should be included in the proper determination of the cost of a bottle of Nola Cola. For example, the president believes there is mutual agreement that such items as syrup, water, carbonation, and bottle caps are properly part of manufacturing costs.

Required: A list of other items that should be included, and to what extent.

C. Improving a cost information and accumulation system. An examination of costing methods and procedures in the Franklin Printing Company reveals the following:

   (a) Costing formulas and ratios prepared a long time ago are still being used by estimators even though prices for materials have increased, overhead is higher, and new machinery has been installed.
   (b) An estimator in the Production Department and a cost clerk in the Cost Department prepare estimates independently from one another, resulting in widely divergent cost figures.
   (c) A profit per individual job or order can never be determined.
   (d) Each job or order is sold with a definite markup. Yet, instead of a profit of $100,000 as the president hoped for, the chief accountant prepared an income statement showing only a $48,000 profit.
   (e) Determining departmental efficiency and control over expenses is not possible.

Required: A statement outlining:
   (1) Possible causes of the existing conditions.
   (2) Possible steps to remedy the situation.

D. Installing a cost information and accumulation system. A textile manufacturer asks advice concerning the installation of a cost system. The manufacturer explains briefly that many different cloths are produced, starting with scoured wool that passes through the following processes before becoming finished cloth: picking and blending, carding, spinning, weaving, finishing, and dyeing. The company's sales representatives take orders considerably in advance of the actual production of the cloth, using samples produced during a special period set aside each season for the manufacture of samples. Competition is keen and the profit margin is low. Financing is received through bank loans.

Required:
   (1) The principal advantages of installing a cost system.
   (2) The principal additions or alterations necessary to operate a cost system. (The present accounting system is designed for the purpose of preparing annual financial statements.)
   (3) An explanation of how matters can be arranged in order to find the cost of the principal stages of manufacture, such as carding, spinning, weaving, etc. (The carding machines operate three shifts per day; the spinning machines, two shifts; and the weaving machines, one shift.)

E. Designing cost accumulation procedures. A client has asked advice as to a satisfactory system of factory costs for a factory that is divided into two main divisions:

   (a) *Machine Shop.* This division makes steel molds used in the manufacture of plastic articles. These molds require careful precision work; and frequently, one person is employed at machining one mold for several weeks. The finished molds are used by the Plastics Division of the company. In addition, some other machine work is done for customers, although this forms the smaller portion of the shop's output.
   (b) *Plastics Division.* This division manufactures plastic articles including ash trays, buttons, knobs, etc. The process of manufacture consists of placing chemical powders in a mold,

which is then placed under a steam press where pressure is applied for a few minutes. The chemical powders are the only materials used and are not processed before being placed in the mold. After being pressed, a certain amount of finishing and inspection labor is necessary to complete the articles.

It is ascertained that:

(a) The company has had no previous cost records.
(b) Production in both divisions is controlled by job order tickets.
(c) Materials are kept in one place, but no record has been kept of withdrawals.
(d) Labor is paid at hourly rates, and a time clock at the factory entrance is used for determining the hours worked in any day.
(e) Employees have been preparing satisfactory time tickets showing the hours worked on each job and, in the case of the Plastics Division, the number of units produced; but this record has never been balanced against the wages paid nor the record of production.
(f) Spoilage is a substantial factor in both divisions.
(g) The Machine Shop and the Plastics Division are in separate parts of the one building.
(h) The company has a satisfactory system of general ledger accounting.

Required: A method or methods for obtaining factory costs, explaining why they are considered the most satisfactory under the circumstances.

(CICA adapted)

6 Process Costing
Cost of Production Report
Lost Unit Calculations

Cost accumulation procedures used by manufacturing concerns are classified as either (1) job order costing or (2) process costing. The preceding chapter discussed procedures applicable to job order costing. It is important to understand that, except for some modifications, the accumulation of materials costs, labor costs, and factory overhead also applies to process costing.

Process costing methods are used for industries producing chemicals, petroleum, textiles, steel, rubber, cement, flour, pharmaceuticals, shoes, plastics, sugar, and coal. This type of costing is also used by firms manufacturing items such as rivets, screws, bolts, and small electrical parts. A third type of industry using process costing methods is the assembly-type industry which manufactures such things as typewriters, automobiles, airplanes, and household electric appliances (washing machines, refrigerators, toasters, irons, radios, television sets, etc.). Finally, certain service industries, such as gas, water, and heat, cost their products by using process costing methods. Thus, process costing is used when products are manufactured under conditions of continuous processing or under mass production methods. In fact, process costing procedures are often termed "continuous or mass production" cost accounting procedures.

The type of manufacturing operations performed determines the cost procedures that must be used. For example, a company manufacturing custom machinery will use job order costing, whereas a chemical company will use process costing. In the case of the machinery manufacturer, a job order cost sheet is prepared for each order, accumulating the costs of materials, labor, and factory overhead. In contrast, the chemical company cannot identify materials, labor, and factory overhead with each order, since each order is part of a batch or a continuous process. The individual order identity is lost, and the cost of a completed unit must be computed by dividing total cost incurred during a period by total units completed. The summarization of the costs takes place via the cost of production report, which is an extremely efficient, economical, and timesaving device for the collection of large amounts of data.

The entire process costing discussion is presented in this and the following two chapters. This chapter considers the (1) cost of production reports, (2) calculation of departmental unit costs, (3) costing of work in process, (4) computation of costs transferred to other departments or to the finished goods storeroom, and (5) effect of lost units on unit costs. Chapter 7 deals with (1) special problems involved in adding materials in departments other than the first, (2) problems connected with the beginning work in process, and (3) the possibility of using costing methods other than those previously discussed. Chapter 8 discusses the costing of by-products and joint products.

CHARACTERISTICS AND PROCEDURES OF PROCESS COSTING

The characteristics of process costing are:

1. A cost of production report is used to collect, summarize, and compute total and unit costs.
2. Production is accumulated and reported by departments.
3. Costs are posted to departmental work in process accounts.
4. Production in process at the end of a period is restated in terms of completed units.
5. Total cost charged to a department is divided by total computed production of the department in order to determine a unit cost for a specific period.
6. Costs of completed units of a department are transferred to the next processing department in order to arrive at the total costs of the finished products during a period. At the same time, costs are assigned to units still in process.

The procedures of process costing are designed to:

1. Accumulate materials, labor, and factory overhead costs by departments.
2. Determine a unit cost for each department.
3. Transfer costs from one department to the next and to finished goods.
4. Assign costs to the inventory of work still in process.

If accurate unit and inventory costs are to be established by process cost-ing procedures, costs of a period must be identified with units produced in the same period.

COSTING BY DEPARTMENTS

The nature of manufacturing operations in firms using process or job order cost procedures is usually such that work on a product takes place in several departments. With either procedure, departmentalization of materials, labor, and factory overhead costs facilitates application of responsibility ac-counting. Each department performs a specific operation or process towards the completion of the product. For example, after the Blending Department has completed the starting phase of work on the product, units are transferred to the Testing Department, after which they may go to the Terminal Depart-ment for completion and transfer to the finished goods storeroom. Both units and costs are transferred from one manufacturing department to another. Sep-arate departmental work in process accounts are used to charge each depart-ment for the materials, labor, and factory overhead used to complete its share of a manufacturing process.

Process costing involves averaging costs for a particular period in order to obtain departmental and cumulative unit costs. The cost of a completed unit is determined by dividing the total cost of a period by the total units produced during the period. Determining departmental production for a period includes evaluating units still in process. The breakdown of costs for the computation of total unit costs and for costing units transferred and departmental work in process inventories is also desirable for cost control purposes.

Departmental total and unit costs are determined by the use of the cost of production report, which is described and illustrated in detail in later sections of this chapter. Most of the activity in process costing involves the accumula-tion of data needed for the preparation of these cost reports.

PRODUCT FLOW

A product can flow through a factory in numerous ways. Three product flow formats associated with process costing — sequential, parallel, and se-lective — are illustrated here to indicate that basically the same costing pro-cedures can be applied to all types of product flow situations.

Sequential Product Flow

In a sequential product flow, each item manufactured goes through the same set of operations, as illustrated at the top of the next page. Materials are placed into production in the Blending Department, and labor and factory overhead are added. When the work is finished in the Blending Department, it

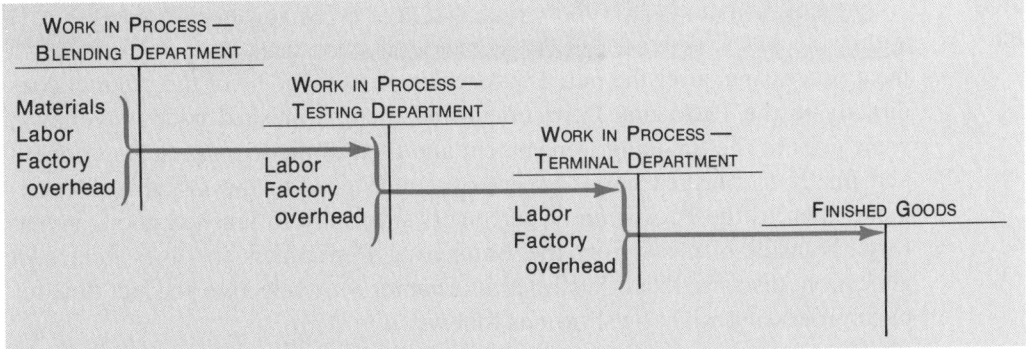

moves to the Testing Department. The second process, and any succeeding processes, may add more materials or simply work on the partially completed input from the preceding process, adding only labor and factory overhead, as in this example. After the product has been processed by the Terminal Department, it is a completed product and becomes a part of finished goods inventory.

In a parallel product flow, certain portions of the work are done simultaneously and then brought together in a final process or processes for completion and transfer to finished goods inventory. As in the previous illustration, materials may be added in subsequent processes. Pictorially, this might be shown as:

Parallel Product Flow

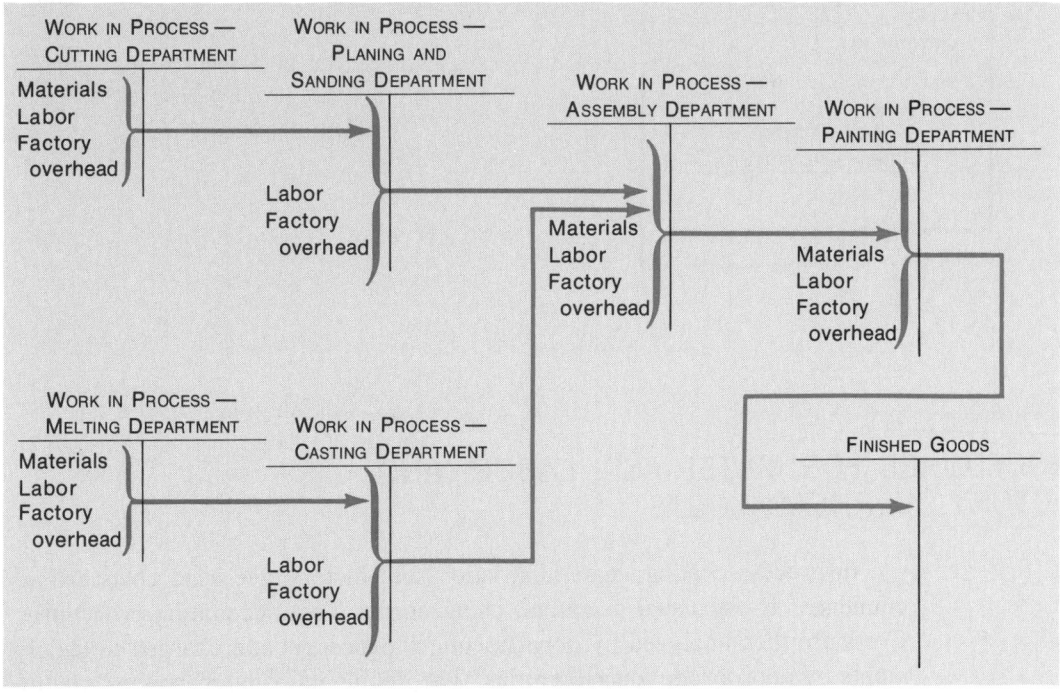

Selective Product Flow

In a selective product flow, the product moves to different departments within the plant, depending upon the desired final product. For example, in meat processing, after the initial butchering process, some of the product goes directly to the Packaging Department and then to finished goods inventory; some goes to the Smoking Department and then to the Packaging Department and finally to finished goods inventory; some goes to the Grinding Department, then to the Packaging Department, and lastly to finished goods inventory. Transfer of costs from the Butchering Department involves joint cost allocation, discussed and illustrated in Chapter 8. A selective product flow for meat processing might be shown as follows:

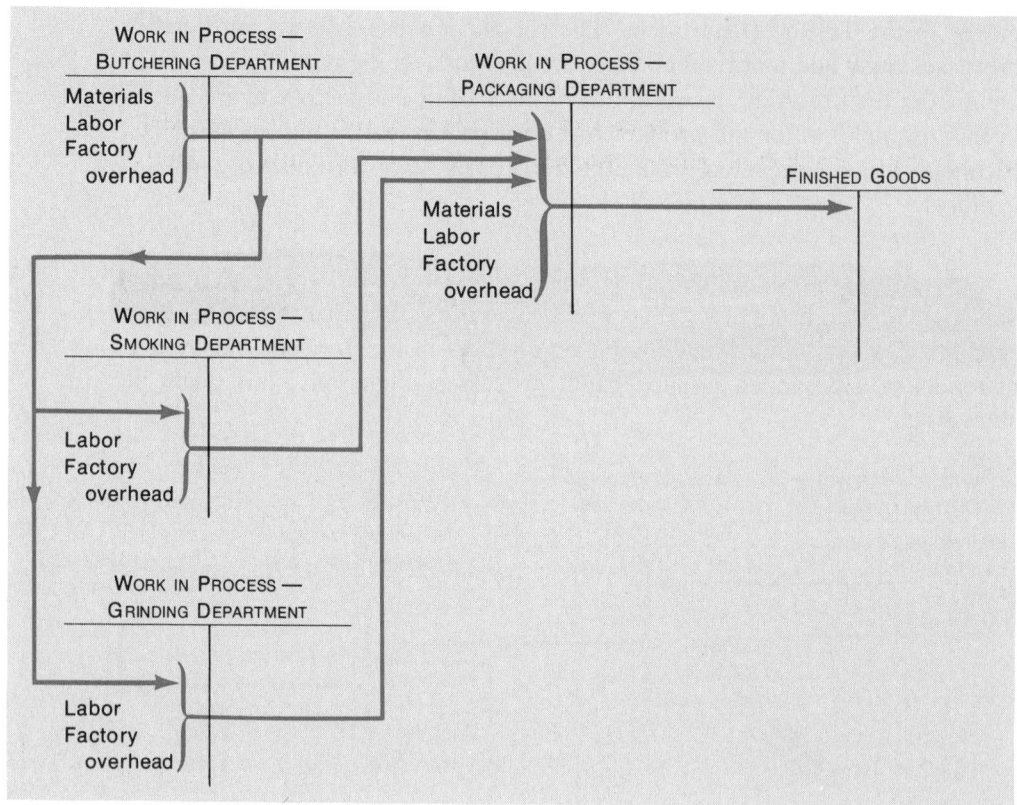

PROCEDURES FOR MATERIALS, LABOR, AND FACTORY OVERHEAD COSTS

In process costing, materials, labor, and factory overhead costs are accumulated in the usual accounts, using normal cost accounting procedures. Costs are then analyzed by departments or processes and charged to departments by appropriate journal entries. The details involved in process costing are usually fewer than those in job order costing, where accumulation of costs for many orders can become unwieldy.

Materials Costs

In job order costing, materials requisitions are used to charge jobs for direct materials used. If requisitions are used in process costing, details are considerably reduced because materials are charged to departments rather than to jobs, and the number of departments using materials is usually less than the number of jobs a firm might handle at a given time. Frequently materials are issued only to the process-originating department; subsequent departments add labor and factory overhead. If materials are needed in a department other than the first, they are charged to that department performing the specific operation.

For materials control purposes, materials need not always be priced individually on requisition forms. The cost of materials used can be determined at the end of the production period through *inventory difference* procedures, i.e., adding purchases to beginning inventory and then deducting ending inventory. Or consumption reports which state the cost of materials or quantity of materials put into process by various departments can be used. Costs or quantities charged to departments by consumption reports may be based on formulas or prorations. Formulas specify the type and quantity of materials required in the various products and are applied to finished production in order to calculate the materials consumed. Chemical and pharmaceutical industries use such procedures, particularly when more than one product is manufactured by a department. Frequently the cost of materials used by a department must be prorated to different products on various estimated bases. This proration is described in Chapter 8 as joint costing.

For any of the materials cost computation methods discussed, a typical journal entry charging direct manufacturing materials used during a period is:

Work in Process — Blending Department	24,500	
Materials		24,500

The source of the cost figures for the above entry as well as the entries for labor and factory overhead is the cost of production report which is discussed beginning on page 123.

Labor Costs

Labor costs are identified by and charged to departments in process costing, thus eliminating the detailed clerical work of accumulating labor costs by jobs. Daily time tickets or weekly time clock cards are used instead of job time tickets. Summary labor charges are made to departments through an entry which distributes the direct manufacturing payroll:

Work in Process — Blending Department	29,140	
Work in Process — Testing Department	37,310	
Work in Process — Terminal Department	32,400	
Payroll		98,850

**Factory
Overhead
Costs**

Factory overhead incurred in process costing as well as in job order costing should be accumulated in the factory overhead subsidiary ledger for producing and service departments. This procedure is consistent with requirements for responsibility accounting and responsibility reporting.

The factory overhead chapters emphasize and recommend the use of predetermined overhead rates for charging overhead to jobs and products. However, in various process and job order cost procedures, actual overhead rather than applied overhead is sometimes used for product costing. This practice is feasible when production remains comparatively stable from period to period, since factory overhead will then remain about the same from one month to the next. The use of actual overhead can also be justified when factory overhead is not an important part of total cost. However, predetermined overhead rates for producing departments should be used if:

1. Production is not stable.
2. Factory overhead, especially fixed overhead, is a significant cost.

Fluctuations in production can lead to the unequal incurrence of actual factory overhead from month to month. In such cases, factory overhead should be applied to production using predetermined rates, so that units produced receive proper charges for factory overhead. Similarly, if factory overhead — especially fixed factory overhead — is significant, it is desirable to allocate factory overhead on the basis of normal or uniform production using predetermined rates. Indeed, the use of predetermined rates is highly recommended for improving cost control and facilitating cost analysis.

Prior to charging factory overhead to departments via their respective work in process accounts, expenses must be accumulated in a factory overhead control account. As expenses are incurred, the entry is:

Factory Overhead Control	XXXXX	
Accounts Payable..		XXXXX
Accumulated Depreciation — Machinery		XXXXX
Prepaid Insurance..		XXXXX
Materials		XXXXX
Payroll		XXXXX

The use of a factory overhead control account requires a subsidiary ledger for factory overhead, with departmental expense analysis sheets to which all expenses are posted (see Chapter 10). Service department expenses are kept in like manner and distributed later to producing departments. At the end of each period, departmental expense analysis sheets are totaled. These totals, which also include distributed service department costs, represent factory overhead for each department. By debiting the actual cost incurred or by using the predetermined rates multiplied by the respective actual activity base (e.g., direct labor hours) for each producing department, the entry charging these expenses to work in process is as follows:

Work in Process — Blending Department	28,200	
Work in Process — Testing Department	32,800	
Work in Process — Terminal Department........................	19,800	
Factory Overhead Control		80,800

THE COST OF PRODUCTION REPORT

A departmental cost of production report shows all costs chargeable to a department. It is not only the source for summary journal entries at the end of the month but also a most convenient vehicle for presenting and disposing of costs accumulated during the month.

A cost of production report shows (1) total and unit costs transferred to it from a preceding department; (2) materials, labor, and factory overhead added by the department; (3) unit costs added by the department; (4) total and unit costs accumulated to the end of operations in the department; (5) the cost of the beginning and ending work in process inventories; and (6) cost transferred to a succeeding department or to a finished goods storeroom.

It is customary to divide the cost section of the report into two parts: one showing costs for which the department is accountable, including departmental and cumulative total and unit costs, the other showing the disposition of these costs. A quantity schedule showing the total number of units for which a department is accountable and the disposition made of these units is also part of each department's cost of production report. Information in this schedule, adjusted for equivalent production, is used to determine the unit costs added by a department, the costing of the ending work in process inventory, and the cost to be transferred out of the department.

A cost of production report determines periodic total and unit costs. However, a report that would merely summarize the total costs of materials, labor, and factory overhead and show only the unit cost for the period would not be satisfactory for controlling costs. Total figures mean very little; cost control requires detailed data. Therefore, in most instances, the total cost is broken down by cost elements for each department head responsible for the costs incurred. Furthermore, detailed departmental figures are needed because of the various completion stages of the work in process inventories.

Either in the cost of production report itself or in the supporting schedules, each item of material used by a department is listed; every labor operation is shown separately; factory overhead components are noted individually; and a unit cost is derived for each item. To condense the illustrated cost of production reports, only total materials, labor, and factory overhead charged to departments are considered; and unit costs are computed only for each cost element rather than for each item.

The reports of The Clonex Corporation, which manufactures one product in three producing departments (Blending, Testing, and Terminal), are used to illustrate the details involved in the preparation of cost of production reports.

Blending Department

The cost of production report of the Blending Department, the originating department of The Clonex Corporation, is shown below. It illustrates the detailed computations needed to complete a cost of production report.

The Clonex Corporation
Blending Department
Cost of Production Report
For the Month of January, 19--

Quantity Schedule

Units started in process..		50,000
Units transferred to next department...	45,000	
Units still in process (all materials — ½ labor and factory overhead).	4,000	
Units lost in process	1,000	50,000

Cost Charged to the Department

	TOTAL COST	UNIT COST
Cost added by department:		
Materials..	$24,500	$ .50
Labor	29,140	.62
Factory overhead..	28,200	.60
Total cost to be accounted for	**$81,840**	**$1.72**

Cost Accounted for as Follows

Transferred to next department (45,000 × $1.72)		$77,400
Work in process — ending inventory:		
Materials (4,000 × $.50)	$ 2,000	
Labor (4,000 × ½ × $.62)...	1,240	
Factory overhead (4,000 × ½ × $.60)..	1,200	4,440
Total cost accounted for		**$81,840**

ADDITIONAL COMPUTATIONS:

Equivalent production: Materials = 45,000 + 4,000 = 49,000 units

$$\text{Labor and factory overhead} = 45,000 + \frac{4,000}{2} = 47,000 \text{ units}$$

$$\text{Unit costs: Materials} = \frac{\$24,500}{49,000} = \$.50 \text{ per unit}$$

$$\text{Labor} = \frac{\$29,140}{47,000} = \$.62 \text{ per unit}$$

$$\text{Factory overhead} = \frac{\$28,200}{47,000} = \$.60 \text{ per unit}$$

The quantity schedule of the cost report shows that the Blending Department put 50,000 units in process, with units reported in terms of finished product. Finished units could be stated in pounds, feet, gallons, barrels, etc. If materials issued to a department are stated in pounds and the finished product is reported in gallons, units in the quantity schedule will be in terms of the finished product, gallons. A product conversion table would be used to determine the number of units for which the department is accountable. The quantity schedule of the Blending Department's report shows that of the 50,000 units for which the department was responsible, 45,000 units were transferred to the next department (Testing), 4,000 units are still in process, and 1,000 units were lost in processing.

Equivalent Production. Costs charged to a department come from an analysis of materials used, payroll distribution sheets, and departmental expense analysis sheets. The Blending Department's unit cost amounts to $1.72: $.50 for materials, $.62 for labor, and $.60 for factory overhead.

Computation of individual unit costs requires an analysis of the ending work in process to determine its stage of completion. This analysis is usually made by a supervisor or is the result of using predetermined formulas. Materials, labor, and factory overhead have been used on the 4,000 units in process but not in an amount sufficient for completion. To assign costs equitably to in-process inventory and transferred units, units still in process must be restated in terms of completed units, which is 4,000 units for materials cost but less than 4,000 for labor and overhead costs. The figure for partially completed units in process is added to units actually completed in order to arrive at the *equivalent production* figure for the period. This equivalent production figure represents the number of units for which sufficient materials, labor, and overhead were issued or used during a period. Materials, labor, and overhead costs are divided by the appropriate equivalent production figure to compute unit costs by elements. Should a cost element be at a different stage of completion with respect to units in process, then a separate equivalent production figure must be computed.

In many manufacturing processes, all materials are issued at the start of production. Unless stated otherwise, the illustrations in this discussion assume such a procedure. Therefore, the 4,000 units still in process have all the materials needed for their completion but not all labor and factory overhead. Only 50 percent of the labor and factory overhead needed to complete the units has been used. In terms of equivalent production, labor and factory overhead in process are sufficient to complete 2,000 units. The illustrations in this chapter do not include the beginning work in process, a consideration deferred to the next chapter.

Unit Costs. Departmental cost of production reports indicate the cost of units as they leave each department. These individual departmental unit costs are accumulated into a completed unit cost for the period. The report for the Blending Department shows a materials cost of $24,500, labor cost of $29,140, and factory overhead of $28,200. The materials cost of $24,500 is sufficient to complete 49,000 units (the 45,000 units transferred out of the department as well as the work in process for which enough materials are in process to complete 4,000 units). The unit materials cost is, therefore, $.50 ($24,500 ÷ 49,000). A similar computation determines the number of units actually and potentially completed with the labor cost of $29,140 and the factory overhead of $28,200. The 2,000 equivalent units in process are added to the 45,000 units completed and transferred to obtain a total equivalent production figure of

47,000 units for both labor and factory overhead. When the equivalent production figure of 47,000 units is divided into the monthly labor cost of $29,140, a unit cost for labor of $.62 ($29,140 ÷ 47,000) is computed. The unit cost for factory overhead is $.60 ($28,200 ÷ 47,000). The unit cost added by the department is $1.72, which is the sum of the materials, labor, and overhead unit costs — $.50, $.62, and $.60. This departmental unit cost figure cannot be determined by dividing the total departmental cost of $81,840 by a single equivalent production figure, because no such figure exists; units in process are at different stages of completion as to materials, labor, and factory overhead.

Disposition of Departmental Costs. In the departmental cost report, the section titled "Cost Charged to the Department" shows a total departmental cost of $81,840. The section titled "Cost Accounted for as Follows" shows the disposition of this cost. The 45,000 units transferred to the next department have a cost of $77,400 (45,000 units × $1.72). The balance of the cost to be accounted for, $4,440 ($81,840 − $77,400), is the cost of work in process.

The inventory figure must be broken down into its component parts: materials, labor, and factory overhead. These individual costs are easily determined. The cost of materials in process is obtained by multiplying total units in process by the materials unit cost (4,000 × $.50 = $2,000). The costs of labor and factory overhead in process are similarly calculated. The amount of labor and overhead in process is sufficient to complete only 50 percent, or 2,000, of the units in process. Therefore, the cost of labor in process is $1,240 (2,000 × $.62) and factory overhead in process is $1,200 (2,000 × $.60).

Lost Units. Continuous processing leads to the possibility of waste, seepage, shrinkage, and other factors which cause loss or spoilage of production units. Management is interested not only in the quantities reported as completed production, units in process, and lost units but also in a comparison of planned and actual results. In verifying reported figures, the accountant must reconcile quantities put into process with quantities reported as completed and lost. One method of making such reconciliations is to establish the process yield, i.e., the finished production that should result from processing various materials. This yield is computed as follows:

$$\text{Percent yield} = \frac{\text{Weight of finished product}}{\text{Weight of materials charged in}} \times 100$$

The yield figure is useful to management for controlling materials consumption and ties in closely with a firm's quality control procedures. Various yields are established as normal. Yields below normal are measures of inefficiencies and are sometimes used to compute lost units. Frequently quality control data are used to compute production costs, since the use of incorrect quantities would result in incorrect unit costs.

Units Lost in the First Department. Lost units reduce the number of units over which total cost can be spread, causing an increase in unit costs. The 1,000 units lost in the Blending Department increase the unit costs of materials, labor, and factory overhead. Had these units not been lost, the equivalent production figure would be 50,000 units for materials and 48,000 for labor and factory overhead. The unit cost for materials would be $.49 instead of $.50; labor, $.607 instead of $.62; and factory overhead, $.588 instead of $.60. In the first department, the only effect of losing units is an increase in the unit cost of the remaining good units. In this situation, the loss is assumed to apply to all good units and to be within normal tolerance limits. The treatment of excess or abnormal loss is discussed on pages 131–132.

The Blending Department transferred 45,000 units to the Testing Department, where labor and factory overhead were added before the units were transferred to the Terminal Department. Costs incurred by the Testing Department resulted in additional departmental as well as cumulative unit costs.

Testing Department

The cost of production report of the Testing Department, shown on page 128, differs from that of the Blending Department in several respects. Several additional calculations are made, for which space has been provided on the report. The additional information deals with (1) cost received from the preceding department, (2) an adjustment of the preceding department's unit cost because of lost units, and (3) cost received from the preceding department to be included in the cost of the ending work in process inventory.

The quantity schedule for the Testing Department shows that the 45,000 units received from the Blending Department were accounted for as follows: 40,000 units sent to the Terminal Department, 3,000 units still in process, and 2,000 units lost. An analysis of the work in process indicates that units in process are but one-third complete as to labor and factory overhead. Unit costs, $.91 for labor and $.80 for factory overhead, were calculated as follows: equivalent production of the Testing Department is 41,000 units [40,000 + ⅓(3,000)], the labor unit cost is $.91 ($37,310 ÷ 41,000), and the factory overhead unit cost $.80 ($32,800 ÷ 41,000). There is no materials unit cost, since no materials were added by the department. The departmental unit cost is $1.71, the sum of the labor unit cost of $.91 and the factory overhead unit cost of $.80.

The Testing Department is responsible for labor and factory overhead used as well as for the cost of units received from the Blending Department. This latter cost is inserted as a cost charged to the department under the title "Cost from preceding department," which is immediately above the section of the report dealing with cost added by the department. The cost transferred in was $77,400, previously shown in the cost report of the Blending Department as cost transferred out of that department by this entry:

Work in Process — Testing Department 77,400
    Work in Process — Blending Department   77,400

The work in process account of the Testing Department is charged with cost received from the preceding department and with $70,110 of departmen-

The Clonex Corporation
Testing Department
Cost of Production Report
For the Month of January, 19--

Quantity Schedule

Units received from preceding department		45,000
Units transferred to next department	40,000	
Units still in process (⅓ labor and factory overhead)....................	3,000	
Units lost in process...	2,000	45,000

Cost Charged to the Department	TOTAL COST	UNIT COST
Cost from preceding department:		
Transferred in during the month (45,000 units)	$ 77,400	$1.72
Cost added by department:		
Labor...	$ 37,310	$ .91
Factory overhead	32,800	.80
Total cost added	$ 70,110	$1.71
Adjustment for lost units...		.08
Total cost to be accounted for...	$147,510	$3.51

Cost Accounted for as Follows

Transferred to next department (40,000 × $3.51)............................		$140,400
Work in process — ending inventory:		
Adjusted cost from preceding department [3,000 × ($1.72 + $.08)]..	$ 5,400	
Labor (3,000 × ⅓ × $.91)	910	
Factory overhead (3,000 × ⅓ × $.80)..	800	7,110
Total cost accounted for...		$147,510

ADDITIONAL COMPUTATIONS:

Equivalent production: Labor and factory overhead = $40,000 + \dfrac{3,000}{3} = 41,000$ units

Unit costs: Labor = $\dfrac{\$37,310}{41,000} = \$.91$ per unit

Factory overhead = $\dfrac{\$32,800}{41,000} = \$.80$ per unit

Adjustment for lost units:

Method No. 1 — $\dfrac{\$77,400}{43,000} = \$1.80$; $\$1.80 - \$1.72 = \$.08$ per unit

Method No. 2 — 2,000 units × $1.72 = $3,440; $\dfrac{\$3,440}{43,000} = \$.08$ per unit

tal labor and factory overhead, a total cost of $147,510 to be accounted for by the department.

Units Lost in Departments Subsequent to the First. The Blending Department's unit cost was $1.72 when 45,000 units were transferred to the Testing Department. However, because 2,000 of these 45,000 units were lost during processing in the Testing Department, the $1.72 unit cost figure no longer applies and must be adjusted. The total cost of the units transferred remains at $77,400, but 43,000 units must now absorb this total cost, causing an increase of $.08 in the cost per unit due to the loss of 2,000 units in the Testing Department.

The lost unit cost can be computed by one of two methods. Method No. 1 determines a new unit cost for work done in the preceding department and subtracts the preceding department's old unit cost figure from the adjusted unit cost figure. The difference between the two figures is the additional cost due to the lost units. The $1.80 new adjusted unit cost for work done in the preceding department is obtained by dividing the remaining good units, 43,000 (45,000 − 2,000), into the cost transferred in, $77,400. The old unit cost figure of $1.72 is subtracted from the revised unit cost to arrive at the adjustment of $.08.

Method No. 2 determines the lost units' share of total cost and allocates this cost to the remaining good units. Total cost previously absorbed by the units lost is $3,440, which is the result of multiplying the 2,000 lost units by their unit cost of $1.72. The $3,440 cost must now be absorbed by the remaining good units. The additional cost to be picked up by each remaining good unit is $.08 ($3,440 ÷ 43,000 units).

The lost unit cost adjustment must be entered in the cost of production report. The $.08 is entered on the "Adjustment for lost units" line. The departmental unit cost of $1.71 does not have to be adjusted for units lost. In the Testing Department, the cost of any work done on lost units has automatically been absorbed in the departmental unit cost by using the equivalent production figure of 41,000 instead of 43,000 units. The $1.72 unadjusted unit cost for work done in the preceding department, the $1.71 departmental unit cost, and the $.08 adjustment for lost units are totaled in order to obtain the $3.51 cumulative unit cost for work done up to the end of operations in the Testing Department.

Timing of Lost Units. Lost units may occur at the beginning, during, or at the end of a process. For purposes of practicality and simplicity, it is ordinarily assumed that units lost at the beginning or during a process were never put in process. The cost of units lost is spread over the units completed and units still in process.

When units are lost or are identified as lost at the end of a process, the cost of the lost units is charged to completed units only. No part of the loss is charged to units still in process. Assume that the 2,000 units lost by the Testing Department were the result of spoilage found at final inspection by the Quality Control Department; their cost would be charged only to the 40,000 finished units, as illustrated on page 130 in the cost of production report for the Testing Department.

A comparison of the differences between the two cost of production reports for the Testing Department as to amounts for costs of units transferred and work in process inventory is shown below the production report on the next page. Note the offsetting increases and decreases.

The Clonex Corporation
Testing Department
Cost of Production Report
For the Month of January, 19—

Quantity Schedule

Units received from preceding department		45,000
Units transferred to next department	40,000	
Units still in process (⅓ labor and factory overhead).....................	3,000	
Units lost in process (at end of process)..	2,000	45,000

Cost Charged to the Department	TOTAL COST	UNIT COST
Cost from preceding department:		
Transferred in during the month (45,000 units)	$ 77,400	$1.72
Cost added by department:		
Labor..	$ 37,310	$ .87
Factory overhead	32,800	.76
Total cost added	$ 70,110	$1.63
Total cost to be accounted for...	$147,510	$3.35

Cost Accounted for as Follows

Transferred to next department [40,000 units × ($3.35 + $.1675)]*..		$140,720
Work in process — ending inventory:		
From preceding department (3,000 × $1.72)..............................	$ 5,160	
Labor (3,000 × ⅓ × $.87)	870	
Factory overhead (3,000 × ⅓ × $.76)..	760	6,790
Total cost accounted for..		$147,510

ADDITIONAL COMPUTATIONS:

$$\text{Equivalent production: Labor and factory overhead} = 40,000 + \frac{3,000}{3} +$$

$$2,000 \text{ lost units} = 43,000 \text{ units}$$

$$\text{Unit costs: Labor} = \frac{\$37,310}{43,000} = \$.87 \text{ per unit}$$

$$\text{Factory overhead} = \frac{\$32,800}{43,000} = \$.76 \text{ per unit}$$

Lost unit cost = $3.35 × 2,000 units = $6,700; $6,700 ÷ 40,000 units = $.1675 per unit to be added to $3.35 to make the transfer cost $3.5175.

*40,000 units × $3.5175 = $140,700. To avoid a decimal discrepancy, the cost transferred is computed: $147,510 − $6,790 = $140,720.

Cost of units transferred:		Work in process inventory:	
On page 128	$140,400	On page 128	$7,110
On this page..................	140,720	On this page...................	6,790
Increase	$ 320	Decrease	$ 320

In this illustration, the assumption has been made that the lost units, identified at the end of the process, were complete as to all costs. In some companies, members of the Quality Control or Inspection Departments make production checks prior to the end of the process. Such a procedure uncovers lost units that are not complete when the loss is incurred or the spoilage discovered and yet the loss may pertain only to units completed and not to units still in process. In such a case the lost units should be adjusted for their equivalent stage of completion. For instance, 2,000 units lost at the 90 percent stage of conversion would appear as 1,800 equivalent units with regard to labor and factory overhead costs.

Normal vs Abnormal Loss of Units. Units are lost through evaporation, shrinkage, substandard yields, spoiled work, poor workmanship, or inefficient equipment. In many instances the nature of operations makes certain losses normal or unavoidable, because they are considered within normal tolerance limits for human and machine errors. The cost of these normally lost units does not appear as a separate item of cost but is spread over the remaining good units.

A different situation is created by abnormal or avoidable spoilage or losses that are not expected to arise under normal, efficient operating conditions. The cost of such abnormal spoilage or losses is charged either to Factory Overhead, as shown below, thereby appearing as an additional unfavorable factory overhead variance, or directly to a current period expense account and reported as a separate item in the cost of goods sold statement.

	SUBSIDIARY RECORD	DR.	CR.
Factory Overhead Control		6,700	
Lost Units	6,700		
Work in Process — Testing Department ..			6,700

The cost of production report would show the abnormal spoilage or loss as follows:

Transferred to next department (40,000 units × $3.35) $134,020*
Transferred to factory overhead [(40,000 units × $.1675) or
  (2,000 lost units × $3.35)]   6,700

*40,000 units × $3.35 = $134,000. To avoid decimal discrepancy, the cost transferred is computed: $147,510 − $6,790 ending inventory − $6,700 = $134,020.

If the lost units were only partially complete, equivalent production calculations should consider their stage of completion when lost or spoiled, and the costing of the abnormal loss should be weighted accordingly. If one part of the loss is normal and another part abnormal, each portion must be treated in accordance with the above discussion. The critical factor in distinguishing between normal and abnormal spoilage or loss is the degree of controllability. Normal or unavoidable spoilage or loss is produced by the process under efficient operating conditions, referred to as uncontrollable. Abnormal or avoidable spoilage or loss is considered unnecessary, because the conditions resulting in the loss are controllable. For this reason, within the limits set by the state of the art of production, the difference is a short-run condition; in the long run, management should adjust and control all factors of production and eliminate all abnormal conditions.

Disposition of Testing Department Costs. The cost of production report on page 128 shows a total cost of $147,510 to be accounted for by the Testing Department. The department completed and transferred 40,000 units to the Terminal Department at a cost of $140,400 (40,000 × $3.51). The remaining cost is assigned to the work in process inventory. This balance is broken down by the various costs in process. When computing the cost of the ending work in process inventory of any department subsequent to the first, costs received from preceding departments must be included.

The 3,000 units still in process, completed by the Blending Department at a unit cost of $1.72, were later adjusted by $.08 (to $1.80) because of the loss of some of the units transferred. Therefore, the Blending Department's cost of the 3,000 units still in process is $5,400, the result of multiplying the 3,000 units by the $1.80 adjusted unit cost. The $5,400 figure is not broken down further, since such information is not pertinent to the Testing Department's operations. However, the amount is listed separately in the cost of production report, because it is part of the Testing Department's ending work in process inventory.

Materials (if any), labor, and factory overhead added by a department are costed separately in order to arrive at total work in process. In the Testing Department, no materials were added to the units received; thus, the ending inventory shows no materials in process. However, labor and factory overhead costs were incurred. The work in process analysis stated that labor and factory overhead used on the units in process were sufficient to complete 1,000 units. The cost of labor in process is $910 (1,000 × $.91) and factory overhead in process is $800 (1,000 × $.80). The total cost of the 3,000 units in process is $7,110 ($5,400 + $910 + $800). This cost, added to that transferred to the Terminal Department, $140,400, accounts for the total cost of $147,510 charged to the Testing Department.

Terminal Department   The cost of production report of the third or Terminal Department is illustrated on page 133. Total and unit cost figures were derived by using procedures discussed for the cost of production report of the Testing Department. The work completed is transferred to the finished goods storeroom; thus, the title "Transferred to finished goods storeroom" is used in place of the title "Transferred to next department." Costs charged to the Terminal Department come from the payroll distribution and the department's expense analysis sheet. The journal entry transferring costs from the Testing Department follows:

Work in Process — Terminal Department	140,400	
Work in Process — Testing Department		140,400

The Clonex Corporation
Terminal Department
Cost of Production Report
For the Month of January, 19--

Quantity Schedule

Units received from preceding department		40,000
Units transferred to finished goods storeroom...............................	35,000	
Units still in process (¼ labor and factory overhead).....................	4,000	
Units lost in process..	1,000	40,000

Cost Charged to the Department

	TOTAL COST	UNIT COST
Cost from preceding department:		
Transferred in during the month (40,000 units)	$140,400	$3.51
Cost added by department:		
Labor..	$ 32,400	$ .90
Factory overhead	19,800	.55
Total cost added	$ 52,200	$1.45
Adjustment for lost units...		.09
Total cost to be accounted for...	**$192,600**	**$5.05**

Cost Accounted for as Follows

Transferred to finished goods storeroom (35,000 × $5.05)............		$176,750
Work in process — ending inventory:		
Adjusted cost from preceding department [4,000 × ($3.51 + $.09)]..	$ 14,400	
Labor (4,000 × ¼ × $.90)	900	
Factory overhead (4,000 × ¼ × $.55).....................................	550	15,850
Total cost accounted for..		**$192,600**

ADDITIONAL COMPUTATIONS:

Equivalent production: Labor and factory overhead $= 35,000 + \dfrac{4,000}{4} = 36,000$ units

Unit costs: Labor $= \dfrac{\$32,400}{36,000} = \$.90$ per unit

Factory overhead $= \dfrac{\$19,800}{36,000} = \$.55$ per unit

Adjustment for lost units:

Method No. 1 — $\dfrac{\$140,400}{39,000} = \$3.60;\ \$3.60 - \$3.51 = \$.09$ per unit

Method No. 2 — 1,000 units × $3.51 = $3,510; $\dfrac{\$ 3,510}{39,000} = \$.09$ per unit

The entry to transfer finished units to the finished goods storeroom is presented below:

Finished Goods...	176,750	
Work in Process — Terminal Department.......................		176,750

Combined Cost of Production Reports

The three cost of production reports for The Clonex Corporation have been discussed and computed separately. These reports would most likely be consolidated in a single report summarizing manufacturing operations of the firm for a specified period. Such a report, as illustrated below, should be reviewed in order to observe the interrelationship of the various departmental reports.

The Clonex Corporation
Cost of Production Report
All Producing Departments
For the Month of January, 19--

	BLENDING		TESTING		TERMINAL	
Quantity Schedule						
Units started in process....................	50,000					
Units received from preceding department.................................			45,000		40,000	
Units transferred to next department.................................	45,000		40,000			
Units transferred to finished goods storeroom............................					35,000	
Units still in process	4,000		3,000		4,000	
Units lost in process	1,000	50,000	2,000	45,000	1,000	40,000
	TOTAL COST	UNIT COST	TOTAL COST	UNIT COST	TOTAL COST	UNIT COST
Cost Charged to the Department						
Cost from preceding department: Transferred in during the month...			$ 77,400	$1.72	$140,400	$3.51
Cost added by department:						
Materials...	$24,500	$ .50				
Labor..	29,140	.62	$ 37,310	$ .91	$ 32,400	$ .90
Factory overhead...........................	28,200	.60	32,800	.80	19,800	.55
Total cost added	$81,840	$1.72	$ 70,110	$1.71	$ 52,200	$1.45
Adjustment for lost units..................				.08		.09
Total cost to be accounted for .	$81,840	$1.72	$147,510	$3.51	$192,600	$5.05
Cost Accounted for as Follows						
Transferred to next department.......	$77,400		$140,400			
Transferred to finished goods storeroom............................					$176,750	
Work in process — ending inventory:						
Adjusted cost from preceding department.................................			$ 5,400		$ 14,400	
Materials...	$ 2,000					
Labor..	1,240		910		900	
Factory overhead...........................	1,200	4,440	800	7,110	550	15,850
Total cost accounted for		$81,840		$147,510		$192,600

DISCUSSION QUESTIONS

1. What is the primary objective in process costing?

2. Job order and process costing procedures are used by different types of industries. Discuss the procedure appropriate for each type.

3. For the following products indicate whether job order or process cost procedures would be required:

   (a) Gasoline   (e) Dacron yarn
   (b) Sewing machines   (f) Cigarettes
   (c) Chocolate syrup   (g) Space capsules
   (d) Textbooks   (h) Men's and women's suits

4. What are the distinguishing characteristics of process cost procedures?

5. Discuss three product flow formats.

6. Compare the cost accumulation and summarizing procedures of job order costing and process costing.

7. Can predetermined overhead rates be used in process costing?

8. Would one expect to find service departments in a firm using process costing? If so, how would they be handled? Would cost of production reports be used for service departments?

9. What is the purpose of a cost of production report?

10. What are the various sections of a cost of production report?

11. Separate cost of production reports are prepared for each producing department. Why is this method used in preference to one report for the entire firm?

12. Are month-to-month fluctuations in average unit costs computed in a cost of production report meaningful data in attempting to control costs?

13. What is equivalent production? Explain in terms of its effect on computed unit costs.

14. In process costing, physical inventories of work in process must be taken at the end of each accounting period. Ordinarily, all department heads are responsible for their own inventories, and the methods they use to determine such data are crude by comparison with procedures used for determining year-end physical inventory. It is not unusual for a department head to estimate rather than count inventory in process. Consequently, figures are bound to have errors. Is this good practice or should more accurate methods be used, such as having inventory teams determine inventories?

15. What is the justification for spreading the cost of lost units over the remaining good units? Should the cost of these units ever be charged to overhead? Will the answer be different if units are lost (a) in the originating department, (b) at the beginning of a department's operations, (c) during operations, or (d) at the end of operations?

16. (a) Distinguish between normal (unavoidable) spoilage and abnormal (avoidable) spoilage. (b) Explain how both should be reported for management purposes.

(AICPA adapted)

17. Select the answer which best completes the statement:

(a) A characteristic which applies to process costing but not to job order costing is: (1) identifiable batches of production; (2) equivalent units of production; (3) averaging process; (4) use of standard costs.

(b) In processing goods through a factory, materials are successively run through producing Departments A, B, and C. For product costing purposes, Department B should treat items received from Department A as: (1) materials; (2) work in process; (3) finished goods; (4) equivalent units.

(c) The type of spoilage that should *not* affect the recorded cost of inventories is: (1) abnormal spoilage; (2) normal spoilage; (3) seasonal spoilage; (4) standard spoilage.

(d) Transferred in costs in a cost of production report are most similar to: (1) materials added at the beginning of the process; (2) conversion costs added during the process; (3) costs transferred to the next process; (4) costs included in beginning inventory.

(AICPA adapted)

EXERCISES

Round off all amounts to three decimal places.

1. Cost of production report. A company's Department 2 costs for June were:

Cost from Department 1	$16,320
Cost added in Department 2:	
Materials	43,415
Labor	56,100
Factory overhead	58,575

The quantity schedule shows 12,000 units were received during the month from Department 1; 7,000 units were transferred to finished goods; and 5,000 units in process at the end of June were 50% complete as to materials cost and 25% complete as to conversion cost.

Required: Cost of production report.

2. Costing of units transferred; lost units. Read, Inc., instituted a new process in October, during which it started 10,000 units in Department A. Of the units started, 1,000 units, a normal number, were lost during the process; 7,000 were transferred to Department B; and 2,000 remained in work in process inventory at the end of the month, 100% complete as to materials and 50% complete as to conversion cost. Materials and conversion costs of $27,000 and $40,000, respectively, were charged to the department in October.

Required: Total cost transferred to Department B.

(AICPA adapted)

3. Cost of production report; normal loss. For December, the Production Control Department of Carola Chemical, Inc., reported the following production data for Department 2:

Transferred in from Department 1	55 000 liters
Transferred out to Department 3	39 500 liters
In process at end of December (with ⅓ labor and factory over-	
head)	10 500 liters

All materials were put into process in Department 1.

The Cost Department collected these figures for Department 2:

Unit cost for units transferred in from Department 1	$1.80
Labor cost in Department 2	$27,520
Applied factory overhead	15,480

Required: A cost of production report for Department 2 for December.

4. Cost of production report. Brooks, Inc., uses process costing. The costs for Department 2 for April were:

Cost from preceding department		$20,000
Cost added by department:		
Materials	$21,816	
Labor	7,776	
Factory overhead	4,104	33,696

The following information was obtained from the department's quantity schedule:

Units received	5,000
Units transferred out	4,000
Units still in process	1,000

The degree of completion of the work in process as to costs originating in Department 2 was: 50% of the units were 40% complete; 20% were 30% complete; and the balance were 20% complete.

Required: The cost of production report for Department 2 for April.

5. Equivalent production. During April, 20,000 units were transferred in from Department A at a cost of $39,000. Materials cost of $6,500 and conversion cost of $9,000 were added in Department B. On April 30, Department B had 5,000 units of work in process 60% complete as to conversion costs. Materials are added in the beginning of the process in Department B.

Required:
(1) Equivalent production computations.
(2) The cost per equivalent unit for conversion costs.

(AICPA adapted)

6. Costing of units transferred out; abnormal loss. During February, the Assembly Department received 60,000 units from the Cutting Department at a unit cost of $3.54. Costs added in the Assembly Department were: materials, $41,650; labor, $101,700; and factory overhead, $56,500. There was no beginning inventory. Of the 60,000 units received, 50,000 were transferred out; 9,000 units were in process at the end of the month (all materials, ⅔ converted); 1,000 lost units were ½ complete as to materials and conversion costs. The entire loss is considered abnormal and is to be charged to factory overhead.

Required: Cost of production report.

7. Cost of production report; normal and abnormal spoilage. The Sterling Company uses process costing. In Department B, conversion costs are incurred uniformly throughout the process. Materials are added at the end of the process, following inspection. Normal spoilage is expected to be 5% of good output.

The following information related to Department B for January:

	UNITS	DOLLARS
Received from Department A	12,000	$84,000
Transferred to finished goods	9,000	
Ending inventory (70% complete)	2,000	
Cost incurred:		
Materials		18,000
Labor and factory overhead		45,600

Required: Cost of production report for Department B.

8. Cost of production report; normal and abnormal spoiled units. The Curtis Company uses process costing in accounting for its production department which uses two materials. Material A is added at the beginning of the process and is inspected at the 90% stage; Material B is then added to the good units. Normal spoilage units amount to 5% of good output.

Company records contain the following information for January:

Started during the period	10,000 units
Material A	$13,370
Material B	$ 4,500
Direct labor cost	$37,580
Factory overhead	$46,975
Transferred to finished goods	7,000 units
Ending inventory (95% complete, including Material B)	2,000 units

Required: Cost of production report.

9. Cost of production report; spoiled units — normal and abnormal. Hettinger, Inc., uses process costing in its two producing departments. In Department 2, inspection takes place at the 96% stage of completion, after which materials are added to good units. A spoilage rate of 3% of good output is considered normal.

Department 2 records for April show:

Received from Department 1	30,000 units
Cost	$135,000
Materials	$ 12,500
Conversion cost	$139,340
Transferred to finished goods	25,000 units
Ending work in process inventory (50% complete)	4,200 units

Required: Cost of production report.

10. Computation of equivalent production. Pietra-Gonatas, Inc., uses process costing to account for the costs of its only product, Product D. Production takes place in three departments: Fabrication, Assembly, and Packaging.

At the end of the fiscal year, June 30, the following inventory of Product D is on hand:

(a) No unused raw materials or packaging materials.
(b) Fabrication Department: 300 units, ⅓ complete as to raw materials and ½ complete as to direct labor.
(c) Assembly Department: 1,000 units, ²/₅ complete as to direct labor.
(d) Packaging Department: 100 units, ¾ complete as to packaging materials and ¼ complete as to direct labor.
(e) Shipping or finished goods area: 400 units.

Required:
(1) The number of equivalent units of raw materials in all inventories at June 30.
(2) The number of equivalent units of the Fabrication Department's direct labor in all inventories at June 30.
(3) The number of equivalent units of packaging materials in all inventories at June 30.

(AICPA adapted)

PROBLEMS

Round off all amounts to three decimal places.

6-1. Cost of production report; normal spoilage. Malamud Company uses process costing. All materials are added at the beginning of the process. The product is inspected when it is 80% converted, and spoilage is identified only at that point. Normal spoilage is expected to be 5% of good output.

During March, 10,500 units were put into process. Current costs were $52,500 for materials; $39,770 for labor; and $31,525 for factory overhead. The 3,000 units still in process at the end of March were estimated to be 90% complete. All spoilage was normal. A total of 7,000 units were transferred to finished goods.

Required: A cost of production report for March.

6-2. Cost of production report; spoilage at end of process, all normal. Primakoff, Inc., uses process costing in its two producing departments. Materials are added at the end of the process after quality control inspection; no abnormal spoilage occurred during the month.

During October, 2,500 units were received from Department 1 at a cost of $50,000. Costs incurred by Department 2 during October were:

Materials	$ 8,000
Conversion costs	36,000

A total of 2,000 units were transferred to finished goods inventory.

The 300 units still in process at the end of October were ⅔ complete as to conversion costs.

Required: Cost of production report for Department 2.

6-3. Cost of production report; spoilage at end of process, both normal and abnormal. The Gassert Company uses process costing in its two producing departments. The following information pertains to Department 2 for November.

Normal spoilage is 5% of output; inspection and identification of spoilage take place at the end of the process; materials are added after inspection.

Department 2 received 14,000 units from Department 1 at a cost of $140,000. Department 2 costs were $12,000 for materials and $90,000 for conversion costs.

A total of 8,000 units were completed and transferred to finished goods. At the end of the month, 5,000 units were still in process, estimated to be 60% complete as to conversion costs.

Required: Cost of production report for Department 2.

6-4. Quantity and equivalent production schedules; adjustment for lost units. Biological Laboratories, Inc., produces an antibiotic product in its three producing departments. The following quantitative and cost data have been made available:

	DEPARTMENT		
	Blending	Testing	Terminal
Production data:			
Started into production	8 000 kg	5 400 kg	3 200 kg
Transferred to next department	5 400	3 200	
Transferred to finished goods storeroom			2 100
In process (100% materials, ⅓ labor and overhead)	2 400	1 800	
In process (100% materials, ⅔ labor and overhead)			900
Cost charged to departments:			
Materials	$20,670	$ 7,980	$14,400
Labor	11,160	5,016	11,520
Factory overhead	5,580	2,280	5,040
Total	$37,410	$15,276	$30,960

Lost units are normal and apply to all production.

Required:
(1) A quantity schedule for each of the three departments.
(2) An equivalent production schedule for each of the three departments.
(3) The unit cost of factory overhead in the Blending Department.
(4) The lost unit cost in the Testing Department if the unit cost transferred in from the Blending Department is $5.35.

6-5. Equivalent production and cost computations; evaluation of report. The Moderna Company employs departmental budgets and performance reports in planning and controlling its operations. Department A's budget for January was for the production of 1,000 units of equivalent production, a normal month's volume.

The following performance report was prepared for January by the company's accountant:

Variable costs:	Budget	Actual	Variance
Direct materials	$20,000	$23,100	$3,100 (unfavorable)
Direct labor	10,000	10,500	500 (unfavorable)
Indirect labor	1,650	1,790	140 (unfavorable)
Power	210	220	10 (unfavorable)
Supplies	320	330	10 (unfavorable)
Total	$32,180	$35,940	$3,760
Fixed costs:			
Rent	$ 400	$ 400	
Supervision	1,000	1,000	
Depreciation	500	500	
Other	100	100	
Total	$ 2,000	$ 2,000	
Total variable and fixed costs	$34,180	$37,940	$3,760

Direct materials are introduced at various stages of the process. All conversion costs are incurred uniformly throughout the process. Because production fluctuates from month to month, the fixed overhead is applied at the rate of $2 per equivalent unit as to conversion costs.

Actual variable costs are applied monthly as incurred.

There was no beginning inventory at January 1. Of the 1,100 new units started during January, 900 were completed and shipped. There was no finished goods inventory at January 31. Units in process at January 31 were estimated to be 75% complete as to direct materials and 80% complete as to conversion costs. There was no shrinkage, spoilage, or waste of materials during January.

Required:
(1) A schedule of equivalent production for January.
(2) A schedule computing the amount of over- or underapplied overhead at January 31.
(3) A schedule computing the cost of goods shipped and the cost of the work in process inventory at January 31 at *actual* cost.
(4) Comments on the performance report, and specific conclusions, if any, to be drawn from the report.

(AICPA adapted)

6-6. Cost of production report. The Anderson Company manufactures a mechanical device known as "Klebo," and uses process costing. The manufacturing operations take place in one department, as described below.

Material K, a metal, is stamped to form a part which is assembled with one of the purchased parts "X." The unit is then machined and cleaned, after which it is assembled with two units of part "Y" to form the finished "Klebo." Spray priming and enameling is the final operation.

Time-and-motion studies indicate that of the total time required for the manufacture of a unit, the first operation requires 25% of the labor cost; the first assembly, an additional 25%; machining and cleaning, 12.5%; the second assembly, 25%; and painting, 12.5%. Factory overhead is considered to follow the same pattern of operations as labor.

The following data apply to October, the first month of operations:

Units finished and sent to finished goods warehouse	67,000
Units assembled but not painted	5,000
Units ready for the second assembly	3,000
Inventories at the end of the month:	
Material K (kg)	5 800
Part X (units of part X)	5,000
Part Y (units of part Y)	6,000
Klebos in process (units)	8,000
Units in finished goods inventory	7,500

Material K purchased — 100 000 kilograms	$25,000
Part X purchased — 80,000 units	16,000
Part Y purchased — 150,000 units	15,000
Primer and enamel used	1,072
Direct labor	45,415
Factory overhead	24,905

Required: A cost of production report showing total cost, equivalent production, unit cost, cost of goods finished, and work in process inventories.

(AICPA adapted)

CASES

A. Accounting for spoiled units. The Household Aids Company assembles clip clothespins in three sections, and uses process costing. Under normal operating conditions, each section has a spoilage rate of 2%. However, spoilage can go as high as 5% and is usually discovered when a faulty pin enters process or on final completion by a section.

The spring mechanism is the only material which can be saved from a spoiled unit. The production supervisor assigns a worker once or twice a week to remove the springs from spoiled units. The salvaged springs are placed in bins at the assembly tables in Section No. 1 to be used again. No accounting entry is made of this salvage operation.

In the past, the controller has made no attempt to account for spoilage separately. Lost unit costs have been absorbed by the units transferred out of the section and those remaining in process. However, because spoilage is increasing, a different method is needed.

Required: A recommended solution to the problem.

B. Inventory costing for financial statements. The United Fiber Corporation mines and sells a fibrous mineral. On December 31, 19D, the inventory amounted to 25,000 tons of fiber; all this inventory was produced during 19D and is costed at $19.88 per ton, the average cost per ton produced in 19D. Production and costs in other years were as follows:

Tons Produced and Average Costs

YEAR	TONS PRODUCED	COST PER TON
19A	170,000	$14.65
19B	180,000	14.85
19C	175,000	15.06
19D	110,000	19.88

Production Costs

	AMOUNTS		PER TON	
	19C	*19D*	*19C*	*19D*
Tons produced	175,000	110,000		
Direct labor	$ 472,500	$ 401,500	$ 2.70	$ 3.65
Indirect labor	346,500	286,000	1.98	2.60
Supplies and other production expenses	708,750	479,600	4.05	4.36
Depletion	262,500	165,000	1.50	1.50
Salaries (superintendents, factory clerks, security guards)	217,000	233,200	1.24	2.12
Depreciation	227,500	247,500	1.30	2.25
Other fixed expenses	400,750	374,000	2.29	3.40
Total	$2,635,500	$2,186,800	$15.06	$19.88

Indirect labor, supplies, and other production expenses are considered variable costs. There are no semivariable costs. Depletion is computed at $1.50 per ton mined, and depreciation on machinery and equipment is computed on a straight-line basis. Due to an extended strike in 19D, much less of the fibrous mineral was mined than during the three preceding years in which production was considered normal. The management explained that the rise in 19D unit labor costs was caused by general increases of from 33% to 40% in hourly wage rates. The increase in the unit cost of supplies and other production expenses is accounted for by an increase in prices of about 10%. All increases took place at the beginning of the year.

Required:
(1) A discussion as to whether the pricing of the ending inventory on December 31, 19D, at $19.88 per ton, is acceptable for financial statement purposes.
(2) A presentation with full calculations as to how the ending inventory price should be adjusted and dealt with in the statements, assuming that the price of $19.88 per ton is not acceptable for financial purposes.
(3) A brief discussion of the classification of fixed and variable costs.

(AICPA adapted)

Process Costing
Addition of Materials
Average and Fifo Costing

In numerous industries, all materials needed for the product are put in process in the first department. However, additional materials might be required in subsequent departments in order to complete the units. The addition of such materials has two possible effects on units and costs in process:

1. The additional materials increase the unit cost, since these materials become a part of the product manufactured, but do not increase the number of final units. For example, in a finishing plant of a textile company, the material added is often a bleach; in a wire company, a plating mixture; in an automobile assembly plant, additional parts. These materials are needed to give the product certain specified quantities, characteristics, or completeness; or

2. The added materials increase the number of units and also cause a change in unit cost. In processing a chemical, water is often added to a mixture, causing an increase in the number of units and a spreading of costs over a greater number of units.

INCREASE IN UNIT COST DUE TO ADDITION OF MATERIALS

In the simplest case, added materials, such as parts of an automobile, do not increase the number of units but increase total cost and unit costs. A materials unit cost must be computed for the department, and a materials cost must be included in the work in process inventory.

The cost of production report of the Terminal Department of the Clonex Corporation (page 133) is used to illustrate the different effects of the addition of materials on total and unit costs of a department. Assume that additional materials costing $17,020 are placed in process and charged to the Terminal Department. Assume further that the materials in work in process are sufficient to complete 2,000 of the 4,000 units; that is, units are 50 percent complete as to materials cost. The effect of the additional materials cost is shown in the cost report below.

The Clonex Corporation
Terminal Department
Cost of Production Report
For the Month of January, 19--

Quantity Schedule

Units received from preceding department		40,000
Units transferred to finished goods storeroom.............................	35,000	
Units still in process (½ materials — ¼ labor and factory overhead)..	4,000	
Units lost in process..	1,000	40,000

Cost Charged to the Department

	Total Cost	Unit Cost
Cost from preceding department:		
Transferred in during the month (40,000 units)	$140,400	$3.51
Cost added by department:		
Materials	$ 17,020	$ .46
Labor...	32,400	.90
Factory overhead	19,800	.55
Total cost added	$ 69,220	$1.91
Adjustment for lost units..		.09
Total cost to be accounted for..	$209,620	$5.51

Cost Accounted for as Follows

Transferred to finished goods storeroom (35,000 × $5.51)............		$192,850
Work in process — ending inventory:		
Adjusted cost from preceding department (4,000 × $3.60)	$ 14,400	
Materials (4,000 × ½ × $.46)...	920	
Labor (4,000 × ¼ × $.90)	900	
Factory overhead (4,000 × ¼ × $.55)...	550	16,770
Total cost accounted for..		$209,620

ADDITIONAL COMPUTATIONS:

$$\text{Equivalent production: Materials} = 35,000 + \frac{4,000}{2} = 37,000 \text{ units}$$

$$\text{Labor and factory overhead} = 35,000 + \frac{4,000}{4} = 36,000 \text{ units}$$

$$\text{Unit costs: Materials} = \frac{\$17,020}{37,000} = \$.46 \text{ per unit}$$

$$\text{Labor} = \frac{\$32,400}{36,000} = \$.90 \text{ per unit}$$

$$\text{Factory overhead} = \frac{\$19,800}{36,000} = \$.55 \text{ per unit}$$

Adjustment for lost units:

$$\text{Method No. 1} - \frac{\$140,400}{39,000} = \$3.60; \$3.60 - \$3.51 = \$.09 \text{ per unit}$$

$$\text{Method No. 2} - 1,000 \text{ units} \times \$3.51 = \$3,510; \frac{\$ 3,510}{39,000} = \$.09 \text{ per unit}$$

The only differences in the two cost reports (pages 133 and 144) are the $17,020 materials cost charged to the department and the $.46 materials unit cost ($17,020 ÷ 37,000). The additional materials cost is also reflected in the total cost to be accounted for, in the cost of units transferred to finished goods, and in the ending work in process inventory.

INCREASE IN UNITS AND CHANGE IN UNIT COST DUE TO ADDITION OF MATERIALS

When additional materials result in additional units, different computations are necessary. The greater number of units causes a decrease in unit cost which necessitates an adjustment of the preceding department's unit cost, since the increased number of units will absorb the same total cost transferred from the preceding department.

To illustrate the situation of additional units resulting from the addition of materials, assume Terminal Department costs for labor and factory overhead of $32,400 and $19,800, respectively, an additional materials cost of $17,020, and an increase of 8,000 units as the result of added materials. The effect of these assumptions on the Terminal Department's cost of production report is shown on page 146.

The additional 8,000 units are entered in the department's quantity schedule as "Additional units put into process." The quantity schedule reports that 44,000 units were completed and transferred to the finished goods storeroom and that 4,000 units are still in process, 50 percent complete as to materials and 25 percent complete as to labor and factory overhead. Therefore, equivalent production is 46,000 units for materials and 45,000 for labor and factory overhead. Dividing departmental materials, labor, and factory overhead costs for the period by these production figures results in a unit cost of $.37 ($17,020 ÷ 46,000) for materials, $.72 ($32,400 ÷ 45,000) for labor, and $.44 ($19,800 ÷ 45,000) for factory overhead.

These computations do not differ from those already discussed. Peculiar to this situation of additional materials is the adjustment of the preceding department's unit cost. Total cost charged to the Terminal Department as cost transferred in from the preceding department must now be allocated over a greater number of units, thereby reducing the unit cost of work done in the preceding department.

In the illustration on page 144, the $140,400 cost transferred to the Terminal Department was absorbed by 40,000 units, resulting in a unit cost of $3.51. Because of the 8,000 increase in units, the $140,400 cost must now be spread over 48,000 units, resulting in a unit cost for the preceding department of $2.925. This adjusted cost is inserted in the production report on page 146 as "Adjusted unit cost of units transferred in during the month" and is added to departmental unit costs to arrive at the unit cost accumulated to the end of operations in the Terminal Department.

The Clonex Corporation
Terminal Department
Cost of Production Report
For the Month of January, 19—

Quantity Schedule

Units received from preceding department	40,000	
Additional units put into process	8,000	48,000
Units transferred to finished goods storeroom	44,000	
Units still in process (½ materials — ¼ labor and factory overhead)	4,000	48,000

Cost Charged to the Department

	TOTAL COST	UNIT COST
Cost from preceding department:		
Transferred in during the month (40,000 units)	$140,400	$3.510
Cost added by department:		
Materials	$ 17,020	$ .370
Labor	32,400	.720
Factory overhead	19,800	.440
Total cost added	$ 69,220	$1.530
Adjusted unit cost of units transferred in during the month		2.925
Total cost to be accounted for	$209,620	$4.455

Cost Accounted for as Follows

Transferred to finished goods storeroom (44,000 × $4.455)		$196,020
Work in process — ending inventory:		
Adjusted cost from preceding department (4,000 × $2.925)	$ 11,700	
Materials (4,000 × ½ × $.370)	740	
Labor (4,000 × ¼ × $.720)	720	
Factory overhead (4,000 × ¼ × $.440)	440	13,600
Total cost accounted for		$209,620

ADDITIONAL COMPUTATIONS:

Equivalent production: Materials $= 44,000 + \dfrac{4,000}{2} = 46,000$ units

Labor and factory overhead $= 44,000 + \dfrac{4,000}{4} = 45,000$ units

Unit costs: Materials $= \dfrac{\$17,020}{46,000} = \$.370$ per unit

Labor $= \dfrac{\$32,400}{45,000} = \$.720$ per unit

Factory overhead $= \dfrac{\$19,800}{45,000} = \$.440$ per unit

Adjustment for additional units: $\dfrac{\$140,400}{48,000} = \$2.925$ per unit

When additional materials increase the number of units being processed, it is still possible to have lost units. However, should increased and lost units occur, no separate calculation is required for the lost units; only net units added are used. In the illustration above, 8,000 additional units resulted from added materials. It is quite possible, though, that the materials added should have yielded 10,000 additional units. The difference between the 8,000 units and the anticipated 10,000 units could be due to the loss of 2,000 units. If this is the case, the effect of the lost units is similar to that of units lost in the first department; that is, the cost is absorbed within the department as an increase in unit costs. However, if desired, it is also possible to report the effect of these lost units separately. If 10,000 additional units should have resulted, the effect of losing 2,000 units can be determined as follows: (1) compute the unit cost of work done in preceding departments and in the Terminal Department as if no loss had occurred; (2) compute the loss by multiplying the unit cost obtained in the preceding computation by the 2,000 lost units.

BEGINNING WORK IN PROCESS INVENTORIES

The cost of production reports illustrated in Chapter 6 list ending work in process inventories. These inventories become beginning inventories of the next period.

Several methods are used in accounting for these beginning inventory costs. Two methods are illustrated here:

1. *Average costing.* Beginning inventory costs are added to the costs of the new period.
2. *First-in, first-out (fifo) costing.* Beginning inventory costs are kept sep- arate and the new costs necessary to complete the work in process inventory are computed.

When beginning work in process inventory costs are merged with costs of the new period, the problem is essentially one of securing representative average unit costs. Ordinarily, the averaging process is quite simple.

Average Costing

The February cost reports of the three departments reviewed in Chapter 6 are used to illustrate the treatment of beginning work in process inventory and to show the relationship of costs from one period to the next. Ending invento- ries in January departmental cost reports become beginning work in process inventories for February. Computations begin with this January work in pro- cess inventory data:

	BLENDING	TESTING	TERMINAL
Units	4,000	3,000	4,000
Cost from preceding depart- ment...............................	—	$5,400	$14,400
Materials in process..............	$2,000	—	—
Labor in process..................	1,240	910	900
Factory overhead in process....	1,200	800	550

Blending Department. The beginning work in process inventory of the Blending Department shows a $2,000 materials cost, a $1,240 labor cost, a $1,200 factory overhead cost, and 4,000 units in process. During February, additional charges to the department are: materials, $19,840; labor, $24,180; and factory overhead, $22,580. The additional materials put into process are for the production of 40,000 units. Therefore, units to be accounted for total 44,000 (4,000 + 40,000). Of the total units put into process, 39,000 are completed; 38,000 of the completed units were transferred to the Testing Department; and the other 1,000, although completed, are still on hand awaiting transfer. At month-end, 3,000 units are in process, 100 percent complete as to materials but only 66⅔ percent complete as to labor and overhead. During the month, 2,000 units were lost. The above facts are illustrated on the following page in the cost of production report of the Blending Department.

The unit cost of work done in the Blending Department is $1.72, consisting of $.52 for materials, $.62 for labor, and $.58 for factory overhead. The $.52 unit cost for materials is computed by adding the materials cost in the beginning work in process to the materials cost for the month ($2,000 + $19,840) and dividing the $21,840 total by an equivalent production figure of 42,000 units. The 42,000 figure consists of 38,000 units completed and transferred, 1,000 units completed but still on hand, and 3,000 units in process, complete as to materials. It is important to note that the cost of materials already in process is added to the materials cost for the month before dividing by the equivalent production figure. This method results in an average unit cost for work done in the current and preceding periods.

The same procedure is followed in computing unit costs for labor and factory overhead. The $.62 unit cost for labor is the result of dividing equivalent production of 41,000 units [39,000 + (⅔ × 3,000)] into the sum of the beginning work in process labor cost of $1,240 and the departmental labor cost of $24,180 for the month. The factory overhead unit cost is $.58 [($1,200 + $22,580) ÷ 41,000].

Total cost charged to the department is disposed of as follows: $65,360 is transferred to the Testing Department and $5,680 is assigned to the ending work in process. The work in process inventory consists of $1,720 (1,000 units × $1.72) for units completed but on hand and of the following costs assigned to units still in process: $1,560 (3,000 units × $.52) for materials; $1,240 (2,000 units × $.62) for labor; and $1,160 (2,000 units × $.58) for factory overhead.

The 1,000 units completed but on hand are listed as work in process in the Blending Department, although all operations in that department have been performed on these units. These units remain in the work in process inventory of the Blending Department to assign it responsibility for this part of total work in process. The cost transfer entry for the 38,000 units transferred to the next department is:

Work in Process — Testing Department 65,360
   Work in Process — Blending Department   65,360

Testing Department. Accounting for beginning work in process inventory costs in departments other than the first requires additional calculations because

The Clonex Corporation
Blending Department
Cost of Production Report — Average Costing
For the Month of February, 19—

Quantity Schedule

Units in process at beginning (all materials — ½ labor and factory overhead)	4,000	
Units started in process	40,000	44,000
Units transferred to next department	38,000	
Units completed and on hand	1,000	
Units still in process (all materials — ⅔ labor and factory overhead)	3,000	
Units lost in process	2,000	44,000

Cost Charged to the Department

	TOTAL COST	UNIT COST
Cost added by department:		
Work in process — beginning inventory:		
Materials	$ 2,000	
Labor	1,240	
Factory overhead	1,200	
Cost added during period:		
Materials	19,840	$ .52
Labor	24,180	.62
Factory overhead	22,580	.58
Total cost to be accounted for	$71,040	$1.72

Cost Accounted for as Follows

Transferred to next department (38,000 × $1.72)		$65,360
Work in process — ending inventory:		
Completed and on hand (1,000 × $1.72)	$ 1,720	
Materials (3,000 × $.52)	1,560	
Labor (3,000 × ⅔ × $.62)	1,240	
Factory overhead (3,000 × ⅔ × $.58)	1,160	5,680
Total cost accounted for		$71,040

ADDITIONAL COMPUTATIONS:

Equivalent production: Materials = 38,000 + 1,000 + 3,000 = 42,000 units
Labor and factory overhead = 38,000 + 1,000 + (⅔ × 3,000)
= 41,000 units

Unit costs: Materials = $2,000 + $19,840 = $21,840; $\frac{\$21,840}{42,000}$ = $.52 per unit

Labor = $1,240 + $24,180 = $25,420; $\frac{\$25,420}{41,000}$ = $.62 per unit

Factory overhead = $1,200 + $22,580 = $23,780; $\frac{\$23,780}{41,000}$ = $.58 per unit

part of the cost assigned to the work in process inventory is classified as cost from a preceding department. When the ending work in process inventory was computed, part of the cost of this inventory came from costs added by the preceding department. It is this part of the inventory which now requires separate treatment.

Because costs assigned to the beginning work in process inventory are added to costs incurred during the period and these totals are divided by equivalent production figures to secure average unit cost figures, the beginning work in process inventory of departments other than the first must be split into two parts:

1. That part consisting of work which was done in preceding departments.
2. That part representing costs added by the department itself.

The portion of the work in process inventory representing the cost of work done in preceding departments is entered in the section of the cost report titled "Cost from preceding department." It is added to the cost of transfers received from the preceding department during the current period. An average unit cost for work done in preceding departments is then computed. The other portion of the inventory, which represents costs added by the Testing Department, is entered as a departmental cost to be added to other departmental costs incurred during the period. Average unit costs are then computed.

The cost of production report of the Testing Department presented on page 151 illustrates both of the aforementioned procedures. The analysis of the beginning work in process of this department (page 147) lists 3,000 units in process with a cost of $5,400 from the preceding department, a labor cost of $910, and $800 for factory overhead. The following costs pertain to February: cost from the preceding department, $65,360; labor, $34,050; factory overhead, $30,018. Units completed and transferred to the Terminal Department totaled 36,000; 4,000 units are in process 50 percent complete as to labor and factory overhead; 1,000 units were lost in process.

The $5,400 portion of the beginning work in process inventory, which is cost from the preceding department, is entered in the current month's cost report as work in process — beginning inventory. It is added to the $65,360 of cost transferred during the month to the Testing Department from the Blending Department. The average unit cost for work done in the preceding department is $1.726, computed by dividing total cost received from the Blending Department, $70,760 ($5,400 + $65,360), by 41,000 units. These units consist of 3,000 units in the beginning work in process inventory and 38,000 units received during the month. The unit cost is a *weighted average*, since it considers all units and costs received from the preceding department. It is not the average of the two unit costs, $1.80 and $1.72. Such an average would be inaccurate, since there are more units with a unit cost of $1.72 (38,000 units) than with a unit cost of $1.80 (3,000 units). Instead, the total cost is divided by the total units.

Departmental unit costs for labor and factory overhead are computed as explained in discussing the cost report of the Blending Department. The $910 of labor in process at the beginning is added to labor put in process during the

The Clonex Corporation
Testing Department
Cost of Production Report — Average Costing
For the Month of February, 19--

Quantity Schedule

Units in process at beginning (⅓ labor and factory overhead)	3,000	
Units received from preceding department	38,000	41,000
Units transferred to next department	36,000	
Units still in process (½ labor and factory overhead)....................	4,000	
Units lost in process...	1,000	41,000

Cost Charged to the Department

		TOTAL COST	UNIT COST
Cost from preceding department:			
Work in process — beginning inventory (3,000 units)...............		$ 5,400	$1.800
Transferred in during this period	(38,000 units)..............	65,360	1.720
Total	(41,000 units)..............	$ 70,760	$1.726
Cost added by department:			
Work in process — beginning inventory:			
Labor...		$ 910	
Factory overhead..		800	
Cost added during period:			
Labor...		34,050	$ .920
Factory overhead..		30,018	.811
Total cost added..		$ 65,778	$ 1.731
Adjustment for lost units			.043
Total cost to be accounted for		**$136,538**	$ 3.500

Cost Accounted for as Follows

Transferred to next department (36,000 × $3.500).........................		$126,000
Work in process — ending inventory:		
Adjusted cost from preceding department [4,000 × ($1.726 + $.043)]..	$ 7,076	
Labor (4,000 × ½ × $.920)	1,840	
Factory overhead (4,000 × ½ × $.811)...................................	1,622	10,538
Total cost accounted for..		**$136,538**

ADDITIONAL COMPUTATIONS:

Unit cost from preceding department $= \dfrac{\$70,760}{41,000} = \$1.726$ per unit

Equivalent production: Labor and factory overhead $= 36,000 + \dfrac{4,000}{2} = 38,000$ units

Unit costs: Labor $= \$910 + \$34,050 = \$34,960;\ \dfrac{\$34,960}{38,000} = \$.920$ per unit

Factory overhead $= \$800 + \$30,018 = \$30,818;\ \dfrac{\$30,818}{38,000} = \$.811$ per unit

Adjustment for lost units:

Method No. 1 $- \dfrac{\$70,760}{40,000} = \$1.769;\ \$1.769 - \$1.726 = \$.043$ per unit

Method No. 2 $-$ 1,000 units $\times \$1.726 = \$1,726;\ \dfrac{\$1,726}{40,000} = \$.043$ per unit month, $34,050; and the total of these two labor costs, $34,960, is divided by an equivalent production figure of 38,000 units [36,000 + (4,000 ÷ 2)] to arrive at the $.920 unit cost. The factory overhead unit cost of $.811 is the result of dividing total factory overhead, $30,818 ($800 + $30,018), by equivalent production of 38,000 units. The departmental unit cost is the sum of these two unit costs, $1.731.

The lost unit cost adjustment figure of $.043 is computed on the assumption that units lost cannot be identified as coming from units in process at the beginning or from units received during the period; units are assumed to have been lost from both sources. The lost unit cost is computed by dividing total preceding department cost, $70,760, by remaining good units, 40,000, and subtracting from this adjusted unit cost of $1.769 the previous average unit cost figure of $1.726. The adjustment because of lost units is $.043. The lost unit adjustment can also be determined by multiplying the 1,000 lost units by the preceding department's average unit cost, $1.726, for a total cost of $1,726, which must be absorbed by the 40,000 remaining good units. The lost unit cost adjustment is added to the $1.731 departmental unit cost and to the unadjusted average preceding department unit cost of $1.726 to give a cumulative unit cost figure of $3.50.

The total cost to be accounted for is $136,538. Of this total, $126,000 is the cost of the 36,000 units completed and transferred. The balance is cost assigned to the work in process inventory. The entry for the cost of the 36,000 units transferred to the next department is:

> **Work in Process — Terminal Department**......................   126,000
>   **Work in Process — Testing Department**   126,000

Terminal Department. To complete this discussion of operations for February, the cost of production report of the Terminal Department is shown on page 153. The entry to transfer the cost of the 36,000 finished units is:

> **Finished Goods**...   182,160
>   **Work in Process — Terminal Department**.................   182,160

Combined Cost of Production Report — Average Costing. Although the cost reports of each department are presented separately, operations for the month would also be combined in a single cost report as illustrated on page 154.

First-In, First-Out (Fifo) Costing

The preceding discussion describes the average costing method of accounting for beginning work in process inventory costs in process costing. It is also possible to keep beginning work in process costs separate rather than average them in with the additional new costs incurred in the next period. This procedure gives separate unit costs (1) for beginning work in process units completed and (2) for units started and finished in the same period.

Some accountants believe that the beginning work in process costs should be kept intact, adding only that portion of additional costs required to com-

The Clonex Corporation
Terminal Department
Cost of Production Report — Average Costing
For the Month of February, 19--

Quantity Schedule

Units in process at beginning (¼ labor and factory overhead)......	4,000	
Units received from preceding department	36,000	40,000
Units transferred to finished goods storeroom...............................	36,000	
Units still in process (⅓ labor and factory overhead).....................	3,000	
Units lost in process..	1,000	40,000

Cost Charged to the Department

	Total Cost	Unit Cost
Cost from preceding department:		
Work in process — beginning inventory (4,000 units)...............	$ 14,400	$ 3.60
Transferred in during this period (36,000 units)..............	126,000	3.50
Total (40,000 units)..............	$140,400	$ 3.51
Cost added by department:		
Work in process — begining inventory:		
Labor..	$ 900	
Factory overhead...	550	
Costs added during period:		
Labor..	33,140	$ .92
Factory overhead...	19,430	.54
Total cost added...	$ 54,020	$ 1.46
Adjustment for lost units		.09
Total cost to be accounted for	194,420	$ 5.06

Cost Accounted for as Follows

Transferred to finished goods storeroom (36,000 × $5.06)............		$182,160
Work in process — ending inventory:		
Adjusted cost from preceding department [3,000 × ($3.51 + $.09)]..	$ 10,800	
Labor (3,000 × ⅓ × $.92)	920	
Factory overhead (3,000 × ⅓ × $.54)..	540	12,260
Total cost accounted for..		**$194,420**

ADDITIONAL COMPUTATIONS:

Unit cost from preceding department $= \dfrac{\$140,400}{40,000} = \$3.51$ per unit

Equivalent production: Labor and factory overhead $= 36,000 + \dfrac{3,000}{3} = 37,000$ units

Unit costs: Labor $= \$900 + \$33,140 = \$34,040; \dfrac{\$34,040}{37,000} = \$.92$ per unit

Factory overhead $= \$550 + \$19,430 = \$19,980; \dfrac{\$19,980}{37,000} = \$.54$ per unit

Adjustment for lost units:

Method No. 1 $- \dfrac{\$140,400}{39,000} = \$3.60; \$3.60 - \$3.51 = \$.09$ per unit

Method No. 2 $- 1,000 \times \$3.51 = \$3,510; \dfrac{\$3,510}{39,000} = \$.09$ per unit

The Clonex Corporation
All Producing Departments
Cost of Production Report — Average Costing
For the Month of February, 19—

	BLENDING		TESTING		TERMINAL	
Quantity Schedule						
Units in process at beginning	4,000		3,000		4,000	
Units started in process	40,000	44,000				
Units received from preceding department			38,000	41,000	36,000	40,000
Units transferred to next department	38,000		36,000			
Units transferred to finished goods storeroom					36,000	
Units completed and on hand	1,000					
Units still in process	3,000		4,000		3,000	
Units lost in process	2,000	44,000	1,000	41,000	1,000	40,000

	TOTAL COST	UNIT COST	TOTAL COST	UNIT COST	TOTAL COST	UNIT COST
Cost Charged to the Department						
Cost from preceding department:						
Work in process — beginning inventory.			$ 5,400	$1.800	$ 14,400	$3.60
Transferred in during this period			65,360	1.720	126,000	3.50
Total			$ 70,760	$1.726	$140,400	$3.51
Cost added by department:						
Work in process — beginning inventory:						
Materials	$ 2,000					
Labor	1,240		$ 910		$ 900	
Factory overhead	1,200		800		550	
Cost added during period:						
Materials	19,840	$ .52				
Labor	24,180	.62	34,050	$ .920	33,140	$ .92
Factory overhead	22,580	.58	30,018	.811	19,430	.54
Total cost added	$71,040	$1.72	$ 65,778	$1.731	$ 54,020	$1.46
Adjustment for lost units				.043		.09
Total cost to be accounted for	**$71,040**	**$1.72**	**$136,538**	**$3.500**	**$194,420**	**$5.06**

Cost Accounted for as Follows						
Transferred to next department	$65,360		$126,000			
Transferred to finished goods storeroom					$182,160	
Work in process — ending inventory:						
Completed and on hand	$ 1,720					
Adjusted cost from preceding department			$ 7,076		$ 10,800	
Materials	1,560					
Labor	1,240		1,840		920	
Factory overhead	1,160	5,680	1,622	10,538	540	12,260
Total cost accounted for		**$71,040**		**$136,538**		**$194,420**

plete units in the beginning work in process. Under the first-in, first-out costing method, the cost of completing units in process at the beginning of the period is computed first, followed by the computation of the cost of units started and finished within the period. This procedure leads to at least two different unit costs for work completed within a specific period. The averaging process produces only one completed unit cost.

To permit the comparison of the two costing procedures, figures in the cost of production reports illustrated previously are used to explain the details of the fifo method. The illustrations indicate that the two methods of costing do not result in significantly different unit costs, since in general, manufacturing operations in process cost type industries are more or less uniform from period to period. Each firm should select that costing method which can be applied easily and conveniently and which, at the same time, offers reliable figures for management's guidance.

Blending Department. The February cost of production report of the Blending Department, pages 156 and 157, uses the fifo method and should be compared with the cost of production report on page 149, which illustrates the average costing method. At the beginning of operations, 4,000 units are in process, 100 percent complete as to materials and 50 percent complete as to labor and factory overhead.

The cost report form remains the same, but the following differences exist in the methods of computing unit costs and of determining costs to be transferred under the fifo method:

1. The beginning work in process cost of $4,440 is kept separate and is not broken down into its component parts as in average costing.
2. The degree of completion of the beginning work in process must be stated in order to compute completed unit costs; average costing does not require the degree of completion of the beginning work in process.

Under fifo costing, the cost of completing the 4,000 units in process at the beginning must be computed first. No additional materials were needed; but since the units in process at the beginning were only 50 percent complete as to labor and factory overhead, more labor and overhead cost must be added to complete these units. To determine costs expended in completing the beginning work in process units and to arrive at the cost of units started and finished within this period, unit costs are computed for materials, labor, and factory overhead added during the period. Materials added during February cost $19,840, sufficient to complete an equivalent production of 38,000 units. Of the 38,000 units transferred, 34,000 were started and completed during the period, 3,000 units were in process at month-end with all the necessary materials, and 1,000 units were complete but still on hand. Therefore, the unit cost for materials is $.522 ($19,840 ÷ 38,000).

Labor cost for February is $24,180. The labor unit cost is computed after determining the number of units that could have been completed from this total labor cost. The labor cost was sufficient to complete (1) 50 percent or 2,000 of the 4,000 units in the beginning inventory; (2) 34,000 units started and completed this period; (3) 1,000 units still on hand; and (4) ⅔ or 2,000 of the 3,000 units still in process. Therefore, the equivalent production for labor is 39,000 units and the unit cost for labor is $.620 ($24,180 ÷ 39,000). The same analysis gives a unit cost for factory overhead of $.579 ($22,580 ÷ 39,000). The current period unit cost for the department is $1.721, and total cost to be accounted for is $71,040.

The Clonex Corporation
Blending Department
Cost of Production Report — Fifo Costing
For the Month of February, 19—

Quantity Schedule

Units in process at beginning (all materials — ½ labor and factory overhead)...	4,000	
Units started in process	40,000	44,000
Units transferred to next department	38,000	
Units completed and on hand	1,000	
Units still in process (all materials — ⅔ labor and factory overhead)..	3,000	
Units lost in process...	2,000	44,000

Cost Charged to the Department	Total Cost	Unit Cost
Work in process — beginning inventory	$ 4,440	
Cost added by department:		
Materials...	$19,840	$ .522
Labor..	24,180	.620
Factory overhead	22,580	.579
Total cost added..	$66,600	1.721
Total cost to be accounted for	$71,040	

Cost Accounted for as Follows

Transferred to next department —			
From beginning inventory:			
Inventory cost...	$4,440		
Labor added (4,000 × ½ × $.620).....................	1,240		
Factory overhead added (4,000 × ½ × $.579)..............	1,158	$ 6,838	
From current production:			
Units started and finished (34,000 × $1.721)..............		58,517*	$65,355
Work in process — ending inventory:			
Completed and on hand (1,000 × $1.721)		$ 1,721	
Materials (3,000 × $.522)..		1,566	
Labor (3,000 × ⅔ × $.620)......................................		1,240	
Factory overhead (3,000 × ⅔ × $.579).......................		1,158	5,685
Total cost accounted for....................................			$71,040

*34,000 units × $1.721 per unit = $58,514. To avoid a decimal discrepancy, the cost transferred from current production is computed as follows: $71,040 − ($6,838 + $5,685) = $58,517.

ADDITIONAL COMPUTATIONS:

	MATERIALS	LABOR AND FACTORY OVERHEAD
Equivalent production:		
Transferred out..	38,000	38,000
Less beginning inventory (all units)	4,000	4,000
Started and finished this period	34,000	34,000
Add beginning inventory (work this period)	–0–	2,000
Add ending inventory:		
Completed and on hand	1,000	1,000
Still in process (work this period)	3,000	2,000
	38,000 units	39,000 units

Unit costs: Materials $= \dfrac{\$19,840}{38,000} = \$.522$ per unit

Labor $= \dfrac{\$24,180}{39,000} = \$.620$ per unit

Factory overhead $= \dfrac{\$22,580}{39,000} = \$.579$ per unit

In average costing, the cost of the units transferred to the next department was computed by multiplying the number of units transferred by the final unit cost. This procedure cannot be followed under fifo costing. Units in process at the beginning must be completed first and will usually have a completed unit cost that is different from the unit cost for work started and finished during the period. In any event, two separate computations determine total cost transferred to the next department. The completed cost pertaining to units in the beginning work in process is computed separately from the cost of the units started, finished, and transferred during the period.

To determine the cost of completing the beginning work in process, the cost of labor and factory overhead used during the period in completing the beginning work in process units is added to the $4,440 already included as a cost of such units. Labor and overhead were added at unit costs of $.620 for labor and $.579 for factory overhead to complete the equivalent of 2,000 of the 4,000 units in process. Labor added was $1,240 (2,000 × $.620) and factory overhead, $1,158 (2,000 × $.579). Therefore, the total cost of the 4,000 units completed and transferred was $6,838 ($4,440 + $1,240 + $1,158). The other 34,000 units were transferred at a unit cost of $1.721, or at a total of $58,517. The balance of the cost to be accounted for is in work in process at the end of the period and is computed as shown on the cost of production report, page 156. The entry to transfer the total cost is:

Work in Process — Testing Department 65,355
Work in Process — Blending Department   65,355

Testing Department. The cost report of the Testing Department is illustrated on pages 158 and 159. Although two separate computations were made to calculate cost transferred out of the Blending Department, the total cost transferred into the Testing Department is shown as only one amount in its cost report. The unit cost of $1.72 is obtained by dividing the 38,000 total units received into the total cost received of $65,355 ($6,838 + $58,517). This procedure seems to cancel out the apparent advantages of the fifo method and has been criticized by some writers. It is certain that the method has little to recommend it; however, as long as CPA examination problems continue to require a knowledge of the fifo method, it is advisable to study this procedure.

The Clonex Corporation
Testing Department
Cost of Production Report — Fifo Costing
For the Month of February, 19—

Quantity Schedule

Units in process at beginning (⅓ labor and factory overhead).	3,000	
Units received from preceding department	38,000	41,000
Units transferred to next department	36,000	
Units still in process (½ labor and factory overhead)	4,000	
Units lost in process	1,000	41,000

Cost Charged to the Department	Total Cost	Unit Cost
Work in process — beginning inventory	$ 7,110	
Cost from preceding department:		
Transferred in during the month (38,000 units)	$ 65,355	$1.720
Cost added by department:		
Labor	$ 34,050	$ .920
Factory overhead	30,018	.811
Total cost added	$ 64,068	$1.731
Adjustment for lost units		.046
Total cost to be accounted for	$136,533	$3.497

Cost Accounted for as Follows

Transferred to next department —			
From beginning inventory:			
Inventory cost	$7,110		
Labor added (3,000 × ⅔ × $.920)	1,840		
Factory overhead added (3,000 × ⅔ × $.811)	1,622	$ 10,572	
From current production:			
Units started and finished (33,000 × $3.497)		115,435*	$126,007
Work in process — ending inventory:			
Adjusted cost from preceding department [4,000 × ($1.72 + $.046)]		$ 7,064	
Labor (4,000 × ½ × $.920)		1,840	
Factory overhead (4,000 × ½ × $.811)		1,622	10,526
Total cost accounted for			$136,533

*33,000 units × $3.497 per unit = $115,401. To avoid a decimal discrepancy, the cost transferred from current production is computed as follows: $136,533 − ($10,572 + $10,526) = $115,435.

ADDITIONAL COMPUTATIONS:

	LABOR AND FACTORY OVERHEAD
Equivalent production:	
Transferred out..	36,000
Less beginning inventory (all units)..	3,000
Started and finished this period...	33,000
Add beginning inventory (work this period)..	2,000
Add ending inventory	2,000
	37,000 units

Unit costs: Labor $= \dfrac{\$34,050}{37,000} = .920$ per unit

Factory overhead $= \dfrac{\$30,018}{37,000} = \$.811$ per unit

Adjustment for lost units:

Method No. 1 $- \dfrac{\$65,355}{38,000 - 1,000} = \$1.766; \ \$1.766 - \$1.720 = \$.046$ per unit

Method No. 2 $-$ 1,000 units $\times \$1.720 = \$1,720; \ \dfrac{\$1,720}{37,000} = \$.046$ per unit

The balance of the report is consistent with the fifo method of costing. The beginning work in process inventory, valued at \$7,110, is shown in total and is not broken down into its component parts. Labor and factory overhead costs needed to complete the beginning in-process units are added to this figure to determine the completed cost of these units to be transferred to the next department. The \$.920 unit cost for labor and the \$.811 unit cost for factory overhead are computed by dividing the equivalent production figure of 37,000 units for labor and factory overhead into the labor cost of \$34,050 and factory overhead of \$30,018, respectively. The equivalent production figure of 37,000 units consists of (1) 2,000 units of beginning inventory completed; (2) 33,000 units started and finished this period; and (3) 2,000 of the 4,000 units in the ending work in process inventory. The labor cost added to the beginning work in process was \$1,840 (2,000 × \$.920) and factory overhead added was \$1,622 (2,000 × \$.811). These two amounts are added to the beginning work in process cost of \$7,110 to give a total cost of \$10,572. This is the completed cost of the 3,000 units in the beginning work in process transferred to the Terminal Department.

The departmental unit cost is \$1.731. Because 1,000 units were lost during February, computation of the cost accumulated to the end of operations in the Testing Department requires an adjustment of \$.046 for lost units. The adjustment is determined by dividing the previous department's total cost of \$65,355 by the good units (37,000) of the period, and subtracting from this new unit cost of \$1.766 the old unit cost of \$1.720. In fifo costing, the lost units must be identified as either beginning work in process units or new units started during the period. The identification is needed to determine which unit cost should be adjusted. In either case it means that due to lost units, total costs incurred must be spread over a smaller number of units. In the case of both the Testing and Terminal Departments, it is assumed that units lost came from those placed in process during the period; that is, from units received in each department in February.

A total of 36,000 units is transferred out of the department, of which 3,000 units came from units in process at the beginning of the period. The cost of the 3,000 units is $10,572. The remaining 33,000 units came from units started and finished during the month. These units are transferred at a cumulative unit cost of $3.497 and a total cost of $115,435. The entry to transfer the cost of the 36,000 units to the next department is:

Work in Process — Terminal Department.........................	126,007	
Work in Process — Testing Department		126,007

The balance of the cost to be accounted for is the ending work in process inventory which is computed in the conventional manner.

Terminal Department. To complete this discussion of fifo costing, the cost of production report of the Terminal Department is presented below and on page 161. Based on this report, the entry to transfer the cost of the 36,000 finished units is:

Finished Goods..	182,166	
Work in Process — Terminal Department......................		182,166

The Clonex Corporation
Terminal Department
Cost of Production Report — Fifo Costing
For the Month of February, 19--

Quantity Schedule

Units in process at beginning (¼ labor and factory overhead).	4,000	
Units received from preceding department................................	36,000	40,000
Units transferred to finished goods storeroom...........................	36,000	
Units still in process (⅓ labor and factory overhead)...............	3,000	
Units lost in process	1,000	40,000

Cost Charged to the Department	TOTAL COST	UNIT COST
Work in process — beginning inventory....................................	$ 15,850	
Cost from preceding department:		
Transferred in during the month (36,000 units)......................	$126,007	$3.500
Cost added by department:		
Labor	$ 33,140	$ .921
Factory overhead...	19,430	.540
Total cost added	$ 52,570	$1.461
Adjustment for lost units..		.100
Total cost to be accounted for..	$194,427	$5.061

Cost Accounted for as Follows

Transferred to next department —
From beginning inventory:

Inventory cost	$15,850	
Labor added (4,000 × ¾ × $.921)	2,763	
Factory overhead added (4,000 × ¾ × $.540)	1,620	$ 20,233

From current production:

Units started and finished (32,000 × $5.061)	161,933*	$182,166

Work in process — ending inventory:

Adjusted cost from preceding department [3,000 × ($3.50 + $.10)]	$ 10,800	
Labor (3,000 × ⅓ × $.921)	921	
Factory overhead (3,000 × ⅓ × $.540)	540	12,261
Total cost accounted for		**$194,427**

ADDITIONAL COMPUTATIONS:

	LABOR AND FACTORY OVERHEAD
Equivalent production:	
Transferred out	36,000
Less beginning inventory (all units)	4,000
Started and finished this period	32,000
Add beginning inventory (work this period)	3,000
Add ending inventory (work this period)	1,000
	36,000 units

Unit costs: Labor $= \dfrac{\$33,140}{36,000} = \$.921$ per unit

Factory overhead $= \dfrac{\$19,430}{36,000} = \$.540$ per unit

Adjustment for lost units:

Method No. 1 — $\dfrac{\$126,007}{36,000 - 1,000} = \$3.60;\ \$3.60 - \$3.50 = \$.100$ per unit

Method No. 2 — $1,000 \times \$3.50 = \$3,500;\ \dfrac{\$3,500}{35,000} = \$.100$ per unit

*32,000 × $5.061 per unit = $161,952. To avoid a decimal discrepancy, the cost transferred from current production is computed as follows: $194,427 − ($20,233 + $12,261) = $161,933.

Combined Cost of Production Report — Fifo Costing. The illustration on page 162 is a combined cost of production report for February, using fifo costing. To observe the differences between the two costing methods discussed, this report should be compared with the cost of production report on page 154, in which average costing is used.

Both average costing and fifo costing have certain advantages. It would be arbitrary to state that one method is either simpler or more accurate than the other. The selection of either method depends entirely upon management's opinion regarding the most appropriate and practical cost determination procedures.

Average Costing vs Fifo Costing

The Clonex Corporation
All Producing Departments
Cost of Production Report — Fifo Costing
For the Month of February, 19—

	BLENDING		TESTING		TERMINAL	
Quantity Schedule						
Units in process at beginning	4,000		3,000		4,000	
Units started in process	40,000	44,000				
Units received from preceding department			38,000	41,000	36,000	40,000
Units transferred to next department	38,000		36,000			
Units transferred to finished goods storeroom					36,000	
Units completed and on hand	1,000					
Units still in process	3,000		4,000		3,000	
Units lost in process	2,000	44,000	1,000	41,000	1,000	40,000

	TOTAL COST	UNIT COST	TOTAL COST	UNIT COST	TOTAL COST	UNIT COST
Cost Charged to the Department						
Work in process — beginning inventory	$ 4,440		$ 7,110		$ 15,850	
Cost from preceding department:						
Transferred in during the month			$ 65,355	$1.720	$126,007	$3.500
Cost added by department:						
Materials	$19,840	$ .522				
Labor	24,180	.620	$ 34,050	$ .920	$ 33,140	$ .921
Factory overhead	22,580	.579	30,018	.811	19,430	.540
Total cost added	$66,600	$1.721	$ 64,068	$1.731	$ 52,570	$1.461
Adjustment for lost units				.046		.100
Total cost to be accounted for	$71,040	$1.721	$136,533	$3.497	$194,427	$5.061

	BLENDING		TESTING		TERMINAL	
Cost Accounted for as Follows						
Transferred to next department —						
From beginning inventory:						
Inventory cost	$ 4,440		$ 7,110		$ 15,850	
Labor added	1,240		1,840		2,763	
Factory overhead added	1,158	$ 6,838	1,622	$ 10,572	1,620	$ 20,233
From current production:						
Units started and finished		58,517		115,435		161,933
		$65,355		$126,007		$182,166
Work in process — ending inventory:						
Completed and on hand	$ 1,721					
Adjusted cost from preceding department			$ 7,064		$ 10,800	
Materials	1,566					
Labor	1,240		1,840		921	
Factory overhead	1,158	5,685	1,622	10,526	540	12,261
Total cost accounted for		$71,040		$136,533		$194,427

The basic difference between the two methods concerns the treatment of beginning work in process inventory. The averaging method adds beginning work in process inventory costs to the preceding department's materials, labor, and factory overhead costs incurred during a period. Unit costs are determined by dividing these costs by equivalent production figures. Units and costs are transferred to the next department as one cumulative figure.

The fifo method retains the beginning work in process inventory cost as a separate figure. Costs necessary to complete the beginning work in process units are added to this total cost. The sum of these two cost totals is transferred to the next department. Units started and finished during the period have their own unit cost which is usually different from the completed unit cost of units in process at the beginning of the period. The fifo method thus separately identifies for management the current period unit cost originating in a department. Unfortunately, the costs are averaged out in the next department, resulting in a loss of much of the value associated with the use of the fifo method.

If the fifo method is used, units lost during a period must be identified as to whether they came from units in process at the beginning or from units received during the period. Also, in computing equivalent production figures in fifo costing, the degree of completion of both the beginning and ending work in process inventories must be considered.

The principal disadvantage of fifo costing is that if several unit cost figures are used at the same time, extensive detail is required within the cost of production report, which can lead to complex procedures and even inaccuracy. Whether the extra detail yields more representative unit costs than the average costing method is debatable, especially in a firm using process costing where production is continuous and more or less uniform and appreciable fluctuations in unit costs are not expected to develop. Under such conditions, the average costing method leads to more satisfactory cost computations.

DIFFICULTIES ENCOUNTERED IN PROCESS COST ACCOUNTING PROCEDURES

Certain difficulties likely to be encountered in actual practice should be mentioned with regard to process cost accounting procedures:

1. The determination of production quantities and their stages of completion presents problems. Every computation is influenced by these figures. Since the data generally come to the cost department from operating personnel often working under circumstances that make a precise count difficult, a certain amount of doubtful counts and unreliable estimates are bound to exist. Yet, the data submitted form the basis for the determination of inventory costs.
2. Materials cost computations frequently require careful analysis. In the illustrations, materials cost is generally part of the first department's

cost. In certain industries, materials costs are not even entered on production reports. When materials prices are influenced by fluctuating market quotations, the materials cost may be recorded in a separate report designed to facilitate management decisions in relation to the materials market.

3. The discussion of lost units caused by shrinkage, spoilage, or evaporation indicates that the time when the loss occurs influences the final cost calculation. Different assumptions concerning the loss would result in different departmental unit costs which, in turn, affect inventory costs, the cost of units transferred, and the completed unit cost. Another consideration involves the possibility of treating cost attributable to avoidable loss as an expense of the current period.

4. Industries using process cost procedures are generally of the multiple product type. Joint processing cost must be allocated to the products resulting from the processes. Weighted unit averages or other bases are used to prorate the joint cost to the several products. If units manufactured are used as a basis for cost allocation, considerable difficulties arise in determining accurate unit costs. Additional clerical expenses are necessary if the labor-hour or machine-hour basis is used for charging overhead to work in process. Management must decide whether economy and low operational cost are compatible with increased information based on additional cost computations and procedures.

It should be noted that some companies use both job order and process costing procedures for various purposes in different departments. This is particularly true when a parallel or selective cost flow format is required. Each system or method employed by a company must be based on reliable production and performance data which, when combined with output, budget, or standard cost data, will provide the foundation for effective cost control and analysis.

DISCUSSION QUESTIONS

1. How does the fifo method differ from the average method of process costing?

2. Why are units completed and on hand in a processing department included in the department's work in process?

3. How are equivalent production figures computed when fifo costing is used?

4. A certain factory transferred out 8,800 completed units during its second period of operation. The period was begun with 400 units 75% completed and ended with 800 units 50% completed. Assuming that the fifo method is used, what was the equivalent production for the period?

5. In another factory, the equivalent production (using the fifo method) was 7,000 units during a period in which 500 units, 60% complete, were on hand at the start and 600 units, 75% complete, were on hand at the end of the period. How many units were fully completed?

6. What are some of the disadvantages of the fifo costing method?

7. Enumerate several of the basic difficulties frequently encountered in process costing.

8. Express an opinion as to the usefulness of data, derived from process costing, for the control of costs.

9. Select the answer which best completes the statement:

(a) During 19B, the Novo-Minetto Company had a total manufacturing cost of $180,000. The business completed 14,000 units of product, of which 4,000 units were one-half completed in 19A, and started production on an additional 6,000 units that were one-half completed at the end of 19B. For 19B, the production cost per unit was: (1) $18; (2) $16.36; (3) $12; (4) $9.

(b) When materials are added in a department subsequent to the first department and additional units result, it affects the unit cost in a cost of production report by causing: (1) an increase in the preceding department's unit cost, which necessitates an adjustment of the transferred-in unit cost; (2) a decrease in the preceding department's unit cost, which necessitates an adjustment of the transferred-in unit cost; (3) an increase in the preceding department's unit cost, but does not necessitate an adjustment of the transferred-in unit cost; (4) a decrease in the preceding department's unit cost, but does not necessitate an adjustment of the transferred-in unit cost.

(c) Materials are added at the beginning of a process. The beginning work in process inventory was 30% complete as to conversion cost. Using the fifo method, the total equivalent units for materials for this process during this period are equal to the: (1) beginning inventory this period; (2) units started this period; (3) units started this period plus the beginning inventory; (4) units started this period plus 70% of the beginning inventory.

(AICPA adapted)

EXERCISES

1. Computation of equivalent production — average vs fifo. On November 1, Yankee Company had 20,000 units of work in process in Department A, 100% complete as to materials cost and 20% complete as to conversion cost. During November, 160,000 units were started in Department A and 170,000 units were transferred to Department B. The work in process on November 30 was 100% complete as to materials cost and 40% complete as to conversion cost.

Required: Equivalent production for Department A, using (1) the average method, and (2) the fifo method.

(AICPA adapted)

2. Computation of equivalent production. The M & U Company operates two producing departments whose quantity reports appear as follows:

	DEPARTMENT 1	DEPARTMENT 2
Beginning inventory	200	80
Department 1 — all materials, 25% conversion cost		
Department 2 — 60% conversion cost		
Started in process.....................................	2,260	2,160
	2,460	2,240

	DEPARTMENT 1	DEPARTMENT 2
Transferred out	2,160	2,000
Ending inventory......................................	300	240
Department 1 — all materials, 60% conversion cost		
Department 2 — 80% conversion cost		
	2,460	2,240

Required: Equivalent production figures for each department, using:
(1) The average method.
(2) The fifo method.

3. Computation of equivalent production. The Production Control Department of a plant that uses process costing sent the following production data for one of the four producing departments to the Cost Department:

Product received from previous department	100 000 kilograms
Product finished and sent to next department	71 840 kilograms
Product finished and remaining in this department..........	4 160 kilograms
Product unfinished in this department..............................	24 000 kilograms

In this department, additional materials are added to the work received from the preceding department. Three distinctly different types of materials are used at three separate stages of production in this department:

Material A is added at the beginning of the process.
Material B is added when the process is ¼ completed.
Material C is added when the process is ¾ completed.

Labor and factory overhead are incurred at a uniform rate throughout the manufacturing process in this department.

Examination of the unfinished work discloses that: ¼ was ⅞ completed; ½ was ½ completed; ¼ was ⅙ completed.

There was no beginning work in process inventory.

Required:
(1) The equivalent production figures for each of the materials.
(2) The equivalent production figures for labor and factory overhead.

4. Computation of equivalent production. The following data originate from four different situations. Stages of completion of inventories apply to all cost elements.

(1) Started in process, 13,000 units; transferred, 11,000 units; in process, 800 units, ½ completed and 1,200 units, ¼ completed.
(2) Beginning inventory, 12,500 units, ⅖ completed; started in process, 50,000 units; transferred, 52,500; in process at end of period, 6,000 units, ½ completed and 4,000 units, ¼ completed.
(3) Beginning inventory, 9,000 units, ⅓ completed and 6,000 units, ½ completed; started in process, 37,500 units; transferred, 45,000; in process at end of period, 3,000 units, ½ completed and 4,500 units, ⅓ completed.
(4) Beginning inventory, 12,000 units, ⅓ completed; started in process, 26,000 units; lost in processing, 1,000 units from production started this period (loss was normal and occurred throughout the manufacturing process); transferred, 28,000; in process at end of period, 6,000 units, ½ completed and 3,000 units, ⅔ completed.

Required: The equivalent production figures in each situation, using:
(1) Fifo costing.
(2) Average costing.

5. Cost assigned to work in process inventory. The manager of a company requested the work in process inventory figures on (a) the average cost basis and (b) the first-in, first-out basis. The data are:

Units in beginning inventory, 8,000; all materials, 50% labor and overhead.
Cost of beginning inventory: materials, $3,984; labor, $2,148; overhead, $2,148.
Placed in process, 40,000 units. Cost: materials, $24,000; labor, $19,968; overhead, $19,968.
Units completed and transferred, 42,000.
Units in process at the end, 6,000; all materials, 60% labor and overhead.

Required: The costs assigned to the work in process inventory.

6. Cost of production report; materials added. Monnier, Inc., produces a cologne, Mon Roi, which requires processing in three departments. In the third department, materials are added, doubling the number of units. The following data pertain to the operations of Department 3 for March:

Units received from Department 2	20,000
Units transferred to finished goods storeroom	32,000
The balance of the units are still in process — 100% complete as to materials, 50% complete as to labor and overhead.	
Cost transferred from Department 2	$30,000
Cost added by the department:	
Materials	$8,800
Labor	9,000
Factory overhead	7,200 $25,000

There was no beginning work in process inventory.

Required: A cost of production report for Department 3 for March.

7. Cost of production report — average method. The Millwood Supply Company manufactures a single product on a continuous plan in three departments. On November 1, the work in process inventory in Department 2 was:

Cost in preceding department	$13,130
Materials — Department 2	None
Labor — Department 2	$ 500
Factory overhead — Department 2	$ 50
Units in process	5,000

Costs in Department 2 during November were:

Labor	$14,200
Factory overhead	$ 3,450

During November, 70,000 units were received from Department 1 at a unit cost of $2.641; 68,000 units were completed in Department 2, of which 60,000 were transferred to Department 3, and 8,000 were on hand in Department 2 at the end of the month. Four thousand units were still in process, estimated to be one-half complete as to labor and factory overhead. The balance was lost within the department; its cost is to be absorbed by all the finished and unfinished production of the department.

Required: A November cost of production report for Department 2, using the average costing method for beginning work in process inventories.

8. Cost of production report — fifo method. French Creek Ceramics, Inc., operates three producing departments — Molding, Painting, and Firing. During August, the Painting Department transferred 12,400 units to the Firing Department, lost 500 units, and had 800 units in process at the end of August. There were 2,400 units in process on August 1 in the Painting Department. The remaining units started in the Painting Department during August were received from the Molding Department. The costs incurred in the Painting Department during August were: materials, $5,886; labor, $7,830; and factory overhead, $1,134. The work in process inventory on August 1 was $6,656. The costs transferred to the Painting Department from the Molding Department amounted to $23,797.80. The Painting Department work in process inventory was three-fourths complete on August 1 and one-fourth complete on August 31.

Required: The August cost of production report for the Painting Department, using the first-in, first-out method of accounting for beginning inventories. (Carry unit cost computations to four decimal places.)

9. Computation of equivalent production — fifo method; materials added. Poole, Inc., produces a chemical compound in two departments, A and B, using the following procedure:

The chemical compound requires one pound of Chemical X and one pound of Chemical Y. One pound of Chemical X is processed in Department A and transferred to Department B, where one pound of Chemical Y is added when the process is 50% complete. When the processing is complete in Department B, the finished chemical compound is transferred to finished goods. The process is a continuous 24-hour-a-day operation. Normal spoilage occurs in Department A, where 5% of Chemical X is lost in the first few minutes of processing. Department A's conversion cost is incurred uniformly throughout the process and is allocated to good pounds produced, since spoilage is normal. Department B's conversion cost is allocated equally to each equivalent pound of output. No spoilage occurs in Department B.

Data available for October are:

	DEPARTMENT A	DEPARTMENT B
Work in process, October 1	8,000 pounds	10,000 pounds
Stage of completion of beginning inventory (one batch per department)............	$3/4$	$3/10$
Started or transferred in............................	50,000 pounds	?
Transferred out	46,500 good pounds	?
Work in process, October 31	?	12,000 pounds
Stage of completion of ending inventory (one batch per department)...................	$1/3$	$1/5$
Total equivalent pounds of material added in Department B..........................		44,500 pounds

Required:
(1) A quantity schedule for each department.
(2) An equivalent production schedule for each department, using the fifo method.

(AICPA adapted)

PROBLEMS

7-1. Cost of production report; materials added. Andersen, Inc., manufactures a product in two departments. Materials are added in each department, increasing the number of units manufactured. A summary of the cost information for the company's first month of operations (January) is as follows:

	DEPARTMENT No. 1	DEPARTMENT No. 2
Materials	$ 90,000	$ 67,500
Labor..	39,000	41,400
Factory overhead	7,800	20,700
Total	$136,800	$129,600

The production supervisor reports that 300,000 units were put into production in Department 1. Of this quantity, 75,000, a normal number, were lost in production; and 180,000 were completed and transferred to Department 2. For the balance in process at the end of the month, all materials had been added, but only one third of the labor and factory overhead had been applied.

In Department 2, 45,000 units of materials were purchased outside and added to the units received from Department 1; 195,000 units were completed and transferred to finished goods inventory. The remainder were in process at the end of the month, with all materials added, but only 40% complete for labor and factory overhead.

Required: A cost of production report for January. (Carry unit cost computations to three decimal places.)

7-2. Cost of production report — average and fifo; lost units; materials added. Drilprodco, Inc., manufactures a single product that passes through three processing departments. Average costing is used in Departments 1 and 2; fifo costing in Department 3. February data follow:

Quantity schedule:

	DEPARTMENT 1	DEPARTMENT 2	DEPARTMENT 3
Units in process at beginning	3,000	2,000	2,000
Units started in process	61,000	—	15,000*
Units received from preceding department	—	50,000	45,000
	64,000	52,000	62,000
Units completed and transferred .	50,000	45,000	55,000
Units completed and on hand	5,000	—	—
Units lost in process.....................	1,000 (beginning)	2,000 (during)	1,000 (at end)
Units still in process.....................	8,000	5,000	6,000
	64,000	52,000	62,000

*Materials added in Department 3 result in an increase in the number of units.

	DEPARTMENT 1	DEPARTMENT 2	DEPARTMENT 3
Stage of completion of units in process at beginning of period:			
Materials	100%	100%	100%
Labor and factory overhead ..	50	25	20
Stage of completion of units in process at close of period:			
Materials	100%	100%	100%
Labor and factory overhead ..	50	20	50
Cost data:			
Work in process — beginning inventory:			
Cost from preceding department.....................................		$ 1,600	$ 2,875
Materials	$ 749	158	2,630
Labor.......................................	837	325	5,280
Factory overhead	1,061	481	6,360
Cost added during period:			
Materials	12,481	3,092	8,400
Labor.......................................	16,273	4,045	15,236
Factory overhead	18,409	4,579	22,854

Required:
(1) Equivalent production calculations.
(2) Cost of production report for February. (Carry unit cost computations to three decimal places.)

7-3. Process costing — fifo method. Dornal Motors is engaged in the production of a standard type of electric motor. Manufacturing costs for April totaled $66,000. At the beginning of April, inventories appeared as follows:

Motors in production, estimated 80% completed.......... 2,500 units $32,000
Motors on hand, completed .... 1,200 units $19,200

During the month, 5,500 completed units were placed in finished stock. At the end of April, inventories were:

Motors in production, estimated 50% completed........................... 1,000 units
Motors on hand, completed.. 1,400 units

The company uses the fifo method for process costing and for costing goods sold. In costing finished goods, the unit cost for units completed from beginning work in process inventory is kept separate from the unit cost of motors started and completed during the month.

Required:
(1) The cost assigned to the ending work in process inventory.
(2) The cost assigned to the ending finished goods inventory.
(3) The cost of goods sold.

(CGAA adapted)

7-4. Cost of production report — fifo method; spoiled units cost charged to factory overhead. At the beginning of October, the accountant for the O'Connor-Bradley Company drew up a new form to be used for the cost of production statement for the month. Inserted in the form was the ending work in process inventory figure for September in the amount of $3,144. This inventory consisted of 160 units, with all materials included but only 50% of the labor and overhead.

During October, the Cost Department gathered and recorded the following production and cost data and other information:

Purchases of materials:		Materials used for:	
Invoice cost	$82,600	Production	$84,868
Freight in	13,444	Equipment maintenance	1,940
Total materials cost	$96,044	Factory supplies	8,636
		Total cost of materials used	$95,444

Payroll:		Other factory overhead:	
Direct labor	$56,760	Heat	$ 480
Supervision	5,800	Payroll taxes	2,800
Indirect labor	6,048	Rent of building	2,400
Equipment maintenance	1,360	Power	3,208
Total payroll	$69,968	Tools	4,000
		Equipment depreciation	8,000
		Total factory overhead	$20,888

Production data for October:

In process, October 31: 168 units, all materials, $3/7$ labor and overhead.
Started: 6,928 units, all materials placed in production.
Spoiled: 128 units, all materials, $3/4$ labor and overhead; these spoiled units have no salvage value. The materials and labor costs spent on these spoiled units are added to the factory overhead.
Finished: 6,792 good units.

Inventories are costed by the fifo method.
Twenty percent of the building is occupied by and charged to the Sales Department as heat and rent expense.

Required:
(1) Equivalent production figures.
(2) A cost of production report.
(3) The unit cost for the three elements of cost.

7-5. Cost of production report — fifo method. Deterra, Inc., uses three departments to produce a detergent. The Finishing Department is the third and last step before the product is transferred to storage.

All materials needed to give the detergent its final composition are added at the beginning of the process in the Finishing Department. Any lost units occur only at this point.

The company uses the fifo method. The following data for the Finishing Department for October have been made available:

Production data:

In process, October 1 (labor and factory overhead, ¾ complete) 10,000 gals.
Transferred in from preceding department.................................. 40,000 gals.
Finished and transferred to storage... 35,000 gals.
In process, October 31 (labor and factory overhead, ½ complete) .... 10,000 gals.

Additional data:

Work in process inventory, October 1:
   Cost from preceding department.. $ 38,000
   Cost from this department:
      Materials 21,500
      Labor... 39,000
      Factory overhead 42,000
   Total work in process inventory, October 1 .... $140,500

Transferred in during October $140,000

Cost added in this department:
   Materials .... $ 70,000
   Labor.. 162,500
   Factory overhead 130,000
   Total cost added $362,500
Total cost to be accounted for... $643,000

Required: A cost of production report for October.   (AICPA adapted)

7-6. Average costing method; normal spoilage during production. The Manayunk Paper Company manufactures a high-quality paper box. The Box Department applies two separate operations — cutting and folding. The paper is first cut and trimmed to the dimensions of a box form by one machine group. One square foot of paper is equivalent to four box forms. The trimmings from this process have no scrap value. Box forms are then creased and folded (i.e., completed) by a second machine group. Any partially processed boxes in the Box Department are cut box forms that are ready for creasing and folding. These partly processed boxes are considered 50% complete as to labor and factory overhead. The Materials Department maintains an inventory of paper in sufficient quantities to permit continuous processing, and transfers to the Box Department are made as needed. Immediately after folding, all satisfactory boxes are transferred to the Finished Goods Department

During June, the Materials Department purchased 1,210,000 square feet of unprocessed paper for $244,000. Conversion cost for June was $226,000. A quantity equal to 30,000 boxes was spoiled during paper cutting, and 70,000 boxes were spoiled during folding. All spoilage has a zero salvage value, is considered normal, and cannot be reprocessed. All spoilage loss is allocated between the completed units and partially processed boxes. The company applies the weighted average costing method to all inventories. Inventory data for June are:

Inventory	Physical Unit	JUNE 1 Units on Hand	Cost	June 30 Units on Hand
Materials Department:				
Paper..	square feet	390,000	$76,000	200,000
Box Department:				
Boxes cut (not folded)	number	800,000	55,000*	300,000
Finished Goods Department:				
Completed boxes on hand	number	250,000	18,000	50,000

*Materials............................... $35,000
Conversion cost................... 20,000
               $55,000

Required:

(1) A report of cost of paper used in June by the Materials Department.
(2) A schedule showing the physical flow of units (including beginning and ending inventories) in the Materials Department, in the Box Department, and in the Finished Goods Department.
(3) A schedule showing the computation of equivalent units produced in June for materials and conversion cost in the Box Department.
(4) A schedule of the computation of unit costs for the Box Department.
(5) A report of inventory cost and cost of completed units for the Box Department.
(6) A schedule showing the computation of unit costs for the Finished Goods Department. (Carry computation to five decimal places.)
(7) A report of inventory cost and cost of units sold for the Finished Goods Department.

(AICPA adapted)

7-7. Cost of production report — fifo and average costing methods. The Rex Processing Company manufactures one product through two processes. For each unit of Process No. 1 output, 2 units of Material X are put in at the start of processing. For each unit of Process No. 2 output, 3 cans of Material Y are put in at the end of processing. Two pounds of Process No. 1 output are placed in at the start of Process No. 2 for each unit of finished goods started.

Spoilage generally occurs in Process No. 2 when processing is approximately 50% complete. Work in process accounts are maintained for materials, conversion cost, and prior department cost. The company uses fifo costing for Process No. 1 and average costing for Process No. 2.

Data for March:

(a) Units transferred:
  From Process No. 1 to Process No. 2 .... 2,200 pounds
  From Process No. 2 to finished goods .... 900 gallons
  From finished goods to cost of goods sold .... 600 gallons
(b) Units spoiled in Process No. 2, 100 gallons.
(c) Materials unit costs: X, $1.51 per unit; Y, $2 per can.
(d) Conversion costs: Process No. 1, $3,334; Process No. 2, $4,010.
(e) Spoilage recovery: $100 (treated in Process No. 2 as cost reduction which came from Process No. 1).
(f) Inventory data:

	PROCESS NO. 1		PROCESS NO. 2	
	Beginning	Ending	Beginning	Ending
Units..	200	300	200	300
Fraction complete, conversion cost..........	½	⅓	½	⅔
Costs:				
Materials...	$560			
Conversion cost......................................	108		$ 390	
Prior department cost............................			2,200	

Required: A cost of production report with a quantity schedule for March.   (AICPA adapted)

7-8. Fifo method. In the course of an examination of the financial statements of the Zaranka Corporation for the year ended December 31, the auditors ascertained the following information concerning the corporation's manufacturing operations.

Zaranka has two producing departments, Fabricating and Finishing. In the Fabricating Department, Polyplast is prepared from Miracle Mix and Bypro. In the Finishing Department, each unit of Polyplast is converted into six Tetraplexes and three Uniplexes. Service departments provide services to both producing departments.

The Fabricating and Finishing Departments use process cost procedures. Actual production costs, including factory overhead, are allocated monthly.

Service department expenses are allocated to producing departments as follows:

EXPENSES	FABRICATING	FINISHING
Building maintenance...................................	$30,000	$15,000
Timekeeping and personnel	16,500	11,000
Others...	19,500	19,500

These expenses are not included in the departmental factory overhead below.

Materials inventory and work in process are priced on a fifo basis.

The Fabricating Department's records for December show:

Quantities (units of Polyplast):	
In process, December 1...	3,000
Started in process...	25,000
Total units to be accounted for	28,000
Transferred to Finishing Department..	19,000
In process, December 31...	6,000
Normal losses throughout the process...	3,000
Total units accounted for..	28,000

Cost of work in process, December 1:	
Materials..	$ 13,000
Labor...	17,500
Factory overhead	21,500
	$ 52,000
Direct labor cost	$154,000
Departmental factory overhead..	$132,000

Polyplast work in process at the beginning and end of the month was partially completed as follows:

	MATERIALS	LABOR AND FACTORY OVERHEAD
December 1	66⅔%	50%
December 31	100%	75%

Materials inventory records for December indicate:

	MIRACLE MIX		BYPRO	
	Quantity	Amount	Quantity	Amount
Balance, December 1	62,000	$62,000	265,000	$18,550
Purchases:				
December 12	39,500	49,375		
December 20	28,500	34,200		
Fabricating Department usage..............	83,200		50,000	

Required:
(1) The equivalent number of units of Polyplast for materials and conversion costs.
(2) (a) Total Fabricating Department cost to be accounted for.
  (b) Unit costs for materials and conversion cost.
  (c) Cost of units transferred to Finishing Department, and cost of the ending work in process inventory in the Fabricating Department.

(AICPA adapted)

7-9. Cost of production report — fifo method; materials added. Eckert-LaBour, Inc., produces a chemical agent for commercial use. The company accounts for production in two cost centers: (1) Cooking and (2) Mix-Pack. In the first cost center, liquid substances are combined and boiled in large cookers, which causes a normal decrease in volume from evaporation. After cooking, the chemical is transferred to Mix-Pack, where an equal quantity of alcohol is added before being mixed and bottled in one-liter containers.

Materials are added at the beginning of production in each cost center, and labor is added equally during production in each cost center. The process is "in control" as long as the yield ratio for the Cooking Department is not less than 78%.

The fifo method is used to cost work in process inventories, and transfers are at an average unit cost, i.e., the total cost transferred divided by the total number of units transferred.

The following information is available for October:

COST INFORMATION	COOKING DEPARTMENT	MIX-PACK DEPARTMENT
Work in process, October 1:		
Materials	$ 990	$ 120
Labor	100	60
Overhead	80	48
Prior department cost		426
Month of October:		
Materials	$39,600	$15,276
Labor	10,050	16,000
Overhead	8,040	12,800

Inventory and production records show that the Cooking Department had 1 000 liters 40% processed on October 1 and 800 liters 50% processed on October 31; the Mix-Pack Department had 600 liters 50% processed on October 1 and 1 000 liters 30% processed on October 31.

Production reports for October show that the Cooking Department started 50 000 liters into production and completed and transferred 40 200 liters to Mix-Pack, and Mix-Pack completed and transferred 80,000 one-liter containers of the finished product to the distribution warehouse.

Required:
(1) A quantity report for the Cooking and the Mix-Pack cost centers, accounting for both actual units and equivalent unit production.
(2) A cost of production report for each of the two cost centers, computing total cost and cost per unit for each element of cost in inventories, for October production, and for transfers.
(3) The yield ratio for Cooking, indicating whether the process was "in control" during October.

(AICPA adapted)

7-10. Fifo method. The Suyama Corporation uses process costing to accumulate costs for its product, SUYA. Materials and units are costed on the fifo method. Inventories, costs, and production data for October are:

	SEPT. 30	OCT. 31
Materials	100,000 lbs.	80,000 lbs.
Materials cost	$ 100,000	
Work in process inventories:		
All materials, 40% complete as to labor and factory overhead	20,000 units	
Cost	$ 84,000	
All materials, 33⅓% complete as to labor and factory overhead		30,000 units
Finished goods inventory	40,000 units	24,000 units
Cost	$ 448,000	
Purchases of materials	440,000 lbs. @ $1.10 per lb.	
Transferred to production	460,000 lbs.	
Production ratio — 2 lbs: 1 unit of SUYA		
Completed during the month	220,000 units	
Direct labor	$1,198,800	
Factory overhead	421,800	

Required:
(1) Equivalent production units for materials, labor, and factory overhead.
(2) Unit costs for the three cost elements. (Round off unit costs to five decimal places.)
(3) Cost of units transferred to finished goods inventory, using the fifo method. (Round off total costs to the nearest dollar.)
(4) Cost of the ending work in process inventory, in detail.
(5) Number of units sold and the cost of the finished goods inventory on October 31, using the fifo method and the average cost method and indicating cost difference per unit and in total.

(AICPA adapted)

7-11. Fifo method; units lost at end of process. In the process of verifying the pricing of the company's inventory of work in process and finished goods recorded on the company's books, the auditor finds:

Finished goods inventory, 110,000 units.. $504,900
Work in process inventory, 90,000 units, 50% completed.................. 330,480

The company follows the practice of pricing the above inventories at the lower of cost or market on a first-in, first-out basis. Materials are added to the production line at the start of the process, and overhead is applied to the product at the rate of 75% based on direct labor dollars. The auditor also learns that the market value of the finished goods inventory and the work in process inventory is greater than the amounts shown above, with the exception of the defective units in the ending inventory of finished goods, the market value of which amounts to $1.00 per unit. The difference between the market value and the assigned cost is expensed.

A review of the company's cost records shows:

	Units	AMOUNTS Materials	Labor
Beginning inventory, January 1, 19--, 80% completed........	100,000	$100,000	$160,000
Additional units started in 19--...	500,000		
Materials cost incurred..		550,000	
Labor cost incurred			997,500
Units completed in 19--:			
Good units...	500,000		
Defective units...	10,000		

Finished goods inventory at December 31, 19--, includes 10,000 defective units.
Defective units occur at the end of the process, at the point of final inspection.

Required:
  (1) Schedules indicating:
   (a) Effective or equivalent production.
   (b) Unit costs of materials, labor, and factory overhead of current period production. (Carry unit cost computations to three decimal places.)
   (c) Costing of inventories of finished goods, defective units, and work in process.
  (2) The necessary journal entry(ies), if any, to state correctly the inventory of finished goods and work in process.

(AICPA adapted)

8

By-Product and
Joint Product Costing

Many industrial concerns are confronted with the difficult and often rather complicated problem of assigning costs to their by-products and/or joint products. Chemical companies, coke manufacturers, refineries, flour mills, coal mines, lumber mills, gas companies, dairies, canners, meat packers, and many others produce in their manufacturing or conversion processes a multitude of products to which some costs must be assigned. Assignment of costs to these various products enhances equitable inventory costing for income determination and financial statement purposes. An even more important aspect of by-product and joint product costing is that it furnishes management with data for use in planning maximum profit potentials and evaluating actual profit performance.

DIFFICULTIES IN COSTING BY-PRODUCTS AND JOINT PRODUCTS

By-products and joint products are difficult to cost because a true joint cost is indivisible. For example, an ore might contain both lead and zinc. In the raw state, these minerals are joint products, and until they are separated by reduction of the ore, the cost of finding, mining, and processing is a joint cost; neither lead nor zinc can be produced without the other prior to the split-off stage. The cost accumulated to the split-off stage must be borne by the difference between the selling price and the cost to complete and sell each mineral after the split-off point.

Joint costs are frequently confused with *common costs*. However, there is a significant difference between the two: a joint cost is indivisible and common costs are divisible. Common costs are allocable among products or ser-

176

vices because each of the products or services could have been obtained separately. Therefore, any shared costs of obtaining them can be allocated on the basis of relative usage of common facilities. For example, the cost of fuel or power may be allocated to products on the basis of production volumes or metered usage. The indivisibility characteristic of a joint cost is not always easy to comprehend, since in some cases a joint cost can be divided among joint products in accordance with a common cost-causing characteristic. However, the result of such a division is of limited use to management for decision making.

Because of the indivisibility of a joint cost, cost allocation and apportionment procedures used for establishing the unit cost of a product are far from perfect and are, indeed, quite arbitrary. The costing of joint products and by-products highlights the problem of assigning costs to products whose origin, use of equipment, share of raw materials, share of labor costs, and share of other facilities cannot truly be determined. Whatever methods of allocation are employed, the total profit or loss figure is not affected — provided there are no beginning or ending inventories — by allocating costs to the joint products or by-products, since these costs are recombined in the final income statement. However, a joint cost is ordinarily allocated to the products on some acceptable basis to determine product costs needed for inventory carrying costs. For this reason, there is an effect on periodic income, because different amounts may be allocated to inventories of the numerous joint products or by-products under various allocation methods. In addition, product costs may be required for such special purposes as justifying selling prices before governmental regulatory bodies. However, the validity of splitting a joint cost to determine fair regulated prices for joint products has been questioned by both accountants and economists.

JOINT PRODUCTS AND COST DEFINED

Joint products are produced simultaneously by a common process or series of processes, with each product possessing more than a nominal value in the form in which it is produced. The definition emphasizes the point that the manufacturing process creates products in a definite quantitative relationship. An increase in one product's output will bring about an increase in the quantity of the other products, or vice versa, but not necessarily in the same proportion.

A *joint product cost* may be defined as that cost which arises from the common processing or manufacturing of products produced from a common raw material. Whenever two or more different products are created from a single cost factor, a joint product cost results. A joint cost is incurred prior to the point at which separately identifiable products emerge from the same process.

The flowchart shown below depicts the production of coke, for which coal is the original raw material. In addition to coke as its major product, the process produces sulfate of ammonia, light oil, crude tar, and gas. The greater quantity of gas is not sold but is used to fire the coke ovens and the boilers in the power plant. The coke ovens are the split-off point for cost assignments. The cost of each product consists of a pro rata share of the joint cost plus any separable or subsequent costs incurred in order to put the products into salable condition.

Coke and Its
Associated
Products

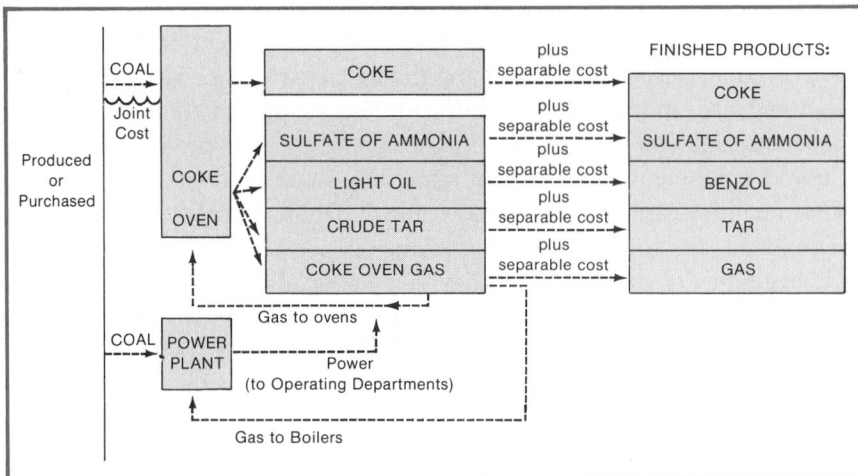

BY-PRODUCTS DEFINED

The term *by-product* is generally used to denote one or more products of relatively small total value that are produced simultaneously with a product of greater total value. The product with the greater value, commonly called the "main product," is usually produced in greater quantities than the by-products. Ordinarily, the manufacturer has only limited control over the quantity of the by-product that comes into existence. However, the introduction of more advanced engineering methods, such as in the petroleum industry, has permitted greater control over the quantity of residual products. In fact, one company, which formerly paid a trucker to haul away and dump certain waste materials, discovered that the waste was valuable as fertilizer, and this by-product is now an additional source of income for the entire industry.

NATURE OF BY-PRODUCTS

The accounting treatment of by-products necessitates a reasonably complete knowledge of the technological factors underlying their manufacture, since the origins of by-products may vary. By-products arising from the cleansing of the main product, such as gas and tar from coke manufacture, generally have a residual value. In some cases, the by-product is leftover scrap or waste, such as sawdust in lumber mills. In other cases, the by-product may not be the result of any manufacturing process but may arise from preparing raw materials before they are used in the manufacture of the main product. The separation of cotton seed from cotton, cores and seeds from apples, and shells from cocoa beans are examples of this type of by-product.

By-products can be classified into two groups according to their marketable condition at the split-off point: (1) those sold in their original form without need of further processing and (2) those which require further processing in order to be salable.

METHODS OF COSTING BY-PRODUCTS

The accepted methods for costing by-products fall into two categories:

1. A joint production cost is not allocated to the by-product. Any revenue resulting from sales of the by-product is credited either to income or to cost of the main product. In some cases, costs subsequent to split-off may be offset against the by-product revenue. For inventory costing, an independent value may be assigned to the by-product. The methods most commonly used in industry are:

   Method 1. Revenue from sales of the by-product is listed on the income statement as:
   a. Other income.
   b. Additional sales revenue.
   c. A deduction from the cost of goods sold of the main product.
   d. A deduction from the total manufacturing cost of the main product.

   Method 2. Revenue from sales of the by-product less the costs of placing the by-product on the market (marketing and administrative expenses) and less any additional processing cost of the by-product is shown on the income statement in a manner similar to that indicated in Method 1.

   Method 3. The replacement cost method.

2. Some portion of the joint production cost is allocated to the by-product. Inventory costs are based on this allocated cost plus any subsequent processing cost. In this category, the following method is used:

   Method 4. The market value (reversal cost) method.

Method 1: Recognition of Gross Revenue

Method 1 is a typical noncost procedure in which the final inventory cost of the main product is overstated to the extent that some of the cost belongs to the by-product. However, this shortcoming is somewhat removed in Method 1 (d), although a sales value rather than a cost is deducted from the production cost of the main product.

By-Product Revenue as Other Income. To illustrate this procedure, the following income statement is presented:

Sales (main product, 10,000 units @ $2).....................................		$20,000
Cost of goods sold:		
Beginning inventory (1,000 units @ $1.50).............................	$ 1,500	
Total production cost (11,000 units @ $1.50).........................	16,500	
Cost of goods available for sale...	$18,000	
Ending inventory (2,000 units @ $1.50)................................	3,000	15,000
Gross profit..		$ 5,000
Marketing and administrative expense......................................		2,000
Operating income...		$ 3,000
Other income: Revenue from sales of by-product		1,500
Income before income tax...		$ 4,500

By-Product Revenue as Additional Sales Revenue. In this case, the income statement above would show the $1,500 revenue from sales of the by-product as an addition to sales of the main product. As a result, total sales revenue would be $21,500, and gross profit and operating income would increase accordingly. All other figures would remain the same.

By-Product Revenue as a Deduction from the Cost of Goods Sold. In this case, the $1,500 revenue from the by-product would be deducted from the $15,000 cost of goods sold figure, thereby reducing the cost and increasing the gross profit and operating income. The income before income tax remains at $4,500.

By-Product Revenue Deducted from Production Cost. In this case, the $1,500 revenue from by-product sales is deducted from the $16,500 total production cost, giving a new production cost of $15,000. This revised cost results in a new average unit cost of $1.3625 for the main product. The final inventory will consequently be $2,725 instead of $3,000. The income statement would appear as follows:

Sales (main product, 10,000 units @ $2)................................			$20,000
Cost of goods sold:			
Beginning inventory (1,000 units @ $1.35)............................		$ 1,350	
Total production cost (11,000 units @ $1.50).............	$16,500		
Revenue from sales of by-product	1,500		
Net production cost.......................................		15,000	
Cost of goods available for sale (12,000 units @ $1.3625 average cost)...		$16,350	
Ending inventory (2,000 units @ $1.3625)............................		2,725	13,625
Gross profit..			$ 6,375
Marketing and administrative expense......................................			2,000
Operating income...			$ 4,375

The preceding methods require no complicated journal entries. The revenue received from by-product sales is debited to Cash (or Accounts Receivable). In the first three cases, Income from Sales of By-Product is credited; in the fourth case, the production cost of the main product is credited.

Method 2 recognizes the need for assigning some cost to the by-product. It does not attempt, however, to allocate any main product cost to the by-product. Any expenses involved in further processing or marketing the by-product are recorded in separate accounts. All figures are shown on the income statement, following one of the procedures described in Method 1.

Method 2: Recognition of Net Revenue

Journal entries in Method 2 would involve charges to by-product revenue for the additional work required and perhaps for factory overhead. The marketing and administrative expense might also be allocated to the by-product on some predetermined basis. Some firms carry an account called By-Product to which all additional expenses are debited and all income is credited. The balance of this account would be presented in the income statement, following one of the procedures outlined in Method 1. However, accumulated manufacturing costs applicable to by-product inventory should be reported on the balance sheet.

The replacement cost method ordinarily is applied by firms whose by-products are used within the plant, thereby avoiding the necessity of purchasing certain materials and supplies from outside suppliers. The production cost of the main product is credited for such materials, and the offsetting debit is to the department that uses the by-product. The cost assigned to the by-product is the purchase or replacement cost existing in the market. This method is common in the steel industry. Although many by-products are sold in the open market, other products, such as blast furnace gas and coke oven gas, are mixed and used for heating in open-hearth furnaces. The waste heat from open hearths is used again in the generation of steam needed by the various producing departments. The resourceful use of these by-products and their accounting treatment are indicated by the following procedure used by a steel company:

Method 3: Replacement Cost Method

1. Coke oven by-products are credited to the cost of coke at the average sales price per unit for the month.
2. Coke oven and blast furnace gas are credited respectively to the cost of coke and the cost of pig iron at a computed value based on the cost of fuel oil yielding equivalent heat units.
3. Tar and pitch used as fuel are credited respectively to the cost of coke at a computed value based on the cost of fuel oil yielding equivalent heat units.
4. Scrap steel remelted is credited to the cost of finished steel at market cost of equivalent grades purchased.
5. Waste heat from furnaces used to generate steam is credited to the steel ingot cost at a computed value based on the cost of coal yielding equivalent heat units.[1]

---

[1] Howard C. Greer, "Accounting for By-Products and Joint Products," *NA(C)A Bulletin,* Vol. XVII, No. 24, Section 1, p. 1413.

Method 4: Market Value Method

The market value (reversal cost) method is basically similar to the last technique illustrated in Method 1. However, it reduces the manufacturing cost of the main product, not by the actual revenue received, but by an estimate of the by-product's value at the time of recovery. This estimate must be made prior to split-off from the main product. Dollar recognition depends on the stability of the market as to price and salability of the by-product; however, control over quantities is important. The by-product account is charged with this estimated amount and the production (manufacturing) cost of the main product is credited. Any additional costs of materials, labor, or factory overhead incurred after the by-product is separated from the main product are charged to the by-product. The marketing and administrative expense might also be allocated to the by-product on some equitable basis. The proceeds from sales of the by-product are credited to the by-product account. The balance in this account can be presented on the income statement in one of the ways outlined for Method 1, except that the manufacturing cost applicable to by-product inventory should be reported in the balance sheet.

The market value (reversal cost) method of ascertaining main product and by-product costs may be illustrated as shown below:

ITEM	MAIN PRODUCT	BY-PRODUCT
Materials	$ 50,000	
Labor	70,000	
Factory overhead..............................	40,000	
Total production cost (40,000 units)	$160,000	
Market value (5,000 units @ $1.80)		$9,000
Estimated gross profit consisting of:		
(20% of selling price, assumed)	$1,800	
Marketing and administrative expense		
(5% of selling price)	450	2,250
		$6,750
Estimated production costs after split-off:		
Materials	$1,000	
Labor	1,200	
Factory overhead............................	300	2,500
Estimated value of by-product at split-off to be credited to main product......	4,250	$4,250
Net cost of main product	$155,750	
Add back *actual* production cost after split-off		2,300
Total...		$6,550
Total number of units.........................	40,000	5,000
Unit cost	$ 3.894	$ 1.31

This illustration indicates that an estimated value of the by-product at the split-off point results when estimated gross profit and production cost after split-off are subtracted from the by-product's ultimate market value. Alternatively, if the by-product has a market value at the split-off point, the by-product account is charged with this market value and the main product's production cost would be credited. It is also possible to use the total market values of the main product and the by-product at the split-off point as a basis for assigning a share of the prior-to-split-off cost to the by-product, applying the offsetting credit to the production cost of the main product. In any event, subsequent-to-split-off cost related to the by-product would be charged to the by-product.

Method 4 is based on the theory that the cost of a by-product is related to its sales value. It is a step toward the recognition of a by-product cost prior to its split-off from the main product. It is also the nearest approach to methods employed in joint product costing.

CHARACTERISTICS OF JOINT PRODUCTS AND COST

Many products or services are linked together by physical relationships which necessitate simultaneous production. To the point of split-off or to the point where these several products emerge as individual units, the cost of the products forms a homogeneous whole.

The classic example of joint products is found in the meat-packing industry, where various cuts of meat and numerous by-products are processed from one original carcass with one lump-sum cost. Another example of joint product manufacturing is the production of gasoline, where the derivation of gasoline inevitably results in the production of such items as naphtha, kerosene, and distillate fuel oils. Other examples of joint product manufacturing are the simultaneous production of various grades of glue and the processing of soybeans into oil and meal. Joint product costing is also found in industries that must grade raw material before it is processed. Tobacco manufacturers (except in cases where graded tobacco is purchased) and virtually all fruit and vegetable canners face the problem of grading. In fact, such manufacturers have a dual problem of joint cost allocation: (1) materials cost is applicable to all grades; (2) subsequent manufacturing costs are incurred simultaneously for all the different grades.

The chief characteristic of the joint product cost is the fact that the cost of these several different products is incurred in an indivisible sum for all products, rather than in individual amounts for each product. The total production cost of multiple products involves both joint cost and separate, individual product costs. These separable product costs are identifiable with the individual product and, generally, need no allocation. However, the joint production cost requires allocation or assignment to the individual products.

METHODS OF ALLOCATING THE JOINT PRODUCTION COST

The allocation of the joint production cost incurred up to the split-off point can be made by:

1. The market or sales value method, based on the relative market values of the individual product.
2. The quantitative or physical unit method, based on some physical measurement unit such as weight, linear measure, or volume.
3. The average unit cost method.
4. The weighted average method, based on a predetermined standard or index of production.

Market or Sales Value Method

This method enjoys great popularity because of the argument that the market value of any product is a manifestation of the cost incurred in its production. The contention is that if one product sells for more than another, it is because more cost was expended to produce it. Therefore, the way to prorate the joint cost is on the basis of the respective market values of the items produced. The method is really a weighted market value basis using the total market or sales value of each unit (quantity sold times the unit sales price).

To illustrate, assume that joint products A, B, C, and D are produced at a total joint production cost of $120,000. Quantities produced are: A, 20,000 units; B, 15,000 units; C, 10,000 units; and D, 15,000 units. Product A sells for $.25; B, for $3; C, for $3.50; and D, for $5. These prices are market or sales values for the products at the split-off point; i.e., it is assumed that they can be sold at that point. Management may have decided, however, that it is more profitable to process certain products further before they are sold. Nevertheless, this condition does not destroy the usefulness of the sales value at the split-off point for the allocation of the joint production cost. The proration of this joint cost is made in the following manner:

Joint Products	No. of Units Produced	Market Value per Unit	Total Market Value	Ratio of Product Value to Total Market Value	Apportionment of the Joint Production Cost
A	20,000	$ .25	$ 5,000	3.125%	$ 3,750
B	15,000	3.00	45,000	28.125	33,750
C	10,000	3.50	35,000	21.875	26,250
D	15,000	5.00	75,000	46.875	56,250
Total...	60,000		$160,000	100.000%	$120,000

The same results can be obtained if the total joint production cost ($120,000) is divided by the total market value of the four products ($160,000). The resulting 75 percent is the percentage of joint cost in each individual market value. By multiplying each market value by this percentage, the joint cost will be apportioned as shown in the preceding chart.

Proponents of the market or sales value method state that the joint cost should be assigned to products in accordance with their sales value because, were it not for such a cost, a sales value would not exist. Under this method, each joint product yields the same unit gross profit percentage, assuming that the units are sold without further processing. This can be illustrated as follows, assuming no beginning inventories:

	TOTAL	A	B	C	D
Sales — units	52,000	18,000	12,000	8,000	14,000
Ending inventories	8,000	2,000	3,000	2,000	1,000
Sales — dollars	$138,500	$ 4,500	$36,000	$28,000	$70,000
Production cost	$120,000	$ 3,750	$33,750	$26,250	$56,250
Less ending inventory	16,125	375*	6,750	5,250	3,750
Cost of goods sold	$103,875	$ 3,375	$27,000	$21,000	$52,500
Gross profit	$ 34,625	$ 1,125	$ 9,000	$ 7,000	$17,500
Gross profit percentage	25%	25%	25%	25%	25%

*$3,750 production cost ÷ 20,000 units produced = $.1875; $.1875 × 2,000 units in ending inventory = $375.

Consideration of Cost After Split-Off. Products not salable in their stage of completion at the split-off point and therefore without any market value require additional processing to place them in marketable condition. In such cases, the basis for allocation of the joint production cost is a hypothetical market value at the split-off point. To illustrate the procedure, the assumptions listed below are added to the preceding example:

PRODUCT	ULTIMATE MARKET VALUE PER UNIT	PROCESSING COST AFTER SPLIT-OFF
A	$ .50	$ 2,000
B	5.00	10,000
C	4.50	10,000
D	8.00	28,000

To arrive at the basis for the apportionment, it is necessary to use a working-back procedure whereby the after-split-off processing cost is subtracted from the ultimate sales value to find a hypothetical market value. The exhibit on the top of page 186 indicates the steps to be taken.

If in a given situation, certain of the joint products are salable at the split-off point while others are not, the market values at the split-off point would be used for the former group; for the latter group, hypothetical market values would be required. In developing hypothetical market values, the after-split-off manufacturing cost may be considered, as well as the after-split-off marketing and administrative expense traceable to specific products, and an allowance for profit.

PRODUCT	ULTI-MATE MARKET VALUE PER UNIT	UNITS PRO-DUCED	ULTIMATE MARKET VALUE	PROCESSING COST AFTER SPLIT-OFF	HYPO-THETICAL MARKET VALUE*	APPORTION-MENT OF JOINT PRODUCTION COST**	TOTAL PRODUCTION COST	TOTAL PRODUCTION COST PERCENT-AGE***
A	$ .50	20,000	$ 10,000	$ 2,000	$ 8,000	$ 4,800	$ 6,800	68.0
B	5.00	15,000	75,000	10,000	65,000	39,000	49,000	65.3
C	4.50	10,000	45,000	10,000	35,000	21,000	31,000	68.8
D	8.00	15,000	120,000	28,000	92,000	55,200	83,200	69.3
Total			$250,000	$50,000	$200,000	$120,000	$170,000	68.0

*At the split-off point
**Percentage to allocate joint production cost (using the joint cost total determined on page 184):

$$\frac{\text{Joint production cost}}{\text{Hypothetical market value}} = \frac{\$120,000}{\$200,000} = .60 = 60\%;$$

60% × hypothetical market value = apportionment of joint production cost
***The production cost percentage is calculated by dividing total production cost by the ultimate market value; e.g., $\frac{\$49,000}{\$75,000} = .653 = 65.3\%$ for Product B, and $\frac{\$170,000}{\$250,000} = .68 = 68\%$ for all products combined.

The following illustration uses the same number of units sold as was used in the preceding illustration.

	TOTAL	A	B	C	D
Sales — units	52,000	18,000	12,000	8,000	14,000
Sales — dollars	$217,000	$ 9,000	$60,000	$36,000	$112,000
Cost of goods sold:					
Joint production cost	$120,000	$ 4,800	$39,000	$21,000	$ 55,200
Further processing cost	50,000	2,000	10,000	10,000	28,000
Total	$170,000	$ 6,800	$49,000	$31,000	$ 83,200
Less ending inventory	22,211	680*	9,795	6,192	5,544
Cost of goods sold	$147,789	$ 6,120	$39,205	$24,808	$ 77,656
Gross profit	$ 69,211	$ 2,880	$20,795	$11,192	$ 34,344
Gross profit percentage	32%	32%	35%	31%	31%

*$6,800 production cost ÷ 20,000 units produced = $.34; $.34 × 2,000 units in ending inventory = $680.

Since the statement has often been made that every joint product should be equally profitable, the following modification of the sales value technique has been suggested. The overall gross profit percentage (32 percent) is used to determine the gross profit for each product. The gross profit is deducted from sales value to find the total cost, which is reduced by each product's further processing cost to find the joint cost allocation for each product.

	TOTAL	A	B	C	D
Ultimate sales value	$250,000	$10,000	$75,000	$45,000	$120,000
Less 32% gross profit	80,000	3,200	24,000	14,400	38,400
Total cost	$170,000	$ 6,800	$51,000	$30,600	$ 81,600
Further processing cost	50,000	2,000	10,000	10,000	28,000
Joint cost	$120,000	$ 4,800	$41,000	$20,600	$ 53,600

If sales value, gross profit percentage, or further processing costs are estimated, the balance labeled "Joint cost" would serve as the basis for allocating the actual joint cost to the four products.

Quantitative Unit Method

This method attempts to distribute the total joint cost on the basis of some unit of measurement, such as pounds, gallons, tons, or board feet. Of course, the joint products must be measurable by the basic measurement unit. If this is not possible, the joint units must be converted to a denominator common to all units produced. For instance, in the manufacture of coke, products such as coke, coal tar, benzol, sulfate of ammonia, and gas are measured in different units. The yield of these recovered units is measured on the basis of the quantity of product extracted per ton of coal.

The following table illustrates the use of weight as a quantitative unit method of joint cost allocation:

PRODUCT	YIELD IN POUNDS OF RECOVERED PRODUCT PER TON OF COAL	DISTRIBUTION OF WASTE TO RECOVERED PRODUCTS	REVISED WEIGHT OF RECOVERED PRODUCTS	MATERIALS COST OF EACH PRODUCT PER TON OF COAL
Coke.............	1,320.0 lbs.	69.474 lbs.*	1,389.474 lbs.	$13.895**
Coal tar.........	120.0	6.316	126.316	1.265
Benzol	21.9	1.153	23.053	.230
Sulfate of ammonia	26.0	1.368	27.368	.275
Gas	412.1	21.689	433.789	4.335
Waste (water).	100.0			
Total.........	2,000.0 lbs.	100.000 lbs.	2,000.000 lbs.	$20.000

*$[1,320 \div (2,000 - 100)] = 69.474$
**$(1,389.474 \div 2,000) \times \$20 = \$13.895$

Average Unit Cost Method

This method attempts to apportion total joint production cost to the various products on the basis of a predetermined standard or index of production. An average unit cost is obtained by dividing the total number of units produced into the total joint production cost. As long as all units produced are measured in terms of the same unit and do not differ greatly, the method can be used without too much misgiving. When the units produced are not measured in like terms, the method cannot be applied. Using the figures in the market value example, the procedure can be illustrated as follows:

$$\frac{\text{Total joint production cost}}{\text{Total number of units produced}} = \frac{\$120,000}{60,000} = \$2 \text{ per unit}$$

PRODUCT	UNITS	JOINT PRODUCTION COST ALLOCATED
A	20,000	$ 40,000
B	15,000	30,000
C	10,000	20,000
D	15,000	30,000
		$120,000

Companies using this method argue that all products turned out by the same process should receive a proportionate share of the total joint production cost based on the number of units produced.

Weighted Average Method

In many industries, the previously described methods do not give a satisfactory answer to the joint cost apportionment problem. For this reason, weight factors are often assigned to each unit, based upon size of the unit, difficulty of manufacture, time consumed in making the unit, difference in type of labor employed, amount of materials used, etc. Finished production of every kind is multiplied by weight factors to apportion the total joint cost to individual units.

Using figures from the previous example, weight factors assigned to the four products might be as follows:

> Product A — 3   points
> Product B — 12   points
> Product C — 13.5 points
> Product D — 15   points

The joint production cost allocation would result in these values:

PRODUCT	UNITS ×	POINTS =	WEIGHTED UNITS	COST PER × UNIT* =	JOINT PRODUCTION COST
A	20,000	3	60,000	$.20	$ 12,000
B	15,000	12	180,000	.20	36,000
C	10,000	13.5	135,000	.20	27,000
D	15,000	15	225,000	.20	45,000
			600,000		$120,000

$$* \quad \frac{\text{Total joint production cost}}{\text{Total number of weighted units}} = \frac{\$120,000}{600,000} = \$.20 \text{ per unit.}$$

FEDERAL INCOME TAX LAWS AND THE COSTING OF JOINT PRODUCTS AND BY-PRODUCTS

Federal income tax laws concerning the costing of joint products and by-products are not numerous. Legislators recognize the impossibility of establishing a specific code of law for every conceivable situation involving this type of cost problem. Consequently, the written pronouncement of the law does not precisely establish the boundaries of acceptable procedures. A digest of legal viewpoint is given in the Federal Income Tax Regulations, which state the following:

> *Inventories of miners and manufacturers.* A taxpayer engaged in mining or manufacturing who by a single process or uniform series of processes derives a product of two or more kinds, sizes, or grades, the unit cost of which is substantially alike, and who in conformity to a recognized trade practice allocates an amount of cost to each kind, size, or grade of product,

which in the aggregate will absorb the total cost of production, may, with the consent of the Commissioner, use such allocated cost as a basis for pricing inventories, provided such allocation bears a reasonable relation to the respective selling values of the different kinds, sizes, or grades of product.

The above quotation does not fully and unequivocally authorize the utilization of the market value theory of costing joint products and by-products. The words "in conformity to a recognized trade practice" and "with the consent of the Commissioner" clearly imply that the multiplicity of conceivable situations is far too great to be covered by definite rules that allow or prohibit a particular costing procedure. Thus, when the size of the business warrants the trouble and expense and before any joint product and by-product inventories are assigned costs for income tax purposes, the commissioner must study the proposed costing program and inform the producer whether it will be allowed. It is a genuine problem for the commissioner to decide whether a cost policy conforms closely enough to the accepted standards of the industry, or whether the alleged cost of a joint product or a by-product is reasonably related to the market values. So much depends upon the judgment of the commissioner that a person might justifiably claim that in joint product and by-product costing disputes, the commissioner is virtually the enactor of the law. Of course, decisions may be appealed, but the higher tribunals find themselves beset by the same vague, general statute; and thus they too must rely almost entirely upon their own independent discretion and practically make the law.

Clearly, tax laws have not solved the problem of costing joint products and by-products for the accountant and the manufacturer. Tax officials find themselves in exactly the same predicament as any coke producer, petroleum refiner, or chemical manufacturer, even though their immediate objective may be limited to collecting a proper tax. The necessity of defining and interpreting accepted practices in a given industry proves, at least partially, that if the present income tax law on joint product and by-product costing — with its implication that the market value method is desirable — is unfair or manifestly inaccurate and illogical, it can and will be changed if industry and the accounting profession can offer better reasons for the use of other procedures.

JOINT COST ALLOCATION IN THE PETROLEUM INDUSTRY

The allocation of joint cost plays a significant role in the determination of prices in the petroleum industry. Oil and gas are often joint products, with one third of all gas produced by oil wells. The wildcatter drilling a well generally cannot know whether oil and/or gas will be discovered. Obviously, there is a substantial joint cost, and this cost relates to both crude oil and natural gas. Traditionally, accounting in the oil industry looked upon gas as a by-product, and no serious effort was made to separate gas costs from the total joint cost. With the building of long-distance pipe lines as a result of a dramatic increase in natural gas demand, however, natural gas emerged as a full joint product.

In past years, the problem of allocating joint cost between crude oil and natural gas was intensified due to the Federal Power Commission's role in attempting to establish just and reasonable prices for natural gas. A landmark court decision required the FPC to consider gas costs, at least as a basis for comparison with other regulatory methods. Accordingly, accountants representing the FPC, the gas producers, and the gas distributors have searched for a solution to a problem which theoretically is incapable of other than an arbitrary solution, i.e., splitting a joint cost for the purpose of setting a selling price for one of the products, based on actual costs. Despite the best efforts of accountants and economists, the basic problem remains.

The following methods have been used or suggested in order to arrive at some answer to this vexing problem of joint costing:

1. The sales realization method, often referred to as the sales allocation or the Federal Trade Commission method.
2. The BTU (British Thermal Units) allocation method.
3. The relative cost method.

Sales Realization Method

The sales realization method divides the joint cost between oil and gas by first recognizing the existence of two types of costs: (1) annual cost and (2) return on investment. Annual cost, which includes operating cost, depreciation, depletion, exploration, and development, is allocated according to the revenue received from the products during a recent test year. The return on investment (a percentage of total net plant and working capital) is allocated between oil and gas according to the "actual average remaining reserve realization ratio." This ratio takes into account the value of the reserves remaining in the ground in the test year, using prices realized by the company in the test year. In short, annual cost (including exploration) is allocated in proportion to the value of annual sales, and return on investment is allocated in proportion to the value of the remaining reserves.

The sales realization method, which uses prices to determine prices, has been criticized by both the Federal Power Commission and the gas producers as being a circular method. Cost depends on sales value which depends on prices set on the basis of cost. When the method is applied the first time, the cost is based on the present sales prices. In subsequent price determinations, the new cost will be determined in part by the prices previously set.

BTU Method

The BTU method uses the relative heat content of oil and gas, expressed in British Thermal Units. A *BTU* is the amount of heat required to raise the temperature of one pound of water one degree Fahrenheit. Equivalent BTU content ratios of gas to oil used range from between 4.8 and 6 million cubic feet to 1 barrel of oil. The joint cost is allocated in proportion to BTU content of the products and can be applied to the output of the test year as well as to the average remaining reserves. The rationale of the method is that the consumer is interested in energy, not in gas, oil, or coal. The BTU method allocates the joint cost based on readily ascertainable physical data and can be applied to all the products connected with gas and oil.

The BTU method has been criticized for not properly reflecting the value of all the joint products produced. Only a part of the products resulting from crude oil are valuable for BTU content alone. Gasoline is valuable because of its form. Various modifications of the basic BTU formula have been suggested to give proper weighting to energy form.

Relative Cost Method

Under the relative cost method, which has been accepted by the Federal Power Commission, the production cost from a joint product lease is allocated to the oil and gas produced on the basis of the relationship between the cost actually incurred in producing the same products from single product leases (i.e., leases from which only oil or only gas is produced).

This method has considerable appeal when the company has sufficient single product leases for computing representative single product costs. In addition, the company should be large enough to assume an averaging of economic and geological lease characteristics. Of course, this method does not provide for allocation of exploration expenditures, which represent a significant portion of total costs and are incurred on a company-wide basis.

JOINT PRODUCT COST ANALYSIS FOR MANAGERIAL DECISIONS AND PROFITABILITY ANALYSIS

The Securities and Exchange Commission requires that annual reports to stockholders include data by lines of business. Likewise, the Federal Trade Commission requests that certain businesses furnish cost and profit data for a wide range of specific product categories. The Financial Accounting Standards Board requires business enterprises, excluding nonpublic enterprises, to report in their annual external financial statements the revenue, operating profit or loss (revenue less operating expense), as well as identifiable assets of each significant industry segment of their operations. "Significant" generally means 10 percent or more of the total of the respective amounts. Aggregate depreciation, depletion, amortization expenses, and the amount of capital expenditures must also be reported for each segment. Furthermore, the FASB requires information about foreign operations, export sales, and major customers, who need not be identified. Also, methods used for cost allocations to segments must be disclosed. Interim financial statements are exempt from these requirements.[2] The SEC's disclosure requirements are consistent with the provisions contained in FASB statements, yet they call for more information than the FASB.

Companies generally resist such requirements. One of their main arguments is that cost allocation today is fraught with great danger of improper interpretation caused by an arbitrarily allocated joint cost. Of course, as this chapter indicates, there are acceptable ways of allocating joint product cost. Yet, the choice of method makes a difference. The decision determines the degree of profitability of the various individual products.

Joint cost allocation methods indicate only too forcefully that the amount of the cost to be apportioned to the numerous products emerging at the point of split-off is difficult to establish for any purpose. Furthermore, the acceptance of an allocation method for the assignment of the joint production cost does not solve the problem. The thought has been advanced that no attempt should be made to determine the cost of individual products up to the split-off point; rather, it seems important to calculate the profit margin in terms of total combined units. Of course, costs incurred after the split-off point will provide management with information needed for decisions relating to the desirability of further processing to maximize profits.

Production of joint products is greatly influenced by both the technological characteristics of the processes and by the markets available for the products. This establishment of a product mix which is in harmony with customer demands appears profitable but is often physically impossible. It is interesting to note that cost accounting in the meat-packing industry serves primarily as a guide to buying, for aggregate sales realization values of the various products that will be obtained from cutting operations are considered in determining the price that a packer is willing to pay for livestock. Sales realization values are also considered when deciding to sell hams or other cuts in a particular stage or to process them further.

A joint cost is often incurred for products that are either interchangeable or not associated with each other at all. Increasing the output of one will in most joint cost situations unavoidably increase to some extent the output of the other. These situations fall into the category of the cost-volume-profit relationship and differential cost analysis (Chapters 24 and 25). Evaluation of many alternative combinations of output can lead to time-consuming computations. Often such evaluations are carried out on a computer using sophisticated simulation techniques. Developments in operations research procedures have provided techniques helpful in solving such problems (Chapter 28 on linear programming).

---

[2]*Statement of Financial Accounting Standards, No. 14*, "Financial Reporting for Segments of a Business Enterprise" (Stamford: Financial Accounting Standards Board, 1976); *Statement of Financial Accounting Standards, No. 18*, "Financial Reporting for Segments of a Business Enterprise — Interim Financial Statements" (Stamford: Financial Accounting Standards Board, 1977); and *Statement of Financial Accounting Standards, No. 21*, "Suspension of the Reporting of Earnings per Share and Segment Information by Nonpublic Enterprises" (Stamford: Financial Accounting Standards Board, 1978).

For profit planning, and perhaps as the only reliable measure of profitability, management should consider a product's contribution margin after separable or individual costs are deducted from sales. This contribution margin allows management to predict the amount that a segment or product line will add to or subtract from company profits. This margin is not the product's net profit figure. It only indicates relative profitability in comparison with other products. "Net profit determined by allocating to segments an 'equitable' share of all costs, both separable and joint, associated with the group of segments is not a reliable guide to profit planning decisions because these data cannot be used for predicting the outcome of decisions in terms of the change in aggregate net profit."[3] For these reasons, attempts to allocate joint marketing cost to products and customers by time studies of salespersons' activities, as well as attempts to allocate the joint production cost, often yield results which are unreliable for appraising segment profitability.

DISCUSSION QUESTIONS

1. (a) Distinguish between joint products and by-products.
   (b) Describe and briefly discuss the appropriateness of two acceptable methods of accounting for the by-product in the determination of the cost of the main products.
   (c) Assuming proper treatment of the by-product costs, describe two acceptable methods of allocating to joint products the cost of the initial producing department.

(AICPA adapted)

2. How may the revenue from the sale of by-products be shown on the income statement?

3. Does the showing of revenue from by-products on the income statement influence the unit cost of the main product?

4. By what method can production cost be relieved of the value of a by-product that can be further utilized in production processes? Explain.

5. Are by-products ever charged with any cost? Explain.

6. By-products which require no additional processing after the point of separation are often accounted for by assigning to them a cost of zero at the point of separation and crediting the cost of production of the main product as sales are made.
   (a) Justify the above method of treating by-products.
   (b) Discuss the possible shortcomings of the treatment.

(AICPA adapted)

---

[3]Walter B. McFarland, *Concepts for Management Accounting* (New York: National Association of Accountants, 1966), p. 49.

7. Name four methods for apportioning the total joint production cost to joint products.

8. Why is the market value method for joint cost allocation so often used by industry?

9. Oregon Logging Company obtains its cost information by dividing total cost by the number of board feet of lumber produced. The president states that money is lost on every foot of low grade lumber sold but is made up on the high grades. Appraise the statement.

10. Discuss the advantages and disadvantages of the market value and average unit cost methods of joint cost allocation.

(CMA adapted)

11. What is the chief difference between the quantitative unit method and the average unit cost method of joint cost allocation?

12. Does the Internal Revenue Service prescribe any definite joint product or by-product cost allocation methods for tax purposes? Explain.

13. Select the answer which best completes the statement:
    (a) When two products are manufactured during a common process, the factor determining whether the products are joint products or one main product and one by-product is the: (1) potential marketability for each product; (2) amount of work expended in the production of each product; (3) relative total sales value of each product; (4) management policy.
    (b) If a company obtains two salable products from refining one ore, the refining process must be accounted for as a(n): (1) mixed cost process; (2) joint process; (3) extractive process; (4) reduction process.
    (c) A joint cost should be allocated: (1) to by-products; (2) on the basis of costs after separation; (3) on an authoritatively selected and consistently applied basis; (4) on the basis of the selling price of all products.
    (d) The method of accounting for joint product cost that will produce the same gross profit rate for all products is the: (1) market value method; (2) physical measure method; (3) actual costing method; (4) split-off costing method.
    (e) A by-product: (1) is produced from material that would otherwise be of no value; (2) has a lower selling price than the main product; (3) is created along with the main product, but its sales value does not cover its production cost; (4) usually produces a smaller amount of revenue than the main product.
    (f) The Baylor Company manufactures two joint products at a joint cost of $100,000. These products can be sold when split off or when further processed at an additional cost and sold as higher quality items. The decision to sell at the split-off point or to process further should be based on the: (1) assumption that the joint cost is irrelevant; (2) allocation of the joint cost using the market value or sales value method; (3) assumption that the joint cost must be allocated using a quantitative or physical unit method; (4) allocation of the joint cost using any equitable and rational allocation basis.
    (g) The primary purpose for allocating to various products the joint cost of a processing center is to: (1) develop accurate processing cost variances by product; (2) report more correct standard product costs for comparative analysis; (3) establish inventory cost assigned to unsold units; (4) record accurate cost of sales by product line.

(h) A joint process produces three products, A, B, and C, that may be sold at the split-off point or processed further. Additional processing costs are entirely variable and are traceable to the respective products produced. A joint product cost of $50,000 was allocated by the market value method. Relevant data are:

Product	Units Produced	Sales Value at Split-Off	Additional Cost	Sales Value
A	20,000	$ 45,000	$20,000	$ 60,000
B	15,000	75,000	20,000	98,000
C	15,000	30,000	18,000	62,000
		$150,000	$58,000	$220,000

The columns "Additional Cost" and "Sales Value" fall under the heading: ADDITIONAL COST AND SALES VALUE IF PROCESSED FURTHER

To maximize profits, the products that should be processed further are:
(1) A only; (2) C only; (3) B and C only; (4) none, because of the joint cost.
(AICPA and CMA adapted)

EXERCISES

1. **By-product costing and entries.** The Doar Company produces a product known as Doaron. In the manufacture of this chemical, a by-product results which can be sold as is for $.25 per kilogram or be processed further and sold for $.60 per kilogram. The additional processing for each kilogram of by-product requires $.10 for materials, $.12 for labor, and $.11 for factory overhead.

Production costs of the main product to the point of separation were: materials, $111,000; labor, $90,500; and factory overhead, $75,700. During the month, 170 000 kilograms of Doaron and 26 000 kilograms of by-product were produced.

Required: Journal entries for the by-product when it is:
(1) Stored without assigning it any cost and later sold on account at $.25 per kilogram, with no additional costs incurred.
(2) Stored and costed at $.25 per kilogram, reducing the main product cost by the amount allocated to the by-product.
(3) Further processed and stored, with no cost prior to separation allocated to it.
(4) Further processed and stored, the cost prior to separation being allocated to it using the market values at the point of separation for cost allocation, with the cost of the main product being reduced by the cost allocated to the by-product and the main product selling at $2 per kilogram.

2. **Reversal cost method for by-products.** Lawlor, Inc., manufactures one main product and two by-products. Data for July are:

	MAIN PRODUCT	BY-PRODUCT A	BY-PRODUCT B
Sales..	$150,000	$12,000	$7,000
Manufacturing cost before separation......	75,000	—	—
Manufacturing cost after separation.........	23,000	2,200	1,800
Marketing and administrative expense.....	12,000	1,500	1,100

Required: An income statement, assuming no beginning or ending inventories and using the reversal cost method for the by-products, allowing a 15% operating profit for By-Product A and a 12% operating profit for By-Product B.

3. **Cost allocation for by-products and joint products.** The cost accountant of the Magill Company prepared the income statement reproduced on page 196, with Magic as the main product, Ligam as the by-product, and by-product revenue treated as other income.

Magill Company
Income Statement
For Year Ended September 30, 19--

Sales (85,000 lbs. @ $5.20)		$442,000
Cost of goods sold:		
Magic (Process 1)	$221,400	
Magic finishing (Process 2)	101,700	
Total manufacturing cost	$323,100*	
Less inventory of finished Magic (5,000 lbs.)	17,950**	305,150
Gross profit		$136,850
Marketing and administrative expense		113,000
Operating income		$ 23,850
Other income:		
Sales of Ligam (48,000 lbs. @ $.85)		$ 40,800
Less: Ligam finishing cost (Process 3)	$11,440*	
Inventory of finished Ligam (7,000 lbs.).	1,456***	
	$ 9,984	
Ligam marketing expense	9,000	18,984	21,816
Income before income tax		$45,666

*Includes beginning inventory

**Inventory of finished Magic: $\frac{\$323,100}{90,000} \times 5,000 = \$17,950$

***Inventory of finished Ligam: $\frac{\$11,440}{55,000} \times 7,000 = \$1,456$

Required:
(1) Characteristics of Ligam, if any, which justify its treatment as a by-product.
(2) Characteristics of Ligam, if any, which justify its treatment as a joint product.
(3) If Ligam is treated as a by-product, an explanation of why cost should be associated with the inventory of finished Ligam at September 30, 19--.
(4) Both products are manufactured in part simultaneously from the same raw materials. Separation occurs at the end of Process 1. Compute the Process 1 cost allocation to Magic and Ligam as joint products on the sales value basis if Process 1 — Magic sells for $3 per lb. and Process 1 — Ligam sells for $.45 per lb. Production at the end of Process 1 was 108,000 lbs., of which $5/9$ became Magic and $4/9$ Ligam. (Round off all amounts to three decimal places.)

4. Joint cost allocation — market value method; by-product allocation — market value (reversal cost) method. The Tracy Company manufactures joint products X and Y as well as by-product Z. Cumulative cost data for the period show $204,000 representing 20,000 completed units processed through the Refining Department at an average cost of $10.20. Costs are assigned to X and Y by the market value method which considers further processing costs in subsequent operations. To determine the cost allocation to Z, the market value (reversal cost) method is used. Additional data:

	Z	X	Y
Quantity processed	2,000 units	8,000 units	10,000 units
Sales price per unit	$5	$20	$25
Further processing cost per unit	1	5	7
Marketing and administrative expense per unit	1	—	—
Operating profit per unit	1	—	—

Required: Cumulative cost allocated to Z, X, and Y.

5. Joint cost allocation — market value and weighted average methods. The Buildon Company produces three joint products: Buildon, Buildeze, and Buildrite. Total joint production cost for November was $21,600.

The units produced and unit sales prices at the split-off point were:

PRODUCT	UNITS	UNIT SALES PRICE
Buildon	6,000	$2.20
Buildeze	8,000	1.25
Buildrite	10,000	1.28

In determining costs by the weighted average method, each unit is weighted as follows:

PRODUCT	PER UNIT WEIGHTING
Buildon	6
Buildeze	4
Buildrite	4

Required: Allocation of the production cost, using:
(1) The market value method.
(2) The weighted average method.

6. Cost allocation — weighted average method. A department's equivalent production schedules show 10,000 units of Article X and 8,000 units of Article Y. Both articles are made from the same raw materials, but a unit of Article X and Article Y require estimated quantities of materials in the ratio of 3:2, respectively. Both articles pass through the same conversion process, but Article X and Article Y require estimated production times per unit in the ratio of 5:4, respectively.

Required: A computation of the unit materials and conversion costs for each product if the total costs are: materials, $92,000; conversion cost, $41,000.

7. Allocation of joint cost by relative weights. The product engineering staff of the Pyramid Company prepared the following analysis of relative weights for cost elements in the manufacture of joint products A, B, and C in Department 10:

PRODUCT	OUTPUT FOR EACH UNIT OF MATERIALS INPUT	OUTPUT FOR EACH HOUR OF LABOR CREW TIME	FACTORY OVERHEAD
A	3	1	The engineers deter-
B	4	1$^1/_6$	mined that twice as
C	2	1$^1/_6$	much weight should
			be given to time spent
			in production as is
			given to size. Prod-
			ucts A and B are the
			same total weight and
			shape, but product C
			is in total twice as
			heavy and twice as
			bulky.

Joint costs incurred in Department 10 in March:

Materials	$220,000
Labor	190,000
Factory overhead	170,000
Total	$580,000

Required: Allocation of joint cost to the three products by relative weights.

8. Joint cost allocation — market value method. The Skantz Company manufactures three different products from a single raw material. A summary of production costs shows:

	PRODUCT			
	S	K	A	Total
Output in kilograms	80 000	200 000	160 000	440 000
Selling price per kilogram	$.75	$1.00	$1.50	—

	SEPARABLE COSTS			
	S	K	A	Total Cost
Production costs:				
Materials	—	—	—	$ 90,000
Direct labor	$ 3,000	$20,000	$30,000	80,000
Variable factory overhead	2,000	10,000	16,000	45,000
Fixed factory overhead	15,000	34,000	30,000	115,000

All separable costs have been assigned to products but the joint cost has not been allocated. All of the year's output was sold.

Required: The gross profit for each product, allocating the joint cost by the market value method.

(CGAA adapted)

9. Joint cost allocation using market value method; sell or process further. The Domecq Company produces three products, A, B, and C, as the result of initial joint processing plus separable processing after the split-off point. Records for July show the following:

	A	B	C	TOTAL
Materials used	—	—	—	$150,000
Joint processing cost	—	—	—	170,000
Separable processing costs	$50,000	$80,000	$70,000	—
Units produced	6,000	12,000	6,250	—
Units sold	4,000	9,000	4,250	—
Unit sales price	$50.00	$37.50	$40.00	—

Required:
(1) The cost assigned to ending inventory for each product and in total, assuming no beginning inventory and using the market value method for joint cost allocation. In completing this requirement, disregard the information given in requirement (2).
(2) The difference in operating profit if Domecq accepts an offer from a prospective customer who would be willing to buy all the output of Product B at the split-off point for $30 per unit.

(CGAA adapted)

10. Allocation of joint cost — market value method. The CBA Company produces three joint products, C, B, and A. During February, the following information was recorded:

	C	B	A	TOTAL
Joint materials	—	—	—	$ 5,000
Joint processing	—	—	—	$23,000
Separable processing	$8,000	$5,000	$2,000	$15,000
Output in kilograms	2 000 kg	5 000 kg	3 000 kg	10 000 kg
Sales in kilograms	1 500 kg	4 200 kg	2 400 kg	8 100 kg
Sales price per kilogram	$10	$6	$7	—

Required:
(1) Total cost for each product, using the market value method.
(2) Justification for treating a joint product as a by-product.

(CGAA adapted)

11. Market value at the split-off point for joint cost allocation. Miller Company buys Zeon for $.80 a gallon. At the end of processing in Department 1, Zeon splits off into Products A, B, and C. A is sold at the split-off point with no further processing; B and C require further processing before they can be sold; B is processed in Department 2; and C is processed in Department 3. The following is a summary of costs and other related data for the year ended June 30, 19B:

	DEPARTMENT		
	1	*2*	*3*
Cost of Zeon	$96,000	—	—
Direct labor	14,000	$45,000	$65,000
Factory overhead	10,000	21,000	49,000

	PRODUCT		
	A	*B*	*C*
Gallons sold	20,000	30,000	45,000
Gallons on hand at June 30, 19B	10,000	—	15,000
Sales (in dollars)	$30,000	$96,000	$141,750

There were no inventories on hand at July 1, 19A, and there was no Zeon on hand at June 30, 19B. All gallons on hand at June 30, 19B, were complete as to processing. There were no factory overhead variances. Miller uses the market value at split-off point to allocate joint cost.

Required:
(1) The market value at the split-off point for Product A total units produced for the year.
(2) The total joint cost for the year ended June 30, 19B, to be allocated.
(3) The cost of Product B sold for the year ended June 30, 19B.
(4) The cost assigned to the Product A ending inventory.

(AICPA adapted)

12. Joint cost allocation — average unit cost and market value methods. Vreeland, Inc., manufactures three products, X, Y, and Z, from a joint process. The joint cost totals $60,000. Additional information follows:

			ADDITIONAL COST AND MARKET VALUE IF PROCESSED FURTHER	
Product	*Units Produced*	*Market Value at Split-Off*	*Additional Cost*	*Market Value*
X	6,000	$40,000	$9,000	$55,000
Y	4,000	35,000	7,000	45,000
Z	2,000	25,000	5,000	30,000

Required:
(1) Total cost for each product, using the average unit cost method.
(2) Total cost for each product, using the market value method.

(AICPA adapted)

13. Joint cost allocation; sell or process further. The Newport Chemical Company manufactures three products, R, S, and T. During November, the following joint costs were incurred: materials, $180,000; direct labor, $100,000; factory overhead, $70,000. Quantities jointly produced were: R, 20,000; S, 50,000; T, 30,000. Additional costs after split-off were:

	DIRECT LABOR	FACTORY OVERHEAD
R	$25,000	$15,000
S	35,000	25,000
T	18,000	12,000

Unit sales prices are: R, $7; S, $5; T, $8.

Required:
(1) Gross profit for each product, assuming that all units produced were sold and that joint cost is allocated using the market value method.
(2) A decision as to whether Product R should be sold at the split-off point for $4.50 per unit or processed further and sold for $7 per unit.

(CGAA adapted)

PROBLEMS

8-1. Cost allocation — joint products and by-products. The Harrison Corporation produces three products, Alpha, Beta, and Gamma. Alpha and Gamma are joint products while Beta is a by-product of Alpha. No joint cost is to be allocated to the by-product. The production processes for a given year are as follows:

(a) In Department 1, 110,000 pounds of material, Rho, are processed at a total cost of $120,000. After processing, 60% of the units are transferred to Department 2 and 40% of the units (now Gamma) are transferred to Department 3.

(b) In Department 2, the material is further processed at a total additional cost of $38,000. Seventy percent of the units (now Alpha) are transferred to Department 4 and 30% emerge as Beta, the by-product, to be sold at $1.20 per pound. The marketing expense related to Beta is $8,100.

(c) In Department 4, Alpha is processed at a total additional cost of $23,660. After processing, Alpha is ready for sale at $5 per pound.

(d) In Department 3, Gamma is processed at a total additional cost of $165,000. In this department, a normal loss of units of Gamma occurs which equals 10% of the good output of Gamma. The remaining good output is sold for $12 per pound.

Required:

(1) A schedule showing the allocation of the $120,000 joint cost between Alpha and Gamma, using the market value at split-off point and treating the net realizable value of Beta as an addition to the sales value of Alpha.

(2) A statement of gross profit for Alpha, independent of the answer to requirement (1), assuming that:

(a) $102,000 of total joint cost was appropriately allocated to Alpha.

(b) 48,000 pounds of Alpha and 20,000 pounds of Beta were available to sell.

(c) During the year, sales of Alpha were 80% of the pounds available for sale. There was no beginning inventory.

(d) The net realizable value of Beta available for sale is to be deducted from the cost of producing Alpha. The ending inventory of Alpha is to be based on the net cost of production.

(e) All other costs, selling prices, and marketing expenses are those presented in the facts of the original problem.

(AICPA adapted)

8-2. Inventory cost determination; management processing decision. The Laverock Company's joint cost of producing 1,000 units of Product A, 500 units of Product B, and 500 units of Product C is $100,000. The unit sales values of the three products at the split-off point are: A — $20; B — $200; C — $160. Ending inventories include 100 units of A, 300 units of B, and 200 units of C.

Required:

(1) The amount of joint cost that would be included in the ending inventory of the three products (a) using the market value method and (b) using the average unit cost method.

(2) The relative merits of each of these two bases of joint cost allocation (a) for financial statement purposes and (b) for decisions about the desirability of selling joint products at the split-off point or processing them further.

(AICPA adapted)

8-3. Cost of production report — fifo method; joint products and by-products. The data at the top of page 201 were gathered from the records of the Rodholmes Company for February.

Materials are issued in Process 1. At the end of processing in Process 1, the by-product appears and the balance of production is transferred to Process 2 for additional processing of one main product and to Process 3 for additional processing of the other main product.

The joint cost of Process 1, less the market value of the by-product, is apportioned to the main products using the market value method at the split-off point. Selling prices for the finished products of Processes 2 and 3 are $10 and $15, respectively. The by-product sells for $2. The company uses the fifo costing method.

| | PROCESS | | |
	1	2	3
Unit data:			
Beginning work in process inventory (⅓ completed in Processes 2 and 3)...	—	3,000	3,000
Started or received	32,000	10,000	20,000
	32,000	13,000	23,000
Transferred to Process 2	10,000	—	—
Transferred to Process 3	20,000	—	—
Transferred to finished goods storeroom	—	9,000	20,000
Transferred out as by-product	2,000	—	—
Normal loss...	—	—	1,000
Ending work in process inventory (¼ completed in Process 2 and ½ completed in Process 3)	—	4,000	2,000
	32,000	13,000	23,000
Partial summary of costs:			
Beginning work in process inventory..............................	—	$ 8,000	$14,500
Cost added by department:			
Materials	$58,000	—	—
Labor and factory overhead..	30,000	18,000	60,000
	$88,000		
Less market value of by-product	4,000		
	$84,000		

Required: A departmental cost of production report for February. (Carry unit cost computations to four decimal places and round off the unit cost adjustment for lost units to the nearest cent.)

8-4. Joint product and by-product cost allocation. Enid Chemical Company manufactures several products in its three departments:

(a) In Department 1, the raw materials amanic acid and bonyl hydroxide are used to produce Amanyl, Bonanyl, and Am-Salt. Amanyl is sold to others, who use it as a raw material in the manufacture of stimulants. Bonanyl is not salable without further processing. Although Am-Salt is a commercial product for which there is a ready market, the company does not sell this product, preferring to submit it to further processing.

(b) In Department 2, Bonanyl is processed into the marketable product, Bonanyl-X. The relationship between Bonanyl used and Bonanyl-X produced has remained constant for several months.

(c) In Department 3, Am-Salt and the raw material colb are used to produce Colbanyl, a liquid propellant. As an inevitable part of this process, Demanyl is also produced. Demanyl was discarded as scrap until discovery of its usefulness as a catalyst in the manufacture of glue. For two years, Enid has been able to sell all of its Demanyl production.

In its financial statements, the company states inventory at the lower of cost (on the first-in, first-out basis) or market. Unit costs of the items most recently produced must therefore be computed. The cost allocated to Demanyl is computed so that after allowing $.04 per pound for packaging and selling costs, no profit or loss will be recognized on sales of this product.

Certain data for October follow:

RAW MATERIALS:	POUNDS USED	TOTAL COST
Amanic acid...	6,300	$5,670
Bonyl hydroxide.................................	9,100	6,370
Colb...	5,600	2,240

CONVERSION COSTS (LABOR AND FACTORY OVERHEAD): TOTAL
                                                 COST
Department 1..$33,600
Department 2...   3,306
Department 3... 22,400

	Pounds Produced	INVENTORIES, POUNDS		Sales Price per Pound
		September 30	October 31	
Amanyl	3,600	—	—	$ 6.65
Bonanyl	2,800	210	110	—
Am-Salt.........................	7,600	400	600	6.30
Bonanyl-X	2,755	—	—	4.20
Colbanyl	1,400	—	—	43.00
Demanyl	9,800	—	—	.54

Required: Schedules for the items listed below for October with supporting computations prepared in good form and answers rounded to the nearest cent.
(1) Cost per pound of Amanyl, Bonanyl, and Am-Salt produced, using the market or sales value method.
(2) Cost per pound of Amanyl, Bonanyl, and Am-Salt produced, using the average unit cost method.
(3) Cost per pound of Colbanyl produced, assuming that the cost per pound of Am-Salt produced was $3.40 in September and $3.50 in October.

(AICPA adapted)

8-5. Cost of production report for joint products and by-products. The Constantine Chemical Company produces two principal products known as XO and MO. Incidental to the production of these products, it produces a by-product know as Bypo. The company has three producing departments which it identifies as Departments 101, 201, and 301. Raw materials A and B are started in process in Department 101. Upon completion of processing in that department, one fifth of the material is by-product and is transferred directly to stock. One third of the remaining output of Department 101 goes to Department 201 where it is made into XO, and the other two thirds goes to Department 301 where it becomes MO. The processing of XO in Department 201 results in a 50% gain in weight of materials transferred into the department due to the addition of water at the start of the processing. There is no gain or loss of weight in the other processes.

The company considers the income from Bypo, after allowing $.05 per pound for estimated selling and delivery costs, to be a reduction of the costs of the two principal products. The company assigns Department 101 costs to the two principal products in proportion to their net sales value at point of separation, computed by deducting costs to be incurred in subsequent processes from the sales value of the products.

The following information concerns operations during April:

INVENTORIES:	MARCH 31		APRIL 30
	Quantity (Pounds)	Cost	Quantity (Pounds)
Department 101..	—	—	—
Department 201..	800	$17,160	1,000
Department 301..	200	2,340	360
Finished stock — XO.................................	300	7,260	80
Finished stock — MO	1,200	18,550	700
Finished stock — Bypo	—	—	—

Inventories in process are estimated to be one-half complete in Departments 201 and 301, both at the beginning and at the end of the month. The company uses the fifo method for inventory costing.

Costs:	Materials Used	Labor and Factory Overhead
Department 101..................................	$134,090	$87,418
Department 201..................................	—	31,950
Department 301..................................	—	61,880

The materials used in Department 101 weighed 18,000 pounds.

Sales prices:
XO   — $29.50 per pound
MO   — 17.50 per pound
Bypo —   .50 per pound

Prices as of April 30 are unchanged from those in effect during the month.

Required: A departmental cost of production report for April. (Carry unit cost computations to three decimal places and round off total amounts to the nearest dollar.)

(AICPA adapted)

CASE

Theory of joint product cost allocation methods; product mix and gross profit analysis. Vidrio, Inc., manufactures two plate glass sizes that are produced simultaneously in the same manufacturing process. Since the small sheets of plate glass are cut from large sheets with flaws, the joint cost is allocated equally to each good sheet produced, large and small. The difference in after-split-off costs for large and small sheets is considerable.

Last year the company decided to increase its efforts to sell the large sheets because they produced a larger gross profit than the small sheets. Accordingly, the amount of the fixed advertising budget devoted to large sheets was increased; and the amount devoted to small sheets was decreased. However, no changes in sales prices were made.

By midyear, the Production Planning Department had increased the monthly production of large sheets in order to stay above the minimum inventory level. However, it also had cut back the monthly production of small sheets because the inventory ceiling had been reached.

At the end of last year, the net result of the change in product mix was a decrease of $112,000 in gross profit. Although sales of large sheets had increased 34,500 units, sales of small sheets had decreased 40,200 units.

Required:
(1) Difference between joint product cost and:
   (a) After-split-off cost.
   (b) Fixed cost.
   (c) Prime cost.
(2) The propriety of allocating joint product cost for general purpose financial statements on the basis of:
   (a) Physical measures, such as weight or units.
   (b) Relative sales or market value.
(3) In allocating joint cost to joint products, the advantages in reducing the relative sales value of each joint product by its after-split-off cost.
(4) The mistake made by Vidrio, Inc., in deciding to change its product mix, explaining why it caused a smaller gross profit last year.

(AICPA adapted)

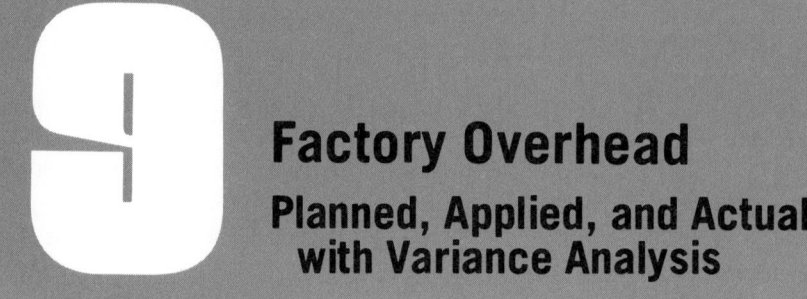

Part Three
Planning and Control of Factory Overhead

9

Factory Overhead
Planned, Applied, and Actual with Variance Analysis

The use of a predetermined factory overhead rate for the purpose of charging a fair share of factory overhead to products was introduced briefly in earlier chapters. This chapter (1) discusses the methods, procedures, and bases available for applying factory overhead; (2) describes methods and procedures for classifying and accumulating actual factory overhead; (3) shows computations for over- or underapplied factory overhead; and (4) analyzes the total net variance, showing the spending and idle capacity variances. Chapter 10 discusses (1) the departmentalization of factory overhead, (2) the creation and use of separate departmental overhead rates, and (3) departmentalization in nonmanufacturing businesses and nonprofit institutions and organizations. Chapter 11 discusses (1) the relationship of product costing to responsibility accounting, (2) the allocation of service center costs, using the maintenance department and its cost as an example, and (3) monthly overhead variance analysis for use in responsibility accounting and reporting for producing and service departments.

Factory overhead is generally defined as indirect materials, indirect labor, and all other factory expenses that cannot conveniently be identified with nor charged directly to specific jobs or products or final cost objectives, such as government contracts. Other terms used for factory overhead are *factory burden, manufacturing expense, manufacturing overhead, factory expense*, and *indirect manufacturing cost*.

Factory overhead possesses two characteristics that require consideration if products are to be charged with a fair share of this expense. These characteristics deal with the particular relationship of factory overhead to (1) the product itself and (2) the volume of production. Unlike direct materials and direct labor, factory overhead is an invisible part of the finished product. No materials requisition or labor time ticket can indicate the amount of overhead, such as factory supplies or indirect labor, that enters into a job or product. Yet factory overhead is as much a part of a product's manufacturing cost as direct materials and direct labor. Because of the impossibility of tracing factory overhead to specific jobs or specific products, an arbitrary overhead allocation must be made. A predetermined factory overhead rate permits an equitable and logical allocation, therewith abandoning the use of actual cost for costing purposes.

The second characteristic deals with the change that many items of overhead undergo with a change in production volume. First, the total amount of fixed overhead remains relatively constant regardless of changes in production volume, while the fixed overhead per unit of output varies inversely with production volume; second, the semivariable cost varies but not in proportion to units produced; and finally, only the variable cost varies proportionately with production output (see chart below). Therefore, as production volume changes, the combined effect of these different overhead patterns can cause unit manufacturing cost to fluctuate considerably unless some method is provided to stabilize overhead charged to the units produced.

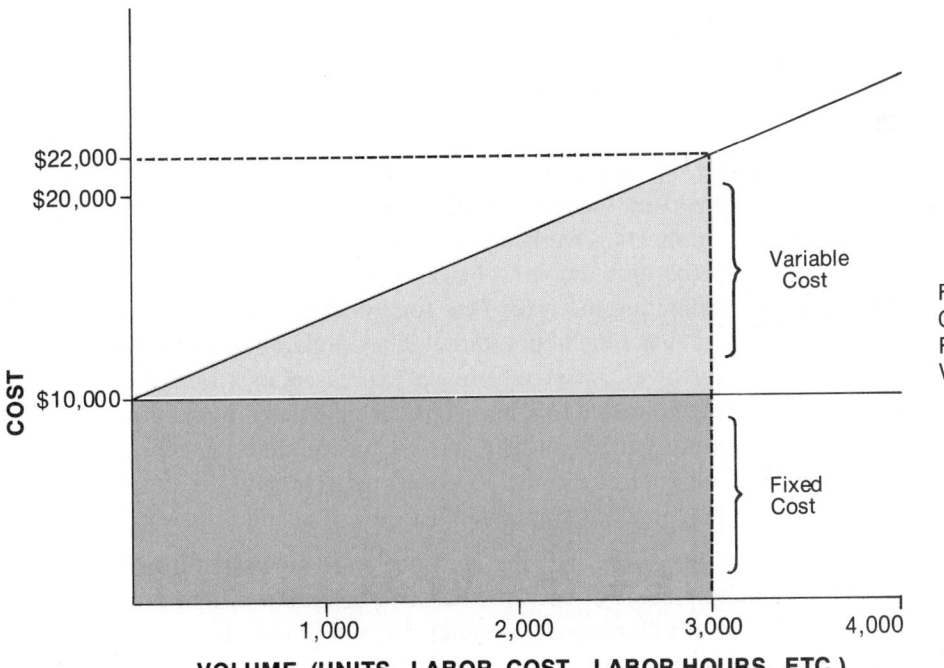

Fixed-Variable Cost Relationship to Volume

FACTORY OVERHEAD — PREDETERMINED

A predetermined overhead rate provides the only feasible method of computing product overhead costs promptly enough to serve management needs, identify inefficiencies, and smooth out uncontrollable and somewhat illogical month-to-month fluctuations in unit costs. For example, the various overhead expenses must be charged to all work done during any period. How can such a charge be made? It is possible to allocate actual overhead to all work completed during the month, using a base such as actual direct labor dollars, direct labor hours, machine hours, or some other base. As long as the volume of work completed each month is the same, and costs are within control limits, this method might be accurate. As variations occur, work completed during different months would receive a greater or a smaller charge — an inequitable situation.

For example, costing problems would result if actual costs incurred for repairs and maintenance were charged directly to a job or product. It is unreasonable to charge them to work in process during the month when repairs are made. Ordinarily, repairs are necessary because of wear and tear over a much longer period than one month and are made to permit continuous operations in any month. Since overhead cost needs to be assigned promptly to production and inefficiencies need to be identified, factory overhead is usually charged to work done on an estimated basis. However, the use of estimates can cause certain difficulties because underlying data are the result of opinions and judgments. Consequently, estimates must be the outcome of careful studies.

The Use of a Predetermined Factory Overhead Rate

Predetermined factory overhead rates are used for both job order and process cost accumulation procedures.

Job Order Costing. Actual costs of direct materials and direct labor used on a job are determined from materials requisitions and time cards and are entered on job order cost sheets. Overhead costs have been predetermined from cost data to arrive at the total amount of overhead estimated for the activity level to be used in computing the rate. This total cost is then related to estimated direct labor hours, machine hours, direct labor dollars, or some other base for the same activity level, ultimately to be expressed in a rate. For example, factory overhead applicable to a job would be calculated by multiplying actual direct labor hours incurred on the job by the predetermined rate, and the amount would be entered on the job order cost sheet. The cost of a job is known at the time the job is completed.

Process Costing. In process costing, unit costs are computed by dividing total weekly or monthly costs of each process by the output of that process. While process costing could produce product costs without the use of overhead rates, predetermined overhead rates are recommended, since they speed up unit product cost calculations and offer other distinct advantages when cost or production levels are subject to wide fluctuations. The use of overhead rates for process costing is similar to that for job order costing.

The types of overhead rates used differ not only from company to company but also from one department, cost center, or cost pool to another within the same company. The type, significance, and use of factory overhead items must be considered when deciding upon applicable rates. At least five main factors influence the selection of overhead rates:

Factors To Be Considered in Selection of Overhead Rates

FACTORS INFLUENCING SELECTION OF OVERHEAD RATES

I. Base to be used
   a. Physical output
   b. Direct materials cost
   c. Direct labor cost
   d. Direct labor hours
   e. Machine hours

II. Activity level selection
   a. Normal capacity
   b. Expected actual capacity

III. Including or excluding of fixed overhead
   a. Absorption costing
   b. Direct costing

IV. Use of a single rate or several rates
   a. Plant-wide or blanket rate
   b. Departmental rates
   c. Cost center or cost pool rates

V. Use of separate rates for service activities

Base To Be Used. The primary objective in selecting a base is to insure the application of factory overhead in a reasonable proportion to the beneficial or causal relationship to jobs, products, or work performed. Ordinarily, the base selected should be closely related to functions represented by the overhead cost being applied. If, for example, factory overhead is predominantly labor oriented, such as supervision and indirect labor, the proper base is probably direct labor cost or direct labor hours. If overhead items are predominantly investment oriented, related to the ownership and operation of machinery, then a machine-hour basis is probably most appropriate. If overhead is mainly materials-oriented overhead, such as costs associated with the purchasing and handling of materials, then the materials cost might be considered as the base.

A secondary objective in selecting a base is to minimize clerical cost and effort. When two or more bases provide approximately the same applied overhead cost to specific units of production, the simplest base should be used. Although the cost of administering the various methods differs from one company to another, the direct labor cost basis or the direct materials cost basis seems to cause the least clerical effort and cost. The labor and machine hour bases generally require additional clerical work and expense.

Factory overhead rates are stated as percentages or as an amount per hour, unit, pound, product, etc. The following bases are used for applying factory overhead: (1) physical output, such as number of units, weight, or volume of the output, (2) direct materials cost, (3) direct labor cost, (4) direct labor hours, and (5) machine hours.

Physical Output. The *physical output* or *units of production* basis, the simplest and most direct method of applying factory overhead, is computed as follows:

$$\frac{\text{Estimated factory overhead}}{\text{Estimated units of production}} = \text{Factory overhead per unit}$$

If the estimated expense is $300,000 and the company intends to produce 250,000 units during the next period, each completed unit would be charged with $1.20 ($300,000 ÷ 250,000 units) as its share of factory overhead. An order with 1,000 completed units would be charged with $1,200 (1,000 units × $1.20) of factory overhead.

The physical output basis is satisfactory when a company manufactures only one product; otherwise, the method is either unsatisfactory or subject to arbitrary allocation procedures. However, if the several products manufactured are alike or closely related, their difference being merely one of weight or volume, application of factory overhead can be made on a weight, volume, or point basis. The weight basis applies overhead according to the weight of each unit of product, as illustrated below:

	PRODUCT		
	A	*B*	*C*
Estimated number of units manufactured .	20,000	15,000	20,000
Unit weight of product	5 lbs.	2 lbs.	1 lb.
Estimated total weight produced	100,000 lbs.	30,000 lbs.	20,000 lbs.
Estimated factory overhead per pound ($300,000 ÷ 150,000)........................	$2	$2	$2
Estimated factory overhead for each product	$200,000	$60,000	$40,000
Estimated factory overhead per unit	$10	$4	$2

If the weight or volume basis does not seem to yield a just apportionment of overhead, the method can be improved by assigning a certain number of points to each unit to compensate for differences. For example, a company manufacturing Products L, S, M, and F computes an overhead rate per product as follows:

PRODUCT	ESTIMATED QUANTITY	POINTS ASSIGNED	ESTIMATED TOTAL POINTS	ESTIMATED FACTORY OVERHEAD PER POINT	ESTIMATED FACTORY OVERHEAD FOR EACH PRODUCT	ESTIMATED FACTORY OVERHEAD COST PER UNIT
L	2,000	5	10,000	$3	$ 30,000	$15
S	5,000	10	50,000	3	150,000	30
M	3,000	8	24,000	3	72,000	24
F	4,000	4	16,000	3	48,000	12
			100,000		$300,000	

If products are different in any respect, such as time to produce or method of production not considered in the allocation basis, a uniform charge based on physical output may result in incorrect costing. Other methods must be adopted in such instances.

Direct Materials Cost Basis. In some companies, a study of past costs will reveal a correlation between direct materials cost and factory overhead. The study might show that factory overhead has remained approximately the same percentage of direct materials cost. Therefore, a rate based on materials cost might be applicable. In such instances, the charge is computed by dividing total estimated factory overhead by total direct materials cost expected to be used in the manufacturing processes:

$$\frac{\text{Estimated factory overhead}}{\text{Estimated materials cost}} \times 100 = \frac{\text{Percentage of overhead}}{\text{per direct materials cost}}$$

If the estimated expense is $300,000 and the estimated materials cost is $250,000, each job or product completed would be charged with an additional 120 percent [($300,000 ÷ $250,000) × 100] of its materials cost as its share of factory overhead. For example, if the materials cost of an order is $5,000, the order would receive an additional charge of $6,000 ($5,000 × 120%) for factory overhead.

The materials-related cost basis has only limited use, because in most cases no logical relationship exists between the direct materials cost of a product and factory overhead used in its production. One product might be made from high-priced materials, another from less expensive materials; yet, both products might require the same manufacturing process and thus incur approximately the same amount of factory overhead. If the materials cost basis is used to charge overhead, the product using expensive materials will, in this case, be charged with more than its share. To overcome this unfairness, two overhead rates might be calculated: one for items that are materials oriented, such as purchasing, receiving, inspecting, handling, and storage costs; the other for the remaining overhead costs.

The CASB advocates in its "Indirect Cost Allocation" proposal the allocation of overhead based on prime cost or total direct cost. A prime cost base (direct labor and direct materials costs) or a total direct cost base (direct labor, direct materials, and other direct costs) may be used if the constituent elements of the prime cost or the total direct cost are in about the same proportions among the cost objectives.

Direct Labor Cost Basis. The direct labor cost basis seems to be the most widely used method of applying overhead to jobs or products. Estimated factory overhead is divided by estimated direct labor cost to compute a percentage:

$$\frac{\text{Estimated factory overhead}}{\text{Estimated direct labor cost}} \times 100 = \text{Percentage of direct labor cost}$$

If estimated factory overhead is $300,000 and total direct labor cost for the next period is also estimated at $300,000, the overhead rate would be 100 percent [($300,000 ÷ $300,000) × 100]. A job or product with a direct labor cost of $3,000 would be charged with $3,000 ($3,000 × 100%) for factory overhead.

Analysis of this method of applying factory overhead indicates a step in the direction of charging overhead equitably to products manufactured. Factory overhead items that are used over a period of time must be taken into consideration. The direct labor cost basis does so, since the labor cost is computed by multiplying the number of work-hours by an hourly wage rate; the more hours worked, the higher the labor cost, the greater the use of time-related items, and the greater the charge for factory overhead.

The direct labor cost basis is relatively easy to use, since information needed to apply overhead is readily available. Its use is particularly favored when (1) a direct relationship between direct labor cost and factory overhead exists and (2) the rates of pay per hour for similar work are comparable. The weekly payroll provides the direct labor cost without any additional record keeping. As long as economy in securing underlying information remains a main prerequisite, the direct labor cost basis can be accepted as the best and quickest of the available methods of applying factory overhead.

On the other hand, this method can be objected to for two reasons:

1. Factory overhead must be looked upon as adding to the value of a job or product. The added value often comes about through depreciation charges of high-cost machinery, which might not bear any relationship to direct labor payroll.
2. Total direct labor cost represents the sum of wages paid to high- and low-wage production workers. By applying overhead on the basis of direct labor cost, a job or product is charged with more overhead when a high-wage operator performs work. Such a method can lead to incorrect distribution of factory overhead particularly when numerous operators, with different hourly rates in the same department, perform similar operations on different jobs or products.

The direct labor hour basis is designed to overcome the latter disadvantage.

Direct Labor Hour Basis. Computation of this rate is:

$$\frac{\text{Estimated factory overhead}}{\text{Estimated direct labor hours}} = \text{Rate per direct labor hour}$$

If estimated factory overhead is $300,000 and total direct labor hours are estimated to be 200,000 hours, an overhead rate based on direct labor hours would be $1.50 per hour of direct labor ($300,000 ÷ 200,000 hours). A job that required 400 direct labor hours would be charged with $600 (400 hours × $1.50) for factory overhead.

The use of this method requires accumulation of direct labor hours by job or product. Timekeeping forms and records must be organized to provide the additional data. The use of the direct labor hour basis requires first a direct relationship between direct labor hours and factory overhead and, second, different rates of pay per hour for similar work, caused by seniority rather than increased output. As long as labor operations are the chief factor in production processes, the direct labor hour method is acceptable as the most equitable basis for applying overhead. However, if shop or factory departments use machines extensively, the direct labor hour method might lead to an inaccurate costing. This disadvantage is overcome through the use of the machine hour method.

Machine Hour Basis. This method is based on time required to perform identical operations by a machine or group of machines. Machine hours expected to be used are estimated and a machine hour rate determined as follows:

$$\frac{\text{Estimated factory overhead}}{\text{Estimated machine hours}} = \text{Rate per machine hour}$$

If factory overhead is estimated to be $300,000 and assuming that 300,000 machine hours will be used, the rate is $1 per machine hour ($300,000 ÷ 300,000 machine hours). Work that required 120 machine hours would be charged with $120 (120 hours × $1) for factory overhead.

This method requires additional clerical work. A reporting system must be designed to assure correct accumulation of all required data for proper overhead accounting. Generally, shop personnel, supervisors, or timekeepers collect machine hour data needed to charge overhead to jobs, products, or work performed. The machine hour method is considered the most accurate method of applying overhead if the overhead cost is comprised predominantly of facility-related costs, such as depreciation, maintenance, and utilities.

Factory overhead rates are also used for estimating purposes. When materials and labor costs have been estimated, knowledge of the overhead distribution base quantity needed can be translated easily and efficiently into a factory overhead cost to arrive at total estimated cost. Selection of the correct basis for applying overhead is of utmost importance if a cost system is to provide proper and accurate costs and if management is to receive meaningful and valuable data.

Activity Level Selection. In calculating an overhead rate, a great deal depends on the activity level selected. The greater the assumed activity, the lower the fixed portion of the overhead rate, because fixed overhead will be spread over a greater number of direct labor dollars, hours, etc. The variable portion of the rate will tend to remain constant at various activity levels. Determination of estimates used in deriving a factory overhead rate depends on whether a long- or a short-range viewpoint is adopted, i.e., whether the activity level used is normal capacity, expected actual capacity, or some other capacity level (Chapter 18).

Normal Capacity. The long-range or long-term planning and control approach, the *normal capacity concept*, advocates an overhead rate in which expenses and production are based on average utilization of the physical plant over a time period long enough to level out the highs and lows that occur in every business venture. A rate based on normal capacity should not change sporadically because of changes in actual production; therefore, a more useful unit cost results. The rate will be changed when prices of certain expense items change or when fixed costs increase or decrease. A normal capacity rate concept assumes that the rate should not be changed because existing plant facilities are used to a greater or lesser degree. A job or product should not cost more to produce in any one accounting period just because production was lower and fixed charges were spread over a fewer number of units. The calculation of a normal capacity rate follows procedures described above. Factory overhead and bases used are estimated in terms of normal production figures.

In most instances, the use of a normal rate causes applied expenses to differ from actual expenses incurred. The possibility of such a difference or variance must be recognized but should not serve to discourage the use of an overhead rate nor encourage the change of this rate. In fact, when this variance, generally called over- or underapplied factory overhead, is further analyzed, it reveals useful management information (pages 219–226).

Expected Actual Capacity. The short-range or short-term planning and control approach, the *expected actual capacity* concept, advocates a rate in which overhead and production are based on the expected actual output for the next production period. This method usually results in the use of a different predetermined rate for each period, depending on increases or decreases in estimated factory overhead and production figures. The use of a predetermined rate based on expected actual production is often due to the difficulty of judging current performance on a long-range or normal capacity level. The fact that at times the factory overhead charged to production approaches the expense actually incurred often makes the use of the expected actual factory overhead rate seem logical and acceptable even though the expense is not representative of normal operations.

The following example of product costing uses overhead rates based on both activity levels. Assume that the normal capacity for a company is 150,000 direct labor hours. For the past year, the actual capacity attained was 116,000 hours. The management believes that 120,000 hours will be worked during the coming year. The fixed expense for either capacity level is $120,000, and the variable expense is $.50 per direct labor hour.

The predetermined factory overhead rate based on normal capacity is $1.30 per direct labor hour, and the overhead rate based on expected actual capacity is $1.50 per direct labor hour, calculated as shown on page 213. The difference in the two rates lies in the fixed overhead rate. The expected actual capacity method increases the rate by $.20 per hour, resulting in a greater product cost than with the normal capacity rate. Since fixed expenses are the same for both levels, it must be assumed that management anticipated a volume of business requiring such an amount of fixed cost. It is executive man-

	NORMAL CAPACITY	EXPECTED ACTUAL CAPACITY
Fixed expense	$120,000	$120,000
Variable expense:		
150,000 hours × $.50.................	75,000	
120,000 hours × .50.................		60,000
Total estimated overhead..............	$195,000	$180,000
Estimated direct labor hours..........	150,000	120,000
Factory overhead rate per hour......	$1.30	$1.50
Fixed overhead rate per hour........	$ .80	$1.00

agement's task to reach that level of operation which will assure a profitable and competitive position.

Including or Excluding of Fixed Overhead Items. Ordinarily, cost accounting procedures apply all factory costs to the output of a period. Under these procedures, called *absorption costing*, *conventional costing*, or *full costing*, both fixed and variable expenses are included in overhead rates. Another method of costing, termed *direct costing*, is sometimes used, chiefly for internal management purposes. Under this method of costing, only variable overhead is included in overhead rates. The fixed expense does not become a product cost but is treated as a period cost, meaning that it is charged off in total each period as is the marketing and administrative expense. It is not included in either work in process or finished goods inventories.

Absorption and direct costing are the results of two entirely different cost concepts with respect to product cost, period cost, gross profit, and operating income. The two methods result in different inventory costs and different period profits. Direct costing is discussed in detail in Chapter 22.

Each of the various bases discussed for applying overhead may be used with absorption or direct costing, with rates based on normal or expected actual capacity.

Of the five main factors influencing the selection of overhead rates outlined at the beginning of this section, two have not been discussed, namely, the use of a single factory rate or individual, departmental rates and the use of separate rates for service activities. These methods are discussed in the next two chapters.

Calculating a factory overhead rate involves estimating the activity level and classifying expenses.

The Calculation of a Factory Overhead Rate

Estimating the Activity Level and Expenses. The first step in calculating the overhead rate is to determine the activity level to be used for the base selected and then estimate or budget each individual expense at the estimated activity level in order to arrive at the total estimated factory overhead.

The following list shows the estimated factory overhead for De Witt Products for a normal capacity level estimated at 200,000 direct labor hours.

De Witt Products
Estimated Factory Overhead For 19—

EXPENSE	AMOUNT
Supervisors	$ 70,000
Indirect labor	75,000
Overtime premium	9,000
Factory supplies	23,000
Repairs and maintenance	12,000
Electric power	20,000
Fuel	6,000
Water	1,000
FICA tax	18,000
Unemployment taxes	5,000
Workmen's compensation	3,000
Hospitalization insurance	2,000
Pensions	15,000
Vacations and holidays	12,000
Group insurance	4,000
Depreciation — building	5,000
Depreciation — equipment	13,000
Property tax	4,000
Insurance (fire)	3,000
Total estimated factory overhead	$300,000

Classifying Expenses as Fixed or Variable. The classification of expenses according to changes in volume attempts to establish a variability pattern for each expense item. This classification must, in turn, consider certain specific assumptions regarding plant facilities, prices, managerial policy, and the state of technology. Once the classification has been decided upon, the expense may remain in this category for a limited period of time. Should underlying conditions change, the original classification must be reviewed and expenses reclassified as necessary.

Variable expenses change with production volume and are considered a function of volume; that is, the amount of variable expense per unit is constant. Fixed expenses, on the other hand, are just the opposite. The total amount is fixed, but the expense per unit is different for each production level. Increased production causes a decrease in fixed expense per unit. Knowledge of the effect of fixed and variable expenses on the product unit cost is highly important in any study of factory overhead. A knowledge of the behavior of all costs is fundamental to the planning and analytical processes for decision-making purposes.

An examination of fixed and variable expenses indicates the difficulty of segregating all expenses as either fixed or variable. Some expenses are partly fixed and partly variable; some are fixed to a certain production level and then increase as production increases. Also, costs may change in step-like fashion at various production levels. Such expenses are classified as semivariable.

Because expenses are to be classified as either fixed or variable, the fixed portion of any semivariable expense and the degree of change in the variable part must be determined. Several methods are available to aid in finding the constant portion and the degree of variability in the variable portion. These procedures determine the relationship between increases in production and increases in total and individual expenses. For example, when production is expected to increase 10 percent, it is possible to determine the corresponding increase in total expense as well as the increase in individual expenses such as supplies, power, or indirect labor. A detailed illustration and discussion of such procedures are presented in Chapter 18.

The expenses for De Witt Products total $300,000. In the illustration below, these expenses are classified as either fixed or variable.

De Witt Products
Estimated Factory Overhead For 19--

EXPENSE	FIXED	VARIABLE	TOTAL
Supervisors	$ 70,000		$ 70,000
Indirect labor	9,000	$ 66,000	75,000
Overtime premium		9,000	9,000
Factory supplies	4,000	19,000	23,000
Repairs and maintenance	3,000	9,000	12,000
Electric power	2,000	18,000	20,000
Fuel	1,000	5,000	6,000
Water	500	500	1,000
FICA tax	3,000	15,000	18,000
Unemployment taxes	1,500	3,500	5,000
Workmen's compensation	500	2,500	3,000
Hospitalization insurance	500	1,500	2,000
Pensions	2,000	13,000	15,000
Vacations and holidays	2,000	10,000	12,000
Group insurance	1,000	3,000	4,000
Depreciation — building	5,000		5,000
Depreciation — equipment	13,000		13,000
Property tax	4,000		4,000
Insurance (fire)	3,000		3,000
Total estimated factory overhead	$125,000	$175,000	$300,000

Establishing the Factory Overhead Rate. After the activity level for the selected base and the factory overhead have been estimated, the overhead rates can be computed. Assuming that the direct labor hour base is used and direct labor hours for the coming year are estimated to be 200,000 (normal capacity level), the factory overhead rate at this selected activity level would be:

$$\text{Factory overhead rate} = \frac{\text{Estimated factory overhead}}{\text{Estimated direct labor hours}} = \frac{\$300,000}{200,000} = \frac{\$1.50 \text{ per}}{\text{direct labor hour}}$$

This rate should be used to charge overhead to jobs, products, or work performed. Amounts applied are first entered in subsidiary ledgers such as job order cost sheets and cost of production reports. Direct labor hours, direct labor cost, or other similar data already recorded determine the amount of overhead chargeable to each job or product.

The factory overhead rate can be further broken down into its fixed and variable components:

$$\frac{\$125,000 \text{ Estimated fixed factory overhead}}{200,000 \text{ Estimated direct labor hours}} = \$ .625 \text{ Fixed portion of the factory overhead rate}$$

$$\frac{\$175,000 \text{ Estimated variable factory overhead}}{200,000 \text{ Estimated direct labor hours}} = \$ .875 \text{ Variable portion of the factory overhead rate}$$

$$\text{Total factory overhead rate} = \underline{\underline{\$1.500}} \text{ per direct labor hour}$$

FACTORY OVERHEAD — ACTUAL

Deciding upon the base and activity level to be utilized, estimating the factory overhead, and calculating the overhead rate take place prior to the incurrence or recording of the actual expenses. Factory overhead is applied as soon as the necessary data, in this case direct labor hours, have been made available. Each day, however, as actual overhead items are purchased, requisitioned, or used, the actual transactions are recorded in general and subsidiary ledgers independent of the application of factory overhead based on the predetermined overhead rate.

Accumulation of Actual Factory Overhead for Control

Factory overhead includes numerous items which can be classified in many different ways. Every firm, because of its own manufacturing peculiarities, will devise its own particular accounts and methods of classifying them. However, regardless of these possible variations, expenses are usually summarized in a factory overhead control account kept in the general ledger. Details of this general ledger account are kept in a subsidiary overhead ledger. This subsidiary ledger also can take many forms, and it may be difficult to recognize it as such, particularly when electronic data processing equipment is used. A subsidiary ledger will group various expense items together under significant selective titles as to kinds of expenses and will also detail the expenses chargeable to individual producing and service departments, thereby permitting stricter control over factory overhead.

The accumulation of factory overhead in accounting records presents several distinct problems. Due to the many varied potential requests and uses of factory overhead data for managerial decision-making purposes, it is almost impossible to set up an all-purpose system for accumulating factory overhead.

A basic objective for accumulating factory overhead is the gathering of information for purposes of control. Control, in turn, requires (1) reporting costs to the individual department heads responsible for them and (2) making comparisons with amounts budgeted for the level of operations achieved. The mechanics for collecting overhead items are based on the chart of accounts, which indicates the accounts to which various factory overhead items are to be charged.

Overhead items are ultimately identified with specific producing departments. At the end of the month or year, applied factory overhead and actual factory overhead are analyzed. The comparison between actual and applied figures might lead to computation of the spending and the idle capacity variances (pages 221–223).

Factory overhead accounts are kept in a subsidiary ledger, often utilizing punched cards, tapes, or magnetic disks. The company's chart of accounts will define the accounts to be used. The overhead accounts shown below comprise a partial list of accounts used:

Steps in Accounting for Actual Factory Overhead

Supervisors' Salaries	Workmen's Compensation
Indirect Labor	Hospitalization Insurance
Overtime Premium	Pensions
Factory Supplies	Vacations and Holidays
Repairs and Maintenance	Group Insurance
Electric Power	Depreciation — Building
Fuel	Depreciation — Equipment
Water	Property Tax
FICA Tax	Insurance (fire)
Unemployment Taxes	

Each of the above expenses may be departmentalized, as discussed in the next chapter.

The steps involved in accounting for factory overhead transactions are:

1. Analysis.
2. Journalizing.
3. Posting to the factory overhead subsidiary ledger and the factory overhead general ledger control account.

Principal Original Records

Some overhead items are vouchered and paid for during the month; others are the result of current journal entries for factory supplies and indirect labor used; still others are adjustments made at the end of a fiscal period. The principal source documents used for recording overhead in the journals are (1) purchase vouchers, (2) materials requisitions, (3) labor time tickets, and (4) general journal vouchers.

Underlying source documents provide a record of the overhead information which must be analyzed and accumulated in proper accounts. To obtain accurate and useful information, each transaction must be properly classified at its inception. Those responsible for this identification must be thoroughly familiar with names and code numbers of cost accounts as well as with the purpose and function of each account.

Purchase Vouchers. Factory overhead items recorded on purchase vouchers are supported by vendors' invoices, which are analyzed and classified in accordance with the chart of accounts. The specific account charged is indicated by an account number.

Materials Requisitions. Materials requisitions contain all charges for indirect materials and supply items drawn from storerooms. Requisitions specify the account, code number, and department to which the cost is to be charged. Accounts affected by transactions involving materials requisitions are Indirect Materials, Factory Supplies, Fuel, Lubricants, Maintenance Supplies, and Miscellaneous Operating Supplies.

Labor Time Tickets. Labor time tickets are used for indirect labor. Supervisors, timekeepers, or the shop personnel themselves enter pertinent data on the time tickets so that proper factory overhead accounts can be charged. The data to be included are the indirect labor operational code, the worker's name and code number, and the department to which indirect labor is to be charged.

General Journal Vouchers. A general journal voucher is used for making entries in the general journal. Journal entries are principally used for end-of-month adjustments. Typical overhead items involved in such transactions are depreciation, fire insurance, and property tax.

Books of Original Entry

The books of original entry used to accumulate factory overhead costs are (1) the accounts payable register and/or the cash payments journal, (2) the general journal, and (3) the factory journal. The format for the books of original entry depends on the basic plan for accumulation of factory overhead items in the accounts.

Accounts Payable Register and/or Cash Payments Journal. Transactions with outsiders are usually recorded in the accounts payable register and/or cash payments journal. Items are journalized from prepared vouchers based on the original source documents, discussed in Chapter 4.

General Journal. Factory overhead transactions are also accumulated in the general journal with perhaps a special column for factory overhead. To avoid the recording of too many items in a general journal, special journals, such as materials requisitioned and payroll journals, are used.

Factory Journal. The factory journal facilitates the posting process when cost accounts are kept in a separate ledger rather than in the general ledger. In such instances, all cost transactions involving factory cost accounts are entered in the factory journal using factory journal vouchers. The factory journal is posted to the factory ledger. To avoid duplication and to provide self-balancing, reciprocal accounts are used. Use of the reciprocal accounts was described in Chapter 4.

Factory Overhead Control Account

Overhead accounts are kept in the general ledger only when accounts are not too numerous; otherwise, the system becomes unwieldy. Because the number of expense accounts is ordinarily quite large, it is customary to have a factory overhead control account in the general ledger and the individual overhead accounts in a factory overhead subsidiary ledger. The relationship between the factory overhead control account and its subsidiary ledger is the same as that between the accounts receivable control account and its subsidiary ledger.

When all postings have been made to the factory overhead control account from the various journals, the debit side represents total actual factory overhead incurred during the period. The credit side of the account represents the overhead applied during the period. The illustration below indicates that actual factory overhead for the period was $292,000. (The total of the factory overhead subsidiary ledger equals the amount of the debit to Factory Overhead Control.) Applied factory overhead was $285,000, based on 190,000 actual direct labor hours worked during the period (capacity utilized) and a predetermined factory overhead rate of $1.50 per direct labor hour.

FACTORY OVERHEAD CONTROL

| Dec. 31 | 292,000 | Dec. 31 (190,000 × $1.50) | 285,000 |

TOTAL ACTUAL OVERHEAD
INCURRED DURING PERIOD

OVERHEAD *APPLIED*
DURING PERIOD

FACTORY OVERHEAD — APPLIED, OVER- OR UNDERAPPLIED, AND VARIANCE ANALYSIS

This section presents the mechanics of applying factory overhead, discusses the meaning of the difference between the debits and the credits in the factory overhead control account, and analyzes the difference to determine the spending and idle capacity variances.

The job order cost sheets or the departmental cost of production reports receive postings as soon as direct materials or direct labor data become available. Factory overhead is applied to the work done after the direct materials and the direct labor costs have been recorded. If direct labor hours or machine hours are the basis for overhead charges, these data must also be available to the cost department. A special section of a job order cost sheet used for factory overhead is shown below. This is a reproduction of part of the illustration on page 95.

The Mechanics of Applying Factory Overhead

APPLIED FACTORY OVERHEAD					
DATE	DEPARTMENT	BASIS OF APPLICATION	HOURS	RATE	COST
11/15	Cutting	$3 per direct labor hour	20	$3.00	$ 60.00
11/15	Planing	$4 per direct labor hour	50	4.00	200.00
11/22	Assembly	$2 per direct labor hour	100	2.00	200.00
11/29	Upholstery	100% of direct labor cost	--	--	1,200.00
		Total Applied Factory Overhead			$ 1,660.00

Section of Job Order Cost Sheet Showing Applied Factory Overhead

The journal entry for summarizing factory overhead charges to job order cost sheets or departmental cost of production reports is:

Work in Process 285,000
    Applied Factory Overhead 285,000

Charges made to subsidiary records (the job order cost sheets or departmental cost of production reports) list in detail applied factory overhead charged to jobs or process costing departments. The debit to the work in process control account brings total applied overhead into the general ledger or into the factory ledger if factory cost accounts are kept there. The applied factory overhead account is subsequently closed to the factory overhead control account by the following entry:

Applied Factory Overhead 285,000
    Factory Overhead Control 285,000

It is common practice to use an applied factory overhead account because it keeps applied costs and actual costs in separate accounts. However, some companies post the credit directly to Factory Overhead Control.

Debits to the factory overhead control account are for actual expenses incurred during the period, while credits are for applied expenses. There may also be credit adjustments (e.g., the return of supplies to the storeroom) which reduce total actual factory overhead. Since the debits and credits are seldom equal, there is usually a debit or credit balance in the account. A debit balance indicates that overhead has been underapplied; a credit balance means that overhead has been overapplied. These over- or underapplied balances must be analyzed carefully, because they are the source of much information needed by management for controlling and judging the efficiency of operations and the use of available capacity during a particular period.

Overapplied and Under-applied Factory Overhead

In the factory overhead control account on page 219, actual factory overhead incurred during the period is $7,000 more than total applied factory overhead. Therefore, factory overhead for the period was $7,000 underapplied. If applied overhead had exceeded actual overhead, overhead would have been overapplied. In either case, the difference must be analyzed to determine the reason or reasons for the over- or underapplied factory overhead. Two separate variances are computed in making the analysis:

1. *Spending variance* — a variance due to budget or expense factors.
2. *Idle capacity variance* — a variance due to volume or activity factors.

Variance Analysis

The analysis can be made in the following manner, using the factory overhead rates given on pages 215 and 216:

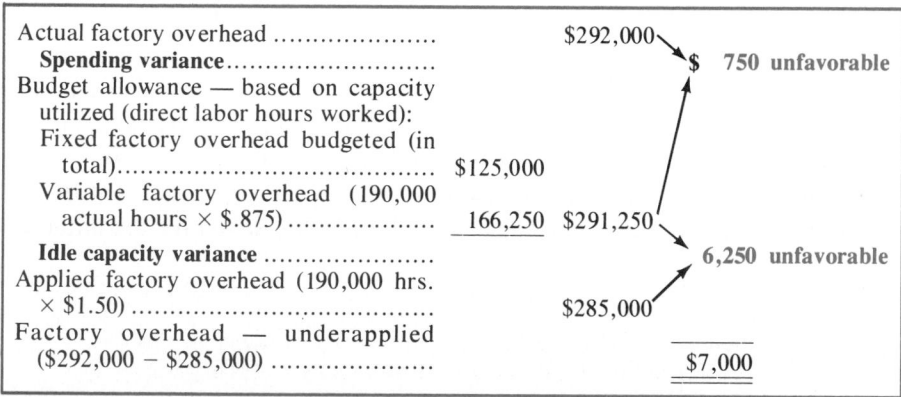

The analysis can also be made in columnar form as follows:

(1) ACTUAL FACTORY OVERHEAD	(2) BUDGET ALLOWANCE (BASED ON CAPACITY UTILIZED)		(3) APPLIED FACTORY OVERHEAD	(1–3) TOTAL OVERHEAD VARIANCE	(1–2) SPENDING VARIANCE	(2–3) IDLE CAPACITY VARIANCE
$292,000	Fixed	$125,000	$285,000**	$7,000	$750	$6,250***
	Variable	166,250*			Unfavorable	Unfavorable
	Total	$291,250				

*190,000 direct labor hours × variable overhead rate of $.875 per direct labor hour.
**190,000 direct labor hours × total overhead rate of $1.50 per direct labor hour.
***Proof: 10,000 idle hours × fixed overhead rate of $.625 per direct labor hour.

Spending Variance. The $750 spending variance is the difference between the actual factory overhead incurred and the budget allowance estimated for the capacity utilized, i.e., for the actual activity of 190,000 direct labor hours worked. The spending variance can also be computed as follows:

Actual factory overhead incurred during the period......................	$292,000
Less budgeted fixed overhead..	125,000
Actual variable expense incurred during the period......................	$167,000
Variable overhead applied during the period (190,000 hours × $.875)...	166,250
Spending variance — unfavorable	$ 750

If actual overhead had been less than budgeted, the spending variance would have been favorable. Any difference between actual and budgeted fixed overhead would be included as part of the spending variance.

A breakdown of the $750 spending variance, as well as a comparison of each actual expense with its budgeted figure, is useful. Details of the actual expenses are recorded in the factory overhead subsidiary ledger. Comparison of actual with budgeted overhead for capacity worked (190,000 direct labor hours) is illustrated on page 222.

The budgeted figures utilize the concept of the flexible budget discussed in Chapter 18. Basically, the budget figures represent the budget for the level of activity attained. For example, from the estimates for indirect labor on page 215, fixed overhead is $9,000; and the variable part of the overhead cost is $.33 per hour ($66,000 estimated variable indirect labor ÷ 200,000 estimated direct labor hours). The budgeted indirect labor for the activity level attained is $9,000 plus $62,700 (190,000 direct labor hours × $.33), or $71,700.

Some of the actual expenses exceed while others are less than the budgeted figures. Each difference must be analyzed, the reason for the difference

De Witt Products
Comparison of Actual and Budgeted Factory Overhead for 19——
(Capacity Utilized: 190,000 Direct Labor Hours = 95% of Normal)

	BUDGETED	ACTUAL	OVER	UNDER
Variable overhead:				
Indirect labor	$ 62,700	$ 63,550	$ 850	—
Overtime premium	8,550	8,700	150	—
Factory supplies	18,050	18,720	670	—
Repairs and maintenance	8,550	7,200	—	$1,350
Electric power	17,100	17,650	550	—
Fuel	4,750	4,300	—	450
Water	475	500	25	—
FICA tax	14,250	14,450	200	—
Unemployment taxes	3,325	3,425	100	—
Workmen's compensation	2,375	2,400	25	—
Hospitalization insurance	1,425	1,435	10	—
Pensions	12,350	12,550	200	—
Vacations and holidays	9,500	9,300	—	200
Group insurance	2,850	2,820	—	30
Total	$166,250	$167,000	$2,780	$2,030
Fixed overhead:				
Supervisors	$ 70,000	$ 70,000	—	—
Indirect labor	9,000	9,000	—	—
Factory supplies	4,000	4,000	—	—
Repairs and maintenance	3,000	3,000	—	—
Electric power	2,000	2,000	—	—
Fuel	1,000	1,000	—	—
Water	500	500	—	—
FICA tax	3,000	3,000	—	—
Unemployment taxes	1,500	1,500	—	—
Workmen's compensation	500	500	—	—
Hospitalization insurance	500	500	—	—
Pensions	2,000	2,000	—	—
Vacations and holidays	2,000	2,000	—	—
Group insurance	1,000	1,000	—	—
Depreciation — building	5,000	5,000	—	—
Depreciation — equipment	13,000	13,000	—	—
Property tax	4,000	4,000	—	—
Insurance (fire)	3,000	3,000	—	—
Total	$125,000	$125,000	—	—
Total overhead	$291,250	$292,000	$2,780	$2,030
Spending variance — unfavorable			$ 750	

must be determined, and discussion must be initiated with the individual responsible for its incurrence. Corrective action should be taken where called for; likewise, effective and efficient performance should be recognized and rewarded. Observe that even underexpenditures may be undesirable. For example, the $1,350 underspent repairs and maintenance amount may suggest insufficient attention to preventive maintenance.

Idle Capacity Variance. The rate used for applying factory overhead is $1.50 per direct labor hour, which is based on 200,000 normal capacity hours. However, direct labor hours worked during the period totaled only 190,000 hours; capacity not used was 10,000 direct labor hours. The capacity attained was 95 percent (190,000 ÷ 200,000) of normal.

The $1.50 overhead rate is considered the proper costing price for each direct labor hour used. The fact that operations were at a level below normal should not increase the factory overhead cost of each unit. The cost of idle capacity should be recorded separately and considered a part of total manufacturing cost. The $6,250 idle capacity variance arises because 10,000 available hours were not used; it is computed as follows:

Budget allowance (based on capacity utilized).....................	$291,250
Applied factory overhead..	285,000
Idle capacity variance — unfavorable	$ 6,250

The idle capacity variance can also be computed by multiplying the 10,000 idle hours by the $.625 fixed expense rate or by multiplying the total budgeted fixed expense of $125,000 by 5 percent (100% − 95%).

Responsibility for the idle capacity variance rests with executive management, inasmuch as this variance indicates the under- or overutilization of plant and equipment. The cause of a capacity variance, whether favorable or unfavorable, should always be determined and possible reasons for the variance discovered. One cause may be a lack of proper balance between production facilities and sales. On the other hand, it might be due to a favorable sales price that recovers fixed overhead at an unusually low volume level.

Disposition of Over- or Underapplied Factory Overhead. Because of its importance, the analysis of the over- or underapplied factory overhead is presented in detail. Disposition of this figure is generally quite simple. Although total over- or underapplied overhead is analyzed, showing spending and idle capacity variances, it need not be journalized and posted in two parts. At the end of the fiscal period, overhead variances may be (1) treated as a period cost or (2) divided between inventories and cost of goods sold.

For financial reporting purposes, the procedure often used for disposing of over- or underapplied overhead is to close it to Cost of Goods Sold or directly to Income Summary, thereby treating the over- or underapplied factory overhead as a period cost. The entries are at the top of page 224.

Cost of Goods Sold... 7,000
    Factory Overhead Control   7,000

or

Income Summary.. 7,000
    Factory Overhead Control   7,000

The over- or underapplied figure is closed to the cost of goods sold account or to the income summary account depending on whether management considers such a variation a manufacturing or a managerial cost. If the variance is closed to the cost of goods sold account, it will appear in the cost of goods sold statement. If it is closed to the income summary account, it will appear in the income statement. The results of both procedures are shown in the statements illustrated on page 225.

Internal Revenue Service regulations require that inventories include an allocated portion of significant annual overhead variances. When the amount involved is not significant in relation to total actual factory overhead, an allocation is not required unless such allocation is made for financial reporting purposes. Also, the taxpayer must treat both over- and underapplied overhead consistently. The regulations, however, do permit expensing of the idle capacity variance.

Regardless of the disposition made of the over- or underapplied figure, the computation, analysis, and reporting of both the spending and idle capacity variances are significant and important. In the disposition of over- or underapplied factory overhead for financial reporting purposes, companies should generally follow the same procedures at interim dates as are followed at year-end. Variances that occur at an interim date and that are expected to be absorbed prior to year-end should be deferred rather than disposed of immediately.[1] Further discussion of disposition of variances is reserved for the standard cost chapter (Chapter 20).

INCORRECT OVERHEAD RATES

An overhead rate may be incorrect because of misjudgments regarding estimated overhead or anticipated activity. A large over- or underapplied overhead figure does not necessarily mean that the overhead rate was wrong. As mentioned, use of a normal overhead rate is purposely designed to show spending variances as well as the extent to which normal capacity is or is not used. Likewise, when an overhead rate based on expected actual conditions is used, seasonal variations may lead to large over- or underabsorbed overhead which will tend to even itself out during a full year. The best way to detect an incorrect overhead rate is to analyze the factors used in its predetermination. Since a rate is an estimate, small errors should be expected, and the rate need not be changed for such errors.

---

[1]*Opinions of the Accounting Principles Board, No. 28*, "Interim Financial Reporting" (New York: American Institute of Certified Public Accountants, 1973), par. 14.

De Witt Products
Income Statement
For Year Ended December 31, 19—

Sales		$1,600,000
Less: Cost of goods sold at normal	$1,195,000	
Underapplied factory overhead	7,000	1,202,000
Gross profit		$ 398,000
Less: Marketing expense	$ 150,000	
Administrative expense	100,000	250,000
Income before income tax		$ 148,000

De Witt Products
Cost of Goods Sold Statement
For Year Ended December 31, 19—

Direct materials used	$ 400,000
Direct labor used	500,000
Applied factory overhead (see Schedule B-1)	285,000
Total manufacturing cost	$1,185,000
Less work in process inventory change	20,000
Cost of goods manufactured at normal	$1,165,000
Plus finished goods inventory change	30,000
Cost of goods sold at normal	$1,195,000
Plus underapplied factory overhead	7,000
Cost of goods sold at actual	$1,202,000

De Witt Products
Schedule B-1
Factory Overhead for 19—

Supervisors	$ 70,000
Indirect labor	72,550
Overtime premium	8,700
Factory supplies	22,720
Repairs and maintenance	10,200
Electric power	19,650
Fuel	5,300
Water	1,000
FICA tax	17,450
Unemployment taxes	4,925
Workmen's compensation	2,900
Hospitalization insurance	1,935
Pensions	14,550
Vacations and holidays	11,300
Group insurance	3,820
Depreciation — buildings	5,000
Depreciation — equipment	13,000
Property tax	4,000
Insurance (fire)	3,000
Total actual factory overhead	$292,000
Less underapplied factory overhead	7,000
Applied factory overhead	$285,000

CHANGING OVERHEAD RATES

Overhead rates are usually reviewed annually. This procedure helps level out costing through the year and ties overhead control in with budget control. If rates are changed during a fiscal or budget period, meaningful comparisons will be difficult. Changes in production methods, prices, efficiencies, and sales expectancy make review and, possibly, revision of overhead rates a necessity at least annually. Revisions should be based on a complete review of all factors involved. The extent to which a company revises its overhead rates depends on frequency of changes, on factors which affect overhead rates, and on management's need and desire for current costs and realistic overhead variance information.

GRAPHIC PRESENTATION OF FACTORY OVERHEAD

This chapter's discussion of estimating, accounting for, and analyzing factory overhead is presented diagrammatically below:

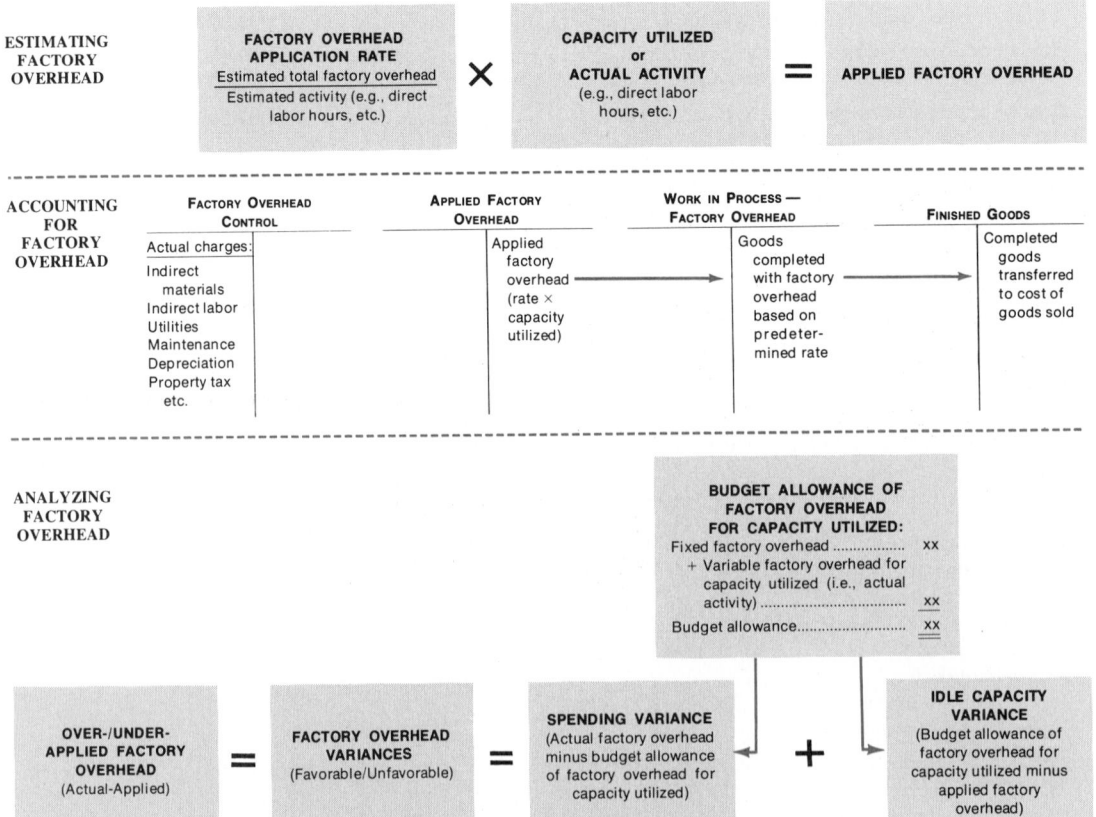

Estimating, Accounting for, and Analyzing Factory Overhead

DISCUSSION QUESTIONS

1. State some of the main expenses that are considered to be factory overhead.

2. Should the wages of an apprentice or trainee be charged to a job or considered as overhead?

3. Factory overhead constitutes a much larger proportion of total manufacturing cost today than in the past, and is expected to continue to do so. Why?

4. Why will a department's factory overhead vary from month to month?

5. When and why must predetermined factory overhead rates be used? Indicate the impracticalities and inaccuracies of charging actual overhead to jobs and products.

6. Should predetermined factory overhead rates be used in process costing? Explain.

7. Name five bases used for applying factory overhead. What factors must be considered in selecting a particular basis?

8. Why is the selection of a proper predetermined rate so essential to accurate costing? Explain.

9. How does the selection of normal or maximum capacity affect operating profit in setting the factory overhead rate?

10. What are the steps involved in accounting for factory overhead?

11. What is the purpose of each of the following items in job order costing? How do they relate to each other?
    (a) Factory overhead control account.
    (b) Job order cost sheet.
    (c) Work in process — factory overhead.
    (d) Applied factory overhead.

12. The factory overhead control account has a credit balance at the end of the period. Was overhead over- or underapplied?

13. Over- or underapplied overhead can be analyzed into two parts called variances. Name these variances, state the reason(s) for their titles, and show their computations.

14. A company's normal capacity is 10,000 units per month. At normal capacity, fixed factory overhead is estimated to be $15,000 and variable factory overhead is estimated to be $35,000. During August, the company produced 7,700 units. What is the idle capacity variance?

15. A company applies factory overhead to production on the basis of direct labor dollars. At the end of the year, factory overhead has been overapplied to the extent of $60,000. Name at least five factors which would cause this situation and explain how the credit balance should be treated.

16. Production for Dietary Beverages shows a pronounced seasonal fluctuation. Should factory overhead variances be shown as adjustments to the cost of goods sold on the company's monthly income statements? If not, what alternative is possible?

17. If large underabsorbed (underapplied) factory overhead variances occur month after month, the factory overhead rate should be revised to make unit costs more accurate. Comment.

18. Select the answer which best completes the statement:
    (a) Overapplied factory overhead will always result when a predetermined factory overhead rate is employed and: (1) production is greater than defined capacity; (2) actual overhead costs are less than expected; (3) defined capacity is less than normal capacity; (4) overhead incurred is less than applied overhead.
    (b) The difference over a period of time between actual factory overhead and applied factory overhead will usually be minimal when the predetermined overhead rate is based on: (1) normal capacity; (2) designed capacity; (3) direct labor hours; (4) machine hours.
    (c) If a predetermined factory overhead rate is not employed and the volume of production is reduced from the level planned, the cost per unit would be expected to: (1) remain unchanged for fixed cost and increase for variable cost; (2) increase for fixed cost and remain unchanged for variable cost; (3) increase for fixed cost and decrease for variable cost; (4) decrease for fixed cost and decrease for variable cost.
    (d) A spending variance for factory overhead is the difference between actual factory overhead cost and factory overhead cost that should have been incurred for the actual hours worked and results from: (1) price differences for factory overhead costs; (2) quantity differences for factory overhead costs; (3) price and quantity differences for factory overhead costs; (4) differences caused by production volume variation.
    (e) Factory overhead should be allocated on the basis of: (1) an activity basis which relates to cost incurrence; (2) direct labor hours; (3) direct labor cost; (4) machine hours.
    (f) If over- or underapplied factory overhead is interpreted as an error in allocating actual costs against the production for the year, this suggests to an accountant that the over- or underapplied factory overhead for the year should be: (1) carried forward in the factory overhead account from year to year; (2) eliminated by changing the predetermined factory overhead rate in subsequent years; (3) apportioned among the work in process inventory, the finished goods inventory, and the cost of goods sold; (4) treated as a special gain or loss occurring during the year.
    (g) Underapplied factory overhead costs are: (1) fixed factory costs not allocated to units produced; (2) factory overhead costs not allocated to units produced; (3) excess variable factory overhead costs; (4) costs that cannot be controlled.
    (h) A company found that the differences in product costs resulting from the application of predetermined factory overhead rates rather than actual factory overhead rates were immaterial even though actual production was substantially less than planned production. The most likely explanation is that: (1) factory overhead was composed chiefly of variable costs; (2) several products were produced simultaneously; (3) fixed factory overhead was a significant cost; (4) costs of factory overhead items were substantially larger than anticipated.
    (i) When a manufacturing company has a highly automated manufacturing plant producing many different products, the most appropriate basis for

applying factory overhead to work in process is: (1) direct labor hours; (2) direct labor dollars; (3) machine hours; (4) cost of materials used.

(j) According to Internal Revenue Service regulations, significant underapplied factory overhead resulting from unanticipated price increases should be disposed of by: (1) decreasing cost of goods sold; (2) increasing cost of goods sold; (3) decreasing cost of goods sold, work in process inventory, and finished goods inventory; (4) increasing cost of goods sold, work in process inventory, and finished goods inventory.

(k) If a company uses a predetermined rate for application of factory overhead, the idle capacity variance is the: (1) over- or underapplied fixed cost element of overhead; (2) over- or underapplied variable cost element of overhead; (3) difference in budgeted costs and actual costs of fixed overhead items; (4) difference in budgeted costs and actual costs of variable overhead items.

(AICPA and CMA adapted)

EXERCISES

1. Factory overhead application. On November 30, the work in process account of the Bee Dee Company showed:

WORK IN PROCESS

Materials	20,800	Finished	
Direct		goods	45,600
labor	20,160		
Factory			
overhead	15,840		

Materials charged to the work still in process amounted to $4,560. Factory overhead is a fixed percentage of direct labor cost.

Required: The individual amounts of factory overhead and direct labor charged to work still in process. (Round off all amounts to four decimal places.)

2. Variance analysis. A company's books indicate that actual factory overhead was $43,296 (123% of the budget allowance based on capacity utilized) and applied factory overhead was $37,350, based on a normal capacity predetermined factory overhead rate. The estimates for fixed and variable factory overhead were $10,500 and $28,500, respectively, based on the levels of activity the company had expected to achieve during the month.

Required: The amount of the spending and idle capacity variances.

3. Calculation of estimated labor hours. The Millan Company employs 150 people who work 8 hours a day, 5 days a week. Normal capacity for the firm is based on the assumption that the equivalent of 47 weeks of work can be expected from an employee.

Required:
(1) The number of direct labor hours to be used in setting up the firm's factory overhead rate based on normal capacity.
(2) The number of direct labor hours if management and workers agree on a 10-hour, 4-day workweek.

4. Various predetermined factory overhead rates. The Carrcroft Company estimates its factory overhead for the next period at $54,000. It is estimated that 36,000 units will be produced at a materials cost of $45,000. Production will require 24,000 direct labor hours at an estimated cost of $120,000. The machines will run about 1,600 hours.

Required: The predetermined factory overhead rate based on:

(1) Materials cost.   (4) Direct labor cost.
(2) Units of production.   (5) Direct labor hours.
(3) Machine hours.

5. Factory overhead application and analysis. Normal capacity of the Duro Company is set at 90,000 direct labor hours. The expected operating level for the period just completed was 72,000 hours. At this expected actual capacity level, the variable expense was estimated to be $54,000 and the fixed expense, $36,000. Actual results show 75,000 hours were worked during the period.

Required:

(1) The predetermined overhead rate based on normal capacity.
(2) The predetermined overhead rate based on expected actual capacity.
(3) The amount of factory overhead applied to production if the company used the normal overhead rate.
(4) The amount of factory overhead applied to production if the company used the expected actual overhead rate.
(5) Variance computations to show whether there would be a favorable idle capacity variance if the normal capacity rate were used.
(6) Variance computations to show whether there would be a favorable idle capacity variance if the expected actual rate were used.

6. Factory overhead rates and variances on various capacity levels. The accountant of the Cordell Company is asked by management to compute factory overhead rates based on (a) normal capacity, (b) expected actual capacity, (c) theoretical capacity, and (d) average sales for the previous three years. The accountant prepared the following summary:

	EXPECTED ACTUAL	AVERAGE SALES	NORMAL CAPACITY	THEORETICAL CAPACITY
Capacity levels	80%	85%	90%	100%
Direct labor hours......................	27,200	28,900	30,600	34,000
Factory overhead:				
Fixed..	$102,000	$102,000	$102,000	$102,000
Variable....................................	136,000	144,500	153,000	170,000
Total......................................	$238,000	$246,500	$255,000	$272,000

Required:

(1) Factory overhead rates per direct labor hour for each of the four capacity levels. (Round off all amounts to two decimal places.)
(2) The amount of over- or underabsorbed factory overhead for the other three levels if actual hours worked and actual factory overhead incurred were identical with the estimated hours and the estimated overhead of the expected actual capacity level.

7. Entries for factory overhead. Speedo Co. assembles and sells electric mixers. All parts are purchased and labor is paid on the basis of $32 per mixer assembled. The cost of the parts per mixer totals $40. As the company handles only this one product, the unit cost basis for applying factory overhead is used. Estimated factory overhead for the coming period, based on a production of 30,000 mixers, is as follows:

Indirect materials	$220,000
Indirect labor..	240,000
Light and power...	30,000
Depreciation...	25,000
Miscellaneous	55,000

During the period, 29,000 mixers were assembled and actual factory overhead was $565,300. These units were completed but not yet transferred to the finished goods storeroom.

Required:

(1) Journal entries to record the above information.
(2) The amount of over- or underapplied factory overhead..

8. Variance analysis procedure. The Kreiter Company was totally destroyed by fire during June; however, certain fragments of its cost records were recovered with the following data: idle capacity variance, $1,266 favorable; spending variance, $779 unfavorable; and applied factory overhead, $16,234.

Required:
   (1) Budget allowance, based on capacity utilized.
   (2) Actual factory overhead.

9. Variance analysis. The Henkel Company made the following data available from its accounting records and reports:

   (a) $\dfrac{\$600,000 \text{ estimated factory overhead}}{200,000 \text{ estimated direct labor hours}}$ = $3.00 predetermined factory overhead rate
   (b) Further analysis indicates that one third of the rate is variable-cost oriented.
   (c) During the year, the company worked 210,000 direct labor hours, and actual factory overhead expenditures were $631,000.

Required: The spending and idle capacity variances.

10. Factory overhead variance analysis. Normal operating capacity of a company's power plant is estimated to be 4 750 000 kilowatt-hours per month. At this level of activity, fixed overhead is estimated to be $171,000 and variable overhead, $209,000. During November, the power plant produced 5 000 000 kilowatt-hours. Actual overhead for the month totaled $393,000.

Required:
   (1) Over- or underapplied overhead. (Carry all computations to three decimal places.)
   (2) Spending and idle capacity variances.

PROBLEMS

9-1. Journal entries; job order costing. The Evert Company uses job order costing. The following data were obtained from the company's cost records as of June 30:

Job No.	Direct Materials	Direct Labor Hours
1001	$16,300	2,300
1002	23,600	4,700
1003	24,500	4,200
1004	15,400	2,500
1005	18,200	3,200
1006	13,700	1,980

Direct labor is charged to jobs at an average cost of $6 per direct labor hour.

Factory overhead is charged to jobs on the basis of $3 per direct labor hour. Actual overhead totaled $58,000.

During June, Jobs 1001, 1002, 1003, 1004, and 1005 were completed. Jobs 1001 and 1002 were shipped out, and the customers were billed in the amounts of $48,000 and $82,000 respectively.

Required: General journal entries to summarize the transactions for June. Over- or underapplied factory overhead is not closed out until the end of the year.

9-2. Journal entries for monthly transactions. Shapiro, Inc., uses job order costing and applies factory overhead on the basis of direct labor hours.

Transactions for July were:

   (a) Materials purchased on account, $10,000.
   (b) Shop supplies purchased on account, $5,000.
   (c) Materials requisitioned, $10,000, of which $7,000 was direct materials.
   (d) Recorded liability, paid and distributed payroll: direct labor, $15,000; indirect labor, $5,000; employee income tax withheld, $2,000; FICA tax, $1,200.

(e) Employer factory payroll taxes for the month, $1,800.
(f) Factory overhead paid: repairs, $175; rent, $300; power and light, $400.
(g) Depreciation of machinery and equipment, $625.
(h) Expired insurance on machinery, $50.
(i) Paid marketing and administrative expense, $1,100.
(j) Factory overhead applied to production at the rate of 75% of direct labor cost.
(k) Inventories at the end of the month: work in process, $9,000; finished goods, $6,000.
(l) Sales on account, $50,000.

The trial balance as of July 1 is shown below:

Shapiro, Inc.
Trial Balance
July 1, 19--

Cash	20,000	
Notes Receivable	10,000	
Accounts Receivable	28,000	
Allowance for Doubtful Accounts		1,900
Finished Goods	5,000	
Work in Process	10,000	
Materials	15,000	
Prepaid Insurance on Machinery	500	
Factory Overhead Control	8,500	
Machinery and Equipment	75,000	
Accumulated Depreciation — Machinery and Equipment		25,000
Accounts Payable		10,000
Employees Income Tax Payable		2,000
Accrued Payroll Taxes		900
Common Stock		100,000
Retained Earnings		32,200
Total	172,000	172,000

Required: General journal entries to record the transactions (a) through (l), using a factory overhead control account (not closed until the end of the year) to record both actual and applied overhead.

9-3. Factory overhead application to jobs. The Tristate Company has been in business for only a short period of time. During the past month, the firm had the following costs, as shown by its books and records:

Materials used	$19,500
Direct labor	24,000
Indirect materials used in plant	3,000
Indirect plant labor	4,000
Supervisor's salary, plant	3,000
Labor fringe cost, plant	2,800
Depreciation of plant	1,000
Depreciation of factory machinery	2,000
Property tax on plant	300
Marketing and administrative expense	3,500
Insurance on plant	200
Miscellaneous factory overhead	1,200
Power and light for plant	500
Advertising	1,500

The company has not set up a predetermined rate for applying factory overhead. It intends to wait until the end of each month to charge actual overhead incurred during the month to jobs worked on during that month. Labor pay rates vary considerably among the various labor skills employed in the plant. There is also a wide variation in the proportionate use made of labor skills on each job order.

During the past month, the company worked on three orders, two of which were completed. Costs and other pertinent data in connection with these orders are:

	JOB 301	JOB 302	JOB 303
Materials cost	$6,000	$ 8,000	$5,500
Direct labor hours	2,000	3,000	1,000
Machine hours	1,200	1,800	600
Direct labor cost	$8,000	$12,000	$4,000

Required:
 (1) The cost of each job, using as the basis for charging factory overhead: (a) direct labor cost, (b) direct labor hours, (c) machine hours.
 (2) The recommended method of applying factory overhead, assuming that costs and operations will remain in the same proportions.

9-4. Factory overhead rates and application. The Cost Department of the Bundy Company made the following estimates for the coming year: factory overhead, $425,000; materials cost, $850,000; production, 20,800 cases; labor cost, $250,000; labor hours, 106,250.

Required:
 (1) The factory overhead rate based on (a) labor cost, (b) labor hours, and (c) materials cost.
 (2) The amount of overhead to be charged to Job 465 by each rate in (1) above. (Job 465: materials cost, $21,000; labor cost, $14,800 for 3,700 hours.)

9-5. Factory overhead analysis. The Pepper Company's factory overhead rate is $3 per hour. Budgeted overhead for 3,000 hours per month is $16,000 and at 7,000 hours is $24,000. Actual factory overhead for the month is $18,000, and actual volume is 5,000 hours.

Required:
 (1) Variable overhead in overhead rate.
 (2) Budgeted fixed overhead.
 (3) Normal volume or normal capacity hours.
 (4) Applied factory overhead.
 (5) Over- or underabsorbed factory overhead.
 (6) Spending variance.
 (7) Idle capacity variance.

9-6. Variance analysis. The Duncan Company's factory overhead for April is summarized below. Normal capacity is used as the activity level for computing the predetermined factory overhead rate.

Factory Overhead — April
(Actual Activity — 80% of Normal)

EXPENSE	ESTIMATED FACTORY OVERHEAD AT 100% (NORMAL)	ESTIMATED FACTORY OVERHEAD AT 80% OF NORMAL	ACTUAL FACTORY OVERHEAD
Superintendence	$1,100	$1,100	$1,100
Depreciation	650	650	650
Property tax	720	720	720
Rent	900	900	900
Power	600	480	530
Maintenance labor	840	672	790
Insurance	350	350	350
Factory supplies	480	384	425
Indirect labor	960	768	710
Payroll taxes	280	224	234
Total	$6,880	$6,248	$6,409

Required:
 (1) The over- or underapplied factory overhead.
 (2) The idle capacity variance.
 (3) The spending variance, in total and by individual expenses.

9-7. Budgeted overhead and variance analysis. In June, the idle capacity variance of Carmichael, Inc., was zero, and the spending variance was $6,000 unfavorable. In July, the idle capacity variance was $8,000 unfavorable, but the spending variance was zero. In June, actual overhead expense was $70,000 for an output of 8,000 tons. July's expense was $56,000, and output was 6,000 tons. In August, output was 9,000 tons, and actual overhead expense was $71,000.

Required:
    (1) Factory overhead budgeted (estimated) for 9,000 tons.
    (2) Factory overhead applied in August.
    (3) Variances for August.

9-8. Inventory costing; overhead analysis; statement of cost of goods sold. The Cost Department of the Inman Company received the following monthly data, pertaining solely to manufacturing activities, from the general ledger clerk:

Work in process inventory, January 1	$ 32,500
Materials inventory, January 1	21,000
Direct labor	128,000
Materials purchased	108,000
Materials returned to suppliers	5,050
Supervision	18,500
Indirect labor	29,050
Heat, light, and power	8,700
Depreciation — factory buildings	7,500
Property tax	4,000
Insurance on factory buildings	3,000
Research and development cost (factory overhead)	14,100
Transportation in (factory overhead)	6,500
Repairs and maintenance — factory equipment	8,250
Depreciation — factory equipment	7,500
Miscellaneous factory overhead	9,900
Finished goods inventory, January 1	18,000
Applied factory overhead	115,200

Additional data:
    (a) Physical inventory taken January 31 shows $9,000 of materials on hand.
    (b) The January 31 work in process and finished goods inventories show the following direct materials and direct labor contents:

	DIRECT MATERIALS	DIRECT LABOR
Work in process	$ 9,000	$ 8,000 (2,000 hrs.)
Finished goods	10,000	20,000 (5,000 hrs.)

    (c) Factory overhead is applied to these two ending inventories on the basis of a factory overhead rate of $3.60 per direct labor hour.

Required:
    (1) The cost assigned to the ending work in process and finished goods inventories, including factory overhead.
    (2) A schedule of the total actual factory overhead for the month.
    (3) An analysis of the over- or underapplied factory overhead, assuming that the predetermined factory overhead rate was based on the following data:

Variable factory overhead	$70,875
Fixed factory overhead	$42,525
Direct labor hours	31,500

    (4) A detailed cost of goods sold statement, assuming that over- or underapplied overhead is closed to the cost of goods sold account.

10

Factory Overhead
Departmentalization for Product Costing and Cost Control

The preceding chapter discussed the establishment and use of one factory-wide predetermined overhead rate, the accumulation of actual factory overhead in books and records, and the analysis of over- or underapplied factory overhead. These phases are now expanded through the use of predetermined departmental factory overhead rates, which improves the charging of overhead to jobs and products, leads to cost control via responsibility accounting, and provides useful data for planning and analytical decision-making processes.

Methods for the control of materials and labor costs are discussed in other chapters. However, because each product manufactured requires a certain minimum amount of materials and labor, there is a limit to the amount of cost reduction for materials and labor which can be realized through the use of such methods. The situation is different for factory overhead. The departmentalization of factory overhead facilitates the responsible control which is so necessary if unit and total costs are to stay within predetermined or budgeted ranges.

THE CONCEPT OF DEPARTMENTALIZATION

Departmentalization of factory overhead means dividing the plant into segments called departments, cost centers, or cost pools, to which expenses are charged. For accounting purposes, dividing a plant into separate departments provides more accurate costing of jobs and products and responsible control of overhead costs.

More accurate costing of jobs and products is possible because departmentalization uses different departmental overhead rates for applying factory overhead. A job or product going through a department is charged with factory overhead for work done in that department, using the department's predetermined overhead rate. Depending on the type and number of departments through which they pass, jobs or products are charged with varying amounts of factory overhead, rather than with a single plant-wide overhead rate.

Responsible control of overhead costs is possible because departmentalization makes the incurrence of expenses the responsibility of a supervisor or manager. Expenses which originate directly and completely in a department are identified with the individual responsible for the supervision of the department.

Computation of predetermined overhead rates requires a series of departmental allocation processes with respect to estimated expenses. These allocations are limited to those necessary for computing overhead rates prior to the beginning of the fiscal period. Actual overhead accumulated during the month or year should remain with the individual department until the end of the accounting period.

Computing complete product costs involves recognizing all manufacturing costs regardless of their direct or indirect relationship to a given department or product. In addition to its direct costs, each product must bear an equitable share of indirect costs such as utilities, materials handling, inspection, storage, and general factory expenses. The selection of the best overhead allocation methods is important in determining product costs.

The entire process of departmentalizing factory overhead is an extension of methods previously discussed. Estimating or budgeting expenses and selecting a proper basis for applying them is still necessary; but, in addition, departmentalizing overhead requires separate estimates or budgets for each department. Actual expenses of a period must still be recorded in a factory overhead control account and a factory overhead subsidiary ledger for each department, according to the nature of the expense. This procedure permits comparison of actual departmental expenses with departmentally applied factory overhead. Over- or underapplied factory overhead is computed departmentally and analyzed separately to determine departmental spending and idle capacity variances.

PRODUCING AND SERVICE DEPARTMENTS

Departments are classified as either producing or service departments. A *producing department* engages in the actual manufacture of the product by changing the shape, form, or nature of the material worked upon, or by assembling the parts into a finished article. A *service department* renders a service that contributes in an indirect manner to the manufacture of the product but which does not itself change the shape, form, or nature of the material that is converted into the finished product. The following table lists examples of producing and service departments:

PRODUCING		SERVICE	
Cutting	Mill Room	Utilities	Shipping
Planing	Plating	Materials Handling	Medical
Assembly	Knitting	Inspection	Production Control
Upholstery	Mixing	Storage	Personnel
Finishing	Refining	Plant Security	Maintenance
Machining		Purchasing	Cafeteria
		Receiving	General Factory Cost Pool

A manufacturing company is usually organized along departmental lines for production purposes. Manufacturing processes dictate the type of organization needed to handle the different operations efficiently, to obtain the best production flow, and to establish responsibility for physical control of production. **Selection of Producing Departments**

The cost information system is designed to fit the departmentalization required for production purposes. The system accumulates manufacturing costs according to such departmentalization whether operations are of the job type or the continuous process type. Factors to be considered in deciding the kinds of departments required for establishing accurate departmental overhead rates with which to control costs are:

1. Similarity of operations, processes, and machinery in each department.
2. Location of operations, processes, and machinery.
3. Responsibilities for production and costs.
4. Relationship of operations to flow of product.
5. Number of departments or cost centers.

The establishment of producing departments for the purpose of costing and controlling expenses is a problem for the management of every company, for which no hard and fast rules can be given. The most common approach divides the factory along lines of functional activities with each activity or group of activities constituting a department. Division of the factory into separate, interrelated, and independently governed units is important for the proper control of factory overhead and the accurate costing of jobs and products.

The number of producing departments used depends on the emphasis the cost system puts on cost control and the development of overhead rates. If the emphasis is on cost control, separate departments might be established for the plant manager and for each superintendent or supervisor. When the development of departmental overhead rates emphasizes accurate costing, fewer departments might be used. Sometimes the number of departments needed for cost control is larger than that needed for overhead rates. In such cases, the cost control system can be adapted to proper overhead rates by combining departments, thus reducing the number of rates used without sacrificing control of costs.

In certain instances, particularly when different types of machines are used, departments are further subdivided for cost control and overhead rate purposes. This results in a refinement in applying and controlling overhead with respect to the jobs or products passing through a department.

Selection of Service Departments   The selection and designation of service departments has considerable bearing on effective costing and control. Services available for the benefit of producing departments and other service departments can be organized in several ways by (1) establishing a separate service department for each function, (2) combining several functions into one department, or (3) placing service costs in a department called "general factory cost pool." The specific service is not identified if service costs applicable to producing and service functions are accumulated in a general factory cost pool.

Determination of the kinds and number of service departments should consider the number of employees needed for each service function, the cost of providing the service, the importance of the service, and the assignment of supervisory responsibility. Establishing a separate department for every service function is rarely done even in large companies. When relatively few employees are involved and activities are closely related, service functions are generally combined for the sake of economy and expediency. Decisions with respect to combining service functions are governed by the individual circumstances existing in each company. Since factory overhead rates for job and product costing are calculated for producing departments only, service department expenses are transferred ultimately to producing departments for rate setting and variance analysis.

DIRECT DEPARTMENTAL EXPENSES IN PRODUCING AND SERVICE DEPARTMENTS

The majority of direct departmental overhead costs can be categorized as follows:

1. Supervision, indirect labor, and overtime.
2. Labor fringe benefits.
3. Indirect materials and factory supplies.
4. Repairs and maintenance.
5. Equipment depreciation.

These expense categories are generally readily identified with the originating department, whether producing or service. In the discussion that follows, detailed attention is given to each of the categories of direct departmental overhead costs.

These factory labor categories, in contrast to direct labor, do not alter the shape or content of a product; they are auxiliary to its manufacture. It is important to realize that any factory labor not classified as direct labor is automatically classified as factory overhead.

Supervision, Indirect Labor, and Overtime

Inasmuch as overhead is allocated to all products, a lax or incorrect classification would cause direct labor that applies to only one product to be allocated as indirect labor in the form of overhead to other products, thereby understating the one product cost and overstating the others. Thus, decisions on whether or not to classify costs as direct labor can have an important effect on overhead rates, since direct labor cost is often used as the base for determining the rates. In such a case, a decision to classify certain labor as indirect reduces the denominator and increases the numerator of the ratio (factory overhead ÷ direct labor cost) used to compute overhead rates. The following illustration points out the possible effect of incorrect identification of $1,000 of direct labor as indirect labor:

	CORRECTLY IDENTIFIED AS DIRECT LABOR	INCORRECTLY IDENTIFIED AS INDIRECT LABOR
Direct labor...	$6,000	$5,000
Factory overhead:		
Indirect labor	$5,000	$6,000
Other overhead......................................	1,000	1,000
Total factory overhead	$6,000	$7,000
Factory overhead rates $= \dfrac{\text{Factory overhead}}{\text{Direct labor cost}}$	$\dfrac{\$6,000}{\$6,000} = 100\%$	$\dfrac{\$7,000}{\$5,000} = 140\%$

The premium portion of overtime paid should generally be charged as overhead to the departments in which the overtime occurred. This method should be followed for all labor except for special cases discussed in the labor chapters. However, the straight-time portion of overtime paid to direct labor employees should be charged to direct labor.

Labor fringe benefits include such costs as vacation and holiday pay, FICA tax, state and federal unemployment taxes, workmen's compensation insurance, pension costs, hospitalization benefits, and group insurance. In theory, these labor fringe benefits are additional labor costs and should — when they pertain to direct labor employees — be added to the direct labor cost. In practice, such a procedure is usually impractical; therefore, these costs that pertain to direct as well as to other factory workers are generally included in factory overhead and become part of the factory overhead rate.

Labor Fringe Benefits

Incorrectly distinguishing between direct and indirect materials (the latter being part of overhead) has the same adverse effects on product costing as failure to make proper distinction between direct and indirect labor. However, distinguishing between direct and indirect materials is usually not as difficult. In a manufacturing operation, direct materials are those which are

Indirect Materials and Factory Supplies

changed in form through processing and become an integral part of the end product. Indirect materials, often referred to as factory supplies, are auxiliary to the processing operations and do not become an essential part of the end product.

There are two basic methods of accounting for the cost of supplies: (1) as a direct departmental charge or (2) as a charge to inventory.

Direct Departmental Charge. An easy, though not the most effective, way to account for factory supplies is to charge the expense to the department that originated the purchase request. This procedure assumes that the department supervisor has the authority to purchase and that the cost of the purchase stays within departmental budget limits. At the end of the accounting period, an adjusting entry should be made, so that the cost of any unused supplies is deferred as inventory on the balance sheet. This adjusting entry would be reversed at the beginning of the next accounting period.

Charge to Inventory. When closer control of supplies is required or when more than one department uses certain supplies, it is not practical or correct to charge only one department at the time of purchase. In such cases, supplies purchased are charged to an inventory account at the time of purchase, and departments using the supplies are charged when supplies are issued.

When an inventory account is used, consumption may be determined by one of two methods. First, if the supply is used only in one department, it is possible to determine the amount to be charged to that department by (1) taking a physical inventory at the end of each month, (2) adding purchases for the month to the cost of the beginning inventory, and (3) from this total, subtracting the final cost assigned to physical inventory at month-end to determine the usage for the month.

A second method of accounting for the cost of supplies through an inventory account involves the use of materials requisitions. Requisitions approved by authorized employees permit charging a department with the proper cost and thereby provide better control over the use of materials than the physical inventory method. However, additional clerical work is required, since requisitions must be prepared, priced, and summarized.

Repairs and Mainte- nance   With respect to repairs and maintenance costs, it is essential to establish control over the total cost incurred by the repairs and maintenance department and to devise effective means for charging maintenance costs to departments receiving the service.

As a rule, the work of repair and maintenance crews is supervised by a maintenance superintendent. If possible and practical, all actual maintenance costs should be charged to a maintenance department, so that the total cost is controlled by the maintenance superintendent and kept within a maintenance budget. However, since maintenance is a service function, its costs must be distributed to departments that receive the service.

Most maintenance work performed for departments is generally of a recurring nature, and charges are incurred evenly throughout the year. However, certain types of maintenance work, such as breakdowns and overhauls, occur at irregular intervals and often involve large expenditures. In such cases, companies using departmental budgets may spread major repair costs over the year by making monthly charges to operations, based on a predetermined rate. These rates are commonly derived from previous years' experience. Monthly provisions are charged to Maintenance Expense and credited to an allowance account. Actual repair costs are charged to the allowance account. In this manner, large maintenance costs are charged to operations in direct proportion to the operating rate and presumably approximate the actual deterioration of the equipment.

Equipment Depreciation

Depreciation is usually a cost not controllable by departmental supervisors. However, their use of equipment influences maintenance and depreciation costs. This is true with respect to all types of depreciable assets — machinery and equipment, buildings, vehicles, and furniture and fixtures. For effective costing and controlling, depreciation is usually identified with the departments using the assets, and the cost is charged directly to departments. The recommended method is to compute depreciation by departments, based on the cost of equipment as recorded on detailed plant asset records. When no records are available or equipment is used by more than one department, depreciation is frequently accumulated in the general factory cost pool.

INDIRECT DEPARTMENTAL EXPENSES

Expenses such as power, light, rent, and depreciation of factory, when shared by all departments, are not charged directly to a department. These expenses do not originate with any specific department. They are incurred for all to use and must, therefore, be prorated to any or all departments using them.

The Cost Accounting Standards Board Disclosure Statement requires that covered federal government contractors identify and describe allocation bases for all factory overhead, service center, and general and administrative cost pools used by the contractor. Selecting appropriate bases for the distribution of these indirect departmental expenses is difficult and, in some instances, rests on an arbitrary decision. To charge every department with its fair share of an expense, a basis using some factor common to all departments must be found. For example, square footage may be used for prorating such expenses as rent. In plants with departments occupying parts of the factory with ceilings of unequal height, cubic measurement rather than square footage might be used. Areas occupied by stairways, elevators, escalators, corridors, and aisles must also be considered.

Some of the indirect departmental expenses that require prorating, together with the bases most commonly used, are:

INDIRECT DEPARTMENTAL EXPENSES	DISTRIBUTION BASIS
Factory rent	Square footage
Property tax	Square footage
Depreciation — buildings	Square footage
Insurance (fire)	Square footage
Building repairs	Square footage
Heat	Square footage
Superintendence	Number of employees
Telephone and telegraph	Number of employees or number of telephones
Workmen's compensation insurance	Department payroll
Light	Kilowatt-hours
Freight in	Materials used
Power	Horsepower-hours

After the distribution bases have been selected, a survey of the factory must be made to secure the information needed to permit the distribution. Information such as total square footage and its breakdown by departments, number of employees in each department, investment in machinery by departments, and estimates of kilowatt-hours (kwh) and horsepower hours (hph) are items listed in the survey.

ESTABLISHING DEPARTMENTAL OVERHEAD RATES

Factory overhead is usually applied on the basis of direct labor cost or hours when one factory overhead rate is used for the entire plant, since this procedure is considered most convenient and acceptable. The use of departmental rates requires a distinct consideration of each producing department's overhead, which often results in the use of different bases for applying overhead for different departments. For example, it is possible to use a direct labor hour rate for one department and a machine hour rate for another. A further refinement might possibly lead to different bases and rates for cost centers within the same producing department.

Since all factory overhead, whether of a general nature or from service departments, must be included in producing departments, the establishment of departmental factory overhead rates proceeds in the following manner:

1. Estimating or budgeting total direct factory overhead of producing and service departments at the selected activity levels; determining, if possible, the fixed (F) and variable (V) nature of each expense category.
2. Preparing a factory survey for the purpose of distributing indirect factory overhead and service department costs.
3. Estimating or budgeting total indirect factory overhead, such as electric power, fuel, water, building depreciation, property tax, and fire

insurance at the selected activity levels; allocating these costs, based on selected methods.

4. Distributing service department costs.
5. Calculating departmental factory overhead rates.

These procedures are illustrated with the total estimated factory overhead for DeWitt Products (page 215), which has now been departmentalized. The figures have been modified for ease in calculating departmental rates, but the fixed-variable cost classification has been retained. The illustration uses four producing departments: Cutting, Planing, Assembly, and Upholstery; and four service departments: Materials Handling, Inspection, Utilities, and General Factory.

Materials handling involves the operation of equipment such as cranes, trucks, fork lifts, and loaders. Since many departments are served by this function, a preferred method of organization establishes a separate service department for materials handling activities. All handling costs are charged to this department, with a supervisor responsible for their control. Costs charged to such a service department are the same as those charged to any department and include wages and labor fringe costs of the department's employees; supplies, such as batteries and gasoline; and repairs and maintenance of the equipment. In addition to centralizing responsibility for materials handling operations, departmentalization has the advantage of collecting all materials handling costs in one place.

For cost control, inspection costs are treated in the same manner as other service department costs. However, in certain instances, a special work order may require additional inspection or testing. This type of inspection cost is chargeable to the order and must be so identified. To accumulate these specific charges, separate cost centers may be established for the purpose of charging time and materials for special inspections.

Power and fuel are consumed for two major purposes: for operating manufacturing facilities such as machines, electric welders, and cranes, and for what might be termed "working condition" purposes, such as lighting, cooling, and heating. In most instances, a single billing is received for electric power or natural gas, because it is not possible or practical to determine directly the consumption for each of the above purposes — to say nothing of the consumption by specific departments, cost centers, or functions.

However, a direct departmental allocation is often desirable and possible. A common method used is to install separate meters to measure power or fuel consumed by specific types of equipment. In other instances, separate power sources (fuel, natural gas, coal, or electricity) may be used for different facilities or equipment, making it possible to determine an individual utility cost by department.

For purposes of departmental and product costing, two methods of accounting for costs of utilities are recommended:

1. Charge all power and fuel costs to a separate utilities department; then allocate to the benefiting departments.
2. Charge specific departments with power or fuel cost if separate meters are provided, and charge the remaining power and fuel costs to a separate utilities department or to a general plant; this remainder is then allocated to the benefiting departments.

Allocation of utilities costs to specific departments is based on special studies that determine such information as each department's horsepower of machines and the number of machines.

Certain expenses other than those discussed above come under the category "general factory," because they represent a variety of miscellaneous factory services. Therefore, a separate general factory cost pool is established to accumulate and control such expenses. Such an organizational unit is usually the direct responsibility of the plant superintendent. Salaries of management personnel directly concerned with production are charged to this cost pool if they cannot be charged to specific departments except by arbitrary allocations. Janitor labor and supplies may be charged to general factory unless charged to maintenance or to a department called "building occupancy." Unless separate service departments for plant security and yard operation are established, these costs are also examples of charges to general factory services.

Estimating Direct Departmental Expenses

Estimating or budgeting the direct expenses of producing and service departments (Exhibit 1, page 245) is a joint undertaking of department heads, supervisors, and members of the budget or cost department of the company. Labor fringe costs are calculated by the office personnel, since the individual supervisor has little influence or knowledge with respect to the underlying rates and figures. Costs of indirect labor and indirect materials are of greater interest to the supervisor. Repairs and maintenance costs are often disputed items unless a definite maintenance program has been established. Departmental depreciation charges are based on management's decision regarding depreciation methods and rates. In the illustration, depreciation of equipment is charged directly to the departments on the basis of asset values and rates set by the controller. The plant manager, working with budget personnel, estimates and supervises the general factory costs.

Factory Survey

Before indirect departmental and service department expenses can be prorated to benefiting and ultimately to producing departments, certain underlying data must be obtained. A survey of factory facilities and records usually produces the information needed, such as rated horsepower of equipment in each department, estimated kilowatt-hour consumption, number of employees in each department, estimated payroll costs, square footage, estimated materials consumption, and asset values. Functions performed by each service department must be studied carefully to determine the most equi-

DeWitt Products
Estimated Departmental Factory Overhead
For the Year 19—

Cost Accounts	F or V	Total	Producing Departments				Service Departments			
			Cutting	Planing	Assembly	Upholstery	Materials Handling	Inspection	Utilities	General Factory
Direct departmental exp.:										
Supervisors	F	$ 70,000	$ 9,000	$ 8,000	$ 8,000	$ 8,000	$10,000	$ 6,000	$ 9,000	$12,000
Indirect labor	F	9,000	1,000	2,000	1,000	1,500	1,000	500	1,000	1,000
Labor fringe costs	V	66,000	9,000	3,000	5,000	5,500	11,000	8,500	10,000	14,000
	F	10,000	1,500	1,000	1,000	1,000	2,000	1,000	1,500	1,000
Indirect materials	V	47,000	10,500	11,800	9,400	8,200	1,800	1,400	1,900	2,000
	F	4,000	500	500	800	1,200	300	200	200	300
Repairs and maintenance	V	19,000	2,500	2,500	3,200	4,800	1,700	800	1,800	1,700
	F	3,000	600	500	700	600			300	300
Depreciation — equipment	V	9,000	1,400	1,500	1,300	1,800	500	200	1,700	600
	F	13,000	1,500	3,500	1,000	3,000				4,000
Total direct departmental expenses		$250,000	$37,500	$34,300	$31,400	$35,600	$28,300	$18,600	$27,400	$36,900
Indirect departmental exp.:										
Electric power	F	$ 2,000							$ 2,000	
	V	20,000							20,000	
Fuel	F	1,000							1,000	
	V	10,000							10,000	
Water	F	1,000							1,000	
	V	4,000							4,000	
Depreciation — buildings	F	5,000	$ 1,250	$ 1,000	$ 1,500	$ 1,250				
Property tax	F	4,000	1,000	800	1,200	1,000				
Insurance (fire)	F	3,000	750	600	900	750				
Total indirect departmental expenses		$ 50,000	$ 3,000	$ 2,400	$ 3,600	$ 3,000			$38,000	
Total departmental factory overhead		$300,000	$40,500	$36,700	$35,000	$38,600	$28,300	$18,600	$65,400	$36,900
Total fixed factory overhead		$125,000	$17,100	$17,900	$16,100	$18,300	$13,300	$ 7,700	$16,000	$18,600
Total variable factory overhead		$175,000	$23,400	$18,800	$18,900	$20,300	$15,000	$10,900	$49,400	$18,300

Exhibit 1

table basis for distributing their expenses. The factory survey for DeWitt Products appears as follows:

DeWitt Products
Factory Survey Prepared at the Beginning of the Year

Producing Departments	Number of Employees	%	Kilo-watt-Hours	%	Horse-power-Hours	%	Floor Area (sq. ft.)	%	Cost of Materials Requisi-tioned	%
Cutting.........	30	20	12 800	20	200,000	40	5,250	25	$180,000	45
Planing........	25	17	6 400	10	120,000	24	4,200	20	40,000	10
Assembly.....	45	30	19 200	30	80,000	16	6,300	30	40,000	10
Upholstery...	50	33	25 600	40	100,000	20	5,250	25	140,000	35
Total.............	150	100	64 000	100	500,000	100	21,000	100	$400,000	100

Schedule A

Estimating and Allocating Indirect Expenses

Indirect departmental expenses, such as heat, electric power, fuel, water, and building depreciation, must be estimated and then allocated to either producing and service departments or perhaps only to producing departments. The method depends upon management's decision. In Exhibit 1, indirect departmental expenses are prorated in two ways: (1) electric power, fuel, and water are charged to Utilities, from which a distribution is made; (2) depreciation of building, property tax, and fire insurance are prorated only to producing departments on the basis of floor area as shown in the Factory Survey (Schedule A); e.g., 25 percent of $5,000, or $1,250, is charged to the Cutting Department for building depreciation. However, as an alternative, these costs could also be allocated to service departments as well as to producing departments.

Distributing Service Department Costs

The number and types of service departments in a company depend on its operations and the degree of expense control desired. As shown in Exhibit 1, each service department of DeWitt Products is charged with its direct overhead. These costs and any indirect departmental expenses charged to the service departments should be distributed equitably to either producing departments and service departments or just to producing departments, again depending on management's decision. The distribution might be based on number of employees, kilowatt-hour consumption, horsepower-hour consumption, floor space, asset value, or cost of materials to be requisitioned. The expenses of service departments must ultimately be transferred to producing departments to establish predetermined factory overhead rates and to analyze variances.

General Rules for Distributing Service Department Overhead. Certain rules are followed for the transfer of service department overhead to benefiting departments. One rule states that service department expenses should be transferred on the basis of producing and other service departments' use of the respective services. To use this rule, a decision must be made with respect to the service department which should be closed first, since services are received not only by producing departments but also by other service departments. Thus, instead of closing all service department overhead directly to producing departments, some overhead may first be charged to other service departments. In some companies (as illustrated in Exhibit 2, page 248), service department expenses are transferred only to producing departments. This procedure avoids much clerical work. It can be justified for product costing if there is no material difference in the final costs of a producing department when the expenses of a service department are not prorated to other service departments. However, this procedure fails to measure the total cost for individual service departments when such information is needed for cost planning and control.

When following the rule that service department expenses should be transferred on the basis of services used by all benefiting departments, the usual procedure is to transfer these expenses stepwise in the order of the amount of service rendered. Expenses of the department rendering the greatest amount of service are transferred first.

When service rendered by a department cannot be determined accurately, it is possible to distribute first the expenses of the service department which has the largest total overhead. This rule assumes that the department with the largest amount of expense rendered the greatest amount of service. Once costs for a service department are distributed, that department is considered closed and no further distributions are made to it, whether the amount of service or the amount of expense determines the order of distribution.

The distribution of estimated service department costs is shown in Exhibit 2, page 248. Since the illustration shows no transfer of service department costs to other service departments, the order of distribution does not matter. The distribution is made by starting with Materials Handling. The overhead of this department is distributed on the basis of the estimated cost of materials requisitioned per Schedule A; e.g., 45 percent of $28,300 = $12,735 to the Cutting Department. The Inspection cost is transferred to the producing departments Assembly and Upholstery on a 50-50 basis, because these two departments are the only ones receiving this type of service and they receive it in equal amounts.

The Utilities cost is transferred in a threefold manner: 20 percent of the cost based on kilowatt-hours; 50 percent, on horsepower-hours; and 30 percent, on floor area. The amount of $13,080 represents 20 percent of $65,400, the total cost of the department. According to Schedule A, 20 percent of $13,080, or $2,616, is distributed to the Cutting Department. The same method is followed for the other costs and departments. General Factory is distributed on the basis of number of employees, e.g., 20 percent of $36,900, or $7,380, is distributed to the Cutting Department.

The distribution of these service department costs is based on percentages in the Factory Survey, page 246. Some accountants proceed in a different manner by calculating a rate per square foot, per kilowatt-hour, or per em-

DeWitt Products
Distribution of Estimated Service Department Costs
and
Calculation of Departmental Factory Overhead Rates
For the Year 19—

Cost Accounts	Total	Producing Departments				Service Departments			
		Cutting	Planing	Assembly	Upholstery	Materials Handling	Inspection	Utilities	General Factory
Total departmental factory overhead before distribution of service depts.	$300,000	$40,500	$36,700	$35,000	$38,600	$28,300	$18,600	$65,400	$36,900
Distribution of service department costs:									
Materials handling (Base: estimated cost of materials requisitioned)		$12,735	$2,830	$2,830	$9,905	(28,300)			
Inspection (Base: equally to assembly and upholstery departments)				9,300	9,300		(18,600)		
Utilities: (Bases: 20% on kwh		2,616	1,308	3,924	5,232			(13,080)	
50% on hph		13,080	7,848	5,232	6,540			(32,700)	
30% on floor area)		4,905	3,924	5,886	4,905			(19,620)	
General factory (Base: no. of employees)		7,380	6,273	11,070	12,177				(36,900)
Total service dept. costs distributed		$40,716	$22,183	$ 38,242	$48,059				
Total departmental factory overhead after distribution of service depts.	$300,000	$81,216	$58,883	$ 73,242	$86,659				
Bases: Direct labor hours		40,608	18,400	$122,000	48,140				
Machine hours			18,400						
Direct labor cost				$122,000					
Rates		$2.00 per direct labor hour	$3.20 per machine hour	60% of direct labor cost	$1.80 per direct labor hour				

ployee. The amount of General Factory cost transferred to the Cutting Department is determined as follows:

$$\frac{\$36,900 \text{ General Factory cost}}{150 \text{ employees}} = \$246 \text{ per employee}$$

$$\$246 \times 30 \text{ employees in the Cutting Department} = \$7,380.$$

Algebraic Method for Overhead Distribution. The proration of service department expenses to other service departments may be incomplete if a department provides service to a department from which it receives service. Consider a case in which Service Department Y provides service to Service
Department Z and, in turn, Z renders service to Y. The incompleteness in
proration arises because, using the rules discussed earlier, one department
would be closed out before the other and therefore before receiving any expense proration from the other. If greater exactness is desired, the technique
illustrated below can be followed.[1]

DEPARTMENT	DEPARTMENTAL OVERHEAD BEFORE DISTRIBUTION OF SERVICE DEPARTMENTS	SERVICES PROVIDED Dept. Y	SERVICES PROVIDED Dept. Z
Producing — A	$ 6,000	40%	20%
Producing — B	8,000	40	50
Service — Y	3,630	—	30
Service — Z	2,000	20	—
Total departmental overhead ...	$19,630	100%	100%

Cost allocation by algebra:

Let: $Y = \$3,630 + .30 Z$
            $Z = \$2,000 + .20 Y$

Substituting: $Y = \$3,630 + .30 (\$2,000 + .20Y)$

Solving: $Y = \$3,630 + \$600 + .06Y$
            $.94Y = \$4,230$
            $Y = \$4,500$

Substituting: $Z = \$2,000 + .20 (\$4,500) = \$2,000 + \$900 = \$2,900$

DISTRIBUTION OF FACTORY OVERHEAD	PRODUCING DEPARTMENTS A	PRODUCING DEPARTMENTS B	SERVICE DEPARTMENTS Y	SERVICE DEPARTMENTS Z	TOTAL
Departmental overhead before distribution of service de-partments	$6,000	$ 8,000	$3,630	$2,000	$19,630
Distribution of:					
Department Y....................	1,800	1,800	(4,500)	900	
Department Z....................	580	1,450	870	(2,900)	
Total departmental overhead ...	$8,380	$11,250			$19,630

---

[1]This illustration uses an algebraic method. Matrix algebra can also be used. See Thomas H. Williams and
Charles H. Griffin, "Matrix Theory and Cost Allocation," *The Accounting Review*, Vol. XXXIX, No. 3, pp.
671–678 and John L. Livingstone, "Matrix Algebra and Cost Allocation," *The Accounting Review*, Vol. XLIII,
No. 3, pp. 503–508.

The mechanics of the technique are greatly facilitated by use of the computational capability and speed offered by the computer.

Calculating Departmental Overhead Rates

After service department expenses have been distributed, producing department overhead rates can be calculated in terms of direct labor hours, direct labor cost, machine hours, or some other appropriate basis. In Exhibit 2, three different bases are used: direct labor hours, machine hours, and direct labor cost.

USE OF DEPARTMENTAL FACTORY OVERHEAD RATES

During the fiscal year, as information becomes available at the end of each week or month, factory overhead is applied to a job or product by inserting the applied overhead figure in the overhead section of a job sheet or production report. Amounts applied must be summarized periodically for entry in the general journal. The summary entry applicable to DeWitt Products would appear as follows:

Work in Process	285,000	
Applied Factory Overhead — Cutting Department (42,010 direct labor hours × $2)		84,020
Applied Factory Overhead — Planing Department (17,000 machine hours × $3.20)		54,400
Applied Factory Overhead — Assembly Department ($111,700 direct labor cost × 60%).............................		67,020
Applied Factory Overhead — Upholstery Department (44,200 direct labor hours × $1.80)...........................		79,560

Separate applied factory overhead accounts have been used here. Entries could also have been made directly to each departmental factory overhead control account.

ACTUAL FACTORY OVERHEAD — DEPARTMENTALIZED

Actual factory overhead is summarized in the factory overhead control account in the general ledger. Details are entered in the factory overhead subsidiary ledger. Departmentalization of actual factory overhead also involves the detailed adaptation of previously outlined procedures for handling actual factory overhead. The extra detail can become quite extensive and unduly burdensome unless care is taken to organize the flow of work efficiently.

Departmental Expense Analysis Sheets

Departmentalization of factory overhead requires that each expense be charged to a department as well as to a specific expense account. Such charges are collected on departmental expense analysis sheets. A portion of the form used for both producing and service departments is reproduced on the top of the following page.

DEPARTMENTAL EXPENSE ANALYSIS SHEET

Department No. _1--Cutting_   For _March, 19--_

Explanation	Date	411	412	413	421	433	451	453	Summary

In this form, each column represents a certain class of factory overhead that will be charged to the department. For example, the column coded 411 represents supervisors, and 412 represents indirect labor. Entries to departmental expense analysis sheets are facilitated by combining department numbers and expense codes. A code such as 1412 indicates that Department No. 1 (Cutting) is charged with indirect labor (Code 412). Similar combinations are used for other departments. The chart of accounts establishes the codes.

The subsidiary ledger must also include a sheet for each indirect factory expense not originally charged to a department so that the total of the subsidiary overhead ledger will equal the total in the factory overhead control account.

At the end of the fiscal period, actual costs of producing and service departments, as well as those of a general indirect nature, are again assembled in the same manner as for estimated factory overhead at the beginning of the year. When all overhead has been assembled in the producing departments, it is then possible to compare actual with applied overhead and to determine the over- or underapplied factory overhead. The procedures are summarized as follows:

Steps and Procedures at End of Fiscal Period

1. Preparing a summary of the actual direct departmental factory overhead of producing and service departments. (See Exhibit 3 on page 252.)
2. Preparing a second factory survey based on the actual data experienced during the year. (See Schedule B on page 254.)
3. Allocating actual indirect factory overhead to producing and service departments based on the results of the factory survey at the end of the year. (See Exhibit 3 and Schedule B.)
4. Distributing actual service department costs on the basis of the end-of-the-year factory survey. (See Exhibit 4 on page 253 and Schedule B.)
5. Comparing actual total and departmental factory overhead with the total and departmental factory overhead applied to jobs and products during the year, and determining the total and departmental over- or underapplied factory overhead. (See Exhibit 4.)

DeWitt Products
Actual Departmental Factory Overhead
For the Year 19—

COST ACCOUNTS	F or V	TOTAL	Cutting	Planing	Assembly	Upholstery	Materials Handling	Inspection	Utilities	General Factory
			PRODUCING DEPARTMENTS				SERVICE DEPARTMENTS			
Direct departmental expenses:										
Supervisors	F	$ 70,000	$ 9,000	$ 8,000	$ 8,000	$ 8,000	$10,000	$ 6,000	$ 9,000	$12,000
Indirect labor	F	9,000	1,000	2,000	1,000	1,500	1,000	500	1,000	1,000
	V	63,000	9,800	2,800	4,200	6,000	10,000	7,300	9,000	13,900
Labor fringe costs	F	10,000	1,500	1,000	1,000	1,000	2,000	1,000	1,500	1,000
	V	45,000	10,000	11,400	9,700	8,000	1,700	1,300	1,600	1,300
Indirect materials	F	4,000	500	500	800	1,200	300	200	200	300
	V	23,000	4,300	3,600	2,900	5,400	1,800	1,200	2,100	1,700
Repairs and maintenance	F	3,000	600	500	700	600	600	300	300	300
	V	12,000	1,700	1,800	2,000	2,100			2,500	1,000
Depreciation — equipment	F	13,000	1,500	3,500	1,000	3,000				4,000
Total direct departmental expenses		$252,000	$39,900	$35,100	$31,300	$36,800	$27,400	$17,800	$27,200	$36,500
Indirect departmental expenses:										
Electric power	F	$ 2,000							$ 2,000	
	V	14,000							14,000	
Fuel	F	1,000							1,000	
	V	7,000							7,000	
Water	F	1,000							1,000	
	V	3,000							3,000	
Depreciation — buildings	F	5,000	$ 1,250	$ 1,000	$ 1,500	$ 1,250				
Property tax	F	4,000	1,000	800	1,200	1,000				
Insurance (fire)	F	3,000	750	600	900	750				
Total indirect departmental expenses		$ 40,000	$ 3,000	$ 2,400	$ 3,600	$ 3,000			$28,000	
Total actual departmental factory overhead before distribution of service departments		$292,000	$42,900	$37,500	$34,900	$39,800	$27,400	$17,800	$55,200	$36,500

Exhibit 3

DeWitt Products
Distribution of Actual Service Department Costs
and
Computation of Departmental Over- or Underapplied Factory Overhead
For the Year 19—

Cost Accounts	Total	Producing Departments				Service Departments			
		Cutting	Planing	Assembly	Upholstery	Materials Handling	Inspection	Utilities	General Factory
Total actual departmental factory overhead before distribution of service departments.	$292,000	$42,900	$37,500	$34,900	$39,800	$27,400	$17,800	$55,200	$36,500
Distribution of service department costs:									
Materials handling (Base: actual cost of materials requisitioned)		$12,330	$ 2,740	$ 3,014	$ 9,316	(27,400)			
Inspection (Base: equally to assembly and upholstery departments)				8,900	8,900		(17,800)		
Utilities: (Bases: 20% on kwh / 50% on hph / 30% on floor area)		2,870 / 11,592 / 4,140	883 / 6,072 / 3,312	2,760 / 4,968 / 4,968	4,527 / 4,968 / 4,140			(11,040) / (27,600) / (16,560)	
General factory (Base: number of employees)		8,760	6,205	10,220	11,315				(36,500)
Total service department costs distributed		$39,692	$19,212	$34,830	$43,166				
Total actual departmental factory overhead after distribution of service departments	$292,000	$82,592	$56,712	$69,730	$82,966				
Total applied factory overhead	285,000	84,020	54,400	67,020	79,560				
(Over-) or underapplied factory overhead	$ 7,000	$ (1,428)	$ 2,312	$ 2,710	$ 3,406				

Exhibit 4

DeWitt Products
Factory Survey — December 31, 19--

PRODUCING DEPARTMENTS	NUMBER OF EMPLOYEES	%	KILO-WATT-HOURS	%	HORSE-POWER-HOURS	%	FLOOR AREA (SQ. FT.)	%	COST OF MATERIALS REQUISI-TIONED	%
Cutting.........	35	24	16 978	26	210,000	42	5,250	25	$193,500	45
Planing........	25	17	5 224	8	110,000	22	4,200	20	43,000	10
Assembly.....	40	28	16 325	25	90,000	18	6,300	30	47,300	11
Upholstery...	45	31	26 773	41	90,000	18	5,250	25	146,200	34
Total............	145	100	65 300	100	500,000	100	21,000	100	$430,000	100

Schedule B

OVER- OR UNDERAPPLIED FACTORY OVERHEAD

With the year-end overhead distribution sheet completed, total actual departmental factory overhead can now be transferred to the individual departmental factory overhead control accounts. Using the figures provided by the overhead distribution sheet (Exhibit 4), the following entry can be made:

Factory Overhead — Cutting Department..........................	82,592	
Factory Overhead — Planing Department.........................	56,712	
Factory Overhead — Assembly Department	69,730	
Factory Overhead — Upholstery Department....................	82,966	
Factory Overhead Control		292,000

A comparison of actual and applied overhead of each producing department as well as of the total overhead of the company results in the following (over-) underapplied factory overhead:

TOTAL	CUTTING	PLANING	ASSEMBLY	UPHOLSTERY
$7,000	$(1,428)	$2,312	$2,710	$3,406

SPENDING AND IDLE CAPACITY VARIANCE ANALYSIS

In the previous chapter, page 221, the $7,000 underapplied factory overhead was analyzed and a $750 unfavorable spending variance and a $6,250 unfavorable idle capacity variance were determined. The $1.50 overhead rate used there and based on 200,000 direct labor hours is not applicable for the departmentalized illustration. New rates with different bases have been created. However, it is possible to analyze each departmental over- or underapplied figure and determine a departmental spending and idle capacity variance. What is particularly needed is the amount of overhead budgeted for the level of operation attained (capacity utilized), which, in turn, requires a knowledge of the fixed and variable overhead in each producing department. To develop the budget allowance, the estimates shown in the summaries of the departmental factory overhead (Exhibit 1) and the distribution of service department costs (Exhibit 2) are examined. Exhibit 1 indicates the fixed and variable departmental costs at the bottom line of the estimates. The service department costs distributed to the producing departments, as shown in Exhibit 2, are considered variable costs for the producing departments. The fixed-variable classification does not apply after the distribution.

The spending and idle capacity variance analysis reproduced below and on the next page is prepared for executive management on the basis of the actual annual data after the books have been closed. However, the middle- and operating-management levels require current cost control information at least once a month. With ever greater emphasis placed upon the control of costs by responsible supervisory personnel, procedures must communicate to all levels of management the control information in a manner that permits the charging and discharging of responsibility of cost incurrence. This approach is discussed in Chapter 11.

CALCULATION OF ESTIMATED FIXED AND VARIABLE OVERHEAD RATES

	PRODUCING DEPARTMENTS			
	Cutting	*Planing*	*Assembly*	*Upholstery*
Fixed departmental overhead	$17,100	$17,900	$ 16,100	$18,300
Variable departmental overhead.......	$23,400	$18,800	$ 18,900	$20,300
Variable service department costs	40,716	22,183	38,242	48,059
Total variable overhead	$64,116	$40,983	$ 57,142	$68,359
Bases:				
Direct labor hours	40,608			48,140
Machine hours..........................		18,400		
Direct labor cost			$122,000	
Fixed overhead rate......................	$ .42	$ .97	13%	$ .38
Variable overhead rate	1.58	2.23	47	1.42
Total overhead rate:				
Per direct labor hour	$2.00			
Per machine hour		$3.20		
Of direct labor cost....................			60%	
Per direct labor hour				$1.80

CALCULATION OF BUDGET ALLOWANCES*

	PRODUCING DEPARTMENTS			
	Cutting	*Planing*	*Assembly*	*Upholstery*
Fixed overhead.............................	$17,100	$17,900	$ 16,100	$18,300
Variable overhead:				
42,010 direct labor hours × $1.58 ..	66,376			
17,000 machine hours × $2.23.......		37,910		
$111,700 direct labor cost × 47%...			52,499	
44,200 direct labor hours × $1.42 ..				62,764
Total budget allowance..................	$83,476	$55,810	$ 68,599	$81,064

*Based on capacity utilized, i.e., actual activity.

	SPENDING AND IDLE CAPACITY VARIANCE ANALYSIS					
PRODUCING DEPART- MENTS	(1) ACTUAL OVERHEAD	(2) BUDGET ALLOWANCE	(3) APPLIED OVERHEAD	TOTAL VARIANCE (1)–(3)	SPENDING VARIANCE (1)–(2)	IDLE CAPACITY VARIANCE (2)–(3)
Cutting......	$ 82,592	$ 83,476	$ 84,020	$(1,428)	$ (884)	$ (544)
Planing......	56,712	55,810	54,400	2,312	902	1,410
Assembly ..	69,730	68,599	67,020	2,710	1,131	1,579
Upholstery	82,966	81,064	79,560	3,406	1,902	1,504
Total........	$292,000	$288,949	$285,000	$ 7,000	$3,051	$3,949

OVERHEAD DEPARTMENTALIZATION IN NONMANUFACTURING BUSINESSES AND NONPROFIT ORGANIZATIONS

The responsible control of departmental expenses is equally essential in nonmanufacturing activities. The following large complex entities should be divided into administrative and supervisory departments, sections, or service units for cost planning and control:

Nonmanufacturing segments of manufacturing concerns (e.g., marketing departments — see Chapter 23)
Retail or department stores
Financial institutions (banks, savings and loan associations, and brokerage houses)

Insurance companies
Educational institutions (public school systems, colleges, and universities)
Service organizations (hotels, motels, hospitals, and nursing homes)
Federal, state, and local governments (and their agencies)

Retail or department stores have practiced departmentalization for many years by grouping their organizations under the following typical headings: administration, occupancy, sales promotion and advertising, purchasing, selling, and delivery. These groups incur costs similar to those in manufacturing businesses. The group "Occupancy" is almost identical with General Factory, and includes such expenses as building repairs, rent and taxes, insurance on buildings and fixtures, light, heat, power, and depreciation on buildings and fixtures. Again, similar to factory procedures, group costs are prorated to revenue-producing sales departments via a charging or billing rate.

Financial institutions (banks, savings and loan associations, and brokerage houses) should departmentalize their organizations in order to control expenses and establish a profitability rating of individual activities. The size of the institution and the types of services offered determine the number of departments. The accumulation of departmental costs again follows factory procedure: (1) direct expenses, such as salaries, supplies, and depreciation of equipment, are charged directly; (2) general expenses, such as light, heat, and air conditioning, are prorated to the departments on appropriate bases. As income and expenses are ascertained, it is possible to create a work cost unit that permits the charging of accounts for services rendered and the analysis of an account's profitability.

The work of *insurance companies* is facilitated by dividing the office into departments. Some departments have several hundred clerks, and the work is highly organized. Insurance companies were one of the first businesses to install large-scale digital computers to reduce the clerical costs connected with the insurance business and to calculate new insurance rates and coverage on a more expanded basis for greater profitability. This quite detailed departmentalization might include actuarial, premium collection, group insurance, policyholders' service, registrar, medical, and legal information. While some costs are unique to the individual group, most are identical with expenses experienced in any office department.

Educational institutions (such as public school systems, colleges, and universities) and *service organizations* (such as hotels, motels, hospitals, and nursing homes) find it increasingly necessary to budget their expenses on a departmental basis in order to control expenses and be able to charge an adequate cost recovering fee for their services. The extended services of social security via Medicare have made a knowledge of costs mandatory in hospitals and nursing homes. Departmentalization will assist management in creating a costing or charging rate for short- or long-term care, for special services, for nurses' instruction, and for professional services (surgical, medical, X-rays, laboratory examinations, and filling of prescriptions).

The *federal government* employs a great number of people in a vast number of departments and agencies. A similar situation exists in *state and local governments*. This discussion uses the municipality as an example, since its varied services are better known to the public. Some common services or departments are street cleaning, street repairing and paving, public works projects, police and fire departments, city hospitals, sewage disposal plants, and trash and garbage collection. These services should be budgeted and their costs controlled on a responsibility accounting basis. Since the costs incurred are generally not revenue- but service-benefit-oriented, an attempt should be made to measure the operating efficiency of an activity based on some unit of measurement such as per capita (police), per mile (street paving and cleaning), and per ton (trash and garbage collection). Ever-increasing costs require additional revenue, which means additional taxes. Taxpayers, however, expect efficient service in return for their tax money.

The state and federal goverments must be made equally aware of the need for responsible cost control methods, so that services may be rendered at the lowest cost with greatest efficiency. The federal government, particularly with its many departments and agencies and a huge sum budgeted for all of these units, must ensure that these activities are being administered by cost-conscious and service-minded people. The departmentalization process helps to assure the achievement of such a goal in any governmental unit.

DISCUSSION QUESTIONS

1. State reasons for the preference of departmental overhead rates over a single plant-wide rate.

2. The statement has been made that the entire process of departmentalizing factory overhead is an extension of methods used when a single overhead rate is used. Explain.

3. For effective control of overhead, a supervisor, superintendent, manager, or department head can be held accountable for more than one cost center; but responsibility for a single cost center should not be divided between two or more individuals. Discuss.

4. What is a producing department? A service department? Give illustrations of each.

5. What are some of the factors that must be considered in deciding the kinds and number of departments required to control costs and to establish accurate departmental overhead rates?

6. State reasons for using a general factory cost pool for certain types of overhead instead of allocating it directly to producing and service departments.

7. Justify classifying overtime premiums and rework labor as factory overhead. List some of the difficulties in estimating these items in the creation of predetermined overhead rates.

8. Most companies keep plant asset records to identify equipment and its original cost by location or department. However, charges for depreciation, property tax, and fire insurance are often accumulated in general factory accounts and charged to departments on the basis of equipment values. Is this the best method for controlling such costs? If not, suggest possible improvements.

9. What are the several steps followed in establishing departmental factory overhead rates?

10. What are the important factors involved in selecting the rate to be used for applying the factory overhead of a producing department?

11. What are some of the practices with respect to the sequence used in distributing service department overhead to producing departments? What bases should be used to transfer the overhead of the following service departments?

Production Control	Maintenance
Purchasing	Utilities
Medical	Cafeteria
Payroll	Accounting
Storeroom	Personnel

12. Procedures followed in computing departmental factory overhead rates determine the accounting for actual factory overhead. Explain. What are departmental expense analysis sheets, and how are they used? Trace a requisition for indirect materials through the departmentalization of factory overhead process.

13. A company uses departmental factory overhead rates based on direct labor hours. Would the sum of departmental over- or underapplied overhead be any

different if a plant-wide or blanket rate were used? Would the costs of goods sold and inventory be different?

14. Describe how departmental over- or underapplied overhead is determined, and explain the computations of departmental spending and idle capacity variances.

15. Overhead control in a nonmanufacturing business can be achieved through departmentalization. Explain.

16. Federal, state, and local governments should practice cost control via responsibility accounting. Discuss.

EXERCISES

1. Cost classification. The management of Meinhart, Inc., believes that costs can be kept at budgetary levels by assigning cost responsibility to specific individuals.

Required: Classification of the following items according to specific departments (cost centers or cost pools):
- (a) Factory wages
- (b) Depreciation of machinery
- (c) Purchasing of raw materials
- (d) Factory supplies used
- (e) Plant manager's salary
- (f) Sales manager's salary
- (g) Cost of operating power plant which serves entire plant
- (h) Data processing

2. Types of factory overhead rates. Linkevich, Inc., engages the services of a CPA firm for the installation of a cost system. Preliminary investigation of manufacturing operations discloses these facts:

- (a) The company makes a line of light fixtures and lamps. The materials cost of any particular item ranges from 15% to 60% of total factory cost, depending on the kind of metal and fabric used.
- (b) The business is subject to wide cyclical fluctuations, since the sales volume follows new housing construction.
- (c) About 60% of the manufacturing is normally finished during the first quarter of the year.
- (d) For the whole plant, the wage rates range from $3.25 to $7.75 an hour. However, within each of the eight individual departments, the spread between the high and low wage rate is less than 5%.
- (e) Each product requires the use of all eight of the manufacturing departments, but not proportionately.
- (f) Within the individual manufacturing departments, factory overhead ranges from 30% to 80% of conversion cost.

Required: A letter to the president of Linkevich, Inc., explaining whether its cost system should use the following procedures, and including the reasons supporting each of these recommendations:
- (1) A predetermined overhead rate or an actual overhead rate — departmental or plant-wide.
- (2) A method of factory overhead distribution based on direct labor hours, direct labor cost, or prime cost.

(AICPA adapted)

3. Entries with overhead subsidiary ledger. The general ledger of the Fletcher Company contains a factory overhead control account supported by a subsidiary ledger showing details by departments. The plant has one service department and three producing departments. The table on page 260 shows details with respect to these departments.

	MACHINING DEPT.	PAINTING DEPT.	ASSEMBLY DEPT.	GENERAL FACTORY COST POOL
Building space (sq. ft.)..............................	10,000	4,000	4,000	2,000
Value of machinery.................................	$30,000	$10,000	$6,000	$2,000
Horsepower rating	100	–0–	10	15
Compensation insurance rate (per $100)...	$1.50	$1.50	$1.00	$1.00

During January, certain assets expired and some liabilities accrued as outlined below:

(a) Depreciation on buildings, 3% per year; cost, $60,000.

(b) Depreciation on machinery based on 10-year life; machinery cost, $48,000.

(c) Property tax for the year ending December 31 is estimated to be $1,200 (60% on buildings and 40% on machinery).

(d) Fire insurance in the amount of $100,000 is carried on buildings and machinery, and the rate is $.60 per $100 of coverage. Sixty percent of this insurance applies to buildings. The prepaid fire insurance account shows a balance of $300 at January 31 before adjustment.

(e) Compensation insurance for January is based on the following earnings of factory employees: Machining Department, $3,000; Painting Department, $1,200; Assembly Department, $1,600; and General Factory Cost Pool, $600.

(f) The power meter reading at January 31 shows 12 500 kilowatt-hours consumed. The rate is $.03 per kilowatt-hour.

(g) The heat and light bill for January is $300.

(h) Supplies requisitions show $180 used in the Machining Department, $230 in the Assembly Department, and $410 in the General Factory Cost Pool.

Required: Journal entries with details entered in the factory overhead subsidiary ledger.

4. Allocation of service department costs. The factory overhead work sheet for the Chattanooga Products Company had the following columnar totals after the actual direct charges and the indirect departmental expense allocations had been made: Service departments: A — $12,480, B — $14,000, and C — $11,000; Producing departments: X — $50,000 and Y — $60,000.

Required: Completion of the work sheet (rounding to the nearest dollar) if the service department costs are allocated as follows:
Dept. A costs: 40% to B, 10% to C, 30% to X, and 20% to Y.
Dept. B costs: 40% to C, 30% to X, and 30% to Y.
Dept. C costs: 50% to X and 50% to Y.

5. Distribution of service department expenses. The Martin Company has four producing departments and three service departments. The following information for October is available:

DEPARTMENT	ACTUAL EXPENSES	SQUARE FEET	EMPLOYEES	INVESTMENT IN EQUIPMENT
Grinding..	$10,000	3,000	30	$20,000
Forming.......................................	14,000	1,500	20	10,000
Machining....................................	4,000	2,500	30	12,000
Finishing......................................	8,000	1,000	10	4,000
Building Service..........................	6,000	500	15	600
Health and Recreation................	5,000	2,000	5	1,600
Repairs and Maintenance..........	3,000	2,000	10	2,400
Total	$50,000	12,500	120	$50,600

The order and bases for distributing expenses of the service departments are: Building Service, area; Health and Recreation, number of employees; Repairs and Maintenance, investment in equipment. The company assigns service department expenses to other service departments; however, after a department's expenses have been allocated, no expenses are assigned back to it.

Required: Distribution of service department expenses, based on the data given.

6. Overhead distribution and rate calculation. The Torresdale Company has four producing departments and three service departments. The estimated annual overhead for these seven departments is as follows:

ESTIMATED EXPENSES	PRODUCING DEPARTMENTS				SERVICE DEPARTMENTS		
	01	02	03	04	Main-tenance	Tool-room	Store-room
Fixed factory overhead	$36,000	$48,000	$45,000	$30,000	$15,000	$10,500	$12,000
Variable factory overhead	24,000	22,000	20,000	20,000	10,800	10,500	3,000
Total	$60,000	$70,000	$65,000	$50,000	$25,800	$21,000	$15,000

Management decided to distribute the service department costs on a dual basis: (a) fixed overhead on a standby or ready-to-serve basis and (b) variable overhead on a billing or charging rate basis.

The fixed overhead of the three service departments is to be distributed as follows:

SERVICE DEPARTMENTS	TOTAL	01	02	03	04
Maintenance....................................	$15,000	$5,000	$4,000	$3,000	$3,000
Toolroom	10,500	3,500	2,500	2,500	2,000
Storeroom......................................	12,000	6,000	3,000	2,000	1,000

The variable overhead of the service departments is distributed on the basis of the following data:

DEPARTMENT	MAINTENANCE (AREA IN SQUARE FEET)	TOOLROOM (NUMBER OF EMPLOYEES)	STOREROOM (NUMBER OF MATERIALS REQUISITIONS)
No. 01	12,000	50	30,000
No. 02	10,000	40	30,000
No. 03	9,000	30	28,000
No. 04	5,000	30	12,000
Maintenance..........................	5,000	10	
Toolroom.............................	3,000	5	
Storeroom............................	1,000	5	

No service department's cost is to be prorated to other service departments.

Required:
(1) A factory overhead distribution sheet on the basis of the data and instructions given.
(2) Factory overhead rates for the four producing departments, based on the following predetermined machine hours, direct labor hours, and direct labor cost:

DEPARTMENT No.	
01	33,000 machine hours
02	32,000 machine hours
03	39,070 direct labor hours
04	$59,960 labor cost

7. Transfer entries and variance analysis. A distribution of a company's actual factory overhead for the past year is given at the top of page 262. Budgeted factory overhead for the four producing departments (including apportioned service department overhead) is also given for two levels of activity. The company uses a predetermined rate for each producing department based on labor hours at the normal capacity level. Actual hours worked last year were 17,000 hours for Department A and 18,000 hours for B.

ACTUAL FACTORY OVERHEAD

	A	B	C	D	X	Y	Z	Total
Actual expenses..........	$10,000	$16,000	$4,000	$8,000	$3,000	$5,000	$6,000	$52,000
Z's expenses	1,500	750	1,250	500	1,000	1,000	6,000	
Y's expenses	1,800	1,200	1,800	600	600	$6,000		
X's expenses	2,000	1,000	1,200	400	$4,600			
Total...........................	$15,300	$18,950	$8,250	$9,500				$52,000

BUDGETED FACTORY OVERHEAD

	20,000 hours (Normal)	16,000 Hours
Department A...	$17,800	$15,000
Department B	20,200	17,800
Department C	10,600	9,400
Department D	10,600	9,400
Total...	$59,200	$51,600

Required:
(1) Entries to record:
   (a) The transfer of the actual factory overhead to producing departments, assuming that the actual factory overhead was accumulated in a single factory overhead control account.
   (b) The applied factory overhead of Departments A and B.
(2) Computation of the spending and idle capacity variances for Departments A and B.

8. Overhead analysis and causes for variances. The Skinner Company uses predetermined departmental overhead rates. The rate for the Fabricating Department is $4 per direct labor hour. Direct labor employees are paid $6.50 per hour. A total of 15,000 direct labor hours were worked in the department during the year. Total overhead charged to the department for supervisors' salaries, indirect labor, labor fringe benefit costs, indirect materials, and service department costs was $65,000.

Required:
(1) The over- or underapplied factory overhead.
(2) The effect on the amount of over- or underapplied factory overhead in each of the following situations. Discuss each item separately as though the other factors had not occurred.
   (a) Direct laborers worked one hundred overtime hours for which time-and-a-half was paid. Overtime premium, the amount in excess of the regular rate, is charged as overhead to the department in which the overtime is worked.
   (b) A $.35 per hour wage increase was granted November 1. Direct labor hours worked in November and December totaled 2,500.
   (c) The company cafeteria incurred a $1,500 loss, which was distributed to producing departments on the basis of number of employees. Nine of the 120 employees work in the Fabricating Department. No loss was anticipated when predetermined overhead rates were computed.

9. Algebraic distribution of factory overhead. The Holmes Company has decided to distribute the costs of service departments by the algebraic method. The producing departments are P1 and P2, the service departments are S1 and S2, and the monthly data are:

	ACTUAL FACTORY OVERHEAD COSTS BEFORE DISTRIBUTION	SERVICES PROVIDED BY	
		S1	S2
P1	$84,000	40%	50%
P2	58,000	50	30
S1	20,000	—	20
S2	17,600	10	—

Required: Total factory overhead of producing department P1 after distribution of service department costs.

10. Algebraic distribution of factory overhead. A company's two service departments serve not only the two producing departments but also one another. The relationships between the four departments can be expressed as follows:

	PERCENTAGES OF SERVICES CONSUMED BY DEPARTMENTS				
SERVICE DEPARTMENTS	Producing		Service		SERVICE COSTS TO BE DISTRIBUTED
	A	B	Y	Z	
Y	50%	40%		10%	$10,000
Z	40%	40%	20%		8,800

Required:
(1) The amount of service costs applicable to each department.
(2) The total factory overhead in each producing department if primary overhead amounts to $22,000 in Department A and $29,000 in Department B.

11. Algebraic distribution of factory overhead. The estimated departmental factory overhead for Producing Departments S and T and Service Departments E, F, and G (before any service department allocations) are:

PRODUCING DEPARTMENTS		SERVICE DEPARTMENTS	
S....................	$60,000	E.................	$20,000
T....................	90,000	F.................	20,000
		G.................	10,000

The interdependence of the departments is tabulated as follows:

Departments	SERVICES PROVIDED		
	E	F	G
Producing — S	—	30%	40%
Producing — T	50%	40	30
Service — E	—	20	—
Service — F...	20	—	—
Service — G...	30	10	—
Marketing...	—	—	20
General Office	—	—	10
	100%	100%	100%

Required:
(1) The final amount of estimated overhead of each service department after reciprocal transfer costs have been calculated algebraically.
(2) The total factory overhead of each producing department and the amount of Department G cost assigned to the Marketing Department and to General Office.

12. Overhead distribution. Nash, Inc., has two producing departments and three service departments. A summary of costs and other data for each department prior to allocation of service department costs for the year ended June 30, 19--, shows:

	PRODUCING DEPARTMENTS		SERVICE DEPARTMENTS		
	Fabrication	Assembly	General Factory Cost Pool	Maintenance	Cafeteria
Direct labor cost....................	$1,950,000	$2,050,000	$90,000	$82,100	$87,000
Direct materials cost.............	3,130,000	950,000	—	65,000	91,000
Factory overhead cost	1,650,000	1,850,000	70,000	56,100	62,000
Direct labor hours	562,500	437,500	31,000	27,000	42,000
Number of employees..........	280	200	12	8	20
Square footage occupied	88,000	72,000	1,750	2,000	4,800

The costs of General Factory Cost Pool, Maintenance, and Cafeteria are allocated on the basis of direct labor hours, square footage occupied, and number of employees, respectively. There are no factory overhead variances.

Required:
  (1) The amount of Maintenance cost allocated to Fabrication, assuming that the company elects to distribute service department costs directly to the producing departments without inter-service-department cost allocation.
  (2) The amount of General Factory Cost Pool cost allocated to Assembly, assuming the same policy of allocating service departments to producing departments only.
  (3) Assuming that the company elects to distribute service department costs to other service departments (starting with the service department with the greatest total cost) as well as to the producing departments and that once a service department's cost has been allocated, no subsequent service department cost is recirculated back to it:
     (a) The amount of Cafeteria cost allocated to Maintenance.
     (b) The amount of Maintenance cost allocated to Cafeteria.

                                                              (AICPA adapted)

PROBLEMS

10-1. Overhead distribution sheet. Hamlin, Inc., applies factory overhead on the following bases: in Department A, 35% of A's materials cost; in Department B, $4.00 per direct labor hour in B.

The following accounts and their balances at the end of the month have been taken from the books and records:

Work in Process — Materials	$46,000
Work in Process — Direct Labor	29,450
Work in Process — Applied Factory Overhead	27,550
Indirect Labor	17,400
Factory Office	3,200
Building Charges (including depreciation, insurance, etc.)	4,000
Powerhouse Expenses (coal, labor, etc.)	2,800

Additional information:

	PRODUCING DEPARTMENTS		
	A	B	Powerhouse
Direct materials	$33,000	$13,000	
Direct labor	11,780	17,670	
Direct labor hours	3,500	4,000	
Power used	60%	40%	
Floor space occupied	750 sq. ft.	750 sq. ft.	500 sq. ft.

Indirect labor and factory office are apportioned in direct ratio to the cost of direct labor.

Required:
  (1) A distribution sheet showing the distribution of factory overhead costs to producing departments and the powerhouse.
  (2) The total and departmental over- or underapplied factory overhead after the powerhouse expenses have been allocated to the producing departments.

10-2. Overhead distribution sheet and rate calculation. The president of the Bellows Products Company has been critical of the product costing methods whereby factory overhead is charged to products on a factory-wide overhead rate. The chief accountant suggested a departmentalization of the factory for the purpose of calculating departmental factory overhead rates, accumulating the following estimated direct departmental overhead data on an annual basis:

OVERHEAD ITEMS	PRODUCING DEPARTMENTS			SERVICE DEPARTMENTS		
	Dept. 10	Dept. 12	Dept. 14	Store-room	Repairs and Maintenance	General Factory Cost Pool
Supervision............................	$12,500	$16,000	$14,000	$ 7,200	$ 8,000	$24,000
Indirect labor	5,400	6,000	8,000	6,133	7,200	18,000
Indirect supplies....................	4,850	5,600	5,430	1,400	3,651	1,070
Labor fringe benefits.............	6,872	9,349	10,145	640	760	2,100
Equipment depreciation.......	6,000	8,000	10,000	560	1,740	1,100
Property tax, depreciation of buildings, etc.						20,000
Total......................................	$35,622	$44,949	$47,575	$15,933	$21,351	$66,270

The annual light and power bill is estimated at $9,300 and is allocated on the basis of electricity usage.

The order and bases of distribution of service department expenses are as follows:

(a) General Factory Cost Pool — area occupied
(b) Storeroom expenses — estimated requisitions
(c) Repairs and maintenance — estimated repairs and maintenance hours

The following departmental information is provided:

	DEPT. 10	DEPT 12	DEPT. 14	STORE-ROOM	REPAIRS AND MAINTENANCE	GENERAL FACTORY COST POOL
Percentage of usage of electricity..	20%	25%	30%	3%	12%	10%
Area occupied (sq. ft.)...................	21,000	25,200	29,400	3,360	5,040	—
Estimated number of requisitions	124,200	81,000	40,500	—	24,300	—
Estimated number of repairs and maintenance hours...................	4,800	4,200	6,000	—	—	—
Estimated direct labor hours........	80,000	90,000	80,000	—	—	—

Required: A factory overhead distribution sheet with calculation of overhead rates for the producing departments based on direct labor hours.

10-3. Overhead distribution sheet and rate calculation. Cassel Chemical Co. consists of three producing departments and four service departments. For the purpose of creating factory overhead rates, the accountant prepared the cost distribution sheet shown below. It contains operational data gathered by the accountant.

DATA	TOTAL	PRODUCING DEPARTMENTS			SERVICE DEPARTMENTS			
		Preparation	Mixing	Packaging	Utilities	Maintenance	Materials Handling	Factory Office
Operational data:								
Floor space — sq. ft.	53,000	10,000	12,000	16,000	3,000	3,000	5,000	4,000
Maintenance hours..............	6,820	1,860	2,480	930	620		620	310
Metered hours in hundreds	4,000	1,400	1,600	320		200	320	160
Expenses:								
Indirect labor......	$22,000	$ 3,800	$ 2,600	$ 2,400	$3,500	$4,000	$3,300	$2,400
Payroll taxes.......	2,522	440	532	420	230	355	320	225
Indirect materials.........	5,703	700	938	2,300	920	150	150	545
Depreciation.......	850	100	150	50	100	200	200	50
Total	$31,075	$ 5,040	$ 4,220	$ 5,170	$4,750	$4,705	$3,970	$3,220

For the distribution of expenses of the service departments, the following procedures had been decided upon:

(a) Utilities: 80% on metered hours — power
                              20% on floor square footage
(b) Maintenance: Maintenance hours excluding utilities
(c) Materials Handling: 48% to Preparation, 32% to Mixing, and 20% to Packaging;
                              pounds handled — 395,300 in Preparation, 262,850 in Mixing
(d) Factory Office: Preparation, 40%; Mixing, 30%; Packaging, 30%

Required:
(1) Completion of the cost distribution sheet. No reciprocal charging should take place. (Round off all amounts to the nearest dollar.)
(2) Factory overhead rates based on pounds handled in Preparation and Mixing and on direct labor cost of $86,000 in Packaging. (Round off to the nearest cent.)

10-4. Journal entries; revision of overhead rates. The Yonkers Furniture Company manufactures laboratory benches in three producing departments: Cutting, Assembling, and Finishing. All overhead costs are charged directly to producing departments without the use of auxiliary or service departments.

For the first six months of the calendar year, management had approved the following predetermined factory overhead rates:

Cutting .... $1.50 per machine hour
Assembling .... 1.90 per direct labor hour
Finishing .... 100% of direct labor cost

Factory overhead costs for the first six months were:

Cutting $16,950
Assembling....................................... 12,143
Finishing... 8,405

For the same period the following data were also accumulated:

Cutting .... 12,900 machine hours
Assembling.............................. 8,100 direct labor hours
Finishing.................................. $9,100 direct labor

As of June 30, the company revised its budget in the light of experience to that date and projections for the remainder of the year. Data on factory overhead from the new budget follow:

	CUTTING	ASSEMBLING	FINISHING
Total budgeted factory overhead	$26,975	$20,160	$14,805
Application basis (estimated)	20,750 machine hours	12,600 direct labor hours	$16,450 direct labor

Required: Journal entries to record:
(1) Incurred and applied overhead for the first six months.
(2) Adjustment of the applied overhead based on the new rates, retroactive to January 1. Analysis of the job cost sheets shows the total overhead adjustment should be distributed 5% to work in process, 35% to finished goods, and 60% to cost of goods sold.

10-5. Cost center rates and variance analysis. The Cost Department of the Vulcan Co. applies factory overhead to jobs and products on the basis of predetermined cost center overhead rates. In each of the two producing departments, two cost centers have been set up. For the coming year, the following estimates and other data have been made available:

DEPARTMENT 10:	ESTIMATED ANNUAL FACTORY OVERHEAD			ESTIMATED ANNUAL MACHINE HOURS
	Fixed	Variable	Total	
Cost Center 10-1...................	$14,040	$23,400	$37,440	15,600
Cost Center 10-2...................	26,910	43,290	70,200	23,400

DEPARTMENT 20:	ESTIMATED ANNUAL FACTORY OVERHEAD			ESTIMATED ANNUAL DIRECT LABOR HOURS
	Fixed	*Variable*	*Total*	
Cost Center 20-1..................	$ 8,320	$21,580	$29,900	26,000
Cost Center 20-2..................	6,240	19,760	26,000	20,800

Required:

(1) The annual normal cost center overhead rates based on the estimated machine hours in Department 10 and the estimated direct labor hours in Department 20.

(2) Application of factory overhead to the four cost centers on the basis of these actual machine or labor hours used or worked during the month of February:

COST CENTERS	10-1	10-2	20-1	20-2
Machine hours..............	1,220	2,000		
Labor hours...................			2,250	1,650

(3) The spending and the idle capacity variances for the two producing departments. Actual factory overhead in Department 10 amounted to $9,630 and in Department 20 to $4,205.

(4) Analysis of the total idle capacity variance of Department 10, determining the idle capacity variances of the two cost centers. Use $1/12$ of the total annual estimated hours as normal monthly hours.

10-6. Allocation of personnel department costs. Bracken, Inc., has 1,000 employees — 600 factory workers, 300 clerks, and 100 managers. Of that number, Department A, a producing department, has 60 factory, 30 clerical, and 10 managerial employees.

During the past year, Bracken's Personnel Department incurred the following expenses charged to six functional categories:

		EXPENSES				
FUNCTIONAL CATEGORY	Salaries	Advertising and Recruiting	Rent	Depreciation	Supplies and Miscellaneous	Total
Placement and separation..................	$ 30,000	$12,800	$ 2,400	$ 168.00	$ 600	$ 45,968.00
Labor relations..............	17,625	200	1,530	153.25	275	19,783.25
Benefits...........................	22,875	1,000	1,890	142.00	745	26,652.00
Management development..............	30,000	500	2,640	182.25	185	33,507.25
Safety	13,375	500	1,110	94.25	70	15,149.25
Wage and salary administration...........	26,125	–0–	2,430	260.25	125	28,940.25
Total	$140,000	$15,000	$12,000	$1,000.00	$2,000	$170,000.00

The following criteria are used for allocating the functionally categorized costs to benefiting departments:

(a) Placement and separation — 90% placement related, 10% separation related. Cost of placing and separating a manager is five times that for other employees.

(b) Labor relations — the average number of factory workers.

(c) Benefits — the average number of employees.

(d) Management development — the average number of managers.

(e) Safety — 90% factory worker related; 10% clerical and managerial related.

(f) Wage and salary administration — the average number of employees.

The past year was stable in terms of the total work force, with the same number of employees at the end of the year as at the beginning. During the year, Bracken placed and separated 60 factory, 30 clerical, and 10 management employees. Of this number, 20% of the factory workers, 20% of the clerical employees, and one manager were from Department A.

Required: The allocation of the Personnel Department costs to Department A. (Round off all amounts to the nearest cent.)

10-7. Algebraic distribution of actual factory overhead. The controller of the Plotkin Corporation instructs the cost supervisor to use an algebraic procedure for allocating service department costs to producing departments. The corporation's three producing departments are served by three service departments, each of which consumes part of the services of the other two. After primary but before reciprocal distribution, the account balances of the service departments and the interdependence of the departments were tabulated as follows:

DEPARTMENT	DEPARTMENTAL OVERHEAD BEFORE DISTRIBUTION OF SERVICE DEPARTMENTS	SERVICES PROVIDED Powerhouse	Personnel	General Factory
Mixing...................	$125,000	25%	35%	25%
Refining...............	90,000	25	30	20
Finishing	105,000	20	20	20
Powerhouse........	16,000	—	10	20
Personnel	29,500	10	—	15
General Factory..	42,000	20	5	—
	$407,500	100%	100%	100%

Required:
(1) The final amount of overhead of each service department after reciprocal transfer costs have been calculated algebraically.
(2) The total factory overhead of each producing department.

10-8. Algebraic distribution; make-or-buy decision for a service department. The Capettini Company has three service departments (Water, Steam, and Electric Power) and one producing department. The technical relationships between the service departments are that it requires 0.8 kilowatt-hours of electricity to pump one gallon of water, .5 gallons of water to generate one cubic foot of steam, and .15 cubic feet of steam to generate one kilowatt-hour of electricity. Each unit of producing department output requires .6 gallons of water, .9 cubic feet of steam, and 4.8 kilowatt-hours of electricity. The output of the producing department is 100,000 units.

Cost data before service department cost allocations are:

DEPARTMENT	VARIABLE COST PER UNIT OF SERVICE DEPARTMENT OUTPUT	FIXED COSTS AT VARIOUS SERVICE DEPARTMENT OUTPUT LEVELS 0–50,000	50,001– 100,000	100,001– 300,000	300,001– 800,000
Water..........................	$ .0133	$4,000	$ 6,000	$ 8,000	Not Applicable
Steam........................	.1000	5,000	10,000	12,000	Not Applicable
Electric Power..........	.0100	6,000	8,000	8,500	$9,000

The company can purchase electric power externally for $.03 per kilowatt-hour.

Required: Calculations (with the aid of the algebraic method for allocating service department costs) to support a recommendation as to whether the company should continue generating electric service internally or acquire it externally.

10-9. Hospital cost allocation methods. Inter-Urban Hospital completed its first year of operation as a qualified institutional provider under the health insurance (HI) program for the aged and wishes to receive maximum reimbursement from the government for its allowable costs. The hospital compiled the following financial, statistical, and other information:

(a) For the first year, the reimbursement settlement for inpatient services may be calculated at the option of the provider under either of the following apportionment methods:
(1) *Departmental RCC (Ratio of Cost Centers) Method* — provides for listing on a departmental basis the ratios of beneficiary inpatient charges to total inpatient charges with each departmental beneficiary inpatient charge ratio applied to the allowable total cost of the respective department.
(2) *Combination Method (With Cost Finding)* — provides that the cost of routine services be apportioned on the basis of the average allowable cost per day for all inpatients

applied to total inpatient days of beneficiaries. The residual part of the provider's total allowable cost attributable to ancillary (nonroutine) services is to be apportioned in the ratio of the beneficiaries' share of charges for ancillary services to the total charges for all patients for such services.

(b) The hospital's charges and allowable costs for departmental inpatient services were as follows:

DEPARTMENT	CHARGES FOR HI PROGRAM BENEFICIARIES	TOTAL CHARGES	TOTAL ALLOWABLE COSTS
Inpatient routine services (room, board, nursing)	$425,000	$1,275,000	$1,350,000
Inpatient ancillary service departments:			
X-ray	$ 56,000	$ 200,000	$ 150,000
Operating room	57,000	190,000	220,000
Laboratory	59,000	236,000	96,000
Pharmacy	98,000	294,000	207,000
Other	10,000	80,000	88,000
Total ancillary	$280,000	$1,000,000	$ 761,000
Total	$705,000	$2,275,000	$2,111,000

(c) Statistical and other information:
   (1) Total inpatient days for all patients 40,000
   (2) Total inpatient days applicable to HI beneficiaries (1,200 aged patients with average stay of 12.5 days) 15,000
   (3) A fiscal intermediary acting on behalf of the government's Medicare program negotiated a fixed allowance rate of $45 per inpatient day, subject to retroactive adjustment, as a reasonable cost basis for reimbursing the hospital for services covered under the HI program. Interim payments based on an estimated 1,000 inpatient days per month were received during the 12-month period, subject to an adjustment for the provider's actual cost experience.

Required:
   (1) Schedules computing the total allowable cost of inpatient services for which the provider should receive payment under the HI program, and the remaining balance due for reimbursement under:
      (a) The Departmental RCC Method.
      (b) The Combination Method (With Cost Finding).
   (2) The method under which the hospital should elect to be reimbursed for its first year under the HI program, assuming that the election can be changed for the following year with the approval of the fiscal intermediary. Explain.
   (3) The hospital administration wishes to compare its charges to HI program beneficiaries with published information on national averages for charges for hospital services.
      (a) The average total hospital charge for an HI inpatient.
      (b) The average charge per inpatient day for HI inpatients (with computations).

(AICPA adapted)

CASES

A. Cost accounting records; overhead distribution; ledger accounts. Lankford, Inc., uses job order costing that has been kept rather inadequately by the former accountant, who left in the middle of September. The company's president asks for assistance in getting the books and records in an acceptable order. The company's cost system includes a general ledger and a factory ledger with reciprocal control accounts. A trial balance of the factory ledger at September 1 is shown on the top of page 270.

Materials	30,000	
Store Supplies	10,000	
Work in Process	20,000	
General Ledger Control		60,000
	60,000	60,000

After reviewing the work done up to September 1, information is gathered for September from the following sources:

				WORK IN PROCESS				
					Service Depts.		Producing Depts.	
	GENERAL LEDGER		STORE		Power	General	Pattern	Machine
SOURCES OF INFORMATION	CONTROL	MATERIALS	SUPPLIES	Total	Plant	Plant	Foundry	Shop
From cash payments journal:								
Purchases	$(27,150)*	$20,000	$ 7,150					
Direct labor	(6,150)			$ 6,150	$300	$ 350	$ 2,200	$ 3,300
Direct factory overhead	(2,300)			2,300	50	175	730	1,345
Assets acquired	(9,400)							
Prepaid insurance	(3,000)							
From general ledger entries:								
Depreciation	(1,100)			1,100	140	80	**	**
Property tax	(250)			250	40	20	**	**
Expired insurance	(500)			500	100	25	**	**
Repairs to power plant	(320)			320	320			
From requisitions:								
Materials		(27,000)		27,000	500	1,000	15,500	10,000
Store supplies	150		(15,150)	15,000	150	1,350	9,000	4,500
From cost of finished jobs report:								
Shipped to customers	45,000			(45,000)				
For company's own use	2,460			(2,460)				
Bases for distribution of costs:								
Power plant							50%	50%

General plant on the basis of store supplies issued to producing departments.
Indirect costs of producing departments on the basis of each department's direct labor cost.

*( ) denotes credit balance.
**Balance on the basis of direct labor cost.

Required: On a work sheet, using the same headings as those appearing in this information:
 (1) The direct, indirect, and total costs that should be debited to the work in process account for September.
 (2) Distribution of service department costs to the producing departments as per instructions.
 (3) The September 30 balances of the following factory ledger accounts: General Ledger Control; Materials; Store Supplies; Work in Process.

(AICPA adapted)

B. Assigning costs to activity centers in a data processing department. Rubinoff Associates recently reorganized its computer and data processing activities. In the past, small computer units were located in accounting departments at the firm's plants and subsidiaries. These units have been replaced with a single electronic data processing department at corporate headquarters. The new department has been in operation for two years, regularly producing reliable and timely data for the past twelve months.

Because the department has focused its activities on converting applications to the new system and producing reports for the plant and subsidiary managements, little attention has been devoted to data processing costs. Now that the department's activities are operating relatively smoothly, company management has requested that the departmental manager recommend a cost accumulation system to facilitate cost control and the development of suitable service charging rates.

For the past two years, the data processing costs have been recorded in one account. The costs have then been allocated to user departments on the basis of computer time used. The schedule below reports the costs and charging rate for 19––:

Electronic Data Processing Department
Costs for the Year Ended December 31, 19––

(a) Salaries and benefits	$ 622,600
(b) Supplies	40,000
(c) Equipment maintenance contract	15,000
(d) Insurance	25,000
(e) Heat and air conditioning	36,000
(f) Electricity	50,000
(g) Equipment and furniture depreciation	285,400
(h) Building improvement depreciation	10,000
(i) Building occupancy and security	39,300
(j) Corporate administrative charge	52,700
Total cost	$1,176,000
Computer hours for user processing*	2,750
Hourly rate ($1,176,000 ÷ 2,750)	$428

*Use of available computer hours:

Testing and debugging programs	250
Set-up of jobs	500
Processing jobs	2,750
Downtime for maintenance	750
Idle time	742
Total	4,992

The department manager recommends that the data processing costs be accumulated by five activity centers within the department: Systems Analysis, Programming, Data Preparation, Computer Operations (processing), and Administration. The Administration activity cost should be allocated to the other four activity centers before a separate rate for charging users is developed for each of the first four activities.

The manager noted that the subsidiary accounts within the department contained the following charges:

(a) Salaries and benefits — the salary and benefit costs of all employees in the department.
(b) Supplies — punch card cost, paper cost for printers, and a small amount for miscellaneous other costs.
(c) Equipment maintenance contracts — charges for maintenance contracts covering all equipment.
(d) Insurance — cost of insurance covering the equipment and the furniture.
(e) Heat and air conditioning — a charge from the corporate heating and air conditioning department estimated to be the differential costs which meet the special needs of the Data Processing Department.
(f) Electricity — the charge for electricity, based upon a separate meter within the department.
(g) Equipment and furniture depreciation — the depreciation charges for all owned equipment and furniture within the department.

(h) Building improvement depreciation — the depreciation charges for the building changes which were required to provide proper environmental control and electrical service for the computer equipment.

(i) Building occupancy and security — the department's share of the depreciation, maintenance, heat, and security costs of the building; these costs are allocated to the department on the basis of square feet occupied.

(j) Corporate administrative charge — the department's share of the corporate administrative cost which is allocated to the department on the basis of number of employees in the department.

Required:

(1) Whether each of the ten cost items (lettered a through j) should be allocated to the five activity centers, and for each cost item which should be distributed, the basis upon which the distribution should be made. Justify your answer in each case, including an indication as to whether the cost would be included in a rate designed to include only variable costs as opposed to a full cost rate.

(2) The total number of hours that should be employed to determine the charging rate for Computer Operations (processing), using the analysis of computer utilization shown as a footnote to the department cost schedule, and assuming that the Computer Operations (processing) activity cost will be charged to the user departments on the basis of computer hours. Explain.

(CMA adapted)

C. Comparing cost systems for inventory costing and income determination. The Manhattan Company is engaged in manufacturing items to fill specific orders received from its customers. While at any given time it may have substantial inventories of work in process and finished goods, all such amounts are assignable to firm sales orders.

The company's operations, including the administrative and sales functions, are completely departmentalized. Its cost system is on a job order cost accumulation basis. Direct materials and direct labor are identified with jobs by the use of materials issue tickets and daily time cards. Overhead costs are accumulated for each factory service, administrative, and marketing department. These overhead costs, including administrative and marketing expenses, are then allocated to producing departments and an overhead rate computed for each producing department. This rate is used to apply overhead to jobs on the basis of direct labor hours. The result is that all costs and expenses incurred during any month are charged to the work in process accounts for the jobs.

Required:

(1) Comparison of this system, as it affects inventory costing, with the usual system for manufacturing businesses.

(2) Criticism of the system as it affects inventory costing and income determination.

(3) Justifications for the use of the company's system.

(AICPA adapted)

D. Decision regarding depreciation on old and new building. Ullman, Inc., owned one factory building with a net depreciated cost of $90,000. Machinery and equipment was carried at $120,000. Because of expanding business, a new building was built at a cost of $150,000 and $210,000 of equipment was installed. During the next several years, some new equipment was put in the old building and both plants continued to operate. Depreciation has been computed on a straight-line basis.

Recently the old plant was shut down because of lack of orders. The sales manager proposes that the company should no longer take depreciation on the old building and machinery, which is not in use and is not wearing out. To take depreciation on it increases cost, overstates inventory, and places the company in a poor competitive position to bid for business, since its costs are high.

Required: A full discussion of this proposal.

(AICPA adapted)

11 Factory Overhead
Responsibility Accounting and Responsibility Reporting

Direct materials and direct labor are generally identifiable directly with specific products, jobs, or processes. Factory overhead, however, consisting of indirect supplies, indirect labor, labor-related payroll taxes, and numerous factory expense items such as power, water, utilities, repairs and maintenance, property tax, insurance, and depreciation, creates two distinct problems:

1. Allocation to products for the purpose of inventory costing and profit determination, and
2. Control of factory overhead with the aid of responsibility accounting.

The well-designed information system should yield product costs for inventory costing and profit determination. It should also provide a control mechanism encompassing *responsibility accounting* and make meaningful cost data available for setting policies and making decisions. The predetermined or budgeted revenue and expense items form the foundation for comparison with actual results, leading to variance analysis or the management by exception principle.

The establishment of such a system allows and maintains the most efficient and profitable balance between manufacturing and marketing. On the one hand, management needs to decide the kinds and costs of its products; on the other hand, it must decide the prices of its products. The greatest profit results from the proper balance of these considerations. For these reasons, product costs must be fairly accurate, include all relevant costs, and recognize cost differentials between products.

RESPONSIBILITY ACCOUNTING AND CONTROL OF FACTORY OVERHEAD

Webster's dictionary defines being *responsible* as "liable to be called upon to answer." Kohler's *A Dictionary for Accountants* defines *responsibility* as "the obligation prudently to exercise assigned or imputed authority attaching to the assigned or imputed role of an individual or group participating in organizational activities or decisions." The N.A.(C.)A. Research Series, No. 22, says: "A responsibility may be defined as an organizational unit having a single head accountable for activities of the unit."

Responsibility Accounting — Basic Concepts

The concepts enumerated below are prerequisites to the initiation and maintenance of a responsibility accounting system.

1. Responsibility accounting is based on a classification of managerial responsibilities (departments) at every level in the organization for the purpose of establishing a budget for each. The individual in charge of each responsibility classification should be responsible and accountable for the expenses of his or her activity. This concept introduces the need for the classification of costs into controllable and not controllable by a department head. Generally, costs charged directly to a department, with the exception of fixed costs, are controllable by the department's manager.
2. The starting point for a responsibility accounting information system rests with the organization chart in which the spheres of jurisdiction have been determined. Authority leads to the responsibility for certain costs and expenses which, with the knowledge and cooperation of the supervisor, department head, or manager, are presented in the budget.
3. Each individual's budget should clearly identify the costs controllable by that person. The chart of accounts should be adapted to permit recording of controllable or accountable expenses within the jurisdictional framework.

Personal Factors in Responsibility Accounting

A program to develop management accounting controls must be considered a prime responsibility of executive management with the accounting department providing technical assistance. To assure the follow-through of the program and its ultimate success, management must provide a complete clarification of the objectives and responsibilities of all levels of the organization. This prerequisite requires an understanding by middle and operating management of executive management's goals. The acceptance of responsibility for certain costs and expenses does not always follow the issuance of directives and orders. Supervisory personnel, particularly at the foreman level, need guidance and training to achieve the control and/or profit results expected from them. Control responsibility does not happen naturally, but requires a certain fundamental attitude or frame of mind for the task.

One of the most beneficial influences is executive management's own exemplary adherence to the cost-and-profit responsibility it created. Of equal importance is the motivation for corrective action by the responsible individual. The issuance of reports based on the organization's responsibility concept is not sufficient. The successful achievement of effective management control depends upon the lines of communication between the accounting department, the responsible supervisors, and their superiors. Responsibility accounting requires teamwork in the truest sense of the word.

As the preceding factory overhead chapters indicate, many overhead items are directly chargeable to a given department and become the direct responsibility of the departmental supervisor. Allocated or distributed overhead causes problems in assigning cost responsibility. To calculate a departmental factory overhead rate, these costs must be allocated so that all costs can be charged to a job, a product, or the work performed. The allocation procedure, however, is not necessary for cost control; that is, for responsibility accounting. Any allocated charges, shown on the report furnished to the supervisor, should be limited to those expenses for which control and responsibility have been assumed. The procedure depends a great deal upon the methods of cost accumulation and allocation used by a firm. Certain expenses (e.g., electricity), when metered for a department, could be considered direct departmental overhead. When these expenses, together with others, are collected first in an account or in a cost pool such as General Factory or Utilities, the allocation takes place on a preestablished basis. Differences between actual and allocated or charged-out costs in these accounts or departments should not be shown on the reports for the departments served; the control or responsibility phase should stay with the originating department.

Responsibility for Overhead Costs

The Billing or Sold-Hour Rate of a Service Department. The cost system provides for a normal volume distribution of service hours, use hours, and/or maintenance hours to producing or other service departments. The distribution can be looked upon as a purchase by the recipient center or a sale by the servicing center. The distribution to the recipient center is based on what is termed a *billing rate*, a *sold-hour rate*, a *charging rate*, or a *transfer rate*. The method is based on the idea that these departments or centers purchase the services in the same manner as direct materials and direct labor. For these cost elements, quantities and costs are controlled and differences noted. The consuming department's supervisor is responsible for the number of hours worked, or kilowatt-hours purchased, and the cost incurred in the department.

The determination of the rate follows the procedures discussed in the previous factory overhead chapters:

1. Estimating or budgeting costs of any service department or cost pool according to their nature (supervision, supplies, electricity, etc.).
2. Classifying costs as fixed or variable. This classification often leads to the realization that many costs of service departments or cost pools are fixed over fairly wide ranges of service volume.

3. Determining a rate by dividing total estimated departmental cost by the number of hours the service is expected to be needed. The establishment of the use hours is as important here as it is in factory overhead rate determination. The hours can be based either on past experience in a representative period or on future activity or volume as expressed in the budget. A refinement of the rate is the apportionment of fixed costs to cost centers on a readiness-to-serve basis. As some departments would require more service than others, the initial cost proration is made on that basis. The remaining cost is then divided by the budgeted hours of the recipient departments.[1]

4. Comparing actual service department costs incurred in the department with estimated or budgeted costs. This comparison is made (1) in the service department to which the expenses are originally charged — actual costs are compared with charged-out or sold-out amounts; and (2) in the benefiting (recipient) departments in which the charges for service departments' services are linked with the budget allowances. This step is the control phase of the service department's charging-out procedure. The supervisor of the service department is responsible for the actual cost versus the cost or hours charged out. The benefiting department supervisor is responsible for the number of hours or the cost charged for service. Comparison will also lead to the calculation of variances for service and producing departments.

Billing Rates for Electronic Data Processing Services. Electronic data processing (EDP) services offer an excellent illustration of the need for careful attention to the use of appropriate billing rates. EDP services usually start as a support group, with costs classified as general overhead and a possible allocation to broad functional classifications such as manufacturing (factory overhead), marketing, and administrative expenses. As data processing matures and becomes an integral part of the organization's operations, more precise cost accounting mechanisms are considered. The EDP center might apportion costs to users on the basis of a percentage of general utilization; e.g., assigning ten percent of the costs to one department, fifteen percent to another, and so forth. This approach has limitations, because it fails to contribute to efficient use of the EDP facility and does not aid the recipient in making selective judgments about the application requested. Users need to understand the cost and value of the services which they require.

The electronic data processing department should develop a price (charge) for the services which users can include in their departmental budgets. The price of a given system is usually a fixed amount plus a variable amount per transaction, the volume of which would affect the total processing time. The difference between actual price and actual cost provides one measure of the data processing department's efficiency.[2]

The general, one-rate allocation to the broad classification may be superseded by the partitioning of the computer into cost centers with major ex-

[1]An example of more sophisticated allocation procedures is found in Daniel L. Jensen's "A Class of Mutually Satisfactory Allocations," *The Accounting Review*, Vol. LII, No. 4, pp. 842–856.
[2]Adapted from "The Fair Measure," *Data Processor*, Vol. 18, No. 2, pp. 10–13.

penses classified as a direct expense to a cost center. To illustrate, Exhibit 1, page 278, is a budget for a data processing department which has been partitioned into eight cost centers.[3]

The "percent utilization expected" is important to a data processing department. Experience indicates that available hours are often utilized only at a 70 to 80 percent rate. The difference between utilized and available hours represents nonproductive activity which, for a systems analyst or a programmer, consists of vacation, holiday, illness, training, staff meetings, administrative tasks, professional societies, initial examination of requests and other miscellaneous tasks. Operation codes should be assigned for situations such as idle time, downtime, and preventive maintenance. Time recording procedures established in all cost centers would allow the data processing administration to:

1. Keep a close watch over the productive utilization percentage and take action if and when it gets out of line.
2. Calculate the cost of each project or system based on actual time incurred multiplied by the budgeted hourly rates.
3. Compare the actual productive hours to budgeted productive hours, and be aware of variances on a weekly or monthly basis.
4. Note the variance between total actual monthly data processing cost and the summation of project and system costs.
5. For subsequent years, estimate more accurately the expected productive hours by cost centers.

The development and maintenance of job cost procedures incorporating budgeted hourly rates provide the following benefits:

1. Aid in controlling or reducing data processing costs.
2. Permit accurate and realistic costing of all work performed by project, system, user department, and/or line of business served.
3. Provide realistic rates to be used in estimating the cost of requested or proposed projects.
4. Permit a comparison of actual costs of processing a system to those costs which were estimated prior to implementation.
5. Aid in the evaluation of operating efficiency of a data processing installation.
6. Provide one measure of profitability for each data processing cost center and for the entire department in those cases where services are charged to a user or customer.

Maintenance Costs and Responsibility Accounting. Maintenance expense, like any other indirect factory cost, must be charged to producing departments in order to be included in the calculation of overhead rates. The basic problem is assigning cost responsibility for this expense. Maintenance engineers often believe that their department really incurs no cost at all, since any cost incurrence is for the benefit and at the request of other departments. Factory su-

---

[3]Adapted from "Costing in the Data Processing Department" by John E. Finney, *Management Accounting*, Vol. LVI, No. 4, pp. 29–35.

DATA PROCESSING BUDGET BY COST CENTER

Item	Annual Budget	Systems	Programming	Computer Background	Computer Foreground 1	Computer Foreground 2	Off-Line Devices	Data Entry	Data Control
Data processing administration	$ 48,000	$ 7,400	$ 5,200	$ 4,700	$ 8,900	$ 5,600	$ 500	$ 13,000	$ 2,700
Group managers and secretaries	82,000	20,000	15,000	5,000	10,000	10,000	2,000	10,000	10,000
Other salaries and fringe benefits	528,300	114,000	84,000	10,000	23,000	15,000	4,000	230,000	48,300
Training costs	11,000	3,500	3,500	300	900	500	200	1,600	500
Supplies	34,600	2,300	1,700	1,000	8,000	12,600	2,000	6,000	1,000
Travel expenses	7,700	4,000	2,000	500	700	500			
Consulting fees	9,000	6,000	3,000						
Rent, insurance and utilities	78,000	13,500	13,500	8,000	11,000	9,000	2,000	17,000	4,000
Equipment rental and depreciation	356,000			80,000	150,000	77,000	1,000	47,000	1,000
Equipment maintenance	30,700			8,000	12,000	10,000	500		200
Depreciation on furniture and fixtures	6,100	1,700	1,700	200	400	400	300	400	1,000
Employment agency fees	7,000	4,000	3,000						
Dues and subscriptions	1,600	1,000	600						
Total budgeted cost	$1,200,000	$177,400	$133,200	$117,700	$224,900	$140,600	$ 12,500	$325,000	$ 68,700
Available or purchased hours		14,560	14,560	7,488	7,488	7,488	1,040	60,320	12,480
Percent utilization expected		70	80	35	60	20	85	86	80
Expected productive hours		10,192	11,648	2,621	4,493	1,498	884	51,875	9,984
Budgeted hourly rate		$ 17.41	$ 11.44	$ 44.91	$ 50.06	$ 93.86	$ 14.14	$ 6.27	$ 6.88

Exhibit 1

pervisors, on the other hand, may argue that they have no influence on either personnel or machinery costs of the maintenance department. The control is in reality twofold: the factory supervisors control the amount of maintenance work, while maintenance engineers or supervisors control the quantity of people and materials required to serve the various departments. Since maintenance work is done at the request of production supervisors, the problem arises as to whether control should be exercised at the source level or the recipient level.

At the source level, service and maintenance labor is organized and supervised. Control at this point requires predetermination of labor-hour requirements in each of the producing and service departments for each service or maintenance function. At the recipient level, the cost system establishes budget allowances for this indirect cost. Budget allowances based on planned levels of production permit the determination of the labor-hour budgets and advance scheduling of the work force of each shop service or maintenance unit. Preplanning is the heart of the control, providing an opportunity for corrective action before the hours are worked. Maintenance and service department supervisors are apprised of the maintenance allowance or budgeted service for individual recipient cost centers, but the distribution or scheduling of the work is left to their discretion.

Preventive Maintenance. One major problem, however, is how much maintenance or repair work is needed in a department. The solution may be determined by the executive management group. When a factory is laid out and the machinery installed, a maintenance program should be planned. The size of the maintenance department, the type or class of workers (carpenters, plumbers, electricians, pipefitters, masons, millwrights, machinists, etc.), and the kind of equipment and tools are greatly influenced by early decisions. On the other hand, experience indicates that such maintenance objectives are lacking in many companies due to management's own lack of interest as well as alleged difficulties in planning, measuring, and controlling the maintenance function. Although many organizations engage the services of outside firms for part or all of their maintenance, the need for careful planning and control of maintenance cost is not negated.

When management and the supervisors of the producing, service, and maintenance engineering departments agree on a preventive maintenance program, their objective is to keep equipment in such condition that breakdowns and the need for emergency repairs are at a minimum. Preventive maintenance facilitates the scheduling of maintenance work and helps to obtain better utilization of the maintenance work force and the productive equipment. It also reduces operating losses due to machine breakdowns, extensive damage, or serious injuries to personnel.

A preventive maintenance program can work automatically so that inspection, minor repairs, adjustments, and lubrication are completed as a matter of course. The method further provides for a check on the effectiveness of the maintenance work by the supervisor of the serviced or buying unit. The maintenance supervisor, in turn, is responsible for the inspection and the upkeep of the facilities.

The discussion has intentionally dealt with factory overhead items only, since their assignment and control occupies the attention of many executives, department heads, and supervisors. However, other departments and functions in administration and marketing also require supervision and control by responsible managers.

Responsi-bility for Direct Materials and Direct Labor

Basically, the best approach to assigning responsibility for any cost element is to identify those individuals who are in the most favored position to keep the costs under control. The assignment of responsibility for overhead expenses to supervisors and department heads provides a certain degree of control. Admittedly, however, certain expenses (e.g., maintenance expenses) are often troublesome. In the direct materials and direct labor areas, many individuals may be assigned the responsibility for costs incurred, and this responsibility often becomes very obscure and nearly impossible to identify. Of course, it seems advisable to insist upon the assignment on the basis of relative control rather than absolute control.

In the direct materials area, the variances or deviations from a predetermined norm or standard will result in (1) materials price variances, (2) materials quantity, or mix and yield variances, and/or (3) excessive defective work, rejects, or scrap costs. In the direct labor area, the variances or deviations from a predetermined norm or standard will result in (1) pay rate variations, (2) efficiency variations, (3) and/or overtime costs.

Other cost elements also may be subject to change for which a manager may be held responsible. In later chapters, the deviations from budgeted gross or net profit figures require explanation. The changes in sales prices, sales volume, and sales mix are the responsibility of the marketing department. Yet the gross profit figure contains elements of cost as well, so that a further investigation is warranted.

Cost Control Character-istics

An effective cost control system has two major characteristics:

1. A sound technical design with goals set at a challenging but attainable performance level and with a reporting system that distinguishes controllable costs within each managerial responsibility from costs controllable elsewhere in the organization.
2. A managerial style sensitive to the behavior of people in a particular organizational setting; this requires a proper blend of:
   (a) Involvement by managers in setting goals for their own activities.
   (b) Leadership provided by executive management.
   (c) Open communication channels through which individual managers feel their views receive serious consideration.
   (d) Review procedures which disclose and discourage suboptimization and individual gains at the expense of the whole organization.

Cost control techniques are effective only with sufficient managerial appreciation of the behavioral aspects of control systems.[4]

Today with the emphasis on responsible control of financial results via the return-on-capital-employed concept, assets, liabilities, net worth, revenue, and costs form a vast area in which the entire management spectrum from the top executive to the supervisor holds some share of responsibility. Like blocks within a pyramid (page 288), the responsibility travels from the lowest to the highest level of supervision. All supervisors are responsible for costs incurred by their subordinates.

Variance Analysis for Responsibility Accounting

To exercise this control, the cost and/or budget department should issue monthly reports that compare actual results with predetermined amounts or budget allowances. An analysis prepared at the end of the annual fiscal period, as shown in Chapter 10, is not very helpful for immediate control actions. Reports on a monthly or more frequent basis are advisable to allow short-range comparisons of those costs for which operating management is responsible.

The illustrative problem beginning on page 282 assumes that variable expenses are controllable at the departmental level while fixed expenses are not. These assumptions apply to almost all costs in most situations. In some circumstances, certain variable expenses may be controlled at a higher level in the organization; e.g., employee fringe benefits may be determined by negotiations between executive management and the labor union or by government regulations. Such costs should be analyzed and separately identified to relieve a department manager of this responsibility. Conversely, a department manager may have some control over certain fixed costs — those that involve a long-term commitment (sometimes called *committed fixed expenses*), such as equipment depreciation or lease expense, and those that can be readily changed in the short run (sometimes called *programmed fixed expenses*), such as the number of foremen in the department. These costs should be individually identified as controllable by the manager of the department. Whether fixed or variable, some costs may be joint with respect to two or more departments and thus require arbitrary allocation. Accordingly, their controllability by a single department manager is restricted.

Attention must be called to the fact that in the long run all costs are controllable. Variable costs are generally controllable over short time periods. Some fixed costs, such as supervisory labor or equipment rental, can also be terminated on short notice while other fixed costs, such as depreciation of plant assets or a long-term lease agreement, involve a fixed commitment over a long period of time. Finally, some costs possess a dual short- and long-run controllability characteristic. For example, a five-year contract as to the price of a raw material, representing a long-run commitment, is not immediately controllable and the contract may be negotiable only at a higher management

---

[4]Walter B. McFarland, *Manpower Cost and Performance Measurement* (New York: National Association of Accountants, 1977), p. 101.

level. However, waste and spoilage of the same material is immediately controllable by the department. Generally, department managers should be well enough informed to explain cost variances even though the control or certain aspects of the control do not fall within their scope of authority and responsibility.

The data, steps, and methods presented below are based on the illustration in Chapter 10. There the annual factory overhead of the four producing departments and four service departments of DeWitt Products was estimated, and product costing rates (factory overhead rates) were calculated after the indirect departmental expenses and service department costs had been apportioned and distributed. At the end of the year, annual actual factory overhead was compared with applied factory overhead, and departmental spending and idle capacity variances were determined.

At this point the analysis moves into a monthly comparison. To keep the illustration compact, the four producing departments and only one service department, Utilities, are used. Some of the data previously presented must now be modified to serve this control responsibility phase. For product costing purposes, four departmental factory overhead rates have been computed and are listed below.

Cutting Department ...... $2.00 per direct labor hour
Planing Department ...... $3.20 per machine hour
Assembly Department... 60% of direct labor cost
Upholstery Department . $1.80 per direct labor hour

At the end of January the following actual data are assembled:

DEPARTMENTS	ACTUAL HOURS (LABOR OR MACHINE) OR LABOR COST	ACTUAL CONSUMPTION FOR THE MONTH		ACTUAL DEPARTMENTAL OVERHEAD BEFORE BILLING OUT UTILITIES
		kwh	hph	
Cutting............	3,046 direct labor hours	1 180	19,000	$3,575
Planing............	1,620 machine hours	700	10,800	3,125
Assembly	$11,400 direct labor cost	1 700	7,000	2,900
Upholstery.......	4,100 direct labor hours	1 980	8,000	3,570
Utilities...........				5,860
		5 560	44,800	

Based on the actual production and cost data, the cost department would apply the following amounts of factory overhead to products passing through the four departments:

Cutting Department, 3,046 direct labor hours × $2.00.................... $6,092
Planing Department, 1,620 machine hours × $3.20........................ 5,184
Assembly Department, $11,400 direct labor cost × 60%................. 6,840
Upholstery Department, 4,100 direct labor hours × $1.80 7,380

To determine and analyze the amount of over- or underapplied factory overhead, service department costs must be added to the actual direct and indirect departmental overhead to put actual and applied figures on a comparable basis. These procedures were presented in Chapter 10.

In responsibility accounting, the emphasis rests upon the comparison of actual departmental expenses with budgeted or estimated costs exclusive of service department costs. Many accountants believe that only the variable overhead (i.e., the controllable expenses for which the department head is responsible) should be compared and not the total overhead. Naturally, the procedures for different organizations vary.

Spending Variance on a Departmental Basis

In this example, both procedures are illustrated for the four producing departments and one service department. The first computation shows total actual departmental overhead, both fixed and variable, compared with budgeted or predetermined departmental overhead. The second computation shows only variable or controllable actual departmental overhead compared with its budgeted or predetermined amount. The service department cost is excluded in both situations.

Computation 1

	DEPARTMENTS				
	Cutting	*Planing*	*Assembly*	*Upholstery*	*Utilities*
Actual departmental overhead	$3,575	$3,125	$2,900	$3,570	$5,860
Budget allowances:					
Fixed expenses ($^1/_{12}$ annual fixed costs; e.g., $17,100* ÷ 12 = $1,425)...	$1,425	$1,492	$1,342	$1,525	$1,333
Variable expenses:					
3,046 hours × $.5762**	1,755				
1,620 hours × $1.0217**		1,655			
$11,400 × 15.5%**			1,767		
4,100 hours × $.4217**				1,729	
5 560 kwh × $.1544**					858
44,800 hph × $.0494**					2,213
1,750 sq. ft.*** × $.7057**					1,235
Budget allowances.......	$3,180	$3,147	$3,109	$3,254	$5,639
Spending variances	$ 395	$ (22)	$(209)	$ 316	$ 221
	unfav.	fav.	fav.	unfav.	unfav.

*Estimated fixed cost for the Cutting Department, page 245.
**Variable cost rate, as calculated on page 284.
***1,750 sq. ft. is $^1/_{12}$ of 21,000 sq. ft. (to convert to a one-month period), as shown on page 246.

Computation 2

	DEPARTMENTS				
	Cutting	*Planing*	*Assembly*	*Upholstery*	*Utilities*
Actual variable departmental overhead (e.g., $3,575 − $1,425 fixed costs)	$2,150	$1,633	$1,558	$2,045	$4,527
Budgeted variable expenses....	1,755	1,655	1,767	1,729	4,306
Spending variances	$ 395	$ (22)	$(209)	$ 316	$ 221
	unfav.	fav.	fav.	unfav.	unfav.

The variable cost rates for the producing departments are calculated by dividing the variable departmental overhead, before service department distribution, by the predetermined or estimated direct labor hours, direct labor cost, or machine hours, using data from pages 245 and 248:

| | ESTIMATED VARIABLE DEPARTMENTAL OVERHEAD | ÷ | Estimated | | | = | VARIABLE DEPARTMENTAL COST RATES |
			DIRECT LABOR HOURS	DIRECT LABOR COST	MACHINE HOURS		
Cutting............	$23,400		40,608				$ .5762
Planing............	$18,800				18,400		$1.0217
Assembly	$18,900			$122,000			15.5%
Upholstery.......	$20,300		48,140				$ .4217

In the producing departments, actual hours or actual costs for the month are multiplied by the variable cost rate to arrive at the budgeted or estimated variable cost. The variable rates for Utilities (using data from pages 245 and 248) are calculated as follows:

Total departmental cost $65,400
Less fixed expense.......................... 16,000
Total variable expense.................... $49,400

$49,400 × 20% = $9,880 ÷ 64 000 kwh = $.1544 variable rate per kwh
$49,400 × 50% = $24,700 ÷ 500,000 hph = $.0494 variable rate per hph
$49,400 × 30% = $14,820 ÷ 21,000 sq. ft. = $.7057 variable rate per sq. ft.

The estimated allowance for Utilities is based on the actual monthly consumption figures multiplied by the corresponding variable rates.

Idle Capacity Variance on a Departmental Basis

Responsibility accounting stresses the control of variable expenses and the calculation of the departmental spending variance. It is possible, however, to continue the analysis and calculate an idle capacity variance based entirely on departmental costs without any allocation of service department costs or charges. To illustrate, again using data from page 245, the Cutting Department's total estimated overhead cost is $40,500 with $17,100 fixed and $23,400 variable. The variable overhead rate is $.5762 and the fixed rate $.4211 ($17,100 ÷ 40,608 estimated hours), providing a total of $.9973. In the Cutting Department, a factory overhead rate of $2 per direct labor hour is used for product costing purposes; the difference of $1.0027 ($2.00 − $.9973) is accounted for by service department costs assigned to this department.

The analysis is shown below:

(1) ACTUAL OVERHEAD	(2) BUDGET ALLOWANCE	(3) APPLIED OVERHEAD	(4) TOTAL VARIANCE (1)–(3)	(5) SPENDING VARIANCE (1)–(2)	(6) IDLE CAPACITY VARIANCE (2)–(3)
$3,575	$3,180	$3,038*	$537 unfav.	$395 unfav.	$142** unfav.

*3,046 actual hours × $.9973
**3,384 (40,608 hours ÷ 12 months) predetermined hours − 3,046 actual hours = 338 idle hours × $.4211

A similar analysis can be made for the service department, Utilities:

(1) ACTUAL OVERHEAD	(2) BUDGET ALLOWANCE	(3) UTILITIES COST CHARGED OUT	(4) TOTAL VARIANCE (1)–(3)	(5) SPENDING VARIANCE (1)–(2)	(6) IDLE CAPACITY VARIANCE (2)–(3)
$5,860	$5,639	$5,701*	$159 unfav.	$221 unfav.	$(62) fav.

*The amount of cost charged out is based on the total predetermined cost of $65,400 which was to be distributed 20% or $13,080 based on kwh, 50% or $32,700 on hph, and 30% or $19,620 on floor area, resulting in these charging rates: $.2044 ($13,080 ÷ 64 000 kwh); $.0654 ($32,700 ÷ 500,000 hph); and $.9343 ($19,620 ÷ 21,000 sq. ft.). The $5,701 is the result of:

$$5\ 560 \text{ actual kwh} \times \$.2044 = \$1,136$$
$$44,800 \text{ actual hph} \times \$.0654 = 2,930$$
$$1,750 \text{ sq. ft. } (^{1}/_{12} \text{ of } 21,000 \text{ sq. ft.}) \times \$.9343 = \underline{1,635}$$
$$\underline{\underline{\$5,701}}$$

While the responsibility for the cost incurred is, generally speaking, easily identifiable in the producing departments, a service department's cost variances need a great deal of additional investigation. With a service department such as Utilities, the analysis is not so easy because:

1. Utilities can be charged accurately to consuming departments only when departmental or cost center meters are used.
2. Even with meters, the quantity used might differ from the quantity produced due to line losses. The pinpointing of the responsibility for these losses is often impossible.
3. Since any utility can often be either purchased from outside or manufactured inside, it could be possible that the interchangeable use of one source with another will give rise to variances for which the cause is also difficult to detect.

Similar difficulties regarding the pinpointing of responsibility for the cost incurrence and the resulting variance are experienced with any service department. The maintenance department has already been cited as an example. In many instances, service department costs are largely fixed, at least over a relevant range of activity or volume. For this reason, responsibility is difficult to establish. The idle capacity variance is particularly troublesome when calculated on a monthly basis. The spending variance is somewhat more meaningful since actual and budgeted costs can be compared with their increases and decreases.

As a rule, the manager of the service department is responsible for the variance between the actual cost and the cost based on the number of hours or service units charged out or sold. The manager of the producing or services received department, together with the service department supervisor, is responsible for the number of hours or service units consumed in the department. This statement indicates that a kind of dual responsibility exists between the charges to the services received departments and the credits to the services rendered departments. The consuming department's cost must be compared with the allowed or budgeted service cost to determine the cost increase or decrease in that department, while the service department must examine its cost on the basis of the quantity consumed or sold.

RESPONSIBILITY REPORTING

Responsibility accounting is a program encompassing all operating management for which the accounting, cost, or budget divisions provide technical assistance in the form of daily, weekly, or monthly control reports. Responsibility reporting includes the reporting phase of responsibility accounting. In fact, the terms "responsibility accounting" and "responsibility reporting" are generally considered synonymous.

Reporting to the various levels of management can be divided into responsibility-performance reporting and information reporting. A clear distinction between the two is important; each serves different goals or objectives. *Responsibility-performance reports* are accountability reports with two purposes:

1. To inform managers and superiors of their performance in responsible areas.
2. To motivate managers and superiors to generate the direct action necessary to improve performance.

Information reports are issued for the purpose of providing managers with information relevant to their areas of interest, although not necessarily associated directly with their specific responsibility for performance. Information reports serve a broader and different set of goals than performance reports. In the short view, responsibility-performance reports are more important than information reports because of the immediate and pressing needs to keep the business on course. However, from the long view, information reports bearing on the progress and growth of the business are also important.

Fundamentals of Responsibility-Performance Reports

Responsibility-performance reports should be based on certain fundamental qualities and characteristics:

1. Reports should fit the organization chart; that is, they should be addressed to the individuals responsible for controlling the items covered by the reports. Managers must be educated to use the results of the reporting system.
2. Reports should be consistent in form and content each time they are issued. Changes should be made only for good reasons and with clear explanations to users.
3. Reports should be prompt and timely. Prompt issuance of a report requires that cost records be organized so that information is available when it is needed.
4. Reports should be issued with regularity. Promptness and regularity are closely tied in with the mechanical aids used to assemble and issue reports.

5. Reports should be easy to understand. Often they contain accounting terminology that managers with little or no accounting training find difficult to understand, and vital information may be incorrectly communicated. Therefore, accounting terms should be explained or modified to fit the user. Management should have some knowledge of the kind of items chargeable to an account as well as the methods used to compute overhead rates, allocate costs, and analyze variances.

6. Reports should convey sufficient but not excessive detail. The amount and nature of the detail depend largely on the management level receiving the report. Reports to management should neither be flooded with immaterial facts nor so condensed that management lacks vital information essential to carrying out its responsibilities.

7. Reports should give comparative figures (a comparison of actual with budgeted figures, or of predetermined standards with actual results) and should isolate variances.

8. Reports should be analytical. Analysis of underlying papers, such as time tickets, scrap tickets, work orders, and materials requisitions, provides reasons for poor performance which might have been due to power failure, machine breakdown, an inefficient operator, poor quality of materials, or other similar factors.

9. Reports for operating management should be stated in physical units as well as in dollars, since dollar information may be irrelevant to a supervisor not trained in the language of the accountant.

10. Reports may tend to highlight supposed departmental efficiencies and inefficiencies. Care should be exercised to see that such reports do not encourage departmental activities aimed at "making a good showing" regardless of the effect on the entire organization.

To be of value, information must be used; to be used, it must be understood by both accounting and nonaccounting personnel. Effective information usage depends on the form and method of the reporting techniques, whether written, oral, or visual.

The two principal written reporting techniques are charts or graphs and tabular presentation. Narrative reports are useful for conveying qualitative information that is difficult to quantify. Supplementary oral and visual presentations have been used effectively in chart rooms, which offer opportunities for groups to receive information, raise questions, and voice opinions.

Responsibility-Reporting Systems Illustrated

The illustrations presented on pages 288 and 289 depict the pyramid structure of the reporting procedure for responsibility accounting. The first system is employed in a manufacturing concern; the second, in a bank.

The first step in a responsibility-reporting system is the establishment of lines of responsibility and responsibility areas. Each block in a company's organization chart represents a segment (cost center, division, department, etc.) that is reported upon and that receives reports on the functions responsible to it. Any report prepared according to this concept easily fits into one of the blocks illustrated in the organization chart at the top of page 288.

Organization
Chart for a
Manufacturing
Concern

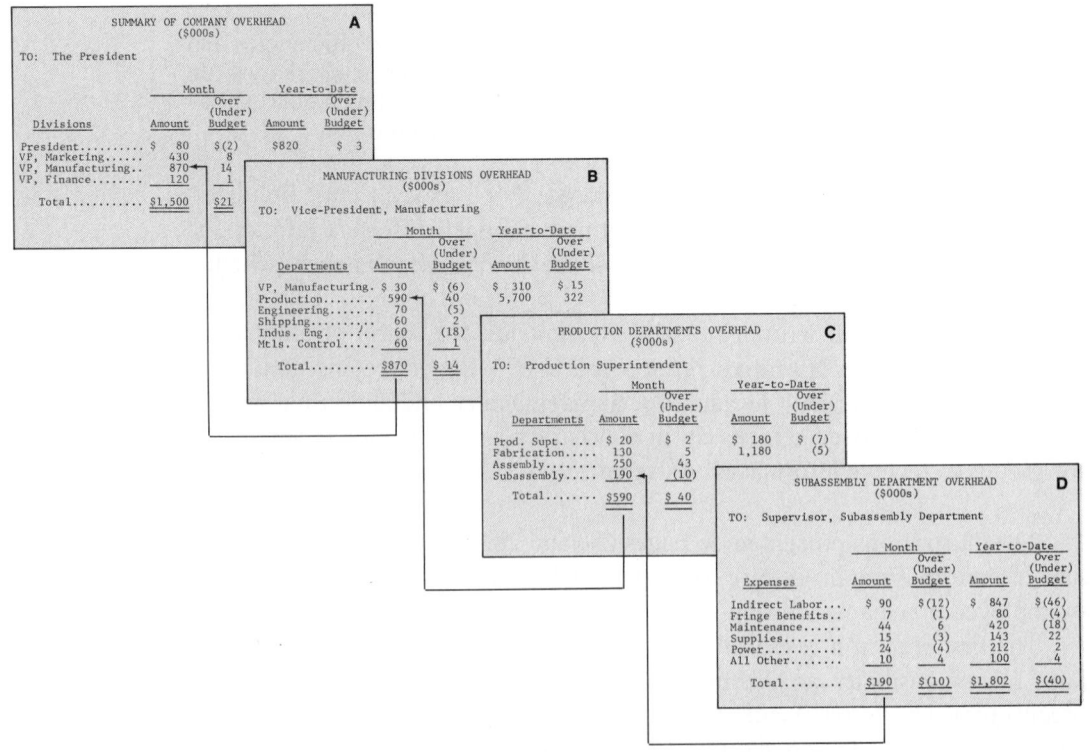

The following reports illustrate the factory overhead reporting structure for each level of responsibility and the relationship of each report to the next higher echelon of responsibility.[5] Starting with Report D (bottom of the pyramid), the Subassembly Department supervisor is provided with the factory overhead expenses for this area. The supervisors for the Fabrication and Assembly Departments also receive similar reports. The supervisors of these three departments are responsible to the production superintendent. Report C summarizes the overhead expenses for the production superintendent and the

Flow of Responsibility Reporting in a Manufacturing Concern

---

[5]James D. Willson, "Human Relations and More Effective Reporting," *NAA Bulletin*, Vol. XLII, No. 9, pp. 13–24.

RESPONSIBILITY EXPENSE SYSTEM: REPORTING FLOW   EXHIBIT A

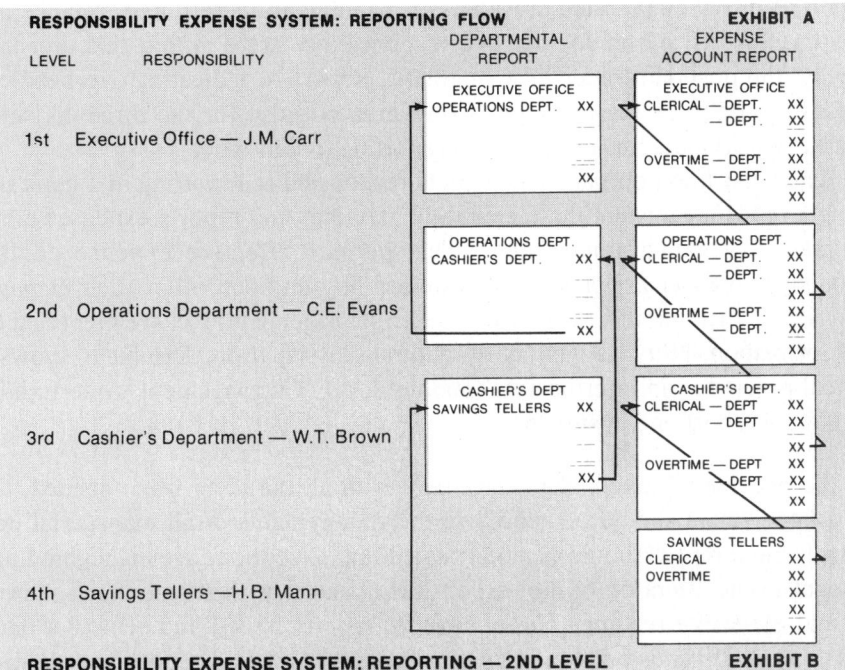

LEVEL	RESPONSIBILITY
1st	Executive Office — J.M. Carr
2nd	Operations Department — C.E. Evans
3rd	Cashier's Department — W.T. Brown
4th	Savings Tellers —H.B. Mann

Responsibility Reporting in a Bank

RESPONSIBILITY EXPENSE SYSTEM: REPORTING — 2ND LEVEL   EXHIBIT B
OPERATING PERFORMANCE REPORT

DEPARTMENT NAME: OPERATIONS DEPARTMENT				RESPONSIBILITY OF: C. E. EVANS	FOR PERIOD ENDING: APRIL 30, 19XX			
CURRENT PERIOD				RESPONSIBILITY AREA	YEAR TO DATE			
TOTAL	VARIABLE	FIXED	UNFAVORABLE* VS PLAN		TOTAL	VARIABLE	FIXED	UNFAVORABLE* VS PLAN
$ 35,000	$ 10,000	$ 25,000	$2,000*	OPERATIONS ADMINISTRATION	$ 140,000	$ 40,000	$ 100,000	$ 8,000*
130,000	120,000	10,000	5,000*	CASHIER'S DEPARTMENT	520,000	480,000	40,000	20,000*
120,000	105,000	15,000	4,000	DATA PROCESSING	480,000	420,000	40,000	16,000
55,000	45,000	10,000	1,000	DEPOSIT ACCOUNTING	220,000	180,000	40,000	4,000
•	•	•	•		•	•	•	•
$375,000	$305,000	$ 70,000	$3,000*	TOTAL PERSONNEL EXPENSE	$1,500,000	$1,220,000	$ 280,000	$12,000*
$ 25,000	$ 10,000	$ 15,000	$3,000	OPERATIONS ADMINISTRATION	$ 100,000	$ 40,000	$ 60,000	$12,000
20,000	5,000	15,000	4,000	CASHIER'S DEPARTMENT	80,000	20,000	60,000	16,000
210,000	35,000	175,000	5,000*	DATA PROCESSING	840,000	140,000	700,000	20,000*
15,000	5,000	10,000	3,000*	DEPOSIT ACCOUNTING	60,000	20,000	40,000	12,000*
•	•	•	•		•	•	•	•
$290,000	$ 60,000	$230,000	$2,000*	TOTAL NON-PERSONNEL EXPENSE	$1,160,000	$ 240,000	$ 920,000	$ 8,000*
$665,000	$365,000	$300,000	$5,000	TOTAL DEPARTMENTAL EXPENSES	$2,660,000	$1,460,000	$1,200,000	$20,000*

RESPONSIBILITY EXPENSE SYSTEM: REPORTING — 4TH LEVEL   EXHIBIT C
OPERATING PERFORMANCE REPORT

DEPARTMENT NAME: SAVINGS TELLERS				RESPONSIBILITY OF: H. B. MANN	FOR PERIOD ENDING: APRIL 30, 19XX			
CURRENT PERIOD				RESPONSIBILITY ACCOUNT	YEAR TO DATE			
TOTAL	VARIABLE	FIXED	UNFAVORABLE* VS PLAN		TOTAL	VARIABLE	FIXED	UNFAVORABLE* VS PLAN
$ 3,200		$3,200	$ 200	ADMINISTRATION	$ 12,800		$12,800	$ 800
900		900	100*	STAFF	3,600		3,600	400*
30,000	$30,000		2,000*	CLERICAL	120,000	$120,000		8,000*
300	300		200*	OVERTIME PREMIUM	1,200	1,200		800*
$34,400	$30,300	$4,100	$2,100*	TOTAL PERSONNEL EXPENSE	$137,600	$121,200	$16,400	$8,400*
$ 4,800		$4,800	$ 200	EQUIPMENT RENTALS	$ 19,200		$19,200	$ 800
200	$ 200		100*	SUPPLIES	800	$ 800		400*
300		300	100	TELEPHONE	1,200		1,200	400
700	700		400	OTHER MISC. EXPENSES	2,800	2,800		1,600*
$ 6,000	$ 900	$5,100	$ 200*	TOTAL NON-PERSONNEL EXPENSE	$ 24,000	$ 3,600	$20,400	$ 800*
$40,400	$31,200	$9,200	$2,300*	TOTAL DEPARTMENTAL EXPENSES	$161,600	$124,800	$36,800	$9,200*

three departments for which the production superintendent is accountable. Report B provides the vice-president of manufacturing with performance figures for this office and for the five responsibility areas within this division. Finally, the president receives a summary, Report A, indicating overhead expenses not only for the president's own area but also for the three divisions (Marketing, Manufacturing, Finance) reporting to that office.

The illustration on page 289 depicts responsibility reporting in a bank utilizing a reporting system that accurately identifies and reports expenses along the bank's organizational lines.[6] This permits effective expense control through the proper assignment of responsibility and control at each management level. In Exhibit A, expenses at each management level are identified by area of responsibility as well as by natural classification. Exhibit B shows a typical report for an intermediate (middle) level of management while Exhibit C shows a report of a cost center.

Reviewing the Reporting Structure

To provide all levels of management with all the facts when needed, the reporting system should be geared to the requirements of all managerial personnel. Each report should be so arranged that exceptions are highlighted and brought to the attention of the responsible manager without too much searching and extensive reading. The number of reports issued and sent to a manager also needs constant examination. Too many times a reporting system is cluttered with old, detailed, and voluminous reports without consideration of the cost of their preparation or their justification. No reporting system is ever perfect. It requires continuous checking and examination in the light of changing times and the vicissitudes of business itself.

DISCUSSION QUESTIONS

1. Explain responsibility accounting and the classification of revenues and expenses under this concept.

2. Responsibility accounting does not involve a drastic change in accounting theory or principles. Discuss.

3. What is the significance of controllable as compared to uncontrollable costs?

4. Enumerate a few general requirements that are absolutely necessary for a successful responsibility accounting system.

5. Enumerate some of the benefits that should result from responsibility accounting.

6. Why is some knowledge of human relations important to responsibility accounting?

---

[6]William E. Ellingson, Edward T. Kennedy, and Paul W. Landgren, Jr., "Computer-Based Bank Financial Information Systems," *The Arthur Andersen Chronicle*, Vol. 29, No. 2, p. 28.

7. The departmentalization of factory overhead is essential for maximum control of overhead. Explain in terms of responsibility reporting.

8. Overhead control reports received by department heads should include only those items over which they have control. Explain.

9. Why must service department overhead be included in the overhead rates? Why should actual service department overhead be accumulated in service department accounts instead of being charged directly to production department accounts?

10. Although service department overhead must be included in departmental overhead rates, actual overhead of these departments need not be distributed to departments serviced each period. Explain.

11. The three charges listed below are found on the monthly report of a division which manufactures and sells products primarily to outside companies. State which, if any, of these charges are consistent with the responsibility accounting concept. Support each answer with a brief explanation.

    (a) A charge for general corporation administration at 10% of division sales.
    (b) A charge for the use of the corporate computer facility. The charge is determined by taking the actual annual Computer Department cost and allocating an amount to each user on the ratio of its use to total corporation use.
    (c) A charge for goods purchased from another division. (The charge is based upon the competitive market price for the goods.)

    (CMA adapted)

12. The electric bill of the Emmons Company increased from $5,000 to $7,500 between January and February. As a bill is received, its cost is allocated to various departments on the basis of actual usage.

    (a) What factors may have caused the increase?
    (b) Is this an effective way of handling this cost? If not, suggest a better procedure.

13. Discuss the information which a well-designed cost report should give to the management from the point of view of production and of control. Is there any other information with which the cost figures should be amplified? In what terms should such information be given?

14. On what fundamentals should the method of presenting cost data to management be based?

15. Why is usefulness of the figures so important in accounting?

16. A frequent complaint made by management is that cost reports arrive too late to be of any value to the executives. What are the main contributing causes of this condition, and how can it be remedied?

17. Select the answer which best completes the statement:

    (a) Which of the following should not be on a monthly cost control report of a department manager? (1) departmental labor cost; (2) departmental supplies cost; (3) depreciation on departmental equipment; (4) cost of materials used in the department.
    (b) Periodic internal performance reports based upon a responsibility accounting system should not: (1) distinguish between controllable and uncontrollable costs; (2) be related to the organization chart; (3) include

allocated fixed overhead in determining performance evaluation; (4) include variances between actual and controllable costs.

(c) The concept of management by exception refers to management's: (1) lack of a predetermined plan; (2) consideration of only rare events; (3) consideration of items selected at random; (4) consideration of only those items which vary materially from plans.

(d) Of most relevance in deciding how or which costs should be assigned to a responsibility center is the degree of: (1) avoidability; (2) causality; (3) controllability; (4) variability.

(e) Of most relevance in deciding how indirect costs should be assigned to a product is the degree of: (1) avoidability; (2) causality; (3) controllability; (4) linearity.

(f) The most desirable measure for evaluating the performance of the departmental manager is departmental: (1) revenue less controllable departmental expenses; (2) net income; (3) contribution to indirect expenses; (4) revenue less departmental expenses.

(g) The term that identifies an accounting system in which the operations of the business are broken down into cost centers and the control function of the supervisor or the manager is emphasized is: (1) responsibility accounting; (2) operations-research accounting; (3) control accounting; (4) budgetary accounting.

(h) A desirable characteristic of a factory overhead control report for a production manager is that: (1) it is more important that the report be precise than timely; (2) the report should include information on all costs chargeable to the department, regardless of their origin or control; (3) the report should be stated in dollars rather than in physical units, so that the department head knows the financial magnitude of any variances; (4) the report should specify those costs controllable by the department head.

(AICPA and CMA adapted)

EXERCISES

1. Maintenance charging rate. A charging rate is frequently used to charge Maintenance Department overhead to departments using its services. The charge is determined by multiplying the number of labor hours of service by a charging rate which is computed by the following formula:

$$\frac{\text{Total actual Maintenance Department overhead}}{\text{Total labor hours worked}}$$

The superintendent of the Stamping Department was upset by a $15,000 maintenance charge for work that involved approximately the same number of labor hours as work done in a previous month when the charge was $12,000.

Required:
(1) Factors which might have caused the increased charge.
(2) Improvements to be made in the distribution of this company's Maintenance Department overhead.

2. Transfer rates and variance analysis. The Hogan Company uses predetermined departmental overhead rates to apply factory overhead. In computing these rates, every attempt is made to transfer service department overhead to producing departments on the most equitable bases. Budgeted overhead and other data for the Maintenance Department and General Factory are:

	Maintenance Dept.	General Factory
Monthly fixed overhead........	$7,500	$30,000
Variable overhead.................	$1.00 per mainte-nance labor hour	$20.00 per employee (producing departments only)
Average hourly wage rate	$7.50	—
Normal level of activity.........	15,000 maintenance hours per month	1,000 producing department employees
Actual November results:		
Total overhead...................	$27,000	$53,000
Actual level of activity.......	14,000 maintenance hours	980 producing department em-ployees

Required:
(1) Charging or billing rates to be used to transfer estimated maintenance and general factory overhead to other departments, together with a description of the method used.
(2) Spending and idle capacity variances for the service departments.

3. Billing rate and variance analysis. The Laubach Company operates its own power-generating plant. Power cost is distributed to the producing departments by charging the fixed cost according to the standby capacity provided and the variable cost on the basis of a predetermined rate multiplied by actual consumption. The rated standby capacity of Departments A, B, and C is 50 000, 37 500, and 12 500 kwh respectively per month.

The following information relates to the producing departments and the power plant for January through May:

	Consumption in Kilowatt-Hours			Power Plant	
	Dept. A	Dept. B	Dept. C	Fixed	Variable
January	45 000	40 000	10 000	$20,000	$19,600
February.........	55 000	35 000	11 000	20,000	20,000
March.............	47 500	38 000	11 000	20,000	19,800
April................	53 800	37 000	12 500	20,000	21,800
May.................	44 000	33 000	13 000	20,000	19,000

Predetermined variable power costs are based on $.20 per kwh.

Required:
(1) Power cost chargeable to each department for each of the five months.
(2) The over- or underdistributed variable cost of the power plant for each of the five months.

4. Power plant charging rate. During November, the actual expense of operating a power plant was $9,300, of which $2,500 was considered a fixed cost.

	Producing Departments		Service Departments	
Schedule of Horsepower-Hours	A	B	X	Y
Needed at capacity production.......................	10,000	20,000	12,000	8,000
Used during November....................................	8,000	13,000	7,000	6,000

Required:
(1) The dollar amounts of the power plant expense to be allocated to each producing and service department. The fixed cost is assigned on the basis of the power plant's readiness to serve.
(2) Reasons for allocating one service department's cost to other service departments as well as to producing departments.

(AICPA adapted)

5. Service departments sold-hour rates; variance analysis. A company's two service departments provide the following data:

SERVICE CENTER	MONTHLY BUDGET	SERVICE-HOURS AVAILABLE	ACTUAL MONTHLY EXPENSE
Carpenter Shop	$20,000	4,000	$19,300
Electricians	30,000	5,000	28,400

The two service departments serve three producing departments that show the following budgeted and actual cost and service-hours data:

Department No.	ESTIMATED SERVICES REQUIRED		ACTUAL SERVICES USED	
	Carpenter Shop	Electricians	Carpenter Shop	Electricians
1..................	1,200 hrs.	1,800 hrs.	800 hrs.	2,000 hrs.
2..................	1,500 hrs.	2,000 hrs.	1,600 hrs.	1,700 hrs.
3..................	1,300 hrs.	1,200 hrs.	900 hrs.	1,100 hrs.

Required:
(1) The sold-hour rates for the two service departments.
(2) The amounts charged to the producing departments for services rendered.
(3) The spending variances for the two service departments, assuming that 70% of the budgeted expense is fixed in Carpenter Shop and 80% in Electricians.

6. Billing rates; variance analysis. The management of the Dyson Company wishes to secure greater control over service departments and decides to create a billing rate for the Maintenance and Payroll Departments. For September, the following predetermined and actual operating and cost data have been made available:

Maintenance Department:
Predetermined data (beginning of the month):
Normal level of maintenance hours per month 3,200
Average hourly rate for maintenance worker................................... $8.70
Other maintenance costs:

	FIXED COST PER MONTH	VARIABLE COST PER MAINTENANCE LABOR HOUR
Supervision.............	$9,800	$.50
Tools and supplies.	2,300	.75
Other miscella- neous items.........	700	.05

Actual data (end of the month):
Maintenance hours worked... 3,455
Maintenance workers' earnings...................................... $29,610
Other costs (supervision, etc.)... $16,390

Payroll Department:
Predetermined data (beginning of the month):
Average number of employees in factory and office...................... 1,200
Budgeted cost for department.......................... $12,000 *plus* $2 for each
employee in factory and
office

Actual data (end of the month):
Number of employees in factory and office..................................... 1,165
Total cost in the Payroll Department $14,375

Required:
(1) The billing rate for the two departments.
(2) A variance analysis for the two departments for September.

7. Overhead analysis; report to supervisor. The cost and operating data on April factory overhead for Department 10 are shown at the top of page 295.
Required:
(1) A variance analysis of the factory overhead for Department 10.
(2) A departmental report for the supervisor of Department 10 with explanations regarding the format used.

	BUDGETED FACTORY OVERHEAD	ACTUAL FACTORY OVERHEAD
Variable departmental overhead:		
Supplies	$ 2,000	$ 1,700
Repairs and maintenance.............	800	600
Indirect labor	4,000	3,600
Power and light	1,200	1,150
Heat	400	350
Total..........................	$ 8,400	$ 7,400
Fixed departmental overhead:		
Building expense..........	$ 800	$ 840
Depreciation — machinery.................	2,400	2,400
Taxes and insurance....	400	420
Total..........................	$ 3,600	$ 3,660
Total departmental overhead	$12,000	$11,060
Operating data:		
Normal capacity hours.	8,000	
Factory overhead rate per hour.....................	$1.50	
Actual hours.................		6,400

PROBLEMS

11-1. Overhead rates; variance analysis in producing and service departments. Management control of the Santelani Products Co. prepared the budgeted and actual data shown below.

	BUDGETED DATA, 19--				ACTUAL DATA MARCH, 19--		
Departments	Direct Labor Cost	Direct Labor Hours	Factory Overhead Fixed	Variable	Direct Labor Cost	Direct Labor Hours	Factory Overhead Cost
Machining	$132,000	22,000	$12,840	$14,400	$12,780	2,130	$3,186*
Assembly	168,000	28,000	14,100	18,300	13,860	2,310	3,741*
Tools and Supplies.....	-0-	-0-	3,600	5,600	-0-	-0-	919
Materials Handling	-0-	-0-	5,700	6,000	-0-	-0-	1,080

*Includes service departments

The fixed overhead of the service departments is apportioned to the producing departments on a 60:40 basis and the variable overhead on the basis of direct labor hours. Budgeted direct labor hours are based on normal capacity utilization. Factory overhead is applied on the basis of direct labor hours.

Required:
(1) Departmental factory overhead rates for producing departments, based on (a) direct labor cost and (b) direct labor hours. (Round off all amounts to three decimal places.)
(2) Spending and idle capacity variances of producing and service departments, including total over- or underabsorbed factory overhead for March. (Round off calculations to three decimal places.)

11-2. Variance analysis in producing and service departments based on responsibility reporting. Congo Floors, Inc., has four producing departments and three service departments. Departmental overhead rates are established at the beginning of the fiscal year to aid in costing completed products. Actual factory overhead is accumulated and monthly budget reports are sent to each department supervisor for the purpose of responsibility accounting. On the basis of predetermined departmental expenses and after the allocation of the three service departments' costs, the following overhead rates for the four producing departments were calculated:

| | | PRODUCING DEPARTMENTS | | |
	Forming	Molding	Finishing	Packing and Shipping
Departmental expenses:				
Variable expense...............	$19,500	$120,000	$22,400	$16,000
Fixed expense....................	19,500	77,000	15,820	7,000
Total direct departmental expense............................	$39,000	$197,000	$38,220	$23,000
Distributed service departments' costs:				
Machine Shop....................	6,200	14,800		
Hydraulic Power................	1,400	15,600		
General Plant	5,400	28,600	5,780	7,000
Total departmental overhead......................................	$52,000	$256,000	$44,000	$30,000
Factory overhead rates.........	$4 per direct labor hour	$8 per machine hour	275% per direct labor cost	$2 per 100 units

Actual departmental production and cost data at the end of the budget period are:

| | PRODUCING DEPARTMENTS | | | | SERVICE DEPARTMENTS | | |
	Forming	Molding	Finishing	Packing and Shipping	Machine Shop	Hydraulic Power	General Plant
Departmental expenses:							
Variable expense.....	$21,800	$116,000	$20,780	$19,300	$ 8,100	$ 5,000	$12,880
Fixed expense.........	19,500	77,000	15,820	7,000	14,000	12,000	36,000
Total actual expense..	$41,300	$193,000	$36,600	$26,300	$22,100	$17,000	$48,880
Production data:							
Direct labor hours...	13,150						
Machine hours		30,900					
Direct labor cost......			$18,100				
Units shipped				1,588,000			

Required:
(1) The amount of factory overhead applied in each of the four producing departments.
(2) The spending and idle capacity variances for the Forming and Molding Departments before service department costs are allocated. (Carry all computations to five decimal places.)
(3) The amount of departmental overhead variance for which each departmental supervisor is responsible, considering only variable costs for all departments. Assume that the use of service department facilities was exactly the same as the amount budgeted when the producing department overhead rates were calculated. (Round off all amounts to three decimal places.)

11-3. Variance analysis of producing and service departments overhead. Midwest Products, Inc., decided to push for a greater amount of cost consciousness and cost responsibility among its departmental supervisors. The allocation of service department costs to the producing departments, using predetermined rates, has been in use for some time. Now the management asks the Cost Department, with the cooperation of the departmental supervisors, not only to prepare departmental budgets but also to give the supervisors monthly reports for cost control information.

The company operates with three producing departments, A, B, and C, and two service departments, Repairs and Maintenance, and Utilities. For the year 19--, the Cost Department had prepared the following departmental factory overhead budgets and determined the factory overhead rates based on direct labor hours:

	PRODUCING DEPARTMENTS			SERVICE DEPARTMENTS	
Expenses	A	B	C	Repairs and Maintenance	Utilities
Total budgeted expense*	$52,000	$52,450	$41,900	$56,000	$49,000
Allocation of service depts.:					
Utilities (based on kilowatt-hours).................................	14,000	15,750	12,250	7,000	(49,000)
Repairs and maintenance (based on direct labor hours).................................	18,000	27,900	17,100	(63,000)	
Total.....................................	$84,000	$96,100	$71,250		
Bases:					
Kilowatt-hours	40 000	45 000	35 000	20 000	
Direct labor hours	20,000	31,000	19,000		
Service department allocation rates.....................................				$.90 per direct labor hour	$.35 per kilowatt-hour
Departmental overhead rates..	$4.20 per direct labor hour	$3.10 per direct labor hour	$3.75 per direct labor hour		

*The amounts used to arrive at these figures have been omitted.

Actual cost and operating data before allocation of service department costs at the end of the budget period are:

	PRODUCING DEPARTMENTS			SERVICE DEPARTMENTS	
Expenses	A	B	C	Repairs and Maintenance	Utilities
Total actual expense*	$56,220	$52,850	$42,580	$55,320	$49,240
Operating data:					
Direct labor hours...........	20,480	29,850	20,100		
Kilowatt-hours.................	39 300	46 200	35 800	18 950	

*The amounts used to arrive at these figures have been omitted.

Required:
(1) The amount of factory overhead applied for each of the three producing departments.
(2) The amount of over- or underapplied factory overhead for each of the three producing departments, charging them with service department costs on the basis of actual kilowatt-hours or labor hours multiplied by the billing rate.
(3) The total variance for each of the two service departments.

11-4. Billing rates; estimated factory overhead and variance analysis. Herramienta Tool Co. has two producing departments, Planers and Radial Drills, and two service departments, Maintenance and Utilities. The Cost Department collected the data shown at the top of page 298.

Required:
(1) The billing (or charging) rate for each of the two service departments.
(2) The total predetermined factory overhead for each of the two producing departments and their departmental factory overhead rates based on direct labor hours. Service department expenses are to be distributed on the basis of the billing rates calculated in (1) above. (Carry all computations to three decimal places.)
(3) An analysis of the over- or underapplied factory overhead of each of the two producing departments for January, including the spending and idle capacity variances. Service de-

	PRODUCING DEPARTMENTS		SERVICE DEPARTMENTS	
	Planers	Radial Drills	Maintenance	Utilities
Estimated Data for 19––:				
Factory overhead:				
Fixed overhead	$18,000	$15,000	$ 6,000	$ 4,800
Variable overhead	15,000	9,000	4,500	3,600
Total	$33,000	$24,000	$10,500	$ 8,400
Direct labor hours.............	12,000	7,500		
Maintenance hours...........	2,500	1,000	3,500	
Kilowatt-hours...................	45 000	25 000		70 000
Actual data for January 19––:				
Factory overhead:				
Fixed overhead	$ 1,500	$ 1,250	$ 500	$ 400
Variable overhead	1,620	1,050	670	310
Total	$ 3,120	$ 2,300	$ 1,170	$ 710
Direct labor hours.............	1,020	680		
Maintenance hours...........	320	80	400	
Kilowatt-hours...................	4 000	2 000		6 000

partment expenses are to be charged on the basis of actual hours (maintenance or kilo-watt) multiplied by the billing rate. This method treats these expenses as being wholly vari-able.

(4) A calculation and analysis of the over- or underdistributed factory overhead in each of the two service departments, including the spending and idle capacity variances. (Round off all amounts to four decimal places.)

11-5. Budget allowance; variance analysis based on responsibility reporting. The controller of the Tippens Corporation prepared the following forecast income statement for the year 19––:

	AMOUNT	UNIT
Sales (60,000 units)	$600,000	$10.00
Cost of goods sold (Schedule I)...	384,000	6.40
Gross profit...	$216,000	$ 3.60
Operating expenses:		
Marketing expense $80,000		
Administrative expense 70,000	150,000	2.50
Income before income tax...	$ 66,000	$ 1.10
Schedule I — Estimated cost of goods sold:		
Direct materials...	$102,000	$ 1.70
Direct labor..	162,000	2.70
Factory overhead	120,000	2.00
Total	$384,000	$ 6.40

The product's manufacturing processes require two producing departments that make use of the services of Department 76, Maintenance, and Department 95, Janitorial. To charge the products moving through the two departments, the cost accountant has prepared an overhead distribution sheet and calculated predetermined factory overhead rates for product costing as shown on page 299.

The Department 76 cost was allocated to the two producing departments on the basis of the direct labor hours. The Department 95 cost was prorated 50% to the factory and 50% to the general offices. The two producing departments shared the 50% factory allocation on a 40:60 basis, respectively.

For January, the Planning Department scheduled 5,000 units. At the end of the month, sales and production showed the following results:

Sales	4,900 units
Production — completed in both departments........................	5,200 units

	PRODUCING DEPARTMENTS		SERVICE DEPARTMENTS	
	Dept. 10	Dept. 12	Dept. 76 Maintenance	Dept. 95 Janitorial
Production units	60,000	60,000		
Direct labor hours	15,000	12,000		
Direct labor cost.......................	$90,000	$72,000		
Factory overhead:				
Variable overhead	$27,000	$22,800	$ 5,100	$2,700
Fixed overhead	17,520	34,230	8,400	7,200
Share of Department 76.......	7,500	6,000	$13,500	$9,900
Share of Department 95.......	1,980	2,970		4,950
Total factory overhead............	$54,000	$66,000		
To marketing and administrative expenses				$4,950
Factory overhead rate (based on direct labor hours)	$3.60	$5.50		

Actual hours and costs at the end of the month:

	DEPT. 10	DEPT. 12	DEPT. 76	DEPT. 95
Hours worked...................	1,340	1,030		
Actual factory overhead:				
Variable overhead	$2,700	$2,240	$495	$340
Fixed overhead.............	1,500	3,000	700	600

Required:
(1) The budget allowance for each of the two producing departments for January based on (a) scheduled production hours and (b) actual production hours.
(2) The spending and idle capacity variances for each of the two producing departments based on actual production hours.
(3) The spending variance for each of the two service departments. (Round off all amounts to three decimal places.)

CASES

A. Cost responsibility and the attitude of managers. Declining profits compelled the management of the Olinvelte Corporation to approach employees to work for production economy and increased productivity. Production managers were promised a monetary incentive based on cost reductions.

The production managers responded with (1) an increased rate of production; (2) a higher rejection rate for quantities of raw materials and parts received from the storeroom; (3) a postponement of repairs and maintenance work; and (4) a reliance on quick emergency repairs to avoid breakdowns.

The repair and maintenance policy is causing serious conflicts. The maintenance supervisor argues that the postponement of certain repairs in the short run and the use of emergency repair techniques could result in increased costs later and, in some instances, could reduce the life of machines as well as machine safety.

Even more serious is the growing bitterness caused by pressures placed on the maintenance managers by individual production managers to obtain service. Also, in several instances, some production departments whose production has been halted due to machine breakdown have had to wait while another production department, with an aggressive manager, has received repair service on machines not needed in the current production run. Furthermore, the demand for immediate service sometimes results in substandard repair work.

The production departments are charged with the actual cost of the repairs. A record of the repair work conducted in individual production departments is prepared by the maintenance managers. This record, when completed in the Accounting Department, shows the repair hours, the hourly rate of the maintenance worker, the maintenance overhead charge, and the cost of any parts. The record serves as the basis for the charges to production departments. Production managers have complained about the charging system, claiming that charges depend upon which maintenance worker does the work (hourly rate and efficiency), when the work is done (the production department is charged for the overtime premium), and how careful the worker is in recording the time on the job.

Required:
  (1) Identification and a brief explanation of the motivational factors which may cause friction between the production and maintenance managers.
  (2) A report which revises the system employed to charge production departments for repair costs, so that the production departments' complaints are eliminated or reduced.

(CMA adapted)

B. Analysis of operating costs in a university. Regional University has a total enrollment of 5,000 full-time students and a faculty of 350. It is state supported, with appropriations as the sole source of operating funds and all tuition and fees remitted to the state treasurer. The 19-- operating appropriation was $12.5 million, which represents an average cost of $2,500 per student.

The basic product of the university is the granting of degrees to students who complete degree requirements in a particular program. The departments granting degrees are somewhat analogous to producing departments, and the various support departments (i.e., facilities services, academic support services, administrative services) are similar to overhead departments in a manufacturing environment.

The administration has implemented a model used by a nearby university to analyze operating costs. The new cost model will provide information which will be helpful in assessing the effectiveness of internal resource utilization, in assisting budget preparation and the related budget justification before the legislature, and in providing data for examining options for allocating funds based upon current program costs and projected university enrollments. The cost model is designed to provide information about the traceable direct costs incurred by academic departments and the allocated support costs charged to academic departments. The sum of the traceable direct and allocated support costs is considered the total cost of an academic department. Various cost measures are calculated for each academic department and for the student degree programs (majors) offered by each department.

Schedules 1 and 2 for the Electrical Engineering Department of Regional University's College of Engineering have been prepared according to the new cost model. Similar schedules are prepared for all academic departments and degree programs in the university. The following definitions for student activity measures assist in the interpretation of the cost data:
  (a) Student Credit Hour (SCH) — the standard measure of instructional activity which is the equivalent of one student enrolled in an academic course for which one credit hour is granted, e.g., a three-credit-hour course with 20 students equals 60 SCH of instructional activity.
  (b) Full-Time Student — a student enrolled for 30 credit hours in an academic year.
  (c) Equivalent Full-Time Students — number of credit hours taken by students divided by 30 credit hours.

Schedule 1 presents the total instructional cost (traceable direct and allocated support) and the instructional cost per SCH taught by the Electrical Engineering Department. Schedule 2 presents the traceable direct and total cost of the electrical engineering degree program (major); the cost per SCH taken and per student major is also presented there.

Schedule 1:

Regional University — College of Engineering
Instructional Costs for the Electrical Engineering Department
For the 19–– Academic Year

	TOTAL COST (000S OMITTED)	COST PER SCH TAUGHT[1]
Traceable direct costs:		
Salaries and benefits	$ 600	$ 73.20
Travel expenses...............................	25	3.00
Printing and advertising	3	.40
Supplies	29	3.50
Equipment	16	1.90
Rentals	12	1.50
Total direct cost...........................	$ 685	$ 83.50
Allocated support costs:		
Facilities services (utilities, building and grounds, etc.)[2]...............	$ 180	$ 22.00
Academic support services (library, computer, etc.)[3]	206	25.10
Administrative services (admissions, placement, etc.)[3].............	103	12.60
Office of Engineering Dean[3]	15	1.80
Total allocated support cost.......	$ 504	$ 61.50
Total department instructional cost...	$1,189	$145.00

[1]Student credit hours (SCH) taught in the Electrical Engineering Department totaled 8,200.
[2]Cost allocated on the basis of square feet occupied.
[3]Cost allocated on the basis of the number of student majors.

Schedule 2:

Regional University — College of Engineering
Program Costs of Students Majoring In Electrical Engineering
For the 19–– Academic Year

DEPARTMENT PROVIDING INSTRUCTION	TRACEABLE DIRECT COST[1]		TOTAL COST[1]	
Chemical	($92.90 × 200)	$ 18,580	($169.60 × 200)	$ 33,920
Civil...	($69.80 × 100)	6,980	($147.30 × 100)	14,730
Electrical	($83.50 × 6,500)	542,750	($145.00 × 6,500)	942,500
Mechanical............................	($74.80 × 1,150)	86,020	($126.50 × 1,150)	145,475
All nonengineering[2]		112,500		202,500
Cost associated with students enrolled as electrical engineering majors.................................		$766,830		$1,339,125
Electrical engineering degree program cost per SCH taken[3]		$ 49.60		$ 86.70
Electrical engineering degree program cost per student[4]		$ 1,489		$ 2,600

[1]The costs of each academic department used by students majoring in electrical engineering are determined by multiplying the cost per SCH taught in that department by the number of SCH taken by students enrolled in the electrical engineering degree program from that department.
[2]Students majoring in electrical engineering were enrolled in 7,500 SCH from various nonengineering departments. Each nonengineering department has its own traceable direct and total costs per SCH and the cost to the electrical engineering program is charged according to these rates. However, the detail of these charges has been omitted from this schedule.
[3]A total of 15,450 SCH were taken by students in the electrical engineering degree program.
[4]The electrical engineering degree program has 515 equivalent full-time students.

Required:

  (1) (a) The total traceable direct cost per SCH taught in the Electrical Engineering Department is $83.50 (Schedule 1). Is this an approximation of the variable cost per SCH taught in that department?

     (b) The annual traceable direct cost per student majoring in electrical engineering is $1,489 (Schedule 2). Is this an approximation of the annual variable cost per student major in electrical engineering?

     (c) The allocated support cost per SCH taught is $61.50 for the Electrical Engineering Department and $76.70 for the Chemical Engineering Department. Does this mean that more support costs were allocated to the Chemical Engineering Department?

  (2) Should traceable direct and total department instructional costs per SCH taught (as presented in Schedule 1) be used by the Electrical Engineering Department in preparing its budget for presentation to the university administration?

  (3) The cost model as employed by Regional University generates data regarding the traceable direct and total program costs in terms of dollars, SCH taken, and student majors for degree programs (Schedule 2 is an example of these cost measures for the electrical engineering degree program). Could Regional University use these data, when available for all academic departments:

     (a) To measure the cost effectiveness of programs offered by departments?

     (b) To justify different tuition rates for different degree programs?

(CMA adapted)

C. Reviewing the reporting structure. Wright Company employs a computer-based data processing system for maintaining all company records. The present system was developed in stages over the past five years and has been fully operational for the last 24 months.

When the system was being designed, all department heads were asked to specify the types of information and reports they would need for planning and controlling operations. The Systems Department attempted to meet the specifications of each department head. Company management specified that certain other reports be prepared for department heads. During the five years of systems development and operations, there have been changes in the department head positions due to attrition and promotions. New department heads have often requested additional reports according to their specifications; the Systems Department has complied with all of these requests. Consequently, the data processing system has generated a large quantity of reports each reporting period. Occasionally, a report has been discontinued upon request by a department head but only if it was not a standard report required by executive management.

Company management became concerned about the quality of information being produced by the system and the Internal Audit Department was asked to evaluate the effectiveness of these reports. The audit staff noted the following reactions to this information overload:

     (a) Many department heads would not act on certain reports during periods of peak activity. The department head would let these reports accumulate with the hope of catching up during a subsequent lull.

     (b) Some department heads had so many reports that they did not act at all upon the information or made incorrect decisions because of misuse of the information.

     (c) Frequently action required by the nature of the report data was not taken until the department head was reminded by someone who needed the decision. These department heads did not appear to have developed a priority system for acting on the information produced by the data processing system.

     (d) Department heads often would develop the information they needed from alternative, independent sources, rather than utilize the reports generated by the data processing system. This was often easier than trying to search among the reports for the needed data.

Required:

  (1) An explanation of whether each of the observed reactions is a functional or dysfunctional behavioral response.

  (2) Recommendations for procedures that the company could employ to eliminate any dysfunctional behavior and to prevent its recurrence.

(CMA adapted)

Part Four
Planning and Control of Materials and Labor

12
Controlling and Costing Materials

Effective materials management is essential in order to (1) provide the best service to customers, (2) produce at maximum efficiency, and (3) manage inventories at predetermined levels to stabilize investments in inventories. Successful materials management requires the development of a highly integrated and coordinated system involving sales forecasting, purchasing, receiving, storage, production, shipping, and actual sales. Both the theory of costing materials and inventories and the practical mechanics of cost calculations and record keeping must be considered.

Costing materials presents some important, often complex, and sometimes highly controversial questions concerning the costing of materials used in production and the cost of inventory remaining to be consumed in a future period. In financial accounting, the subject is usually presented as a problem of inventory valuation; in cost accounting, the primary problem is the determination of the cost of various materials consumed in production and a proper charge to cost of goods sold. The discussion of materials management in this chapter deals with:

1. Procedures for materials procurement and use.
2. Materials costing methods.
3. Cost of materials in inventory at the end of a period.
4. Costing procedures for scrap, spoiled goods, and defective work.

PROCEDURES FOR MATERIALS PROCUREMENT AND USE

Although production processes and materials requirements vary, the cycle of procurement and use of materials usually involves the following steps:

1. *Engineering, planning*, and *routing* determine the design of the product, the materials specifications, and the requirements at each stage of operations. Engineering and planning not only determine the maximum and minimum quantities to run and the bill of materials for given products and quantities but also cooperate in developing standards where applicable.
2. The *production budget* provides the master plan from which details concerning materials requirements are eventually developed.
3. The *purchase requisition* informs the purchasing agent concerning the quantity and type of materials needed.
4. The *purchase order* contracts for appropriate quantities to be delivered at specified dates to assure uninterrupted operations.
5. The *receiving report* certifies quantities received and may report results of inspection and testing for quality.
6. The *materials requisition* notifies the storeroom or warehouse to deliver specified types and quantities of materials to a given department at a specified time or is the authorization for the storeroom to issue materials to departments.
7. The *materials ledger cards* record the receipt and the issuance of each class of materials and provide a perpetual inventory record.

Accounting procedures for materials procurement and use involve forms and records necessary for general ledger financial accounting as well as those necessary for costing a job, process, or department, and for maintaining perpetual inventories and other statistical summaries. The purchase requisition, purchase order, receiving report, materials requisition, bill of materials, scrap report, returned materials report, materials ledger cards, and summary of materials used are some of the forms used for materials control under a cost system. The purchases journal, the cash payments journal, the general journal, and the general ledger control accounts are also used.

The discussion in this section is not based on any particular type or size of industry. It is, rather, a general description of the accounting and controlling procedures involved in the procurement and use of materials. The flowchart on page 305 shows procedures for purchasing, receiving, recording, and paying for materials, i.e., the procurement phase.

Purchases of Productive Materials   The actual purchase of all materials is usually made by the purchasing department headed by a general purchasing agent. In some small and medium-size companies, however, department heads or supervisors have authority to purchase materials as the need arises. In any case, systematic procedures should be in writing in order to fix responsibility and to provide full information regarding the ultimate use of materials ordered and received.

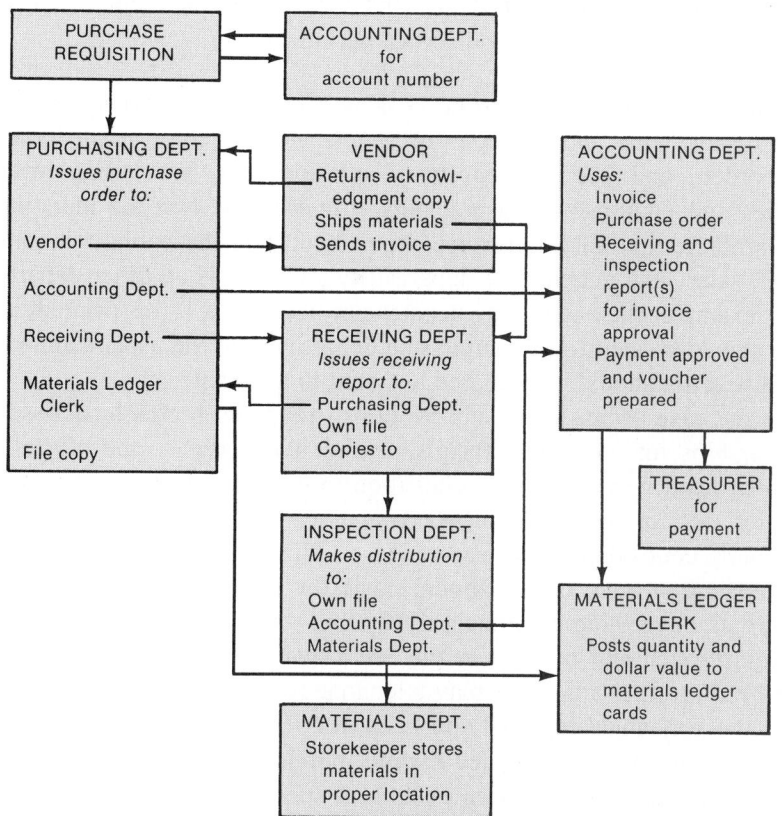

Flowchart for
Purchasing,
Receiving,
Recording, and
Paying for
Materials

The purchasing department should (1) receive purchase requisitions for materials, supplies, and equipment; (2) keep informed concerning sources of supply, prices, and shipping and delivery schedules; (3) prepare and place purchase orders; and (4) arrange for adequate and systematic reports between the purchasing, the receiving, and the accounting departments. An additional function of the purchasing department in many enterprises is to verify and approve for payment all invoices received in response to purchase orders placed by the department. This procedure has the advantage of centralizing the verification and approval of invoices in the department that originates the purchases and that has complete information concerning items and quantities ordered, prices, terms, shipping instructions, and other conditions and details of the purchases. However, invoice verification and approval by the purchasing department may violate sound procedures and principles of internal control, particularly if the same individual prepares an order and later approves the invoice. Consequently, invoice audit and approval in many instances have been made a function of the accounting department, which receives a copy of the purchase order. The purchase order carries all necessary information regarding price, discount agreement, and delivery stipulations, as well as the number of the account to which the order is to be charged. Furthermore, the centralization of invoice approval in the accounting department helps avoid delaying payments beyond the discount period.

Purchases of Supplies, Services, and Repairs

The procedure followed in purchasing productive materials should apply to all departments and divisions of a business. Purchase requisitions, purchase orders, and receiving reports are appropriate for accounting department supplies and equipment, the company cafeteria, the first aid unit, the treasurer's office, the building service department, and the public relations, personnel, sales, and engineering departments, as well as all other departments. If, for example, the accounting department needs new forms printed, a requisition should be sent to the purchasing department in the usual manner, and a purchase order should be prepared and sent to the printer.

In the case of magazine subscriptions, trade and professional association memberships for company officials, and similar services, the official or department head may send in a requisition in the usual manner. A requisition, an order, and an invoice for all goods and services purchased are a necessity in properly controlling purchases.

Repair contracts on an annual basis for typewriters, calculators, electronic data processing equipment, and some types of factory equipment may be requisitioned and ordered in the usual manner. In other cases, a department head or other employee may telephone for service and shortly thereafter may have a machine repaired and back in operation. In such cases, the purchasing agent issues a so-called blanket purchase order that amounts to approval of all repair and service costs of a specific type without knowing the actual amount charged. When the repair bill is received, the invoice clerk checks the amount of the bill with the head of the department where the repairs took place and then approves the invoice for payment.

Purchasing Forms

The principal forms required in purchasing are the purchase requisition and the purchase order.

Purchase Requisition. The *purchase requisition* originates with (1) a stores or warehouse clerk who observes that the quantity on hand is at a set ordering minimum, (2) a materials ledger clerk who may be responsible for notifying the purchasing agent when to buy, (3) a works manager who foresees the need for special materials or unusual quantities, (4) a research or engineering department employee who needs materials or supplies of a special nature, or (5) a computer that has been programmed to produce replenishment advice for the purchasing department. For standard materials, little information other than the stock number may be needed, and the purchasing agent uses judgment concerning where to buy and the quantity to order. For other purchase requests, it may be necessary to give meticulous descriptions, blueprints, catalog numbers, weights, standards, brand names, exact quantities to order, and suggested prices.

A purchase requisition is illustrated below. One copy remains with the originating employee, and the original is sent to the purchasing department for execution of the request.

PURCHASE REQUISITION	No. **07615**

TO: Purchasing Department

| | Mo. | Day | Yr. |

DELIVER
  TO:_____   DATE REQUIRED:_____
  _____ JOB NO./DEPT. NO.:_____
                      ACCT. NO.:_____

SUGGESTED
  SUPPLIER:_____
PLEASE ORDER THE ITEMS LISTED BELOW:

Quantity	Item No.	Description	Unit Price	Amount

BUDGET CONTROL	

Allowance For Period $ _____	Balance Available $ _____	Ordered By_____
	Amt. This Purchase $ _____	
	Remaining Balance $ _____	Approved By_____

Purchase Order. The *purchase order*, signed by the purchasing agent or other official, is a written authorization to a vendor to supply specified quantities of described goods at agreed terms and at a designated time and place. As a convenience, the vendor's order forms may be used; but in typical practice, the order forms are prepared by the purchasing company, and the form is adapted to the particular needs of the purchaser. As a matter of record and for accounting control, a purchase order should be issued for every purchase of materials, supplies, or equipment. When a purchase commitment is made by mail, telephone, or a sales representative, the purchase order serves as confirmation to the vendor and places the required documents in the hands of those concerned in the purchasing company.

The purchase order gives the vendor a complete description of the goods and services desired, the terms, the prices, and the shipping instructions. When necessary, the description may refer to attached blueprints and specification pages. The original and an acknowledgment copy are sent to the vendor. The acknowledgment copy is a necessary form for contract procedure, because other copies are distributed as shown in the flowchart on page 305. The vendor is asked to sign and return the copy to the purchaser, indicating that the order was received and will be delivered according to the specifications enumerated in the purchase order.

Receiving   The function of the receiving department is to: unload and unpack incoming materials; check quantities received against the shipper's packing list; identify goods received with descriptions on the purchase order; prepare a receiving report; notify the purchasing department of discrepancies discovered; arrange for inspection when necessary; notify the traffic department and the purchasing department of any damage in transit; and route accepted materials to the appropriate factory location.

The *receiving report* shows the purchase order number, the account number to be charged, the name of the vendor, details relating to transportation, and the quantity and type of goods received. The form also provides a space for the inspection department to note either the complete approval of the shipment or the quantity rejected and the reason for the rejection. If inspection does not take place immediately after receipt of the materials, the receiving report is distributed as follows: (1) the receiving department keeps one copy and sends another copy to the purchasing department as notice of the arrival of the materials; (2) all other copies go to the inspection department, and are distributed when inspection is completed. After inspection, one copy of the receiving report, with the inspection result noted thereon, is sent to the accounting department, where it is matched with the purchase order and the vendor's invoice and then paid. Other copies go to various departments such as materials and production planning. One copy accompanies the materials, so that the storekeeper knows the quantity and the kind of materials received.

Invoice Approval and Data Processing   By the time materials reach the receiving department, the company usually will have received the invoice from the vendor. This invoice and a copy of the purchase order are filed in the accounting department. When the receiving report with its inspection report arrives, the receiving report and the invoice are compared to see that materials received meet purchase order specifications as to items, quantities, prices, price extensions, discount and credit terms, shipping instructions, and other possible conditions. If the invoice is found to be correct or has been adjusted because of rejects as noted by the inspection department, the invoice clerk approves it, attaches it to the purchase order and the receiving report, and sends these papers to another clerk for the preparation of the voucher.

Invoice approval is an important step in materials control procedure, since it certifies that the goods have been received as ordered and that payment can be made. The invoice approval information is often built into a rubber stamp, as shown on page 309, and each invoice is stamped. The verification procedure is handled by responsible invoice clerks, thus assuring systematic examination and handling of the paper work necessary for adequate control of materials purchases. The preparation of the voucher is based on the information taken from the invoice approval stamp.

The voucher data are entered first in the purchases journal and are posted to the subsidiary records. They are then entered in the cash payments journal according to the due date for payment. The original voucher and two copies are sent to the treasurer for issuance of the check. The treasurer mails the check with the original voucher to the vendor, files a voucher copy, and returns one voucher copy to the accounting depart-

INVOICE APPROVAL
Purchase Order No. _____   Invoice Date _____
Vchr. No. _____   Date Paid _____
Vchr. Date _____   Check No. _____
ACCOUNTS CHARGED AND CODES: $
_____
_____
_____
Gross Amount .... $
...% Discount on $ _____
Net Amount Payable .... $ _____
Approved By _____   Posted By _____

Invoice Approval Stamp

ment for the vendor's file. Purchase transactions entered in the purchases journal affect the control accounts and the subsidiary records as shown in the chart below.

TRANSACTION	GENERAL LEDGER CONTROL		SUBSIDIARY RECORDS
	Debit	Credit	
Materials purchased for stock	Materials	Accounts Payable	Entry in the Received section of the materials ledger card
Materials purchased for a particular job or department	Work in Process	Accounts Payable	Entry in the Direct Materials section of the production or job order
Materials and supplies purchased for factory overhead purposes	Materials	Accounts Payable	Entry in the Received section of the materials ledger card
Supplies purchased for marketing and administrative offices	Materials Marketing Expenses Control Administrative Expenses Control	Accounts Payable	Entry in the Received section of the materials ledger card or in the proper columns of the marketing or administrative expense analysis sheets
Purchases of services or repairs	Factory Overhead Marketing Expenses Control Administrative Expenses Control	Accounts Payable	Entry in the proper account columns of the expense analysis sheets
Purchases of equipment	Equipment	Accounts Payable	Entry on the equipment ledger card

Correcting Invoices

When the purchase order, receiving report, and invoice are compared, various adjustments may be needed as a result of the circumstances described below.

1. Some of the materials ordered are not received and are not entered on the invoice. In this case no adjustment is necessary, and the invoice may be approved for immediate payment. On the purchase order the invoice clerk will make a notation of the quantity received in place of the quantity ordered. If the vendor is out of stock or otherwise unable to deliver specified merchandise, an immediate ordering from other sources may be necessary.
2. Items ordered are not received but are entered on the invoice. In this situation the shortage is noted on the invoice and is deducted from the total before payment is approved. A letter to the vendor explaining the shortage is usually in order.
3. The seller ships a quantity larger than called for on the purchase order. The purchaser may keep the entire shipment and add the excess to the invoice, if not already invoiced; or the excess may be returned or held, pending instructions from the seller. Some companies issue a supplementary purchase order that authorizes the invoice clerk to pay the overshipment.
4. Materials of a wrong size or quality, defective parts, and damaged items are received. If the items are returned, a correction on the invoice should be made before payment is approved. It may be advantageous to keep damaged or defective shipments if the seller makes adequate price concessions, or the items may be held subject to the seller's instructions.
5. It may be expedient for a purchaser to pay transportation charges, even though delivered prices are quoted and purchases are not made on this basis. The amount paid by the purchaser is deducted on the invoice, and the paid freight bill is attached to the invoice as evidence of payment.

Electronic Data Processing for Materials Received and Issued

The preceding description of invoice approval and payment was for a manual operation performed by an accounts payable clerk or an invoice clerk. In an electronic data processing (EDP) system, the computer — to a great extent — replaces the clerk. Upon receipt of the invoice (the source document), the accounts payable clerk enters the account distribution on the invoice. The data are then directly inputted from the invoice to the computer data bank via a terminal device. The data are edited, audited, and merged with the purchase order and the receiving order data, both of which have been stored in the computer data bank. The common matching criterion on all documents is the purchase order number. Quantities, dollar values, due dates, terms, and unit prices are matched. When in agreement, the cost data are entered in the accounts payable computer file with a date for later payment, or a printout of a check is transmitted for payment.

The above procedure deals with the accounts payable phase of a purchase transaction. Of equal importance is the need for posting the data in quantities and dollar values to the materials inventory file in the EDP system. The information enters the EDP system from either the invoice or the invoice approval form, which would have to include all computer-necessary data. The internal computer program updates the materials inventory file. The program applicable to a purchase transaction for materials can be depicted in the flowchart below. The withdrawal of materials could also be programmed, so that manual postings to the materials inventory file would be eliminated.

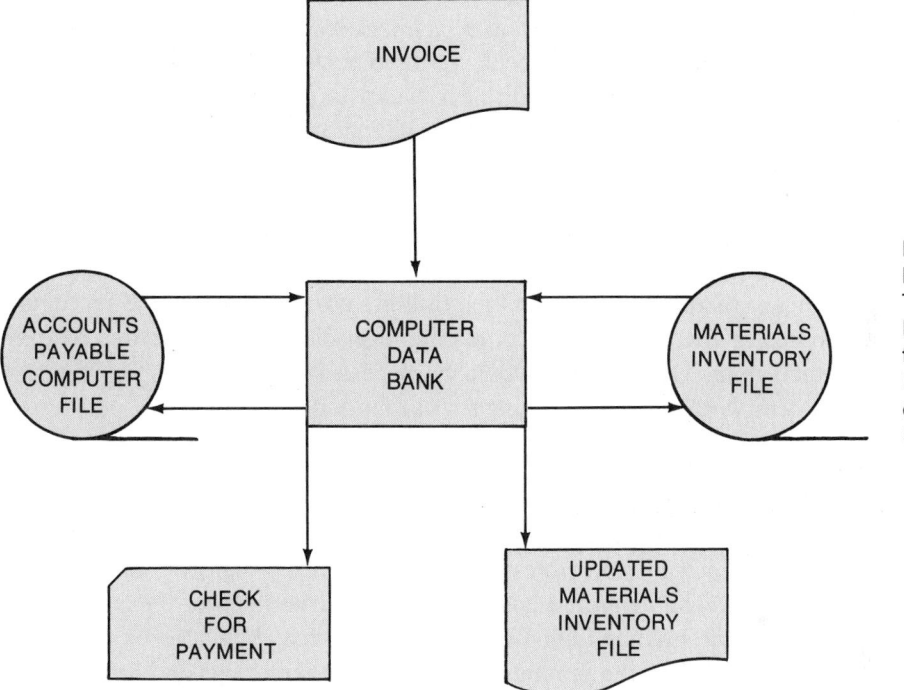

Integration of a Purchase Transaction for Materials into the Accounts Payable Phase of an EDP System

A guiding principle in accounting for the cost of materials is that all costs incurred in entering a unit of materials into factory production should be included. Acquisition costs, such as the vendor's invoice price and transportation charges, are visible costs of the purchased goods. Less obvious costs of materials entering factory operations are costs of purchasing, receiving, unpacking, inspecting, insuring, storing, and general and cost accounting.

Cost of Acquiring Materials

Controversial concepts and certain practical limitations result in variations in implementing the principles of costing materials even with respect to easily identified acquisition costs. Calculating a number of cost additions and adjustments to each invoice involves clerical expenses which may be greater than benefits derived from the increased accuracy. Therefore, materials are commonly carried at the invoice price paid the vendor, although all acquisition costs and price adjustments affect the materials cost. As a result, acquisition costs are generally charged to factory overhead when it is not practical to follow a more accurate costing procedure.

Purchases Discount. The handling of discounts on purchases is one major problem in accounting for materials costs. Trade discounts and quantity discounts normally are not on the accounting records but are treated as price reductions. Cash discounts should be handled as price adjustments but often are accounted for as other income, although income is not produced by buying. A lower purchase cost may well widen the margin between sales price and cost, but it takes the sale to produce income. When the vendor quotes terms such as 2/10, n/30 on a $100 invoice, is the sales price $100 or $98? The purchaser has two dates to make payment: on the tenth day, which allows time to receive, unpack, inspect, verify, voucher, and pay for the goods; or twenty days later. For the additional twenty days an additional charge or penalty of 2 percent is assessed. If regarded as interest, the extra charge is 36 percent per year [(360 days ÷ 20 days) × 2%]. On these terms the seller is pricing on essentially a cash basis, and the purchaser has no reasonable choice except to buy on the cash basis.

Although the nature of a purchases discount is readily understood, for practical reasons the gross materials unit cost of the invoice is commonly recorded in the materials account; the cash discount is recorded as a credit account item. Otherwise it would be necessary to compute the discount on each item, with unit costs having four or more decimal places.

Freight In. Freight or other transportation charges on incoming shipments are obviously costs of materials, but differences occur in the allocation of these charges. A vendor's invoice for $600 may show 25 items weighing 1,700 pounds shipped in five crates, with the attached freight bill showing a payment of $48. The delivered cost is $648. But how much of the freight belongs to each of the invoice items, and what unit price should go on the materials ledger card? When the purchased units are not numerous and are large in size and unit cost, computation of actual amounts of freight may be feasible; otherwise, some logical, systematic, and expedient procedure is necessary.

If freight charges are debited to Materials, the total amount should be added proportionately to each materials card affected. This might be done by assuming that each dollar of materials cost carries an equal portion of the freight. For example, freight of $48 on materials costing $600 would add $.08 ($48 ÷ $600) to each dollar on the invoice. The relative weight of each item on the invoice might be determined and used as a basis for calculating the applicable freight. If an invoice item is estimated to weigh 300 pounds, then $8.47 [(300 ÷ 1,700) × $48] would be added for freight. This procedure is also likely to result in unit costs having four or more decimal places on the materials ledger cards. To simplify procedures, all freight costs on incoming materials and supplies may be charged to Freight In. As materials are issued for production, an applied rate for freight in might be added to the unit price on the ledger cards. The same amount is included in the debit to Work in Process or Factory Overhead (Indirect Materials), and Freight In is credited. Any balance in Freight In at the end of a period is closed to Cost of Goods Sold or prorated to Cost of Goods Sold and inventories.

Another often advocated method of accounting for incoming freight costs on materials is to estimate the total for an accounting period and include this amount in computing the factory overhead rate. Freight In would then become one of the accounts controlled by Factory Overhead. For materials or supplies used in marketing and administrative departments, freight, transportation, or delivery costs should be charged to the appropriate nonmanufacturing account.

Applied Acquisition Costs. If it is decided that the materials cost should include incoming freight charges and other acquisition costs, an applied rate might be added to each invoice and to each item instead of charging these costs directly to factory overhead. A single rate for these costs can be used, but a more accurate method is to use separate rates for each class of costs, as shown below:

$$\frac{\text{Estimated purchasing department cost for budget period}}{\text{Estimated number of purchases or estimated amount of purchases}} = \begin{array}{c}\text{Rate per}\\ \text{purchase or}\\ \text{rate per dollar}\\ \text{purchased}\end{array}$$

$$\frac{\text{Estimated receiving department cost for budget period}}{\text{Estimated number of items to be received during period}} = \text{Rate per item}$$

$$\frac{\text{Estimated materials department cost for budget period}}{\text{Estimated number of items, feet of space, dollar value, etc.}} = \begin{array}{c}\text{Rate per item,}\\ \text{cubic foot,}\\ \text{dollar stored,}\\ \text{etc.}\end{array}$$

$$\frac{\text{Estimated applicable accounting department cost for budget period}}{\text{Estimated number of transactions}} = \begin{array}{c}\text{Rate per}\\ \text{transaction}\end{array}$$

This procedure results in the following accounting treatment:

Materials	xxx	
Applied Purchasing Department Expenses		xxx
Applied Receiving Department Expenses		xxx
Applied Materials Department Expenses		xxx
Applied Accounting Department Expenses..............................		xxx

Actual expenses incurred by each of the departments for which applied rates are used will be debited to the applied accounts. Differences between the expenses incurred by the departments during the period and the expenses applied to the materials cost would represent over- or underapplied expenses and would be closed to Cost of Goods Sold or prorated to Cost of Goods Sold and inventories.

Imputed Interest. A company making an inventory purchase with a non-interest-bearing note or a note with an interest rate that varies from prevailing interest rates should classify the effective interest imputed to the note as interest expense, rather than as a cost of the materials. For example, assume that a $100,000, 6-month, non-interest-bearing note is used to purchase materials. If the company can borrow at a short-term credit rate of 8%, the inventory should be costed at $96,154 ($100,000 × .96154, the present value of $1 at 8% for 6 months). The difference of $3,846 should be debited to Interest Expense.[1]

Storage and Use of Materials

Materials, together with a copy of the receiving report, are forwarded to the storeroom from the receiving or inspection department. The storekeeper and assistants are responsible for safeguarding the materials, which means that materials and supplies are placed in proper bins or other storage spaces, that they are kept safely until required in production, and that all materials taken from the storeroom are properly requisitioned. It is good policy to restrict admittance to the storeroom to employees of that department only and to have these employees work behind locked doors, issuing materials through cage windows.

Since the cost of storing and handling materials may be a substantial amount, careful design and arrangement of storerooms can result in significant cost savings. Materials can be stored according to (1) the materials account number; (2) the frequency of use of the item; (3) the factory area where the item is used; or (4) the nature, size, and shape of the item. In practice, no single base is likely to be suitable, but the size and shape of materials usually dictate the basic storeroom arrangement. Variations can then be introduced, such as placing most frequently used items nearest the point of issue and locating materials used primarily in one factory area nearest that area.

Bin cards or *stock cards* are effective ready references that may be attached to storage bins, shelves, racks, or other containers. Bin cards usually show quantities of each type of material received, issued, and on hand. They are not a part of the accounting records as such, but they show the quantities on hand in the storeroom at all times and should agree with the quantities on the materials ledger cards in the accounting department. The design of a bin card is not limited to the size or shape illustrated at the right.

BIN CARD

STORES NO. 565   UNIT _____
LOCATION Bin No.10   MAXIMUM 2,000
    MINIMUM 200
DESCRIPTION 3/4" valves

DATE	QUANTITY RECEIVED	QUANTITY ISSUED	BALANCE	CONDITION OR REMARKS
8-21	500		500	
8-24		200	300	

Issuing and Costing Materials into Production

To control the quantity and cost of materials, supplies, and services requires a systematic and efficient system of purchasing, recording, and storing. Equally necessary is a systematic and efficient procedure for issuing materials and supplies.

[1]For further discussion, see *Opinions of the Accounting Principles Board, No. 21,* "Interest on Receivables and Payables" (New York: American Institute of Certified Public Accountants, 1971).

Materials Requisition. The *materials requisition*, illustrated below, is a written order to the storekeeper to deliver materials or supplies to the place designated or to give the materials to the person presenting a properly executed requisition. It is drawn by someone who has the authority to requisition materials for use in the department. The authorized employee may be a production control clerk, a department head, a supervisor, a group leader, an expediter, or a materials release analyst. In a computerized system, the computer program will often prepare the requisition in the form of a tabulating card.

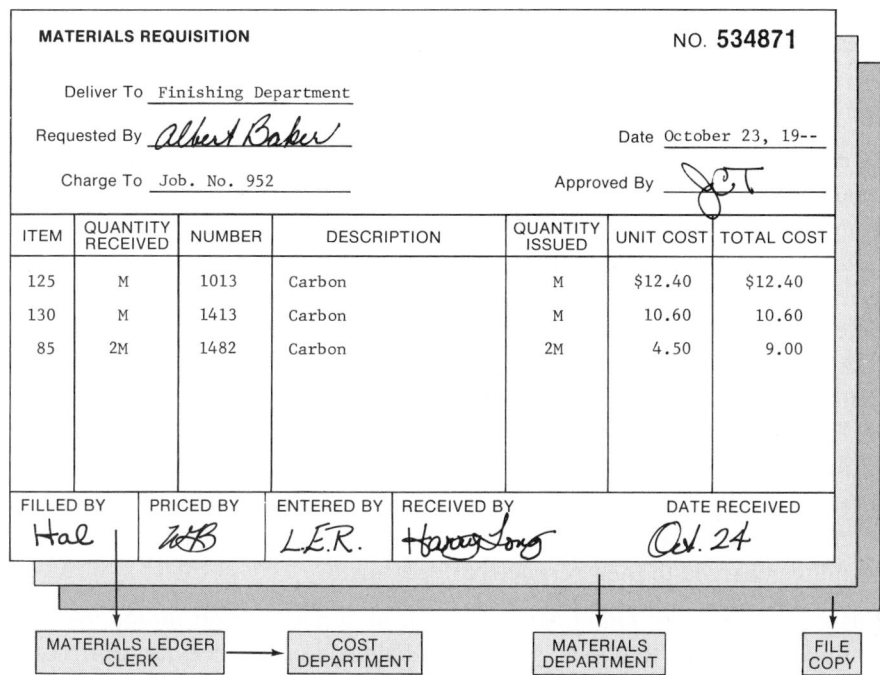

The materials requisition is the basic form used to withdraw materials from the storeroom. Its preparation results in entries in the Issued section of the materials ledger cards and in postings to the job order cost sheets, production reports, or the various expense analysis sheets for individual departments. All withdrawals result in debits to Work in Process or to control accounts for factory overhead, marketing expenses, or administrative expenses, and in credits to Materials.

Materials Requisitioned Journal. With the posting to the materials ledger cards, the job order cost sheets, the production reports, and the expense analysis sheets completed, it is still necessary to post the materials withdrawals to the proper ledger control accounts. This task is greatly facilitated by the use of a *materials requisitioned journal.* This journal is a form of materials summary, an example of which is shown on page 316. At the end of the month, the totals of the various columns are posted directly to the ledger accounts, except for the Sundries column from which items are posted individually.

					Debits						
Date	Credit Materials	Description	Req. No.	Job or Acct. No.	Work in Process	Factory Overhead Control	Marketing Expenses Control	Administrative Expenses Control	Sundries		
									Acct. No.	Post. Ref.	Amount
19-- Oct. 1	600 00	Direct materials	4101	5317	600 00						
1	225 00	Indirect materials	4102	411		225 00					
3	1,800 75	Direct materials	4103	5318	1,800 75						
3	195 50	For installation	4104						135	√	195 50
4	75 00	Supplies	4105	630				75 00			
4	112 80	Supplies	4106	530			112 80				
	41,160 90				36,400 00	2,280 00	1,525 40	760 00			195 50

MATERIALS REQUISITIONED JOURNAL

Tabulating Cards as Materials Requisitions. Tabulating cards are convenient input or output devices for computer operations. To produce the card, the computer is instructed by the console operator to perform certain materials issuance transactions for jobs or products. The card serves as authority for the storekeeper to issue the materials. Internal computer operations will update the materials data bank and eventually produce output reports including totals that will be entered in the general ledger accounts, unless those accounts are also part of the EDP system.

Indirect materials or supplies for factory or office use will also be stored in the inventory data bank of the computer. When such materials are needed, a request will inform the computer as to type, quantity, and requesting department. Supplies requisitioned for marketing and administrative departments would be charged to their respective departments.

Bill of Materials. The *bill of materials*, a kind of master requisition, is a printed or duplicated form that lists all the materials and parts necessary for a typical job or production run. Time is saved and efficiency is promoted through the use of a bill of materials. When a job or production run is started, all the materials listed on the bill of materials are sent to the factory or are issued on a prearranged time schedule. As the bill of materials is a rather cumbersome medium for posting purposes, however, data processing improves the procedure by simultaneously preparing tabulating cards for materials requisitions. While the storekeeper issues the materials as stated on the bill of materials, the tabulating cards can be processed in the materials ledger section and in the cost department at almost the same time as the materials are used in the factory. A computer program will provide the printouts of the bill of materials and process the information internally to update the accounting records.

Materials Ledger Card — Perpetual Inventory

As purchased materials go through the systematic verification of quantities, prices, physical condition, and other checks, the crux of the accounting procedure is to establish a perpetual inventory — maintaining for each type of material a record showing quantities and prices of materials received, issued, and on hand. Materials ledger cards or stock ledger sheets constitute a subsidiary materials ledger controlled by the materials or inventory accounts in the general ledger or in the factory ledger.

Materials ledger cards commonly show the account number, description or type of material, location, unit measurement, and maximum and minimum quantities to carry. These cards are the *materials ledger*, with new cards prepared and old ones discarded as changes occur in the types of materials carried in stock. The ledger card arrangement is basically the familiar debit, credit, and balance columns under the description of Received, Issued, and Balance. A materials ledger card is illustrated below:

MATERIALS LEDGER CARD

Piece or Part No._____   Reorder Point_____

Description_____   Reorder Quantity_____

Maximum Quantity_____

RECEIVED				ISSUED				BALANCE		
Date	Rec. No.	Qty.	Amount	Date	Req. No.	Qty.	Amount	Quantity	Unit Cost	Amount

The approved invoice with supporting documents, such as the purchase order and receiving report, goes to the materials ledger clerk. These documents enable the clerk to make the necessary entries in the Received section of the materials ledger card. Each receipt increases the balance on hand, and the new balance is extended upon entry of the receipt.

Unsatisfactory goods or defective units should be detected by the inspection department before being stored or even paid for. The receiving report should show materials actually accepted, and the ledger entries are made after all adjustments. However, goods accepted in the storeroom may be found unsatisfactory after part of a shipment has been used in the factory, and the balance may then be returned to the vendor. Since these units were entered in the Received and Balance sections of the materials ledger card when they were placed in the storeroom, an adjustment must be made. The recommended procedure is to enter the quantity and the value of the returned shipment in red in the Received section and to reduce the balance accordingly.

When the storekeeper issues materials, a copy of the requisition is sent to the materials ledger clerk, who then makes an entry in the Issued section of the materials ledger card showing the date, requisition number, job, lot, or department number, quantity, and cost of the issued materials. The new balance is computed and entered in the Balance column. As already explained, these manual operations can be performed in an EDP system based on the computer program designed for materials transactions.

MATERIALS COSTING METHODS

The ultimate objective in cost accounting is to produce accurate and meaningful figures. These figures can be used for purposes of control and analysis and eventually matched against revenue produced in order to determine operating income.

After the unit cost and total cost of incoming materials are entered in the Received section of a materials ledger card, the next step is to cost these materials as they move either from storeroom to factory as direct or indirect materials or from storeroom to marketing and administrative expense accounts as supplies. The more common methods of costing materials issued and inventories are:

1. First-in, first-out (fifo).
2. Average cost.
3. Last-in, first-out (lifo).
4. Other methods — such as month-end average cost, last purchase price or market price at date of issue, and standard cost.

These methods relate to assumptions as to flow of costs. The physical flow of units may coincide with the method of cost flow, though such a condition is not a necessary requirement. Although this discussion deals with materials inventory, the same costing methods are also applicable to work in process and finished goods inventories.

The illustrations discussed below assume a perpetual inventory system; i.e., an entry is made each time the inventory is increased or reduced. Such a procedure is a desirable characteristic of most cost accounting systems. The alternative to a perpetual inventory system is the physical inventory system whereby purchases are added to the beginning inventory, the ending (remaining) inventory is counted and costed, and the difference is considered the cost of materials issued. Even with physical inventory costing, a perpetual inventory of units only may be maintained by using bin cards for physical control and other inventory management purposes.

First-In, First-Out (Fifo) Method of Costing

The first-in, first-out (fifo) method of costing is used to introduce the subject of materials costing. This illustration is based on the following transactions:

Feb.   1. Beginning balance: 800 units @ $6 per unit.
         4. Received 200 units @ $7 per unit.
       10. Received 200 units @ $8 per unit.
       11. Issued 800 units.
       12. Received 400 units @ $8 per unit.
       20. Issued 500 units.
       25. Returned 100 excess units from the factory to the storeroom to be recorded at the latest issued price.
       28. Received 600 units @ $9 per unit.

Calculations for the above transactions would be as follows:

FIFO COSTING METHOD ILLUSTRATED

Feb. 1. Beginning balance.........................	800 units @ $6 =	$4,800	
4. Received....................................	200	@ $7 =	1,400	
10. Received....................................	200	@ $8 =	1,600	$7,800
11. Issued	800	@ $6 =		4,800
Balance	⎰200	@ $7 =	1,400	
	⎱200	@ $8 =	1,600	3,000
12. Received....................................	400	@ $8 =	3,200	6,200
20. Issued	⎰200	@ $7 =	1,400	
	⎱300	@ $8 =	2,400	3,800
Balance	300	@ $8 =	2,400	
25. Returned to storeroom...................	100	@ $8 =	800	
28. Received....................................	600	@ $9 =	5,400	8,600
Balance	⎰400	@ $8 =	3,200	
	⎱600	@ $9 =	5,400	$8,600

The fifo method of costing issued materials follows the principle that materials used should carry the actual experienced cost of the specific units used. The method assumes that materials are issued from the oldest supply in stock and that the cost of those units when placed in stock is the cost of those same units when issued. However, fifo costing may be used even though physical withdrawal is in a different order. Advantages claimed for the fifo costing method are:

1. Materials used are drawn from the cost records in a logical and systematic manner.
2. Movement of materials in a continuous, orderly, single-file manner represents a condition necessary to and consistent with efficient materials control, particularly for materials subject to deterioration, decay, and quality or style changes.

The fifo method is recommended whenever (1) the size and cost of materials units are large, (2) materials are easily identified as belonging to a particular purchased lot, and (3) not more than two or three different receipts of the materials are on a materials card at one time. Fifo costing is definitely awkward if frequent purchases are made at different prices and if units from several purchases are on hand at the same time. Added costing difficulties arise when returns to vendors or to the storeroom occur.

Average Costing Method

Issuing materials at an average cost assumes that each batch taken from the storeroom is composed of uniform quantities from each shipment in stock at the date of issue. Often it is not feasible to mark or label each materials item with an invoice price in order to identify the used unit with its acquisition cost. It may be reasoned that units are issued more or less at random as far as the specific units and the specific costs are concerned and that an average cost of all units in stock at the time of issue is a satisfactory measure of materials cost. However, average costing may be used even though the physical withdrawal is in an identifiable order. If materials tend to be made up of numerous small items low in unit cost and especially if prices are subject to frequent change, average costing is advantageous because:

1. It is a realistic costing method useful to management in analyzing operating results and appraising future production.
2. It minimizes the effect of unusually high or low materials prices, thereby making possible more stable cost estimates for future work.
3. It is a practical and less expensive perpetual inventory system.

The average costing method divides the total cost of all materials of a particular class by the number of units on hand to find the average price. The cost of new invoices is added to the total in the Balance column; the units are added to the existing quantity; and the new total cost is divided by the new quantity to arrive at the new average cost. Materials are issued at the established average cost until a new purchase is recorded. Although a new average cost may be computed when materials are returned to vendors and when excess issues are returned to the storeroom, for practical purposes it seems sufficient to reduce or increase the total quantity and cost, allowing the unit price to remain unchanged. When a new purchase is made and a new average is computed, the discrepancy created by the returns will be absorbed.

Using the data of the fifo illustration (page 318), the transactions can be summarized in this manner:

AVERAGE COSTING METHOD ILLUSTRATED

				Average Cost
Feb. 1. Beginning balance	800 units @ $6	= $4,800		
4. Received	200	@ $7	= 1,400	
Balance	1,000		6,200	$6.20
10. Received	200	@ $8	= 1,600	
Balance	1,200		7,800	6.50
11. Issued	800	@ $6.50 =	5,200	
Balance	400		2,600	6.50
12. Received	400	@ $8	= 3,200	
Balance	800		5,800	7.25
20. Issued	500	@ $7.25 =	3,625	
Balance	300		2,175	7.25
25. Returned to storeroom	100		725	
Balance	400		2,900	7.25
28. Received	600	@ $9	= 5,400	
Balance	1,000		$8,300	8.30

Last-In, First-Out (Lifo) Method of Costing

The last-in, first-out (lifo) method of costing materials issued is based on the premise that materials units issued should carry the cost of the most recent purchase, although the physical flow may actually be different. The method assumes that the most recent cost (the approximate cost to replace the consumed units) is most significant in matching cost with revenue in the income determination procedure.

Under lifo procedures, the objective is to charge the cost of current purchases to work in process or other operating expenses and to leave the oldest costs in the inventory. Several alternatives can be used to apply the lifo method. Each procedure results in different costs for materials issued and the ending inventory, and consequently in a different profit. It is mandatory, therefore, to follow the chosen procedure consistently.

To illustrate lifo costing, the transactions for the fifo illustration on page 318 are used here:

LIFO COSTING METHOD ILLUSTRATED

Feb. 1. Beginning balance........................... 800 units @ $6 = $4,800
       4. Received..................................... 200   @ $7 = 1,400
      10. Received..................................... 200   @ $8 = 1,600 $7,800
      11. Issued .... { 200   @ $8 = 1,600
                                                          { 200   @ $7 = 1,400
                                                          { 400   @ $6 = 2,400   5,400
          Balance 400   @ $6 = 2,400
      12. Received..................................... 400   @ $8 = 3,200   5,600
      20. Issued .... { 400   @ $8 = 3,200
                                                          { 100   @ $6 =   600   3,800
          Balance 300   @ $6 = 1,800
      25. Returned to storeroom.................... 100   @ $6 =   600
      28. Received..................................... 600   @ $9 = 5,400   7,800
          Balance .... { 400   @ $6 = 2,400
                                                       { 600   @ $9 = 5,400 $7,800

The basic difference between the various applications of the lifo method is the time interval between inventory computations. In the preceding illustration of lifo costing, a new inventory balance is computed after each receipt and each issue of materials, with the ending inventory consisting of 1,000 units valued at $7,800. If, however, a physical rather than a perpetual costing procedure is used, whereby the issues are determined at the end of the period by ignoring day-to-day issues and by subtracting total ending inventory from the total of the opening balance plus the receipts, the ending inventory would consist of:

      800 units @ $6, on hand in the beginning inventory......... $4,800
      200 units @ $7, from the oldest purchase, Feb. 4............ 1,400
    1,000 units, lifo inventory at the end of February.............. $6,200

Both procedures are appropriate applications of the lifo method, even though the cost of materials used and the ending inventory figures differ. Such a difference does not occur in fifo costing.

Regardless of the cost flow assumption, this latter procedure is particularly appropriate in process costing where individual materials requisitions are seldom used and the materials move into process in bulk lots, as in flour mills, spinning mills, oil refineries, and sugar refineries. The procedure also functions smoothly for a company that charges materials to work in process from month-end consumption sheets which provide the cost department with quantities used.

The advantages of the lifo costing method are:

1. Materials consumed are priced in a systematic and realistic manner. It is argued that current acquisition costs are incurred for the purpose of meeting current production and sales requirements; therefore, the most recent costs should be charged against current production and sales.
2. Unrealized inventory gains and losses are minimized, and reported operating profits are stabilized in industries subject to sharp materials price fluctuations.
3. Inflationary prices of recent purchases are charged to operations in periods of rising prices, thus reducing profits, resulting in a tax saving, and therewith providing a cash advantage through deferral of income tax payments. The tax deferral creates additional working capital as long as the economy continues to experience an annual inflation rate increase.

The disadvantages of the lifo costing method are:

1. The election of lifo for income tax purposes is binding for all subsequent years unless a change is authorized or required by the Internal Revenue Service (IRS).
2. Lifo is a "cost only" method with no write-down to the lower of cost or market allowed for income tax purposes. Furthermore, the IRS requires that when lifo is adopted, an adjustment must be made to restore any previous write-downs from actual cost. Should the market decline below lifo cost in subsequent years, the business would be at a tax disadvantage. When prices drop, the only option may be to charge off the older (higher) costs by liquidating the inventory. However, liquidation for income tax purposes must take place at the end of the year. According to IRS regulations, liquidation during the fiscal year is not acceptable if the inventory returns to its original level at the end of the year. Interim external financial reporting principles impose a similar requirement when inventory is expected to be replaced by the end of the annual period.
3. Lifo must be used in financial statements if it is elected for income tax purposes. However, for financial reporting purposes, the lower of lifo cost or market can be used without violating IRS lifo conformity rules.
4. Record keeping requirements under lifo, as well as fifo, are substantially greater than those under alternative costing and pricing methods.
5. Inventories may be depleted due to unavailability of materials to the point of consuming inventories costed at older or perhaps the oldest prices. This situation will create a mismatching of current revenue and cost. Sometimes companies using lifo counteract this problem by establishing an allowance for replacement of the lifo inventory account. Cost of Goods Sold is charged with current cost. The allowance account is credited for the excess of the current replacement cost over the lifo carrying cost for the inventory temporarily liquidated. When this inventory is replenished, the temporary allowance (credit) is removed and the goods acquired are placed in inventory at their old lifo cost.

6. In Standard No. 411, "Accounting for Acquisition Costs of Materials," the Cost Accounting Standards Board (CASB) precludes the use of lifo except when applied currently on a specific identification basis. As a result, the use of the lifo method, when an annual lifo adjustment is made, is ruled out for government contracts to which CASB regulations apply.[2]

The decision to adopt the lifo method has had increased appeal in the last few years, due to an accelerated rate of inflation; however, its adoption should not be automatic. Long-range effects as well as short-term benefits must be considered.

Although fifo, average cost, and lifo are commonly used methods of costing materials units into work in process, various other methods exist.

Other Materials Costing Methods

Month-End Average Cost. To insure quick costing and early reporting of completed jobs or products, some companies at the close of each month establish an average cost for each kind of material on hand and use this cost for all issues during the following month. When perpetual inventory costing procedures are not used, a variation of this method is to wait until the end of a costing period to compute the cost of materials consumed. The cost used is obtained by adding both quantities and dollars of purchases to beginning inventory figures, thus deriving an average cost.

Market Price at Date of Issue. Materials precisely standardized and traded on commodity exchanges, such as cotton, wheat, copper, or crude oil, are sometimes costed into production at the quoted price at date of issue. In effect, this procedure substitutes replacement cost for experienced or consumed cost and has the virtue of charging materials into production at a current and significant price. This method of materials costing and that of using the last purchase price are often used for small, low-priced items.

Standard Cost. This method charges issued materials at a predetermined or estimated price reflecting a normal or an expected future price. Receipts and issues of materials are recorded in quantities only on the materials ledger cards or in the computer data bank, thereby simplifying the record keeping and reducing clerical or data processing costs.

In recording materials purchases, the difference between actual and standard cost is recorded in a purchase price variance account. The variance account enables management to observe the extent to which actual materials costs differ from planned objectives or predetermined estimates. Materials are charged into production at the standard price, thereby eliminating the erratic costing inherent in the actual cost methods. Standard quantities for normal production runs at standard prices enable management to detect trouble areas and take corrective action immediately. Materials pricing under standard costs is discussed in Chapters 19 and 20.

[2]*Standards, Rules and Regulations, Part 411*, "Accounting for Acquisition Costs of Materials" (Washington, D.C.: Cost Accounting Standards Board, 1975), p. 229.

Analysis and Comparison of Costing Methods

The several methods of costing materials represent industry's intense effort to measure costs. Undoubtedly, there is no one best method applicable to all situations. Methods may vary even within the same company, and the same method need not be used for the entire inventory of a business. Whichever method of costing is chosen, it should be followed consistently from period to period.

The various costing methods represent different views of the cost concept. The best method to use is the one that most clearly reflects periodic income when consumed cost is subtracted from current revenue. Perhaps no costing method will reflect consumed materials cost with complete accuracy at all times in all situations. The most appropriate method will, as nearly as possible, (1) relate current cost to current sales; (2) reflect the procurement, manufacturing, and sales policies of a particular company; and (3) carry forward to the new fiscal period a previously incurred residual cost which will be consumed in subsequent periods.

Adequate comparison of the various methods of costing is difficult and involved. The ending inventory figures of the previous illustrations indicate:

Fifo costing $8,600
Average costing...................... 8,300
Lifo costing........................... 7,800 (or $6,200, depending upon the timing of the costing procedure)

Certain generalizations can be made relative to the use of fifo, average cost, and lifo. In periods of rising prices, fifo costing will result in materials being charged out at lowest costs; lifo will result in materials being charged out at highest costs; and average costing will result in a figure between the two. In a period of falling prices, the reverse situation will develop — with fifo showing the highest cost of materials consumed, lifo showing the lowest cost of materials used, and average cost showing a result between the other two methods.

CASB Costing of Materials

In accounting for government contracts to which CASB regulations apply, materials may be charged directly to a contract if the contract is specifically identified at the time of purchase or manufacture. Materials drawn from company-owned inventory can be priced using fifo, lifo, average, or the standard costing method. However, the method(s) selected must be used consistently for similar categories of materials. Furthermore, the contractor must prepare in writing the procedure for accumulating and allocating the cost of materials.[3]

COST OF MATERIALS IN INVENTORY AT THE END OF A PERIOD

When the cost basis is used in costing inventories for financial statements and income tax returns, the sum total of the materials ledger cards must agree

[3]Ibid., p. 226

with the general ledger materials control account which, in turn, is the materials inventory figure on the balance sheet. Unless a shift from the cost basis is made in valuing the year-end inventory, the method used for costing materials issued is the method used for assigning dollars to inventory.

American accounting tradition follows the practice of pricing year-end inventories at *cost or market, whichever is lower*. This departure from any experienced cost basis is generally defended on the grounds of conservatism. A more logical justification for cost or market inventory valuation is that a full stock is necessary to expedite production and sales. If physical deterioration, obsolescence, and price declines occur, or if stock when finally utilized cannot be expected to realize its stated cost plus a normal profit margin, the reduction in inventory value is an additional cost of the goods produced and sold during the period when the decline in value occurred.

Inventory Valuation at Cost or Market, Whichever Is Lower

The American Institute of Certified Public Accountants (AICPA) moved away from the traditional *cost or market, whichever is lower* principle of valuing inventories. After defining inventory and reiterating that the major objective of accounting for inventories is the proper determination of income through the process of matching appropriate costs against revenue, the AICPA states:

AICPA Cost or Market Rules

> The primary basis of accounting for inventories is cost, which has been defined generally as the price paid or consideration given to acquire an asset. As applied to inventories, cost means in principle the sum of the applicable expenditures and charges directly or indirectly incurred in bringing an article to its existing condition and location.[4]

The AICPA takes the position that cost may properly be determined by any of the common methods of costing already discussed in this chapter. The position of the AICPA is clearly stated in the following sentence: "In keeping with the principle that accounting is primarily based on cost, there is a presumption that inventories should be stated at cost." Having advocated the basic cost principle, the AICPA then reverts at least part way to the traditional cost or market rule.

The AICPA in effect says it is mandatory that cost be abandoned in valuing inventory when the usefulness of goods is no longer as great as its cost. This, then, becomes a principle of *cost or residual useful cost, whichever is lower*, as described below:

> A departure from the cost basis of pricing the inventory is required when the utility of the goods is no longer as great as its cost. Where there is evidence that the utility of goods, in their disposal in the ordinary course of

---

[4]*Accounting Research and Terminology Bulletins — Final Edition* (New York: American Institute of Certified Public Accountants, 1961), p. 28.

business, will be less than cost, whether due to physical deterioration, obso-lescence, changes in price levels, or other causes, the difference should be recognized as a loss of the current period. This is generally accomplished by stating such goods at a lower level commonly designated as *market*.[5]

The last sentence returns to the traditional meaning of cost or market, whichever is lower by saying that the residual useful cost is "market," which in turn is defined as "replacement cost." In the AICPA's cost or market ap-proach to inventory valuation, it is clear that the Institute does not hold that a replacement cost should be used for inventory value merely because it is lower than the acquisition cost figure. The real test is the usefulness of the inventory (whether it will sell at its cost). The AICPA is more precise in stating which figure should be used in case the inventory cost cannot be re-covered:

> As used in the phrase *lower of cost or market*, the term *market* means current replacement cost (by purchase or by reproduction, as the case may be) except that:
>
> 1. Market should not exceed the net realizable value (i.e., estimated sell-ing price in the ordinary course of business less reasonably predict-able costs of completion and disposal); and
> 2. Market should not be less than net realizable value reduced by an allowance for an approximately normal profit margin.[6]

The position of the AICPA in regard to inventory valuation may be inter-preted as follows:

1. In principle, inventories are to be priced at cost.
2. Where cost cannot be recovered upon sale in the ordinary course of business, a lower figure is to be used.
3. This lower figure is normally market replacement cost, except that the amount should not exceed the expected sales price less a deduction for costs yet to be incurred in making the sale. On the other hand, this lower market figure should not be less than the expected amount to be realized in the sale of the goods, reduced by a normal profit margin.

To illustrate the preceding narrative, assume that a certain commodity sells for $1; the marketing expense is 20 cents; the normal profit is 25 cents. The lower of cost or market as limited by the foregoing concepts is developed in each case as illustrated at the top of the following page.[7]

The lower of cost or market procedure may be applied to each inventory item, to major inventory groupings, or to the inventory as a whole. Applica-tion of this procedure to the individual inventory items will result in the lowest inventory value. However, application to inventory groups or to the inventory as a whole may provide a sufficiently conservative valuation with less effort. The application method selected by a company must be followed

[5]*Ibid.*, p. 30.
[6]*Ibid.*, p. 31.
[7]Adapted from Harry Simons, Jay M. Smith, Jr., and K. Fred Skousen, *Intermediate Accounting*, 6th ed. (Cincinnati: South-Western Publishing Co., 1977), pp. 215–216.

			MARKET			
CASE	COST	REPLACE-MENT COST	FLOOR (ESTIMATED SALES PRICE LESS COSTS OF COMPLETION AND DISPOSAL AND NORMAL PROFIT)	CEILING (ESTIMATED SALES PRICE LESS COSTS OF COMPLETION AND DISPOSAL)	MARKET (LIMITED BY FLOOR AND CEILING VALUES)	LOWER OF COST OR MARKET
A	$.65	$ .70	$.55	$.80	$.70	$.65
B	.65	.60	.55	.80	.60	.60
C	.65	.50	.55	.80	.55	.55
D	.50	.45	.55	.80	.55	.50
E	.75	.85	.55	.80	.80	.75
F	.90	1.00	.55	.80	.80	.80

A: Market is not limited by floor or ceiling; cost is less than market.
B: Market is not limited by floor or ceiling; market is less than cost.
C: Market is limited to floor; market is less than cost.
D: Market is limited to floor; cost is less than market.
E: Market is limited to ceiling; cost is less than market.
F: Market is limited to ceiling; market is less than cost.

consistently from year to year. Work in process and finished goods inventories are also subject to the lower of cost or market principle.

Adjustments for Departures from the Costing Method Used

The problem of year-end inventory valuation is primarily a question of the materials cost consumed in products manufactured and sold to customers and the cost assignable to goods in inventory ready to move into production and available for sales the next fiscal period. This question is important, because the materials ledger cards would have to be adjusted for any change in unit prices if there is a departure from the commonly used costing method. Since the new unit price could not be made available to the materials ledger clerk for some time after the year-end inventory was taken and priced, the detailed task of changing hundreds and even thousands of cards would be cumbersome and time consuming. Therefore, instead of adjusting the ledger cards, companies may create an inventory valuation account, as illustrated by the following journal entry:

	SUBSIDIARY RECORD	DR.	CR.
Cost of Goods Sold (or Factory Overhead Control)..		5,000	
Inventory Adjustment — Lower of Cost or Market.........................	5,000		
Materials — Allowance for Inventory Decline to Market...............................			5,000

In the subsequent fiscal period, Materials — Allowance for Inventory Decline to Market is closed out to Cost of Goods Sold to the extent necessary to bring the materials consumed that are still carried at a higher cost to the desirable lower cost level.

Use of the valuation account retains the cost of the inventory and at the same time reduces the materials inventory for statement purposes to the desired cost or market, whichever is lower valuation without disturbing the materials ledger cards. The preceding entry should result in the following balance sheet presentation:

Materials, at cost	$100,000	
Less allowance for inventory decline to market......................	5,000	
Materials, at cost or market, whichever is lower......................		$95,000

The net charge to Cost of Goods Sold may be shown in the cost of goods sold statement or deducted from the ending inventory at cost, thus increasing the cost of materials used.

Whenever the lower of cost or market procedure is applied to each inventory item and the adjustment of materials ledger cards to a lower market figure is not burdensome and the data are available early in the next year, the adjustment should be accomplished by dating the entry with the last day of the fiscal period just ended and entering in the Balance section the units on hand at the unit price determined for inventory purposes. In such a case, the credit portion of the adjusting entry would be to the materials account.

Inventory Pricing and Interim Financial Reporting

Companies should generally use the same inventory pricing methods and make provisions for write-downs to market at interim dates on the same basis as used at annual dates when preparing published financial statements. However, the following exceptions are appropriate at interim reporting dates:

1. Some companies use estimated gross profit rates to determine the cost of goods sold during interim periods or use other methods different from those used at annual inventory dates. These companies should disclose the method used at the interim date and any significant adjustments that result from reconciliations with the annual physical inventory.
2. Companies that use the lifo method may encounter a liquidation of base period inventories at an interim date that is expected to be replaced by the end of the annual period. In such cases the inventory at the interim reporting date should not give effect to the lifo liquidation, and cost of sales for the interim reporting period should include the expected cost of replacement of the liquidated lifo base.[8]

Thus, if the liquidation of base period inventories is considered temporary and is expected to be replaced prior to year-end, the company should charge Cost of Goods Sold at current prices. The difference between the carrying value of the inventory and its current replacement cost is a current liability for replace-

---

[8]*Opinions of the Accounting Principles Board, No. 28*, "Interim Financial Reporting" (New York: American Institute of Certified Public Accountants, 1973), par. 14.

ment of temporarily depleted lifo base inventory. When the liquidated inventory is replaced, inventory is debited for the original lifo value, and the liability is removed from the books.

> 3. Inventory losses from market declines should not be deferred beyond the interim period in which the decline occurs. Recoveries of such losses on the same inventory in later interim periods of the same fiscal year through market price recoveries should be recognized as gains in the later interim period. Such gains should not exceed previously recognized losses. Some market declines at interim dates, however, can reasonably be expected to be restored in the fiscal year. Such *temporary* market declines need not be recognized at the interim date since no loss is expected to be incurred in the fiscal year.[9]

Transfer of Materials Cost to Finished Production

The ultimate, intended destination of direct materials is finished products delivered to customers. The cost of materials used on each job or in each department is transferred from the materials requisition to the job order cost sheet or to the cost of production report. When the job or process is completed, the effect of materials used, as well as labor distributed and factory overhead applied, is expressed in this entry:

Finished Goods... xxxx
   Work in Process xxxx

In production devoted to filling specific orders, cost sheets should provide sufficient information relative to the cost of goods sold. If a considerable portion of production is to be used for stock, a finished goods ledger is advantageous in maintaining adequate and proper control over the inventory. The finished goods ledger, controlled by the finished goods account in the general ledger, is similar in form and use to materials ledger cards.

Some production may consist of components manufactured for use in subsequent manufacturing operations. If the units move directly into these operations, the transfer is simply from one departmental work in process account to the next. However, if the components must be held in inventory, their cost should be debited to Materials and credited to Work in Process.

Physical Inventory

Even with a perpetual inventory system, periodic physical counts are necessary to discover and eliminate discrepancies between the actual count and the balances on materials ledger cards. These discrepancies may be due to: errors in transferring invoice data to the cards; mistakes in costing requisitions; unrecorded invoices or requisitions; or spoilage, breakage, and theft. In some enterprises, plant operations are suspended periodically during a seasonal low period or near the end of the fiscal year while a physical inventory is taken. In others, an inventory crew or members of the internal audit department make a count of one or more stock classes every day throughout the year, presumably on a well-planned schedule, so that every materials item will be inventoried at least once during the year.

---

[9]*Ibid.*

Adjusting Materials Ledger Cards and Accounts to Conform to Inventory Count

When the inventory count differs from the balance on the materials ledger card, the ledger card is adjusted to conform to the actual count. If the ledger card balance shows more materials units than the inventory card, an entry is made in the Issued section; and the Balance section is reduced to equal the verified count. In case the materials ledger card balance is less than the physical count, the quantity difference may be entered in the Received section or may be entered in red in the Issued section with the Balance section being increased to agree with the actual count.

In addition to the corrections on the materials ledger cards, the materials account must be adjusted for the increase or decrease. If the inventory count is less than that shown on the materials ledger card, the following entry should be recorded:

	SUBSIDIARY RECORD	DR.	CR.
Factory Overhead Control		xxxx	
Inventory Adjustment to Physical Count...	xxxx		
Materials			xxxx

COSTING PROCEDURES FOR SCRAP, SPOILED GOODS, AND DEFECTIVE WORK

Generally, manufacturing operations cannot escape the occurrence of certain losses or output reduction due to scrap, spoilage, or defective work. Management and the entire personnel of an organization should cooperate to reduce such losses to a minimum. As long as they occur, however, they must be reported and controlled.

Scrap and Waste

In many manufacturing processes, waste and scrap result from (1) the processing of materials, (2) defective and broken parts, (3) obsolete stock, (4) revisions or abandonment of experimental projects, and (5) worn out or obsolete machinery. This scrap should be collected and placed in storage for sale to scrap dealers. At the time of sale, the following entry may be made:

Cash (or Accounts Receivable)	xxxx	
Scrap Sales (or Factory Overhead Control)		xxxx

The amount realized from the sale of scrap and waste can be treated in two ways with respect to the income statement:

1. The amount accumulated in Scrap Sales may be closed directly to Income Summary and shown on the income statement under Other Income.
2. The amount may be credited to Factory Overhead Control, thus reducing the total factory overhead expense and thereby the cost of goods manufactured.

When scrap is collected from a job or department, the amount realized from the sale of scrap is often treated as a reduction in the materials cost charged to the individual job or product. In this case, the entry to record the sale would be:

Cash (or Accounts Receivable) xxxx
   Work in Process xxxx

When the quantity and value of scrap material is relatively high, it should be stored in a designated place under the supervision of a storekeeper. A scrap report (as shown below) is generally prepared in duplicate to authorize

---

DEPARTMENT __Fabricating__

WEEKLY SCRAP REPORT

FOR WEEK ENDING __November 10, 19--__

PART NO.	DESCRIPTION	UNITS USED	SCRAPPED	% SCRAP	COST	REASON
115b	Braces	7,200	108	1.50	$ 7.00	
115e	Fins	9,400	305	3.23	30.50	
115s	Guides	15,600	520	3.33	41.40	Defective
115k	Supports	8,500	42	.50	25.30	parts

TOTAL FOR WEEK .... $ 104.20

SCRAP COST—YEAR TO DATE .... $ 4,533.75

PREDETERMINED SCRAP ALLOWANCE FOR THE YEAR ...... $ 5,000.00

---

transfer and receipt of the scrap. The original is forwarded to the materials ledger clerk, and a copy remains on file in the department in which the scrap originated. The materials ledger clerk can follow two procedures:

1. *Open a materials ledger card, filling in the quantity only.* The dollar value would not be needed. When the scrap is sold, the entries and treatment of the income item might be handled as discussed previously.

2. *Record not only the quantity but also the dollar value of the scrap delivered to the storekeeper.* The value would be based on scrap prices quoted on the market at the time of entry. The entry would be:

Scrap Materials xxxx
   Scrap Sales (or Work in Process or Factory Overhead
     Control) xxxx

When the scrap is sold, the entry would be:

Cash (or Accounts Receivable) xxxx
   Scrap Materials xxxx

Any difference between the price at the time the inventory is recorded and the price realized at the time of sale would be a plus or minus adjustment in the scrap sales account, the work in process account, or the factory overhead control account, consistent with the account credited in the first entry.

To reduce accounting for scrap to a minimum, often no entry is made until the scrap is actually sold. At that time, Cash or Accounts Receivable is debited while Scrap Sales is credited. This method is expedient and is justified when a more accurate accounting becomes expensive and burdensome, the scrap value is relatively small, or the price is uncertain.

Proceeds from the sale of scrap are in reality a reduction in production cost. As long as the amounts are relatively small, the accounting treatment is not a major consideration. What is important is an effective scrap control system based on periodic reporting to responsible supervisory personnel. Timely scrap reports for each producing department call attention to unexpected items and unusual amounts and should induce prompt corrective action.

Spoiled Goods

Cost accounting should provide product costs and cost control information. In the case of spoilage, the first requirement is to know the nature and cause of the spoiled units. The second requirement, the accounting problem, is to record the cost of spoiled units and to accumulate spoilage costs and report them to responsible personnel for corrective action.

Attaining the degree of materials and machine precision and the perfection of labor performance necessary to eliminate spoiled units entirely would involve costs far in excess of a normal or tolerable level of spoilage. If spoilage is normal and happens at any time and at any stage of the productive process, its cost should be treated as factory overhead, included in the predetermined factory overhead rate, and prorated over all production of a period. If, on the other hand, normal spoilage is caused by exacting specifications, difficult processing, or other unusual and unexpected factors, the spoilage cost should be charged to that order. In either case, the cost of abnormal spoilage should be charged to factory overhead.

Spoiled Materials Charged to Total Production. The Nevada Products Company has a monthly capacity to manufacture 125,000 three-inch coil springs for use in mechanical brakes. Production is scheduled in response to orders received. Spoilage is caused by a variety of unpredictable factors and averages $.05 per spring. During November, 100,000 springs were produced with a materials cost of $.40 per unit, a labor cost of $.50 per unit, and factory overhead charged to production at a rate of 150% of the direct labor cost. This rate is based on an estimate that includes $.05 per spring for spoilage. The entry to record work put into production during the month is:

Work in Process — Materials.....................................	40,000	
Work in Process — Labor	50,000	
Work in Process — Factory Overhead............................	75,000	
Materials		40,000
Payroll		50,000
Applied Factory Overhead		75,000

On the last working day of the month, the entire day's production of 4,000 units is spoiled due to improper heat treatment; however, these units can be sold for $.50 each in the secondhand market. To record this normal loss on spoiled goods and the possible resale value, the entry that charges all production during the period with a proportionate share of the spoilage is:

	SUBSIDIARY RECORD	DR.	CR.
Spoiled Goods		2,000	
Factory Overhead Control		4,600	
Loss on Spoiled Goods	4,600		
Work in Process — Materials...............			1,600
Work in Process — Labor			2,000
Work in Process — Factory Overhead.....			3,000

The materials, labor, and factory overhead in the spoiled units reduced by the recovery or sales value of these units ($1,600 materials + $2,000 labor + $3,000 factory overhead − $2,000 cost recovery = $4,600 spoilage loss) is relocated or transferred from Work in Process to Factory Overhead Control. Each of the 96,000 good units produced during the month has a charged-in cost of $.05 for spoilage (96,000 × $.05 = $4,800); the actual spoilage during the period is $4,600.

The good units produced during the week or on the order where spoilage did occur carry a cost of $.40 for materials, $.50 for labor, and $.75 for overhead because spoilage is charged to all production — not to the lot or order which happens to be in process at the time of spoilage. In other words, the $165,000 monthly production cost less the $6,600 credit resulting from spoiled units leaves $158,400 to be divided by the 96,000 good units manufactured during the month at a cost of $1.65 per good unit. The entry transferring the good units to Finished Goods is:

Finished Goods...	158,400	
Work in Process — Materials......................................		38,400
Work in Process — Labor		48,000
Work in Process — Factory Overhead...........................		72,000

During the month, the amounts charged to Factory Overhead Control represent the depreciation, insurance, taxes, indirect materials, and indirect labor actually experienced, along with the $4,600 spoilage cost. All production during the month is charged with overhead of $.75 per unit. Overhead analysis reveals a $200 favorable variance ($4,600 actual minus $4,800 applied) attributable to the spoilage units. Any difference between the price when the inventory was recorded and the price realized at the time of sale would be a plus or minus adjustment to Factory Overhead Control (Loss on Spoiled Goods).

For effective cost control, normal spoilage rates and amounts should be established for each department and for each type or class of materials. Weekly or monthly spoilage reports similar to the scrap report illustrated on page 331 should be reviewed by an individual who has the responsibility and authority to initiate corrective action where needed.

Spoiled Materials Charged to a Particular Job. The Nevada Products Company has a contract to manufacture 10,000 heavy-duty coil springs for the Tri-State Supply Company. This order requires a steel wire that is harder and slightly heavier than stock normally used, but the production process, as well as labor time and overhead factors, is identical with the standard product. Materials cost for each of these springs is $.60. This special order requires exacting specifications, and normal spoilage is to be charged to the order. The $.05 per unit spoilage factor is now eliminated from the overhead rate, and 140% of direct labor cost, or $.70 per unit, is the rate used on this job. The order is put into production the first day of December, and sampling during the first hour of production indicates that eleven units of production are required to secure ten good springs. Entries to record costs placed into production for 11,000 units are:

Work in Process — Materials..	6,600	
Work in Process — Labor	5,500	
Work in Process — Factory Overhead................................	7,700	
Materials		6,600
Payroll		5,500
Applied Factory Overhead		7,700

One thousand units did not meet specifications and are spoiled but can be sold as seconds for $.45 per unit. The entry to record the spoilage is:

Spoiled Goods..	450	
Work in Process — Materials..		150
Work in Process — Labor		125
Work in Process — Factory Overhead.............................		175

$$\frac{\$ \ 450 \ \text{Sales recovery}}{\$1,800 \ \text{Cost of 1,000 units}} = 25\%$$

$$25\% \times \begin{cases} \$600 \ \text{Materials} & = \$150 \\ \$500 \ \text{Labor} & = \$125 \\ \$700 \ \text{Factory overhead} & = \$175 \end{cases}$$

OR

$$\frac{\$ \ 6,600 \ \text{Materials}}{\$19,800 \ \text{Total job cost}} \times \$450 \ \text{sales recovery} = \$150$$

$$\frac{\$ \ 5,500 \ \text{Labor}}{\$19,800 \ \text{Total job cost}} \times \$450 \ \text{sales recovery} = \$125$$

$$\frac{\$\ 7,700\ \text{Factory overhead}}{\$19,800\ \text{Total job cost}} \times \$450\ \text{sales recovery} = \$175$$

The entry transferring the completed order to Finished Goods would be:

Finished Goods...	19,350	
Work in Process — Materials.......................................		6,450
Work in Process — Labor		5,375
Work in Process — Factory Overhead............................		7,525

The net result of this treatment is to charge the spoilage loss of $1,350 ($1,800 − $450 cost recovery) to the 10,000 good units that are delivered at the original contract price. The unit cost of completed springs is $1.935 ($19,350 ÷ 10,000 units).

Any difference between the price when the inventory was recorded and the price realized at the time of sale should be an adjustment to Work in Process, Finished Goods, or Cost of Goods Sold, depending on the completion status of the particular job order. As an expedient, the difference might be closed to Factory Overhead Control.

In the manufacturing process, imperfections may arise because of faults in materials, labor, or machines. If the unit can be reprocessed in one or more stages and made into a standard salable product, it is often profitable to rework the defective unit. Although spoiled work cannot usually be made into a first-class finished unit without uneconomical expenditures, defective work can be corrected to meet specified standards by adding materials, labor, and factory overhead.

Defective Work

Two methods of accounting for the added cost to upgrade defective work are appropriate, depending upon circumstances:

1. If defective work is experienced in regular manufacturing, the additional cost to correct defective units (based on previous experience) is included in the predetermined factory overhead and in the resulting factory overhead rate. Actual rework cost is charged to Factory Overhead Control.

    To illustrate, assume that a company has an order for 500 units of a product that has direct production costs of $5 for materials and $3 for labor, with factory overhead charged to production at 200% of labor cost. Fifty units are found to be defective and are to be reworked at a total cost of $30 for materials, $60 for labor, and overhead at 200% of direct labor cost. The entries are:

Work in Process — Materials.................................	2,500	
Work in Process — Labor	1,500	
Work in Process — Factory Overhead.....................	3,000	
Materials		2,500
Payroll		1,500
Applied Factory Overhead		3,000

	Subsidiary Record	Dr.	Cr.
Factory Overhead Control		210	
Defective Work	210		
Materials			30
Payroll			60
Applied Factory Overhead			120
Finished Goods.............................		7,000	
Work in Process — Materials........			2,500
Work in Process — Labor			1,500
Work in Process — Factory Over-head			3,000

The unit cost of the completed units is $14 ($7,000 ÷ 500 units).

2. Suppose, however, that the same company received a special order for 500 units with the agreement stating that any defective work is chargeable to the contract. During production, 50 units are improperly assembled. The total cost to correct these defective units is $30 for materials, $60 for labor, and 200% of the direct labor cost for factory overhead. The entries in this case are:

Work in Process — Materials....................................	2,500	
Work in Process — Labor	1,500	
Work in Process — Factory Overhead........................	3,000	
Materials		2,500
Payroll		1,500
Applied Factory Overhead		3,000
Work in Process — Materials....................................	30	
Work in Process — Labor	60	
Work in Process — Factory Overhead........................	120	
Materials		30
Payroll		60
Applied Factory Overhead		120
Finished Goods..	7,210	
Work in Process — Materials.............................		2,530
Work in Process — Labor		1,560
Work in Process — Factory Overhead.....................		3,120

The unit cost in this case is $14.42 instead of $14.

Whenever the defective work cost is charged directly to the job, a slight overcharge of factory overhead results because of the inclusion of rework cost in the factory overhead rate. One remedy to correct this discrepancy would be either to create a new independent overhead rate or to separate costs for the special job.

SUMMARY OF MATERIALS MANAGEMENT

Materials managers are constantly confronted with these problems and requirements:

1. Inventories account for a large portion of the working capital requirements of most businesses. This fact makes materials and/or inventory

management a major problem requiring constant attention by all three management levels.
2. At present, the problem of materials management has become even more acute due to market conditions and inflation.
3. Effective materials management and materials control is found in an organization in which individuals have been vested with responsibility for, and authority over, the various details of procuring, maintaining, and disposing of inventory. Such a person or persons must have the ability to obtain, coordinate, and evaluate the necessary facts and to take action when and where needed.

DISCUSSION QUESTIONS

1. List the forms more frequently used in the procurement and use of materials.

2. Should formal purchase requisitions and purchase orders be prepared for the purchase of incidental supplies, services, and repairs? Explain.

3. How is an invoice approved for payment?

4. In a electronic data processing system, the computer replaces the accounting clerk to a great extent. Explain.

5. An invoice for materials shows a total of $5,400; terms: 3/10, n/30. If the purchaser elects to pay the invoice at the end of 30 days, what is the effective interest cost resulting from failure to take the discount?

6. A client who wishes to include as a part of the cost of materials all of the cost of acquiring and handling incoming materials wants to know:
   (a) The principal items that may enter into the cost of materials acquisition and handling.
   (b) The arguments favoring the inclusion of these items as a part of materials in storage.
   (c) The arguments against inclusion of these items as a part of the cost of materials in storage.

   (AICPA adapted)

7. During periods of rapid increase in materials prices, which costing method might result in a more desirable figure for cost of goods manufactured and sold?

8. To effect an approximate matching of current cost with related sales revenue, the last-in, first-out (lifo) method of pricing inventories has been developed.
   (a) Describe the establishment of lifo and the subsequent pricing procedures when lifo is applied to units of product with a periodic inventory system in use.
   (b) Discuss the general advantages and disadvantages claimed for the lifo method.

   (AICPA adapted)

9. The lifo vs fifo controversy has spanned a number of decades. Proponents of each of the inventory procedures ascribe certain merits to each. Identify the inventory procedure, lifo or fifo, to which the following features are attributed:
(a) Matches actual physical flow of goods.
(b) Matches old costs with new prices.
(c) Costs inventory at approximate replacement cost.
(d) Matches new costs with new prices.
(e) Emphasizes the balance sheet.
(f) Emphasizes the income statement.
(g) Opens door for profit manipulation.
(h) Understates the current ratio in a period of inflation.
(i) Overstates inventory turnover in a period of inflation.
(j) Gives higher profits in a period of inflation.
(k) Matches current cost with current revenue.
(l) Reflects more accurately the profit available to owners.
(m) Gives lower profits in a period of deflation.
(n) Results in a procession of costs in the same order as incurred.
(CGAA adapted)

10. Does the method of inventory costing have its principal effect on the balance sheet or on the income statement?

11. A company's own power plant uses coal as the principal fuel. Coal is delivered by rail and stored in an open field close to the powerhouse from which it is fed into furnaces by conveyor belts. What method should be used to determine coal consumption during a time period and the coal on hand at the end of the period?

12. At times physical quantities of materials as determined by actual count and inspection do not agree with the figures in materials ledger cards. What may cause such discrepancies? What accounting steps are taken to adjust the differences?

13. In charging out materials, how should the cost of waste, such as scraps in suit and dress factories, be accounted for?

14. Several methods of accounting for scrap materials are discussed in this chapter. Which method could be regarded as most accurate?

15. In the control of materials cost, why is the knowledge that there is excessive waste likely to be of greater value than the income derived from the sale of scrap?

16. What procedures should be adopted in order to deal with the following items listed in the materials ledger cards?
(a) Scrap delivered to the storeroom.
(b) Return of materials to storage in excess of production requirements.
(c) Gain or loss in weight through climatic conditions while in storage.
(d) Short lengths of cut material become waste during the productive operations.
(e) Breakage in the storeroom.

17. In some situations, labor and materials costs incurred on spoiled or defective work are treated as factory overhead. In other cases the cost of perfecting defective work is charged directly to the job. Explain the appropriate use of each accounting treatment.

18. Select the answer which best completes the statement:
   (a) An item of inventory purchased this period for $15 has been written down to its current replacement cost of $10. It sells for $30 with a disposal cost of $3 and a normal profit of $12. Which of the following statements is not true? (1) The cost of goods sold of the following year will be understated. (2) The current year's income is understated. (3) The ending inventory of the current year is understated. (4) Income of the following year will be understated.
   (b) Which of the following statements is true in applying the lower-of-cost-or-market rule to work in process inventory? (1) This category is an exception, and the rule does not apply. (2) The cost of completing the inventory is added to the cost of disposal, and both are deducted from the estimated sales price when computing realizable value. (3) Market value cannot ordinarily be determined. (4) Equivalent production is multiplied by the sales price.
   (c) The method of inventory costing which most nearly approximates the actual flow of costs and units in most manufacturing situations is: (1) average; (2) first-in, first-out; (3) last-in, first-out; (4) standard.
   (d) If a unit of inventory has declined in value below original cost but the market value exceeds net realizable value, the amount to be used for purposes of inventory valuation is: (1) net realizable value; (2) original cost; (3) market value; (4) net realizable value less normal profit margin.
   (e) When evaluating materials inventory at cost or market, whichever is lower, the term "market" means: (1) net realizable value; (2) net realizable value less a normal profit margin; (3) replacement cost; (4) discounted present value.
   (f) Which statement is not valid as it applies to inventory costing methods? (1) If inventory quantities are to be maintained, part of the earnings must be invested (plowed back) in inventories when fifo is used during a period of rising prices. (2) Lifo tends to smooth out the income pattern, since it matches the current cost of goods sold with current revenue, and inventories remain at constant quantities. (3) When a firm using the lifo method fails to maintain its usual inventory position (reduces stock on hand below customary levels), there may be a matching of old costs with current revenue. (4) Unlike lifo, the use of fifo permits some control by management over the amount of income for a period through controlled purchases.
   (g) If inventory levels are stable or increasing, an argument which is not in favor of the lifo method as compared to fifo is: (1) income tax tends to be reduced in periods of rising prices; (2) cost of goods sold tends to be stated at approximately current cost in the income statement; (3) cost assignments typically parallel the physical flow of goods; (4) income tends to be smoothed as prices change over a period of time.
   (h) An inventory costing procedure in which the oldest costs incurred rarely have an effect on the ending inventory is: (1) fifo; (2) lifo; (3) conventional retail; (4) average.
   (i) A company's inventory cost on its balance sheet was lower using fifo than lifo. Assuming no beginning inventory, the direction of movement of the cost of purchases during the period was: (1) up; (2) down; (3) steady; (4) undeterminable.

                                                                  (AICPA adapted)

EXERCISES

1. Materials costing methods. The Meltzer Company made the following materials purchases and issues during January:

Inventory:	January 1.	500 units @ $1.20	
Receipts:	January 6.	200	@ 1.25
	10.	400	@ 1.30
	25.	500	@ 1.40
Issues:	January 15.	560	
	27.	500	

Required: The cost of materials consumed and the cost assigned to the inventory at the end of the month, using a perpetual inventory system and:
  (1) Average costing, rounding unit costs to the nearest cent.
  (2) Fifo costing.
  (3) Lifo costing.

2. Materials costing methods. The following information is to be used in costing inventory on October 31:

October 1. Beginning balance: 800 units @ $6
       5. Purchased 200 units @ $7
       9. Purchased 200 units @ $8
    16. Issued 400 units
    24. Purchased 300 units @ $9
    27. Issued 500 units

Required: The cost of materials used and the cost assigned to the October 31 inventory by each of these perpetual inventory costing methods:
  (1) First-in, first-out.
  (2) Last-in, first-out.
  (3) Average, using a materials ledger card and rounding unit costs to the nearest cent.
  (4) Most recent purchase price.

3. Materials costing methods. The Kentucky Respiratory Clinic makes the following purchases and issues of replaceable tubes for portable respirator machines:

Inventory:	January 1.	400 units @ $1.40	
Receipts:	January 6.	500	@ 1.31
	10.	200	@ 1.24
	25.	700	@ 1.23
Issues:	January 15.	600	
	27.	500	

Required: The cost of tubes issued and the cost assigned to the January 31 inventory by each of these perpetual inventory costing methods:
  (1) Fifo.
  (2) Lifo.
  (3) Average, rounding unit costs to five decimal places.

4. Allocation of freight. An invoice for materials A, B, and C is received from the Lawson Company. The invoice totals are: A, $15,000; B, $8,000; and C, $22,000. The freight charge on this shipment weighing 9 000 kilograms is $990. Shipping weights for the respective materials are 2 900, 2 400, and 3 700 kilograms.

Required:
  (1) The cost per kilogram to be entered on the materials ledger cards for A, B, and C if each dollar of invoice cost is assigned an equal portion of the freight charge. (Round off unit costs to three decimal places.)
  (2) The cost per kilogram to be entered on the materials ledger cards for each material if the freight cost is assigned on a basis of shipping weight for each material.

5. Ledger accounts for materials cost flow. During one week of operations, a materials ledger card reflected the following transactions:

1st day	Beginning balance: 1,400 pounds @ $4.60 per lb.
2d	Received 1,000 pounds @ $4.80 per lb.
3d	Issued 800 pounds.
4th	Issued 800 pounds.
5th	Received 1,200 pounds @ $5.00 per lb.
6th	Issued 800 pounds.

Other costs for the week were direct labor, $4,800, and factory overhead, $4,360; 1,700 units of product were completed, and 1,500 were sold. There was no beginning inventory of finished goods, and no work was in process over the weekend.

Required:
(1) Ledger accounts for Materials, Work in Process, Finished Goods, and Cost of Goods Sold, using (a) fifo costing and (b) lifo costing. A perpetual inventory system is used. (Round off unit costs to three decimal places.)
(2) The final inventory by the lifo costing method if inventory is taken at the end of the week and day-to-day issues are ignored.

6. Correcting perpetual inventory cards. The following differences were reported in reconciling the physical inventories of materials with the materials ledger cards. The physical inventory has been verified and is correct in each case.

MATERIAL	PHYSICAL INVENTORY	MATERIALS LEDGER BALANCE	DIFFERENCE REPORTED
1	2,000 units	2,100 units	The accountant neglected to record an issue of direct materials to production. Average cost per unit, $2.
2	500 units	400 units	An invoice and receiving report for 100 units purchased at $3 per unit has not been recorded.
3	1,000 gals.	1,030 gals.	The shrinkage is a normal condition of storage and issue of this material. Average cost per gallon, $.30.
4	900 lbs.	930 lbs.	Shortage due to negligence. Average cost per pound, $10.

Required:
(1) A separate correcting entry in general journal form for each transaction.
(2) The procedure necessary to correct or adjust the materials ledger card for each difference.

7. Lower of cost or market inventory valuation. Moore Corporation has two products in its ending inventory, each accounted for at the lower of cost or market. A profit margin of 30% on the sales price is considered normal for each product. Specific data with respect to each product are:

	PRODUCT 1	PRODUCT 2
Historical cost..	$17.00	$ 45.00
Replacement cost...	15.00	46.00
Estimated cost to dispose	5.00	26.00
Estimated sales price......................................	30.00	100.00

Required: The unit values to be assigned in costing the ending inventory of each product, using the lower of cost or market.

(AICPA adapted)

8. Inventory valuation — AICPA rule. The AICPA's position regarding inventory valuation was under discussion in an accounting seminar. The members were asked to decide on the proper valuation for the following situations with these pertinent factors and simplified figures:

	SITUATION				
	1	2	3	4	5
Cost	$100	$100	$100	$40	$100
Net realizable value*	80	80	80	80	80
Net realizable value less normal profit**	50	50	50	50	50
Market (replacement cost)	60	90	40	30	110

*Market is not to exceed this amount (upper limit of market).
**Market is not to be less than this amount (lower limit of market).

Required: The inventory value for each situation, based on the AICPA rule.

9. Inventory valuation at cost or market, whichever is lower. The following information has been gathered for four inventory items:

ITEM	ORIGINAL COST	REPLACEMENT COST	SALES PRICE	ESTIMATED COST TO COMPLETE AND SELL	NORMAL PROFIT MARGIN
Delta	$ .67	$ .62	$ .72	$ .04	$ .08
Sigma	2.20	2.12	2.22	.12	.08
Beta	.19	.20	.24	.03	.01
Nu	.93	.87	.97	.05	.04

Required: The unit value that would be assigned to each item for inventory valuation purposes, using the lower of cost or market as defined by the AICPA.

10. Journal entries to correct materials accounts. The following transactions were completed by the Patterson Company:
  (a) The inventory of materials on the average costing basis was $4,200 and represented a book quantity of 8,000 units. An actual count showed 7,780 units.
  (b) Materials of $150 issued to Job 182 should have been charged to the Repair Department.
  (c) Excess materials returned from the factory amounted to $382 for Job 257.
  (d) Materials returned to vendor amounted to $165. Freight out on this shipment, to be borne by the Patterson Company, was $14, paid in cash.
  (e) Finished goods returned by customers: cost, $1,500; sales price, $2,100.
  (f) Materials requisitions totaled $4,814.50, of which $214.50 represented supplies used.
  (g) Materials purchased and placed in stockroom, $6,150, of which $500 represented supplies. Freight in paid, applicable to direct materials, was $70.
  (h) Supplies returned to the storeroom, $150.
  (i) Scrap materials sent to the storeroom valued at sales price (debit Scrap Materials):

        From direct materials.................. $190
        From supplies.............................   10

  (j) Spoiled work received in storeroom: original cost, $60; sales value, $20. Loss is charged to total production.
  (k) Scrap was sold for $250 cash; the book value of the scrap was $200 [see transaction (i)].

Required: The general ledger entries or adjustments, if any, that should be made for each of the above transactions. (Carry all computations to three decimal places.)

11. Fifo, lifo, and cash flow. Due to rising prices for materials, the problem of using the most appropriate inventory costing method has become acute. With the wide variety of methods available to account for inventories, it is important to select one that will be the most beneficial for a company. To illustrate, assume that two companies are almost identical except that one uses fifo and the other lifo costing. Both companies have a beginning inventory of 200 units @ $2 per unit. The ending inventory is 240 units. The price paid for all purchases during the fiscal period was $2.40, and sales totaled 180 items at a sales price of $3.60. The income tax rate is 50% for both companies.

Required:
  (1) The amount of total materials available for sale.
  (2) Income statements showing after-tax earnings for both companies.
  (3) Cost assigned to the ending inventory based on the fifo and lifo costing methods.
  (4) The cash position at the end of the fiscal year, assuming that all transactions, materials purchases, sales, and income tax were paid in cash.
  (5) A brief evaluation of the results.

12. Accounting for spoiled work. Lot 201 called for the making of 3,500 suits with these unit costs:

Direct materials	$19.60
Direct labor	17.20
Factory overhead (includes a $1 allowance for spoiled work)	14.80
	$51.60

When the lot was completed, 175 rejected units, a normal number, were sold for $15.60 each. A separate work in process account is used for each cost element.

Required:
  (1) Entries if the loss is charged to all production.
  (2) Entries if the loss is charged to Lot 201. (Round off all amounts to the nearest dollar.)

13. Defective and spoiled production. Mixwell, Inc., received an order for 25 automatic mixing machines. Because of the order's exacting specifications, it is anticipated that defective and spoiled work will exceed the normal rate. The materials cost per unit is $80; labor cost, $194; and factory overhead for this order is to be applied at 100% of the labor cost. During production, 5 units were found to be defective and required the following total additional costs: materials, $97, labor, $125, and factory overhead at the 100% rate. On final inspection, 2 units were classified as seconds and sold for $400 each, the proceeds being credited to the order. The purchaser has agreed to accept the 23 machines, although the acceptable units are fewer than the number ordered.

Required: Unit cost of the completed units.

14. Error corrections; entries for scrap, spoiled and defective units. The following data relate to transactions not yet recorded for the current accounting period:
  (a) Materials costing $600 and used in production were erroneously charged to factory supplies.
  (b) Scrap materials sent to the storeroom and valued at estimated sales price: from job orders, $250; from factory supplies and indirect materials, $50.
  (c) In the final processing, 100 units of an order, a normal number, were spoiled; their estimated sales value is $4 per unit. These units had been charged with $500 of materials, $300 of labor, and $200 of factory overhead, which included a $20 allowance for spoiled units. The following alternative assumptions may be made:
     Assumption 1: Spoilage cost is charged to the specific job.
     Assumption 2: Spoilage cost is spread over all production.
  (d) While producing 1,000 units of a job order, 30 units were incorrectly assembled. The cost to rework the 30 units was $150 for materials, $110 for labor, and $125 for factory overhead, which includes a $5 allowance for rework of defective units. The following alternative assumptions may be made:
     Assumption 1: Rework cost is charged to the specific job.
     Assumption 2: Rework cost is spread over all production.
  (e) Goods costing $1,200 were returned by a customer and were debited to Materials and credited to Accounts Receivable at the cost figure. The sales price of the returned merchandise was $1,800.

Required: All necessary general journal entries, including those related to alternative assumptions. No subsidiary ledger accounts are needed. A single work in process account is used and perpetual inventory accounts are maintained.

PROBLEMS

12-1. Applied acquisition costs. Zang Industries, Inc., records incoming materials at invoice price less cash discounts plus applied receiving and handling cost. For product Zingo, the following data are available:

	BUDGETED FOR THE MONTH	ACTUAL COST FOR THE MONTH
Freight in and cartage in	$ 1,500	$ 1,580
Purchasing Department cost..................................	4,800	4,500
Receiving Department cost	3,900	4,200
Storage and handling	4,200	3,800
Testing, spoilage, and rejects	2,600	3,120
Total	$17,000	$17,200

The purchasing budget shows estimated net purchases of $136,000 for the month; actual invoices net of discounts total $141,500 for the month.

Required:
(1) The applied acquisition costing rate for the month.
(2) The amount of applied cost added to materials purchased during the month.
(3) The possible disposition to be made of the variance.

12-2. Ledger cards for materials. Records of the Summit Company show the following purchases and issues of materials during October:

October 1. Beginning balance: 2,800 units @ $12.00 per unit.
      4. Issued 1,200 units.
      6. Received 1,000 units @ $13.30 per unit.
      8. Issued 1,000 units.
     14. Received 400 units @ $14.00 per unit.
     17. Issued 800 units.
     20. Received 500 units @ $14.16 per unit.
     25. Issued 900 units.
     27. Received 1,200 units @ $13.00 per unit.

Required:
(1) Materials ledger cards using: (a) fifo costing; (b) lifo costing; (c) average costing.
(2) Cost of materials issued during October for the three methods.
(3) The October 31 inventory if the market price of the materials on that date is $11 per unit.

12-3. Analyzing a company's future plant expansion based on its costing methods. The board of directors of the Williams Corporation is considering the possibility of a plant expansion. After some research and a review of the company's materials costing methods, the president presents the controller with the proposition of using the lifo method instead of the present fifo method because of its apparent tax advantages. A reduction of the company's income tax liability might provide additional capital for the planned expansion. The president requests the controller to study the proposal further. The controller's analysis regarding the inventory is based on these transactions for June:

June 1. Beginning balance: 200 units @ $3.00 per unit.
     2. Purchased 500 units @ $3.20 per unit.
     7. Issued 400 units.
    11. Purchased 300 units @ $3.30 per unit.
    14. Issued 400 units.
    17. Purchased 400 units @ $3.20 per unit.
    21. Issued 200 units.
    24. Purchased 300 units @ $3.40 per unit.
    26. Purchased 400 units @ $3.50 per unit.
    29. Issued 600 units.

Perpetual inventory costing is used.

Sales were 1,600 units @ $7 per unit; marketing and administrative expenses totaled $2,100.

Required:
(1) Comparative income statements based on the transactions for June, using the lifo and fifo methods and a 50% income tax rate.
(2) The cash position of the Williams Corporation at the end of June, assuming that all transactions, purchases, sales, and nonmanufacturing expenses were paid in cash.

12-4. Inventory costing and valuation. Alberta, Ltd., uses perpetual inventory costing for inventory item 407, which it purchases for resale. The company began its operations on January 1, and is in the process of preparing its first financial statements.

Upon examining the inventory ledger and other accounting records, the following information was gathered pertaining to the first four months of operations:

PURCHASES			SALES	
	Units	Cost per Unit		Units
January 2..............	2,000	$5	January 15	500
February 2.............	1,200	6	January 31	700
March 2	1,500	8	February 15..............................	600
April 2....................	1,900	7	February 28..............................	900
			March 15..................................	600
			March 31..................................	800
			April 15....................................	700
			April 30....................................	700

On April 30, the following additional information was obtained:

(a) Current replacement cost, $6.50 per unit.
(b) Net realizable value, $8 per unit.
(c) Net realizable value reduced by a normal profit margin, $5 per unit.

Management has not decided which of the following three inventory costing methods should be selected to evaluate the cost of goods sold:

(a) Average method.
(b) First-in, first-out method.
(c) Last-in, first-out method.

Required:
(1) The perpetual inventory ledger for item 407 using each of the above methods. (Carry all computations to three decimal places.)
(2) A comparative statement showing the effect of each method on gross profit; the sales price is $10 per unit.
(3) The necessary adjusting journal entry under each of the three inventory costing methods, assuming that the company decides to show its April 30 inventory at the lower of cost or market.

(CGAA adapted)

12-5. Inventory valuation. The Hildebrand Company uses one metal casting of a certain kind and weight in processing a "Benn." In January the materials ledger card for these metal castings showed the following data:

RECEIVED			ISSUED		
	Units	Cost per Unit		Requisition Number	Units
Jan. 1. Balance	100	$1.00	Jan. 4.	107	80
10. Purchase	100	.95	11.	216	70
20. Purchase	200	.90	23.	461	60
28. Purchase	100	.88	29.	515	120

Required:
(1) The ending inventory cost, assuming that:
    (a) A perpetual inventory system is used with the lifo costing method.
    (b) A periodic inventory system is used and that the physical inventory is priced by the lifo costing method.
(2) The value to be used in the balance sheet if the lower of cost or market is to be used, the estimated sales price of completed Benns is $1.25 per unit, the estimated cost of completion and disposal is $.25 per unit, the normal profit is $.05 per unit, the assumed fifo cost for this ending inventory is $165, and its replacement cost is $160.
(3) The journal entry necessary to reflect the decline in inventory value computed in (2) if this cost is considered a normal cost of the manufacturing operation.

12-6. Inventory valuation at cost or market, whichever is lower — applied to groups. Weinhaller, Inc., has divided its products into two basic groups with two grades within each group. The lower of cost or market rule has always been applied to the ending inventory of each group of products. The following schedule presents the relevant inventory data as of December 31:

	GROUP A		GROUP B	
	Grade 1	Grade 2	Grade 3	Grade 4
Number of units on hand	50	100	100	200
Sales price per unit	$30	$40	$35	$20
Sales price less cost of completion and disposal per unit	24	36	30	16
Sales price less cost of completion and disposal and normal profit per unit	18	28	23	12
Replacement cost per unit at December 31	20	25	26	17
Cost per unit	19	29	27	15

Required: The value of inventory as of December 31 by applying the lower of cost or market rule to each group of products.

(CMA adapted)

12-7. Inventory valuation at other than cost. In some instances accounting principles require a departure from valuing inventory exclusively at cost.

Required:
(1) The proper inventory price per unit for these cases:

	CASE				
	1	2	3	4	5
Cost	$2.00	$2.00	$2.00	$2.00	$2.00
Net realizable value*	1.30	2.05	1.80	2.40	1.90
Net realizable value less normal profit**	1.10	1.85	1.60	2.20	1.70
Market (replacement cost)	1.20	2.10	1.85	2.15	1.60

*Market is not to exceed this amount (upper limit of market).
**Market is not to be less than this amount (lower limit of market).

(2) The proper inventory price per unit in Case 5, assuming that the item is also in stock at the end of the next fiscal period and that the four values are $2.00, $1.90, $1.70, and $2.05, respectively.
(3) The circumstances under which freight in might be excluded from the determination of inventory cost, with comments on the propriety of the exclusions.
(4) A list of other materials-related costs that might similarly be excluded from inventory cost.

12-8. Spoiled and defective work on government contract; revision of invoice. Stancyk, Inc., produces small motors on special orders. In February a U.S. Air Force contract for the production of 120 motors at cost plus a fixed fee of $2,290 was completed. This invoice was mailed to the contracting officer of the Air Force:

```
                              INVOICE
Direct materials...............................................  $11,814.70
Direct labor...................................................   15,660.22
Factory overhead ..............................................    5,220.08
   Total manufacturing cost ..................................  $32,695.00
Fixed fee......................................................    2,290.00
   Total (for 120 motors) ....................................  $34,985.00
```

The Air Force cost inspector objected to this billing, stating that the spoilage of 5 motors and additional costs for 1 defective motor had been charged directly to the Air Force job, whereas the procedure previously had been to spread such costs over all the jobs. The inspector cited CASB Standard No. 402, "Consistency in Allocating Costs Incurred for the Same Purpose," as applicable to this situation.

The spoiled motors had been sold as scrap for $50 each, and the original scrap value was assigned to them. The defective motor required $30 of additional materials and 5 labor hours to correct its defects. Workers on the contract were paid $6 per hour and had worked a total of 7,200 hours, of which 2,630 hours had been spent on the Air Force contract. The company uses a predetermined factory overhead rate of $2 per labor hour. Each motor requires $95 of direct materials. Spoiled and defective work is discovered during final inspection after all normal labor cost has been incurred.

Required: Assuming that the company's work in process account has not been credited for any work completed during February:
(1) All journal entries that the company has made in connection with this contract.
(2) The journal entries the company should have made for the spoiled and defective work.
(3) The journal entries to correct the books and complete the contract.
(4) A revised invoice for the U.S. Air Force.

12-9. Journal entries for spoiled units. The Gamble Company manufactures Product C at a cost per unit of $6 that consists of $1 for materials, $2 for labor, and $3 for factory overhead. During May, 1,000 units were spoiled that can be sold for $.60 each. The accountant said that the entry for these 1,000 spoiled units could be one of these four:

```
1  Spoiled Goods ...............................................  600
     Work in Process — Materials...............................       100
     Work in Process — Labor...................................       200
     Work in Process — Factory Overhead .......................       300

2  Spoiled Goods ...............................................  600
   Factory Overhead Control....................................  5,400
     Work in Process — Materials...............................     1,000
     Work in Process — Labor...................................     2,000
     Work in Process — Factory Overhead .......................     3,000

3  Spoiled Goods ...............................................  600
   Loss on Spoiled Goods.......................................  5,400
     Work in Process — Materials...............................     1,000
     Work in Process — Labor...................................     2,000
     Work in Process — Factory Overhead .......................     3,000

4  Spoiled Goods ...............................................  600
   Accounts Receivable.........................................  5,400
     Work in Process — Materials...............................     1,000
     Work in Process — Labor...................................     2,000
     Work in Process — Factory Overhead .......................     3,000
```

Required: The circumstances under which each of the above entries would be appropriate.

(AICPA adapted)

CASES

A. Organizing for materials acquisition and distribution. A regional governmental agency serves a nine-county area with small offices located in each county. Each office is responsible for the acquisition and storage of operating supplies used in the respective county. Therefore, each office has leased warehouse space and has one employee in charge of purchasing, warehousing, and record keeping for operating supplies.

The services provided by the governmental unit have increased substantially over the past ten years. Consequently, the use of supplies has increased greatly. The total acquisition cost of supplies reached $5.2 million during the fiscal year. Because the activity relating to operating supplies has become so great, the agency management is considering the establishment of a central purchasing and warehousing function for the nine-county area.

Currently the total inventories for all nine county warehouses average $600,000 during a month. The offices pay from $2.10 to $3.25 per square foot for warehouse space. The total expenditure for warehouse facilities for the fiscal year was $275,000. Utilization of warehouse space averaged 60% of leased space for all offices and ranged from 45% to 70% in the individual cases.

The office in the extreme southwest portion of the region appears to be the most likely choice for the location of the central warehouse and purchasing function at this time. The greatest volume of operating supplies of all offices is used in this county. Warehouse space which should be adequate for the entire region is available because the present facility for this county, only partially leased at the present time, can be leased in its entirety. In addition, the rental fee would drop from $2.85 to $2.40 per square foot.

Required:
  (1) Identification and justification of data to be used in deciding whether to continue with the present system or centralize the purchasing and warehousing function.
  (2) Qualitative factors to be considered by the governmental unit before the decision is made.

(CMA adapted)

B. Materials purchasing function; analysis of systems and control problems. The flowchart on page 349 portrays the materials purchasing function of a medium-sized manufacturing company, from the preparation of initial documents through the vouchering of invoices for payment in accounts payable.

Required: Identification and explanation of the systems and control problems evident from the flowchart, including any internal control weaknesses resulting from activities performed or not performed. All documents are prenumbered.

(AICPA adapted)

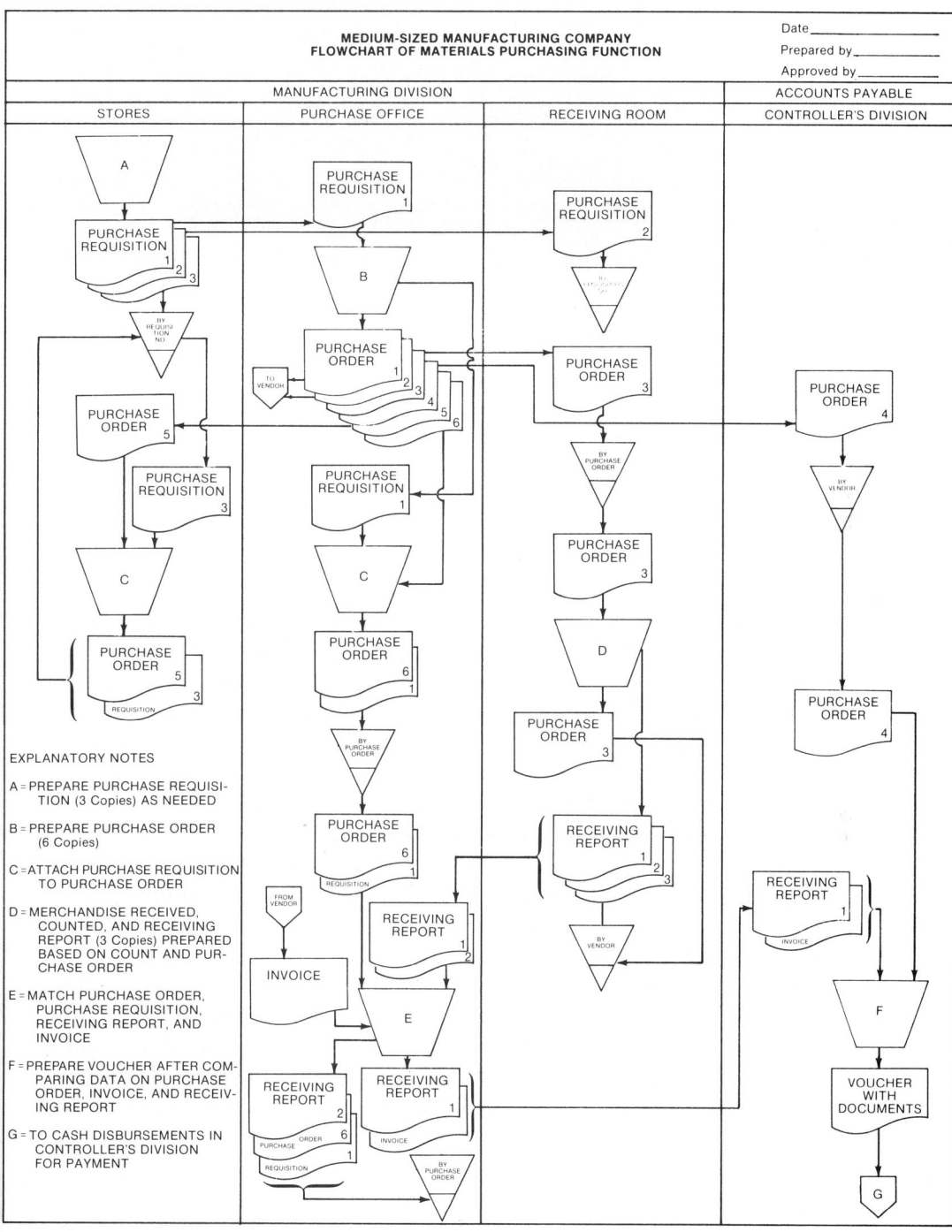

MEDIUM-SIZED MANUFACTURING COMPANY
FLOWCHART OF MATERIALS PURCHASING FUNCTION

Date _____
Prepared by _____
Approved by _____

MANUFACTURING DIVISION — STORES | PURCHASE OFFICE | RECEIVING ROOM

ACCOUNTS PAYABLE — CONTROLLER'S DIVISION

EXPLANATORY NOTES

A = PREPARE PURCHASE REQUISI-
    TION (3 Copies) AS NEEDED

B = PREPARE PURCHASE ORDER
    (6 Copies)

C = ATTACH PURCHASE REQUISITION
    TO PURCHASE ORDER

D = MERCHANDISE RECEIVED,
    COUNTED, AND RECEIVING
    REPORT (3 Copies) PREPARED
    BASED ON COUNT AND PUR-
    CHASE ORDER

E = MATCH PURCHASE ORDER,
    PURCHASE REQUISITION,
    RECEIVING REPORT, AND
    INVOICE

F = PREPARE VOUCHER AFTER COM-
    PARING DATA ON PURCHASE
    ORDER, INVOICE, AND RECEIV-
    ING REPORT

G = TO CASH DISBURSEMENTS IN
    CONTROLLER'S DIVISION
    FOR PAYMENT

13 Quantitative Models for Materials Planning and Control

The planning and control of inventory from product design to final delivery are of considerable strategic significance to management. Inventories serve as a cushion between the production and consumption of goods and exist in various forms: materials awaiting processing; partially completed products or components; and finished goods at the factory, in transit, at warehouse distribution points, and in retail outlets. At each of these stages, a sound economic justification for the inventory should exist, since each additional unit carried in inventory generates some additional costs.

Inventory investment varies with the type of industry and the characteristics of a company. On the average, inventory accounts for about one third of total assets, and for many manufacturers the cost of materials represents about one half of total product cost. Any inventory planning and control method should have but one goal that might be expressed in two ways: (1) to minimize total cost or (2) to maximize profit within specified time and resource allocations. For example, the size of inventory at production sites should reflect the profitability inherent in large production runs, in the economic ordering, handling, and shipping of lots, and in the need for flexibility to meet uncertain future demand.

PLANNING MATERIALS REQUIREMENTS

Materials planning begins with the design of a product. Whether it is a regular product or a special contract, a series of planning stages is necessary to get materials into production. In the preliminary stages, the engineering division studies the proposal, design, blueprints, and other available specifications and prepares a product requirement statement. The tooling department studies the work details necessary to manufacture the product in a particular plant. The manufacturing control division examines production in terms of existing and contemplated production schedules. The materials planning and cost estimating departments study the cumulative information and submit a cost estimate for the production proposal. The long-range or economic planning section suggests a product price based on considerations of present product lines, economic conditions and expectations, company policies, and expansion plans. Executive management must finally decide whether to proceed with, reject, or modify the proposal.

To plan manufacturing requirements, every stock item or class of items must be analyzed periodically to:

1. Forecast demand for the next month, quarter, or year.
2. Determine acquisition lead time.
3. Plan usage during the lead time.
4. Establish quantity on hand.
5. Place units on order.
6. Determine reserve or safety stock requirements.

These six steps are illustrated below in determining the quantity to order in September for a November delivery. In this illustration, the *lead time*, the time between the order and delivery, is two months. The desired inventory cushion or *safety stock* is approximately a two weeks' supply.

Planned or forecast usage from review date:		UNITS
September production		2,500
October production		2,000
November production		2,500
Desired inventory, November 30		1,000
Total to be provided		8,000
Quantity on hand, September 1	1,600	
On order for September delivery	2,000	
On order for October delivery	2,000	5,600
Quantity to order for November delivery		2,400

Future requirements for each purchased or produced item play a central role in materials control. If usage requirements are not accurately planned, even the most elaborate control system will result in the wrong level of inventory during and at the end of a future period.

Materials planning deals with two fundamental factors — the quantity and the time to purchase. Determination of how much and when to buy involves two conflicting kinds of cost — the cost of carrying inventory and the cost of inadequate carrying. The nature of these conflicting costs is indicated in the following comparison.

COST OF CARRYING INVENTORY	ESTI-MATE	COST OF INADEQUATE CARRYING
Interest or investment of working capital....	10.00%	Extra purchasing, handling, and transportation costs
Property tax and insurance.................	1.25	Higher price due to small order quantities
Warehousing or storage.....................	1.80	Frequent stockouts resulting in disruptions of production
Handling......................	4.25	schedules, overtime, and extra setup time
Deterioration and shrinkage of stocks.	2.60	Additional clerical costs due to keeping customer back-order
Obsolescence of stocks	5.20	records
Total........................	25.10%	Inflation-oriented increases in prices when inventory purchases are deferred
		Lost sales and loss of customer goodwill

Inventory Carrying and Ordering Costs for Economic Order Quantity Calculations

The *economic order quantity (EOQ)* is the amount of inventory to be ordered at one time for purposes of minimizing annual inventory cost. If a company buys in large quantities, the cost of carrying the inventory is high because of the sizable investment. If purchases are made in small quantities, frequent orders with correspondingly high ordering costs will result. Therefore, the quantity to order at a given time must be determined by balancing two factors: (1) the cost of possessing (carrying) materials and (2) the cost of acquiring (ordering) materials. Buying in larger quantities may decrease the unit cost of acquisition, but this saving may be more than offset by the cost of carrying materials in stock for a longer period of time.

The six cost factors of carrying an inventory, listed at the top of this page, are expressed as a percentage of the average inventory investment and can be estimated and measured. These cost factors should include only those costs that vary with the level of inventory. For example, in the case of warehousing or storage, only those costs that will vary with changes in the number of units ordered should be included. The cost of labor and equipment used in the storeroom is normally a fixed cost and should not be considered a part of the carrying charge. Similarly, the insurance cost is included only when the company has a monthly reporting type of policy with premiums charged on the fluctuating inventory value. A standard insurance policy for one year or more should be considered a fixed cost that is irrelevant to the decision.

It is difficult to determine the costs of not carrying enough inventory; yet they must be considered in deciding upon order quantities and order points. Such costs include ordering costs, although the fixed cost of placing an order is not relevant. Only the variable or out-of-pocket cost of procuring an order should be included. The costs of processing an order include preparing the requisition and the purchase order, handling the incoming shipment and preparing a receiving report, communicating in case of quantity/quality errors or delays in receipt of materials, and accounting for the shipment and the payment. Other costs of not carrying enough inventory relate to such questions as savings in freight and quantity discounts as well as to the question of when to order, including an appropriate allowance for safety stock.

Depending upon many factors, it may cost from $2 to $20 or more to process an order and from 10 to 35 percent of the average inventory investment to hold materials. Techniques for analyzing cost behavior, described and illustrated in Chapter 18, should facilitate the determination of realistic carrying and ordering cost estimates. Mathematical and statistical techniques permit improved planning and control in an endeavor to maximize profits and minimize costs.

A tabular arrangement of data relative to a materials item allows the determination of an approximate economic order quantity, and thereby the number of orders that need to be placed annually. To illustrate, assume the following data:

Tabular Determination of the Economic Order Quantity

Estimated requirements for next year....................................	2,400 units
Cost of the item per unit	$ 1.50
Ordering cost (per order)	$20.00
Inventory carrying cost (% of average inventory investment).....	10%

Based on these data, various possible order sizes can be evaluated:

QUANTITATIVE DATA

Order size in units	300	400	800	1,200	2,400
Number of orders........................	8	6	3	2	1
Average inventory (order size ÷ 2) .	150	200	400	600	1,200

COST DATA

Average inventory investment	$225.00	$300	$600	$900	$1,800
Total carrying cost (10% of average inventory)...............................	$ 22.50	$ 30	$ 60	$ 90	$ 180
Total ordering cost	160.00	120	60	40	20
Cost to order and carry	$182.50	$150	$120	$130	$ 200

Of the order sizes calculated, 800 is the most economical; thus, an order should be placed every four months. However, the most economical order size may not have been calculated; there may be some unit quantity between 400 and 800 or between 800 and 1,200 with a cost to order and carry that is lower than $120.

The graph on page 354 shows the lowest point of the total-cost-to-order-and-carry curve, about $120, and the most economic order quantity of about 800 units. The ideal order size is the point where the sum of the ordering and carrying costs is at a minimum, i.e., where the total cost curve is at its lowest. This point occurs where the annual carrying charges equal the ordering charges, i.e., where these two cost lines intersect.

Graphic Determination of the Economic Order Quantity

Graphic
Determination
of the
Economic
Order Quantity

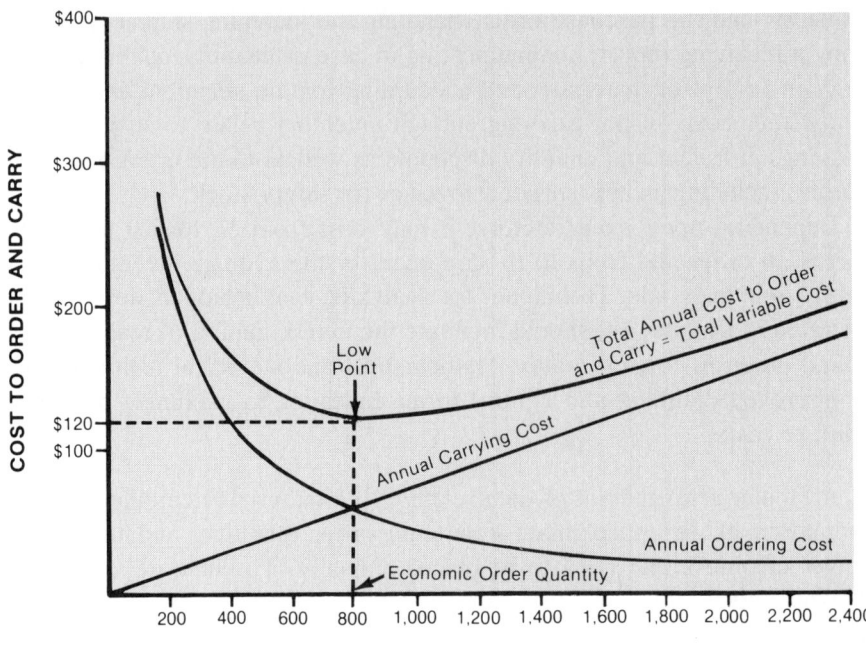

**The
Economic
Order
Quantity
Formula**

To determine the economic order quantity by a tabular or graphic method is lengthy and may not provide the most accurate answer. Companies using order-point calculations based upon economic order quantities usually prefer to use a formula. With information such as quantity required, unit price, inventory carrying cost, and cost per order, differential calculus makes it possible to compute economic order quantity by formula. One formula variation follows:

$$\text{Economic order quantity} = \sqrt{\frac{2 \times \text{Annual required units} \times \text{Cost per order}}{\text{Cost per unit of material} \times \text{Carrying cost percentage}}}$$

$$OR \qquad \text{EOQ} = \sqrt{\frac{2 \times \text{RU} \times \text{CO}}{\text{CU} \times \text{CC}}}$$

Given the terms EOQ, RU, CO, CU, and CC as specified, the formula is based on the following relationships:

$$\frac{\text{RU}}{\text{EOQ}} = \text{Number of orders placed annually}$$

$$\frac{\text{RU} \times \text{CO}}{\text{EOQ}} = \text{Annual ordering cost}$$

$$\frac{\text{EOQ}}{2} = \text{Average number of units in inventory at any point in time}$$

$$\frac{\text{CU} \times \text{CC} \times \text{EOQ}}{2} = \text{Annual carrying cost}$$

$$\frac{RU \times CO}{EOQ} + \frac{CU \times CC \times EOQ}{2} = \begin{array}{l} \text{Total annual cost of ordering and carry-} \\ \text{ing inventory, designated as } AC^1 \end{array}$$

This formula for the economic order quantity, or least-cost order quantity in units, is the square root of a fraction whose numerator is twice the product of the annual unit demands and the cost per order and whose denominator is the product of the unit price and the annual carrying rate. The formula assumes a constant rate of materials usage.

Using this formula, the EOQ for the data on page 353 is:

$$EOQ = \sqrt{\frac{2 \times 2,400 \times \$20}{\$1.50 \times 10\%}} = \sqrt{\frac{96,000}{.15}} = \sqrt{640,000} = 800 \text{ units}$$

It is also possible to express EOQ in dollars rather than in units. The following formula is usually employed:

$$EOQ = \sqrt{\frac{2 \times AB}{I}} \quad \text{where } A = \text{Annual requirements in dollars}$$
$$B = \text{Ordering cost (per order)}$$
$$I = \text{Inventory carrying cost (\% of average inventory investment)}$$

Using this formula and the following data from the previous illustration:

A = \$3,600 (or 2,400 units @ \$1.50)
B = \$20
I = 10\% per year

$$EOQ = \sqrt{\frac{2 \times \$3,600 \times \$20}{.10}} = \$1,200 \text{ total cost}$$

The EOQ can be converted to units by dividing the EOQ total cost by the cost per unit (\$1,200 ÷ \$1.50 = 800 units).

---

[1]This latter equation is then solved utilizing differential calculus to determine minimum total annual cost of inventory, AC, represented by the EOQ formula:

$$AC = \frac{RU \times CO}{EOQ} + \frac{CU \times CC \times EOQ}{2}$$

$$AC = RU \times CO \times EOQ^{-1} + \frac{CU \times CC \times EOQ}{2}$$

$$\frac{dAC}{dEOQ} = -RU \times CO \times EOQ^{-2} + \frac{CU \times CC}{2}$$

$$\frac{dAC}{dEOQ} = \frac{-RU \times CO}{EOQ^2} + \frac{CU \times CC}{2}$$

$$\text{Let } \frac{dAC}{dEOQ} = 0 \; ; \frac{-RU \times CO}{EOQ^2} + \frac{CU \times CC}{2} = 0$$

$$\frac{CU \times CC}{2} = \frac{RU \times CO}{EOQ^2}$$

$$EOQ^2 \times CU \times CC = 2 \times RU \times CO$$

$$EOQ^2 = \frac{2 \times RU \times CO}{CU \times CC}$$

$$EOQ = \sqrt{\frac{2 \times RU \times CO}{CU \times CC}}$$

The following example is given to indicate the results when new cost data enter the formula, since any shift in cost data will affect the answer. Again, only those cost components that vary directly with order or production quantities should be used, i.e., the variable costs.

RU = 2,400 units of materials used per year (200 units per month)
CO = $10 ordering cost per order
CU = $1.50 cost per unit of materials
CC = 20% carrying cost as a percent of average inventory investment

$$EOQ = \sqrt{\frac{2 \times 2,400 \times \$10}{\$1.50 \times 20\%}} = \sqrt{\frac{48,000}{.30}} = \sqrt{160,000} = 400 \text{ units}$$

The economic order quantity for the stock item is 400 units, or six orders per year. Other order quantities resulting in more or less than six orders per year are not so economical, as proven by the following table, which is based on $3,600 annual usage of materials.

ORDERS PER YEAR	UNITS PER ORDER	VALUE PER ORDER	ORDERING COST	CARRYING COST	TOTAL COST
1	2,400	$3,600	$10	$360	$370
2	1,200	1,800	20	180	200
3	800	1,200	30	120	150
4	600	900	40	90	130
5	480	720	50	72	122
6	400	600	60	60	120
7	343	515	70	52	122
8	300	450	80	45	125

Quantity Price Discounts

By purchasing in quantities larger than the minimum, quantity price discounts and/or freight savings may be realized, resulting in a lower cost per unit and altering the economic order quantity. However, buying in larger quantities involves a larger investment in inventories. Therefore, larger quantities should be purchased only if an added return on the average added investment is adequate.[2]

The table on page 357 considers the effect of quantity price discounts, using a cost-comparison approach.

The EOQ Formula and Production Runs

The EOQ formula is equally appropriate in computing the optimum size of a production run, in which case CO represents an estimate of the setup cost and CU is the variable manufacturing cost per unit. To illustrate, assume that stock item A86 is manufactured rather than purchased; the setup cost (CO), such as the cost of labor to rearrange and adjust machines, is $62; and the variable manufacturing cost (CU) is $2 per unit. The optimum size of a production run is computed as follows:

$$\sqrt{\frac{2 \times 6,000 \text{ units} \times \$62 \text{ setup cost}}{\$2 \text{ variable manufacturing cost} \times 20\%}} = \sqrt{\frac{744,000}{.4}} = \sqrt{1,860,000} = 1,364 \text{ units}$$

---

[2]For further discussion of quantity discounts in EOQ computations, see Richard I. Levin and Charles A. Kirkpatrick, *Quantitative Approaches to Management*, 3d ed. (New York: McGraw-Hill Book Company, 1975), pp. 192–197.

Number of orders per year	1	2	3	4	5	6	8
Size of order	$3,600	$1,800	$1,200	$ 900	$ 720	$ 600	$ 450
Average inventory	1,800	900	600	450	360	300	225
Quantity discount	8%	6%	5%	5%	4½%	4%	4%
Cost of materials	$3,312	$3,384	$3,420	$3,420	$3,438	$3,456	$3,456
Carrying cost (20% of average)	360	180	120	90	72	60	45
Cost to order ($10 per order)	10	20	30	40	50	60	80
Total cost per year	$3,682	$3,584	$3,570	$3,550	$3,560	$3,576	$3,581

Determining the Time to Order

The EOQ formula answers the quantity problem of inventory control. However, the question of when to order is equally important. This question is controlled by three factors: (1) time needed for delivery, (2) rate of inventory usage, and (3) safety stock. Unlike the economic order quantity, the order point has no generally applicable and acceptable formula. Determining the order point would be relatively simple if *lead time* — the interval between placing an order and having materials on the factory floor ready for production — and the usage pattern for a given item were definitely predictable. For most stock items there is a variation in either or both of these factors, which almost always causes one of three results: (1) if lead time or usage is below expectation during an order period, the new materials will arrive before the existing stock is consumed, thereby adding to the cost of carrying inventory; (2) if lead time or usage is greater than expected, a *stockout* will occur with the resultant incurrence of costs associated with not carrying enough inventory; (3) if average lead time is used to determine an order point, a stockout could be expected on every other order.

Forecasting materials usage requires the expenditure of time and money. In materials management, forecasts are an expense as well as an aid to balancing the cost to acquire and the cost to carry inventory. Since perfect forecasts are rarely possible, an inventory cushion or safety stock is often the least costly device for protecting against a stockout. The basic problem is to determine the safety stock quantity. If the safety stock is greater than needed, the carrying cost will be too high; if too small, frequent stockouts will occur and inconveniences, disruptions, and additional costs will result. The optimum safety stock is that quantity which results in minimal total annual cost of stockouts and safety stock carrying cost. This carrying cost is determined in the same manner as in calculating the economic order quantity. The annual cost of stockouts depends upon their probability and the actual cost of each stockout.

To illustrate, assume that a company uses an item for which it places 10 orders per year, the cost of a stockout is $30, and the carrying cost is $.50 per unit. The following probabilities of a stockout have been estimated for various levels of safety stock:

Probability	Safety Stock Level
40%	0 units
20	50
10	100
5	200

The total carrying cost and stockout cost at each level of safety stock is determined as follows:

EXPECTED ANNUAL STOCKOUTS (PROBABILITY × NUMBER OF ORDERS)	TOTAL STOCKOUT COST	TOTAL CARRYING COST	TOTAL STOCKOUT AND CARRYING COST
4.0	$120	–0–	$120
2.0	60	$ 25	85
1.0	30	50	80
.5	15	100	115

In this illustration, the optimum level of safety stock is 100 units, since the total stockout and safety stock carrying cost is minimized at this level. Such an analysis of important stock items leads to smooth operations and effective materials management.

Order Point Formula

Order points are based on usage during the time necessary to requisition, order, and receive materials, plus an allowance for protection against stockout. The *order point* is reached when inventory on hand and quantities due in are equal to the lead time usage quantity plus the safety stock quantity. In equation form, the order point may be expressed as:

$$I + QD = LTQ + SSQ, \text{ when:}$$

I = Inventory balance on hand

QD = Quantities due in from orders previously placed, materials transfers, and returns to stock

LTQ = Lead time quantity equals average lead time in months, weeks, or days multiplied by average month's, week's, or day's use

SSQ = Safety stock quantity

The following approaches are illustrated, both of which are solved mathematically and graphically:

1. Usage and lead time are known with certainty; therefore, no safety stock is provided.

2. Based on the same figures, a safety stock is injected into the calculation.

Order Point Illustrated – No Safety Stock. Assume the weekly use of 175 units of a stock item (35 units each Monday through Friday, or 25 units seven days a week) and that a lead time of four weeks establishes an order point at 700 units (175 units × 4 weeks). Assuming that the unit cost is $.50, the carrying cost is 20%, the order cost is $24, and annual usage is 9,100 units (175 units × 52 weeks), then the EOQ is computed as follows:

$$\text{EOQ} = \sqrt{\frac{2 \times 9,100 \times \$24}{\$.50 \times 20\%}} = \sqrt{\frac{436,800}{.10}} = \sqrt{4,368,000} = 2,090 \text{ units}$$

Each order provides a 12 weeks' supply (2,090 ÷ 175). Figure 1 shows the control pattern of this item if usage and lead time are definitely known. It is apparent that (1) if lead time is more than four weeks, a stockout will result; and (2) if usage exceeds 700 units in any four-week period following an order point, a stockout is inevitable. Since perfect prediction of usage and lead time is usually unrealistic, a safety stock allowance is needed.

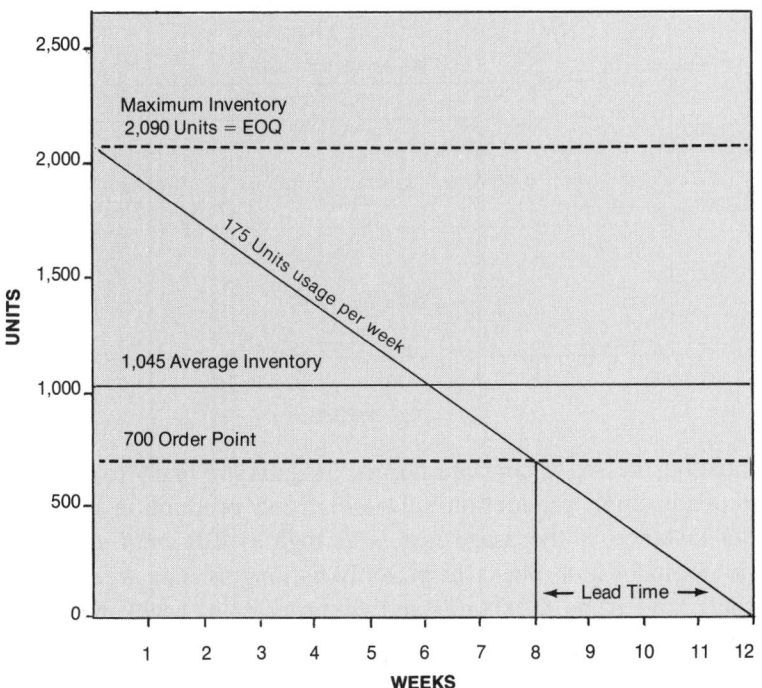

Figure 1 —
Rate of Usage
and Lead Time
Known with
Certainty

Order Point Illustrated – Safety Stock. Assuming the same usage of 175 units per week shown in Figure 1, with a lead time of normally four weeks but possibly as long as nine weeks, the order point would be 1,575 units: 700 units usage during normal lead time (175 units × 4 weeks) plus 875 units safety stock (175 units × 5 weeks). Assuming a beginning inventory of 2,800 units and no orders outstanding, the usage, order schedule, and inventory levels would be:

2,800 units in beginning inventory
1,225 usage to order point (1,255 ÷ 175 weekly usage = 7 weeks)
1,575 order point
  700 usage during normal lead time (700 ÷ 175 weekly usage = 4 weeks)
  875 maximum inventory or safety stock at date of delivery, assuming normal lead time and usage
2,090 EOQ units received
2,965 maximum inventory, assuming normal lead time and usage

The average inventory, assuming normal lead time and usage, is 1,920 units [(2,090 EOQ ÷ 2) + 875 units safety stock]. Figure 2 depicts materials planning under the above assumptions and shows that a stockout would not occur unless lead time exceeds nine weeks, assuming normal usage.

Figure 2 —
Rate of Usage
Known with
Certainty and
Lead Time
Known but
Variable

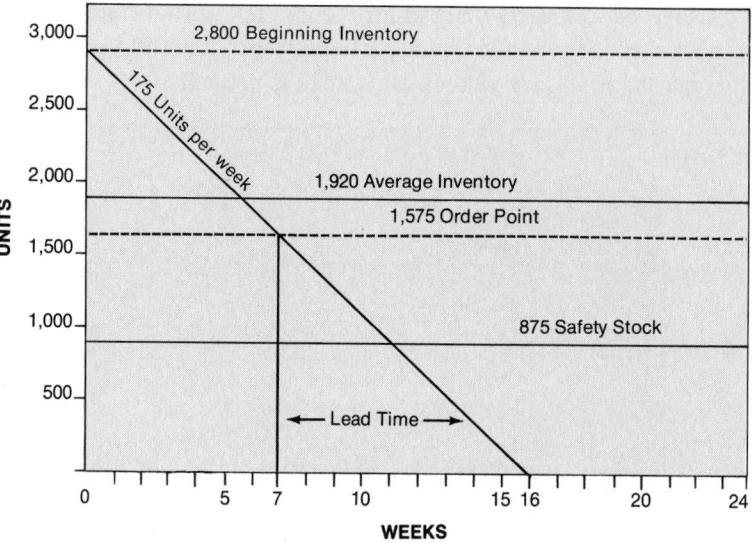

In most businesses, a constant normal usage is not likely to occur because usage depends upon production schedules, and production depends upon sales. For instance, if the usage rate is as high as 210 units per week, with lead time normally four weeks or possibly as long as nine weeks, the safety stock would have to be 1,190 units and the order point 1,890 units, calculated as follows:

Normal usage for normal lead time of four weeks (175 units × 4 weeks)		700 units
Safety stock:		
Normal usage for five weeks' delay (175 units × 5 weeks)	875	
Usage variation [(210 − 175) × 9 weeks]..................	315	1,190
Order point		1,890 units

Assuming a beginning inventory of 2,800 units with no orders outstanding, the usage, order schedule, and inventory levels would be:

2,800 units in beginning inventory
  910 usage to order point (910 ÷ 210 maximum weekly usage = 4.3 weeks)
1,890 order point
  700 normal usage for normal lead time (700 ÷ 175 normal weekly usage = 4 weeks)
1,190 maximum inventory or safety stock at date of delivery, assuming normal lead time and usage
2,090 EOQ units received
3,280 maximum inventory, assuming normal lead time and usage

The average inventory, assuming normal lead time and usage, is 2,235 units [(2,090 EOQ ÷ 2) + 1,190 units safety stock]. Figure 3 shows materials planning under the assumptions that the rate of usage and lead time are known but variable.

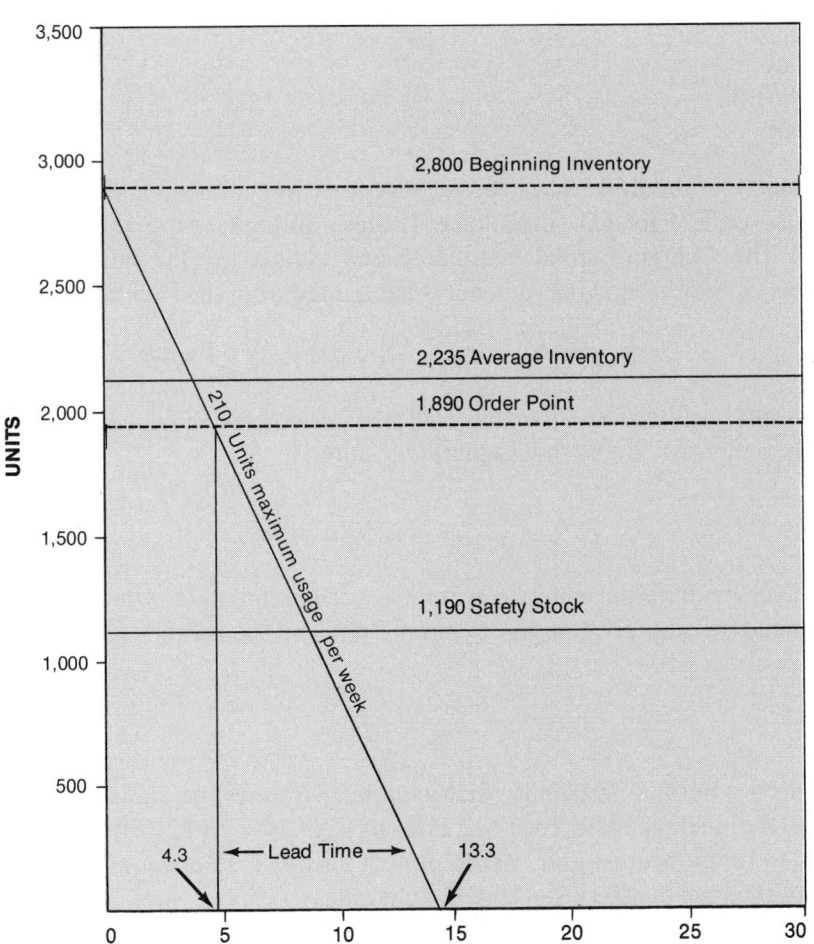

Figure 3 —
Rate of Usage
and Lead Time
Known but
Variable

**Safety
Stock
Calculations
by
Statistical
Methods**

The preceding situations tend to provide a safety stock for the extreme boundaries of usage and lead time variability. In other situations, the amount of safety stock is often calculated by traditional rules of thumb, such as a two weeks' supply. These approaches have given way to statistical techniques which minimize the combined costs of stockouts and carrying inventory. With any increasing complexity of calculations, computer application is inevitable.

The tabulation of an eight months' actual consumption of Material J-2, together with the forecast monthly usage, forms the basis for the following statistical approach:

	(1)	(2)	(3)	(4)
			FORECAST	
		UNITS	MINUS	COLUMN 3
	FORECAST	CONSUMED	UNITS CONSUMED	SQUARED
January	260	250	10	100
February	218	225	− 7	49
March	260	275	−15	225
April	230	240	−10	100
May	275	280	− 5	25
June	270	260	10	100
July	245	240	5	25
August	270	280	−10	100
			−22	724

In Column 3, the differences between forecast requirements and actual usage are derived and totaled. In Column 4, these differences are squared and totaled. The Column 3 total is squared and divided by the number of time periods (8 months) and the quotient is subtracted from the Column 4 total:

$$724 - \frac{(-22)^2}{8} = 724 - \frac{484}{8} = 724 - 60.5 = 663.5$$

The result is divided by the number of time periods minus one, and the square root is computed, giving the standard deviation:

$$\sqrt{\frac{663.5}{8-1}} = \sqrt{94.786} = 9.74$$

The average difference between forecast requirements and actual usage is computed next by dividing the Column 3 total by the number of time periods (months):

$$\frac{-22}{8} = -2.75$$

Based on a normal probability distribution, two times the standard deviation minus the average difference, 22.23 units [2(9.74) − (−2.75)], or 22 when rounded to the nearest unit, would protect against a stockout about 97.5 percent of the time (a safety stock of 22 units).

Here the average difference of −2.75 increases the safety stock because the actual usage is, on the average, greater than the forecast usage. A positive average difference would indicate that, on the average, the actual usage is less than the forecast, thus reducing the safety stock figure.

Three times the standard deviation minus the average difference, approximately 32 units $[3(9.74) - (-2.75)]$ of safety stock, would result in about 99.5 percent protection against stockouts due to variation in usage based upon experience of eight months.

In January, with a usage forecast of 260 units, a lead time of one month, and a safety stock of 22 units, the order point is 282 units for Material J-2. Of course, an additional safety stock allowance may be needed if lead time varies, again giving consideration to the degree of protection desired by management. When the stock reaches the order point level, it should trigger an order for the most economical order quantity.

Lead time units must be the same time period units of measure as those used in computing the standard deviation, e.g., days, weeks, or months. This illustration uses months as time period units and assumes a lead time of one month. When the lead time is not one time period, proper computation of the safety stock requires the multiplication of the desired number of standard deviations, the standard deviation, and the square root of the number of time period units. From this product, the average difference multiplied by the number of time period units is subtracted. Assuming the same standard deviation and average difference as computed on page 362 (two standard deviations and a lead time of four months), the safety stock would be computed as follows:

$$\text{Safety stock} = (2 \times 9.74 \times \sqrt{4}) - (-2.75 \times 4)$$
$$= (19.48 \times 2) + 11$$
$$= 38.96 + 11$$
$$= 49.96 = \text{approximately 50 units for safety stock}$$

Forecasting Usage

The number of units needed during the lead time and the lead time itself are the two variables which influence the when-to-order decision. It is usually possible to estimate fairly accurately the time required to receive materials. It is seldom possible to forecast exactly the materials needed even for a short future period; and when thousands of items are involved, the task becomes prodigious even with the aid of a computer. Some forecasting techniques are briefly mentioned in order to indicate the scope and complexity of the task:

1. Factor listing or barometric methods.
2. Statistical methods.
3. Forecasting surveys.

Factor listing involves enumerating the favorable and unfavorable conditions likely to influence sales of the various divisions or products of a company and relies upon the forecaster's judgment to evaluate the degree of the influence factor. *Barometric methods* result in systematized factor listing.

Statistical methods describe historical patterns in time series. The methods may be simple or complex, but the purpose is to reveal patterns that have occurred in the past and project them into the future. The usual procedure results in plotting time series data (such as total sales, sales of specific lines or products, inventory units or dollars, labor hours, or machine hours) on a graph, thus revealing a trend or a seasonal or cyclical pattern. A moving average may be used to smooth a series and remove irregular fluctuations, but the intent is to describe mathematically the growth or decline over a period of time. Regression analysis usually employs the least-squares method (see Chapter 18) to determine economic relationships between a dependent variable and one or more independent variables, such as sales territory, family incomes, advertising expenditures, and price of the product.

Forecasting surveys are used to avoid complete dependence on historical data. They are commonly made in order to determine consumer buying intentions, opinions, or feelings about the business outlook, and capital investment plans.

General Observations

The primary key to good inventory planning is sufficient knowledge of the fundamental techniques to develop enough self-confidence to permit their practical adaptation to the specific needs of the company. Basically, economic order quantity and computed order points assume:

1. Relatively uniform average demand.
2. Uniform rate of inventory usage.
3. Normal distribution of demand forecast errors.
4. Constant purchase price per unit regardless of order size.
5. Available funds when the order point is reached.
6. Statistical independence of demand for all inventory items.

Circular slide rules made expressly for computing EOQ are available, easy to use, and sufficiently accurate for all practical purposes. The formula can be translated into a logarithmic chart or nomograph, which makes its use mechanical, requiring no mathematical knowledge.

Aside from the technical and mathematical steps, it is important to remember that the following fundamentals largely determine the success of the inventory planning procedures:

1. The order point is a significant factor affecting inventory planning, since it establishes the inventory level. It determines the investment in inventories and the ability to provide satisfactory customer service. The order point is primarily dependent on the accuracy of the sales or usage forecast.
2. Of equal importance is the establishment of unit costs, carrying and ordering costs, and the investment factor. They are involved in determining the economic order quantity.
3. The inventory model should be sensitive and adaptive to seasonal usage variations and other nonstatic data influencing order point quantity computations.

MATERIALS CONTROL

Materials control is accomplished through functional organization, assignment of responsibility, and documentary evidence obtained at various stages of operations. These stages begin with the approval of sales and production budgets and with the completion of products which are ready for sale and shipment to warehouse stocks or to customers.

Two levels of inventory control exist: unit control and dollar control. Purchasing and production managers are primarily interested in unit control; they think, order, and requisition in terms of units instead of dollars. Executive management is primarily interested in the financial control of inventories. These executives think in terms of an adequate return on capital employed; i.e., dollars invested in inventory must be utilized efficiently and effectively. Inventory control is operating successfully when inventory increases or decreases follow a predetermined and predictable pattern, related in amount and time to sales requirements and production schedules.

The control of materials must meet two opposing needs: (1) maintenance of an inventory of sufficient size and diversity for efficient operations and (2) maintenance of a financially favorable inventory. A basic objective of good materials control is the ability to place an order at the right time with the right source to acquire the right quantity at the right price and quality. Effective inventory control should:

1. Provide a supply of required materials and parts for efficient and uninterrupted operations.
2. Provide ample stocks in periods of short supply (seasonal, cyclical, or strike), and anticipate price changes.
3. Store materials with a minimum of handling time and cost and protect them from loss by fire, theft, elements, and damage through handling.
4. Keep inactive, surplus, and obsolete items to a minimum by systematic reporting of product changes which affect materials and parts.
5. Assure adequate inventory for prompt delivery to customers.
6. Maintain the amount of capital invested in inventories at a level consistent with operating requirements and management's plans.

Inventory control systems and techniques should be based on these fundamental principles:

Control Principles

1. Inventory is created by purchasing (a) materials and parts and (b) additional labor and overhead to process the materials into finished goods.
2. Inventory is reduced through sales and spoilage.
3. Accurate sales and production schedule forecasts are essential for efficient purchasing, handling, and materials investment.
4. Management policies, which attempt to balance size and diversity of inventory for efficient operations and cost of maintaining that inventory, are the greatest factor in determining inventory investment.
5. Ordering materials is a response to forecasts; scheduling production controls inventory.

6. Inventory records alone do not achieve inventory control.
7. Control is comparative and relative, not absolute. It is exercised by people with varying experiences and judgment. Rules and procedures guide these individuals in making evaluations and decisions. For example, by establishing closer controls, experts in the field of materials control commonly expect to reduce inventory by 15 percent or more without significantly affecting customer service or production scheduling.

Organizing for Materials Control

Materials control is commonly centralized in one department called the materials management or materials control department. Size of the company, number of purchased items in a finished product, time required to manufacture a product, and physical size, weight, and unit value of items are factors that influence the organization and personnel required for effective materials control. A materials management organization may include some or all of the following sections:

Planning and Scheduling	Warehousing
Purchasing	Packing
Receiving	Traffic
Inspection	Shipping
Stores	Statistical Analysis
Materials Handling	Value Analysis
Finished Goods	New Product Planning

Materials Control Methods

Materials control methods differ primarily in (1) frequency of review of the status of materials and (2) care and cost expended in making the review, especially in estimating future usage of an item. In the case of critical items and high-value materials, it is necessary to make a weekly or even daily review with experienced supervisory personnel. For low-value items, a quarterly, semiannual, or annual review may be adequate. On low-cost items, large safety stocks and large orders of three to six months' supply are appropriate, since carrying costs are usually low and risk of obsolescence is often negligible. Control methods include (1) order cycling, (2) the min-max method, (3) the two-bin system, and (4) the automatic order system.

The *order cycling* or *cycle review method* examines periodically (e.g., each 30, 60, or 90 days) the status of quantities on hand of each item or class. Different companies use different time periods between reviews and may use different cycles for different types of materials. High-value items and items that would tie up normal operations if out of stock usually require a short review cycle. On low-cost and noncritical items, a longer review cycle is common, since these materials would be ordered in large quantities and a stockout would not be as costly. At each review period in the order cycling system, orders are placed to bring quantities up to some determined and desired level. This quantity is often expressed as a number of days' or weeks' supply and can be adjusted to projected sales for seasonal items.

The *min-max method* is based on the premise that the quantities of most stock items are subject to definable limits. A maximum quantity for each item is established. A minimum level provides the margin of safety necessary to prevent stockouts during a reorder cycle. The minimum level sets the order point, and the quantity to order will usually bring inventory to the maximum level.

The *two-bin system* of inventory control separates each stock item into two bins, piles, or bundles. The first bin contains enough stock to satisfy usage that occurs between receipt of an order and the placing of the next order; the second bin contains the normal amount used from order date to delivery date plus the safety stock. When the first bin is empty and the second bin is tapped, a requisition for a new supply is prepared. The second bin or reserve quantity is determined originally by estimating usage requirements and adding a safety stock adequate to cover the time required for replenishing the materials. For example, if monthly usage of an item is ten dozen, a one-month safety stock is desired; and if 30 days are required to place an order and receive delivery, the second bin should contain 20 dozen units. A purchase order must be written when the reserve stock is tapped; otherwise, a stockout is likely to occur. The two-bin or "last bag" system requires little paper work, since reordering takes place when the "last bag" is opened.

The *automatic order* or *order point system* is automatic in the sense that ordering is triggered when a materials ledger card shows that the balance on hand has dropped to the order point. The system is especially advantageous in companies using electronic data processing equipment. The materials control department reviews materials items, forecasts usage and lead time, establishes safety stock requirements, and determines economic order quantities. Thereafter, subject to quarterly or semiannual review, receipts and issues are machine-recorded on the materials cards. When the quantity on hand drops to the established order point, the materials cards are automatically machine-sorted and are routed to order clerks who activate orders for the quantity specified. Companies with computers go even further in their use of the automatic order system. The computer reviews and updates order points, recalculates economic order quantities, and even writes purchase orders.

Inventory Turnover — A Basic Ratio

Meaningful ratios require uniformity and consistency in computing the ratio's underlying data. *Inventory turnover* is the ratio between the cost of goods sold and the average inventory investment, and represents the number of times per accounting period that inventory is physically replaced. For this ratio, the focus must be on specific divisions and products or product groups in order to provide a viable materials control technique employing timely comparison of planned ratios versus actual results.

Selective Control — The ABC Plan

Segregation of materials for *selective control*, called the *ABC plan*, is an analytical approach based upon statistical averages. The ABC plan measures the cost significance of each materials item. "A," or high-value, items would be under the tightest control and the responsibility of the most experienced personnel. "C" items would be under simple physical controls such as the two-bin system with safety stocks. The plan provides an impressive saving in materials cost.

The ABC plan concentrates on important items and is also known as *control by importance and exception (CIE)*. Because it is impractical to give equal attention to all items in inventory, stock items are classified and ranked in descending order on the basis of the annual dollar value of each item, thus providing a proportional value analysis. In most situations, an arbitrary number of items can be selected on a percentage basis to approximate:

10% of the items to equal 70% of the dollar cost of materials used
30% of the items to equal 25% of the dollar cost of materials used
60% of the items to equal 5% of the dollar cost of materials used

The following table suggests the handling of high-, middle-, and low-value items to achieve effective control:

	HIGH-VALUE ITEMS (A)	MIDDLE-VALUE ITEMS (B)	LOW-VALUE ITEMS (C)
Quality of personnel	Best available	Average	Low
Records needed	Complete	Simple	Not essential
Order point and quantity used...........	As guides, frequent review	Infrequent review	Strictly used
Number of orders per year......................	Generally high	Two to six	One or two
Replacement time........	As short as possible	Normal	Can be long
Amount of safety stock	Low	Moderate	High
Inventory turnover	High	Moderate	Low

The procedure for segregating materials for selective control consists of six steps:

1. Determining future use in units over the review forecast period — month, quarter, or year.
2. Determining the price per unit for each item.
3. Multiplying the projected price per unit by the projected unit requirement to determine the total cost of that item during the period.
4. Arranging the items in terms of total cost, listing first the item with the highest total cost.
5. Computing for each item its percentage of the total for (a) units — number of units of each item divided by total units of all items, and (b) total cost — total cost of each item divided by total cost of all materials.
6. Plotting the percentages on a graph.

The table and graph on page 369 demonstrate ABC inventory classification.

ITEM	UNITS	% OF TOTAL		UNIT COST	TOTAL COST	% OF TOTAL	
1	800	8	} 12%	$20.00	$16,000	32.0	} 56% — A
2	400	4		30.00	12,000	24.0	
3	1,600	16		4.50	7,200	14.4	
4	1,400	14	} 42%	5.00	7,000	14.0	} 38% — B
5	1,200	12		4.00	4,800	9.6	
6	2,000	20		1.00	2,000	4.0	
7	1,600	16	} 46%	.50	800	1.6	} 6% — C
8	1,000	10		.20	200	.4	
Total	10,000	100			$50,000	100.0	100%

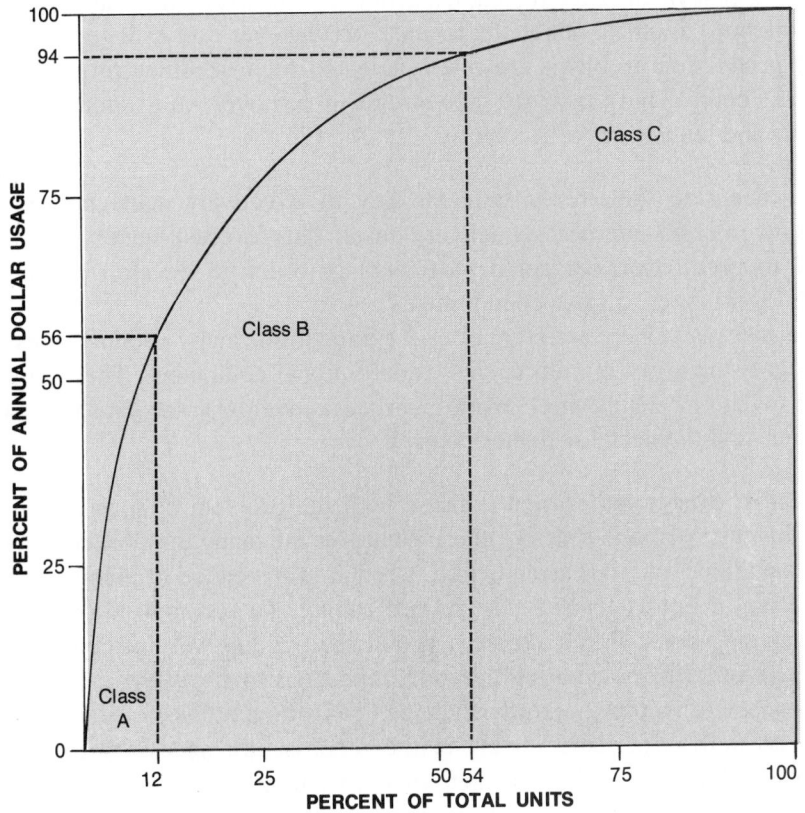

Distribution of
Inventory
Usage Values
(Cumulative
Percentages)

The receiving or inspection department forwards materials to storerooms together with a copy of the receiving report. The storekeeper and assistants are responsible for safeguarding the materials. Materials and supplies are placed in proper bins or other storage spaces until properly requisitioned for production. Admittance to the storeroom should be restricted to employees of that department. These employees often work behind locked doors, issuing materials through cage windows.

Physical Control of Materials in the Storeroom

Controlling Materials in Process

The materials cost control responsibility is not ended when materials are requisitioned for production. Until goods are finished, packed, sold, and shipped, inventory control problems and cost savings potentials exist. This is particularly true of in-process inventories which are intimately related to production processes and schedules, but often are not controlled. Generally, the objective is to maintain inventory levels based either on maximum production or the lowest unit cost.

The computation of turnover rates aids in identifying inventory problems and measuring the effectiveness of control procedures. A computation is usually made for each manufacturing department, cost center, or process by dividing the cost of units transferred to the next department by the average inventory cost of the transferring department. Turnover rates vary from one department to another; hence the focus is on turnover rate changes. Scheduling or production problems are often indicated by a declining turnover rate. For cost control purposes, the downtrend in turnover rates should suggest analysis and induce corrective action.

Controlling Finished Goods

An accurate sales forecast is the key to effectively managing finished goods inventories and meeting delivery dates. This forecast must be communicated to production control departments in order to develop production schedules for meeting sales commitments.

To meet customer preferences and competition, many product lines feature a growing array of colors, sizes, and optional equipment. This results in added inventory items, more work in process inventory and finished subassemblies, and the need for tighter control.

Control of Obsolete and Surplus Inventory

Almost every organization is faced with the problem of surplus and obsolete inventory at one time or other. Whatever the many possible reasons for such conditions may be, some action is required to reduce or eliminate these items from inventory and free the related capital. To accomplish a reduction, management should first make certain that the buildup will not continue due to present ordering policies and, second, take steps to dispose of stock. Accurate perpetual inventory records showing acquisition and issue quantities and dates, as well as periodic review of the records, are necessary to identify obsolete and surplus items. Obsolete inventory usually results from changing a design or dropping a product. Prompt sale of the inventory for the first reasonable offer is usually the best policy.

DISCUSSION QUESTIONS

1. What data are needed in order to exercise effective management of materials cost and inventories?

2. What are some of the costs of not carrying enough inventory? How can these costs be measured?

3. Define and discuss the economic order quantity (EOQ) technique, including assumptions and accounting data used therein.

(AICPA adapted)

4. Inventories usually are an important asset for both manufacturing and merchandising firms. A proper balance of inventory quantities is desirable from several standpoints. Maintaining such a balance is dependent upon a number of factors, including ordering at the proper time and in the correct lot size. Serious penalties may result from both overstocking and stockout situations.

   (a) In connection with inventory ordering and control, certain terms are basic. Explain each of the following: (1) economic order quantity, (2) order point, (3) lead time, and (4) safety stock.

   (b) (1) What are the costs of carrying inventories? Explain. (2) How does overstocking add to the cost of carrying inventories?

   (c) (1) What are the consequences of maintaining minimal or inadequate inventory levels? (2) What are the difficulties of measuring precisely the costs associated with understocking?

   (d) Discuss the propriety of including carrying costs (of normal inventory, overstocking, and understocking) in the inventory cost (1) for external reporting and (2) for internal decision making.

(AICPA adapted)

5. When should inventory be ordered?

6. It is generally true that production and inventory management can be no better than the sales forecast. Name some techniques used to forecast sales.

7. An inventory planning and control system is designed to minimize the total cost of ordering and carrying inventory. Therefore, inventory control is good as long as the investment in inventory is declining. Discuss.

8. Is general management concerned primarily with unit control or financial control of inventory?

9. The control of materials must meet two opposing needs. What are they?

10. What are the principal differences in commonly used control plans?

11. The principle of "exception" should be utilized fully for effective materials control. Explain.

12. In what situation are selective control, automatic control, and bin control of materials effective?

13. What is the key to controlling finished goods inventory in a manufacturing company?

14. Select the answer which best completes the statement:

   (a) Expected annual usage of materials is 2,000,000 units, and the economic order quantity is 10,000 units. The invoice cost of each unit is $500, and the cost to place one purchase order is $80. The average inventory is: (1) 1,000,000 units; (2) 5,000 units; (3) 10,000 units; (4) 7,500 units.

   (b) Based on the information in (a), the estimated annual order cost is: (1) $16,000; (2) $100,000; (3) $32,000; (4) $50,000.

   (c) A sales office has developed the probabilities for daily sales of a perishable product as shown on page 372.

DAILY SALES	PROBABILITIES
100 units	.2
150	.5
200	.2
250	.1
	1.0

The product is restocked at the start of each day. If the company desires a 90% probability of satisfying sales demand, the initial stock balance for each day should be: (1) 250; (2) 160; (3) 200; (4) 150.

(d) Stewart Company has developed an inventory model for Product A and needs a solution for minimizing the total annual inventory cost. Included in A's inventory cost are the costs of holding, ordering and receiving, and incurring stockouts. The solution for minimizing inventory cost would state: (1) at what inventory level and how many units to reorder; (2) either at what inventory level or how many units to reorder; (3) how many units but not at what inventory level to reorder; (4) at what inventory level but not how many units to reorder.

(e) A company's treasurer complains about an excessive investment in inventories. At the same time, the purchasing agent states that large inventory balances are necessary to take advantage of supplier discounts, and the production manager complains that production often is delayed by inventory shortages. The quantitative technique most relevant to this situation is: (1) economic order quantity models; (2) linear programming; (3) payback analysis; (4) probability analysis.

(f) A company places orders for a certain item for which the order size is determined in advance, using the EOQ formula. All orders are the same size. When the policy is implemented, demand per period is only one half of the expected demand when order size was computed. Consequently, the actual total inventory cost will be: (1) larger than if the expected demand per period had occurred, and larger than if the actual demand per period had been used to calculate order size; (2) larger than if the expected demand per period had occurred, and smaller than if the actual demand per period had been used to calculate order size; (3) smaller than if the expected demand per period had occurred, and larger than if the actual demand per period had been used to calculate order size; (4) smaller than if the expected demand per period had occurred, and smaller than if the actual demand per period had been used to calculate order size.

(g) Ignoring safety stocks, a valid computation of the order point is: (1) the economic order quantity; (2) the economic order quantity multiplied by the anticipated demand during the lead time; (3) the anticipated demand during the lead time; (4) the square root of the anticipated demand during the lead time.

(h) For its economic order quantity model, a company has a cost of $10 for placing an order and an annual cost of $2 for carrying one unit in stock. If the cost of placing an order increases by 20%, the annual cost of carrying one unit in stock increases by 25%, and all other considerations remain constant, the economic order quantity will: (1) remain unchanged; (2) decrease; (3) increase; (4) either increase or decrease depending on the order point.

(i) The basic EOQ model assumes demand is determinable and the essence of the model is: (1) to minimize ordering cost or carrying cost and maximize the rate of inventory turnover; (2) to minimize ordering cost or carrying cost, whichever is higher; (3) to order sufficient quantity to meet the next period's demand economically; (4) to minimize the total ordering cost and carrying cost.

(j) In computing economic order quantity, a lifo or fifo inventory method will have the following result: (1) no effect; (2) lifo will increase the order quantity in times of rising prices; (3) lifo will reduce the order quantity in times of rising prices; (4) fifo will increase the order quantity in times of rising prices.

(k) A company has correctly computed its economic order quantity as 500 units. However, management feels it would rather order in quantities of 600 units. The company's total annual ordering cost and total annual carrying cost for an order quantity of 600 units compared to the respective amounts for an order quantity of 500 units would be: (1) a higher ordering cost and a higher carrying cost; (2) a lower ordering cost and a lower carrying cost; (3) a higher ordering cost and a lower carrying cost; (4) a lower ordering cost and a higher carrying cost.

(l) The following data refer to various annual costs relating to the inventory of a single-product company:

Annual interest that could have been earned on
   alternate investment of funds............................. $800
Units required during the year............................... 10,000

	VARIABLE COST PER UNIT
Transportation in on purchases.................	$.20
Storage..	.12
Insurance...	.10

The annual carrying cost per unit is: (1) $.22; (2) $.30; $.42; (4) $.50.

(m) A company has assembled the following data for a given year:

Economic order quantity (standard order
   size) .... 5,000 units
Total cost to place purchase orders for
   the year.. $10,000
Cost to place one purchase order.............. 50
Cost to carry one unit for one year............. 4

Estimated annual usage in units is: (1) 1,000,000; (2) 2,000,000; (3) 4,000,000; (4) not determinable from the data given.

(AICPA adapted)

EXERCISES

1. Planning materials requirements. A company's production schedule calls for 2,300 units of Material A for January operations, 2,100 units for February, and 2,500 units for March. On January 1, the inventory of Material A is 2,000 units; 2,300 units are on order for January delivery and 2,100 units for February delivery. A minimum reserve of 72% of the January 1 inventory is to be maintained throughout the remainder of the year.

Required:
(1) The number of units of Material A to order for March delivery, as of January 1.
(2) The estimated quantity on hand on March 1 and on March 31.

2. Usage forecast and inventory balances. On September 1, a materials analyst is asked to deter-mine the number of units of Material X to order for November delivery. The production schedule calls for 3,500 units of this material for September operations, 2,500 units in October, and 3,600 units in November. On September 1, the inventory shows 4,000 units on hand, 2,000 units on order for September delivery, and 3,000 units on order for October delivery. A 2,000-unit minimum re-serve inventory is maintained.

Required:
(1) Quantity to order for November delivery.
(2) The number of units on hand on (a) November 1 and (b) November 30, if the planned usage occurs and outstanding orders are received on expected delivery dates.

3. Computations and applications of the EOQ formula. (Round off all answers to the nearest whole number.)

(a) Shilders, Inc., has an annual usage of 100 units of Item M with a purchase price of $55 per unit. The following data are applicable to Item M:

Ordering cost.. $5 per order
Carrying cost percentage 15%

Required: The economic order quantity.

(b) Henry Company has developed the following information for one of its inventory items: units required per year, 30,000; cost of placing an order, $400; unit carrying cost per year, $600.

Required: The economic order quantity.

(c) Modern Equipment Company estimates a need for 9,000 Ajets next year at a cost of $3 per unit. The estimated carrying cost is 20%, and the cost to place an order is $12.

Required: The most economical number of units to order at one time.

(d) Trefoil, Inc., requires 27,000 containers next year at a list price of $12 per container. The estimated carrying cost is 25% of average inventory, and the cost to place an order is $20.

Required: The most economical number of units to order at one time.

(e) The Shubert Company estimates that it will need 12,500 cartons next year at a cost of $8 per carton. The estimated carrying cost is 25% of average inventory investment, and the cost to place an order is $20.

Required:
(1) The most economical number of units to order.
(2) The frequency in days that orders should be placed, based on a 365-day year.

(f) Bradley Sporting Goods, Inc., buys baseballs at $20 per dozen from its wholesaler. Bradley will sell 36,000 dozen baseballs evenly throughout the year. The firm desires a 10% return on its average inventory investment. In addition, rent, insurance, and property tax for each dozen baseballs in the average inventory is $.40. The cost involved in handling each pur-chase order is $10.

Required:
(1) The economic order quantity.
(2) The total annual inventory expense to sell 36,000 dozen baseballs if orders are placed at 800 dozen evenly throughout the year.

(g) Pierce Company annually manufactures 10,000 blades for its electric lawn mower division. Blades are used evenly throughout the year. The setup cost each time a production run is made is $80, and the cost to carry a blade in inventory is $.40. Management's objective is to produce the blades at the lowest possible cost.

Required: The most economical number of annual production runs if each run is scheduled for the same number of blades.

    (h) A customer has been ordering 5,000 specially designed metal columns at the rate of 1,000 per order during the past year. The variable production cost is $8 per unit: $6 for materials and labor, and $2 for factory overhead. It costs $1,500 to set up for one run of 1,000 columns, and the inventory carrying cost is 20%. Since this customer may buy at least 5,000 columns per year, the company would like to avoid making five different production runs.

Required: The most economical production run.

    (i) Nussbaum, Inc., manufactures a line of walnut office products. Management estimates the demand for the double walnut letter tray at 6,000 units. The tray sells for $80. The costs relating to the letter tray are: manufacturing cost per tray, $50; cost to initiate a production run, $300; annual cost of carrying the tray in inventory, 20% of manufacturing cost. In prior years, the production for the tray has been scheduled in two equal production runs.

Required: The expected annual cost savings the company could experience if it employed the economic order quantity model to determine the number of production runs which should be initiated during the year. (CMA adapted)

4. Cost resulting from inability to use EOQ. The Electro Company manufactures some of its product lines from raw materials, and for other products assembles purchased parts. For one product, 10,000 subassembled parts at $100 each are purchased annually. The per order and receiving cost is $200, and the carrying cost is 25%.

This is only one of many inventory items the firm must carry, and a capital rationing decision has been made to spend only $10,000 at a time on these subassemblies. Units must be ordered in multiples of 100.

Required:
    (1) Computation of the EOQ.
    (2) The opportunity loss expressed as carrying cost by changing the EOQ and inventory level to the availability of capital.

5. Order point, inventory levels, ordering cost. The Western-Colorado Company has developed the following data to assist in controlling one of its inventory items:

Economic order quantity..............	1 000 liters
Average daily use..........................	100 liters
Minimum daily use........................	80 liters
Maximum daily use	120 liters
Working days per year..................	250 days
Safety stock	400 liters
Cost of carrying inventory............	$1.00 per liter per year
Lead time	7 working days

Required:
    (1) Order point.
    (2) Average inventory.
    (3) Normal maximum inventory.
    (4) Absolute maximum inventory.
    (5) Cost of placing one order.   (CGAA adapted)

6. Economic order quantity, order point, safety stock. The Bolger Company has obtained the following costs and other data pertaining to one of its materials:

Working days per year...	250
Normal use per day..	500 units
Maximum use per day	600 units
Minimum use per day...	100 units
Lead time...	5 days
Variable cost of placing one order......................	$36
Variable carrying cost per unit per year.............	$ 1

Required:
  (1) Economic order quantity.
  (2) Safety stock (maximum).
  (3) Order point.
  (4) Normal maximum inventory.
  (5) Absolute maximum inventory.
  (6) Average inventory, assuming normal lead time and usage.   (CGAA adapted)

7. Safety stock. Harrington & Sons, Inc., would like to determine the safety stock to maintain for a product, so that the lowest combination of stockout cost and carrying cost would result. Each stockout will cost $75; the carrying cost for each safety stock unit will be $1; the product will be ordered five times a year. The following probabilities of running out of stock during an order period are associated with various safety stock levels:

SAFETY STOCK LEVEL	PROBABILITY OF STOCKOUT
10 units	40%
20	20
40	10
80	5

Required: Combined stockout and safety stock carrying cost associated with each level and the recommended level of safety stock.   (AICPA adapted)

8. ABC plan of control. Memphis Industries, Inc., is considering a system of selective control of materials, using the following data:

MATERIALS STOCK NO.	QUARTERLY USAGE IN UNITS	UNIT COST	TOTAL COST
115.24	2,000	$20.00	$ 40,000
115.25	20,400	.25	5,100
115.26	5,600	10.50	58,800
115.27	1,000	30.00	30,000
115.28	18,600	1.00	18,600
115.29	7,560	2.50	18,900
115.30	8,880	3.25	28,860
115.31	4,920	2.00	9,840
115.32	6,840	2.00	13,680
115.33	30,000	.50	15,000
115.34	9,980	1.50	14,970
115.35	8,220	2.50	20,550
Total	124,000		$274,300

Required:
  (1) An arrangement of the data for presentation to management, assuming that the ABC plan of selective control is indicated. (Round off all percentages to two decimal places.)
  (2) A graph to depict the situation.

9. Graphing ABC inventory items. An inventory management group decided to classify and group the items in an inventory by ranking them according to their revenue-producing potentials, since a major portion of sales dollar volume is contributed by a relatively small percentage of items. Based on the ABC plan of selective control, the group established the following volume-cost inventory pattern:

VOLUME-COST GROUP	NUMBER OF ITEMS	PERCENT OF TOTAL NUMBER OF ITEMS	PERCENT OF SALES VOLUME CONTRIBUTED
A	480	23%	78%
B	250	12	12
C	1,370	65	10
Total	2,100	100%	100%

Required: A graph based on the above analysis.

PROBLEMS

13-1. Economic order quantity and quantity discount. McCormick Company, a regional supermarket chain, orders 480,000 cans of frozen orange juice per year from a California distributor. A 24-can case of frozen juice delivered to McCormick's central warehouse costs $4.80, including freight charges. The company borrows funds at a 10% interest rate to finance its inventories.

The McCormick Company's purchasing agent has calculated that it costs $15 to place an order for frozen juice and that the annual variable storage expense (electricity, insurance, handling) is $.08 for each can of juice.

Required:
    (1) The number of cases of frozen juice that McCormick Company should request in each order.
    (2) The order-size decision McCormick should make if the California distributor offers a 10% discount off the delivery price for minimum orders of 72,000 cans.

                                              (CGAA adapted)

13-2. EOQ formula and safety stock. Powell Company sells a number of products to many restaurants in the area. One product is a special meat cutter with a disposable blade. Blades are sold in a package of 12 at $20 per package. It has been determined that the demand for the replacement blades is at a constant rate of 2,000 packages per month. The packages cost the company $10 each from the manufacturer and require a three-day lead time from date of order to date of delivery. The ordering cost is $1.20 per order, and the carrying cost is 10% per annum. The company uses the economic order quantity formula.

Required:
    (1) The economic order quantity.
    (2) The number of orders needed per year.
    (3) The total cost of ordering and carrying blades for the year.
    (4) The date on which the next order should be placed, assuming that there is no reserve (safety stock) and that the present inventory level is 200 packages. (360 days = 1 year.)
    (5) Discussion of the difficulties that most firms would have in attempting to apply the EOQ formula to their inventory problems.

                                              (CMA adapted)

13-3. Establishing safety stock. The Heusen Products Company has been experiencing stockouts on one of its important materials, even though deliveries are dependable within one month from the date of an order. Management asks that a safety stock for this item be established and provides the following record of actual and forecast usage during the past nine months.

MONTH	USAGE	FORECAST	MONTH	USAGE	FORECAST
January..................	475	490	June........................	520	510
February...............	480	490	July.........................	500	510
March	490	475	August....................	490	510
April........................	500	485	September	485	500
May........................	510	500			

It is believed that a 97.5% protection against a stockout is adequate.

Required:
    (1) A schedule showing the safety stock required, using the statistical method. (Round off all amounts to two decimal places.)
    (2) The safety stock required if the normal lead time is two months.

13-4. Order point; safety stock using probabilities. The Starr Company manufactures several products, one of which requires an electric motor. The EOQ formula is used to determine the optimum number of motors to order. Management now wants to determine the required safety stock quantity.

Starr uses 30,000 electric motors annually (300 working days). Using the EOQ formula, the company orders 3,000 motors at a time. The lead time for an order is five days. The annual cost of carrying one motor in safety stock is $10. Management estimates that the cost of being out of stock is $20 for each motor.

The company has analyzed usage during past reorder periods by examining the inventory records which indicate the following usage patterns:

Usage During Lead Time	Number of Times Quantity Was Used
440 units	6
460	12
480	16
500	130
520	20
540	10
560	6
	200

Required:
(1) Order point, disregarding a safety stock allowance.
(2) The level of safety stock of electric motors in order to minimize annual stockout and carrying costs, using probabilities.
(3) The order point, including a safety stock allowance.
(4) Factors Starr Company should have considered in estimating stockout cost.

(CMA adapted)

13-5. Comparison of order quantity methods. Verdon Electronics, Inc., a small manufacturer of electronic instruments, has found that 20% of its inventory items account for 76% of total annual dollar usage and that 50% of its inventory items account for only 6% of total annual dollar usage. Its major competitor applies the ABC item-dollar value concept in determining order quantities in the following manner:

Inventory Category	Percentage of Inventory Items	Order Quantity
A	20%	1 month's usage
B	30	2 months' usage
C	50	6 months' usage

Verdon Electronics' industrial engineers contend that such rules of thumb are quite arbitrary and that more precise techniques are warranted. Their case is supported by the application of the EOQ formula to the following two sets of assumptions:

	High-Dollar Usage Item	Low-Dollar Usage Item
Ordering cost per order...	$5	$5
Inventory carrying cost per year per dollar of inventory...	$.20	$.20
Total yearly usage..	1,200 units	1,200 units
Purchase cost per unit of the item	$20	$.05

Required: The economic order quantity (to the nearest whole number) for the high-dollar and low-dollar usage item and comparison with the order quantities used by the company's competitor.

13-6. EOQ; order point; graphic illustration of materials management. The new financial vice-president of Titan Products Corporation is directing an intensive analysis of working capital management. The objective is to attain more efficient resource allocation and higher earnings from each dollar of assets.

Materials cost of one important manufactured product is $12 per unit; sales average 100 units per month; and the lead time is one month. Calculations show that the variable cost of placing an order and handling the incoming shipment is $50, and the cost of holding units in stock is 25% of the average inventory.

Required:
   (1) The economic order quantity.
   (2) The order point.
   (3) A graphic presentation of materials management.

13-7. Optimum production run size. A manufacturer expects to produce 200,000 Widgets during the year ending June 30, to supply a demand which is uniform throughout the year. The setup cost for each production run of Widgets is $144 and the variable cost of producing each Widget is $5. The cost of carrying one Widget in inventory is $.20 per year. After a batch of Widgets is produced and placed in inventory, it is sold at a uniform rate, and inventory is exhausted when the next batch of Widgets is completed.

Management would like to have an equation to describe the above situation and determine the optimal quantity of Widgets in each production run in order to minimize total production and inventory carrying costs.

   Let: AC = Total annual cost of producing and carrying Widgets in inventory.
   X = Number of Widgets to be produced in each production run.

Required:
   (1) The number of production runs to be made during the fiscal year.
   (2) The total setup cost for the fiscal year.
   (3) The total cost of carrying inventory during the fiscal year.
   (4) The derivation, $\dfrac{dAC}{dX}$, of the equation which determines the optimal quantity of Widgets produced during each production run in the fiscal year.
   (5) The quantity of Widgets (to the nearest whole number) that should be produced in each production run in the fiscal year in order to minimize total cost.

(AICPA adapted)

CASES

A. Improving materials control procedures. A small company manufacturing various commodities for stock, and to a lesser extent for special orders, is faced with difficulties in its materials control procedures.

Under the present system, materials are requested from the storekeeper by production supervisors according to their work needs. Materials requisitions signed by a supervisor and identifying the production or lot number to which they relate are used. The purchasing agent, who is also office manager, orders regular stock items upon notice from the materials ledger clerk that a particular item has reached the order point. Incoming materials are checked in by the storekeeper, who prepares a daily report of materials received.

One of the major difficulties has been coordinating purchasing with accounting. In addition to the purchasing agent, the plant superintendent and some of the supervisors are free to order, especially when supplies and parts are needed which are not regularly carried in the storeroom. As a result of purchases by the superintendent and supervisors, frequently no document for the order is available when a vendor's invoice is received. When goods do not meet specifications, the person upon whose request the goods were ordered proceeds to return the goods to the vendor, and, generally, the Accounting Department is not notified. Sometimes a payment is made for goods which have been returned.

Required: Comments on the basic difficulties in the company's control procedures, and recommended corrective measures.

B. Estimating ordering and carrying costs. Evans, Inc., a large wholesale distributor, deals exclusively in baby shoes. Due to substantial ordering and storing costs, management decided to use the EOQ model to help determine the optimum quantities to order from the different manufacturers. To use the EOQ model, values for two of the costs, ordering cost and carrying cost, must be developed.

As a starting point, management has decided to develop values for the two costs by using cost data from the most recent fiscal year. The company had placed 4,000 purchase orders during the year, the largest of which was 400 orders in June and the smallest, 250 in December. Selected cost data for these two months and for the year were:

	COST FOR HIGH ACTIVITY MONTH (JUNE — 400 ORDERS)	COST FOR LOW ACTIVITY MONTH (DECEMBER — 250 ORDERS)	ANNUAL COST
Purchasing Department:			
Purchasing manager............	$ 1,750	$ 1,750	$ 21,000
Buyers	2,500	1,900	28,500
Clerks	2,000	1,100	20,600
Supplies	275	150	2,500
Accounts Payable Department:			
Clerks	2,000	1,500	21,500
Supplies	125	75	1,100
Data processing...................	2,600	2,300	30,000
Warehouse:			
Supervisor...........................	1,250	1,250	15,000
Receiving clerks..................	2,300	1,800	23,300
Receiving supplies	50	25	500
Shipping clerks....................	3,800	3,500	44,000
Shipping supplies................	1,350	1,200	15,200
Freight out	1,600	1,300	16,800
Total.................................	$21,600	$17,850	$240,000

The Purchasing Department is responsible for placing all orders. The costs listed for the Accounts Payable Department relate only to the processing of purchase orders for payment. The Warehouse costs reflect two operations, receiving and shipping. The receiving clerks inspect all incoming shipments and place the orders in storage. The shipping clerks are responsible for processing all sales orders to retailers.

The company leases space in a public warehouse where the rental fee is priced according to the square feet occupied during a month. The annual charges during the year totaled $34,500. Annual insurance and property tax on the shoes stored in the warehouse were $5,700 and $7,300, respectively. The company pays 8% a year for a small amount of short-term, seasonal bank debt. Long-term capital investments are expected to produce a rate of return of 12% after income tax; the effective income tax rate is 40%.

The inventory balances tend to fluctuate during the year, depending upon the demand for baby shoes. Selected data on inventory balances for the year are:

Inventory, January 1..	$160,000
Inventory, December 31......................................	120,000
Highest inventory balance (June)......................	220,000
Lowest inventory balance (December)..............	120,000
Average monthly inventory	190,000

The boxes in which the baby shoes are stored are all approximately the same size and occupy about the same amount of storage space in the warehouse.

Required:
    (1) Estimated values appropriate for:
        (a) Cost of placing an order (CO).
        (b) Annual carrying cost per dollar of average investment in inventory (CC).
    (2) An explanation as to whether the costs should be developed solely from the historical data used in the EOQ model.   (CMA adapted)

C. Economic order quantity; inventory control. LASI Automobile Supply is both a retail and wholesale auto supply business, selling engine repair parts and a line of accessories. The company also operates a paint and body shop and installs mufflers, shock absorbers, and tail pipes.

Six months ago, LASI was contacted by a national manufacturer of automotive glass about the possibility of becoming an area wholesale distributor of curved windshields. The distributorship was accepted primarily to supply area garages, but soon windshield replacement became a feature of the body shop.

Deciding between weekly and monthly ordering of windshields, the company's accountant obtained the following information:

    (a) Insurance, storage, and handling costs of the windshields are estimated at $432 per year.

    (b) LASI should sell about 300 windshields per month, combining installations in its own shop and sales to repair shops.

    (c) Delivered price of the windshields to LASI is $45 each.

    (d) An agreement between the manufacturer and LASI requires an average inventory of 60 units.

    (e) Cost of placing an order is $15.

Required:

    (1) Advice on the quantity and frequency of orders.

    (2) Recommended procedure for controlling the inventory to assure ordering only those windshields needed to replace the models sold.

14

Controlling and Accounting for Labor Costs

Labor cost represents the human contribution to production and is an important cost factor requiring constant measurement, control, and analysis. The economic advantage of increased production at lower unit costs, along with rising wage rates and ever-increasing fringe benefits, has accelerated the trend toward greater use of automatic equipment to produce more goods in fewer labor hours. Changes in the utilization of a labor force often require changes in methods of compensating labor, followed by changes in accounting for labor costs.

All wage payments are, in the last analysis, directly or indirectly based on and limited by the productivity and skill of the worker. Therefore, proper motivation, control, and accounting for this human cost factor is one of the most important problems in the management of an enterprise. A cooperative and enthusiastic labor force, loyal to the company and its policies, can contribute greatly toward efficient, low-cost operations. Wages are only one element in employer-employee relations, however. Adequate records, easily understood and readily available, are an equally important factor in harmonious relations between management, employees, labor unions, government agencies, and the general public.

BASIS FOR LABOR COST CONTROL

Labor cost control is based on pertinent and timely information transmitted to management. Top executives are often primarily interested in the ratio

382

of labor cost to total cost and in changes in the labor cost ratio. A plant superintendent needs to know details of the labor cost by departments, product lines, by direct and indirect workers, and by jobs or processes. Shop supervisors need similar detailed information applicable to their jurisdiction.

Cost control is often described as an attitude or state of mind as much as an activity. Labor cost control begins with an adequate production planning schedule supported by labor-hour requirements and accompanying labor costs, determined well in advance of production runs. In most manufacturing plants, it is usually possible to establish a reasonably accurate ratio of direct labor hours and number of employees to dollar sales by product lines, and, by relating this ratio to the sales forecast, to predict future labor requirements. The relationship between sales volume and personnel needs is perhaps more direct and predictable in wholesale, retail, financial, and service enterprises. Effective labor cost control is achieved through (1) production planning, (2) use of labor budgets and labor time and wage standards, (3) labor performance reports, and (4) appropriate payment for labor, including wage incentive systems.

PRODUCTIVITY AND EFFICIENCY MEASUREMENT AND LABOR COSTS

Productivity may be defined as the measurement of production performance using the expenditure of human effort as a yardstick. It is the amount of goods and services a worker produces. Perhaps productivity could also be described as the efficiency with which resources are converted into commodities and/or services. Greater productivity can be achieved by better processes, improved or modern equipment, or any other factor that improves the utilization of manpower. When productivity increases, business profits and the real earnings of workers should also increase.

Control of labor costs requires a standard of performance to measure the productivity and efficiency of the work performed and to appraise the differences between expectation and accomplishment. The objective of productivity measurement is to provide management with a concise and accurate index for the comparison of actual results with a standard of performance. Productivity measurement should recognize the individual contribution of factors such as employees (including management), plant and equipment used in production, products and services utilized in production, capital invested, and government services utilized (as indicated by taxes). However, in many productivity statistics, particularly those developed by the Bureau of Labor Statistics of the U.S. Department of Labor, the measurement takes into account only one element of input — labor. It ignores such essential factors as capital and land, thereby assigning the cause of changes in productive efficiency solely to the labor input factor.

At their best, productivity measurement ratios are crude statistical devices. The most generally utilized measurement has been physical output per labor hour — a term considered more descriptive than labor productivity.

The Importance of Measuring Productivity and Efficiency

In today's economy, the need for more and better goods at the lowest possible cost requires greater productivity per labor hour. This does not mean that workers will have to work harder physically, but that management and labor should employ ingenuity and inventive ability to develop methods, machines, and materials that will reduce the number of labor hours required to make a product. This requirement leads to the question: "What is a fair (or standard) day's work?" In many organizations, time studies conducted by industrial engineers provide the answer to this question. A fair day's work is the amount of work expected of an individual in return for the base rate or guaranteed hourly wage. With an incentive wage system, a worker is paid in proportion to output beyond the standard of performance.

Setting a standard of performance is not an easy task, since it is often accompanied by serious disputes between management and labor unions. The pace at which the observed person is working is noted and referred to as a *rating* or *performance rating*. The rating factor is applied to the selected task to obtain a *normal time*, i.e., the time it should take a person working at a normal pace to do the job. Allowances are added for personal time, rest periods, and possible delays. The final result is the *standard time* for the job, expressed in minutes per piece or in units to be produced per hour.

The *productivity-efficiency* ratio measures the output of an individual, relative to the performance standard. This ratio can also be used to measure the relative operating achievement of a machine, an operation, a department, or an entire organization.

Departmental ratios, such as the labor efficiency ratio, assist in judging the efficiency of department heads and supervisors. A *labor efficiency ratio* usually expresses the relative difference or variance between actual hours worked and standard hours allowed for the work performed. For example, if 4,000 hours is standard and if 4,400 hours are used, then there is an unfavorable labor efficiency ratio of 110% (4,400 ÷ 4,000), which indicates that actual labor hours exceeded the standard hours by 10%. If the standard cost for 4,000 hours is $28,000, then the labor efficiency variance is $2,800 (10% × $28,000). The relationship can also be expressed as a ratio of standard labor hours to actual labor hours, which results in an unfavorable labor efficiency ratio of 90.9% (4,000 ÷ 4,400). If 4,400 actual labor hours at the $7 standard rate per hour cost $30,800, the unfavorable labor efficiency variance is approximately $2,800 [(100.0% − 90.9%) × $30,800].

The calculation of labor cost variances is discussed in detail in Chapter 19. At this point it is sufficient to indicate that, based on the above data and on an actual labor rate of $7.25 per hour, the variance analysis would be:

4,400 actual labor hours at $7.25 per hour	$31,900
4,400 actual labor hours at $7 per hour	30,800
Labor rate variance (unfavorable)...	$ 1,100
4,400 actual labor hours at $7 per hour	$30,800
4,000 standard labor hours at $7 per hour	28,000
Labor efficiency variance (unfavorable).......................................	$ 2,800

Base Rate (or Job Rate)

The basic pay for work performed is called the *base rate* or *job rate*. A base rate should be established for each operation in a plant or office and grouped by class of operation. The establishment of equitable compensation for the performance of each occupation and operation in a plant or office is not a simple task. An equitable wage rate or salary structure requires an analysis, description, and evaluation of each job within the plant or office. The value of all jobs must relate to wages and salaries paid for similar work in the community and in the industry or business as a whole. Maintaining competitive wage rates and salaries facilitates the acquisition and retention of quality personnel.

Fringe Costs

Base wages or salaries do not comprise the entire labor cost picture. Supplements, sometimes called *fringe costs* (or fringes), also form a substantial element of labor cost. Fringe costs, such as FICA tax, unemployment taxes, holiday pay, vacation pay, overtime premium pay, pension costs, and cost of living adjustments, must be added to the base rate in order to arrive at the full labor cost. While these fringe costs are generally included in the factory overhead rate, they should not be overlooked in management's planning and control responsibilities, in decision-making analyses, or in labor-management wage arbitration sessions. Workers' demands for a 50¢ per hour increase in pay may result in far greater expenditures by the company when related fringe costs are considered.

LABOR PERFORMANCE REPORTS

Production schedules, performance standards, and labor budgets represent plans and expectations; but effective control of labor efficiency and costs depends upon meaningful and timely performance reports sent to department heads and supervisors who are directly responsible for departmental production. Labor performance reports are designed to compare budgets and standards with actual results attained, thereby pointing to variances from planned performance. The departmental direct labor cost report on page 386, the plant-wide labor cost report issued weekly or monthly, the daily performance report for labor, and the daily idle time reports (page 387) illustrate media used to provide supervisors and plant managers with information needed for effective cost control.

In the report appearing below, the expected direct labor cost for the week is computed from the October labor budget, shown at the bottom of the page, for the Cooler Assembly Department. For example, in motor assembling, the Cooler Assembly Department produced 600 units of Model No. 625 requiring 1.5 hours of budgeted labor per unit, 800 units of Model No. 500 with 1.5 hours of budgeted labor per unit, and 500 units of Model No. 600 with 1.3 hours of budgeted labor per unit; a total of 2,750 budgeted labor hours @ $6 per hour for a total of $16,500.

DEPARTMENTAL DIRECT LABOR COST REPORT

Department __Cooler Assembly__   Supervisor __H. Stevenson__

Production __No. 625--600 units__   Week Ending __October 12, 19--__

__No. 500--800 units__

__No. 660--500 units__

Operation	Actual Cost	Budgeted Cost	Variance	Reasons
Motor.........	$16,925.00	$16,500.00	$425 over 2.6%	Reboring hangers
Fan...........	3,000.00	3,060.00	60 under 2.0%	Good group
Freon.........	5,675.00	5,220.00	455 over 8.7%	Overtime and reweld
Total...	$25,600.00	$24,780.00	$820 over	

LABOR BUDGET

Department __Cooler Assembly__   For __October, 19--__

          Prepared __September 10, 19--__

Model No. or Job No.	Units Scheduled	Budgeted Assembly Hours per Unit			Total Budgeted Direct Labor Hours
		Motor	Fan	Freon	
625	2,000	1.5	.25	.5	4,500
748	1,000	1.5	.30	.6	2,400
500	3,000	1.5	.20	.4	6,300
600	1,500	1.3	.40	.5	3,300
	7,500				16,500

Variable and Fixed Costs	Total Cost	Cost per Unit	No. of Employees*
Variable costs:			
Direct labor -- 16,500 hrs. @ $6	$ 99,000	$13.200	94
Indirect labor -- 1,000 hrs. @ $4.80	4,800	.640	6
Total variable labor budget	$103,800	$13.840	
Fixed costs:			
Supervision -- 700 hrs. @ $7	$ 4,900	$ .653	4
Clerical & Packing -- 350 hrs. @ $4.60 ..	1,610	.215	2
Total fixed labor budget	$ 6,510	$ .868	___
Total for October	$110,310	$14.708	106

*No. of hrs. ÷ 176 (22 days x 8 hrs.)

The plant-wide labor cost report below is sent to executive and plant management to indicate (1) the trend of direct and indirect labor cost in the three departments and (2) the actual cost compared with the estimated cost figures.

LABOR COST REPORT		Actual Labor Cost			Estimated Labor Cost		
Plant Midville							
Week Ending October 12, 19--							
Department	Labor Class	This Week	Last Week	Year to Date	This Week	Last Week	Year to Date
Cutting	Direct....	$28,500	$28,200	$1,174,380	$28,200	$28,000	$1,172,500
	Indirect..	2,200	2,250	81,640	2,240	2,200	81,800
	Total..	$30,700	$30,450	$1,256,020	$30,440	$30,200	$1,254,300
Forming	Direct....	$13,600	$13,400	$ 430,525	$13,750	$13,450	$ 431,000
	Indirect..	1,600	1,600	65,600	1,600	1,620	65,700
	Total..	$15,200	$15,000	$ 496,125	$15,350	$15,070	$ 496,700
Cooler Assembly	Direct....	$25,600	$26,100	$1,152,250	$24,780	$24,000	$1,150,000
	Indirect..	2,825	2,800	117,880	2,750	2,750	117,000
	Total..	$28,425	$28,900	$1,270,130	$27,530	$26,750	$1,267,000

The daily performance report for labor and the daily idle time report[1] below combine three types of daily labor reports: (1) employee performance, (2) departmental performance, and (3) idle time. Physical factors such as hours are coupled with percentages to improve the effectiveness of these reports.

DAILY PERFORMANCE REPORT FOR LABOR

Daily Performance Report by Employees				Daily Performance Report by Departments			
Employee No.	Actual Producing Hours	Standard Hours of Output	Percent Performance	Department	Actual Producing Hours	Standard Hours of Output	Percent Performance
105	8	10	125.0	1	110	90	81.8
110	6	7	116.7	2	280	300	107.1
112	5	4	80.0	3	150	145	96.7

DAILY IDLE TIME REPORT

Department	Total Direct Labor Hours	Productive Direct Labor Hours		Idle Time Due To							
				Maintenance		No Materials		Other		Total	
		Amount	%	Amount	%	Amount	%	Amount	%	Amount	%
1	3,200	2,900	90.6	200	6.2	50	1.6	50	1.6	300	9.4
2	1,300	1,200	92.3	25	1.9	25	1.9	50	3.9	100	7.7
3	600	550	91.7	20	3.3	30	5.0			50	8.3
4	200	180	90.0	10	5.0			10	5.0	20	10.0
Total	5,300	4,830	91.1	255	4.8	105	2.0	110	2.1	470	8.9

[1]William L. Ferrara, "An Integrated Approach to Control of Production Costs," *NAA Bulletin*, Vol. XLI, No. 9, p. 65.

The daily efficiency report, illustrated below, is designed for and issued to shop superintendents to help maintain schedules that depend greatly upon the utmost efficiency of shop personnel. The report shows actual hours, standard hours, and the percent of efficiency of each group.

		DAILY EFFICIENCY REPORT						Date: 5/17/-- Issued: 5/18/--
		Daily Hours		Cumulative Hours		Efficiency %*		
Group	Group Name	Actual	Standard	Actual	Standard	Daily	Cumulative	Remarks
0501	Handling Labor & Mat.	153.1	172.6	752.3	811.9	112.7	107.9	
1001	Shipping	133.6	174.3	1883.2	2604.6	130.5	138.3	
	Total -- Todd Division	291.7	346.9	2635.5	3416.5	118.9	129.6	
5001	Dimension Mill #1	75.6	270.6	1028.7	1044.2	357.9	101.5	
5101	Machine Room #1	16.1	17.1	305.6	341.0	106.2	111.6	
5102	Dimension Mill #2	55.1	72.0	449.5	560.7	130.7	124.7	
5103	Machine Room #2	155.1	174.5	988.7	906.2	112.5	91.7	
5201	Wood Subassembly	148.1	210.8	1153.7	1106.7	142.3	95.9	
5701	Insulation	50.0	44.9	625.9	702.3	89.8	112.2	
8407	Door Frame Paint	11.0	2.4	96.7	47.0	21.8	48.6	

*Standard ÷ Actual

THE COMPUTER'S CONTRIBUTION TO LABOR COST CONTROL

Whenever large numbers of hourly workers perform standardized labor tasks, a computer program can calculate and report each worker's daily earnings and efficiency. Because such a report is too voluminous and impractical for a plant manager or supervisor to use, one procedure is to program for significant unfavorable shifts in performance from one day to the next. This type of report provides for management by exception, whereby the supervisor can work to correct problems of a very few workers and prevent chronic difficulties. With a work force of five hundred employees, a daily report from the computer, identifying significant adverse changes, might appear as shown below. The report is focused on adverse changes in performance from the workers' historical pattern. For example, Perez is a highly efficient performer, but the 81% efficiency rate seems too low for this worker; and management has an opportunity to take early corrective action if needed.

	EMPLOYEE PERFORMANCE REPORT (Significant Adverse Change)								May 19, 19--
Employee	% Efficiency Last Month			% Efficiency Yesterday	Previous Five Days % Efficiency					Number of Times Reported This Month
	Low	High	Average							
BOWAN, T.	72%	84%	78%	64%	76	79	83	81	78	1
DURAM, A.	75	91	83	69	71	73	85	90	90	2
GORDON, E.	70	78	74	31	76	71	75	78	74	1
HOESL, A.	62	88	75	56	80	84	76	65	87	3
PEREZ, G.	86	98	92	81	85	93	97	94	92	1

With daily efficiency performances in computer storage, management can be provided with monthly or quarterly reports on chronically low efficiency workers. The following illustration is indicative of the information needed to increase effectiveness in labor utilization and labor cost control. Even with no knowledge of the situation, a reading of the illustration suggests that Asbury, Clarke, and probably Varney are not likely to be satisfactory workers in this department if 75% of the standard rate is considered minimal. Dettmer and Mayes appear to be new employees and seem to be improving, while Shaw appears capable of attaining the desired productivity level.

EMPLOYEE PERFORMANCE REPORT
(Chronically Low Performance)   November 30, 19--

Employee	% Efficiency Last 12 Months			% Efficiency This Month	Previous Five Months % Efficiency	Number of Times Reported This Year
	Low	High	Average			
ASBURY, M.	33%	43%	38%	40%	42 49 43 51 46	6
CLARKE, G.	42	58	50	52	56 45 51 45 51	7
DETTMER, C.	58	74	66	71	70 68 66 58 63	3
MAYES, W.	60	66	63	66	64 60 56 54 50	2
SHAW, T.	70	84	77	68	70 75 68 75 80	5
VARNEY, M.	45	73	59	64	60 65 68 66 64	4

Effective control is best achieved by careful use of comparisons between actual performance and predetermined standards of performance. Daily or weekly comparisons may be in aggregate (i.e., by department or division), or they may be made for each employee. Departmental labor cost reports can be combined to form a plant summary of operating performance, which is most useful to the plant superintendent and other production officials.

PRODUCTIVITY, INFLATION, AND PRICES

In recent years the topic of inflation has received ever-increasing coverage from TV and news publications, leading to a mounting public and political interest. Inflation erodes the value of savings, reduces purchasing power, and creates serious disparities between individuals on fixed incomes and workers receiving steady pay increases. Some wage earners, whose wages rise faster than prices, are less affected by this inflationary spiral. Individuals whose incomes do not rise as fast as prices are forced to curb their spending habits.

In recent years, productivity has generally been increasing, resulting in more available goods and services. However, the normal productivity gain has fallen below the average gain of the previous decade. Gains in real living standards must come primarily from improved productivity. Without gains in productivity, improvement in real incomes for some citizens can come only at the expense of others.

The slowdown has given rise to increased costs. Whenever output does not keep pace with costs, unit costs — and, therefore, prices — go up. Wage increases, often excessive, have been a significant factor in this wage-price spiral because labor cost forms such a large part of total cost. If prices are to be kept from rising, then wage increases should not exceed an amount that will cause further increases in unit costs. In recent years, employment costs — wages, salaries, and fringes — have risen more than output or production per labor hour, leading to higher prices to meet higher unit labor costs. In some cases, labor cost increased when output per labor hour actually dropped.

To offset or curtail the wage-price spiral requires (1) increased productivity reflected in lower prices rather than higher wages, so that everyone may benefit; (2) wages held at a level that will not cause higher labor cost per unit of product; and (3) reduction in governmental deficit financing.

ORGANIZATION FOR LABOR COST CONTROL

To achieve labor cost control, other departments and functions besides the accounting department are involved, such as personnel, time and motion study, production planning, budgeting, and timekeeping. In fact, the entire control process begins with the design of the product and continues as a cooperative activity until the product is sold.

Personnel Department

The chief function of a personnel department is to provide an efficient labor force. In a general way, this department is responsible for seeing that an entire organization follows good personnel policies; but very little of the real personnel work is done by employees of the personnel department. Personnel relations are personal relations — between department heads and their subordinates, between supervisors and workers, and among all employees.

Personnel functions, dealing with the human resources of the organization, involve recruiting and employment procedures, training programs, job descriptions, job evaluations, and time and motion studies. Hiring of employees may be for replacement or for expansion. Replacement hiring starts with a labor requisition sent to the personnel department by a department head or supervisor. If the original vacancy is for one of the better jobs, that job will usually be filled by promotion, and the replacement requisition will be for the job which is finally vacant. Expansion hiring requires authorization by executive management. Authority to hire results from approval of the labor requirements of a production schedule rather than from separate requisitions to fill individual jobs. The personnel department, in conjunction with the department heads concerned, plans the expansion requirements and agrees upon promotions and promotional transfers to be made, the number and kind of workers to be hired, and the dates at which new recruits will report for work.

Employment practices must comply not only with regulations set forth at the federal level (i.e., the Equal Employment Opportunity Commission; the Department of Health, Education, and Welfare; and the Department of Labor) but also with regulations of human rights commissions in several of the states.

A production planning department is responsible for the scheduling of work, the release of job orders to the producing departments, and the dispatching of work in the factory. The release of orders is generally accompanied by materials requisitions and labor time tickets that indicate the operations to be performed on the product. A specific and understandable listing of detailed operations is important if work is to be performed within the time allowed and with the materials provided. Delays caused by lack of materials, machine breakdowns, or need for additional instructions give rise to complaints by the workers and lead to additional labor costs. Production schedules prepared several weeks in advance, utilizing labor time standards for each producing department, lead to cost control through the use of departmental labor budgets similar to the illustration on page 386.

Production Planning Department

PROCEDURES FOR LABOR COSTING

The aforementioned activities lay the groundwork necessary to account for and control labor costs. The accounting for wages and salaries requires the work of the:

1. Timekeeping department, which gathers and collects total and specific time worked on a job, product, process, or in a department.
2. Payroll department, which determines the gross and net amount of earnings of each worker, computes the total payroll, and keeps earnings records for each employee.
3. Cost department, which charges jobs, products, processes, or departments with the cost applicable as evidenced by the payroll distribution.

In detail, labor costing procedures involve:

1. The employment history of each worker — date hired, wage rate, initial assignment, promotions, tardiness, sickness, and vacations.
2. Adequate information for compliance with union contracts, social security laws, wage and hour legislation, income tax withholdings, and other federal, state, and local government requirements.
3. The time required for each basic manufacturing operation in order to develop efficient methods.
4. The establishment of labor cost standards for comparative purposes.
5. Productivity in relation to type of wage payment, creating the best system of compensation for each kind of work.
6. Each employee's time worked, wage rate, and total earnings for each payroll period.

7. The output or accomplishment of each employee.
8. The amount of direct labor cost and hours to be charged to each job, lot, process, or department, and the amount of indirect labor cost. The direct labor cost or hours information may be used as a basis for factory overhead allocation.
9. Total labor cost in each department for each payroll period.

The accounting principles, procedures, and objectives in labor costing are relatively simple, although considerable difficulty in their application may be experienced with large numbers of workers or when workers shift from one type of work to another under various factory conditions. Basically, two sets of underlying detailed records are kept, one for financial accounting and the other for cost accounting. The procedures for labor accounting are outlined below. The journal entries associated with these procedures, as well as those pertaining to labor-related costs, are discussed and illustrated in the next chapter.

FINANCIAL ACCOUNTING	COST ACCOUNTING
A record is kept of the total time worked and the total amount earned by each worker.	A record is kept of the time worked on each job, process, or department by each worker and the cost thereof.
The daily or weekly amount earned by each worker is entered on the payroll book.	The direct labor hours and cost are entered on the respective job sheets or production reports; the indirect labor cost is entered in the proper column of the departmental expense analysis sheets or standing orders.
Each payroll period the total amount of wages paid to workers results in the following entry: Payroll .... xxx 　Employees Income 　　Tax Payable .... xxx 　FICA Tax Payable...... xxx 　Accounts Payable or 　　Cash xxx	The weekly or month-end entry for labor distribution is: Work in Process.. xxx Factory Over- 　head Control.... xxx 　Indirect 　　Labor......... xxx 　Payroll xxx

Timekeeping Department　　Securing an accurate record of the time purchased from each employee is the first step in labor costing. To do so, it is necessary to provide a:

1. Clock card as unquestionable evidence of the employee's presence in the plant from the time of entry to departure.
2. Time ticket (or job ticket) to secure information as to the type of work performed.

Both forms are supervised, controlled, and collected by the timekeeping department. Since the earnings of the employee depend mainly upon these two forms and the timekeeper processes them in the first step toward final payment, the timekeeping department forms a most valuable link in harmonious labor-management relationships. In fact, to many workers, the timekeeper *is* management. Frequently the timekeeper's performance is the basis for a worker's first opinion of the company.

Clock Card. A *clock card* provides space for the name and number of the employee and usually covers an entire payroll period. When completed, the clock card shows the time a worker started and stopped work each day or shift of the payroll period, with overtime and other premium hours clearly indicated.

The *time clock* (or *time recorder*) is a mechanical instrument for recording employee time in and out of the office and the factory. Under a typical procedure, each employee is assigned a clock number that identifies the department and the employee. The clock number is used for identification on the payroll and in charging labor time to departments and production orders. Usually timekeepers are stationed near the clocks during a change of shifts in order to expedite smooth and rapid movement in and out of the plant and to insure proper clock card procedures.

Clock Card

Time Ticket (or Job Ticket). In accounting for materials, the receiving sheet and the invoice are evidence that the goods have been received and payment is in order. In accounting for labor, the clock card is evidence that time has been purchased and is comparable to the receiving sheet. The *time ticket* (or *job ticket*) shows the specific use that has been made of the time purchased and is comparable to the materials requisition.

When the individual time ticket is used, a new ticket must be made out for each job worked on during the day. Since this procedure leads to many tickets per employee, some plants use a *daily time report* on which the worker lists jobs.

The best procedure for filling in the time tickets depends upon many factors peculiar to shop operations. In some factories, the workers prepare their own time tickets, approved by the supervisor, or the supervisor prepares them. Remote computer terminals enable employees to report time distributions by direct entry to the computer. These entries are later confirmed by the supervisors, based on reports received from the computer center. In other factories, timekeepers, dispatch clerks, and supervisors have desks near the work stations. Employees report to the timekeeper when changing jobs, get a new assignment from the dispatch clerk, secure instructions at the supervisor's desk, get the required tools at the tool crib, and thus shift from one job to another.

Each day, usually after the morning shift has clocked in, the timekeeper collects all the time tickets or the daily time reports of the previous day, together with the clock cards. Before the daily time tickets are sent to the payroll department, the total time reported on each time ticket is compared with the total hours of each employee's clock card. If there is any difference, an adjustment is made. If the clock card shows more hours than the time tickets, the difference is reported as idle time. If the time tickets show more hours than the clock card, the error is corrected in consultation with the supervisor and the worker.

The degree of accuracy in reporting time varies from plant to plant, but in most situations a report to the exact minute is neither necessary nor practical. Many companies find it advantageous to use a decimal system, which is fast and which measures the hour in ten periods of six minutes each rather than the regular clock interval of five-minute periods and twelve periods per hour. On a decimal system, a job started at 9:23 a.m. and finished at 11:38 a.m. would be reported at 9.4 and 11.6 with an elapsed time of 2.2 hours.

Time tickets form the basis for calculating bonuses under a wage incentive plan. When wages are based on hours worked, the time tickets provide a means of auditing the clock cards and a source of data concerning efficient utilization of labor.

Payroll Department   The work of the payroll department follows two basic steps: (1) computation of the payroll and (2) distribution of the payroll to jobs, processes, and departments. The work, procedures, and functions of this department depend upon the size and complexity of a company. Some companies require only a simple payroll department staffed by one or two payroll clerks who perform the work manually; others require an elaborate payroll department with many employees and computerized procedures. In any case, the payroll department is responsible for the important task of recording the job classification, department, and wage rate for each employee. It records hours worked and wages earned, makes payroll deductions, determines the net amount due each employee, maintains a permanent earnings record for each employee, and prepares the paycheck or provides the cashier's or treasurer's office with the necessary records to make the payments.

The company's payroll is prepared from clock cards, time tickets, or computer printouts. The final computed payroll may be recorded in a payroll journal, payroll record, payroll report, or payroll sheet. The record may be a bound book with sheets ruled for the special needs of a company; it may be a loose-leaf book, cards, or sheets for filing; or it may be produced on sheets or rolls through the use of payroll machines or computerized methods. A record of individual employee earnings and deductions must also be maintained. Practically all large enterprises and many smaller ones use a computerized system for payroll preparation.

Payroll Payments. If the number of employees is not large, all workers are usually paid on the same day, which may be weekly, semimonthly, or monthly. Some companies stagger the payroll during the week in order to give an even flow to the work of the payroll department. If workers are paid in cash, it is necessary to transport the payroll cash from a bank to the payroll office, to prepare pay envelopes for each worker, and to arrange them alphabetically or by clock number for distribution.

In most instances employees are paid by check. Payroll checks may be drawn against the regular checking account or a special payroll deposit. The special payroll bank account is especially advantageous with large numbers of workers. When a payroll fund is deposited in the bank, the payroll department certifies the amount required for a particular payment date, a voucher is drawn for the specified amount, and a check is drawn against the regular deposit account and is deposited in the payroll fund. By utilizing this procedure, only one check, drawn on the general bank account, appears in the cash payments journal each payroll period. For each employee, the paymaster prepares a check drawn against the special payroll account. When machine methods are used for payroll accounting, the payroll journal, the checks, the check register, and the employees' earnings records are commonly prepared in one simultaneous operation.

Payroll Distribution. The individual time ticket or daily time report shows the use made of the time purchased from each factory employee. The tickets for each employee must agree with the employee's total earnings for the week. Time tickets are sorted by jobs, departments, and types of indirect labor to permit the distribution of the total payroll to Work in Process and to the departmental expense analysis sheets controlled by Factory Overhead Control. Distribution of the payroll is speeded up when automated methods are used. If the payroll department does not prepare the distribution summary, the time tickets are sent to the cost department, which must perform this task. Labor costs distributed to jobs, processes, or departments must agree with the total amount recorded in the payroll account. The distribution summary may also show the labor hours when they are the basis for the application of factory overhead.

Cost Department

On the basis of the labor distribution summary or the time tickets, the cost department records the direct labor cost on the appropriate job cost sheets or production reports, and the indirect cost on the departmental expense analysis sheets. In some factories, cost accounting activities are decentralized, and cost work becomes largely a matter of organization and direction in carrying out a system for recording payroll information and labor costs. In such a supervisory capacity, cost clerks may be stationed in producing departments to assist in accumulating and classifying labor costs, using the summarized time tickets to compute production costs and services by job orders, units of output, departmental operations, and product types. In other factories, the cost department may be highly centralized and may not direct and control any timekeeping or payroll preparation.

Summary

The organization chart on the following page summarizes the departmental interrelationships required for effective labor cost control and accounting.

The preceding labor costing procedures have emphasized manufacturing labor. Labor costing of nonmanufacturing labor, such as marketing and administrative employees, also requires the same detailed cost accumulation and distribution procedures.

COMPUTERIZED PAYROLL PROCEDURES

The preceding discussion of labor and payroll procedures was based on manual and/or semi-mechanical operations. Yet almost from the very moment that electronic computers were invented and used in business, payroll procedures were among the first to be programmed for these new machines. The reason for this immediate acceptance was that businesses had definitive payroll accounting procedures which lent themselves to computer adaptation. Consequently, payroll accounting procedures can be computerized to the extent that the need for manual processing is virtually eliminated.

The preparation of labor performance reports was discussed and illustrated earlier in this chapter. However, their presentation is made possible because computerized labor accounting begins the day an employee is hired and the data for the employee's name, number, job classification, shift, department, direct/indirect pay rate, deductions, etc., are entered in the em-

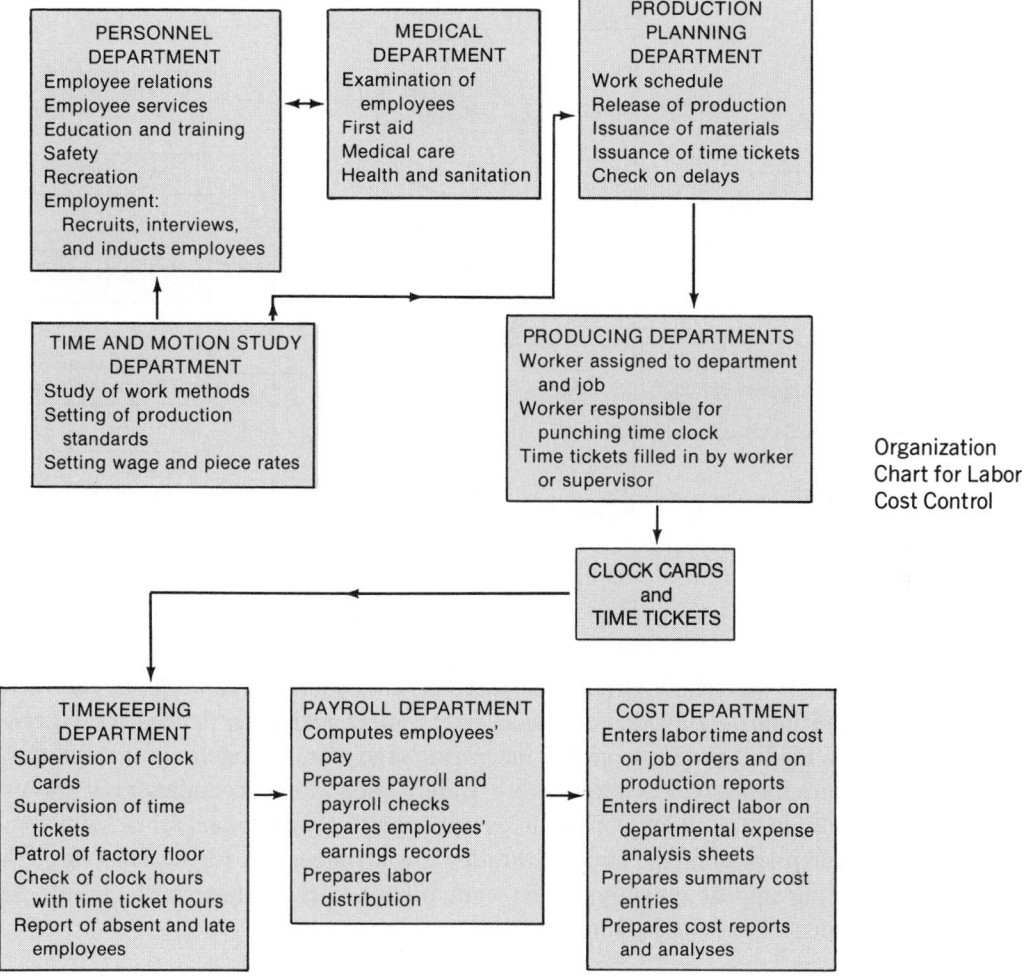

Organization Chart for Labor Cost Control

ployee's master file. From that moment on, the employee's activities and those of every other employee are inputted for payroll data, labor distribution, and a permanent employment data bank. Computerized labor and payroll procedures are depicted in the flowchart on page 398.

INCENTIVE WAGE PLANS

In the modern industrial enterprise of mass production and many employees, a worker's wage is based on negotiated labor contracts, productivity studies, job evaluation, profit sharing, incentive wage plans, and guaranteed annual wages. Because all wages are paid for work performed, an element of incentive is present in all wage plans. In contrast with pay by the hour, week, or month, an incentive wage plan should reward workers in direct proportion

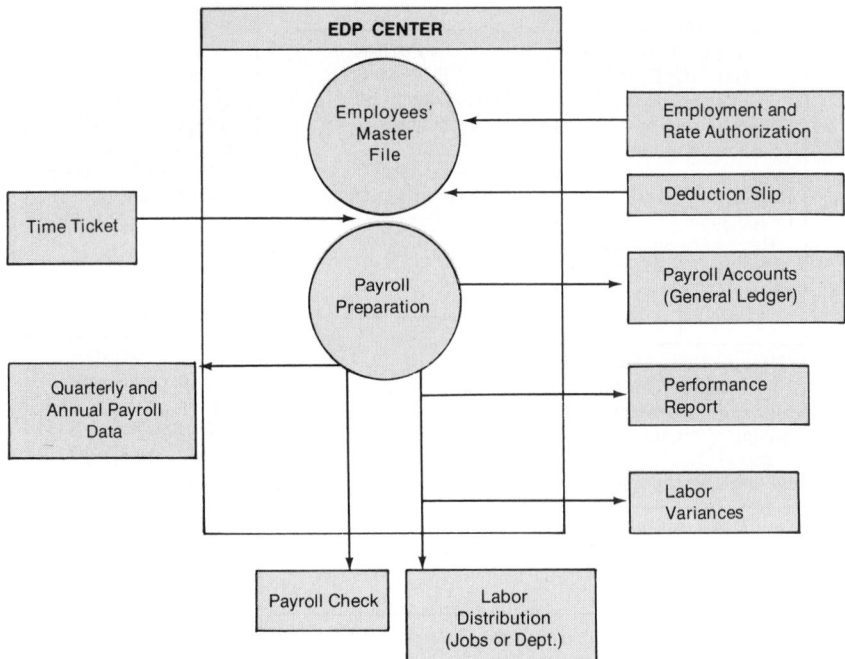

Flowchart of
Computerized
Labor and
Payroll
Procedures

to their increased output. As stated earlier, a fair day's work standard should be established so that the worker can meet and even exceed it, thereby receiving full benefit from the incentive wage plan. At one time, incentive wage plans for factory workers were widely used. Recent studies now show that about half of all large companies use incentive wage plans for at least some of their work centers. Union attitudes toward incentive wage plans vary. Some unions oppose incentive plans while others, such as those in the textile, shoe, and steel industries, support them.

Requirements of an Incentive Wage Plan

To be successful, an incentive wage plan must meet certain requirements: (1) applicability to situations in which a worker can increase output, (2) provision for proportionately more pay for output above standard, (3) setting fair standards so that extra effort will result in bonus pay, and (4) immediate reward every payday. Along with these essentials, the plan needs to be reasonably simple and understandable to workers as well as to managers.

Purpose of an Incentive Wage Plan

The primary purpose of an incentive wage plan is to induce a worker to produce more, to earn a higher wage, and at the same time to reduce unit costs. The plan seeks to insure greater output, to increase control over labor cost by insuring more uniform unit costs, and to change the basis for reward from hours served to work accomplished. Naturally, producing more in the same period of time should result in higher pay for the worker. Because of the greater number of units produced, it should also result in a lower cost per unit for factory overhead and labor cost combined.

For example, assume that a factory operation takes place in a building that is rented for $2,400 per month (or $80 per day or $10 per hour) and that insurance, taxes, and depreciation amount to $64 per day or $8 per hour. Assume further that 10 workers on an 8-hour day are paid $6 per hour and that each worker produces 40 units of product per day (an individual production rate of 5 units per hour). The workers and the management agree that a rate of $6.60 per hour will be paid if a worker produces 48 units per day, thereby increasing the hourly output from 5 to 6 units.

The following illustration shows the cost per hour and cost per unit for two systems, and indicates how a wage incentive can reduce unit costs and at the same time provide the worker with a higher income.

ORIGINAL SYSTEM, $6 PER HOUR (10 workers)				NEW SYSTEM, $6.60 PER HOUR (10 workers)			
COST FACTOR	AMOUNT PER HOUR	UNITS PER HOUR	UNIT COST	COST FACTOR	AMOUNT PER HOUR	UNITS PER HOUR	UNIT COST
Labor	$60	50	$1.20	Labor	$66	60	$1.1000
Rent	10	50	.20	Rent	10	60	.1667
Depreciation, insurance, and taxes ..	8	50	.16	Depreciation, insurance, and taxes ..	8	60	.1333
Total...........	$78	50	$1.56	Total...........	$84	60	$1.4000

Effect of an Incentive Wage Plan on Unit Costs

Although the hourly labor cost of the work crew increases from $60 to $66, the cost of a complete unit of product is reduced from $1.56 to $1.40. The unit cost decrease is caused by two factors: (1) unit output per worker is increased 20 percent with a 10 percent increase in wages and (2) the same amount of factory overhead is spread over 60 instead of 50 units of product an hour. For greater precision, such an analysis should also include labor-related costs, such as employer's payroll taxes, as well as any other relevant factory overhead that would influence the unit cost.

These general principles have been applied to most discussions on incentive wage plans. However, the lowering of conversion or manufacturing cost resulting from an incentive wage plan, illustrated here on a cost per unit basis, could be explained in terms of differential (marginal or incremental) cost analysis (Chapter 25).

> If the introduction of an incentive wage system results in greater labor productivity, the desirability of achieving this increased productivity may be evaluated by the net incremental change in *total* revenues and/or costs. Since total fixed costs, by definition, are not expected to change in response to (small) changes in production volume, these cost elements should be ignored in the analysis, and attention directed to the other items sensitive to volume changes.

If the market will absorb additional output, the marginal revenue [and costs] of this output becomes important in the evaluation. If the market is saturated, or if other capacity restrictions preclude an increase in volume, the revenue side may be ignored and then the increased productivity anticipated would provide benefits to the extent that the labor formerly devoted to production could be eliminated or used in some alternative way, i.e., the appropriate benefit is the labor's opportunity cost, and any concurrent reduction in time-related variable costs. The benefits derived from these items must, of course, be reduced by any increases resulting from extra incentive payments to employees and extra costs involved in administering a more complex compensation plan.[2]

Types of Incentive Wage Plans

In actual practice, time wages and output wages are not clear-cut and distinct. Incentive plans typically involve wage rates based upon various combinations of output and time. Many wage incentive systems retain the names of industrial engineers and efficiency experts who originated the plans — the Taylor Differential Piece-Rate Plan, the Halsey Premium Plan, the Bedaux Point System, the Gantt Task and Bonus Plan, and the Emerson Efficiency Bonus Plan. Most of these plans — like obsolete machinery — are no longer used, but many adaptations are still in use.

An employee's earnings are determined by (1) the ratio of a worker's production to standard production, (2) the hourly base rate for the job classification, and (3) the incentive wage plan in use. To demonstrate the operation of incentive wage plans, the straight piecework plan, the 100 percent bonus plan, and the group bonus plan are discussed as representative examples.

Straight Piecework Plan. The *straight piecework plan*, one of the simplest incentive wage plans, pays wages above the base rate for production above the standard. The production standard is computed in minutes per piece and is then translated into money per piece. If time studies determine that 2.5 minutes is to be the standard time required for producing one unit, the standard rate is 24 pieces per hour. If a worker's base pay rate is $7.44 per hour, the piece rate is $.31. Workers are generally guaranteed a base pay rate, even if they fail to earn that amount in terms of output. If a worker's production exceeds 24 pieces per hour, the $.31 per unit still applies. In the table on page 401, with standard production of 24 pieces per hour and with a guaranteed hourly rate, the labor cost per unit of output declines until the standard is reached and then remains constant at any level of output above standard.

While piece rates reflect an obvious cause-effect relationship between output and pay, the incentive is effective only when workers can control their rates of output. Piece rates would not, of course, be effective when output is machine paced. As previously stated, modification of production standards and labor rates becomes necessary when increases in output are the result of the installation of new and better machines.

---

[2]Werner G. Frank, "Evaluation of Wage Incentives: Fixed Costs, Revisited," *The Accounting Review*, Vol. XLVII, No. 1, p. 156.

Units per Hour	Guaranteed Hourly Rate	Piece Rate	Earned per Hour	Labor Cost per Unit	Overhead per Hour	Overhead per Unit	Conversion Cost per Unit
20	$7.44	$ 0	$7.44	$.372	$4.80	$.240	$.612
22	7.44	0	7.44	.338	4.80	.218	.556
24	7.44	.31	7.44	.310	4.80	.200	.510
26	7.44	.31	8.06	.310	4.80	.185	.495
28	7.44	.31	8.68	.310	4.80	.171	.481
30	7.44	.31	9.30	.310	4.80	.160	.470
32	7.44	.31	9.92	.310	4.80	.150	.460

Straight Piecework Plan

100 Percent Bonus Plan. The *100 percent bonus plan* is a variation of the straight piecework plan. It differs in that standards are never stated in terms of money, but in time per unit of output. Instead of a price per piece, a standard time is allowed to complete a job or unit; and the worker is paid for the standard time at the hourly rate if the job or unit is completed in standard time or less. Thus, if a worker produces 100 units in an 8-hour shift and the standard time is 80 units per shift (or 10 units per hour), the worker would be paid the hourly rate for 10 hours. In other variations of the 100 percent bonus plan, savings are shared with the supervisor and/or the company.

Each payroll period, a production indicator must be figured for every worker before earnings can be computed. Production standards in units of output per hour are set by industrial engineers. Hours of work and units produced are reported to the payroll department, where the reported hours worked are multiplied by the hourly production standard to determine the standard units. The worker's hourly production is then divided by the standard quantity, resulting in the production indicator, or efficiency ratio. The efficiency ratio multiplied by the worker's base rate results in the hourly earnings for the period. The table below illustrates how earnings are computed, assuming that standard production is 15 units per hour.

Worker	Hours Worked	Output Units	Standard Units	Efficiency Ratio	Base Rate	Base × Efficiency Ratio	Total Earned	Labor Cost per Unit	Overhead per Hour	Overhead per Unit	Conversion Cost per Unit
Abrams	40	540	600	90	$3.75	—*	$150.00	$.2778	$5.40	$.4000	$.6778
Gordon	40	660	600	110	3.75	4.1250	165.00	.2500	5.40	.3273	.5773
Hanson	40	800	600	133	3.75	4.9875	199.50	.2494	5.40	.2700	.5194
Jonson	38	650	570	114	3.80	4.3320	164.62	.2533	5.40	.3157	.5690
Stowell	40	750	600	125	4.00	5.0000	200.00	.2667	5.40	.2880	.5547
Wiebold	40	810	600	135	3.86	5.2110	208.44	.2573	5.40	.2667	.5240

*When the efficiency ratio is less than 100, no bonus is earned.

100 Percent Bonus Plan

The 100 percent bonus plan has gained in popularity because of the frequency of wage increases. The standards, stated in terms of time and output quantity, need no adjustment when wage rates change. Since the system emphasizes time rather than money, the plan lends itself to the development of controls and efficiency standards.

Group Bonus Plan. Industry uses a great variety of incentive wage plans, some of which depend upon a superior productive performance of a whole department or an entire factory. Factory operations often require employees to work in groups or crews using large machines. Although the work of each employee is essential to the machine operation, it is frequently impossible to separate the work of one member of a crew. A worker on an assembly line cannot increase output without the cooperation of the entire group. Group bonus plans have proven successful in such situations.

Group bonus plans, like those designed for individual incentive, are intended to encourage production at rates above a minimum standard. Each worker in the group receives an hourly rate for production up to the standard output. Units produced in excess of the standard are regarded as time saved by the group, and each worker is in effect paid a bonus for time saved as well as being paid for time worked. Usually, the bonus earned by the group is divided among the group members in accordance with their respective base rates.

Group plans reduce the amount of clerical work necessary to compute labor cost and payrolls and the amount of supervision necessary to operate the incentive system. Group plans may also contribute to better cooperation among workers, and good workers are likely to bring pressure to bear upon poor workers who might jeopardize the group bonus. Group plans quite often lead to the reduction of accidents, spoilage, waste, and absenteeism. For example, a bonus may be paid to a crew or department which has not had an accident for a specified period of time, or which has a reject rate in units of output below a specified ratio.

The following table illustrates the operation of a 100 percent group bonus plan. A crew of 10 workers uses costly equipment, and each is paid $5 an

Units Produced	Standard Hours for Units Produced	Actual Hours	Regular Group Wage	Bonus (Hrs. Saved @ $5)	Total Group Earnings	Labor Cost per Unit	Over-head Cost per Unit	Conversion Cost per Unit
350	70	80	$400	$ 0	$400	$1.143	$.914	$2.057
400	80	80	400	0	400	1.000	.800	1.800
425	85	80	400	25	425	1.000	.753	1.753
450	90	80	400	50	450	1.000	.711	1.711
475	95	80	400	75	475	1.000	.674	1.674
500	100	80	400	100	500	1.000	.640	1.640

100 Percent Group Bonus Plan

hour for a regular 8-hour shift. Standard production is 50 units per hour, or 400 units per shift; overhead is $320 per 8-hour shift, or $40 per hour.

The installation and successful operation of incentive wage plans require not only the combined efforts of the personnel department, labor unions, factory engineers, and accountants but also the cooperation and willingness of each worker. Wage incentives are:

General Observations Regarding Incentive Wage Plans

> . . .based on the premise that monetary bonuses will, in fact, motivate workers to achieve higher production rates. While this seems a reasonable assumption, the writing of behavioral scientists and the empirical research that has been carried out suggest that the relationship between monetary incentives and increased production is not a simple or unambiguous one. William F. Whyte, a behavioral scientist, notes in a study of the effect of piecework on productivity, 'It is only in a fraction of the jobs . . . that the piecework provides an incentive to tap the full productive capacities of workers.' After describing in detail a number of case situations, he concludes, 'Management should recognize that financial incentives are both a technical engineering and a human relations problem.' This suggests that management should approach the design, evaluation, and implementation of such plans with the awareness of their possible behavioral, as well as economic, implications.[3]

WAGE INCENTIVE TIME STANDARDS VIA LEARNING CURVE THEORY

Incentive wage plans assume that monetary bonuses will motivate workers to achieve higher productivity rates. In turn, the greater the output, the lower the conversion cost per unit. Yet, the previous discussion also stresses the fact that motivation is not always based on financial rewards. Furthermore, an incentive wage plan based on fixed time standards — no matter how scientifically engineered — often does not appear to motivate workers.[4] Even with such drawbacks, many current incentive wage plans still use fixed time standards for rewarding individual performance through bonus payments; however, the deficiencies existing in such wage incentive standards have been remedied by means of the learning curve theory.

The *learning curve theory* stipulates that every time the cumulative quantity of units produced is doubled, the cumulative average time per unit is reduced by a given percentage. If it is assumed that this reduction is 20 percent, it means that the second unit requires 80 percent of the cumulative average time per unit required for the first unit; the fourth unit, 80 percent of the second; the eighth unit, 80 percent of the fourth; and so on. Based on this theory, the following table of values for an 80 percent learning curve can be

---

[3]*Ibid.*, pp. 159–160.
[4]A fixed time standard is best explained by referring to the 100 percent bonus plan (page 401), in which the standard is fixed at 80 units per day (or 10 units per hour).

computed, assuming that 10 direct labor hours are required to produce the first unit:[5]

UNITS ×	CUMULATIVE AVERAGE REQUIRED LABOR HOURS PER UNIT =	ESTIMATED TOTAL HOURS NEEDED TO PERFORM THE TASK
1	10.0 hours	10.0 hours
2	8.0 (10.0 × 80%)	16.0
4	6.4 (8.0 × 80%)	25.6
8	5.1 (6.4 × 80%)	40.8
16	4.1 (5.1 × 80%)	65.6
32	3.3 (4.1 × 80%)	105.6
64	2.6 (3.3 × 80%)	166.4

The results indicate that the rate is constant at each doubling of the accumulated number of times the task is performed. The figures in the third column are the cumulative average hours times the number of units. To estimate the total time needed to perform the task the first 32 times, the calculation would be $32 \times 3.3 = 105.6$ hours.

Generally, as tasks become more complicated in terms of labor skill, there is more room for learning to occur and, therefore, a greater likelihood of a lower labor input percentage as production increases. Of course, such factors as improvements in engineering design, equipment, and techniques may account for labor savings as well.

The 80 percent learning curve is used here for illustrative purposes. The 80 percent rate is frequent among industries, and the percentage typically is no lower than 60 nor higher than 85. The actual percentage will depend on the particular situation. At the extremes, the actual percentage could range from 100 percent (if no learning occurs) to 50 percent. At the latter extreme, if the average accumulated time for the first unit is 100 minutes, then the time for the second unit must equal zero (i.e., 100 minutes × 50% = 50 minutes — accumulated average time per task unit at the 2 task units level, or a total of 100 minutes for the 2 units). Thus, the 50 percent rate is an upper limit of learning — one that can never be reached. If the production period is long or the labor operations are routine, a point in production is reached when any improvement through repetition would become imperceptible; the learning curve would level out to a steady-state condition.[6]

After the learning curve percentage has been empirically determined for a specific operation, estimates for successive increments in output can be estimated as long as conditions remain the same.

> Conditions which may cause deviations from times predicted by an established learning curve include changes in product design, changes in proportions of manufactured and purchased components, and changes in equipment.

---

[5]James A. Broadston, "Learning Curve Wage Incentives," *Management Accounting*, Vol. XLIX, No. 12, pp. 15–23.
[6]For further discussion of learning curves, see Leonard W. Hein, *The Quantitative Approach to Managerial Decisions* (Englewood Cliffs, N.J.: Prentice-Hall, Inc., 1967), pp. 90–113.

When production is discontinuous with comparatively long lapses of time and changes in personnel, . . . relearning will be required. Learning curves are not useful when operations are machine-paced because machines do not learn.[7]

By means of the learning curve, the time standard or unit standard used for determining a worker's earnings has now changed to a variable time instead of the fixed time standard. The variable time standard meets the need of an incentive wage system more equitably.

The improvement phenomenon, as well as its mathematical model, the learning curve, provides an insight into human capabilities that bears directly upon the ability of workers to do work and the time required for them to learn new skills. An actual learning curve may show small irregularities; yet it will eventually follow an underlying natural characteristic of group or individual human activity.[8]

As soon as workers have passed the learning stage and begin to produce the expected number of units (i.e., reach the standard proficiency), they will begin to draw bonus pay for doing the operation in less than standard time. They may even slow down a little and yet perform the operation in standard time or better, drawing the bonus pay but working less hard for it.

Government procurement agencies have used the learning curve as a tool for cost evaluation in negotiating prices for contracts. When a bid on a contract is entered, the unit labor cost is usually estimated. The learning curve permits the determination of lot costs for various stages of production. As production progresses, the cumulative average unit labor cost should decrease.

By comparing the budgeted cost with the experienced labor cost in the initial stages of production, the trend of the labor cost can be determined. If, for example, an average labor cost of $20 per unit is to be achieved, the following output and cost table with 80, 85, and 90 percent learning curves can be predetermined:[9]

CUMULATIVE QUANTITY	LEARNING CURVE 80%	85%	90%
25	$61.02	$45.36	$33.22
50	48.82	38.56	30.47
100	39.06	32.78	27.43
200	31.25	27.68	24.69
400	25.00	23.53	22.22
800	20.00	20.00	20.00

The learning curve allows projection of the cumulative average unit cost at any stage of production. It also predicts labor hours with accuracy and

[7]Walter B. McFarland, *Manpower Cost and Performance Measurement* (New York: National Association of Accountants, 1977), p. 43.
[8]Broadston, *op. cit.*, p. 15.
[9]William H. Boren, "Some Applications of the Learning Curve to Government Contracts," *NAA Bulletin,* Vol. XLVI, No. 2, pp. 21–22.

reliability, establishes work load, and allows production control to take advantage of reducing time per unit by increasing lot sizes, thereby maintaining a level work force. It also provides a basis for standard cost variance calculations (Chapter 19), allows judgment of a manager's performance relative to the department's target, and provides a basis for cost control through analysis of undesirable shifts of the curve.

UNION CONTRACTS

Many possible provisions relative to wages, hours, and working conditions are always present when a labor contract is negotiated. The employer and employee have a mutual interest in the terms of a contract and a mutual responsibility for carrying out the agreement.

Since the union serves as the employees' representative and the agreement is signed by both union and company officials, the contract is likely to be printed for distribution to all interested parties. Provisions of a typical contract involve the personnel department in the hiring, promotion, and dismissal of employees; the payroll department in the determination of regular wages, premium pay for overtime, holidays, vacations, night shifts, and premium rates or bonus payments under incentive wage plans; and the cost department, since a contract represents the terms and price of labor to be purchased during the life of a contract. It is important that managers of these departments become thoroughly familiar with provisions of the contract and that all procedures in connection with labor accounting be designed and executed in harmony with its provisions. Grievances leading to stoppages and strikes can be caused by poorly understood or poorly executed union agreements.

DISCUSSION QUESTIONS

1. Is it generally true that all wage payments are ultimately limited by and are usually based, directly or indirectly, on the productivity of the worker?
2. The basis for labor cost control is the provision of pertinent and timely information to management. What kind of information is needed by executive management as compared with department managers?
3. Define productivity.
4. What is meant by performance rating?
5. How can labor efficiency be determined or measured?
6. Why has the subject of inflation been receiving ever-increasing attention throughout the nation and the world?

7. In what way are the creation and maintenance of an efficient labor force a cooperative effort?

8. It is frequently stated that accurate cost accounting is of great value in wage negotiations. How may cost records contribute to settlement of wage disputes?

9. Accounting for labor has a two-fold aspect: financial accounting and cost accounting. Differentiate between the two.

10. What is the purpose of determining the labor hours (a) worked by each employee; (b) worked on each job, or in each department?

11. In accounting for and controlling labor costs, what is the function of the (a) timekeeping department, (b) payroll department, and (c) cost accounting department?

12. What purpose is served by the (a) clock card; (b) time ticket?

13. If employees' clock cards show more time than their time tickets, how is the difference reconciled?

14. What is the purpose of an incentive wage plan?

15. In most incentive wage plans, does production above standard reduce the labor cost per unit of output? Discuss.

16. Wage incentive plans are successful in plants operating near full capacity.
    (a) Discuss the desirability of using these plans during periods of curtailed production.
    (b) Is it advisable to install an incentive wage plan in a plant operating at 60% of capacity? Discuss.

17. Is it necessary to record the time spent by pieceworkers on their various jobs or operations? Give reasons.

18. Differentiate between wages based on the straight piecework plan, the 100 percent bonus plan, and the group bonus plan.

19. Because of faulty determination of piecework rates, workers' earnings in a particular plant have been unduly high. Sales volume and prices are declining, and it is necessary to reduce production costs. What solution could be suggested?

20. A company's management established a plan in which a bonus is paid to any supervisor within a specific department, based on the net saving made in the department. The company does not pay out the entire bonus but pays part in cash and places the remainder in a fund. The fund acts as a reserve against which negative variances are charged during the year. At the end of February, a certain department's net saving for the month is $680. Of this amount, 20% is distributed to the supervisory staff. The department employs a supervisor and an assistant. The method of sharing the bonus is on a point basis with 100 points assigned to the supervisor and 60 points to the assistant. How much bonus is each supervisor entitled to receive?

21. State the basic concept underlying the relationship involved in the learning curve theory.

22. Name some situations for the application of the learning curve theory.

23. A factory supervisor discharged an hourly worker but did not notify the Payroll Department. The supervisor then forged the worker's signature on time cards and work tickets. When the payroll checks were given out, the checks drawn for the discharged worker were diverted to the supervisor's own use. Select the statement that would be the most effective method for preventing dishonesty in payroll procedures:

(a) Require a written authorization for each employee added to or removed from the payroll.

(b) Have a paymaster with no other payroll responsibility than that of distributing payroll checks.

(c) Have someone other than persons who prepare or distribute the payroll obtain custody of unclaimed payroll checks.

(d) From time to time, rotate persons distributing the payroll.

(AICPA adapted)

EXERCISES

1. Production planning and control reports. Lippincott, Inc., a supplier of bulk metals and alloys, recently negotiated to supply 3,000 sections of aluminum air-conditioning ductwork for an office building under construction. The order required fabricating, cutting, and assembly. Based on experience, the supervisor prepared the following daily budget:

DEPARTMENT	SECTIONS SCHEDULED	HOURS BUDGETED
Fabricating	100	50
Cutting	100	30
Assembly	100	25

Realizing the need for up-to-the-minute production information, the supervisor obtained the following results for the first two days:

	DEPARTMENT	SECTIONS PRODUCED	HOURS REQUIRED
First day:	Fabricating	112	48
	Cutting	81	30
	Assembly	77	22
Second day:	Fabricating	120	49
	Cutting	96	30
	Assembly	96	23

Required:

(1) Action to be taken by the supervisor, based on the first day's report.

(2) Action needed according to the results on the second day's report.

2. Labor performance variances. Trainor, Inc., whose largest selling product is Trak, prepares monthly production budgets for its three departments. Budgeted and actual amounts for April are as shown below.

DEPARTMENT	BUDGETED HOURS	ACTUAL LABOR COST	UNITS PRODUCED
Mixing	1,100	$ 6,532	740
Processing	3,320	18,850	615
Packaging	580	2,544	800

The following standards have been adopted for this product:

DEPARTMENT	STANDARD HOURS PER UNIT	STANDARD LABOR COST PER HOUR
Mixing......................................	1.5	$6.10
Processing............................	5.0	6.50
Packaging.............................	0.5	6.00

Required: A labor cost control report for April.

3. 100 percent bonus plan. Mary Martin, employed by the Ocean City Canning Company, submitted the following labor data for the first week in June:

	UNITS	HOURS
Monday............................	270	8
Tuesday............................	210	8
Wednesday.......................	300	8
Thursday..........................	240	8
Friday...............................	260	8

Required: A schedule showing Mary's weekly earnings, the effective hourly rate, and the labor cost per unit, assuming a 100 percent bonus plan with a base wage of $6 per hour and a standard production rate of 30 units per hour. (Round off the bonus percentage to two decimal places.)

4. 100 percent bonus plan. West-Chester, Inc., produces printed circuits for the electronics industry. The firm has recently initiated a 100 percent bonus plan with standard production set at 50 units per hour.

The company employs 10 workers on an 8-hour shift at $8 per hour. Depreciation on plant equipment is $9.00 per hour, and other overhead is applied at $7.00 per hour.

Production for the first week under the 100 percent bonus plan was:

	UNITS
Monday...............................	3,800
Tuesday..............................	4,500
Wednesday.........................	4,600
Thursday............................	4,500
Friday.................................	4,400

Management is interested in appraising the results of the new incentive wage plan.

Required: A schedule showing employee earnings, unit labor cost, unit overhead cost, and conversion cost per unit. (Round off unit costs to three decimal places.)

5. Incentive wage plan. Scan-Electro Company, a relatively small supplier of computer-oriented parts, is currently engaged in producing a new component for the computer sensory unit.

The company has been producing 150 units per week; factory overhead (all fixed) was estimated to be $1,200 per week. The following is a schedule of the pay rates of three workers properly classified as direct labor:

EMPLOYEE	HOURLY RATE
Clancy, D.	$6.00
Luken, T.	8.00
Schott, J.	7.00

Customers have been calling in for additional units, but management does not want to work more than 40 hours per week. To motivate its workers to produce more, the company decided to institute an incentive wage plan. Under the plan, the workers would be paid a base rate per hour, as shown in the following schedule, and a premium of $1 per unit when the total number of units exceeds 150.

EMPLOYEE	BASE RATE
Clancy, D.	$3.50
Luken, T.	5.50
Schott, J.	4.50

The first week the plan was put into operation, production increased to 165 units. The shop superintendent studied the results and considered the plan too costly; production had increased 10%, but the labor cost had increased by approximately 23.2%. The superintendent requested permission to redesign the plan in order to make the labor cost increase proportionate to the productivity increase.

Required:

(1) The dollar amount of the 23.2% labor cost increase.
(2) An opinion, supported by figures, as to whether the shop superintendent was correct in assuming that the incentive wage plan was too costly, and a discussion of other factors to be considered.

6. Incentive plans. Standard production for an employee in the Assembly Department is 20 units per hour in an 8-hour day. The hourly wage rate is $7.50.

Required: The employee's earnings under each of the following conditions (carrying all computations to three decimal places):

(1) If an incentive plan is used, with the worker receiving 80% of the time saved each day, and records indicate:

	UNITS	HOURS
Monday	160	8
Tuesday..................	170	8
Wednesday	175	8

(2) If the 100 Percent Bonus Plan is used and 880 units are produced in a 40-hour week.
(3) If an incentive plan is used, providing an hourly rate increase of 5% for all hours worked each day that quota production is achieved, and records indicate:

	UNITS	HOURS
Monday	160	8
Tuesday..................	168	8
Wednesday	175	8

7. Learning curve and production cost. A company's new process will be carried out in one department. The production process has an expected learning curve of 80%. The cost subject to the learning effect for the first batch produced by the process was $10,000.

Required: The cumulative average cost per batch subject to the learning effect after the 16th batch has been produced, using the learning curve function.

(AICPA adapted)

8. Learning curve. The Greeley Company uses labor standards in the manufacturing of its products. Based upon past experience, the company considers the effect of an 80% learning curve when developing standards for direct labor costs.

The company is planning the production of an automatic electrical timing device requiring the assembly of purchased components. Production is planned in lots of five units each. A steady-state production phase with no further increases in labor productivity is expected after the eighth lot. The first production lot of 5 units required 90 hours of direct labor time at a standard rate of $6 per hour.

Required:

(1) The standard amount the company should establish for the total direct labor cost required for the production of the first 8 lots.
(2) Discussion of the factors that should be considered in establishing the direct labor standards for each unit of output produced beyond the first 8 lots.

(CMA adapted)

PROBLEMS

14-1. Planning labor costs. Messmer, Inc., a relatively new company in the environmental control industry, is experiencing tremendous growth in product demand. To meet customers' increasing demands, the management is considering the addition of a nighttime production shift beginning October 1.

Production takes place in three departments: Assembly, Molding, and Finishing. Standard time in the Molding Department is 10 minutes per unit produced, while the Finishing Department averages 12½ items per hour. Employees in these two departments are paid $8 per hour. Two people are needed in the Assembly Department, each with a monthly salary of $1,400, to serve the extra shift. Five cleanup employees are needed, and one supervisor for each 19 workers (including cleanup employees) is required in the Molding and Finishing Departments. Supervisors are paid $1,800 per month, and each member of the cleanup crew is paid $5.50 per hour.

Under normal conditions, the company schedules 20 workdays per month, with a standard monthly production of 120,000 units.

Required: A monthly labor budget for the extra shift, showing the time required in each department, the labor cost for each department and service, the unit labor cost, and the number of employees required. (Round off unit costs to four decimal places.)

14-2. Labor performance report; efficiency variances. The Elting Company is interested in improving its control over labor costs. The Accounting Department assembled the following data for September:

LABOR ACTIVITY	ACTUAL HOURS	ACTUAL EXPENSE
Productive labor time	8,000	$63,900
Setup time	200	1,554
Cleanup time	110	662
Downtime	350	2,776

A predetermined standard of 7,700 hours of productive labor has been provided. Statistical analysis has established that setup time, cleanup time, and downtime should be 3%, 1%, and 4%, respectively, of standard production time allowed. The standard labor rate is $8 per hour.

Required:
(1) A labor performance report for September, including total variances and labor efficiency variances, to be sent to the plant manager.
(2) An explanation and analysis for any difference between the labor efficiency variance and the total labor variance.

14-3. Incentive wage plans. Standard production for a worker is 10 units per hour or 400 units per workweek. The hourly wage rate is $8 and factory overhead is $4 per direct labor hour.

Required:
(1) The following schedule, assuming that the Halsey Premium Plan is used, with the worker receiving 75% of the labor cost value of the time saved. (Round off unit costs to three decimal places.)

NO. OF UNITS	DAILY WAGE	UNITS ABOVE STANDARD	HOURS SAVED	VALUE OF TIME SAVED	PREMIUM 75%	TOTAL PAY PER HOUR	CONVERSION COST PER UNIT
80	$64	0					
90	64	10					
110	64	30					

(2) A schedule, using the format shown on the bottom of page 401, assuming that the 100 Percent Bonus Plan is used and the worker produced 450 units in 40 hours. (Round off unit costs to three decimal places.) (continued)

(3) The following schedule, assuming that the Measured Daywork incentive plan is in effect, with a daily quota of 80 units and the hourly wage rate increased 5% if the quota is met or exceeded:

DAY	UNITS	WAGE RATE PER HOUR	AMOUNT EARNED	LABOR COST PER UNIT	CONVERSION COST PER UNIT
Monday	80				
Tuesday	90				

14-4. Group bonus plan. Employees of Frenkel and Frey Enterprises work in groups of five, plus a group leader. Standard production for a group is 400 units for a 40-hour week. The workers are paid $6 an hour until production reaches 400 units; then a bonus of $1.20 per unit is paid, with $1 being divided equally among the five workers and the remainder passing to the group leader (who is also paid a weekly salary of $300). Factory overhead is $6 per direct labor hour and includes the group leader's earnings.

The production record of a group for one week shows:

	HOURS WORKED	UNITS PRODUCED
Monday	40	72
Tuesday	40	81
Wednesday	40	95
Thursday	40	102
Friday	40	102

Required:
(1) The week's earnings of the group (excluding the leader), the labor cost per unit, the overhead cost per unit, and the conversion cost per unit, based upon the above data. (Round off unit costs to four decimal places.)
(2) A schedule showing daily earnings of the group (excluding the leader), unit labor cost, unit overhead cost, and the conversion cost per unit, assuming that the company uses the group bonus plan.

14-5. Quarterly bonus allotment. Fitts and Preucel, Inc., manufacturers of standard pipe fittings for water and sewage lines, pay a bonus to their employees, based upon the production recorded each calendar quarter. Normal production is set at 240,000 units per quarter. A bonus of $.25 per unit is paid for any units in excess of the normal output for each quarter. Distribution of the bonus is made on the following point basis:

EMPLOYEES PARTICIPATING	POINTS ALLOWED FOR EACH EMPLOYEE
1 Works manager	250
2 Production engineers	200
5 Shop supervisors	200
1 Storekeeper	100
5 Factory office clerks	10
150 Factory workers	20

The employees' earnings are not penalized for any month in which the actual output falls below the monthly average of the normal quarterly production. In such a case, the deficiency is deducted from any excess in subsequent months before any bonus is earned by and paid to the employees.

At the end of March, cumulative actual production amounted to 270,000 units.

Required:
(1) A calculation showing the amount of bonus payable to each group of employees (Carry all calculations to four decimal places.)
(2) Journal entries at the end of each month on the basis of the following production figures: January, 75,000 units; February, 94,000 units; March, 101,000 units.
(3) A statement as to whether this bonus is considered a direct labor cost or a factory overhead item and its position on the income statement.

14-6. Incentive wage plans. The company's union steward complained to the payroll department that several union members' wages had been miscalculated in the previous week. The schedule below indicates the wages and conditions of the earnings of the workers involved:

Worker	Incentive Wage Plan	Total Hours	Down-time Hours	Units Pro-duced	Stan-dard Units	Base Rate	Gross Wages per Books
Dodd	Straight piecework	40	5	400	—	$6.00	$284.00
Hare	Straight piecework	46	—	455*	—	6.00	277.20
Lowe	Straight piecework	44	4	420**	—	6.00	302.20
Ober	Percentage bonus plan	40	—	250	200	6.00	280.00
Rupp	Percentage bonus plan	40	—	180	200	5.00	171.00
Suggs	Emerson Efficiency	40	—	240	300	5.60	233.20
Ward	Emerson Efficiency	40	2	590	600***	5.60	280.00

*Includes 45 pieces produced during the 6 overtime hours.
**Includes 50 pieces produced during the 4 overtime hours. The overtime, brought about by the downtime, was necessary to meet a production deadline.
***Standard units for 40 hours production.

The company's union contract contains the following description of the systems for computing wages in various departments of the company. The minimum wage for a worker is the base rate, which is also paid for any downtime when the worker's machine is under repair or there is no work. Workers are paid 150% of base rates for overtime production in a standard workweek of 40 hours.

(a) Straight piecework. The worker is paid at the rate of $.66 per piece produced.
(b) Percentage bonus plan. Standard quantities of production per hour are established by the Engineering Department. The worker's average hourly production, determined from the total hours worked and the worker's production, is divided by the standard quantity of production to determine an efficiency ratio. The efficiency ratio is then applied to the base rate to determine the worker's hourly earnings for the period.
(c) Emerson Efficiency system. A minimum wage is paid for total hours worked. A bonus, calculated from the following table of rates, is paid when the worker's production exceeds $66\frac{2}{3}\%$ of standard output or efficiency. The bonus rate is applied only to wages earned during productive hours.

Efficiency	Bonus
Up to $66\frac{2}{3}\%$	0
$66\frac{2}{3}$ – 79%	10%
80 – 99%	20
100 – 125%	45

Required: A schedule comparing each individual's gross wages per books with the gross wages calculated.

(AICPA adapted)

14-7. Computation of learning curve and other program costs deferred. A company that produces large special-purpose computers has introduced a new model of an existing product. The new machine represents a significant technological advancement, and substantial learning curve costs are expected. Based on extensive studies, the company has determined that it is reasonable to forecast a market of at least 200 units for the new computer. Accordingly, the company has calculated its estimated average cost of sales per machine as follows:

Initial tooling and other production costs	$ 2,000,000
Estimated production cost (200 units × $90,000)	18,000,000
Total estimated production cost	$20,000,000
Number of units to be produced and sold	200
Average cost per unit ($10,000 initial cost + $90,000 production cost)	$100,000

At the balance sheet date, the company has received firm orders for 150 computers. As of this same date, the company has delivered and installed 45 computers; 35 additional units are in production and are estimated to represent 15 equivalent completed units. The total cost incurred at the balance sheet date, including initial tooling and other production costs, was $9,350,000.

Required: The amount to be reported as production learning curve and other program costs deferred.

CASES

A. Setting productivity standards. Anvil, Inc., intends to expand its Punch Press Department with the purchase of three new presses from Presco, Inc. Mechanical studies indicate that for Anvil's intended use, the output rate for one press should be 1,000 pieces per hour. The company has similar presses now in operation that average 600 pieces per hour. This average is derived from these individual outputs:

WORKER	DAILY OUTPUT (IN PIECES)
Allen, W.	750
Miller, G.	750
Salermo, J.	600
Velasquez, E.	500
Underwood, P.	550
Keppinger, J.	450
Total.....................................	3,600
Average daily output...............	600

Anvil's management also plans to institute a standard cost accounting system in the very near future. The company's engineers are supporting a standard based upon 1,000 pieces per hour; the Accounting Department, a standard based upon 750 pieces per hour; and the Punch Press Department supervisor, a standard based upon 600 pieces per hour.

Required:
(1) Arguments which each proponent could use.
(2) The alternative which best reconciles the needs of cost control and the motivation of improved performance, with an explanation for the choice made.

(CMA adapted)

B. Designing a compensation plan. Fabray, Inc., manufactures and sells costume jewelry and men's and women's toiletries. Sales are seasonal, with the major sales volume to retailers occurring in the months preceding Mother's Day, Father's Day, and Christmas. The company is planning to revise its method for compensating its sales force in an attempt to encourage the salespeople to increase their sales efforts.

One compensation system under consideration is a combination salary, commission, and bonus plan. Each salesperson would receive a monthly (base) salary on the first of each month and would earn a 5% commission on all sales. The commission would be earned in two installments: half in the month of delivery and the remaining half in the month of collection. The applicable commission earned in the month would be paid on the 15th of the following month. In addition, sales personnel could earn a bonus if the sales for the month exceeded the monthly sales quota. The bonus would be equal to 2% of the commission earned for sales delivered during the month and would be paid on the 15th of the following month.

The base salary and sales quotas will be established at the beginning of the year. The base salary will be reevaluated annually for each salesperson, considering such factors as cost of living, performance, and length of service. An annual sales quota will be prepared for each sales territory, based upon management's expectations for sales in that territory. The monthly sales quota for each territory will then be determined by dividing the annual sales quota by 12.

Required:
    (1) The factors to be considered when designing a compensation plan for employees.
    (2) Identification and discussion of the strengths and weaknesses of the company's compensation plan in terms of:
        (a) The company's attempt to encourage its sales force to increase its sales efforts.
        (b) The behavioral and motivational factors that influence employees' actions.

(CMA adapted)

C. Controlling hiring practices and payroll procedures. The Ballard Corporation employs about fifty production workers. The factory supervisor interviews applicants and either hires or rejects them. When hired, the applicant prepares a W-4 form (Employee's Withholding Exemption Certificate) and gives it to the supervisor, who writes the hourly rate of pay in the corner of the W-4 form. The form is then given to a payroll clerk as notice that the worker has been employed. The supervisor verbally advises the Payroll Department of rate adjustments.

A supply of blank time cards is kept in a box near the entrance to the factory. Each worker takes a time card on Monday morning, fills in his or her name, and notes daily arrival and departure times in pencil. At the end of the week, the worker drops the time card in a box near the factory door.

The completed time cards are taken from the box on Monday morning by a payroll clerk. Two payroll clerks divide the time cards alphabetically, one taking the A to L section of the payroll and the other taking the M to Z section. Each clerk is fully responsible for a section of the payroll, computing the gross pay, deductions, and net pay, posting the details to the employees' earnings records, and preparing and numbering the payroll checks. Employees are automatically removed from the payroll when they fail to turn in a time card.

The payroll checks are manually signed by the chief accountant and given to the supervisor, who distributes the checks to the workers in the factory and arranges for the delivery of the checks to absent workers. The payroll bank account is reconciled by the chief accountant, who also prepares the various quarterly and annual payroll tax reports.

Required: Suggestions for improving the Ballard Corporation's system of internal control for factory hiring practices and payroll procedures.

D. Control of computerized payroll procedures. The Wayne Corporation has been in business for the past eighteen years and has grown from a very small family-owned operation to a medium-sized manufacturing concern with several departments. A substantial number of the procedures employed by Wayne Corporation have been in effect since the business was started.

Recently the corporation has computerized its payroll function. All workers pick up weekly time cards on Monday morning and write in their names and identification numbers. These cards are kept near the factory entrance. The workers write the time of their daily arrival and departure on the cards. Each Monday, the factory supervisors collect the completed time cards for the previous week and send them to the Data Processing Department.

In Data Processing the time cards are used to prepare the weekly time file which is processed with the master payroll file maintained on magnetic tape according to worker identification number. The checks are written by the computer on the regular checking account and imprinted with the treasurer's signature. After the payroll file is updated and the checks are prepared, the checks are sent to the factory supervisors, who distribute them to the workers or hold them for the workers to pick up later if they are absent.

The supervisors notify Data Processing of new employees and terminations. Any changes in hourly pay rates or any other changes affecting payroll are usually communicated to Data Processing by the supervisors.

The workers also complete a time ticket for each individual job worked on each day. These are collected daily and sent to Cost Accounting to prepare a cost distribution analysis.

Further analysis of the payroll function reveals the following:

(a) A worker's gross wage never exceeds $300 per week.
(b) Raises never exceed $.55 per hour for the factory workers.
(c) No more than 20 hours of overtime are allowed each week.
(d) The factory employs 150 workers in ten departments.

The payroll function has not been operating smoothly for some time, but new problems have surfaced since the payroll was computerized. The supervisors have indicated that they would like a weekly report indicating worker tardiness, absenteeism, and idle time, so that they can determine the amount of productive time lost and the reason for the lost time. The following errors and inconsistencies have been encountered the past few pay periods:

(a) A worker's paycheck was not processed properly because of transposing two numbers of the identification number when filling out the time card.
(b) A worker was issued a check for $1,531.80 when it should have been $153.81.
(c) One worker's paycheck was not written, and this error was not detected until the paychecks for that department were distributed by the supervisor.
(d) Part of the master payroll file was destroyed when the tape reel was inadvertently mounted on the wrong tape drive and used as a scratch tape. Data Processing attempted to reestablish the destroyed portion from original source documents and other records.
(e) One worker received a paycheck for an amount considerably larger than earned. Further investigation revealed that 84 had been punched instead of 48 for hours worked.
(f) Several records on the master payroll file were skipped and not included on the updated master payroll file. This was not detected for several pay periods.
(g) In processing nonroutine changes, a computer operator included a pay rate increase for a friend in the factory. This was discovered by chance by another employee.

Required: A discussion of control weaknesses in the payroll procedure and in the computer processing as it is now conducted and recommended changes necessary to correct the system.

(CMA adapted)

15

Accounting for Labor-Related Costs

Fundamentally, a labor cost consists of the hourly rate, the daily or weekly wage, or the monthly salary paid to an employee. Yet, in addition to the basic earnings computed on hours worked or units produced, many other cost elements enter into labor cost: overtime earnings; premium pay for work on holidays, Saturdays, and Sundays when overtime is not involved; shift bonuses or differentials; production incentives such as an attendance bonus, length-of-service bonus, nonaccident bonus, and Christmas or year-end bonus; paid vacations; apprenticeship or trainee costs and training programs for the hard-core unemployed; dismissal or severance pay; and retirement pensions. In addition to these elements, labor cost usually includes paid holidays; unemployment compensation; FICA tax; other insurance such as life, accident, and workmen's compensation; hospital, surgical, and dental benefits for employees and their dependents; and in some companies, jury service pay and even free lunches. The total cost to keep an employee at work for an hour or a full day will include some or all of these fringe benefits. For factory workers, labor and labor-related costs may be classified as direct labor or factory overhead; for sales personnel, as marketing expense; and for office and administrative personnel, as administrative expense.

OVERTIME EARNINGS

The Fair Labor Standards Act of 1938, commonly referred to as the Federal Wage and Hour Law, established a minimum wage per hour with time and a half for hours worked in excess of 40 in one week. Subsequently the Act has been amended, broadening the coverage and raising the minimum wage.[1] Some types of organizations and workers are exempt from the provisions of the Act and its amendments, or have lower minimums.

A number of payroll practices are mandatory to comply with the Federal Wage and Hour Law. For each employee, records must show:

1. Hours worked each working day and the total hours worked during each workweek.
2. Basis on which wages are paid.
3. Total daily or weekly earnings at straight time.
4. Total extra pay for overtime worked each week.
5. Total wages paid during each pay period, the date of payment, and the work period covered by the payment.

Overtime earnings consist of two elements: (1) the regular pay due for the employee's work and (2) the overtime premium pay, which is an additional amount for work done beyond the 40-hour workweek or a regular workday (as specified in some labor union contracts). For most workers, an employer must pay as a minimum the regular rate plus one half the rate for overtime employment. For example, if an employee is paid $8 per hour for a regular workweek of 40 hours, but works 45 hours, the gross earnings are:

Regular workweek	40 hours @ $8 =	$320
Overtime	5 hours @ 8 =	40
Overtime premium	5 hours @ 4 =	20
Gross earnings		$380

Charging overtime premium pay to a specific job or product or to factory overhead depends primarily upon the reason for the overtime work. The contract price of a particular job, taken as a rush order with the foreknowledge that overtime will be necessary, may include the premium wage factor, which should be charged to the specific job. When orders cannot be completed in the regular working hours, the overtime premium pay should be included in the predetermined factory overhead rate as factory overhead, because it cannot properly be allocated to work that happens to be in process during overtime hours.

BONUS PAYMENTS

Bonus payments may be a fixed amount per employee or job classification, a percentage of profits, a fraction of one month's wages, or some other

---

[1]In 1980, the minimum wage is $3.10 per hour; in subsequent years, it is scheduled to be increased.

calculated amount. The amount of bonus for each employee may be a fixed and long-established tradition of a company, or the amount may vary from year to year. Bonus payments are a production cost, a marketing expense, or an administrative expense. If a factory worker's average weekly earnings are $250 and the company intends to pay two weeks' pay as a bonus at the end of the year, then earnings actually amount to $260 per week, but the additional $10 per week is paid in a lump sum of $500 ($10 × 50 weeks, assuming two weeks of vacation time) at the end of the year. To spread the bonus cost over production throughout the year via the predetermined factory overhead rate, the weekly entry would be:

	SUBSIDIARY RECORD	DR.	CR.
Work in Process		250	
Factory Overhead Control		10	
Bonus Pay	10		
Payroll			250
Liability for Bonus			10

When the bonus is paid, the liability account is debited and Cash and the withholding accounts are credited.

In theory, this and other direct-labor-related costs are additional labor costs that should be charged to Work in Process the same as the employees' gross wages. In practice, such a procedure usually is impractical, and these costs are generally included in the predetermined factory overhead rate.

VACATION PAY

Vacation pay presents cost problems similar to those of bonus payments. When a shop employee is entitled to a paid vacation of 2 weeks, the total wages earned during 50 weeks of productive labor are paid over a period of 52 weeks. For example, assume that an employee has a base wage of $200 per week and is entitled to a paid vacation of 2 weeks. The cost of labor is $200, plus $8 per week. In 50 weeks at $8 per week, the deferred payment of $400 will equal the expected vacation pay. The entry to set up the weekly labor cost including the provision for vacation pay would be:

	SUBSIDIARY RECORD	DR.	CR.
Work in Process		200	
Factory Overhead Control		8	
Vacation Pay	8		
Payroll			200
Liability for Vacation Pay			8

When the vacation is taken, the liability account is debited and Cash and the withholding accounts are credited. Similarly, accrual should be made for employer liability pertaining to sick leave, holidays, jury duty, military training, or other personal activities for which employees receive compensation.

Salaried employees usually receive two or more weeks of vacation. Vacation pay of salaried workers, as well as payment for other absences, should also be considered to accrue during the time these employees perform their duties. If it becomes necessary to hire temporary employees to perform the duties of salaried personnel who are absent, this additional expense is rightfully charged to the departmental salary accounts.[2]

GUARANTEED ANNUAL WAGE PLANS

While a guaranteed annual wage plan for all industrial workers is far from realization, a step in that direction has been taken in labor contracts that provide for the company to pay employees who are laid off. In one industry's plan, for example, the unemployed worker is guaranteed 60 to 65 percent of normal take-home pay, beginning the second week of layoff and continuing for as long as 26 weeks. The company pay is a supplement to the state unemployment insurance. To provide funds from which payments can be made during unemployment periods, a specified amount such as $.10 an hour for each worker is paid into a fund by the company.

In principle, if it is assumed that layoffs will eventually occur, it is clear that the employee while working is earning $.10 an hour that is not included in the paycheck at the end of the payroll period. This amount is held in reserve by the company in order to make payments during unemployment periods. For a factory worker whose base pay rate is $5 an hour, the cost effect of unemployment pay for a 40-hour week is illustrated by this entry:

	SUBSIDIARY RECORD	DR.	CR.
Work in Process		200	
Factory Overhead Control		4	
Unemployment Pay	4		
Payroll			200
Liability for Unemployment Pay.............			4

Another version of this plan is one which guarantees that a worker's weekly paycheck will not fall below a minimum figure and sets no upper limit on earnings during other weeks of the pay period. This plan amounts to a

---

[2]The accrual of employer obligations for labor-related costs for personal absence is required in accounting for government contracts to which CASB regulations apply. *Standards, Rules and Regulations, Part 408*, "Accounting for Costs of Compensated Personal Absence" (Washington, D.C.: Cost Accounting Standards Board, 1974).

As this text goes to press, the FASB is proposing that employers should accrue the liability for vacation pay and other future payments attributable to employees' current service. *Proposed Statement of Financial Accounting Standards* "Accounting for Compensated Absences" (Stamford: Financial Accounting Standards Board, December 17, 1979).

floor placed under weekly earnings to keep them above a predetermined minimum. Employees are paid their actual earnings each pay period; the guarantee comes into effect only when earnings drop below the minimum.

APPRENTICESHIP AND TRAINING PROGRAMS

In many plants, new workers receive some preliminary training before they become economically productive. The portion of the wages paid in excess of the average or standard paid for the productive output, plus the cost of instruction, is an indirect labor cost to be charged to the total annual output through inclusion in the factory overhead rates. When unusual training programs are needed as a result of the opening of a new plant or the activating of a second or third shift, a case can be made for treating the training cost as development or starting load cost and deferring a portion of the cost over a period of time.

HUMAN RESOURCE ACCOUNTING

In annual reports, management often speaks in glowing terms of its employees as the company's most valuable asset. Yet management makes little effort to assess the value of this asset, and the company's accounting system does little to provide any assistance. For example, many firms invest heavily in personnel training programs without evaluating the expected payoff or the return on such investments. A firm is apt to send its managers to a variety of executive development programs whose value is essentially taken on faith and which are discontinued when profits cannot afford them.

Human resource accounting is the process of developing financial assessments of people or groups of people within organizations and society and of monitoring these assessments over time. It deals with the value of investments in human beings and with the related economic results. Managers are being asked to give more serious consideration to human resource investment decisions and to the human resource impact of all their decisions. Thus, the personnel function within an organization may serve more efficiently its role of acquisition, development, and utilization of human resource potential.

A human resource accounting system needs to identify incurred human resource costs that are to be separated from the firm's other costs. The techniques and procedures used should distinguish between the asset and expense components of human resource costs. The resulting human resource assets would then be classified into functional categories, such as recruiting, hiring, training, development, and familiarization. Such information would purportedly enable management to make decisions based on a realistic cost/benefit analysis and cost amortization and would provide investors with an improved basis to assess the value of an enterprise.

The quantification of human resources appears to be the first stumbling block for the creation of human resource accounting. All companies have methods of measuring sales, profits, investments in plant and equipment, and investments in inventories. Similarly, incurred human resource costs, such as training programs, can be measured, although determining the time period for amortization may be difficult. But beyond the possibility of capitalizing certain incurred human resource costs, how does a company set a quantitative value for such attributes as loyalty, skills, morale, decision-making ability, and intelligence? Since it seems difficult to quantify these human factors, it seems equally difficult to assign asset status to human resources except when measured incurred costs can be identified. The justification for measuring an asset value is based on the economic concept that an asset is capable of providing future benefits to the firm. Since the employee group is important to the future success of the company, it has value that should be reported as an asset on the balance sheet. Asset determination for human resources is particularly meaningful for professional sports franchises where a superstar is essentially the asset that creates gate receipts. As with any other asset, the professional athlete can be sold or traded, which increases the litigation involving current player contracts.

In spite of the difficulties, a number of proposals have attempted to utilize human resource accounting. Some proposals focus on incurred costs only, while others encompass estimated values. These proposals are:

1. *Capitalizing salaries* — whereby a firm assumes that what the employees are doing will be of some future benefit to the firm and that appropriate rates of capitalization can be determined.

2. *Capitalizing the cost of acquiring an employee* — a plan that would require collecting the costs of acquiring, hiring, and training. (A precedent for this method exists in professional sports.)

3. *Capitalizing startup costs* — involves not only capitalizing startup costs but goes one step further by considering the synergistic components of cost and time required for members of a firm to establish effective cooperative working relationships.

4. *Behavioral variables approach* — involves periodic measurements of the key causal and intervening variables for the corporation as a whole. Statistical variation in leadership styles and technical proficiency levels (causal variables) and the resulting changes in subordinate attitudes, motivations, and behavior (intervening variables) can establish relationships between such variables. These changes would produce changes in the end-result variables such as productivity, innovation, and human resource developments; and trends in earnings could then be predicted. These forecasts are discounted to find the present value of the human resources.

5. *Opportunity costs* — suggest that investment center managers are encouraged to bid for any scarce employee they desire. The winning

manager includes the bid in the investment base. The division's benefit is the increased profit produced by the new employee.

6. *Economic value approach* — compares differences in present and future earnings of similar firms in the same industry. Ostensibly, the differences are due to human organization. Future earnings are forecast and discounted to find their present value. A portion thereof is allocated to human resources based on their contribution.

7. *Present value method* — involves determining wage payments over perhaps a five-year period, and then discounting these payments at the rate of return of owned assets in the economy for the most recent year. This calculation yields the present value of the future five-years' wage payments based on this year's return.

8. *Stochastic rewards valuation model* — involves a stochastic process defined as a natural system that changes in time in accordance with the law of probability. To measure an individual's value to an organization requires:

(a) An estimate of the time interval during which an individual is expected to render services to the organization, and

(b) A measure of the services expected to be derived from the individual during this interval.

The resource's expected value is then multiplied by a discount factor to arrive at the present value of expected future services.[3]

Human resource data may be part of a large-scale accounting system or merely part of a specific project application. Although the human resource accounting movement might gain an aura of respectability from inclusion in external reports, these data seem more useful for managerial decisions, i.e., an internal reporting focus.

At present, the value of human resource accounting systems for specific purposes must be determined by designing models and methods which can be empirically tested. Research is required to demonstrate both the feasibility and the effects of human resource accounting on management's attitude, behavior, and decisions. Unless empirical data from organizations using such systems are collected, analyzed, and published, current theoretical arguments may soon lose their glamour.[4]

PENSION PLANS

A *pension plan* is an arrangement whereby a company provides retirement benefit payments for all employees in recognition of their work contribution to the company. A pension plan is probably the most important as well as the most complicated factor associated with labor and labor costs. It influ-

---

[3]Roger Jauch and Michael Skigen, "Human Resources Accounting: A Critical Evaluation," *Management Accounting*, Vol. LV, No. 11, pp. 33–36.

[4]For an example of empirical research, see Lawrence A. Tomassini, "Assessing the Impact of Human Resource Accounting: An Experimental Study of Managerial Decision Preferences," *The Accounting Review*, Vol. LII, No. 4, pp. 904–913. In this study, human resource accounting cost data caused different preferences to be expressed between the experimental and control group subjects.

ences personnel relations, company financing, income determination, income tax considerations, and general economic conditions. It must also comply with governmental regulations.

Pension Cost Estimate

The ultimate cost of a company pension plan depends upon several related factors:

1. The number of employees reaching retirement age each year.
2. The average benefit to be paid to each retired employee.
3. The average period over which benefits will be paid.
4. Income from pension fund investments.
5. Income tax allowances.
6. Expense of administration.
7. Treatment of benefits to employees who leave the company before reaching the pension age.

When a pension plan is initiated, the amount necessary to provide pensions for all employees who are expected to stay until retirement is the product of (1) the number of employees eventually to retire, (2) the average benefit, and (3) the average period of payment. To illustrate, assume that a company has 100 employees who are each to be paid $6,000 per year for an average of 10 years for an estimated eventual cost of $6,000,000. If each employee who retires has worked an average of 30 years, the average annual cost is $200,000 ($6,000,000 ÷ 30 years). The annual cost per employee would then be $2,000 ($200,000 ÷ 100 employees). If each employee works 40 hours per week and 50 weeks per year, the pension cost of each of the 2,000 hours worked is $1. While this procedure ignores administrative cost and the earnings from funds invested, it is indicative of a method that may be used to convert the pension cost to an hourly basis.

Pension Cost Allocation

In the case of bonuses and paid vacations, part of the total earnings of an employee is withheld or accrued for a period of months and then paid in a lump sum. In the case of pension payments, the wage is earned and the labor cost is incurred many years before the payment is made. As a matter of principle, if an employee is paid a base wage of $320 for a 40-hour week and if the retirement payments to be made will amount to $1 an hour, the pension cost incurred is $40 per week and is chargeable to factory overhead, marketing expense, or administrative expense.[5]

Employee Retirement Income Security Act of 1974

The Employee Retirement Income Security Act of 1974 (more commonly known as ERISA or the Pension Reform Act of 1974) was enacted in order to make certain that promised pensions are actually paid at retirement. This Act sets minimum government standards for vesting, participation, funding, management, and a variety of other matters. The Act also covers a wide range of

---

[5]For an extensive study of accounting for pension plans, refer to: *AICPA Research Study No. 8* (1965) by E. L. Hicks; *APB Opinion No. 8* (1966); *FASB Interpretation No. 3* (1974); *CASB Standard No. 412* (1975) and *Standard No. 413* (1977).

employee welfare plans for health, accident, and death benefits. In addition, it covers pension or retirement plans and establishes both labor standards (administered by the Secretary of Labor) and tax standards (administered by the Secretary of the Treasury). The labor and tax standards taken together form a common body of legislation pertaining to practically all employee benefit plans not specifically exempted from the Act.

Virtually every private pension, profit-sharing, thrift, or savings plan has been amended in recent years in order to comply with the Pension Reform Act of 1974. All plans must contend with increased record keeping, compliance, and reporting. Many plans are burdened with increased costs and/or funding obligations. Plans most likely to be affected are those that (1) have not provided for a substantial degree of vesting prior to retirement, (2) have not been funding past service costs or have operated on a pay-as-you-go basis, and (3) have had restrictive criteria as to age and years of service as a condition for participation.

The Pension Reform Act of 1974, a vast and momentous piece of legislation, should be studied by every accounting student.[6] The presentation here enumerates only a few matters relevant to labor-related costs. Among the more important changes and new requirements affecting employers and employees are:

1. New employees cannot be denied participation for more than one year unless an employee is under twenty-five years of age or benefits are fully vested at the end of a three-year waiting period. The law prohibits a plan from excluding an employee because of advanced age if employment began at least five years prior to normal retirement age.
2. An employer's minimum annual contribution generally must include the normal cost for the year plus amortization of initial past service liabilities, liabilities resulting from plan amendments, and experience gains and losses. Amortization payments must be calculated on a level payment basis. The amortization period for initial past service costs is forty years for existing plans and thirty years for new plans. The periods for liabilities resulting from plan amendments and experience gains and losses are thirty years and fifteen years, respectively.
3. In case the assets of a terminated plan are not sufficient to pay the insured benefits, the Pension Benefit Guaranty Corporation (PBGC) guarantees vested benefits of terminated plans up to $750 per month for each participant or beneficiary of plans with more than 25 participants over a five-year period. To finance this insurance program the PBGC collects a premium from all covered plans. The annual premium is $2.60 per participant.
4. Descriptions of the plan and annual financial, actuarial, and other information must be provided to participants and beneficiaries, the Secretaries of Labor and the Treasury, and the PBGC.

Vesting. A participant of a pension plan is assured of receiving future benefits under a plan when rights to the benefits become vested. *Vesting* means that

---

[6]The student is encouraged to refer to *Explanation of Pension Reform Act of 1974* (P. L. 93–406), Commerce Clearing House, Inc.; Pamphlet No. 4891 (1974), pp. 1–96.

benefits cannot be forfeited even in the event of dismissal or discontinuance of company operations. Employees who resign will still be entitled upon reaching retirement age to receive the benefits in which their rights were vested. The Pension Reform Act of 1974 sets minimum vesting standards that must be met by all plans subject to the participation standards. To protect participants and beneficiaries against a possible loss of pension benefits arising from plan termination, the Act created the aforementioned Pension Benefit Guaranty Corporation within the Department of Labor.

Funding. The Pension Reform Act of 1974 established minimum funding standards for certain defined benefit plans. The effect of these standards is to impose time limitations for accumulating sufficient assets to pay retirement benefits to participants. Generally, employers must contribute currently the normal cost of the plan for the plan year plus a level funding, including interest, of past service costs and certain other costs. Each plan must establish and maintain a funding standard account. A plan satisfies the minimum funding deficiency at the end of the year, as reflected in its funding standard account. An accumulated funding deficiency is the excess of the total charges over the total credits to the funding standard account. The law will not permit the use of the so-called pay-as-you-go method, whereby employers would make periodic pension payments directly to retired employees.

Present Value (PV). Basic to all funding methods is the concept of present value (PV), sometimes referred to as capitalized value. The *present value* principle permits the value at any given point of time to be expressed as the equivalent value at a different point of time under a set of future conditions. The principle is particularly useful in dealing with financial transactions involving a time series, such as periodic contributions and retirement annuities. It permits the computation of an entire series of financial transactions over a period of time to be expressed as a single value at any point of time.

The Role of the Actuary. Computations relating to pension plan costs, contributions, and benefits are made by an *actuary*, an expert in pension, life insurance, and related matters involving life contingencies. An actuary employs mathematical, statistical, financial, and other techniques to compute costs or benefits, to equate costs with benefits, and to evaluate and project actuarial experience under a plan. Membership in the American Academy of Actuaries, or one of the other recognized actuarial organizations, identifies a person as a member of the actuarial profession.

Administrative Problems. The Pension Reform Act of 1974 mandates sweeping changes in the structure and administration of all types of qualified employee benefit plans. In addition, the Pension Reform Act of 1974 creates a staggering number of complicated requirements in such areas as disclosure, reporting, investments, and insurance. For example, an employer must report to four main government agencies: The Department of Labor, the Pension Benefit

Guaranty Corporation (for plans covered by termination insurance), the Internal Revenue Service, and the Secretary of Labor. A Summary Description Report must also be prepared and sent to all participants and beneficiaries.

For many businesses, the new and more rigid requirements for eligibility, vesting, and funding mean dramatically increased pension costs. Pension costs (excluding social security costs) are now running from 5 percent to 10 percent of a company's annual payroll, a level often equivalent to 25 percent or more of its annual profit. It may be only a matter of time before pension costs rise to at least 20 percent of a company's annual payroll. This increase will in turn be translated into price increases that will fuel further wage increases and lead to even higher pension costs.

In 1975, the Cost Accounting Standards Board promulgated Standard No. 412, "Cost Accounting Standards for Composition and Measurement of Pension Cost," establishing the components of pension cost, the bases for measuring such cost, and the criteria for assigning pension cost to cost accounting periods. This standard is to be used in accounting for government contracts to which CASB regulations apply. The CASB asserts that its standard is compatible with the requirements of the Pension Reform Act of 1974, although certain provisions of its standard are more restrictive than the Pension Reform Act. Furthermore, the CASB, while attempting to stay within the general constraints of APB Opinion No. 8, "Accounting for the Cost of Pension Plans," specifies certain features of the Opinion which it feels are not appropriate for government contract costing purposes. In 1977, CASB Standard No. 413, "Adjustment and Allocation of Pension Cost," declared that actuarial gains and losses should be calculated and gave criteria for assigning pension expense to accounting periods and to segments, as well as for valuing pension fund assets.

ADDITIONAL LEGISLATION AFFECTING LABOR-RELATED COSTS

Costing labor and keeping payroll records were relatively simple prior to the first social security act. This legislation made it necessary for many employers to initiate or redesign payroll procedures in order to account accurately for payroll deductions. Later, other state and federal legislation imposed additional requirements affecting the accounting for wages and salaries. For example, the Federal Insurance Contributions Act, federal and state unemployment tax laws, and workmen's compensation laws require periodic reports.[7] As a result of the multiplicity of forms and regulations, competent personnel are needed in a company's payroll department.

---

[7]These pages summarize the major provisons. U.S. Treasury Department Internal Revenue Service Circular E entitled "Employer's Tax Guide" is an excellent source for a more comprehensive coverage of these regulations. A free copy of the current edition can be obtained by writing to the nearest District Director, Internal Revenue Service.

**Federal
Insurance
Contribu-
tions Act
(FICA)**

This legislation is administered and operated entirely by the federal government. Originally enacted in August of 1935 and operative January 1, 1936, the Act provided that employers in a covered industry must withhold 1 percent of the wages paid to each employee up to $3,000 of earnings in any one year, which amounted to a maximum of $30 of FICA tax. The employer was required to contribute an equal amount. Employees in several types of work, such as agricultural workers, domestic services, federal, state, and municipal employees, nonprofit organizations, self-employed persons, and a variety of others, were specifically excluded in the 1935 Act.

The Federal Insurance Contributions Act has been amended many times since 1935, the amendments tending to bring more employees under the Act, and to increase the benefits, the tax rate, and the wage base upon which the tax is levied. Under the 1965 FICA amendments, the long-debated Hospital Insurance Program (Medicare) was enacted.[8]

Records Necessitated by the FICA. The Federal Insurance Contributions Act requires that employers who are subject to its provisions keep records providing:

1. The name, address, and social security account number of each employee.
2. The total amount and the date of each remuneration payment and the period of service covered by such payment.
3. The amount of such remuneration payment that constitutes taxable wages.
4. The amount of tax withheld or collected.

Although the legislation does not order, suggest, or recommend forms or details for securing the required information, the employer must keep records that will enable a government agency to ascertain whether the taxes for which the employer is liable are correctly computed and paid. These records must be kept for at least four years after the date the tax becomes due or the date the tax is paid, whichever is later. Employees are not required to keep records, but the Act recommends that each employee keep accurate and permanent records showing the name and address of each employer, dates for beginning and termination of employment, wages earned, and tax withheld during employment.

Collection and Payment of the FICA Tax. Employers other than those in excluded classes of employment are required to pay a tax on wages paid, equal to the amount paid by the employees. The employer is further required to collect the FICA tax from employees by deducting the current percent from the wages paid each payday up to the current annual limit or base to which the tax applies.

---

[8]Although 6.5 percent for FICA tax is not the current rate at publication date, it is used in the illustrations and in the end-of-chapter material. The actual rate changes from time to time. The wage base to which the tax applies, assumed in this textbook to be annual wages up to $25,000 per employee, is also subject to change.

Federal income tax withheld and employee and employer FICA taxes must be deposited with either an authorized commercial bank depository or a Federal Reserve Bank on a periodic basis, depending on the amount of taxes to be remitted. On or before the last day of the month following each calendar quarter (April 30, July 31, October 31, and January 31), the employer is required to file a quarterly return, remitting the FICA and withheld federal income taxes applicable to the expired quarter, reduced by any deposits made. Ten additional days are allowed for filing the quarterly report if all deposits are made on time.

Unemployment compensation insurance is another phase of social security legislation affecting labor costs and payroll records. Unlike FICA, which is strictly a federal program, FUTA provides for cooperation between state and federal governments in the establishment and administration of unemployment insurance. When the initial legislation was enacted in August, 1935, by the federal government, provisions of FUTA forced various states to pass adequate unemployment laws.

Federal Unemployment Tax Act (FUTA)

Under the Federal Unemployment Tax Act, an employer in covered employment must pay an unemployment insurance tax to the federal government. The annual earnings base is $6,000 of each employee's wages paid with .7 percent payable to the federal government and 2.7 percent to the state.[9]

While the federal legislation provides for 3.4 percent employer payroll tax, most states provide an experience rating plan under which an employer who stabilizes employment may pay less than 2.7 percent to the state agency, with zero as a possible payment. A few states use an earnings base of more than $6,000 in determining the state tax. Most states provide for maximum unemployment insurance rates above 2.7 percent, with rates tending toward a maximum of 4 to 5 percent. While the federal act requires no employee contribution, some states levy an unemployment insurance tax on the employee.

Records Necessitated by the FUTA. Every employer subject to unemployment taxes must keep records providing:

1. The total amount of remuneration paid to each employee during the calendar year.
2. The total amount of such remuneration that constitutes taxable wages.
3. The amount of contributions paid into each state unemployment compensation fund, showing separately (a) payments made and not deducted from the remuneration of employees and (b) payments made and deducted from the remuneration of employees.
4. All information required to be shown on the prescribed tax return.

As with the FICA tax, the Federal Unemployment Tax Act does not prescribe or recommend forms or procedures for securing the required information. Each employer is expected to use accounting procedures and to maintain

[9]The $6,000 base and the rates of .7 percent (federal) and 2.7 percent (state) are current under the federal legislation at the time of publication and are used in the illustrations and in the end-of-chapter material.

records that will enable the Internal Revenue Service to determine whether the tax is correctly computed and paid.

Payment of the FUTA Tax. The federal portion of the unemployment tax is payable quarterly. However, if the employer's tax liability (plus any accumulated tax liability for previous quarters) is $100 or less for the fiscal year, only one payment is required by January 31 of the following year. The related tax return, due January 31, is sent to the IRS regional service center of the employer's principal place of business.

State Unemployment Reports and Payments. The various state unemployment compensation laws require reports from employers to determine their liability to make contributions, the amount of taxes to be paid, and the amount of benefit to which each employee is entitled if unemployment occurs. While the reports and report forms vary from state to state, the more important requirements are:

1. *Status Report.* The status report determines whether an employer is required to make contributions to the state unemployment insurance fund.
2. *Contribution and Wage Report.* All employers covered by the state unemployment compensation laws are required to file quarterly tax returns, commonly called the Contribution and Wage Report. The report provides a summary statement of wages paid during the quarter, a computation of the tax, names of employees, and wages paid to each during the quarter.
3. *Separation Report.* When it becomes necessary to lay off workers, printed materials prepared by the State Employment Commission are provided, informing employees how to secure new employment and how to make an application for unemployment benefits. An employee who quits without good cause or before working a certain number of weeks, is discharged for ample reason, or has been unemployed for a short period may be ineligible for unemployment payments. In these cases, an employer files a separation notice with the State Employment Commission. Since any unemployment benefits paid to a former employee may increase the employer's state rate, the separation notice is filed in order to prevent the charge-back that the State Employment Commission would otherwise make.

Workmen's Compensation Insurance

Workmen's compensation insurance laws provide insurance benefits for workers or their survivors for losses caused by accidents and occupational diseases suffered in the course of employment. These are all state laws and in most states have been in effect for many years. While the benefits, premium costs, and various other details vary from state to state, the total insurance cost is borne by the employer. The employer may have the option of insuring with an approved insurance company or through a state insurance fund. In some cases, if the size and the financial resources are sufficient, the enterprise may carry its own risk.

The employer is required to withhold federal income tax — and state income and city wage taxes if applicable — from salary and wage payments to employees and to furnish information to the Internal Revenue Service and to state and city taxing authorities, showing the amount of remuneration paid each employee and the amount of income taxes withheld. The collection of income taxes from employees and the remittance of these taxes affect payroll accounting. Before new employees begin work, they are required to fill out a withholding exemption certificate (W-4 form).

Withholding of Federal Income Tax, State Income Tax, and City Wage Tax

Income taxes are withheld from each wage payment in accordance with the amount of the employee's earnings and the exemptions claimed on the W-4 form. Employers are required to furnish a written statement or receipt to each employee from whom taxes have been withheld, showing the total wages earned and the amount of taxes withheld (income taxes and FICA) during a calendar year. This withholding statement (W-2 form) must be delivered to the employee on or before January 31 of the following year. If employment is terminated before December 31, the W-2 form must be furnished within 30 days from the last payment of wages.

Each employer must deposit federal income tax withheld and file a quarterly return in the manner described in the discussion of collection and payment of the FICA tax on page 429. A reconciliation of the quarterly returns with duplicate copies of the W-2 forms furnished employees must accompany the fourth-quarter return each year. Therefore, payroll records must show the names of persons employed during the year, the periods of employment, the amounts and dates of payment, and the taxes withheld each payroll date.

The state may also levy an income tax that must be withheld from employees' wages. The tax withheld must be remitted to the taxing authorities along with the required reports. Information must also be supplied to the employee.

A city or municipality may levy a wage earnings tax on an employee working within its boundaries even though the employee is not a resident. Here, too, not only must reports and payments be made to the local taxing authority, but information must also be supplied to the employee.

LABOR-RELATED DEDUCTIONS

In addition to compulsory payroll deductions, a variety of other deductions may be withheld from take-home pay with the consent of the employee.

Many companies provide various benefits for their employees, such as health, accident, hospital, and life insurance. It is common for the company and the employees to share the cost, with the employees' share being deducted from wages each payroll period or at regular intervals. If the company has paid insurance premiums in advance, including the employees' share, an

Insurance

asset account, such as Prepaid Health and Accident Insurance, will be debited at the time that the payments are made. The employer's share will be subsequently credited to the asset account and debited to expenses, and the asset account will be credited for the employees' share of the premiums when the payroll deductions are made. In this payroll deduction, as in all similar cases, a subsidiary ledger showing the contributions of each employee is necessary, and one or more general ledger accounts are maintained.

Union Dues   Many enterprises employing union labor agree to a union shop and to a deduction of initiation fees and regular membership dues from the wages of each employee. To account for these deductions, a column is provided in the payroll journal; and a general ledger account entitled Union Dues Payable shows the liability for amounts withheld from the employees. At regular intervals, the company prepares a report and remits the dues collected to the union treasurer.

U.S. Savings Bonds   To cooperate with the federal government, an employer and an employee frequently agree to some systematic plan of withholding from wages a fixed amount for the purpose of purchasing U.S. Savings Bonds. A deduction column is provided in the payroll journal, and a general ledger account entitled U.S. Savings Bonds Payable is set up to show the liability for wages withheld for this purpose. When the accumulated amount withheld from a given employee is sufficient to purchase a bond, an entry is made debiting U.S. Savings Bonds Payable and crediting Cash.

Payroll Advances   For a variety of reasons, payroll advances may be made to officers, sales representatives, and factory workers. The advances may be in the form of cash, materials, or finished goods. To provide control, an advance authorization form should be executed by a responsible official and should be sent to the payroll department. The asset account debited for all advances represents a receivable to the company and may be entitled Salary and Wage Advances.

When the advances take the form of merchandise, Materials or Finished Goods is credited. If the merchandise is charged to the employee at a figure above cost, Sales may be credited. When the price is above cost but substantially less than the regular sales price, an account entitled Sales to Employees might be maintained. At the regular payroll date, the employee's earnings are entered in the payroll journal as usual, and the advance is deducted from wages to be paid. The amount of the advance being deducted is credited to Salary and Wage Advances.

SUMMARY OF LABOR-RELATED COSTS

The hourly wage or monthly salary which an employer agrees to pay is only a portion of the total wage cost involved. The U.S. Chamber of Commerce surveyed 748 companies and reported that the cost of fringe benefits was 36.7 percent of private industry's salary and wage costs during 1977, up from 35.4 percent in 1975. In 1977, these costs averaged $4,692 per employee, up from $3,984 in 1975.

The following is a list of labor-related costs that could be incurred by an employer, but would not be included in the basic wages:

FICA tax for employees' old-age, survivors, and disability insurance and the hospital insurance program.. 6.5%
Federal unemployment insurance tax (FUTA) 7
State unemployment insurance (representing a typical rate with most companies paying less than the 2.7% maximum)............................. 2.0
State workmen's compensation insurance (rates vary with the hazards — a fraction of 1% to 3% and over)....................................... 1.0
Vacation pay and paid holidays (two weeks of vacation and 7 to 10 holidays in relation to 52 weeks of 40 hours).................................. 8.0
Contributions to pension fund (probable average) 10.0
Recreation, health services, life insurance, medical care 4.0
Contributions to unemployment pay funds 3.5
Time off for voting, jury duty, grievance meetings 1.3
Services related to parking lots, income tax, legal advice, meal money, uniforms... 1.5

Typical total labor-related costs expressed as a percentage of straight-time earnings.. 38.5%

RECORDING LABOR COSTS

Many methods of recording wage transactions exist, depending in part upon the entries that are posted from the payroll journal itself. It is worth repeating that the basic principle of labor costing is simple and straightforward. A record of the labor time "purchased" is made through use of the clock card; a record of the performance received is made through the use of time tickets or the daily time report. The accounting entries required, therefore, are:

1. To record wage payments due employees and the liability for all amounts withheld from wages.
2. To charge the total labor cost to appropriate jobs, processes, and departments.

Weekly, semimonthly, monthly, or as often as a payroll is met, the total amount earned by workers is debited to Payroll with credits to Accrued Payroll and to the withholding accounts. The cost of labor purchased is summarized and recorded as debits to Work in Process, Factory Overhead Control, Marketing Expenses Control, and Administrative Expenses Control and as a credit to Payroll. Employer payroll taxes are recorded, and at appropriate times, payments are made to discharge payroll-related liabilities.

The accounting for labor costs and payroll liabilities is illustrated in general journal form on pages 435 and 436, based upon these assumptions:

1. The payroll period is for January, 19B.

2. The payroll is paid on January 9, 19B, and on January 23, 19B, covering wages earned through the preceding Saturday. Note that the wages of the last week

JANUARY, 19B						
Sun	Mon	Tue	Wed	Thu	Fri	Sat
		1	2	3	4	5
6	7	8	9	10	11	12
13	14	15	16	17	18	19
20	21	22	23	24	25	26
27	28	29	30	31		

of December, 19A, would be paid on January 9 and that the payment of January 23 would cover work done through January 19.

3. Payroll figures for wages earned during January are:

Direct factory labor $38,500
Indirect factory labor 18,000
Sales salaries 20,000
Office and administrative salaries 12,000
Total payroll $88,500

4. Wages paid during January, 19B: $50,000 on January 9, and $40,000 on January 23. Of the federal income tax withheld, $4,800 is on the payroll of January 9 and $3,700 on that of January 23.

5. Wages earned and unpaid on December 31, 19A, total $26,000. On January 31, the amount is $24,500.

6. The cost of the employer's payroll taxes is recorded when the month-end labor cost distribution entry is made, with separate liability accounts for federal and state agencies. Employees' FICA taxes are recorded as a liability when they are withheld at the payroll date, in compliance with the regulations.

Added assumptions:

Unemployment insurance: .7% federal; 2.7% state.
Workmen's compensation: 1% of total payroll.
Pension cost estimated to be $4,000 per month, divided as follows: direct labor, $1,540; indirect labor, $900; sales salaries, $1,000; office and administrative salaries, $560.
Payroll advances, $2,200 deducted on January 9 payroll.
Union dues collected, $1,000 each payroll period.
Savings bonds deductions, $1,200 on January 9 and $900 on January 23.
Health and accident insurance, 1% of payroll, shared equally — employees' share as wages paid, employer's share as wages earned.
Cost for estimated unemployment payments under guaranteed annual wage plan, 2% of factory labor earned.

This illustration records the employer's payroll taxes as a liability when the wages are earned, which follows the accrual concept of accounting. As a practical matter, many employers do not accrue payroll taxes at the end of each fiscal period because the legal liability does not occur until the next period when the wages are paid. This latter practice may be considered acceptable if it is consistently applied or if the amounts are not material; it is, however, required for income tax purposes.

		SUBSIDIARY RECORD	DR.	CR.
	Reversing entry for wages payable as of December 31:			
Jan. 2	Accrued Payroll		26,000.00	
	Payroll			26,000.00
9	Payroll		50,000.00	
	Accrued Payroll			37,300.00
	Employees Income Tax Payable			4,800.00
	FICA Tax Payable			3,250.00
	Salary and Wage Advances			2,200.00
	Union Dues Payable			1,000.00
	U.S. Savings Bonds Payable			1,200.00
	Prepaid Health and Accident Insurance			250.00
9	Accrued Payroll		37,300.00	
	Cash			37,300.00
23	Payroll		40,000.00	
	Accrued Payroll			31,600.00
	Employees Income Tax Payable			3,700.00
	FICA Tax Payable			2,600.00
	Union Dues Payable			1,000.00
	U.S. Savings Bonds Payable			900.00
	Prepaid Health and Accident Insurance			200.00
23	Accrued Payroll		31,600.00	
	Cash			31,600.00
31	Payroll		24,500.00	
	Accrued Payroll			24,500.00
31	Work in Process — Labor		38,500.00	
	Factory Overhead Control		6,699.00	
	FICA Tax	2,502.50		
	Unemployment Insurance Taxes	1,309.00		
	Workmen's Compensation	385.00		
	Pension Expense	1,540.00		
	Health and Accident Insurance	192.50		
	Estimated Unemployment Expense	770.00		
	Payroll			38,500.00
	FICA Tax Payable			2,502.50
	Federal Unemployment Tax Payable			269.50
	State Unemployment Tax Payable			1,039.50
	Prepaid Workmen's Compensation			385.00
	Liability for Pensions			1,540.00
	Prepaid Health and Accident Insurance			192.50
	Liability for Unemployment Pay			770.00

			Subsidiary Record	Dr.	Cr.
Jan. 31	Factory Overhead Control......................................			21,312.00	
		Indirect Labor	18,000.00		
		FICA Tax	1,170.00		
		Unemployment Insurance Taxes	612.00		
		Workmen's Compensation	180.00		
		Pension Expense	900.00		
		Health and Accident Insurance	90.00		
		Estimated Unemployment Expense..............	360.00		
		Payroll			18,000.00
		FICA Tax Payable......................................			1,170.00
		Federal Unemployment Tax Payable..................			126.00
		State Unemployment Tax Payable			486.00
		Prepaid Workmen's Compensation			180.00
		Liability for Pensions			900.00
		Prepaid Health and Accident Insurance			90.00
		Liability for Unemployment Pay........................			360.00
31	Marketing Expenses Control...............................			23,280.00	
		Sales Salaries..	20,000.00		
		FICA Tax	1,300.00		
		Unemployment Insurance Taxes	680.00		
		Workmen's Compensation	200.00		
		Pension Expense	1,000.00		
		Health and Accident Insurance	100.00		
		Payroll			20,000.00
		FICA Tax Payable......................................			1,300.00
		Federal Unemployment Tax Payable..................			140.00
		State Unemployment Tax Payable			540.00
		Prepaid Workmen's Compensation			200.00
		Liability for Pensions			1,000.00
		Prepaid Health and Accident Insurance			100.00
31	Administrative Expenses Control			13,928.00	
		Office and Administrative Salaries	12,000.00		
		FICA Tax	780.00		
		Unemployment Insurance Taxes	408.00		
		Workmen's Compensation	120.00		
		Pension Expense	560.00		
		Health and Accident Insurance	60.00		
		Payroll			12,000.00
		FICA Tax Payable......................................			780.00
		Federal Unemployment Tax Payable..................			84.00
		State Unemployment Tax Payable			324.00
		Prepaid Workmen's Compensation			120.00
		Liability for Pensions			560.00
		Prepaid Health and Accident Insurance			60.00

1. The hourly wage of an employee is $5.50, but the labor cost of the employee is considerably more than $5.50 an hour. Explain.

2. Discuss the accounting treatment of fringe benefits to factory employees.

3. An important function of cost accounting is accounting for labor costs and related fringe benefits.
   (a) Define direct labor and indirect labor.
   (b) Discuss reasons for distinguishing between direct and indirect labor.
   (c) Give three costing methods of accounting for the premium costs of overtime direct labor. State circumstances under which each method would be appropriate.
   (d) A company has expensed vacation pay on the cash basis in prior years and is considering changing to the accrual basis in the next fiscal period. What would be the effects of this change upon the next fiscal period's annual financial statement?

   (AICPA adapted)

4. For many years a company has paid all employees one week's wages as a Christmas bonus. It is also company policy to give 2-week paid vacations. What accounting procedures should be followed with respect to the bonus and vacation pay?

5. The productive efficiency of a company depends upon superior group leaders. The company management suggests that group leaders and selected workers organize a class in personnel administration and group leadership. The class is set up at a nearby university with one of the regular professors in charge. The employees attend the class at night on their own time, but the company pays the tuition charges. How should the company account for this cost?

6. A company has a straight hourly wage rate system with the hourly rates ranging from $4.75 to $7.25, depending solely on the length of the employee's service with the company. Sometimes, unusually high or unusually low labor cost occurs on a job or in a department, depending upon the seniority of the workers who draw the production assignment. The company does not wish to change its wage policy but also does not want per-unit labor cost to depend on the seniority of workers on a particular job or in a particular department. How might the company accomplish both of these objectives?

7. In recent years, the concept of human resource accounting has been theorized in management and accounting literature.
   (a) Define this theory.
   (b) What are the objectives of the concept?
   (c) State the theoretical proposals that have been made in favor of human resource accounting.
   (d) What are some of the more serious drawbacks of this concept?

8. The increasing amount of fringe benefits has focused the attention of accountants on these costs. One of the principal costs is that of pension plans. The total cost of contributions that must be paid ultimately to provide pen-

sions for the present participants in a plan cannot be determined precisely in advance; however, reasonably accurate estimates can be made by the use of actuarial techniques. List the factors entering into the determination of the ultimate cost of a funded pension plan.

(AICPA adapted)

9. The term "pension plan" has been referred to as a formal arrangement for employee retirement benefits, whether established unilaterally or through negotiation, by which specific or implied commitments have been made and used as the basis for estimating costs. Explain the preferable procedure for computing and accruing the costs under a pension plan.

(AICPA adapted)

10. Select the answer which best completes the statement. Past service benefit costs incurred upon the adoption of a pension plan should be charged (debited) to: (a) the current period; (b) retained earnings; (c) current and future periods benefited; (d) future periods benefited.

(AICPA adapted)

11. Define vesting.

12. What is meant by the experience-rating provisions of the unemployment compensation laws of various states?

Unless otherwise directed, use the following rates in the exercises and problems: FICA tax, 6.5%; FUTA tax, .7%; state unemployment insurance tax, 2.7%.

EXERCISES

1. Entries and distribution of payroll. The general ledger of the Ames Company showed these balances at the end of November: direct labor, $24,000; indirect labor, $5,500; sales salaries, $6,000; and office salaries, $4,500. Federal and state unemployment insurance rates apply to only 20% of the payroll in each department. Due to an excellent employment record, the company pays 1% state unemployment insurance tax. Income tax to be withheld is $5,350; there is a city wage tax of 1% on employee gross earnings.

Required:
  (1) The entry to record payroll liability.
  (2) The entry to distribute the payroll cost and to record the employer's payroll taxes.

2. Payroll entries. A company is preparing its monthly payroll for October. The following data apply to Carin Savage, a full-time marketing supervisor:
  (a) Year to date, through September:

Gross pay	$12,000
FICA tax withheld	780
Federal income tax withheld	1,600
Net pay	9,620

  (b) Savage's October earnings were $1,500. Income tax to be withheld is $200.

Required: Entries to record and distribute the payroll and to record the employer's payroll taxes. The state unemployment insurance tax rate is 2%.

3. Recording overtime premium. An employee of the Machining Department is paid $7.50 per hour for a regular week of 40 hours. During the week ended October 18, the employee worked 48 hours and earned time and a half for overtime hours.

Required:
   (1) Entry to distribute the labor cost if the overtime premium is charged to the jobs worked on during the overtime hours.
   (2) Entry to distribute the labor cost if the overtime premium is not charged to specific jobs.

4. Bonus and vacation pay liability. A production worker earns $1,150 per month and the company pays the worker a year-end bonus equal to one month's wages. The worker is also entitled to a half-month paid vacation per year. Company policy dictates that bonus and vacation benefits be treated as indirect costs and accrued during the 11½ months the employee is at work.

Required: The journal entry to record and distribute (simultaneously) the labor cost of the production worker for a month. Assume there are no deductions from gross wages.

5. Bonus and vacation pay liability. Four factory workers and a supervisor comprise a team in the Machining Department. The supervisor earns $10 per hour and the combined hourly direct wages of the four workers is $32. Each employee is entitled to a two-week paid vacation and a bonus equal to four weeks' wages per year. Vacation pay and bonuses are treated as an indirect cost and are accrued over the 50-week work year. A provision in the union contract does not allow these employees to work in excess of 40 hours per week.

Required: The journal entry to record the bonus and vacation liability applicable to one week's production.

6. Pension cost estimation and allocation. The Algonquin Company has just installed a pension plan for its employees. The company operates, on the average, 50 weeks out of the year for 40 hours each week. After an average of 25 years, each of the approximately 100 workers is to receive a pension averaging $10,000 a year for an average of 10 years. For March, the number of direct labor hours was 16,000. The pension cost is recorded monthly on the basis of direct labor hours.

Required:
   (1) Pension cost per direct labor hour for March, assuming that earnings from pension fund investments will provide 50% of the required fund.
   (2) Total pension cost for March.

7. Employer's payroll taxes. A company's earnings records contain the following data for four employees:

CLASSIFICATION	WAGES PAID JANUARY 1 TO MARCH 31	APRIL WAGES
Direct laborer...	$5,700	$1,400
Production supervisor...	6,600	1,600
Salesperson..	5,400	1,100
General accountant	6,300	1,500

Required: Journal entry to record employer's payroll tax accrual for April, assuming that payroll taxes are treated as indirect costs.

8. Fringe benefits. A production worker earns $1,242 a month, and the company pays one month's salary as a bonus at the end of the year. The worker is also entitled to a half-month paid vacation, and the company pays $517.50 a year into a pension fund for the worker. All labor-related fringe benefits for production workers are treated as factory overhead. Bonus, vacation pay, and pension costs are charged to production during the 11½ months the employee is at work. The state unemployment insurance tax rate is 1.6%. The employer's share of FICA tax is $80.73.

Required: The journal entries to record the February payroll distribution and the cost of fringe benefits. Subsidiary ledger accounts are to be omitted.

9. Payroll, tax deductions, and payroll distribution. The information on page 440, taken from the daily time tickets of a producing department, summarizes time and piecework for the week ended April 30.

EMPLOYEE	CLOCK No.	JOB No	HOURS WORKED	PRODUCTION PIECES	HOURLY RATE	PIECE RATE
Belcastro, V.	90	641	40	960	—	$.30
Cherpack, C.	91	—	46	—	$7.00	—
Meadows, A.	92	638	40	—	5.80	—
Smeltzer, S.	93	—	40	—	7.20	—

The company operates on a 40-hour week and pays time and a half for overtime. Additional information:

(a) A FICA tax deduction should be made for each employee.
(b) An advance of $20 was made to Belcastro on April 26.
(c) A 2% deduction is to be made from each employee's wage for the company's employee health and hospital benefit plan.
(d) Cherpack works in the storeroom issuing materials; Smeltzer is the supervisor; the others work directly on special orders as noted.
(e) Use 10% in computing income tax withheld. State unemployment insurance is 2%.

Required:
(1) Each employee's gross pay, deductions, and net pay.
(2) Journal entries to (a) set up the accrued payroll and other liabilities, (b) pay the payroll, and (c) distribute the payroll and record the employer's payroll taxes.

10. Cost principles and cost determination. As a subcontractor under a prime contract with a government agency, a company operating a machine shop undertook to produce certain parts on a cost-plus-fixed-fee basis. The hours of operation were about evenly divided between the above contract and the regular business of the company.

Each day the work required for the regular company business was completed first. The remainder of the day, with whatever overtime was necessary, was given over to production under the contract. During the contract period, overtime hours represented a substantial portion of the total hours worked. Under an agreement with the employees, time and a half was paid for all hours over eight worked each day.

Job sheets recorded the actual costs of materials and direct labor, including any overtime premium paid. Factory overhead was applied on the basis of the labor cost so recorded, and the job sheets were adjusted each month to eliminate any balance in the overhead variance account.

Required:
(1) Objections to the cost accounting principles applied.
(2) Reasons for any incorrectness of the client's statements.
(3) Procedure for making a revised cost determination.   (AICPA adapted)

PROBLEMS

15-1. Entries for payroll and payroll taxes. The general ledger accounts of the Arzee Company contained these credit balances for the period October 1 through November 30:

Employees Income Tax Payable...........	$8,500	Federal Unemployment Tax Payable...	$ 290
FICA Tax Payable.................................	2,940	State Unemployment Tax Payable.......	608

For the December 1–15 payroll, which totaled $28,000, employees' FICA deductions amounted to only $1,230, since some of the employees had already earned the maximum applicable during the year. For the same period, income tax withheld totaled $2,372.

The company apportions employer FICA taxes as follows: 60% to Factory Overhead, 30% to Marketing Expense, and 10% to General Office Expense. The state unemployment insurance tax rate is 2%, and only $5,000 of the payroll (all factory employees) is subject to this tax, since all other employees had earned more than $6,000 by December 1. The company closed for the year on December 15 and had no more payroll expenses.

Required:
(1) The entry to record the payroll for the period December 1–15.
(2) The entry to pay the payroll of December 1–15.
(3) The entry to record the employer's payroll taxes for the period December 1–15.
(4) The entry to record payment of all taxes due governmental agencies for the period October 1 through December 31.

15-2. Payroll taxes, vacation pay, and payroll. The normal workweek at Gabler Publishing, Inc., is Monday through Friday, with payday being the following Tuesday. On November 1, after the reversing entry was posted, the payroll account showed a $2,230 credit balance, representing labor purchased during the last two days of October.

Deductions for FICA tax and 10% for income tax are withheld from each payroll check.

The labor summary for November shows $16,400 of direct labor and $5,600 of indirect labor. Vacation pay is charged to current production at a rate of 4% of total payroll.

Payrolls were: November 7 .... $5,890
14 4,920
21 5,900
28 4,880

NOVEMBER						
Sun	Mon	Tue	Wed	Thu	Fri	Sat
			1	2	3	4
5	6	7	8	9	10	11
12	13	14	15	16	17	18
19	20	21	22	23	24	25
26	27	28	29	30		

Required:
(1) Entries to record each payroll.
(2) The entry on November 30 to distribute the payroll and to record the employer's payroll taxes, treating the employer's payroll taxes and vacation pay as factory overhead. The state unemployment tax rate is 2%.
(3) Ledger accounts for Payroll and Accrued Payroll and the entry to record accrued wages at the end of November.

15-3. Payroll entries — general and factory office. National Sensors, Inc., a manufacturer of air pollution control devices, maintains factory records at each plant location. At the Lansdale factory, where there are four producing departments, a payroll journal is maintained as a book of original entry for the factory employees, even though salaries of personnel in the Shipping Department and Finished Goods Stockroom are charged to marketing expense. Payroll checks are prepared at the home office and sent to the factory for delivery to the factory employees. Overtime premium wages are treated as factory overhead. The liability for payroll taxes is kept on the general office books. Factory payroll taxes are charged to factory overhead.

For the week ended May 30, the following factory payroll summary was prepared:

DEPARTMENT	LABOR HOURS	PAYROLL (EARNED HOURS)	OVERTIME PREMIUM	FEDERAL INCOME TAX WITHHELD (10%)	FICA TAX (6.5%)	NET PAY
Casting..................................	240	$ 1,620	$108	$ 172.80	$112.32	$1,442.88
Forging	410	2,542	160	270.20	175.63	2,256.17
Machining..............................	560	3,976	120	409.60	266.24	3,420.16
Assembly................................	160	960	—	96.00	62.40	801.60
Toolroom	84	428	16	44.40	28.86	370.74
Storeroom..............................	82	410	8	41.80	27.17	349.03
Stockroom	40	180	—	18.00	11.70	150.30
Shipping	40	192	—	19.20	12.48	160.32
Total.....................................	1,616	$10,308	$412	$1,072.00	$696.80	$8,951.20
Sales Office	—	$ 2,200	—	$ 220.00	$143.00	$1,837.00
General Office	—	1,550	$150	170.00	110.50	1,419.50

Required: Entries in journal form for the factory office and general office books to record:
(1) Preparation of the payroll.
(2) Payment of the payroll.

(continued)

(3) Distribution of the payroll.

(4) Recording of the employer's payroll taxes. (State unemployment insurance is 1.6% of the payroll.)

15-4. Pension plans. The Deleplano Corporation adopted a pension plan for its employees on January 1, 19E. A trial balance of the records of the plan at December 31, 19F, follows:

Cash	400	
Investments (at cost)	3,400	
Bone, Equity		1,590
Cohan, Equity		1,060
Dohler, Equity		850
Income from Investments (received in 19F)		300
	3,800	3,800

The following data pertain to the corporation's employees for 19F:

	DATE EMPLOYED	DATE TERMINATED	SALARY PAID IN 19F
Bone	Dec. 8, 19A	—	$17,900
Cohan	Feb. 1, 19C	—	14,100
Dohler	Dec. 8, 19C	April 9, 19F	3,500
Kolman	Sept. 15, 19D	—	8,000
Jones	Sept. 21, 19F	Dec. 22, 19F	3,000
Lohman	May 6, 19F	—	5,500
Total			$52,000

The provisions of the plan include the following:

(a) The corporation shall contribute 10% of its income before deducting income tax and the contribution, but not in excess of 15% of the total salaries paid to the participants in the plan who are in the employ of the corporation at year-end. The employees make no contributions to the plan.

(b) An employee shall be eligible to participate in the plan on January 1 following the completion of one full year of employment.

(c) The corporation's contribution shall be allocated to the participants' equities on the following point system:
   (1) For each full year of employment — 2 points.
   (2) For each $100 of salary paid in the current year — 1 point.

(d) Participants shall have a vested interest of 10% of their total equity for each full year of employment. Forfeitures shall be distributed to the remaining participants in proportion to their equities in the plan at the beginning of the year. Terminated employees shall receive their vested interests at year-end.

(e) Income from the plan's investments shall be allocated to the equities of the remaining participants in proportion to their equities at the beginning of the year.

The Deleplano Corporation's income in 19F before income tax and the contribution to the plan was $73,250.

Required:

(1) A schedule computing the corporation's contribution to the plan for 19F.

(2) A schedule computing the vested interests of the participants terminating their employment during 19F.

(3) A schedule showing the allocation of the corporation's 19F contribution to each participant.

(4) A schedule showing the allocation of the plan's 19F income on investments and forfeitures by terminated participants.

(AICPA adapted)

15-5. Payroll cycle. The payroll department of the Cordero Company, Inc., prepares its monthly and biweekly payroll on the following payroll data:

(a) The payroll period deals with August and September; the last payment was made on August 25.

AUGUST						
Sun	Mon	Tue	Wed	Thu	Fri	Sat
		1	2	3	4	5
6	7	8	9	10	11	12
13	14	15	16	17	18	19
20	21	22	23	24	25	26
27	28	29	30	31		

SEPTEMBER						
Sun	Mon	Tue	Wed	Thu	Fri	Sat
					1	2
3	4	5	6	7	8	9
10	11	12	13	14	15	16
17	18	19	20	21	22	23
24	25	26	27	28	29	30

(b) The workweek is Monday through Friday; paychecks are distributed on the Friday following the close of the two weeks. The company pays its factory, marketing, and office and administrative personnel on a biweekly basis. Executives, superintendents, and department heads are paid on a monthly basis on the first Friday following the last day of the month. The 4th of September is Labor Day; all employees will be paid but the direct labor cost is charged to factory overhead.

(c) The payroll is based on these data:

Monthly salaries:
2 executives.. $3,000 each per month
3 superintendents .... 2,500 each per month
2 department heads .... 2,000 each per month

Hourly workers:
Direct factory labor ...   200 employees; 40 hours per week; average pay, $6 per hour
Indirect factory labor   30 employees; 40 hours per week; average pay, $4 per hour

Weekly rates:
Marketing personnel ....   12 employees; average pay, $350 per week
Office and administrative personnel......   9 employees; average pay, $305 per week

(d) Additional assumptions:
Federal income tax withheld: 15% on monthly salaries
                                  10% on all others
FICA tax: 6.5% (maximum $25,000 earnings per year)
Federal unemployment tax: .7% up to $6,000 per employee
State unemployment tax: 2.7% up to $8,000 per employee; the state in which the Cordero Company is located set an $8,000 limit for this tax.

The FICA tax is recorded as a liability when it is withheld at the payroll date, in compliance with regulations. The employer's payroll taxes are recorded when the cost distribution entry is made; separate liability accounts are kept for federal and state agencies; month-end payroll accrual entries are made only at the end of the calendar year.

Workmen's compensation insurance: 1% of total payroll.
Pension cost: 5% for monthly salaries, with equal contribution by these employees deducted from their paychecks; 3% for all other employees, with no contribution by them.
Union dues: $.50 deducted each payday from each hourly worker.
Health insurance: 1% of earnings, shared equally between employees and employer.

Required:
(1) Journal entries with all applicable deductions for the monthly salaries to be paid in September. Distribution to be made as follows: 2 executives to administration; 3 superintendents to factory; 1 department head to marketing; 1 department head to administration (office).
(2) Journal entries with all applicable deductions for factory, marketing, and office employees on a biweekly basis for the earnings to be paid in September. Distribution to be made on the basis of the four categories.
(3) Journal entries for one direct laborer for the first of the two-week payroll periods in order to illustrate the procedure required for an individual employee.

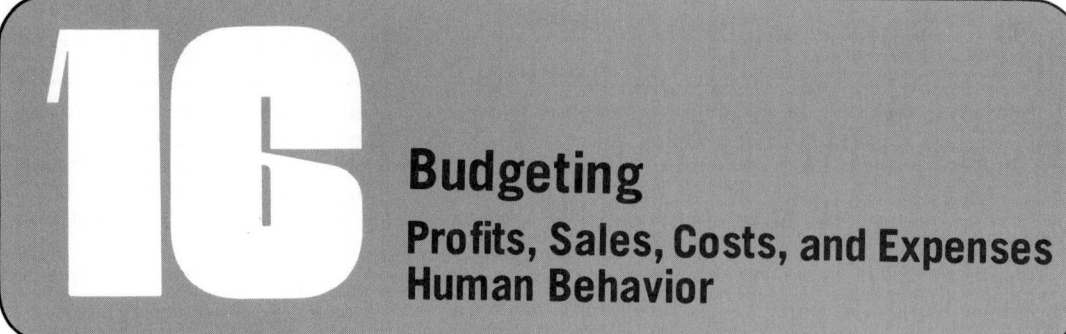

Part Five   Planning of Profits, Sales, and Costs

16   Budgeting
Profits, Sales, Costs, and Expenses
Human Behavior

Effective planning and control of operations depend upon cost accounting, which provides management with detailed statements of the actual cost of materials, labor, factory overhead, marketing expenses, and administrative expenses. Comparisons and analyses of these actual costs with estimates and standards prepared in advance of production and sales enable management to identify the reasons for any differences. Management can then formulate intelligent production plans and sales policies for achieving the organization's objectives.

PROFIT PLANNING

The terms "profit planning" and "budgeting" can be viewed as synonymous. *Profit planning* is a well thought-out operational plan with its financial implications expressed in the form of long- and short-range income statements, balance sheets, and cash and working capital projections. A budget is simply a plan expressed in financial and other quantitative terms. Profit planning is directed to the ultimate objectives of the organization and serves as a guide to maintaining a definite course of activity.

Sound and intelligent planning of profits is a difficult task, because technology changes rapidly, and social and political factors exert strong influences on business. To accomplish this task, managers must be motivated to strive for attainment of their personal objectives in congruence with the organization's objectives.

Fundamentally, three different procedures can be followed in setting profit objectives:

1. The *a priori* method, in which the profit objectives take precedence over the planning process. At the outset, management specifies a given rate of return, which it seeks to realize in the long run by means of planning toward that end.
2. The *a posteriori* method, in which the determination of profit objectives is subordinated to the planning, and the objectives emerge as the product of the planning itself.
3. The *pragmatic* method, in which management uses a profit standard that has been tested empirically and sanctioned by experience. By using a target rate of profit derived from experience, expectations, or comparisons, management establishes a relative profit standard which is considered satisfactory for the company.[1]

In setting profit objectives, management needs to consider the following factors:

1. Profit or loss resulting from a given volume of sales.
2. Sales volume required to recover all consumed costs, to produce a profit adequate to pay dividends on preferred and common stock, and to retain sufficient earnings in the business for future needs.
3. Break-even point.
4. Sales volume that the present operating capacity can produce.
5. Operating capacity necessary to attain the profit objectives.
6. Return on capital employed.

Public expectations with regard to social responsibilities compel companies to also consider the social consequences of profit objectives. Increasingly, important actions must be evaluated in a context that includes social as well as economic impacts. Potential social impacts specifically pertain to ". . . environmental pollution, the consumption of nonrenewable resources, and other ecological factors; the rights of individuals and groups; the maintenance of public service; public safety; health and education; and many other social concerns."[2]

In recent years, business has become increasingly aware of a need to develop long-range profit plans or forecasts. Long-range planning has been defined as "the continuous process of making present decisions systematically and, with the best possible knowledge of their futurity, organizing systematically the efforts needed to carry out these decisions and measuring the results of these decisions against the expectations through organized, systematic feedback."[3] Long-range plans are not stated in precise terms, nor are they expected to be completely coordinated future plans. They deal rather

[1]*Research Report No. 42*, "Long-Range Profit Planning" (New York: National Association of Accountants, 1964), pp. 60–65.
[2]Robert K. Elliott, "Social Accounting and Corporate Decision-Making," *Management Controls*, Vol. XXI, No. 1, p. 2.
[3]Peter F. Drucker, "Long-Range Planning," *Management Science*, Vol. 5, No. 3, p. 240.

with specific areas such as sales, capital expenditures, extensive research and development activities, and financial requirements.

In long-range profit planning, management attempts to find the most probable course of events. Long-range planning does not eliminate risk, for risk-taking is the essence of economic activity. An end result of successful long-range profit planning is a capacity to take a greater risk, which is a fundamental way to improve entrepreneurial performance.

Market trends and economic factors, growth of population, personal consumption expenditures, and indexes of industrial production form the background for long-range planning. Quantitative and dollar sales estimates for a three- to five-year forecast may be developed from this information. A prospective income statement can then be prepared, showing anticipated sales, variable costs, contribution margin, fixed factory overhead, fixed marketing and administrative expenses, and operating income by years. A balance sheet by years should indicate anticipated cash balances, inventory levels, accounts receivable balances, and liabilities. This financial long-range plan might also be supported by a cash flow statement.

The rate of return on capital (total assets) employed is an important statistic in long-range profit planning and in setting profit objectives. To measure the effectiveness with which management is likely to use the assets, rates of return are computed for each individual year covered in the long-range plan. These figures show whether planned increases in total net income will keep pace with increases in assets at the corporate as well as divisional or operating levels. Though return on capital employed is the basic measure of profit performance (discussed in detail in Chapter 27), companies typically use several other measures, such as the ratio of net income to sales, the ratio of sales to shareholders' capital, and earnings per common share.[4]

Short-Range Plans or Budgets   Management's long-range plans can only be achieved through successful long-run profit performance, which requires growth and a reasonably high and stable level of profit. Long-range plans with their future expectancy of profits and growth must, however, be incorporated into a shorter-range budget for both planning and control of the contemplated course of action. Although one year is the usual planning period, the short-range budget may cover periods of three, six, or twelve months, depending upon the nature of the business. For efficient planning, the annual budget should be expanded into an eighteen-month budget, allowing for a three-month period at the end of the old year, twelve months for the regular budget period, and an additional three months into the third year. These overlapping months are needed in order to allow transition from year to year and to make adjustments based on prior months' experience. The budget period should:

1. Be divided into months.
2. Be long enough to complete production of the various products.

[4]*Research Report No. 42, loc. cit.*

3. Cover at least one entire seasonal cycle for a business of a seasonal nature.
4. Be long enough to allow for the financing of production well in advance of actual needs.
5. Coincide with the financial accounting period to compare actual results with budget estimates.

Some organizations use a continuous budget, by which a month or quarter in the future is added as the month or quarter just ended is dropped, and the budget for the entire period is revised and updated as needed. This procedure forces management to think continuously about its short-range plans.

Profit planning, or budgeting, has the advantages of:

Advantages of Profit Planning

1. Providing a disciplined approach to the solution of problems.
2. Obliging management to make an early study of its problems and instilling into an organization the habit of careful study before making decisions.
3. Developing throughout the organization an atmosphere of profit-mindedness, and encouraging an attitude of cost-consciousness and maximum resource utilization.
4. Enlisting the aid and coordinating the operating plans of the diverse segments of the entire management organization so that the final decisions and contingency plans represent the total organization in the form of an integrated, comprehensive plan.
5. Affording the opportunity of appraising systematically every facet of the organization as well as examining and restating periodically its basic policies and guiding principles.
6. Coordinating and correlating all efforts, since no management activity reveals weaknesses in organization as quickly as the orderly procedure necessary for systematic budgeting.
7. Aiding in directing capital and effort into the most profitable channels.
8. Encouraging a high standard of performance by stimulating competition, providing a sense of purpose, and serving as an incentive to perform more effectively.
9. Providing yardsticks or standards for measuring performance and gauging the managerial judgment and ability of the individual executive.

While the advantages of profit planning are unquestionably impressive and far reaching, certain limitations and pitfalls need to be mentioned:

Limitations of Profit Planning

1. Forecasting is not an exact science; a certain amount of judgment is present in any budgetary plan. A revision or modification of estimates should be made when variations from the estimates warrant a change of plans.
2. A profit planning program needs the cooperation and participation of all members of management. Basic for success is executive management's sustained adherence to and enthusiasm for the budget plan. Too often a budgetary plan has failed because executive management has paid only lip service to its execution.

3. Profit planning does not eliminate nor take over the role of administration. Executives should not feel restricted by the budget. Rather, the budgetary plan is designed to provide detailed information that allows the executives to operate with strength and vision toward achievement of the organization's objectives.
4. Installation takes time. Management often becomes impatient and loses interest because it expects too much too soon. The budget plan must first be sold to the responsible people; and they, in turn, must then be guided, trained, and educated in the fundamental steps, methods, and purposes of a budgetary system.

PRINCIPLES OF BUDGETING

A company's organization chart and its chart of accounts form the basic framework on which to build a coordinated and efficient system of managerial planning and budgetary control. The organization chart defines the functional responsibilities of executives and thereby justifies their budgets. Although final responsibility for the budget rests with executive management, all managers are responsible for the preparation and execution of their departmental budgets. If a budgetary control system is to be successful, these managers must fully cooperate and must understand their role in making the budget system successful.

The Budget Committee

The budgeting process is usually directed by a budget committee, which is composed of the sales manager, the production manager, the chief engineer, the treasurer, and the controller. The principal functions of the budget committee are to:

1. Decide on general policies.
2. Request, receive, and review individual budget estimates.
3. Suggest revisions in individual budget estimates.
4. Approve budgets and later revisions.
5. Receive and analyze budget reports.
6. Recommend actions designed to improve efficiency where necessary.

In performing these functions, the budget committee becomes a management committee. It is a powerful force in coordinating the various activities of the business and in controlling operations.

Budget Development and Implementation

The procedure used in developing a budget may be as important as its content and should include these fundamental principles:

1. Provide adequate guidance so that all management levels are working on the same assumptions, targeted objectives, and agenda. All managers should understand the limitations and constraints of their participation and the bounds of their decision making. Participants should be told, prior to the time the budget is established, how their activities will fit into the entire organization and what constraints will be placed upon them and their activities by upper-level administrative decisions.

2. Encourage participation in the budgeting process at each level within the organization. Structure the activity of developing the budget to involve the people who will be responsible for implementing the budget and who will be rewarded according to its accomplishments.
3. Structure the climate of budget preparation to eliminate anxiety and defensiveness. Individuals should have the freedom and authority to influence and accept their own performance levels, and should assume the responsibility for accomplishment. Budget preparation should be oriented to the problems and opportunities of the participants.
4. Structure the preparation of the budget so that there is a reasonably high probability of successful attainment of objectives. When challenging but attainable objectives are achieved, feelings of success, confidence, and satisfaction are produced and aspiration levels are raised. If objectives are not accomplished, the reasons for this failure should be clear. A careful distinction should be made between controllable factors for which individuals should be responsible and for uncontrollable factors for which they are not.[5]

If the proper procedure for developing a budget has been followed, implementation difficulties are minimized. Proper budget implementation requires adherence to the following principles:

1. Establish rewards and reward contingencies that will lead to achieving the organizational objectives. Too often, the budgeting process does not provide sufficient rewards to induce employees to accomplish organizational objectives.
2. The organization should focus on rewarding achievement rather than punishing failure. Feelings of success or failure largely determine attitudes toward the budget and the level of performance to which employees will aspire.
3. Provide rapid feedback on the performance of each work team or individual. This principle necessitates the use of reports and reporting procedures that are understandable to workers and supervisors at the department level, so that they can analyze their results and initiate corrective action.[6]

Budgeting and Human Behavior

Anyone who has ever been charged with the task of creating a budget and establishing budget figures, particularly of departmental overhead, must be aware of the irrational and often obstinate behavior of certain supervisors with respect to the contemplated budget program.[7] In some firms, budgeting is perhaps the most unpopular management and/or accounting device for planning and control.

In recent years, considerable attention has been given to the behavioral implications of providing managers with the data required for planning, coordinating, and controlling activities. Cost accounting and budgeting play an im-

---

[5]J. Owen Cherrington and David J. Cherrington, "Budget Games for Fun and Frustration," *Management Accounting*, Vol. LVII, No. 7, p. 32.
[6]*Ibid.*
[7]Chris Argyris, *The Impact of Budgets on People* (New York: Financial Executives Research Foundation; formerly Controllership Foundation, Inc., 1952).

portant role in influencing individual and group behavior at all of the various stages of the management process including: (1) setting goals; (2) informing individuals what they must do to contribute to the accomplishment of these goals; (3) motivating desirable performance; (4) evaluating performance; and (5) suggesting when corrective action must be taken. In short, accountants cannot ignore the behavioral sciences (psychology, social-psychology, and sociology) because the ''information for decision making'' function of accounting is essentially a behavioral function.[8]

For budget building, James L. Peirce suggests:

> In the field of cost control, use the budget as a tool to be placed in the foremen's hands — not as a club to be held over their heads. To implement this rule, it may be a good idea to design an educational program. Meetings attended by line and staff supervisors may prove an effective vehicle. Cost reduction must be placed on the basis of mutual effort toward a common aim. The creation of this atmosphere is an essential, definite step in budget practice.[9]

An individual manager's attitude toward the budget will depend greatly upon the existing good relationship within the management group. Guided by the company plan, with an opportunity for increased compensation, greater satisfaction, and eventually promotion, the middle and lower management group might achieve remarkable results. A discordant management group, unwilling to accept the budget's underlying figures, might show such poor accomplishment that the administration is compelled ''to defer trying the planning and control idea until it has put its house in order.''[10] Peirce further states that:

> We are beginning to learn that no tool can be used effectively unless the hand that guides it is rightly motivated. Like all other techniques of business, the budget should be a door open to more satisfying and profitable work — not an instrument of torture.
>
> Then it will be known that what you can do without a budget you can do better with one. It will be seen that the entire planning and control procedure is a device for freeing men to do their best work — not a machine of restriction and condemnation.
>
> Planning is but another word for the vision that sees a creative achievement before it is manifest. Control is but a name for direction. The genius of management cannot fail to turn the budget idea finally into positive channels, so that people individually as well as business leadership generally will reap the harvest that it promises.[11]

The remarks quoted from Peirce's article indicate that no budget can be successful as long as people are unwilling to accept it. The problem of mo-

---

[8]For references explaining behavioral implications of accounting in some detail, see:
William J. Bruns, Jr., and Don T. DeCoster, *Accounting and Its Behavioral Implications* (New York: McGraw-Hill Book Company, 1969).
Edwin H. Caplan, *Management Accounting and Behavioral Science* (Reading, Mass.: Addison-Wesley Publishing Co., Inc., 1971).
[9]James L. Peirce, ''The Budget Comes of Age,'' *The Harvard Business Review*, Vol. 32, No. 3, p. 65.
[10]*Ibid.*, pp. 58–67.
[11]*Ibid.*, p. 67

tivating a company's personnel, however, is difficult to solve. It was stated in Chapter 14 (page 403) that pay incentives for factory workers do not necessarily lead to greater productivity. Office and/or management personnel, as well as factory workers, might find other reasons or causes that generate employee motivation necessary for achieving excellence in their work standards. An article in *The Journal of Accountancy* suggested these requirements for motivating financial personnel:

1. A compensation system that builds and maintains a clearly understood relationship between results and rewards.
2. A system for performance appraisal that employees understand with regard to their individual effectiveness and key results, their tasks and their responsibilities, their degree and span of influence in decision making, as well as the time allowed to judge their results.
3. A system of communication that allows employees to query their superiors with trust and honest communication.
4. A system of promotion that generates and sustains employee faith in its validity and judgment.
5. A system of employee support through coaching, counseling, and career planning.
6. A system that not only considers company objectives, but also employees' skills and capacities.
7. A system that will not settle for mediocrity, but which reaches for realistic and attainable standards, stressing improvement and providing an environment in which the concept of excellence can grow.[12]

THE COMPLETE PERIODIC BUDGET

A complete set of budgets generally consists of:

1. Sales estimates by:
   a. Territory and product, or
   b. Territory, customer group, and product.
2. Estimates of inventory, production, and purchase requirements.
3. Estimates of materials, labor, and factory overhead combined into a cost of goods sold schedule.
4. Detailed expense budgets for marketing and administrative expenses.
5. A budget of major repairs, replacements, and improvements of plant and machinery, and research and development expenditures.
6. A cash budget showing cash receipts and disbursements.
7. A forecast income statement.
8. A forecast balance sheet showing the estimated financial position of the company at the end of the budget period.

Sales Budget

One of the most important elements in a budgetary control system is a realistic sales forecast that is based on analyses of past sales and the present market. The task of preparing the sales budget is usually approached from two different angles: (1) judging and evaluating external influences and (2)

---

[12]Paul E. Sussman, "Motivating Financial Personnel," *The Journal of Accountancy*, Vol. 141, No. 2, p. 80.

considering internal influences. These two influences are brought together in a workable sales budget. External influences include the general trend of industrial activity, governmental policies, cyclical phases of the nation's economy, purchasing power of the population, population shift, and changes in buying habits and modes of living. Internal influences are sales trends, factory capacities, new products, plant expansion, seasonal products, sales estimates, and establishment of quotas for salespeople and sales territories. The profit desired by the company is a highly significant consideration.

Forecasting Sales. The preparation of sales estimates is usually the responsibility of the marketing manager assisted by individual salespeople and market research personnel. Because of the many dissimilarities in the marketing of products, actual methods used to forecast sales vary widely in various companies. One method used by many companies is the preparation of sales estimates by individual salespeople. All salespeople supply their district managers with estimates of probable sales in their territories. These estimates are consolidated and adjusted by the district marketing manager. They are then forwarded to the general marketing manager, who makes further adjustments. These adjustments include allowances for expected economic conditions and competitive conditions of which salespeople are unaware, as well as allowances for expected canceled orders and sales returns that salespeople would likely disregard because their estimates are based on the orders they expect to procure.

In estimating sales as well as expenditures, the frequent tendency to over- or underestimate plans must be recognized. Individuals tend to be overly pessimistic or optimistic in setting goals and in making plans. Therefore, the budgeting system should be designed to monitor this tendency in order to keep goals and plans within reasonable bounds.[13]

In most large organizations, the forecasting procedure usually starts with known factors; namely, (1) the company's sales of past years broken down by product groups and profit margins, (2) industry or trade sales volume and perhaps profits, and (3) unusual factors influencing sales in the past. The company's past sales figures often require a restudy or reclassification due to changes in products, profit margins, competition, sales areas, distribution methods, or changes within the industry. Industry or trade sales and profits are secured from trade associations, trade publications, and various business magazines. For some industries, the U.S. Department of Commerce publishes information that is useful as background data. Unusual factors influencing past sales are inventory conditions, public economic sentiment, competition, and customer relations. Charting a company's volume in units of various products for a three- to five-year period and comparing it with the industry's volume will disclose the company's sales trend and will pinpoint factors that affected past sales.

---

[13]John W. Hardy and E. Dee Hubbard, "Internal Reporting Guidelines: Their Coverage in Cost Accounting Texts," *The Accounting Review*, Vol. LI, No. 4, p. 918.

Although the feeling frequently exists that the sales forecast is a crystal-ball area, a sound basis for determining future sales may be established by applying probability analysis techniques to the consideration of general business conditions, the industry's prospects, the company's potential share of the total industry market, and the plans of competitive companies.

Seasonal Variations. When the annual sales forecast has been approved, it must be placed on an operating period basis, which is usually a month. The monthly sales budget should show seasonal sales patterns for each product manufactured. These patterns are evident from the company's experience and from records of a product's trend during past years. Any fluctuations in a trend should be considered, as well as the causes of fluctuations, such as customs or habits based on local or national traits, climate, holidays, or even the influences of companies in the firm's own industry.

The seasonal or operating sales budget is of great help in judging the records of individual salespeople. Averaging sales over a budget period is not sufficient to assure success of a sales program. Too many times low sales in one month have been excused with the optimistic statement that sales in the following month will make up the difference. When this does not happen, the sales budget and the entire budget plan suffer.

Sales Budget on a Territory and Customer Basis. A sales budget should not only be placed on a monthly basis for each product, but should also be classified by territories or districts and by types of customers, as illustrated below. The customer classification should show sales to jobbers, wholesalers, retailers, institutions, governmental agencies, schools and colleges, foreign businesses, etc. Such a breakdown indicates the contribution of each territory and customer class to total sales and profits. An analysis of this type often reveals

Product X
Sales Budget
(By Territory and By Customer Group)
For Year Ending December 19--

TERRITORY	CUSTOMER GROUP	JANUARY Qty.	JANUARY Value	FEBRUARY Qty.	FEBRUARY Value	DECEMBER Qty.	DECEMBER Value	TOTAL Qty.	TOTAL Value
North	A	1,440	$ 21,600	1,620	$ 24,300	1,260	$ 18,900	21,600	$ 324,000
	B	960	14,400	1,080	16,200	840	12,600	14,400	216,000
	Total	2,400	$ 36,000	2,700	$ 40,500	2,100	$ 31,500	36,000	$ 540,000
East	A	400	$ 6,000	450	$ 6,750	350	$ 5,250	6,000	$ 90,000
	B	400	6,000	450	6,750	350	5,250	6,000	90,000
	Total	800	$ 12,000	900	$ 13,500	700	$ 10,500	12,000	$ 180,000
South	A	1,440	$ 21,600	1,620	$ 24,300	1,260	$ 18,900	21,600	$ 324,000
	B	1,760	26,400	1,980	29,700	1,540	23,100	26,400	396,000
	Total	3,200	$ 48,000	3,600	$ 54,000	2,800	$ 42,000	48,000	$ 720,000
West	A	640	$ 9,600	720	$ 10,800	560	$ 8,400	9,600	$ 144,000
	B	960	14,400	1,080	16,200	840	12,600	14,400	216,000
	Total	1,600	$ 24,000	1,800	$ 27,000	1,400	$ 21,000	24,000	$ 360,000
Total		8,000	$120,000	9,000	$135,000	7,000	$105,000	120,000	$1,800,000

that certain territories or classes of customers are not given sufficient attention by sales managers and sales representatives. A detailed sales budget can be a strong means for analyzing possible new trade outlets. It also assists in identifying reasons for a drop in sales, in investigating such a decrease, and in taking remedial steps.

Estimating Production and Inventory Requirements. Prior to the final acceptance of a sales budget, the factory's capacity to produce the estimated quantities must be determined. If factory capacity is available, production should be planned at a level that will keep workers and equipment operating all year. Serious fluctuations in employment are expensive and do not promote good labor relations. The production level should also maintain inventories that are sufficient to fulfill the month's sales requirements. At the same time, the investment in inventories should be held to a level consistent with sound financial policy.

If the sales budget indicates that factory employment in certain months would fall below a desirable level, it would be necessary to attempt to increase sales volume or increase inventories. If estimated sales are higher than available capacity, the purchase or rental of new machinery and factory space must be considered as a means of increasing plant capacity.

Sales Forecast Follow-Up. Follow-up review should occur at intervals influenced by the frequency of change in the company, its industry, and general economic conditions. The review should determine (1) the accuracy of past forecasts, (2) location of the major forecast errors, (3) the best method by which to update forecasts, and (4) the steps needed for improvement of the making and monitoring of future forecasts.

Past errors indicate the reliance that can be placed on sales forecasts and provide insight into the company and the personal bias built into the forecast. When forecasts are monitored, comparison with actual results should extend beyond financial results to include consideration of the underlying factors and key assumptions. Such comparisons might require the monitoring of unit sales volumes, prices, production rates, backlogs of sales orders, changes in capacity, and economic indicators.[14]

Production Budget

The production budget deals with the scheduling of operations, the determination of volume, and the establishment of maximum and minimum quantities of materials and finished goods inventories. It provides the basis for preparing the budgets of materials, labor, and factory overhead.

A production budget is stated in physical units. As illustrated on page 455, this budget is frequently the sales budget adjusted for any inventory changes. The production budget, like other budgets, is detailed by months or quarters as well as annually. For comparison with actual production, the detailed bud-

---

[14]Robert S. Savesky, "How Good Is Your Company's Sales Forecast?" *Price Waterhouse & Co. Review*, Vol. 22, No. 2, p. 37.

Product X
Production Budget
For Year Ending December 31, 19––

	JANUARY	FEBRUARY	DECEMBER	YEAR, 19––
Units required to meet sales budget..............................	8,000	9,000	7,000	120,000
Add desired ending inventory	6,400	7,400	4,400	4,400
Total units required	14,400	16,400	11,400	124,400
Less estimated beginning inventory	4,400	6,400	1,400	4,400
Planned production..............	10,000	10,000	10,000	120,000

get should be broken down by work stations. The nature of this division will be determined by plant layout, type of production, and other factors.

Coordination of the production budget with the sales budget is extremely important. Seasonal fluctuations of sales should usually be leveled out in production planning in order to stabilize employment without causing a shortage of finished products, inefficient service to customers, or large inventories. Production facilities that have limited usefulness should also be included in a company's planning. If the products of such facilities are overlooked and sales personnel concentrate on selling high-profit items, the resulting idle capacity may be more costly to the company than the effort needed to sell these products.

For a company that does not manufacture standard products but produces only on orders, a detailed production budget may not be possible. However, if there are standardized parts, production can be budgeted in a manner similar to that used by a company producing standard products. In special-order work, the primary problem is to be prepared for production when orders are received. Work must be routed and scheduled through the factory, so that delays are prevented and production facilities are fully utilized.

No division of a manufacturing business has made so much progress in scientific management as the production department. Constant effort is directed toward devising new ways and shortcuts that will lead to more efficient production and cost savings which will be reflected in earnings. When competition is keen and management is under pressure to cut prices, the possibilities for reducing production costs are the first to be considered. Since labor presses for wage increases and resists cutbacks, these reductions must take the form of labor-saving devices and careful planning, routing, and scheduling.

With the forecast sales translated into physical units in the production budget, the estimated costs of materials, labor, and factory overhead essential to the sales and production program can be computed. These costs, often based on standard costs, are summarized in the manufacturing budget as shown on the next page. The costs are classified as fixed and variable, and are

Manufacturing Budget

Product X
Manufacturing Budget Estimates
For Year Ending December 31, 19--

PRODUCTION	120,000 UNITS	125,000 UNITS
Direct materials cost, $5 per unit........................	$600,000	$625,000
Direct labor cost, $3 per unit............................	360,000	375,000
Variable factory overhead, $1 per unit.................	120,000	125,000
Fixed factory overhead	240,000	240,000
Fixed factory overhead per unit	($2)	($1.92)

reported in the budget according to the axiom that fixed costs are fixed in total, but variable per unit, while variable costs are variable in total, but fixed per unit.

Detailed budgets are prepared for direct materials and direct labor in order to identify these costs with products and responsible managers. The factory overhead is budgeted in detail by responsibility centers or departments. This budget information becomes part of the master budget to be used as a standard or target against which the performance of the individual department is judged and evaluated.

Direct Materials Budget. The first cost budget to be prepared is usually the materials budget, which indicates the quantity and cost of materials required to produce the predetermined units of finished goods. A materials budget (1) permits the purchasing department to set up a purchasing schedule that assures delivery of materials when needed, (2) leads to the determination of minimum and maximum quantities of materials and finished parts that must be on hand, and (3) establishes a means by which the treasurer can gauge the financial requirements of the purchasing department. Although the materials budget usually deals only with direct materials, these factors are also applicable to supplies and indirect materials that are included in the factory overhead budget and the commercial expenses budget.

The production planning department determines the quantity and type of materials required for the various products manufactured by a company. The dollar value of these materials must also be determined. When the direct materials budget is completed, the treasurer can include in the cash budget the necessary funds for periodic purchases as well as for all other cash payments.

Most companies have standard parts lists and bills of materials which detail all materials requirements. These requirements are given to the purchasing department which sets up a buying schedule. This schedule, illustrated on page 457, is based on the objective of providing sufficient materials without overstocking. In preparing a buying schedule, the purchasing department must consider changes in possible delivery promises by the supplier and changes in the rate of materials consumption because of unforeseen circumstances.

The materials ledger cards of many companies include a section which shows the minimum and maximum quantities to be stored. When quantities

Material A
Production, Inventory, and Purchase Requirements Schedule (in units)
For Year Ending December 31, 19--

	JANUARY	FEBRUARY	DECEMBER	TOTAL
Beginning inventory..............	80,000	80,000	80,000	80,000
Purchases	45,000	45,000	50,000	600,000
Materials available	125,000	125,000	130,000	680,000
Ending inventory	80,000	80,000	80,000	80,000
Materials used	45,000	45,000	50,000	600,000

are greater than the maximum or less than the minimum, the stock record clerk should inform the purchasing department or the production planning department. The coordination of materials records with purchasing department data acts as a check on both the overstocking of materials and the danger of a possible shortage.

Direct Labor Budget. The annual budget is the principal tool for the overall planning for human resources. When the budget is completed and approved, it should include a human resources plan that is coordinated with planned sales and production activities as well as the profit goal.[15]

The direct labor budget, based on specifications drawn up by product engineers, guides the personnel department in determining the number and type of workers needed. If the labor force has been with the firm for several years and if the production schedule does not call for additional workers, the task of the personnel department is rather easy. If an increase or decrease in the labor force is required, the personnel department must make plans in advance to assure the availability of workers. Frequently the personnel department must provide a training program which provides workers to the production department at the proper time. When workers are to be laid off, the personnel department must prepare a list of those affected, giving due recognition to skill and seniority rights. In many companies, this schedule is prepared in collaboration with union representatives in order to protect employees from any injustice or hardship.

Indirect labor is included in the factory overhead budget and consists of such employees as helpers in producing departments, maintenance workers, crane operators, materials clerks, and receiving clerks. Labor requirements for marketing and administrative activities must be budgeted as part of the commercial expenses budget.

For each type of labor, the hours or the number of workers must be translated into dollar values. Established labor rates as agreed upon in union contracts are generally used. If conditions indicate that labor rates might change, the new rates should be used, so that the financial budget reflects the most recent figures available.

---

[15]Walter B. McFarland, *Manpower Cost and Performance Measurement* (New York: National Association of Accountants, 1977), p. 27.

Factory Overhead Budget. The factory overhead budget is prepared on the basis of the chart of accounts, which properly classifies expense accounts and details the various cost centers for planning and control and assignment of factory overhead to product cost. As discussed in Chapter 3, expenses can be grouped in several ways:

1. Natural expense classification, such as indirect materials and supplies, indirect labor, freight, light, and power.
2. Departmental or functional classification according to the producing or service department or cost center in which the expense originated.
3. Division of expenses according to variability, i.e., variable and fixed.

The natural expense classification alone is not useful for budget purposes, since expenses are usually incurred by various departments. By classifying expenses according to individual departments, the value and importance of budgetary control for expenses becomes significant.

Preparation of any expense budget should be guided by the principle that every expense is chargeable to a department, and that an executive, department head, or supervisor should be held accountable and responsible for expenses incurred. Those expenses for which the department supervisor is directly responsible should be identified in the supervisor's budget. Allocated expenses for which the supervisor has little or no responsibility should also be identified.

If department supervisors accept the budget, they are more likely to cooperate in its execution. Therefore, supervisors should be asked to prepare their own estimates of departmental expenses, based on the department's projected activity for the budget period. These estimates and any revisions should be reviewed and coordinated with other budgets before they are incorporated into the overall budget.

The factory overhead budget of a department is generally prepared as a report which enables executive management and individual department supervisors to make monthly comparisons of budgeted and actual expenses. The report illustrated below presents end-of-month analysis.

Molding Department
Factory Overhead Budget
For July, 19——

	BUDGETED	ACTUAL	OVER	UNDER
Indirect labor	$ 930	$ 900		$ 30
Oil	10	10		
Fuel	30	35	$ 5	
Tools	50	25		25
Heat	50	20		30
Power and light	180	180		
Repairs to machinery	100	50		50
Supervisor	900	900		
Depreciation	100	100		
Spoiled work	50	20		30
	$2,400	$2,240	$ 5	$165

The Budgeted column indicates expenses allowed for July. The Actual column shows amounts actually spent during the month. The last two columns indicate amounts by which actual expenses are above or below budgeted figures. This type of monthly or seasonal budget is highly valuable if expenses are to be analyzed for a period shorter than twelve months. Each item of expense should be considered on a volume-of-activity basis, using flexible budgeting (Chapter 18), in order to make the monthly budget as nearly accurate as possible.

Among the expenses commonly included in a departmental overhead budget are machinery repair costs, which are based on the budget of the maintenance department. These costs are difficult to control, because breakdowns are unpredictable and occur irregularly and their causes are not easily determined. Therefore, the economical use of plant and equipment must be the joint responsibility of production and maintenance personnel.

Budgeting Commercial Expenses

The company's chart of accounts is also the basis for budgetary control of commercial expenses, which include both marketing (selling or distribution) and administrative expenses. These expenses may be classified by primary accounts and by functions.

Budgeting and analyzing commercial expenses by primary accounts is the simplest method of classification. This method stresses the nature or the type of expenditure, such as salaries, commissions, repairs, light and heat, rent, telephone and telegraph, postage, advertising, travel expenses, sales promotion, entertainment, delivery expense, freight out, insurance, donations, depreciation, taxes, and interest. As expenses are incurred, they are recorded in primary expense accounts, posted to ledger accounts, and then taken directly to the income statement. No further allocation is made. At the end of an accounting period, actual expenses are compared with either budgeted expenses or expenses of the previous month or year.

To control commercial expenses effectively, it is necessary to group them by functional activities or operating units. Classification by function emphasizes departmental activities, such as selling, advertising, warehousing, billing, credit and collection, transportation, accounting, purchasing, engineering, and financing. Such a classification is consistent with the concept of responsibility accounting and may be compared to collecting factory overhead by departments or cost centers. A departmental classification adds to rather than replaces the process of classifying expenses by primary accounts, because primary account classifications are maintained within each department.

When a departmental classification system is used, it is important that each expense be charged to a department, and that the classification conforms to the company's organization chart at the corporate level as well as each marketing territory level. However, it is impossible to suggest exact classifications, since organizational structures vary so much in business organizations. Departments known by the same name may perform widely differing functions.

Commercial expenses grouped by department may be subclassified as direct and indirect expenses. Direct expenses, such as salaries and supplies, are charged directly to a department. Indirect expenses are general or service department expenses that are prorated to benefiting departments. Expenses such as rent, insurance, and utilities, when shared by several departments, constitute this type of expense.

To identify an outlay of cash or the incurrence of a liability with a function requires considerably more work than is required by the primary account method. However, the chart of accounts will normally provide the initial breakdown of expenses. Usually the allocation of expenses to departments and the identification of the primary account classification within each department can be made when the voucher is prepared. This procedure requires coding the expenditure when it is requisitioned for purchase. Any increase in expenses caused by the use of this functional method is more than offset by the advantages of improved cost control.

Marketing Expenses Budget. A company's marketing activities can be divided into two broad categories:

1. Obtaining the order — involves the functions of selling, advertising, and market analysis.
2. Filling the order — involves the functions of warehousing, order assembly, packing, shipping, transportation, billing, and credit and collection.

The supervisors of functions connected with marketing activities should prepare budget estimates of these costs. Some estimates are based on individual judgment, while others are based on the costs experienced in previous years, modified by expected sales volume. Expenses such as depreciation and insurance depend upon the policy established by management.

Administrative Expenses Budget. Administrative expenses include some costs which are peculiar to the administrative function, such as directors' fees, franchise taxes, capital stock taxes, and professional services of accountants, lawyers, and engineers. Other expenses, such as purchasing, engineering, personnel, and research, are shared by the production and marketing as well as the administrative functions.

As a result of the problem of classifying certain expenses, the budgeting and control of administrative expenses is often quite difficult. The difficulty is increased because the persons responsibile for the control of such expenses as food services, patents, or donations to the United Fund may not be identifiable. However, an attempt should be made to place every item of expense under the jurisdiction and control of an executive, such as the chief executive, treasurer, controller, general accounting supervisor, or office manager. This person should be responsible for estimating the administrative expenses of a specific section or division, and should have authority to control the incurrence of the division's expenses. For example, the office manager should supervise filing clerks, mail clerks, librarians, stenographers, secretaries, and receptionists. This arrangement permits better control and more intense utilization of personnel in clerical jobs, where overlapping and overexpansion are common.

COMPUTERIZED BUDGETING[16]

The time required to assemble the periodic budget and to achieve a consensus of the managers involved is so great that the budgeting process is often inhibited. Time constraints may be handled more effectively, however, by converting the elements of the conventional budgeting process into a functional planning tool through the use of computer modeling techniques. Tedious arithmetic can be eliminated by converting budgeting procedures into a computerized set of straightforward algebraic formulas. The resulting computerized model entails the following primary components:

1. A line-by-line outline which describes the format of the desired output of budget schedules and statements.
2. A structure of algebraic logic or procedures which demonstrates the computational processes in simple formulas.
3. Elements of data which, when passed through the computational process, will generate the desired output.

The development of a computerized budgeting process can result in substantial benefits. These benefits include:

1. Shortening the planning cycle time. By reducing computational effort, it is frequently possible to delay the start of budget preparation until more accurate inputs are available. Thus the quality of sales forecasts and cost estimates may be improved.
2. Reconsidering planning assumptions. Time savings make it feasible to reconsider planning assumptions early in the budgeting process. Cost and profit implications of various assumptions can be estimated before any commitment is made.
3. Continuous budgeting. Plans can be updated continuously throughout the budget period and, in some cases, planning horizons can be extended beyond the current budget period.
4. Operating analysis capability. If procedures and data are maintained in current form, the computerized model is available to produce instant answers to "what if" questions. More alternatives can be evaluated when such a model is used.
5. Discipline. Development of a model requires precise understanding and definition of the organization and its accounting system. Therefore, the discipline of developing the relationships inherent in a computerized budgeting model is of itself a valuable learning experience.

---

[16]This discussion adapted from Richard C. Murphy, "A Computerized Model Approach to Budgeting," *Management Accounting*, Vol. LVI, No. 12, pp. 34–36, 38.

DISCUSSION QUESTIONS

1. How is management's function of control executed through a budgetary control system?

2. Profit planning includes a complete financial and operational plan for all phases and facets of the business. Discuss.

3. Discuss the three different procedures that a company's management might follow to set profit objectives.

4. Differentiate between long-range profit planning and short-range budgeting.

5. Discuss the relationship between budgets and human behavior.

6. The human factors in budget preparation are more important than its technical intricacies. Explain.

7. Can a budgetary control system lead to results which are against the best interests of the company as a whole? Discuss.

8. The accountant must be skilled in accounting as well as in communications and human relations. Discuss.

9. While the budget is usually thought to be an important and necessary tool for management, it has been subject to some criticism from managers and researchers studying organizations and human behavior.
   (a) Describe and discuss the benefits of budgeting from the behavioral point of view.
   (b) Describe and discuss the criticisms leveled at the budgeting processes from the behavioral point of view.
   (c) What solutions are recommended to overcome the criticisms described in (b)?

   (CMA adapted)

10. The development of a budgetary control program requires specific systems and procedures needed in carrying out management's functions of planning, organizing, and controlling. Enumerate these steps.

11. State the fundamental axiom of fixed and variable costs of the product.

12. Commercial expenses are generally identified as marketing and administrative expenses. How should these expenses be grouped for budgetary purposes?

EXERCISES

1. Forecast cost of goods sold statement. Marquette, Inc., with $20,000,000 of par stock outstanding, plans to budget earnings of 6%, before income tax, on this stock.

The Marketing Department budgets sales at $12,000,000.

The budget director approves the sales budget and expenses as follows:

Marketing..	15% of sales
Administrative..	5%
Financial	1%

Labor is expected to be 50% of the total manufacturing cost; materials issued for the budgeted production will cost $2,500,000; therefore, any savings in manufacturing cost will have to be in factory overhead.

Inventories are to be as follows:

	BEGINNING OF YEAR	END OF YEAR
Finished goods	$800,000	$1,000,000
Work in process	100,000	300,000
Materials	500,000	400,000

Required: The projected cost of goods sold statement, showing the budgeted purchases of materials and the adjustments for inventories of materials, work in process, and finished goods.

2. Quarterly sales budget by districts; inventory schedule. Estimated sales percentages for the first three-month period of the coming year of the Midlands Company are:

DISTRICT	JANUARY	FEBRUARY	MARCH	TOTAL
Colorado	50%	30%	20%	100%
Kansas	55	30	15	100
Nebraska	50	25	25	100
Missouri	50	25	25	100

Estimated unit sales (at $2 per unit) by districts for the three months are:

DISTRICT	UNIT SALES
Colorado	20,000
Kansas	30,000
Nebraska	10,000
Missouri	40,000
Total	100,000

Company policy expects an inventory of 10,000 units at the beginning and at the end of each three-month period. The production schedule is:

January	55%
February	30%
March	15%

Required:
(1) An estimate of sales by units and dollars for each of the first three months for each district and in total.
(2) A schedule of the end-of-month inventories by units.

3. Sales budgets by territories and product lines. Yost Electronics Corporation has two product lines, high-speed printers and electronic typewriters. The company's Market Research Department prepared the following sales forecast for the coming year:

	HIGH-SPEED PRINTERS	ELECTRONIC TYPEWRITERS
Industry's total sales forecast	25,000	90,000
Company's share of the market	20%	10%
Sales price per unit	$1,800	$500

The sales representatives submitted these territorial sales estimates:

New England	1,200	2,000
Middle Atlantic	3,000	4,000
Southern States	1,800	2,000
Total	6,000	8,000

To establish an acceptable forecast, the budget director averages the two estimates. The resulting forecast is then broken down by territories in the same ratio as reflected in the estimates of the sales force.

Required: A sales forecast showing unit sales and total sales revenue by sales territory and by product lines.

4. Production budget. The Harrison Company's sales forecast for the next quarter, ending June 30, indicates the following:

PRODUCT	EXPECTED SALES
Ceno	21,000 units
Nepo	37,500
Teno	54,300

Inventories at the beginning and desired quantities at the end of the quarter are as follows:

PRODUCT	MARCH 31	JUNE 30
Ceno	5,800 units	6,200 units
Nepo	10,600	10,500
Teno	13,000	12,200

Required: A production budget for the second quarter.

5. Production budget. The Padre Island Canning Company produces frozen and condensed soup products. Frozen soups come in three principal varieties: snapper, shrimp, and pea. The condensed soups come in two principal varieties: tomato and chicken noodle. The Sales Division prepared the following tentative sales budget for the first six months of the coming year:

PRODUCT	BUDGETED FOR SALES
Frozen soups:	
Snapper	250,000 cans
Shrimp	150,000
Pea	350,000
Condensed soups:	
Tomato	1,000,000
Chicken noodle	750,000

The following inventory levels have been decided upon:

	WORK IN PROCESS				FINISHED GOODS	
	Beginning		Ending		Beginning	Ending
	Units	% Processed	Units	% Processed	Units	Units
Frozen soups:						
Snapper	5,000	80	4,000	75	15,000	20,000
Shrimp	3,000	70	3,000	75	8,000	5,000
Pea	4,000	75	5,000	80	20,000	20,000
Condensed soups:						
Tomato	25,000	80	40,000	75	75,000	60,000
Chicken noodle.	15,000	60	25,000	80	30,000	20,000

Required: A production budget for the six-month period.

6. Production, inventory, and purchase requirements. The following estimates and information have been gathered as part of the budget preparation of the Hobbycraft Co. The company manufactures a hobby shop sales item, consisting of two types of material which the company precuts and preshapes for sale to hobbyists. The sales for the second and third quarter of the coming year have been estimated as follows:

	SECOND QUARTER	THIRD QUARTER
Massachusetts	10,000 kits	35,000 kits
Vermont	8,000	25,000
New Hampshire	5,000	20,000
Total	23,000 kits	80,000 kits

It is decided that finished kits inventories are to be 25,000 at the end of the second quarter and 5,000 at the end of the third quarter. The inventory at the beginning of the second quarter will consist of 8,000 finished kits.

Each kit is packaged in a colorful cardboard box and contains 2 units of Material A and 5 units of Material B. The inventory of materials at the beginning of the second quarter will be:

Boxes	125,000
Material A	15,000 units
Material B	45,000 units

There are sufficient boxes on hand for both quarters; none will be purchased during the two periods. Material A can be bought whenever needed and in any quantity desired. The 15,000 units on hand is considered to be the ideal inventory quantity. Material B must be purchased in quantities of 10,000 or multiples of 10,000. At the end of both the second and third quarters, a minimum quantity of 30,000 units should be on hand, or as close thereto as the standard purchase quantity will permit.

Required:
(1) Schedule of ending inventories and budgeted production of kits for each quarter.
(2) Schedule of production requirements and purchase requirements for each quarter for each of the three types of materials.

7. Production budget, purchase requirements, and manufacturing budget. The Amsterdam Company prepared the following figures as a basis for its 19—— budget.

			REQUIRED MATERIALS PER UNIT	
PRODUCT	EXPECTED SALES	ESTIMATED PER UNIT SALES PRICE	A	B
Tribolite	80,000 units	$1.50	1 kg	2 kg
Polycal	40,000	2.00	2	—
Powder X	100,000	.80	—	1

Estimated inventories at the beginning and desired quantities at the end of 19—— are:

MATERIAL	BEGINNING	ENDING	PURCHASE PRICE PER KILOGRAM
A	10 000 kg	12 000 kg	$.20
B	12 000	15 000	.10

PRODUCT	BEGINNING	ENDING	DIRECT LABOR HOURS PER 1,000 UNITS
Tribolite	5,000 units	6,000 units	50.0
Polycal	4,000	2,000	125.0
Powder X	10,000	8,000	12.5

The direct labor cost is budgeted at $8 per hour and variable factory overhead at $6 per hour of direct labor. Fixed factory overhead, estimated to be $40,000, is a joint cost and is not allocated to specific products in developing the manufacturing budget for internal management use.

Required:
(1) Production budget.
(2) The budgeted quantities and dollar amounts of purchase requirements for each material.
(3) Manufacturing budget, by product and in total.

8. Labor cost budget. The Galway Company produces numerous related small parts. Its Cost Department has always prepared a labor budget in dollars only, since no information regarding the number of parts manufactured is available. During the past year, direct labor costs by quarters were reported as follows:

QUARTERS	MACHINING DEPARTMENT		FINISHING DEPARTMENT		TOTAL
First	$15,813	21%	$ 4,416	23%	$20,229
Second	18,072	24	4,608	24	22,680
Third	20,331	27	4,992	26	25,323
Fourth	21,084	28	5,184	27	26,268
Total	$75,300	100%	$19,200	100%	$94,500

The ratios of direct labor to total manufacturing cost during the past year averaged:

Machining Department... 23.75%
Finishing Department 25.00%

These ratios are expected to remain the same for the coming year. The manufacturing cost excluding direct labor has been budgeted for the coming year, with $244,000 for the Machining Department and $90,000 for the Finishing Department. The percentage distribution of labor requirements for each quarter will be the same for the coming year.

Required: The direct labor cost requirements for each quarter of the coming budget period.

PROBLEMS

16-1. Sales, materials, labor, and inventory budgets. The Budget Department gathered the following data concerning future sales and budget requirements:

ANTICIPATED SALES FOR 19--			EXPECTED INVENTORIES JANUARY 1, 19--	DESIRED INVENTORIES DECEMBER 31, 19--
Product	Units	Price		
A	20,000	$55	8,000 units	10,000 units
B	50,000	50	15,000	15,000
C	30,000	80	6,000	6,000

Materials used in manufacture:

		AMOUNT USED PER UNIT OF PRODUCT		
STOCK NO.	UNIT	A	B	C
110	Each	3		5
50	Each	2	1	3
41	Kilograms		2	
30	Kilograms		3	
40	Meters	5		4

	ANTICIPATED PURCHASE PRICE FOR MATERIALS	EXPECTED INVENTORIES JANUARY 1, 19--	DESIRED INVENTORIES DECEMBER 31, 19--
110	$3.00 each	21,000 each	25,000 each
50	2.00 each	17,000 each	23,000 each
41	2.50 per kilogram	10 000 kilograms	15 000 kilograms
30	4.00 per kilogram	18 000 kilograms	18 000 kilograms
40	3.25 per meter	25 000 meters	30 000 meters

Direct labor requirements and rates:

PRODUCT	HOURS PER UNIT	RATE PER HOUR
A	4	$4.00
B	5	3.00
C	5	4.20

Overhead is applied at the rate of $2 per direct labor hour.

Required:
(1) Sales budget (in dollars).
(2) Production budget (in quantities).
(3) Direct materials budget (in quantities).
(4) Direct materials purchases budget (in dollars).
(5) Direct labor budget (in dollars).
(6) Finished goods inventory, December 31, 19-- (in dollars).

16-2. Manufacturing budget; overhead rate. Techni-Toy, Inc., manufactures a variety of children's toys. The initial survey of the company's budget committee indicates an annual sales forecast of 95,000 plastic dolls. Management also plans to produce 5,000 dolls for stock. The purchasing agent indicates that economic lot purchases of 3 500 kilograms of plastic @ $2 per kg and 2 000 liters of paint @ $6 per liter are required to produce the 100,000 units.

Budgeted factory overhead expenses for this production schedule are:

Fixed factory overhead:
Depreciation — buildings...............................	$ 500
Depreciation — equipment............................	800
Supervision..	3,200
Insurance...	220

Variable factory overhead:
Indirect labor...	$ .250 per direct labor hour
Indirect supplies..	.004 per unit
General factory..	.050 per direct labor hour

Labor hours and rates for the two operations are:

Plastic Molder	2,000 hours @ $6.20 per hour
Painter	1,200 hours @ 6.00 per hour

Required:
(1) A manufacturing budget.
(2) The factory overhead rate based on direct labor hours.

16-3. Materials budget. The Press Company manufactures and sells industrial components. Its Whitmore Plant is responsible for producing two components, AD-5 and FX-3, using plastic, brass, and aluminum.

For budgeting purposes, Press Company has adopted a thirteen-period reporting cycle in all of its plants. Each period is four weeks long and has 20 working days. The projected inventory levels for AD-5 and FX-3 at the end of the current (seventh) period and the projected sales for these two products for the next three four-week periods are presented below:

	PROJECTED INVENTORY LEVEL END OF SEVENTH PERIOD	PROJECTED SALES		
		Eighth Period	*Ninth Period*	*Tenth Period*
AD-5	3,000 units	7,500 units	8,750 units	9,500 units
FX-3....................	2,800	7,000	4,500	4,000

Past experience has shown that adequate inventory levels for AD-5 and FX-3 can be maintained if 40% of the next period's projected sales are on hand at the end of a reporting period. Based on this experience and the projected sales, the Whitmore Plant has budgeted production of 8,000 AD-5 and 6,000 of FX-3 in the eighth period. Production is assumed to be uniform for both products within each four-week period.

The materials specifications for AD-5 and FX-3 are as follows:

	AD-5	FX-3
Plastic..	2.0 lbs.	1.0 lb.
Brass	.5	—
Aluminum..	—	1.5

Data relating to the purchase of materials are:

	PURCHASE PRICE PER POUND	STANDARD PURCHASE LOT	ORDER POINT	PROJECTED INVENTORY STATUS AT THE END OF THE SEVENTH PERIOD		LEAD TIME IN WORKING DAYS
				ON HAND	ON ORDER	
Plastic.......	$.40	15,000 lbs.	12,000 lbs.	16,000 lbs.	15,000 lbs.	10 days
Brass.........	.95	5,000	7,500	9,000	—	30
Aluminum .	.55	10,000	10,000	14,000	10,000	20

The sales of AD-5 and FX-3 do not vary significantly from month to month. Consequently, the safety stock incorporated into the order point for each of the materials is adequate to compensate for variations in the sales of the finished products. The order point for each of the materials denotes the inventory balance at which to order and includes consideration of quantities due in, of lead time, and of safety stock.

Materials orders are placed the day the quantity on hand falls below the order point. Whitmore Plant's suppliers are very dependable, so that the given lead times are reliable. The outstanding orders for plastic and aluminum are due to arrive on the tenth and fourth working days of the eighth period, respectively. Payments for all materials orders are remitted in the month of delivery.

Required: For the eighth period:
(1) Projected quantities (in pounds) of each material to be issued to production.
(2) Projected quantities (in pounds) of each material ordered and the date (in terms of working days) the order is to be placed.
(3) The projected inventory balance (in pounds) of each material at the end of the period.
(4) The payments for purchases of each material.

(CMA adapted)

16-4. Materials purchases, production, and inventory budgets. The purchasing agent and the chief accountant of Toyland, Inc., are trying to solve the problem of scheduling purchases in connection with a planned expansion in the production of rocking horses. All lumber used is procured in a standard size, of which the following amounts, which include a due allowance for waste, are used in one complete rocking horse:

> Oak   — 2 board feet
> Pine — 5 board feet
> Maple — 10 board feet

A sales budget has been approved, and the following production schedule has been drawn up for 19A:

QUARTER	ROCKING HORSES
1st	75
2d	150
3d	175
4th	200

The production schedule for the first quarter of 19B calls for approximately 220 rocking horses.

Delivery of lumber is slow and uncertain; but by ordering early, delivery can be assured during the quarter desired. Lumber must be purchased in quantities that are multiples of 300 board feet of each kind of lumber; but since there is a very good discount for purchases of 1,500 board feet lots for all kinds of lumber combined, such purchases are made whenever possible. Otherwise, the minimum requirements are always purchased. In determining minimum requirements, it is necessary to have on hand at the beginning of a quarter sufficient materials to take care of production for that quarter.

Purchases of 1,500 board feet lots are restricted because of limited storage facilities. At the present time, there is sufficient space to store 3,000 board feet of all types of lumber combined. During the early part of the year, a new shed will be constructed to store an additional 1,200 board feet, making a total storage space of 4,200 board feet available prior to the end of the second quarter.

Inventory of lumber on January 1, 19A, is as follows:

> Oak   — 150 board feet
> Pine — 600 board feet
> Maple — 900 board feet

Required: Schedule, or schedules, indicating the materials production requirements, materials purchases, and materials inventories for each type of lumber, by quarter for 19A, expressed in board feet.

16-5. Sales forecasts; purchases and materials requirements. The management of Consumer Food Products decided to install a budgetary control system under the supervision of a budget director and a committee. Among its products, the company manufactures a patented breakfast food that is sold in packages of two sizes — 1 lb. and 2 lb. The cereal is made from two types of grain, called R (rye) and S (soy) for this purpose. There are two operations: (a) processing and blending and (b) packaging. The grains are purchased by the bushel measure, a bushel of R containing 70 lbs. and a bushel of S containing 80 lbs. Three bushels of grain mixed in the proportion of 2R:1S produce 198 lbs. of finished product; the entire loss occurs in the first department.

To prepare estimated sales figures for the first six months of the coming year, the budget committee first asked the salespeople to prepare sales estimates in units. The following was submitted:

| | TERRITORIES | | | | |
	I	II	III	Other	6-Month Total
1-lb. package	10,000	15,000	12,000	613,000	650,000
2-lb. package	12,000	18,000	12,000	783,000	825,000
Total	22,000	33,000	24,000	1,396,000	1,475,000

The figures submitted are analyzed by the budget committee in the light of general business conditions. The company uses the Federal Reserve Board Index together with its own trade index to prepare a trend percentage that exists in the business. The trend percentage indicates that a .90 general index figure should be applied to the estimates in order to arrive at the final sales figures. The monthly sales figure is to be set up as one sixth of the total figure finally computed. The finished goods inventory is to be kept at zero if possible; the work in process inventory is to be kept near the present level, which is about 160,000 lbs. of blended material.

Factory facilities permit processing sales requirements as stated in the sales budget. The production manager decided to accept the monthly sales figures for the production budget.

Purchases of grains in bushels have been arranged as follows:

| | TYPE R | | TYPE S | |
	Quantity	Price	Quantity	Price
January..	5,000 bu.	$1.30	2,000 bu.	$1.20
February..	2,000	1.40	1,000	1.20
March	–0–	–0–	3,000	1.25
April	8,000	1.50	3,000	1.00
May..	3,000	1.50	–0–	–0–
June...	4,000	1.60	4,000	1.00
Beginning inventory, January 1	10,000	1.20	3,000	1.00

Materials are charged into production on the fifo basis.

Required:
  (1) A revised sales forecast based on the index.
  (2) A sales forecast on a dollar basis, assuming that the 1-lb. package sells for $.25 and the 2-lb. package for $.50.
  (3) A schedule of materials purchases.
  (4) A computation of materials requirements for production. (Round off to the nearest whole amount.)
  (5) A schedule of the materials account (fifo basis), indicating beginning inventory, purchases, usage, and ending inventory for the six-month period taken as a whole.

CASES

A. Corporate goals. Duval, Inc., a large publicly held corporation, has always had good profit margins and excellent earnings. However, in the past two years, Duval has experienced a leveling of sales and a reduced market share, resulting in a stabilization of profits rather than growth. Despite these trends, the firm has maintained an excellent cash and short-term investment position. The president has called a meeting of the treasurer and the vice-presidents for sales and production in order to develop alternative strategies for improving Duval's performance.

The sales vice-president suggests that sales levels can be improved by presenting the company's product in a more attractive and appealing package, increasing the advertising, and maintaining the current price, which would be lower than that of most other competing products.

The treasurer is skeptical of maintaining the present price when others are increasing prices, since this will curtail revenue, unless this policy provides a competitive advantage. The repackaging will increase costs in the near future, at least, because of the start-up costs of a new packaging process. Increasing advertising outright would have a doubtful short-run benefit.

The sales vice-president replies that increased, or at least redirected, advertising is necessary to promote price stability and to take advantage of the new packaging, thus providing the company with a competitive advantage. The president adds that the advertising should be studied closely to determine the type to be used — television, radio, newspaper, magazine. In addition, if television is used, attention must be directed to the type of programs to be sponsored — children's, family, sporting events, news specials, etc.

The production vice-president suggests several possible production improvements, such as a systems study of the manufacturing process to identify changes in the work flow, which would cut costs, and purchasing new equipment in order to reduce operating costs. The product could be improved by employing a better grade of materials and by engineering changes in its fabrication. When queried by the president on the impact of the proposed changes, the production vice-president indicates that the primary benefit would be product performance, but that appearance and safety would also be improved. According to the sales vice-president and treasurer, this would result in increased sales.

The treasurer notes that all of the production proposals would increase immediate costs, resulting in lower profits. If profit performance is going to be improved, the price structure should be examined closely. The current level of capital expenditures should be maintained unless substantial cost savings can be obtained.

The treasurer further believes that expenditures for research and development should be decreased, since previous outlays have not prevented a decrease in Duval's share of the market. The production vice-president agrees that the research and development activities have not proven profitable, due to application in the wrong area. The sales vice-president cautions against any drastic reductions, because the packaging change will only provide a temporary advantage in the market, necessitating more effort in product development.

Focusing on the use of liquid assets and the present high yields on securities, the treasurer suggests improving the firm's profitability by shifting funds from the presently held short-term marketable securities to longer term, higher yield securities. Cost reductions would provide more funds for investments, but the restructuring of the investments from short-term to long-term would hamper flexibility.

In summarizing, the president, aware that they have a good start and that the ideas provide some excellent alternatives, states, "I think we ought to develop these ideas further and consider other ramifications. For instance, what effect would new equipment and the systems study have on the labor force? Shouldn't we also consider the environmental impact of any plant and product change? We want to appear as a leader in our industry — not a follower. I note that none of you considered increased community involvement through such groups as the Chamber of Commerce and the United Fund. These additional points plus the factors you mentioned should all be considered in our decision on the final course of action."

Required:
    (1) The implied corporate goals expressed by each of the following: (a) treasurer; (b) sales vice-president; (c) production vice-president; (d) president.
    (2) The type of goals discussed above compared with the corporate goal(s) postulated by the classical economic theory of the firm.   (CMA adapted)

B. Evaluation of budget procedures. Clarkson Company, a large multidivision firm with several plants in each division, uses a comprehensive budgeting system for planning operations and measuring performance. The annual budgeting process commences in August, five months prior to the beginning of the fiscal year. At this time, the division managers submit proposed budgets for sales, production and inventory levels, and expenses. Capital expenditure requests also are formalized at this time. The expense budgets include direct labor and all factory overhead items, separated into fixed and variable components. Direct materials are budgeted separately in developing the production and inventory schedules.

The expense budgets for each division are developed from each plant's results, as measured by the percent variation from an adjusted budget in the first six months of the current year, and a target expense reduction percentage established by the corporation.

To determine plant percentages, the plant budget for the just completed half-year period is revised to recognize changes in operating procedures and costs outside the control of plant management (e.g., labor wage rate changes and product style changes). The difference between this revised budget and the actual expenses is the controllable variance, expressed as a percentage of the actual expenses. If unfavorable, this percentage is added to the corporate target expense reduction percentage. A favorable plant variance percentage is subtracted from the corporate target. If a plant had a 2% unfavorable controllable variance and the corporate target reduction was 4%, the plant's budget for next year should reflect costs approximately 6% below this year's actual costs.

Next year's final budgets for the corporation, its divisions, and plants are adopted after corporate analysis of the proposed budgets and a careful review with each division manager of the changes made by corporate management.

Division profit budgets include allocated corporate costs, and plant profit budgets include allocated division and corporate costs.

Required: Evaluation of the budget procedures of Clarkson Company with respect to its effectiveness for planning and controlling operations.

(CMA adapted)

C. The budget and human behavior. Drake, Inc., is a multiproduct firm with several manufacturing plants. Management generally has been pleased with the operation of all the plants but the Swan Plant, whose poor operating performance has been traced to poor control over plant costs. Four plant managers have resigned or been terminated during the last three years.

David Green was appointed the new manager of the Swan Plant on February 1, 19B. Green is a young and aggressive individual who had progressed rapidly in Drake's management development program and had performed well in lower level management positions.

Green had been recommended for the position by Susan Bradley, Green's immediate supervisor. Bradley was impressed by Green's technical ability and enthusiasm. Bradley explained to Green that the assignment as Swan Plant manager was approved despite the objections of some of the other members of the executive management team. Bradley told Green that she had complete confidence in him and his ability and was sure that Green wanted to prove that she had made a good decision. Therefore, Bradley expected Green to have the Swan Plant on budget by June 30.

As a result of Swan Plant's past difficulties, Susan Bradley has had responsibility for formulating the last four annual budgets for the plant. The 19B budget was prepared during the last six months of 19A before Green had been appointed plant manager. The budget report covering the three-month period ended March 31, 19B, showed that Swan's costs were slightly over budget. At a meeting with Bradley, Green described the changes he had instituted during the last month. Green was confident that the costs would be held in check with these changes and the situation would get no worse for the rest of the year.

Bradley repeated that she not only wanted the cost controlled but she expected Swan Plant to be on budget by June 30. Green pointed out that the Swan Plant had been in poor condition for three years. He further stated that, while he appreciated the confidence Bradley had in him, he had only been in charge two months.

Susan Bradley then replied, "I am expected to meet my figures. The only way that can occur is if my subordinates exercise control over their costs and achieve their budgets. Therefore, to assure that I achieve my goals, get the Swan Plant on budget by June 30 and keep it on budget for the rest of the year."

Required:
(1) A critical evaluation of the budget practices described in the problem.
(2) The likely immediate and long-term effects on David Green and Drake, Inc., if the present method of budget administration is continued.   (CMA adapted)

D. Time budget, billing rates, and budgeted income statement. In June, 19A, after ten years with a large CPA firm, Anna B. Johnson, CPA, opened an office as a sole practitioner.

In 19C, Walter L. Smith, CPA, joined Johnson as a senior accountant. The partnership of Johnson and Smith was organized July 1, 19H, and a fiscal year ending June 30 was adopted and approved by the Internal Revenue Service.

Continued growth of the firm has required additional personnel. The current complement, including approved salaries for the fiscal year ending June 30, 19N, is as follows:

Partners:
Anna B. Johnson, CPA	$24,000
Walter L. Smith, CPA	18,000

Professional staff:
Supervisor:
Harold S. Vickers, CPA	17,500

Senior Accountant:
Duane Lowe, CPA	12,500

Assistants:
James M. Kennedy	10,500
Viola O. Quinn	10,500

Secretaries:
Livia A. Garcia	7,800
Johnnie L. Hammond	6,864
Mary Lyons	6,864

During a severe illness which kept Johnson away from the office for over four months in late 19L, the firm suffered, mainly because other personnel lacked knowledge about the practice. After Johnson's return, a plan was developed for delegation of administrative authority and responsibility and for standardization of procedures. The goals of the plan included income objectives, standardized billing procedures (with flexibility for adjustments by the partners), and assignment schedules to eliminate overtime and to allow for nonchargeable time such as vacations and illness. The firm plans a 52-week year with five-day, forty-hour weeks.

The partners have set an annual income target for the firm of at least $55,000 (after partners' salaries). The budget for fiscal year 19N is 700 hours of chargeable time at $45 per hour for Johnson and 1,100 hours at $40 per hour for Smith. Johnson and Smith are to devote all other available time, except as specified below, to administration. The billing rates for all other employees including secretaries are to be set at a level to recover their salaries plus the following overhead items: fringe benefits of $15,230, other operating expenses of $49,380, and a contribution of $20,500 to target income.

The partners agree that salary levels are fair bases for allocating overhead in setting billing rates, with the exception of salary costs of the secretaries' nonchargeable time, which are to be added to overhead to arrive at total overhead to be allocated. Thus, the billing rates for each secretary will be based upon the salary costs of chargeable time plus a share of the total overhead. No portion of total overhead is to be allocated to partners' salaries.

The following information is available for nonchargeable time:
(a) Because of the recent illness, Johnson expects to be away an additional week. Smith expects no loss of time from illness. All other employees are to be allowed one illness day per month.
(b) Allowable vacations are as follows:

Johnson	1 month (173 hours)
Smith	1 month (173 hours)
Vickers	3 weeks
Garcia	3 weeks
All other employees	2 weeks

(c) If any of the holidays observed (7 annually) falls on a weekend, the office is closed the preceding Friday or following Monday.

(d) Kennedy and Quinn should each be allotted three days to sit for the November 19M CPA examination.

(e) Hours are budgeted for other miscellaneous activities of the personnel as follows:

	Johnson	Smith	Vickers	Lowe	Kennedy	Quinn	Garcia	Hammond	Lyons
Firm projects...........................		100	40	40	40		200		
Professional development ...	80	80	56	40	40	50	24	16	24
Professional meetings..........	184	120	40	40	16	16	24	8	8
Firm meetings......................	48	48	48	24	24	24	48	8	8
Community activities............	80	40	40	24	16	16	12		
Office time other than firm administration			84	72			1,000	716	808
Total other miscellaneous....	392	388	308	240	136	106	1,308	748	848

(f) Unassigned time should be budgeted for Lowe, Kennedy, and Quinn as 8, 38, and 78 hours, respectively.

Required:

(1) A time allocation budget for Johnson, Smith, and each employee, ending with budgeted chargeable time for the year ending June 30, 19N.

(2) A schedule computing billing rates by employee for the year ending June 30, 19N, independent of the solution to requirement (1) and assuming the data below as to budgeted chargeable hours. The schedule should show the proper allocation of appropriate expenses and target income contribution to salaries applicable to chargeable time in accordance with the objective established by the partners. (Round billing rate calculations to the nearest dollar.)

	BUDGETED CHARGEABLE HOURS
Vickers	1,600
Lowe..	1,650
Kennedy	1,550
Quinn...	1,450
Garcia..	500
Hammond	1,150
Lyons...	1,200

(3) A condensed statement of budgeted income for the year ending June 30, 19N, independent of solutions to requirements (1) and (2) and assuming the following data as to budgeted chargeable hours and billing rates:

	BUDGETED CHARGEABLE HOURS	BUDGETED HOURLY BILLING RATE
Johnson..	700	$45
Smith..	1,100	40
Vickers...	1,600	32
Lowe	1,650	25
Kennedy...	1,550	15
Quinn	1,450	17
Garcia	500	5
Hammond	1,150	7
Lyons	1,200	7

(AICPA adapted)

17

Budgeting
Expenditures and Cash
Nonmanufacturing Businesses and Nonprofit Organizations
PERT/Cost

Budgeting usually is an iterative process. Budgets are prepared, reviewed, and revised until executive management is satisfied that the result represents the best plans that can be devised under existing circumstances. Furthermore, management may develop contingency plans for dealing with various eventualities. As the planning period unfolds, budget revisions may be required, and such revisions will be facilitated if management has anticipated alterations called for by changing circumstances and conditions.

This chapter discusses specific budgets, such as capital expenditures and research and development budgets, which play a significant part in the long- and short-range plans of any management. Closely related thereto is the cash budget that reveals excesses and/or shortages of funds. The forecast annual statements serve as a master budget and final check on the ultimate results expected from the combined sales-cost-profit plan. Financial forecasts for external users, budgeting for nonmanufacturing businesses and nonprofit organizations, zero-base budgeting, PERT and PERT/cost, and probabilistic budgets conclude the presentation.

CAPITAL EXPENDITURES BUDGET

Capital expenditures are long-term commitments of resources to realize future benefits. Budgeting capital expenditures is one of the most important areas of managerial decision. Facility improvements and plant expansion programs must be geared to a limited supply of funds from internal operations and external sources. The magnitude of funds involved in each expenditure and the length of time required to recover the investment call for penetrating analysis and capable judgment. Decisions regarding current manufacturing operations can always be changed, but because the benefits of a capital expenditure will be reaped over a fairly extended length of time, managerial errors could be quite costly.

To minimize the number of capital expenditure errors, many firms have established definite procedures for evaluating the merits of a project before funds are released. True control of capital expenditures is exercised in advance by requiring that each request be based on evaluation analyses. Managerial control requires facts regarding engineering estimates, expected sales volumes, production costs, and marketing costs. Management usually has a firm conviction as to what is consistent with the long-range objectives of the business. It is fundamentally interested in making certain that the project will contribute to the earnings position of the company.

Evaluating Capital Expenditures

Capital expenditure programs involve both short- and long-range projects. Provisions must be made in the current budget for short-range capital expenditures. These short-range projects must be examined in the light of their economic worth as compared with other projects seeking final approval. The process of budgeting provides the only opportunity to examine projects side by side and to evaluate their contribution to future periods.

Short- and Long-Range Capital Expenditures

Long-range projects which will not be implemented in the current budget period need only be stated in general terms, since the exchange and addition of capital assets are only significant in the current budget period. In the main, long-range capital expenditure plans are a management responsibility and are translated into budget commitments only as the opportune time for their implementation approaches. Timing is most important to the achievement of the most profitable results in planning and budgeting capital expenditures.

RESEARCH AND DEVELOPMENT BUDGET

Research and development activities have been defined as follows:

1. *Research* is planned search or critical investigation aimed at discovery of new knowledge with the hope that such knowledge will be useful in developing a new product or service (hereinafter "product") or a new process or technique (hereinafter "process") or in bringing about a significant improvement to an existing product or process.
2. *Development* is the translation of research findings or other knowledge into a plan or design for a new product or process or for a significant improvement to an existing product or process whether intended for sale or use. It includes the conceptual formulation, design, and testing of product alternatives, construction of prototypes, and operation of pilot plants. It does not include routine or periodic alterations to existing products, production lines, manufacturing processes, and other ongoing operations even though those alterations may represent improve-

ments and it does not include market research or market testing activities.[1]

The managements of many firms are acutely aware of the increased necessity for and rapid growth of research and development activities and of the need to consider their costs from both the long- and short-range points of view. From the long-range viewpoint, management must assure itself that a program is in line with future market trends and demands and that the future cost of a program is not at odds with forecast economic and financial conditions. From the short-range viewpoint, management must be assured that experimental efforts are being expended on programs which promise a satisfactory rate of return on the dollars invested.

Research and development projects compete with other projects for available financial resources. The value of the research and development program must be shown as clearly as possible, so that management can compare it with similar programs and other investment opportunities. Therefore, the motivation and intent of experimental activities must be carefully identified.

The research and development budget involves identifying program components and estimating their costs. Other planning devices are used at times, but the budget is considered best for (1) balancing the research and development program, (2) coordinating the program with the company's other projects, and (3) checking certain phases of nonfinancial planning. The budget forces management to think in advance about planned expenditures, both in total amounts and in sphere of effort. It helps achieve coordination, because it presents an overall picture of proposed research and development activities which can be reviewed and criticized by other operating managers. Exchange of opinions and information at planning meetings is management's best control over the program.

Another important purpose of research and development budgeting is to coordinate these plans with the immediate and long-term financial plans of the company. The budget also forces the research and development director and staff to think in advance about major aspects of the program: personnel requirements, individual or group work loads, equipment requirements, special materials, and necessary facilities. These phases of the research and development program are often overlooked or duplicated.

Forms of a Research and Development Budget

Management expects the research and development staff to present ideas along with a complete and detailed budget which can be evaluated as part of the entire planning program. The controller's staff may assist in the preparation of budgets with clearly defined goals and properly evaluated cost data.

Submission of data takes many forms. Information regarding segmentation and allocation of time and effort to various phases of the program is of

---

[1]*Statement of Financial Accounting Standards, No. 2*, "Accounting for Research and Development Costs" (Stamford: Financial Accounting Standards Board, 1974), par. 8.

particular interest to executive management as well as to divisional managers. The following example of a research and development balance sheet has been proposed:[2]

RESEARCH AND DEVELOPMENT BALANCE SHEET
PROGRAM PLANNED FOR 19--
(Percentages of Total Effort by Area of Inquiry and by Phase)

PHASE	COST REDUCTION			IMPROVED PRODUCTS			NEW PRODUCTS			TOTAL
	A*	B	C	A	B	C	A	B	C	
Applied research .	4%	3%	3%	2%	4%	4%	1%	1%	3%	25%
Development......	5	12	3	4	1		2		3	30
Basic research	7	6	2	5			10		15	45
Total by product lines	16%	21%	8%	11%	5%	4%	13%	1%	21%	100%
Total by area of inquiry		45%			20%			35%		

*A, B, and C refer to product lines.

The overall research and development program should be supported by a specific budget request which indicates the jobs or steps within each project, the necessary labor hours, the service department time required, and required direct departmental funds. Each active project should be reviewed monthly, comparing projected plans with results attained.

Research and development costs generally should be expensed in the period incurred because of the uncertainty of the extent or length of future benefit to the company. An exception to the expensing requirement applies to costs of research and development expenditures that are (1) conducted for others, (2) unique to extractive industries, or (3) incurred by a government-regulated enterprise, such as a public utility, which often defers research and development costs because of the rate-regulated aspects of its business. Equipment and purchased intangibles having alternative future uses should be recorded as assets and expensed through depreciation or amortization. Research and development costs, when expensed, should be reported as one item in the operating expense section of the income statement.[3]

Accounting for Research and Development Costs

CASH BUDGET

A *cash budget* involves detailed estimates of anticipated cash receipts and disbursements for the budget period or some other specific period. It has gen-

---

[2]J. B. Quinn, "Study of the Usefulness of Research and Development Budgets," *NAA Bulletin*, Vol. XL, No. 1, pp. 79–90.
[3]*Statement of Financial Accounting Standards, No. 2, op. cit.*, pars. 2, 3, and 11–14.

erally been recognized as an extremely useful and essential management tool. Planning and controlling cash is basic to good management. Even if a company does not prepare extensive budgets for sales and production, it should set up a budget or estimate of cash receipts and disbursements as an aid to cash management.

Purpose and Nature of a Cash Budget

A cash budget:

1. Indicates the effect on the cash position of seasonal requirements, large inventories, unusual receipts, and slowness in collecting receivables.
2. Indicates the cash requirements needed for a plant or equipment expansion program.
3. Shows the need for additional funds from sources such as bank loans or sales of securities and the time factors involved. In this connection, it might also exert a cautionary influence on plans for plant expansion, leading to a modification of capital expenditure decisions.
4. Indicates the availability of cash for taking advantage of discounts.
5. Assists in planning the financial requirements of bond retirements, income tax installments, and payments to pension and retirement funds.
6. Shows the availability of excess funds for short-term or long-term investments.
7. Serves as a basis for evaluating the actual cash management performance of responsible individuals, using measurement criteria such as the target average daily balance as compared with the actual average daily balance in each cash account.

The period of time covered by a cash budget varies with each type of business. A cash budget is generally quite accurate when it covers a short period, but it requires constant attention. A yearly cash budget should usually be prepared by months, with changes made at the end of each month in order to (1) incorporate deviations from the previous forecast and (2) add a month to replace the month just passed, so that a *rolling cash budget* covering the next twelve months is always available. As the coming month or week moves closer, weekly or even daily cash receipts and disbursements schedules are necessary for prudent and efficient cash management.

A cash budget includes no accrual items. For example, assume that payroll accrued at the beginning and end of a month is $4,800 and $3,300, respectively, and the budget shows that $18,000 in wages and salaries will be earned by employees. The treasurer computes the monthly cash requirement for the payroll as follows:

Accrued payroll at beginning of month	$ 4,800
Add payroll earned as per budget	18,000
	$22,800
Deduct accrued payroll at end of month	3,300
Amount of cash to be paid out	$19,500

Additional adjustments are necessary for deductions from employees' earnings when these deductions are not remitted in the months withheld.

Preparation of a cash budget may follow either of two generally accepted procedures:

Preparation of a Cash Budget

1. The cash receipts and disbursements method.
2. The adjusted income method.

Cash Receipts and Disbursements Method. In this method, all anticipated cash receipts, such as cash sales, cash collections on accounts receivable, dividends, interest on notes and bonds, proceeds from sales of assets, royalties, bank loans, and stock sales, are carefully estimated. Likewise, cash requirements for materials purchases, supplies, payroll, repayment of loans, dividends, taxes, and purchases of plant or equipment must be determined.

The primary sources of cash receipts are cash sales and collections of accounts receivable. Estimates of collections of accounts receivable are based on the sales budget and on the company's collection experience. A study is made of a representative period to determine how customers pay their accounts, how many take the discount offered, and how many pay within 10 days, 30 days, and so forth. These experiences are set up in a schedule of anticipated collections from sales. Collections during a month will be the result of (1) this month's sales and (2) accounts receivable of prior months' sales. Seasonal variations should also be considered if they affect the collections pattern. To illustrate, assume that during each month, collections on accounts receivable show the following pattern:

From this month's sales...	10.8%
From prior months' accounts receivable:	
Last month's sales..	78.2
2 months old	6.3
3 months old	2.1
4 months old	1.2
Cash discounts taken	1.2
Doubtful accounts	.2
	100.0%

On the basis of these percentages, collections for the month of July are computed as follows:

MONTH	CREDIT SALES	%	COLLECTIONS
July	$160,000	10.8	$ 17,280
June	200,000	78.2	156,400
May................................	175,000	6.3	11,025
April...............................	180,000	2.1	3,780
March............................	178,000	1.2	2,136
Total collections for July			$190,621

Estimated cash disbursements are computed from the:

1. Materials budget, which shows planned purchases.
2. Labor budget, which indicates wages earned.

3. Various types of expense budgets, both manufacturing and commercial, which indicate expenses expected to be incurred. Noncash expenses such as depreciation are excluded.
4. Plant and equipment budget, which details cash needed for the purchase of new equipment or replacements.
5. Treasurer's budget, which indicates requirements for items such as dividends, interest and payments on loans and bonds, donations, and income taxes.

Adjusted Income Method. In this method of preparing the cash budget, cash estimates come from the forecast income for the period, adjusted for noncash transactions and for expected cash-oriented changes in asset and liability accounts not affected by income calculations. The noncash transactions are added back to income for the period. Noncash items are depreciation, doubtful accounts receivable, expired insurance premiums, accruals for warranties or guarantees, and income tax accruals. The next step is to add anticipated decreases in assets or increases in liabilities and to deduct anticipated increases in assets or decreases in liabilities. The expected cash position at the end of a period is the cash balance at the beginning of the period plus or minus the net cash increase or decrease as indicated by the analysis of the forecast income and other cash transactions. This method is not as effective a planning and control technique as is the cash receipts and disbursements method, because it is usually in terms of aggregate cash flows rather than in terms of detailed cash receipts and disbursement components.

Electronic Cash Management

The basic premise of cash management is that dollars in transit are not earning assets. They cannot be utilized until they are available as deposits. Similarly, cash lying idle in checking accounts contributes nothing to corporate profitability.

Organizations with multiple, geographically dispersed units, or firms with a widespread customer base making individual payments to dispersed collecting units can especially benefit from electronic cash management systems. The system involves cash concentration by means of nationwide electronic transfers which accelerate the collection of deposits from local banks into a central account on a same-day basis. By drawing checks on its centrally located account, the firm has the additional advantage of *float* for the time it takes the check to be cleared back to the central bank account.[4] Such procedures enhance efficient and effective cash management.

PROJECTED OR FORECAST INCOME STATEMENT

A *projected income statement* contains summaries of the sales, manufacturing, and expense budgets. It projects net income, the goal toward which all efforts are directed, and it offers management the opportunity to judge the

---

[4]George H. Denniston, Jr., "Cash Management and Corporate Profitability," *Flying Colors*, Vol. 6, No. 8, p. 32.

accuracy of the budget work and investigate causes for variances. No new estimates are actually made; figures taken from various budgets are merely arranged in the form of an income statement, as illustrated below. The sales budget gives expected sales revenue; the manufacturing budget furnishes manufacturing costs and cost of goods sold which, when deducted from sales, give the estimated gross profit. Estimates from the marketing and administrative expense budgets are subtracted from estimated gross profit to arrive at income from operations. Other income and expense items are either added or deducted to determine income before income tax. Finally, the provision for income tax is deducted to determine net income. These income statement

Projected Income Statement
By Months for Year Ending December, 19--

	JANUARY	FEBRUARY	DECEMBER	TOTAL
Sales	$ 480,000	$ 540,000	$420,000	$7,200,000
Cost of goods sold:				
Materials used	$ 180,000	$ 180,000	$200,000	$2,400,000
Direct labor	90,000	90,000	100,000	1,200,000
Factory overhead:				
Fixed	49,500	49,500	49,500	594,000
Variable	54,000	54,000	60,000	720,000
Cost of goods manufactured	$ 373,500	$ 373,500	$409,500	$4,914,000
Add beginning finished goods inventory (fifo)	630,000	667,500	491,400	630,000
Cost of goods available for sale	$1,003,500	$1,041,000	$900,900	$5,544,000
Less ending finished goods inventory	667,500	664,000	614,250	614,250
Cost of goods sold	$ 336,000	$ 377,000	$286,650	$4,929,750
Gross profit	$ 144,000	$ 163,000	$133,350	$2,270,250
Commercial expenses:				
Marketing expenses:				
Fixed	$ 25,000	$ 25,000	$ 25,000	$ 300,000
Variable	12,000	13,500	10,500	180,000
Administrative expenses:				
Fixed	20,000	20,000	20,000	240,000
Variable	8,000	9,000	7,000	120,000
Total commercial expenses	$ 65,000	$ 67,500	$ 62,500	$ 840,000
Income from operations	$ 79,000	$ 95,500	$ 70,850	$1,430,250
Other expenses:				
Uncollectible accounts expense	$ 4,800	$ 5,400	$ 4,200	$ 72,000
Interest on notes payable	500	500	500	6,000
Total	$ 5,300	$ 5,900	$ 4,700	$ 78,000
Other income:				
Interest income			1,250	7,500
Other expenses (net)	$ 5,300	$ 5,900	$ 3,450	$ 70,500
Income before income tax	$ 73,700	$ 89,600	$ 67,400	$1,359,750
Less provision for income tax	36,850	44,800	33,700	679,875
Net income	$ 36,850	$ 44,800	$ 33,700	$ 679,875

details may be segmented by individual products or product groups and by individual marketing territories.

PROJECTED OR FORECAST BALANCE SHEET

A *projected balance sheet* for the beginning of the budget period is the starting point for the preparation of a forecast balance sheet for the end of the budget period. As illustrated below, it incorporates all changes in assets, liabilities, and capital in the budgets submitted by the various departments, functions, or segments.

Projected Balance Sheet By Months for Year Ending December, 19––				
Assets	JANUARY 1	JANUARY 31	FEBRUARY 28	DECEMBER 31
Cash	$ 400,000	$ 173,000	$ 99,300	$ 245,675
Accounts receivable	250,000	153,400	180,100	149,500
Less allowance for doubtful accounts	(2,500)	(1,300)	(700)	(2,500)
Inventories:				
Finished goods	630,000	667,500	664,000	614,250
Materials	320,000	320,000	320,000	320,000
Plant and equipment	3,000,000	3,000,000	3,000,000	3,000,000
Less accumulated depreciation	(600,000)	(616,850)	(633,950)	(815,400)
Other assets	202,500	200,650	198,550	167,100
U.S. Government bonds				500,000
Interest receivable				7,500
Total assets	$4,200,000	$3,896,400	$3,827,300	$4,186,125
Liabilities and Capital				
Current liabilities	$ 770,000	$ 231,000	$ 77,000	
Accounts payable (purchases)		32,400	32,400	$ 36,000
Accounts payable (factory overhead and marketing and administrative expenses)		134,800	136,800	137,600
Interest payable		500	1,000	
Income tax payable		33,850	75,050	118,650
Long-term debt	120,000	120,000	120,000	
Common stock	960,000	960,000	960,000	960,000
Retained earnings	2,350,000	2,383,850	2,425,050	2,933,875
Total liabilities and capital	$4,200,000	$3,896,400	$3,827,300	$4,186,125

Numerous advantages result from the preparation of a forecast balance sheet. One advantage is that a forecast balance sheet discloses unfavorable ratios which management may wish to change for various reasons. Unfavorable ratios can lower credit ratings or cause a drop in the value of the corporation's securities. A second advantage is that a forecast balance sheet serves as a check on the accuracy of all other budgets. Still another advantage is that a return-on-investment ratio can be computed by relating net income to capital employed. An inadequate return on investment would suggest a need for budget changes.

FINANCIAL FORECASTS FOR EXTERNAL USERS

Recent years have seen increasing recognition of the importance of financial forecasts for external users, because investors and potential investors seek to enhance the process of predicting the future. What has happened in the past, as reported in the financial statements, may be looked to as an indicator of the future. Often, however, past results may not be indicative of future expectations and may need to be tempered accordingly.

The question of whether forecasts should be included in external financial statements is controversial. Opponents point out that the uncertainty of forecasts and the potential dangers of undue reliance upon them could result in added legal liability, a drop in credibility, or both. These concerns and potentially advantageous disclosures to competitors have been cited as causes of widespread opposition by management.

On the positive side, it has been argued that the inclusion of forecasts in external financial statements "should be provided when they will enhance the reliability of users' predictions."[5] Furthermore, the assertion has been made that:

1. Forecasts . . . should be presented with their significant underlying assumptions, so that each user can evaluate them in the context of his own needs. The underlying assumptions supporting forecasts, however, should not be presented in such detail that they affect adversely the enterprise's competitive position.
2. The use of ranges to supplement single numbers may be appropriate . . . The limits of the range would indicate the uncertainty inherent in the forecast.
3. Forecasts . . . should be updated periodically and ultimately compared with actual accomplishments. . . . The preparer should explain . . . significant differences between the original and revised forecasts and between forecasts and actual results.[6]

In 1975, the American Institute of Certified Public Accountants issued a statement setting forth guidelines for published financial forecasts which are "an estimate of the most probable financial positions, results of operations, and changes in financial position for one or more future periods." The AICPA excluded projections defined as estimates of financial results which are based on "what-would-happen-if" assumptions. Primarily, the AICPA recommends that:

1. Financial forecasts be presented in the same format as historical financial statements.
2. Accounting principles used in the forecast be consistent with those expected to be used in the historical statements for the forecast period.
3. Forecast amounts should represent the single most probable forecast result, but supplementary ranges or probability statements for key items are encouraged.

[5]Report of the Study Group on the Objectives of Financial Statements, *Objectives of Financial Statements* (New York: American Institute of Certified Public Accountants, 1973), p. 46.
[6]*Ibid*., p. 47.

4. Crucial assumptions in the forecast and key factors in the financial results be disclosed.[7]

Securities and Exchange Commission regulations presently encourage but do not require inclusion of financial forecasts in external financial reports. SEC guidelines are in harmony with AICPA recommendations.

PLANNING AND BUDGETING FOR NONMANUFACTURING BUSINESSES AND NONPROFIT ORGANIZATIONS

Many industrial concerns still pay only lip service to the suggested steps, methods, and procedures of budgeting. To an even greater extent, nonmanufacturing businesses — and especially nonprofit organizations — generally lack effective planning and control mechanisms. However, examples of effective budgeting do exist.

Nonmanu-facturing Businesses

Under the guidance of the National Retail Merchants Association, department stores have followed merchandise budget procedures that have a long and quite successful history. A budget for a retail store is a necessity, inasmuch as the profit per dollar of sales is generally low — usually from 1 to 3 percent. Planning, budgeting, and control administration is strongly oriented toward profit control on the total store as well as on a departmental basis. The merchandise budget shows predetermined sales and profits, generally on a six-month basis following the two merchandising seasons: spring-summer and fall-winter. The merchandise budget includes sales, purchases, expenses, capital expenditures, cash, and annual statements.

Although it is logical for a department store or a wholesaler to plan and budget its activities, banks, savings and loan associations, and insurance companies should also create a long-range profit plan coordinating long-term goals and objectives of the institution. In these businesses, forecasting would deal with deposit size and mix, number of insured and mix of policies, capital requirements, types of earning assets, physical facilities, personnel requirements, operational changes, and new, additional, or changed depositor or client services. The long-range goal should be translated into short-range budgets, starting at the lowest level of responsibility, building and combining the various organizational units into a whole.

Nonprofit Organiza-tions

Annual budgets for government at all levels in the United States now approximate one trillion dollars — an enormous sum of money. Yet, in spite of the many decades in which governmental budgeting has been practiced, the general public is increasingly critical of services received for money spent. While the federal government might be under more obvious attack, state, county, and municipal governments are equally criticized not only for the lack

[7]*Statement of Position, No. 75-4,* "Presentation and Disclosure of Financial Forecasts" (New York: American Institute of Certified Public Accountants, August, 1975), pp. 3–5.

of a satisfactory control system, but also for the ill-conceived procedure for planning the costs and revenues needed to govern. Therefore, a budget based on a managerial approach would go a long way toward pacifying taxpayers.

The difficulty of planning and budgeting in governments and nonprofit organizations is measuring the benefits or outputs of programs. A private enterprise measures its benefits in terms of increased revenue or decreased cost. In the public sector, however, the social problem complicates the measurement of benefits. Consequently, such endeavors have often resulted in relatively meaningless monetary outcome data. For governmental as well as other nonprofit organizations, program performance evaluation is needed. Problems encountered in monetary output measurements suggest that monetary inputs (costs) might be more meaningfully related to nonmonetary outcomes for specific programs.[8]

The concept of a planning, programming, budgeting system, commonly referred to as PPBS, had its origin in the Defense Department's attempt to quantify huge expenditures in terms of benefits derived from activities and programs of the public sector. PPBS might be defined as an analytical tool to assist management (1) in the analysis of alternatives as the basis for rational decision making and (2) in allocating resources to accomplish stated goals and objectives over a designated time period. The analysis technique is closely related to cost-benefit analysis, focusing upon the outputs or final results, rather than the inputs or the initial dollars expended. The outputs are directly relatable to the planned objectives through the use of performance budgets.

The idea that governmental programs should be undertaken in the light of final benefits has caused agencies in the field of health, education, and welfare services to examine the application of PPBS to their activities and programs. However, PPBS has been critized because its required specification of objectives cannot be transformed readily into operational outcome quantities or statistics. At federal, state, and local government levels, PPBS, if effective, needs a great deal of refinement and innovation, an understanding of its aims and methods, and active participation of executive and middle management.

Another example of a governmental planning system is the Integrated Financial Management System (IFMS) implemented in 1977 by a major U.S. city. IFMS is a comprehensive system of budgeting, accounting, and reporting with the use of computers and more up-to-date systems management. It is expected to bring spending by the city's far-flung bureaucracy under firm central control for the purpose of achieving financial controls through budgeting. If successful, this city, as well as others, will be helped in solving its fiscal problems.

In the same way that governmental units have become budget and cost conscious, nonprofit organizations, such as hospitals, churches, school districts, colleges, universities, fraternal orders, libraries, and labor unions, are

[8]For additional discussion and illustration, see James E. Sorensen and Hugh D. Grove, "Cost-Outcome and Cost-Effectiveness Analysis: Emerging Nonprofit Performance Evaluation Techniques," *The Accounting Review*, Vol. LII, No. 3, pp. 658–675.

adopting strong measures of budgetary control. In the past, efforts to control costs were generally exercised through pressure to reduce budget increases rather than through methods improvements or program changes. Long-range planning was seldom practiced.

Basically, the objectives of nonprofit organizations are directed toward the economic, social, educational, or spiritual benefit of individuals or groups who have no vested interest in such organizations in the form of ownership or investment. The presidents, boards of directors, trustees, or administrative officers, like their counterparts in profit-seeking enterprises, are charged with the stewardship of economic resources, except that their job is primarily to use or spend these resources instead of trying to derive monetary gain. It is expressly for this nonprofit objective that these organizations should install adequate and effective methods and procedures in planning, budgeting, and cost control. Personnel practices, such as programs to train and improve the performance of the administrative personnel, should also be made effective within these institutions.

ZERO-BASE BUDGETING

Customarily, those in charge of an established budgetary program are required to justify only the increase sought above last year's appropriation. What they are already spending is usually accepted as necessary, with little or no examination.

In the late 1960s, the concept of zero-base budgeting was introduced in some governmental and business organizations and more recently has received increased attention. *Zero-base budgeting* is a budget-planning procedure for the reevaluation of an organization's program and expenditures. It requires each manager to justify the entire budget request in detail and places the burden of proof on the manager to justify why authorization to spend any money at all should be granted. It starts with the assumption that zero will be spent on each activity — thus, the term "zero-base." What a manager is already spending is not accepted as a starting point.

Managers are asked to prepare for each activity or operation under their control a "decision package" that includes an analysis of cost, purpose, alternative courses of action, measures of performance, consequences of not performing the activity, and benefits. The zero-base budgeting approach asserts that in building the budget from zero, two types of alternatives should be considered by managers: (1) different ways of performing the same activity and (2) different levels of effort in performing the activity.

Success in implementing zero-base budgeting requires:

1. Linkage of zero-base budgeting to the long-range planning process.
2. Sustained support and commitment from executive management.
3. Innovation among the managers who make up the budget decision packages.

4. Sale of the procedure to the people who must perform the work necessary to keep the concept vigorous.

Sound budgeting procedures should always require a careful evaluation of all operating facts each time the budget is prepared. Therefore, the zero-base budgeting procedure is new and unique mainly in approach rather than in basic planning and control philosophy.[9]

PERT AND PERT/COST — SYSTEMS FOR PLANNING AND CONTROL

The accountant's involvement in management planning and control has led to the use of the network analysis systems for planning, measuring progress to schedule, evaluating changes to schedule, forecasting future progress, and predicting and controlling costs. These systems are variously referred to as PERT (Program Evaluation and Review Technique) or CPM (Critical Path Method). The origin of PERT is military; it was introduced in connection with the Navy Polaris program. CPM's origin is industrial.

Many companies have been using these methods in planning, scheduling, and costing such diverse projects as constructing buildings, installing equipment, and research and development. There is also an opportunity for using PERT in business administration tasks, such as scheduling the closing of books, revising standard cost data, scheduling the time elements for the preparation of departmental budgets, cash flows, and preparing the annual profit plan, as well as for audit planning and control.[10] In conjunction with PERT and critical path techniques, computer systems are providing executive management with far better means for directing large-scale, complex projects. Management can now measure cost, time, and technical performance on an integrated basis. Actual results can be compared with the network plan and revisions made as needed.

PERT is a probabilistic diagram of the interrelationships of a complex series of activities. Whether a military, industrial, or business administration task, time is the fundamental element of any of these activities. The major **The PERT System**

---

[9]For a comprehensive treatment of zero-base budgeting, see:
Peter A. Pyhrr, *Zero-Base Budgeting: A Practical Management Tool for Evaluating Expenses* (New York: John Wiley & Sons, Inc., 1972).
Paul J. Stonich, *Zero-Base Planning and Budgeting* (Homewood, Illinois: Dow Jones-Irwin, 1977).
James W. Pattillo, *Zero-Base Budgeting: A Planning, Resource Allocation and Control Tool* (New York: National Association of Accountants, 1977).

[10]For discussion of such uses of PERT, see:
Robert L. Shultis, "Applying PERT to Standard Cost Revisions," *NAA Bulletin*, Vol. XLIV, No. 3, pp. 35–43.
James G. Case, "PERT — A Dynamic Approach to Systems Analysis," *NAA Bulletin*, Vol. XLIV, No. 9, pp. 27–38.
Gordon B. Davis, "Network Techniques and Accounting — With an Illustration," *NAA Bulletin*, Vol. XLIV, No. 11, pp. 11–18.
A. H. Russell, "Cash Flows in Networks," *Management Science*, Vol. 16, No. 5, pp. 357–373.
Jack L. Krogstad, Gary Grudnitski, and David W. Bryant, "PERT and PERT/Cost for Audit Planning and Control," *The Journal of Accountancy*, Vol. 144, No. 5, pp. 82–91.

burden of PERT is the determination of the longest time duration for the completion of the entire project. This calculation is based on the length of time required for the longest sequence of activities.

All of the individual tasks to complete a given job or program must be visualized in a *network* of events and activities. An *event* represents a specified accomplishment at a particular instant in time, such as B or E in the network chart below. An *activity* represents the time and resources necessary to move from one event to another, e.g., B → E in the chart. Some of the activities may be in series; e.g., market research cannot be performed before the research design is planned. Other activities may be parallel; e.g., the engines for a ship can be built at the same time the hull is being constructed.

Time estimates for PERT are made for each activity on a three-way basis, i.e., optimistic (t_o), most likely (t_m), and pessimistic (t_p). In the network below, the three time estimates, expressed in units of one week, are indicated under each activity line. From these estimates an expected time (t_e) is calculated for each activity, generally based on the formula:

$$t_e = \frac{t_o + 4t_m + t_p}{6}$$

For example, the activity D-F has a value of $t_e = 7$, determined as follows:

$$\text{If: } t_o = 5$$
$$t_m = 6$$
$$t_p = 13$$

$$\text{Then: } t_e = \frac{5 + 4(6) + 13}{6} = \frac{42}{6} = 7$$

Pert Network with Time Estimates in Weeks

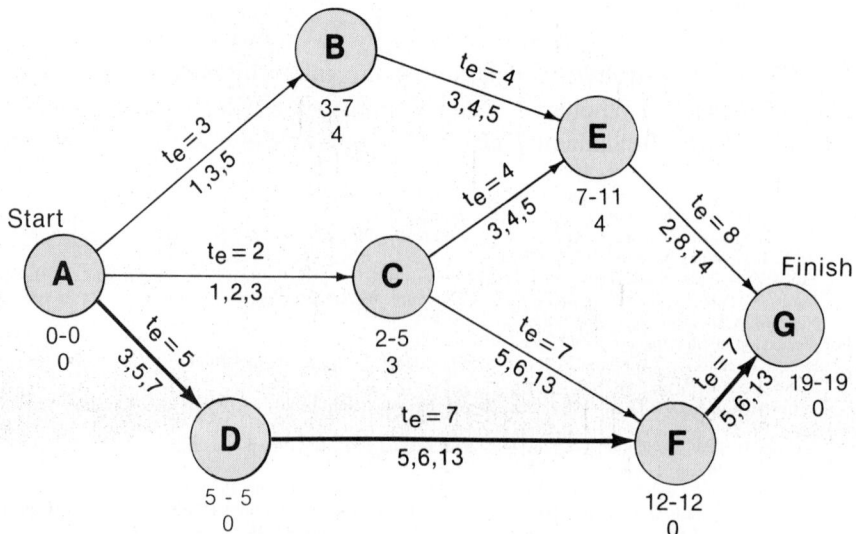

Below each event in the network are noted the earliest expected and latest allowable times, and below these two numbers, the slack time is shown. The *earliest expected time* is the earliest time that an activity can be expected to start, because of its relationship to pending activities. The *latest allowable time* is the latest time that an activity may begin and not delay completion of the project.

The Critical Path. The longest path through the network is known as the *critical path* and is denoted on the flowchart by the arrows connecting A-D-F-G. Shortening of total time can be accomplished only by shortening the critical path. However, if the critical path A-D-F-G is shortened from nineteen weeks to fifteen weeks, A-C-F-G (assuming F-G remains unchanged) would then become the critical path because it would be the longest.

Slack Time. Activities along the critical path (A-D-F-G) have a slack of zero. All noncritical activities have positive slack. The less the amount of slack time, the more critical an activity or path, and vice versa.

Slack is computed by subtracting the earliest expected time from the latest allowable time. It is determinable only in relation to an entire path through the network. When multiple activities lead to an event, the event's earliest expected starting time is always the largest sum of expected times of the preceding activities. When multiple activities lead from an event, the latest allowable time at that event is always the smallest figure found by subtracting from total project time the sum of expected times of subsequent network activities. For example, path A-C-E-G at event C has an earliest expected time of two weeks and a latest allowable time of five weeks [19 − (7 + 7)], for a slack time of three weeks. At event E, the earliest expected time is seven weeks (3 + 4) and the latest allowable time is eleven weeks (19 − 8), for a slack time of four weeks. However, if any slack time is used up, that is if a noncritical activity utilizes more than the expected time, the slack times for subsequent activities must be recomputed. Recomputation would also be necessary when less than the expected times are required.

Slack allows management some flexibility. If available slack time is not exceeded, noncritical activities can be delayed without delaying the project's completion date. Slack time information provides useful data for initial planning and continuous project monitoring when the project's status is compared with the plan.

The PERT/Cost System

PERT/cost is an integrated management information system designed to furnish management with timely information for planning and controlling schedules and costs of projects. The PERT/cost system is really an expansion of PERT. It assigns cost to time and activities, thereby providing total financial planning and control by functional responsibility.

The predetermination of cost is in harmony with the accountant's budgeting task and follows the organizational and procedural steps used in responsibility accounting. The PERT/cost estimates are activity- or project-oriented, and the addition of the cost component permits analyses involving time/cost tradeoffs. Each activity is defined at a level of detail necessary for individual job assignments and supervisory control. Control is on scheduled tasks, with time and cost as the common control factors. Cost accumulation methods must be devised to be compatible with PERT/cost control concepts.

In the network chart below, the activities noted by the dark green circles — A, B, C, and D — represent completed events. The dollar figures in the white blocks represent estimated costs, e.g., $30,000 for activity F-G. Figures in the light green blocks to the right of the estimates are actual costs. Estimated times (t_e) and actual times (t_a) are shown below the activity lines.

Activities A-B, A-C, and A-D have been completed. A-B required one half week more time than planned; however, it is not on the critical path and will not affect total project duration. If excess time were such that another path became long enough to be the critical path, then total time would be involved.

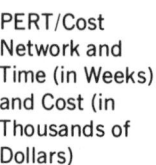

PERT/Cost
Network and
Time (in Weeks)
and Cost (in
Thousands of
Dollars)

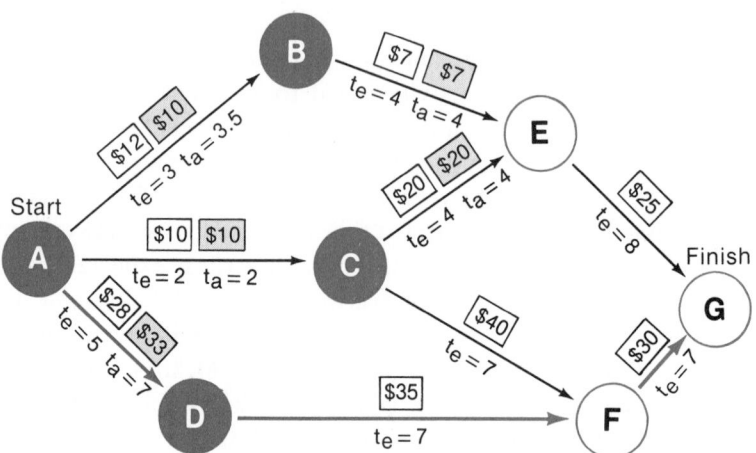

The actual activity cost of $10,000 for A-B compared to a budget of $12,000 indicates an underrun of $2,000. Activity A-C budget and actual figures coincide for time and cost. A-D had an overrun of $5,000 and a two-week slippage. The slippage requires immediate attention because A-D is on the critical path. Immediate investigation and corrective action seem needed for B-E and C-E. According to the present status report, both activities have consumed the budgeted time and cost and are not yet completed.

While comparison of actual versus planned time and cost figures is essential, comparison alone is not enough to evaluate a project. Evaluation of performance is needed to complete the process. For example, a project is not necessarily in financial trouble when actual expenditures exceed budgeted; progress may be correspondingly ahead of schedule. Nor is a project necessarily meeting performance standards when it is within the budget. To evaluate the true status, management needs to study performance, cost, and timing.

PROBABILISTIC BUDGETS

The budget may be developed based on one set of assumptions as to the most likely performance in the forthcoming period. However, there is increasing evidence that several sets of assumptions are evaluated by management before the budget is finalized. One possibility is the PERT-like three-level estimates — optimistic, most likely, and pessimistic. This involves estimating each budget component assuming each of the three conditions. Probability trees can be used in which several variables can be considered in the analysis, e.g., number of units sold, sales price, and variable manufacturing and marketing costs.

To each discrete set of assumptions a probability can be assigned, based on past experience and management's best judgment about the future, thus revealing to management not only a range of possible outcomes but also a probability associated with each. Further statistical techniques can then be applied, including an expected (weighted, composite) value, the range, and the standard deviation for the various budget elements, such as sales, manufacturing cost, and marketing cost. For example, the expected value for sales may be $960,000 with a range from a low of $780,000 to a high of $1,200,000 and a standard deviation of $114,600.

The computational capability of the computer facilitates the consideration of complex sets of assumptions and permits the use of simulation programs, making it possible to develop more objectively determined probabilities.[11]

DISCUSSION QUESTIONS

1. What is meant by a capital expenditure? How does it differ from a revenue expenditure?

2. Name some purposes of and some reasons for a research and development program.

3. Research and development expenditures form a major element of cost in many firms. These research and development expenditures are not necessarily governed by current operating requirements or business volume but can

---

[11]An exhaustive treatment of these techniques is beyond the scope of this discussion. For expanded discussion and illustrations, see:

William L. Ferrara and Jack C. Hayya, "Toward Probabilistic Profit Budgets," *Management Accounting*, Vol. LII, No. 3, pp. 23–28.

Belverd E. Neddles, Jr., "Budgeting Techniques: Subjective to Probabilistic," *Management Accounting*, Vol. LIII, No. 6, pp. 39–45.

Edmund J. Hall and Richard J. Kolkmann, "A Vote for the Probabilistic Pro Forma Income Statement," *Management Accounting*, Vol. LVII, No. 7, pp. 45–48.

Davis L.S. Chang and Shu S. Liao, "Measuring and Disclosing Forecast Reliability," *The Journal of Accountancy*, Vol. 143, No. 5, pp. 76–87, (Monte Carlo simulation).

be expanded or contracted as management sees fit. Companies should establish budgetary procedures that are to provide control and accounting systems for research and development expenditures. What are such procedures specifically designed to achieve?

4. Managers of industrial or commercial enterprises consider a cash budget an extremely useful management tool. Why?

5. The cash budget assists management in making more effective use of money and capital markets. Comment.

6. Name the two methods used for the preparation of a cash budget.

7. The forecast income statement may be viewed as the apex of budgeting. Explain this statement.

8. The projected balance sheet may indicate an unsatisfactory financial condition. Discuss.

9. What governing criterion has been suggested for determining whether to include forecasts in external financial statements?

10. Discuss the need for planning and budgeting in (a) nonmanufacturing businesses and (b) nonprofit organizations.

11. What is the objective of the control concept generally referred to as PPBS?

12. What is the basic idea involved in zero-base budgeting?

13. Define and discuss the Program Evaluation and Review Technique (PERT), including assumptions and accounting data used therein.

(AICPA adapted)

14. Explain the computation of slack in the PERT network.

15. State the relationship between PERT and PERT/cost systems.

16. Contrast the probabilistic budget and the traditional budget in terms of information provided to management.

EXERCISES

1. Cash receipts and disbursements. Wayne Corporation has estimated its activity for December. Selected data from these estimated amounts are as follows:

(a) Sales $350,000
Gross profit (based on sales)... 30%
Increase in trade accounts receivable during month (net of allowance for
doubtful accounts).. $ 10,000
Change in accounts payable during month .... none
Increase in inventory during month.. $ 5,000

(b) Variable marketing, general, and administrative expenses include a charge for doubtful accounts of 1% of sales.

(c) Marketing, general, and administrative expenses total $35,500 per month plus 15% of sales.

(d) Depreciation expense of $20,000 per month is included in fixed marketing, general, and administrative expenses.

Required:
(1) Estimated December cash receipts from operations.
(2) Estimated December cash disbursements from operations.   (AICPA adapted)

2. Cash budget for a manufacturer. The January 1 cash balance of the Cowan Company is $5,000. Sales for the first four months of the year are expected to be as follows: January, $65,000; February, $54,000; March, $66,000; and April, $63,000. On January 1, uncollected accounts for November and December of the previous year are $13,500 and $39,150, respectively. Collections from customers follow this pattern: 55% in the month of sale, 30% in the month following the sale, 13% in the second month following the sale, and 2% uncollectible.

Materials purchases for December were $10,000. Forecast purchases for the coming year are: January, $12,500; February, $16,500; March, $13,000; and April, $14,000. Purchases are usually paid by the 10th of the month following the month of purchase. Other cash expenditures of $41,000 are forecasted for each month.

Required:
(1) Expected cash collections during February.
(2) Expected cash balance, February 1.
(3) Expected cash balance, February 28.

3. Cash budget for a retailer. Prentiss, Inc., provides the following actual data for 19A and budgeted data for 19B.

	DECEMBER 31, 19A	DECEMBER 31, 19B
Trade accounts receivable................	$ 84,000	$ 78,000
Merchandise inventory......................	150,000	140,000
Accounts payable — merchandise....	(95,000)	(98,000)

Budgeted sales for 19B are $1,200,000; sales for 19A were $1,100,000. Cash sales average 20% of total sales each year.

Cost of goods sold for 19B is estimated to be $840,000.

Budgeted 19B variable general and administrative expenses are $120,000. They vary in proportion to sales and are paid 50% in the year incurred and 50% the following year. Unpaid variable expenses are not included in accounts payable above.

Fixed general and administrative expenses, including $35,000 depreciation and $5,000 uncollectible accounts expense, total $100,000 per year. Such expenses involving cash payments are paid 80% in the year incurred and 20% the following year. Unpaid fixed expenses are not included in accounts payable above.

Required:
(1) Cash collected in 19B resulting from sales in 19A and 19B.
(2) Cash disbursed in 19B for purchases of merchandise.
(3) Cash disbursed in 19B for variable and fixed general and administrative expenses.

(AICPA adapted)

4. Forecast income statement. The Schmidt Company has just received a franchise to distribute air conditioners. The company commenced business on January 1, 19––, with the following assets:

Cash...	$ 45,000
Inventory	94,000
Warehouse, office, and delivery facilities and equipment..............	800,000

All facilities and equipment have a useful life of 20 years and no residual value. First quarter sales are expected to be $360,000 and should be doubled in the second quarter. Third quarter sales are expected to be $1,080,000. One percent of sales are considered to be uncollectible. The gross profit margin should be 30%. Variable marketing expenses (except uncollectible accounts) are budgeted at 12% of sales and fixed marketing expenses at $48,000 per quarter, exclusive of depreciation. Variable administrative expenses are expected to be 3% of sales and fixed administrative expenses should total $34,200 per quarter, exclusive of depreciation.

Required: Forecast income statement for the second quarter.   (CGAA adapted)

5. Forecast income statement. The president of a hardware manufacturing company has asked the controller to prepare an income forecast for the next year by quarters, with sales reported for each of the two major segments — commercial and government.

The Marketing Department provided the following sales estimates:

	1st QUARTER	2d QUARTER	3d QUARTER	4th QUARTER
Commercial sales...	$250,000	$266,000	$275,000	$300,000
Government sales...	100,000	120,000	110,000	115,000

The controller's office assembled these figures:

  (a) Cost of goods sold: 46% of total sales.
  (b) Advertising expenditures: $4,000 each quarter.
  (c) Selling expenses: 10% of total sales.
  (d) Administrative expenses: 16.8% of gross profit.
  (e) General office expenses: 12% of gross profit.
  (f) Other income: $8,000 per quarter.
  (g) Corporate income tax rate: 40%.

Required:
  (1) A forecast income statement, by quarters and in total. All figures should be shown in thousands of dollars and rounded to the nearest thousand, adding four quarters across to obtain total figures.
  (2) An analysis of the effect of a 5% increase in commercial sales revenue, using the same income statement format as for (1) above.

6. Departmental forecast budget. The plant manager of a company requests advice about a department manufacturing machine tools of varying sizes. The figures shown below are the actual results for the years indicated. The manager is concerned with the recent decline in output and profit and the recent increases in factory overhead. It has been company practice to use the actual factory overhead to direct labor percentages of each year for costing products made in the following year. Production for the next year will be 180,000 units. The unit sales price, materials prices, and wage rates are expected to remain the same as for last year.

	LAST YEAR	PREVIOUS YEAR	BEST YEAR	NORMAL YEAR
Materials used...	$ 30,000	$ 45,000	$ 40,000	$ 36,000
Direct labor...	60,000	90,000	80,000	72,000
Factory overhead...	50,000	67,500	52,000	48,000
Total...	$140,000	$202,500	$172,000	$156,000
Departmental profit for year...	2,500	7,500	28,000	15,000
Sales value of output...	$142,500	$210,000	$200,000	$171,000
Output...	200,000 units	300,000 units	400,000 units	360,000 units
Rate of factory overhead — to direct labor cost...	83.3%	75%	65%	66.7%
Estimated amount of fixed overhead included in above factory overhead...	$ 15,000	$ 15,000	$ 12,000	$ 12,000

Required:
  (1) A departmental budget for the coming year, with the estimated profit. (Carry all computations to four decimal places.)
  (2) An opinion on the factory overhead rate to be used.
  (3) Any other comments of interest to the manager.

7. PERT network. The Shelton Construction Company has decided that a PERT network will help in planning a new job. The network for the new project is shown on the next page, with optimistic, most likely, and pessimistic time estimates, in days, shown on the connecting lines between events.

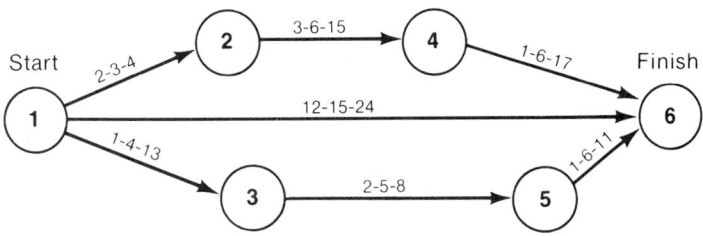

Required: The critical path.   (CGAA adapted)

8. PERT network. A budget department prepared the following time estimates for a contemplated project with 36 days as the target date:

EVENT	ACTIVITY	t_o	t_m	t_p
2	1–2	1	2	3
3	1–3	8	9	10
4	1–4	4	6	20
5	2–5	4	7	10
6	3–6	3	6	45
6	4–6	2	3	10
8	5–8	4	8	24
5	6–5	1	3	5
7	6–7	3	4	5
8	7–8	6	10	14

Required:
    (1) A calculation of t_e (expected time) for each activity.
    (2) Total t_e for each path and identification of the critical path for the project.
    (3) The PERT network for the above data, including slack at each event.

9. PERT network. A new product is to be introduced by a company. An examination of the activities to be carried out and the probable elapsed time for each are shown in the following table:

JOB CODE	ACTIVITY	TIME (IN WEEKS)
A	Prepare manufacturing procedures	1
B	Prepare quality control procedures	3
C	Determine equipment requirements	3
D	Prepare engineering design of equipment	5
E	Select plant site	5
F	Requisition equipment	2
G	Have equipment delivered	6
H	Requisition materials	2
I	Have materials delivered	2
J	Produce initial quantities	2
K	Deliver finished product to warehouse	2

Required:
    (1) A PERT network for these activities, assuming that the site must be selected before the equipment is requisitioned.
    (2) The critical path.
    (3) Slack times available for Jobs B and E.   (CGAA adapted)

10. PERT network for auditing liabilities. All audits have a critical path, but auditors seldom recognize it as such without the aid of network analysis. In the auditing of liabilities, the following activities and estimated times have been identified:

		TIME ESTIMATE (HOURS)
ACTIVITY CODE	ACTIVITY	
6.10–6.11	Obtain schedule of liabilities	2
6.11–6.12	Mail confirmations	12
6.12–6.16	Process confirmations	39
6.16–6.17	Investigate debit balances	5
6.11–6.13	Vouch selected liabilities	64
6.13–6.14	Test accruals and amortization	4
6.11–6.14	Test pension plan	4
6.14–6.15	Reconcile interest expense to debt	8
6.15–6.17	Verify debt restriction compliance	5
6.17–6.18	Review subsequent payments	10

Required: The PERT network, identifying the critical path and including slack times.

PROBLEMS

17-1. Cash and purchases budget for a manufacturer. Tomlinson Company seeks assistance in developing cash and other budget information for May, June, and July. On April 30, the company had cash of $5,500, accounts receivable of $437,000, inventories of $309,400, and accounts payable of $133,055. The budget is to be based on the following assumptions:

Sales:

(a) Each month's sales are billed on the last day of the month.
(b) Customers are allowed a 3% discount if payment is made within 10 days after the billing date. Receivables are recorded at the gross selling price.
(c) Sixty percent of the billings are collected within the discount period; 25% by the end of the month; 9% by the end of the second month; and 6% prove uncollectible.

Purchases:

(a) Fifty-four percent of all purchases of materials and a like percentage of marketing, general, and administrative expenses are paid in the month purchased, with the remainder paid in the following month.
(b) Each month's units of ending materials inventory are equal to 130% of next month's production requirement.
(c) The cost of each unit of inventory is $20.
(d) Wages and salaries earned each month by employees total $38,000.
(e) Marketing, general, and administrative expenses (of which $2,000 is depreciation) are equal to 15% of the current month's sales.

Actual and projected sales are as follows:

March	$354,000	June	$342,000
April	363,000	July	360,000
May	357,000	August	366,000

Actual and projected materials needed for production:

March	11,800 units	June	11,400 units
April	12,100	July	12,000
May	11,900	August	12,200

Accrued payroll at the end of each month is as follows:

March	$3,100	June	$3,400
April	2,900	July	3,000
May	3,300	August	2,800

Required:
(1) Budgeted cash disbursements during June.
(2) Budgeted cash collections during May.
(3) Budgeted units of inventory to be purchased during July.   (AICPA adapted)

17-2. Cash forecast. The Barker Corporation manufactures and distributes wooden baseball bats. The business is seasonal with most of its sales made in late winter and early spring. Therefore, the production schedule for the last quarter of the year is rather heavy in order to build up inventory to meet expected sales volume.

The company experiences a temporary cash strain during this heavy production period. The payroll cost increases during the last quarter because overtime is scheduled to meet the increased production needs. Collections from customers are low because the fall season produces only modest sales. This year the company concern is intensified because of the rapid increases in prices during the current inflationary period. In addition, the Sales Department forecasts sales of less than one million bats for the first time in three years, a decrease caused by the popularity of aluminum bats.

The cash account builds up during the first and second quarters as sales exceed production. The excess cash is invested in U.S. Treasury bills and other commercial paper. During the last half of the year, the temporary investments are liquidated to meet cash needs. In the early years of the company, short-term borrowing was used to supplement the funds released by selling investments, but this has not been necessary in recent years. Because costs are higher this year, the treasurer asks for a forecast for December to judge if the $40,000 in temporary investments will be adequate to carry the company through the month with a minimum balance of $10,000. Should this amount ($40,000) be insufficient, negotiations for a short-term loan must be initiated.

The unit sales volume for the past two months and the estimates for the next four months are:

October (actual)...................	70,000 units	January (estimated)	90,000 units
November (actual)	50,000	February (estimated)........	90,000
December (estimated)	50,000	March (estimated)............	120,000

The bats are sold for $3 each. All sales are made on account. One half of the accounts are collected in the month of the sale, 40% are collected in the month following the sale, and the remaining 10% in the second month following the sale. Customers who pay in the month of the sale receive a 2% cash discount.

The production schedule for the six-month period beginning with October reflects the company's policy of maintaining a stable, year-round work force by scheduling overtime to meet production schedules:

October (actual)...................	90,000 units	January (estimated)	90,000 units
November (actual)	90,000	February (estimated)........	100,000
December (estimated)	90,000	March (estimated)............	100,000

The bats are made from wooden blocks that cost $6 each. Ten bats can be produced from each block. The blocks are acquired one year in advance, so that they can be properly aged. Barker pays the supplier one twelfth of the cost of this material each month until the obligation is retired. The monthly payment is $60,000.

The plant is normally scheduled for a 40-hour, five-day workweek, except during the busy production season, when the workweek may be increased to six 10-hour days. Each worker can produce 7.5 bats per hour, with a total plant normal monthly output of 75,000 bats. Factory employees are paid $4.00 per hour (up $.50 from last year) for regular time, and time and one half for overtime.

Other manufacturing costs consist of variable factory overhead of $.30 per unit and annual fixed factory overhead of $280,000, including depreciation of $40,000. Marketing expenses comprise the variable cost of $.20 per unit and annual fixed cost of $60,000. The fixed administrative cost is $120,000 annually. All fixed costs are incurred and paid uniformly throughout the year.

The controller has accumulated the following additional information:

(a) The balances of selected accounts as of November 30, 19A, are as follows:

Cash	$ 12,000
Marketable Securities (cost and market are the same)	40,000
Accounts Receivable	96,000
Prepaid Expense	4,800
Accounts Payable (arising from materials purchases)	300,000
Accrued Vacation Pay	9,500
Note Payable (equipment)	102,000
Accrued Income Tax Payable	50,000

(b) Interest to be received from the company's temporary investments is estimated at $500 for December.

(c) Prepaid expense of $3,600 will expire during December, and the balance of the prepaid account is estimated at $4,200 for the end of December.

(d) Baker purchased new machinery in 19A as part of a plant modernization program. The machinery was financed by a 24-month note of $144,000. The terms call for equal principal payments over the next 24 months, with interest paid at the rate of 1% per month on the unpaid balance at the first of the month. The first payment was made May 1, 19A.

(e) Old equipment with a book value of $8,000 is to be sold during December for $7,500.

(f) Each month the company accrues $1,700 for vacation pay by charging Vacation Pay Expense and crediting Accrued Vacation Pay. The plant closes for two weeks in June when all plant employees take a vacation.

(g) Quarterly dividends of $.20 per share will be paid on December 15 to stockholders of record. Barker Corporation has authorized 10,000 shares; the company has issued 7,500 shares, and 500 shares of these are classified as treasury stock.

(h) The quarterly income tax payment of $50,000 is due on December 15, 19A.

Required:

(1) A schedule which forecasts the cash position at December 31, 19A, and suggestions of action, if any, required to maintain a $10,000 cash balance.

(2) An indication of changes Barker might consider in its methods of conducting business in order to reduce or eliminate the need for short-term borrowing, without prejudice to requirement (1) and assuming that Barker regularly needs to arrange short-term loans during the November-to-February period.   (CMA adapted)

17-3. Projected income statements and cash budgets. David Construction, Inc., builds heavy construction equipment for commercial and government purposes. Because of two new contracts and the anticipated purchase of new equipment, management needs certain projections for the next three years.

The following information was obtained from the company's records and personnel:

(a) The firm uses the completed-contract method of accounting, whereby construction costs and all general and administrative expenses are capitalized until the contract is completed.

(b) The December 31, 19B, balance sheet shows:

Assets

Cash		$ 72,000
Progress billings receivable		—
Costs of uncompleted contracts in excess of billings		—
Property, plant, and equipment	$2,800,000	
Less accumulated depreciation	129,600	2,670,400
Total assets		$2,742,400

Liabilities and Stockholders' Equity

Loans payable	—
Accrued construction cost	$ 612,400
Accrued income tax payable	65,000
Common stock ($10 par)	500,000
Paid-in capital in excess of par	100,000
Retained earnings	1,465,000
Total liabilities and stockholders' equity	$2,742,400

(c) Two contracts will be started in 19C — Contract X and Contract Y — to be completed in December 19D and December 19E, respectively. No other contracts will be started until after their completion. All other outstanding contracts were completed in 19B.

Total estimated revenue for Contract X is $2,000,000 and for Contract Y is $1,500,000. The estimated cash collections per year are:

	19C	19D	19E
Contract X	$ 800,000	$1,200,000	—
Contract Y	300,000	450,000	$750,000
	$1,100,000	$1,650,000	$750,000

Estimated construction costs to be incurred per contract per year are:

	CONTRACT X	CONTRACT Y
19C	$ 720,000	$ 250,000
19D	1,000,000	400,000
19E	—	650,000
	$1,720,000	$1,300,000

Depreciation is included in these estimated construction costs. For 19C, 10%, and for 19D and 19E, 15% of the estimated construction costs represent depreciation. The cash portion of these estimated construction costs is paid 70% in the year incurred and 30% in the following year.

(d) Total general and administrative expenses (not included in construction costs) consist of a fixed portion each year for each contract, and a variable portion which is a function of cash collected each year. For the two prior years, cash collected and total general and administrative expenses (based on one contract each year) were:

	CASH COLLECTED	TOTAL GENERAL AND ADMINISTRATIVE EXPENSES
19B	$1,350,000	$27,250
19A	1,180,000	24,700

These general and administrative expenses are paid in the year incurred.

(e) Dividends are expected to be distributed as follows:
19C: Stock — 10% of common shares outstanding (estimated fair market value is $15 per share)
19D: Stock split — 2-for-1 (par value to be reduced to $5 per share)
19E: Cash — $1.00 per share

(f) In 19D, a new asset will be acquired for $700,000, to be paid that year.

(g) When the cash balance falls below $70,000, short-term loans in multiples of $10,000 are obtained. For purposes of this problem, ignore interest on short-term loans and any repayments on these loans.

(h) Assume that income tax is paid in full the following year.

Required:
(1) Projected income statements for each of the calendar years 19D and 19E (when contracts are to be completed). The income tax rate is 40%, and the company uses the same methods for accounting and tax purposes.
(2) Cash budgets for each of the calendar years 19C, 19D, and 19E, using this format:

Cash (beginning of year) .... $
Plus collections ....
Less disbursements (enumerated) ....
Plus borrowing (if any) ....
Cash (end of year) .... $

(AICPA adapted)

17-4. Projected income statement; impact of price and volume change. The Metropolitan News, a daily newspaper, serves a community of 100,000. The paper has a circulation of 40,000, with 32,000 copies delivered directly to subscribers. The rate schedule for the paper is:

Single issue price:	
Daily..	$ .15
Sunday	.30
Weekly subscription (includes daily and Sunday)	1.00

The paper has experienced profitable operations for the year just ended, as shown in the following income statement:

The Metropolitan News
Income Statement
For the Year Ended December 31, 19A
(000s omitted)

Revenue:		
Newspaper sales...	$2,200	
Advertising sales..	1,800	$4,000
Costs and expenses:		
Personnel costs:		
Commissions:		
Carriers...	$ 292	
Sales	73	
Advertising	48	
Salaries:		
Administration...	250	
Advertising	100	
Equipment operators...	500	
Newsroom	400	
Employee benefits...	195	$1,858
Newsprint..		834
Other supplies..		417
Repairs..		25
Depreciation..		180
Property tax..		120
Building rental..		80
Automobile leases..		10
Other..		90
Total..		$3,614
Income before income tax...		$ 386
Income tax		154
Net income..		$ 232

The Sunday edition usually has twice as many pages as the daily editions. Analysis of daily edition variable costs for 19A is shown in the schedule below:

	COST PER ISSUE	
	Daily	*Sunday*
Newsprint..	$.050	$.100
Other supplies..	.025	.050
Carrier and sale commissions	.025	.025
	$.100	$.175

For next year, several changes in operations are scheduled and some costs are expected to increase:

  (a) The building lease expired on December 31, 19A, and has been renewed with a change in the rental fee provisions from a straight fee to a fixed fee of $60,000 plus 1% of newspaper sales.

(b) The Advertising Department will eliminate the payment of a 4% advertising commission on contracts sold by its employees. An average of two thirds of the advertising has been sold on a contract basis in the past. The salaries of the four people who solicit advertising will be raised from $7,500 each to $21,000 each.

(c) Automobiles will no longer be leased. Employees whose jobs require automobiles will use their own and be reimbursed at $.15 per mile. The leased cars were driven 80,000 miles in 19A and it is estimated that the employees will drive some 84,000 miles next year on company business.

(d) Cost increases estimated for next year:
 (1) Newsprint, $.01 per daily issue and $.02 for the Sunday paper.
 (2) Salaries:

Equipment operators	8%
Other employees	6%

 (3) Employee benefits: from the present 15%, to 20% of personnel costs, excluding carrier and sales commissions.

(e) Circulation increases of 5% in newsstand and home delivery are anticipated.

(f) Advertising revenue is estimated at $1,890,000, with $1,260,000 from employee-solicited contracts.

Required:
(1) A projected income statement for the Metropolitan News for 19B, using a format which shows the total variable cost and total fixed cost (in thousands of dollars) for the newspaper. (Round calculations to the nearest thousand dollars.)
(2) The effect on projected 19B income if the following proposed rates are implemented in 19B:

Single issue price:	
Daily	$ .20
Sunday	.40
Weekly subscription (includes daily and Sunday)	1.25

Initiation of this change is estimated to cause a 10% decline in currently anticipated newsstand and home delivery sales units.

(CMA adapted)

17-5. Budget for a college. Delmarua College has asked for assistance in developing its budget for the coming 19A–B academic year. The following data for the current year are supplied:

	LOWER DIVISION (FRESHMAN-SOPHOMORE)	UPPER DIVISION (JUNIOR-SENIOR)
Average number of students per class	25	20
Average salary of faculty member	$20,000	$20,000
Average number of credit hours carried each year per student	33	30
Enrollment, including scholarship students	2,500	1,700
Average faculty teaching load in credit hours per year (10 classes of 3 credit hours)	30	30

For 19A–B, lower-division enrollment is expected to increase by 10%, while the upper division's enrollment is expected to remain stable. Faculty salaries will be increased by a standard 5%, and additional merit increases to be awarded to individual faculty members will be $90,750 for the lower division and $85,000 for the upper division.

The current budget is $210,000 for operation and maintenance of plant and equipment, including $90,000 for salaries and wages. Experience of the past three months suggests that the current budget is realistic, but increases of 5% in salaries and wages and $9,000 in other expenditures for operation and maintenance of plant and equipment are to be expected in 19A–B.

The budget for the remaining expenditures for 19A–B is as follows:

Administrative and general	$240,000
Library	160,000
Health and recreation	75,000
Athletics	120,000
Insurance and retirement	265,000
Interest	48,000
Capital outlay	300,000

The college expects to award 25 tuition-free scholarships to lower-division students and 15 to upper-division students. Tuition is $42 per credit hour, with no other fees.

Budgeted revenues for 19A–B are as follows:

Endowments	$114,000
Net income from auxiliary services	235,000
Athletics	180,000

The college's remaining source of revenue is an annual support campaign held during the spring.

Required:
  (1) A schedule computing for 19A–B, by division (a) the expected enrollment, (b) the total credit hours to be carried, and (c) the number of faculty members needed.
  (2) A schedule computing the budget for faculty salaries, by division, for 19A–B.
  (3) A schedule computing the tuition revenue budget, by division, for 19A–B.
  (4) A schedule computing the amount which must be raised during the annual support campaign in order to cover the 19A–B expenditures budget, assuming that the faculty salaries budget computed in requirement (2) was $4,600,000 and that the tuition revenue budget computed in requirement (3) was $5,000,000.

(AICPA adapted)

17-6. Revenue projection for a school system. The Beaver County School Board bases its revenues budget for the fiscal year ending July 31, 19B, on projections of receipts for the fiscal year ending July 31, 19A. The receipts are summarized by type and source as follows:

Beaver County School Board
Actual Revenues Received
For Fiscal Year Ending July 31, 19A

Type and Source	Sales Tax	State Grants	Federal Grants	Allocation of Federal Revenue Sharing
City A	$ 300,000			$ 250,000
City B	450,000			300,000
All other cities	210,000			200,000
Unincorporated areas	150,000			
Federal government			$750,000	
State government	300,000	$200,000		1,000,000
Total	$1,410,000	$200,000	$750,000	$1,750,000

These actual revenues represent receipts as of April 30, 19A, only. Projected receipts for the remainder of the fiscal year ending July 31, 19A, are: (a) sales tax collections should continue at the same rate; (b) additional state grants are expected to total $50,000; (c) no more federal funds of any kind are forthcoming until after July 31, 19A.

Revenues for 19B are expected to change as follows: (a) sales tax collections are projected to increase by 10%; (b) state grants will remain the same; (c) federal grants will be cut by two thirds; (d) federal revenue-sharing allocations should increase by 10%.

Required:
  (1) A schedule of actual and projected revenues (by type and source) for the fiscal year ending July 31, 19A.
  (2) A schedule of projected revenues (by type and source) for the fiscal year ending July 31, 19B.

17-7. PERT/cost network. Late in 19A, the Connors Instrument Company was the successful bidder on a contract to design and produce the instrument panel for a new fighter plane. The price agreed upon in the bid was $475,000, and the work was to be completed by June 30, 19B.

Work on the contract was scheduled to begin on February 27, 19B, and management decided to utilize PERT/cost techniques to control production time and cost. Analysis of the contract showed the following tasks with estimates of time and cost.

	TIME ESTIMATES (WEEKS)			COST ESTIMATES	
TASK	Optimistic	Most Likely	Pessimistic	Variable per Week	Fixed Cost
Design instrumentation (DI).......	6	7	8	$ 7,500	$18,500
Design panel (DP)........................	2	3	10	8,000	8,000
Design power system (DPS).......	3	4	5	28,000	4,000
Build instrumentation (BI)..........	4	5	12	18,000	12,000
Build panel (BP).........................	3	5	7	4,500	2,500
Build power system (BPS)	4	6	8	4,800	1,200
Assemble and ship (A&S)...........	1	2	3	4,000	2,000

Three special considerations applied to the sequence of the scheduling:
(a) The designing of the instrumentation and the panel had to be completed before the designing of the power system could begin.
(b) The designing of the instrumentation and the panel had to be completed before the building of the instrumentation could begin.
(c) The building of the panel had to be completed before the building of the power system could begin.

At the end of the week beginning April 3, 19B, the following data were assembled concerning the status of the work on the contract as of that date:

TASK	WEEKS	COST		WORK COMPLETED
Design instrumentation	6	$63,000		100 %
Design panel.............................	4	41,000		100
Build instrumentation	1	13,000	Variable	16⅔
Design power system................	1	30,000	Cost	25
Build panel.................................	1	3,000	Only	20

Required:
(1) The PERT/cost network as of the beginning of the contract, February 27, 19B, showing the critical path and slack times.
(2) An updated PERT/cost network at the end of the week of April 3, 19B.
(3) A report for management as of the end of the week of April 3, 19B, showing the schedule status and the cost status of the contract.

17-8. Use of PERT network. Edna Jones is responsible for finding a suitable building and establishing a new convenience grocery store for Thrift-Mart, Inc. Jones enumerated the specific activities which had to be completed and the estimated time to accomplish each activity, preparing a network, which appears below, to aid in the coordination of activities.

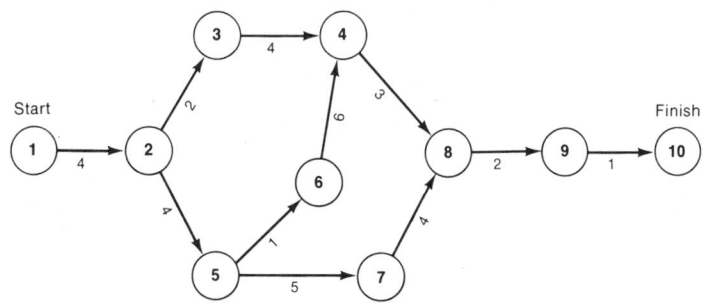

The list of activities to locate a building and establish a new store is as follows:

Activity Number	Description of Activity	Estimated Time Required (in weeks)
1–2	Find building	4
2–3	Negotiate rental terms	2
3–4	Draft lease	4
2–5	Prepare store plans	4
5–6	Select and order fixtures	1
6–4	Have fixtures delivered	6
4–8	Install fixtures	3
5–7	Hire staff	5
7–8	Train staff	4
8–9	Receive inventory	2
9–10	Stock shelves	1

Required:
(1) The critical path for finding and establishing the new convenience store.
(2) An explanation of the necessity for delivery of the fixtures in four weeks instead of six, if the sole objective is to open the store two weeks earlier.
(3) Additional information needed to administer the proposed project properly, since a program, such as the one illustrated by the network for the new convenience store, cannot be implemented unless the required resources are available at the required dates.

(CMA adapted)

CASES

A. Projected statement of financial position. The Breckenridge Institute is a nonprofit foundation that undertakes scientific research on a contract basis for federal, state, and local governments as well as for business firms. The objectives of the institute as established by the board of trustees are to operate a financially sound organization and to provide quality research service at reasonable cost for the government and business community. The board is also committed to operate with a minimum amount of debt.

Pursuant to these objectives, management is endeavoring to serve its clients without using outside consultants or subcontracting work to other laboratories. The institute has gained an excellent reputation for its research capabilities and for the economical manner in which it is operated.

The statement of financial position for the institute at April 30, 19A, the statement of revenues and expenses showing the actual results for the year ended April 30, 19A, and the budgeted amount for the coming year ending April 30, 19B, appear on the next page. The statement of cash receipts and disbursements presenting actual results and budgeted figures for the years ending April 30, 19A and 19B, respectively, appears on page 506.

During the construction of the budget, the following additional information was developed:

(a) Purchases of materials and supplies were budgeted at $610,000.
(b) Write-offs of specific accounts receivable are estimated as follows:
    (1) $8,000 of the accounts receivable balance at April 30, 19A.
    (2) Uncollectible accounts of $12,000 from fiscal 19B sales to be written off in fiscal 19B.
(c) The unusually large budgeted expenditure for capital equipment is part of a three-year program begun in 19A to enable the institute to enter new areas of scientific research. Similar amounts will be spent in the next two years for additional equipment. Increased revenues from the new capabilities will not be significant until 19D.
(d) The increased level of consultant fees is expected to continue until the capital expansion program is complete.

Required:
(1) A projected statement of financial position (in thousands of dollars) as of April 30, 19B, for presentation to the board of trustees.

(2) A report which identifies the financial difficulties the institute's management will face in the next several years in fulfilling the objectives established by the board of trustees.

(CMA adapted)

Breckenridge Institute
Statement of Financial Position
April 30, 19A
(000s omitted)

Assets				Liabilities and Equities		
Current assets:				Current liabilities:		
Cash			$ 110	Accounts payable		$ 120
Marketable securities			80	Accrued payroll, payroll taxes,		
Accounts receivable:				and benefits		46
Government contracts	$230			Due to outside consultants		20
Private contracts	$150			Interest payable		16
Less allowance for				Current portion of long-term		
doubtful accounts	10	140	370	debt		60
Materials and supplies			64	Total current liabilities		$ 262
Prepaid insurance			6	Long-term debt		240
Total current assets			$ 630	Total liabilities		$ 502
Plant and equipment (net of depreciation)			1,200	Original capital	$1,000	
				Accumulated excess of revenues		
Total assets			$1,830	over expenditures	328	1,328
				Total liabilities and equities		$1,830

Breckenridge Institute
Statement of Revenues and Expenses
(000s omitted)

	ACTUAL RESULTS FOR THE YEAR ENDED 4/30/A	BUDGET FOR THE YEAR ENDING 4/30/B
Revenues from operations:		
Federal government	$1,500	$1,650
State and local government	224	250
Private (less allowance for doubtful accounts of $19 and $25)	1,216	1,335
Interest	4	2
Total revenues	$2,944	$3,237
Operating expenses:		
Personnel:		
Salaries	$1,390	$1,300
Wages	175	200
Employee benefits and payroll taxes	273	300
Consultants	35	250
Employee training	20	35
Materials and supplies	548	600
Utilities	60	60
Insurance	20	20
Depreciation	160	165
Other expenses	117	123
Interest charges	16	14
Total operating expenses	$2,814	$3,067
Excess of revenues over expenses	$ 130	$ 170

Breckenridge Institute
Cash Receipts and Disbursements
(000s omitted)

	ACTUAL RESULTS FOR THE YEAR ENDED 4/30/A	BUDGET FOR THE YEAR ENDING 4/30/B
Receipts:		
Contracts:		
Federal, state, and local governments..................	$1,700	$1,820
Private...	1,200	1,300
	$2,900	$3,120
Interest	4	2
Sales of marketable securities (no gain or loss on sale)	—	50
Total receipts...	$2,904	$3,172
Disbursements:		
Salaries and wages	$1,560	$1,510
Employee benefits...	260	300
Consultant fees	15	230
Employee training programs................................	20	35
Materials and supplies...	540	575
Utilities	55	65
Insurance	20	22
Other expenses	117	123
Interest	18	16
Retirement of debt	60	60
Purchases of capital equipment	80	315
Total disbursements	$2,745	$3,251
Increase (decrease) in cash	$ 159	$ (79)

B. Sales and production schedules; income statement. A1 Sound Systems manufactures speakers for component stereo systems. Three models are produced: Model 150, Model 100, and Model 50. The speakers are marketed in two regions, the South and Southwest. The production departments are designated Cutting, Assembling, and Finishing. Lumber, speakers, and a finishing compound are the materials used in the production of the speakers.

The management and department heads have made the following estimates for the coming year:

(a) Sales forecast:

MODEL	SOUTH	SOUTHWEST	SALES PRICE
150	3,000 units	4,000 units	$175 per unit
100	5,000	7,000	120
50	7,000	8,000	90

(b) Inventories (fifo):

MATERIALS	BEGINNING INVENTORY		ENDING INVENTORY	
	Units	Unit Cost	Units	Unit Cost
Lumber (board feet) ...	40,000	$ .75	30,000	$ .75
Speakers......................	10,000	15.00	8,000	15.00
Finish (pints)..............	1,500	2.00	2,000	2.00

Work in process: None at the beginning or end of the period.

Finished goods:

MODEL	BEGINNING INVENTORY		ENDING INVENTORY	
	Units	Unit Cost	Units	Unit Cost
150...........................	200	$98.00	200	$105.50
100...........................	300	62.00	400	66.75
50...........................	400	47.00	300	50.25

(c) Materials requirements:

MODEL	LUMBER (BOARD FEET)	SPEAKERS	FINISH (PINTS)
150..	12	5	2
100..	8	3	1
50..	6	2	1

(d) Estimated materials cost:
Lumber, $.75 per board foot.
Speakers, $15 per speaker.
Finish, $2 per pint.

(e) Estimated labor cost:

	CUTTING	ASSEMBLING	FINISHING
Rate per hour................................	$6.00	$5.00	$4.00

Estimated labor time requirements:

MODEL	CUTTING	ASSEMBLING	FINISHING
150..	.375 hours	2.0 hours	.375 hours
100..	.375	1.5	.250
50..	.375	1.5	.250

(f) Overhead budgets have been prepared that show the following unit overhead rates:

MODEL	CUTTING	ASSEMBLING	FINISHING
150..	$1.00	$2.00	$.75
100..	1.00	1.50	.50
50..	1.00	1.50	.50

(g) Marketing expenses: $500,000.
Administrative expenses: $300,000.
Income tax rate: 50%.

Required: Annual budget schedules utilizing the budget estimates provided above. The schedules should be designed to provide essential data in an easily understood form. Titles and schedule numbers to be used are listed below. Cross-references should be made using schedule numbers.

SCHEDULE	TITLE
(1)	Sales budget — by models, by sales regions.
(2)	Production budget — by models, by units.
(3)	Direct materials budget — by materials, by models, and in units.
(4)	Purchases budget — by materials, by cost.
(5)	Cost of materials for production — by materials, by models.
(6)	Schedule of beginning and ending inventories — by materials, by models.
(7)	Direct labor budget — by models, by departments.
(8)	Factory overhead budget (applied overhead) — by models, by departments.
(9)	Cost of goods manufactured and sold statement.
(10)	Income statement — with each item shown as a percentage of sales. (Round off percentages to the nearest tenth of a percent.)

18

Budgeting
The Flexible Budget
Cost Behavior Analysis
Statistical Correlation Analysis

Budgets are based on certain definite assumed conditions and results. The budgets discussed and illustrated in Chapters 16 and 17 are known as fixed or forecast budgets, while the budgets discussed in this chapter are known as flexible budgets. The term "fixed" is misleading, however, since a fixed budget is subject to revision. *Fixed* merely denotes that the budget is not adjusted to actual volume attained. It represents a prefixed point of sales and cost estimates with which actual results are compared. A flexible budget, however, is adjusted to actual volume.

Both fixed and flexible budgets provide management with information necessary to attain the major objectives of budgetary control, which include:

1. An organized procedure for planning.
2. A means for coordinating the activities of the various divisions of a business.
3. A basis for cost control.

Planning is one of the primary functions of management. The fixed budget provides an organized method of planning and a procedure for measuring the nature and the extent of deviations from the preconceived plan. It is the organized means for formalizing and coordinating plans of the many individuals whose decisions influence the conduct of a business.

A budget plan requires the coordination of all management levels of a business. Production must be planned in relation to expected sales; materials must be acquired in line with expected production requirements; facilities must be expanded as foreseeable future needs justify; and finances must be planned in relation to the funds needed for the expected volume of sales and production.

Cost control is predicated on the idea that actual costs will be compared with budgeted costs, relating what did happen with what should have happened. To accomplish this, an acceptable measure of what costs should be under any given set of conditions must be available.

THE FLEXIBLE BUDGET

When a company's activities can be estimated within close limits, the fixed budget is satisfactory. However, completely predictable situations exist in only a few cases. If business conditions change radically, causing actual operations to differ widely from fixed budget plans, this management tool is not reliable or effective. The fact that costs and expenses are affected by fluctuations in volume limits the use of the fixed budget and leads to the use of the flexible budget. To illustrate, the cost of operating an automobile per mile depends on the number of miles driven. The more a car is used per year, the more it costs to operate it but the less it costs per mile. If the owner prepares an estimate of the total cost and compares actual expenses with the budget at year-end, success in keeping expenses within the allowed limits cannot be determined without accounting for the mileage factor. The reason for this lies in the nature of the expenses, some of which are fixed while others are variable or semivariable. Insurance, taxes, registration, and garaging are fixed costs, which remain the same whether the car is operated 1,000 or 20,000 miles. The costs of tires, gas, oil, and repairs are variable costs, which depend largely upon the miles driven. Obsolescence and depreciation result in a semivariable cost, which fluctuates to some degree but does not vary directly with the usage of the car.

The underlying principle of a flexible budget is the need for some norm of expenditures for any given volume of business. This norm should be known beforehand in order to provide a guide to actual expenditures. To recognize this principle is to accept the fact that every business is dynamic, ever-changing, and never static. It is erroneous, if not futile, to expect a business to conform to a fixed, preconceived pattern.

The preparation of a flexible budget results from the development of formulas for each department and for each account within a department or cost center. The formula for each account indicates the fixed amount and/or a variable rate. The fixed amount and variable rate remain constant within prescribed ranges of activity. The variable portion of the formula is a rate expressed in relation to a base such as direct labor hours, direct labor cost, or machine hours.

The application of the formulas to the level of activity actually experienced produces the allowable expenditures for the volume of activity attained. These budget figures are compared with actual costs in order to measure the performance of each department. This ready-made comparison makes the flexible budget a valuable instrument for cost control, because it assists in evaluating the effects of varying volumes of activity on profits and on the cash position.

Originally, the flexible budget idea was applied principally to the control of departmental factory overhead. Now, however, the idea is applied to the entire budget, so that production as well as marketing and administrative budgets are prepared on a flexible budget basis.

CAPACITY AND VOLUME

The discussion of the actual preparation of a flexible budget must be preceded by a basic understanding of the term "capacity." The terms "capacity" and "volume" (or activity) are used in connection with the construction and use of both fixed and flexible budgets. *Capacity* is that fixed amount of plant and machinery and number of personnel for which management has committed itself and with which it expects to conduct the business. *Volume* is the variable factor in business. It is related to capacity by the fact that volume (activity) attempts to make the best use of existing capacity.

Any budget is a forecast of sales, costs, and expenses. Materials, labor, factory overhead, marketing expenses, and administrative expenses must be brought into harmony with the sales volume. Sales volume is measured not only by sales the market could absorb, but also by plant capacity and machinery available to produce the goods. A plant or a department may produce 1,000 units or work 10,000 hours, but this volume (or activity) may not be compatible with the capacity of the plant or department. The production of 1,000 units or the working of 10,000 hours may be greater or smaller than the amount of sales the company can safely expect to achieve in a given market during a given period.

Capacity Levels

The following terms are used in referring to capacity levels: *theoretical, practical, expected actual*, and *normal*. Current Internal Revenue Service regulations permit the use of practical, expected actual, or normal capacity in assigning factory overhead costs to inventories.

Theoretical Capacity. The theoretical capacity of a department is its capacity to produce at full speed without interruptions. It is achieved if the plant or department produces at 100 percent of its rated capacity.

Practical Capacity. It is highly improbable that any company can operate at theoretical capacity. Allowances must be made for unavoidable interruptions, such as time lost for repairs, inefficiencies, breakdowns, setups, failures, unsatisfactory materials, delays in delivery of materials or supplies, labor shortages and absences, Sundays, holidays, vacations, inventory taking, and pattern and model changes. The number of work shifts must also be considered. These allowances reduce theoretical capacity to the practical capacity level. This reduction is caused by internal influences and does not consider the chief external cause, lack of customers' orders. Reduction from theoretical to practical capacity typically ranges from 15 percent to 25 percent, which results in a practical capacity level of 75 percent to 85 percent of theoretical capacity.

Expected Actual Capacity. Expected actual capacity is based on a short-range outlook. The use of expected actual capacity is feasible with firms whose products are of a seasonal nature, and market and style changes allow price adjustments according to competitive conditions and customer demands.

Normal Capacity. Firms may modify the above capacity levels by considering the utilization of the plant or various departments in the light of meeting average sales demands over a period long enough to level out the peaks and valleys which come with seasonal and cyclical variations. Finding a satisfactory and logical balance between plant capacity and sales volume is one of the important problems of business management.

Once the normal (or average) capacity level has been established, overhead costs can be estimated and factory overhead rates computed. The use of these rates will cause all overhead of the period to be absorbed, provided normal capacity and normal expenses prevail during the period. Any deviation from normal capacity and/or normal overhead will result in the variances discussed in Chapters 9, 10, and 11. The ease and speed with which the actual results may be compared with budgeted figures make the flexible budget of inestimable value in analyzing end-of-period deviations.

Purposes of Establishing Normal Capacity. Although there may be some differences between a normal long-run volume and the sales volume expected in the next period, normal capacity is useful in establishing sales prices and controlling costs. It is the basis for the entire budget system, and it can be used for the following purposes and aims:

1. Preparation of departmental flexible budgets and computation of predetermined factory overhead rates.
2. Compilation of the standard cost of each product.
3. Scheduling production.
4. Assigning cost to inventories.
5. Measurement of the effects of changing volumes of production.
6. Determination of the break-even point.

Although other capacity assumptions are sometimes used due to existing circumstances, normal capacity fulfills both long- and short-term purposes. The long-term utilization of the normal capacity level relates the marketing phase and therewith the pricing policy of the business to the production phase over a long period of time, leveling out fluctuations that are of short duration and of comparatively minor significance. The short-term utilization relates to management's analysis of changes or fluctuations that occur during an operating year. This short-term utilization measures temporary idleness and aids in an analysis of its causes.

Factors Involved in Determining Normal Capacity. In determining the normal capacity of a plant, both its physical capacity and average sales expectancy must be considered; neither plant capacity nor sales potential alone is sufficient. As previously mentioned, sales expectancy should be determined for a period long enough to level out cyclical variations rather than on the sales expectancy for a short period of time. It should also be noted that outmoded machinery and machinery bought for future use must be excluded from the considerations which lead to the determination of the normal capacity level.

Calculation of the normal capacity of a plant requires many different judgment factors. Normal capacity should be determined first for the business as a whole and then broken down by plants and departments. Determination of a departmental capacity figure might indicate that for a certain department the planned program is an overload while in another it will result in excess capacity. The capacities of several departments will seldom be in such perfect balance as to produce an unhampered flow of production. For the department with the overload, often termed the "bottleneck" department, actions such as the following might have to be taken:

1. Working overtime.
2. Introducing an additional shift.
3. Temporarily transferring operations to another department where spare capacity is available.
4. Subcontracting the excess load.
5. Purchasing additional equipment.

On the other hand, the excess facilities of other departments might have to be reduced. Or the sales department might be asked to search for additional orders to utilize the spare capacity in these departments.

Effect of Capacity on Overhead Rates

The effect of the various capacity levels on predetermined factory overhead rates is illustrated below. If the 75 percent capacity level is considered to be the normal operating level, the overhead rate is $2.40 per direct labor hour.

ITEM	NORMAL CAPACITY	PRACTICAL CAPACITY	THEORETICAL CAPACITY
EFFECT OF VARIOUS CAPACITY LEVELS ON PREDETERMINED FACTORY OVERHEAD RATES			
Percentage of production capacity	75%	85%	100%
Direct labor hours	7,500 hrs.	8,500 hrs.	10,000 hrs.
Budgeted factory overhead:			
Fixed.................................	$12,000	$12,000	$12,000
Variable	6,000	6,800	8,000
Total.................................	$18,000	$18,800	$20,000
Fixed factory overhead rate per direct labor hour	$1.60	$1.41	$1.20
Variable factory overhead rate per direct labor hour	.80	.80	.80
Total factory overhead rate per direct labor hour	$2.40	$2.21	$2.00

At higher capacity levels the rate is lower, because the fixed overhead is spread over more hours.

A distinction must be made between idle and excess capacity. *Idle capacity* results from the temporary idleness of production or distribution facilities due to a lack of orders. Idle facilities are restored to full use as soon as the need arises. Their cost is usually part of the expense total used in setting up the overhead rate and is at all times a part of the product cost. However, as explained in the factory overhead and standard cost chapters, the cost of idle capacity can be isolated both for control purposes and for the guidance of management.

Idle Capacity vs Excess Capacity

Excess capacity, conversely, results either from greater productive capacity than the company could ever hope to use, or from an imbalance in equipment or machinery. This imbalance involves the excess capacity of one machine in contrast with the output of other machines with which it must be synchronized. Any expense arising from excess capacity should be excluded from the factory overhead rate and from the product cost. The expense should be treated as a deduction in the income statement. In many instances, it may be wise to dispose of excess plant and equipment.

ANALYSIS OF COST BEHAVIOR

The success of a flexible budget depends upon careful study and analysis of the relationship of expenses to volume of activity or production and results in classifying expenses as fixed, variable, and semivariable.

A *fixed expense* remains the same in total as activity increases or decreases. Fixed factory overhead includes conventional items such as straight-line depreciation, property insurance, and real estate taxes. Other expenses not inherently fixed acquire the fixed characteristic through the dictates of management policy.

Fixed Expenses

The classification of an expense as fixed is valid only on the assumption that the underlying conditions remain unchanged. Thus, there is really nothing irrevocably fixed with respect to any expense classified as fixed. In the long run, all expenses are variable. In the short run, some fixed expenses, sometimes called *programmed fixed expenses*, will change because of changes in the volume of activity or for such reasons as changes in the number and salaries of the management groups. Other fixed expenses (e.g., depreciation or a long-term lease agreement) may commit management for a much longer period of time; therefore, they have been labeled *committed fixed expenses*.

A *variable expense* is expected to increase proportionately with an increase in activity and decrease proportionately with a decrease in activity. Variable expenses include the cost of supplies, indirect factory labor, receiving, storing, rework, perishable tools, and maintenance of machinery and tools. A measure of activity — such as direct labor hours or dollars, or ma-

Variable Expenses

chine hours — must be selected as an independent variable for use in estimating the variable expense, the dependent variable, at specified levels of activity. A rate of variability per unit of activity is thus determined.

Variable expenses are subject to certain fundamental assumptions if they are to remain so classified. For instance, it is assumed that prices of supplies or indirect labor do not change, that manufacturing methods and procedures do not vary, and that efficiencies do not fluctuate. If conditions change, the need for and use of variable expense items also change. For these reasons, variable expenses require constant attention so that revisions can be instigated from time to time.

Semivariable Expenses

A *semivariable expense* displays both fixed and variable characteristics. Examples of such expenses are the salaries of supervisors, accountants, buyers, typists, clerks, and janitors; employees' insurance and pension plans; maintenance of buildings and grounds; and power, water, gas, telephone and telegraph, office machine rentals, coal, fuel oil, some supplies, and even membership dues in trade, professional, and recreational organizations and clubs.

Three reasons for this semivariable characteristic of some expenses are:

1. A minimum organization may be needed, or a minimum quantity of supplies or services may need to be consumed, in order to maintain readiness to operate. Beyond this minimum cost, which is fixed, additional cost varies with volume.
2. Accounting classifications, based upon the object of expenditure or function, commonly group fixed and variable items together. As an example, the cost of steam may be charged to one account, although the cost of steam used for heating is dependent upon weather while the cost of steam used in the manufacturing process varies closely with volume of production in the factory.
3. Production factors are divisible into infinitely small units. When such costs are charted against their volume, their movements appear as a series of steps rather than as a continuous straight line. This situation is quite noticeable in moving from a one-shift to a two-shift or from a two-shift to a three-shift operation. Such moves result in definite steps in the cost line because a complete set of workers must be added at one point.[1]

The cost line of a semivariable expense is depicted graphically on page 515. The graph illustrates that the fixed portion of this expense is at $200 (Line A). The variable portion increases in a straight line (Line B), indicating that for each increase in volume (the independent variable), there is a corresponding increase in the variable portion of the expense (the dependent variable).

Relevant Range

The cost line of a semivariable expense (Line B in the graph) is often stated as being in linear or proportional relationship to the base. This linearity is used and accepted in most cost studies, even though the rate of variability of many semivariable and variable expenses does not fluctuate indiscriminately from zero to 100 percent. But the degree of error is negligible as long as

---

[1]*NA(C)A Bulletin*, Vol. 30, No. 20, pp. 1224–1225.

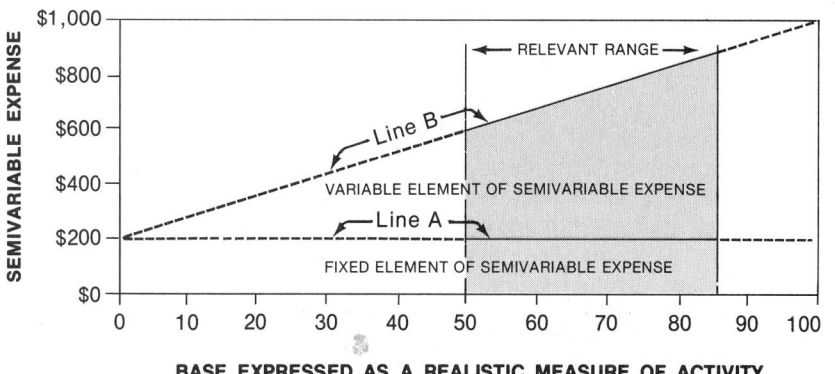

Fixed and Variable Elements of a Semivariable Expense

activity remains within a reasonably relevant range, as illustrated on the graph. The *relevant range* is the range of activity over which the amount of fixed expense and the rate of variability remain unchanged. It applies to expenses that are either all fixed, all variable, or semivariable.

The expense at zero activity is a fixed expense only if the linear relationship found in the range of observations extends back to zero activity. Otherwise, the expense figure calculated at the zero activity level is merely the value resulting from finding the point at which the regression line computed from the available data intersects the vertical expense line. In such a case, a given expense may be more accurately described, for example, as fixed at $1,000 up to an activity level of 2,000 direct labor hours, with additional activity within a relevant range having a variable rate of $.60 per direct labor hour.

Analysis of Direct Materials and Direct Labor

The analysis of cost behavior discussed in this chapter focuses on factory overhead costs. However, the flexible budget for a producing department may include direct materials and direct labor, which also have cost behavior characteristics. Direct materials are viewed as varying directly with changes in the level of production. Although direct labor costs are similarly viewed, they tend to be fixed when there is a stable labor force with no overtime work and when the cost of idle time is likely to be charged to factory overhead or a current period variance account. If a relatively stable labor force is maintained, but overtime is worked and/or extra workers are employed when activity reaches a certain level, the direct labor cost is fixed up to a point, beyond which it will vary in steps and behave like a semivariable expense.

DETERMINING THE FIXED AND VARIABLE ELEMENTS OF A SEMIVARIABLE EXPENSE

The determination of the fixed and variable elements of a semivariable expense and the creation of itemized as well as total fixed and total variable costs is necessary in order to plan, analyze, control, measure, or evaluate:

1. Departmental expenses allowed at various levels of activity.
2. Operating efficiency of a department.
3. Contribution margin and direct costing.
4. Marketing profitability of territories, products, and customers.
5. Break-even point and cost-volume-profit situations.
6. Utilization of facilities.
7. Company profit structure.
8. Differential and comparative cost decisions.
9. Effect of alternative courses management might wish to follow.
10. Proposed capital expenditures.

The following statistical methods are used in determining the fixed and variable elements of a semivariable expense: (1) high and low points method, (2) statistical scattergraph method, and (3) method of least squares. These methods are also used in determining the rate of variability of expenses that are entirely variable. In such cases, a variable rate is found, and the computed fixed portion is zero. Moreover, an entirely fixed expense would yield a fixed portion, with a zero variable rate.

Since the statistical methods deal primarily with past costs, the values determined thereby might not fit the situation expected to exist in the coming month or year. Therefore, findings should be adjusted when future conditions point to a change, and unusual conditions should be eliminated to assure the reliability and comparability of data. Industrial engineers and operating personnel working with the controller's staff should study each function (activity, job) to determine (1) the necessity of the function, (2) the most efficient method to do the job, and (3) the proper cost of performing the work at various levels of production. The close scrutiny of every expense item will frequently reveal conditions allowed to exist in the past without being known or questioned.

High and Low Points Method

This technique can best be explained by using an example. To establish the fixed and variable elements of the machine repair cost for a producing department, actual expenses incurred during two different periods are listed in the table below. The periods (data points) selected from the historical data

---

MACHINE REPAIR EXPENSE FOR A PRODUCING DEPARTMENT

	ACTIVITY LEVEL — DIRECT LABOR HOURS		EXPENSE
High	6,840 hours	100%	$2,776
Low	2,736	40	1,750
Difference	4,104 hours	60%	$1,026

Variable rate = $1,026 ÷ 4,104 hours = $.25 per direct labor hour

	HIGH	LOW
Total expense	$2,776	$1,750
Variable expense ($.25 per direct labor hour)	1,710	684
Fixed element	$1,066	$1,066

being analyzed are the high and low periods as to activity level. These periods are usually, but not necessarily, also the highest and lowest figures for the expense being analyzed. If the periods having the highest or lowest activity levels are not the same as those having the highest or lowest expense being analyzed, the activity level should govern in making the selection. The high and low periods are selected because they represent conditions at two different activity levels, but care must be taken not to select data points distorted by abnormal conditions.

The 60 percent difference between the activity levels selected in the example is 4,104 hours, with a cost variation of $1,026. The variable rate is determined by dividing $1,026 by the 4,104 hours, arriving at a variable costing rate of $.25 per direct labor hour. The fixed portion in the total expense is found by subtracting the figure obtained by multiplying high activity hours (6,840) times the variable hourly rate ($.25) from the high activity cost ($2,776). The same answer is obtained when low activity hours and cost are used.[2]

With variable and fixed elements established, the expense totals for various levels of activity can be calculated. This factor is important in the construction of the flexible budget and in the determination of the budget allowance in standard cost accounting.

Expense levels may also be determined by the use of graphs such as the one shown below. The graph shows the total expense and its fixed and vari-

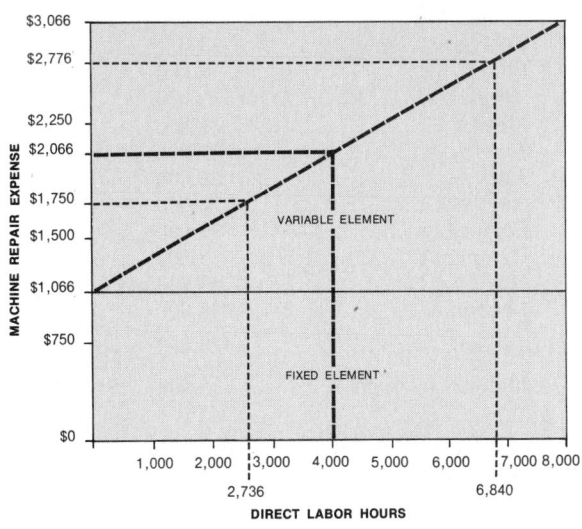

Fixed and Variable Elements in Machine Repairs

---

[2]The high and low points method is equivalent to solving two simultaneous equations, based on the assumption that both points fall on the locus of the true variable cost line. Using the above figures, equations could be set up and solved as follows:

$$F + 6,840V = \$2,776$$
$$-F - 2,736V = -1,750$$
$$\overline{4,104V = \$1,026}$$
$$V = \frac{\$1,026}{4,104} = \$.25 \text{ per direct labor hour}$$

able elements, and it also permits the quick calculation of any budget allowance within the relevant range of activity; e.g., for 4,000 hours, the total expense is $2,066, composed of $1,066 fixed cost and $1,000 variable cost. The budget allowance could also be computed as follows: 4,000 hours × $.25 (the variable rate per hour) + $1,066 (fixed cost) = $2,066.

The high and low points method is simple, but it has the disadvantage of using only two data points to determine cost behavior, and it is based on the assumption that the other data points lie on a straight line between the high and low points. Because it uses only two data points, it may not yield answers that are as accurate as those derived by other methods that consider a larger number of points.

Statistical Scattergraph Method

A technique widely used for analyzing semivariable expenses is the statistical scattergraph method. In this method, various costs (the dependent variable) are plotted on a vertical line — the *y-axis* — and measurement figures (the independent variable, e.g., direct labor dollars, direct labor hours, units of output, or percentage of capacity) are plotted along a horizontal line — the *x-axis*.

To illustrate this method, the following data are taken from a company's records for a previous year:

MONTH	DIRECT LABOR HOURS	ELECTRICITY EXPENSE
January	34,000	$ 640
February	30,000	620
March	34,000	620
April............................	39,000	590
May.............................	42,000	500
June	32,000	530
July	26,000	500
August	26,000	500
September	31,000	530
October.........................	35,000	550
November	43,000	580
December......................	48,000	680
Total........................	420,000	$6,840
Monthly average	35,000	$ 570

These data are then plotted on the graph on the next page. Each point on the graph represents the electricity expense for a particular month. For instance, the point labeled "Nov." represents the electricity expense for November, when 43,000 direct labor hours were worked. The x-axis shows the direct labor hours, and the y-axis shows the electricity expense. Line B is plotted by visual inspection. This line represents the trend shown by the majority of data points. Generally, there should be as many data points above as below the line. Another line (Line A) is drawn parallel to the base line from the point of

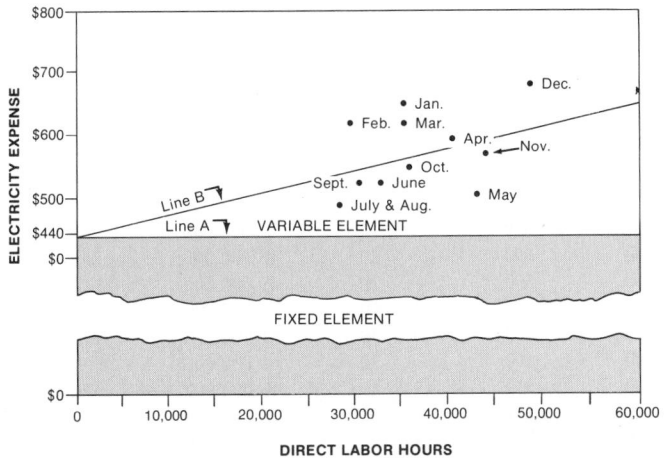

Statistical Scattergraph Representing the Fixed and Variable Elements for Electricity Expense

intersection on the y-axis, which is read from the scattergraph as approximately $440. This line represents the fixed element of the electricity expense for all activity levels within the relevant range.

The triangle formed by Lines A and B shows the increase in electricity expense as direct labor hours increase. This increase, based on direct labor hours, is computed as follows:

$$\begin{array}{ccc} \text{Average monthly} \\ \text{expense} \end{array} - \begin{array}{c} \text{Fixed} \\ \text{element} \end{array} = \begin{array}{c} \text{Average monthly variable} \\ \text{element of expense} \end{array}$$

$$\$570 \qquad - \qquad \$440 \qquad = \qquad \$130$$

$$\frac{\text{Average monthly variable element of expense}}{\text{Average monthly direct labor hours}} = \begin{array}{c} \text{Variable cost per} \\ \text{direct labor hour} \end{array}$$

$$\frac{\$130}{35{,}000 \text{ hours}} = \$.0037 \text{ per direct labor hour}$$

Thus, the electricity expense consists of $440 fixed expense per month and of a variable factor of $.0037 per direct labor hour.

Method of Least Squares

In the graph above, Line B is drawn as a straight line even though the points do not follow a perfect linear pattern. In most analyses, a straight line is adequate, because it is a reasonable approximation of cost behavior within the relevant range. However, mathematicians have worked out a technique, the method of least squares, for computing a more exact straight line, called a *regression line*.

The *method of least squares* (sometimes called *simple regression analysis*) determines mathematically a line of best fit or a linear regression line drawn through a set of plotted points, so that the sum of the squared deviations of each actual plotted point from the point directly above or below it on the regression line is at a minimum. To illustrate this method, the data from page 518 are used in completing the following table:

MONTH	(1) DIRECT LABOR HOURS	(2) DIFFERENCE FROM AVERAGE OF 35,000 HOURS	(3) ELEC-TRICITY EXPENSE	(4) DIFFERENCE FROM AVERAGE OF $570 ELECTRICITY EXPENSE	(5) (2) SQUARED	(6) (2) × (4)	(7) (4) SQUARED
January	34,000	− 1,000	$ 640	+ $ 70	1,000,000	− $ 70,000	$ 4,900
February	30,000	− 5,000	620	+ 50	25,000,000	− 250,000	2,500
March.........	34,000	− 1,000	620	+ 50	1,000,000	− 50,000	2,500
April...........	39,000	+ 4,000	590	+ 20	16,000,000	+ 80,000	400
May............	42,000	+ 7,000	500	− 70	49,000,000	− 490,000	4,900
June	32,000	− 3,000	530	− 40	9,000,000	+ 120,000	1,600
July	26,000	− 9,000	500	− 70	81,000,000	+ 630,000	4,900
August	26,000	− 9,000	500	− 70	81,000,000	+ 630,000	4,900
September ...	31,000	− 4,000	530	− 40	16,000,000	+ 160,000	1,600
October.......	35,000	0	550	− 20	0	0	400
November ...	43,000	+ 8,000	580	+ 10	64,000,000	+ 80,000	100
December....	48,000	+ 13,000	680	+ 110	169,000,000	+ 1,430,000	12,100
	420,000	0*	$6,840	0*	512,000,000	$2,270,000	$40,800

*The sum of these columns is always zero, except for rounding differences.

To prepare this table, the following steps are required:

1. First, determine the average direct labor hours and electricity expense. The total direct labor hours are 420,000 which, when divided by 12, results in an average of 35,000 hours per month. The total expense is $6,840, or an average of $570 per month ($6,840 ÷ 12).
2. Compute the differences between actual monthly figures and the average monthly figures computed in Step 1. These differences are entered in Columns 2 and 4.
3. Two multiplications must be made: differences computed in Column 2 are squared and entered in Column 5; the same differences are multiplied by differences in Column 4 and entered in Column 6. A third multiplication made at this time is to be used in computing the coefficient of correlation (page 523): differences computed in Column 4 are squared and entered in Column 7.
4. Compute a variable rate for electricity expense:

$$\frac{\text{Column 6}}{\text{Column 5}} = \frac{\$2,270,000}{512,000,000} = \$.0044 \text{ or } .44\% \text{ or } \$.44 \text{ per 100 direct labor hours}$$

5. Compute the fixed expense, using the equation for a straight line, $y = a + bx$, where y is the total expense at activity level x, a is the y intercept (or fixed expense), and b is the slope of the line (degree of variability, or variable rate):

$$y = a + bx$$
$$\$570 = a + \$.0044(35,000)$$
$$\$570 = a + \$154$$
$$a = \$416 \text{ fixed element of electricity expense per month}$$

The answer above differs somewhat from the figure determined by the scattergraph method, because visual inspection is not as accurate as the mathematical procedure. This preciseness injects a higher degree of objectivity and lack of bias into the figures. Many accountants and industrial engineers responsible for budget preparations prefer this more scientific technique. However, it is still useful to plot the data first, as illustrated on page 519, in order to verify visually the existence of a reasonable degree of correlation. Whatever method is used, abnormal data should be excluded, and a sufficient number of data points should be included in order to represent a full range of usual operating conditions. In this illustration, the sample size was small in order to simplify the computations.

Standard Error of the Estimate. The application of the method of least squares resulted in an estimated monthly fixed electricity expense of $416 and a variable electricity expense rate of $.0044 per direct labor hour. These are average expenses based on a calculated regression line (designated y_c) and are used to predict electricity expense for specified levels of direct labor hours. The visual scatter around the regression line portrayed in the graph on page 519 indicates the likelihood that actual electricity expense will vary from what might be estimated using the calculated fixed expense and variable expense rate. Because some variation can be expected, management should determine an acceptable range of tolerance for use in exercising control over expenses. Expenses within the limits of variation can be accepted. Expenses beyond the limits should be investigated, and any necessary corrective action should be taken.

The *standard error of the estimate* is defined as the standard deviation about the regression line. Management can use this concept to develop a confidence interval which, in turn, can be used to decide whether a given level of expense is indicative of a need for management action. To illustrate, the following table can be prepared from the data on page 518:

MONTHS	(1) DIRECT LABOR HOURS	(2) ELECTRICITY EXPENSE	(3) EXPECTED AVERAGE ELECTRICITY EXPENSE*	(4) DIFFERENCE (2) − (3)	(5) (4) SQUARED
January	34,000	$ 640	$ 566	+ $ 74	$ 5,476
February	30,000	620	548	+ 72	5,184
March	34,000	620	566	+ 54	2,916
April.......................	39,000	590	588	+ 2	4
May........................	42,000	500	601	− 101	10,201
June	32,000	530	557	− 27	729
July	26,000	500	530	− 30	900
August	26,000	500	530	− 30	900
September	31,000	530	552	− 22	484
October..................	35,000	550	570	− 20	400
November	43,000	580	605	− 25	625
December................	48,000	680	627	+ 53	2,809
	420,000	$6,840	$6,840	0**	$30,628

*Calculated regression line (y_c) values, (direct labor hours × $.0044) + $416, rounded to the nearest dollar.
**The sum of this column is always zero, except for rounding differences.

The standard error of the estimate is then calculated as follows:

$$\sqrt{\frac{\Sigma(y-y_c)^2}{n-2}} = \sqrt{\frac{\text{Column 5}}{n-2}} = \sqrt{\frac{\$30,628}{12-2}} = \sqrt{\$3,062.80} = \underline{\underline{\$55.34}}$$

In accordance with normal curve distribution probabilities, approximately 68 percent of the data points lie within plus and minus one standard error (standard deviation) from the regression line. Similarly, two standard errors approximate 95 percent of the data points and three standard errors, 99 percent. Thus, assuming normal error distribution, probability statements can be made concerning the reliability of estimates based on the regression equation.

In this illustration, approximately two thirds (68 percent) of the electricity expense observations lie within plus and minus one standard error from the regression line, or between $55.34 above and below the regression line. For example, if 39,000 direct labor hours of activity occur in a future month, the electricity expense, estimated to be $588 [(39,000 × $.0044) + $416], can be expected to lie between $532.66 ($588.00 − $55.34) and $643.34 ($588.00 + $55.34) about two thirds of the time. Electricity expense outside these limits could occur because of random chance about one third of the time. If the expense is outside the limits for reasons other than random chance, management may be required to take corrective action.

If management desires more confidence that an expense is not outside acceptable tolerance limits simply because of random chance, the limits must be extended. For example, there is approximately a 95 percent probability that the electricity expense will lie within plus and minus two standard errors or, in this example, between $477.32 [$588.00 − (2 × $55.34)] and $698.68 [$588.00 + (2 × $55.34)]. Using two standard errors, electricity expense outside these limits could occur because of random chance only about 5 percent of the time, increasing the likelihood that factors requiring management action account for the expense being outside the computed limits.

This discussion assumes an equal dispersion and thus an equal standard error of the estimate at all points along the regression line. However, at the extremes the data may be more widely dispersed than at the middle portion of the range. As a result, the confidence interval band is not parallel to the regression line. In general, there is more risk and thus a wider confidence interval at the extremes of the range.[3]

---

[3]The appropriate correction factor for use in estimating the confidence intervals at the extremes of the range, as well as at other portions, is:

$$\sqrt{1+\frac{1}{n}+\frac{(x-\bar{x})^2}{\Sigma(x-\bar{x})^2}}$$

where x is the specified independent variable data point (say a future period in which activity is 43,000 direct labor hours), $\bar{x}$ is the average or mean of the independent variables (35,000 direct labor hours in the example), and $\Sigma(x-\bar{x})^2$ is the difference of each x variable in the sample from the average squared and summed (Column 5 from p. 520). Thus:

$$\sqrt{1+\frac{1}{12}+\frac{(43,000-35,000)^2}{512,000,000}} = \sqrt{1+\frac{1}{12}+\frac{64,000,000}{512,000,000}} = \sqrt{1+.0833+.1250} = \sqrt{1.2083} = \underline{\underline{1.1}}$$

The standard error of the estimate would then be multiplied by the computed correction factor ($55.34 × 1.1) and the result of $60.87 would be used as the adjusted standard error of the estimate for setting electricity expense tolerance limits when direct labor hours are 43,000. The adjustment factor can be similarly computed and used for greater precision in estimating a confidence interval for other specified values of the independent variable (direct labor hours).

Correlation Analysis. The application of the statistical scattergraph method accomplishes visual verification of a reasonable degree of correlation. *Correlation* means establishing the relationship between the values of two attributes — the independent variable (x, or direct labor hours in the illustration) and the dependent variable (y, or electricity expense in the illustration) — before arriving at the fixed cost and the variable rate for semivariable expenses, or the variable rate for entirely variable expenses. If all plotted points fell on the regression line, perfect correlation would exist.

Mathematical measurements may be used to quantify correlation. In statistical theory, the *coefficient of correlation*, denoted "r," is a measure of the extent to which two variables are related linearly. When $r = 0$, there is no correlation; and when $r = \pm 1$, the correlation is perfect. As r approaches $+ 1$, the correlation is positive, which means that the dependent variable (y) increases as the independent variable (x) increases, and the regression line slopes upward to the right. As r approaches $- 1$, the correlation is negative or inverse, which means that the dependent variable (y) decreases as the independent variable (x) increases, and the regression line slopes downward to the right.

The *coefficient of determination*, r^2, is found by squaring the coefficient of correlation. The coefficient of determination is considered easier to interpret than the coefficient of correlation (r), because it represents the percentage of explained variance in the dependent variable. The larger the coefficient of determination, the closer it comes to the coefficient of correlation until both coefficients equal 1. The word "explained" means that the variations in the dependent variable are related to, but not necessarily caused by, the variations in the independent variable.

The formula for calculating the coefficient of correlation is:

$$r = \frac{\Sigma(x - \bar{x})(y - \bar{y})}{\sqrt{\Sigma(x - \bar{x})^2 \, \Sigma(y - \bar{y})^2}}$$

where $x - \bar{x}$ is the difference between each independent variable (direct labor hours in the illustration on page 518) and the average of the independent variables; and $y - \bar{y}$ is the difference between each dependent variable (electricity expense) and the average of the dependent variables. The coefficient of correlation (r) and the coefficient of determination (r^2) for the data on page 518 are calculated as follows:

$$r = \frac{\Sigma(x - \bar{x})(y - \bar{y})}{\sqrt{\Sigma(x - \bar{x})^2 \, \Sigma(y - \bar{y})^2}} = \frac{\text{Column 6}}{\sqrt{(\text{Column 5})(\text{Column 7})}}$$

$$= \frac{2{,}270{,}000}{\sqrt{(512{,}000{,}000)(40{,}800)}} = \frac{2{,}270{,}000}{\sqrt{20{,}889{,}600{,}000{,}000}}$$

$$= \frac{2{,}270{,}000}{4{,}570{,}514.2} = \underline{\underline{+.49666}}$$

$$r^2 = \underline{\underline{.24667}}$$

The coefficient of determination of less than .25 means that less than 25% of the change in electricity expense is related to the change in direct labor hours. The conclusion is that the cost is related not only to direct labor hours but to other factors as well, such as the time of day for production or the season of the year. Furthermore, some other independent variable, such as machine hours, may afford a better correlation.

To illustrate a case in which a high degree of correlation exists, the cost of electricity from the previous example is slightly altered, with direct labor hours remaining on the same level. The solution below indicates an almost perfect correlation between the two attributes, which means that this relationship could be accepted as the basis for calculating the factory overhead rate and constructing the flexible budget.

	(1)	(2)	(3)	(4)	(5)	(6)	(7)
MONTH	DIRECT LABOR HOURS	DIFFERENCE FROM AVERAGE OF 35,000 HOURS	ELEC- TRICITY EXPENSE	DIFFERENCE FROM AVERAGE OF $655 ELECTRICITY EXPENSE	(2) SQUARED	(2) × (4)	(4) SQUARED
January	34,000	− 1,000	$ 660	+ $ 5	1,000,000	− $ 5,000	$ 25
February	30,000	− 5,000	590	− 65	25,000,000	325,000	4,225
March.........	34,000	− 1,000	660	+ 5	1,000,000	− 5,000	25
April...........	39,000	+ 4,000	680	+ 25	16,000,000	100,000	625
May............	42,000	+ 7,000	740	+ 85	49,000,000	595,000	7,225
June	32,000	− 3,000	610	− 45	9,000,000	135,000	2,025
July	26,000	− 9,000	580	− 75	81,000,000	675,000	5,625
August........	26,000	− 9,000	550	− 105	81,000,000	945,000	11,025
September ...	31,000	− 4,000	630	− 25	16,000,000	100,000	625
October.......	35,000	0	640	− 15	0	0	225
November ...	43,000	+ 8,000	750	+ 95	64,000,000	760,000	9,025
December....	48,000	+ 13,000	770	+ 115	169,000,000	1,495,000	13,225
	420,000	0	$7,860	0	512,000,000	$5,120,000	$53,900

$$ r = \frac{\Sigma(x - \bar{x})(y - \bar{y})}{\sqrt{\Sigma(x - \bar{x})^2 \, \Sigma(y - \bar{y})^2}} = \frac{\text{Column 6}}{\sqrt{(\text{Column 5})(\text{Column 7})}} $$

$$ = \frac{5,120,000}{\sqrt{(512,000,000)(53,900)}} = \frac{5,120,000}{\sqrt{27,596,800,000,000}} $$

$$ = \frac{5,120,000}{5,253,265.7} = \ +.97463 $$

$$ r^2 = .94991 $$

Method of Least Squares for Multiple Independent Variables. Typically, cost behavior is shown as dependent on a single measure of volume or on some other independent variable. In the discussion above, for example, the behavior of the dependent variable, electricity expense, was described by the independent variable, direct labor hours. However, a cost may vary because of more than one factor.

Multiple regression analysis is a further application and expansion of the method of least squares, permitting the consideration of more than one independent variable. In multiple regression analysis, the simple least-squares equation for a straight line, $y = a + bx$, is expanded to include more than one independent variable. For example, in the equation $y = a + bx + cz$, c is the degree of variability for an additional independent variable z.

The least-squares concept is fundamentally the same for several independent variables as it is for only one. Although the cost relationship can no longer be shown on a two-dimensional graph and the arithmetical computations become more complex, the widespread availability of computer programs makes the use of multiple regression analysis more feasible.

If the cost behavior of a group of expenses in one or more expense accounts is being described, an alternate to multiple variables (and hence to the considerations necessitated by multiple variables when applying the least squares method) may be possible. That is, expenses may be grouped and classified in sufficient detail so that expenses in a particular group are all largely related to only one independent variable. This would allow the use of the method of least squares as earlier illustrated, i.e., simple regression analysis. If this approach is not feasible, i.e., if more than one independent variable is still required to describe the cost behavior, then multiple regression analysis should be employed.[4]

PREPARING A FLEXIBLE BUDGET

Considerable discussion has been devoted to the development of the underlying details necessary for the preparation of a flexible budget. It is not intended to convey the idea, however, that the factory overhead budget outranks the budgets for other functions of the business, because these other functions can also utilize the flexible budget concept. Any increase or decrease in business activity must be reflected throughout the enterprise. In some activities or departments, changes will be greater or smaller than in others. Certain departments have the ability to produce more without much additional cost, while in others costs increase or decrease in more or less direct proportion to production increases or decreases. The flexible budget attempts to deal with this problem.

When the fixed dollar amount and the variable rate of an expense have been determined, budget allowances for any level within a relevant range of activity can be computed without difficulty. Illustrated on page 526 is a budget

[4]For a comprehensive treatment, see Chapter 13, "Regression and Correlation — Curvilinear and Multivariate Analysis," Charles T. Clark and Lawrence L. Schkade, *Statistical Analysis for Administrative Decisions* (Cincinnati: South-Western Publishing Co., 1979).

allowances schedule, based on normal capacity, for the Machining Department of a manufacturing company.

BUDGET ALLOWANCES FOR MACHINING DEPARTMENT

Activity Base: Normal capacity, 4,000 direct labor hours per month = 80% of rated capacity

EXPENSE	FIXED EXPENSE	VARIABLE RATE PER DIRECT LABOR HOUR
Indirect labor	$ 600	$ .175
Clerical help	100	.050
Setup crew	800	.070
Rework operations	100	
Supervision	1,200	
Factory supplies	200	.055
Total controllable by department head	$ 3,000	$ .350
Insurance — fire, etc.	$ 80	
Taxes — state and local	50	
Depreciation	500	
Total noncontrollable	$ 630	
Maintenance	$ 600	$ .20
Building occupancy	780	.10
Gas, water, steam, and air	540	.30
General expenses	450	.05
Total service departments (apportioned)	$ 2,370	$ .65
Total	$ 6,000	$1.00

Summary:

Fixed expense	$ 6,000
Variable expense, 4,000 direct labor hours @ $1 per hour	4,000
Total cost at normal capacity	$10,000
Factory overhead rate of Machining Department at normal capacity ($10,000 ÷ 4,000 hours)	$2.50 per direct labor hour

The schedule of budget allowances is the basis for the flexible budget on page 527. In this budget, the factory overhead rate declines steadily as production moves to the 90 percent operating level. As production approaches theoretical capacity, the overhead rate increases, because items such as rework operations and supervision increase faster than at lower levels and overtime premiums and night premiums are introduced. While such cost increases are revealed through the flexible budget, the situation indicates a possible departure from the use of the equation for a straight line, $y = a + bx$, or $6,000 fixed expense + $1.00(x) for all levels of activity. However, it must be emphasized that one definite level must be agreed upon and used for setting the predetermined factory overhead rate for applying overhead cost to production. Costs, the base selected, and the resulting rate will lead to spending and idle capacity variances that might warrant a rate change in the next period for the sake of more meaningful cost control and pricing procedures. In any case, the effective use of cost data for planning, control, and decision-making purposes requires reasonably accurate knowledge of cost behavior.

FLEXIBLE BUDGET FOR MACHINING DEPARTMENT

Operating level:				
Based on direct labor hours	3,500	4,000*	4,500	5,000
Percentage of rated capacity	70%	80%	90%	100%
Monthly allowances for expenses:				
Indirect labor	$1,212.50	$ 1,300.00	$ 1,387.50	$ 1,475.00
Clerical help	275.00	300.00	325.00	350.00
Setup crew	1,045.00	1,080.00	1,115.00	1,150.00
Rework operations	100.00	100.00	100.00	135.00
Supervision	1,200.00	1,200.00	1,200.00	1,400.00
Factory supplies	392.50	420.00	447.50	475.00
Overtime premium	—	—	—	500.00
Night premium	—	—	—	100.00
Total controllable by department head	$4,225.00	$ 4,400.00	$ 4,575.00	$ 5,585.00
Insurance — fire, etc.	$ 80.00	$ 80.00	$ 80.00	$ 80.00
Taxes — state and local	50.00	50.00	50.00	50.00
Depreciation	500.00	500.00	500.00	500.00
Total noncontrollable	$ 630.00	$ 630.00	$ 630.00	$ 630.00
Maintenance	$1,300.00	$ 1,400.00	$ 1,500.00	$ 1,600.00
Building occupancy	1,130.00	1,180.00	1,230.00	1,280.00
Gas, water, steam, and air	1,590.00	1,740.00	1,890.00	2,040.00
General expenses	625.00	650.00	675.00	700.00
Total service departments	$4,645.00	$ 4,970.00	$ 5,295.00	$ 5,620.00
Total factory overhead	$9,500.00	$10,000.00	$10,500.00	$11,835.00
Factory overhead rate per direct labor hour	$2.714	$2.500	$2.333	$2.367

*Normal capacity.

In the flexible budget for the Machining Department, the factory overhead rate based on direct labor hours means that all variable expenses are related to this activity base. In many instances, however, the activity base is not uniform for all overhead items. Certain departments within a firm may have different bases, and a single department may require different bases and rates for different groups of expenses. Within a department, only a low correlation or none at all may exist between some of the expenses and the activity base selected. It is therefore essential to study the correlation of volume in physical terms, such as units produced, labor hours worked, or machine hours used, with the dollar cost for each item or group of items. Such studies quite often indicate that a new base must be chosen for some or all of the expenses to arrive at the most acceptable separation of fixed and variable expenses. The use of statistical correlation analysis is suggested to discover the correct volume base to be used before attempting to separate the fixed and variable elements of the many expense items that are semivariable in nature and before describing the rate of variability of entirely variable expenses.

FLEXIBLE BUDGETING THROUGH ELECTRONIC DATA PROCESSING AND STEP CHARTS

The determination of the fixed and variable elements in each departmental expense is a time-consuming task, particularly when computations, calculations, and analyses are performed either manually or by a desk calculator. The application of data processing techniques can eliminate this tedious chore and at the same time provide the necessary tools for budgetary control and responsibility reporting throughout the year.

Predetermined rates are usually used; however, when increases or decreases in certain expenses are anticipated due to a change in the product or a change in processing, the projected overhead amounts are adjusted accordingly. Some expenses are budgeted on a step-chart basis which is in harmony with the relevant range idea mentioned previously.[5]

The step chart below indicates the allowance for nonproduction personnel at various levels of production activity. Each bisected square is an indication as to the number of nonproduction personnel (upper left-hand corner) and salary levels allowable (lower right-hand corner) at each step. The levels are based on the number of production workers. In a step chart for a service

Step Chart for a Producing Department

Department _____

MONTHLY DEPARTMENTAL ALLOWANCE FOR NONPRODUCTION PERSONNEL

NUMBER OF PRODUCTION PERSONNEL From	To	DEPARTMENT HEAD	SUPERVISOR	ASSISTANT SUPERVISOR	MFG. QUALITY ANALYST					
0	10	1 / 1674								
11	20	1 / 1674	1 / 1000		1 / 1050					
21	30	1 / 1674	2 / 2000		1 / 1050					
31	40	1 / 1674	4 / 4000		2 / 2100					
41	50	1 / 1674	5 / 5000	1 / 1200	2 / 2100					
51	60	1 / 1674	5 / 5000	1 / 1200	3 / 3150					
61	70	1 / 1674	6 / 6000	1 / 1200	3 / 3150					
71	80	1 / 1674	6 / 6000	1 / 1200	4 / 4200					
81	90	1 / 1674	7 / 7000	1 / 1200	4 / 4200					
91	100									

---
[5]Eugene J. McNaboe, "Flexible Budgeting Through Electronic Data Processing," *Management Accounting*, Section 1, Vol. XLVII, No. 7, pp. 9–17.

department, the levels might be based on the total number of production hours in all producing departments. Such detailed data enhance the development of monthly departmental budgets by subexpense classifications.

FLEXIBLE BUDGET FOR A SERVICE DEPARTMENT

Flexible budgets for service departments permit (1) comparison of actual expenses with allowed expenses at the prevailing level of operations and (2) establishment of a fairer use rate or sold-hour rate by charging operating departments with fixed expenses regardless of activity and with a variable cost based on departmental activity. In the flexible budget for the Maintenance Department of a company, illustrated below, the expenses of the department are estimated at a fixed amount of $4,200. At 80 percent capacity, the total expense is $27,000. Assuming that the company has two producing departments and two service departments to which a fixed cost of $1,200, $2,000, $600, and $400, respectively, is charged as the readiness-to-serve cost of the Maintenance Department, the remaining balance of $22,800 is divided by the total number of maintenance hours, 2,400, to arrive at a variable rate of $9.50 per hour.

FLEXIBLE BUDGET FOR MAINTENANCE DEPARTMENT

Operating level:				
Maintenance hours	2,100	2,400	2,700	3,000
Percentage of plant capacity	70%	80%	90%	100%
Monthly allowances for expenses:				
Artisans	$12,600	$14,400	$16,200	$18,000
Supervision	2,000	2,000	2,000	2,000
Factory supplies	5,950	6,800	7,650	8,500
Tools	1,400	1,600	1,800	2,000
Depreciation	1,400	1,400	1,400	1,400
Building occupancy	800	800	800	800
Total expense	$24,150	$27,000	$29,850	$32,700
Fixed expense	$ 4,200	$ 4,200	$ 4,200	$ 4,200
Variable expense	19,950	22,800	25,650	28,500
Variable charging rate per maintenance hour	$9.50	$9.50	$9.50	$9.50

FLEXIBLE MARKETING AND ADMINISTRATIVE BUDGETS

In contrast to the factory overhead budget, which bases its expense levels in most cases on direct labor hours, machine hours, or direct labor dollars, the budget for commercial expenses is often based on net sales, as illustrated on page 530. This practice has been criticized, and other methods are suggested in Chapter 23.

FLEXIBLE MARKETING AND ADMINISTRATIVE BUDGET

Net sales		$600,000	$700,000	$800,000	$900,000	$1,000,000
Monthly allowances for marketing expenses:	**BASED ON SALES**					
Sales salaries	5%	$30,000	$35,000	$40,000	$45,000	$50,000
Advertising	1%	6,000	7,000	8,000	9,000	10,000
Sales expenses	2%	12,000	14,000	16,000	18,000	20,000
Misc. expenses	.5%	3,000	3,500	4,000	4,500	5,000
Depreciation	Fixed	10,000	10,000	10,000	10,000	10,000
Total marketing		$61,000	$69,500	$78,000	$86,500	$95,000
Monthly allowances for administrative expenses:	**BASED ON SALES**					
Executives' salaries	Fixed	$20,000	$20,000	$20,000	$30,000	$50,000
General expenses	3%	18,000	21,000	24,000	27,000	30,000
Depreciation	Fixed	5,000	5,000	5,000	5,000	5,000
Insurance	Fixed	3,000	3,000	3,000	3,000	3,000
Taxes	Fixed	4,000	4,000	4,000	4,000	4,000
Total administrative		$50,000	$53,000	$56,000	$69,000	$92,000

DISCUSSION QUESTIONS

1. Name some relative advantages in the use of a flexible budget over a fixed budget.

2. What is the underlying principle of a flexible budget?

3. A company has been operating a budget system for a number of years. Production volume fluctuates widely, reaching its peak in the fall, but is quite low during the rest of the year. Manufacturing for stock during the dull period as a means of smoothing out the volume fluctuations is impractical because of frequent and sudden changes in specifications prescribed by the customers. Actual annual volume has been substantially below normal. The budget produces large unfavorable capacity variances since overhead rates are computed from normal volume and are inadequate to absorb the overhead which should be charged into production during the low-volume periods. This fixed type of budget based on an unrealistic normal production volume fails to serve its planning and control purpose. As a consultant, diagnose the situation and offer advice.

4. Differentiate between (a) theoretical capacity, (b) practical capacity, (c) expected actual capacity, and (d) normal capacity.

5. (a) What situations give rise to idle capacity costs? (b) How and why should such costs be accounted for? (c) What is excess capacity cost?

6. Explain the difference between variable, fixed, and semivariable factory overhead.

7. Why should semivariable expenses be separated into their fixed and variable elements?

8. What methods are available for separating semivariable expenses?

9. Define and discuss the method of least squares with reference to assumptions, accounting data used, and single and multiple independent variables.

(AICPA adapted)

10. The least-squares relationship between electric power consumed, y (e), and production, x, was computed to be: y (e) = 10,000 + 50x. Determine the predicted electric power demands for the coming week if the planned production is 500 units.

(CGAA adapted)

11. Define the standard error of the estimate and explain its use in setting tolerance limits.

12. Explain the purpose of statistical correlation analysis in cost behavior analysis.

13. Can service departments' expenses be set up using flexible budget procedures? What makes the situation difficult? Suggest how the expenses can be allocated meaningfully to producing departments.

14. An analysis of the relationship of total factory overhead to changes in direct labor hours is expressed as: y = $1,000 + $2x.
Select the answer which best completes the statement:
(a) The above equation was probably found through the use of the mathematical technique known as: (1) linear programming; (2) multiple regression analysis; (3) the method of least squares (simple regression analysis); (4) dynamic programming.
(b) The relationship shown above is: (1) parabolic; (2) curvilinear; (3) linear; (4) probabilistic.
(c) The "y" in the above equation is an estimate of: (1) total variable cost; (2) total factory overhead; (3) total fixed cost; (4) total direct labor hours.
(d) The $2 in the above equation is an estimate of: (1) total fixed cost; (2) variable cost per direct labor hour; (3) total variable cost; (4) fixed cost per direct labor hour.

(CMA adapted)

15. Select the answer which best completes the statement:
(a) Flexible budgeting is a reporting system wherein the: (1) budget standards may be adjusted at will; (2) reporting dates vary according to the activity levels reported upon; (3) statements included in the budget report vary from period to period; (4) planned activity level is adjusted to the actual activity level before the budget comparison report is prepared.
(b) The budget for a specific cost during a fiscal period was $80,000, while the actual cost for the same period was $72,000. Considering these facts, it can be stated that the plant manager has done a better than expected job in controlling the cost if: (1) the cost is variable and actual production was 90% of budgeted production; (2) the cost is variable and actual production has equaled budgeted production; (3) the cost is variable and actual production was 80% of budgeted production; (4) none of the above.

(c) The primary difference between a fixed budget and a flexible budget is that a fixed budget: (1) includes only fixed costs, while a flexible budget includes only variable costs; (2) is concerned only with future acquisitions of plant assets, while a flexible budget is concerned with expenses that vary with sales; (3) cannot be changed after a fiscal period begins, while a flexible budget can be changed after a fiscal period begins; (4) is a budget for a single level of some measure of activity, while a flexible budget consists of several budgets or a range of budgets based on some measure of activity.

(d) Application rates for factory overhead best reflect anticipated fluctuations in sales over a cycle of years when they are computed under the concept of: (1) theoretical capacity; (2) normal capacity; (3) practical capacity; (4) expected actual capacity.

(e) The variable factory overhead rate under the practical capacity, expected actual capacity, and normal capacity levels would be the: (1) same except for normal capacity; (2) same except for practical capacity; (3) same except for expected actual capacity; (4) same for all three levels.

(f) A fixed cost: (1) may change in total when such change is unrelated to changes in production; (2) will not change in total because it is unrelated to changes in production; (3) is constant per unit for each unit of change in production; (4) may change in total, depending on production within the relevant range.

(g) The term "relevant range" as used in cost accounting means the range: (1) over which costs may fluctuate; (2) over which cost relationships are valid; (3) of probable production; (4) over which relevant costs are incurred.

(h) The total cost for Gallop, Inc., is budgeted at $230,000 for 50,000 units and at $280,000 for 60,000 units of output. Because of the need for additional facilities, the budgeted fixed cost for 60,000 is 25% more than for 50,000 units. Gallop's budgeted variable cost per unit of output is: (1) $1.60; (2) $1.67; (3) $3.00; (4) $5.00.

(i) The following relationships pertain to a year's budgeted activity for the Smythe Company:

Direct labor hours	300,000	400,000
Total cost	$129,000	$154,000

The budgeted fixed cost for the year is: (1) $25,000; (2) $54,000; (3) $75,000; (4) $100,000.

(j) In the attempt to establish a means of predicting the total cost per desk, production management has found that total direct labor hours per unit correlate very highly with the total incurred cost per desk. Management proposes the use of simple regression analysis as a means of predicting the cost to manufacture a desk. Which of the following statements is *not* true of this technique? (1) An equation of the form $y = a + bx$ results; (2) The coefficient of correlation will be greater than 1; (3) The predicted value is known as the dependent variable; (4) The method of least squares can be used in the determination.

(k) A plant superintendent has noticed that spoiled units occur in the manufacturing process on Monday more than on any other day of the week. If appropriate data to determine the relationship between spoiled units and the day of the week are collected, the resultant number: (1) provides a measure of the extent to which the day of the week accounts for the variability in the spoiled units; (2) provides a measure of the extent to which the spoiled units account for the variability in the day of the week; (3) establishes that one variable is the cause of another variable; (4) establishes that the day of the week is the cause of the spoiled units.

(l) A retail store is interested in the relationship between sales (independent variable) and theft losses (dependent variable). Using the proper formula, the coefficient of correlation is computed to be .95. Concerning these factors (sales and theft losses), a definite conclusion is that: (1) an increase in sales causes an increase in theft losses; (2) movement of these factors is in opposite directions; (3) movement of these factors is entirely unrelated; (4) movement of these factors is in the same direction.

(m) The appropriate range for the coefficient of correlation (r) is:

   (1) $0 \leq r \leq 1$; (2) $-1 \leq r \leq 1$; (3) $-100 \leq r \leq 100$; (4) $-\text{infinity} \leq r \leq \text{infinity}$.

(AICPA and CMA adapted)

EXERCISES

1. Critique of performance report. The Chan Company uses a fixed or forecast budget to measure its performance against the objectives set by the forecast and to help in controlling costs. At the end of a month, management received the following report, which compares actual performance with budgeted figures:

ITEMS OF COST	ACTUAL	BUDGET
Units produced	73,500	75,000
Direct materials	$37,020	$39,000
Direct labor	5,950	6,000
Factory supplies	1,550	1,500
Indirect labor	710	726
Repairs and maintenance	2,300	2,250
Insurance and property tax	350	355
Rent	2,000	2,000
Depreciation	2,200	2,200
Total	$52,080	$54,031

Required: Conclusions to be drawn from this report, indicating weaknesses, if any, of this type of budget.

2. Flexible budget for performance evaluation. The University of Boyne offers an extensive continuing education program in many cities throughout the state. For the convenience of its faculty and administrative staff and to save costs, the university employs a supervisor to operate a motor pool. The motor pool operated with 20 vehicles until February, when an additional automobile was acquired. The motor pool furnishes gasoline, oil, and other supplies for its automobiles. A mechanic does routine maintenance and minor repairs. Major repairs are done at a nearby commercial garage.

Each year, the supervisor prepares an operating budget, which informs the university administration of the funds needed for operating the pool. Depreciation (straight-line) on the automobiles is recorded in the budget in order to determine the cost per mile.

The schedule on the next page presents the annual budget approved by the university, with March's actual costs compared to one twelfth of the annual budget.

University Motor Pool
Budget Report for March

	ANNUAL BUDGET	ONE-MONTH BUDGET	MARCH ACTUAL	(OVER) UNDER
Gasoline...	$ 42,000	$3,500	$ 4,300	$(800)
Oil, minor repairs, parts, and supplies...............	3,600	300	380	(80)
Outside repairs..	2,700	225	50	175
Insurance...	6,000	500	525	(25)
Salaries and benefits..	30,000	2,500	2,500	—
Depreciation..	26,400	2,200	2,310	(110)
	$110,700	$9,225	$10,065	$(840)
Total miles...	600,000	50,000	63,000	
Cost per mile...	$.1845	$.1845	$.1598	
Number of automobiles.......................................	20	20	21	

The annual budget was constructed upon these assumptions:

(a) 20 automobiles in the pool.
(b) 30,000 miles per year per automobile.
(c) 15 miles per gallon per automobile.
(d) $1.05 per gallon of gasoline.
(e) $.006 per mile for oil, minor repairs, parts, and supplies.
(f) $135 per automobile for outside repairs.

The supervisor is unhappy with the monthly report comparing budget and actual costs for March, claiming it presents an unfair picture of performance. A previous employer used flexible budgeting to compare actual costs to budgeted amounts.

Required:
(1) A report showing budgeted amounts, actual costs, and monthly variations for March, using flexible budget techniques. (Round off computations to four decimal places.)
(2) An explanation of the basis of the budget figure for outside repairs.

(CMA adapted)

3. Factory overhead rates; unabsorbed fixed overhead. Hawkins Company management is considering the use of a flexible budget for variable factory overhead and wishes a study of its operations based on the following data:

	80%	90%	100%
Capacity...	80%	90%	100%
Direct labor hours..	48,000	54,000	60,000
Variable factory overhead.................................	$96,000	$108,000	$120,000

Fixed factory overhead is budgeted at $250,000 for each of the three levels of activity.

Required:
(1) The total factory overhead rate at each capacity level, based on direct labor hours. (Round off computations to three decimal places.)
(2) The variable factory overhead rate for each level.
(3) The amount of unabsorbed fixed overhead if the company operates at 80% of capacity, yet applies a rate based on the 100% capacity level.

4. Flexible budget. Operating at normal capacity, the Elgar Company employs 20 production workers in the Assembly Department, working 8 hours per day, 20 days per month at a wage rate of $9 per hour. Normal capacity is 3,800 units of production per month. Supplies average $.23 per direct labor hour, indirect labor cost is ⅛ of direct labor cost, and other charges are $.18 per direct labor hour. The flexible budget at the normal capacity activity level follows:

Direct materials	$ 4,760
Direct labor	28,800
Fixed factory overhead	670
Supplies	736
Indirect labor	3,600
Other charges	576
Total	$39,142
Cost per unit	$10.30

Required: The flexible budget at 60% and 75% capacity.

5. Flexible budget. Corvallis, Inc., employs 10 production workers, working 8 hours a day, 20 days per month, at a normal capacity of 2,400 units. The direct labor wage rate is $6.30 per hour; direct materials are budgeted at $2 per unit produced. Fixed factory overhead is $960; supplies average $.25 per direct labor hour; indirect labor is $1/6$ of direct labor cost; and other charges are $.45 per direct labor hour.

Required: The flexible budget at 60%, 80%, and 100% of normal capacity, showing itemized manufacturing costs, total manufacturing cost, and total manufacturing cost per unit.

6. Determining variable and fixed factory overhead budget allowances. The following information has been used by the Prince Edward Island Company in preparing its budgets for January and February:

	JANUARY	FEBRUARY
Units to be sold	9,000	11,000
Units to be produced	12,000	10,000
Direct labor hours	24,000	20,000
Insurance on factory	$ 2,000	$ 2,000
Sales salaries	13,000	15,000
Depreciation (factory building and machinery)	10,000	10,000
Light and heat (factory)	340	300
Advertising	15,000	15,000
Indirect factory labor	3,800	3,300
Factory supplies	3,000	2,500
Direct materials used	60,000	50,000
Lubricants for factory machinery	1,800	1,500

Required:
(1) The variable budget allowance per direct labor hour for each factory overhead expense. (Carry computations to three decimal places.)
(2) The fixed budget allowance for each factory overhead expense.   (CGAA adapted)

7. Separating fixed and variable costs; standard error of the estimate; correlation analysis. A controller is interested in an analysis of the fixed and variable costs of electricity as related to direct labor hours. The following data have been accumulated:

MONTH	ELECTRICITY COST	DIRECT LABOR HOURS
November	$1,548	297
December	1,667	350
January	1,405	241
February	1,534	280
March	1,600	274
April	1,600	266
May	1,613	285
June	1,635	301

Required:
(1) The amount of fixed overhead and the variable cost ratio, using (a) the high and low points method, (b) a scattergraph with trend line fitted by inspection, and (c) the method of least squares. (Round off computations to three decimal places.)

(2) The standard error of the estimate.
(3) The standard error of the estimate correction factor when direct labor hours are 300.
(4) The coefficient of correlation (r) and the coefficient of determination (r^2).

8. Separating fixed and variable expenses; standard error of the estimate; correlation analysis.
The custodial supplies expense and guest days of occupancy at Hotel Excelsior for a 6-month
period are:

	CUSTODIAL SUPPLIES EXPENSE	GUEST DAYS OF OCCUPANCY
January	$9,255	21,500
February	9,170	21,000
March	9,561	23,300
April	8,949	19,700
May	9,017	20,100
June	9,493	22,900

Required:
(1) The amount of fixed and variable custodial supplies expense per guest day of occupancy,
using (a) the high and low points method, (b) a scattergraph with trend line fitted by inspection, and (c) the method of least squares.
(2) The standard error of the estimate.
(3) The coefficient of correlation (r) and the coefficient of determination (r^2).

9. Fixed-variable cost analysis; standard error of the estimate; correlation analysis. A company
making tubing from aluminum billets uses a process in which the billets are heated by induction to
a very high temperature before being put through an extruding machine that shapes the tubing
from the billets. The inducer, a very large coil into which the billet is placed, must sustain a great
flow of current to heat the billets to the desired temperature. Regardless of the number of billets to
be processed, the coil is kept on during the entire operating day because of the time involved in
starting it up. The Cost Department wants to charge the variable electricity cost to each billet and
the fixed electricity cost to factory overhead. The following data have been assembled:

MONTH	NUMBER OF BILLETS	COST OF ELECTRICITY	MONTH	NUMBER OF BILLETS	COST OF ELECTRICITY
January	2,000	$400	July	1,400	$340
February	1,800	380	August	1,900	390
March	1,900	390	September	1,800	380
April	2,200	420	October	2,400	440
May	2,100	410	November	2,300	430
June	2,000	400	December	2,200	420

Required:
(1) A fixed-variable expense analysis using the method of least squares.
(2) A graph indicating the results calculated.
(3) The standard error of the estimate.
(4) The coefficient of correlation (r) and the coefficient of determination (r²).

10. Cost variability; standard error of the estimate; correlation analysis. Clinton Hospital is interested in an analysis of the fixed and variable cost of supplies as related to patient days of occupancy. The following data have been accumulated:

MONTH	COST OF SUPPLIES	PATIENT DAYS OF OCCUPANCY
November	$2,153	1,164
December	2,201	1,405
January	2,060	885
February	2,009	910
March	2,040	995
April	2,015	927
May	1,997	874
June	2,098	1,140

Required:
   (1) The fixed and variable cost elements included in the cost of supplies, using (a) the high and low points method, (b) a scattergraph with trend line fitted by inspection, and (c) the method of least squares. (Round off computations to three decimal places.)
   (2) The standard error of the estimate.
   (3) The standard error of the estimate correction factor when patient days of occupancy are 1,350.
   (4) The coefficient of correlation (r) and the coefficient of determination (r²).

11. Cost behavior analysis; standard error of the estimate; correlation analysis. A company's cost department has compiled weekly records of production volume (in units), electric power used, and direct labor hours employed. The range of output for which the following statistics were computed is from 500 to 2,000 units per week:

ELECTRIC POWER	DIRECT LABOR
$y = 1,000 + .4x$	$y = 100 + 1.2x$
where y is electric power and x is units of production	where y is direct labor hours and x is units of production
Standard error of the estimate: 100	Standard error of the estimate: 300
Coefficient of correlation: .45	Coefficient of correlation: .70

Required:
   (1) The best estimate of the additional number of required direct labor hours, if production for the next period should be 500 units greater than production in this period.
   (2) Comments on the reliability of the above equations for estimating electric power and direct labor requirements, together with the necessary assumptions if the estimating equations are to be used to predict future requirements. An interpretation of the standard error of the estimate and the coefficient of correlation should be included.

(CGAA adapted)

PROBLEMS

18-1. Budget planning and performance comparison. Metzger, Inc., produces farm equipment at several plants. The business is seasonal and cyclical in nature. The company has attempted to use budgeting for planning and controlling activities, but the variable nature of the business has caused some company officials to be skeptical of its usefulness. The chief accountant for the Adrian Plant has been using a flexible budget to help plant management control operations.

The president asks for an explanation of flexible budgeting, its application, and its possible use for the entire company. The chief accountant presents the following data:

Budget data for 19––:
   Normal monthly capacity of the plant in direct labor hours ....   10,000 hours
   Materials cost (6 lbs, @ $1.50)... $ 9 per unit
   Labor cost (2 hours @ $6)... $12 per unit

Estimated factory overhead at normal monthly capacity:
   Variable factory overhead:
      Indirect labor .... $ 6,650
      Indirect materials...   600
      Repairs   750
         Total variable factory overhead.............................. $ 8,000

   Fixed factory overhead:
      Depreciation .... $ 3,250
      Supervision...   3,000
         Total fixed factory overhead .... $ 6,250

   Total fixed and variable factory overhead .... $ 14,250

Planned units for January	4,000
Planned units for February	6,000

Actual data for January:

Hours worked..	8,400
Units produced..	3,800

Costs incurred:

Materials (24,000 lbs.)	$ 36,000
Direct labor..	50,400
Indirect labor	6,000
Indirect materials...	600
Repairs	1,800
Depreciation	3,250
Supervision..	3,000
Total...	$101,050

Required:
(1) A manufacturing budget for January.
(2) A report for January, comparing actual and budgeted costs for the month's actual activity, assuming that the units produced are to be the measure of activity used in preparing the flexible budget.
(3) Explanation of the possibility of applying flexible budgeting to the nonmanufacturing activities of Metzger, Inc.

(CMA adapted)

18-2. Flexible budget; overhead rate. The controller of the Nogales Corporation decided to prepare a flexible factory overhead budget ranging from 80% to 100% of capacity for the next year with 50,000 hours as the 100% level. The data available are based on either past experiences, shop supervisors' figures, or management's decisions. For expenses of a semivariable nature, the fixed amount and the variable rate are determined via the high and low points method. The direct labor rate is $7.50 per hour. Additional data for factory overhead are:

Annual fixed expenses:

Depreciation..	$ 9,000
Insurance..	1,500
Maintenance cost (including payroll taxes and fringe benefits)..	24,000
Property tax...	1,500
Supervisory staff (including payroll taxes and fringe benefits)..	36,000

Variable expenses:

Shop supplies..	$.10 per direct labor hour
Indirect labor (excluding inspection)....................	$.45 per direct labor hour
Payroll taxes and fringe benefits..........................	18% of labor cost, direct and indirect

Semivariable expenses (from previous five years):

YEAR	DIRECT LABOR HOURS	POWER AND LIGHT	INSPECTION (INCLUDING PAYROLL TAXES AND FRINGE BENEFITS)	OTHER SEMI-VARIABLE EXPENSES
19A	44,000	$1,500	$ 9,200	$8,000
19B	40,000	1,400	9,000	7,500
19C	45,000	1,600	9,200	8,200
19D	49,000	1,650	10,000	8,800
19E	50,000	1,700	10,200	8,900

Required:
(1) A flexible factory overhead budget ranging from 80% to 100% of capacity, with 10% intervals.

(2) The total factory overhead rate, variable cost rate, and fixed cost rate for 100% of capacity. (Round off to two decimal places.)

18-3. Flexible budget. Department A, one of 15 departments in the manufacturing plant, is involved in the production of all of the six products manufactured by Augustin Products, Inc. Because Department A is highly mechanized, its output is measured in direct machine hours. Flexible budgets are utilized throughout the plant in planning and controlling costs, but here the focus is upon the application of flexible budgets in Department A only.

On March 15, 19A, the following flexible budget was approved for Department A to be used throughout the fiscal year 19A-B, beginning on July 1, 19A. This flexible budget was developed through the cooperative efforts of Department A's manager, the supervisor, and members of the Budget Department.

Flexible Budget for Department A
For Fiscal Year 19A-B

Controllable Costs	Fixed Amount per Month	Variable Rate per Direct Machine Hour
Employees' salaries	$ 9,000	
Indirect wages	18,000	$.07
Indirect materials		.09
Other costs	6,000	.03
Total	$33,000	$.19

On May 5, 19A, the annual sales plan and the production budget were completed. To continue preparation of the annual profit plan, which was detailed by month, the production budget was translated to planned activity for each of the 15 departments. The planned activity for Department A was:

	For Twelve Months Ending June 30, 19B				
	Year	July	August	September	October–June
Planned output in direct machine hours	325,000	22,000	25,000	29,000	249,000

On August 31, 19A, Department A's manager was informed that the planned September output had been revised to 34,000 direct machine hours. On September 30, 19A, Department A's accounting records showed the following actual data for September:

Actual output in direct machine hours	33,000
Actual controllable costs incurred:	
Employees' salaries	$ 9,300
Indirect wages	20,500
Indirect materials	2,850
Other costs	7,510
Total	$40,160

The requirements below and on page 540 relate primarily to the potential uses of the flexible budget for the period March through September, 19A.

Required:
(1) An explanation of how the range of the activity base to which the variable rates per direct machine hour are relevant should be determined.
(2) An illustration of the application of the high and low points method of determining the fixed and variable components of indirect wage costs for Department A. Assume that the high and low values for indirect wages are $19,400 at 20,000 direct machine hours and $20,100 at 30,000 direct machine hours. *(continued)*

(3) An explanation and illustration of the use of the flexible budget in:
     (a) Budgeting costs when the annual sales plan and production budget are completed (about May 5, 19A, or shortly thereafter).
     (b) Budgeting a cost revision based upon a revised production budget (about August 31, 19A, or shortly thereafter).
     (c) Preparing a cost performance report for September, 19A.

                                                    (AICPA adapted)

18-4. Fixed and variable cost analysis; standard error of the estimate; correlation analysis. The management of the Roberts Hotel is interested in an analysis of the fixed and variable costs in the electricity used relative to hotel occupancy. The data shown below have been gathered from books and records for the year.

	GUEST DAYS	ELECTRICITY COST
January	1,000	$ 400
February	1,500	500
March	2,500	500
April	3,000	700
May	2,500	600
June	4,500	800
July	6,500	1,000
August	6,000	900
September	5,500	900
October	3,000	700
November	2,500	600
December	3,500	800
Year total	42,000	$8,400

Required:
(1) The fixed and variable elements of the electricity cost, using (a) the method of least squares, (b) the high and low points method, and (c) a scattergraph with trend line fitted by inspection. (Round off the variable rate to four decimal places.)
(2) The other elements, besides occupancy, which might affect the amount of electricity used in any one month.
(3) The standard error of the estimate.
(4) The standard error of the estimate correction factor when guest days are 2,000.
(5) The coefficient of correlation (r) and the coefficient of determination (r^2).

18-5. Method of least squares; standard error of the estimate; correlation analysis. The Ramon Company manufactures a wide range of electrical products at several different plant locations. Due to fluctuations, its Franklin plant has been experiencing difficulties in estimating the level of monthly overhead.

Management needs more accurate estimates to plan its operational and financial needs. A trade association publication indicates that for companies like Ramon, overhead tends to vary with direct labor hours. Based on this information, one member of the accounting staff proposes that the overhead cost behavior pattern be determined in order to calculate the overhead cost in relation to budgeted direct labor hours. Another member of the accounting staff suggests that a good starting place for determining the cost behavior pattern of the overhead cost would be an analysis of historical data to provide a basis for estimating future overhead costs.

Data on direct labor hours and the respective factory overhead costs for the past two years are shown on the next page.

Required:
(1) The amount of fixed factory overhead and the variable cost ratio, using the method of least squares. (Round fixed factory overhead to the nearest dollar and the variable cost ratio to the nearest cent.)
(2) The standard error of the estimate.
(3) The coefficient of correlation (r) and the coefficient of determination (r^2). (Round off to four decimal places.)   (CMA adapted)

| | 19A | | 19B | |
	Direct Labor Hours	Factory Overhead Costs	Direct Labor Hours	Factory Overhead Costs
January	2,000	8,500	2,100	8,700
February	2,400	9,900	2,300	9,300
March	2,200	8,950	2,200	9,300
April	2,300	9,000	2,200	8,700
May	2,000	8,150	2,000	8,000
June	1,900	7,550	1,800	7,650
July	1,400	7,050	1,200	6,750
August	1,000	6,450	1,300	7,100
September	1,200	6,900	1,500	7,350
October	1,700	7,500	1,700	7,250
November	1,600	7,150	1,500	7,100
December	1,900	7,800	1,800	7,500

18-6. Correlation analysis. The Cost Department of the Freed Electric Company attempts to establish a flexible budget to assist in the control of marketing expenses. An examination of individual expenses shows:

ITEM	FIXED PORTION	VARIABLE PORTION
Sales staff:		
Salaries	$1,200	none
Retainers	2,000	none
Commissions	none	4% on sales values
Advertising	5,000	none
Travel expense	?	?

Statistical analysis is needed to split the travel expense satisfactorily into its fixed and variable portions. Before beginning such an analysis, it is thought that the variable portion of the travel expense might vary in accordance either with the number of calls made on customers each month or the value of orders received each month. Records reveal the following details over the past twelve months:

MONTH	CALLS MADE	ORDERS RECEIVED	TRAVEL EXPENSE
January	410	$53,000	$3,000
February	420	65,000	3,200
March	380	48,000	2,800
April	460	73,000	3,400
May	430	62,000	3,100
June	450	67,000	3,200
July	390	60,000	2,900
August	470	76,000	3,300
September	480	82,000	3,500
October	490	62,000	3,400
November	440	64,000	3,200
December	460	80,000	3,400

Required:

(1) The coefficient of correlation and coefficient of determination between (a) the travel expense and the number of calls made and (b) the travel expense and orders received. (Round off to four decimal places.)

(2) A comparison between the answers obtained in (1a) and (1b).

CASES

A. Flexible vs fixed budget. L'Argonne County Hospital is located in the county seat. The county, a well-known summer resort area, doubles its population during the vacation months, May–August, and hospital activity more than doubles during that period. The hospital is relatively small, but its pleasant surroundings have attracted a well-trained and competent medical staff.

One year ago an administrator was hired to improve the business and accounting activities of the hospital. Among the new ideas introduced was responsibility accounting leading to departmental quarterly cost reports. Previously, cost data were presented to department heads infrequently. The announcement of the new procedure and the accompanying report received by the supervisor of the Laundry Department contained this information:

> The hospital has adopted a responsibility accounting system. From now on you will receive quarterly reports comparing the costs of operating your department with budgeted costs. The reports will highlight the differences (variations) so you can zero in on the departure from budgeted costs. Responsibility accounting means you are accountable for keeping the costs in your department within the budget. The variations from the budget will help you identify which costs are out of line and the size of the variation will indicate which are the most important. Your first such report accompanies this announcement.

L'Argonne County Hospital
Performance Report — Laundry Department
July–September, 19--

	BUDGET	ACTUAL	(OVER) UNDER BUDGET	PERCENT (OVER) UNDER BUDGET
Patient days	9,500	11,900	(2,400)	(25)
Pounds processed — laundry	125,000	156,000	(31,000)	(25)
Costs:				
Laundry labor	$ 9,000	$12,500	$(3,500)	(39)
Supplies	1,100	1,875	(775)	(70)
Water, water heating, and softening	1,700	2,500	(800)	(47)
Maintenance	1,400	2,200	(800)	(57)
Supervisor's salary	3,150	3,750	(600)	(19)
Allocated administration cost	4,000	5,000	(1,000)	(25)
Equipment depreciation	1,200	1,250	(50)	(4)
Total cost	$21,550	$29,075	$(7,525)	(35)

Administrator's comments: Costs are significantly above budget for the quarter. Particular attention needs to be paid to labor, supplies, and maintenance.

The annual budget for 19-- was constructed by the new administrator, who compiled it from an analysis of the prior three years' costs. Quarterly budgets were computed as one fourth of the annual budget, which showed that all costs increased each year with more rapid increases between the second and third year. The administrator considered establishing the budget at an average of the prior three years' costs, hoping that the installation of the system would reduce costs to this level. However, in view of rapidly increasing prices, last year's costs less 3% were used for the 19-- budget. The activity level measured by patient days and pounds of laundry processed was set at last year's volume, which was approximately equal to the volume of each of the past three years.

Required:
(1) Comments on the method used to construct the budget.
(2) Information to be communicated by variations from the budget.
(3) Reasons for or against the report's effective communication of the level of efficiency of the Laundry Department. (CMA adapted)

B. Cost behavior and the flexible budget. The Boggs Company has a contract with a labor union guaranteeing a minimum wage of $500 per month to each direct labor employee with at least twelve years of service. At present, 100 employees qualify for this coverage. All direct labor employees are paid $5 per hour.

The direct labor budget for 19-- was based on the annual usage of 400,000 direct labor hours × $5, or a total of $2,000,000. Of this amount, $50,000 (100 employees × $500) per month (or $600,000 for 19--) was regarded as fixed expense. Thus, the budget for any specific month was determined by the formula: $50,000 + $3.50 × direct labor hours worked.

Data on the performance for the first three months of 19–– are:

	JANUARY	FEBRUARY	MARCH
Direct labor hours worked	22,000	32,000	42,000
Direct labor cost — flexible budget	$127,000	$162,000	$197,000
Direct labor cost incurred	110,000	160,000	210,000
Variance (U — unfavorable; F — favorable)	$ 17,000 F	$ 2,000 F	$ 13,000 U

The factory manager was perplexed by the results that showed favorable variances when production was low and unfavorable variances when production was high, believing that control over labor cost was consistently good.

Required:
(1) An explanation and illustration of variances, using amounts and diagrams as necessary.
(2) An explanation of this direct labor flexible budget as a basis for controlling direct labor cost, indicating changes that might improve control over direct labor cost and facilitate performance evaluation of direct labor employees.

(AICPA adapted)

C. Regression and correlation analysis — utility and implementation. Naomi McCarty, controller of The Arkansas Distribution Company, is responsible for development and administration of the company's internal information system as well as the coordination of the company's budget preparation.

At a meeting with Don Tuma, the Vice-President, McCarty proposed that the company employ regression analysis (the least-squares method) and correlation analysis as a standard part of its internal information system relating to sales and expenses. She felt that such analyses, including projections, would be significant decision-making aids.

Tuma admitted that he had forgotten the exact mechanics of regression and correlation analysis. However, he did remember enough about it to comment that:

(a) Regression and correlation calculations for weekly or monthly amounts would involve enormous numbers of calculations because the company's budget and control system uses weekly amounts for sales and some expenses and monthly amounts for other expenses.
(b) A great deal of caution must be exercised when relying on predictions calculated by regression analysis techniques.

McCarty agreed that a large number of calculations would be required, but felt that this problem might be overcome by computerizing the analysis. The computerized analysis would have to suit the company's budget and control system and cover all significant sales and expense accounts, of which there are about 100.

The company's computer is not large and operates only with card and magnetic tape input/output. No standard computer programs are available for this kind of analysis. Therefore, a program must be specially written, its accompanying data gathered, and the processing problems solved.

To pursue her idea, McCarty decided to obtain sample data regarding sales and related selling expense for the past five years. Using regression analysis, she predicted sales of $30,500,000 for the coming year and calculated a coefficient of correlation of .4 between sales and the selling expense.

Required:
(1) The advantages and limitations of using regression and correlation analysis according to McCarty.
(2) A statement pointing out those matters that should be considered before the regression analysis is made, based on the sample data collected.
(3) An outline of the programming and operating problems that might be encountered if the analysis is computerized using the available computer.

(CICA adapted)

19

Standard Costing
Setting of Standards
and Analysis of Variances

A *standard cost* is the predetermined cost of manufacturing a single unit or a number of product units during a specific period in the immediate future. It is the planned cost of a product under current and/or anticipated operating conditions.

A standard cost has two components: a standard and a cost. A standard is like a norm and whatever is considered normal can generally be accepted as standard. For example, if a score of 72 is the standard for a golf course, a golfer's score is judged on the basis of this standard. In industry, the standards for making a desk, assembling a radio, refining crude oil, or manufacturing railway cars are based on carefully determined quantitative and qualitative measurements and engineering methods. A standard must be thought of as a norm in terms of specific items, such as pounds of materials, hours of labor required, and percentage of plant capacity to be used. In many firms, a standard can be operative for a long time. A change is needed only when production methods or the products themselves have become obsolete or undesirable.

PURPOSES OF STANDARD COSTS

Standard cost systems aid in planning operations and gaining insights into the probable impact of managerial decisions on cost levels and profits. Standard costs are used for:

1. Establishing budgets.
2. Controlling costs and motivating and measuring efficiencies.
3. Promoting possible cost reduction.
4. Simplifying costing procedures and expediting cost reports.
5. Assigning costs to materials, work in process, and finished goods inventories.
6. Forming the basis for establishing bids and contracts and for setting sales prices.

The effectiveness of controlling costs depends greatly upon a knowledge of expected costs. Standards serve as measurements which call attention to cost variations. Executives and supervisors become cost-conscious as they become aware of results. This cost-consciousness tends to reduce costs and encourages economies in all phases of the business.

The use of standard costs for accounting purposes simplifies costing procedures through the reduction of clerical labor and expense. A complete standard cost system is usually accompanied by standardization of productive operations. Standard production or manufacturing orders, calling for standard quantities of product and specific labor operations, can be prepared in advance of actual production. Materials requisitions, labor time tickets, and operation cards can be prepared in advance of production, and standard costs can be compiled. As orders for a part are placed in the shop, previously established requirements, processes, and costs will apply. The more standardized the production, the simpler the clerical effort. Reports can be systematized to present complete information regarding standards, actual costs, and variances. Reports that are integrated and tied in with the financial accounts through journal entries are discussed in Chapter 20.

A complete standard cost file by parts and operations simplifies assigning costs to materials, work in process, and finished goods inventories. The use of standard costs stabilizes the influence of materials costs. Placing bids, securing contracts, and establishing sales prices are greatly enhanced by the availability of reliable standards and the continuous review of standard costs.

The standard cost system may be used in connection with either the process or job order cost accumulation method. However, it is more often used in process costing because of the greater practicality of setting standards for a continuous flow of like units than for unique job orders.

COMPARISON OF BUDGETS AND STANDARDS

The budget is one method of securing reliable and prompt information regarding the operation and control of an enterprise. When manufacturing budgets are based on standards for materials, labor, and factory overhead, a strong team for possible control and reduction of costs is created.

Standards are almost indispensable in establishing a budget. Because both standards and budgets aim at the same objective — managerial control — it is often felt that the two are the same and cannot function independently. This opinion is supported by the fact that both use predetermined costs for the coming period. Both budgets and standard costs make it possible to prepare reports which compare actual costs and predetermined costs for management.

Building budgets without the use of standard cost figures can never lead to a real budgetary control system. The figures used in the illustrations in the budget chapters are only fair estimates, even though they have been set with great care and the cooperation of those responsible. Under such conditions, the budget can hardly be considered the basis against which actual results are to be measured. This shortcoming is recognized by adding the flexible budget as a refinement. With the use of standard costs, the preparation of budgets for any volume and mixture of products is more reliably and speedily accomplished, and a budget becomes a summary of standards for items of cost.

The principal difference between budgets and standard costs lies in their scope. The budget, as a statement of expected costs, acts as a guidepost which keeps the business on a charted course. Standards, on the other hand, do not tell what costs are expected to be, but rather what they will be if certain performances are achieved. A budget emphasizes the volume of business and the cost level which should be maintained if the firm is to operate as desired. Standards stress the level to which costs should be reduced. If costs reach this level, profits will be increased.

SETTING STANDARDS

Calculation of a standard cost is based on physical standards, two types of which are often discussed: basic and current. A *basic standard* is a yardstick against which both expected and actual performances are compared. It is similar to an index number against which all later results are measured. *Current standards* are of three types:

1. The *expected actual standard* is a standard set for an expected level of operation and efficiency. It is a reasonably close estimate of actual results.
2. The *normal standard* is a standard set for a normal level of operation and efficiency, intended to represent challenging yet attainable results.
3. The *theoretical standard* is a standard set for an ideal or maximum level of operation and efficiency. Such standards constitute goals to be aimed for rather than performances that can be currently achieved.

Materials and labor costs are generally based on normal, current conditions, allowing for alterations of prices and rates and tempered by the desired efficiency level. Factory overhead is based on normal conditions of efficiency and volume.

Standards must be established for a definite period of time to be effective in the control and analysis of costs. Standards are usually computed for a six- or twelve-month period, although a longer period is sometimes used.

The success of a standard cost system depends on the reliability, accuracy, and acceptance of the standards. Extreme care must be taken to be sure that all factors are considered in the establishment of standards. In certain cases, a sampling of averages derived from the records of previous periods are used as standards. However, the most effective standards are set by the industrial engineering department on the basis of careful studies of products and operations, using appropriate sampling techniques and including participation by those individuals whose performance is to be measured by the standards.

Standards must be set, and the system implemented, in an atmosphere that gives full consideration to behavior characteristics of managers and workers. In the long run, workers and plant management will tend to react negatively if they feel threatened by imposed standards. If they participate in setting standards, they can more readily identify with the standard costing procedure and the standards could become their personal goals.

Standards which are too loose or too tight will generally have a negative impact on worker motivation. If standards are too loose, workers will tend to set their goals at this low rate, thus reducing productivity below what is obtainable. If the standard is too tight, workers realize the impossibility of attaining the standard, become frustrated, and will not attempt to meet the standard. A reasonable standard which can be attained under normal working conditions is likely to contribute to the worker's motivation to achieve the designated level of activity or productivity.

Once standards are set, it is important to provide the proper standard cost cards, on which the itemized cost of each materials part, labor operation, and overhead cost is shown. A master standard cost card, illustrated below, gives the standard unit cost of a product.

Date of Standard July 1, 19--   STANDARD COST CARD FOR PRODUCT Alpac

	ITEM CODE	QUAN-TITY	STANDARD UNIT PRICE	DEPARTMENT 1	2	3	4	5	TOTALS
DIRECT MATERIALS	2-234	4	$3.00/pc.		$12.00				
	3-671	24	1.00/doz.			$2.00			
	5-489	2	2.50/pc.					$ 5.00	
	5-361	8	1.50/pc.					12.00	
	TOTAL DIRECT MATERIALS COST								$ 31.00

	OPERA-TION NUMBER	STANDARD HOURS	STANDARD RATE PER HOUR	DEPARTMENT 1	2	3	4	5	
DIRECT LABOR	2-476	3	$6.00		$18.00				
	2-581	11½	6.40		73.60				
	3-218	4	6.30			$25.20			
	5-420	2½	6.20					$15.50	
	TOTAL DIRECT LABOR COST								132.30

	STANDARD HOURS	RATE PER DIRECT LABOR HOUR		DEPARTMENT 1	2	3	4	5	
FACTORY OVERHEAD	14½	$1.80			$26.10				
	4	2.00				$8.00			
	2½	1.50						$3.75	
	TOTAL FACTORY OVERHEAD.................								37.85
	TOTAL MANUFACTURING COST PER UNIT								$201.15

Standard Cost
Card

The master standard cost card is supported by individual cards that indicate how the standard cost was compiled and computed. Each subcost card represents a form of standard cost card.

MATERIALS COST STANDARDS

Two standards must be developed for direct materials costs:

1. A materials price standard.
2. A materials quantity (or usage) standard.

Materials Price Standard and Variance

Price standards permit (1) checking the performance of the purchasing department and the influence of various internal and external factors and (2) measuring the effect of price increases or decreases on the company's profits. Determining the price or cost to be used as the standard cost is often difficult, because the prices used are controlled more by external factors than by a company's management. Prices selected should reflect current market prices and are generally used throughout the forthcoming fiscal period.

If the actual price paid is more or less than the standard price, a price variance occurs. Price increases or decreases occurring during the fiscal period are recorded in the materials price variance account(s). Price standards are revised at inventory dates or whenever there is a major change in the market price of any of the principal materials or parts.

To illustrate the computation of a price variance, assume that 5,000 pieces of Item 5-489 on the standard cost card for Alpac (page 547) are purchased at a unit price of $2.47. The *materials purchase price variance* is computed as follows:

	Pieces	×	Unit Cost	=	Amount
Actual quantity purchased	5,000		$2.47 actual		$12,350
Actual quantity purchased	5,000		2.50 standard		12,500
Materials purchase price variance	5,000		$(.03)		$ (150) fav.

The $150 materials purchase price variance is favorable because the actual price is less than the standard price, and $.03 expresses the unit cost difference. As an alternative, the materials purchase price variance can be recognized when the materials are used rather than when they are purchased and is then called the *materials price usage variance* (Chapter 20).

Materials Quantity Standard and Variance

Quantity or usage standards are generally developed from materials specifications prepared by the departments of engineering (mechanical, electrical, or chemical) or product design. In a small or medium-sized company, the superintendent or even the foremen will state basic specifications regarding type, quantity, and quality of materials needed and operations to be performed.

Quantity standards should be set after the most economical size, shape, and quality of the product and the results expected from the use of various kinds and grades of materials have been analyzed. The standard quantity should be increased to include allowances for acceptable levels of waste, spoilage, shrinkage, seepage, evaporation, and leakage. The determination of the percentage of spoilage or waste should be based on figures that prevail after the experimental and developmental stages of the product have been passed.

The *materials quantity variance* is computed by comparing the actual quantity of materials used with the standard quantity allowed, both priced at standard cost. The standard quantity allowed is determined by multiplying the quantity of materials that should be required to produce one unit (the standard quantity per unit) times the actual number of units produced during the period. The units produced are the equivalent units of production for the materials cost being analyzed.

The materials quantity (or usage) variance for Item 5-489, of which 3,550 pieces are used in producing 1,750 equivalent units of Alpac, is computed as follows:

	PIECES ×	UNIT COST	=	AMOUNT
Actual quantity used....................	3,550	$2.50 standard		$8,875
Standard quantity allowed.............	3,500	2.50 standard		8,750
Materials quantity variance	50	2.50 standard		$ 125 unfav.

The standard quantity allowed is the result of multiplying 1,750 units of Alpac by the standard quantity of two pieces per unit. The $125 materials quantity (or usage) variance is unfavorable because the actual quantity used exceeded the standard quantity by 50 units.

LABOR COST STANDARDS

Two standards must also be developed for direct labor costs:
1. A rate (wage or cost) standard.
2. An efficiency (time or usage) standard.

Labor Rate Standard and Variance

In many plants, the standard is based on rates established in collective bargaining agreements that define hourly wages, piece rates, and bonus differentials. Without a union contract, rates are based on the earnings rate as determined by agreement between the employee and the personnel department at the time of hiring. Since rates are generally based on definite agreements, labor rate variances are not too frequent. If they occur, they are generally due to unusual short-term conditions existing in the factory.

To assure fairness in rates paid for each operation performed, job rating has become a recognized procedure in industry. When a rate is revised or a change is authorized temporarily, it must be reported promptly to the payroll department to avoid delays, incorrect pay, and faulty reporting. Any difference between the standard and actual rates results in a *labor rate* (wage or cost) *variance*.

To illustrate the computation of the labor rate variance for Operation 2-476 on the standard cost card for Alpac (page 547), assume that 1,880 hours are worked at a rate of $6.50 per hour to produce 530 equivalent units of Alpac. The labor rate variance is computed as follows:

	TIME ×	RATE	=	AMOUNT
Actual hours worked	1,880	$6.50 actual		$12,220
Actual hours worked	1,880	6.00 standard		11,280
Labor rate variance	1,880	$ .50		$ 940 unfav.

The labor rate variance of $940 is unfavorable. The difference in terms of the rate is $.50 per hour.

Labor Efficiency Standard and Variance

Determination of labor efficiency standards is a specialized function; therefore, they are usually established by industrial engineers using time and motion studies. Standards are set in accordance with scientific methods and accepted practices. They are based on actual performance of a worker or group of workers possessing average skill and using average effort while performing manual operations or working on machines operating under normal conditions. Time factors for acceptable levels of fatigue, personal needs, and delays beyond the control of the worker are studied and included in the standard. Such allowances are an integral part of the labor standard, but time required for setting up machines, waiting, or a breakdown is included in the factory overhead standard.

The establishment of time standards requires a detailed study of manufacturing operations. Standards based on operations should be understood by supervisors and used to enhance labor efficiency. However, time standards are of limited use "where operating times are strongly influenced by factors which cannot be standardized and controlled by management or where output from highly mechanized work is a function of machine time and speed rather than of labor hours worked."[1]

When a new product or process is started, the labor efficiency standard for costing and budget development should be based on the learning curve phenomenon (Chapter 14). The learning curve may well be, at least in part, an explanation of the labor efficiency variance associated with employees assigned to existing tasks that are new to them. Labor-related factory overhead costs and perhaps materials usage might also be affected.

The *labor efficiency variance* is computed at the end of any reporting period (day, week, or month) by comparing actual hours worked with standard hours allowed, both at the standard labor rate. The standard hours allowed figure is determined by multiplying the number of direct labor hours established or predetermined to produce one unit (the standard labor hours per unit) times the actual number of units produced during the period for which the variances are being computed. The units produced are the equivalent units of production for the labor cost being analyzed.

The labor efficiency variance for Operation 2-476 is computed as follows:

[1]Walter B. McFarland, *Manpower Cost and Performance Measurement* (New York: National Association of Accountants, 1977), p. 60.

	TIME ×	RATE	=	AMOUNT
Actual hours worked	1,880	$6 standard		$11,280
Standard hours allowed	1,590	6 standard		9,540
Labor efficiency variance	290	6 standard		$ 1,740 unfav.

The standard hours allowed is the result of multiplying 530 units of Alpac by three standard hours per unit. The unfavorable labor efficiency variance of $1,740 is due to the use of 290 hours in excess of standard hours allowed.

FACTORY OVERHEAD COST STANDARDS

Procedures for establishing and using standard factory overhead rates are similar to the methods discussed in Chapters 9 and 10, dealing with the estimated direct and indirect factory overhead and its application to jobs and products. An overhead budget for rate calculation provides a budget allowance for a specific, predetermined level of activity, while a flexible budget provides allowances for various levels of activity. Both types of budgets aim for the control of factory overhead. Control is achieved by keeping actual expenses within ranges established by the budget. The maximum limit of a range is the amount set up in the flexible budget. However, for costing jobs or products it is necessary to establish a normal overhead rate based on total estimated factory overhead at normal capacity volume.

The effect of volume on overhead cost per unit is illustrated below:

Production volume (units)	80,000	90,000	100,000	110,000
Factory overhead:				
Variable	$112,000	$126,000	$140,000	$154,000
Fixed	60,000	60,000	60,000	60,000
Total	$172,000	$186,000	$200,000	$214,000
Factory overhead per unit:				
Variable	$1.40	$1.400	$1.40	$1.400
Fixed	.75	.667	.60	.545
Total unit overhead cost	$2.15	$2.067	$2.00	$1.945

The illustration indicates the basic pattern of overhead behavior. Fixed expenses remain fixed, within a normal range of activity, as volume (output) changes, but they vary per unit. The greater the number of units, the smaller the amount of fixed overhead expense per unit. Variable expenses, on the other hand, increase proportionately with each increase of volume (output) and remain fixed per unit.

This characteristic of overhead behavior is important in establishing a standard factory overhead rate. Overhead absorption is accomplished by selecting a plant capacity as the base for charging variable and fixed overhead to jobs or products.

Variable expenses should be measured and controlled at any volume by the supervisors with the aid of a flexible budget. The variable expenses in the flexible budget correspond to applied variable overhead, and *variable over-*

head variances result from a comparison of actual variable costs with the flexible budget (applied) variable factory overhead.

Fixed expenses can be absorbed fully only by operating at the volume on which the rate is based. If the base set for overhead absorption is reached, budgeted and absorbed cost figures will be identical. Since this is highly improbable, a difference occurs between budgeted fixed expenses and absorbed fixed overhead, and *fixed overhead variances* result from an analysis of this difference. For purposes of analysis, budgeted fixed overhead is used. Any difference that might occur between budgeted and actual fixed overhead becomes a part of the variable overhead variances in the methods of analysis presented in this chapter. Alternatively, this difference can be identified as a separate variance, called the *fixed spending variance*.

The variances associated with variable and fixed factory overhead permit management to measure the success or failure of its control of overhead and utilization of facilities.

The Standard Factory Overhead Rate

The *standard factory overhead rate* is a predetermined rate that is usually based on direct labor hours. Other bases may also be used, e.g., direct labor dollars or machine hours. The use of direct labor dollars, however, may cause some distortion in the variances computed, because the actual direct labor dollar figure includes any labor rate variations from the standard labor rate.

The data from the following flexible budget for Department 3, which is involved in producing Alpac, are used to illustrate the computation of the standard overhead rate and the overhead variances.

DEPARTMENT 3
MONTHLY FLEXIBLE BUDGET

	80%	90%	100%	
Capacity.....................................	80%	90%	100%	
Standard production	800	1,000	1,200	
Direct labor hours	3,200	4,000	4,800	
Variable factory overhead:				
Indirect labor	$1,600	$2,000	$2,400	$ .50 per dlh
Indirect materials	960	1,200	1,440	.30
Supplies	640	800	960	.20
Repairs	480	600	720	.15
Power and light......................	160	200	240	.05
Total variable factory overhead	$3,840	$4,800	$5,760	$1.20 per dlh
Fixed factory overhead:				
Supervisor.............................	$1,200	$1,200	$1,200	
Depreciation of machinery	700	700	700	
Insurance	250	250	250	
Property tax..........................	250	250	250	
Power and light......................	400	400	400	
Maintenance	400	400	400	
Total fixed factory overhead.....	$3,200	$3,200	$3,200	$3,200 per month
Total factory overhead	$7,040	$8,000	$8,960	$3,200 per month
				+ $1.20 per dlh

Assuming that the 90% column represents normal capacity, the standard factory overhead rate is computed as follows:

$$\frac{\text{Total factory overhead}}{\text{Direct labor hours}} = \frac{\$8,000}{4,000} = \$2 \text{ per standard direct labor hour}$$

At the 90% capacity level, the rate consists of:

$$\frac{\text{Total variable factory overhead}}{\text{Direct labor hours}} = \frac{\$4,800}{4,000} = \$1.20 \text{ variable factory overhead rate}$$

$$\frac{\text{Total fixed factory overhead}}{\text{Direct labor hours}} = \frac{\$3,200}{4,000} = .80 \text{ fixed factory overhead rate}$$

Total factory overhead rate at normal capacity .... $\underline{\$2.00}$ per standard direct labor hour

Jobs or processes are charged with costs on the basis of standard hours allowed multiplied by the standard factory overhead rate. The standard hours allowed figure is determined by multiplying the labor hours required to produce one unit (the standard labor hours per unit) times the actual number of units produced during the period. The units produced are the equivalent units of production for the departmental factory overhead cost being analyzed. At the end of each month, overhead actually incurred is compared with the expenses charged into process using the standard factory overhead rate. The difference between these two figures is called the *overall* (or *net*) *factory overhead variance*.

Factory Overhead Variances

At the end of a month, the data for Department 3 are as follows:

Actual overhead.. $7,384
Standard hours allowed for actual production .... 3,400 hours*
Actual hours used .... 3,475 hours

*850 equivalent units produced × 4 standard direct labor hours per unit of production.

The overall factory overhead variance is computed below:

Actual departmental overhead $7,384
Overhead charged to production (3,400 standard hours allowed
   × $2 standard overhead rate).. 6,800
Overall (or net) overhead variance...................................... $\underline{\$\ \ 584}$ unfav.

This unfavorable overall overhead variance needs further analysis to reveal detailed causes for the variance and to guide management toward remedial action. This analysis may be made by using (1) the two-variance method, (2) the three-variance method, or (3) the four-variance method.

Two-Variance Method. The two variances are the (1) controllable variance and (2) volume variance. The *controllable variance* is the difference between actual expenses incurred and the budget allowance based on standard hours allowed for work performed. The *volume variance* represents the difference between the budget allowance and the standard expenses charged to work in process (standard hours allowed × standard overhead rate).

Controllable Variance. The controllable variance is the responsibility of the department managers to the extent that they can exercise control over the costs to which the variances relate. It is computed as shown below:

Actual factory overhead		$7,384
Budget allowance based on standard hours allowed:		
Fixed expense budgeted	$3,200	
Variable expense (3,400 standard hours allowed ×		
$1.20 variable overhead rate)............................	4,080	7,280
Controllable variance...		$ 104 unfav.

The controllable variance consists of variable expense only and can also be computed as follows:

Actual variable expense ($7,384 actual factory overhead −	
$3,200 of fixed expense budgeted)......................................	$4,184
Variable expense for standard hours allowed	4,080
Controllable variance..	$ 104 unfav.

Volume Variance. The volume variance indicates the cost of capacity available but not utilized or not utilized efficiently and is considered the responsibility of executive and departmental management. It is computed as shown below:

Budget allowance based on standard hours allowed	$7,280
Overhead charged to production	6,800
Volume variance..	$ 480 unfav.

This variance consists of fixed expense only and can also be computed as follows:

Normal capacity hours	4,000
Standard hours allowed for actual production	3,400
Capacity hours not utilized, or not utilized efficiently	600
Volume variance (600 hours × $.80*)	$ 480 unfav.

*Fixed expense rate at normal capacity.

Three-Variance Method. The three variances are the (1) spending variance, (2) idle capacity variance, and (3) efficiency variance. The *spending variance* is the difference between actual expenses incurred and the budget allowance based on actual hours worked. The *idle capacity variance* is the difference between the budget allowance based on actual hours and actual hours worked multiplied by the standard overhead rate. These two variances are identical with the spending and idle capacity variances discussed in Chapters 9 and 10. The *efficiency variance* is the difference between actual hours worked multiplied by the standard overhead rate and the standard hours allowed times the standard overhead rate.

Spending Variance. The spending variance is the responsibility of the department manager, who is expected to keep actual expenses within the budget. It is computed as follows:

Actual factory overhead		$7,384
Budget allowance based on actual hours worked:		
Fixed expense budgeted	$3,200	
Variable expense (3,475 actual hours × $1.20 variable overhead rate)..	4,170	7,370
Spending variance...		$ 14 unfav.

The spending variance consists of variable expense only and can also be computed as follows:

Actual variable expense ($7,384 actual factory overhead − $3,200 fixed expense budgeted)..	$4,184
Allowed variable expense for actual hours	4,170
Spending variance...	$ 14 unfav.

By basing the budget allowance on actual hours instead of on standard hours allowed as shown in the controllable variance, the department manager receives a more favorable budget allowance, which reduces the variance from $104 to $14. This reduction is caused by the influence of efficiency (or, in this case, inefficiency), which is identified separately as the variable expense portion of the efficiency variance.

Idle Capacity Variance. The idle capacity variance is the responsibility of executive management, and is computed as shown below:

Budget allowance based on actual hours worked	$7,370
Actual hours (3,475) × standard overhead rate ($2).................	6,950
Idle capacity variance	$ 420 unfav.

This variance consists of fixed expense only and can also be computed as follows: (4,000 normal capacity hours − 3,475 actual hours) × $.80 fixed expense rate = $420. It indicates the amount of overhead that is either under- or overabsorbed because actual hours are either less or more than the hours on which the overhead rate was based. Department 3 operated at 86.875% of normal capacity based on actual hours.

Efficiency Variance. The efficiency variance is the responsibility of department management, and is caused by inefficiencies, inexperienced labor, changes in operations, new tools, and different types of materials. It is computed as shown below:

Actual hours (3,475) × standard overhead rate ($2).................	$6,950
Overhead charged to production	6,800
Efficiency variance...	$ 150 unfav.

This variance can also be computed as follows: (3,475 actual hours − 3,400 standard hours allowed) × $2 = $150. It consists of fixed and variable expenses and results when actual hours used are more or less than standard hours allowed. When labor hours are the basis for applying factory overhead, this variance and its cause reflect the effect of the labor efficiency variance on factory overhead. When machine hours are the basis, the variance relates to efficiency of machine usage.

Four-Variance Method. The four variances — (1) spending variance, (2) variable efficiency variance, (3) fixed efficiency variance, and (4) idle capacity variance — add to the three-variance method an analysis which divides the efficiency variance into its fixed and variable components.

Spending Variance. The spending variance is identical with that of the three-variance method, and is computed as follows:

Actual factory overhead	$7,384
Budget allowance based on actual hours worked	7,370
Spending variance	$ 14 unfav.

Variable Efficiency Variance. The variable efficiency variance is computed as follows:

Budget allowance based on actual hours worked	$7,370
Budget allowance based on standard hours allowed	7,280
Variable efficiency variance	$ 90 unfav.

This variance recognizes the difference between the 3,475 actual hours worked and the 3,400 standard (or allowed) hours for the work performed. Multiplying the difference of 75 hours times $1.20 (variable expense rate) results in $90. The sum of the spending and variable efficiency variances equals the controllable variance, $104, of the two-variance method.

Fixed Efficiency Variance. The fixed efficiency variance is computed as follows:

Actual hours (3,475) × fixed overhead rate ($.80)	$2,780
Standard hours allowed (3,400) × fixed overhead rate ($.80)	2,720
Fixed efficiency variance (75 hours × $.80)	$ 60 unfav.

When the variable efficiency variance and the fixed efficiency variance are combined, they equal the efficiency variance of the three-variance method.

Idle Capacity Variance. This variance is identical with the idle capacity variance of the three-variance method and represents the idle or unused capacity, i.e., the difference between budgeted (normal) capacity and actual capacity. It is computed as follows:

Normal capacity hours (4,000) × fixed overhead rate ($.80)	$3,200
Actual hours worked (3,475) × fixed overhead rate ($.80)	2,780
Idle capacity variance (525 hours × $.80)	$ 420 unfav.

The fixed efficiency variance and the idle capacity variance are split-offs of the $480 unfavorable volume variance of the two-variance method, which was computed by multiplying the 600 hours not utilized by the $.80 fixed overhead rate. The fixed efficiency variance indicates how effectively or ineffectively available capacity was used. In this illustration, it informs management that 525 hours otherwise available and expected to be used, costing $420 in terms of fixed expense, remained idle during the month.

Summary. Although all methods of factory overhead variance analysis are commonly used, the two-variance method seems to be favored. It should be noted that at times the methods are intermingled, and are given different titles, and involve additional analyses. A summary of the three methods described in this chapter is given on pages 558 and 559.

MIX AND YIELD VARIANCES

Basically, the establishment of a standard product cost requires the determination of price and quantity standards. In many industries, particularly of the process type, materials mix and materials yield play significant parts in the final product cost, in cost reduction, and in profit improvement.

Materials specification standards are generally set up for various grades of materials and types of secondary materials. In most cases, specifications are based on laboratory or engineering tests. Comparative costs of various grades of materials are used to arrive at a satisfactory materials mix, and changes are often made when it seems possible to use less costly grades of materials or substitute materials. In addition, a substantial cost reduction might be achieved through the improvement of the yield of good product units in the factory. At times, trade offs may occur; e.g., a cost saving resulting from use of a less costly grade of materials may result in a poorer yield, or vice versa. A variance analysis program identifying and evaluating the nature, magnitude, and causes of mix and yield variances is an aid to operating management.

Mix Variance

After the standard specification has been established, a variance representing the difference between the standard cost of formula materials and the standard cost of the materials actually used can be calculated. This variance is generally recognized as a *mix* (or *blend*) *variance*, which is the result of mixing basic materials in a ratio different from standard materials specifications. In a woolen mill, for instance, the standard proportions of the grades of wool for each yarn number are reflected in the standard blend cost. Any difference between the actual wool used and the standard blend results in a blend or mix variance.

Industries like textiles, rubber, and chemicals, whose products must possess certain chemical or physical qualities, find it quite feasible and economical to apply different combinations of basic materials and still achieve a perfect product. In cotton fabrics, it is common to mix cotton from many parts of the world with the hope that the new mix and its cost will contribute to improved profits. In many cases, the new mix is accompanied by either a favorable or unfavorable yield of the final product. Such a situation may make it difficult to judge correctly the origin of the variances. A favorable mix variance, for instance, may be offset by an unfavorable yield variance, or vice

SUMMARY OF FACTORY OVERHEAD

METHOD	(1) ACTUAL FACTORY OVERHEAD	(2) BUDGET ALLOWANCE FOR FACTORY OVERHEAD (ACTUAL HOURS WORKED)	(3) BUDGET ALLOWANCE FOR FACTORY OVERHEAD (STANDARD HOURS ALLOWED)	(4) ACTUAL HOURS × STANDARD OVERHEAD RATE*
Two-Variance Method	$7,384		$7,280	
Three-Variance Method	$7,384	$7,370		$6,950
Four-Variance Method	$7,384	$7,370	$7,280	$6,950

*3,475 actual hours worked × $2 standard factory overhead rate.

versa. Thus, any apparent advantage created by one may be canceled out by the other.

Yield Variance

Yield can be defined as the amount of prime product manufactured from a given amount of materials. The *yield variance* is the result of obtaining a yield different from the one expected on the basis of input. In a gray iron foundry, the materials charged into the cupola include coke, flux material, and all alloy materials and innoculants used as ladle additions. Cupola operation involves the application of heat to melt the metal as well as a complex thermochemical reaction. This process results in yield, meaning good castings made from the melted metal, expressed as a percent of total metal charged.

In sugar refining, a normal loss of yield develops because, on the average, it takes approximately 102.5 pounds of sucrose in raw sugar form to produce 100 pounds of sucrose in refined sugars. Part of this sucrose emerges as black-strap molasses, but a small percentage is completely lost.

In the canning industry, it is customary to estimate the expected yield of grades per ton of fruit purchased or delivered to the plant. The actual yield

VARIANCE ANALYSIS METHODS

(5)

FACTORY OVERHEAD CHARGED TO PRODUCTION**	VARIANCES FOR EACH METHOD		OVERALL (OR NET) FACTORY OVERHEAD VARIANCE (UNFAVORABLE)
$6,800	Controllable variance (Col. 1 − Col. 3)	$104	$584
	Volume variance (Col. 3 − Col. 5)	$480	
$6,800	Spending variance (Col. 1 − Col. 2)	$ 14	$584
	Idle capacity variance (Col. 2 − Col. 4)	$420	
	Efficiency variance (Col. 4 − Col. 5) ...	$150	
$6,800	Spending variance (Col. 1 − Col. 2)	$ 14	$584
	Variable efficiency variance (Col. 2 − Col. 3)..	$ 90	
	Fixed efficiency variance***	$ 60	
	Idle capacity variance****	$420	

**3,400 standard hours allowed × $2 standard factory overhead rate.
***(3,475 actual hours worked − 3,400 standard hours allowed) × $.80 fixed factory overhead rate.
****(4,000 normal capacity hours − 3,475 actual hours worked) × $.80 fixed factory overhead rate. This variance can also be computed by subtracting Column 4 from Column 2.

should be compared to the one expected and should be evaluated in terms of cost. If the actual yield deviates from predetermined percentages, cost and profit will differ.

Since the final product cost contains not only materials but also labor and factory overhead, a yield variance for labor and factory overhead should be determined when the product is finished. The actual quantities resulting from the processes are multiplied by the standard cost, which includes all three cost elements. A labor yield variance must be looked upon as the result of the quality and/or quantity of the materials handled, while the factory overhead yield variance is due to the greater or smaller number of hours worked. It should be noted that the overhead yield variance may have a significant effect on the amount of over- or underabsorbed factory overhead.

To illustrate the calculation of mix and yield variances, assume that the Springmint Company, a manufacturer of chewing gum, uses a standard cost system. Standard product and cost specifications for 1,000 lbs. of chewing gum are as follows:

Illustration of Variances

	QUANTITY	×	PRICE	=	COST
Gum base ..	800		$.25 per lb.		$200
Corn syrup	200		.40		80
Sugar........	200		.10		20
Input	1,200 lbs.				$300; $300 ÷ 1,200 lbs. = $.25 per lb.*
Output ...	1,000 lbs.				$300; $300 ÷ 1,000 lbs. = $.30 per lb.*

*Weighted averages.

The production of 1,000 lbs. of chewing gum requires 1, 200 lbs. of raw materials. Hence, the expected yield is 1,000 lbs. ÷ 1,200 lbs., or $^5/_6$ of input.

Materials records indicate:

	BEGINNING INVENTORY	PURCHASES IN JANUARY	ENDING INVENTORY
Gum base	10,000 lbs.	162,000 lbs. @ $.24	15,000 lbs.
Corn syrup.............................	12,000	30,000 @ .42	4,000
Sugar.....................................	15,000	32,000 @ .11	11,000

To convert 1,200 lbs. of raw materials into 1,000 lbs. of finished product requires 20 hours at $6 per hour, or $.12 per lb. of finished product. Actual direct labor hours and cost for January are 3,800 hours at $23,104.

Factory overhead is applied on a direct labor hour basis at a rate of $5 per hour ($3 fixed, $2 variable), or $.10 per lb. of finished product. Normal overhead is $20,000 with 4,000 direct labor hours. Actual overhead for the month is $22,000. Actual finished production for January is 200,000 lbs.

The standard cost per pound of finished chewing gum is:

Materials	$.30 per lb.
Labor	.12
Factory overhead	.10
	$.52 per lb.

Materials Variances. The materials variances for January consist of (1) price variances, (2) a mix variance, (3) a yield variance, and (4) quantity variances. The company computes the materials price variances as follows, using the procedure illustrated on page 548, and recognizes these variances when the materials are purchased.

MATERIAL	QUANTITY	ACTUAL PRICE	STANDARD PRICE	UNIT PRICE VARIANCE	PRICE VARIANCE
Gum base	162,000	$.24	$.25	$(.01)	$(1,620)
Corn syrup.............	30,000	.42	.40	.02	600
Sugar....................	32,000	.11	.10	.01	320
Net materials purchase price variance					$ (700) fav.

The materials mix variance results from combining materials in a ratio different from the standard materials specifications. It is computed as follows:

Actual quantities at individual standard materials costs:

Gum base   —   157,000 lbs. @ $.25............................. $39,250
Corn syrup —   38,000   @ $.40............................. 15,200
Sugar   —   36,000   @ $.10............................. 3,600 $58,050
            ───────
            231,000 lbs.

Actual quantity at weighted average of standard materials
cost input (231,000 lbs. × $.25) 57,750*

Materials mix variance .... $ 300   unfav.

*This figure can also be determined by multiplying the standard (expected) output from actual
input (192,500 lbs., or ⁵/₆ of 231,000 lbs.) by $.30 weighted average of standard materials cost
output.

The yield variance is computed as follows:

Actual quantity at standard materials cost $57,750
Actual output quantity at standard materials cost (200,000 lbs. ×
$.30) 60,000*

Materials yield variance .... $(2,250) fav.

*This figure can also be determined by multiplying the input needed to produce 200,000 lbs.
(240,000 lbs.) by $.25.

The yield variance occurred because the actual production of 200,000 lbs.
exceeded the expected output of 192,500 lbs. (⁵/₆ of 231,000 lbs.) by 7,500 lbs.
The yield difference multiplied by the standard weighted materials cost of $.30
per output pound equals the favorable yield variance of $2,250.

The materials quantity variance can be computed for each item as follows, using the procedure illustrated on page 549.

		UNIT	×	STANDARD UNIT COST	=	AMOUNT	MATERIALS QUANTITY VARIANCE
Gum base:	Actual quantity used	157,000 lbs.		$.25		$39,250	
	Standard quantity allowed	160,000 lbs.*		.25		40,000	$ (750) fav.
Corn syrup:	Actual quantity used	38,000 lbs.		$.40		$15,200	
	Standard quantity allowed	40,000 lbs.**		.40		16,000	(800) fav.
Sugar:	Actual quantity used	36,000 lbs.		$.10		$ 3,600	
	Standard quantity allowed	40,000 lbs.***		.10		4,000	(400) fav.
Total materials quantity variance							$(1,950) fav.

*An output of 200,000 lbs. should require an input of 240,000 lbs., with a standard yield of 1,000 lbs. output for each
1,200 lbs. input. Then the 240,000 lbs. × (800 lbs. ÷ 1, 200 lbs.) gum base portion of the formula = 160,000 lbs.
**The 240,000 lbs. × (200 lbs. ÷ 1,200 lbs.) corn syrup portion of the formula = 40,000 lbs.
***The 240,000 lbs. × (200 lbs. ÷ 1,200 lbs.) sugar portion of the formula = 40,000 lbs.

The total materials quantity variance can also be determined by comparing actual quantities at standard prices, $58,050 ($39,250 + $15,200 + $3,600),
to actual output quantity at standard materials cost, $60,000 (200,000 lbs. ×
$.30) for a total favorable variance of $1,950. The mix and yield variances
separate the materials quantity variance into two parts:

Materials mix variance .... $ 300   unfav.
Materials yield variance....................... (2,250) fav.
Materials quantity variance .... $(1,950) fav.

The influence of individual raw materials on the total materials mix variance can be computed in the following manner:

Material	Actual Quantity	Standard Formula	× Total Actual Quantity =	Actual Quantity Using Standard Formula	Quantity Variation ×	Standard Unit Price	Materials Mix = Variance
Gum base	157,000 lbs.	$\frac{800}{1,200}$	231,000 lbs.	154,000 lbs.	3,000 lbs.	$.25	$750
Corn syrup...	38,000	$\frac{200}{1,200}$	231,000	38,500	(500)	.40	(200)
Sugar	36,000	$\frac{200}{1,200}$	231,000	38,500	(2,500)	.10	(250)
	231,000 lbs.			231,000 lbs.	–0–		$300

Labor Variances. The expected output of 192,500 lbs. of chewing gum should require 3,850 standard labor hours (20 hours per thousand pounds of chewing gum produced). Similarly, the actual output of 200,000 lbs. of chewing gum should require 4,000 standard labor hours.

The labor variances are the (1) rate variance, (2) efficiency variance, and (3) yield variance. The computation of these variances for January is as follows:

Actual payroll...	$23,104
Actual hours (3,800) × standard labor rate ($6)	22,800
Labor rate variance	$ 304 unfav.
Actual hours × standard labor rate	$22,800
Standard hours allowed for expected output (3,850) × standard labor rate ($6)...	23,100
Labor efficiency variance..	$ (300) fav.
Standard hours allowed for expected output × standard labor rate	$23,100
Standard hours allowed for actual output (4,000) × standard labor rate ($6)...	24,000
Labor yield variance...	$ (900) fav.

The labor rate variance is computed as shown on page 550. The traditional labor efficiency variance, as illustrated on page 550, is computed as follows:

	Time	× Rate =	Amount
Actual hours worked................................	3,800	$6	$22,800
Standard hours allowed	4,000	6	24,000
Labor efficiency variance.........................	(200)	6	$(1,200) fav.

The labor yield variance identifies the portion of the labor efficiency variance attributable to obtaining an unfavorable or, as in this illustration, a favorable yield [(3,850 standard hours allowed for expected output − 4,000 standard hours allowed for actual output) × $6 standard labor rate = $900].

The favorable labor efficiency variance of $300 is the portion of the traditional labor efficiency variance that is attributable to factors other than yield. The sum of the two variances, $900 plus $300, equals the $1,200 traditional labor efficiency variance.

Factory Overhead Variances. A yield variance can also be computed for factory overhead. When the three-variance method is used, the overhead variances consist of the (1) spending variance, (2) idle capacity variance, (3) efficiency variance, and (4) yield variance. These variances are computed as follows:

THREE-VARIANCE METHOD ADAPTED TO COMPUTE A YIELD VARIANCE

Actual factory overhead		$22,000	
Budget allowance (based on actual hours):			
Fixed expense budgeted	$12,000		
Variable expense (3,800 hours × $2)	7,600	19,600	
Spending variance		$ 2,400	unfav.
Budget allowance (based on actual hours)		$19,600	
Actual hours (3,800) × standard overhead rate ($5)..................		19,000	
Idle capacity variance		$ 600	unfav.
Actual hours × standard overhead rate.....................................		$19,000	
Standard hours allowed for expected output (3,850) × standard overhead rate ($5)		19,250	
Overhead efficiency variance..		$ (250)	fav.
Standard hours allowed for expected output × standard overhead rate		$19,250	
Standard hours allowed for actual output (4,000) × standard overhead rate ($5)		20,000	
Overhead yield variance...		$ (750)	fav.

The spending and idle capacity variances are computed in the same manner as discussed on page 555. The overhead efficiency variance and the overhead yield variance, when combined, equal the efficiency variance discussed earlier in this chapter. The overhead yield variance measures that portion of the total overhead variance resulting from a favorable yield [(3,850 hours − 4,000 hours) × $5 = $750].

When the two-variance method is used, the overhead variances are the (1) controllable variance, (2) volume variance, and (3) yield variance. These variances are computed as shown on page 564.

The $2,300 unfavorable controllable variance equals the unfavorable spending variance, $2,400, combined with the $100 variable part of the favorable overhead efficiency variance [(3,800 hours − 3,850 hours) × $2]. The $450 unfavorable overhead volume variance equals the unfavorable idle capacity variance, $600, combined with the $150 fixed part of the favorable overhead efficiency variance [(3,800 hours − 3,850 hours) × $3].

TWO-VARIANCE METHOD ADAPTED TO COMPUTE A YIELD VARIANCE

Actual factory overhead		$22,000
Budget allowance (based on standard hours allowed for expected output):		
Fixed expense budgeted	$12,000	
Variable expense (3,850 hours × $2)	7,700	19,700
Controllable variance		$ 2,300 unfav.
Budget allowance (based on standard hours allowed for expected output)		$19,700
Standard hours allowed for expected output (3,850) × standard overhead rate ($5)		19,250
Overhead volume variance..		$ 450 unfav.
Standard hours allowed for expected output × standard overhead rate		$19,250
Standard hours allowed for actual output (4,000) × standard overhead rate ($5)		20,000
Overhead yield variance		$ (750) fav.

The favorable overhead yield variance is the same as for the three-variance method and can be viewed as consisting of $300 variable cost [(3,850 standard hours allowed for expected output − 4,000 standard hours allowed for actual output) × $2], and $450 fixed cost [(3,850 − 4,000) × $3].

MANAGERIAL USEFULNESS OF VARIANCE ANALYSIS

Costs of production are affected by internal factors over which management has a large degree of control. An important job of executive management is to help the members of various management levels understand that all of them are part of the management team. Standard costs and their variances are an aid to keeping management informed of the effectiveness of production effort as well as that of the supervisory personnel.

Supervisors who often handle two thirds to three fourths of the dollar cost of the product are made directly responsible for the variances which, as the chapter discussion indicates, show up as materials variances (price, quantity, mix, and yield) or as direct labor variances (rate and efficiency). Materials and labor variances can be computed for each materials item, for each labor operation, and for each worker. Factory overhead variances (spending, controllable, idle capacity, volume, and efficiency) indicate the failures or successes of the control of variable and fixed overhead expenses in each department.

Variances are not ends in themselves but springboards for further analysis, investigation, and action. Variances also permit the supervisory personnel to defend themselves and their employees against failures that were not their fault. A variance provides the yardstick to measure the fairness of the standard, allowing management to redirect its effort and to make reasonable adjustments. Action to eliminate the causes of undesirable variances and to encourage and reward desired performance lies in the field of management, but supervisory and operating personnel rely on the accounting information system for facts which facilitate intelligent action toward the control of costs.

DISCUSSION QUESTIONS

1. (a) Define standard costs.
   (b) Name some advantages of a standard cost system.

2. A team of management consultants and company executives concluded that a standard cost installation was a desirable vehicle for accomplishing the objectives of a progressive management. State some uses of standard costs that can be associated with the above decision.

3. Does a standard cost system increase or decrease the amount of accounting and clerical effort and expense required to prepare cost reports and financial statements?

4. Is a standard cost system equally applicable to job order costing and process costing?

5. A conference speaker discussing budgeted and standard costs made the following statement: "Budgets and standards are not the same thing. They have different purposes and are set up and used in different ways; yet a specific relationship exists between them."
   (a) Identify distinctions or differences between budgets and standards.
   (b) Identify similarities between budgets and standards.

6. The use of standard costs in pricing and budgeting is quite valuable since decisions in the fields of pricing and budgetary planning are made before the costs under consideration are incurred. Discuss.

7. Explain how materials, labor, and factory overhead standards are set, including the types of people involved and the methods used.

8. What types of variances are computed for materials, labor, and factory overhead?

9. In a paper mill, materials specification standards are set up for various grades of pulp and secondary furnish (waste paper) for each grade and kind of paper produced. Yet at regular intervals the cost accountant is able to determine a materials mix variance. Why does a mix variance occur?

10. How does the calculation of a mix variance differ from that of a quantity variance?

11. A cost standard in a process industry is often based on an assumed yield rate. Any difference in actual yield from standard yield will produce a yield variance. Express this variance in formula form.

12. Select the answer which best completes the statement:
   (a) A purpose of standard costing is to: (1) determine the break-even production level; (2) control costs; (3) eliminate the need for subjective decisions by management; (4) allocate cost more accurately.
   (b) A company employing very tight (theoretical) standards in a standard cost system should expect that: (1) a large incentive bonus will be paid; (2) most variances will be unfavorable; (3) employees will be strongly motivated to attain the standards; (4) costs will be controlled better than if lower standards were used.

(c) Of the different types of standards listed below, the one which best describes labor costs that should be incurred under forthcoming efficient operating conditions is: (1) ideal; (2) basic; (3) maximum efficiency; (4) normal.

(d) In standard costing, standard hours allowed is a means of measuring: (1) standard output at standard hours; (2) actual output at standard hours; (3) standard output at actual hours; (4) actual output at actual hours.

(e) In preparing the cost report at standard for process costing: (1) equivalent units are *not* used; (2) equivalent units are computed using an approach that ignores inventories; (3) the actual equivalent units are multiplied by the standard cost per unit; (4) the standard equivalent units are multiplied by the actual cost per unit.

(f) In a standard cost system, the materials purchase price variance is obtained by multiplying the: (1) actual price by the difference between actual quantity purchased and standard quantity allowed; (2) actual quantity purchased by the difference between actual price and standard price; (3) standard price by the difference between standard quantity purchased and standard quantity allowed; (4) standard quantity purchased by the difference between actual price and standard price.

(g) A favorable labor efficiency variance indicates: (1) the average wage rate paid was less than the standard rate; (2) the standard labor hours allowed for the units produced were greater than actual labor hours used; (3) the actual total labor cost incurred was less than the standard labor cost allowed for the units produced; (4) the number of units produced was less than the number of units budgeted for the period.

(h) Given below are notations and their respective meanings:
   AH = Actual hours
   SHA = Standard hours allowed for actual production
   AR = Actual rate
   SR = Standard rate
The formula that represents the calculation of the labor efficiency variance is: (1) SR × (AH − SHA); (2) AR × (AH − SHA); (3) AH × (AR − SR); (4) SHA × (AR − SR).

(i) The standard cost variance representing the difference between actual factory overhead incurred and budgeted factory overhead based on actual hours worked is the: (1) volume variance; (2) spending variance; (3) efficiency variance; (4) quantity variance.

(j) The fixed portion of the standard factory overhead application rate is a function of a predetermined "normal" activity level. If standard hours allowed for good output equal this "normal" activity level for a given period, the volume variance will be: (1) zero; (2) favorable; (3) unfavorable; (4) either favorable or unfavorable, depending on the budgeted overhead.

(AICPA adapted)

EXERCISES

Whenever variances are required in the following exercises, indicate whether they are favorable or unfavorable.

1. Materials variance analysis. The Schlosser Lawn Furniture Company uses 12 meters of aluminum pipe at $.80 per meter as standard for the production of its Type A lawn chair. During one month's operations, 100 000 meters of the pipe were purchased at $.78 a meter, and 7,200 chairs were produced using 87 300 meters of pipe. The materials price variance is recognized when materials are purchased.

Required: The materials price and quantity variances.

2. Materials variance analysis. The standard price for Material 3-291 is $3.65 per liter. During November, 2 000 liters were purchased at $3.60 per liter. The quantity of Material 3-291 issued during the month was 1 775 liters and the quantity allowed for November production was 1 825 liters.

Required: Materials price variance, assuming that:
(1) It is recorded at the time of purchase.
(2) It is recorded at the time of issue.

3. Labor variance analysis. The processing of a product requires a standard of .8 direct labor hours per unit for Operation 4-802 at a standard wage rate of $6.75 per hour. The 2,000 units actually required 1,580 direct labor hours at a cost of $6.90 per hour.

Required: The labor rate and efficiency variances.

4. Factory overhead variance analysis. The Osage Company uses a standard cost system. The factory overhead standard rate per direct labor hour is:

$$\text{Fixed:} \quad \frac{\$4,500}{5,000 \text{ hours}} = \$ \ .90$$

$$\text{Variable:} \quad \frac{\$7,500}{5,000 \text{ hours}} = \frac{1.50}{\$2.40}$$

For October, actual factory overhead was $11,000, actual labor hours worked were 4,400, and the standard hours allowed for actual production were 4,500.

Required: Factory overhead variance analysis using the two-, three-, and four-variance methods.

5. Actual hours worked; standard hours allowed. The following information relates to the Finishing Department of Bourne Company for the fourth quarter:

Total actual overhead....................................$178,500
Budget allowance formula...........................$110,000 plus $.50 per direct labor hour
Predetermined factory overhead rate..........$1.50 per direct labor hour
Spending variance...$8,000 unfavorable
Efficiency variance ....$9,000 unfavorable

The total factory overhead variance is divided into three variances — spending, idle capacity, and efficiency.

Required:
(1) Actual direct labor hours worked in the Finishing Department during the fourth quarter.
(2) Standard direct labor hours allowed for production in the Finishing Department during the fourth quarter.

(AICPA adapted)

6. Factory overhead controllable and volume variances. The following data are available:

	PRODUCT A	PRODUCT B
Standard cost per direct labor hour:		
Fixed factory overhead..	$1.00	$1.00
Variable factory overhead	1.50	2.00
Actual data:		
Sales..	10,000 units	12,000 units
Production...	8,000 units	14,000 units

Each product unit requires two hours of direct labor when operating at standard; fixed factory overhead was budgeted at $40,000; actual factory overhead was $125,000.

Required:
  (1) Factory overhead controllable and volume variances.
  (2) Additional information required to compute factory overhead variances using the three- and four-variance methods.

7. Factory overhead variance analysis. The normal capacity of a plant is 20,000 direct labor hours per month. At normal capacity, the budgeted factory overhead is $2.10 per direct labor hour, consisting of $12,000 fixed expense and $1.50 per hour variable expense. During June, the plant operated 18,000 direct labor hours, with actual factory overhead of $40,000. The standard for the capacity attained is 17,500 hours.

Required: An analysis of factory overhead using the two-, three-, and four-variance methods.

8. Variance analysis: materials, labor, factory overhead. The DeVries Company has a budgeted normal monthly capacity of 10,000 labor hours, with a standard production of 8,000 units at this capacity. Standard costs are:

Materials...2 kilograms @ $.50	
Labor...$9 per hour	
Factory overhead at normal capacity:	
Fixed expense $5,000	
Variable expense..$1.50 per labor hour	

During May, actual factory overhead totaled $17,550 and 9,000 labor hours cost $76,500. During the month, 7,000 units were produced using 14 400 kg of materials at a cost of $.51 per kg.

Required: Two variances for materials, two variances for labor, and variances for factory overhead, using the two-, three-, and four-variance methods.

9. Variance analysis: materials, labor, and factory overhead; process costing. The Redman Company manufactures a product whose standard unit cost is as follows:

Direct materials: 24 kilograms (kg) @ $3.00	$ 72.00
Direct labor: 6 hours @ $6.50	39.00
Factory overhead: 6 hours @ $.75...	4.50
Total unit standard cost...	$115.50

The factory overhead was based on the following flexible budget, in which 90% is normal capacity.

	80%	90%	100%
Hours (direct labor)	40,000	45,000	50,000
Variable expenses	$20,000	$22,500	$25,000
Fixed expenses...	11,250	11,250	11,250
Total factory overhead	$31,250	$33,750	$36,250

Actual data for November:

  Planned production, 7,500 units.
  Materials put into production, 192 410 kg @ $3.04 (average cost).
  Direct labor, 46,830 hours @ $6.60 average labor cost.
  Actual factory overhead, $36,340.

Other data:

  Beginning inventory, work in process, 80 units, all materials, 50% converted.
  Ending inventory, work in process, 100 units, all materials, 50% converted.
  Started in process during November, 7,850 units.

Required: A variance analysis of (1) direct materials, (2) direct labor cost, and (3) factory overhead (two-variance method).

10. Price, mix, and yield variances. Malmuta Company uses a standard cost system. The standard cost card for one of its products shows the following materials standards:

MATERIAL	POUNDS	×	STANDARD PRICE PER POUND	=	AMOUNT
A	20		.70		$14
B	5		.40		2
C	25		.20		5
Total materials cost per unit...					$21

The standard 50 lb. mix cost per lb. is $.42 ($21 ÷ 50 lbs.). The standard mix should produce 40 lbs. of finished product, and the standard cost of finished product per lb. is $.525 ($21 ÷ 40 lbs.).

Materials of 500,000 lbs. were used as follows:

Material A...230,000 lbs. @ $.80		
Material B... 50,000 @ $.35		
Material C...220,000 @ $.25		

The output of the finished product was 390,000 lbs.

Required: Product analysis showing materials price, mix, and yield variances.

11. Price, mix, and yield variances. Cordell Chemical, Inc., produces Petrochloronal, using the following standard proportions and costs of materials:

	KILOGRAMS	COST PER KILOGRAM	AMOUNT
Material A...	50	$5.00	$250.00
Material B...	40	6.00	240.00
Material C...	60	3.00	180.00
	150	4.4667	$670.00
Standard shrinkage (33⅓%)	50		
Net weight and cost	100	6.70	$670.00

A recent production run yielding 100 output kilograms required an input of:

	KILOGRAMS	COST PER KILOGRAM
Material A...	40	$5.15
Material B...	50	6.00
Material C...	65	2.80

Required: Materials price, mix, and yield variances.

12. Price, mix, and yield variances. The standard mix for producing 8,000 bottles of Product X is:

Material A: 1 000 liters @ $.10
Material B: 2 000 @ $.40

During May, 10,000 bottles of Product X were produced from an input of:

Material A: 1 500 liters @ $.11
Material B: 3 300 @ $.37

Required: Materials price, mix, and yield variances for May.

13. Price, mix, and yield variances. The standard product mix for making 12,500 tubes of liquid solder is:

Material A: 1 500 kilograms @ $.06..	$ 90	
Material B: 625 @ .40..	250	
Material C: 1 000 @ .25..	250	

During April, 77,500 tubes of solder were produced from an input of:

Material A: 8 750 kilograms @ $.056..	$ 490	
Material B: 3 750 @ .380..	1,425	
Material C: 6 250 @ .280..	1,750	

Required: Materials price, mix, and yield variances, including an analysis of the portion of the mix variance attributable to each material.

PROBLEMS

Whenever variances are required in the following problems, indicate whether they are favorable or unfavorable.

19-1. Standard cost sheet; labor variance analysis. Olano, Inc., plans to sell its new skin care lotion, Lanosof, in a 4-ounce bottle at a suggested retail price of $1. Cost and production studies show these standard costs:

Container:

ITEM NO.	DESCRIPTION	COST	ALLOWANCE FOR WASTE AND BREAKAGE
2147	4-oz. bottle	$5.75 per gross	2%
315	Label	3.30 per 1,000	4%

Materials:

ITEM NO.	DESCRIPTION	COST	QUANTITY USED PER 125 GALLON BATCH*
4247	Compound 34A	$40 per 100 lbs.	70 lbs.
3126	Alcohol and glycerin	40 per 100 lbs.	68
4136B	Perfume oil		4

*One gallon contains 128 oz.

Standard costs of a 90 lb. batch of perfume oil are as follows:

Ingredients	$2,169.95
Direct labor: 4.4 hours @ $9.12	40.13
Factory overhead: $7.50 per batch plus $1.95 per standard labor hour.	

Allowance for lost materials:

Allow 5% of standard materials cost for overfilling, waste, and breakage.

Direct labor per gross:

Compounding	0.15 hours	@ $7.60
Filling and packing	1.00	@ $7.00

Factory Overhead:

Compounding .... $3.00 per standard labor hour
Filling and packing .... $1.75 per standard labor hour plus $.95 per gross

Required:

(1) A standard cost sheet for one gross of this product, arranging the data under the five subheadings listed above. (Calculations should be made to the nearest cent per gross.)

(2) An analysis of the labor variance from standard, assuming that the company expected to produce 1,000 gross of Lanosof Lotion in its first week of production, but actually produced only 850 gross, and its direct labor cost for 825 hours of filling and packing was $5,871.

(AICPA adapted)

19-2. Variance analysis. On May 1, Bovar Company began the manufacture of a new mechanical device known as "Dandy." The company installed a standard cost system in accounting for manufacturing costs. The standard costs for a unit of Dandy are:

Materials: 6 lbs. at $1 per lb.	$ 6.00
Direct labor: 1 hour at $4 per hour...	4.00
Factory overhead: 75% of direct labor cost	3.00
	$13.00

The following data were obtained from Bovar's records for May:

Actual production of Dandy	4,000 units
Units sold of Dandy..	2,500
Sales..	$50,000
Purchases (26,000 pounds)	27,300

Materials price variance (applicable to May purchases)	$1,300 unfav.
Materials quantity variance...	1,000 unfav.
Direct labor rate variance...	760 unfav.
Direct labor efficiency variance..	800 fav.
Factory overhead total variance	500 unfav.

Required:
(1) Standard quantity of materials allowed (in pounds).
(2) Actual quantity of materials used (in pounds).
(3) Standard hours allowed.
(4) Actual hours worked.
(5) Actual direct labor rate.
(6) Actual total factory overhead.   (AICPA adapted)

19-3. Variance analysis — materials, labor, and factory overhead. The Organet Stamping Company manufactures a variety of products made of plastic and aluminum components. During the winter months, substantially all of the production capacity is devoted to the production of lawn sprinklers for the following spring and summer. Other products are manufactured during the remainder of the year. Because a variety of products are manufactured throughout the year, factory activity is measured by production labor hours rather than units of product.

Production and sales volume have grown steadily for the past several years as can be seen from the following schedule of standard production labor content of annual output:

YEAR	HOURS
19A..	26,000
19B..	28,000
19C..	27,000
19D..	30,000
19E..	32,000

The company has developed standard costs for its several products, setting the costs for each year in the preceding October. The standard cost of a sprinkler for 19F is $2.50, computed as follows:

Direct materials:	
Aluminum: .2 lb. @ $.40..	$ .08
Plastic: 1.0 lb. @ $.38...	.38
Production labor: .3 hr. @ $4.00	1.20
Factory overhead (calculated using 30,000 annual production labor hours as normal capacity):	
Variable: .3 hr. @ $1.60..	.48
Fixed: .3 hr. @ $1.20	.36
Total	$2.50

During February 19F, 8,500 good sprinklers were manufactured. Due to plastic shortages, the purchasing agent had to purchase lower grade plastic than called for in the standards, causing an increase in the number of sprinklers rejected by quality control. The following costs were incurred:

Materials requisitioned for production:	
Aluminum: 1,900 lbs. @ $.40	$ 760
Plastic:	
Regular grade: 6,000 lbs. @ $.38...	2,280
Low grade: 3,500 lbs. @ $.38..	1,330
Production labor:	
Straight time: 2,300 hrs. @ $4.00	9,200
Overtime: 400 hrs. @ $6.00...	2,400
Factory overhead:	
Variable	5,200
Fixed...	3,100
Cost charged to production..	$24,270

Materials price variations are not charged to production but to a materials price variance account when the invoice is entered. All materials are carried in inventory at standard prices. Materials purchases for February were:

Aluminum: 1,800 lbs. @ $.48		$ 864
Plastic:		
Regular grade: 3,000 lbs. @ $.50		1,500
Low grade: 6,000 lbs. @ $.29		1,740

Required: Two variances each for materials, production labor, and factory overhead.

(CMA adapted)

19-4. Equivalent production and standard costing. The standard cost card for Trico Company's product is:

Materials: 7 liters @ $.50	$3.50
Labor: ½ hr. @ $6.00	3.00
Variable factory overhead: ½ hr. @ $2.00	1.00
Fixed factory overhead: ½ hr. @ $4.00	2.00
Standard product cost per unit	$9.50

Data for November:

(a) 1,000 units (40% converted) were in process at the beginning of the month.
　　5,050 units were started during the month.
　　5,000 units were transferred to finished goods.
　　800 units (25% converted) were in process at the end of the month.
(b) Materials are all added at the beginning of the process. Conversion costs are incurred evenly throughout the process. Inspection takes place when the units are 80% converted. Under normal conditions, no spoilage should occur.
(c) 40 000 liters of materials were purchased for $19,200 and were charged to inventory at standard cost.
(d) 37 000 liters of materials were issued to production.
(e) Direct labor payroll was $15,600 for 2,400 hours.
(f) Actual factory overhead costs were:

Indirect labor (variable)		$ 4,000
Supervision		4,000
Depreciation (based on time)		2,500
Supplies		1,000
Heat, light, and power (variable)	$ 300	
(fixed)	1,200	1,500
Property tax		200
Insurance		500
		$13,700

(g) Marketing and administrative expenses were: variable, $1.00 per unit sold; fixed, $13,500.
(h) Normal output for a month is 4,000 units.

Required:
(1) November equivalent production for materials and for conversion costs.
(2) Standard cost of:
　　(a) Units transferred to finished goods.
　　(b) Abnormal spoilage.
　　(c) Ending inventory of work in process.
(3) Materials price and quantity variances.
(4) Labor rate and efficiency variances.
(5) Factory overhead variances, using the four-variance method.　　　　(CGAA adapted)

19-5. Standard process costing: cost of production report at standard; variance analysis. The Ritter Company uses a standard process costing system in accounting for its one product, which is produced in one department. All materials are added at the beginning of the process. Inspection takes place at the end of the process, and any spoiled units revealed by inspection are considered abnormal and completed as to all cost elements.

Standard cost per unit:

Materials: 3 square meters @ $.60	$1.80
Direct labor: ¼ hour @ $10.00	2.50
Variable factory overhead: ¼ hour @ $2.00	.50
Fixed factory overhead: ¼ hour @ $2.80	.70
Total	$5.50

Normal capacity is 8,750 direct labor hours per month.
Actual data for November:
   (a) Beginning work in process inventory — 5,000 units (40% converted).
   (b) Started in process during the month — 30,000 units.
   (c) Spoiled during November — 1,000 units.
   (d) Ending work in process inventory — 2,000 units (80% converted).
   (e) Actual costs incurred:

Materials purchased	100 000 square meters @ $.64, recorded at standard cost
Materials used	92 000 square meters
Direct labor	8,000 hours @ $10.60
Variable factory overhead	$17,000
Fixed factory overhead	$25,000

Required:
   (1) Cost of production report, at standard, for November.
   (2) Two variances each for materials and direct labor and three for factory overhead.

(CGAA adapted)

19-6. Variance analysis; unit manufacturing cost. Edgmand Company manufactures a fuel additive with a stable sales price of $40 per drum. Since the company lost a government contract, it has been producing and selling 80,000 drums per month (50% of normal capacity). For the coming fiscal year, management expects to increase production to 140,000 drums per month.
   The following facts about the company's operations are available:

(a) Standard costs per drum of product manufactured:

Materials:	
8 gallons of Miracle Mix @ $2	$16
1 empty drum	1
	$17
Direct labor — 1 hour	$ 5
Factory overhead	$ 6

(b) Costs and expenses during September:

Miracle Mix:
   500,000 gallons purchased @ $950,000; 650,000 gallons used
Empty drums:
   94,000 purchased @ $94,000; 80,000 used
Direct labor:
   82,000 hours worked @ $414,100
Factory overhead:

Depreciation of building and machinery (fixed)	$210,000
Supervision and indirect labor (semivariable)	460,000
Other factory overhead (variable)	98,000
Total factory overhead	$768,000

(c) Other factory overhead was the only actual factory overhead cost that varied from the overhead budget allowance for the September level of actual production; it was budgeted at $90,000.

(d) At a normal capacity of 160,000 drums per month, supervision and indirect labor costs are expected to be $570,000. All cost functions are linear.

(e) None of the September cost variances are expected to occur proportionally in future months. For the coming fiscal year, the Cost Standards Department expects the same standard usage of materials and direct labor hours. The average prices expected are $2.10 per gallon of Miracle Mix, $1 per empty drum, and $5.70 per direct labor hour. The current flexible budget of factory overhead costs is considered applicable to future periods without revision.

(f) September production was 80,000 drums.

Required:

(1) Variance analyses for September: (a) materials purchase price variance, (b) materials quantity (or usage) variance, (c) labor rate variance, (d) labor efficiency (time or usage) variance, (e) controllable variance, and (f) volume variance for factory overhead.

(2) The actual manufacturing cost per drum of product expected at production of 140,000 drums per month, using these cost categories: materials, direct labor, fixed factory overhead, and variable factory overhead.

(AICPA adapted)

19-7. Reconstruction of records; variance analysis; standard cost sheet. The Leftwich Company lost most of its factory cost records early in February 19B, due to a fire.

The trial balance of the factory ledger at December 31, 19A follows:

Inventories: Finished Goods	$ 65,900	
Work in Process	–0–	
Materials	54,000	
General Ledger		$119,900
	$119,900	$119,900

All payments on behalf of the factory are made by the home office.

A copy of the January 19B standard cost variance report showed the following data:

		UNFAVORABLE	FAVORABLE
Materials	— price variance		$2,000
	— quantity variance	$ 480	
Direct labor	— rate variance	3,000	
	— efficiency variance		4,000
Factory overhead	— spending variance		1,000
	— idle capacity variance	3,000	
	— efficiency variance		1,000

The executive to whom the variance report had been sent noted beside the spending variance "Budget Allowance for January, $27,000" and wrote on the top of the report "January Production, 25,000 units."

The following additional facts are made available:

(a) Standard costs are revised annually at the beginning of each fiscal year. The figures in the trial balance reflect 19B standards.

(b) The actual direct labor cost for January 19B was $99,000 based on 12,000 actual hours worked. This information, as well as the fact that actual hours or production represent 80% of normal hours or production, was obtained from the Payroll Department of the home office.

(c) The supplier of the materials mailed copies of the January invoices indicating that 25,000 units had been purchased at a cost of $38,000. One unit of production requires two units of materials.

(d) Materials are carried at standard cost. No change was made at January 1, 19B.

(e) Overhead is applied to production on the basis of standard direct labor hours.

(f) Sales in January 19B were 28,000 units.

(g) All production was completed in January 19B, and forwarded to the finished goods warehouse.

Required:
(1) A detailed variance analysis of the three cost elements.
(2) The budget allowance if the two-variance analysis method for factory overhead had been used.
(3) The 19B product standard cost sheet.

19-8. Standard cost for lots; variance analysis. Vincenti Shirts, Inc., manufactures short- and long-sleeved shirts for large stores. It produces a single quality shirt in lots to each customer's order and attaches the store's label to each. The standard costs for a dozen long-sleeved shirts are:

Direct materials: 24 meters @ $.55	$13.20
Direct labor: 3 hours @ $7.50	22.50
Factory overhead: 3 hours @ $2.25	6.75
Standard cost per dozen	$42.45

During October, Vincenti worked on three orders for long-sleeved shirts. Job cost records for the month disclose the following:

Lot	Units in Lot	Materials Used	Hours Worked
30	1,000 dozen	24 100 meters	3,000 hours
31	1,650	40 440	5,130
32	1,200	28 750	2,870

The following information is also available:

(a) Vincenti purchased 96 000 meters of materials during October at a cost of $53,200. The materials price variance is recorded when goods are purchased and all inventories are carried at standard cost.
(b) Direct labor incurred amounted to $85,800 during October. According to payroll records, production employees were paid $7.80 per hour.
(c) Overhead is applied on the basis of direct labor hours. Factory overhead totaling $25,500 was incurred during October.
(d) A total of $324,000 was budgeted for factory overhead for the year, based on estimated production at the plant's normal capacity of 48,000 dozen shirts per year. Overhead is 40% fixed and 60% variable at this level of production.
(e) There was no work in process at October 1. During October, Lots 30 and 31 were completed; all materials were issued for Lot 32, which was 80% complete as to labor.

Required:
(1) A schedule computing the standard cost of Lots 30, 31, and 32 for October.
(2) A schedule computing the materials price variance for October.
(3) For each lot produced during October, schedules computing the (a) materials quantity variance in meters; (b) labor efficiency variance in hours; and (c) labor rate variance in dollars.
(4) A schedule computing the total controllable and volume overhead variances for October.
(AICPA adapted)

19-9. Price, mix, and yield variances. Chocolate manufacturing operations require close control of daily production and cost data. The computer printout for a batch of one ton of cocoa powder indicates the following materials standards:

Ingredients	Quantities (Pounds)	Unit Cost	Mix Cost
Cocoa beans	800	$.45	$ 360
Milk	3,700	.50	1,850
Sugar	500	.25	125
Total batch	5,000	$.467 (weighted average)	$2,335

On December 7, the company's Commodity Accounting and Analysis Section reported the following production and cost data for the December 6 operations:

Ingredients put in process:

Cocoa beans:	225,000 lbs. @ $.425	$ 95,625
Milk:	1,400,000 lbs. @ $.533	746,200
Sugar:	250,000 lbs. @ $.240	60,000
	1,875,000 lbs.	$901,825

Transferred to cocoa powder inventory: 387 tons. There was no work in process inventory.

Required: Materials price, mix, and yield variances.

19-10. Materials, labor, and overhead variances; mix and yield variances. The Century Cement Company uses a standard cost system for its production of cement. Cement is produced by mixing two major components, A (lime) and B (clay), with water and by adding a third component, C, quantitatively insignificant.

Materials standards and costs for the production of 100 tons of output are:

COMPONENTS	TONS	COST	PERCENT OF INPUT QUANTITY	AMOUNT
Material A	55	$43.00	50%	$2,365
Material B	44	35.00	40	1,540
Material C	11	25.00	10	275
Input	110		100%	$4,180 = $38.00 per ton
Output	100			$4,180 = $41.80 per ton

The monthly factory overhead budget for a normal capacity level of 16,500 direct labor hours is as follows:

	FIXED OVERHEAD	VARIABLE OVERHEAD
Plant manager	$ 2,000	
Supervisors	1,800	
Indirect labor	2,220	$ 810
Indirect supplies	850	2,040
Power and light	300	2,200
Water	480	2,000
Repairs and maintenance	500	1,200
Insurance	450	
Depreciation — production facilities	3,775	
Total	$12,375	$8,250

To convert 110 tons of materials into 100 tons of finished cement requires 500 direct labor hours at $7.50 per hour or $37.50 per ton. Factory overhead is applied on a direct labor hour basis.

Actual data for April:

In producing 3,234 tons of finished cement, the following costs were incurred:

Direct labor	15,800 hrs. @ $7.95
Fixed factory overhead	$11,075
Variable factory overhead	$ 8,490

	MATERIALS PURCHASED		MATERIALS REQUISITIONED
	Quantity	Price per Ton	Quantity
Material A	2,000 tons	$44	1,870 tons
Material B	1,200	37	1,100
Material C	500	24	440

There were no inventories of materials or work in process at the beginning of April. The materials price variance is recognized at time of purchase.

Required:
(1) Materials price, mix, and yield variances.
(2) Direct labor rate, efficiency, and yield variances.
(3) Factory overhead spending, idle capacity, efficiency, and yield variances.

19-11. Materials, labor, and overhead variances; mix and yield variances. Bowman Crunchies, Inc., manufactures breakfast cereal, using the following proportion of ingredients:

	QUANTITY	PRICE	COST
Wheat germ	25 lbs.	$2.00	$ 50
Barley	100	1.00	100
Oats	125	.80	100
Input...	250 lbs.		$250 = $1.00 per lb.
Output...	200 lbs.		$250 = $1.25 per lb.

Materials records for October indicate:

	BEGINNING INVENTORY	PURCHASES	PURCHASE PRICE	ENDING INVENTORY
Wheat germ....................................	2,000 lbs.	8,000 lbs.	$2.05 per lb.	1,200 lbs.
Barley	5,000	35,000	1.10	5,300
Oats	4,000	45,000	.75	7,000

The materials price variance is recognized when the materials are purchased.

The conversion of 250 pounds of materials into 200 pounds of finished product requires 25 direct labor hours at $8.00 per hour. The actual direct labor for the month was 8,000 hours and cost $64,800.

Factory overhead is applied on a direct labor hour basis at a rate of $3 per hour ($1 fixed, $2 variable). Normal capacity overhead is $30,000 with 10,000 direct labor hours. Actual overhead for October was $28,000. Actual finished production for the month was 70,000 pounds.

Required:
(1) Materials purchase price, mix, and yield variances; materials quantity variance for each material.
(2) Labor rate, efficiency, and yield variances.
(3) Factory overhead:
   (a) Spending, idle capacity, efficiency, and yield variances.
   (b) Controllable, volume, and yield variances.

CASES

A. Effect of assumed standard levels. Harden Company has experienced increased production costs. The primary area of concern identified by management is direct labor. The company is considering adopting a standard cost system to help control labor and other costs. Useful historical data are not available because detailed production records have not been maintained.

To establish labor standards, Harden Company has retained an engineering consulting firm. After a complete study of the work process, the consultants recommended a labor standard of one unit of production every 30 minutes, or 16 units per day for each worker. The consultants further advised that Harden's wage rates were below the prevailing rate of $7 per hour.

Harden's production vice-president thought that this labor standard was too tight, and from experience with the labor force, believed that a labor standard of 40 minutes per unit or 12 units per day for each worker would be more reasonable.

The president of Harden Company believed the standard should be set at a high level to motivate the workers and to provide adequate information for control and reasonable cost comparisons. After much discussion, management decided to use a dual standard. The labor standard of one unit every 30 minutes, recommended by the consulting firm, would be employed in the plant as a motivation device, while a cost standard of 40 minutes per unit would be used in reporting. Management also concluded that the workers would not be informed of the cost standard used for reporting purposes. The production vice-president conducted several sessions prior to implementation in the plant, informing the workers of the new standard cost system and answering questions. The new standards were not related to incentive pay but were introduced when wages were increased to $7 per hour.

The new standard cost system was implemented on January 1, 19--. At the end of six months of operation, these statistics on labor performance were presented to executive management:

	JANUARY	FEBRUARY	MARCH	APRIL	MAY	JUNE
Production (units).................................	5,100	5,000	4,700	4,500	4,300	4,400
Direct labor hours................................	3,000	2,900	2,900	3,000	3,000	3,100
Quantity variances:						
Variance based on labor standard (1						
unit each 30 minutes)........................	$3,150 U*	$2,800 U	$3,850 U	$5,250 U	$5,950 U	$6,300 U
Variance based on cost standard (1						
unit each 40 minutes)........................	$2,800 F	$3,033 F	$1,633 F	-0-	$ 933 U	$1,167 U

*U, unfavorable; F, favorable.

Materials quality, labor mix, and plant facilities and conditions have not changed to any great extent during the six-month period.

Required:
(1) A discussion of the impact of different types of standards on motivation, and specifically the likely effect on motivation of adopting the labor standard recommended for Harden Company by the engineering firm.
(2) An evaluation of Harden Company's decision to employ dual standards in its standard cost system.

(CMA adapted)

B. Factory overhead variance analysis. Strayer Company uses a standard cost system and budgets the following sales and costs for 19--:

Unit sales...	20,000
Sales...	$200,000
Total production cost at standard	130,000
Gross profit...	70,000
Beginning inventories...	None
Ending inventories	None

The 19-- budgeted sales level was the normal capacity level used in calculating the factory overhead predetermined standard cost rate per direct labor hour.

At the end of 19--, Strayer Company reported production and sales of 19,200 units. Total factory overhead incurred was exactly equal to budgeted factory overhead for the year and there was underapplied total factory overhead of $2,000 at December 31. Factory overhead is applied to the work in process inventory on the basis of standard direct labor hours allowed for units produced. Although there was a favorable labor efficiency variance, there was neither a labor rate variance nor materials variances for the year.

Required: An explanation of the underapplied factory overhead of $2,000, being as specific as the data permit and indicating the overhead variances affected. Strayer uses a three-variance method to analyze the total factory overhead.

(AICPA adapted)

20 Standard Costing
Accumulating and Evaluating Costs and Variances

Some companies prefer to keep standard costs for statistical purposes only. However, the incorporation of standard costs into the regular accounting system permits the most efficient use of a standard cost system and leads to savings and increased accuracy in clerical work. In either case, variances can be analyzed for cost control, and standard costs can be used in developing budgets, bidding on contracts, and setting prices.

STANDARD COSTING METHODS

Standard costs should be viewed as costs which pass through the data processing system into financial statements. However, variations exist in the methods of accumulating these costs. Some systems employ the partial plan, others the single plan. Both plans center around the entries to the work in process account, as illustrated below. Under either plan, the work in process account can be broken down by individual cost elements (materials, labor, and factory overhead) and/or by departments.

The Partial Plan

WORK IN PROCESS

Actual cost	Standard cost

The Single Plan

WORK IN PROCESS

Standard cost	Standard cost

The Partial Plan

In the *partial plan*, the work in process account is debited for the actual cost of materials, labor, and factory overhead and is credited at standard cost when goods are completed and transferred to finished goods inventory. Any balance remaining in the work in process account consists of two elements: (1) the standard cost of work still in process and (2) the variances between actual and standard costs. To isolate these variances, additional analysis is needed.

The Single Plan

Since timely identification and reporting are major control features of standard cost accounting, prompt communication for very short time frames may be required. The *single plan* debits and credits the work in process account at standard costs only, and variances are recorded in separate variance accounts. These entries are periodic (often monthly) summaries of standard costs, actual costs, and resulting variances. They are discussed in detail in the following pages and are used in the exercises and problems of this chapter.

STANDARD COST ACCOUNTING PROCEDURES FOR MATERIALS

The recording of materials purchased can be handled by three different methods:

1. *Record the price variance when materials are received and placed in stores*. The general ledger control account, Materials, is debited at standard cost and the materials ledger cards are kept in quantities only. A standard price is noted on the card when the standards are set. As purchases are made, no prices are recorded on these cards. This procedure results in clerical savings and speedier postings.
2. *Record the materials at actual cost when received, and determine the price variance when the materials are requisitioned for production*. The general ledger control account, Materials, is debited at actual cost and the materials ledger cards show quantities and dollar values as in a historical cost system.
3. *Use a combination of methods (1) and (2)*. Calculate price variances when the materials are received, but defer charging them to production until the materials are actually placed in process. At that time, only the price variance applicable to the quantity used will appear as a current charge, the balance remaining as a part of the materials inventory. This method results in two types of materials price variances: (1) a materials purchase price variance originating when materials purchases are first recorded, and (2) a materials price usage variance when materials are used. The occurrence of the materials price usage variance is a reduction of the materials purchase price variance.

For control purposes, the price variance should be determined when the materials are received. If it is not computed and reported until the materials are requisitioned for production, then remedial action is difficult because the time of computation is so far removed from the time of purchase. Also, the problem of deciding which actual cost is applicable is again present.

These methods for recording materials purchased are illustrated below, using the following data from Chapter 19:

Standard unit price as per standard cost card	$2.50
Purchases	5,000 pieces @ $2.47
Requisitioned	3,550 pieces
Standard quantity allowed for actual production	3,500 pieces

Method 1

The journal entry when materials are received is:

Materials	12,500	
Accounts Payable		12,350
Materials Purchase Price Variance		150

When materials issued to the factory are recorded, the entry is:

Work in Process	8,750	
Materials Quantity Variance	125	
Materials		8,875

Method 2

When materials are received, no variance is computed and the entry is:

Materials	12,350	
Accounts Payable		12,350

When materials issued are recorded, the entry is:

Work in Process	8,750.00	
Materials Quantity Variance	125.00	
Materials		8,768.50
Materials Price Usage Variance		106.50

Computations for this entry are:

	PIECES ×	UNIT COST	=	AMOUNT
Actual quantity used	3,550	$2.47 actual		$8,768.50
Actual quantity used	3,550	2.50 standard		8,875.00
Materials price usage variance	3,550	$(.03)		$ (106.50) fav.

	PIECES ×	UNIT COST	=	AMOUNT
Actual quantity used	3,550	$2.50 standard		$8,875.00
Standard quantity allowed	3,500	2.50 standard		8,750.00
Materials quantity variance ...	50	2.50 standard		$ 125.00 unfav.

For this computation, the cost used is $2.47 per piece, since no other actual cost is available and no other purchases were made. In practice, the actual cost used would depend upon the type of inventory costing method employed, such as fifo, lifo, or average costing.

In this method, the materials price usage variance account appears on the books after the materials are issued, and then only for the quantity issued — not for the entire purchase. The price variance occurred because the materials were purchased at $.03 less than the standard price; the quantity variance, because 50 pieces were used in excess of the standard quantity allowed.

Method 3

This entry, identical with the first entry in Method 1, would be made when the materials are received:

Materials	12,500	
Accounts Payable		12,350
Materials Purchase Price Variance		150

When the materials issued are recorded, two entries are made. The following entry, identical with the second entry in Method 1, recognizes the 50 pieces used beyond the standard quantity:

Work in Process	8,750	
Materials Quantity Variance	125	
Materials		8,875

The next entry transfers $106.50 from the purchase price variance account to the price usage variance account.

Materials Purchase Price Variance	106.50	
Materials Price Usage Variance		106.50

In Method 3, any balance remaining in the materials purchase price variance account at the end of the accounting period is used to adjust the inventory to actual cost. This balance takes on the aspect of a valuation account and is shown in the balance sheet as follows:

Materials (at standard cost)	$3,625.00
Less materials purchase price variance	43.50
Materials (adjusted to actual)	$3,581.50

STANDARD COST ACCOUNTING PROCEDURES FOR LABOR

The payroll is computed on the basis of clock cards, job tickets, and other labor time information furnished to the payroll department. In a standard cost system, these basic records supply the data for the computation of labor variances.

The necessary journal entries are illustrated with the following data from Chapter 19:

Actual hours worked	1,880
Actual rate paid per hour	$6.50
Standard hours allowed for actual production	1,590
Standard rate per hour	$6.00

The following journal entry records the total actual direct labor payroll, assuming that there were no payroll deductions:

Payroll	12,220	
Accrued Payroll		12,220

To distribute the payroll and to set up the variance accounts, the journal entry is:

Work in Process	9,540	
Labor Rate Variance	940	
Labor Efficiency Variance	1,740	
Payroll		12,220

STANDARD COST ACCOUNTING PROCEDURES FOR FACTORY OVERHEAD

The close relationship between standard costs and budgetary control methods is particularly important for the analysis of factory overhead. Actual factory overhead is measured not only against the applied overhead cost, but also against a budget based on the capacity at which a company expects to operate during a period and a budget based on actual and standard activity allowed for actual production.

The following data from Chapter 19 are used to illustrate the journal entries for the two-variance, three-variance, and four-variance methods.

Normal capacity (in direct labor hours)		4,000 hours
Total overhead at normal capacity:		
Fixed	$3,200	
Variable	4,800	$8,000
Overhead rate per direct labor hour:		
Fixed	$ .80	
Variable	1.20	$2.00
Actual overhead		$7,384
Actual direct labor hours		3,475 hours
Standard hours allowed for actual production		3,400 hours

Two-Variance Method

The entry to record the actual factory overhead is:

Factory Overhead Control	7,384	
Various Credits		7,384

When overhead is applied to work in process:

Work in Process	6,800	
Factory Overhead Control		6,800

(If the applied factory overhead account is used, it is subsequently transferred to the factory overhead control account.)

The factory overhead control account now has a debit balance of $584, which can be analyzed and closed out as follows:

Factory Overhead Controllable Variance	104	
Factory Overhead Volume Variance	480	
Factory Overhead Control		584

Three-Variance Method

The entry to record the actual factory overhead is:

Factory Overhead Control	7,384	
Various Credits		7,384

When overhead is applied to work in process:

Work in Process	6,800	
Factory Overhead Efficiency Variance	150	
Factory Overhead Control		6,950

The factory overhead control account now has a debit balance of $434, which can be analyzed as to spending and idle capacity variances and closed as follows:

Factory Overhead Spending Variance	14	
Factory Overhead Idle Capacity Variance	420	
Factory Overhead Control		434

As an alternative, the second entry may be recorded as a debit to Work in Process and as a credit to Factory Overhead Control for $6,800. The balance of $584 in Factory Overhead Control would then be closed as follows:

Factory Overhead Spending Variance	14	
Factory Overhead Efficiency Variance	150	
Factory Overhead Idle Capacity Variance	420	
Factory Overhead Control		584

Four-Variance Method

The entry to record the actual factory overhead is:

Factory Overhead Control	7,384	
Various Credits		7,384

When overhead is applied to work in process:

Work in Process	6,800	
Factory Overhead Variable Efficiency Variance	90	
Factory Overhead Fixed Efficiency Variance	60	
Factory Overhead Control		6,950

The factory overhead control account has a debit balance of $434, which can be analyzed as to spending and idle capacity variances and closed as follows:

Factory Overhead Spending Variance	14	
Factory Overhead Idle Capacity Variance	420	
Factory Overhead Control		434

As an alternative, the second entry may be recorded as a debit to Work in Process and as a credit to Factory Overhead Control for $6,800. The balance of $584 in Factory Overhead Control would then be closed as follows:

Factory Overhead Spending Variance..	14	
Factory Overhead Variable Efficiency Variance	90	
Factory Overhead Fixed Efficiency Variance	60	
Factory Overhead Idle Capacity Variance	420	
Factory Overhead Control		584

STANDARD COST ACCOUNTING PROCEDURES FOR COMPLETED PRODUCTS

The completion of production requires the transfer of cost from the work in process account of one department to the work in process account of another department, or, in the case of the last department, to the finished goods account. The cost transferred is the standard cost.

The journal entry for the transfer of finished products is as follows:

Finished Goods (at standard cost)	xxxx	
Work in Process (at standard cost).......................................		xxxx

The finished goods ledger card will show quantities only, because the standard cost of the units remains the same during a period unless severe cost changes occur. When goods are shipped to customers, the entry is:

Cost of Goods Sold (at standard cost)	xxxx	
Finished Goods (at standard cost)		xxxx

JOURNAL ENTRIES FOR MIX AND YIELD VARIANCES

The journal entries for the mix and yield variances computed in the previous chapter are:

Materials

To record materials purchases:

Materials	55,700	
Accounts Payable...		55,000
Materials Purchase Price Variance...............................		700

To charge materials into production:

Work in Process	57,750	
Materials Mix Variance...	300	
Materials		58,050

To transfer materials cost to finished goods:

Finished Goods...	60,000	
Materials Yield Variance		2,250
Work in Process		57,750

Labor

To set up payroll liability:

Payroll	23,104	
Accrued Payroll..		23,104

To transfer payroll to work in process and to isolate variances:

Work in Process	23,100	
Labor Rate Variance	304	
Labor Efficiency Variance.............................		300
Payroll		23,104

To transfer labor cost to finished goods:

Finished Goods..	24,000	
Labor Yield Variance		900
Work in Process		23,100

Factory Overhead (Two-Variance Method)

To record actual overhead:

Factory Overhead Control	22,000	
Various Credits		22,000

To apply factory overhead to products:

Work in Process	19,250	
Factory Overhead Control		19,250

To set up controllable and volume variances:

Factory Overhead Controllable Variance............................	2,300	
Factory Overhead Volume Variance.................................	450	
Factory Overhead Control		2,750

To transfer factory overhead to finished goods:

Finished Goods..	20,000	
Factory Overhead Yield Variance.................		750
Work in Process		19,250

It should be noted that Work in Process is debited for the standard production that should be attained from the input into the system and not for the standard for the amount of actual production. The resulting difference is the yield variance for each cost element.

When the transfer of the finished products to the warehouse or stockroom is reported to the cost department, one compound journal entry could be made, as shown below, in place of the three individual entries for each element.

Finished Goods (200,000 lbs. × $.52).............................	104,000	
Work in Process (192,500 lbs. expected yield × $.52)		100,100
Yield Variance (7,500 lbs. gain × $.52).......................		3,900

The $3,900 favorable yield variance is comprised of:

Materials yield variance..	$2,250 fav.
Labor yield variance..	900 fav.
Factory overhead yield variance	750 fav.

Expressed as a percentage, the yield gain is 3.90 percent:

$$\frac{7,500 \text{ lbs.}}{192,500 \text{ lbs.}} \times 100 = 3.90\%$$

RESPONSIBILITY AND CONTROL OF VARIANCES

Management scrutinizes variances in an attempt to determine why they occur, what corrective action can be taken, and how efficient and effective performance should be rewarded. Of course, there is no substitute for competent supervision, but variance reporting should be an aid to the supervisor in carrying out control responsibilities. However, management should recognize that explanations of the reasons for variances have limited usefulness in improving future control of costs, because the explanations seldom suggest corrective action. Consequently, the results of implemented corrective action must be measured and reported if cost control is to be effective.

The extent of variance investigation should be based on the estimated cost of making the investigation versus the value of the anticipated benefits. To be of greatest value, variances should be identified quickly and reported as frequently as possible (in some instances, daily), since the closer the reporting to the point of incurrence, the greater the chance for control and remedial action. Also, variances should be reported in physical units as well as dollars.

Causes of Variances

A variance is a symptom. Every significant variance, whether favorable or unfavorable, should be investigated and critically analyzed, either because performance has deviated from the standard or the standard itself is wrong. Perhaps standards are out-of-date. For example, the manufacturing process may change, thus changing physical standards, or rapidly rising materials prices may cause monetary standards to be out-of-date. Perhaps a favorable variance is more than offset by a related unfavorable variance (e.g., low-cost materials of poor quality), or necessary activities such as maintenance of equipment are being neglected, causing lower expenditures and a favorable variance. Of course, management should use the occurrence of desirable favorable variances as an opportunity to recognize the efficient performance of responsible managers and workers.

The purchasing department carries the primary responsibility for materials price variances, and control is obtained by getting several quotations, buying in economical lots, taking advantage of cash discounts, and selecting the most economical means of delivery. However, economic conditions and unexpected price changes by suppliers may be outside the limits of the department's control. Internal factors, such as costly rush orders requiring materials at special prices, would not be the fault of the purchasing department.

Materials quantity variances may result from many causes, which must be identified if the variances are to have meaning. If the materials are of poor quality, the fault may be with the individual who prepared the purchase requisition informing the purchasing department about the quality of materials to be purchased. If the materials purchased varied from the purchase requisition specifications, the fault may lie with the purchasing department. Or perhaps the faulty materials went unnoticed during inspection when received. Other causes include inexperienced or inefficient workers, poor equipment, changes in production methods, or faulty blueprints.

Labor rate variances tend to be fairly minor because labor rates are usually based on union agreements. Rate variances may occur, however, because of the use of a single average rate for a department, operation, or craft, while several different rates exist for the individual workers. Then, too, a worker may be assigned to a task that normally pays a different rate. In this case, the planning or scheduling of work assignments would be the cause of the variance.

Labor efficiency variances may occur for a multitude of reasons. These reasons include a lack of materials or faulty materials, inexperienced workers and the related learning curve phenomenon (pages 403–406), poor equipment and breakdowns, changes in production methods, incorrect scheduling, or faulty blueprints.

Factory overhead variances relate to the variable and the fixed factory overhead. The portion of the spending variance attributable to each expense category can be determined as discussed on pages 221–223. The spending or controllable variance is basically the responsibility of the department head, but differences between the actual cost and the allowed budget figure may be caused by higher prices or different labor rates. The idle capacity or volume variance is generally ascribed to executive management levels. The decision with regard to the utilization of plant capacity and the setting of the predetermined overhead rate's volume base rests with the planning group. Within the range of fixed costs, however, changes occur due to changes in depreciation rates, increases in insurance premiums, or increases in salaries of top-level managers. The responsibility for overhead efficiency variances, including both the fixed and variable components, is generally attributed to the department manager.

Tolerance Limits for Variance Control

The control of standard cost variances is the responsibility of a designated manager. However, some variance in cost measurements can be expected, due to the factors employed in creating the basic physical and economic standards and due to the nature of the variance. With an expected variance in mind, the question must be asked, "How large a variance from standard should be tolerated before it is considered abnormal?" In other words, some tolerance limit or range should be established, so that if the cost variance falls within this range, it can be considered acceptable. If the variance is outside the range, an investigation should be made if the cost of doing so is reasonable.

Each variance should be highlighted in a manner indicating whether the variance is within the control limit. Such information enables the responsible manager or supervisor to accept deviations from the standard as a valuable tool for the control of costs and lessens the dangers of their being more averse to risk than upper-level managers prefer. A manager who is unduly concerned about the penalty for even small variances may perform in a manner that hampers rather than enhances efficient operations.

Past data on established operations, tempered by estimated changes in the future, usually furnish reliable bases for estimating expected costs and calculating control limits that serve to indicate good as well as poor operation. The standard error of the estimate (pages 521–522) may be used in setting tolerance limits for standard cost variance control. In setting and applying tolerance limits, it is important to recognize that the relative magnitude of a variance is more significant than its absolute value.

To illustrate the use of tolerance limits, assume that $10,000 appears in a factory overhead budget for maintenance expense. A significant range should be established, since the actual maintenance cost will likely differ from the budget figure. Based on past experience and future expectations, assume again that the range should be ± $2,000.

At the end of the month, the actual maintenance expense is $14,000, indicating a variance of $4,000 ($14,000 − $10,000). Such a result might call for further investigation into the causes of the variance. Suppose, however, that the actual expense is only $10,900. Then the variance is $900. This is an acceptable deviation requiring no further investigation, at least at this time. If the unfavorable variance persists in subsequent report periods, the causes, which in the long run may be significant, should be examined.

In this example, maintenance expense is classified as a fixed cost, since no deviation from the basic amount is expected as a result of a change in the level of activity. However, this cost is generally classified as a semivariable expense, i.e., a fixed amount plus a variable rate which depends, in this case, on direct labor hours as the source of activity or volume. Thus, a relationship between the variance and volume must be established for the maintenance expense.

To modify the previous example, assume a tolerance limit of $3,000 when activity is 10,000 direct labor hours. When direct labor hours increase or decrease, the tolerance limit is $3,000 ± $.05 per hour for any difference in 10,000 direct labor hours and the standard hours allowed for actual production. Assuming that $10,000 is the budget allowance for 12,700 direct labor hours and the actual cost of $14,000 was incurred when standard direct labor hours allowed were 12,700, the tolerance limit would be $3,135 [$3,000 + ($.05 × 2,700)]. This amount would be used to evaluate the $4,000 variance.

DISPOSITION OF VARIANCES

Variances may be disposed of in either of the following ways: they may be (1) closed to Income Summary or (2) treated as adjustments to Cost of Goods Sold and to inventories.

Variances Closed to Income Summary

Stating the work in process and finished goods inventories and the cost of goods sold at standard costs allows comparison of sales revenue and standard cost by product class. At the end of the month or year, the procedure for handling cost variances is to consider them as profit or loss items. Unfavorable (or debit) manufacturing cost variances are deducted from the gross profit calculated at standard cost. Favorable (or credit) variances are added to the gross profit computed at standard cost. The treatment of manufacturing cost variances using this method is depicted in the following income statement, which should be supported by a variance analysis report.

Income Statement
For Year Ended December 31, 19—

		DEBIT BALANCES	
Sales			$52,000
Cost of goods sold (at standard) — see Schedule 1			24,000
Gross profit (at standard)			$28,000
Adjustments for standard cost variances:			
Materials purchase price variance		$ 1,200	
Labor efficiency variance		600	
Factory overhead controllable variance		720	
Factory overhead volume variance		1,200	
Total debit variances			3,720
Gross profit (adjusted)			$24,280
Less: Marketing expenses		$12,000	
Administrative expenses		6,000	18,000
Operating income			$ 6,280

Schedule 1
Cost of Goods Sold
For Year Ended December 31, 19—

Materials purchased	$20,000	
Less ending inventory	4,000	
Materials used		$16,000
Direct labor		10,000
Factory overhead		20,000
		$46,000
Less ending work in process		16,000
Cost of goods manufactured		$30,000
Less ending finished goods inventory		6,000
Cost of goods sold		$24,000

At the end of the period, variance accounts are closed to the income summary account:

Income Summary..	3,720	
Materials Purchase Price Variance..................................		1,200
Labor Efficiency Variance...		600
Factory Overhead Controllable Variance...........................		720
Factory Overhead Volume Variance.................................		1,200

As an alternative, if variances are considered a manufacturing function responsibility, they are closed to the cost of goods sold account, rather than directly to the income summary account. The total amount in Cost of Goods Sold (the standard cost of units sold plus the variances) would then be closed to Income Summary. Variances closed to the cost of goods sold account will appear in the cost of goods sold statement; variances closed to the income summary account will appear in the income statement.

Accountants who use these procedures believe that only standard costs should be considered the true costs. Variances are not treated as increases or decreases in manufacturing costs but as deviations from contemplated costs, due to abnormal inactivity, extravagance, inefficiencies or efficiencies, or other changes of business conditions. This viewpoint leads to the closing of all variances to the income summary account, which is an acceptable procedure as long as standards are reasonably representative of what costs ought to be. However, some proponents of this procedure suggest that the unused portion of the materials purchase price variance should be linked with materials still on hand and shown on the balance sheet as part of the cost of the ending materials inventory.

If an adjustment is made for the materials purchase price variance, whereby a part of the variance is attached to the materials inventory, the following computation would be made in this example:

Balance in materials inventory = $4,000 or 20% of purchases made
Materials purchase price variance = $1,200
Variance transferred to the materials account = $240 (20% of $1,200)

The materials account would be increased and the amount closed to Income Summary would be decreased, thereby increasing the operating income from $6,280 to $6,520. The journal entry to close the variance accounts would be:

Income Summary..	3,480	
Materials	240	
Materials Purchase Price Variance..................................		1,200
Labor Efficiency Variance...		600
Factory Overhead Controllable Variance...........................		720
Factory Overhead Volume Variance.................................		1,200

A second method used for the distribution of variances allocates them to Cost of Goods Sold and inventories. *Accounting Research Bulletin No. 43* states with respect to the cost of inventories that:

> Standard costs are acceptable if adjusted at reasonable intervals to reflect current conditions so that at the balance-sheet date standard costs reasonably approximate costs computed under one of the recognized bases. In such cases descriptive language should be used which will express this relation-

Variances Allocated to Cost of Goods Sold and Inventories

ship, as, for instance, "approximate costs determined on the first-in, first-out basis," or, if it is desired to mention standard costs, "at standard costs, approximating average costs."[1]

Cost Accounting Standards Board regulations require that significant standard cost variances be included in inventories. Current Internal Revenue Service regulations also require the inclusion of a portion of significant variances in inventories. When the amount involved is not significant in relation to total actual factory overhead for the year, an allocation is not required by the IRS unless such allocation is made for financial reporting purposes. Also, the taxpayer must treat both favorable and unfavorable variances consistently. Regulations, however, do permit expensing of the idle capacity variance.

To illustrate the allocation of variances, the percentage of cost elements in the inventories and cost of goods sold of the previous example are:

	MATERIALS		LABOR		FACTORY OVERHEAD	
ACCOUNT	Amount	%	Amount	%	Amount	%
Work in Process	$ 6,000	37.5	$ 2,000	20	$ 8,000	40
Finished Goods	2,000	12.5	2,000	20	2,000	10
Cost of Goods Sold	8,000	50.0	6,000	60	10,000	50
Total	$16,000	100.0	$10,000	100	$20,000	100

The allocation of the variances shown on page 590 is summarized in the table below. The materials purchase price variance of $960 ($1,200 − $240 allocated to Materials) is multiplied by the respective percentage of materials in the inventory and cost of goods sold account (37.5%, 12.5%, and 50.0%). The labor and factory overhead variances are allocated in a similar manner.

ACCOUNT	TOTAL AMOUNT	WORK IN PROCESS	FINISHED GOODS	COST OF GOODS SOLD
Materials Purchase Price Variance	$ 960	$ 360	$120	$ 480
Labor Efficiency Variance	600	120	120	360
Factory Overhead Controllable Variance	720	288	72	360
Factory Overhead Volume Variance	1,200	480	120	600
Total	$3,480	$1,248	$432	$1,800

The proration of these variances to Work in Process, Finished Goods, and Cost of Goods Sold results in the income statement illustrated below.

Income Statement
For Year Ended December 31, 19--

Sales		$52,000
Cost of goods sold (standard adjusted to actual) — Schedule 1		25,800
Gross profit (actual)		$26,200
Less: Marketing expenses	$12,000	
Administrative expenses	6,000	18,000
Operating income		$ 8,200

[1]*Accounting Research Bulletin, No. 43*, "Inventory Pricing" (New York: American Institute of Certified Public Accountants, 1953), Chapter 4, par. 6.

Schedule 1
Cost of Goods Sold
For Year Ended December 31, 19--

	STANDARD	VARIANCE	ACTUAL
Materials available	$20,000		$21,200
Materials purchase price variance		$1,200	
Less materials inventory (ending)	4,000		4,240
Materials purchase price variance		240	
Materials used	$16,000		$16,960
Materials purchase price variance		$ 960	
Direct labor	10,000		10,600
Efficiency variance		600	
Factory overhead	20,000		21,920
Controllable variance		720	
Volume variance		1,200	
Total manufacturing cost	$46,000	$3,480	$49,480
Less ending work in process inventory	16,000	1,248	17,248
Cost of goods manufactured	$30,000	$2,232	$32,232
Less ending finished goods inventory	6,000	432	6,432
Cost of goods sold	$24,000	$1,800	$25,800

The adjusted operating income is $8,200 compared to the operating income of $6,280 shown in the income statement on page 590. The difference of $1,920 is summarized as follows:

Cost added to:	Materials	$ 240
	Work in process	1,248
	Finished goods	432
	Total	$1,920

Entries transfer the prorated amounts to the respective accounts in the general ledger only. Subsidiary inventory accounts and records are not adjusted. The various adjustment accounts could be shown on the balance sheet as valuation or contra accounts against standard inventory values, or combined with them to form one amount. At the beginning of the next period, the portion of these proration entries that affects inventory accounts is reversed in order to return beginning inventories to standard costs. At the end of that period, the amount reversed plus new variances are allocated in the same manner as before, based on ending inventory and cost of goods sold account balances.

In connection with closing variances, a problem arises in the allocation of variances to product or commodity groups. Preferably, standard cost variances are shown as deductions in total and are not allocated to major commodity groups to determine the profit and loss per commodity. Experience has shown that it is almost impossible to do otherwise. The basic idea of variance analysis is misconstrued when such prorations are attempted. The isolation of variances is for the purpose of controlling costs and determining what the variances are, where they occurred, and what caused them.

The treatment of variances depends upon the (1) type of variance (materials, labor, or factory overhead), (2) size of variance, (3) experience with standard costs, (4) cause of variance (e.g., incorrect standards), and (5) timing of the variance (e.g., an unusual variance caused by seasonal fluctuations). Therefore, determining the most acceptable treatment requires consideration of more than the argument that only actual costs should be shown in the financial statements. The determination of an actual cost may be impossible, and to argue that charging off variances in the period in which they arise might distort the operating income reveals a misunderstanding of standard costs.

One view of the disposition of variances has been expressed as follows:

1. Where the standards are current and attainable, companies would "state their inventories at standard cost and charge the variances against the income of the period in which the variances arise. They justify this practice on the grounds that variances represent inefficiencies, avoidable waste not recoverable in the selling price, and random fluctuations in actual cost."

2. Where standards are not current, "the general practice is to divide the variances between inventories and cost of goods sold or profit and loss thereby converting both inventories and cost of sales to approximate actual costs."[2]

Another view asserts that:

1. Any variances which are caused by inactivity, waste, or extravagance (outside acceptable tolerance limits) should be written off, since they represent losses. They should not be deferred by capitalizing them in the inventory accounts. This would include quantity variances on materials and labor as well as idle time (capacity) and efficiency variances on overhead. To assign a portion of such costs to inventory may cloud the product pricing decision. For example, "the inclusion of idle capacity costs in product costs has the effect of raising [inventory] costs when it is most difficult to raise prices [low volume periods] and lowering [inventory] costs when it is easiest to ask for higher prices [high volume periods]."[3]

2. An inventory reserve account should be established and charged with part of the price (spending and rate) variances (and quantity, capacity, and efficiency variances within acceptable tolerance limits) to an extent which would bring the materials, work in process, and finished goods inventories up to, but not in excess of, current market values. The rest of the price (spending and rate) variance amounts (as well as those variances described in (1) above) should be written off, since they represent excess costs. In this way, the inventory accounts themselves will be valued at standard cost while the inventories on the balance sheet will, as a whole, be shown at reasonable values through the use of the inventory reserve account. In addition, losses caused by

[2]*NAA Research Report, Nos. 11–15*, "How Standard Costs Are Being Used Currently" (New York: National Association of Accountants, 1948), pp. 65–66.
[3]Edwin Bartenstein, "Different Costs for Different Purposes," *Management Accounting*, Vol. LX, No. 2, p. 46.

excessive costs and inefficiencies will be shown in the operating statement for the period in which they occur.[4]

The AICPA takes the following position concerning variance disposition for interim financial reporting in published financial statements:

> Companies that use standard cost accounting systems for determining inventory and product costs should generally follow the same procedures in reporting purchase price, wage rate, usage or efficiency variances from standard cost at the end of an interim period as followed at the end of a fiscal year. Purchase price variances or volume or capacity cost variances that are planned and expected to be absorbed by the end of the annual period, should ordinarily be deferred at interim reporting dates. The effect of unplanned or unanticipated purchase price or volume variances, however, should be reported at the end of an interim period following the same procedures used at the end of a fiscal year.[5]

Disposition of Variances and Interim Financial Reporting

REVISION OF STANDARD COSTS

Standards should be changed only when underlying conditions change or when they no longer reflect the original concept. The idea that standards should be changed more than once a year weakens their effectiveness and increases operational details. However, standard costs require continuous review and, at times, frequent change.

Events, rather than time, determine whether standard costs should be revised. These events may be classified as internal or external. Technological advances, design revisions, method changes, labor rate adjustments, and changes in physical facilities are among the internal conditions. External events include materials price changes, market trends, specific customer requirements, and changes in the competitive situation.

When standard costs are changed, any adjustment to inventory should be made with care so that inventories are not written up or down arbitrarily. The National Association of Accountants has made the following comments concerning whether the ending inventory should be adjusted for such changes:

1. If the new standard costs reflect conditions which affected the actual cost of the goods in the ending inventory, most firms adjust inventory to the new standard cost and carry the contra side of the adjusting entry to cost of sales by way of the variance accounts. In effect, this procedure assumes that the standard costs used to cost goods in the inventory have been incorrect and that restatement of inventory cost is needed to bring inventories to a correct figure on the books. Since the use of incorrect standards has affected the variance accounts as well as the inventory, the adjustment is carried to the variance accounts.
2. If the standard costs represent conditions which are expected to prevail in the coming period but which have not affected costs in the past period,

[4]W. Wesley Miller, "Standard Costs and Their Relation to Cost Control," *NA(C)A Bulletin*, Vol. XXVII, No. 15, p. 692.
[5]*Opinions of the Accounting Principles Board, No. 28*, "Interim Financial Reporting" (New York: American Institute of Certified Public Accountants, 1973), par. 14.

ending inventories are costed at the old standards. It appears to be common practice to adjust the detailed inventory records to new standard costs.

In order to maintain the control relationship which the inventory accounts have over subsidiary records, the same adjustment is entered in the inventory control accounts; and the contra entry is carried to an inventory valuation account. Thus, the net effect is to state the inventory in the closing balance sheet at old standard costs. In the next period the inventory valuation account is closed to cost of sales when the goods to which the reserve relates move out of inventories. By use of this technique, the detailed records can be adjusted to new standards before the beginning of the year while at the same time the net charge to cost of sales in the new period is for old standard cost since the latter cost was correct at the time the goods were acquired.[6]

BROAD APPLICABILITY OF STANDARD COSTING

The use of standard costing is not limited to manufacturing situations. This powerful working tool for planning and control can be used in other aspects of business organizations, as discussed in Chapter 23. The nonprofit organization sector (hospitals, governmental agencies, etc.) also affords many opportunities to utilize standard costing concepts and techniques. Though standard costs may not be formally recorded in the accounts, many relatively small organizations, such as automotive repair shops and construction contractors, can utilize the comparison of actual to standard quantities, times, and costs for bidding, pricing of jobs or projects, and the planning and control of routine operating activities.

DISCUSSION QUESTIONS

1. Some firms incorporate standard costs into their accounts; others maintain them only for statistical comparisons. Discuss these different uses of standard costs.

2. Compare the use of actual cost methods to standard costing systems for inventory costing.

3. Name several advantages of using standard costs for finished goods and goods sold.

4. Differences between actual costs and standard costs may be recorded in variance accounts. What considerations might determine the number of variance accounts?

5. In a standard cost system, the computation of variances is a first step. What steps should follow?

---

[6]*NAA Research Report, Nos. 11–15, op. cit.* p. 64.

6. Discuss the meaning of variance control and responsibility by various levels of management.

7. The determination of periodic income depends greatly upon the cost assigned to materials, work in process, and finished goods inventories. What considerations determine the costing of inventories at standard or approximate actual costs by companies using standard costs?

8. Present arguments in support of each of the following three methods of treating standard cost variances for purposes of financial reporting:
   (a) As deferred charges or credits on the balance sheet.
   (b) As charges or credits on the income statement.
   (c) Allocated between inventories and cost of goods sold.

   (AICPA adapted)

9. Select the answer which best completes the statement:
   (a) One of the purposes of standard costs is to: (1) simplify costing procedures and expedite cost reports; (2) replace budgets and budgeting; (3) cost products for external reporting and income tax purposes; (4) eliminate having to account for over- or underapplied factory overhead at the end of the period.
   (b) The statement best characterizing a standard cost system is that: (1) standard costs involve cost control which, in turn, means cost reduction; (2) standards can pinpoint responsibility and help motivate employees; (3) all variances from standard should be reviewed; (4) all significant variances should be reviewed, except significant favorable variances.
   (c) The term best identified with a system of standard costs is: (1) marginal costing; (2) contribution approach; (3) management by exception; (4) standardized accounting system.
   (d) The variance that is least significant for cost control is: (1) labor rate; (2) materials quantity; (3) factory overhead spending; (4) factory overhead volume.
   (e) At the end of the fiscal year, the Rolon Company had several substantial variances from standard variable manufacturing costs. The strongest justification for allocation between inventories and cost of goods sold would be attributable to: (1) additional costs of materials acquired under a speculative purchase contract; (2) a breakdown of equipment; (3) overestimates of production activity for the period, resulting from failure to predict an unusual decline in the market for the company's product; (4) increased labor rates won by the union as a result of a strike during the year.
   (f) Standard costing will produce the same financial statement results as actual or conventional costing when standard cost variances are distributed to: (1) cost of goods sold; (2) an income or expense account; (3) cost of goods sold and inventory; (4) a balance sheet account.
   (g) An unacceptable financial accounting treatment of standard cost variances at an interim reporting date is: (1) apportioning the total only between work in process and finished goods inventories at the end of the interim reporting period; (2) apportioning the total only between that part of the current period's production remaining in inventories at the end of the period and that part sold during the period; (3) carrying forward the total to be offset by opposite balances in later periods; (4) charging or crediting the total to the cost of goods sold during the period.

(h) A departmental supervisor has determined that corrective action to assure normal operations of the department for the following week will cost $500. The excess cost of operating the department inefficiently for one week is $3,000. The department's efficiency variance is $600. If there is a 90% probability that a week in which the department operates inefficiently will be followed by a week in which normal operations occur, the expected cost of *not* taking corrective action is: (1) $.90 \times \$3,000$; (2) $.10 \times \$3,000$; (3) $3,000$; (4) 600.

(AICPA and CMA adapted)

EXERCISES

Whenever variances are required in the following exercises, indicate whether they are favorable or unfavorable.

1. Journal entries; variance analysis. The Parmley Company manufactures a product with the following standard costs:

Materials: 3 sq. ft. @ $2.00	$ 6.00
Direct labor: ½ hour @ $8.00	4.00
Variable factory overhead: ½ hour @ $3.00	1.50
Fixed factory overhead: ½ hour @ $2.00	1.00
	$12.50

Normal capacity is 8,000 units. The following information pertains to actual activity:

9,000 units were produced.
30,000 square feet of materials were purchased at $2.07 per square foot, and the materials price variance is recognized at the time of purchase.
Direct labor payroll was $36,080 for 4,400 hours worked.
28,000 square feet of materials were used.
Variable factory overhead cost, $14,000.
Fixed factory overhead cost, $8,500.
8,200 units were sold at $18.00 per unit.
Marketing and administrative expenses were $20,000.

Required: Journal entries of transactions, identifying three factory overhead variances and two variances each for materials and direct labor. Work in Process is charged with standard costs for actual production.

(CGAA adapted)

2. Journal entries; variance analysis. The Willingham Company makes a product for which the following standards have been set:

Materials: 3 square meters @ $5.00	$15.00	
Direct labor: 2 hours @ $8.00	16.00	
Variable factory overhead: 2 hours @ $1.50	3.00	
Fixed factory overhead: 2 hours @ $2.00	4.00	
	$38.00	
Normal output	5,000	units

Actual data for March:

Production (no work in process inventories)	4,000	units
Sales at $50 per unit	3,000	units
Materials purchased (inventoried at standard cost), actual cost,		
$4.95 per square meter	15 000	m²
Materials used	12 500	m²

| Direct labor at $8.40 per hour.. | 7,800 hours |
| Factory overhead .... | $32,100 |

It was decided that all variances — two variances each for materials and direct labor, four variances for factory overhead — should be closed to Cost of Goods Sold.

Work in Process is charged with standard costs for actual production.

Required: Journal entries to record the above information.   (CGAA adapted)

3. Journal entries; variance analysis. Students' Manufacturing, Inc., produces custom-made, tie-dyed sweat shirts for distribution on college campuses. The following standards have been established:

Materials:	
Cotton cloth: 2 yards @ $1	$2.00
Dyes: 1 pint @ $.50...	.50
Labor: ½ hour @ $6	3.00
Factory overhead: ½ hour @ $1	.50
	$6.00

The yearly production budget is based upon normal plant operations of 20,000 hours, with fixed factory overhead of $6,000.

Inventories at January 1 were:

Cotton cloth (2,000 yards @ $1)...	$2,000
Dye (1,000 pints @ $.50)	500
Work in process (1,000 units; ¼ finished as to conversion; all materials issued)...	3,375
Finished goods (500 @ $6)...	3,000

Production for January:

3,000 units completed
750 units ⅓ converted, all materials added

Transactions for January:

Cotton cloth purchased..	5,000 yds. @ $1.10
Dyes purchased...	2,500 pints @ $.49
Cotton cloth issued to factory	5,600 yards
Dyes issued to factory	2,700 pints
Direct labor payroll..	1,550 hours @ $5.90
Actual factory overhead	$1,520
Sales on account	3,100 sweat shirts @ $9

Required: Journal entries to record the January transactions, accounting for work in process at standard cost and recognizing variances in the proper accounts. Use the two-variance method in computing materials, labor, and factory overhead variances; recognize the materials price variance at the time of purchase. Use separate inventory and variance accounts for each material. Close all variances into Cost of Goods Sold.

4. Journal entries; variance analysis. The Starcraft Company manufactures a single product whose standard cost per unit is:

Materials: 20 kilograms @ $1...	$20.00
Labor: 6 hours @ $6	36.00
Factory overhead: 6 hours @ $1.60..	9.60
	$65.60

Budgeted factory overhead:

Fixed..	$ 8,400	
Variable..	10,800	$19,200
Normal capacity labor hours..		12,000
Factory overhead rate per labor hour ($19,200 ÷ 12,000 hours)		$1.60

During one production period, operations were scheduled for 80% of normal capacity. In this period, 1,400 units were completed with 400 units in process at the end of the period, complete as to materials and ½ complete as to labor and factory overhead. There were no units in process at the beginning of the period.

Work in process is charged and credited at standard costs.

Transactions during the period:

Purchased 40 000 kg of materials at $1.05 per kg.
Issued for production, 35 500 kg of materials.
Labor cost incurred for 9,500 hours, $57,475.
Actual factory overhead, $16,500.

Required: Journal entries to:
(1) Record purchase of the materials, with recognition of the price variance at the time of purchase.
(2) Issue materials to production.
(3) Record distribution of labor in process.
(4) Record actual factory overhead.
(5) Apply factory overhead and set up factory overhead variance accounts, using the two- and three-variance methods.

5. Materials variance analysis and journal entries. Creole Plastics Corporation produces kitchen utensils. It uses a standard cost system for controlling manufacturing costs. One of its finished products is a small salad bowl which is manufactured from three distinct raw plastics — Rexo, Zyco, and Durel. The Materials section of the standard cost card for this product, for use during this cost period, indicated the following standards for the materials necessary to manufacture each job of 1,000 salad bowls.

MATERIAL	STANDARD QUANTITY AND PRICE	TOTAL
Rexo	150 lbs. @ $1	$150
Zyco	250 @ 2	500
Durel	100 @ 3	300
	Total standard materials cost per job...............	$950

During the current cost period, the completed job orders included ten jobs of 1,000 salad bowls each.

Cost data relative to materials for these ten jobs were:

MATERIAL	PURCHASED	CONSUMED
Rexo	1,800 lbs. @ $1.10	1,400 lbs. @ $1.10
Zyco	1,000 @ 1.80	1,000 @ 1.80
Zyco	2,000 @ 2.00	1,600 @ 2.00
Durel	1,200 @ 3.20	850 @ 3.20

Required:
(1) The amount of variations from standard, both price and quantity, for each item of material under each of the following assumptions: (a) price variations are computed on materials purchased and (b) price variations are computed on materials issued to production, using the fifo costing method.
(2) Journal entries for the purchase and issue of materials under the various assumptions given in (1).

6. Price, mix, and yield variances; journal entries. Medicope, Inc., produces an antiseptic powder which is sold in bulk to institutions such as schools and hospitals. The product's mixture is tested at intervals during the production process. Materials are added as needed to give the mixture the desired drying and medicating properties. The standard mixture with standard prices for a 100-lb. batch is as follows:

10 lbs. of hexachlorophene @ $.45
10 lbs. of para-chlor-meta-xylenol @ $.30
30 lbs of bentonite @ $.08
20 lbs. of kaolin @ $.10
50 lbs. of talc @ $.05

During January, the following materials were purchased:

1,500 lbs. of hexachlorophene @ $.47
1,100 lbs. of para-chlor-meta-xylenol @ $.33
4,000 lbs. of bentonite @ $.07
2,500 lbs. of kaolin @ $.11
6,000 lbs. of talc @ $.04

The materials price variance is recorded when materials are purchased. Production for the month consisted of 10,700 lbs. of finished product. There were no beginning or ending inventories of work in process. The following actual materials quantities were put into production:

1,050 lbs. of hexachlorophene
1,125 lbs. of para-chlor-meta-xylenol
3,080 lbs. of bentonite
2,200 lbs. of kaolin
5,300 lbs. of talc

Required:
(1) Calculation of all materials variances (price, mix, and yield).
(2) Journal entries for (a) purchase, (b) usage, (c) completion of materials, and (d) disposition of variances, assuming all completed units were sold.

7. Disposition of variances by adjustments to cost of goods sold and inventories. Esther Corporation uses a standard cost system which records materials at actual cost, records the materials price variance when materials are issued to work in process, and prorates all variances at the end of the year. Variances associated with direct materials are prorated, based on the direct materials balances in the appropriate accounts; and variances associated with direct labor and factory overhead are prorated, based on the direct labor balances in the appropriate accounts.

The following information is available for the year ended December 31:

Materials inventory at December 31	$ 65,000
Finished goods inventory at December 31:	
Direct materials	87,000
Direct labor	130,500
Applied factory overhead	104,400
Cost of goods sold for year ended December 31:	
Direct materials	348,000
Direct labor	739,500
Applied factory overhead	591,600
Direct materials price variance (unfavorable)	10,000
Direct materials quantity variance (favorable)	15,000
Direct labor rate variance (unfavorable)	20,000
Direct labor efficiency variance (favorable)	5,000
Factory overhead incurred	690,000

There were no beginning inventories and no ending work in process inventory. Factory overhead is applied at 80% of standard direct labor.

Required:
(1) The amount of direct materials price variance to be prorated to finished goods inventory at December 31.
(2) The total amount of direct materials in the finished goods inventory at December 31, after all variances have been prorated.
(3) The total amount of direct labor in the finished goods inventory at December 31, after all variances have been prorated.

(continued)

(4) The total cost of goods sold for the year ended December 31, after all variances have been prorated.

(AICPA adapted)

8. Standard cost card; income statement. Sharp, Inc., manufactures a product based on standard specifications and costs. The following information is available for April:

	QUANTITIES	STANDARD COST
Inventories, April 1:		
Finished goods	4,000 units	$112,000
Materials	6,000	12,000

Actual and standard quantities and costs for the month are summarized as follows:

	QUANTITIES		COSTS	
	Actual	Standard	Actual	Standard
Materials purchases (units)	100,000		$193,500	$200,000
Materials requisitions (units)	95,000	94,000		
Direct labor (hours)	46,800	47,000	329,940	329,000
Factory overhead — actual			143,800	

The company's standard factory overhead rate is based on a variable factory overhead rate of $2 per direct labor hour, and fixed factory overhead of $50,000 for 50,000 direct labor hours, which is considered normal capacity. During the month, the company planned 24,000 units, but only 23,500 units were produced and placed into finished goods inventory. There was no work in process at the beginning or the end of the period; 21,000 units were sold for $40 per unit. Marketing and administrative expenses were $185,000.

Required:
(1) The standard manufacturing cost card for the product.
(2) An income statement for the month. Variances for materials, labor, and factory overhead are closed to Cost of Goods Sold. Use the two-variance method for factory overhead.

9. Comparative income statement. The Budget Department of the Florida Products Company prepares a forecast income statement for each month's operations. At the end of the month, a comparative income statement is sent to management. For November, the following statement was received:

Florida Products Company
Comparative Income Statement
For Month Ended November 30

	BUDGET	ACTUAL
Sales (10,000 units)	$180,000	$180,000
Cost of goods sold	122,000	138,308
Gross profit	$ 58,000	$ 41,692
Marketing and administrative expenses	25,000	28,000
Operating income	$ 33,000	$ 13,692

The standard cost of a unit of product is as follows:

Direct materials: 8 items @ $.55	$ 4.40
Direct labor: ¾ hour @ $8.40	6.30
Factory overhead: ¾ hour @ $2	1.50
Total standard product cost per unit	$12.20

The factory overhead rate for a total of 10,000 units of normal production was based on:

Variable expense	$ 6,000
Fixed expense	9,000
	$15,000

Actual results for the month show:
Materials used: 2% above standard requirements; average cost, $.58 per item.
Payroll: $74,880 for 7,800 hours worked.
Factory overhead: $16,100.
All marketing and administrative expenses are variable.
A total of 10,000 units were produced and sold.

Required: A comparative income statement for November, accounting for the difference between the budgeted and the actual operating income.

10. Overhead variance analysis; budget report. The Cost Department of Dover Products, Inc., prepared the following flexible budget for November:

	9,938 units	11,180 units	12,422 units
Production based on standard......................	9,938 units	11,180 units	12,422 units
Labor hours	4,000 hours	4,500 hours	5,000 hours
Capacity percentage.....................................	80%	90%*	100%
*Normal capacity			
Fixed factory overhead:			
Superintendence	$ 6,510	$ 6,510	$ 6,510
Indirect labor...	5,750	5,750	5,750
Manufacturing supplies	3,490	3,490	3,490
Maintenance..	1,680	1,680	1,680
Heat, power, and light...............................	110	110	110
Depreciation...	675	675	675
Insurance...	352	352	352
Total fixed overhead	$18,567	$18,567	$18,567
Variable factory overhead:			
Indirect labor...	$ 1,928	$ 2,169	$ 2,410
Manufacturing supplies	1,720	1,935	2,150
Maintenance..	628	707	785
Heat, power, and light...............................	61	68	76
Total variable overhead	$ 4,337	$ 4,879	$ 5,421
Total factory overhead.............................	$22,904	$23,446	$23,988

At the end of November, cost accounting tabulation showed 9,689 items manufactured, 4,150 labor hours worked, and actual factory overhead as follows:

Superintendence...	$ 6,605
Indirect labor	7,512
Manufacturing supplies...	5,450
Maintenance...	2,317
Heat, power, and light...	195
Depreciation	675
Insurance...	352
Total factory overhead	$23,106

Required:
(1) Overhead variances using (a) the three-variance and (b) the two-variance methods. (Round off overhead rates to four decimal places; round off variances to the nearest dollar.)
(2) An itemized budget report for the spending variance, including actual factory overhead, budgeted factory overhead, and variances.

PROBLEMS

Whenever variances are required in the following problems, indicate whether they are favorable or unfavorable.

20-1. Conversion to standard cost; entries; variances analysis. On May 1, 19--, the trial balance of the factory ledger accounts of the Baldwin Company appeared as follows:

Materials (1 000 kilograms)...	$ 620	
Finished Goods (100 units)	5,600	
General Ledger Control..		$6,220
	$6,220	$6,220

The company desires to install and maintain a system of standard costs, with inventories carried at standard cost. It has made the necessary materials and labor studies which reveal for its only product:

Direct materials: One material is used in the manufacturing process; 20 kg should be used for each unit of finished product and should cost $.60 per kg.

Direct labor: Time studies indicate an allowance of 5 hours of direct labor at an hourly rate of $7.50 for each unit of finished product.

The only data the company has concerning factory overhead are the following for the first four months of 19--:

	DIRECT LABOR HOURS	TOTAL FACTORY OVERHEAD
January	5,000	$ 8,100
February	9,500	9,990
March	13,000	11,460
April	8,000	9,360

The plant had been constructed to provide a normal productive capacity for 2,500 units of finished product per month. The controller suggested that a standard overhead rate be calculated at normal capacity, using a flexible budget based on the data for the first four months of 19--, as determined by the high and low points method.

Operating data for May:
Materials purchased: 60 000 kg @ $.58
Materials used: 48 000 kg
Payroll:
   Direct labor: 12,000 hours at $7.20 per hour
   Indirect labor: 1,000 hours at $6 per hour
Factory overhead charges transferred from the home office: $5,000
Units produced: 2,300
Units sold: 2,200
No work in process inventory at the beginning or end of May.

Required:
(1) A standard cost card for the product.
(2) Entries to record the above data using two materials variances, two labor variances, and two factory overhead variances, including an entry to adjust all beginning inventories to standard cost. Liability accounts and the cost of goods sold account are not a part of the factory ledger.

20-2. Variance analysis: materials, labor, factory overhead; income statement. The following information concerns the Horwitz Company, which manufactures one product and uses a standard costing system.

Standard cost per unit:

Materials: 3 liters @ $2..	$ 6	
Direct labor: 2 hours @ $8...	16	
Variable factory overhead: 2 hours @ $3............................	6	
Fixed factory overhead: 2 hours @ $2................................	4	
	$32	

Other data:

Actual production — 11,000 units
Materials purchased — 50 000 liters @ $1.90; purchases are recorded at standard cost
Direct labor (23,000 hours) — $193,200
Depreciation of factory building and equipment — $10,000

Sales salaries — $10,000
Insurance: factory — $2,000; office — $200
Sales — 9,000 units @ $45
Indirect labor (includes $25,000 fixed) — $60,000
Normal capacity — 10,000 units or 20,000 direct labor hours
Heat and light — office — $800
Heat, light, and power — factory — $11,000 (includes $4,000 fixed)
Advertising — $8,000
Materials used — 35 000 liters
Office supplies used — $500
Administrative salaries — $14,000
Depreciation of office building — $1,000
Indirect factory materials used (variable) — $20,000
Delivery expense — $4,000

Required:
(1) An analysis of the materials, direct labor, and factory overhead variances, using the three-variance method for factory overhead.
(2) Income statement, supported by a schedule of variances and treating all variances as period costs.   (CGAA adapted)

20-3. Journalizing standard cost transactions. The following information pertains to production operations of the Wesjian Company for April:

Inventories:

Work in process: Beginning, 2,000 units, all materials, ½ converted; ending, 3,000 units, all materials, ⅓ converted; no spoilage.
Finished goods: No beginning or ending inventory.

Standard and actual costs:

Materials: Standard quantity, 5 square feet per unit; 50,000 square feet were purchased @ $.52; the unfavorable materials purchase price variance was $1,000; 29,500 square feet of materials were requisitioned from the storeroom.
Labor: Standard per unit, ½ hour at $9 per hour; actual labor rate was $9.05 per hour for 2,600 hours.
Factory overhead: Normal capacity, 2,000 labor hours; fixed factory overhead standard, $2 per unit or $4 per labor hour; actual factory overhead was $5,500 variable and $8,200 fixed; efficiency variance, $600 unfavorable; spending variance, $500 unfavorable.

Five thousand units were sold for cash at $15 each.

Required: Journal entries to record the cost accounting cycle transactions using standard costing, debiting Work in Process for standard costs. Variances will not be disposed of until June, the end of the fiscal year.   (CGAA adapted)

20-4. Equivalent production schedules; analyzing differences of actual and standard materials costs. Central Pharmaceutical Company processes a single product, Mudexin, and uses a standard cost accounting system. The process requires preparation and blending of three materials in large batches with a variation from the standard mixture sometimes necessary to maintain quality. The information that follows is available for the Blending Department.

During October, 410 batches of 500 pounds each of the finished compound were completed and transferred to the Packaging Department.

Blending Department inventories totaled 6,000 pounds at the beginning of the month and 9,000 pounds at the end of the month. These inventories consisted of materials in their standard proportions and were completely processed but not transferred. Inventories are carried in the accounts at standard cost prices.

The standard cost card for a 500-pound batch shows the following standard costs:

	QUANTITY	UNIT PRICE	TOTAL COST	
Materials..				
Mucilloid..	250 pounds	$ .14	$35	
Dextrose...	200	.09	18	
Other ingredients..	50	.08	4	
Total per batch	500 pounds			$ 57
Labor:				
Blending	10 hours	$6.00		60
Factory overhead:				
Variable...	10 hours	$1.00	$10	
Fixed	10	.30	3	13
Total standard cost per 500-pound batch..............				$130

During October, the following materials were purchased and put into production:

	POUNDS	UNIT PRICE	TOTAL COST
Mucilloid...	114,400	$.17	$19,448
Dextrose	85,800	.11	9,438
Other ingredients...	19,800	.07	1,386
Total	220,000		$30,272

Wages paid for 4,212 hours of direct labor at $6.25 per hour were $26,325.

Actual factory overhead costs for the month totaled $5,519.

The standards were established for a normal production volume of 200,000 pounds (400 batches) of Mudexin per month. At this level of production, variable factory overhead was budgeted at $4,000, and fixed factory overhead was budgeted at $1,200.

Required:

(1) A schedule presenting:

    (a) The equivalent production computation for the Blending Department for October production in both pounds and batches.

    (b) The standard cost of October production itemized by components of materials, labor, and factory overhead.

(2) Schedules computing the differences between actual and standard costs, and analyzing the differences as materials variances (for each material) caused by (a) price differences and (b) quantity differences. No labor or overhead variances are to be calculated.

(3) An explanation of how materials variances arising from quantity differences could be further analyzed, with schedules presenting such an analysis. (Carry computations to three decimal places.)   (AICPA adapted)

20-5. Income statement; standard process costing; variance analysis. Gipson Corporation manufactures Product G which sells for $25 per unit. Material M is added before processing starts, and labor and overhead are added evenly during the manufacturing process. Production capacity is budgeted at 110,000 units of G annually. The standard costs per unit of G are:

Direct materials:		
M: 2 pounds @ $1.50		$ 3.00
Direct labor: 1.5 hours at $8 per hour..........................		12.00
Factory overhead:		
Variable...	$1.50	
Fixed...	1.10	2.60
Total standard cost per unit..		$17.60

A process cost system is used. Inventories are valued at standard cost. All variances from standard costs are charged or credited to Cost of Goods Sold in the year incurred.

Inventory data for 19--:

	JANUARY 1	DECEMBER 31
Material M	50,000 pounds	60,000 pounds
Work in process:		
All materials, $^2/_5$ processed	10,000 units	
All materials, $^1/_3$ processed		15,000 units
Inventory, finished goods	20,000 units	12,000 units

During 19--, 250,000 pounds of M were purchased at an average cost of $1.485 per pound; and 240,000 pounds were transferred to work in process inventory. Direct labor costs amounted to $1,313,760 at an average hourly labor rate of $8.16.

Actual factory overhead for 19--:

Variable	$181,500
Fixed	114,000

A total of 110,000 units of G were completed and transferred to finished goods inventory. Marketing and administrative expenses were $651,000.

Required: An income statement for 19--, including all manufacturing cost variances and using the two-variance method for factory overhead.

(AICPA adapted)

20-6. Standard costing in the accounts; variance disposition. Bartlett Company uses a standard cost system. The standards for one unit of its only product, Product A, are:

Direct materials: 10 feet of Item 1 at $.75 per foot; and 3 feet of Item 2 at $1 per foot
Direct labor: 2 hours at $7 per hour
Factory overhead: applied at 150% of standard direct labor cost

There was no inventory at July 1, 19A. A summary of costs and related data for the production of Product A during the year ended June 30, 19B, showed that:

(a) 100,000 feet of Item 1 were purchased at $.78 per foot.
(b) 30,000 feet of Item 2 were purchased at $.90 per foot.
(c) 8,000 units of Product A were produced, requiring 78,000 feet of Item 1, 26,000 feet of Item 2, and 15,500 hours of direct labor at $7.10 per hour.
(d) 6,000 units of Product A were sold.
(e) At June 30, 19B, 22,000 feet of Item 1, 4,000 feet of Item 2, and 2,000 completed units of Product A were on hand. (All purchases and transfers are recorded at standard.)

Required:
(1) The total debits to the materials account for the purchase of Item 1 for the year ended June 30, 19B.
(2) The total debits to the work in process account for direct labor for the year ended June 30, 19B.
(3) The balance in the materials quantity variance account for Item 2.
(4) Assuming that all standard variances are prorated to inventories and Cost of Goods Sold, the amount of: (a) the materials quantity variance for Item 2 to be prorated to materials inventory, and (b) the materials purchase price variance for Item 1 to be prorated to materials inventory.

(AICPA adapted)

20-7. Allocating variances; computing standard and actual manufacturing costs; inventory schedules. The Coolidge Corporation commenced doing business on December 1, 19--. The corporation uses a standard cost system for the manufacturing costs of its only product, Hamex. The standard costs for a unit of Hamex are:

Materials: 10 kilograms @ .70	$ 7
Direct labor: 1 hour @ $8	8
Factory overhead (applied on the basis of $2 per direct labor hour)	2
Total	$17

The following data were extracted from the corporation's books for December:

	UNITS	DEBIT	CREDIT
Budgeted production.....................................	3,000		
Units sold	1,500		
Sales...			$45,000
Sales discounts		$ 500	
Materials price usage variance..................		1,500	
Materials quantity variance......................		660	
Direct labor rate variance.........................		250	
Factory overhead spending variance.........			300
Discounts lost...		120	

The company records purchases of materials net of discounts. The amounts shown above for discounts lost and materials price usage variance are applicable to materials used in manufacturing operations during December.

Inventory data at December 31, 19––, indicate the following inventories were on hand:

Finished goods..	900 units
Work in process...	1,200 units
Materials...	None

The work in process inventory was 100% complete as to materials and 50% as to direct labor and factory overhead. The corporation's policy is to allocate variances to the cost of goods sold and ending inventories, i.e., work in process and finished goods.

Required:

(1) A schedule allocating the variances and discounts lost on purchases to the ending inventories and to cost of goods sold.

(2) A schedule computing the cost of goods manufactured at standard cost and at actual cost for December, 19––. Amounts for materials, labor, and factory overhead should be shown separately.

(3) A schedule computing the actual cost of materials, labor, and factory overhead included in the work in process inventory and in the finished goods inventory at December 31, 19––.

(AICPA adapted)

20-8. Revision of standard costs; new standard costs applied to inventory. The standard cost of Product MSY-2, manufactured by the New Bedford Company, is as follows:

	PRIME COST	FACTORY OVERHEAD (50%)	TOTAL
Material A..	$10.00		$10.00
Material B	5.00		5.00
Material C	2.00		2.00
Direct labor — Cutting............................	8.00	$4.00	12.00
Direct labor — Shaping..........................	4.00	2.00	6.00
Direct labor — Assembling	2.00	1.00	3.00
Direct labor — Boxing	1.00	.50	1.50
Total...	$32.00	$7.50	$39.50

The company manufactured 10,000 units of Product MSY-2 at a total cost of $395,000 for the period under review. Materials A, B, and C are issued in the Cutting Department.

The inventory at the end of the period is as follows:

	UNIT COST	TOTAL
100 units Material A	$10.00	$ 1,000
100 units Material B...	5.00	500
100 units Material C...	2.00	200
200 units Product MSY-2 in process — Cutting.................	29.00	5,800
200 units Product MSY-2 in process — Shaping	35.00	7,000
200 units Product MSY-2 in process — Assembling..........	38.00	7,600
200 units Product MSY-2 finished and boxed	39.50	7,900
Total..		$30,000

The following variance accounts relating to this product appear on the books for the period:

	DEBIT	CREDIT
Materials price variance:		
Due to a favorable purchase of total requirements of Material A........		$19,500
Materials usage variance:		
Excessive waste during period...	$ 6,000	
Labor rate variance:		
5% wage increase to direct workers	7,500	
Labor efficiency variance:		
Due to shutdown caused by strike..	17,000	
Factory overhead variance — fixed overhead:		
Due to shutdown caused by strike..	8,000	
Factory overhead variance — variable overhead:		
Due to permanent savings in costs of certain services........................		18,000

Required:
(1) A schedule of revised standard costs, which will clearly indicate the cumulative standard for each successive operation.
(2) A schedule applying the revised standard costs to the ending inventory.

(AICPA adapted)

CASES

A. Variance control and responsibility. The Stewart Co. utilizes a standard cost system. The variances for each department are calculated and reported to the department manager. It is expected that the managers will use the information to improve their operations and recognize that it is used by their superiors for performance evaluation.

John Daley was recently promoted to manager of the Assembly Department of the company. He has complained that the system as designed is disadvantageous to his department. Included among the variances charged to the department is one for rejected units.

The inspection occurs at the end of processing in the Assembly Department. The inspectors attempt to identify the cause of the rejection in order to charge it to the department where the error occurred. Not all errors can be easily identified with a department. These are totaled and apportioned to the departments according to the number of identified errors. The variance for rejected units in each department is a combination of the errors caused by the department plus a portion of the unidentified causes of rejects.

Required:
(1) The validity of Daley's claim.
(2) Recommended action.

(CMA adapted)

B. Variance analysis; variance control responsibility. Colony Corporation manufactures and sells a single product, using a standard cost system. The standard cost per unit of product is:

Materials: 1 pound of plastic @ $2...	$ 2.00
Direct labor: 1.6 hours @ $4	6.40
Variable factory overhead cost per unit...	3.00
Fixed factory overhead cost per unit..	1.45
	$12.85

The factory overhead cost per unit was calculated from the following annual overhead cost budget for a 60,000 unit volume:

Variable factory overhead cost:
Indirect labor (30,000 hours @ $4)	$120,000
Supplies (oil — 60,000 gallons @ $.50)	30,000
Allocated variable service department cost	30,000
Total variable factory overhead cost	$180,000

Fixed factory overhead cost:
Supervision	$ 27,000
Depreciation	45,000
Other fixed costs	15,000
Total fixed factory overhead cost	$ 87,000
Total budgeted annual factory overhead cost for 60,000 units	$267,000

The charges to the Manufacturing Department for November, when 5,000 units were produced, were:

Materials (5,300 pounds @ $2)	$10,600
Direct labor (8,200 hours @ $4.10)	33,620
Indirect labor (2,400 hours @ $4.10)	9,840
Supplies (oil — 6,000 gallons @ $.55)	3,300
Allocated variable service department cost	3,200
Supervision	2,475
Depreciation	3,750
Other fixed costs	1,250
Total	$68,035

The Purchasing Department normally buys about the same quantity as is used in production during a month. In November, 5,200 pounds were purchased at a price of $2.10 per pound.

The company has divided its responsibilities so that the Purchasing Department is responsible for the price at which materials and supplies are purchased, while the Manufacturing Department is responsible for the quantities of materials used.

The Manufacturing Department manager performs the timekeeping function and, at various times, an analysis of factory overhead and direct labor variances has shown that the manager has deliberately misclassified labor hours (e.g., direct labor hours might be classified as indirect labor hours and vice versa), so that only one of the two labor variances is unfavorable. It is not economically feasible to hire a separate timekeeper.

Required:

(1) Calculation of these variances from standard costs for the data given: (a) materials purchase price variance; (b) materials quantity variance; (c) direct labor rate variance; (d) direct labor efficiency variance; (e) total factory overhead variance for 5,000 units of production, analyzed for each expense classification.

(2) An explanation of whether the division of responsibilities should solve the conflict between price and quantity variances.

(3) A report which details the factory overhead budget variance. The report, which will be given to the Manufacturing Department manager, should display only that part of the variance that is the manager's responsibility and should highlight information useful to that manager in evaluating departmental performance and in considering corrective action.

(4) A solution to the company's problem involving the classification of labor hours.

(CMA adapted)

C. In-depth analysis of labor variances. The Felton Company manufactures a complete line of radios. Because a large number of models have plastic cases, the company has its own molding department for producing them. The month of April was devoted to the production of the plastic case for one of the portable radios — Model SX76.

The Molding Department has two operations — molding and trimming; there usually is no interaction of labor in these two operations. The standard labor cost for producing 10 plastic cases for Model SX76 is as follows:

Molding: ½ hour @ $6...	$3.00
Trimming: ¼ hour @ $4...	1.00
	$4.00

During April, 70,000 plastic cases were produced in the Molding Department; however, 10% of these cases had to be discarded because they were found to be defective at final inspection. The Purchasing Department had changed to a new plastic supplier to take advantage of a lower price for comparable plastic. The new plastic turned out to be of a lower quality, resulting in the rejection of the 7,000 cases.

Direct labor hours worked and direct labor costs charged to the Molding Department are shown below:

Molding: 3,800 hours @ $6.25	$23,750
Trimming: 1,600 hours @ $4.15..	6,640
Total labor charges	$30,390

As a result of poor scheduling by the Production Scheduling Department, the supervisor of the Molding Department had to shift molders to the trimming operation for 200 hours during April. The company paid the molding workers their regular hourly rate even though they were performing a lower-rated task. There was no significant loss of efficiency caused by the shift. In addition, as a result of unexpected machinery repairs required during the month, 75 hours and 35 hours of idle time occurred in the molding and trimming operations, respectively.

The monthly report which compares actual costs with standard cost of output for April shows the following labor variance for the Molding Department:

Actual labor cost for April	$30,390
Standard labor cost of output [63,000 × ($4 ÷ 10)]............................	25,200
Unfavorable labor variance...	$ 5,190

This variance is significantly higher than normal.

Required:
(1) A detailed analysis of the unfavorable labor variance for the Molding Department, showing the variance resulting from (a) labor rates; (b) labor substitution; (c) material substitution; (d) operating efficiency; and (e) idle time.
(2) Evaluation of the Molding Department supervisor's argument that the variances due to labor substitution and change in raw materials should not be charged to the department.

(CMA adapted)

D. Theoretical discussion of standard cost variances, capacity, and variance allocation. Last year, Schooley Corporation adopted a standard cost system. Labor standards were set on the basis of time studies and prevailing wage rates, and materials standards were determined from materials specifications and prices then in effect. In determining its standard for overhead, Schooley estimated that a total of 6,000,000 finished units would be produced during the next five years to satisfy demand for its product. The five-year period was selected to average out seasonal and cyclical fluctuations and allow for sales trends. By dividing the annual average of 1,200,000 units into the total annual budgeted overhead, a standard cost was developed for factory overhead.

At June 30, the end of the current fiscal year, a partial trial balance revealed the following:

Materials Purchase Price Variance......................................		$25,000
Materials Quantity Variance...	$ 9,000	
Labor Rate Variance...	30,000	
Labor Efficiency Variance...	7,500	
Factory Overhead Controllable Variance.............................	2,000	
Factory Overhead Volume Variance.....................................	75,000	

Standards were set at the beginning of the year and have remained unchanged. All inventories are priced at standard cost.

Required:

(1) Conclusions to be drawn from each of the six variances shown in the Schooley Corporation's trial balance.

(2) A description of each of the following allocation bases and a theoretical argument for each: (a) ideal (or theoretical) capacity, (b) practical capacity, (c) normal capacity, (d) expected actual capacity.

(AICPA adapted)

E. Standard costs in inventory and variance disposition. Standard costs are being used increasingly by manufacturing companies. Many advocates of standard costing take the position that these costs are a proper basis for inventory costing for external reporting purposes. Accounting Research Bulletin No. 43, however, reflects the widespread view that standard costs are not acceptable unless "adjusted at reasonable intervals to reflect current conditions so that at the balance-sheet date standard costs reasonably approximate costs computed under one of the recognized bases."

Required:

(1) The conceptual merits of using standard costs as the basis for inventory costing for external reporting purposes.

(2) General journal entries for three alternative dispositions of a $1,500 unfavorable variance, when all goods manufactured during the period are included in the ending finished goods inventory. Assume that a formal standard cost system is in operation, that $500 of the variance resulted from actual costs exceeding normal (attainable) standard cost, and that $1,000 of the variance resulted from the difference between the theoretical (ideal) standard and a normal standard.

(3) The conceptual merits of each of the three alternative methods of disposition requested in (2) above.

(AICPA adapted)

21

Gross Profit Analysis

Gross profit is the difference between the cost of goods sold and sales. Since the adherence of the actual to the budgeted or standard gross profit figure is highly desirable, a careful analysis of unexpected changes in gross profit is useful to a company's management. These changes are the result of one or a combination of the following:

1. Changes in sales prices of products.
2. Changes in volume sold.
   a. Changes in the number of physical units sold.
   b. Changes in the types of products sold, often called the *product mix* or *sales mix*.
3. Changes in cost elements, i.e., materials, labor, and overhead costs.

PROCEDURES FOR ANALYZING GROSS PROFIT

The determination of the various causes for an increase or decrease in gross profit is similar to the computation of standard cost variances, although gross profit analysis is often possible without the use of standard costs or budgets. In such a case, prices and costs of the previous year, or any year selected as the basis for the comparison, serve as the basis for the computation of the variances. When standard costs and budgetary methods are employed, however, a greater degree of accuracy and more effective results are achieved. Both methods are illustrated on the following pages.

Gross Profit Analysis Based on the Previous Year's Figures

As the basis for illustrating the analysis of gross profit using the previous year's figures, the following gross profit sections of the Marshall Company's operating statements for 19A and 19B are presented:

	19A	19B	CHANGES
Sales (net)	$120,000	$140,000	+$20,000
Cost of goods sold	100,000	110,000	+ 10,000
Gross profit	$ 20,000	$ 30,000	+$10,000 net increase

In comparison with 19A, sales in 19B increased $20,000 and costs increased $10,000, resulting in an increase in gross profit of $10,000.

Additional data taken from various records indicate that the sales and the cost of goods sold figures can be broken down as follows:

		19A SALES		19A COST OF GOODS SOLD	
PRODUCT	QUANTITY	Unit Price	Total	Unit Cost	Total
X	8,000 units	$5.00	$ 40,000	$4.000	$ 32,000
Y	7,000	4.00	28,000	3.500	24,500
Z	20,000	2.60	52,000	2.175	43,500
		Total sales	$120,000	Total cost	$100,000

		19B SALES		19B COST OF GOODS SOLD	
PRODUCT	QUANTITY	Unit Price	Total	Unit Cost	Total
X	10,000 units	$6.60	$ 66,000	$4.00	$ 40,000
Y	4,000	3.50	14,000	3.50	14,000
Z	20,000	3.00	60,000	2.80	56,000
		Total sales	$140,000	Total cost	$110,000

In analyzing the change in the gross profit of the Marshall Company, the sales and costs of 19A are accepted as the basis (or standard) for all comparisons. A sales price variance and a sales volume variance are computed first, followed by the computation of a cost price variance and a cost volume variance. The sales volume variance and the cost volume variance are analyzed further as a third step, which results in the computation of a sales mix variance and a final sales volume variance.

Computation of Sales Price and Sales Volume Variances. The sales price and sales volume variances of the Marshall Company are computed as follows:

Actual 19B sales		$140,000
Actual 19B sales at 19A prices:		
X: 10,000 units @ $5.00	$50,000	
Y: 4,000 @ 4.00	16,000	
Z: 20,000 @ 2.60	52,000	118,000
Favorable sales price variance		$ 22,000
Actual 19B sales at 19A prices		$118,000
Total 19A sales (used as standard)		120,000
Unfavorable sales volume variance		$ 2,000

Computation of Cost Price and Cost Volume Variances. The cost price and cost volume variances are computed as follows:

Actual 19B cost of goods sold......................................			$110,000
Actual 19B sales at 19A costs:			
X: 10,000 units @ $4.000..		$40,000	
Y: 4,000 @ 3.500..		14,000	
Z: 20,000 @ 2.175..		43,500	97,500
Unfavorable cost price variance.................................			$ 12,500
Actual 19B sales at 19A costs			$ 97,500
Cost of goods sold in 19A (used as standard)			100,000
Favorable cost volume variance..................................			$ 2,500

Computation of the Sales Mix and the Final Sales Volume Variances. The results of the preceding computations might explain the reason for the $10,000 increase in gross profit:

Favorable sales prices variance....................................		$22,000
Favorable volume variances (net) consisting of:		
Favorable cost volume variance..............................	$2,500	
Less unfavorable sales volume variance	2,000	
Net favorable volume variance		500
		$22,500
Less unfavorable cost price variance...........................		12,500
Increase in gross profit...		$10,000

The net $500 favorable volume variance is a composite of the sales volume and cost volume variances. It should be further analyzed to determine the more significant sales mix and final sales volume variances. To accomplish this analysis, one additional figure must be determined — the average gross profit realized on the units sold in the base (or standard) year. The computation is:

$$\frac{\text{Total gross profit of 19A sales}}{\text{Total number of units sold in 19A}} = \frac{\$20,000}{35,000} = \$.5714 \text{ per unit}$$

The $.5714 average gross profit per unit sold in 19A is multiplied by the total number of units sold in 19B (34,000 units). The resulting $19,427 is the total gross profit that would have been achieved in 19B if all units had been sold at 19A's average gross profit per unit.

The sales mix and the final sales volume variances can now be calculated:

19B sales at 19A prices..		$118,000
19B sales at 19A costs		97,500
Difference..		$ 20,500
19B sales at 19A average gross profit..........................		19,427
Favorable sales mix variance....................................		$ 1,073
19B sales at 19A average gross profit..........................		$ 19,427
Total 19A sales (used as standard)	$120,000	
Cost of goods sold in 19A (used as standard)	100,000	
Difference..		20,000
Unfavorable final sales volume variance		$ 573

Check: Favorable sales mix variance............................ $ 1,073
　　　　Unfavorable final sales volume variance 573
　　　　Net favorable volume variance .... $ 500

The sales mix variance can be viewed in the following manner:

	(1)	19A SALES		(2)	(3)	(4)	
	19B SALES			19B SALES (IN 19A		19A UNIT GROSS	
PRODUCT	UNITS	Units	%	PROPORTIONS)	(1) − (2)	PROFIT	(3) × (4)
X	10,000	8,000	22.86	7,772*	2,228	$1.000**	$2,228
Y	4,000	7,000	20.00	6,800	(2,800)	.500	(1,400)
Z	20,000	20,000	57.14	19,428	572	.425	243
Total.........	34,000	35,000	100.00	34,000	−0−		

Rounding difference.. 2
Favorable sales mix variance.. $1,073

*34,000 × 22.86% = 7,772
**$5 sales price − $4 cost of goods sold =$1

The final sales volume variance is the difference in the number of units sold for the two years multiplied by the 19A average gross profit per unit.

19B sales units...	34,000
19A sales units...	35,000
Unit sales difference	1,000
Average gross profit per unit	×$.5714
	$571.40
Rounding difference..	1.60
Unfavorable final sales volume variance	$573.00

Recapitulation of Variances. The variances identified in the preceding computations are summarized below:

	GAINS	LOSSES
Gain due to increased sales price...............................	$22,000	
Loss due to increased cost		$12,500
Gain due to shift in sales mix	1,073	
Loss due to decrease in units sold		573
Total...	$23,073	$13,073
Less	13,073	
Net increase in gross profit..	$10,000	

Gross Profit Analysis Based on Budgets and Standard Costs

As the basis for illustrating the analysis of gross profit using budgets and standard costs, three financial statements for Collier, Inc., are presented on page 617:

1. The budgeted income statement prepared at the beginning of the period.
2. The actual income statement prepared at the end of the period.
3. An income statement prepared at the end of the period on the basis of actual sales units at budgeted sales prices and at standard costs.

Statement 1

Collier, Inc.
Income Statement (Budgeted)

PRODUCT	UNITS	SALES		COST		GROSS PROFIT	
		Unit Price	Amount	Unit Cost	Amount	Per Unit	Amount
A	6,000	$15.00	$ 90,000	$12.00	$ 72,000	$3.00	$18,000
B	3,500	12.00	42,000	10.00	35,000	2.00	7,000
C	1,000	10.00	10,000	8.75	8,750	1.25	1,250
	10,500	$13.52*	$142,000	$11.02*	$115,750	$2.50*	$26,250

*Weighted average.

Statement 2

Collier Inc.
Income Statement (Actual)

PRODUCT	UNITS	SALES		COST		GROSS PROFIT	
		Unit Price	Amount	Unit Cost	Amount	Per Unit	Amount
A	5,112	$16.00	$ 81,792	$13.98	$ 71,466	$2.02	$10,326
B	4,208	12.00	50,496	9.72	40,902	2.28	9,594
C	1,105	9.00	9,945	8.83	9,757	.17	188
	10,425	$13.64*	$142,233	$11.71*	$122,125	$1.93*	$20,108

*Weighted average.

Statement 3

Collier, Inc.
Income Statement (Actual Units At Budgeted Prices and Costs)

PRODUCT	UNITS	SALES		COST		GROSS PROFIT	
		Unit Price	Amount	Unit Cost	Amount	Per Unit	Amount
A	5,112	$15.00	$ 76,680	$12.00	$ 61,344	$3.00	$15,336
B	4,208	12.00	50,496	10.00	42,080	2.00	8,416
C	1,105	10.00	11,050	8.75	9,669	1.25	1,381
	10,425	$13.26*	$138,226	$10.85*	$113,093	$2.41*	$25,133

*Weighted average.

According to Statement 1, Collier, Inc., expected a gross profit of $26,250, based on an estimated production of 10,500 units and an average gross profit of $2.50 per unit. As shown in Statement 2, the company actually made a gross profit of only $20,108, or $1.93 per unit. Statement 3 indicates that the average gross profit for the actual units sold would have been $2.41 per unit if the budgeted sales prices and costs per unit had been achieved.

The $6,142 difference between the budgeted gross profit and the actual gross profit is the result of changes in sales prices, sales volume, sales mix, and costs. For example, on the basis of the budget, A is the most profitable product while C is the least profitable per unit. Due to variations in sales price and cost, B is actually the most profitable while C is the least profitable per unit. The dollar effect of such changes is shown by the calculation of the sales price, sales volume, cost price, cost volume, sales mix, and final sales volume variances.

Computation of Sales Price and Sales Volume Variances. Using the figures from the statements on page 617, the sales price and sales volume variances for Collier, Inc., are computed as follows:

Actual sales	$142,233
Actual sales at budgeted prices	138,226
Favorable sales price variance	$ 4,007
Actual sales at budgeted prices	$138,226
Budgeted sales	142,000
Unfavorable sales volume variance	$ 3,774

Computation of Cost Price and Cost Volume Variances. The cost price and cost volume variances are computed as follows:

Cost of goods sold — actual	$122,125
Budgeted cost of actual units sold	113,093
Unfavorable cost price variance	$ 9,032
Budgeted cost of actual units sold	$113,093
Budgeted cost of budgeted units sold	115,750
Favorable cost volume variance	$ 2,657

Computation of the Sales Mix and the Final Sales Volume Variances. In the above calculations, two volume variances appear:

Unfavorable sales volume variance	$3,774
Favorable cost volume variance	2,657
Net unfavorable volume variance	$1,117

The net volume variance should be further analyzed to determine the sales mix and the final sales volume variances. These variances are computed as follows:

Actual sales at budgeted prices		$138,226.00
Budgeted cost of actual units sold		113,093.00
Difference		$ 25,133.00
Budgeted gross profit of actual units sold (10,425 actual units × $2.50 budgeted gross profit per unit)		26,062.50
Unfavorable sales mix variance		$ 929.50
Budgeted gross profit of actual units sold		$ 26,062.50
Budgeted sales	$142,000	
Budgeted cost of budgeted units sold	115,750	
Budgeted gross profit		26,250.00
Unfavorable final sales volume variance		$ 187.50

Check: Unfavorable sales mix variance.................. $ 929.50
        Unfavorable final sales volume variance 187.50
        Net unfavorable volume variance .... $ 1,117.00

Again, the sales mix variance can be viewed in the following manner:

	(1)	(2)		(3)	(4)	
	ACTUAL SALES	BUDGETED SALES		ACTUAL SALES (IN BUDGETED	(1) − (2)	BUDGETED UNIT GROSS	(3) × (4)
PRODUCT	UNITS	*Units*	%	PROPORTIONS)		PROFIT	
A	5,112	6,000	57.14	5,957*	(845)	$3.00	$(2,535.00)
B	4,208	3,500	33.33	3,475	733	2.00	1,466.00
C	1,105	1,000	9.53	993	112	1.25	140.00
Total.........	10,425	10,500	100.00	10,425	–0–		

Rounding difference... (.50)
Unfavorable sales mix variance... $ (929.50)

*10,425 × 57.14% = 5,957.

The final sales volume variance is the difference in the number of actual and budgeted units sold multiplied by the budgeted average gross profit per unit.

Actual sales units 10,425
Budgeted sales units 10,500
Unit sales difference.. 75
Budgeted average gross profit per unit.. ×$2.50
Unfavorable final sales volume variance $187.50

Recapitulation of Variances. The variances identified in the preceding computations are summarized below:

	GAINS	LOSSES
Gain due to increased sales prices	$4,007	
Loss due to increased cost		$ 9,032.00
Loss due to shift in sales mix..................................		929.50
Loss due to decrease in units sold		187.50
Total...	$4,007	$10,149.00
Less		4,007.00
Net decrease in gross profit.....................................		$ 6,142.00

REFINEMENT OF SALES VOLUME ANALYSIS

In the above computation, the sales mix and final sales volume variances were determined with the aid of an average gross profit figure and total figures only. However, it is often necessary to trace the causes for a change to the individual product lines. Using the figures from the income statements of Collier, Inc., an analysis by products can be made as follows:

COLLIER, INC.
ANALYSIS BY PRODUCT

AMOUNTS BASED ON	PRODUCT A		PRODUCT B		PRODUCT C	
	Sales	Cost	Sales	Cost	Sales	Cost
Statement 3..	$76,680	$61,344	$50,496	$42,080	$11,050	$9,669
Statement 1..	90,000	72,000	42,000	35,000	10,000	8,750
Difference....	−$13,320	+$10,656	+$ 8,496	−$ 7,080	+$ 1,050	−$ 919
Net............	−$2,664		+$1,416		+$131	

RECAPITULATION:

	SALES VOLUME	
	Gains	Losses
On Product A		$2,664
On Product B	$1,416	
On Product C	131	
Total..	$1,547	$2,664
Less gain..		1,547
Net loss due to sales mix variance and final sales volume variance		$1,117

USES OF GROSS PROFIT ANALYSIS

The gross profit analysis based on budgets and standard costs depicts the weak spots in the year's performance. Management is now able to outline the remedies that should correct the situation. For Collier, Inc., the gain due to higher prices is more than offset by the increase in cost, the shift to less profitable products, and the decrease in units sold. As the planned gross profit is the responsibility of the marketing as well as the manufacturing departments, the gross profit analysis brings together these two major functional areas of the firm and points to the need for further study by both of these departments. The marketing department must explain the changes in sales prices, the shift in the sales mix, and the decrease in units sold, while the production department must account for the increase in cost. To be of real value, the cost price variance should be further analyzed to determine variances for materials, labor, and factory overhead.

DISCUSSION QUESTIONS

1. Why is the gross profit figure significant?

2. What causes changes in the gross profit?

3. Explain "product mix" or "sales mix."

4. By what methods can a change in the gross profit figure be analyzed?

5. Describe how the sales price variance is determined. If the sales price variance were journalized in the books, how would such an entry vary from the entry for the materials purchase price variance?

6. How are the sales mix and the final sales volume variances computed?

7. What is the significance of the average gross profit figure of the base or standard year?

8. The gross profit analysis based on budgets and standards makes use of three basic statements. Name them.

9. What important information is revealed by a gross profit analysis on a product basis?

10. Whose task is it to see that the planned gross profit is met?

EXERCISES

1. Gross profit analysis. A cost analyst of the Memphis Company has prepared a monthly gross profit analysis, comparing actual to budget for its two products, Alco and Bacco. June budget and actual data show:

| | | SALES | | | COST OF GOODS SOLD | | GROSS PROFIT | |
	Units	Unit Price	Amount	Unit Cost	Amount	Per Unit	Amount
Budget:							
Alco	8,000	$20.00	$160,000	$16.00	$128,000	$4.00	$32,000
Bacco	4,200	14.00	58,800	12.00	50,400	2.00	8,400
Total budget	12,200	$17.9344*	$218,800	$14.6229*	$178,400	$3.3115*	$40,400
Actual:							
Alco	7,500	$21.00	$157,500	$16.50	$123,750	$4.50	$33,750
Bacco	4,500	13.50	60,750	11.50	51,750	2.00	9,000
Total actual	12,000	$18.1875*	$218,250	$14.625*	$175,500	$3.5625*	$42,750

*Weighted average

Required:
(1) The price and volume variances for sales and cost.
(2) The sales mix and final sales volume variances.

2. Gross profit analysis. The Summers Sporting Goods Shop presents the following data for two types of racquetball gloves, leather and fabric, for 19A and 19B:

| | 19A | | | 19B | | |
	Units	Per Unit	Amount	Units	Per Unit	Amount
Sales:						
Leather racquetball gloves	8,000	$8.00	$64,000	12,000	$10.00	$120,000
Fabric racquetball gloves	8,000	4.00	32,000	20,000	6.00	120,000
			$96,000			$240,000
Cost of goods sold:						
Leather racquetball gloves	8,000	$6.00	$48,000	12,000	$ 9.00	$108,000
Fabric racquetball gloves	8,000	3.00	24,000	20,000	5.00	100,000
			$72,000			$208,000
Gross profit	16,000	$1.50	$24,000	32,000	$ 1.00	$ 32,000

Required:
1. (1) The price and volume variances for sales and cost.
2. (2) The sales mix and final sales volume variances.

3. Gross profit analysis. Actual and budget data for 19-- for the Deerfield Distributing Company are:

	PRODUCT A	PRODUCT B	TOTAL
Actual sales..	60,000 units @ $1.00	20,000 units @ $2.00	$100,000
Actual cost of goods sold	60,000 @ .80	20,000 @ 1.85	85,000
Budgeted sales	50,000 @ 1.25	35,000 @ 2.50	150,000
Budgeted cost of goods sold.............	50,000 @ 1.00	35,000 @ 2.00	120,000

Required:
1. (1) The computations of the following variances: (a) sales price; (b) sales volume; (c) cost price; (d) cost volume.
2. (2) The sales mix and final sales volume variances. (Round off computations to three decimal places.)

4. Gross profit analysis. Bates Brothers Clothiers handles two lines of men's suits — The Bostonian and The Varsity. On these suits, the store realized a gross profit of $159,300 in 19A and $159,570 in 19B. The store manager was puzzled because the dollar sales volume and the number of suits sold were higher for 19B than for 19A, yet the gross profit had remained about the same. The firm's accounting records provided the following detailed information:

	THE BOSTONIAN			THE VARSITY		
YEAR	Suits	Cost	Sales Price	Suits	Cost	Sales Price
19A..........................	1,650	$105	$175	1,460	$70	$100
19B	1,320	114	190	1,975	80	110

Required:
1. (1) The price and volume variances for sales and cost.
2. (2) The sales mix and final sales volume variances. (Round off the 19A average gross profit per unit to three decimal places.)

5. Sales mix variance. The following data for the Rosenman Company are available for 19--:

	BUDGET		ACTUAL	
	Product A	Product B	Product A	Product B
Quantity..................................	100 units	200 units	200 units	125 units
Sales price	$50	$40	$49	$42
Cost	25	30	26	25

Required: Sales mix variance.

6. Gross profit analysis based on inpatient service days. The controller of Langwood Hospital prepared the following statement of operations, comparing 19B to 19A.

	19B	19A
Inpatient service days..	330,000	300,000
Patient service revenues	$13,860,000	$12,000,000
Cost of services rendered:		
Medicines, linens, and other supplies.........................	$ 1,400,000	$ 1,000,000
Salaries — nurses, interns, residents, staff	9,000,000	7,500,000
Patient service overhead...	1,500,000	1,500,000
Total cost of services rendered..............................	$11,900,000	$10,000,000
Gross profit..	$ 1,960,000	$ 2,000,000
Administrative expenses	2,013,000	1,800,000
Excess of revenues over expenditures..........................	$ (53,000)	$ 200,000

Required: An analysis of the gross profit, including the revenue rate (price), revenue volume, cost price, cost volume, revenue mix, and final revenue volume variances. (Round off computations to the nearest thousand.)

7. Gross profit analysis for one product. The president of the McLachlan Wholesale Company, which markets a single product, requests an explanation for the gross profit decline for 19B. The following information is available:

| | 19A | | | 19B | | |
	Units	Per Unit	Total	Units	Per Unit	Total
Sales..	25,000	$3.00	$75,000	24,000	$2.75	$66,000
Cost of goods sold	25,000	$2.38	59,500	24,000	$2.40	57,600
Gross profit...........................			$15,500			$ 8,400

Required: Gross profit analysis.

8. Gross profit analysis for one product. The 19A income statement of the Broome Corporation showed:

Sales (90,500 units)..	$760,200
Cost of goods sold...	452,500
Gross profit...	$307,700

For 19B, the management forecast a sales volume of 100,000 units at a sales price of $8.20 per unit. For this range of activity, the variable cost is estimated to be $4.80 per unit. No fixed cost is included in the cost of goods sold.

Required: An analysis of the variation in gross profit between the two years, indicating the effects of changes in sales prices, sales volume, cost price, and cost volume.

(AICPA adapted)

PROBLEMS

21-1. Gross profit analysis. The Beisswanger Shoe Company manufactures a wide line of ladies' footwear. Sales volume has increased rapidly over the past seven years. However, after a change in executive management, the new president believed that sales volume should increase at an even faster rate. The plan is to increase volume, with the price level remaining the same or declining. After lengthy discussions with the plant manager and the sales manager, a mutually agreeable plan was formulated, whereby the volume was expected to increase with a decrease in the sales price. At the time of this proposal, both the plant manager and the sales manager believed that the existing level of gross profit could be maintained.

In 19A, the last year before adoption of the new plan, the following company data had been recorded with respect to two lines of ladies' footwear — Loafers and Sandals.

	LOAFERS	SANDALS
Shoes sold	10,000	5,000
Revenue...	$200,000	$150,000
Gross profit..	70,000	60,000

The proposed plan did have the desired effect on 19B gross profit. The president was quite enthusiastic over the success of the plan but wanted to know if the increased gross profit was attributable to increased sales or reduced costs.

Data for 19B:

	LOAFERS	SANDALS
Shoes sold	12,000	6,000
Revenue...	$208,000	$144,000
Cost of goods sold...	124,000	86,000
Gross profit..	$ 84,000	$ 58,000

Required: An analysis to indicate the underlying reasons for the change in gross profit.

21-2. Gross profit analysis. Tribal Products, Inc., was organized ten years ago by James Littlebear for the purpose of making and selling souvenirs to tourists in Southwestern Arizona. After much experimentation, the product line has been limited to five products: moccasins, strings of beads, rawhide vests, leather belts, and feathered headdresses. All transactions take place in two small buildings located on tribal land.

After a slow start, the business for the past six years has been extremely profitable, growing at an average annual rate of 12%. In 19B, despite an increase in the total number of units sold, the gross profit of the firm dropped. As a result, Littlebear tentatively blamed the drop in profit on a change in the sales mix.

The accountant has been given the task of analyzing the gross profit of the past two years, shown below, in an attempt to pin down the cause of the loss in profits.

				19A		
	Quantity	Unit Cost	Total Cost	Unit Price	Total Sales	Gross Profit
Moccasins	1,000	$2.50	$ 2,500	$5.00	$ 5,000	$ 2,500
Beads	6,000	.20	1,200	.50	3,000	1,800
Vests	1,500	1.75	2,625	3.50	5,250	2,625
Belts	4,000	.45	1,800	1.00	4,000	2,200
Headdresses	500	4.00	2,000	7.50	3,750	1,750
Total	13,000		$10,125		$21,000	$10,875

				19B		
	Quantity	Unit Cost	Total Cost	Unit Price	Total Sales	Gross Profit
Moccasins	1,100	$2.60	$2,860	$5.00	$ 5,500	$ 2,640
Beads	6,800	.20	1,360	.50	3,400	2,040
Vests	1,200	1.80	2,160	3.50	4,200	2,040
Belts	4,200	.50	2,100	1.00	4,200	2,100
Headdresses	350	3.80	1,330	7.50	2,625	1,295
Total	13,650		$9,810		$19,925	$10,115

Required: An analysis of the gross profit decline from 19A to 19B. (Round off the 19A average gross profit per unit to four decimal places.)

21-3. Gross profit analysis for one product. The Alba Mining Company mines Almet. For 19A and 19B, the company's comparative report of operations showed:

	19A	19B	INCREASE (DECREASE)
Net sales	$ 840,000	$891,000	$ 51,000
Cost of goods sold	945,000	688,500	(256,500)
Gross profit (loss)	$(105,000)	$202,500	$ 307,500

Additional information:

(a) On January 1, 19B, Almet's sales price was increased from $8 to $11 per ton.
(b) On the same day, new machinery was placed in operation, reducing the cost of mining from $9 to $8.50 per ton.
(c) Ending inventories, costed on the lifo basis, did not change.

Required: A gross profit analysis accounting for the effects of the changes in price and volume factors upon (1) sales and (2) cost of goods sold.

(AICPA adapted)

21-4. Gross profit analysis for one product. The president of the Bivert Company, which manufactures one product, requests an analysis of the causes of change in gross profit. An investigation reveals the following information:

	19B		19A	
	Amount	*Per Unit*	*Amount*	*Per Unit*
Sales...................................	$122,400	$10.20	$100,000	$10.00
Cost of goods sold................	70,080	5.84	60,000	6.00
Gross profit...........................	$ 52,320	$ 4.36	$ 40,000	$ 4.00

Required: A detailed analysis of the causes for the change in gross profit.

(AICPA adapted)

21-5. Final sales volume and sales mix variances using contribution margin. Marak Co. makes three grades of indoor-outdoor carpets. The sales volume for the annual budget is determined by estimating the total market volume for indoor-outdoor carpet and then applying the company's prior year market share, adjusted for planned changes due to company programs for the coming year. The volume is apportioned between the three grades, based upon the prior year's product mix, again adjusted for planned changes due to company programs for the coming year.

Given below are the company's budgeted income statement and the results of operations for the current year.

Income Statement (Budgeted)
(in thousands of dollars)

	GRADE 1	GRADE 2	GRADE 3	TOTAL
Sales units...	1,000 rolls	1,000 rolls	2,000 rolls	4,000 rolls
Sales dollars...	$1,000	$2,000	$3,000	$6,000
Variable expense.....................................	700	1,600	2,300	4,600
Contribution margin..............................	$ 300	$ 400	$ 700	$1,400
Traceable fixed expense.......................	200	200	300	700
Traceable margin..................................	$ 100	$ 200	$ 400	$ 700
Marketing and administrative expenses..				250
Operating income.................................				$ 450

Income Statement (Actual)
(in thousands of dollars)

	GRADE 1	GRADE 2	GRADE 3	TOTAL
Sales units...	800 rolls	1,000 rolls	2,100 rolls	3,900 rolls
Sales dollars...	$810	$2,000	$3,000	$5,810
Variable expense.....................................	560	1,610	2,320	4,490
Contribution margin..............................	$250	$ 390	$ 680	$1,320
Traceable fixed expense.......................	210	220	315	745
Traceable margin..................................	$ 40	$ 170	$ 365	$ 575
Marketing and administrative expenses..				275
Operating income.................................				$ 300

Industry volume was estimated at 40,000 rolls. Actual industry volume for the year was 38,000 rolls.

Required:
(1) The final sales volume variance, using budgeted contribution margins.
(2) The effect of the present condition of the carpet industry on the final sales volume variance.
(3) The dollar impact on profits (using budgeted contribution margins) of the shift in product mix from the budgeted mix.

(CMA adapted)

CASE

Gross profit analysis of time-sharing computer programs. The senior systems analyst of Tyrene, Inc., Bob Canedy, developed in his spare time three unique packages of computer programs: Package 1, Inventory Control; Package 2, Sales Analysis; Package 3, Report Preparation. After realizing their marketability, he struck out on his own, forming Data-Pack Co., a computer time-sharing service bureau. He rented an adequate computer and leased some data communication lines and terminals, then placed the packages on-line. Once operational, he planned to sell the use of his packages to industrial customers by the system-connect-hour, i.e., total time elapsing while the customer's terminal is directly connected to the central computer.

In the process of establishing profitable sales prices, Canedy decided to project costs for the first year. Using processing information provided by the computer sales representative, he allocated the total cost to the packages as follows:

	COMPUTER RENTAL ($56,000)		OTHER COMMON COSTS ($14,000)					
	(1)		(2)					
PACKAGE	Core Requisitions (000s Bits)	% of Total Core Requisitions	CPU* Hrs. ÷ System Connect Hrs.	% of Total CPU to System Connect Hrs.	WEIGHTED AVERAGE [4 × COL. (1) + COL. (2)] ÷ 5	COMMON COST ALLOCATION	TRACE-ABLE COST	TOTAL COST
1	80	60%	.18	10%	50%	$35,000	$10,000	$ 45,000
2	33	25	.90	50	30	21,000	14,000	35,000
3	20	15	.72	40	20	14,000	6,000	20,000
Total	133	100%	1.80	100%	100%	$70,000	$30,000	$100,000

*Central Processing Unit.

Working from expected costs, Canedy computed the desired markup for each of the packages. Since he knew that the useful lives of the programs were only a few years, he decided to recoup the investment in time that he had spent on developing the programs by using that criterion in computing a sales price, as follows:

PACKAGE	WORKDAYS SPENT IN DEVELOPING PROGRAMS	(1) % OF TOTAL DEVELOPMENT	PROJECTED SALES (HRS.)	(2) HOURLY COST (PER UNIT)	UNIT MARKUP (1) × (2)	UNIT SALES PRICE	TOTAL SALES (HRS. × SALES PRICE)
1	27	15%	900	$50	$ 7.50	$57.50	$ 51,750
2	108	60	1,000	35	21.00	56.00	56,000
3	45	25	500	40	10.00	50.00	25,000
Total	180	100%	2,400				$132,750

After the first year of operation, Data-Pack's income statement appeared as follows:

Sales:
Package 1: 1,200 hrs. @ $53 .... $63,600
Package 2:   900   @   58 52,200
Package 3:   700   @   46 .... 32,200 $148,000

Cost of goods sold:	COMMON COST	TRACEABLE COST	TOTAL COST	
Package 1	$40,000	$14,000	$54,000	
Package 2	24,000	12,000	36,000	
Package 3	16,000	5,000	21,000	111,000
Operating income				$ 37,000

Although the firm exceeded planned profits by $4,250, it was evident that changes in demand for the packages and changes in costs and sales prices made this gain only coincidental.

Required: A gross profit analysis to determine the effects of demand and fluctuating prices on sales revenue, so that a new price for the most profitable package can be established.

22

Direct Costing and the Contribution Margin

The factory overhead chapters presented the use of the factory overhead rate for product costing and pricing. All factory overhead costs were combined into a composite rate. When this rate is constructed, a capacity, volume, or activity level must be selected, so that all costs and expenses can be expected to be recovered over a certain period of time. This type of costing, known as *absorption, full*, or *conventional costing*, assigns direct materials and direct labor costs and a share of both fixed and variable factory overhead to units of production.

At the end of each month or year, differences between actual and applied overhead cause fluctuations in the unit product costs. These fluctuations are influenced by the fixed costs included in over- or underapplied factory overhead. The unit product cost will also fluctuate in cases in which the capacity level used to calculate the factory overhead rate is different from one period to the next, because the fixed part of the rate will be higher when a lower capacity level is used and lower when a higher level is used. Failure to use a predetermined factory overhead rate also causes even wider unit product cost fluctuations because fixed overhead is then allocated to production based on the actual activity level for the accounting period.

In responsibility accounting, the division of factory overhead into fixed and variable elements aids management in placing cost accountability on those individuals responsible for the incurrence of these costs. The factory overhead rate used for product costing, however, still includes both variable and fixed elements.

In standard cost accounting, dual factory overhead rates, one for variable cost and one for fixed cost, can be employed. Both rates are used in costing products; however, the unit standard as to fixed cost with its overhead based on standard volume will remain stable, and the standard cost of goods sold will generally be proportional to sales volume.

When a short-run standard volume is compared with the long-run or normal capacity concept of the standard cost system, the difference is the volume variance or idle capacity and fixed efficiency variances. If it could be expected that such favorable or unfavorable variances would balance out in the long run, they could be deferred, and the fixed costs included in the periodic cost of goods sold would vary directly and proportionately with sales volume. In such cases, the fixed overhead behaves like the unit variable cost. However, if variances are expensed each period, fluctuations in the unit product cost occur.

Information accumulated in NAA research studies over a period of years indicates that the concept of long-range normal or standard unit cost for costing production, sales, and inventory is not often applied in practice. The reasons for this failure are:

1. Long-range normal or standard volume cannot be reliably determined. First, this is a consequence of the fact that long-range volume for a growing company with indefinite future life cannot be defined in concrete terms capable of being implemented by measurement techniques. Second, long-range forecasts of future volume have, at best, a wide and unknown margin of error.

2. The services of manufacturing facilities and organizations tend to expire with the passage of time whether or not utilized to produce salable goods. Consequently, the period costs of these services also expire with time. To carry such costs forward to future periods results in mismatching of costs with revenues because no benefits from such costs will be received in the future and nothing is contributed by the cost toward production of future revenues. Thus, the practice of charging unabsorbed period cost against revenues of the current period has been justified by reasoning that this charge measures cost of idle capacity and not cost of production. Similarly, apportionment of large overabsorbed balances reflects the opinion that unit product costs based on standard volume have been overstated.[1]

The NAA study concludes that "the concept of long-run unit cost of production is unsatisfactory in measuring short period income. The fault in this case is that the wrong cost concept was chosen for the purpose — i.e., the long-run concept of cost was used to measure short-run operations."[2]

It has been emphasized that the normal capacity concept used for establishing overhead rates is long-range in nature. Management, on the other hand, wants monthly and even weekly earnings reports. They want to know what was earned last month. They do not ask for a profit figure covering the firm's entire production and sales cycle. Although the usefulness of costing methods for managerial purposes has been aided immeasurably through the use of factory overhead rates and flexible budgets, management always asks for more direct and understandable answers. Direct costing seeks to satisfy these demands.

[1]NAA Research Report, No. 37, "Applications of Direct Costing" (New York: National Association of Accountants, 1961), pp. 72–73.
[2]Ibid., p. 73.

DIRECT COSTING DEFINED

Direct costing charges products with only those manufacturing costs that vary directly with volume. Only prime costs (direct materials and direct labor) plus variable factory overhead expenses are assigned to inventories, both work in process and finished goods, and to the cost of goods sold. Thus, these variable costs are charged to the product while fixed manufacturing costs are totally expensed in the current period. Manufacturing costs such as depreciation, insurance, and taxes that are a function of time rather than of production are excluded from the cost of the product. Also excluded are salaries of factory supervisors and office employees as well as wages of certain factory employees, such as maintenance crews and guards, which are considered period costs rather than product costs.

FACETS OF DIRECT COSTING

Direct costing focuses attention on the product and its costs. This interest moves in two directions: (1) to internal uses of the fixed-variable cost relationship and the contribution margin concept; and (2) to external uses involving the costing of inventories, income determination, and financial reporting. The internal uses deal with the application of direct costing in profit planning, product pricing, other phases of decision making, and in cost control. Diagrammatically, these facets of direct costing can be presented as illustrated below:

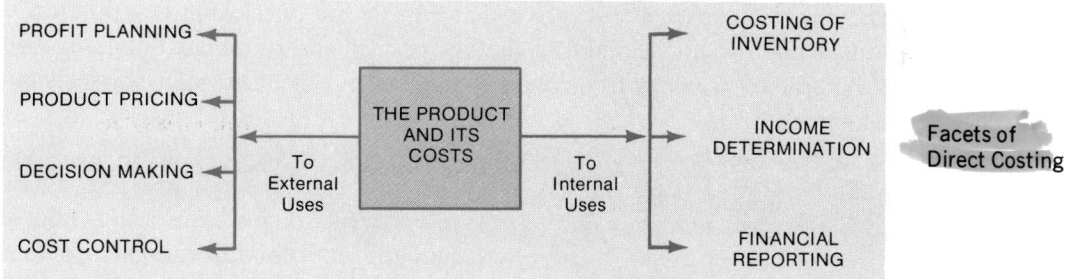

Facets of Direct Costing

Executive management, including marketing executives, production managers, and cost analysts, has generally praised the planning, control, and analytical potentialities of direct costing. Fixed costs calculated on a unit cost basis tend to vary. On the other hand, direct unit costs and the contribution margin per unit tend to remain constant for various volumes of production and sales.

Internal Uses of Direct Costing

The *contribution margin* or *marginal income* is the result of subtracting all variable costs from sales revenue. In direct costing, an income per unit is not calculated; only an income on total sales of all products is determined by subtracting the total fixed cost from the contribution margin, as shown in the illustration below. In this illustration, the figures are based on the assumption that the total variable cost is perfectly variable, with the unit variable cost remaining at the $42 figure, and that the fixed cost is perfectly fixed in total.

	PER UNIT	TOTAL	PERCENTAGE OF SALES
Sales (10,000 units)	$70	$700,000	100
Less variable cost	42	420,000	60
Contribution margin	$28	$280,000	40
Less fixed cost		175,000	25
Operating income		$105,000	15

Direct Costing as a Profit-Planning Tool. A *profit plan*, often called a *budget* or *plan of operations*, covers all phases of future operations to attain a stated profit goal. Although such a plan includes both long- and short-range operations, direct costing is quite useful in planning for short periods, in pricing special orders, or in making current operating decisions. With its separation of variable and fixed costs and the calculation of the contribution margin figure, direct costing facilitates analysis of the cost-volume-profit relationship. Direct costing aids in identifying the relevant analytical data for determining the break-even point, the rate of return on investment, the contribution margin by a segment of total sales, and the total profit from all operations based on a given volume.

The variable cost and the contribution margin allow quick and fairly reliable profit approximations for making decisions in the short run. In such situations, it is assumed that the change or shift of a small segment within the total volume does not require major changes in capacity, which would change fixed or period costs. Period costs that are specific or relevant to a product, a product line, or any segment of the business should be isolated and attached to the product in order to increase the usefulness of these costs for decision-making purposes.

Direct costing also aids management in planning and evaluating the profit resulting from a change of volume, a change in the sales mix, make-or-buy situations, and the acquisition of new equipment. A knowledge of the variable or out-of-pocket costs, fixed costs, and the contribution margin provides guidelines for the selection of the most profitable products, customers, territories, and other segments of the entire business. These uses are discussed in later chapters.

Direct Costing as a Guide to Product Pricing. The economist uses the term "monopolistic competition," a hybrid of pure competition and monopoly, to describe a market that has certain characteristics: (1) many firms sell the same or similar products, differentiated only by name, by real or alleged quality, or by service, rather than by price; (2) a firm cannot change the price without considering the reactions of its competitors; and (3) a firm has little difficulty entering or leaving the market. These characteristics are typical for most company situations. How do these features of monopolistic competition affect pricing?

The best or optimum price is that which will yield the maximum excess of total revenue over total cost. The volume at which the increase in total cost due to the addition of one more unit of volume is just equal to the increase in total revenue, or a zero increase in total profit, is the optimum volume. The price at which this volume can be obtained is the optimum price. A higher price will lower the quantity demanded and decrease total profit. A lower price will increase the quantity sold but decrease total profit.

In a highly competitive market, prices may be regulated through supply and demand. Management regulates supply and attempts to stimulate demand. The primary influence on demand, however, is the consumer. These aspects of pricing and pricing methods are discussed in Chapter 27.

In multiproduct pricing, management needs to know whether each product can be priced competitively in the industry and still contribute sufficiently to the contribution margin for fixed cost recovery and profit. In making pricing decisions, the useful part of a unit cost is the direct cost segment, since it consists of those cost elements that are comparable among firms in the same industry. A long-run pricing policy should, however, make use of a full product cost, i.e., a product cost which includes that portion of fixed (capacity) cost instrumental in the manufacturing process.

Direct Costing for Managerial Decision Making. Installation of a direct costing system requires a study of cost trends and a segregation of fixed and variable costs. The classification of costs as either fixed or variable, with semivariable expenses properly subdivided into their fixed and variable components, provides a framework for the accumulation and analysis of costs. This also provides a basis for the study of contemplated changes in production levels or proposed actions concerning new markets, plant expansion or contraction, or special promotional activities. Of course, it is important to recognize that a study of cost behavior that identifies fixed and variable costs can be accomplished without the use of a formal direct costing system.

In NAA Research Report No. 37, findings on this phase of direct costing are summarized as follows:

> Companies participating in this study generally feel that direct costing's major field of usefulness is in forecasting and reporting income for internal management purposes. The distinctive feature of direct costing which makes it useful for this purpose is the manner in which costs are matched with revenues.
>
> The marginal income [contribution margin] figure which results from the first step in matching costs and revenues in the direct costing income statement is reported to be a particularly useful figure to management because it can be readily projected to measure increments in net income which accompany increments in sales. The theory underlying this observed usefulness of the marginal income figure in decision making rests upon the fact that, within a limited volume range, period costs tend to remain constant in total when

volume changes occur. Under such conditions, only the direct costs are relevant in costing increments in volume.

The tendency of net income to fluctuate directly with sales volume was reported to be an important practical advantage possessed by the direct costing approach to income determination because it enables management to trace changes in sales to their consequence in net income. Another advantage attributed to the direct costing income statement was that management has a better understanding of the impact that period costs have on profits when such costs are brought together in a single group.[3]

Direct Costing as a Control Tool. The direct costing procedure is said to be the product of an allegedly incomprehensible income statement prepared for management. The possible inverse fluctuations of production costs and sales figures due to fixed manufacturing cost allocations between inventories and cost of goods sold require a different type of costing procedure. By adopting direct costing, management and marketing management in particular believe that a more meaningful and understandable income statement can be furnished by the accountant. However, reports issued should serve not only the marketing department but all divisions of an enterprise. It seems appropriate, therefore, to prepare reports for all departments or responsibility centers based on standard costs, flexible budgets, and a division of all costs into their fixed and variable components.

The marketing manager should receive a statement placing sales and production costs in direct relationship to one another. Differences between intended sales and actual sales caused by changes in sales price, sales volume, or sales mix, which are the direct responsibility of the marketing manager, are detailed for analysis as discussed in Chapter 21.

Other managers can examine and interpret their reports with respect to the cost variances originating in their respective areas of responsibility. The production manager is able to study the materials quantity variance, the labor efficiency variance, and the controllable overhead variance. Variable expenses actually incurred can be analyzed by comparing them with the allowable budget figure for work performed. The purchasing agent or manager evaluates the purchase price variance. The personnel manager can be held accountable for labor rate variances. General management, which originally authorized and approved plant capacity in the form of labor and machines, is primarily responsible for utilization of existing facilities. In direct costing, however, no variances result with respect to fixed expenses, since all fixed costs are charged currently against revenue instead of to the product.

Reports constructed on the direct costing basis and augmented by the additional information described become valuable control tools. A profit-responsible management group is continually reminded of the original profit objective for the period. Subsequent approved deviations from the objective are reappraised in light of the current performance. Accounting by organizational

---

[3]*Ibid.*, pp. 84–85.

lines makes it possible to direct attention to the appropriate responsibility. Performance is no longer evaluated on the basis of last month or last year, since each period now has its own standard.

The proponents of direct costing believe that the separation of fixed and variable expenses, and the accounting for each according to some direct costing plan, simplifies both the understanding of the income statement and the assignment of costs to inventories.

External Uses of Direct Costing

To keep fixed overhead out of the reported product costs, variable and fixed expenses should be recorded in separate accounts. Therefore, the chart of accounts should be expanded so that every natural classification has two accounts — one for the variable and one for the fixed portion of the expense. Also, instead of one overhead control account, two should be used: Factory Overhead Control — Variable Expenses and Factory Overhead Control — Fixed Expenses. When a predetermined overhead rate is used to charge variable expenses to work in process, an applied overhead account labeled Variable Applied Factory Overhead is credited. Differences between actual and applied variable overhead constitute controllable or spending and variable efficiency variances when a standard cost system is used and a spending variance when standard costing is not used. Because fixed expenses are not charged to work in process, they are excluded from the predetermined overhead rate. The total fixed expense accumulated in the account, Factory Overhead Control — Fixed Expenses, is charged directly to Income Summary.

To illustrate the effects of direct costing for external uses, assume that the normal capacity of a plant is 20,000 units per month, or 240,000 units a year. Variable costs per unit are: direct materials, $3; direct labor, $2.25; and variable factory overhead, $.75 — a total of $6. Fixed factory overhead is $300,000 per year, $25,000 per month, or $1.25 per unit at normal capacity. The units of production basis is used for applying overhead. Fixed marketing and administrative expenses are $5,000 per month, or $60,000 a year; and variable marketing and administrative expenses are $3,400, $3,600, $4,000, and $3,000 for the first, second, third, and fourth months, respectively.

Actual variable factory overhead is not given. Actual and applied variable overhead are assumed to be the same; otherwise, variable overhead variances could be computed. Likewise, no materials or labor variances are assumed. All these variances would be the same in either the absorption costing method or the direct costing method.

There is no work in process inventory; standard costs are assigned to finished goods only. If work in process inventories were present, they would also be assigned standard costs. If standard costs are not used, then an assumption as to flow of costs must be followed in costing inventories, e.g., average, fifo, or lifo.

The sales price per unit is $10, and actual production, sales, and finished goods inventories in units are:

	FIRST MONTH	SECOND MONTH	THIRD MONTH	FOURTH MONTH
Units in beginning inventory.........			3,000	1,000
Units produced.........................	17,500	21,000	19,000	20,000
Units sold...............................	17,500	18,000	21,000	16,500
Units in ending inventory.............		3,000	1,000	4,500

From this information, the income statements below and on page 635 can be prepared. The first income statement — based on absorption costing — includes the fixed factory overhead in the unit cost and also in the costs assigned to inventory. The second income statement — based on direct costing — excludes the fixed factory overhead from the unit cost and from the costs assigned to inventory.

Income Statement — Absorption Costing

	FIRST MONTH	SECOND MONTH	THIRD MONTH	FOURTH MONTH
Sales	$175,000	$180,000	$210,000	$165,000
Direct materials...	$ 52,500	$ 63,000	$ 57,000	$ 60,000
Direct labor...	39,375	47,250	42,750	45,000
Variable factory overhead...................................	13,125	15,750	14,250	15,000
Fixed factory overhead..	21,875	26,250	23,750	25,000
Cost of goods manufactured..............................	$126,875	$152,250	$137,750	$145,000
Beginning inventory...			21,750	7,250
Cost of goods available for sale.........................	$126,875	$152,250	$159,500	$152,250
Ending inventory..		21,750	7,250	32,625
Cost of goods sold..	$126,875	$130,500	$152,250	$119,625
Fixed (over-) or underapplied factory overhead .	3,125	(1,250)	1,250	
Cost of goods sold at actual..............................	$130,000	$129,250	$153,500	$119,625
Gross profit	$ 45,000	$ 50,750	$ 56,500	$ 45,375
Marketing and administrative expenses.............	8,400	8,600	9,000	8,000
Operating income for the month........................	$ 36,600	$ 42,150	$ 47,500	$ 37,375

Costs Assigned to Inventory. The illustrations show the following ending inventories:

	FIRST MONTH	SECOND MONTH	THIRD MONTH	FOURTH MONTH
Absorption costing	–0–	$21,750	$7,250	$32,625
Direct costing............................	–0–	18,000	6,000	27,000
Differences	–0–	$ 3,750	$1,250	$ 5,625

The differences are caused by the elimination of fixed manufacturing expenses from inventories in direct costing. In absorption costing, these fixed expenses form part of the predetermined factory overhead rate and are included in inventories. The exclusion of this overhead from inventories and its offsetting effect on periodic income determination has been particularly criticized by opponents of direct costing.

	FIRST MONTH	SECOND MONTH	THIRD MONTH	FOURTH MONTH
Sales	$175,000	$180,000	$210,000	$165,000
Direct materials	$ 52,500	$ 63,000	$ 57,000	$ 60,000
Direct labor	39,375	47,250	42,750	45,000
Variable factory overhead	13,125	15,750	14,250	15,000
Variable cost of goods manufactured	$105,000	$126,000	$114,000	$120,000
Beginning inventory			18,000	6,000
Variable cost of goods available for sale	$105,000	$126,000	$132,000	$126,000
Ending inventory		18,000	6,000	27,000
Variable cost of goods sold	$105,000	$108,000	$126,000	$ 99,000
Gross contribution margin	$ 70,000	$ 72,000	$ 84,000	$ 66,000
Variable marketing and administrative expenses	3,400	3,600	4,000	3,000
Contribution margin	$ 66,600	$ 68,400	$ 80,000	$ 63,000
Less fixed expenses:				
Factory overhead	$ 25,000	$ 25,000	$ 25,000	$ 25,000
Marketing and administrative expenses	5,000	5,000	5,000	5,000
Total fixed expenses	$ 30,000	$ 30,000	$ 30,000	$ 30,000
Operating income for the month	$ 36,600	$ 38,400	$ 50,000	$ 33,000

Income
Statement —
Direct Costing

It has been observed that the amount of fixed cost charged to inventory is affected not only by the quantities produced but by the inventory costing method employed — a fact which is largely overlooked. It is often correct but not universally valid to say that when production exceeds sales, absorption costing shows a higher profit than does direct costing; or when sales exceed production, absorption costing shows a lower profit than does direct costing. In relation to four methods of inventory costing — average costing, fifo, lifo, and standard costing — an analysis of the differences in operating income under absorption costing and direct costing has shown that the usual generalizations about full and direct costing hold only under the lifo and the standard costing methods. However, under the fifo and the average costing methods, the results are more complex than those considered by the usual generalizations which therefore do not apply.[4]

As explained previously, managers favor direct costing because sales figures guide cost figures. The variable cost of goods sold varies directly with sales volume, and the influence of production on profit is eliminated. The idea of "selling overhead to inventories" might sound plausible and appear pleasing at first; but when the prior month's inventories become this month's beginning inventories, the apparent advantages cancel out. The results of the second month with absorption costing offer a good example of the effects of large production with cost being deferred in inventories into the next period.

[4]Yuji Ijiri, Robert K. Jaedicke, and John L. Livingstone, "The Effect of Inventory Costing Methods on Full and Direct Costing," *Journal of Accounting Research*, Vol. 3, No. 1, pp. 63–74.

The absorption costing income statement also demonstrates the effect of expensing the fixed over- or underapplied factory overhead resulting from production fluctuations.

Operating Profits. The inclusion or exclusion of fixed expenses from inventories and cost of goods sold causes the gross profit to vary considerably from the gross contribution margin. The gross contribution margin (sales revenue − variable manufacturing cost) in direct costing is greater than the gross profit in absorption costing. This difference has also resulted in some criticism of direct costing. It is argued that a greater gross contribution margin might mislead the marketing department into asking for lower prices or demanding higher bonuses or benefits. In defense of direct costing, however, it is well to recognize that sales prices and bonuses are in most cases based not on gross profit but on operating income.

The income statements on pages 634 and 635 also show differences in operating income. As illustrated below, these differences are attributable to the fixed cost charged to inventory.

	First Month	Second Month	Third Month	Fourth Month
Absorption Costing:				
Operating income for the month..............	$36,000	$42,150	$ 47,500	$37,375
Direct Costing:				
Operating income for the month..............	36,600	38,400	50,000	33,000
Difference...	–0–	$ 3,750	$ (2,500)	$ 4,375
Absorption Costing:				
Inventory change (ending less beginning inventory), increase (decrease)	–0–	$21,750	$(14,500)	$25,375
Direct Costing:				
Inventory change (ending less beginning inventory), increase (decrease)	–0–	18,000	(12,000)	21,000
Difference (inventory change in units × fixed portion of overhead rate $1.25)	–0–	$ 3,750	$ (2,500)	$ 4,375

The inventory change in this illustration is for finished goods only; however, if there were work in process inventories, they too would be included in the inventory change in order to reconcile the difference in operating income. Also, any over- or underapplied fixed factory overhead deferred on the balance sheet rather than being currently expensed would be a reconciling item in explaining the difference in operating income.

The operating income will be the same in each method when no inventories exist or when no change in the total cost assigned to inventory occurs from the beginning to the end of the period. Although the two illustrations are on a monthly basis, they could just as well be quarterly or annual. The shorter period is chosen to indicate more forcefully the effects of each method.

Financial Reporting. The use of direct costing for financial reporting is not accepted by the American Institute of Certified Public Accountants, the Internal Revenue Service, or the Securities and Exchange Commission, nor has it been endorsed by the Financial Accounting Standards Board. The position of these groups is generally based on their opposition to excluding fixed costs from inventories.

The Position of the AICPA. The basis for the AICPA's position on direct costing is Accounting Research Bulletin No. 43. Its "Inventory Pricing" chapter begins by stressing that "a major objective of accounting for inventories is the proper determination of income through the process of matching appropriate costs against revenues."

The Bulletin continues by stating that "the primary basis of accounting for inventories is cost, which has been defined generally as the price paid or consideration given to acquire an asset. As applied to inventories, cost means in principle the sum of the applicable expenditures and charges directly or indirectly incurred in bringing an article to its existing condition and location." In discussing the second point, the Bulletin states quite emphatically that "it should also be recognized that the exclusion of all overheads from inventory costs does not constitute an accepted accounting procedure." This last statement seems to apply to direct costing. Proponents of direct costing might argue, however, that while the exclusion of all overhead is not acceptable, by inference the exclusion of some is acceptable. This argument might sound true, but it does not seem to have any bearing on the Institute's acceptance of direct costing, since in an earlier discussion of cost, the Bulletin states that "under some circumstances, items such as idle facility expense, excessive spoilage, double freight, and rehandling costs may be so abnormal as to require treatment as current period charges rather than as a portion of the inventory cost." This appears to be the type of overhead that the AICPA recognizes as excludable from inventories.

IRS Regulations. Section 471 of the Internal Revenue Code provides two tests which each inventory must meet: (1) it must conform as nearly as possible to the best accounting practice in the trade or business and (2) it must clearly reflect income. The regulations define inventory cost in the case of merchandise produced to be: "(1) the cost of raw materials and supplies entering into or consumed in connection with the product, (2) expenditures for direct labor, and (3) indirect production costs incident to and necessary for the production of the particular article, including in such indirect production costs an appropriate portion of management expenses. . . ." A 1973 amendment to Section 471 specifically identifies the direct costing method as "not in accord with the regulations."

The Position of the SEC. The SEC's refusal to accept annual financial reports prepared on the basis of direct costing is generally the result of (1) its policy to favor consistency among reporting companies as far as possible and (2) its attitude that direct costing is not generally accepted accounting procedure. In filing reports with the SEC, a firm that uses direct costing must adjust its inventories and reported income to what they would have been had absorption costing been used.

Adjustment of Direct Costing Figures for External Reporting. Research studies conducted by the National Association of Accountants and the Financial Executives Research Foundation indicate that an ever-increasing number of companies use direct costing for internal responsibility reporting while others use it for profit planning, short-range price setting, and management control. The management services divisions of CPA firms have been extremely active in installing direct costing systems for internal management purposes. The auditors of these firms adjust the year-end figures for income tax returns and external reporting in harmony with the requirements of the IRS and the SEC.

Company practice indicates that comparatively simple procedures are employed to determine the amount of periodic adjustment. According to NAA Research Report No. 37, one company reported that at the end of each reporting period, manufacturing costs for the period are divided by actual production to create a costing rate which is applied to the units on hand. Another company expresses period expenses as a rate per dollar of direct labor and direct expenses at normal volume. The dollar amount of direct labor and direct expenses in the ending inventory is then multiplied by the foregoing rate to arrive at the period expense component.

A third company allocates all manufacturing overhead to production departments with the result that period manufacturing cost is collected in pools which correspond to the company's major product lines. However, the period costs are not allocated to individual products. At the end of each month, period cost is transferred from inventory to the cost of goods sold on the basis of the relative amounts of direct cost in production and sales. The segregation by product lines for external reporting purposes is desirable because the amount of period cost associated with the several product lines varies widely.[5]

DISCUSSION QUESTIONS

1. Differentiate between direct costs and direct costing.

2. Distinguish between period costs and product costs.

3. Why does the direct costing theorist exclude fixed manufacturing costs from inventories?

4. In the process of determining a proper sales price, what kind of cost figures are likely to be most helpful?

[5]NAA Research Report, No. 37, *op. cit.*, pp. 94–95.

5. Why is it said that an income statement prepared by the direct costing procedure is more helpful to management than an income statement prepared by the absorption costing method?

6. Why should the chart of accounts be expanded when direct costing is used?

7. A manufacturing concern follows the practice of charging the cost of direct materials and direct labor to Work in Process but charges off all indirect costs (factory overhead) directly to Income Summary. State the effects of this procedure on the concern's financial statements and comment on the acceptability of the procedure for use in preparing financial statements.

(AICPA adapted)

8. Has the Internal Revenue Service approved direct costing for tax purposes? Explain.

9. A speaker remarked that even though direct costing has attractive merits, there are certain items that should be considered before converting the present system. What hidden dangers are present in direct costing?

10. List the arguments for and against the use of direct costing.

11. Select the answer which best completes the statement:
   (a) The term meaning that all manufacturing costs (direct and indirect, fixed and variable) which contribute to the production of the product are traced to output and inventories is: (1) job order costing; (2) process costing; (3) absorption costing; (4) direct costing.
   (b) The term that is most descriptive of the type of cost accounting often called direct costing is: (1) out-of-pocket costing; (2) variable costing; (3) relevant costing; (4) prime costing.
   (c) Costs treated as product costs under direct costing are: (1) prime costs only; (2) variable production costs only; (3) all variable costs; (4) all variable and fixed manufacturing costs.
   (d) The basic assumption made in direct costing with respect to fixed costs is that a fixed cost is: (1) a controllable cost; (2) a product cost; (3) an irrelevant cost; (4) a period cost.
   (e) Operating income computed using direct costing would generally exceed operating income computed using absorption costing if: (1) units sold exceed units produced; (2) units sold are less than units produced; (3) units sold equal units produced; (4) the unit fixed cost is zero.
   (f) A company has operating income of $50,000 using direct costing for a given period. Beginning and ending inventories for that period were 13,000 units and 18,000 units, respectively. If the fixed factory overhead application rate is $2 per unit, the operating income using absorption costing is: (1) $40,000; (2) $50,000; (3) $60,000; (4) not determinable from the information given.
   (g) Absorption costing differs from direct costing in the: (1) fact that standard costs can be used with absorption costing but not with direct costing; (2) kinds of activities for which each can be used to report; (3) amount of costs assigned to individual units of product; (4) amount of fixed costs that will be incurred.
   (h) When a firm uses direct costing: (1) the cost of a unit of product changes because of changes in the number of units manufactured; (2) profits fluctuate with sales; (3) an idle capacity variance is calculated by a direct costing system; (4) product costs include variable administrative costs.

(i) Operating income under absorption costing can be reconciled to operating income determined under direct costing by computing the difference between: (1) inventoried fixed costs in the beginning and ending inventories and any deferred over- or underapplied fixed factory overhead; (2) inventoried discretionary costs in the beginning and ending inventories; (3) gross profit (absorption costing method) and contribution margin (direct costing method); (4) sales as recorded under the direct costing method and sales as recorded under the absorption costing method.

(j) Under the direct costing concept, unit product cost would most likely be increased by: (1) a decrease in the remaining useful life of factory machinery depreciated by the units-of-production method; (2) a decrease in the number of units produced; (3) an increase in the remaining useful life of factory machinery depreciated by the sum-of-the-years-digits method; (4) an increase in the commission paid to salespersons for each unit sold.

(k) When using direct costing information, the contribution margin discloses the excess of: (1) revenue over fixed cost; (2) projected revenue over the break-even point; (3) revenue over variable cost; (4) variable cost over fixed cost.

(AICPA and CMA adapted)

EXERCISES

1. Inventoriable unit cost under direct costing. Milner Company uses a standard costing system and manufactures one product whose standard cost is as follows:

Direct materials..	$18
Direct labor	24
Total factory overhead (the ratio of variable cost to fixed cost is 3 to 1).	20
Variable marketing, general, and administrative expenses......................	12
Fixed marketing, general, and administrative expenses..........................	7
Total unit cost...	$81

Required: The inventoriable unit cost for internal reporting purposes under direct costing, based on the standard costs.

(AICPA adapted)

2. Inventory costs — absorption vs direct costing. The following information is available for Keller Corporation's new product line:

Sales price per unit..	$ 15
Variable manufacturing cost per unit of production	8
Total annual fixed manufacturing cost..	25,000
Variable administrative cost per unit of production	3
Total annual fixed marketing and administrative expenses...............	15,000

There was no inventory at the beginning of the year. Normal capacity is 12,500 units. During the year, 12,500 units were produced and 10,000 units were sold.

Required:
(1) Ending inventory, assuming the use of direct costing.
(2) Ending inventory, assuming the use of absorption costing.
(3) Total variable cost charged to expense for the year, assuming the use of direct costing.
(4) Total fixed cost charged to expense for the year, assuming the use of absorption costing.

(AICPA adapted)

3. Income statements — absorption costing vs direct costing. The Denton Corporation produced 24,000 units (normal capacity) of product during the first quarter of the year; 20,000 units were sold at $22 per unit. The costs of this production were:

Materials..	$ 60,000
Direct labor	60,000
Factory overhead:	
Variable cost	120,000
Fixed cost...	96,000

Marketing and administrative expenses for the quarter total $70,000; all are fixed expenses.

Required:
   (1) An income statement using absorption costing.
   (2) An income statement using direct costing.

4. Direct costing income statement. The Prakash Company is comparing its present absorption costing practices with direct costing methods. An examination of its records produced the following information:

Maximum plant capacity..	40,000 units
Normal capacity..	36,000
Fixed factory overhead	$54,000
Fixed marketing and administrative expenses	20,000
Sales price per unit...	10
Standard variable manufacturing cost per unit......................	4
Variable marketing expense per unit sold	1

For the year, the following data are available:

Budgeted production..	36,000 units
Actual production...	30,000
Sales..	28,000
Finished goods inventory, January 1.......................................	1,000
Unfavorable variances from standard variable manufacturing costs	$ 5,000

All variances are written off directly at year-end as an adjustment to Cost of Goods Sold.

Required:
   (1) Direct costing income statement.
   (2) Operating income if absorption costing had been used.

(CGAA adapted)

5. Comparative income statements — absorption costing vs direct costing. On January 2, the Alabama Pulley Company began production of a new model. First quarter sales were 20,000 units and second quarter sales were 26,000 units at $10 each.

Unit product costs each quarter were: direct materials, $1; direct labor, $2; and variable factory overhead, $1.50. Fixed factory overhead was $62,440 each quarter and under absorption costing was applied using an actual overhead rate. During the first quarter, 28,000 units were produced and during the second quarter, 22,000 units were produced.

Marketing and administrative expenses consisted of $15,000 fixed each quarter, and the variable portion was 5% of sales.

The fifo inventory method is used and inventory unit costs are rounded to the nearest cent.

Required:
   (1) Comparative income statements for each quarter using (a) the absorption costing method and (b) the direct costing method.
   (2) Computations explaining the differences in operating income for each quarter.

6. Absorption costing vs direct costing; income statements. The following data pertain to the operations of the McDougal Company for the year:

Sales in kilograms: 75 000
Finished goods inventory, January 1: 12 000 kilograms
Finished goods inventory, December 31: 17 000 kilograms
Sales price: $10 per kilogram

Manufacturing costs:
    Variable cost per kilogram of production: $4
    Fixed factory overhead: $160,000 (normal capacity: 80 000 kilograms)
Marketing and administrative expenses:
    Variable cost per kilogram of sales: $1
    Fixed marketing and administrative expenses: $150,000
A standard costing system is used.

Required:
(1) The year's income statement under the (a) absorption costing method and (b) direct costing method.
(2) An explanation of the difference in operating income under the two concepts.

7. Direct costing statements; analysis of profit differences. The Jarvis Company's Cost Department prepares quarterly income statements based on absorption costing. For the last two quarters of last year and the first quarter of this year, the following income statements were sent to management:

	3D QUARTER	4TH QUARTER	1ST QUARTER
Sales ($20 per unit)	$1,600,000	$1,600,000	$1,600,000
Cost of goods sold (at standard)	$1,200,000	$1,200,000	$1,200,000
Fixed marketing and administrative expenses	250,000	250,000	250,000
Factory overhead volume variance	100,000	250,000	(50,000)
Total cost	$1,550,000	$1,700,000	$1,400,000
Operating income (loss)	$ 50,000	$ (100,000)	$ 200,000

Other cost, sales, and production data are:

Beginning inventory, 3d quarter	40,000 units
Standard variable manufacturing cost	50% of sales price
Normal sales demand	100,000 units per quarter
Standard productive capacity utilization	100,000 units per quarter

Actual sales and production in the three quarters:

QUARTERS	SALES	PRODUCTION
Third	80% of normal	80% of normal
Fourth	80	50
First	80	110

Required:
(1) Income statements for the three quarters based on direct costing procedures.
(2) An explanation for the differences in operating income for each quarter under absorption costing and direct costing.

8. Income statements — absorption costing vs direct costing; analysis of profit differences. The following annual flexible budget has been prepared by Accuro, Inc., for use in making decisions relating to its Product X.

	100,000 UNITS	150,000 UNITS	200,000 UNITS
Sales	$800,000	$1,200,000	$1,600,000
Manufacturing costs:			
Variable	$300,000	$ 450,000	$ 600,000
Fixed	200,000	200,000	200,000
Total manufacturing cost	$500,000	$ 650,000	$ 800,000
Marketing and other expenses:			
Variable	$200,000	$ 300,000	$ 400,000
Fixed	160,000	160,000	160,000
Total marketing and other expenses	$360,000	$ 460,000	$ 560,000
Operating income (loss)	$ (60,000)	$ 90,000	$ 240,000

The 200,000-unit budget has been adopted and will be used for allocating the fixed manufacturing cost to units of Product X. At the end of the first six months, the following information is available:

Production completed......................	120,000 units
Sales @ $8 per unit...........................	60,000 units

All fixed costs are budgeted and incurred uniformly throughout the year, and all costs incurred coincide with the budget.

The over- and underapplied fixed manufacturing cost is deferred on the balance sheet until the end of the year.

Required:
(1) The amount of fixed manufacturing cost applied to production during the first six months under absorption costing.
(2) In income statement format (including ending inventory), (a) the operating income (loss) for the first six months under absorption costing; (b) the operating income (loss) for the first six months under direct costing.
(3) Computations explaining the difference in operating income (loss).

(AICPA adapted)

PROBLEMS

22-1. Unit product costs and comparative gross profit statements based on absorption costing and direct costing. The Accounting Department of the Kimbrell Corporation gathered the following cost and other data:

Normal annual activity: 40,000 direct labor hours
Annual total fixed manufacturing cost: $60,000
Hours required to produce a unit of product: 5
Direct materials and direct labor cost per unit of product: $28
Variable factory overhead per unit of product: $5 (5 hrs. @ $1 per hour)
Sales price per unit of product: $45

Required:
(1) Using the plant's normal activity level as the base, the total manufacturing cost per unit of product based on (a) absorption costing and (b) direct costing.
(2) Comparative gross profit statements using (a) absorption costing and (b) direct costing, based on the following four situations:

YEAR	PRODUCED	SOLD
1st	8,000 units	7,000 units
2d	10,000	6,000
3d	7,000	7,000
4th	4,000	9,000

22-2. Income statements — absorption costing vs direct costing. The management of Murley Company uses the following unit costs for the one product it manufactures:

	PROJECTED COST PER UNIT
Direct materials (all variable)..	$30.00
Direct labor (all variable)	19.00
Factory overhead:	
Variable cost	6.00
Fixed cost (based on 10,000 units per month)	5.00
Marketing, general, and administrative:	
Variable cost (per unit sold)...	4.00
Fixed cost (based on 10,000 units per month)	2.80

The projected sales price is $80 per unit. The fixed costs remain fixed within the relevant range of 4,000 to 16,000 units of production and sales.

Management has projected the following unit data for June:

Beginning inventory	2,000 units
Production	9,000
Available	11,000 units
Sales	7,500
Ending inventory	3,500 units

Required:

(1) An income statement for June, using absorption costing, with all variances charged to Cost of Goods Sold each month.

(2) An income statement for June, using direct costing.

(3) Reconciliation of the operating income difference.　　　　　(AICPA adapted)

22-3. Income statements — absorption costing vs direct costing. Sales and operating profits of the Nantucket Company for the first two quarters of the year were as follows:

	First Quarter	Second Quarter
Sales	$300,000	$450,000
Operating profit	55,000	57,000

The directors were concerned that a 50% increase in sales resulted in only a small increase in operating profit. Using the data below, the chief accountant explained that unabsorbed factory overhead was charged to second-quarter operations.

	First Quarter	Second Quarter
Sales in units	20,000	30,000
Production in units	30,000	24,000
Ending inventory in units	10,000	4,000
Sales price per unit	$ 15	$ 15
Variable manufacturing cost per unit	5	5
Fixed manufacturing cost	180,000	180,000
Fixed factory overhead rate per unit	6	6
Marketing and administrative expenses ($25,000 fixed)	25,000	27,000

All over- and underapplied factory overhead is closed to the cost of goods sold account at the end of each quarter.

Required:

(1) An income statement for the second quarter, using the method now employed by the Nantucket Company.

(2) A direct costing income statement for the second quarter.

(3) Explanation of the difference in the requirement (1) and (2) answers.

(4) Operating profit for the second quarter under each method if production in that period had been 30,000 units. Explain the difference, if any.　　　　　(CGAA adapted)

22-4. Income statements — absorption costing vs direct costing; analysis of profit differences. The Vandergouw Company is a specialty glass company that makes glass equipment for scientific research. Its main product is Dewar flasks used for storing liquid nitrogen and helium, which evaporate rapidly at warmer temperatures. The Dewar flask is a continuous tube of glass forming a U-shape, with a short stand on the bottom, and it functions much like a thermos bottle.

The Vandergouw Company uses highly skilled glassblowers to make the flasks by hand. A tube of glass is heated and bent into the U-shape. While the bottom of the U is still hot, the foot or stand is blown. The inside of the tube is then silvered, the air evacuated, and the ends sealed off. The silvering and the vacuum serve to reduce heat transfer and deflect light, so that when a liquid gas is poured into the container and the lid (purchased elsewhere by the user) is sealed in place, the element will remain liquid for several hours.

This small company accounts for production costs on an absorption costing basis. Vandergouw, however, the president and a glassblower by trade, has difficulty understanding how the cost of tools, lights, protective glasses, and other fixed factory overhead items can become inventory, and feels that the business could be managed better if only direct materials and labor and variable factory overhead were to be assigned to inventory and all fixed factory overhead charged to expense as it occurs. The standard cost of one Dewar flask, as used in the firm's standard costing system, is:

Glass..	$ 2.00
Silver (1.5 ounces @ $2.00)	3.00
Direct labor (3 hours @ $8.00)	24.00
Variable factory overhead ($.50 per dlh)............................	1.50
Fixed factory overhead ($1.00 per dlh)............................	3.00
	$33.50

Other data for April are:

Sales price, $50.00
Sales, 175 units
Production, 184 units, which equals the normal capacity activity level
April 30 inventory of Dewar flasks, 20 units
Favorable materials variance (glass), $18.40
Silver prices have been going up and the average price of all silver used last month was $2.15 per ounce. But, in an effort to save on the increase in price, only 98% of the standard quantity was used.
Actual factory overhead was $950.
Administrative expenses have been running about 5% of sales revenue.

Required: Income statements for April, using the absorption costing method and the direct costing method, with a reconciliation of any profit difference. The firm closes all standard cost variances to the cost of goods sold account.

22-5. Comparative statement of cost of goods sold; variance analysis. The standard cost card of the product Molen of the Molenger Company shows the following details:

Direct materials, 4 units of Olme @ $2...................................	$ 8
Direct labor, 2 hours per finished product...	9
Factory overhead, $3 per direct labor hour	6
Total manufacturing cost	$23

The $3 factory overhead rate is based on $120,000 fixed cost and a $2 variable rate per direct labor hour.

Molenger's Cost Department reports that process costing with the fifo method for work in process inventory is used. The inventory, cost, and production data for the year are as follows:

Units in process:
  January 1:   2,000 units, all materials, 50% processed
  December 31: 1,000 units, all materials, 50% processed
Other data:
  Finished goods: January 1, 1,000 units; December 31, 1,500 units
  Materials put in process: 260,000 units of Olme
  Actual factory overhead: $398,700 including an increase of $15,000 in fixed overhead during the year.
  A total of 66,000 units of Molen were transferred to the warehouse.

The company's management stated that the present absorption standard cost system should be changed to a direct standard cost system. Variable cost variances are to be charged or credited to Cost of Goods Sold.

Required: A comparative cost of goods sold statement, using absorption standard costing and direct standard costing.

22-6. Entries based on absorption costing and direct costing. The Oregon Company uses a standard cost accounting system with absorption costing. The company manufactures one product, the standard cost of which is calculated as follows:

Direct materials gross weight allowed	4¹/₆ lbs.	@ $1.92	=	$ 8.00
Allowance for inherent loss (4%)...	¹/₆ lb.			
Weight of finished product...	4 lbs.			
Direct labor...	3 hours	@ 7.20	=	21.60
Factory overhead..	3 hours	@ 2.00	=	6.00
Total standard cost per unit of product...................................				$35.60

In developing the annual budget and standards, company officials planned to produce 41,000 units of product requiring 123,000 standard direct labor hours in 246 operating days. The annual factory overhead was analyzed as follows:

Nonvariable with production...	$110,700	$ .90 per hour
Variable directly with production in labor hours............................	135,300	1.10
Total factory overhead anticipated...	$246,000	$2.00 per hour

The following account balances, among others, are in the general ledger at May 31. All of the external transactions for May have been journalized and posted, as have all accruals, deferrals, and other internal transactions except those relating to Work in Process, Finished Goods, variances, and Cost of Goods Sold.

Finished Goods...	$ 89,000	
Work in Process..	22,960	
Materials	74,310	
Sales ($50 per unit)		$810,000
Cost of Goods Sold..	437,880	
Direct Labor..	80,640	
Factory Overhead...	22,375	
Materials Price Variance..	476	
Materials Quantity Variance..		960
Direct Labor Rate Variance..		30
Direct Labor Efficiency Variance...	180	
Factory Overhead Spending Variance	50	
Factory Overhead Efficiency Variance...	200	
Factory Overhead Idle Capacity Variance...................................		450

The company carries materials inventory at actual cost and records the variances when charging Work in Process.

Production plans for May called for 11,000 direct labor hours in 22 working days. On this basis, a flexible budget for factory overhead for the month had been drawn as follows:

Fixed overhead (22 days @ $450 per day)*...................................	$ 9,900
Variable overhead (11,000 hours @ $1.10 per hour)......................	12,100
	$22,000

*The company divides the total fixed cost by the number of working days in the year and charges overhead each month on the basis of the budgeted number of working days rather than on the basis of ¹/₁₂ of the annual amount.

May production obtained, in terms of complete units:

Units in process May 1 (materials complete, ¾ converted)............................	800
Units finished	3,800
Units in process May 31 (materials complete, ½ converted).........................	1,000

Direct materials put into production weighed 16,580 lbs. and cost $32,082.
Actual direct labor hours totaled 11,200.

Required:
(1) Journal entries to complete the general ledger record at May 31. (Round off amounts to the nearest dollar.)
(2) Journal entries to complete the general ledger record, assuming that the company had been using direct costing instead of absorption costing. Do not include entries to change May 1 balances from absorption to direct costing.

22-7. Absorption costing vs direct costing. Martin Corporation is considering changing its method of inventory costing from absorption to direct costing and wants to determine the effect of the proposed change on its financial statements.

The firm manufactures Gink, which is sold for $20 per unit. A raw material, Marsh, is added before processing starts; labor and factory overhead are added evenly during the manufacturing process. Production capacity is budgeted at 110,000 units of Gink annually. The standard costs per unit of Gink are:

Marsh (2 lbs. @ $1.50)	$ 3.00
Labor	6.00
Variable factory overhead	1.00
Fixed factory overhead	1.10
Total unit cost	$11.10

Process costing is used with standard costs. Variances from standard costs are now debited or credited to Cost of Goods Sold. If direct costing were adopted, only variances resulting from variable costs would be debited or credited to Cost of Goods Sold.

Inventory data for the year are as follows:

	JANUARY 1	DECEMBER 31
Marsh	50,000 lbs.	40,000 lbs.
Work in process:		
²/₅ processed	10,000 units	
¹/₃ processed		15,000 units
Finished goods	20,000	12,000

During the year, 220,000 lbs. of Marsh were purchased, and 230,000 lbs. were transferred to work in process inventory. Also, 110,000 units of Gink were transferred to finished goods inventory. Annual fixed factory overhead, budgeted and actual, was $121,000. There were no variances between standard and actual variable costs during the year.

Required:
(1) Schedules for the computation of (a) equivalent units of production for materials, labor, and factory overhead for the year; (b) number of units sold during the year; (c) standard unit costs under direct costing and absorption costing; (d) over- or underapplied fixed factory overhead, if any, for the year.
(2) A comparative cost of goods sold statement for the year, using standard direct costing and standard absorption costing.   (AICPA adapted)

22-8. Comparative income statements; income reconciliation; direct costing advantages and disadvantages. Hamm Company uses direct costing for its internal management purposes and absorption costing for external reporting. Thus, at the end of each year, financial data must be converted from direct costing to absorption costing in order to satisfy external requirements.

At the end of 19A, the company anticipated that sales would increase 20% next year. Therefore, production was increased from 20,000 units to 24,000 units to meet this expected demand. However, economic conditions kept the sales level at 20,000 units for each year.

The following data pertain to 19A and 19B:

	19A	19B
Sales price per unit	$30	$30
Sales (units)	20,000	20,000
Beginning inventory (units)	2,000	2,000
Production (units)	20,000	24,000
Ending inventory (units)	2,000	6,000
Total unfavorable materials, labor, and variable factory overhead variances	$5,000	$4,000

Standard variable costs per unit for 19A and 19B are:

Materials	$ 4.50
Labor	7.50
Variable factory overhead	3.00
Total	$15.00

Annual fixed costs for 19A and 19B (budgeted and actual) are:

Production	$ 90,000
Marketing and administrative	100,000
Total	$190,000

The factory overhead rate under absorption costing is based on practical plant capacity, which is 30,000 units per year. All variances and over- or underabsorbed factory overhead are closed to Cost of Goods Sold. Income tax is to be ignored.

Required:
   (1) Income statements for 19B, based on (a) direct costing and (b) absorption costing. (The beginning and ending inventories need not be shown on the income statements, i.e., show cost of goods sold as one figure.)
   (2) An explanation of the difference, if any, in the operating income figures and the entry, if necessary, to adjust the book figures to the financial statement figures.

(CMA adapted)

CASES

A. Sales and production volume effects — absorption vs direct costing. Sun Company, a wholly-owned subsidiary of Guardian, Inc., produces and sells three main product lines. The company employs a standard cost accounting system for record-keeping purposes.

At the beginning of the year, the president of Sun Company presented the budget to the parent company and accepted a commitment to contribute $15,800 to Guardian's consolidated profit in 19--. The president has been confident that the year's profit would exceed the budget target, since the monthly sales reports have shown that sales for the year will exceed the budget by 10%. The president is both disturbed and confused when the controller presents an adjusted forecast as of November 30, indicating that profit will be 11% under budget. The two forecasts are presented below:

	FORECASTS AS OF	
	January 1	November 30
Sales	$268,000	$294,800
Cost of goods sold at standard	212,000*	233,200
Gross profit at standard	$ 56,000	$ 61,600
Less underapplied fixed factory overhead	—	6,000
Gross profit at actual	$ 56,000	$ 55,600
Marketing expenses	$ 13,400	$ 14,740
Administrative expenses	26,800	26,800
Total commercial expenses	$ 40,200	$ 41,540
Income from operations	$ 15,800	$ 14,060

*Includes fixed factory overhead of $30,000.

There have been no sales price changes or product mix shifts since the January 1 forecast. The only cost variance on the income statement is the underapplied factory overhead. This arose because the company used only 16,000 standard machine hours (budgeted machine hours were 20,000) during the year as a result of a shortage of raw materials. Fortunately, Sun Company's finished goods inventory was large enough to fill all sales orders received.

Required:
   (1) Analysis and explanation of the forecast profit decline, in spite of increased sales and good cost control.
   (2) Explanation and illustration of an alternative internal cost reporting procedure which would avoid the confusing effect of the present procedure.

(CMA adapted)

B. Contribution margin; standard cost variance analysis; direct costing's income statement effect. The Charlestown Company manufactures and sells one product. The income statement in its master budget for the year just ended was:

Sales (80,000 units @ $8.50)		$680,000
Cost of goods sold:		
Materials (140,000 lbs. @ $1.00)	$140,000	
Direct labor and fringe benefits (32,000 hours @ $5.00)	160,000	
Variable factory overhead (50% of materials cost)	70,000	
Fixed factory overhead	150,000	
		$520,000
Gross profit		$160,000
General and marketing expenses:		
Variable (5% of sales revenue)	$ 34,000	
Fixed	98,000	
		$132,000
Operating income budgeted		$ 28,000

The company uses direct standard costing for its cost records, and since there have never been any significant beginning or ending inventories of finished goods, those same records have been used in the preparation of the company's year-end financial statements.

During the year just ended, the company, reacting to an expanding market, produced 120,000 finished units. However, only 90,000 units were sold. Even at that, sales were higher than the master budget plan. The company's flexible budget showed an expected operating income of $62,500 at a production and sales level of 90,000 units per year. At the end of the year, the controller said, "I'm certainly glad that generally accepted accounting principles don't agree with the use of direct costing for financial reporting purposes, because our records, based on our standard direct costing system, indicate that we had a loss of $18,500 for this year. However, if I used standard absorption costing instead, developing the standards for inventory costing from the year's master budget and leaving any variances in cost of goods sold as we've always done in our direct costing system, I can instead show an operating profit of $37,750. That's better than the master budget profit, though not as good as the flexible budget profit, and it's certainly better than an $18,500 loss!"

Data for the year's actual sales and costs are:

Sales (90,000 units @ $8.50)	$765,000
Materials used (200,000 lbs. @ $1.25)	250,000
Direct labor and fringe benefits (51,000 hrs. @ $5.00)	255,000
Variable factory overhead	109,000
Fixed factory overhead	157,000
Variable general and marketing expenses	38,250
Fixed general and marketing expenses	113,000

Required:
(1) Explanation of the differences between:
    (a) The master budget income of $28,000 and the flexible budget income of $62,500.
    (b) The flexible budget income of $62,500 and the loss of $18,500 determined by the company's standard direct costing system. Identify manufacturing and general marketing expenses variances, including a factory overhead controllable variance.
    (c) The $18,500 loss according to the company's standard direct costing system and the $37,750 income the controller says would result if standard absorption costing were used instead. Assume the 80,000-unit capacity level is used for calculating the fixed portion of the standard factory overhead rate.
(2) A discussion of inventory costing, including an explanation for the preference of absorption costing and a description of any safeguards against abuse.
(3) An explanation of other acceptable computations of income or loss figures, using absorption costing.   (CICA adapted)

Part Seven Cost and Profit Analysis

23 Marketing Cost and Profitability Analysis

Marketing is the matching of a company's products with markets for the satisfaction of customers at a reasonable profit for the firm. Marketing managers must decide the (1) product selection, design, color, size, and packaging, (2) prices to be charged, (3) advertising and promotion needed, and (4) physical distribution to be followed. These numerous decisions require organization, planning, and control. Marketing activities are usually organized by product or brand lines or by territories or districts. The planning and control phases should be based on a well-structured marketing cost and profitability analysis system.

The preparation of budgets and the need for budgeting in planning and controlling the marketing activity of a firm are discussed in Chapter 16. At the end of each month, budget reports are issued that indicate the success or failure of the budgetary boundaries. However, the problems associated with marketing costs do not end with these budgetary procedures. Cost control at the departmental level is the important feature of any cost improvement program. In marketing, the emphasis ordinarily rests on selling rather than on costs. To limit marketing costs unreasonably might lead to a curtailment of sales activities, which in turn could mean the gradual deterioration or elimination of certain types of sales; conversely, indiscriminate and wasteful spending should not be sanctioned.

It is important to note that general and administrative expenses and research and development costs should also be planned, analyzed, and controlled. Department stores and other merchandising businesses recognized the functional cost control concept many years ago. The financial success of these firms is in no small measure due to the control and reduction of costs on a departmental-functional line basis. In fact, the same concepts and techniques are applicable to costs experienced in local, state, and federal units and in other nonbusiness organizations where functional cost control and analysis are not only possible but necessary. For example, municipal functions such as trash collection or street cleaning should be placed on a departmental budget basis, with a supervisor responsible for the efficient operation of the function and accountable for the cost control within the limits of the budget.

SCOPE OF MARKETING COSTS

The control and analysis of marketing costs must extend beyond the departmental budget. This phase of cost accounting calls for the determination of marketing costs for managerial decisions, thereby making it an integral part of business planning and policy formulation. Management requires meaningful marketing cost information in order to determine and analyze the profitability of (1) a territory or territories; (2) certain classes of customers, such as wholesalers, retailers, institutions, and governmental units; (3) products, product lines, or brands; and (4) promotional efforts by salespersons, telephone, mail, television, or radio.

Control and analysis of marketing costs complement each other. Control begins with the assignment of marketing expenses to various costing groups such as territories, customers, and products. However, assigned costs must be controlled through analysis within the jurisdictional function in order to hold each marketing activity to the predetermined profitability level. Control and analysis are enhanced by (1) predetermining costs allowed for marketing efforts and (2) establishing functional costing rates based on standards and budgets.

The scope of today's marketing activities includes not only the fulfilling of existing demands, but also the creation and discovery of new demands for a company's products and services. This outlook requires the best available working tools for management's use. In many organizations, the marketing activity has always received management's attention, and in some cases even more attention than that rendered to other business operations. In today's economy, the strategic importance and magnitude of marketing costs merit still greater attention.

COMPARISON OF MARKETING AND MANUFACTURING COSTS

The control and analysis of marketing costs present certain complexities. First of all, logistic systems are many and varied. Manufacturers of certain products use basically the same materials and machinery. However, these companies may use vastly different channels of distribution, ranging from a simple, direct distribution to a complex marketing system, with promotional efforts directed to narrow or broad customer groups. Therefore, a meaningful comparison of the marketing costs of one company with another is almost impossible.

Not only do distribution methods vary, but they are also extremely flexible. A company may find that a change in market conditions necessitates a change in its channels of distribution. Distribution standards must be revised with every change in the method of distribution, so tactics may change several times before the best method is found. Such changes would be disastrous in production, however. Once a factory is set up, management is not likely to change its manufacturing techniques to any great extent; therefore, standards set for a particular machine do not require much revision.

The psychological factors present in selling a product are perhaps the main reasons for differences between manufacturing and marketing costing. Management can control the cost of labor, hours of operation, and number of machines operated; but management cannot tell what the customer will do. Various salespersons may have different effects on a customer, who responds to varying appeals. Customer resistance is the enigma in marketing cost analysis. The customer is a controlling rather than a controllable factor, whose wishes and peculiarities govern the method of doing business. Some tentative work has been done in improving the examination and prediction of customer behavior. As an example, a mathematical technique called the *Markov chain* has seen limited use in predicting customer brand loyalty. This process analyzes the current movement of some variable in an effort to predict future movements of that same variable.[1]

The attitudes of marketing and manufacturing management also differ. Although factory managers are eager to measure their accomplishments in terms of reduced cost per unit, most sales managers consider sales the yardstick for measuring their efficiency, although increased sales do not always mean greater profits.

Cause and effect, generally obvious in the factory, are not so readily discernible in the marketing processes. For example, many promotional costs are incurred for future results, creating a time lag between cause and effect. Conversely, the effects of manufacturing changes are usually felt quickly, and matching between effort and result can usually be achieved. Furthermore, manufacturing results are more readily quantified than are marketing costs.

---

[1]Richard I. Levin and C. A. Kirkpatrick, *Quantitative Approaches to Management*, 2d ed. (New York: McGraw-Hill Book Company, 1971), pp. 346–365.

For marketing costs, it is often not easy to identify quantities or units of activity with the cost incurred and results achieved.

Generally accepted accounting practice does not charge Cost of Goods Sold and ending inventories with marketing and administrative expenses. These and other nonmanufacturing expenses usually fall into the category of period costs, even if variable, and as such are charged off in total at the end of the accounting period. Thus, marketing costs are generally charged against the operations of the accounting period in which they are incurred while production costs are held in inventory until the units are sold. This practice is followed because too much uncertainty exists as to the probable results in future periods arising from incurred marketing expenses. Depreciable marketing assets (such as delivery trucks) should, of course, be expensed over their useful lives, not when acquired.

In the field of marketing costs, it is more common to speak of marketing cost analysis rather than of marketing cost accounting. A tie-in of marketing costing with the general accounts, although desirable, is often not necessary. A rate, similar to the factory overhead rate, for charging marketing expenses to operations, is sometimes used but this procedure is not common.

Marketing cost control and analysis deals primarily with historical or past costs, evaluating past performances as related to standards and budgets. In connection with future policies, forecast or predetermined figures are employed. In either case, whether judging past performances or deciding on future activities, the possibility of reducing costs and increasing profits through modern methods applied to the marketing area presents a real challenge to management and the accountant.

The control and analysis of marketing costs should follow methods that are similar to those used for manufacturing costs. The control of marketing costs is aided by the following activities:

1. Departmentalization of activities or functions.
2. Assignment of responsibility for operations.
3. Recognition of direct and indirect departmental expenses.
4. Separation of fixed and variable expenses.
5. Determination and establishment of bases for applying indirect expenses to territories, customers, or products.
6. Comparison of actual with budgeted expenses for continuous control by responsible department supervisors.
7. Use of flexible budgets and standard costs.

MARKETING STUDIES FOR PROFIT PLANNING AND CONTROL

Marketing studies deal with the collection, organization, and analysis of data to solve a wide variety of problems. Some of these problems are identified in the following chart:[2]

---

[2]Adapted from Neil Doppelt, "Marketing Studies," *Arthur Andersen Chronicle*, Vol. XXXVII, No. 1, pp. 31–39.

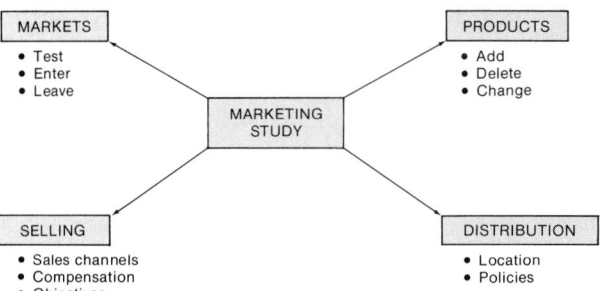

Marketing studies support strategic planning decisions and their control. The skills required for these studies are comparable to those normally needed for the planning, design, and implementation of business information systems in general and include (1) project definition, (2) technical skills, including accounting, (3) analytical and interpretive ability, (4) industry knowledge, and (5) project management — all in the context of relevant data provided by the accounting information system.

MARKETING COST CONTROL

The first step in the control of marketing costs is the classification of natural expenses according to functions or activities. It is essential that each function and its associated expenses be made the responsibility of an individual department head.

Marketing functions are of many types, depending on the nature of the business and its organization, size, and method of operation. Each function should be a homogeneous unit, whose activity can be related to specific items of cost. A function might follow a particular pattern of natural expenses, but most functions will have similar expenses such as salaries, insurance, taxes, heat, light, power, and supplies.

The chart of accounts should be so designed that each function receives directly as many of its charges as possible instead of through allocations. In the chart of accounts illustrated in Chapter 4, marketing expenses have been coded in the 500 series (500–599). However, a three-digit number is ordinarily not sufficient to permit the proper assignment of an expense. For this reason, the original number might be expanded as follows:

DIGITS	CODE	CLASSIFICATION
First two digits	05	Marketing expenses
Third and fourth digits	–01–	Primary or natural expense (e.g., Salaries — Sales Supervision)
Fifth and sixth digits.............	–10–	Function or department
Seventh and eighth digits	–20–	Territory or district
Ninth and tenth digits...........	–30–	Product or product line

The use of a ten-digit code number indicates the great amount of detail required for a meaningful analysis. Electronic data processing equipment permits the use of these and additional code numbers and classifications.

Functional classifications of marketing costs might be structured in the following manner:

1. Selling.
2. Advertising.
3. Warehousing.
4. Packing and shipping.
5. Credit and collection.
6. General accounting (for marketing).

These functional classifications can be grouped into two broad categories: order-getting costs and order-filling costs. Order-getting costs are the costs of activities carried on to bring in the sales orders and include selling and advertising. Order-filling costs are the costs of warehousing, packing and shipping, credit and collection, and general accounting.

A broad category of marketing administration costs may also be identified. This category includes the costs of marketing planning and organization, market research and forecasting, product design and development, and product-line planning.

Direct and Indirect Expenses

Direct expenses are those expenses that can be identified directly with a department, function, or activity, such as the salary of a department manager or the depreciation of a delivery truck. Expenses which can be identified with a territory, customer, product, or definite type of sales outlet may also be considered direct costs. Conversely, indirect expenses are incurred for more than one function or other classification and hence must be allocated. A direct expense may also be allocated when direct identification requires excessive clerical expense.

Marketing expenses may be directly identifiable with functional classifications although indirectly with respect to other classifications such as territories or products, or vice versa, or the expense may be indirect both as to function as well as to other classifications. Thus, the functional classifications may themselves include indirect costs. Expenses of this type include items such as heat, light, maintenance, and the sales manager's salary. Because these expenses cannot be assigned directly, they are recorded in total and then allocated by appropriate bases to various activities.

Functionally classified marketing costs which are indirect with respect to other classifications may be allocated to such classifications as territories and products by (1) using a percentage based on actual sales, manufacturing cost, or some other basis, or (2) creating a standard unit cost for each activity — similar to factory costs. Expenses that are directly identified with one of these other classifications must be excluded from the allocation, otherwise double counting would result.

The assignment of functional marketing expenses as percentages of actual sales or manufacturing costs, or on some other basis, does not offer reliable results. The procedure has been used in the past for want of more satisfactory methods. The determination of a functional standard unit costing rate is a more dependable solution. The charging of marketing expense activities on the basis of a costing rate is a logical extension of widely adopted factory standard costing procedures. Furthermore, the availability of such a rate permits quick and decisive analysis. Actual expenses would be collected in the customary manner and charged to their departmental and natural expense classifications in a subsidiary ledger controlled by a marketing expenses control account in the general ledger.

Selection of Bases for the Allocation of Functional Costs. The apportionment process poses two basic questions: (1) what bases should be used for the allocation and (2) how far should the allocations be carried out? As a solution to the first, statements and opinions stress the fact that the bases used should be fair and equitable; they should be an ideal combination of efforts expended and benefits reaped. The second question occurs because of doubts raised as to the advantages of full allocation of all indirect expenses. Suggestions have been made that certain expenses should be omitted from the allocation procedure when they are not measurable in relation to the function or activity. This is especially true when benefits are so widely dispersed over many functions that any allocation is a mere guess.

Factory overhead rates use a base which most definitely expresses the effort connected with the work of the department, such as labor hours, machine hours, or labor cost. A similar procedure for allocating marketing expenses is to divide the total cost of each marketing function by the units of functional service (the base) to obtain the cost per unit. Either an actual rate or a predetermined standard rate may be used, but the latter is preferable.

The selection of bases or units of measurement requires careful analysis, because the degree to which the final rates represent acceptable costs is greatly dependent upon the adequacy of the bases selected. Each function must be examined with respect to that factor which most influences the volume of its work. Because of the varied services rendered by the numerous functions, different bases are used. It is possible, however, to use one basis for two or more functions. Some of the bases for each function are shown on page 657.

Cost Accounting Standards Board (CASB) Allocation Bases. The CASB has specified methods for allocating certain expenses in costing government contracts. These standards apply to such procedures as the allocation of home office and general and administrative expenses. However, for broader cost accounting system uses, the specified techniques afford useful instruction in determining appropriate bases for allocating costs of various marketing as well as manufacturing functions.

FUNCTION	COST ALLOCATION BASES
Selling............................	Gross sales dollar value of products sold or number of salespersons' calls on customers (based on salespersons' time reports)
Advertising.....................	Quantity of product units sold, relative media circulation, cost of space directly assignable, or not related to orders
Warehousing..................	Size, weight, or number of products shipped or handled
Packing and shipping ...	Number of shipping units, weight, or size of units
Credit and collection.....	Number of customers' orders, transactions, or invoice lines
General accounting.......	Number of customers' orders, transactions, or invoice lines

CASB Standard No. 403, "Allocation of Home Office Expenses to Segments," requires allocation on the basis of the beneficial or causal relationship between supporting and receiving activities. The Standard specifies a hierarchy of allocation techniques:

1. Preferred. *A measure of the activity of the segment performing the function — usually labor oriented, machine oriented, or space oriented.*
2. First alternative. *A measure of the output of the segment performing the function, measured in terms of the units of output of the performing segment.*
3. Second alternative. *A measure of the activity of the segments receiving the service.*

When no identifiable relationship exists, the Standard requires allocation based either on a three-factor formula (payroll dollars, operating revenue, and net book value of tangible capital assets) or on any basis representative of the total activity of the segments.[3] The CASB also requires that general and administrative expenses be allocated using a cost input base that best represents the total activity of the business unit during the cost accounting period.[4] In this way, allocations are more equitable and functional unit costs are more meaningful.

Determination of Functional Unit Cost. The unit cost of an activity is calculated by dividing the total cost of the function by the measurement unit or base selected. A vast amount of information must be collected in order to establish a functional unit costing rate. The tedious assembly of such underlying information is often the reason for the lack of a marketing cost system. When the system is based on standards, the initial work might be more elaborate. However, once the procedure is established, its actual operation should not only be less expensive, but the value derived should far outweigh any previous expenses incurred in establishing the system.

[3]*Cost Accounting Standards* (New York: Price Waterhouse & Co., 1976) pp. 14–15.
[4]*Standards, Rules and Regulations, Part 410*, "Allocation of Business Unit General and Administrative Expenses to Final Cost Objectives" (Washington, D.C.: Cost Accounting Standards Board, 1976).

Fixed and Variable Expenses

Recognition of the fixed-variable cost classification is valuable in controlling marketing costs and in making decisions dealing with the possible opening or closing of a territory, new methods of packaging goods, servicing different types of outlets, or adding or dropping a product line. Fixed marketing expenses include salaries of executive and administrative sales staffs; salaries of warehousing, advertising, shipping, billing, and collection departments; and rent and depreciation of associated permanent facilities. These fixed costs have also been called *capacity costs*.

Variable marketing costs include the expenses of handling, warehousing, and shipping that tend to vary with sales volume. They have been referred to as *volume costs* or as expenses connected with the filling of an order. Another type of variable marketing cost originates in connection with promotional expenses such as salespersons' salaries, travel, and entertainment and some advertising expenses. Management must examine these costs carefully in the planning stage, since sales volume may have little influence upon their behavior. These expenses are variable because of management decisions. In fact, once agreed to by management, these expenses may be fixed, at least for the budget period under consideration.

Flexible Budget and Standards for Marketing Functions

Sales estimates are basically the most important figures in any budget. The accuracy and usefulness of most other estimates depend on them. Methods used in determining sales budget estimates are discussed in Chapter 16. Total sales are ordinarily broken down into the various kinds of products to be sold, into monthly or weekly sales, and into sales by salespersons, territories, classes of customers, and methods of distribution. In each division, quotas may be useful for determining the desirability of cultivating various outlets and for judging the efficiency of sales methods and policies.

Budgets are set up to anticipate the amount of functional expenses for the coming period and to compare them with the actual expenses. Because of the influence of volume and capacity, a comparison of actual costs with predetermined fixed budget figures does not always give a fair evaluation of the activities of a function. Therefore, the use of flexible budgets for the control of marketing costs should be considered.

The flexible budget for a distributive function such as billing might take this form:

FLEXIBLE BUDGET FOR BILLING DEPARTMENT

EXPENSES	FUNCTIONAL UNIT — INVOICE LINE			
	50,000	*55,000*	*60,000*	*65,000*
Clerical salaries	$ 4,000	$ 4,000	$ 4,000	$ 4,000
Supervision	3,000	3,000	3,000	3,000
Depreciation — building	750	750	750	750
Depreciation — equipment	1,250	1,250	1,250	1,250
Supplies	2,500	2,750	3,000	3,250
Total	$11,500	$11,750	$12,000	$12,250

A standard functional unit cost is then established for each activity or function on the basis of normal capacity. These standard unit costs will furnish bases for comparisons with actual costs, and spending and idle capacity variances can be isolated. Using the Billing Department as an example and assuming that 60,000 invoice lines represent normal capacity, the following standard billing rate per invoice line would be computed:

$$\frac{\$12,000}{60,000 \text{ Invoice lines}} = \$.20 \text{ per invoice line}$$

Assuming $9,000 fixed expense and $3,000 variable expense, the variable portion of the rate is:

$$\frac{\$3,000}{60,000 \text{ Invoice lines}} = \$.05 \text{ per invoice line}$$

The cost variances for billing expenses can be computed in a manner similar to that discussed in connection with factory overhead (Chapter 9) and consistent with the basic idea of flexible budgeting. If actual sales required 63,000 invoice lines for a month at a total of $12,500, the variances for the Billing Department would be determined as follows:

Actual expense		$12,500	
Spending variance			$350 unfav.
Budget allowance:			
Fixed expense budgeted	$9,000		
Variable expense ($.05 × 63,000			
invoice lines)	3,150	12,150	
Idle capacity variance			(450) fav.
Standard cost charged in ($.20 ×			
63,000 invoice lines)..................		12,600	

The increased volume leads to a favorable idle capacity variance due to overabsorption of fixed expenses. On the other hand, the supervisor overspent the $12,150 budget allowance by $350.

Accountants usually do not favor carrying this type of variance analysis through ledger accounts. The analysis is usually statistical and is presented to management in report form. However, the following journal entries similar to those for factory overhead could be made:

Billing Expense Charged In	12,600	
Applied Billing Expense...		12,600
Actual Billing Expense	12,500	
Sundry Credits...		12,500
Applied Billing Expense..	12,600	
Billing Expense — Spending Variance	350	
Billing Expense — Idle Capacity Variance......................		450
Actual Billing Expense		12,500

MARKETING PROFITABILITY ANALYSIS

The functional unit costs are used to analyze costs and determine the profitability of territories, customers, products, and salespersons. In most cases, a continuous reshuffling or rearranging of expense items is needed to find the required costs and profits. The possibility of improving marketing cost and profitability analysis has been enhanced by the availability of electronic data processing equipment capable of processing the great amount of quantitative detail so characteristic of these analyses.

Analysis by Territories

Perhaps the simplest analysis of marketing profitability is by territories. When marketing activities are organized on a territorial basis, each identifiable geographical unit can be charged directly with the expenses incurred within its area, thereby minimizing the proration of expenses. Expenses that can be assigned directly to a territory are: salespersons' salaries, commissions, and traveling expenses; transportation cost within the delivery area; packing and shipping costs; and advertising specifically identified with the territory. Expenses that must be prorated to the territory are: general management, general office, general sales manager, credit and collection, and general accounting.

When expenses are identified by territories, a comparative income statement can be prepared, as shown below. This statement permits control and analysis of expenses as well as the computation of profit margins. When sales or expenses seem to be out of line, management can take corrective action.

INCOME STATEMENT BY TERRITORIES

	TERRITORY		
	No. 1	*No. 2*	*No. 3*
Net sales	$210,000	$80,000	$175,000
Cost of goods sold	160,000	60,000	140,000
Gross profit	$ 50,000	$20,000	$ 35,000
Marketing expenses:			
Selling	$ 15,000	$ 8,600	$ 23,900
Warehousing	3,600	1,400	3,100
Packing and shipping	1,500	400	1,900
Advertising	2,000	1,000	500
Credit and collection	800	250	1,200
General accounting	1,200	1,400	1,800
Total marketing expense	$ 24,100	$13,050	$ 32,400
Administrative expenses (equally)	5,000	5,000	5,000
Total marketing and administrative expenses	$ 29,100	$18,050	$ 37,400
Operating income (loss) per territory	$ 20,900	$ 1,950	$ (2,400)

Analysis by Customers

Although most marketing costs can be assigned directly to territories, relatively few of these costs can be traced directly to customers. Perhaps transportation expenses and sales discounts can be considered direct, but all other expenses are allocated on the basis of functional unit costing rates.

The large number of customers makes the allocation and analysis of marketing costs by customers rather cumbersome if not impossible. For this reason, customers are grouped according to certain characteristics to make the analysis meaningful. The grouping may be by (1) territories, (2) amount of average order, (3) customer-volume groups, or (4) kinds of customers.

Analysis of Customers by Territories. This type of analysis reflects territorial cost differences due to the customer's proximity to warehouses, volume of purchases, service requirements, and the kinds of merchandise bought. These factors can make some sales profitable or unprofitable. The analysis proceeds in the same manner outlined for territories, except that the costs would be broken down by customers or kinds of customers within each territory.

Analysis of Customers by Amount of Average Order. The amount of a customer's order is closely related to profitability. An analysis might indicate that a considerable portion of orders comes from customers who cost the company more in selling to them than the orders are worth in terms of gross profit. Companies have therefore resorted to setting minimum dollar values or minimum quantities for orders, thereby reducing the number of transactions and increasing profits. Although selective selling has found much favor among many executives, it requires changes in habits and routines.

To present management with a quick view of the situation regarding the amount of the average order in relation to the number of customers, time spent, and total dollar sales, the chart illustrated below might be helpful.

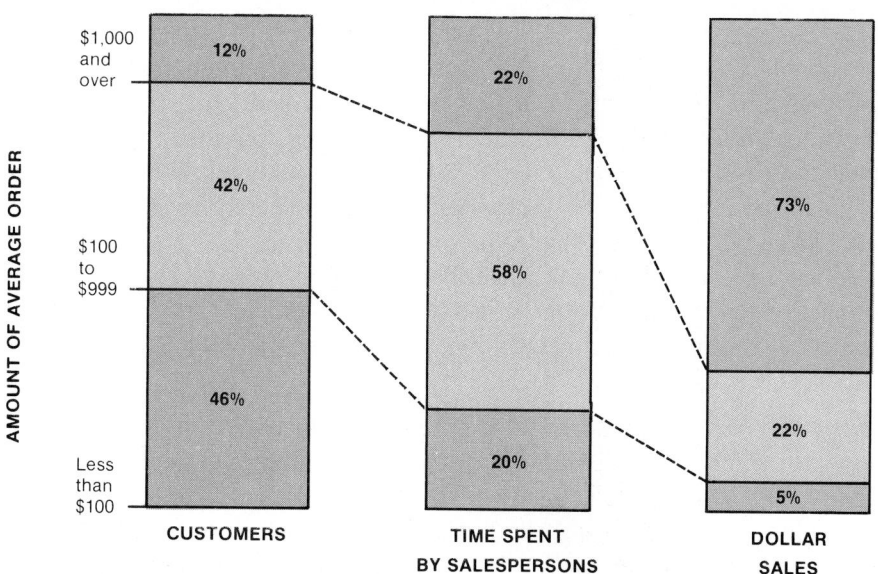

Analysis of
Customers by
Amount of
Average Order

Analysis by Customer-Volume Groups. An analysis of customers by customer-volume groups is similar to that of the amount-of-average-order analysis. Instead of classifying customers by an order's dollar value, however, the customer-volume group analysis is based on an order's quantity or volume. This type of analysis yields information concerning (1) the profitability of various customer-volume groups and (2) the establishment of price differentials.

The analysis shown below indicates that only sales to customers who buy more than 150 units during a week result in a positive contribution margin.

ANALYSIS BY CUSTOMER-VOLUME GROUPS

Customer-Volume Group (Number of Units Purchased During Week)	Customers (% of Total)	Volume (% of Total)	Gross Contribution Margin per 100 Units	Variable Commercial Expenses per 100 Units	Contribution Margin per 100 Units
Customers unsuccessfully solicited...........	17.1%	....	....	....	....
1–25.........................	7.6	0.2%	$1.66	$4.01	$(2.35)
26–50......................	8.3	0.7	1.38	2.55	(1.17)
51–100.....................	12.0	1.9	1.25	1.78	(.53)
101–150....................	9.3	2.4	1.26	1.32	(.06)
151–200....................	7.8	2.9	1.14	1.13	.01
201–250....................	6.4	3.0	1.12	.95	.17
251–500....................	17.1	13.2	1.06	.75	.31
501–1,000.................	12.7	18.6	1.02	.49	.53
1,001–10,000.............	1.7	57.1	.81	.24	.57
Total....................	100.0%	100.0%			

The variable cost of goods sold is subtracted from sales to compute the gross contribution margin, from which the variable commercial (marketing and administrative) expenses are subtracted to compute the contribution margin. Although the customers buying more than 150 units weekly represent only about 46 percent of the customers, they purchase approximately 95 percent of the units sold and thus provide the profits.

In spite of the higher gross contribution margin received from orders by customers who buy less than 150 units, it is not sufficient to cover variable commercial expenses. As a result, the sales to this group provide nothing for fixed expenses and profit.

Analysis by Kinds of Customers. This type of analysis makes a distinction between manufacturers, wholesalers, retailers, government (local, state, and federal), schools, colleges and universities, and hospitals. Prices might be uniform within each customer group but might vary between groups. Different salespersons are often employed for each category; hence their salaries and related expenses can be assigned directly to the group. Delivery to such groups might be different, with one delivery contracted with outside truckers and another made by the firm's own trucks. For analytical purposes, revenue and costs should be related to each kind of customer.

Just as customers are grouped for purposes of analysis, products sold can be grouped according to product lines or brands possessing common characteristics. With the aid of functional costing rates, a product-line (or brand-line) income statement can be prepared for the evaluation of profitable and unprofitable product lines. The statement below relates the actual contribution of each product line to total profits for the year.

Analysis by Products

PRODUCT-LINE INCOME STATEMENT
(CONTRIBUTION MARGIN APPROACH)

	Total	PRODUCT LINE *1*	PRODUCT LINE *2*	PRODUCT LINE *3*
Net sales	$3,100,000	$1,540,000	$1,070,000	$490,000
Less variable cost of goods sold	1,927,000	925,000	590,000	412,000
Gross contribution margin.......	$1,173,000	$ 615,000	$ 480,000	$ 78,000
Less variable marketing expenses:				
Selling..............................	$ 243,300	$ 112,300	$ 89,000	$ 42,000
Warehousing	87,100	48,000	27,500	11,600
Packing and shipping	66,000	39,000	17,800	9,200
Advertising......................	38,000	20,000	12,000	6,000
Credit and collection...........	19,700	12,300	4,200	3,200
General accounting.............	52,200	23,000	16,800	12,400
Total variable marketing expenses.............................	$ 506,300	$ 254,600	$ 167,300	$ 84,400
Margin available for fixed expenses and operating income (contribution margin)	$ 666,700	$ 360,400	$ 312,700	$ (6,400)
Less fixed expense (manufacturing and nonmanufacturing) directly related to individual product lines	120,000	40,000	60,000	20,000
Margin available for common fixed expenses and operating income.............................	$ 546,700	$ 320,400	$ 252,700	$(26,400)
Less common fixed expense (manufacturing and nonmanufacturing)	230,000	Not allocated		
Operating income.................	$ 316,700			

Analysis by Salespersons

The selling function includes costs such as salaries, travel, and other expenses connected with the work of sales representatives. In many instances, salespersons' expenses form a substantial part of the total expense incurred in selling. The control and analysis of these expenses should, therefore, receive management's closest attention. To achieve this control, performance standards and standard costs should be established. These standards are used not only for the control of costs but also for determining the profitability of sales made by salespersons.

Cost Control. The allocation table on page 657 indicates that selling expenses may be allocated on the basis of the number of calls made. A call or visit by a salesperson is usually made for two reasons: to sell and to promote the merchandise or products. The problem is to determine the cost of doing each of these types of work and to compare the actual cost with the standard cost allowed for a call.

A salesperson's call often involves several kinds of work: not only calling on the customer, but also helping the merchant with the display in the store or window. This practice is common in cosmetic, pharmaceutical, and fast-food businesses. Because the salesperson's time is consumed by such activities, a standard time allowed per call is often very difficult to establish. To obtain the necessary statistics for establishing such standards and to make comparisons, the sales representative might be asked to prepare a report providing information regarding the type of calls made as well as the quantity, type, and dollar value of products sold. This information is the basis for much of the analysis discussed previously.

Profitability Analysis. It is also possible to analyze sales in relation to profitability. Sales volume alone does not tell the complete story. High volume does not always insure high profit, and the sales mix plays an important part in the final profit. Although a sales representative might wish to follow the line of least resistance, management must strive to sell the merchandise of all product groups, particularly those with the highest profit margins. Since sales territories are often planned for sales according to product groups, it is necessary that anticipated sales be followed up by analyzing the salespersons' efforts. The table below indicates how such an analysis can be made.

SALES, COSTS, AND PROFITS BY INDIVIDUAL SALESPERSONS
FOR APRIL, 19--

(1)	(2)	(3)	(4)	(5)	(6)	(7)	(8)	(9)	(10)	(11)	(12)
			SALARY		COST	TOTAL			PROFIT,	SHIP-	POTEN-
		%	AND	TRAVEL	OF	COST			% OF	MENTS,	TIAL,
SALES-	SHIP-	OF	COMMIS-	EX-	HANDL-	(4) +	GROSS	PROFIT	SALES	% OF	% OF
PERSON	MENTS	QUOTA	SION	PENSES	ING	(5) + (6)	PROFIT	(8) − (7)	(9) ÷ (2)	TOTAL*	TOTAL*
A	$26,000	80%	$2,000	$3,000	$2,340	$ 7,340	$ 7,540	$ 200	0.8%	6.7%	9.0%
B	26,000	122	1,900	1,800	2,340	6,040	7,800	1,760	6.8	6.7	5.5
C	39,000	100	2,800	2,100	3,500	8,400	11,700	3,300	8.5	10.1	10.5
D	22,000	108	1,800	2,000	1,980	5,780	7,050	1,270	5.8	5.8	5.5
E	21,000	110	1,700	1,700	1,890	5,290	6,720	1,430	6.8	5.4	5.0
F	54,000	125	3,500	3,100	5,700	12,300	14,600	2,300	4.3	14.0	10.0
G	21,000	98	1,600	1,200	1,700	4,500	6,720	2,220	10.6	5.5	5.5
H	46,000	101	3,400	1,000	4,100	8,500	13,800	5,300	11.5	12.0	12.0

*For 8 salespersons out of a total of 15 salespersons.

THE CONTRIBUTION MARGIN APPROACH

Generally, the income statement shows a profit figure after all marketing and administrative expenses have been deducted. The total cost and profit approach assigns all the expenses, direct or indirect, fixed or variable, to each segment analyzed. This procedure is commonly used, since management is familiar with it and believes that no profit is realized until all manufacturing and nonmanufacturing expenses have been recovered.

Marketing cost analysis attempts to allocate marketing expenses to territories, customers, products, or salespersons. However, because these marketing costs contain direct, indirect, fixed, and variable amounts, allocations are extremely difficult and the end results very doubtful. It has been suggested that only the variable manufacturing cost be subtracted from each segment's sales, thus arriving at a figure described as "gross contribution margin." (The conventional income statement deducts all manufacturing costs in arriving at a figure described as "gross profit.") Furthermore, only the variable nonmanufacturing expense would be subtracted from the gross contribution margin of a territory, customer class, product, or salesperson. Fixed expenses would be shown separately and not allocated unless specifically attributable to a segment. When a territory, customer class, or product group contributes nothing to the recovery of fixed expenses, the situation should be examined and remedial steps taken. The product-line income statement on page 663 illustrates this approach. Moreover, in the case of joint costs, variable as well as fixed costs should be viewed as they relate to the contribution made by the group of products or territories rather than based on arbitrary allocations, e.g., to individual products or territories (pages 191–193). The arbitrary nature of joint cost allocations is also a fundamental reason for criticism of requirements to report segment or product-line revenue, costs, and profits in published financial statements.

Although sales volume is the ultimate goal of most sales managers, the trend has been toward a greater recognition of contribution margin as the basis for judging the success and profitability of marketing activities. The increased use of standard production costs has aided the analysis of gross profit, as discussed in Chapter 21. Even though a manufacturer might know the production costs, the question remains: "How much can the company afford for marketing costs?" The problem of determining allowable marketing expenses is intensified because once a sales program gets under way, the majority of expenses become fixed costs, at least in the short run.

The analysis discussed here combines the fixed and variable costs of each functional group to arrive at a functional unit costing rate per activity. But the allocation of joint expense in any type of analysis is often difficult and uncertain. Proponents of the contribution margin approach point out that only specific and direct costs, whether variable or fixed, should be assigned to territories, customers, product groups, or salespersons, with a clear distinction as to their fixed and variable characteristics. Moreover, for the purpose of identifying costs with responsible managers, it is desirable to identify each reported cost with its controllability by the manager in charge of the reported activity.

The contribution margin approach has influenced the thinking of the volume-minded sales manager or salesperson who must recognize that profit is more beneficial than volume. The contribution margin is a better indicator than sales as to the amount available for recovery of fixed manufacturing costs, fixed marketing and administrative expenses, and a profit.

EFFECT OF THE ROBINSON-PATMAN ACT ON MARKETING COST ANALYSIS

The Robinson-Patman Act of June, 1936, amended Section 2 of the Clayton Act, which was enacted to prevent large buyers from securing excessive advantages over their smaller competitors by virtue of their size and purchasing power. Since the Clayton Act prohibited discrimination only where it had a serious effect on competition in general, and since it contained no other provisions for the control of price discrimination, the Act was amended in order to insure competitive equality of the individual enterprise. The following clause of the Robinson-Patman Act is of special interest in connection with marketing costs:

> To make it unlawful for any person engaged in commerce to discriminate in price or terms of sale between purchasers of commodities of like grades and quality; to prohibit the payment of brokerage or commissions under certain conditions; to suppress pseudo-advertising allowances; to provide a presumptive measure of damages in certain cases; and to protect the independent merchant, the public whom he serves, and the manufacturer who sells him his goods from exploitation by unfair competitors.

The amendment does not imply that price discriminations in the sense of price differentials are entirely prohibited or that a seller is compelled or required to grant any price differential whatever. A vendor may sell to all customers at the same price regardless of differences in the cost of serving them. At the core of the amendment are the provisions that deal with charging different prices to different customers. Differentials granted must not exceed differences in the cost of serving different customers. The cost of serving includes the cost of manufacturing, selling, and delivering, which may differ according to methods of selling and quantities sold. The burden of proof is on both the buyer and the seller and requires a definite justification for the discounts granted and received. It is necessary to prove that no discrimination took place with respect to (1) price differences, (2) discounts, (3) delivery service, (4) allowances for service, (5) advertising appropriations, (6) brokerage or commissions, or (7) consignment policies.

These possibilities for discrimination fall chiefly into the field of marketing costs. Many interesting problems have arisen because of the nature of these costs and the numerous variations and combinations in the manner of sale and delivery. As indicated, it is difficult to apply many marketing costs to particular products. Therefore, it is important for concerns performing distribution functions to accumulate cost statistics regarding their marketing costs, because the Act makes allowances for differences in costs. The Act has increased the interest in marketing cost analysis and its part in the determination of prices. The cost justification study below illustrates this point.

COST JUSTIFICATION STUDY[5]

A producer of a heavy bulk chemical, which sells FOB point of manufacture at $25 a ton in minimum quantities of a full rail carload (approximately 40 tons), is offered a contract for 500 to 1,000 carloads a year if it will reduce its FOB shipping point price by 6 percent. The producer does not want to reduce the selling price to other customers, to whom annual shipments range from 10 to 200 carloads. The only source of cost differences is sales solicitation and service expense.

The sales manager estimates (since exact records are not available) that salespersons typically pursue the following call schedule:

CUSTOMER SIZE (IN CARLOADS)	ANNUAL NUMBER OF SALES CALLS
10–40	12
41–80	24
81–150	36
151 and up	50

The sales manager further estimates that each sales call costs approximately $50–$70 regardless of customer size. After questioning, the manager agrees that study would probably show that calls on large customers (more than 100 carloads) are longer in duration than calls on smaller customers. For study and testing purposes, it was assumed that a call on a small customer costs $60 and a call on a large customer costs $90. The cost-sales relationship illustrated below can now be developed.

DIFFERENTIAL COST
LARGE VS. SMALL CUSTOMERS

	ANNUAL CARLOADS PER CUSTOMER				
	25	50	100	200	500
Sales value......................	$25,000	$50,000	$100,000	$200,000	$500,000
Number of sales calls.........	12	24	36	50	50
Assumed cost per call	$ 60	$ 60	$ 90	$ 90	$ 90
Assumed cost of call per customer	720	1,440	3,240	4,500	4,500
Assumed cost of call as a percent of sales..............	2.9%	2.9%	3.2%	2.25%	0.9%

Since the assumed differential costs are less than the 6 percent proposed discount, it appears obvious that a discount of that magnitude is not susceptible to cost justification. Indeed, it is possible that even a one percent discount to a 500-carload customer might be hard to justify since it is probable that more exact costing would narrow the spread in the percentages among the various classes.

---

[5]Herbert G. Whiting, "Cost Justification of Price Differences," *Management Services*, Vol. 3, No. 4, pp. 31–32. Copyright 1966 by the American Institute of Certified Public Accountants, Inc.

A competitor who believes that discrimination exists must file a complaint substantiated by evidence acquired from published price lists or from other persuasive evidence of this kind. The complaint is valid if all of the following violations have been committed:

1. Price discrimination.
2. Discrimination between competitors.
3. Discrimination on products of like grades and quality.
4. Discrimination in interstate commerce.
5. Injurious effect on competition.

The most effective method for a firm to answer any such complaint is to have a functional unit cost system for marketing costs. In fact, no firm should be placed in a situation of having to make a cost study after being cited. Experience has proven that such belated cost justification studies seldom are successful. Therefore, the firm should (1) establish records that show that price differentials are extended only to the extent justified by maximum allowable cost savings and (2) maintain the cost data currently through spot checks conducted periodically to insure that the price differentials are in conformance with current cost conditions.

In justifying price differentials, marginal costing cannot be utilized; i.e., a plant operating at 80 percent capacity and wishing to add an order to increase its capacity to 90 percent cannot restrict its cost considerations to that incremental element of variable cost due to the volume change.[6] The reduced cost per unit resulting from the greater volume must be spread over all units. Thus, the government, in consistently rejecting the marginal approach, endorses instead a method which is often called fully distributed cost analysis and only these fully distributed or average total costs are acceptable for a cost justification defense under the Robinson-Patman Act. The government has held that only identifiable savings resulting from specific methods or quantities connected with given orders can be properly passed in their entirety to specific customers.[7]

In general, the Robinson-Patman Act seems to be working toward greater equity between prices, inasmuch as pricing schedules appear to be more carefully attuned to differences in marketing costs than they were before the enactment of this particular type of control. The accountant must be prepared to study the subject actively and continuously to help management avoid unintentional price discriminations that might be in violation of the law. The marketing manager must also follow the effect of any pricing policy to determine whether it is profitable and produces the kind of business necessary for the wholesome operation of the enterprise.

[6]John E. Martin, "Use of Costs for Justifying Price Differentials," *Arthur Andersen Chronicle*, Vol. XXIV, No. 4, pp. 33–40.
[7]Itzhak Sharav, "Cost Justification Under the Robinson-Patman Act," *Management Accounting*, Vol. LX, No. 1, p. 18.

ILLUSTRATIVE PROBLEM IN MARKETING COST AND PROFITABILITY ANALYSIS

The Bryan Company manufactures and sells a variety of small power tools, dies, drills, files, milling cutters, saws, and other miscellaneous hardware. The company's catalog lists the merchandise under sixteen major classifications. Customers fall into five categories: retail hardware stores, manufacturers, public school systems, municipalities, and public utilities. Territories include New Jersey and Pennsylvania. The company's president believes that in certain areas the cost of marketing the products is too high, that certain customers' orders do not contribute enough to cover fixed costs and earn a profit, and that certain products are being sold to customers and in territories on an unprofitable basis. Therefore, the president has instructed the controller to review the firm's marketing costs and to study the steps, methods, and procedures necessary to provide more accurate information about the profitability of territories, products, and customers.

The controller has designed and operated a standard marketing cost system which gives management the desired information for the control and analysis of marketing and administrative expenses. The preparation and assembling of statistical and cost data were carried out in the following sequence:

1. Total marketing expenses were estimated (or budgeted).
2. Six marketing functions (selling, warehousing, packing and shipping, advertising, credit and collection, general accounting) were established.
3. Direct or functional (departmental) costs were assigned directly to functions; indirect expenses were allocated via a measurement unit, such as kilowatt-hour, footage, or number of employees.
4. Fixed and variable expenses were determined for each function.
5. Functional unit measurement bases were selected for the purpose of assigning costs to the segments to be analyzed, i.e., territory or product.
6. Functional unit measurements or bases applicable to a territory or a product were determined.
7. Unit standard manufacturing costs and standard product sales prices were established.
8. Data regarding the types and number of units sold in the territories were prepared.
9. Income statements by (a) territories and (b) product lines in one territory were prepared for management.

Exhibit 1 on page 670 summarizes the results of the study prepared by the controller. Column 1 shows the total budgeted expense per function. Each total is supported by a budget showing the amount for each individual expense of the function. Columns 2 and 3 place total expenses in a variable and fixed expense classification. Column 4 indicates the functional unit measurement selected as being reliably applicable to that function. Column 5 lists the quantity or value of the measurement unit used to determine the functional unit costing rate. Columns 6, 7, and 8 indicate the variable, fixed, and total functional unit costing rates.

Exhibits 2 and 3 list the details necessary for the preparation of Exhibits 1, 4, and 5. To simplify the illustration, nonmanufacturing costs other than marketing costs have been excluded.

The product-line income statement for the territory of Pennsylvania (Exhibit 5) indicates that the volume and/or price of Product 1 is not sufficient to result in a profit. In Exhibit 6, this analysis is carried further with the aid of a fixed-variable analysis of manufacturing costs and marketing expenses to determine the contribution made by the product line to the total fixed cost and profit. This exhibit assumes the nonexistence of unallocated joint cost, fixed or variable. The product-line income statement on page 663 illustrates a presentation with unallocated costs.

Next, the steps required to bring about an improvement in the profitability of this product line should be determined. Functional marketing cost analysis permits this type of analysis, which should eventually lead to a selective selling program supported by product break-even analyses and by cost-volume-profit and differential cost analyses (Chapters 24 and 25).

Exhibit 1

DETERMINATION OF FUNCTIONAL UNIT COSTING RATES

FUNCTION	BUDGETED EXPENSES Total (1)	Variable (2)	Fixed (3)	FUNCTIONAL UNIT MEASUREMENT BASE (4)	QUANTITY (5)	FUNCTIONAL UNIT COSTING RATES Variable (6)	Fixed (7)	Total (8)
Selling	$ 95,500	$ 38,200	$ 57,300	Gross sales dollar value of product sold	$1,910,000	2%	3%	5%
Warehousing.............	75,000	45,000	30,000	Weight of units shipped	375 000	$ .12	$ .08	$ .20
Packing and shipping ..	63,000	37,500	25,500	Quantity product units sold	150,000	.25	.17	.42
Advertising...............	54,000		54,000	Quantity product units sold	150,000		.36	.36
Credit and collection...	28,800	18,720	10,080	Number of customers' orders	7,200	2.60	1.40	4.00
General accounting.....	49,200	21,300	27,900	Number of times product items appear on customers' invoices	15,000	1.42	1.86	3.28
Total functional distribution expense..............	$365,500	$160,720	$204,780					

Exhibit 2

DATA CONCERNING PRICE, COST, QUANTITY, WEIGHT, AND TRANSACTIONS OF PRODUCTS

PRODUCT CLASS	PRODUCT 1	PRODUCT 2	PRODUCT 3
Standard product sales price...........................	$10.00	$15.00	$18.00
Unit standard manufacturing cost....................	8.00	11.00	12.00
Quantity of product units sold........................	80,000	50,000	20,000
Weight of units shipped (kilograms)	2.25 kg	2.5 kg	3.5 kg
Number of times product items appear on customers' invoices.......................................	6,400	5,700	2,900
Number of customers' orders	2,400	3,000	1,800

Exhibit 3

DATA CONCERNING TRANSACTIONS IN TERRITORIES

TERRITORY	QUANTITY OF PRODUCTS SOLD			NUMBER OF TIMES PRODUCT ITEMS APPEAR ON CUSTOMERS' INVOICES			NUMBER OF CUSTOMERS' ORDERS		
	Product 1	Product 2	Product 3	Product 1	Product 2	Product 3	Product 1	Product 2	Product 3
Pennsylvania	55,000	30,000	16,000	4,000	2,900	1,000	1,000	1,900	900
New Jersey	25,000	20,000	4,000	2,400	2,800	1,900	1,400	1,100	900

Exhibit 4

INCOME STATEMENT FOR ALL PRODUCT CLASSES IN THE TWO TERRITORIES

		TERRITORY	
	TOTAL	Pennsylvania	New Jersey
Gross sales	$1,910,000	$1,288,000	$622,000
Less cost of goods sold	1,430,000	962,000	468,000
Gross profit	$ 480,000	$ 326,000	$154,000
Less marketing expenses:			
Selling	$ 95,500	$ 64,400	$ 31,100
Warehousing	75,000	50,950	24,050
Packing and shipping	63,000	42,420	20,580
Advertising	54,000	36,360	17,640
Credit and collection	28,800	15,200	13,600
General accounting	49,200	25,912	23,288
Total	$ 365,500	$ 235,242	$130,258
Operating income	$ 114,500	$ 90,758	$ 23,742

Exhibit 5

INCOME STATEMENT BY PRODUCT CLASSES IN THE PENNSYLVANIA TERRITORY

		PRODUCT CLASS		
	TOTAL	Product 1	Product 2	Product 3
Gross sales	$1,288,000	$550,000	$450,000	$288,000
Less cost of goods sold	962,000	440,000	330,000	192,000
Gross profit	$ 326,000	$110,000	$120,000	$ 96,000
Less marketing expenses:				
Selling	$ 64,400	$ 27,500	$ 22,500	$ 14,400
Warehousing	50,950	24,750	15,000	11,200
Packing and shipping	42,420	23,100	12,600	6,720
Advertising	36,360	19,800	10,800	5,760
Credit and collection	15,200	4,000	7,600	3,600
General accounting	25,912	13,120	9,512	3,280
Total	$ 235,242	$112,270	$ 78,012	$ 44,960
Operating income (loss)	$ 90,758	$(2,270)	$ 41,988	$ 51,040

Exhibit 6

INCOME STATEMENT OF PRODUCT CLASS WITH FIXED-VARIABLE ANALYSIS OF MANUFACTURING AND MARKETING COSTS IN THE PENNSYLVANIA TERRITORY

		PRODUCT 1
Gross sales		$550,000
Less cost of goods sold (variable unit cost = 60% of $8)		264,000
Gross contribution margin		$286,000
Less variable marketing expenses:		
Selling	$ 11,000	
Warehousing	14,850	
Packing and shipping	13,750	
Credit and collection	2,600	
General accounting	5,680	47,880
Contribution margin		$238,120
Less fixed costs and expenses:		
Manufacturing cost — fixed	$176,000	
Marketing expenses — fixed:		
Selling	$ 16,500	
Warehousing	9,900	
Packing and shipping	9,350	
Advertising	19,800	
Credit and collection	1,400	
General accounting	7,440	240,390
Operating loss — Product Class 1 — Pennsylvania		$ (2,270)

DISCUSSION QUESTIONS

1. What general principles should be observed in planning a system of control for marketing expenses?

2. How are marketing expenses to be classified in order to find the cost of selling jobs or products?

3. A method still commonly used today in analyzing marketing expenses is to relate them to either the total factory cost or the total sales value. This method is merely a relationship and not a scientific basis. Discuss.

4. On what bases might the following marketing expenses be equitably assigned to different types of commodities sold by a company:

   (a) Sales salaries   (e) Advertising on a national scale
   (b) Sales commissions   (f) Expenses of company's own delivery trucks
   (c) Storing finished goods   (g) Sales manager's salary
   (d) Warehouse expenses   (h) Sales office expenses

5. A firm employing its own transport service delivers its products up to a distance of 130 miles from home in quantities varying from 1 to 20 cwt. On the return trip, empty containers are collected from certain customers and a quantity of materials are picked up from suppliers. How should the cost incurred for these services be distributed?

6. The advertising policy of a company includes exhibition of the plant to customers. Visitors are received and guides are supplied from the production staff.
   (a) How should this cost be treated in the records?
   (b) What adequate control of this expenditure can be provided from the point of view of production and sales promotion?

7. Outline a procedure for determining the marketing costs for a concern manufacturing two products. This organization uses national advertising and assigns salespersons to definite territories for contact with established dealers and also to secure additional retail outlets.

8. What are the objectives of profit analysis by sales territories?

9. (a) On what basis should sales expenses be analyzed in order to enable management to judge the effectiveness of the selling function?
   (b) What cost data should be given to salespersons and for what purpose?

10. A company with a national sales force divides the country into sales territories, which are subdivided into districts. The products are nationally advertised and are sold to retail shops. Assuming 1,000 orders per day with an average of four items per order, what marketing cost system should be installed to accumulate:
    (a) The necessary sales statistics to control sales by territories and lines?
    (b) The expenses of such a sales force?
    (c) Records and statistical analyses for use in the preparation of sales budgets and profit margins?

11. What difficulties may arise if an attempt is made to set standards for marketing expenses?

12. Explain briefly the difference between the profit approach and the contribution margin approach in marketing cost analysis.

13. Why did the Robinson-Patman Act lead to the establishment of marketing cost procedures in business?

EXERCISES

1. **Marketing cost analysis by territories.** The King Air Freshener Company of Waco, Texas, markets a single product in Waco and Dallas.

Marketing expenses for the past year were:

Sales salaries	$ 76,000
Salespersons' expenses	16,200
Advertising	24,000
Delivery expense	25,200
Credit investigation expense	6,800
Collection expense	11,400
Total	$159,600

Additional information:

(a) The company has five salespersons, three in Dallas and two in Waco, and each is paid the same salary.

(b) The salespersons receive equal allowances for expenses, except that the Dallas salespersons each receive $400 per year extra for turnpike toll fees.

(c) All advertising is placed according to the number of subscribers to the Waco and Dallas daily newspapers, 150,000 and 750,000 respectively.

(d) Delivery is made by an outside agency which charges a flat annual fee. The agency made 4,800 deliveries (3,000 in Dallas, 1,800 in Waco) from a centrally located warehouse.

(e) 680 new customers were obtained (400 from Dallas, 280 from Waco).

(f) 6,000 customers' remittances were received (4,500 from Dallas, 1, 500 from Waco).

Required: Marketing cost analysis for the two territories.

2. Territorial income statement: managerial decision-making costs. The Fowler Company manufactures textile equipment. Sales are made by company salespersons directly to textile manufacturers in three sales territories.

The following information concerning territories was obtained from the standard sales and marketing expense budgets for June:

ITEM	TERRITORY 1	TERRITORY 2	TERRITORY 3	TOTAL
Net sales..	$120,000	$100,000	$180,000	$400,000
Sales salaries...	6,000	5,000	9,000	20,000
Sales travel expense.............................	3,650	2,350	5,000	11,000
Warehouse expense...............................	1,200	1,000	3,300	5,500
Delivery..	2,000	3,000	6,000	11,000
Supplies..	1,000	800	1,600	3,400

Other standard marketing expenses and methods used to allocate both standard and actual expenses to territories are as follows: advertising, 5% of net sales; credit and collection, 2% of net sales; sales office, $15,000, distributed equally; general sales salaries, $16,000, distributed on basis of net sales; sales commissions paid to salespersons, 8% of net sales. The cost of manufacturing the equipment sold is 60% of net sales.

Required:

(1) A standard income statement comparing the standard net sales, manufacturing cost, marketing expenses, and operating income or loss for the three territories.

(2) How the figures developed in (1) aid management in determining:

(a) Whether a territory should be dropped or whether attempts should be made to develop further such territory by increased advertising, service, etc.

(b) The responsibility for incurrence of marketing costs.

(c) Whether salespersons should discontinue calling on a certain class of customer.

3. Income statement by customer classes. Shelton Company assembles a washing machine that is sold to three classes of customers. The data with respect to these customers are shown below:

CUSTOMER CLASS	SALES	GROSS PROFIT	NUMBER OF SALES CALLS	NUMBER OF ORDERS	NUMBER OF INVOICE LINES
Department stores	$180,000	$ 26,000	240	120	2,100
Retail appliance stores....	240,000	80,000	360	580	4,600
Wholesalers......................	300,000	71,000	400	300	3,300
Total..............................	$720,000	$177,000	1,000	1,000	10,000

Actual marketing costs for the year are:

FUNCTION	COSTS	MEASURE OF ACTIVITY
Selling	$65,000	Salespersons' calls
Packing and shipping	12,000	Customers' orders
Advertising	10,000	Dollar sales
Credit and collection.............	15,000	Invoice lines
General accounting...............	18,000	Customers' orders

Required: An income statement by customer classes with functional distribution of marketing expenses. (When allocating the advertising expense, round to the nearest $100.)

4. Profitability analysis by channels of marketing; variance analysis. The Lindale Electric Company manufactures small electrical home appliances and distributes them via retailers, wholesalers, and department stores. The company's marketing cost system employs functional standard marketing costs that aid in charging and controlling expenses by channels of distribution.

During December, the Cost Department calculated the following standard unit costs for the coming year:

Selling	$ 1.75 per salesperson's call
Warehousing	12.00 per 1,000 cubic feet of product sold
Packing and shipping	47.00 per 1,000 cubic feet of product sold
Advertising	1.25 per media circulation
Credit and collection	.08 per invoice line
General accounting	.35 per customer order

At the end of the year, actual activity and costs were:

			ACTIVITY		
FUNCTION	TOTAL ACTUAL COSTS	Measure of Activity	Retailers	Whole-salers	Depart-ment Stores
Selling	$187,500	Salespersons' calls.....	75,000	10,000	15,000
Warehousing	12,100	Cu. ft. of product	390,000	160,000	250,000
Packing and shipping...	35,900	Cu. ft. of product	390,000	160,000	250,000
Advertising	11,200	Media circulation........	4,000	1,000	5,000
Credit and collection	23,800	Invoice lines................	115,000	75,000	60,000
General accounting	9,300	Customers' orders......	18,500	2,000	4,500
Other actual data:					
Sales..........			$670,000	$310,000	$405,000
Gross profit percentage			25%	40%	30%

Required: An income statement by channels of marketing with:
(1) Functional marketing expenses at standard and
(2) The variances of actual from standard costs to arrive at actual operating income.

5. Marketing cost control using flexible budget and standards. The Kasrail Company sells various imported products through selected retail outlets. Data relative to standard selling costs for one of the company's salespersons shows:

Standard sales for the year	$180,000
Standard selling cost for the year	21,600
Sales for October	14,000
Selling costs for October:	
Actual cost	1,700
Budgeted cost for $14,000 sales	1,650

Required:
(1) Standard selling cost to be charged if the salesperson reported $5,000 sales the first week of October.
(2) Spending variance for the salesperson's October sales.
(3) October idle capacity variance for the salesperson.

6. Salesperson's performance reports. A corporate budget director designed a control scheme in order to compare and evaluate the efforts of the company's three salespersons and the results attained. Specifically, each salesperson is to make five calls per day; the budget provides for $40 per day per salesperson for travel and entertainment expenses; each salesperson was assigned a sales quota of $400 a day. The Budget Department collects the data on actual performance from the daily sales reports and the weekly expense vouchers and then prepares a monthly report. This report includes variances from standard and performance indexes. For the performance index, standard performance equals 100.

The records for November with 20 working days show:

SALESPERSON	SALES CALLS	TRAVEL EXPENSES	SALES
Palmer, K.	70	$1,000	$14,000
Thompson, J.	100	800	8,400
Miller, O.	120	720	6,000

Required: A monthly report comparing the standard and actual performances of the salespersons, including the performance indexes for (1) sales calls, (2) travel expenses, (3) sales, and (4) sales revenue per call.

7. Cost justification study. Larson-Manss Distributors, Inc., has been accused of discriminating against its small-order customers (25 to 50 cases) in Territory 1 as compared with the same class of customers in Territories 2, 3, and 4. The company has broken down its marketing cost by territories and now desires to allocate the territorial costs among classes of customers within each territory. A tabulation of the average distribution costs per year in Territory 1 shows:

Advertising:	
Direct-to-customer catalog	$ 3,600
Radio and newspapers	9,000
Sales salaries	36,000
Sales commissions	48,000
Delivery	28,800
Sales travel cost...	10,800
Collection cost..	8,400
	$144,600

The Accounting Department has tabulated the following to assist in prorating costs in Territory 1 between small-, medium-, and large-order customers:

	SMALL-ORDER CUSTOMERS	MEDIUM-ORDER CUSTOMERS	LARGE-ORDER CUSTOMERS
Net sales..	$150,000	$220,000	$350,000
Number of sales orders taken	2,500	2,000	1,500
Number of cases of product sold..................................	100,000	150,000	250,000
Relative shipping cost (per order)................................	$1	$2	$3
Number of customers..	1,500	1,500	2,000
Relative number of kilometers traveled per day (per salesperson)...	4	10	16
Number of salespersons...	13	6	5

In the Collection Department, the bookkeeping cost per order handled is about ten cents. Each customer is mailed a statement at the end of the month, and the customers make single monthly remittances on account.

All salespersons are paid the same salary; each salesperson works with a single class of customer.

Required: An allocation of the distribution costs of Territory 1 to the three classes of customers. Indicate the base or bases on which each allocation is made. (Round off all base computations to four decimal places, and all allocated amounts to the nearest dollar.)

PROBLEMS

23-1. Territorial profit contribution report. The Ferguson Company uses a territorial profit contribution report as an effective tool for marketing cost analysis. The report is coordinated with the company's semiannual budget by establishing the profit required from each sales territory to meet all branch and head office operating expenses plus expected operating income for each month.

This procedure gives the sales managers not only a sales budget in both quantity and value but also the estimated profit required from each territory under their supervision.

About two months before the beginning of the semiannual accounting period, the Budget Department prepared the following forecast income statement:

Forecast Income Statement
For Six Months Ending December 31, 19--

Net sales		$10,000,000
Cost of goods sold		6,000,000
Gross profit		$ 4,000,000
Sales territorial expenses:		
Freight to customers	$ 700,000	
Salaries and commissions	1,500,000	
Traveling expenses and miscellaneous	300,000	2,500,000
Territorial profit		$ 1,500,000
General marketing and administrative expenses:		
Marketing	$1,000,000	
Administrative	300,000	1,300,000
Operating income		$ 200,000

The sales forecast broken down by months and territories is as follows:

	TERRITORIES				
MONTH	75	42	55	Others	Total
July	$ 10,000	$ 8,000	$ 8,000	$ 974,000	$ 1,000,000
August	15,000	11,000	12,000	1,462,000	1,500,000
September	15,000	11,000	12,000	1,462,000	1,500,000
October	30,000	22,000	24,000	2,924,000	3,000,000
November	20,000	15,000	16,000	1,949,000	2,000,000
December	10,000	8,000	8,000	974,000	1,000,000
Total	$100,000	$75,000	$80,000	$9,745,000	$10,000,000

According to the income statement, the territories are expected to contribute $1,500,000 (recovery of marketing expenses, $1,000,000; administrative expenses, $300,000; and operating income, $200,000). This profit contribution is prorated to each sales territory on the basis of the estimated sales for the same period.

The budget of the territorial profit contribution for the three territories for the three-month period ending September 30, 19--, showed the following costs and expenses:

TERRITORY	COST OF GOODS SOLD	FREIGHT	SALARIES AND COMMISSIONS	TRAVEL EXPENSES AND MISC.
75	$24,890	$1,820	$6,500	$ 790
42	18,319	1,746	4,250	1,185
55	14,815	3,845	6,200	2,340

Actual results in the three territories for the same period were:

TERRITORY	SALES	COST OF GOODS SOLD	FREIGHT	SALARIES AND COMMISSIONS	TRAVEL EXPENSES AND MISC.
75	$44,250	$27,878	$2,212	$6,100	$1,437
42	33,465	24,710	2,245	3,900	1,420
55	18,865	11,378	3,329	5,820	1,940

Required:

(1) A territorial profit contribution report for the three territories comparing actual gross profit contribution with the budgeted amount, and budgeted contribution to meet marketing and administrative expenses and operating income with actual results. Assume that actual and budgeted marketing and administrative expenses are equal.

(2) Factors or a combination of factors that might have caused a loss or the failure to fulfill budget requirements in any territory.

23-2. Territorial cost report and analysis. The Scott Company sells toiletries to retail stores throughout the United States. For planning and control purposes, the Scott Company is organized into twelve geographic regions with two to six territories within each region. One salesperson is assigned to each territory and has exclusive rights to all sales made in that territory. Merchandise is shipped from the manufacturing plant to the twelve regional warehouses, from which the sales in each territory are shipped. National headquarters allocates a specific amount at the beginning of the year for regional advertising.

The net sales for the Scott Company for the year ended September 30 total $10 million. Costs incurred by national headquarters are:

National administration	$250,000
National advertising	125,000
National warehousing	175,000
	$550,000

The results of operations for the South Atlantic Region for the year ended September 30 are:

Scott Company
Statement of Operations for South Atlantic Region
For the Year Ended September 30, 19--

Sales		$900,000
Costs and expenses:		
Advertising fees	$ 54,700	
Uncollectible accounts expense	3,600	
Cost of goods sold	460,000	
Freight out	22,600	
Insurance	10,000	
Salaries and employee benefits	81,600	
Sales commissions	36,000	
Supplies	12,000	
Travel and entertainment	14,100	
Wages and employee benefits	36,000	
Warehouse depreciation	8,000	
Warehouse operating cost	15,000	
Total cost and expense		753,600
Territory contribution		$146,400

The South Atlantic Region consists of two territories — Green and Purple. The salaries and employee benefits consist of the following items:

Regional vice-president	$24,000
Regional marketing manager	15,000
Regional warehouse manager	13,400
Salespersons (one for each territory with both receiving the same salary base)	15,600
Employee benefits (20%)	13,600
	$81,600

The salespersons receive a base salary plus a 4% commission on all items sold in their territory. Uncollectible accounts expense has averaged .4% of sales in the past. Travel and entertainment costs are incurred by the salespersons in calling upon their customers and are based on a fixed authorized amount per year. Freight out is a function of the quantity of goods shipped and the distance shipped. Thirty percent of the insurance is expended for protection of the inventory while it is in the regional warehouse, and the remainder is incurred for the protection of the warehouse. Supplies are used in the warehouse for packing the merchandise to be shipped. Wages (a variable cost) relate to the hourly employees who fill orders in the warehouse. The warehouse operating cost account contains such costs as heat, light, and maintenance.

The following cost analyses and statistics by territory for the current year are representative of past experience and of expected future operations.

	GREEN	PURPLE	TOTAL
Sales	$300,000	$600,000	$900,000
Cost of goods sold*	184,000	276,000	460,000
Advertising	21,800	32,900	54,700
Travel and entertainment	6,300	7,800	14,100
Freight out	9,000	13,600	22,600
Units sold	150,000	350,000	500,000
Pounds shipped**	210,000	390,000	600,000
Sales travel (miles)	21,600	38,400	60,000

*Use to allocate inventory insurance to territories.
**Use to allocate supplies and wages and employee benefits to territories.

The executive management of Scott Company wants the regional vice-presidents to present their operating data in a more meaningful manner. Therefore, management has requested that the regions separate their operating costs into the fixed and variable components of order-getting, order-filling, and administrative. The data are to be presented in the following format:

	TERRITORY COST		REGIONAL	TOTAL
	Green	Purple	COST	COST
Order-getting				
Order-filling				
Administrative				

Required:

(1) A statement which presents the cost for the region by territory, with the costs separated into variable and fixed categories and using management's suggested format.

(2) Identification of the data presented that are relevant to a decision (either for or against) to split the Purple Territory into two separate territories (Red and Blue), and identification of other data needed to aid management in its decision.

(3) An explanation of the use of standards and flexible budgets for planning and controlling marketing costs, assuming that Scott Company keeps its records in accordance with the classification required in (1).   (CMA adapted)

23-3. Income statements by products and amount-of-order classes. The feasibility of allocating marketing and administrative expenses to products or amount-of-order classes for managerial purposes has been considered by the Yale Co. It is apparent that some costs can be assigned equitably to these classifications; others cannot. The company's cost analyst proposed the following bases for apportionment:

	TYPE OF ANALYSIS	
EXPENSE	By Products	By Amount of Order
Sales salaries	Not allocated	Sales dollars times number of customers in class
Sales travel	Not allocated	Number of customers in class
Sales office	Not allocated	Number of customers in class
Sales commissions	Direct	Direct
Credit management	Volume of sales in dollars	Number of customers in class
Packing and shipping	Weight times number of units	Weight times number of units
Warehousing	Weight times number of units	Weight times number of units
Advertising	Not allocated	Not allocated
Bookkeeping and billing	Volume of sales in dollars	Number of orders
General marketing and administrative	Not allocated	Not allocated

From books, records, and other sources, the following data have been compiled:

AMOUNT OF ORDER	NUMBER OF CUSTOMERS	NUMBER OF ORDERS	COST OF GOODS SOLD	TOTAL SALES	PRODUCT SALES		
					X	Y	Z
Under $25	1,000	6,000	$ 59,000	$ 100,000	$ 35,000	40,000	$ 25,000
$26–$100	250	4,000	177,000	300,000	105,000	120,000	75,000
$101–$200	100	4,000	354,000	600,000	210,000	240,000	150,000
Over $200	50	1,000	236,000	400,000	140,000	160,000	100,000
Total	1,400	15,000	$826,000	$1,400,000	$490,000	$560,000	$350,000

Other data:

PRODUCT	WEIGHT	COST OF GOODS SOLD	UNITS SOLD
X	1 kg	$252,000	98,000
Y	3 kg	294,000	70,000
Z	2 kg	280,000	175,000

Marketing and administrative expenses for the year:

Sales salaries	$ 38,250
Sales travel	28,000
Sales office (variable)	15,400
Sales commissions (5%)	70,000
Credit management...	14,000
Packing and shipping	32,900
Warehousing...	16,450
Advertising	150,000
Bookkeeping and billing...	42,000
General marketing and administrative	80,000
Total	$487,000

Required:

(1) A product income statement showing the allocation of marketing and administrative expenses to each product. (Round off all base computations to five decimal places, and all allocated amounts to the nearest dollar.)

(2) An income statement showing the allocation of marketing and administrative expenses to each order class.

23-4. Standard cost variance analysis; revision of sales prices. Jobe Corporation's actual and standard marketing costs for January are:

	BUDGET AT STANDARD COST	ACTUAL
Sales	$750,000	$750,000
Direct marketing costs:		
Selling	$ 12,000	$ 15,000
Shipping salaries...	21,000	28,350
Indirect marketing costs:		
Order filling...	17,250	21,500
Other costs	2,100	2,500
Total cost..	$ 52,350	$ 67,350

Additional data:

(a) The company sells one product at $10 per unit.

(b) The other indirect marketing costs and shipping salaries are allocated on the basis of shipping hours. January shipping hours are:

Budgeted hours...	3,500
Standard operating level	4,400
Actual hours...	4,500

(c) Order-filling costs are allocated on the basis of sales and are comprised of freight, packing, and warehousing costs. An analysis of the amount of these standard costs by unit order size follows:

| UNIT-VOLUME CLASSIFICATION | ORDER-FILLING STANDARD COSTS CLASSIFIED BY UNIT ORDER SIZE | | | |
	1–15	16–50	Over 50	Total
Freight	$ 1,200	$ 1,440	$ 2,250	$ 4,890
Packing	2,400	3,240	4,500	10,140
Warehousing	600	720	900	2,220
Total	$ 4,200	$ 5,400	$ 7,650	$17,250
Units sold	12,000	18,000	45,000	75,000

Management realizes that the marketing cost per unit decreases with an increase in the size of the order and, hence, wants to revise its unit sales prices upward or downward on the basis of the quantity ordered in proportion to the allocated freight, packing, and warehousing standard costs. Management assumes that the revised unit prices will require no changes in standards for sales volume, the number of units sold in each order-size classification, and the profit per unit sold.

Required:

(1) Computation and analysis of variances from standard cost for (a) other indirect marketing costs and (b) shipping salaries. The analysis should compare actual and standard costs at the standard operating level.
(2) A schedule computing the standard cost per unit for each order-filling cost in each unit-volume classification. Use the same format as in item (c).
(3) A schedule computing the revised unit sales prices for each unit-volume classification.

(AICPA adapted)

23-5. Cost allocations to individual stores; sales expansion decision. McCormick Foods, Inc., a grocery chain consisting of three stores, operates in a state that permits each of its municipalities to levy an income tax on corporations operating within their respective municipalities. This legislation establishes a uniform tax rate that may be levied by the municipality. Regulations also provide that the tax is to be computed on income derived within the taxing municipality after a reasonable and consistent allocation of general overhead expenses, which include warehouse, general office, advertising, and delivery expenses. General overhead expenses have not been allocated previously to McCormick's stores.

Each municipality in which McCormick operates a store has levied the corporate income tax as provided by state legislation, and management is considering two plans for allocating general overhead expenses to each store.

General overhead expenses for the year were as follows:

Delivery and warehousing expenses:		
Delivery expense	$40,000	
Warehouse operations	30,000	
Warehouse depreciation	20,000	$ 90,000
Central office expenses:		
Advertising	18,000	
Central office salaries	37,000	
Other central office expense	28,000	83,000
Total general overhead expense		$173,000

Additional information:

(a) One fifth of the warehouse space is used to house the central office, and depreciation of this space is included in the other central office expense. Warehouse operating expenses vary with the quantity of merchandise sold.
(b) All advertising is prepared by the central office and is distributed in the areas in which stores are located.
(c) As each store was opened, the fixed portion of central office salaries increased by $7,000 while other central office expense increased by $2,500. Basic fixed central office salaries were $10,000 and the basic fixed other central office expense was $12,000. The remainder of central office salaries and the remainder of other central office expense vary with sales.

(d) The delivery expense varies with the distance and the number of deliveries. The distances from the warehouse to each store and the number of deliveries made during the year were:

Store	Miles	Number of Deliveries
Ashville.............................	120	140
Burns................................	200	64
Clinton	100	104

The year's operating results, before deducting general overhead expense and the tax for each store, were:

	STORE			
	Ashville	Burns	Clinton	Total
Net sales	$416,000	$353,600	$270,400	$1,040,000
Less cost of goods sold......................................	215,700	183,300	140,200	539,200
Gross profit..	$200,300	$170,300	$130,200	$ 500,800
Less other local operating expenses:				
Fixed...	$ 60,800	$ 48,750	$ 50,200	$ 159,750
Variable..	54,700	64,220	27,448	146,368
Total...	$115,500	$112,970	$ 77,648	$ 306,118
Operating income before general overhead and income tax...	$ 84,800	$ 57,330	$ 52,552	$ 194,682

Required:

(1) The operating income for each store that would be subject to the municipal tax levy on corporation income under each of the following allocation plans:

Plan 1 .... Allocate all general overhead expenses on the basis of sales volume.

Plan 2 .... First, allocate central office salaries and the other central office expense equally to warehouse operations and to each store.

Second, allocate the resulting warehouse operations expense, warehouse depreciation, and advertising to each store on the basis of sales volume.

Third, allocate delivery expense to each store on the basis of delivery miles × number of deliveries.

(2) A management decision to determine which store should be selected for expansion in order to maximize corporate profits. This expansion will increase McCormick's sales by $50,000 and its local fixed operating expense by $7,500, and it will require ten additional deliveries from the warehouse.

(AICPA adapted)

CASES

A. Cost control and profitability analysis. Fayetteville, Inc., is a closely held company with three owners. The company's management is seeking to improve its cost control and profitability analysis procedures.

The following information is available:

(a) The company is a small supermarket chain with one central warehouse and five retail stores. The stores are located in five small towns at distances of 30 to 80 miles from Fayetteville.

(b) The nearest store is 3 miles from the central warehouse and the farthest is 60 miles from the central warehouse. Approximately 90% of the merchandise sold in each retail store is purchased from the central warehouse and delivered to the store in the company's own trucks. The remaining 10% of goods sold is acquired directly by each store from outside suppliers.

(c) Store managers and the managers of each department within the store (groceries, meat, produce, general merchandise, snack bar) are paid a small salary plus a bonus based on their store's profit.

(d) Goods acquired from the central warehouse by department managers are charged to each store at cost plus a markup of 10%. This markup recovers all purchasing, storing, depreciation, salary, delivery, and other costs of the warehouse and thus allows the warehouse to break even.

(e) Store managers have complete authority and responsibility for their stores, including decisions as to which goods should be stocked, what sales prices should be charged for each, and how much and which type of advertising should be selected. Store managers generally delegate much of the authority and responsibility to individual department managers.

(f) Each store is charged a sum to cover all head office costs. Recently the charge has amounted to 2.5% of sales. This charge and the warehouse charge always draw considerable complaint from store and department managers.

(g) The sales prices in each store are based on between 15% and 60% markups on cost, depending upon the type of item sold and the location of the store.

(h) Three of the five stores encounter some price competition, whereas the other two stores tend to be price leaders in their communities.

(i) Annual sales of the company are approximately $6,000,000, and net profits are usually in the $80,000 to $120,000 range.

(j) At present, a monthly income statement including charges referred to in (d) and (f) is prepared for each store and is distributed to all concerned.

Required: A description of the important features of improved cost control and profitability analysis procedures including reasons for any suggested changes in present practices, using the following major headings:

(1) Performance appraisal
(2) Pricing
(3) Budgets
(4) Delivery charges
(5) Other valid areas for discussion

(CICA adapted)

B. Salespersons — cost control and profitability analysis. Mill Company manufactures and sells two similar types of industrial components which are substitutes for each other. One component is manufactured from plastic, while the other uses metal. The company prepares monthly and annual performance reports for each salesperson. The annual reports for two salespersons — Joan Fowler and Burt Barnes — are reproduced on page 684. Both of these people are assigned to similar territories.

The purpose of the performance reports is to compare each salesperson's performance with their planned activity and to show their contributions toward company profits. All costs and expenses which can be identified with their efforts to generate and produce sales are included on the report. Sales administration and promotion costs (including salaries) are charged to the salespersons according to the number of regular and special-handling orders written. Special-handling orders require approximately twice as much administrative effort as regular orders; consequently, they cost twice as much as regular orders ($16 vs $8). The rate was determined by dividing the amount budgeted for sales administration salaries and sales administration and promotion costs ($160,000) by the estimated total orders (regular, 18,000; special handling, 1,000) weighted by the amount of administrative effort. Special-handling orders comprise approximately 5% of the total orders handled.

Required:

(1) An evaluation, from the company's point of view, of the performance of the two salespersons whose reports are presented, using appropriate numerical data.

(2) Changes, if any, that should be made in the performance report to make it more useful for evaluating salespersons.

(CMA adapted)

Performance Report
Salesperson: Joan Fowler
For the Year Ended December 31, 19--

	BUDGET			ACTUAL RESULTS		
	Plastic	Metal	Total	Plastic	Metal	Total
Sales in units	24,000	16,000	40,000	24,000	17,000	41,000
Sales in dollars......................	$144,000	$160,000	$304,000	$144,000	$161,500	$305,500
Cost of sales at standard	72,000	120,000	192,000	72,000	127,500	199,500
Gross profit at standard........	$ 72,000	$ 40,000	$112,000	$ 72,000	$ 34,000	$106,000
Operating expenses:						
Salary			$ 4,000			$ 4,000
Commissions.....................			9,120			9,165
Employee benefits.............			1,968			1,975
Sales administration and promotion:						
Regular orders.....................			11,400			10,000
Special-handling orders...........			1,200			800
Travel and entertainment			6,250			6,000
Shipping and packing.............			12,000			12,300
Total operating expenses.......			$ 45,938			$ 44,240
Salesperson profit contribution ...			$ 66,062			$ 61,760
Other data:						
Miles traveled						32,000
Number of calls						1,200
Number of regular orders.........						1,250
Number of special-handling orders........						50
Average amount of order.........						$ 235

Performance Report
Salesperson: Burt Barnes
For the Year Ended December 31, 19--

	BUDGET			ACTUAL RESULTS		
	Plastic	Metal	Total	Plastic	Metal	Total
Sales in units	24,000	16,000	40,000	20,000	20,000	40,000
Sales in dollars......................	$144,000	$160,000	$304,000	$120,000	$190,000	$310,000
Cost of sales at standard	72,000	120,000	192,000	60,000	150,000	210,000
Gross profit at standard........	$ 72,000	$ 40,000	$112,000	$ 60,000	$ 40,000	$100,000
Operating expenses:						
Salary			$ 4,000			$ 4,000
Commissions.....................			9,120			9,300
Employee benefits.............			1,968			1,995
Sales administration and promotion:						
Regular orders.....................			11,400			11,600
Special-handling orders...........			1,200			2,400
Travel and entertainment			6,250			7,500
Shipping and packing.............			12,000			12,000
Total operating expenses.......			$ 45,938			$ 48,795
Salesperson profit contribution ...			$ 66,062			$ 51,205
Other data:						
Miles traveled						28,000
Number of calls						1,000
Number of regular orders.........						1,450
Number of special-handling orders........						150
Average amount of order.........						$ 194

C. Commissions for sales force motivation. The Sires Company compensates its field sales force on a commission and year-end bonus basis. The commission is 20% of standard gross profit (sales price minus standard cost of goods sold on a full absorption costing basis), contingent upon collection of the account. The customer's credit is approved by the Credit Department. A year-end bonus of 15% of commissions earned is paid to salespersons who equal or exceed their annual sales target. The annual sales target is usually established by applying approximately a 5% increase to the preceding year's sales.

Required:

    (1) The features of this compensation plan that would seem to be effective in motivating salespersons to accomplish company goals of higher profits and return on investment. Explain.

    (2) The features of this compensation plan that would seem to be counter-effective in motivating the salespersons to accomplish the company goals of higher profits and return on investment. Explain.

(CMA adapted)

D. Marketing strategy. Kline Brothers, a department store dominant in its market area, is easily accessible to public and private transportation, has adequate parking facilities, and is near a large permanent military base. The president seeks advice on a recently received proposal.

A local bank in which the department store has an account recently affiliated with a national credit-card plan and has extended an invitation to Kline Brothers to participate. Under the plan, affiliated banks mail credit-card applications to persons with excellent credit ratings in the community regardless of whether they are bank customers. A recipient wishing to receive a credit card completes, signs, and returns the application and installment credit agreement. Card holders may charge merchandise or services at any participating establishment throughout the nation.

The affiliated banks guarantee payment to participating merchants on all invoices presented that have been properly completed, signed, and validated with the impression of credit cards that are not expired, reported stolen, or otherwise canceled. Merchants may turn in all card-validated sales tickets or invoices to their affiliated bank at any time and receive immediate credits to their checking accounts of 96.5% of the face value of the invoices. Card users paying the bank in full within 30 days for amounts billed will have no added charges levied against them. If payments are made under a deferred payment plan, the bank adds a service charge amounting to an effective interest rate of 18% per annum on unpaid balances. Only the affiliated banks and the franchiser of the credit-card plan share in these revenues.

The 18% service charge approximates what Kline Brothers has been billing its customers who pay their accounts over an extended period on a schedule similar to that offered under the credit-card plan. Participation in the plan does not prevent the store from continuing to conduct its credit business as it has in the past.

Required:

    (1) The positive and negative financial- and accounting-related factors to be considered in deciding whether to participate in this credit-card plan. Explain.

    (2) The income statement accounts and the balance sheet accounts that may change materially as the plan becomes fully operative, if the department store does participate. Explain. (Such factors as market position, sales mix, prices, and markup are expected to remain about the same as in the past.)

(AICPA adapted)

24

Break-Even and Cost-Volume-Profit Analysis

Break-even analysis, the construction of break-even charts, and the related cost-volume-profit analysis constitute another area of cost accounting that provides management with cost-and-profit data for profit planning, policy formulating, and decision making. *Break-even analysis* indicates the point at which the company neither makes a profit nor suffers a loss. *Cost-volume-profit analysis*, integrally related to break-even analysis, is concerned with determining the optimal level and mix of output to be produced with available resources. These analyses focus on the firm's short-run output decisions, as does much of the subject matter presented in Chapter 25 and Chapter 28.

THE NATURE OF BREAK-EVEN ANALYSIS

Break-even analysis determines at what level cost and revenue are in equilibrium. The *break-even point*, obtained directly by mathematical computation, is usually presented in graphic form because it not only shows management the point at which neither a profit nor a loss occurs, but also indicates the possibilities associated with changes in costs or sales. Thus, a *break-even chart* can be defined as a graphic analysis of the relationship of costs and sales to profit. Break-even analysis is generally accomplished with the aid of a break-even chart because it is a compact, readable reporting device.

Data for break-even analysis cannot be taken directly from the conventional or full-cost income statement. The form of the statement and the manner in which data are presented do not permit a convenient and practical analysis for planning, policy making, and profit determination. Therefore, each expense shown in the conventional income statement must be analyzed to determine its fixed and variable portions. Of the three classes of expenses — fixed, semivariable, and variable — the semivariable expenses must be separated into their fixed and variable components. The fixed portion is stated as a total figure; the variable portion as a rate or a percentage. This procedure is demonstrated beginning on page 515.

Break-even analysis may be based on historical data, past operations, or future sales and costs. In the latter case, the starting point of the analysis is the determination of estimated or standard costs for various levels of output, with the help of the flexible budget. The analysis then resolves itself into three major elements: (1) defining volume and sales price, (2) determining fixed and variable costs, and (3) relating cost to volume. The anticipated sales revenue based on market conditions and tempered by plant capacity is determined. Existing flexible budgets are reviewed and revised to incorporate expected changes in prices and operating conditions. Forecast production (in units of product or hours) becomes the basis for establishing standard costing rates for materials, labor, and factory overhead. Values so determined are then incorporated in the budget. Where possible, standards for marketing and administrative activities are also used in constructing the budget, which becomes a summary of standards.

The data in the flexible budget can be used directly and without refinement for break-even analysis or can be converted into a break-even chart. Standard costs, which are a current, accurate, and readily obtainable source of data for various types of cost reports and analyses, form a most valuable tool for the preparation of an analysis designed to indicate future profit possibilities.

To illustrate the calculation of the break-even point, assume the following costs and expenses have been determined by the Webb Company:

Determining the Break-Even Point

	TOTAL	VARIABLE	FIXED
Materials	$1,000,000	$1,000,000	
Labor	1,400,000	1,400,000	
Factory overhead	1,600,000	400,000	$1,200,000
Marketing expenses	350,000	150,000	200,000
Administrative expenses	250,000	50,000	200,000
	$4,600,000	$3,000,000	$1,600,000

The Webb Company has used direct costing in preparing the following income statement, which emphasizes the margin available for fixed costs and profit.

Sales...	$5,000,000
Less variable cost	3,000,000
Contribution margin..........................	$2,000,000
Less fixed cost.............................	1,600,000
Profit[1]	$ 400,000

If net sales are $5,000,000, $.60 of every sales dollar, or 60 percent, is required to pay variable costs. Each dollar of sales contributes $.40, or 40 percent, toward covering all other costs and making a profit. The 40 percent, referred to as the *contribution margin ratio (C/M)*, the *marginal income ratio*, or the *profit-volume ratio*, is determined by dividing the contribution margin (sales minus variable costs) by sales revenue. The total sales dollars required to recover the fixed costs is calculated as follows:

$$\frac{\text{Break-even sales}}{\text{volume in dollars}} = \frac{\text{Fixed costs}}{\text{Contribution margin ratio (C/M)}} = \frac{\$1,600,000}{.40} = \underline{\underline{\$4,000,000}}$$

(*or*)

$$\frac{\text{Break-even sales}}{\text{volume in dollars}} = \frac{\text{Fixed costs}}{1 - \dfrac{\text{Variable costs}}{\text{Sales}}} = \frac{\$1,600,000}{1 - \dfrac{\$3,000,000}{\$5,000,000}}$$

$$= \frac{\$1,600,000}{1 - .60}$$

$$= \frac{\$1,600,000}{.40}$$

$$= \underline{\underline{\$4,000,000}}$$

The resulting $4,000,000 is the break-even point at which neither a profit nor a loss is incurred. This break-even figure can be checked as follows:

Sales..	$4,000,000
Less variable cost (60% of sales)	2,400,000
Contribution margin...	$1,600,000
Less fixed cost...	1,600,000
Profit	–0–

If a sales volume of $5,000,000 can be regarded as normal, the percentage of normal at which the company must operate in order to break even is computed as shown below:

$$\frac{\text{Break-even sales volume in dollars}}{\text{Normal sales volume in dollars}} = \frac{\$4,000,000}{\$5,000,000} = \underline{\underline{80\%}} \text{ break-even capacity percentage}$$

If profits are desired, an activity level higher than the break-even capacity percentage must be reached. For this reason, a business person should not set the break-even point as a goal. Break-even analysis is not an easy mechanical substitute for the complex art of managing an enterprise. Analysis is a means to an end — not an end in itself.

---

[1]The term "profit" in this discussion denotes operating income before income tax.

The break-even point can also be computed in units. With a unit sales price of $4 and variable costs at 60 percent of sales, or $2.40 (60% of $4) per unit, the contribution margin per unit is $1.60 ($4 − $2.40). Dividing the total fixed cost by the contribution margin per unit, the break-even point in units is obtained:

$$\text{Break-even sales volume in units} = \frac{\text{Fixed costs}}{\text{Contribution margin per unit}} = \frac{\$1,600,000}{\$1.60} = \underline{\underline{1,000,000}} \text{ units}$$

When the break-even sales volume in dollars is determined first, break-even units can be found by dividing dollar sales by the unit sales price:

$$\frac{\text{Break-even sales volume in dollars}}{\text{Unit sales price}} = \frac{\$4,000,000}{\$4} = \underline{\underline{1,000,000}} \text{ units}$$

Conversely, when break-even units are computed first, break-even sales dollars can be determined by multiplying break-even units by the unit sales price:

$$\text{Break-even sales volume in units} \times \text{Unit sales price} =$$
$$1,000,000 \text{ units} \times \$4 = \underline{\underline{\$4,000,000}}$$

Break-even computations can be presented in a break-even chart, in which the cost line and the sales line intersect at the break-even point. The information needed to construct this chart is forecast sales and fixed and variable costs.

Constructing a Break-Even Chart

A conventional break-even chart for the Webb Company is constructed at the top of page 690 as follows:
1. A horizontal base line, the x-axis, is drawn and spaced into equal distances to represent the sales volume in dollars or in number of units.
2. A vertical line, the y-axis, is drawn at the extreme left and right sides of the chart. The y-axis at the left is spaced into equal parts and represents sales and costs in dollars.
3. A fixed cost line is drawn parallel to the x-axis at the $1,600,000 point of the y-axis.
4. A total cost line is drawn from the $1,600,000 fixed cost point on the y-axis to the $4,600,000 cost point on the right side of the y-axis.
5. The sales line is drawn from the 0 point at the left (the intersection of the x-axis and y-axis) to the $5,000,000 point on the right y-axis.
6. The total cost line intersects the sales line at the break-even point representing $4,000,000 sales or 1,000,000 units of sales.
7. The shaded area to the left of the break-even point is the loss area while the shaded area to the right is the profit area.

In the conventional break-even chart, the fixed cost line is parallel to the x-axis and the variable costs are plotted above the fixed costs. Such a chart emphasizes fixed costs at a definite amount for various levels of activity. Many analysts, however, prefer an alternative chart in which the variable costs are drawn first, and fixed costs are plotted above the variable cost line. An example of this type of chart is shown at the bottom of page 690, using the Webb Company data.

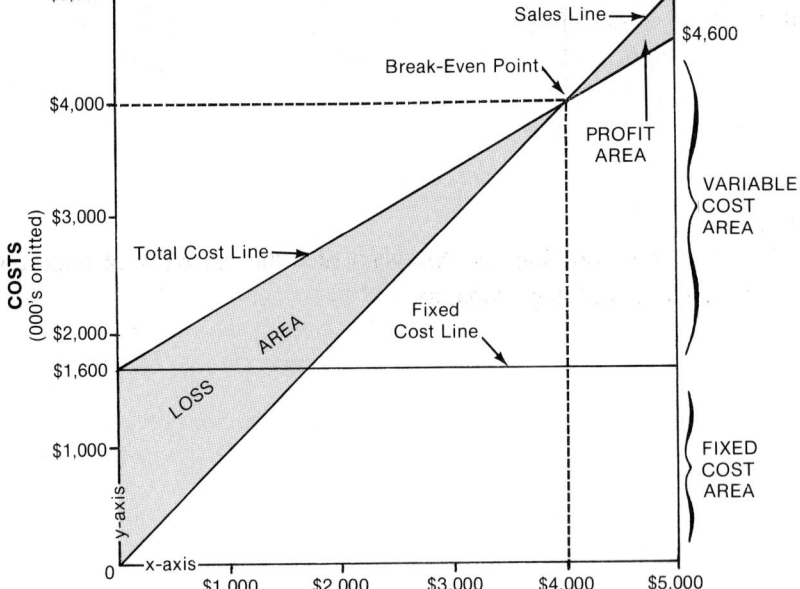

**Break-Even
Chart
(Conventional)**

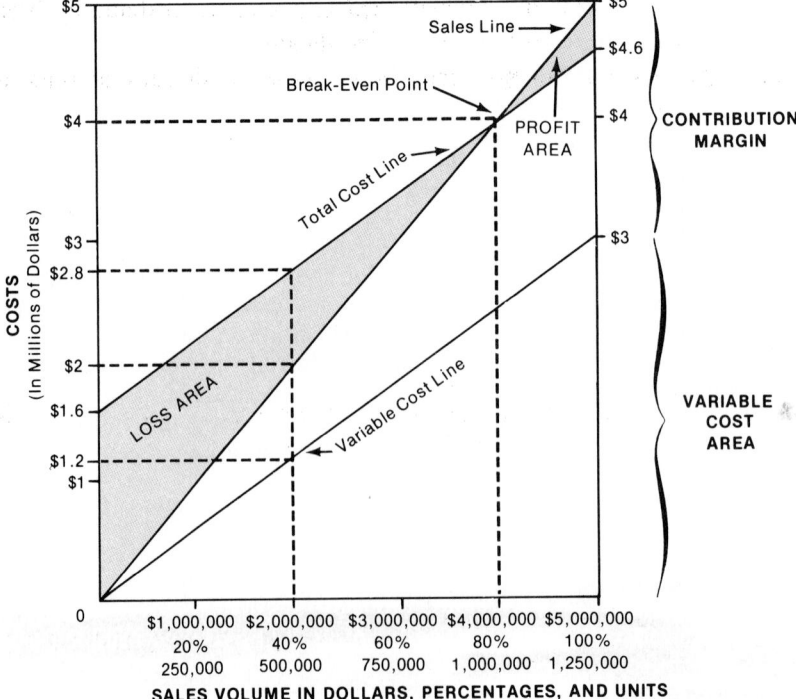

**Break-Even
Chart with
Fixed Costs
Plotted Above
Variable Costs**

The space between the variable cost line and the sales line represents the contribution margin. Where the total cost line intersects the sales line, the break-even point has been reached. The space between the sales line and the total cost line beyond the break-even point represents the profit for the period at any volume. The space between the total cost line and the sales line to the left of the break-even point indicates the fixed costs not yet recovered by the contribution margin and is the loss for the period at any volume below the break-even point.

This alternative break-even chart indicates the recovery of fixed costs at various levels of percentage capacity and at dollar sales or unit sales. If sales, for example, drop to $2,000,000, variable costs would be $1,200,000 (60 percent of $2,000,000) while fixed costs remain at $1,600,000. The loss at this point would be $800,000 [$2,000,000 − ($1,200,000 + $1,600,000)]. The chart shows $2,000,000 on the sales line to be $800,000 below the total cost line. In columnar form, the analysis can be illustrated as follows:

(1)	(2)	(3)	(4)	(5)	(6)
			CONTRIBUTION		PROFIT
NUMBER		VARIABLE	MARGIN	FIXED	(LOSS)
OF UNITS	SALES	COSTS	(2)–(3)	COSTS	(4)–(5)
250,000	$1,000,000	$ 600,000	$ 400,000	$1,600,000	$(1,200,000)
500,000	2,000,000	1,200,000	800,000	1,600,000	(800,000)
750,000	3,000,000	1,800,000	1,200,000	1,600,000	(400,000)
1,000,000	4,000,000	2,400,000	1,600,000	1,600,000	None
1,250,000	5,000,000	3,000,000	2,000,000	1,600,000	400,000

A break-even chart can be constructed in even greater detail by breaking down fixed and variable costs into subclassifications, as shown on page 692. Variable expenses, for example, may be classified as direct materials, direct labor, variable factory overhead, and variable marketing and administrative expenses. Fixed expenses may be divided in a similar manner showing fixed factory overhead and fixed marketing and administrative expenses separately. Even the profit wedge might be subdivided to indicate application of the profit to income tax, interest and dividend payments, and retained earnings.

The accounting data involved, the assumptions made, the manner in which the information is obtained, and the way the data are expressed are limitations that must be considered in connection with the results of break-even analysis. The break-even chart is fundamentally a static analysis. In most cases, changes can only be shown by drawing a new chart or a series of charts. The notion of relevant range as stated in the flexible budget discussion (page 515) is applicable. That is, the amount of fixed and variable costs, as well as the slope of the sales line, is meaningful only in a defined range of activity and must be redefined for activity outside the relevant range. Furthermore, linear cost and sales behavior is assumed and has general acceptance within the relevant range of activity.[2]

Break-Even Analysis for Decision Making

---

[2]Calculus can be employed in dealing with curvilinear functions. See Travis P. Goggans, "Break-Even Analysis with Curvilinear Functions," *The Accounting Review*, Vol. XL, No. 4, pp. 867–871.

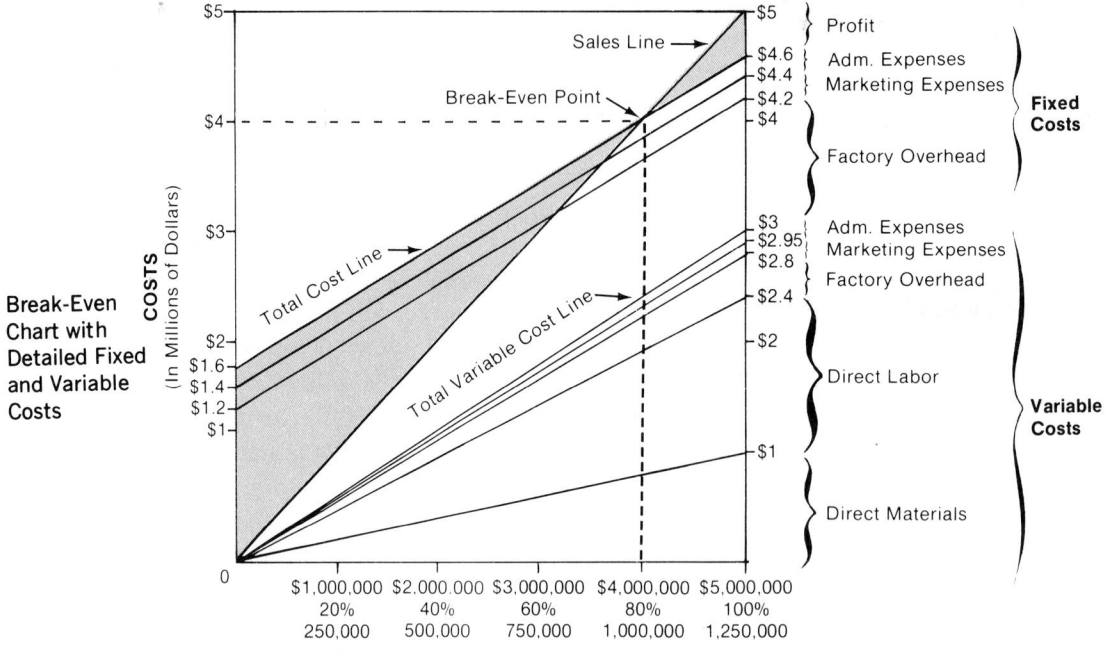

Break-Even Chart with Detailed Fixed and Variable Costs

SALES VOLUME IN DOLLARS, PERCENTAGES, AND UNITS

Despite its limitations, break-even analysis offers wide application for testing proposed actions, for considering alternatives, or for other decision-making purposes. For example, the technique permits determination of the effect on profit of a shift in fixed and/or variable expenses when old machinery is replaced by new equipment. Firms with multiple plants, products, and sales territories may prepare charts which show the effects of the shift in sales quantities, sales prices, and sales efforts. With such information, management is able to direct the firm's operations into the most profitable channels. For a company with numerous divisions, the analysis is particularly valuable in determining the influence on profits of an increase in divisional fixed costs. If, for example, a company's overall contribution margin ratio is 25 percent, a division manager must realize that for every $1 of proposed increase in fixed costs, sales revenue must increase by no less than $4 if the existing profit position is to be maintained ($1 ÷ 25% = $4).

The break-even analysis formula is also useful in projecting sales necessary to realize a projected profit or to minimize a calculated loss. To illustrate, the sales figure necessary to realize a profit objective of $400,000 for the Webb Company is:

$$\frac{\text{Fixed cost} + \text{Profit objective}}{\text{Contribution margin ratio (C/M)}} = \frac{\$1,600,000 + \$400,000}{.40} = \underline{\underline{\$5,000,000}}$$

If management wants to determine the sales level when an operating loss of $200,000 is predicted, then:

$$\frac{\text{Fixed cost} - \text{Estimated loss}}{\text{Contribution margin ratio (C/M)}} = \frac{\$1,600,000 - \$200,000}{.40} = \underline{\underline{\$3,500,000}}$$

These projections can also be read from the break-even charts on page 690.
In using break-even analysis, management should understand that:

1. A change in per unit variable costs changes the contribution margin ratio and the break-even point.
2. A change in sales price changes the contribution margin ratio and the break-even point.
3. A change in fixed costs changes the break-even point but not the contribution margin figure.
4. A combined change in fixed and variable costs in the same direction causes an extremely sharp change in the break-even point.

Effect of Changes in Fixed Costs. If the Webb Company management were able to reduce fixed expenses to $1,450,000, the break-even point would be $3,625,000 ($1,450,000 ÷ .40). If sales remained at the $5,000,000 figure, the profit would increase from $400,000 to $550,000, and the break-even point would be 72.5 percent of sales instead of 80 percent. The change in the break-even point resulting from a reduction in fixed costs is shown by the broken lines in the chart illustrated below. The effects of changes in the per unit variable cost or in the unit sales price could also be charted, thus adding a dynamic dimension to the analysis.

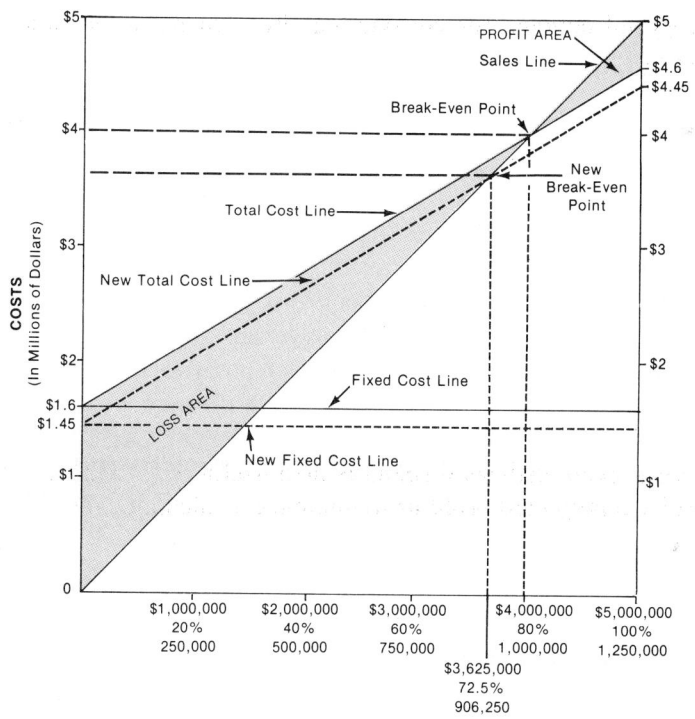

Break-Even
Chart with a
Reduction in
Fixed Costs

SALES VOLUME IN DOLLARS, PERCENTAGES, AND UNITS

Effect of Changes in Sales Mix. When a shift in product sales mix occurs, a change in profit can also be expected unless the same contribution margin ratio is realized on all products. To illustrate, assume that the sales of a high-margin item are reduced for a company that has the following budget:

Sales..		$1,500,000
Variable cost...	$900,000	
Fixed cost...	400,000	1,300,000
Profit		$ 200,000

The break-even sales would be computed as follows:

$$\text{Break-even sales} = \frac{\$400,000}{1 - \dfrac{\$\ 900,000}{\$1,500,000}} = \frac{\$400,000}{1 - .60} = \$1,000,000$$

At the end of the fiscal period (assuming no change occurred in the total fixed cost or in the per unit sales price or variable cost of individual products), the company's income statement shows:

Sales..		$1,420,000
Variable cost...	$908,800	
Fixed cost...	400,000	1,308,800
Profit		$ 111,200

The break-even sales is now $1,111,111, indicating that the decrease in sales of the high-margin item caused an unfavorable increase of $111,111 in the break-even point:

$$\text{Break-even sales} = \frac{\$400,000}{1 - \dfrac{\$\ 908,800}{\$1,420,000}} = \frac{\$400,000}{1 - .64} = \$1,111,111$$

This situation can happen in any business. It illustrates the necessity of taking various sales mixes into account in any break-even analysis. It also stresses the inadequacy of the conventional composite break-even chart in which one product or a consistent average mix of products is considered. When management is interested in break-even analyses for different products, with individual fixed and variable costs, the conventional composite break-even chart is not very helpful. A rule to be followed in the case of multiple products is that changes in break-even points should be the result of changes in sales prices and costs and should not be distorted by an internal mix of products. One way to overcome this difficulty is to have individual break-even analyses and charts for each product; however, if arbitrarily allocated joint costs are included, the results are of limited value.

The Unit Profit Graph. A break-even chart is generally prepared on the basis of total revenue and expenses. These dollar sales and expense figures can be translated into a profit-per-unit graph in order to show more vividly the influence of fixed costs on the product unit cost. Assume, for example, the following: normal capacity, 100 percent; total sales, $50,000 (500 units @ $100); variable cost, $30,000; fixed cost, $15,000; profit, $5,000. The break-even point is $37,500 ($15,000 ÷ .40) or 75 percent of normal capacity ($37,500 ÷ $50,000). The variable cost is $60 per unit, and the fixed cost is $30 per unit if 500 units are made and sold. As volume decreases, the fixed cost per unit increases. This relationship is illustrated in the graph shown below:

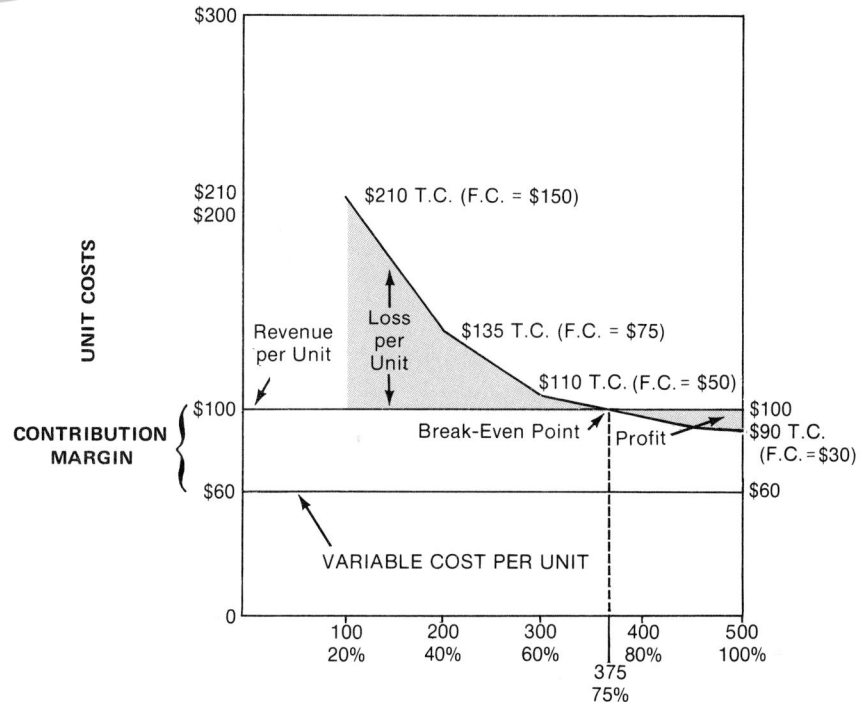

Unit Profit Graph Showing the Influence of Fixed and Variable Costs on Unit Cost

UNITS OF PRODUCT AND PERCENTAGE OF NORMAL CAPACITY

The effect of varying volume on the fixed cost per unit can also be expressed in columnar form:

	UNITS					
	100	200	300	375	400	500
Variable unit cost......................	$ 60	$ 60	$ 60	$ 60	$ 60.00	$ 60
Fixed unit cost............................	150	75	50	40	37.50	30
Total unit cost	$ 210	$135	$110	$100	$ 97.50	$ 90
Unit sales price..........................	100	100	100	100	100.00	100
Profit (loss) per unit.	$(110)	$(35)	$(10)	Break even	$ 2.50	$ 10

The analyses illustrated in the unit profit graph and in the tabular presentation, together with a break-even analysis, are important tools in determining which unit cost(s) should be used in setting sales prices. A break-even chart will help in understanding the effect on total profits when sales prices and fixed and variable costs are related to sales volume.

Unit Cost Formulas. The unit profit graph and the tabular presentation show a total unit cost that varies from a high of $210 per unit to a low of $90 per unit. To obtain a true comparison, unit costs must be judged at all levels of activity. When unit costs of various products are compared, the analyst must observe the production rates of each product, each of which may be at a different level.

New formulas can be developed which aid in determining the effect of changing costs or level of activity. For example, the following formula can be used to determine unit costs under conditions of fluctuating activity levels:

$$\text{Unit cost} = \frac{a + b_1 x}{b_2 x}$$

Where: a = fixed cost
b_1 = variable expense at normal capacity
b_2 = units of production at normal capacity
x = level of activity, expressed as a percentage of normal capacity

Using figures from the example introduced on page 695, the total cost of $45,000 ($15,000 + $30,000) divided by total units (500) gives a unit cost of $90 at the 100 percent level of activity.

To illustrate the utility of the formula, assume that the fixed expense increases to $17,000 and that the variable expense decreases to $27,000 at the 100 percent level of activity. Using these facts, the new break-even point is computed as follows:

New profit = $(sx - b_1x) - a$, where a, b_1, and x are as previously
defined and s = total sales at normal capacity
New profit = $(\$50,000x - \$27,000x) - \$17,000$
New profit = $\$23,000x - \$17,000$

Let new profit equal 0 and solve for x:

$$0 = \$23,000x - \$17,000$$
$$x = \frac{\$17,000}{\$23,000}$$
$$x = .739 \times 100, \text{ or } 74\% \text{ capacity (approximate)}$$

(*or*)

Fixed cost = $17,000
Variable cost = $27,000, or $54 per unit, or 54% of sales
$$\frac{\$17,000}{1 - .54} = \frac{\$17,000}{.46} = \$37,000, \text{ or } 74\% \text{ capacity, or } 370 \text{ units}$$

The unit cost at the new break-even point can then be computed as follows:

$$\text{Unit cost} = \frac{a + b_1x}{b_2x}$$

$$= \frac{\$17,000 + \$27,000(.74)}{500(.74)}$$

$$= \frac{\$17{,}000 + \$19{,}980}{370}$$

$$= \underline{\underline{\$100}} \text{ (approximate)}$$

Assuming the same changes in the fixed and variable expenses, the unit cost at 90 percent of capacity would be determined as shown below:

$$\text{Unit cost} = \frac{\$17{,}000 + \$27{,}000(.90)}{500(.90)}$$

$$= \frac{\$17{,}000 + \$24{,}300}{450}$$

$$= \underline{\underline{\$92}} \text{ (approximate)}$$

The above equations permit the development of unit costs using data included in the budget. They further permit quick and easy computations in connection with problems raised by changing conditions. Budget data expressed in equation form permit quicker analysis of the effects of a variety of changes on unit costs.

Margin of Safety. Information developed from a break-even analysis offers additional useful control data such as the *margin of safety*, which indicates how much sales may decrease from a selected sales figure before the company will break even, i.e., before the company will suffer a loss. From the Webb Company data on page 688, where sales are $5,000,000, the margin of safety is $1,000,000 ($5,000,000 − $4,000,000). The margin of safety expressed as a percentage of sales is called the *margin of safety ratio (M/S)* and is computed as follows:

$$\text{Margin of safety ratio (M/S)} = \frac{\text{Selected sales figure} - \text{Break-even sales}}{\text{Selected sales figure}}$$

$$= \frac{\$5{,}000{,}000 - \$4{,}000{,}000}{\$5{,}000{,}000}$$

$$= \underline{\underline{20\%}}$$

The margin of safety is directly related to profit. Using the same data from page 688, with a contribution margin ratio of 40 percent and a margin of safety ratio of 20 percent, then:

Profit = Contribution margin ratio × Margin of safety ratio
P   = C/M × M/S
P   = 40% × 20%
P   = $\underline{\underline{8\%}}$

If the contribution margin ratio and the profit percentage are known, the margin of safety ratio is:

$$\text{M/S} = \frac{\text{P}}{\text{C/M}} = \frac{8\%}{40\%} = \underline{\underline{20\%}}$$

APPLYING COST-VOLUME-PROFIT ANALYSIS

A cost-volume-profit analysis is generally prepared from annual budget figures, but figures from monthly statements can also be used. Furthermore, the analysis can be applied to a specific product class, to distribution outlets, to methods of sale, and for profit determination. The following illustration shows an analysis based on data from two representative months:

	SALES	TOTAL COSTS	PROFIT
June	$50,000	$40,000	$10,000
May	40,000	36,000	4,000
Difference	$10,000	$ 4,000	$ 6,000

An increase in sales of $10,000 resulted in an increase in costs of $4,000 and an increase in profit of $6,000. This indicates that each dollar increase in sales covered its variable costs of $.40 and contributed $.60 to profit or fixed expenses and profit.

The variable cost factor is found by subtracting the C/M ratio from 100 percent. Since $6,000 ÷ $10,000 = 60 percent (the C/M ratio), the variable cost ratio is 40 percent (100 percent − 60 percent) or, more directly, $4,000 ÷ $10,000 = 40 percent. Knowing the variable cost ratio, the fixed cost in the total cost for June may be found as follows:

Total cost	$40,000
Variable cost ($50,000 × .40)	20,000
Fixed cost	$20,000

For May, the fixed cost is also $20,000, computed as follows: $36,000 − $16,000 ($40,000 sales × .40) = $20,000. This fact is in accordance with the generally accepted validity of the linear relationship of the cost-output figures. The correctness of this assumption can be tested by assuming the following data for October:

Sales	$60,000
Total cost	45,000
Profit	$15,000

Previously, the variable cost ratio was 40 percent, and the fixed cost was $20,000. However, a check shows:

Total actual cost		$45,000
Expected: Variable cost ($60,000 × .40)	$24,000	
Fixed cost	20,000	44,000
Difference		$ 1,000

This difference should be investigated. Fixed and variable costs must be checked to discover any shift of these elements. However, the cause may be a shift of the product mix or numerous other factors.

The C/M ratio permits a profit computation without the necessity of detailed calculations of variable costs. The formula is:

$$\text{Profit} = (\text{Sales} \times \text{C/M}) - \text{Fixed costs}$$

Again using the figures of the Webb Company's income statement on page 688, the profit could be computed as follows:

$$P = (S \times \text{C/M}) - FC$$
$$P = (\$5,000,000 \times .40) - \$1,600,000$$
$$P = \$2,000,000 - \$1,600,000$$
$$P = \underline{\$400,000}$$

The same formula permits the computation of additional figures. If, for example, a company has a fixed cost of $90,000 with sales at $300,000 and a profit of $60,000, the C/M ratio is:

$$P = (S \times \text{C/M}) - FC$$
$$\$60,000 = (\$300,000 \times \text{C/M}) - \$90,000$$
$$\$60,000 + \$90,000 = \$300,000 \times \text{C/M}$$
$$\frac{\$150,000}{\$300,000} = \text{C/M}$$
$$50\% = \text{C/M}$$

If the same company with a C/M ratio of 50 percent suffers a $30,000 loss, the volume of sales is:

$$P = (S \times \text{C/M}) - FC$$
$$-\$30,000 = (S \times .50) - \$90,000$$
$$-\$30,000 + \$90,000 = S \times .50$$
$$\frac{\$60,000}{.50} = S$$
$$\underline{\$120,000} = S$$

The answer can be checked in this manner:

Sales..		$120,000
Variable cost (50% of sales)....................................	$60,000	
Fixed cost..	90,000	150,000
Loss		$(30,000)

While such quick computations are indeed possible and undoubtedly helpful in many circumstances, the fact still remains that the reasonably accurate separation of semivariable expenses into their fixed and variable elements must precede any subsequent use of such figures, if the figures are to be meaningful.

Price Decreases and Volume Increases

In an analysis of the effect of a price decrease on volume, it is often argued that the price decrease will in most instances be offset by an increase in volume, and, therefore, profits will not be reduced and might even be increased. Such an argument seems quite plausible at first. Many business people, however, have found that price reduction does not necessarily lead to the desired increase in volume. If the increase in volume does occur, it is often not large enough to overcome the effect of the price reduction on total profit.

This problem of a possible price reduction being offset by a volume increase was studied by the U.S. Steel Corporation. The purpose of the study was "to ascertain the increase in volume that would have to take place to offset various decreases in steel prices by the United States Steel Corporation subsidiaries, taking into consideration the effect of increased volume on costs, and to estimate the financial gain or loss which would result from price reductions." The study concluded that, because of the low elasticity of demand for steel, the increase in volume resulting from a reduction in price would be less than the increase needed to offset the adverse effects of the lower price on profits. The following data were prepared:

VOLUME INCREASES NEEDED TO COMPENSATE FOR
AVERAGE PRICE DECREASES COMPARED TO
MAXIMUM PROBABLE RESULTING VOLUME INCREASES

% REDUCTION IN PRICE	% OF VOLUME INCREASE REQUIRED TO OFFSET PRICE DECREASE	% OF GREATEST PROBABLE RESULTING VOLUME INCREASE
1%	3.4%	1.0%
5	19.6	5.3
10	48.8	11.1
15	96.7	17.7
20	190.3	25.0

The data indicate that the increase in steel consumption to be expected from a drop in price is not very great. While offsetting volume increases may be more favorable in other types of businesses and industries, they are, in general, hardly enough to overcome reduced prices. In most cases a price reduction must be accompanied not only by increased volume but also by a reduction in the cost of the product.

The Profit-Volume Analysis Graph

Break-even analysis and cost-volume-profit analysis also employ the *profit-volume (P/V) analysis graph*, which relates profit to volume. Using the figures from the income statement on page 688, a P/V analysis graph is shown below.

Profit-Volume Analysis Graph

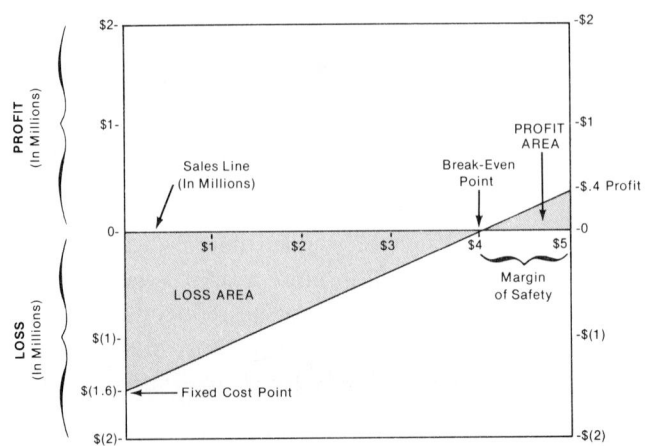

The P/V analysis graph is constructed as follows:

1. The graph is divided into two parts by the sales line.
2. The total fixed cost is marked off below the sales line on the left-hand vertical line. The computed profit or loss figure is located by moving horizontally to the point representing assumed sales dollars, then moving vertically to the point representing the computed profit or loss.
3. Fixed cost and profit points are joined by a diagonal line which crosses the sales line at the break-even point.

When management is considering various courses of action, a tabular report can present the possible results. For example, the effect of possible price increases and decreases for a product are shown in the following report:

| | DECREASE | | NORMAL | INCREASE | |
% CHANGE IN SALES PRICE	*20%*	*10%*	VOLUME	*10%*	*20%*
Units	200,000	200,000	200,000	200,000	200,000
Sales.......................................	$320,000	$360,000	$400,000	$440,000	$480,000
Variable cost...........................	200,000	200,000	200,000	200,000	200,000
Contribution margin..................	$120,000	$160,000	$200,000	$240,000	$280,000
Fixed cost...............................	160,000	160,000	160,000	160,000	160,000
Profit	—	0	$ 40,000	$ 80,000	$120,000
Loss.......................................	$ 40,000	0	—	—	—
Profit per unit..........................	—	—	$.20	$.40	$.60
Loss per unit...........................	$.20	—	—	—	—
% change in profit	−200%	−100%	—	+100%	+300%
Return on investment of $200,000.	− 20%	0%	20%	40%	60%
Break-even point......................	$426,667	$360,000	$320,000	$293,333	$274,286

In this illustration, a 10 percent drop in prices reduces the profit to the break-even point, and a 20 percent drop in prices causes a $40,000 loss. However, the 10 percent and 20 percent price increases cause profits to increase $40,000 and $80,000, respectively. These effects are indicated more effectively, however, in a P/V analysis graph, as shown below.

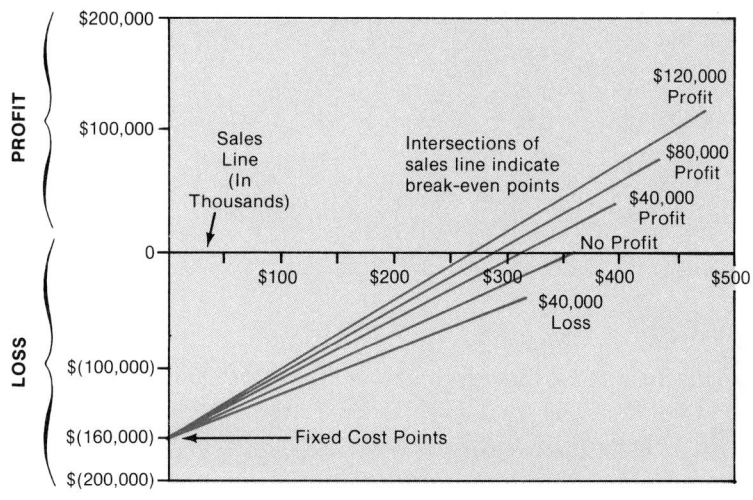

P/V Analysis Graph Illustrating the Effect of Possible Price Changes on Profit

As another example of the use of a P/V analysis graph, assume that a company's management has the following plans regarding sales, costs, volume, and profits:

PLAN 1:		PLAN 2:	
Decrease in price	10%	Increase in price	10%
Increase in volume	12%	Decrease in volume..............	12%
Variable cost increase..........	4%	Variable cost decrease	4%
Fixed cost increase..............	5%	Fixed cost decrease..............	5%

The effect of these plans is summarized below:

COMPOSITE CHANGES	PLAN 1	NORMAL VOLUME	PLAN 2
Units	224,000	200,000	176,000
Sales...	$403,200	$400,000	$387,200
Variable cost...	232,960	200,000	168,960
Contribution margin..	$170,240	$200,000	$218,240
Fixed cost..	168,000	160,000	152,000
Profit	$ 2,240	$ 40,000	$ 66,240
Profit per unit	$.01	$.20	$.3763
% change in profit	−94.4%	....	+65.6%
Return on investment of $200,000........................	1.12%	20%	33.1%
Break-even profit	$397,895	$320,000	$269,677

The graph shown below, based on the summary data, is a composite, highly informative P/V analysis graph.

P/V Analysis Graph Illustrating the Effect of All Profit-Volume Factors

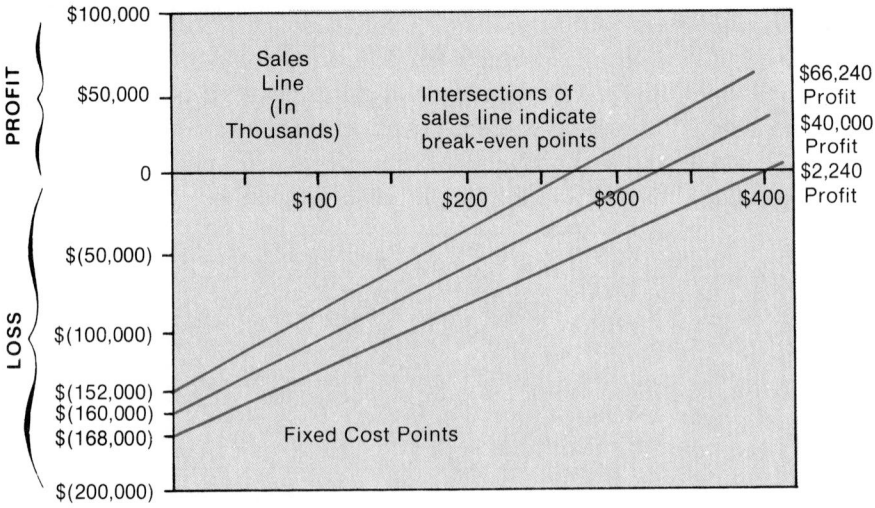

Product Analysis

The discussion so far has dealt with cost-volume-profit relationships based on total cost and total sales revenue. It is much more desirable, however, to investigate these relationships for individual products. A breakdown of costs and sales by products might appear impractical, especially when hundreds of small items are manufactured. In such instances, it is advisable to reduce the large number of products to several major lines. To determine a better product cost for purposes of planning and control, many firms have departmentalized their sprawling factory output. With such departmentalization, the contribution that each product or product group makes to the total contribution margin can be gauged more satisfactorily.

Variable costs used in previous illustrations are a composite of the variable costs of the several manufacturing cost centers, the marketing departments, and administrative divisions. However, it is possible to determine the variable cost of each product line because:

1. Direct materials and direct labor costs can be based on standard costs.
2. Variable factory overhead can be based on normal production hours, labor cost, or machine hours established for the cost centers of the plant. The flexible budget for each cost center serves as an excellent basis for the determination of product factory overhead.
3. Variable marketing and administrative expenses can be charged directly to products or allocated on the basis of the sales value of each product or gross profit return or other bases discussed in Chapter 23. Of course, allocations of either nonmanufacturing or manufacturing costs are arbitrary, a limitation that should not be overlooked.

Once the sales value and the variable cost of each product have been determined, it will be apparent that each product has a different contribution margin and a C/M ratio. To illustrate cost-volume-profit analysis by products, the figures of the Normal Volume column of the summary on page 702 are divided between four products, resulting in data shown below.

PRODUCT	SALES VALUE OF PRODUCTION	VARIABLE COSTS	% OF V.C. TO SALES	CONTRIBUTION MARGIN	C/M RATIO
A	$120,000	$100,000	83%	$ 20,000	17%
B	140,000	60,000	43	80,000	57
C	90,000	30,000	33	60,000	67
D	50,000	10,000	20	40,000	80
Total	$400,000	$200,000	50	$200,000	50
			Less fixed cost....	160,000	
			Profit	$ 40,000	

$$\text{Break-even point} = \frac{\$160,000}{.50} = \$320,000$$

The contribution margin and C/M ratio are shown for each product and in total. The C/M ratio varies from 17 percent for Product A to 80 percent for Product D. If the present sales mix can be altered or if sales can be expanded, products with higher C/M ratios afford greater relative contributions to profit per dollar of sales. But the product's C/M ratio, sales dollars, and contribution margin must be related to facility utilization. The product offering the higher C/M ratio is desirable only if the resulting contribution margin (C/M ratio × sales dollars) is greater than could be achieved by some alternative use of the same limited facilities. If unused or idle facilities are available, perhaps both alternatives can be pursued profitably.

The P/V analysis graph below indicates the profit path for each product, A, B, C, and D.

P/V Analysis
Graph for
Individual
Product
Analysis

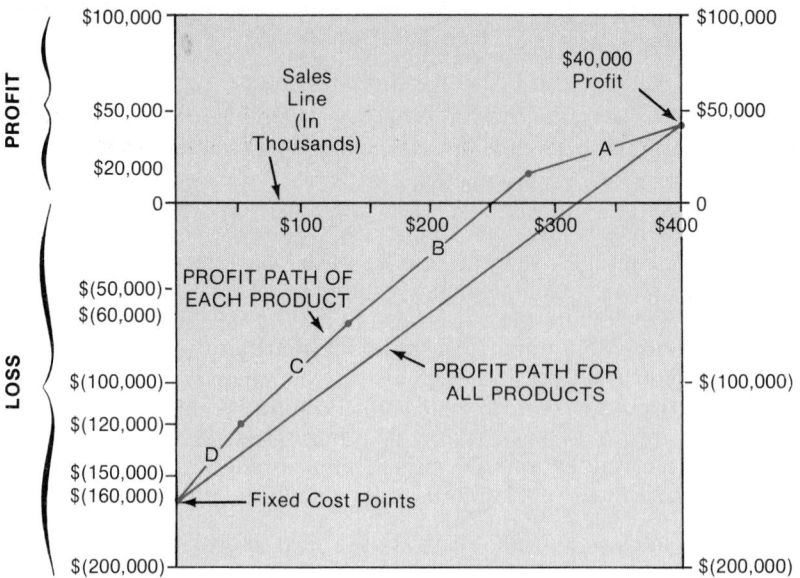

This P/V analysis graph is constructed as follows:

1. The horizontal line 00 represents sales and is marked off from zero to $400,000.
2. The profit path for all products is then drawn, starting at the $(160,000) fixed cost point in the loss area and ending at the $40,000 profit point in the profit area. The break-even point is at the point of crossover from the loss to the profit area.
3. The profit path of each product is plotted next. It starts with the product with the highest C/M ratio, Product D. The line begins at the total fixed cost point and is drawn to the $(120,000) point in the loss area directly below the $50,000 sales volume point. The plotting indicates that $40,000 of the $160,000 fixed cost has been recovered.
4. The profit path of Product C starts at the point where D's path ended. The line for Product C ends opposite the loss figure of $(60,000) and below the sales volume figure of $140,000. The $(60,000) figure shows that $60,000 additional fixed cost was recovered. The $140,000 point on the sales line is the accumulated sales total of Products D and C ($50,000 + $90,000).
5. The profit path for Product B begins at the end of C's path and leads across the sales line into the profit area to the $20,000 profit point immediately above the sales volume figure of $280,000.
6. Product A with the lowest C/M ratio is charted last. It adds $20,000 to the profit, and its path ends at the $40,000 profit figure.

The plotting of the profit path of each product provides management with an interesting pictorial report — the steeper the slope, the higher the C/M ratio. If any product did not have a contribution margin, its path or slope would be downward. Also, the dollar amount of each product's contribution margin can be read from the graph by measuring the vertical distance from one plotted point to the next. Similar graphs can be prepared for the analysis of sales by territories, salespersons, and classes of customers. It is then possible to portray the profitability of territories, the effectiveness of salespersons' selling activities, and the type of customers whose purchases mean greatest profit to the company. In this way, sales effort is measured by marginal contributions toward fixed costs and profit — and not by sales volume.

The Fallacy of Total Cost Analysis

When the profitability of a product is determined by distributing all fixed and variable costs to all products, it is likely that certain products will show a loss, depending on the methods used to allocate fixed cost. For example, the illustration below uses the figures for Products A, B, C, and D, from page 703, and shows the distribution of the fixed cost to each product on the basis of the variable cost ratios. The analysis indicates that Product A is a loss item. Because it also contributes a lower contribution margin and a C/M ratio than the other products, management might want to discontinue it. Product A, however, actually contributes $20,000 to the company's total profit picture.

FIXED COST DISTRIBUTION TO EACH PRODUCT
BASED ON VARIABLE COST RATIOS

PRODUCT	SALES VALUE OF PRODUCTION	TOTAL COST*	PROFIT	PERCENTAGE OF PROFIT TO SALES
A	$120,000	$180,000	−$60,000	−50%
B	140,000	108,000	32,000	22.8
C	90,000	54,000	36,000	40
D	50,000	18,000	32,000	64
Total	$400,000	$360,000	$40,000	10

*Computation of total cost:

Product	Variable Cost	Variable Cost Ratio		Fixed Cost		Fixed Cost Distribution	Total Cost
A	$100,000	$\dfrac{\$100,000}{\$200,000}$	×	$160,000	=	$80,000	$180,000
B	60,000	$\dfrac{60,000}{200,000}$	×	160,000	=	48,000	108,000
C	30,000	$\dfrac{30,000}{200,000}$	×	160,000	=	24,000	54,000
D	10,000	$\dfrac{10,000}{200,000}$	×	160,000	=	8,000	18,000
Total	$200,000						

Most methods used to distribute fixed costs to products confuse cost-volume-profit relations, for they do not recognize the change in costs and profits produced by a change in volume or product mix. This confusion is eliminated by following the contribution margin principle, which sets apart not only the fixed costs that must be allocated, but also those that are directly assignable to a specific product. Attention is then directed to the margin between sales and variable costs, rather than sales and total cost. Products make a favorable contribution as long as the sales revenue exceeds the related variable cost.

An alternative product should replace the existing one only if idle capacity is not available and only if the alternative product will yield a larger total dollar contribution toward recovering the fixed cost and profit for an equal amount of capacity constraint (e.g., machine hours). Since some fixed costs can be changed in the short run, the analysis must consider any change in fixed cost associated with dropping a product or moving from an existing product to an alternative product. It is assumed, of course, that the added product can be marketed without disturbing the market for other products of the company.

In the case of joint products, the variable as well as the fixed joint costs are best viewed in their relationship to the contribution made by the group of joint products rather than on the basis of an arbitrary allocation to each product (pages 191–193).

DISCUSSION QUESTIONS

1. Define break-even point.

2. (a) Why must the conventional income statement be restated for computation of the break-even point? (b) What type of statement is constructed?

3. What is the relationship of budgets and standards to break-even analysis?

4. What is the contribution margin?

5. State the formulas commonly used to determine the break-even point (a) in dollars and (b) in units.

6. A break-even chart, as illustrated below, is a useful technique for showing relationships between costs, volume, and profits.
   (a) Identify the numbered components of the break-even chart.
   (b) Discuss the significance of the concept of the relevant range to break-even analyses.

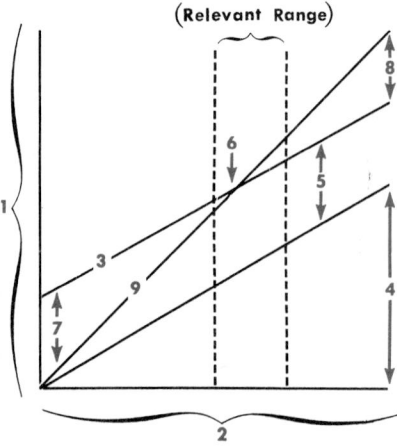

(AICPA adapted)

7. The break-even chart is an excellent planning device. Discuss.

8. Discuss weaknesses inherent in the preparation and uses of break-even point analyses.

9. How does the break-even point move when changes occur in (a) variable expenses? (b) fixed expenses?

10. The break-even chart and the unit profit graph intend to show the same information but seem to differ. How?

11. What is the margin of safety?

12. What is meant by the term "cost-volume-profit relationship"? Why is this relationship important in business management?

13. A price reduction is always accompanied by a proportionate volume increase. Discuss.

14. Use the P/V analysis graph below to select the best answer for (a) and (b).

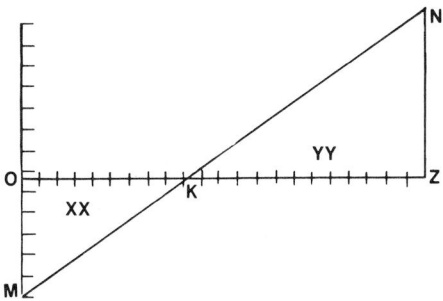

(a) Which of the following statements is correct?
    (1) The areas XX and YY and the point K represent profit, loss, and sales volume at the break-even point, respectively.
    (2) The line O-Z represents the sales volume.
    (3) The line N-Z represents fixed cost.
    (4) The line M-N represents total cost.

(b) The vertical scale represents: (1) sales volume; (2) units produced; (3) the profit area above O and the loss area below O; (4) the contribution margin.

                                                        (CMA adapted)

15. Why is a cost-volume-profit analysis by products valuable to management?

16. Describe how the contribution of each product to the recovery of fixed expenses and to the total profit of a company can be presented in graphic form.

17. Select the answer which best completes the statement:
    (a) Given the notations — SP = selling price per unit; FE = total fixed expense; and VE = variable expense per unit — the break-even sales volume in units is:

    (1) $\dfrac{SP}{FE \div VE}$; (2) $\dfrac{FE}{VE \div SP}$; (3) $\dfrac{VE}{SP - FE}$; (4) $\dfrac{FE}{SP - VE}$

    (b) If the sales price and the variable cost per unit both increase 10% and the fixed cost does not change, the effect on the contribution margin per unit and the contribution margin ratio is that: (1) the contribution margin per unit and the contribution margin ratio both remain unchanged; (2) the contribution margin per unit and the contribution margin ratio both increase; (3) the contribution margin per unit increases and the contribution margin ratio remains unchanged; (4) the contribution margin per unit increases and the contribution margin ratio decreases.

(c) A company increased the sales price for its product from $1.00 to $1.10 per unit when the total fixed cost increased from $400,000 to $480,000 and the variable cost per unit remained unchanged. The effect of these changes on the break-even point is that: (1) the break-even point in units would be increased; (2) the break-even point in units would be decreased; (3) the break-even point in units would remain unchanged; (4) the effect cannot be determined from the information given.

(d) Jarvis Company has a fixed cost of $200,000. Jarvis sells two products, Tetra and Min, at a rate of 2 units of Tetra to 1 unit of Min. The contribution margin is $1 per unit for Tetra and $2 per unit for Min. The units of Min that would be sold at the break-even point are: (1) 44,444; (2) 50,000; (3) 88,888; (4) 100,000.

(e) Information concerning Label Corporation's Product A is as follows:

Sales	$300,000
Variable cost	240,000
Fixed cost	40,000

Assuming that Label increased sales of Product A by 20%, the profit from Product A is: (1) $20,000; (2) $24,000; (3) $32,000; (4) $80,000.

(f) Dallas Corporation is marketing a new product for $1.50 a unit. The fixed cost to manufacture this product is $100,000 for less than 500,000 units and $150,000 for 500,000 or more units. The contribution margin ratio is 20%. The number of units that must be sold to realize a $100,000 operating profit from this product is: (1) 333,333; (2) 500,000; (3) 666,667; (4) 833,333.

(g) The following data apply to Frelm Corporation for a given period:

Total variable cost per unit	$3.50
Contribution margin ÷ sales	30%
Break-even sales (present volume)	$1,000,000

Frelm wants to sell an additional 50,000 units at the same sales price and contribution margin. The amount that fixed costs can increase to generate a profit equal to 10% of the sales value on the additional 50,000 units to be sold is: (1) $57,500; (2) $125,000; (3) $50,000; (4) $67,500.

(h) Cost-volume-profit analysis allows management to determine relative profitability of a product by: (1) highlighting potential bottlenecks in the production process; (2) keeping fixed costs to an absolute minimum; (3) determining the contribution margin per unit and projected profits at various levels of production; (4) assigning costs to a product in a manner that maximizes the contribution margin.

(i) Cost-volume-profit analysis includes some inherent, simplifying assumptions. Which of the following is not one of these assumptions? (1) Cost and revenues are predictable and are linear over the relevant range. (2) Variable costs fluctuate proportionately with volume. (3) Changes in beginning and ending inventory levels are insignificant in amount. (4) Sales mix will change as fixed costs increase beyond the relevant range.

(AICPA adapted)

EXERCISES

Exercises 1–12 cover basic cost accounting procedures and mathematical calculations for break-even and cost-volume-profit analyses.

1. The Salishan Lodge had sales of $4,500,000. The fixed expense was $1,200,000 and the variable expense totaled $1,800,000.

Required:
- (1) Contribution margin ratio (C/M).
- (2) Break-even point.
- (3) Contribution margin.

2. Falk Company budgets June sales at $265,000. The variable expense is expected to be 56% of sales and profit is expected to be $31,768.

Required:
- (1) Break-even point for June.
- (2) June sales if the company made a profit of $10,560.

3. Normal capacity of the Fritz Company is 18,000 units and the unit sales price is $2.50. Costs are:

	VARIABLE (PER UNIT)	FIXED
Direct materials	$.700	—
Direct labor	.800	—
Factory overhead	.150	$3,000
Nonmanufacturing cost	.025	1,290

Required:
- (1) Break-even point in dollars and in units and a proof of the answer.
- (2) Sales dollars required to produce a profit of $8,250.

4. The accounting firm of Smith and Thompson has been studying the sales requirements of the Frisco Bottling Company. In the course of the study, the managing partner submits the following estimated data:

Sales	$900,000	Fixed marketing expenses	$71,000
Direct materials	206,200	Variable marketing expenses	80,000
Direct labor	165,200	Fixed administrative expenses	9,500
Fixed factory overhead	171,896	Variable administrative expenses	4,000
Variable factory overhead	102,600		

Required: The break-even point in dollars.

5. The following data of the Sandmeyer Co. are given for May:

Plant capacity	2,000 units per month
Fixed cost	$4,000 per month
Variable cost	$2.50 per unit
Sales price	$5 per unit

Required:
- (1) The break-even point in dollars.
- (2) The break-even chart. (Use a dollar scale for both the x-axis and y-axis; label and identify each element of the chart.)

6. From the books and records of the Coe Company, the cost analyst determined that sales were $10,000,000 and costs were as follows:

	VARIABLE COSTS	FIXED COSTS	TOTAL
Direct materials	$3,000,000	—	$3,000,000
Direct labor	3,000,000	—	3,000,000
Factory overhead	800,000	$500,000	1,300,000
Marketing expenses	700,000	300,000	1,000,000
Administrative expenses	500,000	200,000	700,000

The company is considering two alternative proposals that would change certain cost items. Proposal 1 would increase fixed costs $100,000, with sales and variable costs remaining the same. Proposal 2 would modernize present equipment at an annual increase of fixed costs of $250,000, with the expectation of saving the same amount in each of the direct materials and the direct labor costs.

Required:
- (1) The current contribution margin ratio (C/M).
- (2) The current break-even point.
- (3) If Proposal 1 is adopted:
  - (a) The break-even point.
  - (b) The profit.
- (4) If Proposal 2 but not Proposal 1 is adopted:
  - (a) The contribution margin ratio (C/M).
  - (b) The break-even point.
  - (c) The profit.

7. The annual budget of The Bond Co. shows:

Sales (40,000 units)		$80,000
Fixed production cost	$20,000	
Fixed marketing and administrative costs	26,200	
Variable production cost	19,000	
Variable marketing and administrative costs	5,000	
Total cost		70,200
Profit from operations		$ 9,800

Required:
- (1) The break-even point in sales dollars, using the figures given in the budget.
- (2) The break-even point in units, using the figures given in the budget.
- (3) The new break-even point in sales dollars, assuming that fixed costs increase $1,867 and variable costs decrease $800 at the $80,000 sales level.
- (4) The increase in sales needed to make the same $9,800 profit, assuming that fixed costs increase by $2,167 and variable costs by $800 at the $80,000 sales level.
- (5) The budgeted profit and the new break-even point in sales dollars assuming that the company revises the annual budget by increasing the unit sales price by 5%, which is expected to decrease volume by 15%, with variable costs bearing the same relationship to sales dollars as in the original annual budget.

8. During the year, Klos Company produced and sold 100,000 units. The unit sales price was $100. Standard and actual costs per unit, based on a production of 100,000 units, were:

Variable cost	$25
Fixed cost	50
Total	$75

Required:
- (1) Operating income according to the direct costing method.
- (2) Break-even point in dollars.
- (3) Margin of safety ratio at the given sales level.

9. The Ringo Ring Company has budgeted sales of $200,000, a profit of $60,000, and fixed expense of $40,000.

Required: The C/M ratio.

10. The Rose Williams Company has a C/M ratio of 36%. Break-even sales are $160,000. The company earned a profit of $28,800 during the year.

Required:
- (1) Fixed expense.
- (2) Sales for the year.
- (3) Variable expense for the year.
- (4) Margin of safety ratio.

11. The Little Rock Company shows fixed expense of $12,150, an M/S ratio of 25%, and a C/M ratio of 30% for one month's operations.

Required:
    (1) The break-even point in dollars.
    (2) Actual sales.
    (3) Profit for the month.

12. Last month the Henke Company had sales of $220,000, a C/M ratio of 40%, and an M/S ratio of 30%. During the current month, a decrease in sales price and a decrease in fixed costs have resulted in a C/M ratio of 36% and an M/S ratio of 24%.

Required:
    (1) The amount sales decreased.
    (2) New break-even point.
    (3) Profit during the current month.
    (4) Decrease in fixed costs.

13. Break-even analysis. The income statement for one of Manhattan Company's products shows:

Sales (100 units at $100 a unit)		$10,000
Cost of goods sold:		
Direct labor	$1,500	
Direct materials used	1,400	
Variable factory overhead	1,000	
Fixed factory overhead	500	
Total cost of goods sold		4,400
Gross profit		$ 5,600
Marketing expenses:		
Variable	$ 600	
Fixed	1,000	
Administrative expenses:		
Variable	500	
Fixed	1,000	
Total marketing and administrative expenses		3,100
Operating income		$ 2,500

Required:
    (1) Break-even point in units.
    (2) Operating income if sales increase by 25%.
    (3) Break-even point in dollars if fixed factory overhead increases by $1,700.

(AICPA adapted)

14. Break-even analysis. The Lublock Specialty Products Company manufactures a product which sells for $5. At present the company produces and sells 50,000 units per year. Unit variable manufacturing and marketing expenses are $2.50 and $.50, respectively. Fixed expenses are $70,000 for factory overhead and $30,000 for marketing and administration.

The sales manager has proposed that the price be increased to $6. To maintain the present sales volume, advertising must be increased. The company's profit objective is 10% of sales.

Required:
    (1) The additional expenditure the company can afford for advertising.
    (2) The new break-even point in units and dollars, using the $6 sales price and the additional advertising expenditure, from requirement (1).

(CGAA adapted.)

15. Break-even analysis. The Carey Company sold 100,000 units of its product at $20 per unit. Variable costs are $14 per unit (manufacturing costs of $11 and marketing costs of $3). Fixed costs are incurred uniformly throughout the year and amount to $792,000 (manufacturing costs of $500,000 and marketing costs of $292,000).

Required:
 (1) The break-even point in units and in dollars.
 (2) The number of units that must be sold to earn an income of $60,000 before income tax.
 (3) The number of units that must be sold to earn an aftertax income of $90,000 if the income tax rate is 40%.
 (4) The number of units required to break even if the labor cost is 50% of variable costs and 20% of fixed costs, and if there is a 10% increase in wages and salaries.

(AICPA adapted)

16. Break-even analysis — hospital operations. The controller of St. Paul's Baptist Hospital analyzed its operations and found this information:

COST	VARIABLE	FIXED
Direct patient supplies	$100,000	—
Direct salaries	754,625	—
Patient service overhead	25,000	$105,000
Administrative expenses	75,000	175,000
Total	$954,625	$280,000

These costs are based on normal inpatient service days of 27,275 in the eighty-bed hospital and on patient service revenues of $1,227,375. Deficits are financed by contributions from the Southern Baptist Convention.

Since the hospital is currently operating at its highest practicable capacity, a proposal has been made for the construction of an additional wing of twenty beds. Fixed costs are expected to increase in about the same ratio as the current fixed-costs-per-bed ratio; the variable-cost-to-sales ratio should remain the same.

Required:
 (1) The current contribution margin ration (C/M). (Compute the answer to 1/100th of 1%.)
 (2) The current break-even point in revenue volume and inpatient service days.
 (3) The current margin of safety ratio (M/S). (Compute the answer to 1/100th of 1%.)
 (4) The new break-even point in revenue volume and inpatient service days, if the additional wing is constructed.

17. Break-even analysis with shifting costs and profits. The Savannah Company provides the following data:

Normal plant capacity	200,000 units
Fixed cost	$120,000
Variable cost	$1.35 per unit
Sales price	$2.25 per unit

Required:
 (1) The break-even point in dollars, in number of units, and in percent of capacity.
 (2) The margin of safety and the margin of safety ratio when operating at normal plant capacity.
 (3) The new break-even point in dollars, if the sales price is reduced to $2 and other data remain the same.
 (4) Volume in dollars required to yield a profit of $30,000 if the calculation is based on (a) the data of (1); (b) the data of (3).
 (5) The break-even point in dollars, in number of units, and in percent of capacity based on the data of (1), except that the fixed cost is reduced by $20,000.
 (6) The expected profit if budgeted sales of $450,000 are realized, costs are the same as at the beginning of the problem, and (a) the sales price per unit is $2.25; (b) the sales price per unit is $2.

18. Break-even analysis, new equipment; new profit goal. The management of the Kent William Company is presently thinking about (1) buying a machine that will reduce the number of production workers and (2) cutting the sales price of the product at the same time. The new machine will increase fixed costs by $10,000 due to depreciation; variable costs will decrease about 25% due to the reduction of direct workers; and the sales price will be reduced by 10%.

Before these changes were under consideration, the company had experienced the following costs and prices:

Sales price per unit	$ 100
Variable cost per unit	60
Total fixed cost	30,000

Required:
(1) Based on the original data:
   (a) The break-even point in number of units.
   (b) The profit if the company operates at a 900-unit volume.
(2) Considering the contemplated changes:
   (a) The new break-even point in number of units.
   (b) The profit if the company retains the 900-unit volume.
   (c) The profit if the company experiences a sales volume of 1,000 units.
(3) The new profit if the company did not buy the new machine and did not lay off any workers, but reduced the price by 10% and increased volume to 950 units.

19. Break-even and patient mix analysis for a hospital. Suver-Neumann Memorial Hospital records provide the following patient mix data for the year:

METHOD OF PAYMENT	PATIENT MIX	AVERAGE DAILY REIMBURSEMENT RATE	AVERAGE DAILY VARIABLE COST
Self-pay	20%	$120	$40
Private insurance	25	120	40
Medicare	30	110	40
Medicaid	25	100	40

The annual fixed cost is $1,000,000.

Required:
(1) The composite break-even point in dollars and inpatient days. (Compute the contribution margin ratio to the nearest percent.)
(2) The composite break-even point in dollars and inpatient days if the patient mix were 50% self-pay and 50% private insurance patients.

20. Price decreases and volume increases — elasticity of demand. Acme Company forecasts next year's sales of Product X to be 50,000 units at a sales price of $10. Management is considering a price reduction to $9 with the expectation that sales and profits will increase. However, the elasticity of demand is questionable, ranging from an estimated low elasticity of only 2,000 additional units sold to a high elasticity of an increase of 30,000 units.

The variable unit manufacturing cost is estimated to be $5 and the variable nonmanufacturing cost is estimated to be 10% of sales revenue. At the high elasticity sales level, annual programmed fixed costs are expected to increase $5,000 and $1,000 for manufacturing and nonmanufacturing costs, respectively.

Required: The change in the contribution to other fixed costs and to income before income tax if the sales price is reduced and the sales volume increases (a) 2,000 units; (b) 30,000 units.

21. Use of limiting constraint. The Pricerite Company presents the following per unit data for two of its products:

	ABITE	BELITE
Sales price	$15.00	$6.75
Variable cost	$ 8.00	$3.00
Fixed cost	4.00	2.75
	$12.00	$5.75
Profit	$ 3.00	$1.00
Units per hour	10	25

Required:
(1) For each product, rounding answers to two decimal places:
   (a) Profit per dollar of sales.   (d) Contribution margin per hour.
   (b) Unit contribution margin.   (e) Profit per hour.
   (c) C/M ratio.
(2) The more profitable product for the company, if there is long-run commitment to the present levels of fixed cost and assuming more units of the products can be sold than can be manufactured with the present labor force and facilities.

PROBLEMS

24-1. Break-even analysis. Columbia Candy Company is a wholesale distributor of candy, serving grocery, convenience, and drug stores in a large metropolitan area. Small but steady growth in sales has been achieved by the company over the past few years while candy prices have been increasing. The company is formulating its plans for the coming fiscal year. Presented below are the data used to project the current year's aftertax net income of $110,400:

Average sales price per box	$ 4.00
Average variable costs per box:	
Cost of candy	$ 2.00
Marketing	.40
Total	$ 2.40
Annual fixed costs:	
Marketing	$160,000
Administrative	280,000
Total	$440,000

Expected annual sales volume (390,000 boxes), $1, 560,000.
Income tax rate, 40%.

Manufacturers of candy have announced that they will increase prices of their products an average of 15% in the coming year due to increases in materials and labor costs. Columbia Candy Company expects that all other costs will remain at the same rates or levels as the current year.

Required:
(1) The break-even point in boxes of candy for the current year.
(2) The sales price per box the company must charge to cover the 15% increase in the cost of candy and still maintain the current contribution margin ratio.
(3) The volume of sales in dollars the company must achieve in the coming year to maintain the same net income as projected for the current year if the sales price of candy remains at $4 per box and the cost of candy increases 15%.

(CMA adapted)

24-2. Break-even analysis. The R.A. Ro Company, a manufacturer of quality handmade pipes, has experienced a steady growth in its sales for the past five years. Increased competition, however, has led the president to believe that an aggressive advertising campaign will be necessary next year to maintain the company's present growth.

To prepare for next year's advertising campaign, the accountant presents the following data for the current year, 19A:

Variable costs:	
Direct labor	$ 8.00 per pipe
Direct materials	3.25
Variable factory overhead	2.50
Total variable cost	$ 13.75 per pipe

Fixed costs:	
Manufacturing	$ 25,000
Marketing	40,000
Administrative	70,000
Total fixed cost	$135,000
Sales price per pipe	$ 25
Expected sales, 19A (20,000 units)	$500,000
Federal income tax rate	40%

The company set the 19B sales target at a level of $550,000, or 22,000 pipes.

Required:
(1) The projected aftertax net income for 19A.
(2) The break-even point in units for 19A.
(3) The aftertax net income for 19B if an additional fixed marketing expense of $11,250 is spent for advertising in 19B (with all other costs remaining constant) in order to attain the 19B sales target.
(4) The break-even point in dollar sales for 19B if the additional $11,250 is spent for advertising.
(5) The required dollar sales to equal 19A's aftertax net income, if the additional $11,250 is spent for advertising in 19B.
(6) The maximum amount that can be spent on additional advertising at a sales level of 22,000 units, if an aftertax net income of $60,000 is desired.

(CMA adapted)

24-3. Product mix ratio and break-even analysis. Break-even analysis has been useful in making product mix decisions. To illustrate, a cost analyst assumed the following situation for a company's three major products:

	PRODUCT		
	A	B	C
Sales price	$10.00	$8.00	$11.00
Variable cost	6.00	5.00	9.00
Contribution margin	$ 4.00	$3.00	$ 2.00

Total fixed cost, $200,000.

Required:
(1) The break-even point (in total and for each product) if the three products are sold in the ratio of 4:3:7 units. (Round the C/M ratio to 1/100th of 1%.)
(2) The new break-even point (in total and for each product) if management decides to concentrate its sales efforts on Product A with its higher contribution margin, resulting in a new sales ratio of 6:3:5 units. (Round the C/M ratio to 1/100th of 1%.)

24-4. Break-even analysis. The Dooley Co. manufactures two products — Baubles and Trinkets. The following data are projected for the coming year:

	BAUBLES		TRINKETS		TOTAL
	Units	Amount	Units	Amount	AMOUNT
Sales	10,000	$10,000	8,000	$10,000	$20,000
Fixed cost		$ 2,000		$ 5,600	$ 7,600
Variable cost		6,000		3,000	9,000
Total cost		$ 8,000		$ 8,600	$16,600
Operating income		$ 2,000		$ 1,400	$ 3,400

Required:
(1) The break-even sales in units for Baubles, assuming that the facilities are not jointly used.
(2) The break-even sales in dollars for Trinkets, assuming that the facilities are not jointly used.

(Continued)

(3) The composite unit contribution margin, assuming that consumers purchase composite units of four Baubles and three Trinkets.

(4) The break-even units for both products, assuming that consumers purchase composite units of four Baubles and three Trinkets.

(5) The composite contribution margin ratio, assuming that a composite unit is defined as one Bauble and one Trinket. (Round to two decimal places.)

(6) The break-even point in dollars, assuming that Baubles and Trinkets become one-to-one complements and there is no change in the company's cost function.   (AICPA adapted)

24-5. Contribution margin; break-even analysis. The president of the Jadlow Company wants guidance on the advisability of eliminating Product C, one of the company's three similar products, or investing in new machinery to reduce the cost of C in the hope of reversing C's operating loss sustained during the year. The products are manufactured in one plant in about the same amount of floor space, and the markets in which they are sold are very competitive.

An income statement for all three products and for Product C only for the year ended October 31 is shown below.

Jadlow Company
Income Statement
For the Year Ended October 31, 19--

	ALL THREE PRODUCTS	PRODUCT C
Sales	$2,800,150	$350,000
Cost of goods sold:		
Materials	$ 565,000	$ 80,000
Labor:		
Direct	1,250,000	150,000
Indirect (fixed)	55,000	18,000
Fringe benefits (15% of labor)	195,750	25,200
Royalties (1% of Product C sales)	3,500	3,500
Maintenance and repairs (fixed)	6,000	2,000
Factory supplies	15,000	2,100
Depreciation (straight-line)	25,200	7,100
Electrical power	25,000	3,000
Scrap and spoilage	4,300	600
Total cost of goods sold	$2,144,750	$291,500
Gross profit	$ 655,400	$ 58,500
Marketing, general, and administrative expenses:		
Sales commissions	$ 120,000	$ 15,000
Officers' salaries	32,000	10,500
Other wages and salaries (fixed)	14,000	5,300
Fringe benefits (15% of wages, salaries, and commissions)	24,900	4,620
Delivery expense	79,500	10,000
Advertising expense (variable)	195,100	26,000
Miscellaneous fixed expense	31,900	10,630
Total marketing, general, and administrative expenses	$ 497,400	$ 82,050
Operating income (loss)	$ 158,000	$ (23,550)

The direct labor cost of Product C could have been reduced by $75,000 and the indirect labor cost by $4,000 by investing an additional $340,000 (financed with 5% bonds) in machinery with a ten-year life and an estimated salvage value of $30,000 at the end of the period. However, the company would have been liable for a total severance pay cost of $18,000 (to be amortized over a five-year period), and the power cost would have increased $500 annually.

Required:

(1) A schedule showing the contribution margin for Product C for the year ended October 31, assuming that each element of cost and expense is entirely fixed or variable within the relevant range and that the change in inventory levels has been negligible.

(2) A schedule computing the break-even point of Product C in terms of annual dollar sales volume, assuming that in the fiscal year the variable costs and expenses of Product C totaled $297,500, fixed costs and expenses were $75,100, and sales were $350,000.

(3) A schedule computing the break-even point of Product C in terms of annual dollar sales volume, assuming the information given in (2) and that the additional machinery had been purchased and installed at the beginning of the year.

(AICPA adapted)

24-6. Hospital department break-even analysis. Hillsboro Hospital operates a general hospital but rents space and beds to separate entities for specialized areas such as pediatrics, maternity, and psychiatric. The hospital charges each separate entity for common services such as patients' meals and laundry and for administrative services such as billings and collections. All uncollectible accounts are charged directly to the entity. Space and bed rentals are fixed for the year.

For the fiscal year ended June 30, 19A, the Pediatrics Department charged each patient an average of $65 per day, had a capacity of 60 beds, operated 24 hours per day for 365 days, and had a revenue of $1,138,800.

Expenses charged by the hospital to the Pediatrics Department for the fiscal year ended June 30, 19A, were:

	BASIS OF ALLOCATION	
	Patient Days (Variable)	Bed Capacity (Fixed)
Dietary...	$ 42,952	
Janitorial...		$ 12,800
Laundry...	28,000	
Laboratory (other than direct charges to patients).....	47,800	
Pharmacy..	33,800	
Repairs and maintenance.....................................	5,200	7,140
General administrative services		131,760
Rent..		275,320
Billings and collections..	40,000	
Uncollectible accounts expense	47,000	
Other expense..	18,048	25,980
	$262,800	$453,000

The only personnel directly employed by the Pediatrics Department are supervising nurses, nurses, and aides. The hospital has minimum departmental personnel requirements based on total annual patient days.

Hospital requirements beginning at the minimum expected level of operations were as follows:

ANNUAL PATIENT DAYS	AIDES	NURSES	SUPERVISING NURSES
10,000–14,000	21	11	4
14,001–17,000	22	12	4
17,001–23,725	22	13	4
23,726–25,550	25	14	5
25,551–27,375	26	14	5
27,376–29,200	29	16	6

The staffing levels represent full-time equivalents, and the Pediatrics Department always employs only the minimum number of required full-time equivalent personnel. Salaries of supervising nurses, nurses, and aides are therefore fixed within ranges of annual patient days. Annual salaries for each class of employee are: supervising nurses, $21,000; nurses, $16,000; and aides, $8,000.

Required: The minimum number of patient days necessary for the Pediatrics Department to break even for the fiscal year ending June 30, 19B. Patient demand is unknown, but assume that revenue per patient day, cost per patient day, cost per bed, and employee salary rates will remain the same as for the fiscal year ended June 30, 19A.

(AICPA adapted)

24-7. Break-even analysis; cash flow analysis. Donna Cooper began the operation of a pizza parlor in 19A. A building was rented for this purpose at $400 per month. Two full-time waiters were hired, and six college students were hired to work 30 hours per week delivering pizza. A public accounting service was employed at $300 per month. The necessary pizza parlor equipment and delivery trucks were purchased with cash. Cooper noticed that expenses for utilities and supplies were reasonably constant.

Cooper's business increased between 19A and 19D. Since 19A, net income for each year more than doubled, but volume has not increased as rapidly.

A projected income statement for 19E prepared by the accounting service is shown below.

Donna's Pizza Parlor
Projected Income Statement
For Year Ending December 31, 19E

Sales		$95,000
Cost of food sold	$28,500	
Wage and fringe benefits — pizza parlor help..	8,150	
Wages and fringe benefits — delivery help..	17,300	
Rent	4,800	
Accounting services...	3,600	
Depreciation — delivery equipment..	5,000	
Depreciation — pizza parlor equipment...	3,000	
Utilities..	2,325	
Supplies (soap, floor wax, etc.)...	1,200	73,875
Income before income tax..		$21,125
Income tax...		6,338
Net income...		$14,787

The average pizza sells for $2.50. Assume that Cooper's income tax rate is 30%.

Required:
(1) The break-even point in the number of pizzas that must be sold.
(2) The cash remaining from the 19E income-producing activities if Cooper withdraws $4,800 for personal use.
(3) The volume that must be reached in the number of pizzas sold in order to obtain a desired aftertax net income of $20,000.
(4) A brief explanation as to why profits have increased at a faster rate than sales.
(5) A brief explanation as to why cash flow for 19E will exceed net income.   (CMA adapted)

24-8. Sales mix and break-even analysis. Rite-Beverage Bottling Company produces a variety of bottled drinks. The company has classified its products into these three basic categories:

BRAND	SALES PRICE PER CASE	VARIABLE COST PER CASE
Trade-Name	$1.50	$1.40
True-Ade.......................................	1.20	1.00
Dietary	1.00	.40

The fixed cost of the company is $37,240 annually and does not change with any change in product mix or with total volume changes of less than 50%. During 19A, sales of Trade-Name accounted for 50% of the company's total sales in cases. Sales of True-Ade were four times that of Dietary. Total sales revenue for the year was $500,000.

Required:
(1) The break-even sales in dollars and units of each product group for 19A, based on the actually experienced sales mix. (Round the contribution margin ratio to two decimal places.)
(2) The amount which could be spent for advertising in 19B to increase sales of the more profitable lines, with the company making a profit of one and one-half times that of 19A on the same total sales revenue, and Tru-Ade sales accounting for 50% of sales in cases; Dietary, 20%; and Trade-Name, 30%.

24-9. Break-even and cost-volume-profit analysis. Hewtex Electronics produces and markets tape recorders and electronic calculators. Its 19A income statement follows:

Hewtex Electronics
Income Statement
For Year Ended December 31, 19A

	TAPE RECORDERS		ELECTRONIC CALCULATORS		
	Total (000s Omitted)	Per Unit	Total (000s Omitted)	Per Unit	Total (000s Omitted)
Sales..	$1,050	$15.00	$3,150	$22.50	$4,200.0
Production costs:					
Materials..............................	$ 280	$ 4.00	$ 630	$ 4.50	$ 910.0
Direct labor	140	2.00	420	3.00	560.0
Variable factory overhead....	140	2.00	280	2.00	420.0
Fixed factory overhead	70	1.00	210	1.50	280.0
Total production cost.......	$ 630	$ 9.00	$1,540	$11.00	$2,170.0
Gross profit.............................	$ 420	$ 6.00	$1,610	$11.50	$2,030.0
Fixed marketing and administrative expenses..					1,040.0
Income before income tax					$ 990.0
Income tax (55%)					544.5
Net income					$ 445.5

The tape recorder business has been fairly stable in recent years, and the company has no plans to change the tape recorder price. However, because of increasing competition and market saturation, management has decided to reduce its calculator price to $20, effective January 1, 19B, and to spend an additional $57,000 in 19B for advertising. As a result, Hewtex estimates that 80% of its 19B revenue will be from electronic calculator sales. The sales units mix for tape recorders and calculators is expected to be 1:2 in 19A and 1:3 in 19B at all volume levels. Materials costs are expected to drop 10% and 20% for the tape recorders and calculators, respectively; however, all direct labor costs are to increase 10%.

Required:
  (1) The number of tape recorders and electronic calculators to break even, using 19A data.
  (2) Sales dollars required to earn an aftertax profit of 9% on sales, using 19B estimates.
  (3) The number of tape recorders and electronic calculators to break even, using 19B estimates.   (CMA adapted)

24-10. Break-even and cost-volume-profit analysis; direct costing. The following data relate to a year's budgeted activity for Crosby Corporation, which manufactures one product:

Beginning inventory...	30,000 units
Production	120,000
Available for sale..	150,000 units
Sales...	110,000
Ending inventory..	40,000 units
Sales price..	$5.00 per unit
Variable manufacturing cost..	1.00
Variable marketing cost...	2.00
Fixed manufacturing cost (based on 100,000 units)..........................	.25
Fixed marketing cost (based on 100,000 units)...................................	.65

A special order is received for 10,000 units to be used in an unrelated market. The total fixed cost remains unchanged within the relevant range of 25,000 units to total capacity of 160,000 units.

Required:
  (1) Projected annual break-even sales in units.
  (2) Projected operating income for the year (a) under direct costing; (b) under absorption costing, charging all variances to Cost of Goods Sold.   *(Continued)*

(3) The price per unit to be charged on the special order, given the original data, so that the operating income will increase by $5,000.

(4) The number of units to be sold to generate a profit equal to 10% of the contribution margin, assuming that the sales price increases by 20%; the variable manufacturing cost increases by 10%; the variable marketing cost remains the same; and the total fixed cost increases to $104,400.   (AICPA adapted)

24-11. Effect of product mix variation. The officers of the Herbert Company reviewed the profitability of the company's four products and the potential effect of several proposals for varying the product mix. An excerpt from the year's income statement and other data follows:

	TOTAL	PRODUCT P	Q	R	S
Sales	$62,600	$10,000	$18,000	$12,600	$22,000
Cost of goods sold	44,274	4,750	7,056	13,968	18,500
Gross profit	$18,326	$ 5,250	$10,944	$ (1,368)	$ 3,500
Operating expense	12,012	1,990	2,976	2,826	4,220
Profit before income tax	$ 6,314	$ 3,260	$ 7,968	$ (4,194)	$ (720)
Units sold		1,000	1,200	1,800	2,000
Sales price per unit		$10.00	$15.00	$7.00	$11.00
Variable cost of goods sold per unit....		$2.50	$3.00	$6.50	$6.00
Variable operating expense per unit....		$1.17	$1.25	$1.00	$1.20

The total fixed cost is not expected to fluctuate as a result of changes under consideration.

Required:

(1) The effect on profit if R is discontinued.

(2) The effect on profit if R is discontinued and if a consequent loss of customers causes a decrease of 200 units in sales of Q.

(3) The effect on profit if R's sales price is increased to $8, and the number of units sold decreases to 1,500 with no effect on the other products.

(4) The effect on profit if a new product, T, is introduced and R is discontinued with no effect on the other products. (The total variable cost per unit of Product T would be $8.05, and 1,600 units can be sold at $9.50 each. The plant in which R is produced can be utilized to produce T.)

(5) The effect on profit if production of P is reduced to 500 units (to be sold at $12 each) and if production of S is increased to 2,500 units (to be sold at $10.50 each). (Part of the plant in which P is produced can easily be adapted to produce S, but changes in quantities make changes in the sales price advisable.)

(6) The effect on profit if production of P is increased by 1,000 units to be sold at $10 each by adding a second shift. (Higher wages must be paid, thus increasing the variable cost of goods sold per unit to $3.50 for each additional unit.)   (AICPA adapted)

24-12. Cost-volume-profit analysis. Three companies are each producing and selling annually 10,000 units of a similar product at a unit sales price of $10. The companies have fixed and variable costs as follows:

COMPANY	FIXED COST	VARIABLE COST PER UNIT
A	$20,000	$6
B	40,000	4
C	60,000	2

Each company contemplates a price cut, from $10 to $8, in the expectation that sales will increase from 10,000 to 15,000 units per year.

Required:

(1) The contribution margin and operating income for each company at the present level of activity.

(2) The contribution margin and operating income for each company at the contemplated price and sales level.

(3) Explanation of the differences in the answers computed in (1) and (2).

                                  (Based on an article in *The Accounting Review*)

24-13. Analysis of price-volume relationships. The income statement for the Woodstock Company for the past year is:

Sales (150,000 units @ $30)		$4,500,000
Cost of goods sold:		
Materials	$1,050,000	
Labor	1,500,000	
Variable factory overhead	450,000	
Fixed factory overhead	500,000	3,500,000
Gross profit		$1,000,000
Variable marketing expenses	$ 135,000	
Fixed marketing expenses	185,000	
Fixed administrative expenses	180,000	500,000
Income before income tax		$ 500,000
Income tax		250,000
Net income		$ 250,000

Woodstock is preparing its budget for the coming year and has made the following predictions about cost increases: materials, 5%; labor, 8%; all other costs (including fixed), 6%.

Productive capacity is 200,000 units.

The president has been offered various proposals by the division managers, as follows:

(a) Maintain the present volume and sales price.
(b) Produce and sell at capacity and reduce the unit price to $28.
(c) Raise the unit price to $32, spend an extra $300,000 on advertising, and produce and sell 180,000 units.

Required: Recommended action, based on quantification of alternatives.

(CGAA adapted)

24-14. Price decreases and volume increases. The following is the income statement of Hansen Company for the year ended December 31, 19A:

Sales (9,600,000 units)		$160,000,000
Cost of goods sold:		
Direct materials	$38,400,000	
Direct labor	28,800,000	
Factory overhead	48,000,000	115,200,000
Gross profit		$ 44,800,000
Marketing and administrative expenses		28,800,000
Operating income		$ 16,000,000

Production capacity of the installed machinery is 12,000,000 units. Company management is conscious of the high degree of underutilized capacity. It is uncertain, however, whether or not the market will absorb more units of product than at present. The task of assessing product demand was assigned to a marketing research consulting firm. Results of the study made by the consultants predicted the following price-volume relationships:

SALES PRICE PER UNIT	QUANTITY DEMANDED
$16.00	10,000,000
15.50	12,000,000
14.50	14,000,000
14.25	18,000,000

An analysis of factory overhead reveals that in 19A, fixed factory overhead was $28,800,000 and fixed marketing and administrative expenses were $19,200,000. If new machinery is to be installed for increasing the production capacity to 18,000,000 units, an additional capital expenditure of $100,000,000 is required, resulting in a fixed factory overhead increase of $10,000,000 per year.

Required: The recommended level of activity.

24-15. Contribution margin and break-even analysis in units. Metal Industries, Inc., operates its Production Department only when orders are received for one or both of its products, two sizes of metal disks. The manufacturing process begins with the cutting of doughnut-shaped rings from rectangular strips of sheet metal; these rings are then pressed into disks. The sheets of metal, each 4 feet long and weighing 32 ounces, are purchased at $1.36 per running foot. The department operated at a loss for the past year, as shown below:

Sales for the year	$172,000
Expense	177,200
Net loss for the department	$ 5,200

The following information is available:

(a) Ten thousand 4-foot pieces of metal yielded 40,000 large disks, each weighing 4 ounces and selling for $2.90, and 40,000 small disks, each weighing 2.4 ounces and selling for $1.40.

(b) The corporation has been producing at less than normal capacity and has had no spoilage in the cutting step of the process. The skeletons remaining after the rings have been cut are sold for scrap at $.80 per pound.

(c) The variable conversion cost is the sum of direct labor and variable overhead. The variable conversion cost of each large disk is 80% of the disk's direct materials cost, and the variable conversion cost of each small disk is 75% of the disk's direct materials cost.

(d) The fixed cost was $86,000.

Required:

(1) A schedule computing for each of the parts manufactured:
  (a) Unit materials cost after deducting the value of salvage.
  (b) Unit variable conversion cost.
  (c) Unit contribution margin.
  (d) Total contribution margin for all units sold.

(2) The number of units the corporation must sell to break even, based on a normal production capacity of 50,000 units, and assuming that the materials cost is $.85 each for large disks and $.51 each for small disks, that no units are spoiled, and that the product mix is one large disk to each small disk.   (AICPA adapted)

24-16. Increase in labor cost and depreciation; new sales price. The management of the Ashton Corporation anticipates a 10% wage increase on January 1 of next year. Presently, labor comprises $12 of the per unit total variable cost. No other cost changes are expected. The management needs assistance to formulate a reasonable product strategy for the next year.

A regression analysis indicates that volume is the primary factor affecting costs. Semivariable costs have been separated into their fixed and variable segments by means of the least-squares method. Beginning and ending inventories never differ materially.

The following current-year data have been assembled for the analysis:

Current sales price per unit	$80
Variable cost per unit	48
Annual volume of sales	5,000 units
Fixed cost (no labor cost included)	$51,000

The management believes that an additional $190,000 in machinery (to be depreciated at 10% annually) will increase present capacity (5,300 units) by 30%.

Required:

(1) The increase in the sales price necessary to cover the 10% wage increase and still maintain the current contribution margin ratio.

(2) The number of units to be sold to maintain the current profit if the sales price remains at $80 and the 10% wage increase goes into effect.

(3) A comparison of the estimated profit before and after capacity is increased, assuming that all units produced can be sold at the present price and that the wage increase goes into effect.   (AICPA adapted)

24-17. Computer marketing, pricing, and financing strategy. North Shore Industries, Inc., recently established the South Bend Division to manufacture and market a new type of computer. North Shore's executive committee is considering financing alternatives.

Engineering estimates indicate that the variable cost of manufacturing a unit will be $20,000, and the variable marketing cost of a unit will be $10,000 with a sales price set at $50,000 per unit. State and federal income taxes are estimated at 55% of income before income tax.

It is further estimated that South Bend will incur fixed costs totaling $4,000,000 per year including depreciation. North Shore must secure an additional $10,000,000 to finance the South Bend Division, and for this it plans to issue at par either stocks or bonds. South Bend must bear the financing cost in addition to other costs.

South Bend will have 72 salespeople. Market surveys indicate that each salesperson must sell an average of one unit every three months if the sales price of the computer is set at $50,000 per unit, and that no one is likely to sell more than one unit in any month.

The market surveys also indicated that each salesperson should be expected to sell one unit every four months if the sales price were set at $60,000 per unit. Reduced sales would cause the variable cost of marketing a unit to increase to $12,000.

Required:
(1) The number of units which must be sold annually at $50,000 per unit to pay all costs, meet any dividend requirement, and comply with the stated objective under each of the following alternatives:
    (a) 6% nonparticipating, cumulative, preferred stock is issued.
    (b) 5% bonds are issued.
    (c) 5% bonds are issued and North Shore requires that South Bend contribute 6% of its sales to be credited to North Shore Industries' retained earnings for internal financing and future expansion.
    (d) 5% bonds are issued and North Shore requires that South Bend contribute annually both $100,000 to be paid out as dividends to North Shore's common stockholders and 6% of South Bend's sales to be credited to North Shore's retained earnings for internal financing and future expansion.
(2) (a) The probability that any one salesperson will sell a computer in any month.
    (b) The average number of units that South Bend can expect to sell per month at $50,000.
(3) (a) A recomputation of requirement (1) (d) under the alternative of increasing the sales price and the variable marketing cost.
    (b) A recommendation for setting the sales price at either $50,000 or $60,000.

(AICPA adapted)

25

Differential Cost Analysis

Many management decisions involve choosing between alternatives such as:

1. Accepting or refusing certain orders.
2. Reducing the price of a single, special order.
3. Making a price cut in a competitive market.
4. Evaluating make-or-buy alternatives.
5. Expanding or reducing plant capacity.
6. Increasing, curtailing, or stopping production of certain products.
7. Replacing present equipment with new machinery.
8. Selecting new sales territories.
9. Spending additional amounts for sales promotion.

Differential cost is the difference in the cost of alternative choices. Differential cost is often referred to as *marginal* or *incremental cost*. The term "marginal cost" is widely used by economists. Engineers generally speak of incremental costs as the added cost incurred when a project or an undertaking is extended beyond its originally intended goal.

Historical costs drawn from the accounting records generally do not give management the differential cost information needed to evaluate alternative courses of action. A flexible budget, however, with its revised costs for each rise in the capacity level, can be useful in some differential cost analyses. The flexible budget shows the various expenses at different levels of production. It indicates that some expenses increase proportionately with an increase in capacity, while other expenses remain comparatively stationary through various levels of activity.

In the flexible budget illustrated on the next page, the $5.40 average unit cost at 60 percent of normal capacity is computed by dividing the total cost at that capacity by the number of units produced ($324,250 ÷ 60,000 units). The total differential cost is determined by subtracting the total estimated cost for one level of activity from that of another level (e.g., $423,400 − $324,250 = $99,150, the differential cost between the 80-percent and 60-percent levels). The differential unit cost is computed by:

1. Subtracting one level of output from the next higher level (80,000 units output at 80 percent minus 60,000 units output at 60 percent = 20,000 units).
2. Dividing the differential cost total between these two levels by the added number of units ($99,150 ÷ 20,000 units = $4.96).

FLEXIBLE BUDGET FOR DIFFERENT RATES OF OUTPUT
(100,000 Units = 100% Normal Capacity)

Capacity	60%	80%	100%	120%
Variable costs:				
Direct manufacturing costs:				
Direct materials	$102,000	$136,000	$170,000	$204,000
Direct labor	93,000	124,000	155,000	186,000
Total	$195,000	$260,000	$325,000	$390,000
Indirect manufacturing costs:				
Heat	$ 720	$ 960	$ 1,200	$ 1,440
Light and power	1,440	1,920	2,400	2,880
Repairs and maintenance	2,460	3,280	4,100	4,920
Supplies	1,260	1,680	2,100	2,520
Indirect labor	9,120	12,160	15,200	18,240
Total	$ 15,000	$ 20,000	$ 25,000	$ 30,000
Commercial expenses:				
Clerical help	$ 11,580	$ 15,440	$ 19,300	$ 23,160
Wages, general	6,960	9,280	11,600	13,920
Supplies	1,260	1,680	2,100	2,520
Total	$ 19,800	$ 26,400	$ 33,000	$ 39,600
Fixed costs (within ranges):				
Manufacturing expenses:				
Foremen	$ 15,250	$ 20,500	$ 20,500	$ 25,750
Superintendent	15,000	15,000	15,000	17,750
Setup crew	5,000	7,500	7,500	8,500
Depreciation and rent	8,000	9,400	9,400	9,400
Insurance	2,600	2,600	2,600	2,600
Total	$ 45,850	$ 55,000	$ 55,000	$ 64,000
Commercial expenses:				
Executives	$ 28,000	$ 35,000	$ 35,000	$ 40,000
Assistants	11,200	16,400	16,400	19,200
Property tax	3,400	3,400	3,400	3,400
Advertising	6,000	7,200	7,200	8,600
Total	$ 48,600	$ 62,000	$ 62,000	$ 71,200
Total cost	$324,250	$423,400	$500,000	$594,800
Units of output	60,000	80,000	100,000	120,000
Average unit cost	$5.40	$5.29	$5.00	$4.96
Differential cost total		$99,150	$76,600	$94,800
Differential cost per unit		$4.96	$3.83	$4.74

The flexible budget also shows that a production increase from 100,000 to 120,000 units means a $94,800 increase in total cost and a $.04 decrease in the average unit cost. The reduced unit cost is due to the absorption of fixed cost by the greater number of units. This type of information from a flexible budget based on standard cost considerably facilitates the solution of differential cost problems.

DIFFERENTIAL COST STUDIES

Differential cost studies deal with the determination of incremental revenue, costs, and margins with regard to alternative uses of fixed facilities or available capacity. In these studies, variable costs are significant, because they usually represent the differential cost. If, however, fixed costs must be increased through the addition of a new machine or rental of additional space, then these costs should be considered differential costs.

The term "fixed" is perhaps a misnomer. If a fixed cost is incurred when additional business, for example, is accepted, it is certainly a variable expense. If it continues, however, it becomes a fixed cost due to its permanent nature. In the latter case, management must be cautioned against a quick decision in favor of additional business, because it might find itself with additional fixed costs and a capacity greater than needed.

Accepting Additional Orders

Differential cost is the cost that must be considered when a decision involves a change in output. The differential cost of added production is the difference between the cost of producing the present smaller output and that of the contemplated, larger output. If available capacity is not fully utilized, a differential cost analysis might indicate the possibility of selling additional output at a figure lower than the existing average unit cost. The new or additional business can be accepted as long as the variable cost is recovered, since any contribution to the recovery of fixed costs and profit is desirable.

To illustrate, assume that a plant has a maximum capacity of 100,000 units, but normal capacity production is set at 80,000 units, or 80 percent of maximum capacity. At this level the predetermined overhead rate is computed so that fixed expenses are fully absorbed when operating at the 80,000-unit level. If fewer units are produced, unabsorbed fixed overhead results; if more units are produced, fixed overhead is overabsorbed. If this company makes only one unit, its cost would be:

Variable cost	$	5 per unit
Total fixed cost		100,000 for this unit
Total		$100,005

At normal capacity, the fixed cost per unit is reduced to $1.25 ($100,000 ÷ 80,000 units), and the total cost per unit is:

Variable cost	$5.00
Share of fixed cost	1.25
Total	$6.25

If additional capacity can be utilized to produce an additional 1,000 units, the unit cost of these units — the differential cost — would be only the $5 variable cost, unless the units required additional fixed expense outlays. An income statement comparing present operating results with the total results after additional units are produced and sold might appear as follows:

	PRESENT BUSINESS	WITH ADDITIONAL BUSINESS
Sales	$720,000	$729,000
Variable cost	400,000	405,000
Contribution margin	$320,000	$324,000
Fixed cost	100,000	100,000
Profit	$220,000	$224,000

The additional business requires variable cost only, inasmuch as the capacity cost (i.e., the fixed cost) indicates that adequate unused capacity is available to handle the additional business. If the 1,000 units are sold at any price above the $5 variable cost, the sale will yield a positive contribution margin.

The illustration above can also be presented in the following manner to highlight the differential revenue of $9,000 and cost of $5,000:

	PRESENT BUSINESS	ADDITIONAL BUSINESS	TOTAL
Sales	$720,000	$9,000	$729,000
Variable cost	400,000	5,000	405,000
Contribution margin	$320,000	$4,000	$324,000
Fixed cost	100,000	–0–	100,000
Profit	$220,000	$4,000	$224,000

Reducing the Price of a Special Order

The differential cost aids management in deciding at what price the firm can afford to sell additional goods. To illustrate, assume that a company manufactures 450,000 units, using 90 percent of its normal capacity. The fixed factory overhead is $335,000, which is $.67 ($335,000 ÷ 500,000 units) for each unit manufactured when operations are at 100 percent of normal capacity. The variable factory overhead rate is $.50 per unit. The direct materials cost is $1.80, and the direct labor cost is $1.40 per unit. Each unit sells for $5. Marketing as well as general and administrative expenses are omitted to simplify the illustration. On the basis of these data, the accountant would prepare the following statement:

Sales (450,000 units @ $5)......................................		$2,250,000
Cost of goods sold:		
Direct materials (450,000 units @ $1.80)	$810,000	
Direct labor (450,000 units @ $1.40)........................	630,000	
Variable factory overhead (450,000 units @ $.50)	225,000	
Fixed factory overhead (450,000 units @ $.67).........	301,500	1,966,500
Income from operations...		$ 283,500
Unabsorbed fixed factory overhead [(500,000 units − 450,000 units) @ $.67]		33,500
Income from operations (adjusted)...........................		$ 250,000

The sales department reports that a customer has offered to pay $4.25 per unit for an additional 100,000 units. To make the additional units, an annual rental cost of $10,000 for new equipment would be incurred. The accountant computes the gain or loss on this order as follows:

Sales (100,000 units @ $4.25)...................................		$425,000
Cost of goods sold:		
Direct materials (100,000 units @ $1.80)	$180,000	
Direct labor (100,000 units @ $1.40)........................	140,000	
Variable factory overhead (100,000 units @ $.50)	50,000	
Fixed factory overhead (100,000 units @ $.67).........	67,000	437,000
Loss on this order		$ 12,000

The accountant's computation would cause management to reject the offer. In this computation, all cost elements use the existing unit costs, and fixed overhead is allocated on the basis of the established rate ($.67 per unit). A second look, however, reveals the effect of the new order on total factory overhead:

Fixed factory overhead (at present)		$335,000
Fixed factory overhead (because of additional business)		10,000
Total fixed factory overhead...................................		$345,000
Fixed factory overhead charged into production:		
For 450,000 units (old business)	$301,500	
For 100,000 units (additional business)	67,000	368,500
Overabsorbed fixed factory overhead........................		$ 23,500

Instead of underabsorbed fixed factory overhead of $33,500, the additional business would result in overabsorbed factory overhead of $23,500 or a net composite gain of $57,000 ($67,000 − $10,000) in absorbed factory overhead. This $57,000 minus the computed $12,000 loss on the order results in a gain of $45,000, as shown in the following statement, which includes only the differential costs and revenue:

Sales (100,000 units @ $4.25)...................................		$425,000
Cost of goods sold:		
Direct materials (100,000 units @ $1.80)	$180,000	
Direct labor (100,000 units @ $1.40)........................	140,000	
Variable factory overhead (100,000 units @ $.50)	50,000	
Additional fixed cost to produce this order	10,000	380,000
Gain on this order		$ 45,000

The unit cost of the additional units can be computed as follows:

$$\frac{\text{Cost of goods sold}}{\text{Additional units}} = \frac{\$380,000}{100,000} = \$3.80 \text{ per additional unit}$$

Whenever a differential cost analysis leads management to accept an additional order at or above the differential cost, it is assumed that the order is not going to disturb the market of the other products being offered. The additional business may involve a product presently marketed by the firm, or a product that can be manufactured with existing facilities and personnel. If these products are placed in a competitive market, they might have to be marketed at established prices. Otherwise, competitors might retaliate by cutting prices to an unprofitable and therefore undesirable level, considering all relevant cost and market factors. The firm must also be careful not to violate the Robinson-Patman Act and other governmental pricing restrictions.

Make-Or-Buy Decisions

Another phase of alternative actions is the problem of whether to make or buy component parts. This problem arises particularly in connection with the possible use of idle equipment, idle space, and even idle labor. In such situations, a manager is inclined to consider making certain parts instead of buying them in order to utilize existing facilities. Faced with a make-or-buy decision, the manager should:

1. Consider the quantity and quality of the parts as well as the technical know-how required, weighing such requirements for both the short-run and long-run period.
2. Compare the cost of making the parts with the cost (or price) of buying them.
3. Compare the making of the parts with possibly more profitable alternative uses that could be made of the firm's own facilities if the parts are purchased.
4. Consider differences in the required capital investment and the timing of cash flows (Chapter 26).
5. Adopt a course of action related to the firm's overall policies. Customers' and suppliers' reactions often play a part in these decisions. Retaliation or ill will could result. Whether it is profitable to make or buy depends upon the circumstances surrounding the individual situation.

The accountant should present a statement that compares the company's cost of making the parts with the vendor's price. The statement should present the differential costs of the part as well as a share of existing fixed expenses and a profit figure that places the total cost on a comparable basis. The budget should also be restated to indicate the effect on total costs and total profit when existing fixed costs are allocated to the additional parts.

A cost study with only the differential costs and with no allocation of existing fixed overhead or of profit is indicative of possible cost savings in the short-run. However, such studies seem to favor the making of the parts in the majority of cases. If management were asked to sell the parts at the differential price, it might be unwilling to do so, since, in the long run, the full cost must be covered and a reasonable profit achieved.

A study by the National Association of Accountants makes the following observations about cost considerations:

> To evaluate the alternatives properly, costs to make vs. costs to buy must be based on the same underlying assumptions. Thus, costs for each of the alternatives must be based on the identical product specifications, quantities, and quality standards.
>
> Determination of the "cost to buy" cannot be limited to existing costs shown on supplier invoices. The competitive nature of supplier pricing requires that current optimum third-party prices based upon identical specifications and quantities be used for evaluation of this alternative. There are many examples of lower prices being obtained from suppliers for larger quantities, standardization of specifications, etc., as well as from the use of competitive bids and/or the threat of self-manufacture. All direct and indirect costs of functions and facilities which are properly allocable to the "buy" alternative, under the "full cost" concept, must be considered. Cost to buy must also include the "full cost" to bring the product to the same condition and location as if self-manufactured — including freight, handling, purchasing, incoming inspection, inventory carrying costs, etc.
>
> Determination of the "cost to make" cannot be limited to those identified as manufacturing costs or used in the valuation of inventories. All direct and indirect costs of functions and facilities which are properly allocable to self-manufacture under the "full cost" concept must be considered.
>
> The long-term nature of most make-or-buy decisions requires that cost determinations not only consider present costs but also projections of future costs resulting from inflationary factors, technological changes, productivity, mechanization, etc. More specifically, the projection of the future cost to make and the cost to buy must give full consideration to what the costs "should be" under obtainable conditions and reflect all possible improvements — not just what may be achieved under existing operating conditions.[1]

Decisions to Shut Down Facilities

Differential cost analysis is also used when a business is confronted with the possibility of a shutdown of both manufacturing and marketing facilities. In the short run, a firm seems to be better off operating than not operating, as long as the products or services sold recover the variable cost and make a contribution toward the recovery of the fixed cost. A shutdown of facilities does not eliminate all costs. Depreciation, interest, property tax, and insurance continue during complete inactivity.

If operations are continued, certain expenses connected with the shutting down of the facilities would be saved. Furthermore, costs that would have to be incurred when a closed facility is reopened can be saved. Management might also consider the investment in the training of the active employees, which would be lost in the event of a shutdown. Morale of other employees, as well as community goodwill, may be adversely affected, and the recruiting and training of new workers would add to present costs. The loss of established markets is also a factor, since reentering a market requires a reeducation of the consumers of the company's products.

---

[1]*NAA Statement, No. 5*, "Criteria for Make-or-Buy Decisions" (New York: National Association of Accountants, June 21, 1973), pp. 5, 7–8.

To orient management regarding the possible steps to be taken, the accountant might again resort to the flexible budget to determine the effects of continuing operations as long as differential costs or any amount above them can be secured. This does not mean, however, that the volume set in the budget should be considered final. In view of probable prices, the most advantageous operating level can be determined only by considering several different volume levels.

While an entire facility may not be closed or eliminated, management may decide to discontinue certain individual products because they are producing no profit or an inadequate profit. Decisions to discontinue products require careful analysis of relevant differential cost and revenue data through a structured and continuous product evaluation program. Several benefits can accrue from an effectively administered evaluation program that has as its objective the timely identification of products that should be eliminated or that can be made more profitable through appropriate corrective action. These benefits include:

Decisions to Discontinue Products[2]

1. Expanded sales.
2. Increased profits.
3. Reduced inventory levels.
4. Executive time freed for more profitable activities.
5. Important and scarce resources, such as facilities, materials, and labor, made available for more promising projects.
6. Greater management concern with why products get into difficulty or fail, thus enabling the institution of policies that will reduce the rate of product failure.

Care must be taken to consider not only the profitability of the product being analyzed but also to evaluate the extent to which sales of other products will be adversely affected when one product is removed. If the sales decrease of related products is severe enough, it might be desirable to retain the product being scrutinized.

Management needs data that will permit development of warning signals for products that may be in trouble. Such warning signals include:

1. Declining sales volume.
2. Product sales volume decreasing as a percentage of the firm's total sales.
3. Decreasing market share.
4. Malfunctioning of the product or introduction of a superior competitive product.
5. Past sales volume not up to projected amounts.
6. Expected future sales and market potential not favorable.
7. Return on investment below minimum acceptable level.
8. Variable costs which approach or exceed revenues.

---

[2]This discussion is adapted from Stanley H. Kratchman, Richard T. Hise, and Thomas A. Ulrich, "Management's Decision To Discontinue a Product," *The Journal of Accountancy*, Vol. 139, No. 6, pp. 50–54.

9. Various costs as a percentage of sales consistently increasing.
10. Increasingly greater percentage of executive time required.
11. Price which must be constantly lowered to maintain sales.
12. Promotional budgets which must be consistently increased to maintain sales.

Studies have shown that firms often do a poor job of identifying products that are in difficulty and that should be eliminated. Probably the major deficiency is the lack of timely, relevant data. To determine what data are required for a successful product monitoring program and its effective implementation and operation, management must draw on the accountant's experience and expertise.

Applications of Differential Cost Analysis

The oil refining industry is characterized by processes that require management to choose between alternatives at various points during the processes. The basic function of oil refining is the separation, extraction, and chemical conversion of the crude oil's component elements, using skillful utilization of heat, pressure, and catalytic principles. The basic petroleum products are obtained through a physical change caused by the application of heat through a wide temperature range. Within a temperature differential of 300° (275° F to 575° F) the different liquid products, called fractions, ends, or cuts, pass off as vapors and are then condensed back into liquids. The initial application of heat drives off the lightest fractions — the naphthas and gasoline; the successively heavier fractions, such as kerosene and fuel oil, follow as the temperature rises. This process of vaporizing the crude oil and condensing the gaseous vapors to obtain the various cuts is commonly referred to as primary distillation.

Certain cuts (such as straight-run gasoline) are marketable with but little treating. Other products may undergo further processing in order to make them more salable. Thus, heavier fractions, such as kerosene and fuel oil, may be subjected to cracking, which will cause them to yield more valuable products such as gasoline. Cracking is a process during which, by the use of high temperatures and pressures and perhaps in the presence of a catalyst, a heavy fraction is subjected to destructive distillation and converted to a lighter hydrocarbon possessing different chemical characteristics, one of which is a lower boiling point. The heaviest of the fractions resulting from primary distillation is known as residuum or heavy bottoms. This residuum, after further processing, treating, and blending, forms lubricating oils and ancillary wax or asphalt products.

The management of a refinery must decide what to do with each distillate or fraction and at what stage of refining each should be sold; whether additional fractions should be bought from other refineries and what price should be paid for the additional units; or whether the company should enlarge the plant in order to handle a greater volume. They must also determine what alternate courses should be taken in order to break into the most profitable market at the moment.

The accountant can help management through the preparation of flexible budgets for the secondary operating departments in which further processing might take place. These departmental flexible budgets are called *cost analysis budgets*. They differ from the flexible budget used for control purposes in several respects: (1) all expenses are included in the analysis budget; (2) budgeted expenses of service departments are allocated to operating departments at corresponding capacity levels; and (3) their aim is to discover the departmental differential costs.

The amounts stated for each class of expense at each production level are computed on separate work sheets where various individual expenses are separated into their fixed and variable elements. This separation is necessary to arrive at the estimated expenses for each level of production.

Analysis budgets for the following departments, which represent secondary processing or finishing operations, are prepared:

Treating	Solvent Extraction
Filters and Burners	Wax Specialties
Cracking	Canning
Solvent Dewaxing	Barrel House

The analysis budget for cracking fuel oil in the Cracking Department is shown below.

ANALYSIS BUDGET

Department: Cracking

Period Budgeted: _____ to _____

Supervisor: _____

Normal Capacity (100%) 100,000 gallons through-put of fuel oil

DEPARTMENT AND/OR EXPENSE ACCOUNT	SHUT-DOWN	60%	80%	100%	120%
Direct expenses	$6,000	$14,000	$16,000	$17,000	$23,000
Allocated expenses (fixed and variable)........................	1,000	2,000	3,000	4,000	6,000
Total cost	$7,000	$16,000	$19,000	$21,000	$29,000
Through-put:					
Total gallons		60,000	80,000	100,000	120,000
Differential gallons		60,000	20,000	20,000	20,000
Differential cost		$9,000	$3,000	$2,000	$8,000
Unit differential cost............		$ .150	$ .150	$ .100	$.4000
Unit average cost		$ .267	$ .238	$ .210	$.2417

Cracking analysis budget:
  Present operations, 80% of normal capacity
  Differential cost (80% to 100%) = $.10 per input gallon
Cracking yields: 75% gasoline; 15% residual fuel oil; 10% loss

---

In the following pages, differential cost analysis is applied to the alternatives which confront the management of an oil refinery. The hypothetical cases illustrate the methods that may be employed in solving such problems.[3]

---

[3]Adapted from a study prepared by John L. Fox, later published in *NA(C)A Bulletin*, Vol. XXXI, No. 4, pp. 403–413, under the title, "Cost Analysis Budget to Evaluate Operating Alternatives for Oil Refiners."

Sell or Process Further. A refiner has on hand 20,000 gallons of fuel oil and must decide whether to sell it as fuel oil or crack it into gasoline and residual fuel. The following facts are available:

Current prices per gallon:
Fuel oil .... $.40
Gasoline... .56

The refiner can then prepare the following differential income computation, utilizing the Cracking Department analysis budget:

Potential revenue — products from cracking:	
Gasoline (15,000 gallons @ $.56)	$8,400
Fuel oil (3,000 gallons @ $.40)	1,200
	$9,600
Less potential revenue — fuel oil (20,000 gallons @ $.40)	8,000
Differential revenue...	$1,600
Less differential cost (20,000 gallons @ $.10).........................	2,000
Loss from cracking of fuel oil	$ 400*

*Not an accounting loss, per se, but a loss of profit that would result from an improper choice of alternatives.

Thus, judging from a quantitative standpoint, it would be more profitable to sell the 20,000 gallons of fuel oil as such rather than process them further.

Choice of Alternate Routings. A refiner is trying to decide whether to treat and sell the kerosene fraction or to crack it for its gasoline content. The current decision involves 10,000 gallons of raw kerosene. Pertinent available information follows (from an analysis budget for cracking kerosene):

Current prices per gallon:	
Kerosene..................................	$.32
Gasoline...................................	.56
Fuel oil	.40
Cracking yields:	
Gasoline...................................	85%
Residual fuel oil	5
Loss	10

Differential costs associated with potential gallons through-put of kerosene:

Cracking............................ $.12 per gallon
Treating .... .04

Using the above amounts, the refiner can prepare the following analysis:

Net potential revenue — products from cracking:		
Gasoline (8,500 gallons @ $.56)...................................	$4,760	
Fuel oil (500 gallons @ $.40).....................................	200	
	$4,960	
Less differential cost (10,000 gallons @ $.12)...............	1,200	$3,760
Net potential revenue — kerosene:		
Total revenue (10,000 gallons @ $.32)	$3,200	
Less differential cost (10,000 gallons @ $.04)..............	400	2,800
Gain from cracking rather than treating		$ 960

In this situation, the more profitable alternative is to crack the kerosene fraction.

Price To Pay for an Intermediate Stock. A refiner has been offered 10,000 gallons of cylinder stock. The usual bargaining process will determine the final price. The would-be purchasers are interested in knowing how high a price they can pay and still make a profit. The stock purchased would be processed into conventional bright stock and sold at that stage, since the blending unit for making finished motor oils is currently working at full capacity. Available information is as follows:

Cylinder stock is of such a quality and type that it will probably yield:
  90% bright stock
  5% petrolatum
  5% loss
Current prices: bright stock, $.50 per gallon; petrolatum — no market

Differential costs associated with processing 10,000 gallons of cylinder stock through several units (from analysis budgets) are:

Solvent dewaxing..................	$.02 per gallon
Solvent extracting	.02
Filtering	.01
Total..............................	$.05 per gallon

Using this information, the refiner's position can be analyzed and a bargaining margin can be determined:

Revenue — bright stock (9,000 gallons @ $.50)............................	$4,500
Differential cost (10,000 gallons @ $.05)	500
Margin...	$4,000
Margin per gallon of cylinder stock...	$ .40

The refiner is now ready to bargain for the purchase of the cylinder stock, knowing that a purchase price of $.40 a gallon represents the break-even point — to pay more would produce a loss, to pay less would result in a gain. Management can then decide how much profit is required to justify the purchase. Here the concept of *opportunity costs* (page 741) also enters into the final decision. If the available capacity could be more profitably used for another purpose, then perhaps the proposed purchase should not be consummated.

Proposed Construction of Additional Capacity. A refiner discovers that the market for finished neutrals is such that present capacity will not satisfy the demand. The refiner feels certain that an addition to the solvent dewaxing and solvent extracting units would prove profitable. The additional wax distillate stock required would be purchased on the open market at the current rate. However, before going ahead with the construction, the chief accountant is consulted and presents the following information:

Unit differential cost:
  Capacity from 100% (normal) to 120% (increase of 10,000 gallons through-put)
    Solvent Dewaxing Department — $.10 per gallon through-put
    Solvent Extracting Department — $.10 per gallon through-put

Assumed yield from wax distillate:
  90% Viscous neutral
  1.5% Paraffin (8 pounds per gallon)
  8.5% Loss

Current market prices:
  Viscous neutrals — $.47 per gallon.
  White crude scale wax — $.08 per pound
  Wax distillate stock — $.35 per gallon*

      *Not a published market price but the price management believes it will have to pay to acquire the stock.

Using this information, the following analysis is prepared:

Differential revenue:		
9,000 gallons viscous neutrals @ $.47............................	$4,230	
1,200 pounds paraffin @ $.08......................................	96	
	$4,326	
Less cost of wax distillate stock (10,000 gallons @ $.35) ..	3,500	
Margin to apply against differential costs		$ 826
Differential costs:		
Solvent Dewaxing Department (10,000 gallons @ $.10)....	$1,000	
Solvent Extracting Department (10,000 gallons @ $.10) ...	1,000	2,000
Potential loss from differential production........................		$1,174

The accountant's analysis indicates that the proposed increase in the productive capacity would not be justified under the stated conditions. Furthermore, even a potential profit should yield a satisfactory return on the additional capital investment.

QUANTITATIVE TECHNIQUES IN DIFFERENTIAL COST ANALYSIS

Differential cost studies must often determine the profitability of the short-run use of available capacity. To aid in these studies, management may use quantitative techniques such as linear programming and probability distributions.

Linear Equations and Linear Programming
Linear equations facilitate the determination of differential costs. If, for instance, y_1 represents the total cost at one level of activity and y_2 the total cost at another level of activity, then $y_2 - y_1$ equals the differential cost. Using the linear equation $y = a + bx$, where a = costs that do not change, b = the 100 percent capacity level of costs that change, and x = percent of capacity, a differential cost equation can be written as follows:

$$\text{Differential cost} = y_2 - y_1 = (a + bx_2) - (a + bx_1)$$
$$= a + bx_2 - a - bx_1$$
$$= bx_2 - bx_1$$
$$= b(x_2 - x_1)$$

Using the flexible budget on page 725, the differential cost between operations at 80% and 100% capacity can be determined as follows (*b* represents the variable costs, $325,000 + $25,000 + $33,000, at the normal capacity level with no change in the fixed cost between these two levels):

$$\text{Differential cost} = \$383,000(1.00 - .8)$$
$$= \$383,000(.2)$$
$$= \underline{\underline{\$\ 76,600}}$$

Often this differential cost does not agree with that shown in the flexible budget because there has been a change in fixed costs or the variable costs may have been treated curvilinearly rather than linearly in preparing the budget. Without a flexible budget, the linear equation method usually offers a quick and reasonably reliable answer.

Incremental analyses may become rather involved due to the multiple constraints on production and the number of products possible. The accountant could try numerous combinations to arrive at the incremental revenue and costs associated with each. However, mathematical or linear programming (Chapter 28) allows the accountant to determine the optimum course of action when the resource allocation problem is complex and its solution is neither obvious nor feasible by trial and error, guess, or intuition.

Probability Distributions

The decision-making process is typically based on a single set of assumptions under conditions of certainty, which, in fact, do not generally exist. The problem is usually handled with business judgment and a "feel" for risk and uncertainty tempering the quantitative analysis of relevant data. Much of the difficulty exists because few managers are willing to estimate a probability distribution. Instead, the manager estimates the future event as a single figure or "best guess." More attention is being given, however, to estimates of a range of possible events and the use of probability estimates to allow for risk and uncertainty in order to indicate the likelihood of the incurrence of these events and to calculate useful statistical data.

In decision-making analyses a wealth of reasonably reliable historical data permits the assignment of fairly objective probabilities, for example, of the rate of materials usage and the lead time for order filling in computing safety stock. In other cases, probability estimates may be much more subjective, resulting in a probability of occurrence for the most probable, pessimistic, and optimistic assumptions.

To illustrate the use of probability distribution data, assume that a company's contribution margin is $10 per unit sold. A study of a 40-month period indicates highly irregular sales and no specific sales trend. The computation on page 738 is based on the results of the study. Assuming that past experience is a reasonable basis for future prediction, each possible total contribution margin (conditional value) at each sales level is multiplied by its respective probability in order to compute an expected contribution margin (expected value).

UNIT SALES PER MONTH	NUMBER OF MONTHS	PROBABILITY
4,000	8	8/40 = .20
5,000	10	10/40 = .25
6,000	12	12/40 = .30
7,000	6	6/40 = .15
8,000	4	4/40 = .10
	40	1.00

UNIT SALES PER MONTH	CONTRIBUTION MARGIN PER UNIT	CONTRIBUTION MARGIN (CONDITIONAL VALUE)	PROBABILITY	EXPECTED CONTRIBUTION MARGIN
4,000	$10	$40,000	.20	$ 8,000
5,000	10	50,000	.25	12,500
6,000	10	60,000	.30	18,000
7,000	10	70,000	.15	10,500
8,000	10	80,000	.10	8,000
Expected contribution margin (expected value).......				$57,000

The expected contribution margin represents the average monthly contribution margin the company should expect, based on past experience. Management is also interested in the risk associated with the expected value. The degree of risk can be measured by computing the standard deviation of the expected value. The *standard deviation* provides a numerical measure of the scatter of the possible values around the average value. The larger the standard deviation, the greater the risk that the actual contribution margin will differ from the expected contribution margin. Computation of the standard deviation is illustrated as follows:

(1) CONTRIBUTION MARGIN (CONDITIONAL VALUE)	(2) DIFFERENCE FROM EXPECTED VALUE ($57,000)	(3) (2) SQUARED	(4) PROBABILITY	(5) (3) × (4)
$40,000	$-17,000	$289,000,000	.20	$ 57,800,000
50,000	-7,000	49,000,000	.25	12,250,000
60,000	3,000	9,000,000	.30	2,700,000
70,000	13,000	169,000,000	.15	25,350,000
80,000	23,000	529,000,000	.10	52,900,000
				$151,000,000

$$\text{Standard deviation} = \sqrt{\text{Col. 3} \times \text{Col. 4}} = \sqrt{\$151,000,000} = \underline{\$12,288}$$

If several expected values are involved, e.g., contribution margins for each of several products, their relative risks cannot be compared by simply looking at the standard deviation of each. This comparison problem can be resolved by computing the *coefficient of variation*, which relates the standard deviation for an estimate to the expected value of that estimate, thus allowing for differences in the relative size of expected values.

Using the illustration on the previous page, the coefficient of variation would be computed as follows:

$$\text{Coefficient of variation} = \frac{\text{Standard deviation}}{\text{Expected contribution margin (expected value)}} = \frac{\$12,288}{\$57,000} = \underline{\underline{.22}}$$

If another product is analyzed, resulting in an expected contribution margin of $100,000 and a standard deviation of $18,000, the relative risk is less, as indicated by the coefficient of variation of .18 ($18,000 ÷ $100,000), even though the standard deviation is greater.

In this illustration, the possible outcomes are relatively few and thus the probability distribution is discrete. When outcomes can take on any value within a certain range, however, a continuous probability distribution may be a better description of the nature of the problem. As a practical matter, the distribution of outcomes would be assumed to have some common (e.g., normal) shape which would again permit calculation of the parameters of the distribution of the outcomes, such as the mean and standard deviation.

Decision Trees. Alternatives and their expected results may be portrayed graphically with the decision tree, especially when sequential decisions are involved. The *decision tree* highlights decision points, alternatives, estimated results, related probabilities, and expected values. Normally, decision trees are restricted to relatively short-term situations involving one or two years. As more decision points and years are added, decision trees become complex. They can be applied to long-term decisions, but in such cases the time value of money should be included in the analysis.

As an example of the use of decision trees, Davis Recreation Enterprises is faced with the problem of deciding where to locate a ski resort. The search has been narrowed to two locations. One is within 50 kilometers (30 miles) of a large city. This accessibility makes the site attractive, but its location at an elevation 1 000 meters (3,000 feet) lower than the second site means that the annual snowfall will be less. The other location is 200 kilometers (125 miles) from the city, but the higher elevation will assure better skiing conditions and a longer season.

For each alternative, the conditional values and the expected value for the first year of operations are:

SKIING WEATHER CONDITIONS	CONTRIBUTION MARGIN (CONDITIONAL VALUE)	PROBABILITY	EXPECTED CONTRIBUTION MARGIN	
Close site:				
Favorable	$120,000	.6	$72,000	
Unfavorable	−20,000	.4	−8,000	
			$64,000	expected value
Distant site:				
Favorable	$ 80,000	.6	$48,000	
Unfavorable	15,000	.4	6,000	
			$54,000	expected value

A one-year decision tree based on these data would appear as follows:

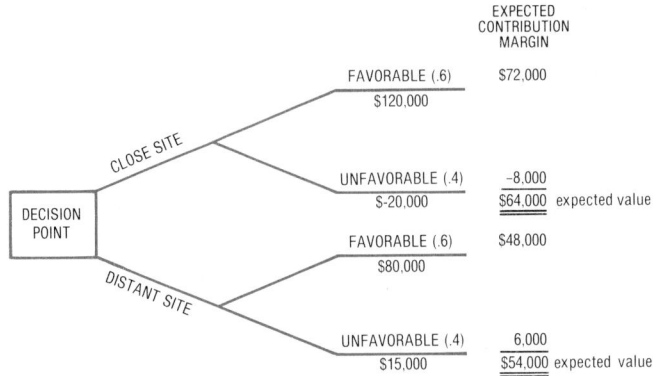

Based on the assumptions and estimates given in the illustration, the company should select the site close to the city, since its expected value is greater than that for the distant site ($64,000 compared to $54,000). However, the decision also will be affected by the decision maker's willingness to accept a negative contribution margin of $20,000 if conditions are unfavorable. The firm may not be in a financial condition that would permit accepting a negative result and, accordingly, may select the lower but safer return of the distant site.

More complex decision trees can be constructed to incorporate additional years and sequential decisions. All sequential decisions are affected by the initial decision. If decisions relating to the second year and beyond can be delayed until more knowledge is available, some of the uncertainty can be eliminated. For example, for the second year, an additional ski lift may be installed at either the close or the distant site, provided favorable skiing weather conditions occurred the first year. If the first year's weather conditions were unfavorable, then funds will be insufficient to permit installing the additional lift, regardless of which site was originally chosen. The decision tree could be extended for the second year with the consideration of (1) a sequential decision as to whether to install an additional lift, assuming favorable weather conditions occurred the first year and (2) continuation through the second year with the existing lift, assuming unfavorable first-year weather conditions.

Monte Carlo Simulation. Monte Carlo simulation is a procedure that utilizes statistical sampling techniques in order to obtain a probabilistic approximation of some mathematical or physical problem. The sampling may be drawn from historical data or from estimates. The method is computer oriented, because without the speed of the computer, most Monte Carlo simulation models become impractical.[4]

---

[4]For a comprehensive discussion of Monte Carlo simulation, see James E. Shamblin and G. T. Stevens, Jr., *Operations Research: A Fundamental Approach* (New York: McGraw-Hill Book Company, 1974), pp. 156–182.

OTHER COST CONCEPTS

In differential cost analysis, care must be taken to avoid action to maximize short-run profits if such action is likely to be detrimental to the overall company profit objective of long-run profit maximization. Walter B. McFarland issued this warning:

> Because overall company profit objectives are usually long-run objectives, it seems advisable to consider long-run implications of decisions which are intended to maximize short-run profits. To illustrate, addition of a product for the purpose of utilizing capacity which is currently excess may preclude more profitable use of the same capacity at a later date. Likewise, at a time when capacity is temporarily inadequate to meet sales demand, actions to maximize short-run profits (e.g., raising profits, dropping low margin products or customers) may be inconsistent with long-run profit objectives.[5]

Not only which but how much information to collect and analyze must also be determined. Too much information is an inefficient use of resources; too little may increase the likelihood of a poor decision. Ideally, one should obtain information if the anticipated value exceeds its anticipated cost. The question centers around obtaining an additional amount of information; and, again, the information should be sought as long as the expected differential information value exceeds its differential cost.[6] Of course, management may be forced to make a decision with less information than it would like simply because there is insufficient time to acquire more information. In some cases information may not be available even though cost-and-time constraints would permit its collection.

To enable management to have useful and meaningful cost data with which to maximize long-run profits, several other cost terms, concepts, and classifications, in addition to differential cost, must be incorporated in the decision-making process. These other costs include opportunity costs, imputed costs, out-of-pocket costs, relevant and irrelevant costs, and sunk costs.

Opportunity Costs

Opportunity costs are the measurable value of an opportunity bypassed by rejecting an alternative use of resources. In the third application of the refinery illustration (page 735), a decision had to be made as to how much profit was required to justify the purchase of the cylinder stock. The concept of opportunity costs enters into the final decision. If the available capacity could be used more profitably for another purpose, then perhaps the intended purchase should not be made. The decision to employ or not to employ the

---

[5]Walter B. McFarland, *Concepts for Management Accounting* (New York: National Association of Accountants, 1966), p. 55.
[6]For further discussion and a quantitative illustration, see ''American Accounting Association Report of Committee on Managerial Decision Models,'' *The Accounting Review*, Supplement to Vol. XLIV (1969), pp. 58–64.

available capacity in favor of one or the other alternative in the future suggests that opportunity costs are also a type of future costs.

Other examples may aid in a better understanding of this concept. The opportunity cost of using a machine to produce one product is the sacrifice of possible earnings from other products that might be produced using the machine. The opportunity costs of the time that owners put into their own businesses are the salaries they could earn elsewhere. Opportunity costs require the measurement of sacrifices associated with alternatives. If a decision requires no sacrifice, there is no opportunity cost.

Imputed Costs

Imputed costs are hypothetical costs representing the cost or value of a resource measured by its use value. Interest on invested capital, rental value of company-owned properties, and salaries of owner-operators of sole proprietorships or partnerships are types of imputed costs. Imputed costs do not involve actual cash outlay, they are not recorded in the books, and they are not considered in a company's regular cost and profit calculations. However, in making comparisons and in reaching a decision, the inclusion of imputed costs is relevant and important.

In contract costing, the Cost Accounting Standards Board provides for inclusion of the imputed cost of capital committed to facilities. Contractors must use an interest rate prescribed by the CASB. The Board's position is that this cost, even though imputed, is relevant for government contract costing. They assert that if contract costs do not include a measure of the imputed cost of money, the result is that cost measurements have made no distinction between contracts with equal amounts of total incurred cost but with vast differences in amounts of facility investments. The imputed interest rate is intended to compensate for the risk-free cost of money and for the impact of inflation. Investment in working capital is excluded, but the CASB is studying techniques for measuring and allocating this cost.[7]

Out-Of-Pocket Costs

While imputed costs do not lead to cash outlays, *out-of-pocket costs* do, either immediately or at some future date. These costs are also often identified as variable or direct costs, because they are the costs relevant to any decision when the total product costs are not pertinent. This cost concept is significant in management's deciding whether a particular venture will at least return the cash expenditures caused by the contemplated business undertaking.

Relevant and Irrelevant Costs

In many instances throughout this text the terms "relevant" or "irrelevant" have been used. The dictionary defines *relevant* as "bearing upon, or properly applying to, the case in hand; of a nature tending to prove or disprove the matters in issue; pertinent." The application of this definition to the

---

[7]*Standards, Rules and Regulations, Part 414*, "Cost of Money as an Element of the Cost of Facilities Capital" (Washington, D.C.: Cost Accounting Standards Board, 1976).

purposes of cost accounting indicates that no single cost figure and concept fits all managerial demands, actions, and decisions. What is necessary is the selection of the appropriate decision model and the kinds of information most useful in implementing the selected model. Differences in the purposes must be recognized and the cost tailored accordingly.

The need for different costs for different purposes is illustrated in Chapter 22 in the discussion of absorption costing and direct costing. This chapter's discussion of cost terms in connection with decision making expresses the relevancy or irrelevancy of a certain cost. Every phase and every decision requires close attention to the inclusion or exclusion of pertinent costs and revenues. The term "relevant," however, is more a statement of the problem than its solution. Costs must be (1) classified in an appropriate manner in order to allow their immediate application to as many situations as feasible, (2) observed and tested in their applicability to a given situation, and (3) perhaps discarded in favor of future costs to permit a comparative analysis for the selection of one alternative in contrast with others.

Sunk Costs

The chances for recovery of expenditures made in the past are almost nil. *Sunk costs* are these irrecoverable costs in a given situation. The meaning of a sunk cost will become particularly apparent when a decision must be reached regarding the exchange of an old asset for a new asset. (See Chapter 26 dealing with investment analysis.) The undepreciated book balance of the old asset is a sunk cost and entirely irrelevant to the decision-making process except in computing the income tax liability; however, the current exchange value is relevant.

Accountants have been reluctant to exclude sunk costs from their traditional mode of analysis. Although sunk costs play a part in reaching the decision to abandon or continue operations, the essential feature of sunk costs in making managerial decisions is that they may be irrelevant either in whole or in part.

DISCUSSION QUESTIONS

1. Suggest a broad definition of the term "differential cost." What other terms are often used and by whom?

2. Distinguish between marginal cost and marginal costing (or direct costing).

3. Differential costs have also been termed alternative costs. In what connections are such alternative costs desirable?

4. Differential costs do not correspond to any possible accounting category. Explain.

5. How does the flexible budget assist in the preparation of differential cost analyses?

6. Differential cost studies deal with alternatives that mean not only increased business but also decreased business or even shutdown conditions. Explain.

7. Why is the variable cost so important in differential cost studies?

8. Discuss explicitly the difference between an analysis based on historical cost data and one based on differential cost procedures. In what respect are they alike? Why is differential cost analysis of greater value to management?

9. When differentially-costed products are marketed, close watch must be kept on their sales trend. Why?

10. Define expected value.

11. Why is the standard deviation of the expected value useful?

12. How is the coefficient of variation used in evaluating the standard deviation?

13. What is the nature of decision trees and how are they used?

14. What is the purpose of Monte Carlo simulation?

15. Define opportunity costs.

16. What are imputed costs?

17. What are sunk costs?

18. Select the answer which best completes the statement:

(a) As part of the data presented in support of a proposal to increase the production of clock radios, the sales manager of Commerce Electronics reported the total additional cost required for the proposed production level. The increase in total cost is known as: (1) controllable cost; (2) differential cost; (3) opportunity cost; (4) out-of-pocket cost.

(b) An item whose entire amount is usually a differential cost is: (1) factory overhead; (2) direct cost; (3) conversion cost; (4) period cost.

(c) Pena Company temporarily has unused production capacity. The idle plant facilities can be used to manufacture a low-margin item. The low-margin item should be produced if it can be sold for more than its: (1) fixed cost; (2) variable cost; (3) variable cost plus any opportunity cost of the idle facilities; (4) indirect cost plus any opportunity cost of the idle facilities.

(d) The effect on a company's profit of discontinuing a department with a contribution to overhead of $16,000 and allocated overhead of $32,000, of which $14,000 cannot be eliminated, would be to: (1) decrease profit by $2,000; (2) decrease profit by $18,000; (3) increase profit by $2,000; (4) increase profit by $16,000.

(e) The use of expected value in evaluating alternative courses of action attempts to deal with: (1) centralization; (2) uncertainty; (3) goal congruence; (4) motivation.

(f) An investor can sell an investment now for $10,000. Another alternative is to hold the investment three days, after which it can be sold, based on the following sales prices and probabilities:

SALES PRICE	PROBABILITY
$ 5,000	.4
8,000	.2
12,000	.3
30,000	.1

Using probability theory, the most reasonable statement is: (1) Hold the investment three days because the expected value of holding exceeds the current price. (2) Hold the investment three days because of the chance of getting $30,000 for it. (3) Sell the investment now because the current sales price exceeds the expected value of holding. (4) Sell the investment now because there is a 60% chance that the sales price will fall in three days.

(g) The Duke Company owns equipment that is used to manufacture important parts for its production process. The company plans to sell the equipment for $10,000 and to select one of the following alternatives: acquire new equipment for $80,000, or purchase the important parts from an outside company at $4 per part. The company should analyze the alternatives by comparing the cost of manufacturing the parts: (1) plus $80,000 with the cost of buying the parts less $10,000; (2) with the cost of buying the parts less $10,000; (3) less $10,000 with the cost of buying the parts; (4) with the cost of buying the parts.

(h) The measurable value of an alternative use of resources is referred to as: (1) opportunity cost; (2) imputed cost; (3) differential cost; (4) sunk cost.

(i) An opportunity cost is usually: (1) relevant, but is not part of traditional accounting records; (2) not relevant, but is part of traditional accounting records; (3) relevant, and is part of traditional accounting records; (4) not relevant, and is not part of traditional accounting records.

(j) Costs that do not appear in accounting records and that do not require dollar outlays but do involve a foregone opportunity by the entity whose costs are being measured are: (1) conversion costs; (2) differential costs; (3) imputed costs; (4) prime costs.

(k) In the development of accounting data for decision-making purposes, relevant costs are defined as: (1) future costs which will differ under each alternative course of action; (2) the change in prime cost under each alternative course of action; (3) standard costs which are developed by time-and-motion-study techniques because of their relevance to managerial control; (4) historical costs which are the best available basis for estimating future costs.

(l) A cost incurred in the past and hence irrelevant for current decision making is a: (1) fixed cost; (2) discretionary cost; (3) sunk cost; (4) direct cost.

(AICPA adapted)

EXERCISES

1. Differential cost of alternative capacities. The Wood River plant of the Union Company has a normal capacity of 90,000 units per month. Monthly production costs are $12 variable per unit and $240,000 fixed. By increasing the fixed cost $10,000 a month, the plant can produce 95,000 units.

Required:
    (1) Differential cost of the production between 80% and 90% of normal capacity.
    (2) Differential cost of producing the 5,000 units above normal capacity.
    (3) Per unit total production cost of the 5,000 units, rounded to the nearest cent.
    (4) Per unit differential production cost of the 5,000 units.

2. New product analysis. Perkins Company is considering the introduction of a new product which will be manufactured in an existing plant; however, new equipment costing $150,000 with a useful life of five years (no salvage value) will be necessary. The space in the existing plant to be used for the new product is currently used for warehousing. When the new product takes over the warehouse space, on which the actual depreciation is $20,000, Perkins Company will rent warehouse space at an annual cost of $25,000. An accounting study produces the following estimates of differential revenue and expense on an average annual basis:

Sales	$500,000
Cost of merchandise sold (excluding depreciation)	385,000
Depreciation of equipment (straight-line)	30,000
Marketing expenses	10,000

The company requires an average annual rate of return of 11% (after income tax) on the average investment in proposals. The effective income tax rate is 46%. (Ignore the time value of money.)

Required:
(1) The average annual differential cost for the first five years (including income tax) which must be considered in evaluating this decision.
(2) The minimum annual net income needed to meet the company's requirement for this proposal.
(3) The estimated annual differential income (after allowing for return on investment in new equipment) resulting from introduction of the new product.
(4) The estimated differential cash flow during the third year.   (AICPA adapted)

3. Analysis of proposed new business. The Saugus Insecticide Company is currently producing and selling 30 000 kilograms of Sta Ded monthly. This volume is 70% of capacity for Sta Ded. A wholesaler outside the Saugus marketing area offers to buy 5 000 kilograms of this product per month on a two-year contract at $1.80 per kilogram, provided the present pinkish color can be changed to green. The product will be marketed under the wholesaler's brand name.

To change the color, a special mixing machine will need to be purchased at a cost of $3,000, but it will have no value at the end of the two-year contract period. Ingredients to change the color in the finished product will cost $.01 per kilogram.

Marketing expenses will not be increased if the new business is accepted, but additional administrative expenses of $150 per month are estimated. No additional cost for supervision or property tax is contemplated. Additional payroll taxes will be $210.

A monthly income statement for the current operations follows:

Saugus Insecticide Company
Income Statement
For Month Ended _____

Sales		$72,000
Cost to manufacture:		
Direct materials	$18,000	
Direct labor	15,000	
Factory overhead:		
Indirect labor	6,000	
Supervisory labor	4,000	
Power ($180 fixed)	780	
Supplies	600	
Maintenance and repair	810	
Depreciation	3,000	
Insurance	210	
Property tax	125	
Payroll taxes	1,250	
Cost of goods produced and sold		49,775
Gross profit		$22,225
Marketing expenses	$11,000	
Administrative expenses	4,500	15,500
Income before income tax		$ 6,725

Required: Differential cost analysis to show whether the company should accept the proposed new business.

4. Acceptance of a special order. Although the Missouri Company has the capacity to produce 16,000 units per month, current plans call for monthly production and sales of only 10,000 units at $15 each. Costs per unit are as follows:

Direct materials	$ 5.00
Direct labor	3.00
Variable factory overhead	.75
Fixed factory overhead	1.50
Variable marketing expense	.25
Fixed administrative expense	1.00
	$11.50

Required:
(1) Recommendation as to whether the company should accept a special order for 4,000 units @ $10.
(2) The maximum price the Missouri Company should be willing to pay an outside supplier who is interested in manufacturing this product.
(3) The unit cost figure the company would use in costing inventory, using direct costing.
(4) The effect on the monthly contribution margin if the sales price were reduced to $14, resulting in a 10% increase in sales volume.

(CGAA adapted)

5. Choice of order to accept. As a result of an expansion program, Whitworth Enterprises, Inc., has excess capacity of 20,000 machine hours, which is expected to be absorbed by the domestic market in a few years.

The company has received inquiries from two companies located in another country. One offers to buy 210,000 units of Product F-W at $.60 per unit; the second offers to buy 300,000 units of Product D-FW at $.70 per unit. Whitworth Enterprises can accept only one of these two offers.

The standard costs for these products are as follows:

	F-W	D-FW
Materials	$.25	$.35
Direct labor	.10	.12
Factory overhead	.20	.28
Total standard cost	$.55	$.75

Factory overhead is applied on a machine-hour basis at $5.60 per hour; 75% of the factory overhead is estimated to be fixed. No marketing and administrative expenses would be applicable to either order; transportation charges are to be paid by the buyer.

Required: The order that should be accepted.

(CGAA adapted)

6. Differential cost analysis for special order. The Detroit sales manager of Brolin Manufacturing, Inc., called the home office stating that a special order involving 3,600,000 gross of Product A could be obtained if it could be sold for 12½% off the list price.

Management contacted the cost analyst, who sent the analysis shown on page 748 to the vice-president in charge of sales with a notation that the profit on this order would be $167,400 ($405,000–$237,600). The vice-president in charge of sales asked for an explanation of this analysis. The cost analyst said that on the basis of the 19–– forecast the company would be operating below its factory overhead absorption volume of 70% of capacity. The special order being above this predetermined volume would cause a swing from underabsorbed to overabsorbed fixed expenses.

Required: An analysis that could have saved the cost analyst much time and have been more helpful and meaningful to the sales executive.

Special Order Cost Analysis

	19-- FORECAST 60% OF CAPACITY		SPECIAL ORDER ADDED TO 19-- FORECAST 80% OF CAPACITY	
	Rate	Amount	Rate	Amount
Sales revenue (10,800,000 gross)	$.140	$1,512,000	$.1400	$1,512,000
Special order (3,600,000 gross).			.1225	441,000
Total.......................................		$1,512,000		$1,953,000
Weighted average rate........	$.140		$.1356	
Standard costs:				
Direct materials.......................	$.040	$ 432,000	$.0400	$ 576,000
Direct labor............................	.021	226,800	.0210	302,400
Variable factory overhead	.010	108,000	.0100	144,000
Fixed factory overhead...........	.020	216,000	.0200	288,000
Variable marketing expenses.	.005	54,000	.0050	72,000
Fixed marketing expenses	.009	97,200	.0090	129,600
Fixed administrative expenses	.007	75,600	.0070	100,800
Total standard cost....................	$.112	$1,209,600	$.1120	$1,612,800
Profit at standard cost...............	$.028	$ 302,400	$.0236	$ 340,200
Volume variances:				
Factory overhead		$ (36,000) unfav.		$ 36,000 fav.
Marketing expenses................		(16,200) unfav.		16,200 fav.
Administrative expenses........		(12,600) unfav.		12,600 fav.
Profit at actual cost		$ 237,600		$ 405,000

7. Make-or-buy decision. Standard costs and other data for two component parts used by Griffon Electronics are presented below:

	PART A4	PART B5
Direct materials...	$ .40	$ 8.00
Direct labor...	1.00	4.70
Factory overhead	4.00	2.00
Unit standard cost...	$5.40	$14.70
Units needed per year..	6,000	8,000
Machine hours per unit	4	2
Unit cost if purchased	$5	$15

In past years, Griffon Electronics has manufactured all of its required components; however, in the current year only 30,000 hours of otherwise idle machine time can be devoted to component production. Accordingly, some of the parts must be purchased from outside suppliers. In producing parts, factory overhead is applied at $1 per standard machine hour. The fixed capacity cost, which will not be affected by any make-or-buy decision, represents 60% of the applied factory overhead.

Required:
  (1) The relevant unit production costs to be considered in the make-or-buy decision to schedule machine time.
  (2) The units of A4 and B5 that Griffon should produce if the allocation of machine time is based on potential cost savings per machine hour.   (AICPA adapted)

8. Make-or-buy decision. Buck Company manufactures Part 1700 for use in its assembly operation. Costs per unit for 5,000 units of Part 1700 are:

Direct materials...	$ 2
Direct labor..	12
Variable factory overhead	5
Fixed factory overhead..	7
Total unit cost..	$26

Hollow Company has offered to sell Buck 5,000 units of Part 1700 for $27 each. If Buck accepts, some of the facilities presently used to manufacture Part 1700 could be used to help with the manufacture of Part 1211, thus saving $40,000 in relevant cost in its manufacture and eliminating $3 per unit of the fixed factory overhead applied to Part 1700.

Required: Make-or-buy decision analysis.

(AICPA adapted)

9. Product alternatives. Schmidt Company sells two products with the following characteristics:

	PRODUCT A	PRODUCT B
Quantity sold	100,000 units	50,000 units
Standard cost per unit:		
Fixed	$10	$20
Variable	10	40
	$20	$60
Sales price per unit	$30	$54

Required:

(1) The profit per unit and in total for each product, assuming that the firm operates at normal capacity and that the standard cost and the actual cost are the same.

(2) A decision as to whether the firm should continue its sales of both products, assuming that the fixed cost (in total) will remain the same.

(3) A decision to either drop Product B or add Product C, assuming that facilities presently committed to B alternatively could be assigned to C, that the two products are mutually exclusive, and that C has the following characteristics:

Quantity sold	25,000 units
Standard cost per unit:	
Fixed	$40
Variable	20
	$60
Sales price per unit	$50

(4) The opportunity cost associated with Product B and with Product C.

10. Proposed new equipment rental vs product discontinuance. Ocean Company manufactures and sells three different products — Ex, Why, and Zee. Projected income statements by product line for the year ending December 31, 19-- are presented below:

	EX	WHY	ZEE	TOTAL
Unit sales	10,000	500,000	125,000	635,000
Revenue	$925,000	$1,000,000	$575,000	$2,500,000
Variable cost of units sold	$285,000	$ 350,000	$150,000	$ 785,000
Fixed cost of units sold	304,200	289,000	166,800	760,000
Gross profit	$335,800	$ 361,000	$258,200	$ 955,000
Variable marketing and administrative expenses	$270,000	$ 200,000	$ 80,000	$ 550,000
Fixed marketing and administrative expenses	125,800	136,000	78,200	340,000
Income (loss) before income tax	$ (60,000)	$ 25,000	$100,000	$ 65,000

Production costs are similar for all three products. The fixed marketing and administrative expenses are allocated to products in proportion to revenue. The fixed cost of units sold is allocated to products by various allocation bases, such as square feet for factory rent and machine hours for repairs.

Management is concerned about the loss for Product Ex and is considering two alternative courses of corrective action.

Alternative A:

Ocean would rent some new machinery for the production of Ex. Management expects that the new machinery would reduce the variable production cost so that the total variable cost for Ex would be 52% of its revenue. The new machinery would increase the total fixed cost allocated to Ex to $480,000 per year. No additional fixed cost would be allocated to Why or Zee.

Alternative B:

Ocean would discontinue the manufacture of Ex. Sales prices of Why and Zee would remain constant. Management expects that Zee production and revenue would increase by 50%. Discontinuance of Ex would reduce the fixed cost (wages) attributable to Ex by $30,000 per year. The remaining fixed cost includes $155,000 of building rent expense per year. The space previously used for Ex can be rented to an outside organization for $157,500 per year.

Required: The effect of Alternative A and Alternative B before income tax.

(AICPA adapted)

11. Sell or process further. In producing Ergon, a by-product, Bygon, is also made and is sold for $20 per ton. The company is considering combining additional chemicals with Bygon to produce low-grade fertilizer, to be called Exton, and sold to wholesalers at $12 per 100 pounds. The chemicals would be added to Bygon at the rate of 40 pounds per 100 pounds of by-product. Additional costs would be:

Chemicals...	$7.00 per 100 pounds of input
Direct labor	3.00 per 100 pounds of output
Variable factory overhead.......................................	1.50 per 100 pounds of output

While present facilities are adequate to produce Exton, $40,000 in additional annual promotion and advertising costs would be incurred. The current volume of Bygon is 2,500,000 pounds, or 1,250 tons.

Required: Recommendation to sell Bygon or process further to produce Exton.

(CMA adapted)

12. Sell or process further. From a particular joint process, Watkins Company produces three products — X, Y, and Z. Each product may be sold at the point of split-off or processed further. Additional processing requires no special facilities, and production costs of further processing are entirely variable and traceable to the products involved. During the past year, these products were processed beyond split-off. The joint production cost for the year was $60,000. Sales value and costs needed to evaluate Watkins' current production policy follow:

PRODUCT	UNITS PRODUCED	SALES VALUE AT SPLIT-OFF	ADDITIONAL COST AND THE NEW SALES VALUE IF PROCESSED FURTHER	
			Sales Value	*Added Cost*
X	6,000	$25,000	$42,000	$9,000
Y	4,000	41,000	45,000	7,000
Z	2,000	24,000	32,000	8,000

The joint cost is allocated to the products in proportion to the relative physical volume of output.

Required:
(1) The unit production cost most relevant to a sell-or-process-further decision for units of Product Z.
(2) The products that the company should subject to additional processing in order to maximize profits.

(AICPA adapted)

13. Choice of production method. PZP Company is evaluating the use of AZ-17 Photo Resist for the manufacture of printed circuit boards. The major advantages in the utilization of this process versus the present silk-screen method are:

(a) Anticipated reduced manufacturing cycle and cost due to elimination of the need for silk circuit screens and shorter operator time to produce circuit boards.
(b) Improved ease of registration between front and back patterns.
(c) The ability to achieve finer line widths and closer spacing between circuit paths.

The proposed AZ-17 process is described as follows:

(a) Fabricate through the completion of the drilling and copper plating of inside holes.
(b) Pressure spray AZ-17 Photo Resist on one side, oven bake for 10 minutes, and repeat for other side.
(c) Use the photo negative and expose each side for seven minutes in a Nu-Arc Printer.
(d) Develop in AZ-17 Developer and proceed through normal operations for making printed circuit board. Total direct labor time to expose a printed wiring board is 30 minutes.

The original silk-screen method uses a wire mesh stencil film, screening ink, and frames. The direct labor time to prepare the screen for each circuit board is 1½ hours. The direct labor time to screen patterns on the printed wire board is 20 minutes.

The hourly direct labor rate is $6.50. The monthly cost for materials and for equipment rental and operation needed for the proposed process is $4,000 greater than for the silk-screen method, excluding direct labor.

The company manufactures 20,000 circuit boards annually.

Required: The annual savings or added cost from changing from the silk-screen method to the new AZ-17 process. (Round off all computations to the nearest dollar.)

14. Expected value of probability distribution. The Stat Company has the following information concerning the demand for one of its products:

Units Demanded	Probability of Unit Demand	Contribution Margin of Units Demanded
0	.10	–0–
1	.15	$1
2	.20	2
3	.40	3
4	.10	4
5	.05	5

Required: The expected contribution margin.   (AICPA adapted)

15. Comparative cost study with probabilities. The owner of the Delicious Donut Shop must decide between the rental of two types of donut-making machines. Machine A, an inexpensive economy model, rents for $1,000 per month, but the variable production cost is $.025 per donut. Machine B rents for $3,000 per month, but the variable production cost is only $.01 per donut. Monthly demand varies between 100,000 and 190,000 donuts according to the following probabilities:

Demand	Probability
100,000	.12
120,000	.17
150,000	.41
170,000	.24
190,000	.06

Required: A cost comparison study of the two machines.

(CGAA adapted)

PROBLEMS

25-1. Acceptance of special order. Akpan company manufactures a product which sells for a well-established price of $15. Under present business conditions, the company is operating at 40% of capacity with production and sales of 6,000 units per month.

An analysis of costs for a recent month shows:

Direct labor*	$13,000
Superintendent's salary*	2,200
Depreciation of building (straight-line)	2,000
Direct materials	8,700
Heat and light	400
Indirect labor*	2,800
Miscellaneous supplies	1,000
Depreciation of machinery (straight-line)	4,500
Machinery repairs	600
Property tax	800
Fire insurance	100
Miscellaneous	1,400
Total	$37,500

*Includes payroll taxes

The total marketing expenses were $30,000, which included $1,800 for packing and shipping. The sales on the special order would require a similar unit cost for packing and shipping. The total administrative and general costs were $4,200.

An offer has been received from a large chain store to purchase 72,000 units to be shipped in equal amounts each month during the coming year. These units would be manufactured with slight immaterial modifications under the chain store's label. The price offered was $8 per unit.

Akpan management does not expect any improvement in business conditions and feels that the chain store's sales will not affect Akpan's sales. The management does not believe that it can afford to accept this offer, feeling that it would reduce the present operating profit.

Required: An analysis comparing the operating results if the order is or is not accepted, assuming that the various items are either completely fixed or variable, depending upon the dominant characteristics of each item and the data given.

(CGAA adapted)

25-2. Differential and opportunity costs. George Jackson owns and operates a small machine shop manufacturing (1) a standard product available from many other similar businesses and (2) products to customer order. An accountant prepared the following income statement for the year:

	CUSTOM SALES	STANDARD SALES	TOTAL
Sales	$50,000	$25,000	$75,000
Materials	$10,000	$ 8,000	$18,000
Labor	20,000	9,000	29,000
Depreciation	6,300	3,600	9,900
Power	700	400	1,100
Rent	6,000	1,000	7,000
Heat and light	600	100	700
Other	400	900	1,300
Total cost	$44,000	$23,000	$67,000
Income before income tax	$ 6,000	$ 2,000	$ 8,000

Depreciation is for machines used in the respective product lines. Power is apportioned on the estimate of power consumption. Rent is for the building space that has been leased for ten years at $7,000 per year. Rent and heat and light are apportioned to the product lines based on amount of occupied floor space. All other costs are variable expenses identified with the product line causing them.

A valued custom-parts customer asks Jackson to manufacture 5,000 special units. The machine shop is working at capacity, and Jackson would have to discontinue the manufacture of other items in order to take this special order. He cannot renege on custom orders already agreed to but could reduce the standard product output by about one half for one year while producing the specially requested custom part. The customer is willing to pay $7 for each part. The materials cost would be about $2 per unit while the labor would be $3.60 per unit. Jackson will have to spend $2,000 for a special device that will be discarded when the job is completed.

Required:
  (1) The following costs related to the 5,000-unit custom order: (a) differential cost of the order; (b) full cost of the order; (c) opportunity cost of taking the order.
  (2) An explanation as to why Jackson should accept or reject the order.   (CMA adapted)

25-3. Differential cost analysis of special order proposal. Anchor Company manufactures several styles of jewelry cases. Management estimates that during the third quarter of this year the company will be operating at 80% of capacity. Because the company desires a higher utilization of plant capacity, it is willing to consider two special order inquiries. The first order is from JCP, Inc., which would like to order a jewelry case similar to one of Anchor's but to be marketed under JCP's own label. JCP has offered Anchor $5.75 each for 20,000 cases to be shipped by October 1. The cost data for the Anchor jewelry case, which would be similar to the specifications of the JCP special order, are:

Regular sales price per case..	$9.00
Cost per case:	
Direct materials	$2.50
Direct labor (.5 hrs @ $6)...	3.00
Factory overhead (.25 machine hrs. @ $4).............................	1.00
Total cost	$6.50

According to the specifications provided by JCP, Inc., the special-order case requires less expensive materials. Consequently, the materials will cost only $2.25 per case. Management has estimated that the remaining cost, labor time, and machine time will be the same as for the Anchor case.

The second special order, submitted by the Krage Co. for 7,500 cases at $7.50 each, would be marketed under the Krage label and must be shipped by October 1. However, the Krage case is different from any in the Anchor line. The estimated costs per case are:

Direct materials...	$3.25
Direct labor (.5 hrs. @ $6)	3.00
Factory overhead (.5 machine hrs. @ $4)	2.00
Total cost...	$8.25

To manufacture these cases, Anchor will incur $1,500 in additional setup cost and will have to purchase a $2,500 special device which will be discarded after the special order is completed.

The Anchor manufacturing capabilities are limited to the total machine hours available. The plant capacity under normal operations is 90,000 machine hours per year or 7,500 machine hours per month. The budgeted fixed factory overhead for the current year is $216,000. Factory overhead cost is applied to production on the basis of machine hours at $4 per hour.

Anchor will have the entire third quarter to work on the special orders. Management does not expect any repeat sales to be generated from either special order. Company practice precludes Anchor from subcontracting any portion of an order when special orders are not expected to generate repeat sales.

Required: An analysis and decision as to whether Anchor Company should accept either special order.
                                                                                                    (CMA adapted)

25-4. Make-or-buy decision. Vernom Corporation, a manufacturer of a highly successful line of summer lotions and insect repellents, has decided to diversify in order to stabilize sales throughout the year. A natural area for the company to consider is the production of winter lotions and creams to prevent dry and chapped skin.

After considerable research, a winter products line has been developed. However, because of the conservative nature of the company's management, Vernom's president has decided to introduce only one new product for the coming winter. If the product is a success, further expansion in future years will be initiated.

The product selected, Chap-Off, is a lip balm in a lipstick-type tube that will be sold to wholesalers in boxes of 24 tubes at $8 per box. Because of available capacity, no additional fixed cost will be incurred to produce Chap-Off. However, a fair share of the company's present fixed cost, $100,000, will be allocated to Chap-Off.

Using the estimated sales and production of 100,000 boxes of Chap-Off as the standard volume, the Accounting Department developed these costs per box:

Direct labor	$2.00
Direct materials	3.00
Total factory overhead	1.50
Total	$6.50

The Vernom Corporation has approached a cosmetics manufacturer to discuss the possibility of purchasing empty tubes for Chap-Off at $.90 per 24 tubes. If the cosmetics manufacturer accepts this purchase proposal, it is estimated that Vernom's direct labor and variable factory overhead costs would be reduced by 10% and that the direct materials cost would be reduced by 20%.

Required:
  (1) A decision as to whether the Vernom Corporation should manufacture or purchase the empty tubes.
  (2) The maximum purchase price acceptable to the Vernom Corporation for the cosmetic manufacturer's empty tubes.
  (3) A decision as to whether the Vernom Corporation should manufacture or purchase the empty tubes, assuming that revised estimates show the sales volume at 125,000 boxes instead of 100,000 boxes. At this new volume, additional equipment — at an annual rental of $10,000 — must be acquired to manufacture the empty tubes.
  (4) The answer to (3) if the company has the option of manufacturing and purchasing the empty tubes at the same time, assuming that 100,000 boxes are to be manufactured and the remainder purchased.
  (5) The nonquantifiable factors to be considered in determining whether the Vernom Corporation should manufacture or purchase the empty tubes.   (CMA adapted)

25-5. Make-or-buy decision involving alternative use of facilities. Virginia Company has manufactured Products P and Z at its Richmond plant for several years. On March 31, 19A, P was dropped from the product line. The company manufactures and sells 50,000 units of Z annually, and this is not expected to change. The unit direct materials and direct labor costs for Z are $12 and $7, respectively.

The Richmond plant is in a leased building renting for $75,000 annually, with the lease expiring on June 30, 19E. The lease provides the company with the right of sublet and with all nonremovable leasehold improvements reverting to the lessor. At the termination of the lease, the company intends to close the Richmond plant, scrapping all of the equipment.

Product P has been manufactured on two assembly lines occupying 25% of the Richmond plant. As of June 30, 19A, the assembly lines will have a book value of $135,000 and a remaining useful life of seven years. This is the only portion of the Richmond plant available for alternative uses.

The company uses one unit of D to produce one unit of Z. Product D is purchased under a contract requiring a minimum annual purchase of 5,000 units. The contract expires on June 30, 19E. A list of D unit costs follows:

ANNUAL PURCHASES (IN UNITS)	UNIT COST
5,000–7,499	$2.00
7,500–19,999	1.95
20,000–34,999	1.80
35,000–99,999	1.65
100,000–250,000	1.35

Alternatives are available for using the space previously used to manufacture P. Some may be used in combination. All can be implemented by June 30, 19A. If no action is taken, the Richmond plant is expected to operate profitably, and factory overhead is not expected to differ materially from past years when P was manufactured. The alternatives are to:

(a) Sell the two P assembly lines for $70,000 to a purchaser who will buy only if the equipment can be acquired from both lines. The purchaser will pay all removal and transportation costs.

(b) Sublet the floor space for an annual rental of $12,100 with a lease requirement that the equipment be removed at a nominal cost and that leasehold improvements costing $38,000 be installed. (Annual indirect costs are expected to increase by $3,500 as a result of the sublease and are to be borne by the Virginia Company.)

(c) Convert one or both P assembly lines to manufacture D at a cost of $45,500 for each line. The converted lines will have a remaining useful life of ten years. Each modified line can manufacture any number of units of D up to a maximum of 37,000 units at unit direct materials and direct labor costs of $.10 and $.25, respectively. Annual factory overhead is expected to increase from $550,000 to $562,000 if one line is converted and to $566,000 if both lines are converted.

Required: A schedule analyzing the best utilization of the following alternatives for the four years ending June 30, 19E (ignore income tax and the time value of money):

(1) Continue to purchase D; sell equipment; rent space.
(2) Continue to purchase D; sell equipment.
(3) Manufacture D on two assembly lines; purchase D as needed.
(4) Manufacture D on one assembly line; purchase D as needed.

(AICPA adapted)

25-6. Evaluating manufacturing alternatives. Arcadia Corporation has its home office in Ohio and leases factory buildings in Texas, Montana, and Maine, all of which produce the same product. Projection of operations for 19B, the forthcoming year, are:

	TOTAL	TEXAS	MONTANA	MAINE
Sales	$4,400,000	$2,200,000	$1,400,000	$800,000
Fixed costs:				
Factory	$1,100,000	$ 560,000	$ 280,000	$260,000
Administration	350,000	210,000	110,000	30,000
Variable cost	1,450,000	665,000	425,000	360,000
Allocated home office cost	500,000	225,000	175,000	100,000
Total	$3,400,000	$1,660,000	$ 990,000	$750,000
Income before income tax	$1,000,000	$ 540,000	$ 410,000	$ 50,000

The sales price per unit is $25.

Because of the marginal results of operations of the factory in Maine, Arcadia has decided to cease operations and sell that factory's machinery and equipment by the end of 19A. Arcadia expects that the proceeds from the sale of these assets would be greater than their book value and would cover all termination costs.

Arcadia, however, would like to continue serving its customers in that area if it is economically feasible and is considering one of the following alternatives:

(a) Expand the operations of the Montana factory by using space presently idle. This move would result in the following changes in that factory's operations:

	INCREASE OVER FACTORY'S CURRENT OPERATIONS
Sales	50%
Fixed costs:	
Factory	20%
Administration	10%

Under this proposal, the variable cost would be $8 per unit for all units sold.

(b) Enter into a long-term contract with a competitor who will serve that area's customers. This competitor would pay Arcadia a royalty of $4 per unit based on an estimate of 30,000 units being sold.

(c) Close the Maine factory and not expand the operations of the Montana factory.

The total home office cost of $500,000 will remain the same under each situation.

Required: A schedule computing Arcadia's total income before income tax that would result from each proposal.

(AICPA adapted)

25-7. Sell or process further. The management of the Bay Company is considering a proposal to install a third production department within its existing factory building. With the present production setup, raw materials are passed through Department 1 to produce Materials A and B in equal proportions. The portions of A and B produced are constant due to the inherent nature of the manufacturing process. Material A is then passed through Department 2 to yield Product C. Material B is presently being sold "as is" at a price of $20.25 per pound. Product C has a sales price of $100 per pound.

The per pound standard costs currently being used by the Bay Company are:

	DEPARTMENT 1 (MATERIALS A & B)	DEPARTMENT 2 (PRODUCT C)	MATERIAL B
Prior department cost	—	$53.03	$13.47
Direct materials	$20.00	—	—
Direct labor	7.00	12.00	—
Variable factory overhead	3.00	5.00	—
Fixed factory overhead:			
Attributable	2.25	2.25	—
Allocated common	1.00	1.00	—
	$33.25	$73.28	$13.47

These per pound standard costs were developed by using an estimated production volume of 200,000 pounds of raw materials input as the normal volume. The Bay Company assigns Department 1 cost to Materials A and B in proportion to their net sales values at the point of separation, computed by deducting subsequent standard production costs from sales prices except that the $300,000 of common fixed factory overhead cost is allocated to the two producing departments on the basis of the space used, a ratio of 2:1.

The proposed Department 3 would occupy the same amount of space as Department 2, and would be used to process Material B into Product D. It is expected that any quantity of Product D can be sold for $30 per pound. Standard costs per pound under this proposal were developed by using 200,000 pounds of raw materials as the normal volume and are:

	DEPARTMENT 1 (MATERIALS A & B)	DEPARTMENT 2 (PRODUCT C)	DEPARTMENT 3 (PRODUCT D)
Prior department cost	—	$52.80	$13.20
Direct materials	$20.00	—	—
Direct labor	7.00	12.00	5.50
Variable factory overhead	3.00	5.00	2.00
Fixed factory overhead:			
Attributable	2.25	2.25	1.75
Allocated common	.75	.75	.75
	$33.00	$72.80	$23.20

Nonmanufacturing costs are expected to be the same for either alternative.

Required: A decision by management as to whether Bay should install Department 3, thereby producing Product D if sales and production levels are expected to remain constant in the foreseeable future and if there are no foreseeable alternative uses for the available factory space. (Show calculations.)

(CMA adapted)

25-8. Sell or process further; shutdown of facilities. Gossett Chemical Company uses comprehensive annual profit planning procedures to evaluate pricing policies, finalize production decisions, and estimate unit costs for its various products. One particular product group involves two joint products and two by-products. This product group is separately analyzed each year to establish appropriate production and marketing policies.

The two joint products, Alchem-X and Chem-P, emerge at the end of processing in Department 20. Both chemicals can be sold at this split-off point — Alchem-X for $2.50 per unit, and Chem-P for $3 per unit. By-product BY-D20 also emerges at the split-off point in Department 20 and is marketable for $.50 per unit without further processing. Unit costs of preparing this by-product for market are $.03 for freight and $.12 for packaging.

Chem-P is sold without further processing, but Alchem-X is transferred to Department 22 for additional processing into a refined chemical labeled as Alchem-XF. No additional materials are added in Department 22. Alchem-XF is sold for $5 per unit. By-product BY-D22 is created by the additional processing in Department 22, and it can be sold for $.70 per unit. Unit marketing costs for BY-D22 are $.05 for freight and $.15 for packaging.

Gossett Chemical Company accounts for by-products by crediting their net realizable value to the production cost of the main products. The market value method is used to allocate the net joint production cost for inventory costing purposes.

A portion of the 19B profit plan established in September, 19A is presented below:

Production budget:

	CHEM-P	ALCHEM-XF
Estimated sales	400,000 units	210,000 units
Planned inventory change	(8,000)	(6,000)
Required production	392,000 units	204,000 units
Minimum production based upon joint output ratio	392,000 units	210,000 units
	BY-D20	BY-D22
By-product output	90,000 units	60,000 units

Manufacturing budget:

	DEPARTMENT 20	DEPARTMENT 22
Materials	$160,000	—
Cost transferred from Department 20*	—	$225,000
Direct labor	170,000	120,000
Variable factory overhead	180,000	140,800
Fixed factory overhead	247,500	188,000
Total	$757,500	$673,800

*The cost transferred to Department 22 is calculated as follows:
Market value of output:

Alchem-X (210,000 × $2.50)	$ 525,000	31%
Chem-X (392,000 × $3.00)	1,176,000	69
Total	$1,701,000	100%
Department 20 cost	$ 757,500	
Less by-product (90,000 × $.35)	31,500	
Net cost	$ 726,000	
Alchem-X	31%	$ 225,000 or $1.07 per unit ($225,000 ÷ 210,000 units)
Chem-X	69	501,000 or $1.28 per unit ($501,000 ÷ 392,000 units)
Allocated net cost	100%	$ 726,000

Marketing expenses budget:

Chem-P	$196,000
Alchem-XF	105,000

Shortly after this budget was compiled, the company learned that a chemical which would compete with Alchem-XF was to be introduced. The Marketing Department estimated that a price reduction to $3.50 a unit would be required for the Alchem-XF to be sold in present quantities.

The market for Alchem-X will not be affected by the introduction of this new chemical. Consequently, the quantities of Alchem-X which are usually processed into Alchem-XF can be sold at the regular price of $2.50 per unit. The cost for marketing Alchem-X is estimated to be $105,000. If the further processing is terminated, Department 22 will be closed and all costs except $74,800 per year will be eliminated.

Required: An analysis indicating whether Gossett should close Department 22 and sell Alchem-X at the split-off point or continue to process it further in Department 22.   (CMA adapted)

25-9. Probability analysis. Vendo, Inc., operates the concession stands at the Tecumseh College football stadium. Tecumseh College has had successful football teams for many years; as a result, the stadium is virtually always filled. From time to time, Vendo has found that its supply of hot dogs is inadequate, while at other times, there has been a surplus. A review of Vendo's sales records for the past ten seasons reveals the following frequency of hot dogs sold:

| | NUMBER OF |
HOT DOGS	GAMES
10,000	5
20,000	10
30,000	20
40,000	15
Total	50

Hot dogs that sell for $.50 each cost Vendo $.30 each. Unsold hot dogs are donated to a local orphanage.

Required:
(1) A table representing the expected value of each of the four possible strategies of ordering 10,000, 20,000, 30,000, or 40,000 hot dogs, assuming that only the four quantities listed were ever sold and that the occurrences were random events. (Ignore income tax.)
(2) The standard deviation (rounded to the nearest whole number) and the coefficient of variation (rounded to two decimal places) for each of the four possible strategies.
(3) The best of the four strategies in (1), based on the expected value.
(4) The dollar value of knowing in advance what the sales level would be at each game.
(5) The standard deviation (rounded to the nearest whole number) and the coefficient of variation (rounded to two decimal places) for the average profit if Vendo knew in advance what the sales level would be at each game.   (CMA adapted)

25-10. Probability analysis: expected contribution margin and expected opportunity cost. A merchant is considering ordering a seasonal item that sells for $10 a unit. This merchandise, with a unit cost of $6, must be sold within the seasonal period, after which it has no market value. The merchant has only one opportunity to place an order, and the following probabilities are associated with the demand:

DEMAND (UNITS)	PROBABILITY
5	.1
6	.2
7	.3
8	.3
9	.1
	1.0

Required:
(1) A contribution margin matrix and the expected contribution margin for each inventory policy.

(2) An opportunity cost matrix and the expected opportunity cost for each inventory policy, assuming that opportunity cost for a contribution margin situation is defined as the difference in the contribution margin resulting because of a difference between the quantity ordered and the quantity sold.

(3) The best strategy.

25-11. Sales probability and contribution margin analysis. Krull Corporation produces a chemical compound which deteriorates and must be discarded if it is not sold by the end of the month during which it is produced. The total variable cost of the manufactured compound is $25 per unit, and it is sold for $40 per unit. The compound can be purchased from a competitor at $40 per unit plus $5 freight per unit. It is estimated that failure to fill orders would result in the complete loss of 8 out of 10 customers placing orders for the compound.

The corporation has sold the compound for the past 30 months. Demand has been irregular and there is no sales trend. During this period, sales per month have been:

UNITS SOLD PER MONTH	NUMBER OF MONTHS
4,000	6
5,000	15
6,000	9

The cost of the primary ingredient used to manufacture the compound is $12 per unit of compound. It is estimated that there is a 60% chance that the primary ingredient supplier may be shut down by a strike for an indefinite period. A substitute ingredient is available at $18 per unit of compound, but the corporation must contract immediately to purchase the substitute or it will be unavailable when needed. A firm purchase contract for either the primary or the substitute ingredient must now be made with one of the suppliers for production next month. If an order were placed for the primary ingredient and a strike should occur, the corporation would be released from the contract and management would purchase the compound from the competitor.

Required:
(1) The probability of sales of 4,000, 5,000, or 6,000 units in any month.
(2) The contribution margin if sales of 4,000, 5,000, or 6,000 units are made in one month and 4,000, 5,000, or 6,000 units are manufactured for sale in the same month (nine possible combinations of units sold and units manufactured), assuming that all sales orders are filled.
(3) The average monthly contribution margin that the corporation should expect over the long run if 5,000 units are manufactured every month and all sales orders are filled.
(4) The standard deviation (rounded to the nearest whole number) and the coefficient of variation (rounded to two decimal places) under the conditions assumed in requirement (3).
(5) The monthly contribution margin from sales of 4,000, 5,000, and 6,000 units if the substitute ingredient is ordered, 5,000 units are manufactured, and all sales orders are filled.
(6) The average monthly contribution margin that the corporation should expect if the primary ingredient is ordered with the existing probability of a strike at the supplier's plant, and assuming that the expected average monthly contribution margin from manufacturing will be $65,000 using the primary ingredient or $35,000 using the substitute, and that the expected average monthly negative contribution margin from purchasing from the competitor will be $25,000.
(7) Reasons for management's ordering the primary or substitute ingredient during the anticipated strike period [under the assumptions stated in (6)].
(8) Justification for management's purchasing the compound from the competitor to fill sales orders when the orders cannot be filled otherwise.

(AICPA adapted)

25-12. Contribution margin and probability analysis. Travis County Simmental, Ltd., a Texas three-year limited partnership, is considering the purchase of 11 first-time-bred Simmental cows at a cost of $10,000 each. The estimated cost of insuring them against disease and theft and of maintaining the herd from date of purchase until they are sold, along with their calves, is $1,000 per cow.

It is estimated, based on industry experience with three-quarter Simmental cows bred for the first time, that two of the calves will be stillborn and these cows will have a rebred sales value of $10,000 each. The other cows, having demonstrated both their fertility and ability to give birth, will have an estimated sales value of $16,000. Their calves, which will be seven-eighths Simmentals and which are sold along with the rebred parent cow, are expected to sell for $20,000 if heifers and $1,250 if bulls.

The probabilities of combinations of heifer and bull calves from nine live births were obtained from the Texas-Oklahoma Simmental Cattlebreeders Association and are as follows:

HEIFERS	BULLS	PROBABILITY
9	0	.002
8	1	.018
7	2	.070
6	3	.164
5	4	.246
4	5	.246
3	6	.164
2	7	.070
1	8	.018
0	9	.002
Total		1.000

Required:

(1) The contribution margin for each combination of heifers and bulls and the expected contribution margin for the proposed transaction, assuming: (a) the facts as stated; (b) that the rebred cows will sell for $7,500 if they produced a stillborn calf, $12,000 if a live calf; and that the calves will sell for $15,000 each if heifers, $940 if bulls.

(2) The standard deviation (rounded to the nearest whole number) and the coefficient of variation (rounded to two decimal places) under the conditions assumed in (1)(b).

25-13. Contribution margin and probability analysis. The Colt-Squeri Company, a wholesale chemical products distributor, ships 10 000 liters of Astrojel per day in an airplane owned by the company. The daily shipment is made to a government-owned military research laboratory in Ohio. The area where the company is located is sometimes fogbound, and shipment can then be made only by rail. The extra cost of preparation for rail shipment reduces the contribution margin of this product from $.40 per liter to $.18 per liter, and there is an additional fixed cost of $3,100 for modification of packaging facilities to convert to rail shipment (incurred only once per conversion).

The fog may last for several days, and Colt-Squeri normally starts shipping by rail only after rail shipments become necessary to meet commitments to the customer, in which case the shipments are still only 10 000 liters per day.

A meteorological report reveals that during the past ten years the area has been fogbound 250 times for at least a day and that of the 250 times, fog continued 100 times for a second consecutive day, 40 times for at least a third consecutive day, 20 times for at least a fourth consecutive day, and 10 times for a fifth consecutive day. Occasions and length of fog were both random. Fog never continued for more than five days, and there were never two separate occurrences of fog in any six-day period.

Required:

(1) The daily contribution margin (ignoring fixed conversion costs) when (a) there is no fog and shipment is made by air and (b) there is fog and shipment is made by rail.

(2) A schedule of the probabilities of the possible combinations of foggy and clear weather on the days following a fogbound day, showing the probability that if fog first occurs on a particular day: (a) the next four days will be foggy; (b) the next three days will be foggy and Day 5 will be clear; (c) the next two days will be foggy and Days 4 and 5 will be clear; (d) the next day will be foggy and Days 3, 4, and 5 will be clear; (e) the next four days will be clear.

(3) A schedule of the three-day contribution (including fixed conversion costs) that should be expected from rail and air shipments if: (a) rail shipments were started on the third consecutive foggy day and the probability that the next two days will be foggy is .25; (b) the probability that the next day will be foggy and Day 5 will be clear is .25; and (c) the probability that the next two days will be clear is .50. Assume that the probability exists that it would be unprofitable to begin shipping 10 000 liters per day by rail on either the fourth or fifth consecutive foggy day, and the company returns immediately to air shipments on the first clear day.

(4) The standard deviation (rounded to the nearest whole number) and the coefficient of variation (rounded to two decimal places) under the conditions assumed in requirement (3).

(5) A discussion of the reliability of the data upon which conclusions are based, including financial data reliability and meteorological data reliability.

(AICPA adapted)

CASES

A. Analysis of differential business. Nubo Manufacturing, Inc., is presently operating at 50% of normal capacity, producing annually about 50,000 units of a patented electronic component. Nubo recently received an offer from a company in Yokohama, Japan, to purchase 30,000 components at $6 per unit, FOB Nubo's plant. Nubo has not previously sold components in Japan. Budgeted production costs for 50,000 and 80,000 units of output follow:

	50,000	80,000
Units		
Costs:		
Direct materials	$ 75,000	$120,000
Direct labor	75,000	120,000
Factory overhead	200,000	260,000
Total cost	$350,000	$500,000
Cost per unit	$7.00	$6.25

The sales manager thinks the order should be accepted, even if it results in a loss of $1 per unit, since the sales may build up future markets. The production manager does not wish to have the order accepted, primarily because the order would show a loss of $.25 per unit when computed on the new average unit cost. The treasurer has made a quick computation indicating that accepting the order will actually increase gross profit.

Required:
(1) Causes of the drop in cost from $7 per unit to $6.25 per unit when budgeted production increases from 50,000 to 80,000 units.
(2) (a) An explanation of whether the production manager and/or the treasurer is correct.
    (b) An explanation of the conclusions of the production manager and the treasurer.
(3) An explanation of how each of the following may affect the decision to accept or reject the special order:
    (a) The likelihood of repeat special sales and/or all sales to be made at $6 per unit.
    (b) Whether the sales are made to customers operating in two separate, isolated markets or whether the sales are made to customers competing in the same market.

(AICPA adapted)

B. Make-or-buy decision. The Utecht Company must decide whether to make or buy certain parts for its products. Until now, the company has made the parts, but the controller has made the following calculation, demonstrating that buying the parts would be cheaper.

Cost to make, per year:

Direct materials	$10,000
Direct labor	10,000
Depreciation of machinery (remaining useful life, 5 years; book value, $25,000)	5,000
Variable factory overhead	4,000
	$29,000
Cost to buy, per year	26,000
Annual advantage to buy	$ 3,000

The production manager does not agree with this calculation, contending that depreciation should not be included in the calculation because the company presently could receive no more than $2,000 for the machines.

Required: Comments on the calculation and the opinion of the production manager.

C. Continuing research project; sunk costs. Management of the Sifri Chemical Company is reviewing a research project that was initiated for the purpose of developing a new product. Expenditures to date on the project total $126,000. The Research and Development Department now estimates that an additional $24,000 will be required to produce a marketable product. Current market estimates indicate a lifetime profit potential having a present value of $40,000 for the product, excluding research and development expenditures.

Required: Advice to management.

26 Capital Expenditures
Planning, Evaluating, and Controlling

Capital expenditure planning, evaluation, and control, sometimes called *capital budgeting*, is the process of planning the continuing investment and reinvestment of an organization's resources and the monitoring of that investment. Capital expenditures involve long-term commitments of resources to realize future benefits. They reflect basic company objectives and have a significant, long-term effect on the economic well-being of the firm.

In the final analysis, a firm must earn a reasonable return on invested funds. Therefore, considerable attention has been devoted to techniques for evaluating capital expenditure proposals. Yet evaluation is only one essential requirement for the effective administration of a capital expenditure program. Equally important is the effective planning and control of such expenditures, because (1) the long-term commitment increases financial risk, (2) the magnitude of expenditures is substantial and the penalties for unwise decisions are usually severe, and (3) the decisions made in this area provide the structure that supports the operating activities of the firm.

PLANNING FOR CAPITAL EXPENDITURES

The phase of planning for capital expenditures consists of relating plans to objectives, structuring the framework, searching for proposals, budgeting the expenditures, and requesting authority for the expenditures.

**Relating
Plans to
Objectives**

Individual projects must be consistent with objectives and must be capable of being blended into a firm's operations. To achieve this consistency, all levels of an organization need to be conscious of objectives and the different roles played by each level relative to these objectives. Ideally, executive management sets broad objectives; managers of functional activities formulate specific policies and programs for action which, when approved, are executed by operating levels of management. The lower the level at which a decision is authorized, the greater the need for guidelines extending to detailed procedures and standards; investment projects not conducive to such detail require handling at a higher level.

**Structuring
the
Framework**

An organization's established capital expenditure framework forms the basis for implementing the capital expenditure program. The framework is important because the very nature of performing tasks implies a sound frame of reference. Several factors influence the molding and revisions of a firm's framework: the company's organizational structure, its philosophy and applications of principles of organization, its size, the nature of its operations, and the characteristics of individual projects.

A company manual may be used to detail policies and procedures and illustrative forms required for administering the capital expenditure program. Such manuals should be stripped down to helpful levels and should (1) encourage people to work on and submit ideas, (2) focus attention on useful analytical tasks, and (3) facilitate rapid project development and expeditious review.

**Searching
for
Proposals**

A capital investment program yields the best results only when the best available proposals are considered and all reasonable alternatives of each proposal have been brought into the analysis for evaluating and screening. Ideas should come from all segments of the enterprise. Persons in the organization should participate in the search activity within the bounds of their technical knowledge and ability, their authority and responsibility, their awareness of operating problems, and existing management guidelines regarding desirable projects. Care must be taken to create and maintain an incentive to search out and bring good projects into the system. This incentive is strong when there is a genuine feeling that all proposals will be reviewed in a fair and objective manner.

**Budgeting
Capital
Expendi-
tures**

The capital expenditures budget is typically prepared for a one-year period. It presents management's investment plans at the time the budget is prepared for the coming period.

Some projects never materialize; others are added through amendments to the budget during the budget year. Thus, the budget must be adaptable to changing needs. The capital expenditures budget is not an authorization to commit funds; it merely affords an opportunity to consolidate plans by looking at projects for the total organization, side by side. The capital expenditures budget should be reconciled with the other periodic budgeting activities of the firm, e.g., expense and cash budgets (Chapters 16 and 17). The annual capital budget should be reconciled with long-range capital investment and operating plans and objectives.

The capital expenditures budget passes through several management levels as it moves toward final approval at the executive management level. It follows that a clear explanation of the content of the approved budget should be transmitted to the various management levels to avoid misunderstandings.

Requesting Authority for Expenditure

The periodic budget is usually an approval of ideas and does not grant automatic approval to commit funds. Authority to commit funds for other than necessary preliminary administrative costs should come by means of an Authority for Expenditure (AFE). The AFE procedure is, in effect, a second look at budgeted projects based on an up-to-date set of documents justifying and describing the expenditure. The AFE and supporting detail should be originated at the level at which the expenditure will occur, with staff assistance if needed.

Approval of the AFE should be delegated to the organizational level having the necessary competence to make the decision, as opposed to requesting executive management's approval for each AFE. The philosophy of companies varies as to the extent of decentralization of approval authority. The amount, type, and significance of the expenditure should be considered in determining the required level of approval. Required approvals also may be governed by whether certain designated evaluation criteria are met.

During the budget year, periodic reports should be prepared by categories, comparing approved AFE expenditures with the budget. The reports should be prepared for use by the organization levels originating the requests for expenditures as well as those granting approval. Higher echelons find summaries helpful, with out-of-line items reported in detail.

EVALUATING CAPITAL EXPENDITURES

Evaluating capital expenditures refers to the basic theory, techniques, and procedures for the appraisal and reappraisal of projects throughout the course of their development. A number of evaluations of a single proposal may be necessary because of:

1. Circumstances that change during the time span from the origin of the project idea to its completion.
2. Alternative solutions of the problem for which the project is designed.
3. Assumptions that vary as to the amount and time pattern of cash flows.

The best available evaluation tools should be used, coupled with an understanding of the risk and danger existing in overreliance on quantitative answers based on many assumptions and estimates. Economic evaluation and related techniques have received prime attention in literature dealing with capital investment programs. The most advanced methods consider the time value of money in computing an estimated return on investment. Many imponderable factors may also affect the decision, e.g., competition, legal requirements, social responsibilities, and emergencies. Furthermore, there is a need to select investments that will keep the firm in balance and be consistent with objectives. The circumstances of each expenditure alternative must be considered in passing judgment on the criteria used. Even then there may be justifiable differences of opinion with respect to governing criteria. The mechanics of various techniques are important, but of still greater importance is their relationship to the overall capital expenditure planning and control process and the need for creative and thoughtful management.

Classification of Capital Expenditures

Capital expenditure projects can be classified as: (1) equipment-replacement expenditures, (2) expansion investments, and (3) improvements of existing products and/or additions of new products. A proposal may involve more than one classification. For example, a firm may consider a proposal to replace a job printing press, whose maintenance cost has become excessive, with a new press that will offer an expanded productive capacity. Also, certain expenditures may be necessary because of tactical or legal requirements rather than for purely economic reasons: a manufacturer may be forced into the production of a less profitable product because of competitive pressure; recreation facilities may be installed for employee use; or air and water pollution regulations may necessitate an expenditure for a waste disposal unit. Certain projects are musts to the point that use of an evaluation technique is superfluous, e.g., the washout of a section of a railway trestle. Other projects, though indicating an acceptable economic return, may be rejected because of lack of funds, failure to fit into overall objectives, failure to meet other evaluation criteria (such as corner locations for gasoline service stations), or external circumstances (such as current economic conditions).

Some projects may not be independent of one another and in such cases should be grouped together for evaluation purposes as a compound project. The following quotation illustrates this point:

> Contingent or dependent projects can arise, for instance, when acceptance of one proposal is dependent on acceptance of one or more other proposals. One simple example would be the purchase of an extra-long boom for a crane which would be of little value unless the crane itself were also purchased; the latter, however, may be justified on its own. When contingent projects are combined with their independent prerequisites, the combination may be called a compound project. Thus, a compound project may be characterized by the algebraic sum of the payoffs and costs of the component projects plus, perhaps, an interaction term.[1]

---

[1] H. Martin Weingartner, "Capital Budgeting of Interrelated Projects: Survey and Synthesis," *Management Science*, Vol. XII, No. 7, p. 492.

Equipment-Replacement Expenditures. These include both like-for-like and obsolescence replacements. The basis for decision making is future or prospective cost savings, i.e., comparing future costs of old equipment with future costs of new equipment. In addition to comparisons of operating costs, the analysis of future costs requires the determination of the prospective purchase price less any ultimate resale or salvage value. The most difficult problem is to estimate the probable economic life of the new equipment. This is the core of any capital expenditure decision. For the present equipment, the future decline in disposal value must be estimated. The original cost of the present facility is a sunk and irrecoverable cost totally irrelevant to the decision-making process. The accumulated depreciation allowance is also independent of the company's real future costs. Book values are not significant for the replacement decision except for the treatment of income tax liability related to plant asset transactions.

Expansion Investments. Expansion investments involve plant enlargement and the invasion of new markets. In these cases the expected results of doing and not doing the job are compared, with the basis for a decision shifted from cost savings to the expected addition to profits, including the consideration of cash inflow. The added profit is estimated by preparing a projected income statement showing additional revenue and expense over the life of the project. The degree of uncertainty in this type of investment is much greater than in the first category.

Improvements of Existing Products and/or Additions of New Products. The basis for a decision on projects in this category is strategic; that is, the relative competitive market position compels the firm to make investments. Failure to keep abreast of competitors can cause deterioration of the market share. Since no historical basis for making the decision exists and the return on such investments must be based on increased profits, a high degree of sound judgment and business insight is required in making a decision.

Cost of Capital

The *cost of capital* represents the expected return that investors demand for a given level of risk. Although this discussion is brief, the cost of capital as related to capital expenditures is a complex concept. It may refer to a specific cost of capital from a particular financing effort to provide funds for a specific project. Such use of the concept connotes the marginal cost of capital and implies linkage of the financing and investment decisions. This view has been challenged as a useful concept for allocating capital, however, and the funds available for one or all projects are more generally considered to be a commingling of more than one source. Therefore, different costs of capital exist, depending upon the sources. A company could obtain funds from (1) bonds, (2) preferred and common stock, (3) use of retained earnings, and (4) loans from banks. If a company obtains funds by some combination of these sources to achieve or maintain a particular capital structure, then the cost of capital (money) is the weighted average cost of each money source. This weighted average considers the joint cost and the desired relative proportions of each type of capital and may be computed as follows:

FUNDS — SOURCE	DESIRED LONG-RUN PROPORTION OF FUNDS TO BE PROVIDED	AFTER-TAX COST	WEIGHTED COST
Bonds............................	.20	.03	.006
Preferred stock	.20	.08	.016
Common stock and retained earnings..........	.60	.13	.078
	1.00	Weighted average cost of capital....	.100 = 10%

The cost of capital for each source is described as follows:

1. The cost of bonds is the aftertax rate of interest.
2. The cost of preferred stock is the dividend per share divided by the present market price.
3. The cost of common stock and retained earnings is the expected earnings per share, after income tax and after preferred dividends are paid, divided by the present market price.[2]

Representative Evaluation Techniques

The following four evaluation techniques are the representative tools in current usage: (1) the payback (or payout) period method, (2) the average annual return on investment method, (3) the present value method, and (4) the discounted cash flow (DCF) method. None of these methods serves every purpose or every firm. The circumstances and needs of a situation determine the most appropriate techniques to be used. A company may use more than one technique (e.g., payback period and DCF) in evaluating each project; however, the same method or methods should be used uniformly for every project throughout the firm. Confusion could arise if Division A used the discounted cash flow method while Division B used the average annual return on investment method.

These evaluation techniques, if thoroughly understood by the analysts who use them, should aid management in exercising judgment and making decisions. Certainly the cost of gathering data and applying the evaluation techniques should be justified in terms of the value to management. Moreover, inaccurate raw data used in the calculations or lack of uniform procedures may yield harmful and misleading conclusions.

For purposes of discussing and illustrating the evaluation methods listed, assume that Shields Company is operating at the limit of the capacity of one of its producing units, and maintenance costs of the existing unit have become excessive. A new unit can be purchased at a cost of $85,796, less trade-in allowance. The old unit has a trade-in value of $3,000, making the net pur-

---

[2]Conflicting opinions exist regarding the treatment of the investors' income tax effect on the cost of equity acquired through the retention of earnings.

chase price $82,796. The expected economic life of the new unit is eight years. Straight-line depreciation is to be used, with an estimated salvage value of $8,300. The old unit has a zero book value (that is, the accumulated depreciation in this situation is assumed to equal the capitalized cost) and its trade-in value will therefore reduce the depreciable basis of the new asset. Such treatment is consistent with the income tax requirement of adjusting the depreciable basis of the new asset for any gain or loss resulting from a replacement in kind.[3] However, if the old asset is sold outright rather than traded in, the aftertax gain or loss would be recognized at the time of the sale. In any case, only the net difference in new versus old depreciation is relevant in computing the income tax savings from depreciation.

The estimated differential aftertax cash flow yielded by the utilized capacity of the new unit is calculated in the table below. In this table, the estimates given in Columns 2 and 3 are uneven numbers, so that the resulting amounts in Column 8 will be easy to use in subsequent computations.

SHIELDS COMPANY — AFTERTAX CASH FLOW

(1) YEAR	(2) ESTIMATED CASH SAVINGS RELATING TO PRESENT CAPACITY (PRIMARILY MAINTENANCE)	(3) ESTIMATED CASH INCOME RELATING TO USE OF INCREASED CAPACITY	(4) (2) + (3)	(5) DEPRE- CIATION*	(6) TAXABLE INCOME (4) − (5)	(7) FEDERAL AND STATE INCOME TAX (6) × 48%	(8) NET AFTERTAX CASH INFLOW (4) − (7)
1	$18,388	$15,324	$33,712	$9,312	$24,400	$11,712	$ 22,000
2	10,707	15,312	26,019	9,312	16,707	8,019	18,000
3	10,188	21,600	31,788	9,312	22,476	10,788	21,000
4	8,265	21,600	29,865	9,312	20,553	9,865	20,000
5	2,496	21,600	24,096	9,312	14,784	7,096	17,000
6	1,923	26,019	27,942	9,312	18,630	8,942	19,000
7	—	26,019	26,019	9,312	16,707	8,019	18,000
8	—	26,019	26,019	9,312	16,707	8,019	18,000
							$153,000
Cash inflow from salvage value at end of economic life							8,300
							$161,300

*Basis of $82,796 − $8,300 salvage value = $74,496; $74,496 ÷ 8 years = $9,312 annual depreciation

Cash flow that will remain unchanged is not relevant in the computations, but cash flow estimates should include an allowance for inflationary influences.

This example involves both a replacement and an expansion investment, in which the cash outlay is restricted to the cost of the plant asset unit. Some

---

[3]If the book value of the old asset is not zero, then the cash invested (net of the trade-in allowance) will be less than the adjusted depreciable basis of the new asset by the amount of the old asset's book value.

projects require the commitment of working capital for inventories, receivables, etc., as well as expenditures that may not be capitalized. When such commitments and expenditures exist, they should be included as part of the initial investment and, to the extent that they are recoverable, should be shown as cash inflow in the recovery years.

The impact of income tax (federal and state) is significant, both as to the amount and the timing of cash flow. Management should take cognizance of income tax in looking at the projected profitability of a proposal, including the income tax treatment of losses and gains resulting from the sale of any displaced assets.[4]

The Payback (or Payout) Period Method. The payback period method is widely used in many firms, if only to serve as an initial screening device or to complement the answers of more sophisticated methods. The technique measures the length of time required by the project to recover the initial outlay.[5] The calculated payback period is compared with the payback period acceptable to management for this particular kind of project. The computation for the Shields Company project is:

YEAR	CASH FLOW	RECOVERY OF INITIAL OUTLAY		PAYBACK YEARS REQUIRED
		Needed	*Balance*	
1	$22,000	$82,796	$60,796	1.0
2	18,000	60,796	42,796	1.0
3	21,000	42,796	21,796	1.0
4	20,000	21,796	1,796	1.0
5	17,000	1,796	—	.1
	Total payback period in years............................			4.1

If the estimated cash flow is uniform for each year, the payback period can be computed by dividing the investment by the annual cash flow. For example, if cash flow equals $22,000 each year, the payback period is 3.8 years ($82,796 ÷ $22,000).

The Average Annual Return on Investment Method. This method is sometimes referred to as the accounting or the financial statement method. When this method is used, an investment proposal is evaluated by comparing the estimated average annual rate of return on the investment with a target rate of return. The estimated rate of return for the Shields Company project may be computed as follows:

Net income without deduction for depreciation (net aftertax cash inflow, excluding salvage value)	$153,000
Less depreciation ($82,796 − $8,300)*	74,496
Net income for economic life...	$ 78,504

---

[4]This discussion does not consider the investment tax credit, which would reduce the cash outflow related to the cost of a capital investment but would not reduce the depreciable basis of the new asset.

[5]The initial outlay used in calculating the payback period should exclude working capital to the extent that the working capital can be recovered through its own liquidation. Investment salvage value at the payback point would further reduce the payback period. Such adjustments result in what is referred to as the "bailout payback."

*Depreciation is assumed to be the only noncash item and is thus the only adjustment required in converting from cash flow to the accrual basis.

$$\text{Average annual return on } \textit{original} \text{ investment} = \frac{\text{Net income}}{\text{Economic life}} \div \text{Original investment}$$

$$= \frac{\$78,504}{8 \text{ years}} \div \$82,796$$

$$= \$9,813 \div \$82,796$$

$$= \underline{\underline{11.85\%}}$$

Another approach to estimating a project's rate of return is to divide the average annual net income by the average investment rather than the original investment. The computation for the Shields Company project is:

Original investment	$82,796
Investment at end of economic life (salvage value)...................	8,300
	$91,096
Average investment ($91,096 ÷ 2)	$45,548*

$$\text{Average annual return on } \textit{average} \text{ investment} = \frac{\text{Net income}}{\text{Economic life}} \div \text{Average investment}$$

$$= \frac{\$78,504}{8 \text{ years}} \div \$45,548$$

$$= \$9,813 \div \$45,548$$

$$= \underline{\underline{21.54\%}}$$

*The original book value and the book value at the end of each year can be averaged if the straight-line depreciation method is not used.

The Present Value Method. A dollar received a year hence is not the equivalent of a dollar received today, becuase the use of money has a value. To illustrate, if $500 can be invested at 20 percent, $600 will be received a year later ($500 + 20% of $500). The $600 to be received next year has a present value of $500 if 20 percent can be earned ($600 ÷ 120% = $500). The difference of $100 ($600 − $500) represents the time value of money. In line with this idea, the estimated results of an investment proposal can be stated at its present value, i.e., as a cash equivalent at the present time.[6]

Present value tables have been devised to facilitate the application of present value theory. The "Present Value of $1" table on page 800 presents computations to three decimal places and shows today's value, or the present

---

[6]The basic formula for present value is:

$$PV = S\frac{1}{(1 + i)^n} \text{ or } \frac{S}{(1 + i)^n} \text{ or } S(1 + i)^{-n}$$

where: PV = present value of future sum of money
S = future sum of money
i = earnings rate for each compounding period
n = number of periods

value, of each dollar to be received or paid in the future for various rates of interest and periods of time.[7] By multiplying the appropriate factor obtained from the table times an expected future cash flow, the present value of the cash flow is easily determined.

The "Present Value of $1 Received or Paid Annually for Each of the Next N Years" table shows the present value of a series of $1 periodic receipts or payments. This table is used when the cash flow is estimated to be the same each period. The relationship between this table and the "Present Value of $1" table is as follows:

PERIOD	PRESENT VALUE OF $1 10%	PRESENT VALUE OF $1 RECEIVED OR PAID ANNUALLY FOR EACH OF THE NEXT N YEARS 10%
1	.909	.909
2	.826	1.736 (.909 + .826)*
3	.751	2.487 (1.736 + .751)
4	.683	3.170
5	.621	3.791
6	.564	4.355
7	.513	4.868
8	.467	5.335

*Difference of .001 results from rounding off the results of the formula.

If the flow is uniform, the flow for one period can be multiplied by the cumulative factor to obtain approximately the same answer as by multiplying the individual factors by the flow for each period and totaling the products. For example, if a project costing $20,000 is expected to yield a uniform annual aftertax cash flow of $5,000 for seven years, then the present value is $5,000 × 4.868, or $24,340, and the net present value is $4,340 ($24,340 − $20,000).

The present value concept can be applied to the Shields Company problem by discounting at the company's 10 percent estimated cost of capital. Some firms may set as their discount rate something in excess of the cost of capital or use different rates that depend on risk and uncertainty and other characteristics of a particular project. However, for the sake of uniformity for comparison purposes, it seems preferable to discount all proposals at a constant rate, the cost of capital. Management can interject an allowance for risk and uncertainty and other characteristics peculiar to each specific proposal in the raw data or in the net present value answer. An allowance for the effect of inflation may be added as well.

The computation for Shields Company follows:

---

[7]Ordinary tables, such as those included in this chapter, assume that all cash flows occur at the end of each period and that interest is compounded at the end of each period. Either or both of these assumptions can be varied by the use of calculus so that, instead of assuming that the cash flows occur at the end of each period, they can be presumed to occur continuously, and interest can be compounded continuously. Although the continuous assumptions often are more representative of actual conditions, the tables in this chapter are more frequently found in practice.

YEAR	CASH (OUTFLOW) INFLOW	PRESENT VALUE OF $1 10%	NET PRESENT VALUE OF CASH FLOW
0	$(82,796)	1.000	$(82,796)
1	22,000	.909	19,998
2	18,000	.826	14,868
3	21,000	.751	15,771
4	20,000	.683	13,660
5	17,000	.621	10,557
6	19,000	.564	10,716
7	18,000	.513	9,234
8	26,300 ($18,000 + $8,300)	.467	12,282
		Net present value....................	$ 24,290

The positive net present value of $24,290 indicates that the true rate of return is greater than the cost of capital discount rate. A net present value of zero would indicate a rate of return of exactly 10 percent.

A project's useful life is one of the uncertainties often associated with capital expenditure evaluations. Equipment obsolescence or shifts in market demands may occur. The conventional payback method determines the time necessary to recover the initial outlay, without regard to present value considerations. However, management may wish to know the minimum necessary life for a project in order to recover the original investment and earn a desired rate of return on the investment. The *present value payback* calculation focuses on this question and is computed for the Shields Company as follows, using the "net present value of cash flow" figures shown above.

YEAR	NET PRESENT VALUE OF CASH FLOW	NEEDED	BALANCE	PRESENT VALUE PAYBACK YEARS REQUIRED
1	$19,998	$82,796	$62,798	1.0
2	14,868	62,798	47,930	1.0
3	15,771	47,930	32,159	1.0
4	13,660	32,159	18,499	1.0
5	10,557	18,499	7,942	1.0
6	10,716	7,942	—	.7
Total present value payback in years.......................................				5.7

Based on the present value of estimated cash flows, 5.7 years will be required to recover the $82,796 original investment and earn a desired 10 percent rate of return on the annual unrecovered investment balance. Additionally, the present value payback will be shortened by the present value of the project's salvage value.

The Discounted Cash Flow (DCF) Method. In the present value method, the discount rate is known or at least predetermined. In the discounted cash flow method, the discount rate is not known but is defined as the rate at which the sum of positive present values equals the sum of negative present values. Present value theory is used, but the analysis is developed further to determine the discounted rate of return, which is then compared with some standard.

The discounted rate of return for the Shields Company can be determined by trial and error, i.e., by computing net present value at various percentages to find the rate at which the net present value is zero. This computation is illustrated in the following table:

YEAR	CASH (OUTFLOW) INFLOW	PRESENT VALUE OF $1 16%	NET PRESENT VALUE OF CASH FLOW	PRESENT VALUE OF $1 18%	NET PRESENT VALUE OF CASH FLOW
0	$(82,796)	1.000	$(82,796)	1.000	$(82,796)
1	22,000	.862	18,964	.847	18,634
2	18,000	.743	13,374	.718	12,924
3	21,000	.641	13,461	.609	12,789
4	20,000	.552	11,040	.516	10.320
5	17,000	.476	8,092	.437	7,429
6	19,000	.410	7,790	.370	7,030
7	18,000	.354	6,372	.314	5,652
8	26,300	.305	8,022	.266	6,996
			$ 4,319		$ (1,022)

The discounted rate is greater than 16 percent and less than, but close to, 18 percent. The trial-and-error search should continue until adjacent rates in the table are found — one rate yielding a positive net present value with another rate yielding a negative net present value, and both as close to zero as possible.

Expanded present value tables permit the determination of a net present value nearer zero. However, an approximation is obtainable by interpolation as follows:

$$16\% + \left(2\% \times \frac{\$4,319}{\$5,341} \right) = 16\% + 2\%(.809) = 16\% + 1.62\% = \underline{17.62\%}$$

The $5,341 is the difference between the net present values at 16% and 18% [$4,319 − (−$1,022)].

The discounted cash flow method permits management to maximize corporate profits by selecting proposals with the highest rates of return as long as the rates are higher than the company's own cost of capital plus management's allowance for risk and uncertainty, project characteristics, and the effect of inflation. In most circumstances, the use of the discounted cash flow instead of the present value method at a given interest rate will not seriously alter the ranking of projects.

Note that the rate of return, using either the discounted cash flow method or the present value method, is computed on the basis of the unrecovered capital from period to period, not on the original investment. In the illustration, the DCF rate of return of 18 percent denotes that over the eight years the aftertax cash inflow equals the recovery of the original investment plus a return of 18 percent on the unrecovered investment from period to period. The net present value of $24,290 (page 773) indicates that over the eight years this additional amount, or a total of $107,086 ($82,796 + $24,290), could have been spent on the machine; and the original investment, plus a return of 10 percent on the unrecovered investment from period to period, could still have been recovered.

If annual cash flows are uniform, the table on page 801 can be used to compute the payback period and find the factor nearest the payback period on the line of the table that represents the stated economic life. The rate of return, located by reading the vertical column heading, is an approximation of the discounted cash flow rate of return. For example, if the economic life of a project is 10 years, the payback period 5.186, and the cash flow uniform, the approximate DCF rate of return would be 14 percent. If desired, a more precise rate of return can be found by interpolation:

PRESENT VALUE FACTOR		PRESENT VALUE FACTOR	
14%..................	5.216	14%..................	5.216
15%..................	− 5.019	Payback period...	− 5.186
	.197		.030

$$\text{Rate of return} = \left(\frac{.030}{.197} \times 1\%\right) + 14\% = \left(.15 \times 1\%\right) + 14\% = .15\% + 14\% = \underline{\underline{14.15\%}}$$

Additionally, and again assuming uniform annual cash flow, the table on page 801 can be used to determine the payback period required to yield a specified DCF rate of return for a project having a prescribed economic life. For example, if a 16% DCF rate of return is desired for a project having an estimated life of 10 years, the required payback period can be read from the table as 4.833 years. A shorter payback period for this project would yield a higher estimated DCF rate of return, and a longer payback period would fail to achieve the desired 16% rate of return. Or, if the project's economic life is unknown, it can be found for a specified DCF rate of return and payback period. As an example, if a 16% DCF rate of return is desired and the payback period is 4.833 years, the table indicates a required project life of 10 years. A longer project life would permit a longer payback period for the same DCF rate of return and a shorter project life would require a shorter payback period. An examination of the table reveals that at the higher rates of return, the required payback periods are relatively insensitive to changes in the rate of return or the project's economic life. If the rate is 25%, for example, it would never be profitable to accept a project with a payback period longer than 4 years.[8] An awareness of these interrelated factors affords rapid analysis of alternative assumptions.

Advantages and Disadvantages of the Evaluation Techniques. The following lists present several advantages and disadvantages of the four evaluation techniques that have been discussed.

---

[8]M. J. Mephan, "A Payback Interpretation of the Annuity Tables," *The Accounting Review*, Vol. L, No. 4, pp. 869–870.

The Payback (or Payout) Period Method

Advantages:

1. It is simple to compute.
2. It may be used to select those investments yielding a quick return of cash, thus placing an emphasis on liquidity.
3. It permits a company to determine the length of time required to recapture its original investment, thus offering an indicator of the degree of risk of each investment. Such an indicator is especially useful when the danger of obsolescence is great.
4. The reciprocal of the payback period may be used under certain conditions as a rough approximation of the rate of return calculated by the discounted cash flow method. The approximation exists when the project's life is long as compared to the length of the payback period (approximately double or more) and when the annual cash inflow is relatively uniform in amount. Although an approximation, the payback period reciprocal always exceeds the DCF rate of return. In the Shields Company example on page 770, the reciprocal is 24 percent (1 ÷ 4.1) and compares to the discounted cash flow computation (page 774) of 18 percent. The lack of uniformity of annual cash flow in this example accounts in large part for the roughness of the approximation. Also, the project's life is only 8 years, compared to a payback period of 4.1 years. If the project's life were longer, the approximation would be closer.
5. It is a widely used method that is certainly an improvement over a hunch, rule of thumb, or intuitive method.

Disadvantages:

1. It ignores the time value of money. To illustrate this disadvantage, assume that the "Net Aftertax Cash Inflow" for the Shields Company had been: Year 1, $55,000; Year 2, $12,000; Year 3, $10,000; Year 4, $5,500; and Year 5, $2,960. The computation would be:

| | | RECOVERY OF INITIAL OUTLAY | | PAYBACK YEARS |
YEAR	CASH FLOW	Needed	Balance	REQUIRED
1	$55,000	$82,796	$27,796	1.0
2	12,000	27,796	15,796	1.0
3	10,000	15,796	5,796	1.0
4	5,500	5,796	296	1.0
5	2,960	296	—	.1
	Total payback period in years......................			4.1

In both this example and the example on page 770, the payback period is 4.1 years; in this example, however, $33,000 more ($55,000 − $22,000) was received in the first year. This situation is more desirable from an investment standpoint because money has a time value; that is, a dollar is worth more the earlier it is received.

2. It ignores income which may be produced beyond the payback period. In the example on page 770, the payback period is 4.1 years, the economic life is 8 years, and the "Net Aftertax Cash Inflow" is $161,300.

Assume that an alternative project indicates a "Net Aftertax Cash Inflow" of $82,796 in the first three years and an economic life of four years with "Net Aftertax Cash Inflow" in the fourth year of $10,000. Although the latter case has a shorter payback period, the original example of a 4.1-year payback and net cash inflow of $161,300 is more desirable when immediate cash problems are not of critical importance.

3. It fails to consider any salvage value.

The Average Annual Return on Investment Method

Advantages:

1. It facilitates expenditure follow-up due to more readily available data from accounting records.
2. It considers income over the entire life of the project.

Disadvantages:

1. It ignores the time value of money. Two projects might have the same average return yet vary considerably in the pattern of flow of cash. In such a case, the recognition of the time value of money would point up the desirability of the alternative having greater cash flow in the earlier periods.
2. The average return on the original investment technique is inapplicable if any of the investment is made after the beginning of the project.

The Present Value Method

Advantages:

1. It considers the time value of money.
2. It considers income over the entire life of the project.

Disadvantages:

1. Some argue that this method is too difficult to use.
2. Management must determine a discount rate to be used. However, a well-informed management should already be aware of its cost of capital that should represent the benchmark for discount rate purposes.
3. If projects being compared involve different dollar amounts of investment, the project with more profitable dollars, as computed by the present value method, may not be the better project if it also requires a larger investment. For example, earning a net present value of $1,000 on an investment of $100,000 is not as economically wise as earning $900 on an investment of $10,000, provided that the $90,000 difference in investments can be used to earn at least $101 in other projects. In this case, a net present value index should be used rather than the net present value dollar figure. This index places all competing projects on a comparable basis for the purpose of ranking them. For the Shields Company, the computation is:

$$\text{Net present value index} = \frac{\text{Net present value}}{\text{Required investment}} = \frac{\$24,290}{\$82,796} = .293$$

This index simplifies finding the optimum solution for competing projects when the total budget for capital outlays is fixed arbitrarily, because it is possible to rank by percentages rather than absolute dollars.

4. It may be misleading when dealing with alternative projects or limited funds under the condition of unequal lives, in that the alternative with the higher net present value may involve longer economic life to the point that it would be less desirable than an alternative having a shorter life. The problem of dealing with alternatives having unequal lives is discussed on the next page.

The Discounted Cash Flow Method

Advantages:

1. It considers the time value of money.
2. It considers income over the entire life of the project.
3. The percentage figure may have more meaning for management than the net present value or net present value index computed by the present value method.
4. The percentage figure allows a generally sound, uniform ranking of projects.

Disadvantages:

1. It is more difficult to use than other methods.
2. It implies that earnings are reinvested at the rate earned by the investment, whereas the present value method implies earnings are reinvested at the rate of discount. It is argued that the latter assumption is more reasonable.

Other Situations and Considerations

The following topics related to evaluating capital expenditure proposals require a brief discussion: the error cushion, alternatives having unequal lives, purchase versus leasing, sensitivity analysis, allowance for risk and uncertainty via probability estimates, and computer usage for evaluation analysis.

The Error Cushion. A project whose estimated desirability is near a cutoff point for the type of project being evaluated affords little cushion for errors. For example, if the management of a chain of automotive muffler shops anticipates that a new location will yield a minimum discounted cash flow of 12 percent, there is obviously a greater cushion for errors when the computed rate of return is 20 percent as opposed to 13 percent. Similarly, when one alternative is clearly superior to others for a particular project, there is a better cushion against errors than when two or more of the best alternatives indicate approximately the same expected results.

Reasonably accurate estimates are desirable in evaluating any project. However, a higher degree of sophistication and care, at a higher cost of obtaining the data, may be necessary to add confidence when the evaluation is close to a cutoff point or when two or more project alternatives yield about the same "best" answer. In many cases, the desirability of a project or the selection from alternatives for a particular project will be so obvious that the costs of making sophisticated data estimates and using evaluation techniques are not justified.

Alternatives Having Unequal Lives. An additional difficulty in capital expenditure evaluation arises when alternatives with different economic lives are compared. To illustrate, a firm may be faced with the problem of acquiring equipment for a manufacturing operation. Two alternatives are available: Equipment A, expected to last 18 years, and Equipment B, expected to last 5 years. There are two ways to deal with this problem:

1. Repeat the investment cycle for Equipment B a sufficient number of times to cover the estimated economic life of Equipment A; in the example, $3^3/_5$ times. An estimate of the salvage value of the fourth equipment investment cycle for Equipment B at the end of the life for Equipment A is needed in order to reflect a common termination date.
2. The period considered can be the life of the shorter-life alternative, Equipment B, coupled with an estimate of the recoverable value of Equipment A at the end of 5 years. The analysis would then cover only the five-year period, with the recoverable value of Equipment A being treated as a cash inflow at the end of the period. A serious difficulty rests in the need to estimate a value of the longer-life asset at the end of 5 years. Such an intermediate recoverable value may not be an adequate measure of the service value of the equipment at that point in its useful life.

Purchase vs Leasing. A lease arrangement may be available as an alternative to investment in a capital asset. This possibility can be evaluated by determining the incremental annual cost of leasing versus purchasing. This cost represents purchasing cost savings which, on an aftertax basis, should be sufficient to yield the desired DCF rate of return on the anticipated purchase price.

In evaluating the leasing and purchasing alternatives, the present value method can be used in either of two ways:

1. The net present value of the purchase price and the associated aftertax savings is computed, with the resulting net present value used to evaluate the attractiveness of purchasing versus leasing.
2. The net present values of the purchasing alternative and the leasing alternative cash flows are computed separately, each on an aftertax basis. The alternative having the more favorable net present value identifies the preferable choice.

Generally, the capital expenditure or investment decision is first justified, followed by the lease or financing decision. The rationale is that the acquisition must be a sound investment before considering the financing strategy.

With a justified capital expenditure in hand, a lease-purchase decision can be made.[9]

Sensitivity Analysis. A comparison of the results of the present value or discounted cash flow techniques with the cost of capital is useful in helping management to arrive at a decision. However, management is never entirely assured, since many estimates enter into quantitative analyses. Any element of the project — revenue, cost, or the investment itself — is subject to variations or changes. Certain estimates are more sensitive to variations than others. Under these circumstances, the analyst must present a variety of possible results using numerous figures so that management can judge the impact of all possibilities. This type of approach, called *sensitivity analysis*, indicates in graphic or tabular form the effect of one project factor on another.

To illustrate, assume that a new Product, X, was developed on the basis of a sales price of $.38 per gallon and at that price the expected DCF rate of return was 26 percent. An expanded analysis showing the rates of return at sales prices ranging from $.34 to $.41 per gallon would be a form of sensitivity analysis. Variations in price, volume, labor cost, materials cost, and project investment are factors usually considered in such calculations. They are varied singly or in combination. For example, assume that the range of DCF rates of return was based on an assumption that the primary raw material, Z, would cost $.28 per gallon. The range of rates of return with the sales price ranging from $.34 to $.41 per gallon could also be computed if the possible costs of the primary raw material were $.29 and $.27.

The graph shown on the next page presents this illustration, assuming that a plant having a capacity of five million gallons per year and an economic life of ten years will require a $600,000 investment. Annual sales volume is also assumed to be five million gallons. The DCF rate of return can be read for the various combinations of Product X sales prices and Material Z costs.

Sensitivity analysis is useful in planning and in a variety of decision-making analyses in which the estimated impact of changed assumptions are relevant, such as in developing long-range plans, the annual budget, break-even and cost-volume-profit analysis, differential cost analysis, and linear programming. The usefulness of data can be further enhanced by injecting probability estimates to allow for risk and uncertainty in order to indicate how likely it appears that the sales price or other factors will vary.

Allowance for Risk and Uncertainty via Probability Estimates. Risk and uncertainty must be considered when cash flows for an investment project are being estimated, because ever-present uncertainty creates a degree of risk in the ultimate occurrence of any set of assumptions used. To assist management in the final decision, the analyst may resort to a presentation of a three-or-more-

---

[9]William L. Ferrara, *The Lease-Purchase Decision: How Some Companies Make It* (New York: National Association of Accountants; Hamilton, Ontario: The Society of Management Accountants of Canada, 1978), p. 7.

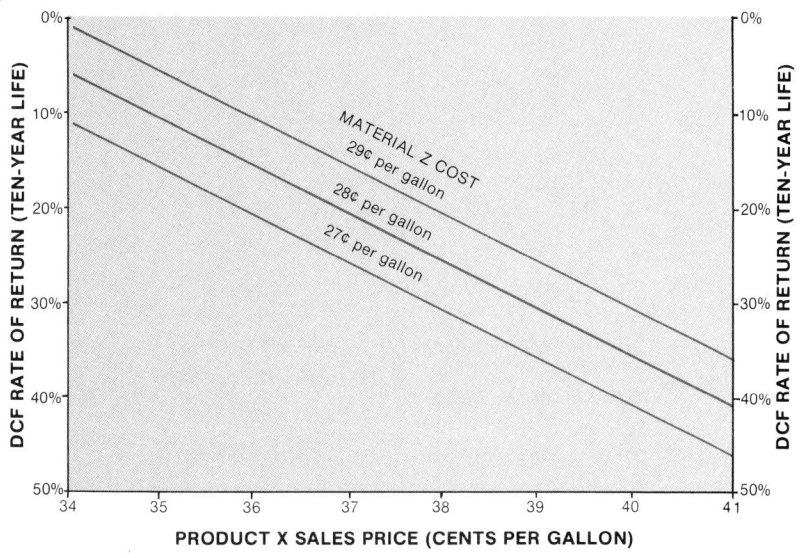

Sensitivity
Analysis Graph

level project estimate to indicate the possible outcomes, with a probability estimate for each. This risk analysis is an extension of sensitivity analysis.

The following procedure is one possible method for dealing with risk and uncertainty:

1. Determine the net present value of the net cash flows for three different assumptions:
   a. Most probable series of events.
   b. A reasonably pessimistic series of events.
   c. A reasonably optimistic series of events.
2. Assign probabilities to the three net present values, using the best information available or standard weights.
3. The sum of the three expected net present values may be used to represent the expected value of the investment, taking risk and uncertainty into consideration to a limited degree.

This procedure is illustrated as follows:

	NET PRESENT VALUE (CONDITIONAL VALUE)	PROBABILITY	EXPECTED NET PRESENT VALUE
Most probable (from page 773)...	$24,290	.50	$12,145
Pessimistic assumptions	5,000	.30	1,500
Optimistic assumptions	35,000	.20	7,000
Expected net present value (expected value)......................			$20,645

The standard deviation and coefficient of variation can be computed as follows:

(1) NET PRESENT VALUE (CONDITIONAL VALUE)	(2) DIFFERENCE FROM EXPECTED VALUE ($20,645)	(3) (2) SQUARED	(4) PROBABILITY	(5) (3) × (4)
$24,290	$ 3,645	$ 13,286,025	.50	$ 6,643,013
5,000	− 15,645	244,766,025	.30	73,429,808
35,000	14,355	206,066,025	.20	41,213,205
				$121,286,026

$$\text{Standard deviation} = \sqrt{\$121,286,026} = \$11,013$$

$$\text{Coefficient of variation} = \frac{\$11,013}{\$20,645} = .53$$

Allowing for risk and uncertainty can be further demonstrated by referring to the illustration introduced on page 780 in the discussion of sensitivity analysis. Assume that probability estimates are made as follows:

MATERIAL Z COST	PROBABILITY OF OCCURRENCE	PRODUCT X SALES PRICE	PROBABILITY OF OCCURRENCE
$.29	20%	$.39	30%
.28	70	.38	30
.27	10	.37	40
	100%		100%

The annual sales volume is expected to be five million gallons. In this example, the sales price variation is assumed to be independent of materials cost and volume; hence, it may increase, remain the same, or decrease at any of the three Material Z costs. Other sales prices and Material Z costs are assumed to have a zero probability of occurrence. The resulting nine possible outcomes for these assumptions and their related probabilities are:

MATERIAL Z (1) Cost	MATERIAL Z (2) Probability	PRODUCT X (3) Sales Price	PRODUCT X (4) Probability	(5) COMBINED PROBABILITY (2) × (4)	(6) DCF RATE OF RETURN* (CONDITIONAL VALUE)	(7) EXPECTED DCF RATE OF RETURN (5) × (6)
$.29	.20	$.39	.30	.06	.26	.0156
	.20	.38	.30	.06	.21	.0126
	.20	.37	.40	.08	.16	.0128
.28	.70	.39	.30	.21	.31	.0651
	.70	.38	.30	.21	.26	.0546
	.70	.37	.40	.28	.21	.0588
.27	.10	.39	.30	.03	.36	.0108
	.10	.38	.30	.03	.31	.0093
	.10	.37	.40	.04	.26	.0104
				1.00		

Expected DCF rate of return (expected value) .... .2500 = 25%

*These rates were read from the graph on page 781.

The standard deviation and coefficient of variation are:

(1) DCF RATE OF RETURN (CONDITIONAL VALUE)	(2) DIFFERENCE FROM EXPECTED VALUE (25%)	(3) (2) SQUARED	(4) PROBABILITY	(5) (3) × (4)
26%	1%	1%	.06	.06%
21	−4	16	.06	.96
16	−9	81	.08	6.48
31	6	36	.21	7.56
26	1	1	.21	.21
21	−4	16	.28	4.48
36	11	121	.03	3.63
31	6	36	.03	1.08
26	1	1	.04	.04
				24.5%

$$\text{Standard deviation} = \sqrt{24.5\%} = \underline{\underline{4.9\%}}$$

$$\text{Coefficient of variation} = \frac{4.9\%}{25\%} = \underline{\underline{.20}}$$

Not only is the expected DCF rate of return of 25 percent useful to management, but the cumulative probabilities of realizing a rate of return at least equal to each of the various rates are also useful. Beginning with the highest rate for the nine possibilities, the following cumulative probabilities can be determined:

DCF RATE OF RETURN	CUMULATIVE PROBABILITY
36%	.03
31	.27 (.03 + .21 + .03)
26	.58 (.27 + .06 + .21 + .04)
21	.92 (.58 + .06 + .28)
16	1.00 (.92 + .08)

Thus, there is a .03 probability that the rate of return will be 36 percent, a .27 probability that the rate will be at least 31 percent, a .58 probability that the rate will be at least 26 percent, etc.

Many economic variables are not independent of one another; e.g., the materials cost may influence the sales price of the finished product. If there is dependence of the variables, computational procedures must be modified by substituting *conditional probabilities*.

The illustration from the previous page can be used to demonstrate variable dependence when the sales price is presumed to be influenced by materials cost. Assume the same probabilities for Material Z cost as before, but assume that the Product X sales price probabilities will be influenced by Material Z cost as follows:

PROBABILITY OF SALES PRICE

PRODUCT X SALES PRICE	Material Z Cost — $.29	Material Z Cost — $.28	Material Z Cost — $.27
$.39	60%	40%	20%
.38	30	40	30
.37	10	20	50
	100%	100%	100%

The resulting nine possible outcomes for these assumptions and their related probabilities are summarized below. Observe that conditional probabilities have been substituted into Column 4.

MATERIAL Z		PRODUCT X		(5) COMBINED PROBABILITY	(6) DCF RATE OF RETURN (CONDITIONAL	(7) EXPECTED DCF RATE OF RETURN
(1)	(2)	(3) Sales	(4) Conditional	PROBABILITY	OF RETURN (CONDITIONAL	OF RETURN
Cost	Probability	Price	Probability	(2) × (4)	VALUE)	(5) × (6)
$.29	⎧.20	$.39	.60	.12	.26	.0312
	⎨.20	.38	.30	.06	.21	.0126
	⎩.20	.37	.10	.02	.16	.0032
.28	⎧.70	.39	.40	.28	.31	.0868
	⎨.70	.38	.40	.28	.26	.0728
	⎩.70	.37	.20	.14	.21	.0294
.27	⎧.10	.39	.20	.02	.36	.0072
	⎨.10	.38	.30	.03	.31	.0093
	⎩.10	.37	.50	.05	.26	.0130
				1.00		

Expected DCF rate of return (expected value) .... .2655 = 26.55%

Again, the standard deviation and coefficient of variation are:

(1) DCF RATE OF RETURN (CONDITIONAL VALUE)	(2) DIFFERENCE FROM EXPECTED VALUE (27%)*	(3) (2) SQUARED	(4) PROBABILITY	(5) (3) × (4)
26%	− 1%	1%	.12	.12%
21	− 6	36	.06	2.16
16	−11	121	.02	2.42
31	4	16	.28	4.48
26	− 1	1	.28	.28
21	− 6	36	.14	5.04
36	9	81	.02	1.62
31	4	16	.03	.48
26	− 1	1	.05	.05
				16.65%

*26.55% rounded = 27%

$$\text{Standard deviation} = \sqrt{16.65\%} = \underline{4.1\%}$$

$$\text{Coefficient of variation} = \frac{4.1\%}{26.55\%} = \underline{.15}$$

Computer Usage for Evaluation Analysis. Electronic data processing equipment offers the analyst an opportunity to expand the investment evaluation analysis beyond a mere handful of manual computations. The computer permits the creation of numerous models that simulate various possibilities of expected results. The main purpose of the simulation process is to improve the quality of management's decisions by offering new and more reliable information and guidance. Whenever the key factors in a business problem are susceptible to various patterns of variations, the use of models and simulation will be especially helpful. It should be understood that even the most sophisticated and computerized analytical methods do not relieve management of the all-important task of making the final decision.

CONTROL OF CAPITAL EXPENDITURES

The control phase consists of (1) control and review of a project while it is in process and (2) follow-up or post-completion audit of project results.

Control While in Process

When a project or a series of projects has finally been approved, methods, techniques, and procedures must be set in motion to permit the control and review of all project elements (costs, time, quality, and quantity) until completion. Control responsibility should be clearly designated, recognizing the necessity of assistance from and coordination with many individuals and groups, including those external to the company. Actual results should be compared with approved plans and evaluation results. Variations or trends toward deviations from plans should be reported promptly to responsible authorities in order to facilitate corrective action as quickly as possible. Day-to-day, on-the-scene observation and up-to-date reports should provide good cost control vehicles. Construction engineers have long used such devices as bar charts for planning and controlling the timing of project activities.

PERT/cost (Chapter 17) utilizes the network scheme to show the interrelationships of the multiple activities required to complete the average to large-scale project. Any project — the installation of a single large machine, a complex of machinery and equipment, or the construction of a new factory or office building — will involve many diverse tasks. Some of them can be done simultaneously; others must await the completion of preceding activities. PERT/cost offers a clear and all-inclusive picture of the operation as a whole in contrast to the bars on a chart. The use of this technique is particularly appropriate for those evaluation cases where more than one estimate is needed due to risk and uncertainty and there is a desire to expedite and increase the reliability of difficult estimates.

The cost of administering the control phase should be commensurate with the value derived. Overcontrol is an inefficient use of administrative resources.

Follow-Up of Project Results

Follow-up or post-completion audit means comparing and reporting results as related to the outcome predicted when the investment project was evaluated and approved. Follow-up affords a test of the existing planning and control procedure and therein the possibility of reinforcing successful projects, salvaging or terminating failing projects, and improving upon future investment proposals and decisions.

The same techniques used to evaluate the proposed project should be used for follow-up. For example, if the DCF rate of return projected in support of a project proposal is compared, in the follow-up procedure, with the actual average annual return on investment, the comparison could be quite misleading. Instead, the projected DCF rate should be compared to a DCF rate based on actual data and a reestimation of future data, thus employing the same evaluation technique in the follow-up as in evaluating the project proposal. It is also important to consider the illusory effect of inflation, which causes the rate of return to be overstated because inflated cash inflows over the project's life are compared to the original investment.

Generally, actual work in the area of follow-up lags behind advances made in other capital expenditure phases. Common hindrances to follow-up procedures are management's unwillingness to incur additional administrative costs, difficulty of quantifying the results of certain types of investments, apparent failure of the accounting or cost system to produce needed information, lack of personnel qualified to perform the follow-up tasks, and resentment of those being audited.

Value received as related to the cost of obtaining the follow-up information should determine the extent of the follow-up. For uniformity, efficiency, and independent review, management should designate a centralized group to prescribe procedures and audit the performance of the follow-up activity. The assembled data should be utilized as a control device and be reported to the controlling levels of management. Out-of-line results should then trigger corrective action in harmony with the management by exception principle.

DISCUSSION QUESTIONS

1. Explain the nature of capital expenditure planning and control.
2. Why are effective planning and control of capital expenditures important?
3. Differentiate between the economic and physical life of a project.
4. Define and discuss the cost of capital.
5. Why would a firm use its weighted average cost of capital as the hurdle rate (minimum rate) for a project investment decision rather than the specific marginal cost of funds?

6. Explain the principal reasons for the difference between the weighted average cost of capital of two firms.

7. Financial accounting data are not entirely suitable for use in evaluating capital expenditures. Explain.   (AICPA adapted)

8. Define the payback (or payout) period method.

9. How do the two average annual return on investment methods differ?

10. Modern capital expenditure evaluation uses the present value concept. Explain this concept.

11. What are the basic differences between the payback method and the present value method?   (AICPA adapted)

12. A manufacturing operation is presently done by hand at an aftertax cash cost for wages and fringe benefits of $1,100 per month. A machine can be purchased to perform this operation at an aftertax cash operating cost of $100 per month. The machine would have an estimated life of 10 years and no scrap value. Money is worth 8%, compounded annually. What is the maximum amount that should be paid for this machine?   (CGAA adapted)

13. Ludington, Inc., purchased a new machine on January 1 for $350,000. The machine is expected to have a useful life of 8 years and no salvage value. Straight-line depreciation is to be used. The present value of the cash flow generated by the machine was calculated to be $371,120 using a time-adjusted rate of return of 14%. What was the annual cash inflow used in calculating the present value?

(AICPA adapted)

14. Discuss the difference between the present value and the discounted cash flow methods.

15. Assuming a uniform cash flow, what is the required payback period in order to yield a 20% DCF rate of return for a project having an estimated economic life of 15 years?

16. Assuming a uniform cash flow, what economic life is required for a project having a DCF rate of return of 15% and a payback period of 5 years?

17. Describe two principal limitations in using the payback period reciprocal as a meaningful approximation of the discounted cash flow rate of return.

18. Both the present value method and the discounted cash flow method assume that the earnings produced by a project are reinvested in the company. However, each approach assumes a different rate of return at which earnings are reinvested. Describe the rate of return assumed in each of the two approaches and discuss which of the assumed rates is more realistic.

(CGAA adapted)

19. Define sensitivity analysis.

20. Distinguish between independent and conditional probabilities.

21. How should a company's analysts follow up and report on the results of capital expenditure decisions?

22. Select the answer which best completes the statement:
    (a) In selecting the purchase of one of two machines to replace an old machine, the management of Ashworth Company should consider as rele-

COST AND PROFIT ANALYSIS

vant: (1) historical costs associated with the old machine; (2) future costs that will be classified as variable rather than fixed; (3) future costs that will be different under the two alternatives; (4) future costs that will be classified as fixed rather than variable.

(b) For a project such as a plant investment, the return that investors demand for investing in a firm is known as: (1) DCF rate of return; (2) net present value; (3) payback; (4) cost of capital.

(c) Jennings Company is planning to purchase a new machine. The payback period is estimated to be 6 years. Project aftertax cash flow is estimated to be $2,000 yearly for the first 3 years and $3,000 yearly for the next 3 years of the payback period. Annual depreciation of $1,500 will be charged to income for each of the 6 years of the payback period. The machine will cost: (1) $15,000; (2) $12,000; (3) $9,000; (4) $6,000.

(d) Ciraulo, Inc., recently acquired a machine at a cost of $64,000. It will be depreciated on a straight-line basis over 8 years, with no estimated salvage value. Ciraulo estimates that this machine will produce an $18,000 annual net cash inflow before income tax. Assuming an income tax rate of 50%, the approximate payback period on this investment is: (1) 3.6 years; (2) 4.9 years; (3) 7.1 years; (4) 12.8 years.

(e) An advantage of using the payback method is that the method is: (1) precise in estimates of profitability; (2) simple to compute; (3) not based on cash flow data; (4) insensitive to the life of the project being evaluated.

(f) The present value and discounted cash flow rate of return methods of evaluating capital expenditure proposals are superior to the payback method in that they: (1) are easier to implement; (2) consider the time value of money; (3) require less input; (4) reflect the effects of depreciation and income tax.

(g) A planned factory expansion project has an estimated initial cost of $800,000. Using a 20% discount rate, the present value of future cost savings from the expansion is $843,000. To yield exactly a 20% time-adjusted rate of return, the actual investment cost cannot exceed the $800,000 estimate by more than: (1) $160,000; (2) $20,000; (3) $43,000; (4) $1,075.

(h) A company bought Machine 1 on March 5, 19A, for $5,000 cash. The estimated salvage value was $200 and the estimated life was 11 years. On March 5, 19B, the company learned that it could purchase a different machine for $8,000 cash. The new machine would save the company an estimated $250 per year compared to Machine 1. The new machine would have no estimated salvage value and an estimated life of 10 years. The company could get $3,000 for Machine 1 on March 5, 19B. Ignoring income tax, the calculation that would best assist the company in deciding whether to purchase the new machine is: (1) present value of $250 for each of the next 10 years + $3,000 − $8,000; (2) present value of $250 for each of the next 10 years − $8,000; (3) present value of $250 for each of the next 10 years + $3,000 − $8,000 − $5,000; (4) present value of $250 for each of the next 10 years + $3,000 − $8,000 − $4,800.

(i) The effectiveness of the present value method has been appropriately questioned as a capital expenditure evaluation technique because: (1) predicting future cash flows is often difficult and clouded with uncertainties; (2) the average return on investment method is usually more accurate and useful; (3) the payback method is theoretically more reliable; (4) the computation involves some difficult mathematical applications that most accountants cannot perform.

(j) Sensitivity analysis is used in capital expenditure evaluation to quantify the: (1) amount that an assumed factor used in evaluating a project could be varied and still produce acceptable results; (2) reaction within the marketplace to a new product; (3) type of capital that must be committed to an anticipated project; (4) relationship between the payback period and the economic lives of the assets used in a project.

(k) The reason for using probabilities in capital budgeting decisions is: (1) risk and uncertainty; (2) cost of capital; (3) time value of money; (4) projects with unequal lives.

(AICPA adapted)

EXERCISES

1. Cost of capital. The Babcock Company wishes to compute a weighted average cost of capital for use in evaluating capital expenditure proposals. Earnings, capital structure, and current market prices of the company's securities are:

Earnings:

Earnings before interest and tax	$ 143,000
Interest expense on bonds	15,000
Pretax earnings	$ 128,000
Income tax (assume 50% tax rate)	64,000
Aftertax earnings	$ 64,000
Preferred stock dividends	14,000
Earnings available to common stockholders	$ 50,000
Common stock dividends	30,000
Retained earnings	$ 20,000

Capital structure:

Mortgage bonds, 5%, 10 years	$ 300,000
Preferred stock, 7%, $100 par	200,000
Common stock, no par, 50,000 shares	350,000
Retained earnings (equity of common stockholders)	150,000
	$1,000,000

Market prices of the company's securities:

Preferred stock	$87.50
Common stock	10.00

Required: Cost of capital using the method illustrated in the chapter.

2. Investment analysis. The Grand Island Company is considering the purchase of a giant press costing $100,000. The estimated cash benefit is:

YEAR	CASH BENEFIT
1	$25,000
2	40,000
3	40,000
4	40,000
5	35,000
6	30,000
7	25,000
8	20,000
9	15,000
10	10,000

The press is to be depreciated on a straight-line basis over a period of 10 years. The salvage value is zero. Assume a 50% tax rate and a cost of capital of 10%.

Required:
- (1) Payback period.
- (2) Average annual return on original investment.
- (3) Average annual return on average investment.
- (4) Net present value.
- (5) Discounted cash flow rate of return.

3. Equipment replacement analysis. The Lubbock Precision Company contemplates the replacement of certain machinery. The annual cost of operating the machinery is $138,600, excluding depreciation, while the estimate for the new machinery is $91,800. Cost of the new equipment is $160,000, net of the trade-in allowance, with a useful life estimate of 8 years and no salvage value. Assume an income tax rate of 50%, an 8% cost of capital, and straight-line depreciation of $20,000 per year. The book value of the old machine is zero.

Required:
- (1) Payback period
- (2) Average annual return on (a) original investment; (b) average investment. (Carry computations to three decimal places.)
- (3) Net present value and net present value index.
- (4) Discounted cash flow rate of return.

4. Present value tables. Heslin, Inc., is considering investing in a machine with a useful life of 5 years and no salvage value. The machine would be depreciated using the straight-line method. The annual cash inflow from operations, net of income tax, is estimated to be $1,000.

Required:
- (1) The amount of the original investment if the DCF rate of return is 12%.
- (2) The net present value, assuming that the firm's cost of capital is 12%, that this rate is used in calculating net present value, and that the amount of the original investment is $3,500.

(AICPA adapted)

5. Effect of depreciation methods on cash flow. Bell Corporation acquired a plant asset at a cost of $100,000. The estimated life was 4 years, and there was no estimated salvage value. Assume a relevant interest rate of 8% and an income tax rate of 40%.

Required: The present value of the income tax benefits resulting from using sum-of-the-years-digits depreciation as opposed to straight-line depreciation on this asset.

(AICPA adapted)

6. Equipment investment analysis. The Unifact Company manufactures one product. The results of its operations for the year are summarized in the following condensed income statement:

Sales		$2,000,000
Less cost of goods sold:		
Fixed cost	$ 250,000	
Variable cost	1,400,000	1,650,000
Gross profit		$ 350,000
Commercial expenses:		
Fixed expense	$ 66,000	
Variable expense	200,000	266,000
Income before income tax		$ 84,000
Income tax		42,000
Net income		$ 42,000

The company is considering the purchase of equipment to replace an existing manual operation. It is estimated that the equipment will effect annual savings of $1,900 in labor and other direct cash costs. The new equipment is estimated to have an installed cost of $10,000 and an economic life of 10 years with no salvage value at the end of its life. Depreciation is computed on a straight-line basis. Assume that the company expects to pay an income tax of 50%.

Required:
(1) Payback period.
(2) Average annual return on original investment.
(3) Average annual return on average investment.
(4) Net present value, rounded to the nearest dollar, assuming that the company wishes to earn 10% on its investment, after income tax.
(5) Present value payback period. (Round computations to the nearest dollar.)
(6) Net present value index.
(7) Discounted cash flow rate of return.

7. Equipment replacement analysis. The Michener Company purchased a special machine one year ago at a cost of $12,500. At that time, the machine was estimated to have a useful life of 6 years and a $500 disposal value. The annual cash operating cost is approximately $20,000.

A new machine that has just come on the market will do the same job but with an annual cash operating cost of only $17,000. This new machine costs $16,000 and has an estimated life of 5 years with a $1,000 disposal value. The old machine could be used as a trade-in at an allowance of $5,000.

Straight-line depreciation is used and the company's income tax rate is 50%.

Required: Recommendation to management based on DCF rate of return computation.
(CGAA adapted)

8. Comparison of equipment alternatives. Two new machines are being evaluated for possible purchase. Forecasts relating to the two machines are:

	MACHINE 1	MACHINE 2
Purchase price	$50,000	$60,000
Estimated life (straight-line depreciation)	4 years	4 years
Estimated scrap value	none	none
Annual cash benefits before income tax:		
Year 1	$25,000	$45,000
Year 2	25,000	19,000
Year 3	25,000	25,000
Year 4	25,000	25,000
Income tax rate	40%	40%

Required: Net present value index for Machine 1 and Machine 2, using an 8% discount rate. (Round off computations to three decimal places.)   (CGAA adapted)

9. Feasibility study. A proposed addition to the Hidden Valley, Colorado, ski lift facilities requires an investment of $1,300,000 and will have a 5-year useful life and no salvage value, and it is estimated that aftertax income over the life of the project will total $600,000, as shown below:

Estimated Revenue and Expenses
(Thousands of Dollars)

	YEAR					
	1	2	3	4	5	Total
Revenue	$ 500	$1,000	$2,000	$2,500	$2,000	$8,000
Expenses: Depreciation.	$ 260	$ 260	$ 260	$ 260	$ 260	$1,300
Other (cash)..	400	750	1,400	1,750	1,400	5,700
	$ 660	$1,010	$1,660	$2,010	$1,660	$7,000
Income before income tax	$ (160)	$ (10)	$ 340	$ 490	$ 340	$1,000
Income tax (40%)	0	0	$ 136	$ 196	$ 136	$ 468
Loss carryforward	0	0	(68)*	0	0	(68)
Income tax	0	0	$ 68	$ 196	$ 136	$ 400
Net income	$ (160)	$ (10)	$ 272	$ 294	$ 204	$ 600

*(160 + $10) × .40 = $68.

Required:
(1) The average annual return on original investment, rounded to the nearest $^1/_{10}$ of 1%.
(2) The average annual return on average investment, rounded to the nearest $^1/_{10}$ of 1%.
(3) The payout period.
(4) The net present value and the net present value index at 8%, rounded to three decimal places.
(5) The discounted cash flow rate of return.

10. Net present value and DCF rate of return reinvestment assumption. Aftertax cash flows for two mutually exclusive projects (with economic lives of 4 years each) are:

YEAR	PROJECT X	PROJECT Y
0	$(12,000)	$(12,000)
1	5,000	0
2	5,000	0
3	5,000	0
4	5,000	25,000

The company's cost of capital is 10%.

Required:
(1) The discounted cash flow rate of return for each project.
(2) The net present value for each project.
(3) The project that should be selected.

(CGAA adapted)

11. Bond redemption analysis. Realm, Inc., is planning to issue new bonds at a lower interest rate in order to cancel currently outstanding bonds. The controller realizes that this decision to redeem bonds and issue new ones can be viewed as a capital expenditure decision. When using capital expenditure evaluation techniques, Realm has adopted the following cutoff points: 8 years for the maximum payback period and 16% for the minimum desired discounted cash flow rate of return.

The net cash investment is estimated to be $550,000, which is the difference between the net cash outflow to redeem the original issue and the amount raised by the new issue. The net cash benefit is estimated to be $120,000 per year for 15 years and is the difference between the annual net cash outlay required on the original issue and the new issue.

Required:
(1) Payback period.
(2) Net present value.
(3) Net present value index, rounded to three decimal places.
(4) Discounted cash flow rate of return.

(AICPA adapted)

12. Purchase vs leasing. Zorba Co. is considering two alternatives for providing additional warehousing space for its department stores. The purchase price of the facility is assumed to be $330,000 with an economic life of 10 years. The estimated salvage value at the end of the economic life is zero, and the straight-line depreciation method is to be used. The irrevocable lease provides that Zorba pay an annual rent of $50,000 for 10 years, payable at the beginning of each year.

Maintenance costs, insurance, etc., are covered in a separate contract with the lessor, whether the asset is purchased or leased. Assume that an income tax of 50% is to be paid at the end of each year and that the taxing authorities will permit taxation of the lease-rental agreement as a lease.

Required: The discounted cash flow rate of return of the aftertax cash savings of purchasing rather than leasing.

13. Purchase vs leasing. Wheary Enterprises plans to operate a sightseeing boat along the Charles River in Boston. In negotiating the purchase of a new vessel from Yachts Dynamic, Inc., Wheary learned that Yachts Dynamic would lease the boat to them as an alternative to selling it outright. Through such an arrangement, Wheary would not pay the $2,200,000 purchase price but would lease for $180,000 annually. Wheary expects the boat to last for 20 years, when its value would be $200,000.

The annual net cash flow, excluding any consideration of lease payments and income tax, is expected to be $600,000. The company's income tax rate is 55% and its cost of capital is 12%. The straight-line depreciation method is to be used.

Required: Recommendation to purchase or lease, using the present value method to evaluate each alternative.

14. Allowing for risk and uncertainty in present value calculations. The administrator of Portland Municipal Hospital is considering the purchase of new operating-room equipment at a cost of $7,500. The surgical staff has furnished the following estimates of useful life and cost savings. Each useful life estimate is independent of each cost savings estimate.

YEARS OF ESTIMATED USEFUL LIFE	PROBABILITY OF OCCURRENCE	ESTIMATED COST SAVINGS	PROBABILITY OF OCCURRENCE
4	.25	$1,900	.30
5	.50	2,000	.40
6	.25	2,100	.30
	1.00		1.00

Required:
(1) The expected net present value, allowing for risk and uncertainty and using a 10% discount rate. (Round computations to the nearest dollar.)
(2) The standard deviation and coefficient of variation (rounded to two decimal places) for the present value calculations of estimated cost savings before deducting the investment.

PROBLEMS

26-1. Cost of capital. Electro Tool Company, a manufacturer of diamond drilling, cutting, and grinding tools, has $1,000,000 of its 8% bond issue maturing next month. To meet this debt, an additional $1,000,000 must be raised, and one proposal under consideration is the sale and lease-back of the company's general office building.

The building would be sold to FHR, Inc., for $1,000,000 and leased back on a 25-year lease with annual payments of $110,168, permitting the lessor to recover its investment and earn 10% on the investment. Electro Tool will pay all maintenance costs, property taxes, and insurance and will reacquire the building at the end of the lease period for a nominal payment.

The current capital structure is:

CAPITAL COMPONENT	AMOUNT	PRETAX COMPONENT COST
Bonds (including amount to be retired next month)	$5,000,000	8.0%
Preferred stock (market value)	1,000,000	9.0
Common stock and retained earnings (market value)	4,000,000	12.5

Electro Tool's income tax rate is 40%.

Required: Weighted average cost of capital before and after bond retirement and sale-leaseback transaction.

(CMA adapted)

26-2. New product investment analysis. The Baxter Company manufactures short-lived fad-type items.

The Research Department has developed an item that would be an interesting promotional gift for office equipment dealers. Agressive efforts by Baxter's sales personnel has resulted in almost firm commitments for this product for the next 3 years. It is expected that the product's value will be exhausted by that time.

To produce the quantity demanded, Baxter will need to buy additional machinery and rent 12,500 square feet of additional space. There is 12,500 square feet of space adjoining the Baxter facility, which Baxter will rent for 3 years at $4 per square foot per year if it decides to make this product.

The equipment will be purchased for about $900,000. It will require $30,000 in modifications, $60,000 for installation, and $90,000 for testing; all of these activities will be done by a firm of engineers hired by Baxter. All of the expenditures will be made on January 1, 19A.

The equipment should have a salvage value of about $180,000 at the end of the third year. No additional general overhead costs are expected to be incurred.

The following estimates of revenue and expenses for this product have been developed for the three years:

	19A	19B	19C
Sales	$1,000,000	$1,600,000	$800,000
Material, labor, and additional factory overhead	$ 400,000	$ 750,000	$350,000
Assigned general overhead	77,500	112,500	72,500
Rent (12,500 square feet of space × $4)	50,000	50,000	50,000
Depreciation	450,000	300,000	150,000
Total expense	$ 977,500	$1,212,500	$622,500
Income before income tax	$ 22,500	$ 387,500	$177,500
Income tax (40%)	9,000	155,000	71,000
Net income	$ 13,500	$ 232,500	$106,500

Required:
(1) A schedule showing the net aftertax cash inflow for this project.
(2) A decision (with supporting computations) as to whether this project should be undertaken if the Baxter Company requires a two-year payback period for its investment.
(3) The aftertax average annual return on average investment for the project.
(4) A decision as to whether the project should be undertaken, using present value analysis and assuming that the Baxter Company requires a 20% aftertax rate of return.

(CMA adapted)

26-3. Equipment investment proposal. Continental Container Company owns and operates a plant whose major product is cardboard six-pack carriers for soft drink bottling companies. This is essentially a large volume, low profit operation, and management is considering further mechanization of the plant's facilities.

The production of the six-pack carriers involves three departments: Printing, Stamping, and Stripping and Packing. In the first department, the bottling company's design is printed on large 10,000-yard rolls of paper. These colored sheets are then sent to the Stamping Department where the rolls are cut into 5' × 6' sheets that are then stamped with the six-pack shape over the printed form. Finally, the Stripping and Packing Department splits off the individual six-packs from the large sheets (12 packs per sheet) with air hammers and the separated packs are packaged in large containers for shipment to the bottling plants.

Plant management feels that the purchase of an additional highly automated machine at a cost of $2,200,000 will allow the plant to handle a larger volume of six-pack business than present capacity permits. In addition, this machine should eliminate the necessity for overtime work during the peak months (May–September) when the bottling companies require a larger supply of packs.

The new machine will necessitate employing two additional machine operators for each shift. The plant should generate enough additional business to keep the machine operating for two shifts, five days per week, fifty weeks per year. Additional factory overhead directly attributable to the machine is $100,000 per year, exclusive of depreciation. The machine can stamp, strip, and pack 5 rolls per 8-hour shift. The cost of training the additional operators, whose average salary will be $9 per hour, is $3,000 per operator. Materials (paper, ink, etc.) and printing costs are estimated to be $80,000 per week if the new machine produces its estimated output. Each pack will sell for $.0338 with approximately 60,000 packs per roll of paper. Overtime that will be avoided is $40,000 per year. The machine has an estimated useful life of 10 years with a salvage value of $200,000. The straight-line depreciation method is to be used. The company's income tax rate is 50%.

Required: The feasibility of this investment, using the present value method and assuming that the company has a cost of capital of 12%.

26-4. Equipment investment related to make-or-buy decision. The Scranton Corporation is a small producer of industrial and commercial chemicals. One of the company's principal products is Quescent Phosphor, which accounts for 30% of total sales volume and 40% of total operating income. The phosphor is used in fluorescent lighting for homes. One of its main ingredients is a chemical called Oxidon, which must be extracted from Oxidon Concentrate. Currently, Scranton purchases all of its concentrate, which is converted into Oxidon by an outside processor. The yield is approximately one kilogram of Oxidon from every one and one-third kilograms of concentrate. Scranton is using, and expects to use, approximately 3 000 kilograms of Oxidon annually. The company pays the processor $35 per kilogram of Oxidon produced in the conversion process.

Scranton's president, in searching for ways to cut production costs, has asked the controller to determine whether the company could realize greater savings over the expected product life of the phosphor by performing the conversion process itself. The controller is aware that the company has the technical ability to perform the conversion and that Quescent Phosphor has an expected future product life of 10 years.

To perform the conversion, Scranton must invest $150,000 to procure and install additional equipment. The equipment is to be depreciated using the straight-line method with an estimated $30,000 salvage value. The company uses an 8% cost of capital criterion for evaluating investment projects.

The controller determined that Oxidon production would incur the following costs each year at the required 3 000 kilogram volume:

Materials:
Oxidon concentrate... $23.40 per kg
Alcohol.. 10.50
Acid 3.90
Sulfate.. 2.40
Additonal direct labor 6.00

Additional factory overhead (excluding depreciation)..................... $15,600

Required: A decision as to whether the company should make the necessary investment to perform the conversion process, using the present value method and assuming that the data will not change over the 10-year period and that the income tax rate is 50%.

26-5. Equipment replacement study. The management of New Brunswick Products, Inc., is considering replacing machinery purchased 8 years ago and costing $80,000 with new machinery costing $130,000. The old machinery has a remaining useful life of 8 years, and its trade-in value is estimated to be $40,000 now, while the trade-in value 8 years hence is estimated to be its book value plus removal cost. Equipment manufacturers advise that both the old and new machinery will probably be obsolete in 8 years to the point that replacement will be mandatory. The proposed new equipment has an estimated life of 8 years, at the end of which its market value is assumed to be equal to its book value at that time with no removal cost to be borne by New Brunswick. Incoming freight and installation costs in connection with the new machinery will be $20,000. A removal cost of $1,000 is anticipated in connection with the old machinery.

The annual costs of operating the old and new machinery are presented on page 796.

	ACTUAL FOR THE OLD MACHINERY	ANTICIPATED FOR THE NEW MACHINERY
Variable cost	$50,000	$15,000
Fixed cost (excluding depreciation) .	11,000	18,500

The desired minimum aftertax rate of return normally required by the company is 12%. The income tax rate applicable throughout is 50%.

Assume, for income tax purposes, that the sum-of-the-years-digits depreciation method is used for the old and new machinery, with a 10% provision for residual value. Any gain or loss on the disposal of the old machinery will serve to adjust the depreciable basis of the new replacement machinery.

Required:
(1) The net aftertax cash flow if the machinery is replaced. (Round computations to the nearest dollar.)
(2) The net present value, the net present value index rounded to three decimal places, and the rate of return on the investment by the discounted cash flow method.
(3) A decision as to whether New Brunswick should replace the existing machinery now.

26-6. Product model change analysis. The Beta Corporation manufactures office equipment and markets its products through wholesale distributors. The company recently learned of a patent on the production of a semiautomatic paper collator that can be obtained at a cost of $60,000 cash. The semiautomatic model is vastly superior to the manual model that the corporation now produces. At a cost of $40,000, present equipment could be modified to accommodate the production of the new semiautomatic model. Such modifications would not affect the remaining useful life of 4 years or the present equipment's salvage value of $10,000. Variable costs, however, would increase by one dollar per unit. Fixed costs, other than relevant amortization charges, would not be affected. If the equipment is modified, the manual model cannot be produced.

The current income statement relative to the manual collator appears as follows:

Sales (100,000 units @ $4)...		$400,000
Variable cost...	$180,000	
Fixed cost*	120,000	
Total cost		300,000
Income before income tax...		$100,000
Income tax (40%)...		40,000
Net income..		$ 60,000

*All fixed costs are directly assignable to the production of the manual collator and include equipment depreciation of $20,000, calculated on the straight-line basis with a useful life of 10 years.

Market research has disclosed three important findings relative to the new semiautomatic model. First, a particular competitor will certainly purchase the patent if Beta Corporation does not. In this case, Beta Corporation's sales of the manual collator would fall to 70,000 units per year. Second, if no increase in the sales price is made, Beta Corporation could sell approximately 190,000 units per year of the semiautomatic model. Third, because of the advances being made in this area, the patent will be completely worthless at the end of 4 years and would be amortized on a straight-line basis.

Because of the uncertainty of the current situation, the materials inventory has been almost completely exhausted. Regardless of the decision reached, substantial and immediate inventory replenishment will be required. The Engineering Department estimates that if the new model is to be produced, the average monthly materials inventory will be $20,000. If the old model is continued, the inventory balance will average $12,000 per month.

Required:
(1) A schedule which shows the differential aftertax cash flows for comparison of the two alternatives, assuming that the corporation will use the sum-of-the-years-digits method for depreciating the cost of modifying the equipment.

(2) A decision as to whether Beta Corporation should undertake the model change, using the present value method, an 18% cost of capital, and assuming that the differential aftertax cash flows and the annual incomes for the two alternatives are as given in the following schedule:

YEAR	DIFFERENTIAL AFTERTAX CASH FLOW (000S OMITTED)	ANNUAL INCOME AFTERTAX (000S OMITTED)	
		Manual	Semiautomatic
0 Investment	− $110	—	—
1	+ 40	$24	$39
2	+ 40	24	39
3	+ 40	24	39
4	+ 50	24	39

(3) A decision as to whether Beta should undertake the model change, using the average annual return on original investment for each alternative, based on the income data in the above schedule.
(4) Additional analytical techniques, if any, to consider before presenting a recommendation to management.
(5) Reservations about using the information, as given in the problem, to reach a decision in this case.   (CMA adapted)

26-7. Purchase vs leasing. Madisons, Inc., has decided to acquire a new machine either by an outright cash purchase at $25,000 or by a leasing alternative of $6,000 per year for the life of the machine. Other relevant information is:

Estimated useful life... 5 years
Estimated salvage value if purchased.. $3,000
Annual cost of maintenance contract to be acquired with either lease or
    purchase $500

Additional information:

(a) Assume a 40% income tax rate and the use of the straight-line method of depreciation.
(b) Assume that the taxing authorities will permit taxation of the lease agreement as a lease.
(c) The company's cost of capital is 10%.

Required:
(1) Under the purchase alternative:
  (a) The present value of the estimated salvage value;
  (b) The annual income tax reduction (cash inflow) related to depreciation;
  (c) The annual aftertax cash outflow for maintenance.
(2) A recommendation to management (with supporting computations), using the present value method to evaluate each alternative. (Round computations to the nearest dollar.)
    (AICPA adapted)

26-8. Purchase vs leasing with options. A manager is interested in evaluating the relative merits of options available under a proposed lease arrangement. The following facts are available:

Purchase. The purchase price of the facility is assumed to be $330,000; the economic life is assumed to be 10 years; and the salvage value at the end of the economic life is zero. Straight-line depreciation is used.
Leasing. The annual rental of the facility is $80,000 for 3 years, payable at the beginning of each year — a 3-year commitment. Thereafter, year-to-year lease renewals at the option of the lessee are available at the rate of $60,000 per year payable at the beginning of each year.
Purchase Option. A purchase option is available with the total purchase price payment due at the end of 3 years when the estimated purchase price and salvage value is $200,000. If the facility is purchased, it can be sold for this same amount at the end of 3 years.
Other Facts. The maintenance costs, insurance, etc., are covered in a separate contract with the lessor whether the asset is purchased or leased. The income tax rate is 50% and is paid at the end of each year. Assume that the taxing authorities will permit taxation of the lease-rental agreement as a lease.

Required:
(1) The discounted cash flow rate of return of the difference between aftertax cash savings of purchasing rather than leasing, assuming that:
  (a) The use of the facility is terminated at the end of 3 years;
  (b) The facility is leased 3 years, at which time the purchase option is exercised;
  (c) The facility is leased for the entire 10 years. (Round computations to the nearest dollar.)
(2) A discussion of how the analysis in (1) can be used in determining whether to purchase or lease the facility.   (Based on an article in *Management Accounting*)

26-9. Equipment feasibility study with allowance for risk and uncertainty. The plant manager of the Fleming Corporation is confronted with a need to purchase a machine.

Machine A will cost $5,000, Machine B's initial cost will be $10,000, and each machine has an estimated life of 3 years. However, an analysis of the operating costs associated with each of the machines reveals that the cost per unit with Machine A is $1 and with Machine B is $.50, excluding depreciation. The product's sales price is $4.

Estimates of the probability of the number of units required for each of the next 3 years, based in part upon analysis of the past and in part on the manager's best appraisal of the future, are as follows:

ANNUAL REQUIREMENTS	PROBABILITY OF OCCURRENCE
2,000	.2
3,000	.6
5,000	.2

Required:
(1) The net present value for each of the three activity levels for Machines A and B, using a discount rate of 6%.
(2) The expected net present value for each machine. (Ignore income tax considerations.)
(3) The standard deviation and coefficient of variation for each machine, rounding data used to the nearest dollar.

26-10. New product analysis considering risk and uncertainty; net present value. Vernon Enterprises designs and manufactures toys. Past experience indicates that the product life cycle of a toy is 3 years. Promotional advertising produces large sales in the early years, but there is a substantial sales decline in the final year of a toy's life.

Consumer demand for new toys placed on the market tends to fall into three classes: 30% of the new toys sell well above expectations; 60% sell as anticipated; and 10% have poor consumer acceptance.

A new toy has been developed, and the following sales projections were made by carefully evaluating its consumer demand:

CONSUMER DEMAND FOR NEW TOY	PROBABILITY OF OCCURRENCE	ESTIMATED SALES IN Year 1	Year 2	Year 3
Above average.......	30%	$1,200,000	$2,500,000	$600,000
Average..................	60	700,000	1,700,000	400,000
Below average.......	10	200,000	900,000	150,000

Variable costs are estimated at 30% of the sales price. Special machinery must be purchased at a cost of $860,000 and will be installed in an unused portion of the factory, which Vernon has unsuccessfully been trying to rent for several years at $50,000 per year with no prospects for future utilization. Fixed costs (excluding depreciation) of a cash-flow nature are estimated at $50,000 per year on the new toy. The new machinery is to be depreciated by the sum-of-the-years-digits method with an estimated salvage value of $110,000 and will be sold at the end of the third year. Advertising and promotional expenses will total $100,000 in the first year, $150,000 in the second year, and $50,000 in the third year. These expenses will be deducted as incurred for income tax reporting. The income tax rate is expected to be 60%.

Required:
  (1) A schedule of the new toy's probable sales for each year.
  (2) A schedule of the new toy's probable net income for each year of its life, assuming that the probable sales are $900,000 in the first year, $1,800,000 in the second year, and $410,000 in the third year.
  (3) A schedule of net cash flows from the new toy's sales for each of the years involved and from disposition of the machinery purchased. [Use the sales data given in (2).]
  (4) A schedule of the net present value of net cash flows computed in (3), assuming a minimum desired rate of return of 10%.

(AICPA adapted)

26-11. Equipment purchase and follow-up analysis. As part of a cost reduction program, the management of Montgomery Products, Inc., is considering the purchase of a new machine tool that will increase productivity through improved performance due to a speed increase of two and a half times over the present equipment.

The Engineering Department proposes the following investment in the new machine tool and its related costs:

New equipment	$91,000
Installation cost	4,000
Relocation, alteration, and rearrangement costs	5,000

All of these costs are to be capitalized. The present equipment is fully depreciated and has a zero trade-in value.

Other annual production and cost data of present and new equipment are estimated as follows:

	PRESENT EQUIPMENT	PROPOSED EQUIPMENT
Machine hours	10,000	4,000
Output	10,000 units	10,000 units
Variable cost ($4 per machine hour)	$40,000	$16,000
Tooling (subcontracted)	8,000	–0–
Annual depreciation (20-year life)		5,000
Other expense		5,000

The machine was purchased, and the actual results at the end of the first year were:

Machine hours	5,000
Output	11,500 units
New equipment	$90,000
Installation cost	6,000
Relocation, alteration, and rearrangement costs	6,000
Variable cost	20,000
Tooling	1,000
Depreciation	5,100
Other expense	6,000

The income tax rate is 50%.

Required:
  (1) The payback period, average annual return on the original investment, and discounted cash flow rate of return, based on the proposal.
  (2) The payback period, average annual return on the original investment, and discounted cash flow rate of return for the actual results at the end of the first year, assuming that these results represent expectations for the life of the project.

PRESENT VALUE OF $1

Future Years	1%	2%	4%	6%	8%	10%	12%	14%	15%	16%	18%	20%	22%	24%	25%	26%	28%	30%	35%	40%	45%	50%
1	.990	.980	.962	.943	.926	.909	.893	.877	.870	.862	.847	.833	.820	.806	.800	.794	.781	.769	.741	.714	.690	.667
2	.980	.961	.925	.890	.857	.826	.797	.769	.756	.743	.718	.694	.672	.650	.640	.630	.610	.592	.549	.510	.476	.444
3	.971	.942	.889	.840	.794	.751	.712	.675	.658	.641	.609	.579	.551	.524	.512	.500	.477	.455	.406	.364	.328	.296
4	.961	.924	.855	.792	.735	.683	.636	.592	.572	.552	.516	.482	.451	.423	.410	.397	.373	.350	.301	.260	.226	.198
5	.951	.906	.822	.747	.681	.621	.567	.519	.497	.476	.437	.402	.370	.341	.328	.315	.291	.269	.223	.186	.156	.132
6	.942	.888	.790	.705	.630	.564	.507	.456	.432	.410	.370	.335	.303	.275	.262	.250	.227	.207	.165	.133	.108	.088
7	.933	.871	.760	.665	.583	.513	.452	.400	.376	.354	.314	.279	.249	.222	.210	.198	.178	.159	.122	.095	.074	.059
8	.923	.853	.731	.627	.540	.467	.404	.351	.327	.305	.266	.233	.204	.179	.168	.157	.139	.123	.091	.068	.051	.039
9	.914	.837	.703	.592	.500	.424	.361	.308	.284	.263	.225	.194	.167	.144	.134	.125	.108	.094	.067	.048	.035	.026
10	.905	.820	.676	.558	.463	.386	.322	.270	.247	.227	.191	.162	.137	.116	.107	.099	.085	.073	.050	.035	.024	.017
11	.896	.804	.650	.527	.429	.350	.287	.237	.215	.195	.162	.135	.112	.094	.086	.079	.066	.056	.037	.025	.017	.012
12	.887	.788	.625	.497	.397	.319	.257	.208	.187	.168	.137	.112	.092	.076	.069	.062	.052	.043	.027	.018	.012	.008
13	.879	.773	.601	.469	.368	.290	.229	.182	.163	.145	.116	.093	.075	.061	.055	.050	.040	.033	.020	.013	.008	.005
14	.870	.758	.577	.442	.340	.263	.205	.160	.141	.125	.099	.078	.062	.049	.044	.039	.032	.025	.015	.009	.006	.003
15	.861	.743	.555	.417	.315	.239	.183	.140	.123	.108	.084	.065	.051	.040	.035	.031	.025	.020	.011	.006	.004	.002
16	.853	.728	.534	.394	.292	.218	.163	.123	.107	.093	.071	.054	.042	.032	.028	.025	.019	.015	.008	.005	.003	.002
17	.844	.714	.513	.371	.270	.198	.146	.108	.093	.080	.060	.045	.034	.026	.023	.020	.015	.012	.006	.003	.002	.001
18	.836	.700	.494	.350	.250	.180	.130	.095	.081	.069	.051	.038	.028	.021	.018	.016	.012	.009	.005	.002	.001	.001
19	.828	.686	.475	.331	.232	.164	.116	.083	.070	.060	.043	.031	.023	.017	.014	.012	.009	.007	.003	.002	.001	
20	.820	.673	.456	.312	.215	.149	.104	.073	.061	.051	.037	.026	.019	.014	.012	.010	.007	.005	.002	.001	.001	
21	.811	.660	.439	.294	.199	.135	.093	.064	.053	.044	.031	.022	.015	.011	.009	.008	.006	.004	.002	.001		
22	.803	.647	.422	.278	.184	.123	.083	.056	.046	.038	.026	.018	.013	.009	.007	.006	.004	.003	.001	.001		
23	.795	.634	.406	.262	.170	.112	.074	.049	.040	.033	.022	.015	.010	.007	.006	.005	.003	.002	.001			
24	.788	.622	.390	.247	.158	.102	.066	.043	.035	.028	.019	.013	.008	.006	.005	.004	.003	.002	.001			
25	.780	.610	.375	.233	.146	.092	.059	.038	.030	.024	.016	.010	.007	.005	.004	.003	.002	.001	.001			
26	.772	.598	.361	.220	.135	.084	.053	.033	.026	.021	.014	.009	.006	.004	.003	.002	.002	.001				
27	.764	.586	.347	.207	.125	.076	.047	.029	.023	.018	.011	.007	.005	.003	.002	.002	.001	.001				
28	.757	.574	.333	.196	.116	.069	.042	.026	.020	.016	.010	.006	.004	.002	.002	.002	.001	.001				
29	.749	.563	.321	.185	.107	.063	.037	.022	.017	.014	.008	.005	.003	.002	.002	.001	.001	.001				
30	.742	.552	.308	.174	.099	.057	.033	.020	.015	.012	.007	.004	.003	.002	.001	.001	.001					
40	.672	.453	.208	.097	.046	.022	.011	.005	.004	.003	.001	.001										
50	.608	.372	.141	.054	.021	.009	.003	.001	.001	.001												

PRESENT VALUE OF $1 RECEIVED OR PAID ANNUALLY FOR EACH OF THE NEXT N YEARS

Future Years	1%	2%	4%	6%	8%	10%	12%	14%	15%	16%	18%	20%	22%	24%	25%	26%	28%	30%	35%	40%	45%	50%
1	.990	.980	.962	.943	.926	.909	.893	.877	.870	.862	.847	.833	.820	.806	.800	.794	.781	.769	.741	.714	.690	.667
2	1.970	1.942	1.886	1.833	1.783	1.736	1.690	1.647	1.626	1.605	1.566	1.528	1.492	1.457	1.440	1.424	1.392	1.361	1.289	1.224	1.165	1.111
3	2.941	2.884	2.775	2.673	2.577	2.487	2.402	2.322	2.283	2.246	2.174	2.106	2.042	1.981	1.952	1.923	1.868	1.816	1.696	1.589	1.493	1.407
4	3.902	3.808	3.630	3.465	3.312	3.170	3.037	2.914	2.855	2.798	2.690	2.589	2.494	2.404	2.362	2.320	2.241	2.166	1.997	1.849	1.720	1.605
5	4.853	4.713	4.452	4.212	3.993	3.791	3.605	3.433	3.352	3.274	3.127	2.991	2.864	2.745	2.689	2.635	2.532	2.436	2.220	2.035	1.876	1.737
6	5.795	5.601	5.242	4.917	4.623	4.355	4.111	3.889	3.784	3.685	3.498	3.326	3.167	3.020	2.951	2.885	2.759	2.643	2.385	2.168	1.983	1.824
7	6.728	6.472	6.002	5.582	5.206	4.868	4.564	4.288	4.160	4.039	3.812	3.605	3.416	3.242	3.161	3.083	2.937	2.802	2.508	2.263	2.057	1.883
8	7.652	7.325	6.733	6.210	5.747	5.335	4.968	4.639	4.487	4.344	4.078	3.837	3.619	3.421	3.329	3.241	3.076	2.925	2.598	2.331	2.108	1.922
9	8.566	8.163	7.435	6.802	6.247	5.759	5.328	4.946	4.772	4.607	4.303	4.031	3.786	3.566	3.463	3.366	3.184	3.019	2.665	2.379	2.144	1.948
10	9.471	8.983	8.111	7.360	6.710	6.145	5.650	5.216	5.019	4.833	4.494	4.192	3.923	3.682	3.571	3.465	3.269	3.092	2.715	2.414	2.168	1.965
11	10.368	9.787	8.760	7.887	7.139	6.495	5.988	5.453	5.234	5.029	4.656	4.327	4.035	3.776	3.656	3.544	3.335	3.147	2.752	2.438	2.185	1.977
12	11.255	10.575	9.385	8.384	7.536	6.814	6.194	5.660	5.421	5.197	4.793	4.439	4.127	3.851	3.725	3.606	3.387	3.190	2.779	2.456	2.196	1.985
13	12.134	11.348	9.986	8.853	7.904	7.103	6.424	5.842	5.583	5.342	4.910	4.533	4.203	3.912	3.780	3.656	3.427	3.223	2.799	2.468	2.204	1.990
14	13.004	12.106	10.563	9.295	8.244	7.367	6.628	6.002	5.724	5.468	5.008	4.611	4.265	3.962	3.824	3.695	3.459	3.249	2.814	2.477	2.210	1.993
15	13.865	12.849	11.118	9.712	8.559	7.606	6.811	6.142	5.847	5.575	5.092	4.675	4.315	4.001	3.859	3.726	3.483	3.268	2.825	2.484	2.214	1.995
16	14.718	13.578	11.652	10.106	8.851	7.824	6.974	6.265	5.954	5.669	5.162	4.730	4.357	4.033	3.887	3.751	3.503	3.283	2.834	2.489	2.216	1.997
17	15.562	14.292	12.166	10.477	9.122	8.022	7.120	6.373	6.047	5.749	5.222	4.775	4.391	4.059	3.910	3.771	3.518	3.295	2.840	2.492	2.218	1.998
18	16.398	14.992	12.659	10.828	9.372	8.201	7.250	6.467	6.128	5.818	5.273	4.812	4.419	4.080	3.928	3.786	3.529	3.304	2.844	2.494	2.219	1.999
19	17.226	15.678	13.134	11.158	9.604	8.365	7.366	6.550	6.198	5.877	5.316	4.844	4.442	4.097	3.942	3.799	3.539	3.311	2.848	2.496	2.220	1.999
20	18.046	16.351	13.590	11.470	9.818	8.514	7.469	6.623	6.259	5.929	5.353	4.870	4.460	4.110	3.954	3.808	3.546	3.316	2.850	2.497	2.221	1.999
21	18.857	17.011	14.029	11.764	10.017	8.649	7.562	6.687	6.312	5.973	5.384	4.891	4.476	4.121	3.963	3.816	3.551	3.320	2.852	2.498	2.221	2.000
22	19.660	17.658	14.451	12.042	10.201	8.772	7.645	6.743	6.359	6.011	5.410	4.909	4.488	4.130	3.970	3.822	3.556	3.323	2.853	2.498	2.222	2.000
23	20.456	18.292	14.857	12.303	10.371	8.883	7.718	6.792	6.399	6.044	5.432	4.925	4.499	4.137	3.976	3.827	3.559	3.325	2.854	2.499	2.222	2.000
24	21.243	18.914	15.247	12.550	10.529	8.985	7.784	6.835	6.434	6.073	5.451	4.937	4.507	4.143	3.981	3.831	3.562	3.327	2.855	2.499	2.222	2.000
25	22.023	19.523	15.622	12.783	10.675	9.077	7.843	6.873	6.464	6.097	5.467	4.948	4.514	4.147	3.985	3.834	3.564	3.329	2.856	2.499	2.222	2.000
26	22.795	20.121	15.983	13.003	10.810	9.161	7.896	6.906	6.491	6.118	5.480	4.956	4.520	4.151	3.988	3.837	3.566	3.330	2.856	2.500	2.222	2.000
27	23.560	20.707	16.330	13.211	10.935	9.237	7.943	6.935	6.514	6.136	5.492	4.964	4.524	4.154	3.990	3.839	3.567	3.331	2.856	2.500	2.222	2.000
28	24.316	21.281	16.663	13.406	11.051	9.307	7.984	6.961	6.534	6.152	5.502	4.970	4.528	4.157	3.992	3.840	3.568	3.331	2.857	2.500	2.222	2.000
29	25.066	21.844	16.984	13.591	11.158	9.370	8.022	6.983	6.551	6.166	5.510	4.975	4.531	4.159	3.994	3.841	3.569	3.332	2.857	2.500	2.222	2.000
30	25.808	22.396	17.292	13.765	11.258	9.427	8.055	7.003	6.566	6.177	5.517	4.979	4.534	4.160	3.995	3.842	3.569	3.332	2.857	2.500	2.222	2.000
40	32.835	27.355	19.793	15.046	11.925	9.779	8.244	7.105	6.642	6.234	5.548	4.997	4.544	4.166	3.999	3.846	3.571	3.333	2.857	2.500	2.222	2.000
50	39.196	31.424	21.482	15.762	12.234	9.915	8.304	7.133	6.661	6.246	5.554	4.999	4.545	4.167	4.000	3.846	3.571	3.333	2.857	2.500	2.222	2.000

27

Profit Performance Measurements
Intracompany Transfer Pricing
Product Pricing Methods

The establishment of a profit goal based on budgets and standards, the delegation of authority and the assignment of responsibility to middle and lower management levels, and finally the creation of decentralized, autonomous divisions of a company lead to the need for measuring the operating and profit performance of top as well as subordinate executives. This chapter discusses the return-on-capital-employed concept, which assists management in appraising company-wide as well as divisional operating performance, and intracompany transfer pricing, which plays a significant role in measuring divisional and departmental results. The chapter also deals with different methods by which management can establish the product prices needed to cover costs and return a profit.

THE RATE OF RETURN ON CAPITAL EMPLOYED

The rate of return on capital employed may be expressed as the product of two factors: the percentage of profit to sales and the capital-employed turnover rate. In equation form, the rate of return is developed as follows:

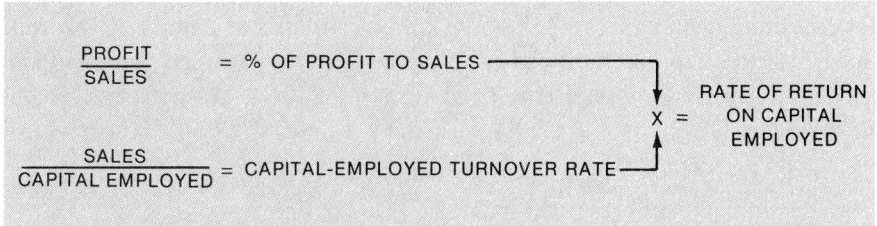

If sales were canceled out in the two fractions, the end result would still be the same. However, the shortened formula does not express the real objective of the concept, which deals with two independent variables — profit on sales and turnover of capital employed. Using the full formula gives management a better comprehension of the elements leading to the final result. The earnings percentage reflects a cost-price relationship, i.e., the success or lack of success of maintaining satisfactory control of costs. The turnover rate reflects the rapidity with which committed assets are employed in the operations.

Because the rate of return on capital employed is the product of two factors, numerous combinations can lead to the same result, as illustrated below for a 20 percent rate of return:

PERCENTAGE OF PROFIT TO SALES	CAPITAL-EMPLOYED TURNOVER RATE	RATE OF RETURN ON CAPITAL EMPLOYED
10%	2.000	20%
8	2.500	20
6	3.333	20
4	5.000	20
2	10.000	20

There is no rate of return on capital employed that is satisfactory for all companies. Manufacturing companies in various industries will have different rates, as will utilities, banking institutions, merchandising firms, and service companies. Management can establish an objective rate by using judgment and experience supported by comparisons with other companies. Every industry has companies with high, medium, and low rates of return. Structure and size of the firm influence the rate considerably. A company with a diversified line of products might have only a fair return rate when all products are pooled in the analysis. In such cases, it seems advisable to establish separate objectives for each line as well as for the total company. Methods for product-line analyses are discussed in a later section of this chapter.

None of the factors or elements that produce the final rate can be disregarded, minimized, or overemphasized without impairing the quality of managerial decisions. Changes in the profit margin can be caused by an increase or decrease in sales or costs. An improved turnover rate with no change in sales **The Formula's Underlying Data** prices indicates that the capital employed is worked harder; that is, more sales are coming out of the same investment. Complete details of the relationships of the capital-employed ratio to the underlying ratios — percentage of profit to sales and capital employed turnover rate — are portrayed in the chart below.

Relationship of Factors Influencing Rate of Return on Capital Employed

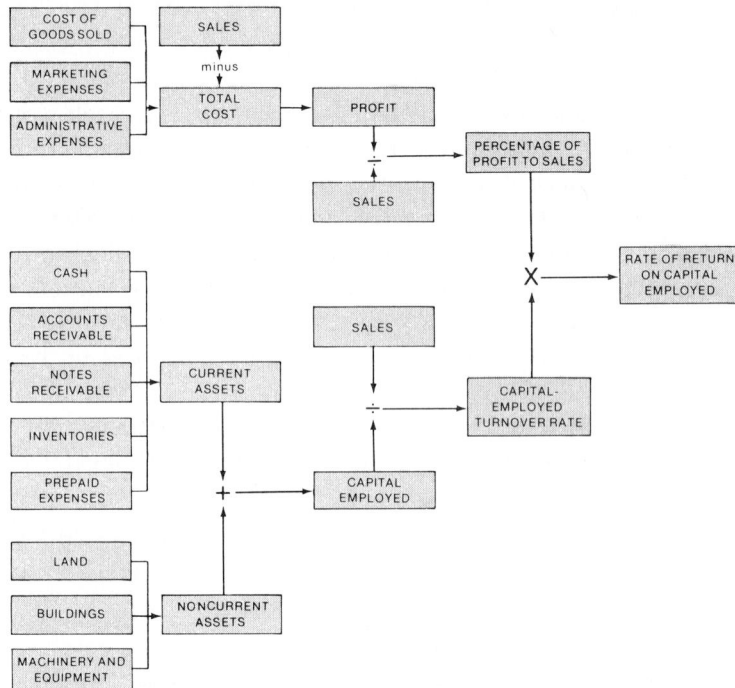

A rate of return on capital employed is computed by using figures from the balance sheet and income statement. Probability estimates can also be incorporated as a part of the computation.[1] The sales figure commonly used is net sales — gross sales less sales returns, allowances, and discounts. No general agreement exists with respect to the profit and capital-employed figures used in computing the rate. Consistency and uniformity are primary requisites, however, since the return on capital employed generally deals with a complexity of operations and/or a great diversity of product lines. Under such circumstances, it seems wise to avoid additional complexity and to seek clarity in the presentation of operating results without sacrifice of substance.

The income statement generally reports several profits such as (1) operating income, which includes cost of goods sold and marketing and administrative expenses but excludes nonoperating income and expenses; (2) income before income tax, which would include the nonoperating income and expense items, and (3) the net income, which is the amount that is transferred to retained earnings. Using operating income means that only transactions of an operating nature should be considered. This profit figure is preferred for divi-

[1]William L. Ferrara, "Probabilistic Approaches to Return on Investment and Residual Income," *The Accounting Review*, Vol. LII, No. 3, pp. 597–604.

sional or department analyses, since nonoperating items are usually the responsibility of the entire company. The use of income before or after income tax is significant when judging the enterprise as a whole. Net income is more defensible because tax money is not available to management, and managerial efficiency should be judged only by the ultimate result.

Capital employed refers to total assets or the sum of current assets and noncurrent assets. In describing capital employed, the word "investment" is intentionally avoided because it is used in connection with capital investment (noncurrent assets) and owner's investment (net worth or equity capital), and its meaning would be confusing.

Many accountants suggest that the amount of capital employed should be averaged over the fiscal period, if possible. Such a procedure tends to equalize unusually high or low year-end asset values or seasonal influences, particularly in divisional comparisons. Also, the sources of funds are not considered in determining the amount of capital employed. Therefore, current and long-term liabilities, which provided the money used in the purchase of assets, are not deducted from the assets. However, some accountants believe that current liabilities should be deducted from current assets to obtain a working capital figure to be used in place of the current assets figure.

Current Assets. The three most significant items classified as current assets are cash, receivables, and inventories. Problems of valuation are connected with each of these assets.

Cash. Ordinarily, the cash shown on the balance sheet is the amount required for total business operations. Cash funds set aside for pensions, taxes, or future expansion or development programs should be excluded. However, some companies believe that if such items are treated uniformly in relation to total cash or assets, no change of the cash balance sheet figure is warranted. On the other hand, certain managers do not accept the stated cash figure but consider a predetermined percentage based on the cost of goods sold or the annual operating expenses.

Receivables. Values used for receivables should be either the gross amount or the net amount after deducting the allowance for doubtful accounts. The procedure should be uniform for all receivables allowances, but when the allowance is in excess of actual needs, an adjustment seems appropriate. The treatment of the allowance will be considered in greater detail in connection with noncurrent assets.

Inventories. Different inventory costing methods, such as fifo, average, or lifo, give rise to some balance sheet and income statement differences. When return ratios of companies in the same industry are compared, an allowance for such differences should be made. Again, if an allowance account is used for lower of cost or market adjustments, the question arises as to whether the inventory should be used as net of the allowance. Here, too, uniformity plays a significant role.

Some companies' inventories are costed on a standard cost or direct costing basis. Use of these two bases will, as in the case of lifo, generally depress inventory values on a company's balance sheet. For internal comparison, however, the use of either method on a uniform basis should not influence results. The same reasoning applies to other deviations from normal procedures.

Noncurrent Assets. In dealing with noncurrent assets, three possible valuation methods have been favored: (1) original cost (original book value), (2) depreciated cost (original cost less the depreciation allowance, i.e., net book value), and (3) estimated replacement cost.

Original Cost. Those accountants favoring the original cost basis argue that:

1. Assets of manufacturing companies, unlike those of mining companies, are considered to be on a continuing rather than on a depleted and abandoned basis.

2. Gross assets of one plant can be compared better with those of another plant, where depreciation practices or the age of the assets may be different.

3. Accumulated depreciation is not deducted from the gross asset value of property, since it represents retention of the funds required to keep the stockholders' original investment intact. Actually, noncurrent assets are used to produce a profit during their entire life; therefore, full cost is considered an investment until the assets are retired from use.

Depreciated Cost. Those accountants who favor the use of the depreciated cost for noncurrent assets state that:

1. While invested capital is conventionally understated at the present time, the wrong method of increasing the original cost cannot be relied on to furnish the correct results. The attempt can only add to the existing confusion in accounting thinking.

2. Cash built up via a depreciation allowance, if added to the gross assets, amounts to overstating the investment. Noncurrent assets are shown at net depreciated costs, thus avoiding duplication of assets.

3. An investment is something separate and distinct from the media through which it is made. The purchase price of a machine should be regarded as the prepaid cost for the number of years of production expected. Each year this number will decline, and the decline should be offset by cash withheld from gross revenue. The function of depreciation accounting is to maintain the aggregate capital by currently providing substitute assets to replace the aggregate asset consumption (depreciation) of the year.

The several acceptable depreciation methods, such as straight-line or the various accelerated methods, result in the balance sheet and income statement differences. When return ratios of companies in the same industry are compared, such differences should be considered.

Replacement Cost and Price-Level-Adjusted Historical Cost. Those accountants who state that noncurrent assets should be included at replacement costs argue that such values are more realistic. They believe that a company receiving a certain and apparently satisfactory return based on book values should recognize the situation as being out-of-step with actual conditions. They further assert that some equalization of facility values of different divisions or companies should be provided, especially between those with old plants that were built at relatively low cost and those with new plants that were built at high cost. This method, of course, poses the serious problem of finding proper values.

Closely allied to any discussion of appropriate noncurrent asset values, and particularly the use of replacement costs, are considerations as to the effect of price-level changes on profits, sales, and capital employed. Sales, profits, and the current assets might be measured in current dollar values while the noncurrent assets and their expired cost might lag years behind. When the noncurrent asset investment is translated into current dollars, the rate of return on capital employed is more realistic.

Departmental Rates of Return

The determination of departmental return on capital is a matter of relating performance to assets placed at the disposal of departmental management. This return is usually expressed as the relationship of operating income to total assets.

The determination of a rate of return on capital employed at the departmental or divisional level involves certain allocation difficulties. Some analysts believe that only a segment's sales, costs, and capital employed should be included in calculating a divisional rate of return, because only these figures are under the control of the divisional manager. Others argue that if certain expenses or capital employed are not allocated, the segments will show a higher return in the aggregate than that of the company. Such a result might create a psychological dilemma which would make it difficult to obtain additional effort from the unit supervisory staff that shows a higher or better return than the company average. Perhaps the best alternative is to calculate a rate of return based on sales, costs, and capital employed specific to the segment, followed by a rate of return calculation that includes a full allocation of total company sales, costs, and capital employed, so that both rates of return are clearly presented.

Sales figures usually can be identified directly with specific segments. The allocation of costs to segments, however, involves the same rationale as the allocation of overhead; i.e., direct departmental expenses are charged to the departments, followed by allocations of general and service department expenses.

The allocation of capital employed that is not directly identified with segments might be achieved as follows:

Cash might be allocated to segments on the basis of (1) gross sales billed, (2) cost of goods sold, (3) a ratio to total product cost, (4) a standard percentage of sales or cost of goods sold, or (5) manufacturing cost less any noncash items.

Accounts Receivable might be allocated to segments or products based on gross sales billed; or allocated on the basis of gross sales for the average number of days reflected in the receivables.

Materials might be allocated on the basis of (1) materials consumed, (2) annual consumption figures, or (3) a ratio to actual or normal usage or standard direct materials cost.

Finished Goods would be directly assigned.

Noncurrent Assets might be allocated on the basis of (1) depreciation for cost purposes or (2) depreciation based on the use of facilities at either normal, standard, or actual volume, preferably to plant operations first and then to product lines. General or service facilities costs, such as powerhouse, hospital, machine shop, and plant laboratory costs, will already have been prorated to products so that the allocation of the investment in these facilities can follow the cost allocation. For instance, the powerhouse cost for steam, electricity, and water will be prorated on the basis of pounds of steam used, kilowatts of electricity used, and gallons of water consumed by each product.

Divisional return-on-capital-employed measures have been criticized as a motivational tool because a division may seek to maximize relative profits rather than absolute profits. Assume that a division which is presently earning 30 percent on capital employed is considering a project whose return would be only 25 percent. The divisional management might decline the project because the return on total divisional capital would decrease. Yet, if the acceptance of the project would make the best use of these divisional resources from a total company point of view, then, with a lower rate of return for the division or for the total company, the project should be accepted.

This suboptimum behavior might be overcome by calculating a *residual income figure* — a division's income less an amount representing the company's cost of capital employed by the division. This additional calculation would emphasize marginal profit dollars above the cost of capital rather than the rate of return on capital employed.

Residual income is a counterpart to the return-on-capital-employed computation and is a dollar measure of profitability. The concept is analogous to the net present value obtained when discounting cash flows. A positive residual income indicates earnings in excess of the desired return, while a negative residual income indicates earnings less than the desired return.[2]

Using the Rate of Return on Capital Employed

The return on capital employed is a measure of profitability for the total company as well as for divisions and individual products. While a company's total analysis and comparison with the industry's ratios are significant for executive management, the real purpose of the return-on-capital-employed ratio is for internal profit measurement and control, with trends more mean-

---

[2]*Ibid.*, p. 599.

ingful than single ratios. It is not a guide for shareholders or investors who measure profitability or earning power by relating profits to equity capital.

Executive management of many companies has shown a growing acceptance of the rate-of-return-on-capital-employed concept as a tool in planning for the future, in establishing sales prices, and in measuring operational profitability. Return-on-capital-employed information is useful to top executives, plant managers, plant engineers, and salespersons. It provides executives with a brief yet comprehensive picture of the true status of all operations in every plant and for every major product line. The plant manager receives a statement which measures the plant's operating results in a single figure. The product engineer's responsibility is to create products which can be manufactured at minimum cost and sold in profitable quantities without abnormal increases in asset investments. The sales staff realizes that price changes, justified as they may seem, are effective only if they contain a profit increment which yields an adequate return.

The return on capital employed not only acts as a measurement of the cooperative efforts of a company's divisions and segments but also shows the extent to which profitable coordination exists. A company's interlocking efforts are most effectively demonstrated by this rate. An appreciation of the concept by all employees will build an organization interested in achieving fair profits and an adequate rate of return.

Budgeting is the principal planning and control technique employed by most companies. Among the multiple phases of budgeting, sales forecasting is still considered the most difficult profit-planning task. Assuming that an acceptable sales budget has been established and production, manufacturing, and commercial expense budgets have been prepared, break-even analyses and return-on-capital-employed ratios are useful in evaluating the entire planning procedure.

Management's objectives with respect to the long-range return, as well as the immediate returns for each division, plant, or product, influence and guide budget-building procedures. As sales, costs, and assets employed are placed in the perspective of the rate of return on capital employed as envisioned by management, there is a marked change in the attitude of the people responsible for assembling the figures. Divisional or departmental budgets are compared with predetermined goals. If too low, examination and revision can perhaps achieve the desired result. If an unusually excellent return is calculated, the reasons for it can be investigated. Management can either accept the situation as is or decide on a temporary modification of its planning goal. At any rate, the return on capital employed offers a satisfactory foundation for the construction of both annual and long-range planning budgets. When considering long-range plans regarding addition of new products, dropping of old products, expansion of production facilities, or investing additional capital in research and development, application of the return on capital employed on any future projects always has a sobering effect if these projects have been conceived haphazardly or overoptimistically.

A successful technique in planning for profit improvement is to (1) define quantitatively (for sales, profits, and capital employed) the gap which exists between performance at present and that represented by long-term objectives, (2) fix the problems precisely by examining the details of each factor, (3) formulate a specific scheduled program of action for each factor, and (4) translate the planned results of each program in terms of its effect upon income and asset accounts. The application of this technique is shown in the following example:

EFFECT OF PLANNED PROGRAMS FOR PROFIT IMPROVEMENT

	PRESENT		CHANGE BY VOLUME	CHANGE BY COST REDUCTION	ASSET CURTAILMENT	FUTURE	
Assets:							
Inventory	$ 500,000				−$100,000	$ 400,000	
Other current assets	200,000		+$ 20,000			220,000	
Noncurrent assets	300,000			+$80,000		380,000	
Total assets	$1,000,000		+$ 20,000	+$80,000	−$100,000	$1,000,000	
Profit:							
Sales billed	$1,000,000	100.0%	+$200,000			$1,200,000	100.0%
Manufacturing cost	$ 770,000	77.0%	+$140,000	−$88,000		$ 822,000	68.5%
Marketing and administrative expenses	130,000	13.0	+ 10,000	− 2,000		138,000	11.5
Total cost and expense	$ 900,000	90.0%	$150,000			$ 960,000	80.0%
Operating profit	$ 100,000	10.0%	+$ 50,000	+$90,000		$ 240,000	20.0%
Return on capital employed:							
%of profit to sales		10.0%					20.0%
Capital-employed turnover rate (times)		1.0					1.2
Return on capital employed (%)		10.0%					24.0%

Advantages of the Use of the Return on Capital Employed. In general, the advantages of the use of the rate of return on capital employed are its tendency to:

1. Focus management's attention upon earning the best profit possible on the capital (total assets) available.
2. Serve as a yardstick in measuring management's efficiency and effectiveness for the company as a whole and its major divisions or departments.
3. Tie together the many phases of financial planning, sales objectives, cost control, and the profit goal.

4. Afford comparison of managerial results both internally and externally.
5. Develop a keener sense of responsibility and team effort in divisional and departmental managers by enabling them to measure and evaluate their own activities in the light of the results achieved by other managers.
6. Aid in detecting weakness with respect to the use or nonuse of individual assets particularly in connection with inventories.

Limitations of the Use of the Return on Capital Employed. The use of the return-on-capital-employed ratio may be subject to some of the following limitations:

1. Lack of agreement on the optimum rate of return might discourage managers who believe the rate is set at an unfair level.
2. Proper allocation requires certain data regarding sales, costs, and assets. The accounting and cost system might not give such needed details.
3. Valuations of assets, particularly with regard to jointly used assets, might give rise to difficulties and misunderstandings.
4. For the sake of making the current period rate of return on capital employed "look good," managers may be influenced to make decisions that are not the best for the long-run interests of the firm.
5. A single measure of performance, such as return on capital employed, may result in a fixation on improving the components of the one measure to the neglect of needed attention to other desirable activities. Product research and development, managerial development, progressive personnel policies, good employee morale, and good customer and public relations are just as important in earning a greater profit and assuring continuous growth.

Multiple Performance Measurements. Many well-managed companies use multiple performance measurements in order to overcome the limitations of a single measure. One company that uses multiple measurements for rating divisional performance describes its method as a quantification of progress against agreed-upon standards. Each year common standards are adopted by agreement of divisional managers and corporate management. Points are assigned to standards, reflecting those areas which require special attention in each division, as determined by management. Performance is measured as follows:

1. Profits for the current year are compared with the profits for the preceding year in absolute dollars, margins, and return on capital employed.
2. Profits are compared with the budget.
3. Cash and capital management measures are employed. Here, the emphasis is on effective management of inventory and receivables.

The claimed advantages of this method are that:

1. Performances of division managers are more fairly measured than would result from using solely a return-on-capital-employed figure.
2. Management can readily see those divisions which are performing well and those which are not.

3. Lost points serve as "red flags" by directing management to areas requiring attention and to the reasons and the corrective actions taken or needed.
4. The system has flexibility as to timely, needed shifting of management emphasis.

In this company, management concludes that it is not enough to tabulate performance statistics. The results must be effectively communicated, corrective action taken, and good performance rewarded. The system must also have the interest and support of division and corporate management.[3]

Graphs as Operating Guides. Sound planning and successful operation must point toward the optimum combination of profits, sales, and capital employed. As stated earlier, the combination will necessarily vary depending upon the characteristics of the product. An industry with products tailor-made to customers' specifications will have different profit margins and turnover ratios compared with industries that mass produce highly competitive consumer goods.

In multiproduct companies, the three basic factors cannot be uniform due to different types of operations. However, a special type of graph can be of assistance in judging the performance of segments or products in their relationship to a desired overall return on capital employed. Such a graph has the advantage of flexibility in appraising profit performance and offers an approach by which performance can be analyzed for improvement.

The graph below shows possible combinations of percentage of profit to sales and capital-employed turnover rate which yield a 20 percent return. When individual divisions, departments, or products are plotted on the graph, the segment's data might appear to the left or right of the basic curve. If on the left, the unit has a capital-employed-return performance below that expected for the company as a whole. A segment whose ratios appear to the right of the basic curve has a return in excess of that expected for the entire

Relationship
Between
Percent of
Profit to
Sales and
Capital-Employed
Turnover Rate

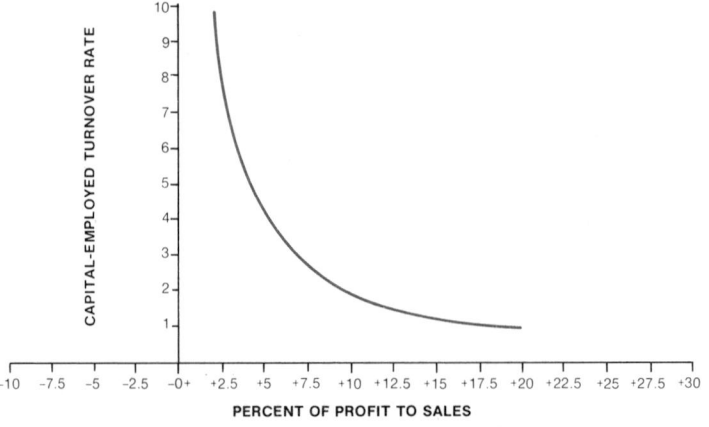

[3]Frank J. Tanzola, "Performance Rating for Divisional Control," *Financial Executive*, Vol. XLIII, No. 3, pp. 20–24.

company. The same interpretation applies when the company's total return is plotted.

INTRACOMPANY TRANSFER PRICING

The effectiveness of the return on capital employed as a device for measuring the performance of divisional segments of a company depends considerably on the accuracy of allocating the costs and assets associated with the unit, segment, or product. In a decentralized multiplant or multiproduct organization, the unit managers are expected to run portions of the enterprise as a semiautonomous business. Thus, a shift to the return-on-capital-employed concept for measuring operational performance requires some rather fundamental policy changes.

As long as a unit, segment, or product is not entirely independent and separable, goods and services are generally transferred from one unit to another, a situation common to integrated corporations. The finished or semifinished product of one or more divisions or subsidiaries frequently becomes the raw material of one or more other divisions. In addition, some service functions are centralized and might conceivably deal with a number of profit centers. When transfers of goods or services are made, a portion of the revenue of one profit center becomes a portion of cost of another, and the price at which transfers are made influences the earnings reported by each profit center. The value of these earnings as a measure of performance depends not only upon the manager's executive abilities but also upon the transfer prices used. Whatever pricing system is used can distort any reported profit and make it a poor guide for operating decisions. In the end, the cost or price used for the transfer will be used in the calculation of the return on capital employed, due to the very nature of the formula.

Years ago transfer pricing played only a minor role in cost control. Today the technique of transfer pricing has expanded into a complex set of procedures in the administration of the decentralized segments of an enterprise. This complexity and the arbitrary nature of intracompany transfer pricing is one reason for criticism of proposals to report segment or product-line revenues and profits in published financial statements. A steel company may operate a coal mine and sell some of its output on the open market but use the remainder in its own steel mills. The coal's transfer price can control whether the mining division shows a large, small, or zero profit.

External factors may influence the transfer price determination. A company with an overseas plant, where tax rates are low, may keep the transfer price high for materials sent to the domestic facility in order to retain profits abroad. Or a company with warehouses in a state with an inventory tax may keep transfer prices low on goods brought into the state in order to reduce its tax bill.[4]

---

[4]"The Numbers Game," *Forbes*, Vol. 114, No. 3, pp. 37–38.

The existence of multiple management objectives makes it extremely difficult for a company to establish logical and sound intracompany transfer
prices. A pricing method can be chosen only after the primary purposes for
the use of the information from transfers have been identified. Therefore, a
transfer pricing system must satisfy these three fundamental criteria: (1) allow
central management to judge as accurately as possible the performance of the
divisional profit center in terms of its separate contribution to the total corporate profit, (2) motivate the divisional manager to pursue the division's own
profit goal in a manner conducive to the success of the company as a whole,
and (3) stimulate the manager's efficiency without losing the division's autonomy as a profit center.[5] The system should also be easy to apply, meet legal
and external reporting requirements, and permit each unit of a company to
earn a profit commensurate with the functions it performs. As a practical matter, these criteria may be difficult to satisfy, because behavioral considerations are of paramount importance. Accordingly, a transfer price should be a
just price to both the selling and buying parties. An advantage gained by one
will be a disadvantage to the other and, in the end, may be detrimental to the
corporate profit goal.

A profit center manager's interest must remain congruent with the firm's
interest. For example, assume that Division X offers its Product A to Division
Y at a transfer price of $14, which includes a $2 profit, a $9 variable cost, and
a $3 fixed cost that presumably will remain unchanged in total as activity
fluctuates. The same product is also available from an outside supplier at $11.
Division Y, acting to minimize its costs, will prefer to purchase Product A at
the lower external price of $11. However, such a decision would not be con-
gruent with the best interests of the total firm, since the $11 external price is
greater than the $9 variable cost which, in this example, is the differential
cost. This analysis assumes that from the total firm point of view, no more
profitable use could be made of the Division X facilities used in supplying
Product A to Division Y.

Four basic methods of pricing intracompany transfers are available: (1)
transfer pricing based on cost, (2) market-based transfer pricing, (3) negotiated transfer pricing, and (4) arbitrary transfer pricing. No one method of
transfer pricing can effectively satisfy all of the requirements, so the best
transfer price can be defined only as it is best for a particular purpose.[6] Regardless of what transfer price is used, the differential cost of goods transferred from division to division should be known and used for decision-making purposes.[7]

[5]Joshua Ronen and George McKinney III, "Transfer Pricing for Divisional Autonomy,"*Journal of Accounting Research*, Vol. 8, No. 1, pp. 99–112.
[6]The transfer pricing methods employed in the meat industry can be studied in the brochure *Financial Planning and Control in the Meat Industry*, prepared by Price Waterhouse & Co. in cooperation with the Accounting Committee, American Meat Institute (Chicago, Illinois, 1967), pp. 142–143.
[7]For further study, the nature and scope of several major transfer pricing models categorized as to (1) the economic theory of the firm, (2) mathematical programming approaches, and (3) other analytical approaches, are covered in A. Rashad Abdel-khalik and Edward J. Lusk, "Transfer Pricing — A Synthesis," *The Accounting Review*, Vol. XLIX, No. 1, pp. 8–23.

In a totally centralized firm, executive management basically makes all decisions with respect to the operations of the divisions. This responsibility makes cost control the basis for measuring a manager's performance. A cost-based transfer price is usually sufficient in this situation. A company without any integration processes might have so little volume of intracompany transfers that it would be too time consuming and costly to price the transfer at other than cost.

The cost figure may be actual, standard, direct, or differential, and the company's cost system should permit the computation of a product's unit cost, even at various stages of production. When service departments are involved in a company's operations, a service charging rate similar to the one described on pages 275–276 should be established in advance of the work performed, so that servicing and benefiting departments or plants know in advance the costs connected with services.

The cost method's primary advantage is simplicity, in that it avoids the elimination of intracompany profits from inventories in consolidated financial statements and income tax returns. Also, the transferred cost can readily be used to measure production efficiency by comparing actual with budgeted costs. Finally, the method allows simple and adequate end-product costing for profit analysis by product lines.

Considering the disadvantages, a transfer price based on cost is not suited to decentralized companies that need to measure the profitability of autonomous units. Also, producing departments may not be sufficiently conscientious in controlling costs that are to be transferred, although the use of standard costs for transfer pricing may alleviate this problem. A transfer price based on cost lacks not only utility for divisional planning, motivating, and evaluating but also the objectivity required of a good performance standard.

Transfer Pricing Based on Cost

The market-based transfer price is usually identical with the one charged to outside customers, although some companies apply a discount to the market price to reflect the economies of intracompany trading. This method is the best profitability and performance measurement because it is objective. It reflects product profitability and division management performance, with divisions operating on a competitive basis. It also aids in future planning and is generally required by foreign tariff laws and income tax regulations.

The most serious drawback to this method is the requirement for a well-developed outside competitive market. Unfortunately, a market price is not always determinable for intermediate products. Also, the market-based price adds an element of profit or loss with each transfer of product. Thus, the determination of the actual cost of the final product is difficult when the product has passed through numerous manufacturing stages.

In analyzing a study made by the National Industrial Conference Board on interdivisional transfer pricing, Itzhak Sharav observes that:

Market-Based Transfer Pricing

In most cases of vertical transfers (between units at different stages of the manufacturing and marketing process), where the transferring division is viewed as a cost center, its transfers will be priced at cost. However, where the transferee is a profit center, . . . the transfer price may include a profit factor thus approximating outside market prices. [However,] . . . horizontal transfers (transferer and transferee are situated at the same stage of the production and marketing process) are usually executed at cost, which may, of course, include freight and handling charges. . . . companies using cost-based transfer prices choose in many cases actual costs which are derived from divisional operating statements and underlying cost records. Often, where available, standard or budgeted costs are employed. In contrast to the preference expressed in the literature, marginal (differential) costs are used by a few companies only. A modified version of cost is the so-called cost-plus transfer price. It is comprised of cost plus a markup that is meant to provide a return on investment in divisional assets. Much less frequently used, this transfer price may be applied in lieu of the hard-to-establish market price.[8]

Statement of Financial Accounting Standards No. 14, "Financial Reporting for Segments of a Business Enterprise," does not specify the transfer pricing method to be used in segment reporting, but it does require disclosure of the method used. A review of 250 annual reports for 1977 indicated that of the surveyed companies which were required to make such a disclosure, 75% used a market-based transfer price.[9] The SEC, however, requires disclosure of:

1. When and where intersegment transfers are made at prices substantially higher or lower than the prevailing market price or the price charged to unaffiliated parties for similar products or services, and
2. The estimated or approximate amounts (or the percentage of increase or decrease in the amounts) of the revenue and operating profit or loss that the particular segments would have had if the intersegment transfers had been made at the prevailing market price.[10]

Negotiated Transfer Pricing

A negotiated transfer price may be used even though competitive outside markets exist. It is felt that the setting of the price by negotiation between buying and selling divisions allows unit managers the greatest degree of authority and control over the profit of their units. A serious problem encountered with this method is that negotiation can not only become time consuming but can also require frequent reexamination and revision of prices. Often the negotiated price diverts the efforts of the manager from activities promoting company welfare to those affecting divisional results only. Furthermore, problems may occur because information is inadequate or conflicting, resulting in a breakdown in negotiations and leading to a need for mediation by executive management or to the use of arbitrary pricing.

Arbitrary Transfer Pricing

An arbitrary transfer price has been used quite frequently in the past and may be employed even when a market-based price is available. A price is established by interaction between buying and selling divisions and is at a

---

[8]Itzhak Sharav, "Transfer Pricing — Diversity of Goals and Practices," *The Journal of Accountancy*, Vol. 137, No. 4, p. 59.
[9]Robert Mednick, "Companies Slice and Serve Up Their Financial Results Under FASB 14," *Financial Executive*, Vol. XLVII, No. 3, p. 54.
[10]*Ibid.*, p. 55.

level considered best for overall company interests, with neither the buying nor selling units having any control over the final decision. The method's disadvantages, however, far outweigh any advantage. It can defeat the most important purpose of decentralizing profit responsibility, i.e., making divisional personnel profit conscious, and it severely hampers the profit incentive of unit managers.

The consuming (buying) and producing (selling) divisions may differ in the purpose a transfer price is to serve. For example, a consuming division may rely on a transfer price in make-or-buy decisions or in determining a final product's sales price based on an awareness of total differential cost. A producing division may use a transfer price to measure its divisional performance and, accordingly, would argue against any price that would not provide a divisional profit. In such circumstances, a company may find it useful to adopt a dual transfer pricing approach in which the: **Dual Transfer Pricing**

1. Producing division uses a market-based, negotiated, or arbitrary transfer price in computing its revenue from intracompany sales.
2. Variable costs of the producing division are transferred to the purchasing division, together with an equitable portion of the fixed cost.
3. Total of the divisional profits will be greater than for the company as a whole, and the profit assigned to the producing division would be eliminated in preparing company-wide financial statements.

Under this system, a producing division would have a profit inducement to expand sales and production, both externally and internally. Yet, the consuming divisions would not be misled; their costs would be the firm's actual costs and would not include an artificial profit. Variable costs, as well as fixed costs, should be associated with the purchase to ensure that the consuming division is aware of the total cost implications. Of course, the benefits from a dual transfer pricing approach can be achieved only if the underlying cost data are accurate and reliable.[11]

PRODUCT PRICING METHODS

Product pricing is a complex subject and is neither a one-person nor a one-activity job. Theorists and practitioners differ on various pricing theories. In practice, the solution to a pricing problem becomes a research job that requires the cooperation and coordination of the economist, statistician, market specialist, industrial engineer, and accountant. Since the determination of a sales price requires consideration of many factors, some of which defy measurement or control, prudent and practical judgment is necessary. Accountants can provide executive management and marketing managers with mileposts to be used as guides when traveling the relatively uncharted road toward successful pricing.

---

[11]Richard B. Troxel, "On Transfer Pricing," *Management Controls*, Vol. XX, No. 7, pp. 160–162.

Costs are generally considered to be the starting point in a pricing situation, even though a rigid relationship is not expected to exist. Prices and pricing policy vary in relation to costs and volume as well as to the selection of a long- or short-range view. The long-run approach allows change in products, manufacturing methods, plant capacity, and marketing and distribution methods. It aims to obtain prices which will return all costs and provide an adequate return on the capital invested. A normal or average product cost is the basis used for long-range pricing. A short-range pricing policy looks toward the recovery of at least part of the total cost in order to meet changing needs resulting from fluctuating sales volume, sales mix, and prices. In such cases, the differential cost of a product may serve as a guide for the determination of prices. Variable costs are the principal source of cost differentials which must be computed in such pricing problems (Chapters 22 and 25).

The relationship between costs and prices is not only one of the most difficult for a business person to determine, but its final determination can have social and even political implications. Price setting is that field of business in which management truly becomes an art. A sales price, generally thought of as the rate of exchange between two commodities, is determined in many industries in a manner that gives individual companies some degree of control over the price. This is particularly true when a company is the sole manufacturer of a product. Even companies that experience a great deal of competition have some measure of control, since products, quality, and/or the services rendered may differ. Although a firm may exercise some control over sales prices, the costs incurred in order to do business are usually more within its control.

Prices may be influenced not only by competition but also by what customers are willing to pay and by governmental regulations and controls. The Robinson-Patman Act must be complied with to avoid alleged price discrimination. Even if a company has little or no control over a sales price, it faces the question of whether it can operate profitably at the price that can be charged. Costs must be known and used as building blocks for determining the minimum price required to justify entering or continuing in a given market.

The accountant's assistance to management in the highly important field of pricing products requires knowledge and recognition of inventory costing methods as well as all cost items as they flow through the cost accounting cycle. The development of an imagination that appreciates and understands the economic and political forces at play is also required. The accountant must be not only an economist but an investment analyst as well and must be able to see problems through management's eyes. By doing so, the accountant becomes a vital part of management with cost accounting as a necessary tool.

Even though price-setting procedures are difficult, methods are available that will assist in their computation and determination. These methods include

(1) profit maximization — relating total revenue to total cost, (2) pricing based on a return on capital employed, (3) conversion cost pricing, (4) the contribution margin and the differential cost approach to pricing, and (5) standard costs for pricing.

Profit Maximization

The objective of most business enterprises is to obtain a price that contributes the largest amount to profit. Economic theorists describe this as *profit maximization*. The profit return on each unit sold is not so important as the total profit realized from all units sold. The price that yields the largest profit at a certain volume is the price to be charged to a consumer.

The schedule below shows the variable cost at $7 per unit with fixed cost at $300,000 for all ranges of output. The most profitable sales price is $14 per unit with a contribution margin of $560,000 and a profit of $260,000, after deducting the fixed cost.

SALES PRICE PER UNIT	NUMBER OF UNITS TO BE SOLD	TOTAL SALES VOLUME	VARIABLE COST ($7 PER UNIT)	FIXED COST	PROFIT (LOSS)
$20	20,000	$ 400,000	$140,000	$300,000	$ (40,000)
18	40,000	720,000	280,000	300,000	140,000
16	60,000	960,000	420,000	300,000	240,000
14	80,000	1,120,000	560,000	300,000	260,000
12	100,000	1,200,000	700,000	300,000	200,000
10	120,000	1,200,000	840,000	300,000	60,000
8	140,000	1,120,000	980,000	300,000	(160,000)

In other situations, the unit variable cost and the total fixed cost may vary according to the total number of units to be sold, thus influencing the most profitable sales price.

Profit maximization is not to be looked upon as the immediate return expected, but rather as a goal to be realized over several months or years. However, during these months and years, sales policies, competition, customer practices, cost changes, and other economic or political influences might radically alter all previous presuppositions.

Pricing Based on a Return on Capital Employed

Some companies attempt to develop prices that will yield a predetermined or desired rate of return on capital employed. The method illustrated below is based on a percentage markup on cost:

$$\frac{\text{Percentage markup}}{\text{on cost}} = \frac{\text{Capital employed}}{\text{Total annual cost}} \times \text{Desired rate of return on capital employed}$$

$$\frac{\text{Percentage markup}}{\text{on cost}} = \frac{\$20,000,000}{\$5,000,000} \times 20\% = \underline{80\%}$$

Sales volume = Total annual cost + (Percentage markup on cost × Total annual cost)

Sales volume = $5,000,000 + (80% × $5,000,000)
        = $5,000,000 + $4,000,000* = $9,000,000

*Or, $4,000,000 = 20% (desired rate of return on capital employed) × $20,000,000 (capital employed)

The formula below gives specific effect to variations in the amount of capital required for supporting differing sales volumes:[12]

$$Price = \frac{\dfrac{Total\ cost + (Desired\ rate\ of\ return \times Noncurrent\ assets)}{Sales\ volume\ in\ units}}{1 - [Desired\ rate\ of\ return \times (Current\ assets \div Sales)]}$$

This formula assumes that the capital employed, particularly cash, accounts receivable, and inventories, varies in direct proportion with sales. NAA Research Report No. 35 states that "a possible objection to the above method is that a change in selling price, by itself, would have no direct effect on the investment in inventory since the latter is stated at cost. This objection can be avoided by introducing inventory as a ratio to factory cost rather than as a ratio to selling price."

The preceding formula can be stated and illustrated in an equivalent yet much simpler form. Assume that a single-product company's total cost is $210,000, total capital employed is $200,000, the sales volume is 50,000 units, and the desired rate of return on capital employed is 20%. The formula used and the determination of the product's sales price would be:

$$Price = \frac{Total\ cost + (Desired\ rate\ of\ return \times Total\ capital\ employed)}{Sales\ volume\ in\ units}$$

$$Price = \frac{\$210,000 + (20\% \times \$200,000)}{50,000\ units} = \frac{\$250,000}{50,000\ units} = \underline{\underline{\$5}}$$

Proof: Sales (50,000 units × $5)	$250,000
Less total cost	210,000
Profit	$ 40,000

Pricing procedures using capital employed as part of the pricing formula may be complex, however. The illustrations assume no change in capital employed. Actually, as prices and costs change, capital employed may be expected to change; with an increase, more cash will be required to serve the business; with higher prices, accounts receivable will be higher, and inventory costs will increase in proportion to increases in factory costs. Decreases would have the reverse effect.

If it is assumed that a firm is in business to maximize its value to the shareholders, then its pricing policy should be based largely on a target rate of return on capital employed. To be effective in its control and analysis, management's pricing decisions should be made after this rate, the standard costs, and the estimated plant capacity have been considered.

Conversion Cost Pricing

Conversion cost pricing attempts to direct management's attention to the amount of labor and factory overhead that products require. To illustrate, assume that a company manufactures two products, each selling for $10. The

---

[12]*NAA Research Report No. 35*, "Return on Capital Employed as a Guide to Managerial Decisions" (New York: National Association of Accountants, December 1, 1959), p. 44.

manufacturing cost for each is $9, resulting in a gross profit of $1 per unit, indicating that from a profit point of view it does not matter which product is promoted. However, a breakdown of the costs reveals the following:

ITEM OF COST	PRODUCT A	PRODUCT B
Direct materials	$ 6	$ 3
Direct labor....................................	2	4
Factory overhead	1	2
Total manufacturing cost	$ 9	$ 9
Sales price	10	10
Gross profit...................................	$ 1	$ 1

The cost breakdown indicates that Product A requires only half the labor and factory overhead that is required for Product B. If it were possible to shift all efforts to A, a greater number of units could be produced and sold with the same gross profit per unit. Marketing costs of A versus B must also be considered. Of course, any volume increase might disturb market equilibrium and even cause a decrease in the price because of increased supply. These difficulties are discussed in Chapter 24.

Contribution Margin Approach to Pricing

In direct costing, the contribution margin figure (excess of sales over variable cost) indicates a product's contribution to the recovery of fixed costs and to profit. The fixed and variable cost classifications permit an evaluation of each product by a comparison of specific contribution margins. While this contribution margin approach might be used for a firm's entire business, it is of even greater value in the analysis of its divisions, plants, products, product lines, customers, and territories. Care must be taken, however, not to confuse contribution with profit, since profit is realized only after all fixed costs are covered.

The differential cost of an order is the variable cost necessary to produce the additional units, plus additional fixed costs (if any) at the new production level. If the cost of additional units is accepted as a basis for pricing them, any price over and above total differential cost would be acceptable. This procedure is, of course, applicable only to the additional units.

To base sales prices on differential cost requires careful scrutiny of all related factors. For example, long-term sales promotion should not be used for a product priced on the basis of differential costs when total cost recovery and a reasonable profit will not result.

Standard Costs for Pricing

If cost estimates used for pricing purposes are prepared on the basis of the standard costs for materials, labor, and factory overhead, the tasks of preparing the estimate and using the data to set the price will be aided considerably. The use of standard costs for pricing purposes makes cost figures more quickly available and reduces clerical detail. Since a standard cost represents the cost that should be attained in an efficiently operated plant at normal capacity, it is essential, once the sales price has been established, that the cost department furnish up-to-the-minute information to all parties to make certain that the cost stays within the rate set by the estimate. Any deviation between actual and standard costs should come to light for quick action through the accounting system.

The National Association of Accountants has stated that companies can be divided into four groups with respect to the type of cost figures which they supply to pricing executives. These groups are composed of:

1. Companies which supply executives with standard costs without the application of any adjustments to the standards.
2. Companies in which the standard costs are adjusted by the ratio of actual costs to standard costs as shown by the variance accounts.
3. Companies which use current market prices for materials, and in a few cases for labor, with standard costs for other elements of product cost.
4. Companies which adjust standard costs to reflect the actual costs anticipated during the period for which the prices are to be in effect.

When standard costs are used for bid prices, they might be based on estimates previously submitted. However, while some materials parts or labor operations might be identical with those used for another product, executives need the most up-to-date information on all cost components in order to set a profitable price. Companies that must present bids adjust the costs developed from the detailed standards to approximate actual costs expected.

DISCUSSION QUESTIONS

1. How is the return on capital employed computed?

2. What management activities are measured by each of the factors involved in determining the rate of return on capital employed?

3. Name some of the factors that will affect the percentage of profit to sales.

4. The term "return on investment" has been confusing because it has been used indiscriminately to describe two different types of financial measurement. Discuss.

5. What items are generally included in the term "capital employed"?

6. In measuring the return on capital, some accountants have argued that capital employed should be measured by gross assets without any deduction for

depreciation. Others believe that only net assets offer the true basis for measuring the investment. Discuss.

7. State two major objectives that management may have in mind when setting up a system for measuring the return on divisional capital employed.

8. From an organizational point of view, two approaches to transfer pricing are (a) to let the managers of profit centers bargain with one another and arrive at their own transfer prices (negotiated transfer pricing) and (b) to have the firm's executive management set transfer prices for transactions between the profit centers (arbitrary transfer pricing). Identify the fundamental advantage and disadvantage of each approach.

(CGAA adapted)

9. Explain the dual transfer pricing approach in intracompany transfer pricing.

10. Discuss the statement, "Price setting is truly an art."

11. What accounting-based methods are available that might assist and permit the computation and determination of a sales price?

12. Discuss the profit maximization method of pricing.

13. Why are standard costs helpful in setting prices?

14. Select the answer which best completes the statement:
    (a) With other variables remaining constant, the rate of return on capital employed of a merchandising company will increase with a decrease in: (1) sales; (2) inventory turnover; (3) the profit margin; (4) the investment in inventory.
    (b) To evaluate the performance of each department, interdepartmental transfers of a product preferably should be made at prices: (1) equal to the market price of the product; (2) set by the receiving department; (3) equal to fully allocated costs to the producing department; (4) equal to variable costs to the producing department.
    (c) A management decision may be beneficial for a given profit center, but not for the entire company. From the overall company viewpoint, this decision would lead to action referred to as: (1) suboptimization; (2) centralization; (3) goal congruence; (4) maximization.
    (d) Mar Company has two decentralized divisions, X and Y. Division X has always purchased certain units from Division Y at $75 per unit. Because Y plans to raise the price to $100 per unit, X desires to purchase these units from outside suppliers for $75 per unit. Y's costs are as follows:

Variable cost per unit	$ 70
Annual fixed cost	$15,000
Annual production of these units for X	1,000 units

If X buys from an outside supplier, the facilities Y uses to manufacture these units would remain idle. If Mar enforces a transfer price of $100 per unit between Divisions X and Y, the result would be that: (1) it would be suboptimization for the company because X should buy from outside suppliers at $75 per unit; (2) it would provide lower overall company net income than a transfer price of $75 per unit; (3) it would provide higher overall company net income than a transfer price of $75 per unit; (4) it would be more profitable for the company than allowing X to buy from outside suppliers at $75 per unit.

(AICPA adapted)

EXERCISES

1. Return on capital employed. During the past year, the Roberts Waterworks Company had a net income of $80,000. Net sales were $400,000 and total capital employed was $800,000.

Required:
    (1) The capital-employed turnover rate.
    (2) The percentage of profit to sales.
    (3) The rate of return on capital employed.

2. Return on capital employed; minimum price. The Victoria Corporation manufactures a highly specialized alloy used in missile skins. Rising materials costs led the company to adopt the lifo method for inventory costing. In 19A the company produced 702 000 kilograms of alloy. New government contracts and other new business should increase volume by about 30%. In spite of increased costs, management felt that it could reduce the sales price from $12.30 per kilogram in 19A to $11.40 in 19B and still maintain the same rate of return on capital employed. However, prices of basic raw materials climbed higher than expected and the desired return and profit did not materialize.

    Data available (000s omitted):

	19A	19B
Sales	$8,450	$8,550
Cost of goods sold and commercial expenses	7,370	7,931
Net income	901	896
Cash	1,200	500
Accounts receivable	1,000	1,000
Inventories	1,750	2,300
Noncurrent assets	6,650	7,400

Required:
    (1) The actual rate of return on capital employed for the past two years.
    (2) The minimum price that the company should have charged.

3. Return on capital employed for product lines. The Boca Raton Company has three lines of products, Mechanical, Household, and Commercial. Sales and cost of goods sold for the past year were:

	MECHANICAL	HOUSEHOLD	COMMERCIAL	TOTAL
Sales	$1,400,000	$750,000	$630,000	$2,780,000
Cost of goods sold	900,000	580,000	415,000	1,895,000
Gross profit	$ 500,000	$170,000	$215,000	$ 885,000

    Marketing and administrative expenses for the year totaled $250,200 and are allocated to product lines on the basis of sales. Income tax is 52%. Average assets employed by the company during the year totaled $2,430,000 and are allocated to the product lines in a ratio of 4:3:2.

Required: For each product line and in total:
    (1) The capital-employed turnover rate, computed to one decimal place.
    (2) The percentage of profit (after income tax) to sales, computed to $1/10$ of one percent.
    (3) The rate of return on capital employed, computed to $1/10$ of one percent.

4. Rate of return on capital employed; payback period; product's rate of return. The management of the Wilkinson Company has been using the return-on-capital-employed method of measuring performance by division and product managers. Recently the management decided to apply the concept to four product groups. The Cost Department assembled the following data from the annual financial statements:

	PRODUCT A	PRODUCT B	PRODUCT C	PRODUCT D
Investment	$ 500,000	$ 300,000	$ 600,000	$ 200,000
Sales volume in dollars	2,000,000	5,000,000	3,000,000	1,800,000
Net income	60,000	45,000	175,000	36,000
Aftertax cash inflows	75,000	60,000	200,000	60,000

The management is further interested in the length of time required for cash produced by the investment to repay the original cash outlay. The management is also aware of the possibility of using the discounted cash flow method, which attempts to show that rate which equates the sum of the present values of a series of future cash flows to the value of the original investment.

Required:
(1) For each product, the (a) capital-employed turnover rate; (b) percentage of profit to sales; and (c) rate of return on capital employed.
(2) The payback period for each of the four products, based on the data given.
(3) The discounted cash flow rate of return for Product D, assuming that the product's life cycle is estimated at 10 years.

5. Division transfer pricing. The Wallach Iron Mill produces high-grade pig iron in its single blast furnace in Bedford, Pennsylvania. Coal from nearby mines is converted into coke in company-owned ovens, and 80% of the coke produced is used in the blast furnace. The management of the mill is experimenting with divisional profit reporting and control and has established the blast furnance as well as the coke-producing activity as profit centers. Coke used by the blast furnace is charged to that profit center at $6 per ton, which approximates the current market price less costs of marketing (including substantial freight costs). The remaining 20% of the coke produced at a normal annual volume output of 80,000 tons is sold to other mills in the area at $7.50 per ton.

Cost of coal and other variable costs of coke production amount to $4.50 per ton. Fixed costs of the coke division amount to $40,000 a year.

The blast furnace manager, with authority to purchase outside, has found a reliable, indepen-dent coke producer who has offered to sell coke at a fixed delivered price of $5 per ton on a long-term contract. The manager of Wallach Iron Mill's coke division claims it cannot match that price and maintain profitable operations.

The manager of the coke division indicates that with an expenditure of $60,000 annually for fixed productive and delivery equipment, the division's entire annual normal output could be sold to outside firms at $6 per ton, FOB the Wallach Iron Mill plant. Other marketing expenses will be $.50 per ton. The increased fixed costs would reduce variable production costs by $1.50 per ton.

Required:
(1) Calculations to guide the coke division manager in deciding whether to accept the offer, assuming that Wallach Iron Mill cannot increase its sales of coke to outsiders above the 20% of normal production.
(2) Calculations to aid executive management in deciding whether to make the additional investment and sell the entire coke division's output to outsiders.

6. Product pricing. Kamm Company is considering changing its sales price of Salien, presently $15. Increases and decreases of both 10% and 25%, as well as increases in advertising and promo-tion expenditures, are being considered, with the following estimated results for 19A and 19B:

	ESTIMATED UNIT SALES		ESTIMATED ADVERTISING AND PROMOTION EXPENDITURES	
PRICE	19A	19B	19A	19B
−25%	190,000	200,000	$200,000	$200,000
−10%	180,000	190,000	250,000	250,000
No change	160,000	170,000	300,000	300,000
+10%	140,000	150,000	400,000	450,000
+25%	130,000	140,000	450,000	550,000

The company has the necessary flexibility in its production capacity to meet these volume levels. The variable manufacturing cost per unit of Salien is estimated to be $7.25 in 19A and $7.80 in 19B.

Required: Recommended sales price.   (CMA adapted)

7. Contribution margin approach to pricing. The Freezex Company is a large manufacturer of refrigeration units. The firm's product line includes refrigerators for homes, industry, and ships.

The firm is composed of three divisions. The Motor Division is responsible for manufacturing the motors for all of the various refrigeration units. In the Shell Division, the refrigerator shells are produced and the motors transferred from the Motor Division are installed. The Marketing Division is responsible for the sale and distribution of the final product.

While a market exists outside the firm for both the motors and shells, the transfer price between divisions is set by executive management. This is done to avoid unnecessary friction, which management feels might impair efficiency and prove wasteful.

Recently the company was asked to submit a bid for 100 refrigeration units for a local ship-building firm. The following unit cost estimate has been prepared:

	MOTOR	SHELL	MARKETING
Manufacturing materials..	$195	$ 180	—
Receiving and handling (60% fixed)	10	25	$ 20
Motor	—	600	—
Refrigeration units..	—	—	1,240
Shipping materials	—	—	30
Direct labor	190	220	35
Factory overhead:			
Fixed	55	45	15
Variable..	100	80	10
General administrative cost..	28	57	67
Transfer price..	600	1,240	—

Prior to submitting its bid, Freezex has learned that its principal competitor has submitted a bid of $1,200 per unit.

Required: An analysis as to whether Freezex can match the competitor's bid.

PROBLEMS

27-1. Rate of return on capital employed. Terrance Corporation's management is concerned over its current financial position and return on capital employed. In a request for assistance in analyzing these financial conditions, the controller provides these statements:

Terrance Corporation
Statement of Working Capital Deficit
December 31, 19A

Current liabilities		$198,625
Less current assets:		
Cash	$ 5,973	
Accounts receivable (net)...	70,952	
Inventory	90,200	167,125
Working capital deficit		$ 31,500

Terrance Corporation
Income Statement
For the Year Ended December 31, 19A

Sales (90,500 units)...	$751,150
Cost of goods sold	451,000
Gross profit..	$300,150
Marketing and general expenses, including $22,980 depreciation	149,920
Income before income tax	$150,230
Less income tax (50%)...	75,115
Net income	$ 75,115

Noncurrent assets consist of land, a building, and equipment, with a book value of $350,000 on December 31, 19A.

Sales of 100,000 units are forecast for 19B. Within this relevant range of activity, costs are estimated as follows (excluding income tax):

	FIXED COST	VARIABLE COST PER UNIT
Cost of goods sold		$4.90
Marketing and general expenses, including $15,450 depreciation	$125,750	1.10
Total...	$125,750	$6.00

The income tax rate is expected to be 50%. Past experience indicates that current assets vary in direct proportion to sales. Management feels that in 19B the market will support a sales price of $8.40 at a sales volume of 100,000 units.

Required:
(1) The 19A inventory turnover rate.
(2) The 19A return-on-capital-employed ratio (after income tax), computed to $^1/_{10}$ of one percent.
(3) The 19B rate of return (after income tax) on book value of total assets, computed to $^1/_{10}$ of one percent.   (AICPA adapted)

27-2. Profit and rate of return on capital employed using various proposals. Safe-for-Kids Toy Company manufactures two specialty children's toys marketed under the trade names of Springy and Leapy. During the year, the following costs, revenue, and capital employed by the company in the production of these two items were:

	SPRINGY	LEAPY
Sales price per unit	$ 1.50	$ 1.95
Sales in units..	280,000	150,000
Materials cost per unit	$ .20	$ .30
Labor cost per unit...	.50	.75
Variable factory overhead per unit.................................	.15	.20
Variable marketing cost per unit....................................	.05	.10
Fixed factory overhead	100,000	30,000
Fixed marketing cost..	30,000	15,000
Variable capital employed	10% of sales	20% of sales
Fixed capital employed...	$148,000	$ 91,500

Fixed administrative and other nonallocable fixed costs amounted to $28,000, and nonallocable capital employed was $25,000.

Management, dissatisfied with the return on total capital employed, is considering a number of alternatives to improve this return.

The market for Springy appears to be underdeveloped, and the consensus is that sales can be increased to 325,000 units at the same price with an increase of $9,500 in the fixed advertising cost. An increase in the production of Springy will require use of some equipment previously utilized in the production of Leapy and a transfer of $10,000 of fixed capital and $5,000 of fixed factory overhead to the production of Springy.

For Leapy, it would mean limiting its production to 100,000 units which could be marketed with the current sales effort at (a) an increase in price of $.15 per unit; (b) without a price increase and with a reduction in current fixed advertising cost of $9,000; or (c) with a $.05 per unit increase in price and a $7,500 reduction in the current fixed advertising cost.

Required:
(1) The income before income tax and the return on capital employed for each product and in total for the year, computed to $^1/_{10}$ of one percent.
(2) The income before income tax and the return on capital employed for each product and in total under each alternative, computed to $^1/_{10}$ of one percent.

27-3. Transfer pricing. A. R. Arnes, Inc., manufactures cologne. The manufacturing process is basically a series of mixing operations with the addition of certain aromatic and coloring ingredients. The finished product is packaged in a company-produced glass bottle and is packed in cases containing six bottles.

Arnes feels that the sale of its product is heavily influenced by the appearance of the bottle and has therefore devoted considerable managerial effort to its production. This has resulted in the development of certain unique bottle production processes.

The areas of cologne production and bottle manufacture have evolved over the years in an almost independent manner; in fact, a rivalry has developed between management personnel as to which division is the most important to the company. This attitude is probably intensified because the bottle manufacturing plant was purchased intact ten years ago, and no real interchange of management personnel or ideas, except at the top corporate level, has taken place.

Since the acquisition, all bottle production has been used by the cologne manufacturing plant. Each area is considered a separate profit center and is evaluated as such. The corporate controller is responsible for the definition of a proper transfer price to use in crediting the bottle production profit center and in debiting the cologne profit center.

At the controller's request, the Bottle Division general manager asks other bottle manufacturers to quote a price for the three possible levels demanded by the Cologne Division. These competitive prices are:

SALES VOLUME (IN EQUIVALENT CASES)*	TOTAL SALES REVENUE	SALES PRICE PER CASE
2,000,000	$ 4,000,000	$2.00
4,000,000	7,000,000	1.75
6,000,000	10,000,000	1.67

*An equivalent case represents six bottles each.

A cost analysis of the internal bottle plant indicates that it can produce bottles at these costs:

SALES VOLUME (IN EQUIVALENT CASES)	TOTAL COST	COST PER CASE
2,000,000	$3,200,000	$1.60
4,000,000	5,200,000	1.30
6,000,000	7,200,000	1.20

The cost analyst explains that these costs represent a fixed cost of $1,200,000 and a variable cost of $1 per equivalent case.

These figures have caused considerable corporate discussion as to the proper price to be used in transferring bottles to the Cologne Division. This interest is heightened because a significant portion of a division manager's income is an incentive bonus based on profit-center results.

The Cologne Division has these costs in addition to the bottle costs:

SALES VOLUME (IN EQUIVALENT CASES)	TOTAL COST	COST PER CASE
2,000,000	$16,400,000	$8.20
4,000,000	32,400,000	8.10
6,000,000	48,400,000	8.07

After considerable analysis, the Marketing Research Department furnishes the following price-demand relationship for the finished product:

SALES VOLUME (IN EQUIVALENT CASES)	TOTAL SALES REVENUE	SALES PRICE PER CASE
2,000,000	$25,000,000	$12.50
4,000,000	45,600,000	11.40
6,000,000	63,900,000	10.65

Required:

(1) The profit for (a) the Bottle Division, (b) the Cologne Division, and (c) the company, using current market transfer prices and assuming a volume of 6,000,000 cases.

(2) Calculations to show whether this production and sales level is the most profitable volume for (a) the Bottle Division, (b) the Cologne Division, and (c) the company.

(3) (a) A definition of a profit center, (b) a discussion of the conditions that should exist for the establishment of a profit center, and (c) an indication as to whether the two divisions should be organized as profit centers.

(CMA adapted)

27-4. Divisional transfer pricing; differential cost analysis. Martin Corporation, a diversified company, recently implemented a decentralization policy under which divisional managers are expected to make their own operating decisions, including whether to do business with other divisions. The performances and year-end bonuses of divisional managers are measured by the return on capital employed of their divisions. Because most divisions have operated at full capacity, it is company policy that all transfers between divisions are to be priced at 120% of standard manufacturing cost (to allow for a "normal" divisional profit margin). This transfer price is not negotiable.

The president of the company is currently faced with a dispute between the general managers of two divisions: the Consumer Products Division and the Engineeering Division. The Consumer Products Division makes and sells several household articles, including a home appliance that has, until recently, been one of the company's steadiest sellers. Recently, this division has had marketing difficulties and has reduced its production of the appliance to 56,000 a year from its usual production at capacity. The unused capacity cannot be utilized for other products. The Engineering Division makes a wide variety of items, including a specialized part (Part TX) that is sold to the Consumer Products Division and to a few small outside companies. The latter buy a steady 12% of the Engineering Division's annual production capacity for the part.

The Consumer Products Division uses four of these parts in each home appliance unit and maintains no significant inventory of unused parts but acquires them from the Engineering Division as needed to meet its production requirements. The parts are not available from any other source.

Because the Consumer Products Division has recently reduced its requirement for Part TX, the Engineering Division has been seeking new customers and has received an offer to buy 100,000 units of the part annually, at a price of $5 each, which is less than the $5.40 each paid by the small outside companies but more than the transfer price paid by the Consumer Products Division. The company making the offer is in a market unrelated to that of either the Consumer Products Division or the small outside companies.

Following are data with respect to Part TX and the home appliance involved in the dispute between the two managers:

	PART TX (ENGINEERING DIVISION)	HOME APPLIANCE (CONSUMER PRODUCTS DIVISION)
Annual production capacity	300,000 units	66,000 units
Unit sales price to outside customers	$5.40	$80.00
Standard manufacturing cost per unit (based on production at full capacity):		
Division's own costs:		
Variable	$2.00	$37.00
Fixed	1.75	13.00
Transfers from the Engineering Division	—	18.00
Standard manufacturing cost per unit	$3.75	$68.00

The manager of the Consumer Products Division has requested that the president instruct the manager of the Engineering Division to refuse the offer received, since (1) no other source for Part TX can be found, (2) the marketing problems with the home appliance are expected to be temporary, and (3) the Engineering Division cannot expand its production capacity for Part TX.

Required:

(1) The action that the manager of the Engineering Division should take as a result of the offer in order to maximize the results of that division. Include calculations of the offer's effect on the Engineering Division.

(2) The overall effect on the company, under existing circumstances, if the Engineering Division's manager accepts the offer.

(3) Factors that the president should consider in deciding whether to intervene in the dispute.

(4) A revised transfer pricing policy to assist the divisional managers in making optimal decisions for the company.

(CICA adapted)

27-5. Differential analysis with probability estimates; return on investment; net present value. The president of Naomi Industries needs assistance in evaluating several financial management problems in the Home Appliances Division as summarized below.

Management wants to determine the best sales price for a new appliance with a variable cost of $4 per unit. The sales manager has estimated these probabilities of achieving annual sales levels for various sales prices:

SALES LEVEL (IN UNITS)	SALES PRICE			
	$4	$5	$6	$7
20,000			20%	80%
30,000		10%	40	20
40,000	50%	50	20	
50,000	50	40	20	

The division's current profit rate is 5% on annual sales of $1,200,000. A $400,000 investment is needed to finance these sales. The company's basis for measuring divisional success is by return on investment.

Management is also considering these two alternative plans submitted by Naomi employees for improving operations in the Home Appliances Division:

Green believes that the division's sales volume can be doubled by greater promotional effort, but this method would lower the profit rate to 4% of sales and would require an additional $100,000 investment.

Hendricks favors eliminating some unprofitable appliances and improving efficiency by adding $200,000 in capital equipment. These methods would decrease the division's sales volume by 10% but would improve the profit rate to 7%.

Black, Jones, and Delozier — three franchised home appliance dealers — have requested short-term financing from the company. These dealers have agreed to repay the loans within three years and to pay Naomi Industries 5% of their profit for the three-year period for use of the funds. The table below summarizes, by dealer, the financing requested and the total remittances (principal plus 5% of profit) expected at the end of each year:

	BLACK	JONES	DELOZIER
Financing requested	$ 80,000	$40,000	$30,000
Remittances expected at the end of:			
Year 1	$ 10,000	$25,000	$10,000
Year 2	40,000	30,000	15,000
Year 3	70,000	5,000	15,000
Total	$120,000	$60,000	$40,000

Management believes that these financing requests should be granted only if the annual pre-tax return to the company exceeds the target internal rate of 20% on investment. Discount factors (rounded) that would provide this 20% rate of return are:

Year 1	.8
Year 2	.7
Year 3	.6

Required:
(1) A schedule of the expected differential profit for each of the sales prices proposed for the new product. Include the expected sales levels in units (weighted according to the sales manager's estimated probabilities), the expected total monetary sales, the expected variable costs, and the expected differential profit.
(2) The company's (a) current rate of return on investment in the Home Appliances Division and (b) the anticipated rates of return under the alternative suggestions made by Green and Hendricks.
(3) The net present value of the investment opportunities of financing Black, Jones, and Delozier. Determine if the discounted cash flows expected from Black, Jones, and Delozier would be more or less than the amounts of Naomi Industries' investment in loans to each of the three dealers.   (AICPA adapted)

27-6. Public utility rate based on capital employed. The Watonga Water Company is a public utility providing water service to 3,000 customers. As a privately owned public utility, its rates are subject to government regulation. Its rate structure is designed to provide a reasonable rate of return, calculated by expressing net income as a percentage of the company's rate base. The rate base, in turn, is the depreciated cost of the utility plant, averaged between the beginning and end of the year.

Operating results for the year were as follows:

Water revenue...		$90,000
Expenses:		
Fixed..	$38,668	
Variable...	12,852	
Depreciation on utility plant..	17,000	68,520
Income before income tax		$21,480
Income tax..		4,510
Net income...		$16,970

Watonga's directors feel the present net income is inadequate and are considering applying for higher rates. At present, each customer is charged a flat rate of $30 per annum.

An analysis of metered water consumption data indicates the following ranges of average monthly usage:

RANGE	CONSUMPTION	NUMBER OF CUSTOMERS
A	0–100 cu. ft. (average: 50 cu. ft.)	900
B	101–500 cu. ft. (average: 300 cu. ft.)	1,800
C	over 500 cu. ft. (average: 700 cu. ft.)	300
		3,000

Other data:

Utility plant in service, January 1	$800,000
Less accumulated depreciation..	200,000
Depreciated cost of utility plant, January 1	$600,000
Utility plant addition during the year...	$ 81,000

The income tax rate on earnings up to $80,000 is unchanged.

Required:
(1) Watonga's rate base and rate of return for the year, computed to $^{1}/_{10}$ of one percent.
(2) Based on the information:
    (a) The flat rate annual customer charge necessary to provide a 10% rate of return.
    (b) For each of the three consumption ranges, the charge per cubic foot of water necessary to provide a 10% rate of return, with the charge for consumption within Range B being double that within Range C, and two thirds of that within Range A; i.e., a customer consuming 150 cu. ft. of water would be billed at the Range A rate for the first 100 cu. ft. and at the lower Range B rate for the additional 50 cu. ft. (Compute answers to nearest $^{1}/_{10}$ of a cent.)   (CGAA adapted)

27-7. Contribution margin approach to pricing. Ed Welsch manufactures custom-made pleasure boats ranging in price from $10,000 to $250,000. For the past thirty years, Welsch has determined each boat's sales price by estimating the costs of materials, labor, and a prorated portion of overhead and by adding 20% to these estimated costs.

For example, a recent price quotation was determined as follows:

Direct materials	$ 5,000
Direct labor	8,000
Overhead	2,000
	$15,000
Plus 20%	3,000
Sales price	$18,000

The overhead figure was determined by estimating the total overhead cost for the year and allocating it at 25% of direct labor.

If a customer rejects the price and business is slack, Welsch is often willing to reduce the markup to as little as 5% over estimated costs. Thus, average markup for the year is estimated at 15%.

Welsch has just completed a pricing course and believes that the company could use some of the modern techniques he has learned. The course emphasized the contribution margin approach to pricing, and Welsch feels that such an approach would be helpful in determining the sales prices of custom-made pleasure boats.

Total overhead (including marketing and administrative expenses for the year) has been estimated at $150,000, of which $90,000 is fixed and the remainder is variable in direct proportion to direct labor.

Required:

    (1) (a) The difference in profit for the year if a customer's offer of $15,000 is accepted.
        (b) The minimum sales price Welsch could have quoted without reducing or increasing profit.
    (2) The advantages that the contribution margin approach to pricing has over the approach used by Welsch.
    (3) The pitfalls, if any, to contribution margin pricing.

                                                                    (CMA adapted)

CASES

A. Return on capital employed as a divisional performance measurement. T Limited consists of a central corporate office and five operating divisions located throughout the country. Each operating division produces and markets its own line of products and sells the product lines of other divisions within its region of the country. Each division prepares its own financial statements, and its manager is evaluated on the basis of the rate earned on its investment. The division's investment figure used in the calculation, has, since the system was started, included all the assets controlled by each divisional manager.

Until last year, the investment figure of each division did not include two classes of assets: the headquarter's assets and the Research Department's assets. The associated headquarter and research expenses were not included in the calculation of return on capital employed (RCE). The headquarter's assets were not material (2% of the company's total assets) since most of the headquarter's facilities were rented. Until recently, research assets also had been small but by the spring of 19-- had grown to just over 10% of the company's total assets. It was expected that more funds would be invested in research facilities in the near future.

In late 19--, the president of T Limited suggested that all the company's assets and expenses should be distributed in some way to all the operating divisions. The president stated that the reported return on investment by the divisions would be more realistic in indicating how well the company was doing as a whole.

Required:
(1) Arguments for and against the use of return on capital employed to measure divisional performance.
(2) Evaluation of the suggestion made by the T Limited president.

(CICA adapted)

B. Divisional performance measurement. Texon Co. is organized into autonomous divisions along regional market lines, with each division manager responsible for sales, cost of operations, acquisition and financing of divisional assets, and working capital management.

The vice-president of general operations for the company will retire in September 19F. To fill the vacancy, a review of the performance, attitudes, and skills of several management employees has been undertaken; interviews with qualified outside candidates also have been held; and the selection committee has narrowed the choice to the managers of Divisions A and F.

Both candidates were appointed division managers in late 19B. The manager of A had been the division's assistant manager for the preceding five years. The manager of F served as Division B's assistant manager before being appointed to F, newly formed in 19A, when its first manager left to join a competitor. The financial results of these divisions' performances in the past three years were (000s omitted):

	DIVISION A			DIVISION F		
	19C	19D	19E	19C	19D	19E
Estimated industry sales — market area........	$10,000	$12,000	$13,000	$5,000	$6,000	$6,500
Division sales..	$ 1,000	$ 1,100	$ 1,210	$ 450	$ 600	$ 750
Variable cost...	$ 300	$ 320	$ 345	$ 135	$ 175	$ 210
Programmed fixed cost	400	405	420	170	200	230
Committed fixed cost.......................................	275	325	350	140	200	250
Total cost..	$ 975	$ 1,050	$ 1,115	$ 445	$ 575	$ 690
Income from operations	$ 25	$ 50	95	$ 5	$ 25	$ 60
Assets employed...	$ 330	$ 340	$ 360	$ 170	$ 240	$ 300
Liabilities incurred	103	105	115	47	100	130
Net investment..	$ 227	$ 235	$ 245	$ 123	$ 140	$ 170
Rate of return on capital employed	11%	21%	39%	4%	18%	35%

Required:
(1) Discussion as to whether it is appropriate to measure the performance of the divisions and the division managers on the basis of their rate of return on capital employed.
(2) Additional measures useful for performance evaluation and reasons for each measure.
(3) The manager to be recommended for vice-president of general operations, giving supporting reasons based on the information given.

(CMA adapted)

C. Divisional transfer pricing. The Defco Division of Gunnco Corporation requests of Ajax Division, operating at capacity, a supply of Electrical Fitting #1726 that is not available from any other source. Ajax Division sells this part to its regular customers for $7.50 each. Defco, operating at 50% capacity, is willing to pay $5 each for this fitting. Defco will put the fitting into a brake unit which it manufactures on essentially a cost basis for a commercial jet plane manufacturer.

Ajax Division produces Electrical Fitting #1726 at a variable cost of $4.25. The cost (and sales price) of the brake unit as it is being built by the Defco Division is:

Purchased parts (outside vendors)	$22.50
Ajax Electrical Fitting #1726	5.00
Other variable costs	14.00
Fixed factory overhead and administrative expenses	8.00
Total	$49.50

Defco believes that the price concession is necessary to obtain the job.

Gunnco uses return on investment and dollar profits in measuring division and division manager performance.

Required:

(1) A recommendation as to whether the Ajax Division should supply Electrical Fitting #1726 to the Defco Division. (Ignore income tax.)

(2) A discussion as to whether it would be to the short-run economic advantage of the Gunnco Corporation for the Ajax Division to supply the Defco Division with Electrical Fitting #1726 at $5 each. (Ignore income tax.)

(3) A discussion of the organizational and managerial behavior difficulties inherent in this situation and a recommendation to Gunnco's president as to how the problem should be handled.

(CMA adapted)

28 Linear Programming for Planning and Decision Making

New tools and techniques are increasingly used by managers as they seek to make intelligent decisions and control operations. At the heart of management's responsibility is the best or optimum use of limited resources that include money, personnel, materials, facilities, and time. *Linear programming*, a mathematical technique, permits determination of the best use of available resources. It is a valuable aid to management because it provides a systematic and efficient procedure which can be used as a guide in decision making.

LINEAR PROGRAMMING AND THE MAXIMIZATION OF CONTRIBUTION MARGIN

The contribution margin is one measure of whether management is making the best use of resources. When the total contribution margin is maximized, management's profit objective should be satisfied.

To illustrate the application of linear programming to the problem of maximizing the contribution margin, assume that a small machine shop manufactures two models, standard and deluxe. Each standard model requires two hours of grinding and four hours of polishing; each deluxe model requires five hours of grinding and two hours of polishing. The manufacturer has three grinders and two polishers; therefore, in a 40-hour week there are 120 hours of grinding capacity and 80 hours of polishing capacity. There is a contribution margin of $3 on each standard model and $4 on each deluxe model and a ready market for both models. To maximize the total contribution margin, the management must decide on (1) the allocation of the available production capacity to standard and deluxe models and (2) the number of units of each model to produce.

To solve this problem, the symbol x is assigned to the number of standard models and y to the number of deluxe models. The contribution margin from making x standard models and y deluxe models is then $3x + $4y. The contribution margin per unit is the sales price per unit less the unit variable cost that is directly traceable to the product. The total contribution margin is the per unit contribution multiplied by the number of units.

The restrictions on machine capacity are expressed in this manner: to manufacture one standard unit requires two hours of grinding time, so that making x standard models uses $2x$ hours. Similarly, the production of y deluxe models uses $5y$ hours of grinding time. With 120 hours of grinding time available, the grinding capacity is written: $2x + 5y \leq 120$ hours of grinding capacity per week. The limitation on polishing capacity is expressed: $4x + 2y \leq 80$ hours per week.

In summary, the relevant information is:

	GRINDING TIME	POLISHING TIME	CONTRIBUTION MARGIN
Standard model...........................	2 hours	4 hours	$3
Deluxe model	5	2	4
Plant capacity............................	120	80	

This information is used in illustrating two basic linear programming techniques — the graphic method and the simplex method.

Graphic Method

When a linear programming problem involves only two variables, a two-dimensional graph can be used to determine the optimal solution. In this example, the x-axis represents the number of standard models, and the y-axis represents the number of deluxe models. The maximum number of each model that can be produced, given the constraints, is determined as follows:

OPERATION	MAXIMUM NUMBER OF MODELS	
	Standard	*Deluxe*
Grinding.................................	$\dfrac{120}{2} = 60$	$\dfrac{120}{5} = 24$
Polishing	$\dfrac{80}{4} = 20$	$\dfrac{80}{2} = 40$

The lowest number in each of the two columns measures the impact of the hours limitations. It appears that at best, the company can produce 20 standard models with a contribution margin of $60 (20 × $3) or 24 deluxe models at a contribution margin of $96 (24 × $4). However, producing a combination of standard and deluxe models may be a better solution.

To determine the combination of production levels in order to maximize the contribution margin, all the constraints are plotted on the graph. In this example, the polishing and grinding constraints are drawn by connecting the points that represent the extremes of production of each model. These points are:

When x = 0: y ≤ 24 grinding constraint
           y ≤ 40 polishing constraint

When y = 0: x ≤ 60 grinding constraint
           x ≤ 20 polishing constraint

The constraints sketched on the graph define the solution space, as shown below:

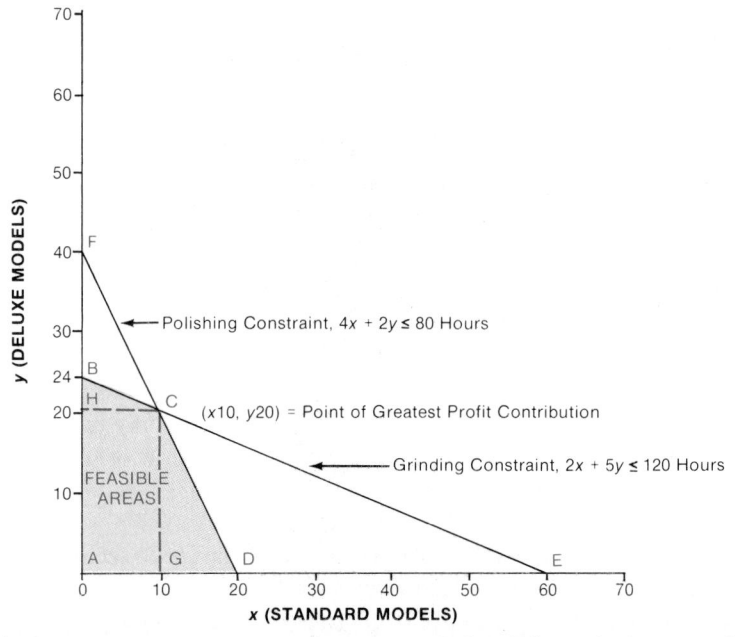

Graph
Depicting
Feasible
Solutions

The solution space represents the area of feasible solutions and is bounded by the lines AB, BC, CD, and AD on the graph. Any combination of standard and deluxe units that falls within the solution space is a feasible solution. However, the best feasible solution, according to mathematical laws, is at one of the four corner points. Consequently, all corner point variables must be examined to find the combination which maximizes the contribution margin (CM) of $3x + $4y.

The x and y corner point values can be read from the graph or computed. The x and y values for the corner points B(24) and D(20) are extreme points that were used in plotting the constraints. Corner point C values can be computed as follows:

Write the constraints as equalities:

$$2x + 5y = 120$$
$$4x + 2y = 80$$

To find the value of y, multiply the first equation by two and subtract the second equation:

$$
\begin{array}{r}
4x + 10y = 240 \\
-4x - 2y = -80 \\
\hline
8y = 160 \\
y = 20
\end{array}
$$

Substitute the value of y in the first equation and solve for x:

$$
\begin{array}{r}
2x + 5(20) = 120 \\
2x = 20 \\
x = 10
\end{array}
$$

The values for x and y and the resulting contribution margin values at each of the corner points are:

A ... ($x = 0$, $y = 0$); \$3(0) + \$4(0) = \$0 CM
B ... ($x = 0$, $y = 24$); \$3(0) + \$4(24) = \$96 CM
C ... ($x = 10$, $y = 20$); \$3(10) + \$4(20) = \$110 CM
D ... ($x = 20$, $y = 0$); \$3(20) + \$4(0) = \$60 CM

The total contribution margin is maximized when 10 standard models and 20 deluxe models are scheduled for production. This solution uses all of the constraint resources:

$$2(10) + 5(20) = 120 \text{ hours grinding constraint}$$
$$4(10) + 2(20) = 80 \text{ hours polishing constraint}$$

Full utilization of all resources will occur, however, only in cases in which the optimal solution is at a point of common intersection of all of the constraint equations in the problem — point C in this example.

Simplex Method

The simplex method is considered one of the basic techniques from which many linear programming techniques are directly or indirectly derived. The *simplex method* is an iterative, stepwise process which approaches an optimum solution in order to reach an objective function of maximization or minimization. Matrix algebra provides the deterministic working tools from which the simplex method was developed, requiring mathematical formulation in describing the problem.

The example described earlier in this chapter is used to illustrate the simplex method.[1] However, before the method can be applied, the following steps must be taken:

---

[1]This presentation is adapted from G. M. F. di Roccaferrera, *Introduction to Linear Programming Processes* (Cincinnati: South-Western Publishing Company, 1967).

1. The relationships which establish the constraints or inequalities must be set up first. Letting x and y be respectively the quantity of items of the standard model and the deluxe model that are to be manufactured, the system of inequalities or the set of constraints is:

$$2x + 5y \leq 120$$
$$4x + 2y \leq 80$$

Both x and y must be positive values or zero ($x \geq 0$; $y \geq 0$). Although this illustration involves only less-than-or-equal-to type constraints, equal-to and greater-than-or-equal-to type constraints can be encountered in maximization problems. All three types of constraints are illustrated in the cost minimization example on pages 845–851.

2. The objective function is the total contribution margin the manager can obtain from the two models. A contribution margin of $3 is expected for each standard model and $4 for each deluxe model. The objective function is CM = $3x + 4y$. The problem is now completely described by mathematical notation.

3. Although the first two steps were the same for the graphic method, the simplex method requires the use of equations, in contrast to the inequalities used by the graphic method. Therefore, the set of inequalities (two less-than-or-equal-to type constraints) must be transformed into a set of equations by introducing slack variables, s_1 and s_2. The use of slack variables involves the addition of an arbitrary variable to one side of the inequality, transforming it into an equality. This arbitrary variable is called a *slack variable*, since it takes up the slack in the inequality. The inequalities rewritten as equalities are:

$$2x + 5y + s_1 = 120$$
$$4x + 2y + s_2 = 80$$

The unit contribution margins of the fictitious products s_1 and s_2 are zero, and the objective equation becomes:

$$\text{Maximize: CM} = 3x + 4y + 0s_1 + 0s_2$$

At this point, the simplex method can be applied and the first matrix or tableau can be set up as shown below:

	MIX		0	3	4	0	0	← OBJECTIVE ROW
		QUANTITY	x	y	s_1	s_2		← VARIABLE ROW
0	s_1	120	2	5	1	0		← PROBLEM ROWS
0	s_2	80	4	2	0	1		←
		0	−3	−4	0	0		← INDEX ROW

OBJECTIVE COLUMN VARIABLE COLUMN QUANTITY COLUMN

First Simplex Tableau and First Solution

Explanation and Computations for the First Tableau. The simplex method records the pertinent data in a matrix form known as the *simplex tableau*. The components of a tableau are described in the following paragraphs.

The *objective row* of the matrix consists of the coefficients of the objective function.

The *variable row* is made up of the notation of the variables of the problem, including slack variables.

The *problem rows* in the first tableau contain the coefficients of the variables in the constraints. Each constraint adds an additional problem row. Variables not included in a constraint are assigned zero coefficients in the problem rows. In subsequent tableaus, new problem row values will be computed.

At each iteration, the *objective column* receives different entries, representing the contribution margin per unit of the variables in the solution.

At each iteration, the *variable column* receives different notations by replacement. These notations are the variables used to find the total contribution margin of the particular iteration. In the first matrix, a situation of no production is considered as a starting point in the iterative solution process. For this reason, only slack variables and *artificial variables* (discussed on page 846) are entered in the objective column, and their coefficients in the objective function are recorded in the variable column. As the iterations proceed, by replacement, appropriate values and notations will be entered in the objective and variable columns.

The *quantity column* shows the constant values of the constraints in the first tableau; in subsequent tableaus, it shows the solution mix.

The *index row* carries values computed by the following steps:

1. Multiply the values of the quantity column and those columns to the right of the quantity column by the corresponding value, by rows, of the objective column.
2. Add the results of the products, by rows, of the matrix.
3. Subtract the values in the objective row from the results in Step 2. For this operation, the objective row is assumed to have a zero value in the quantity column. The contribution margin entered in the cell in the quantity column and the index row is zero, a condition valid only for the first tableau when a situation of no production is considered. In the subsequent matrices, it will be a positive value, denoting the total contribution margin represented by the particular matrix.

The index row for the illustration is determined as follows:

STEPS 1 AND 2	STEP 3
$120(0) + 80(0) = 0$	$0 - 0 =\ \ 0$
$2(0) +\ \ 4(0) = 0$	$0 - 3 = -3$
$5(0) +\ \ 2(0) = 0$	$0 - 4 = -4$
$1(0) +\ \ 0(0) = 0$	$0 - 0 =\ \ 0$
$0(0) +\ \ 1(0) = 0$	$0 - 0 =\ \ 0$

In this first tableau, the slack variables were introduced into the product mix variable column to find an initial feasible solution to the problem. It can be proven mathematically that beginning with positive slack and artificial variables assures a feasible solution. Hence, one possible solution might have s_1 take a value of 120 and s_2 a value of 80. This approach satisfies the constraint but is undesirable since the resulting contribution margin is zero.

It is a rule of the simplex method that the optimum solution has not been reached if the index row carries any negative values at the completion of an iteration. Consequently, this first tableau does not carry the optimum solution since negative values appear in its index row. A second tableau or matrix must now be prepared, step by step, according to the rules of the simplex method.

Explanation and Computations for the Second Tableau. The construction of the second tableau is accomplished through these six steps:

1. Select the *key column*, the one which has the negative number with the highest absolute value in the index row, i.e., that variable whose value will most increase the contribution margin. In the first tableau, the key column is the one formed by the values: 5, 2, and -4.

2. Select the *key row*, the row to be replaced. The key row is the one which contains the smallest positive ratio obtained by dividing the positive numbers in the problem rows of the key column into the corresponding values, by rows, of the quantity column. The smallest positive ratio identifies the equation which operates as the limiting constraint. In the first tableau, the ratios are $\frac{120}{5} = 24$ and $\frac{80}{2} = 40$. Since $\frac{120}{5}$ is the smaller of the two positive ratios, the key row is s_1 — 120, 2, 5, 1, and 0.

	MIX	0	3	4	0	0
		QUANTITY	x	y	s_1	s_2
0	s_1	120	2	5	1	0
0	s_2	80	4	2	0	1
		0	-3	-4	0	0

First Simplex Tableau

3. Select the *key number*, which is the value found in the crossing cell of the key column and the key row. In the example, the key number is 5.

4. Compute the *main row*, which is a computed series of new values replacing the key row of the preceding tableau (in this case, the first tableau). The main row is determined by dividing each amount in Row s_1 (the row being replaced) of the preceding tableau by the key number; i.e., $120 \div 5 = 24$; $2 \div 5 = 2/5$, or 0.4; $5 \div 5 = 1$; $1 \div 5 = 1/5$, or 0.2; $0 \div 5 = 0$. In the second tableau, these are the figures in the Row y, which replaces Row s_1.

5. Compute the amounts in all other rows. In this problem new values are determined for the s_2 row by the following procedure:

$$
\begin{array}{ccccccc}
\text{OLD } s_2 \text{ ROW} & - & \left(\begin{array}{c}\text{OLD } s_2 \text{ ROW AND} \\ \text{y (THE KEY)} \\ \text{COLUMN}\end{array}\right. & \times & \begin{array}{c}\text{y ROW} \\ \text{(SECOND TABLEAU)}\end{array}\left.\begin{array}{c}\\\\\end{array}\right) & = & \begin{array}{c}\text{VALUES OF} \\ \text{NEW } s_2 \text{ ROW}\end{array} \\
\text{(FIRST TABLEAU)} & & & & & & \\
80 & - & (\quad 2 & \times & 24 \quad) & = & 32 \\
4 & - & (\quad 2 & \times & 0.4 \quad) & = & 3.2 \\
2 & - & (\quad 2 & \times & 1 \quad) & = & 0 \\
0 & - & (\quad 2 & \times & 0.2 \quad) & = & -0.4 \\
1 & - & (\quad 2 & \times & 0 \quad) & = & 1
\end{array}
$$

These computations accomplish (1) the substitution of as much of the deluxe model as is consistent with constraints and (2) the removal of as much s_1 and s_2 as is necessary to provide for the insertion of y (deluxe model) units into the solution. The $4 contribution margin of the deluxe model is placed in the objective column of the y row.

6. Finally, compute the index row:

STEPS 1 AND 2	STEP 3
24 (4) + 32 (0) = 96	96 − 0 = 96
0.4(4) + 3.2(0) = 1.6	1.6 − 3 = −1.4
1 (4) + 0 (0) = 4	4 − 4 = 0
0.2(4) + −0.4(0) = 0.8	0.8 − 0 = 0.8
0 (4) + 1 (0) = 0	0 − 0 = 0

When these steps are completed for the contribution margin maximization illustration, the second tableau appears as follows:

Second Simplex Tableau and Second Solution

	MIX	0	3	4	0	0	
		QUANTITY	x	y	s_1	s_2	
4	y	24	0.4	1	0.2	0	← MAIN ROW
0	s_2	32	3.2	0	−0.4	1	
		96	−1.4	0	0.8	0	

This row has been replaced because 24 was the smallest positive ratio computed in Step 2.

This second matrix does not contain the optimum solution since a negative figure, −1.4, still remains in the index row. The contribution margin arising from this model mix is $96 [4(24) + 0(32)], which is an improvement. However, the second solution indicates that some standard models and $1.40 (or 7/5 dollars of contribution margin) can be added for each unit of the standard model substituted in this solution.

It is interesting to reflect on the significance of − 7/5 or −1.4. The original statement of the problem had promised a unit contribution margin of $3 for the standard model. Now the contribution will increase by only $1.40 per unit. The significance of the −1.4 is that it measures the net increase of the per unit contribution margin after allowing for the reduction of the deluxe model represented by y units. That is, all the grinding hours have been committed to produce 24 deluxe models (24 units $\times$ 5 hours grinding time per unit = 120 hours capacity); the standard model cannot be made without sacrificing the deluxe model. The standard model requires 2 hours of grinding time; the deluxe model requires 5 hours of grinding time. To introduce one standard model unit into the product mix, the manufacture of 2/5 (0.4) of one deluxe model units must be foregone. This figure, 0.4, appears in the column headed "x" on the row representing foregone variable (deluxe) models. If more non-slack variables (i.e., more than two products) were involved, the figures for these variables, appearing in Column x, would have the same meaning as 0.4 has for the deluxe models.

Thus, the manufacturer loses 2/5 of $4, or $1.60, by making 2/5 less deluxe models but gains $3 from the additional standard models. A loss of $1.60 and a gain of $3 results in a net improvement of $1.40. The final answer, already known from the graphic method illustration, adds $14 (10 standard models $\times$ 1.4) to the $96 contribution margin that results from producing 24 deluxe models. However, the total contribution margin of $110 results from producing 10 standard models (10 $\times$ $3 = $30) and 20 deluxe models (20 $\times$ $4 = $80). In summary, the -1.4 in the second tableau indicates the amount of increase possible in the contribution margin if one unit of the variable heading that column (x in this case) were added to the solution; and the 0.4 value in Column x represents the production of the deluxe model that must be relinquished.

The quantity column was described for the first tableau as showing the constant values of the constraints, i.e., the maximum resources available (grinding and polishing hours in the illustration) for the manufacture of standard and deluxe models. In subsequent tableaus the quantity column shows the solution mix. Additionally, for a particular iteration in subsequent tableaus, the quantity column shows the constraints that are utilized in an amount different from the constraint's constant value. For example, in the second tableau's quantity column, the number corresponding to the y variable denotes the number of y units in the solution mix (24), and its objective function coefficient of $4 when multiplied by 24 yields $96, the value of the solution at this iteration. The number corresponding to the s_2 variable denotes the difference in total polishing hours and those used in the second tableau solution, i.e., 80 hours of available polishing hours less polishing hours used to produce 24 units of y (24 $\times$ 2), or 80 $-$ 48 = 32. Thus, the number of unused polishing hours is 32. No unused grinding hours, the s_1 variable, are indicated because 24 units of y utilize the entire quantity of available grinding time (24 $\times$ 5 = 120 hours).

While this illustration is of less-than-or-equal-to type constraints, a similar interpretation can be made for equal-to type constraints; i.e., the quantity column denotes the difference in the constant value of the constraint and the value used in the tableau's solution mix. For the greater-than-or-equal-to constraint, the quantity column denotes the amount beyond the constraint's minimum requirement that is satisfied by the particular solution mix.

These constraint utilization or satisfaction differences provide useful information, especially in the optimal solution tableau, because management may wish to make decisions to reduce these differences, e.g., by plans to utilize presently unused capacity associated with less-than-or-equal-to constraints.

Explanation and Computations for the Third Tableau. The third tableau is computed by these steps:

MIX		0	3	4	0	0
		QUANTITY	x	y	s_1	s_2
4	y	24	0.4	1	0.2	0
0	s_2	32	3.2	0	−0.4	1
		96	−1.4	0	0.8	0

Second Simplex Tableau

1. Select the *key column*. This is the column which has the negative number with the highest absolute value in the index row. In the second tableau, the key column is formed by the values 0.4, 3.2, and −1.4.
2. Select the *key row*, s_2, the row to be replaced by x, which is determined as follows: from the second tableau, for the x row, 24 ÷ 0.4 = 60; for the s_2 row, 32 ÷ 3.2 = 10. Since 10 is the smaller positive ratio and comes from the s_2 row, s_2 should be replaced by x.
3. Select the *key number*, which is the value (3.2) located in the crossing cell of the key column and the key row of the preceding (second) tableau.
4. Compute the *main row*. The new x row (old s_2 row) figures are determined by dividing each amount in row s_2 of the second tableau by the amount in the x column in row s_2, the key number. The results are: 32 ÷ 3.2 = 10; 3.2 ÷ 3.2 = 1; 0 ÷ 3.2 = 0; −0.4 ÷ 3.2 = −0.125; 1 ÷ 3.2 = 0.3125.
5. Compute the amounts in all other rows. The new values of the y row are:

OLD y ROW (SECOND TABLEAU)		OLD y ROW AND x (THE KEY) COLUMN		x ROW (THIRD TABLEAU)		VALUES OF NEW y ROW
24	− (	0.4	×	10	) =	20
0.4	− (	0.4	×	1	) =	0
1	− (	0.4	×	0	) =	1
0.2	− (	0.4	×	−0.125	) =	0.25
0	− (	0.4	×	0.3125	) =	−0.125

6. Compute the index row:

STEPS 1 AND 2

20	(4) + 10	(3) = 110
0	(4) + 1	(3) = 3
1	(4) + 0	(3) = 4
0.25 (4) + −0.125	(3) =	0.625
−0.125(4) + 0.3125(3) =		0.4375

STEP 3

110	− 0 = 110
3	− 3 = 0
4	− 4 = 0
0.625	− 0 = 0.625
0.4375 − 0 =	0.4375

The third tableau appears as follows:

	MIX	0	3	4	0	0
		QUANTITY	x	y	s_1	s_2
4	y	20	0	1	0.250	−0.1250
3	x	10	1	0	−0.125	0.3125
		110	0	0	0.625	0.4375

Third Simplex Tableau and Optimal Solution

There are no negative figures in the index row, which indicates that any further substitutions will not result in an increase in the contribution margin; the optimum solution has been obtained. The optimum strategy is to produce and sell 20 deluxe and 10 standard models for a contribution margin of $110.

LINEAR PROGRAMMING AND THE MINIMIZATION OF COST

The previous problem dealt with the maximization of the contribution margin. The simplex method, as well as the graphic method, can also be used in problems whose objective is to minimize the variable cost.

To illustrate a cost minimization problem, assume that a pharmaceutical firm is to produce exactly 40 gallons of a mixture in which the basic ingredients, x and y, cost $8 per gallon and $15 per gallon, respectively. No more than 12 gallons of x can be used, and at least 10 gallons of y must be used. The firm wants to minimize cost.

The cost function objective can be written as:

$$C \text{ (cost)} = 8x + 15y$$

The problem illustrates the three types of constraints, $=$, $\leq$, and $\geq$, as follows:

$$x + y = 40$$
$$x \leq 12$$
$$y \geq 10$$

The optimum solution is obvious. Since x is cheaper, as much of it as possible should be used, i.e., 12 gallons. Then enough y, or 28 gallons, should be used to obtain the desired total quantity of 40 gallons.

In more realistic problems, a solution may not be so obvious, especially if there are many ingredients each having constraints. A simple procedure is

Simplex Method

needed to generate an optimal solution no matter how complex the problem. The steps toward a solution in the cost minimization problem are similar to those taken in the contribution margin maximization example where the simplex method was used and slack variables were introduced in order to arrive at the first feasible solution which gave a zero contribution margin.

In addition to the slack variables, a different type of variable known as an artificial variable is introduced. *Artificial variables* allow two types of restrictions or constraints to be treated: the equal-to type and the greater-than-or-equal-to type. Artificial variables are of value only as computational devices in maximization and minimization problems.

In this minimization problem, an artificial variable, a_1, is introduced in the first constraint, which is of the equal-to type. A new equality is written as follows:

$$x + y + a_1 = 40 \text{ gallons}$$

The new ingredient, a_1, must be thought of as a very expensive item which would not be part of the optimum solution. If a costs \$999 per gallon, for example, 40 gallons would cost \$39,960. This high cost is noted by the coefficient m in the objective function. (For a maximization problem, the notion of a very low contribution margin is denoted by the symbol $-m$.) This symbol is added merely to initiate the simplex method, since the constraint is already an equality.

The second constraint is the less-than-or-equal-to type, and a slack variable, s_1, is added to form an equation: $x + s_1 = 12$ gallons. The s_1 represents the difference between 12 gallons of x and the actual number of gallons of x in the final solution.

The third constraint is the greater-than-or-equal-to type, and a variable, s_2, is introduced to form an equation: $y - s_2 = 10$ gallons. The variable s_2 must be thought of as the amount by which the actual number of gallons of y in the final solution must be reduced to arrive at 10 gallons. For example, if y should be 18 gallons, then s_2 would be 8 gallons ($18 - 8 = 10$ gallons). However, if y appears in the first solution as 0, then $0 - s_2 = 10$ or $s_2 = -10$. This equation is not feasible because -10 gallons of an ingredient is not possible. To prevent s_2 from entering the first solution, in which only slack and artificial variables are introduced, a second artificial variable, a_2, is utilized. Thus, $y - s_2 + a_2 = 10$ gallons. Similar to a_1, a high cost (m) is assigned to a_2 in the objective function.

As a rule, there must be the same number of entries in the variable (mix) column as there are constraints. Before a_2 is introduced in this example, there are three constraints, one artificial variable (a_1), and two slack variables (s_1 and s_2), of which s_2 has a negative coefficient. The introduction of the artificial variable, a_2, gives a set of four variables, from which the three with positive coefficients (s_1, a_1, and a_2) can be chosen to enter into the variable column of the first tableau.

The new cost equation is:

$$C = 8x + 15y - 0s_2 + ma_1 + 0s_1 + ma_2$$

For minimizing cost, the objective function must be multiplied by -1. This transformed function enters the first tableau as the objective row. The resulting equation is:

$$C = -8x - 15y + 0s_2 - ma_1 - 0s_1 - ma_2$$

The new constraints for the simplex solution are:

$$x + y + a_1 = 40$$
$$x + s_1 = 12$$
$$y - s_2 + a_2 = 10$$

The first tableau can be set up as shown below:

	MIX	0	−8	−15	0	−m	0	−m
		QUANTITY	x	y	s_2	a_1	s_1	a_2
−m	a_1	40	1	1	0	1	0	0
0	s_1	12	1	0	0	0	1	0
−m	a_2	10	0	1	−1	0	0	1
		−50m	−m+8	−2m+15	m	0	0	0

First Simplex Tableau and First Solution

Explanation and Computations for the First Tableau. The explanation of the arrangement of the tableau is identical with that given for the first tableau of the maximization model. Observe that variables not included in a constraint are assigned zero coefficients in the problem rows. The index row is computed as follows:

STEPS 1 AND 2	STEP 3
$-m (40) + 0 (12) + (-m) (10) = -50m$	$-50m - 0 = -50m$
$-m (1) + 0 (1) + (-m) (0) = -m$	$- m - (- 8) = -m + 8$
$-m (1) + 0 (0) + (-m) (1) = -2m$	$- 2m - (-15) = -2m + 15$
$-m (0) + 0 (0) + (-m) (-1) = m$	$m - 0 = m$
$-m (1) + 0 (0) + (-m) (0) = -m$	$- m - (- m) = 0$
$-m (0) + 0 (1) + (-m) (0) = 0$	$0 - 0 = 0$
$-m (0) + 0 (0) + (-m) (1) = -m$	$- m - (- m) = 0$

In the simplex method, the optimum solution has not been reached if the index row carries any negative values (except for the quantity column which denotes total cost of this solution) at the completion of an iteration. Consequently, since negative values appear in the index row, the optimum solution has not been found, and a second tableau must be set up.

Explanation and Computations for the Second Tableau. Since the objective is to minimize cost, the key column is found by selecting that column with the negative value having the highest absolute value in the index row, i.e., that variable whose value will most decrease cost. The index row shows only two negative values: $-m + 8$ and $-2m + 15$. Observe that the quantity column value in the index row, $-50m$, is not considered. This figure denotes total cost of this solution and is negative by convention. The negative number with the highest absolute value in the index row is $-2m + 15$; therefore, y is the key column.

	MIX	0	-8	-15	0	$-m$	0	$-m$
		QUANTITY	x	y	s_2	a_1	s_1	a_2
$-m$	a_1	40	1	1	0	1	0	0
0	s_1	12	1	0	0	0	1	0
$-m$	a_2	10	0	1	-1	0	0	1
		$-50m$	$-m+8$	$-2m+15$	m	0	0	0

First Simplex Tableau

The row to be replaced, the key row, is a_2, determined as follows:

a_1 row, $40/1 = 40$
s_1 row, $12/0$ is not considered (not defined mathematically)
a_2 row, $10/1 = 10$

Again, as in the maximization discussion, the smallest positive ratio identifies the equation which operates as the limiting constraint.

Since the key number (the crossing cell of the key column y and the key row a_2) is 1, the values of the main row (y) do not change, as indicated by the following computations: $10/1 = 10$; $0/1 = 0$; $1/1 = 1$; $-1/1 = -1$; $0/1 = 0$; $0/1 = 0$; and $1/1 = 1$.

The values in the other rows are determined as follows:

a_1 Row	s_1 Row
$40 - 1(\,10) = 30$	$12 - 0(\,10) = 12$
$1 - 1(\,0) = 1$	$1 - 0(\,0) = 1$
$1 - 1(\,1) = 0$	$0 - 0(\,1) = 0$
$0 - 1(-1) = 1$	$0 - 0(-1) = 0$
$1 - 1(\,0) = 1$	$0 - 0(\,0) = 0$
$0 - 1(\,0) = 0$	$1 - 0(\,0) = 1$
$0 - 1(\,1) = -1$	$0 - 0(\,1) = 0$

INDEX ROW

Steps 1 and 2		*Step 3*	
$-m(\,30) + 0(12) + (-15)(\,10) =$	$-30m-150$	$(-30m-150) - 0$	$= -30m-150$
$-m(\,1) + 0(\,1) + (-15)(\,0) =$	$-m$	$(-m) \quad - (-\,8) =$	$-m+8$
$-m(\,0) + 0(\,0) + (-15)(\,1) =$	-15	$(-15) \quad - (-15) =$	0
$-m(\,1) + 0(\,0) + (-15)(-1) =$	$-m+15$	$(-m+15) \quad - 0 \quad =$	$-m+15$
$-m(\,1) + 0(\,0) + (-15)(\,0) =$	$-m$	$(-m) \quad - (-m) =$	0
$-m(\,0) + 0(\,1) + (-15)(\,0) =$	0	$(0) \quad - 0 \quad =$	0
$-m(-1) + 0(\,0) + (-15)(\,1) =$	$m-15$	$(m-15) \quad - (-m) =$	$2m-15$

The second tableau appears as follows:

	MIX	0 QUANTITY	-8 x	-15 y	0 s_2	-m a_1	0 s_1	-m a_2	
-m	a_1	30	1	0	1	1	0	-1	
0	s_1	12	1	0	0	0	1	0	Second Simplex Tableau and Second Solution
-15	y	10	0	1	-1	0	0	1	
		-30m-150	-m+8	0	-m+15	0	0	2m-15	

Since negative values appear in the index row, excluding the quantity column, the optimum solution has not yet been found, and a third tableau must be set up.

Explanation and Computations for the Third Tableau. Since $-m + 8$ is the negative number with the highest absolute value in the index row of the second tableau, x is the key column.

The row to be replaced, the key row, is s_1, determined as follows:

$$a_1 \text{ row, } 30/1 = 30$$
$$s_1 \text{ row, } 12/1 = 12$$
$$y \text{ row, } 10/0 \text{ not defined mathematically}$$

The following computations determine the values in the x row that replaces the s_1 row, as well as the values in the other rows:

x Row	a_1 Row	y Row
$12/1 = 12$	$30 - 1(12) = 18$	$10 - 0(12) = 10$
$1/1 = 1$	$1 - 1(1) = 0$	$0 - 0(1) = 0$
$0/1 = 0$	$0 - 1(0) = 0$	$1 - 0(0) = 1$
$0/1 = 0$	$1 - 1(0) = 1$	$-1 - 0(0) = -1$
$0/1 = 0$	$1 - 1(0) = 1$	$0 - 0(0) = 0$
$1/1 = 1$	$0 - 1(1) = -1$	$0 - 0(1) = 0$
$0/1 = 0$	$-1 - 1(0) = -1$	$1 - 0(0) = 1$

INDEX ROW

Steps 1 and 2		*Step 3*		
$-m(18) + (-8)(12) + (-15)(10) =$	$-18m-246$	$(-18m-246) - 0$	$=$	$-18m-246$
$-m(0) + (-8)(1) + (-15)(0) =$	-8	-8	$-(-8) =$	0
$-m(0) + (-8)(0) + (-15)(1) =$	-15	-15	$-(-15) =$	0
$-m(1) + (-8)(0) + (-15)(-1) =$	$-m+15$	$(-m+15)$	-0	$-m+15$
$-m(1) + (-8)(0) + (-15)(0) =$	$-m$	$-m$	$-(-m) =$	0
$-m(-1) + (-8)(1) + (-15)(0) =$	$m-8$	$(m-8)$	$-0 =$	$m-8$
$-m(-1) + (-8)(0) + (-15)(1) =$	$m-15$	$(m-15)$	$-(-m) =$	$2m-15$

The third tableau appears as follows:

MIX		QUANTITY	0 x	−8 y	−15 s_2	0 a_1	−m s_1	0 a_2	−m
−m	a_1	18	0	0	1	1	−1	−1
−8	x	12	1	0	0	0	1	0
−15	y	10	0	1	−1	0	0	1
		−18m−246	0	0	−m+15	0	m−8	2m−15

Third Simplex Tableau and Third Solution

Since a negative value, −m + 15, appears in the index row, excluding the quantity column, the optimum solution has not been found, and a fourth tableau must be set up.

Explanation and Computations for the Fourth Tableau. Since −m + 15 is the only negative number in the index row of the third tableau, excluding the quantity column, s_2 is the key column.

The smallest positive ratio in the following computation identifies the row to be replaced as a_1.

a_1 row, 18/1 = 18
x row, 12/0 is not defined mathematically
y row, 10/−1 = −10

The values in the s_2 row (replacing the a_1 row), the x row, the y row, and the index row are determined as follows:

s_2 Row	x Row	y Row
18/1 = 18	12 − 0 (18) = 12	10 − (−1) (18) = 28
0/1 = 0	1 − 0 (0) = 1	0 − (−1) (0) = 0
0/1 = 0	0 − 0 (0) = 0	1 − (−1) (0) = 1
1/1 = 1	0 − 0 (1) = 0	−1 − (−1) (1) = 0
1/1 = 1	0 − 0 (1) = 0	0 − (−1) (1) = 1
−1/1 = −1	1 − 0 (−1) = 1	0 − (−1) (−1) = −1
−1/1 = −1	0 − 0 (−1) = 0	1 − (−1) (−1) = 0

INDEX ROW

Steps 1 and 2

0 (18) + (−8) (12) + (−15) (28) = −516
0 (0) + (−8) (1) + (−15) (0) = − 8
0 (0) + (−8) (0) + (−15) (1) = − 15
0 (1) + (−8) (0) + (−15) (0) = 0
0 (1) + (−8) (0) + (−15) (1) = − 15
0 (−1) + (−8) (1) + (−15) (−1) = 7
0 (−1) + (−8) (0) + (−15) (0) = 0

Step 3

−516 − 0   = −516
−8 − (− 8) = 0
−15 − (−15) = 0
0 − 0 = 0
−15 − (− m) = m−15
7 − 0 = 7
0 − (− m) = m

The fourth tableau appears as follows:

	MIX	0	−8	−15	0	−m	0	−m
		QUANTITY	x	y	s_2	a_1	s_1	a_2
0	s_2	18	0	0	1	1	−1	−1
−8	x	12	1	0	0	0	1	0
−15	y	28	0	1	0	1	−1	0
		−516	0	0	0	m−15	7	m

Fourth Simplex Tableau and the Optimal Solution

No negative values remain in the index row of the fourth tableau, except the minimum cost figure which is negative (−516) by convention. The following optimum solution has been reached:

$$
\begin{array}{lll}
12 \text{ gals. of } x @ \$\ 8 \text{ per gal.} & = & \$\ 96 \\
+28 \text{ gals. of } y @ \$15 \text{ per gal.} & = & \underline{\ \ 420} \\
\underline{40 \text{ gals. of mixture}} & & \underline{\$516} \text{ the lowest cost combination}
\end{array}
$$

The graphic method can be applied to minimization problems in the same manner as illustrated for maximization problems. Again, the constraints define the solution space when they are plotted on the graph below:

Graphic Method

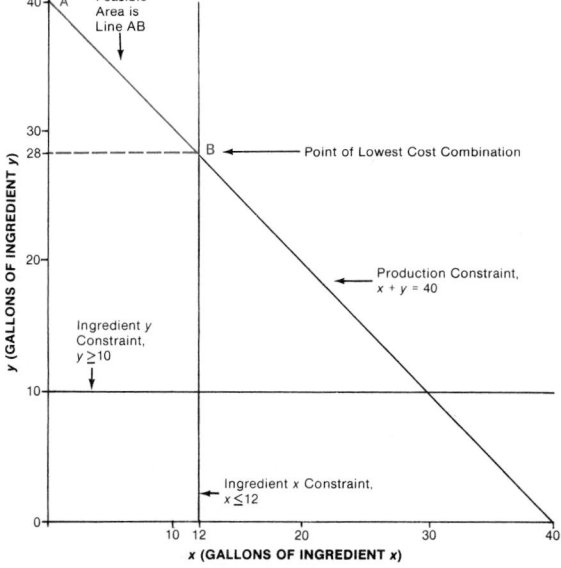

Graph Depicting Feasible Solutions

The solution space indicates the area of feasible solutions represented by the line AB. Any combination of x and y that falls within the solution space (line AB) is a feasible solution. However, the best feasible solution is found at one of the corner points, A or B. Consequently, the corner points must be examined to find the combination that minimizes cost, i.e., $8x + $15y.

The values at each of the two corner points are:

A .... ($x = 0$, $y = 40$); $8(0) + $15(40) = $600 cost
B .... ($x = 12$, $y = 28$); $8(12) + $15(28) = $516 cost

To minimize cost, the company should use 12 gallons of x and 28 gallons of y at a total cost of $516.

SHADOW PRICES

The determination of the optimum mix to maximize the contribution margin or to minimize cost assumes a defined set of constraints. It is useful to consider the sensitivity of the solution if a constraint is relaxed. This effect is often referred to as the *shadow price* and simply shows the change in contribution margin (in a contribution margin maximization problem) or the change in cost (in a cost minimization problem) resulting from relaxing a constraint.

To present the idea of shadow prices, the value of additional grinding or polishing hours (from the contribution margin maximization problem previously discussed) can be considered, i.e., the worth of additional grinding and polishing hours.[2] If the machine shop had more grinding or polishing hours, the contribution margin could be increased by using more of each.

The index row of the third (optimal solution) simplex tableau (page 845) shows the shadow prices in the slack variable columns, which is the location for both $\leq$ and $\geq$ constraints, while the artificial variable column is used for the = constraint, with the m value ignored. In this illustration, only $\leq$ constraints are encountered.

The coefficients under the s_1 (grinding) and s_2 (polishing) slack variable columns give the trade-off in terms of product mix as the constraints are increased or decreased. Thus, one more hour of grinding time will increase the contribution margin by $.625, computed as follows: as one more grinding hour is made available, .25 units of y (deluxe models) with a unit contribution margin of $4 (.25 × $4 = $1) will replace .125 units of x (standard models) with a $3 unit contribution margin (.125 × $3 = $.375), for a net contribution margin of $.625 ($1 − $.375 = $.625).

If additional grinding time could be obtained at no increase in unit variable cost, an increase of $.625 contribution margin per grinding hour would result; and as much as $.625 more than the present unit variable cost of grind-

[2]This discussion adapted from Lanny Gordon Chasteen, "A Graphical Approach to Linear Programming Shadow Prices," *The Accounting Review*, Vol. XLVII, No. 4, pp. 819–823.

ing time could be incurred before reaching a point at which a zero per unit contribution margin would occur. Thus, overtime hours might be considered. The $.4375 has the same meaning for each hour of polishing time, and in each case the observations assume that the sales price per unit remains unchanged.

The range of hours over which the shadow prices of $.625 and $.4375 for grinding and polishing hours are valid can be found as follows:

1. For the lower limit of the range, divide each unit in the solution mix by the coefficients under the slack variable columns, i.e., the s_1 and s_2 columns. The smallest positive number that results in a column is the maximum decrease for that constraint:

	(1)	(2)	(3)	(4)	(5)
				S_1	S_2
		S_1	S_2	GRINDING	POLISHING
PRODUCT	UNITS	GRINDING	POLISHING	(1) ÷ (2)	(1) ÷ (3)
y	20	0.250	−0.1250	80	− 160
x	10	−0.125	0.3125	−80	32

For the grinding constraint, the decrease is 80 hours. Since the original number of hours available was 120, the lower limit is 40 hours. For the polishing constraint, the decrease is 32 hours. Since 80 hours were originally available, the lower limit is 48 hours.

2. For the upper limit of the range, multiply each coefficient by −1 and repeat the Step 1 process. The smallest positive number that results in a column is the maximum increase for that constraint:

	(1)	(2)	(3)	(4)	(5)
				S_1	S_2
		S_1	S_2	GRINDING	POLISHING
PRODUCT	UNITS	GRINDING	POLISHING	(1) ÷ (2)	(1) ÷ (3)
y	20	−0.250	0.1250	−80	160
x	10	0.125	−0.3125	80	− 32

For the grinding constraint, the maximum increase is 80; and since the original number of hours available was 120, the upper limit is 200 hours. For the polishing constraint, the increase is 160, and the upper limit is 240 hours (160 plus the original constraint of 80 polishing hours).

The limits occur for a constraint because increases or decreases beyond the limits will change the shadow price. In summary, the lower and upper constraint limits for this example are:

	LOWER LIMIT	UPPER LIMIT
Grinding hours..	40	200
Polishing hours	48	240

Both the constraints in this example are of the ≤ type. The same method for finding the lower and upper constraint range limits is used for the = type of constraint except that the coefficients under the artificial variable column for the = constraint are used in the computations. For a ≥ constraint, the method for finding the lower and upper constraint range limits differs in that the signs of the coefficients under the slack variable column for the ≥ constraints are changed in Step 1. With this exception, the procedure is the same.

When there is a zero shadow price (not the case in the above example), there is no defined upper limit for the ≤ type of constraint because there is already more of this constraint available than is required. There is no defined lower limit for the ≥ type of constraint because there is already more of this constraint used than is required.

The lower- and upper-limit computations apply, assuming that only one constraint is to be relaxed, and provided there is a unique solution to the linear programming problem. The limits for cases in which two or more constraints are relaxed simultaneously can be computed following a methodology that is beyond the scope of this discussion.[3]

The described method is equally applicable to cost minimization problems. It should also be observed that the shadow price indicates the opportunity cost of using a resource (such as grinding or polishing hours) for some other purpose. For example, if an hour of grinding time could instead be used to produce some other product at a contribution margin greater than $.625 per hour, then use of the grinding hour resource in producing the alternate product would be preferable.

DYNAMIC PROGRAMMING

Dynamic programming is an extension of the basic linear programming technique and involves breaking the problem into a set of smaller problems and then reassembling the results of the analysis. It is best suited for the solution of problems requiring interrelated decisions, i.e., decisions that must be made in sequence and that influence future decisions in the sequence.

The procedure involves partial optimization of a portion of the sequence and then connection of the optimized portion to the next in line until the entire sequence is optimized. Thus, the final result is the sum of the result of the immediate decision plus the optimal result from all future decisions.

Dynamic programming is simple in concept but difficult to apply because of the lack of a clear-cut problem formulation and solution method. Each problem requires unique formulation and solution decisions.[4]

LINEAR PROGRAMMING TECHNIQUES — GENERAL OBSERVATIONS

The maximization and minimization studies, together with the exercises and problems presented in this chapter, are realistic examples of the types of

---

[3]See Harvey M. Wagner, *Principles of Operations Research* (Englewood Cliffs, NJ: Prentice-Hall, Inc., 1969), pp. 132–133.
[4]For a comprehensive treatment of dynamic programming, see James E. Shamblin and G. T. Stevens, Jr., *Operations Research: A Fundamental Approach* (New York: McGraw-Hill Book Company, 1974), pp. 365–389.

problems management faces. By maximizing certain managerial objectives such as contribution margin and utilization of available labor hours or factory capacity, or by minimizing functions such as cost, weight, materials mix, or time, management's goal can be determined quantitatively. To find a feasible solution, it is necessary to state each situation in mathematical notations. Restrictions or constraints must confine the solution within a well-defined area and appear in the form of equations with nonnegative variables. All data must be deterministic, i.e., involve exact relationships and known factors.

For the accounting community, a definite similarity exists between certain managerial problems and mathematical programming techniques. Furthermore, as other chapters have pointed out, the growing need for and involvement of accounting and cost data in management's planning and decision-making processes are supported and enhanced by these techniques.

The methods for determining the most profitable or optimum use of alternative uses of long-life facilities have been presented in Chapter 26. Problems dealing with the short-run uses of facilities or with output having varying combinations of alternative input might be solved by setting down every possible combination of output in order to determine the maximum contribution margin or the minimum cost. Such a procedure, while proven feasible and acceptable, may no longer be necessary. The introduction of newer and more sophisticated decision models, particularly that of linear programming, allows the accountant to administer the implementation of these models by determining the data needed for their application. When the cases move beyond the possibility of being solved manually or by simple desk or hand calculators, the electronic computer aids the accountant in arriving at a correct and immediate solution.

DISCUSSION QUESTIONS

1. Define and discuss the linear programming technique, including assumptions and accounting data used therein.

2. What is meant by the unit cost in linear programming problems?

3. Examine the graph on page 837 and answer the following questions:
   (a) The area bounded by the lines AB, BC, CD, and AD is called the solution space. Why?
   (b) The triangles BCF and CDE are not part of the solution space. Why?
   (c) What does corner point C mean?
   (d) What is the meaning of the perpendicular line CG and the horizontal line CH?

4. Hale Company manufactures Products a and b, each of which requires two processes, grinding and polishing. The contribution margin is $3 for a and $4 for b. A graph showing the maximum number of units of each product that can be processed in the two departments identifies the following corner points: a = 0, b = 20; a = 20, b = 10; a = 30, b = 0. What is the combination of a and b that maximizes the total contribution margin?

(AICPA adapted)

5. Describe the simplex method.

6. The Golden Hawk Company wants to maximize the profits on Products a, b, and c. The contribution margin for each product follows:

PRODUCT	CONTRIBUTION MARGIN
a	$2
b	5
c	4

The production requirements and departmental capacities, by departments, are as follows:

DEPARTMENT	PRODUCTION REQUIREMENT BY PRODUCT (HOURS)			DEPARTMENTAL CAPACITY (TOTAL HOURS)
	a	b	c	
Assembling	2	3	2	30,000
Painting	1	2	2	38,000
Finishing	2	3	1	28,000

Formulate the objective function and the constraints.

7. Formulate the objective function and constraints for a situation in which a company seeks to minimize the total cost of Materials a and b. The per pound cost of a is $25 and of b, $10. The two materials are combined to form a product that must weigh 50 pounds. At least 20 pounds of a and no more than 40 pounds of b can be used.

8. Discuss the components of a simplex tableau.

9. What is the purpose of a slack variable?

10. A partial linear programming maximization simplex tableau for Products x and y and slack variables s_1 and s_2 appears below:

	MIX	QUANTITY	0	6	7	0	0
			x	y	s_1	s_2	
7	y	4	$2/3$	1	$1/3$	0	
0	s_2	4	$4/3$	0	$-1/3$	1	

(a) Compute the index row.
(b) Has an optimum solution been reached? Explain.
(c) Suppose that one unit of s_1 were placed in the solution. What effect would this have on Product y?

11. What is the purpose of an artificial variable?

12. What is a shadow price? Explain its significance.

13. An optimal linear programming simplex tableau appears below for Products x and y and slack variables s_1 and s_2. Both constraints are of the $\leq$ type.

MIX			0	12	14	0	0
		QUANTITY	x	y	s_1	s_2
12	x	3	1	0	$-1/4$	$3/4$
14	y	2	0	1	$1/2$	$-1/2$
		64	0	0	4	2

(a) What is the value of an additional unit of a constraint corresponding to s_1, i.e., what is the shadow price for s_1?

(b) Compute the maximum decrease over which the shadow price for s_2 is valid.

14. Define dynamic programming.

15. Select the answer which best completes the statement:

(a) The simplex method of linear programming is: (1) a general procedure that will solve only two variables simultaneously; (2) a means of determining the objective function in the problem; (3) a means of determining the constraints in the problem; (4) a general procedure for solving all linear programming problems.

(b) A decision model designed to help its user find the best alternative or decision rule according to some criteria is said to be: (1) random; (2) probabilistic; (3) optimizing; (4) satisficing.

(c) The use that is not an application of linear programming is: (1) scheduling flight crews to various flights to minimize costs; (2) routing production to minimize costs; (3) determining the optimum trade-off between time and costs to maximize profits; (4) deciding which warehouses will service which customers to minimize total shipping costs.

(d) Quepea Company manufactures two products, q and p, in a small building with limited capacity. The sales price, cost data, and production time are given below:

	PRODUCT q	PRODUCT p
Sales price per unit...	$20	$17
Variable cost of producing and selling a unit ...	$12	$13
Hours to produce a unit	3	1

Based on this information, the contribution margin maximization objective function for a linear programming solution may be stated as: (1) 20q + 17p; (2) 12q + 13p; (3) 3q + 1p; (4) 8q + 4p.

(e) Globe Manufacturing has several plants in different cities and serves customers in various other cities. Globe wants to know the best way to schedule shipments from various plants to various customers and has been advised that the problem can be solved using linear programming. In a transportation cost minimization problem, the usual coefficients of the objective function would be: (1) usage rates for transportation facilities; (2) restrictions on transportation facilities; (3) shipping costs; (4) time estimates for the critical path.

(f) Fite Company plans to expand its sales force by opening as many as 10 new branch offices and has set $5,200,000 as the capital available for this purpose. Fite will open only two types of branches: 10-person branches (Type a), initial outlay of $650,000 each; and 5-person branches (Type b), initial outlay of $335,000 each. Expected annual aftertax cash inflow for types a and b is $46,000 and $18,000, respectively. No more than 100 employees will be hired for the new branch offices. In a system of inequalities for a linear programming model, the one not representing a constraint is: (1) $a + b \leq 10$; (2) $10a + 5b \leq 100$; (3) $\$46,000a + \$18,000b \leq \$64,000$; (4) $\$650,000a + \$335,000b \leq \$5,200,000$.

(g) In a system of inequalities for a linear programming model, to equalize an inequality such as $3x + 2y \leq 15$: (1) invert the inequality; (2) add a slack variable; (3) add an artificial variable; (4) multiply each element by -1.

(AICPA adapted)

EXERCISES

1. Contribution margin maximization; graphic method. A company has given the following constraints, $8x + 20y \leq 200$ and $4x \leq 60$, and the objective function, $CM = 2x + 10y$.

Required: A graph to determine how many units of x and y to produce to maximize the contribution margin, and the total contribution margin at the optimal solution.

2. Product mix contribution margin. The illustration on page 836 assumes that the market for standard and deluxe models was stable and that the $3 and $4 per unit was maintainable for at least the near future. Increased demand for the deluxe model suggests the desirability of raising the price well above the level that produced the original $4 contribution margin.

Required:
(1) The product mix to be attained if deluxe models are priced to yield a $6 unit contribution margin.
(2) The product mix to be attained if deluxe models are priced to yield a $10 contribution margin.
(3) The contribution margin figure per deluxe model to make it possible to abandon production of standard units and operate at less than full capacity, maintaining maximum profits.

3. Contribution margin maximization; graphic method. The Shamblin Machine Shop currently manufactures two products, a and b. Four types of machines are used, mills, lathes, drills, and welding, with daily shop capacities of 16, 16, 8, and 8 hours, respectively.

Time requirements to produce one unit of each product are:

	PRODUCT	
MACHINE	a	b
Mills	.1067 hours	.0533 hours
Lathes	.0640	.1067
Drills	None	.0800
Welding	.0267	.0320

Each unit of a and b returns a contribution margin of $2.50.

Required: A graph to determine the number of each product to manufacture in order to maximize the contribution margin.

4. Contribution margin maximization. Patsy, Inc., manufactures two products, x and y. Each product must be processed in each of three departments: Machining, Assembling, and Finishing. The hours needed to produce one unit of product per department and the maximum possible hours per department are:

DEPARTMENT	PRODUCTION HOURS PER UNIT		MAXIMUM CAPACITY IN HOURS
	x	y	
Machining	2	1	420
Assembling..........................	2	2	500
Finishing.............................	2	3	600

Other restrictions: $x \geq 50$
$y \geq 50$

The objective function is to maximize the contribution margin where CM $= \$4x + \$2y$.

Required: From the following answers, the feasible solution that will maximize the contribution margin: 150x and 100y, 165x and 90y, 170x and 80y, 200x and 50y.   (AICPA adapted)

5. Opportunity costs; contribution margin maximization — graphic and simplex methods; shadow prices. Walkrite, Inc., produces a quality brand of slippers, x, sold through a large mail-order house. These slippers, produced in lots of 50 or 100 pairs, are sold to the mail-order house at $3.70 per pair. The standard cost card covering the manufacture of a lot of 100 pairs appears as follows:

Direct materials..	$ 20
Direct labor:	
Fabricating — 20 hours at $4 per hour	80
Finishing — 30 hours at $5 per hour...	150
Variable overhead;	
Rate for both Fabricating and Finishing Departments is $2 per hour.........	100
Total (per 100 pairs)	$350

While the company was making plans for next year's production, the mail-order house offered it the opportunity of producing a second line of slippers, y. It offered to pay $4.30 per pair for these slippers. This second line would be produced in the same departments by the same workers who produce the other slippers. The company's management has developed the following standards for this second line for a lot of 100:

Direct materials..	$ 30
Direct labor:	
Fabricating — 40 hours at $4 per hour	160
Finishing — 20 hours at $5 per hour...	100
Variable overhead:	
60 hours at $2 per hour	120
Total (per 100 pairs)	$410

The mail-order house has offered to take as many of each type of slipper as the company cares to produce. Total hours available to the company in both the Fabricating and Finishing Departments are 120 hours per day per department.

The company's accountant attempted to use the simplex method to determine the number of each type of slipper that should be produced per day to realize the highest daily contribution margin. However, the iterations were stopped after producing the second tableau, reproduced on page 860.

Required:
(1) A graph to determine the number of each type of slipper that should be produced per day to realize the highest daily contribution margin.
(2) Completion of the iteration process for the simplex method, showing all calculations.
(3) The shadow prices and their lower and upper constraint range limits.

	MIX	0	20	20	0	0
		QUANTITY	x	y	s_1	s_2
0	s_1	40	0	80/3	1	−2/3
20	x	4	1	2/3	0	1/30
			0	−20/3	0	2/3

6. Contribution margin maximization; graphic and simplex methods; shadow prices. Growfast Nursery is considering the possibility of adding imported fruit trees and oriental yard shrubs to their line of nursery products. The fruit trees have a per unit contribution margin of $6; shrubs, $7. There are 12 square feet available for display. Each tree requires two square feet of space while each shrub occupies three square feet. In addition, two hours each day are needed to prepare each tree for sale and one hour to prepare each shrub. Due to the many jobs to be performed in the nursery, only eight hours are available each day.

Required:
    (1) The number of imported fruit trees and oriental yard shrubs that should be stocked each day to maximize the contribution margin, using the graphic and simplex methods.
    (2) The shadow prices and their lower and upper constraint range limits.

7. Materials allocation; contribution margin maximization — graphic and simplex methods; shadow prices. Cornett Products, Inc., is compelled to curtail manufacturing due to a strike at the mill of one of its suppliers. The company still has the following inventory on hand to permit some production.

                   Material #101-2.................... 12,100 lbs.
                   Material #102-6................... 4,900

Other data:

	MATERIALS	
	#101-2	#102-6
Required per unit of Product a..	.8 lb.	.2 lb.
Required per unit of Product b..	.3	.7
Contribution margin per unit — Product a	$50	
Contribution margin per unit — Product b	80	

Required:
    (1) A graphic and simplex solution regarding the number of units of Products a and b that should be produced in order to maximize the total contribution margin with the available materials while the supplier's employees are on strike.
    (2) The shadow prices and their lower and upper constraint range limits.

8. Impact of constraint change. The Frey Company manufactures and sells two products — a toddler bike and a toy high chair. Linear programming is employed to determine the best mix of bikes and chairs. This approach also allows Frey to speculate on the impact of changes.

    The demand for bikes and chairs is relatively constant throughout the year. The following economic data pertain to the two products:

	BIKE (b)	CHAIR (c)
Sales price per unit	$12	$10
Variable cost per unit..	8	7
Contribution margin per unit...	$ 4	$ 3
Materials required:		
Wood..	1 board foot	2 board feet
Plastic	2 pounds	1 pound
Direct labor required	2 hours	2 hours

Estimates of the resource quantities available in a nonvacation month during the year are:

Wood..	10,000 board feet
Plastic	10,000 pounds
Direct labor...	12,000 hours

The graphic formulation of the constraints of the linear programming model which Frey Company has developed for nonvacation months is presented below:

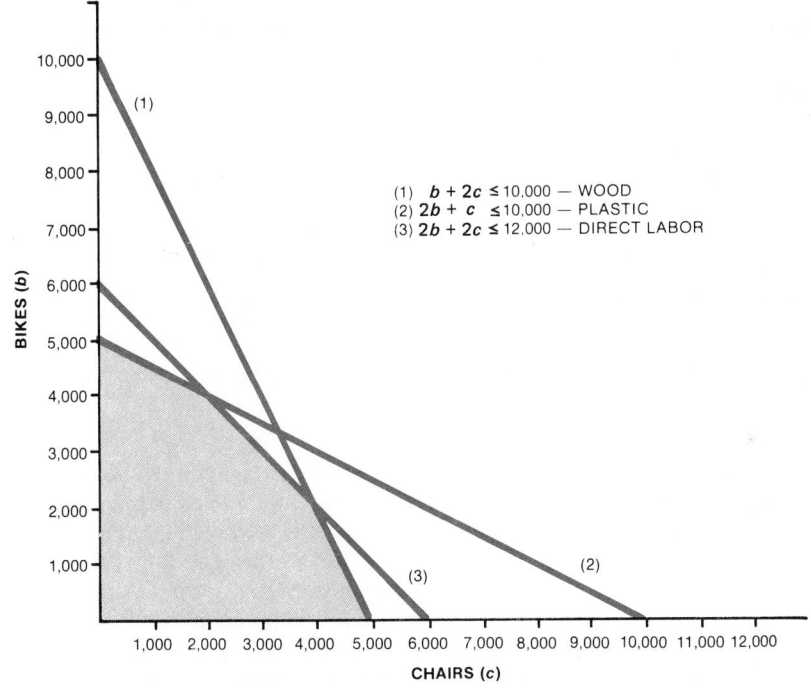

$$\text{(1)} \quad b + 2c \leq 10,000 - \text{WOOD}$$
$$\text{(2)} \quad 2b + c \leq 10,000 - \text{PLASTIC}$$
$$\text{(3)} \quad 2b + 2c \leq 12,000 - \text{DIRECT LABOR}$$

The algebraic formulation of the model for the nonvacation month is:

Objective function: Maximize CM = 4b + 3c

Constraints:

$$b + 2c \leq 10,000 \text{ board feet}$$
$$2b + c \leq 10,000 \text{ pounds}$$
$$2b + 2c \leq 12,000 \text{ direct labor hours}$$
$$b, \ c \geq 0$$

The results from the linear programming model indicate that Frey Company can maximize its contribution margin (and thus profits) for a nonvacation month by producing and selling 4,000 toddler bikes and 2,000 toy high chairs. This sales mix will yield a total contribution margin of $22,000 in a month.

Required: The best product mix and maximum total contribution margin when only 10,000 direct labor hours are available during each of the vacation months of June, July, and August.

(CMA adapted)

9. Cost minimization — graphic and simplex methods; shadow prices. A company produces three products, a, b, and c, which use common materials, x and y. Material x costs \$3 per ton and y \$4 per ton. The amount of materials required per ton of product and the required weight per ton of product are:

MATERIAL	PRODUCT a	PRODUCT b	PRODUCT c
x..	4 lbs.	7 lbs.	1.5 lbs.
y..	8	2	5
Minimum weight required	32	14	15

Required:
- (1) The number of tons of each material needed to meet the requirements at minimum cost by (a) the graphic method and (b) the simplex method.
- (2) The shadow prices and their lower and upper constraint range limits.

10. Cost minimization — graphic and simplex methods; shadow prices. Two additives are mixed with a plastic resin prior to extension into a final product. Over a period of time, empirical relationships were developed to meet quality specifications of the final product. Within the latitude of these relationships, the quantities are varied according to their current cost. Operating costs are not affected by the proportions of the two additives in the product.

The quality relationships per 100 kilograms of product are:

$$\text{For tensile strength} \ldots\ldots\ldots\ldots\ldots\ldots\ldots 2a + b \geq 1.1$$
$$\text{For flexibility} \ldots\ldots\ldots\ldots\ldots\ldots\ldots\ldots\ldots a + 3b \geq 1.5$$

Additive a sells for \$8 per kg, and b for \$5 per kg.

Required:
- (1) The most economical (minimum cost) mixture using the (a) graphic method and (b) simplex method.
- (2) The shadow prices and their lower and upper constraint range limits.

PROBLEMS

28-1. Contribution margin maximization — graphic method. Girth, Inc., makes two kinds of suede leather belts. Belt a is of high quality, while Belt b is of somewhat lower quality. The company earns a contribution margin of \$7 for each unit of a that is sold and \$2 for each unit of b sold. Each unit (belt) of a requires twice as much manufacturing time as a unit of b. Further, if only b is made, Girth has the capacity to manufacture 1,000 units per day. Suede leather is purchased under a long-term contract which makes available enough leather to produce 800 belts per day (a and b combined). Belt a requires a fancy buckle, of which only 400 per day are available; b requires a plain buckle, of which 700 per day are available. The demand for the suede leather belts (a or b) is such that Girth can sell all that it produces.

The graph on page 863 displays the constraint functions based upon the facts presented.

Required:
- (1) The number of units of Belt a and Belt b that should be produced to maximize the daily contribution margin, using the graph.
- (2) The number of units of each of the two belts to be produced each day to maximize the total contribution margin, assuming the same facts except that the sole supplier of buckles for a informs Girth that it will be unable to supply more than 100 fancy buckles per day.
- (3) The number of fancy buckles Girth should buy from Texas Buckles, Inc., assuming the same facts as in (2) except that Texas Buckles could supply Girth with the additional fancy buckles in 100-unit lots only and the price would be \$3.50 more per buckle than Girth is paying now.

(CMA adapted)

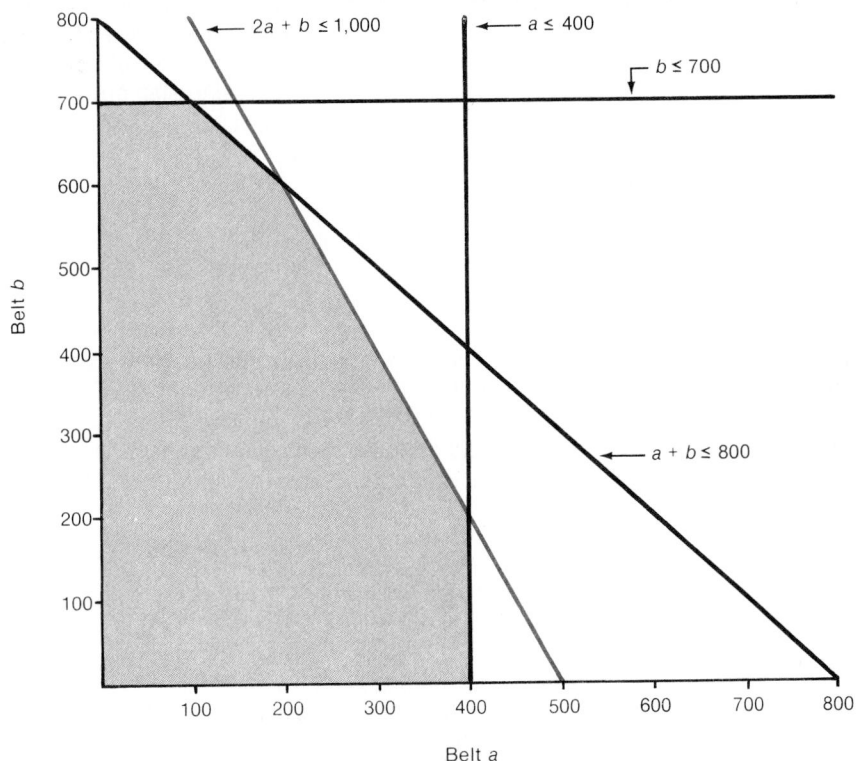

28-2. Contribution margin maximization — graphic and simplex methods; shadow prices. Nikko, Inc., produces two types of promotional fans — oriental and domestic. The contribution margin on oriental fans is $5 per 100; on domestic fans, $4 per 100. Two hundred hours are available for the production of these fans. Two hours are required to produce 100 oriental fans while one hour is required to produce 100 domestic fans. One pound of paper is required for each 100 fans, whether oriental or domestic. Nikko, Inc., has 150 pounds of paper.

Required:
    (1) The product mix that provides the maximum contribution margin, using the graphic and simplex methods.
    (2) The shadow prices and their lower and upper constraint range limits.

28-3. Production planning; contribution margin maximization — graphic and simplex methods; shadow prices. Castelli Corporation manufactures two products, p_1 and p_2, in Departments I, II, and III. The following information concerning departmental hours, product hours, costs, and sales prices is available:

	p_1	p_2	TOTAL HOURS AVAILABLE
Machine hours — Department I	3	5	450
Machine hours — Department II	0	1	60
Machine hours — Department III	5	4	600
Variable manufacturing cost	$ 7	$12	
Sales price per product	11	22	

Required:
    (1) The product mix that provides the maximum contribution margin, using the graphic method and the simplex method.
    (2) The shadow prices and their lower and upper constraint range limits.

28-4. Product mix; contribution margin maximization — graphic and simplex methods; shadow prices. The Sanning Company manufactures two compounds, *m* and *n*. Three processing steps are needed for *m* while two processing steps are needed for *n*. To produce one barrel of each compound, the following percentages of the daily capacities of each processing step are required:

	COMPOUND *m*	COMPOUND *n*
Processing step 1	33⅓%	50 %
Processing step 2	66⅔	33⅓
Processing step 3	100	0

The contribution margin of *m* is $4 per barrel; of *n*, $5 per barrel.

Required:
1. A graphic solution to indicate the maximum total contribution per day from the two compounds.
2. A linear programming simplex analysis to indicate the optimal contribution per compound and the optimal utilization of the available capacities.
3. The shadow prices and their lower and upper constraint range limits.

28-5. Contribution margin maximization — graphic and simplex methods; shadow prices. Trinex Corporation manufactures two products, Trinkets and Gadgets. The information regarding these products is as follows:

PRODUCT	DAILY CAPACITIES IN UNITS		SALES PRICE PER UNIT	VARIABLE COST PER UNIT
	Cutting Department	Finishing Department		
Trinkets..	400	240	$50	$30
Gadgets...	200	320	70	40

The daily capacities of each department represent the maximum production for either Trinkets or Gadgets. However, any combination of Trinkets and Gadgets can be produced as long as the maximum capacity of the deparment is not exceeded; i.e., two Trinkets can be produced in the Cutting Department for each Gadget not produced and three Trinkets can be produced in the Finishing Department for every four Gadgets not produced.

Materials shortages prohibit the production of more than 180 Gadgets per day.

Required:
1. A graph that expresses the production relationships stated in the information given.
2. An identification and a listing of the graphic locations (coordinates) of the:
   (a) Cutting Department's capacity.
   (b) Production limitations for Gadgets because of the materials shortages.
   (c) Area of feasible production combinations.
3. Computation of:
   (a) The contribution margin per unit for Trinkets and Gadgets.
   (b) The total contribution margin for each of the points of intersection of lines bounding the feasible production area.
   (c) The best production alternative.
4. The best production alternative, using the simplex method.
5. The shadow prices and their lower and upper constraint range limits.
6. The kinds of decisions for which the contribution margin data are useful.

(AICPA adapted)

28-6. Scholarship costs; admission policies; cost minimization — simplex method. Due to the budget squeeze, Brook University is faced with the problem of minimizing scholarship expenditures subject to these past traditions and new agreements:

> Out of a class of 1,700 first-year students, the university, for reasons of diversification, admits no more than 800 students who are children of its alumni.

The university will admit at least 250 minority-group students. Any minority-group students having alumni parents are to be counted in the minority group. To encourage universities to admit more minority-group students, the federal government supports the schools with $800 in aid for each minority-group student admitted.

The average scholarship costs to the university before federal aid are:

$1,000 per year for a student whose parent is an alumnus

$2,000 per year for a minority-group student

$1,100 per year for a nonalumnus, nonminority-group student

Required: The number of students to be admitted and the total cost to Brook University, using the simplex method.

28-7. Materials requirements; cost minimization — graphic and simplex methods; shadow prices. Certain animals at the Denver Zoo must receive an adequate amount of two vitamins in their daily food supply. The minimum daily requirement of Vitamin A is 30 units; of Vitamin B, 50 units.

One pound of foodstuff x can provide $3\frac{1}{3}\%$ of the minimum daily requirements of A and 4% of B. One pound of y will supply 10% of A and 2% of B requirements. The costs are: x, $.02 per pound; y, $.05 per pound.

Required:

(1) The least possible cost to provide for the minimum requirements of the two vitamins, using the graphic method and the simplex method.

(2) The shadow prices and their lower and upper constraint range limits.

Index